Jennifer Haworth.

THE NEW ENLARGED
CASSELL'S
GERMAN-ENGLISH
ENGLISH-GERMAN
COMPACT DICTIONARY

THE NEW ENLARGED
GERMAN-ENGLISH
ENGLISH-GERMAN
COMPACT DICTIONARY

*EMBODYING THE LATEST GERMAN ORTHOGRAPHY
AND A PHONETIC KEY TO THE PRONUNCIATION
OF GERMAN WORDS*

TOGETHER WITH APPENDICES CONTAINING
LISTS OF GERMAN AND ENGLISH IRREGULAR
VERBS AND GEOGRAPHICAL AND PROPER NAMES

BY

J. HERON LEPPER, B.A.

BARRISTER-AT-LAW

*Littledale Prizeman ; Stewart Literary Scholar ; Senior
Moderator, Trinity College, Dublin*

CASSELL AND COMPANY, LTD.
London, Toronto, Melbourne and Sydney

First published	September	1925
Second Edition	April	1929
Third Edition	November	1930
Fourth Edition	July	1933
NEW REVISED AND ENLARGED EDITION		
Fifth Edition	March	1936
Sixth Edition	June	1939
Seventh Edition	November	1940
Eighth Edition	January	1943
Ninth Edition	September	1944
Tenth Edition	January	1946
Eleventh Edition	October	1947
Twelfth Edition	August	1952
Thirteenth Edition	August	1954

PRINTED AND BOUND IN ENGLAND BY
HAZELL WATSON AND VINEY LTD
AYLESBURY AND LONDON

THE PRONUNCIATION

The Sounds

The following is a list of the sounds with key words.

Consonants

p	Paar [pa:r]	f	Fuß [fu:s]
b	Bahn [ba:n]	v	wo [vo:]
t	Teil [taɪl]	s	Waſſer ['vasər]
d	dann [dan]	z	ſehen ['ze:ən]
k	kommen ['kɔmən]	ʃ	Schuh [ʃu:]
g	ganz [gants]	ʒ	Etage [e'ta:ʒə]
ʔ	geöffnet [gə'ʔøfnət]	ç	ich [ɪç]
m	Mann [man]	j	ja [ja]
n	neu [nɔy]	x	ach [ax], Buch [bu:x]
ŋ	eng [ɛŋ]	h	Hand [hant]
l	Laut [laʊt]	l̦	Lilie ['li:li̯ə]
r	Rat [ra:t], Wetter ['vɛtər]	ŭ	Statue ['ʃta:tŭə]

Vowels

i	Biene ['bi:nə]	u	Mut [mu:t]
ɪ	bin [bɪn]	y	fühlen ['fy:lən]
e	Ehre ['e:rə]	Y	füllen ['fYlən]
ɛ	gelb [gɛlp], Ähre ['ɛ:rə]	ø	Höhle ['hø:lə]
a	Lamm [lam], lahm [la:m]	ə	gegeben [gə'ge:bən]
ɔ	Sonne ['zɔnə]	ɛ̃	Baſſin [ba'sɛ̃:]
o	wohl [vo:l]	ã	Chance ['ʃã:sə]
ʊ	Mutter ['mʊtər]	õ	Bonbon [bõ'bõ:]

Note.—The sounds [ɛ̃], [ã], [õ] are only used by Germans who are familiar with French, and not by all of these. Most Germans substitute [ɛŋ], [aŋ], [ɔŋ], and pronounce accordingly.

Diphthongs

aɪ	ein [aɪn]	ɔy	Leute ['lɔytə]
aʊ	Haus [haʊs]	uɪ	pfui [pfuɪ]

The Sound Attributes

The following sound attributes are marked in this dictionary:

Full Length of Vowels indicated by : following the vowel letter (examples: lahm [la:m], ſprach [ʃpra:x], compare Lamm [lam], ſchwach [ʃvax]).

Stress, indicated by ' preceding the stressed syllable (examples: leben ['le:bən], lebendig [le'bɛndɪç], jahrelang ['ja:rəlaŋ], Jahrhundert [ja:r'hʊndərt]).

Notes on the Consonants

The following have approximately the same sounds as in English: p b t d k g (hard) m n f v s z h .

[ʔ] is the "glottal stop." In this dictionary it is marked only when occurring in the middle of a word (examples: Verein [fɛr'ʔaɪm], bearbeiten [bə'ʔarbaɪtən].

[ŋ] is the same as the English sound of *ng* in *sing, singer*.

[l] is a "clear" (palatalized) variety.

[r] is normally a rolled consonant.

[v] may always be pronounced as in English.

[s] has a sharper hiss than an English [s].

[ʃ] and [ʒ] are similar to the English *sh* in *ship* and *s* in *measure*.

[ç]. A near approximation to this sound may be acquired by placing the tongue as for the vowel [i] and emitting a strong current of breath.

[j] is the voiced sound corresponding to [ç]. It resembles the English *y* in *yard*.

[x] is approximately the Scotch *ch* in *loch*.

[ĭ] and [ŭ] represent very short non-syllabic [ɪ] and [ʊ].

Notes on the Vowels

[i] resembles the English vowel in *see*.

[ɪ] resembles the English vowel in *bit*.

[e] is unlike any English sound, though it has a resemblance to the English sound in *day*.

[ɛ] is approximately as in the English *get*.

[a] resembles the English [a] in *father*.

[ɔ] resembles the English vowel in *hot*.

[o] resembles the English sound in *go*.

[ʊ] resembles the English vowel in *foot*.

[u] resembles the English vowel in *too*.

[y] has no equivalent in English. It may be acquired by saying [i] through closely rounded lips.

[ʏ] has no equivalent in English. It may be acquired by saying [ɪ] through fairly closely rounded lips.

[ø] has no equivalent in English. It may be acquired by saying [e] through closely rounded lips.

[ə] resembles the English sound of *a* in *along*.

[ɛ̃], [ã], [õ] are nasalized vowels. They may be acquired by attempting to pronounce [ɛ], [a], [o] simultaneously with the consonant [ŋ].

ABBREVIATIONS
Abkürzungen

Acc.	accusative (case), Akkusativ.	f.	substantive of the feminine gender, weibliches Hauptwort.
adj.	adjective, Adjektiv, Eigenschaftswort.		
adv.	adverb, Adverbium, Nebenwort, Umstandswort.	fig.	figuratively, bildlich, figürlich.
Anat.	anatomy, Anatomie.	Fort.	fortification, Befestigungskunst.
Arch.	architecture, Architektur.		
Arith.	arithmetic, Arithmetik.	Gen.	genitive (case), Genitiv, Wesfall.
art.	article, Artikel, Geschlechtswort.		
		Geog.	geography, Geographie.
Artil.	artillery, Artillerie, Geschützkunst.	Geol.	geology, Geologie.
		Geom.	geometry, Geometrie.
Astr.	astronomy, Astronomie, Sternkunde.	Gram.	grammar, Grammatik.
		Hist.	history, Geschichte.
aux. v.	auxiliary verb, Hilfszeitwort.	Horol.	horology, Uhrmacherkunst.
Av.	aviation, das Flugwesen.	Icht.	ichthyology, Fischkunde.
B.	Bible, biblical, Bibel, biblisch.	imp.	impersonal(ly), unpersönlich.
		imperat.	imperative (mood), Imperativ.
Bot.	botany, Pflanzenkunde, Botanik.	ind.	indefinite, unbestimmend.
C.L.	commercial language, kaufmännischer Ausdruck.	indec.	indeclinable, undeklinierbar.
		insep.	inseparable, unzertrennlich.
Carp.	carpentry, Zimmermannskunst.	int.	interjection, Interjektion.
		inter.	interrogative, fragend, Fragewort.
Chem.	chemistry, Chemie, Scheidekunst.		
		inv.	invariable, unveränderlich.
coll.	colloquialism, Ausdruck der Umgangssprache.	ir.	irregular (strong), unregelmäßig (stark).
comp.	comparative (degree), Steigerungsform.	Law.	law-term, juristischer Ausdruck.
Comp(s).	compound word(s), zusammengesetztes Wort.	lit.	literally, buchstäblich.
		m.	substantive of the masculine gender, männliches Hauptwort.
conj.	conjunction, Konjunktion, Bindewort.		
Dat.	dative (case), Dativ, Wemfall.	Mach.	machinery, Maschinenwesen.
		Math.	mathematics, Mathematik.
def.	definite, bestimmt.	Mech.	mechanics, Mechanik.
dem.	demonstrative, demonstrativ, hinweisend.	Med.	medicine, Medizin, Heilkunde.
dial.	dialectal, dialektisch.	Metall.	metallurgy, Metallurgie.
dim.	diminutive, Verkleinerungswort.	Mil.	military term, militärisch.
		Min.	mining, Bergbau; mineralogy, Mineralogie.
Draw.	drawing, Zeichenkunst, Zeichnen.		
		Mus.	music, Musik, Tonkunst.
Eccl.	ecclesiastical, kirchlich.	Myth.	mythology, Mythologie.
Elect.	electricity, Elektrizität.	n.	substantive of the neuter gender, sächliches Hauptwort; see subst. n.; also v.n.
Ellipt.	elliptical(ly), elliptisch.		
Engr.	engraving, Gravierkunst.		
Ent.	entomology, Entomologie.		

Naut.	*nautical term*, Schifferausdruck.
p.	*present participle*, Partizipium der Gegenwart ; *person*, Person.
p.p.	*past participle*, Partizipium der Vergangenheit.
Paint.	*painting*, Malerei.
part.	*particle*, Partikel.
pers.	*personal*, persönlich.
pl.	*plural*, Mehrzahl ; *noun in the plural*, Substantiv im Plural.
Poet.	*poetry*, Poesie, Dichtkunst.
poss.	*possessive*, besitzanzeigend.
pres.	*present tense*, Gegenwart.
Print.	*printing*, Druckerei.
pron.	*pronoun*, Fürwort.
prep.	*preposition*, Verhältniswort.
r.	*reflexive* (verb), Reflexivum.
Railw.	*railways*, Eisenbahnwesen.
reg.	*regular (weak)*, regelmäßig (schwach).
Rel.	*religion*, Religion.
S.	Sache, thing.
s.	*substantive*, Substantiv.
sep.	*separable*, trennbar.
sing.	*singular*, Einzahl.
Sl.	*slang*, Rotwelsch.

subst. n.	*indicates the infinitive used as substantive when it is necessary to distinguish it from* n.=v.n., bezeichnet den substantivisch gebrauchten Infinitiv, wo er vom *n.=v.n.* zu unterscheiden ist.
sup.	*superlative (degree)*, Superlativ.
Surg.	*surgery*, Chirurgie.
Tele.	*telegraphy*, Telegraphie.
th.	*thing*, Ding.
Theat.	*theatre*, Theater, Schauspiel.
Theol.	*theology*, Theologie.
Typ.	*typography*, Typographie, Buchdruckerkunst.
Univ.	*university*, Universität.
v.a.	*active* or *transitive verb*, tätiges oder transitives Zeitwort.
v.aux.	*auxiliary verb*, Hilfszeitwort.
v.imp.	*impersonal verb*, unpersönliches Zeitwort.
v.n.	*neuter* or *intransitive verb*, neutrales oder intransitives Zeitwort.
v.r.	*reflexive verb*, Reflexivum.
Vet.	*veterinary art*, Tierheilkunde.
=	stands for *equality*, *the same as*, gleich.

CASSELL'S
GERMAN-ENGLISH
DICTIONARY

A

A, a [a:], A, a; das A (des A(s), die As) the letter A; the note A or La; A dur, (the key of) A major; A moll, (the key of) A minor.

Aal [a:l], m. (—es, pl. —e, dialectic Äle) eel.

Aar [a:r], m. (—es, pl. —e) eagle.

Aas [a:s], n. (—es, pl. Äser) carcass; carrion.

Ab [ap], I. adv. off; down; away from; from; exit; weit —, far off; Hut — ! off with your hat! — und zu, now and then, sometimes; Strom — (stress on ab, usually spelt stromab), down stream; Berg —, down hill; auf und —, up and down; kurz —, abruptly. II. Separable prefix. When employed as a prefix ab implies separation from, deviation from, disinclination to, and sometimes participation in, similitude.

Abänder—lich ['ap'ɛndərlɪç], adj. alterable. —ung, f. alteration.

Abändern ['ap'ɛndərn], v.a. to alter, to change.

Abart ['ap'a:rt], f. (pl. —en) degeneracy.

Abart—en ['ap'a:rtən], v.n. (aux. f.) to degenerate; to vary. —ung, f. degeneration.

Abbefehlen ['apbəfe:lən], ir.v.a. to countermand.

Abbeizen ['apbaɪtsən], ir.v.a. to remove by caustics.

Abbestell—en ['apbəʃtɛlən], v.a. & n. to countermand. —ung, f. counter-order.

Abbetteln ['apbɛtəln], v.a.; einem etwas —, to obtain something from someone by begging.

Abbiegen ['apbi:gən], ir.v.a. to bend off, turn aside.

Abbild ['apbɪlt], n. (—es, pl. —er) copy; image.

Abbild—en ['apbɪldən], v.a. to portray. —ung, f. illustration; picture; image.

Abbitt—e ['apbɪtə], f. (pl. —en) apology.

Abbitten ['apbɪtən], ir.v.a. to apologize for; to deprecate, beg off.

Abblättern ['apblatərn], v.a. to strip of leaves.

Abblühen ['apbly:ən], v.n. (aux. f. & h.) to droop, fade.

Abborgen ['apborgən], v.a. (einem etwas) to borrow from.

Abbrauchen ['apbrauxən], v.a. to wear out or off.

Abbrechen ['apbrɛçən], ir.v.a. & n. (aux. f. & h.) to break, snap; Zelte —, to strike the tents.

Abbrennen ['apbrɛnən], ir.v.a. to burn off; to burn down.

Abbringen ['apbrɪŋən], ir.v.a. to get off, out, away; to dissuade.

Abbruch ['apbrux], m. (—es, pl. Abbrüche) the act of breaking off, pulling down; damage, injury, loss; abatement (in price).

Abbrüchig ['apbrʏçɪç], adj. brittle; prejudicial.

Abbürsten ['apbʏrstən], v.a. to brush off.

Abbüß—en ['apby:sən], v.a. to atone for, to expiate. —ung, f. atonement, expiation.

Abc, (Abece) [a:be:'tse:], n. abc, alphabet.

Abdächig ['apdɛçɪç], adj. sloping.

Abdämmen ['apdɛmən], v.a. to dam up, off.

Abdampfen ['apdampfən], v.n. (aux. f.) to evaporate.

Abdank—en ['apdaŋkən], v. I. a. to dismiss from service; to discharge; to disband. II. n. (aux. h.) to resign, to retire, to quit the service, to abdicate. —ung, f. resignation, abdication; discharge.

Abdecken ['apdɛkən], v.a. to uncover; to unroof; to clear (the table).

Abdingen ['apdɪŋən], ir.v.a. to beat down in bargaining; to cheapen; einem etwas —, to hire something from someone.

Abdrängen ['apdrɛŋən], v.a. to force away; einem etwas —, to extort something from someone.

Abdreschen ['apdrɛʃən], ir.v.a. to thrash. abgedroschen, p.p. & adj. trite, vulgar.

Abdringen ['apdrɪŋən], ir.v.a. to force away.

Abdruck ['apdruk], m. (—(e)s, pl. Abdrücke) impression; single copy; stamp, stamping; fossil; mark.

Abdrucken ['apdrukən], v.a. to print, to imprint.

Abdrücken ['apdrykən], v.a. to pull the trigger, to fire off (a gun).

Abend ['a:bənt], m. (—s, pl. —e) evening; eve; the west; diesen Abend, this evening; heute abend, to-night; auf heute abend, for this evening; gestern abend, yesterday night; morgen abend, to-morrow night; alle abend or Abende, every evening; am —, zu —, auf den —, in the evening; zu — essen, to sup; guten —, good evening. —lich, adj. evening; western. —s, adv. in the evening, of an evening. —blatt, n. evening (news)paper. —brot, n., —essen, n. supper. —dämmerung, f. evening twilight, dusk. —land, n. occident. —sländer, m. inhabitant of the west; man from the west. —ländisch, adj. occidental, belonging to the west. —mahl, n. supper; das heilige —mahl, the Lord's supper; the holy communion. —rot, n., —röte, f. evening glow, sunset glow.

Abenteuer ['a:bəntɔʏər], n. (—s, pl. —) adventure. —(e)n, to seek adventures. —er, (Abenteurer), m. adventurer. —erin, (Abenteurerin), f. adventuress. —lich, I. adj. adventurous; wonderful; romantic; fantastic. II. adv. adventurously, etc. —lichkeit, f. adventurousness; romance; strangeness.

Aber ['a:bər], I. adv. again, once more; tausend und — tausend, thousands and thousands (lit. a thousand and another thousand). In some cpds. Aber denotes ill, a bad kind of (cp. Ab in Abgott). II. conj. but. —glaube, m. superstition. —gläubisch, adj. & adv. superstitiously. —malig, adj. reiterated, repeated. —mals, adv. again, once more. —witz, m. craziness; —witzig, adj. & adv. crazy, foolish.

Abfahr—en ['apfa:rən], ir.v. I. a. to cart away. II. n. (aux. ʃ.) to set off, to depart. —t ['apfa:rt], f. (pl. —ten) departure; starting time.

Abfall ['apfal], m. (—es, pl. Abfälle) slope; secession, revolt; short-weight; pl. waste, refuse.

Abfallen ['apfalən], ir.v.n. (aux. ʃ.) to fall off; to slope; to decay; to desert, to revolt; der Abgefallene, the apostate.

Abfällig ['apfɛlɪç], adj. sloping; decaying; dissenting.

Abfärben ['apfɛrbən], v.n. (aux. h.) to lose colour; abgefärbt, p.p. & adj. faded, discoloured.

Abfass—en ['apfasən], v.a. to sort or separate; to compose; to write; to draw up. —er, m. (—ers) editor; writer. —ung, f. composition, style, wording.

Abfegen ['apfe:gən], v.a. to sweep off.

Abfertig—en ['apfɛrtɪgən], v.a. to finish; to despatch; to dismiss. —er, m. (—ers, pl. —er) sender. —ung, f. act of finishing; despatch; snub; dismissal.

Abfind—en ['apfɪndən], ir.v. I. a. to satisfy, to compound with (creditors). II. r. to come to terms (mit einem, with someone). —ung, f. settlement; compromise. —ungssumme, f. sum paid in compensation.

Abfliegen ['apfli:gən], ir.v.n. (aux. ʃ.) to fly off; to take off (Av.).

Abfließen ['apfli:sən], ir.v.n. (aux. ʃ.) to run off, to flow off or down; to ebb.

Abfluß ['apflus], m. (—sses, pl. Abflüsse) flowing off; ebb. —graben, m. drain. —röhre, f. waste-pipe, gutter.

Abfolge ['apfɔlgə], f. succession, sequence.

Abforder—n ['apfɔrdərn], v.a. to call away; (einem etwas) to demand from, make a claim against. —ung, f. demand from; recall.

Abforschen ['apfɔrʃən], v.a. (einem etwas) to ascertain by questioning.

Abfragen ['apfra:gən], *v.a.* to inquire of; to ascertain by inquiring.

Abfuhr ['apfu:r], *f.* removal *or* transportation (*of goods*); carting off, carriage.

Abführen ['apfy:rən], *v.a.* to lead away; to carry off, down, away; to export.

Abgabe ['apga:bə], *f.* (*pl.* —n) tax, duty; draft, bill of exchange; delivery. —n, *pl.* fees, dues. —pflichtig, *adj.* assessable, taxable. —n-frei *adj.* duty-free.

Abgang ['apgaŋ], *m.* (—es, *pl.* **Abgänge**) departure; deduction; tare; sale; decease; loss; exit.

Abgäng—ig ['apgɛŋɪç], *adj.* going off, departing; saleable; declining; deteriorating.

Abgeben ['apge:bən], *ir.v.* I. *a.* to give, to deliver; to deliver up; to draw (*a bill*). II. *r.* fich mit jemand(em) —, to frequent someone's company; fich mit etwas —, to occupy oneself with a matter. III. *n.* (*aux.* h.) to deal (*cards*).

Abgebrannt ['apgəbrant], *p.p.* of **abbrennen** & *adj.* burnt out.

Abgebrochen ['apgəbrɔxən], *p.p.* & *adj.* broken off; abrupt. —heit, *f.* abruptness.

Abgedroschen ['apgədrɔʃən], *p.p.* & *adj.* trite.

Abgegriffen ['apgəgrɪfən], *p.p.* of **abgreifen** & *adj.* worn by thumbing.

Abgehen ['apge:ən], *ir.v.n.* (*aux.* f.) to go off, to depart; to go astray; to deviate, digress; to make one's exit.

Abgelebt ['apgəle:pt], *p.p.* & *adj.* worn out; blasé. —heit, *f.* decrepitude.

Abgelegen ['apgəle:gən], *p.p.* & *adj.* remote, distant. —heit, *f.* remoteness.

Abgemacht ['apgəmaxt], *p.p.* & *interj.* settled, agreed.

Abgemessen ['apgəmɛsən], I. *p.p.* & *adj.* measured; slow; formal. II. *adv.* with careful adjustment. —heit, *f.* regularity, exactitude.

Abgeneigt ['apgənaɪkt], *p.p.* & *adj.* disinclined, averse. —heit, *f.* disinclination, repugnance.

Abgenutzt ['apgənʊtst], *adj.* worn out; stale.

Abgeordnete(r) ['apgəʔɔrdnətə(r)], *m.* (—n, *pl.* —n) deputy, political representative. —nhaus, *n.* chamber of deputies.

Abgerechnet ['apgərɛçnət], *p.p.* deducted.

Abgerissen ['apgərɪsən], *p.p.* of **abreißen** & *adj.* torn, ragged, shabby.

Abgesandt ['apgəzant], *p.p.* of **absenden.** —e(r), *m.* (—en, *pl.* —en) ambassador. —e, *f.* ambassadress.

Abgeschieden ['apgəʃi:dən], *p.p.* & *adj.* secluded; separate; dead. —heit, *f.* seclusion.

Abgeschliffen ['apgəʃlɪfən], *p.p.* & *adj.* polished; refined, polite. —heit, *f.* refinement.

Abgeschmackt ['apgəʃmakt], *adj.* tasteless, insipid; absurd; in bad taste. —heit, *f.* absurdity; bad taste.

Abgesehen ['apgəze:ən], *p.p.*; — von, without regard to; apart from; — davon daß, without mentioning that; — auf, (*acc.*) intended for.

Abgesondert ['apgəzɔndərt], *p.p.* & *adj.* separated; separate.

Abgespannt ['apgəʃpant], *p.p.* & *adj.* slackened; tired, low. —heit, *f.* exhaustion; debility; lowness of spirits.

Abgestorben ['apgəʃtɔrbən], *p.p.* & *adj.* paralysed, dead.

Abgestumpft ['apgəʃtʊmpft], *p.p.* & *adj.* blunted; dull.

Abgetan ['apgəta:n], *p.p.* & *adj.* done (away) with, settled, over.

Abgetragen ['apgətra:gən], *p.p.* & *adj.* worn out, threadbare.

Abgewöhnen ['apgəvø:nən], *v.a.* (einem etwas) to disaccustom; to wean from; to break off.

Abgezogen ['apgətso:gən], *p.p.* & *adj.* far off, remote; (C.L.) deducted.

Abglanz ['apglants], *m.* (—es) reflected splendour; reflection.

Ab—gott ['apgɔt], *m.* (—gottes, *pl.* —götter) idol. —göttin, *f.* female idol.

Abgött—erei [apgətə'raɪ], *f.* idolatry. —isch, *adj.* & *adv.* idolatrous.

Abgraben ['apgra:bən], *ir.v.a.* to dig off; to drain.

Abgreifen ['apgraɪfən], *ir.v.a.* to wear out by constant handling; **abgegriffene Bücher**, well-thumbed volumes.

Abgrund ['apgrʊnt], *m.* (—es, *pl.* **Abgründe**) abyss, precipice.

Abgunst ['apgʊnst], *f.* ill-will, envy, spite.

Abgünstig ['apgynstɪç], *adj.* spiteful, envious, grudging.

Abguß ['apgʊs], *m.* (—(ss)es, *pl.*

Abgüsse) pouring off; casting; cast; sink.

Abhalt—en ['aphaltən], *ir.v.a.* to hold off; to restrain; to ward off; to hinder. **—ung**, *f.* hindrance, impediment.

Abhand—eln ['aphandəln], *v.a.* to settle; to bargain for. **—lung**, *f.* discussion; negotiation.

Abhanden [ap'handən], *adj.* not at hand; mislaid, lost; — **kommen**, to get lost.

Abhang ['aphaŋ], *m.* (**—es**, *pl.* **Abhänge**) slope, declivity.

Abhäng—en ['apheŋən], *ir.v.n.* to hang down; to depend on. **—ig**, *adj.* sloping; dependent on, subject to. **—igkeit**, *f.* slope, dependence.

Abhaspeln ['aphaspəln], *v.a.* to unwind from a reel.

Abheben ['aphe:bən], *ir.v.* I. *a.* to lift off; to uncover; to cut (*cards*). II. *r.* to detach itself; to be contrasted.

Abhold ['aphɔlt], *adj.* disinclined, unfavourable.

Abholen ['apho:lən], *v.a.* to fetch off, away; to fetch.

Abhör—en ['aphø:rən], *v.a.* to learn by hearing; **die Zeugen —en**, to examine witnesses. **—ung**, *f.* hearing; trial.

Abhülsen ['aphʏlzən], *v.a.* to shell; to blanch.

Abirr—en ['ap'ɪrən], *v.n.* (*aux.* f.) to lose one's way; to deviate, to err. **—ung**, *f.* deviation.

Abiturient [abiturÏent], *m.* (**—en**, *pl.* **—en**), **—in**, *f.* (*pl.* **—innen**), boy, girl of the top form of a large school (**Gymnasium, Realschule**).

Abkaufen ['apkaufən], *v.a.*; **einem etwas —**, to buy something from someone.

Abkäufer ['apkɔʏfər], *m.* (**—s**, *pl.* **—**) purchaser.

Abkehr ['apke:r], *f.* (*no pl.*) act of turning away, renunciation.

Abkehren ['apke:rən], *v.a.* to turn away; to divert; to brush away.

Abketten ['apkɛtən], *v.a.* to unchain.

Abklang ['apklaŋ], *m.* (**—s**, *pl.* **Abklänge**) dissonance; echo.

Abklär—en ['apklɛ:rən], *v.a.* to clear, clarify. **—ung**, *f.* clarification.

Abklettern ['apklɛtərn], *v.a.* to climb down.

Abknipsen ['apknɪpsən], *v.a.* to clip, snip off.

Abknöpfen ['apknœpfən], *v.a.* to unbutton; **jemandem etwas abknöpfen**, to do someone out of something.

Abknüpfen ['apknʏpfən], *v.a.* to unbind; to undo.

Abkommen ['apkəmən], I. *ir.v.n.* (*aux.* f.) to come away; to deviate; to digress; to be descended from; to fall into disuse. II. *subst.n.* falling into disuse; origin; composition, agreement. **—schaft**, *f.* offspring, posterity.

Abkömmling ['apkœmlɪŋ], *m.* (**—s**, *pl.* **—e**) descendant.

Abkriegen ['apkri:gən], *v.a.* (**einem etwas**) to get something from someone.

Abkühl—en ['apky:lən], *v.a.* & *n.* (*aux.* f.) to cool. **—ung**, *f.* cooling; refreshment.

Abkunft ['apkunft], *f.* (*pl.* **Abkünfte**) descent.

Abkürz—en ['apkʏrtsən], *v.a.* to shorten; to abridge. **—ung**, *f.* abbreviation; abridgment.

Ablage ['apla:gə], *f.* (*pl.* **—en**), laying aside; cloak-room.

Ablaß ['aplas], *m.* (**—sses**, *pl.* **Ablässe**) draining; intermission; (**des Papstes**) indulgence, remission of punishment.

Ablassen ['aplasən], *ir.v.* I. *a.* to drain, let off; to decant; **auf beiden Seiten etwas —**, to split the difference. II. *n.* (*aux.* h.) to leave off, to desist.

Ablauf ['aplauf], *m.* (**—es**) running off; lapse, expiration; wane; ebb; — **eines Wechsels**, maturity of a bill.

Ablaufen ['aplaufən], *ir.v.* I. *n.* (*aux.* f.) to run down; to run off *or* astray; to depart; to expire; to become due. II. *a.* to wear off by running; to get the better of.

Ableg—en ['aple:gən], *v.a.* to put, take off; to lay off, down, aside; **Rechenschaft —en**, to render an account, to account. **—er**, *m.* (**—ers**, *pl.* **—er**) layer; scion.

Ablehn—en ['aple:nən], *v.a.* to remove, keep off; to decline, refuse. **—ung**, *f.* declining, refusal.

Ableist—en ['aplaɪstən], *v.a.*; **einen Eid —en**, to take an oath; to serve (*e.g.* **das Militärjahr**, the year of military service). **—ung**, *f.* serving.

Ableit—en ['aplaɪtən], *v.a.* to divert, lead away; to mislead; to draw off, drain; to derive; to deduce. **—er**, *m.* conductor; channel. **—ung**, *f.* a leading off; derivation.

Ablenk—en ['aplɛnkən], *v.* I. *a.* to divert; to avert; to turn away. II. *n.* (*aux.* ҕ.) to turn off; to swerve. —ung, *f.* diversion.

Ableſen ['aple:zən], *ir.v.a.* to pick off, to gather.

Ableugn—en ['aplɔʏgnən], *v.a.* to deny, disown, disclaim. —ung, *f.* denial, disavowal.

Abliefer—n ['apli:fərn], *v.a.* to deliver (*over*, *up*); to consign. —ung, *f.* delivery.

Abloḩnen ['aplo:nən], *v.a.* to pay off; to discharge.

Ablöſḑen ['apløʃən], *v.a.* to cool, quench; to blot out.

Ablöſ—en ['aplø:zən], *v.* I. *a.* to loosen; to detach; to set a watch; to relieve (*guard*). II. *r.* to be detached; to peel, drop off. —ung, *f.* loosening; amputation; relieving guard; ransom.

Abmaḑ—en ['apmaxən], *v.a.* to undo; to detach; to finish; to settle; **das iſt abgemaḑt!** agreed! it's a bargain! —ung, *f.* arrangement; agreement.

Abmaḩn—en ['apma:nən], *v.a.* to dissuade from; to warn against. —end, *p. & adj.* dissuasive. —ung, *f.* dissuasion.

Abmaß ['apma:s], *n.* measure, dimension.

Abmeſſ—en ['apmɛsən], *ir.v.a.* to measure off; to gauge; to survey; to compare; **ſeine Worte abmeſſen,** to weigh one's words. —er, *m.* (—ers, *pl.* —er) measurer, surveyor. —ung, *f.* measurement; adjustment; survey.

Abmieten ['apmi:tən], *v.a.* to hire from; to farm.

Abnaḩme ['apna:mə], *f.* (*pl.* —n) diminution, decline; decay; wane (*of the moon*); ebb; amputation; sale.

Abneḩm—en ['apne:mən], *ir.v.* I. *a.* to take off; to amputate; to skim (*cream*). II. *n.* (*aux.* ҕ.) to wane; to be lowered; to fail; to shorten. —er, *m.* (—ers, *pl.* —er) buyer, customer.

Abneig—en ['apnaɪgən], *v.* I. *a.* to turn away; to incline; to avert; to render averse. II. *r.* to turn aside from; to incline. —ung, *f.* a turning aside; aversion; declination; divergence.

Abonnent [abɔˈnɛnt], *m.* (—en, *pl.* —en), —in, *f.* (*pl.* —innen) subscriber (*to journal, etc.*).

Abordn—en ['apˀɔrdnən], *v.a.* to delegate, depute; to countermand. —er,

m. constituent, voter. —ung, *f.* delegation, deputation; committee.

Abort ['apˀɔrt], *m.* (—es) W.C., privy; (*rare*) remote place.

Abpflüḑen ['appflʏkən], *v.a.* to pluck off, gather.

Abprägen ['apprɛ:gən], *v.a.* to stamp, to coin.

Abprall—en ['appralən], *v.n.* (*aux.* ſ.) to rebound. —ung, *f.* recoil, rebound.

Abpreſſen ['apprɛsən], *v.a.* to press off; **einem etwas —,** to extort something from someone.

Abraḩmen ['apra:mən], *v.a.* to skim (*milk*).

Abrat—en ['apra:tən], *ir.v.a.* to dissuade from, advise against. —ung, *f.* dissuasion.

Abräum—en ['aprɔʏmən], *v.a.* to clear, to remove. —ung, *f.* clearance; forest clearing.

Abreḑn—en ['aprɛçnən], *v.a. & n.* to settle accounts; to deduct, subtract. —ung, *f.* deduction; discount. —ungs= tag, *m.* settling-day.

Abrede ['apre:də], *f.* (*pl.* —n) agreement; denial.

Abreden ['apre:dən], *v.a.*; **eine S. —,** to agree upon, concert a thing; **einem —,** to dissuade one from.

Abreiben ['apraɪbən], *ir.v.a.* to rub off; **ſiḑ —,** to chafe oneself.

Abreiſe ['apraɪzə], *f.* departure.

Abreiſen ['apraɪzən], *v.n.* (*aux.* ſ.) to set out, to start, to depart.

Abreiſſen ['apraɪsən], *ir.v.* I. *n.* (*aux.* ſ.) to break off; to tear. II. *a.* to tear, break.

Abriḑt—en ['aprɪçtən], *v.a.* to adjust; to regulate; to train. —ung, *f.* training.

Abrinden ['aprɪndən], *v.a.* to peel.

Abrinnen ['aprɪnən], *ir.v.n.* (*aux.* ſ.) to run off.

Abriß ['aprɪs], *m.* (—(ſſ)es, *pl.* —(ſſ)e) hasty sketch; plan; draught.

Abruf ['apru:f], *m.* (—s) recall; proclamation.

Abrufen ['apru:fən], *ir.v.a.* to call away *or* off; to recall.

Abrüſten ['aprʏstən], *v.a.* to disarm.

Abrüſtung ['aprʏstu:ŋ], *f.* disarmament.

Abſage ['apza:gə], *f.* refusal; countermand; disowning; renunciation; defiance, challenge.

Abſagen ['apza:gən], *v.* I. *a.* to

countermand; to refuse. II. *n.* (*aux.* h.) to renounce.

Abfatteln ['apzatəln], *v.* I. *a.* to unsaddle. II. *n.* (*aux.* h.) to dismount.

Abfatz ['apzats], *m.* (—**es**, *pl.* **Abfätze**) pause, stop; sale, market; stanza; ledge; contrast; heel (*of boot, etc.*); paragraph. —**weife**, *adv.* intermittently, by intervals.

Abfchaff—en ['apʃafən], *v.a.* to abolish, repeal; to discharge; to remove. —**ung**, *f.* giving up; abrogation; abolition.

Abfchälen ['apʃɛːlən], *v.a.* to peel; to shell.

Abfcheid—en ['apʃaidən], *ir.v.* I. *a.* to separate; to divide off. II. *n.* (*aux.* f.) to depart; **die Abgeschiedenen**, the departed. III. *subst.n.* (—**ens**) death; parting; separation. —**ung**, *f.* parting, separating.

Abfcheu ['apʃɔy], *m.* (—**s**) abhorrence; abomination; loathing; object of aversion. —**lich** [—'ʃɔylɪç] *adj.* & *adv.* detestable; horrible; loathsome. —**lichfeit**, *f.* abomination; atrocity.

Abfchiden ['apʃikən], *v.a.* to send; to send off.

Abfchieben ['apʃiːbən], *ir.v.a.* to shove off.

Abfchied ['apʃiːt], *m.* (—**(e)s**, *pl.* —**e**) discharge; departure; leave; parting; — **nehmen**, to bid farewell, to take leave. —**s-zeugnis**, *n.* testimonial on leaving.

Abfchießen ['apʃiːsən], *ir.v.a.* to shoot off; to discharge.

Abfchinden ['apʃɪndən], *v.* I. *a.* to skin. II. *r.* to exert oneself to the utmost, work very hard.

Abfchirren ['apʃɪrən], *v.a.* to unharness.

Abfchlag ['apʃlaːk], *m.* (—**(e)s**, *pl.* **Abfchläge**) rebound; fall in price; refusal; **auf** —, in part payment; on account; **mit** — **verfaufen**, to sell at a reduced price.

Abfchlagen ['apʃlaːgən], *ir.v.* I. *a.* to beat off; to strike; to reject. II. *n.* (*aux.* f.) to abate, fall off; to rebound.

Abfchleichen ['apʃlaiçən], *ir.v.n.* & *r.* to slink away.

Abfchließ—en ['apʃliːsən], *ir.v.a.* to lock up; to settle; to balance (*accounts, etc.*); **einen Vertrag —en**, to sign, close an agreement. —**end**, *p.* & *adj.* definitive, final.

Abfchluß ['apʃlus], *m.* (—**ffes**, *pl.*

Abfchlüffe) closing; conclusion; winding up; settlement. —**note**, *f.* contract. —**rechnung**, *f.* balance of account.

Abfchneiden ['apʃnaidən], *ir.v.* I. *a.* to cut off; to clip. II. *n.* (*aux.* h.) to form a contrast, to differ.

Abfchnitt ['apʃnɪt], *m.* (—**es**, *pl.* —**e**) cut; segment; section; paragraph; division; period.

Abfchnitzel ['apʃnɪtsəl], *n.* (—**s**, *pl.* —) snippings, clippings.

Abfchrauben ['apʃraubən], *v.a.* to unscrew.

Abfchreden ['apʃrekən], *v.a.* to frighten, scare away; **abgeschredtes Waffer**, lukewarm water. —**d**, *p.* & *adj.* horrible, forbidding.

Abfchreib—en ['apʃraibən], *ir.v.a.* to write out, transcribe, copy; to deduct; to carry to one's credit. —**er**, *m.* (—**ers**, *pl.* —**er**) copyist; plagiarist. —**erei**, *f.* plagiarism. —**ung**, *f.* copying.

Abfchrift ['apʃrɪft], *f.* (*pl.* —**en**) copy, transcript. —**lich**, *adj.* & *adv.* copied out.

Abfchuß ['apʃus], *m.* (—**ff**)**es**, *pl.* **Abfchüffe**) fall (of water); slope, descent.

Abfchüffig ['apʃʏsɪç], *adj.* steep. —**feit**, *f.* declivity.

Abfchwäch—en ['apʃveçən], *v.* I. *a.* to weaken. II. *r.* to decrease. —**ung**, *f.* weakening, diminution.

Abfchweif ['apʃvaif], *m.* (—**(e)s**) digression, deviation.

Abfchweif—en ['apʃvaifən], *v.n.* (*aux.* f.) to digress; to deviate. —**end**, *p.* & *adj.* digressive. —**ung**, *f.* digression, deviation.

Abfchwemmen ['apʃvemən], *v.a.* to wash away.

Abfchwenfen ['apʃvenkən], *v.r.* to wheel off *or* aside; **rechts (linfs) abgeschwenft!** right (left) wheel!

Abfchwören ['apʃvøːrən], *ir.v.a.* to deny by oath; to abjure.

Abfehbar ['apzeːbaːr], *adj.* & *adv.* visible; within sight; **in** —**er Zeit**, within measurable space of time.

Abfehen ['apzeːən], I. *ir.v.a.* & *n.* to look away from; to perceive; to watch an opportunity; to aim at; **davon abgesehen**, apart from this consideration. II. *subst.n.* design, purpose.

Abfein ['apzain], *ir.v.n.* (*aux.* f.) to be

off, away; **wir find noch weit ab,** we are still at a great distance.

Abseits ['apzaɪts], I. *adv.* aside, apart, aloof ; — **vom Wege,** away from the road. II. *prep.* off from.

Absend—en ['apzɛndən], *ir.v.a.* to send away, to despatch. **—er,** *m.* sender, consignor. **—ung,** *f.* sending off; conveyance.

Absetzbar ['apzɛtsbaːr], *adj.* removable; saleable.

Absetzen ['apzɛtsən], *v.* I. *a.* to set down; to deposit; to depose; to dismiss; **Waren —,** to sell goods. II. *n.* (*aux.* **h.**) to stop, pause. III. *imp.* to result in.

Absicht ['apzɪçt], *f.* (*pl.* **—en**) view; design, purpose, end, aim; **ohne —,** unintentionally. **—slos,** I. *adj.* unpremeditated. II. *adv.* unintentionally.

Absichtlich ['apzɪçtlɪç], *adj. & adv.* intentional, deliberate. **—keit,** *f.* premeditation.

Absingen ['apzɪŋən], *ir.v.a.* to chant; to recite.

Absolut [apzo'luːt], *adj. & adv.* absolute; unconditional.

Absolution [apzolutsi'oːn], *f.* absolution.

Absolvieren [apzɔl'viːrən], *v.a.* to absolve; to complete (*one's studies at college*).

Absonderbar ['apzɔndərbaːr], *adj.* separable.

Absonderlich ['apzɔndərlɪç], I. *adj.* separable; separated, apart; peculiar, singular, odd. II. *adv.* chiefly, expressly. **—keit,** *f.* peculiarity, oddness.

Absonder—n ['apzɔndərn], *v.a.* to separate, to divide; to detach. **—ung,** *f.* separation, division.

Abspannen ['apʃpanən], *v.a.* to unbend; to relax; to unharness; to exhaust utterly; **abgespannt,** *p.p. & adj.* tired out.

Absparen ['apʃpaːrən], *v.a.* to spare from.

Abspenstig ['apʃpɛnstɪç], *adj.* alienated, disloyal; — **machen,** to seduce from allegiance.

Absperr—en ['apʃpɛrən], *v.a.* to barricade; to exclude; to isolate. **—ung,** *f.* act of barring; isolation; solitary confinement; exclusion.

Abspiegel—n ['apʃpiːgəln], *v.* I. *a.* to reflect. II. *r.* to be reflected. **—ung,** *f.* reflection.

Abspruch ['apʃprʊx], *m.* (*pl.* **Absprüche**) verdict, final decision.

Abspülen ['apʃpyːlən], *v.a.* to wash, to rinse.

Abstamm—en ['apʃtamən], *v.n.* (*aux.* **f.**) to descend, to be derived from, to come of. **—ung,** *f.* descent.

Abstatten ['apʃtatən], *v.a.* to pay; to give, render; **einen Besuch —,** to pay a visit; **Bericht —,** to report.

Abstaub—en ['apʃtaʊbən], **Abstäub—en** ['apʃtɔybən], *v.a.* to dust. **—er,** *m.* duster.

Abstehlen ['apʃteːlən], *ir.v.a.* to steal away; **einem etwas —,** to steal something from someone.

Absteig—en ['apʃtaɪgən], *ir.v.n.* (*aux.* **f.**) to descend; to alight; to dismount.

Absterben ['apʃtɛrbən], I. *ir.v.n.* (*aux.* **f.**) to die away *or* out; to wither. II. *subst.n.* death, decay ; extinction.

Abstich ['apʃtɪç], *m.* (**—(e)s,** *pl.* **—e**) copy; contrast.

Abstieg ['apʃtiːk], *m.* (**—(e)s,** *pl.* **—e**) descent, climb down.

Abstimm—en ['apʃtɪmən], *v.* I. *a.* to tune. II. *n.* (*aux.* **h.**) to vote; **über etwas —en lassen,** to put a thing to the vote. **—ig,** *adj.* discordant; disagreeing. **—ung,** *f.* act of voting; dissonance.

Abstoß—en ['apʃtoːsən], *ir.v.* I. *a.* to knock off, to thrust off; to scrape. II. *n.* (*aux.* **h.**) to betake oneself off. **—end,** *adj.* repulsive, repugnant. **—ung,** *f.* repulsion.

Abstrahl ['apʃtraːl], *m.* (**—s,** *pl.* **—en**) reflected ray; splendour.

Abstrahl—en ['apʃtraːlən], *v.* I. *a.* to reflect. II. *n.* (*aux.* **h.**) to be reflected. **—ung,** *f.* reflection.

Abstrakt ['apʃtrakt], *adj. & adv.* abstract.

Abstufung ['apʃtuːfʊŋ], *f.* gradation.

Abstumpf—en ['apʃtʊmpfən], *v.a.* to blunt; to dull; to stupefy. **—end,** *p. & adj.* dulling. **—ung,** *f.* blunting; dulling.

Absturz ['apʃtʊrts], *m.* (**—es,** *pl.* **Abstürze**) waterfall; precipice.

Abstürzen ['apʃtʏrtsən], *v.a.* to precipitate.

Abstutzen ['apʃtʊtsən], *v.a.* to lop; to poll.

Absurd [ap'zʊrt], *adj.* absurd. **—ität** [apzʊrti'teːt], *f.* (*pl.* **—itäten**) absurdity.

Abt [apt], *m.* (**—es.** *pl.* **Äbte**) abbot. **—ei,** *f.* (*pl.* **—eien**) abbey; abbacy.

Abteil ['aptaɪl], *m.* (**—s,** *pl.* **-e**) share; *n.* compartment (*of a railway carriage*).

Abteilen ['aptaɪlən], *v.a.* to divide, share.

Abteilung ['aptaɪluŋ], *f.* division; separation (*from*); section; compartment (*of a railway carriage*). **—ungs-zeichen,** *n.* hyphen.

Äbt—in ['ɛptɪn] (*pl.* **—innen**), **—issin** (*pl.* **—issinnen**), *f.* abbess.

Abtrag ['aptra:k], *m.* (**—(e)s,** *pl.* **Abträge**) payment; compensation.

Abtrag—en ['aptra:gən], *ir.v.a.* to carry away; to pay; to wear out. **—ung,** *f.* carrying off, demolition; payment, liquidation.

Abtrenn—bar, **—lich** ['aptrɛnba:r, —lɪç], *adj.* separable.

Abtrenn—en ['aptrɛnən], *v.a.* to separate; to disunite; to unrip. **—ung, f.** separation.

Abtret—en ['aptre:tən], *ir.v.* I. *a.* to tread off; to resign; to transfer; to abandon. II. *n.* (*aux.* ſ.) to retire; to withdraw. **—ung,** *f.* cession; abdication.

Abtritt ['aptrɪt], *m.* (**—s,** *pl.* **-e**) withdrawal; abdication; exit.

Abtrünnig ['aptrʏnɪç], *adj.* faithless; disloyal, rebellious. **—keit,** *f.* apostasy.

Abtun ['aptu:n], *ir.v.a.* to take, put off; to abolish; to settle; to kill.

Aburteilen ['apʔʊrtaɪlən], *v.a.* & *n.* (*aux.* h.) to decide finally.

Abwandel—bar ['apvandəlba:r], *adj.* declinable. **—ung,** *f.* (*usually* **Abwandlung**) inflection; declension, conjugation.

Abwandeln ['apvandəln], *v.* I. *a.* to conjugate. II. *r.* to be inflected.

Abwärts ['apverts], *prep.* & *adv.* downward; downwards; aside.

Abwechsel—n ['apvɛksəln], *v.* I. *a.* to exchange; to vary. II. *n.* (*aux.* h.) to alternate. **—nd,** I. *p.* & *adj.* changeable; intermittent; alternate. II. *adv.* by turns, alternately. **—ung,** *f.* change; alternation. **—ungsweise,** *adv.* alternately.

Abweg ['apve:k], *m.* (**—(e)s,** *pl.* **-e**) by-way; wrong way.

Abwehr ['apve:r], *f.* defence; repulse; parry. **—mittel,** *n.* means of defence.

Abwehren ['apve:rən], *v.a.* to ward off; to avert.

Abweis—en ['apvaɪzən], *ir.v.a.* to refuse admittance to, reject, send away. **—ung,** *f.* refusal, rejection; disavowal.

Abwend—bar ['apvɛndba:r], *adj.* preventible.

Abwend—en ['apvɛndən], *reg.* & *ir. v.* I. *a.* to avert, prevent; to ward off. II. *r.* to desert. **—ig,** *adj.* alienated. **—ung,** *f.* averting.

Abwesend ['apve:zənt], *adj.* absent.

Abwesenheit ['apve:zənhaɪt], *f.* (*pl.* **—en**) absence.

Abwischen ['apvɪʃən], *v.a.* to wipe off.

Abzahl—en ['aptsa:lən], *v.a.* to pay off; to discharge. **—ung,** *f.* payment in full; instalment; **etwas auf —ung kaufen,** to buy something, paying by instalments.

Abzählen ['aptsɛ:lən], *v.a.* to count out, off; to subtract; to number, reckon.

Abzehr—en ['aptse:rən], *v.* I. *a.* to waste, consume. II. *n.* & *r.* (*aux.* ſ.) to waste away. **—end,** *p.* & *adj.* wasting, consumptive. **—ung,** *f.* emaciation.

Abzeichen ['aptsaɪçən], *n.* (**—s,** *pl.* **—**) badge; *pl.* insignia.

Abzeichn—en ['aptsaɪçnən], *v.a.* to sketch, draw. **—ung,** *f.* sketch; plan.

Abzieh—en ['aptsi:ən], *ir.v.* I. *a.* to draw, pull, take off; to dissuade; to abstract; to subtract; to decant; to sharpen. II. *b.* (*aux.* ſ.) to retire, retreat; to go off guard. **—ung,** *f.* drawing, moving off; diversion; subtraction.

Abzug ['aptsux], *m.* (**—s,** *pl.* **Abzüge**) retreat; drain; deduction; **nach — der Kosten,** expenses deducted. **—s-bogen,** *m.* (**—s,** *pl.* **—**), proof-sheet (*Print.*).

Ach! [ax], *int.* alas! ah!

Achat [a'xa:t], *m.* (**—s,** *pl.* **-e**) agate.

Achse ['aksə], *f.* (*pl.* **—n**) axle, axletree; axis.

Achsel ['aksəl], *f.* (*pl.* **—n**) shoulder. **—grube,** *f.* armpit. **—zucken,** *n.* shrug of the shoulders.

¹ **Acht** [axt], *num. adj.* (sometimes **Achte** *if the numeral stands predicatively*; **es sind ihrer acht(e))** eight; **heute über — Tage,** this day week; **halb —,** half-

past seven; der, die, das, —e, the eighth. —el, n. (—els, pl. —el) eighth part. —ens, adv. eighthly. —erlei, adv. of eight kinds. —fach, —fältig, adj. & adv. eight-fold. —jährig, adj. eight years old. —klang, (Mus.) octave. —mal, adj. eight times. —silbig, adj. octosyllabic. —zehn, num. adj. eighteen. —zehnte, num. adj. eighteenth. —zig, num. adj. eighty. —zigste, num. adj. eightieth.

² Acht [axt], f. attention, care, heed; in — nehmen, to take care of; to mind; gebt —, mark ye! —bar, adj. respectable. —barkeit, f. respectability. —sam, adj. mindful, attentive. —samkeit, f. attention; heedfulness. —los, adj. negligent, inattentive.

³ Acht [axt], f. outlawry. —(s)erklärung, f. outlawing.

Achten ['axtən], v.a. & n. to regard, to esteem; to deem; to pay attention to; dessen ungeachtet, nevertheless, regardless of this. —ung, f. attention; regard.

Ächzen ['ɛçtsən], v.n. to groan heavily.

Acker ['akər], m. —s, pl. Äcker) field, arable land; soil; acre (square measure, pl. Äcker). —bau, m. agriculture. —bestellung, f. tillage. —land, n. arable land. —vieh, n. draught cattle. —wirtschaft, f. agriculture. —zeug, n. agricultural implements.

Ackern ['akərn], v.a. to till, to plough.

Addieren [a'di:rən], v.a. to add, to sum up.

Adel ['a:dəl], m. (—s) nobility; nobleness; von —, of noble birth. —ig, adlig, adj. noble. —s=brief, m. patent of nobility. —stand, m. the nobility.

Ader ['a:dər], f. (pl. —n) vein; lode. —schlag, m. beat of the pulse.

Adler ['a:dlər], m. (—s, pl. —) eagle; —ähnlich, adj. aquiline. —horst, m. aerie.

Admiral [atmɪ'ra:l], m. (—s, pl. —e) admiral. —ität [—ɪ'tɛ:t], f. admiralty.

Adopt—ieren [adop'ti:rən], v.a. to adopt. —iv, adj. adoptive, adopted.

Adresse—e [a'drɛsə], f. (pl. —en) (see Anschrift) address.

Adressieren [adrɛ'si:rən], v.a. to address.

Advent [at'vɛnt], m. (—s) Advent.

Advokat [atvo'ka:t], m. (—en, pl. —en) barrister, advocate.

Aeroplan [a:ero'pla:n], m. (—(e)s, pl. —e) (see Flugzeug) aeroplane.

Aff—en ['ɛfən], v.a. to mock. —erei, f. chaff; mimicry. —isch, adj. apish. —in, f. (pl. —innen) she-ape.

Affe ['afə], m. (—n, pl. —n) ape, monkey. —n=artig, adj. monkeyish. —n=schwanz, m. droll fellow. —n=schande, f. very great shame.

Affig ['afɪç], adj. apish, silly, foolish.

Affizieren [afɪ'tsi:rən], v.a. to affect.

Affodill [afo'dɪl], m. (—s, pl. —e), Affodill=lilie, f. asphodel.

Agent [a'gɛnt], m. (—en, pl. —en) (see Vertreter) agent. —ur [—'tu:r], f. agency.

Agieren [a'gi:rən], v.a. & n. (aux. h.) to act.

Agio ['a:ʒɪo:], n. (—s) agio; exchange; premium.

Agrar— [a'gra:r], (in compounds) agrarian.

Agrarier [a'gra:rɪər], m. (—s, pl. —s) agrarian, agriculturist.

Agrarisch [a'gra:rɪʃ], adj. agrarian.

Ahle ['a:lə], f. (pl. —n) awl, pricker, bodkin.

Ahn [a:n], m. (—s, —en, pl. —en) grandfather, ancestor; pl. ancestors, forefathers. —e, (rare) —in, f. grandmother, ancestress. —lich, adj. ancestral. —en-reihe, f. pedigree. —frau, f. —herr, m. grandparent, ancestor. —herrlich, adj. ancestral.

Ahnd—en ['a:ndən], v.a. to revenge; sometimes = ahnen. —ung, f. resentment, requital; revenge.

Ähneln ['ɛ:nəln], v.n. to bear a likeness to.

Ahn—en ['a:nən], v.a. & n. (aux. h.) to have a presentiment of; to suspect, surmise; es —t mir nichts Gutes, I have a foreboding of evil. —ung, f. foreboding, presentiment; keine —ung haben von, to have not the slightest notion of. —ungs=los, adj. without misgiving; unsuspecting. —ungs=schwer, portentous. —ungs=voll, adj. foreboding; mistrustful.

Ähnlich ['ɛ:nlɪç], adj. similar, like, resembling; analogous to; er sieht seinem Bruder sehr —, he looks very much like his brother. —keit, f. resemblance, similarity, likeness; analogy.

Ahorn ['ahɔrn], m. (—s, pl. —e) maple.

Ähr—e ['ɛ:rə], f. (pl. —en) ear of corn.

Akadem—ie [akade'mi:], f. (pl. —ieen) (see **Hochschule**) academy; university. **—iker** [aka'demɪkər], m. (—ikers, pl. —iker) academician. **—isch**, adj. academic.

Akazie [a'ka:tsɪə], f. (pl. —en) acacia.

Akkurat [aku'ra:t], adj. (see **Genau**) accurate, exact.

Akrostich—on [a'krɔstɪçɔn], n. (—ons, pl. —a) acrostic.

Akt [akt], m. (—es, pl. —e) act; deed, document; **von einer Sache — nehmen**, to take a written note of a fact.

Akte ['aktə], f. (pl. —n) act; deed, bill, document; (pl.) public papers, reports. **—nmensch**, m. (—en, pl. —en) red-tapist.

Akt—ie ['aktsɪə], f. (pl. —ien) share, fund, stock. **—ionär** [—'ne:r], m. (—ionärs, pl. —ionäre) shareholder. **—iengesellschaft**, f. joint-stock company. **—ieninhaber**, m. shareholder.

Aktiv [ak'ti:f], adj. active; effective; actual. **—ität**, f. activity. **—handel**, m. export trade.

Aktuar [aktu'a:r], m. (pl. —e) actuary.

Akust—ik [a'kustɪk], f. acoustics. **—isch**, adj. acoustic.

Akzent [ak'tsɛnt], m. (—s, pl. —e) accent. **—uieren** [—tu'i:rən], v.a. to accentuate.

Alabaster [ala'bastər], m. (—s) alabaster. **—n**, adj. of alabaster.

Alarm [a'larm], m. (—s, pl. —e) alarm; **— blasen** or **— schlagen**, to sound an alarm, beat to arms.

Alaun [a'laun], m. (—s) alum. **—en**, adj. of alum.

Albern ['albərn], adj. & adv. silly, foolish, simple; weak-minded; absurd; **—es Zeug**, nonsense; stuff and nonsense. **—heit**, f. (pl. —heiten) silliness; absurdity; silly action.

Albumin [albu'mi:n], n. (—s) albumen.

Alexandrin—er [aleksan'dri:nər], m. (—ers, pl. —er) Alexandrine.

Algebra ['algebra:], f. algebra. **—isch** [—'bra:ɪʃ] adj. algebraical.

Alkohol ['alkohol], n. (—(e)s, pl. —e) alcohol. **—haltig**, adj. alcoholic. **—iker** [—'ho:lɪkər], m. drunkard. **—isch**, adj. alcoholic.

All [al], I. n. (—s) the universe. II. adj. (—er, —e, —es) used collectively, all, entire, whole; used distributively, every, each, any, all; **—e beide**, both of them; **—e drei Tage**, every third

day; **—e Tage**, every day; **—es**, everything; everybody; **über —es**, above all things; **er kann —es**, he can do anything, is good at everything; **—es Mögliche**, all that is possible; **—es durch einander**, higgledy-piggledy. **—e**, adv. all gone, at an end, exhausted; **ich bin ganz —e**, I am quite exhausted (coll.). **—bekannt**, adj. notorious. **—da**, **—dort**, adv. there. **—gegenwärtig**, adj. omnipresent. **—gemach**, adv. gradually. **—gemein**, adj. & adv. universal, general. **—gewaltig**, adj. omnipotent. **—hier**, adv. here. **—jährlich**, adj. annual; adv. annually. **—mächtig**, adj. omnipotent. **—mählich**, adj. & adv. by degrees, gradual. **—seitig**, adj. versatile. **—tägig**, **—täglich**, adj. daily; common; commonplace. **—tags-kleid**, n. everyday dress. **—tags-mensch**, m. commonplace fellow. **—vater**, m. father of all (God). **—weise**, adj. all-wise. **—wissend**, adj. omniscient. **—wissenheit**, f. omniscience. **—wöchentlich**, adj. & adv. weekly. **—zu**, adv. too, much too, quite too. **—zugleich**, adv. all together. **—zumal**, adv. all at once; all together.

Alle ['alə], in comp.; **—das**, all that; **bei —dem**, for all that; **trotz —dem und —dem**, for all that and all that. **—mal**, adv. always, ever; yet, still, of course; **ein für —mal**, once for all; **—mal wenn**, whenever. **—nfalls**, adv. in any case, at all events; if need be; by chance, possibly, perhaps. **—nthalben**, adv. everywhere, in all places. **—samt**, adv. altogether. **—wege**, adv. everywhere; always; quite; in every way, surely, undoubtedly. **—weile**, adv. always; just now. **—zeit**, adv. always; at all times.

Allee [a'le:], f. (pl. —n) alley, walk, avenue.

Allein [a'lain], I. indec. adj. & adv. alone, sole, single; solitary, apart, by oneself. II. adv. only, merely. III. conj. only, but. **—ig**, adj. & adv. exclusive, only, unique.

Aller ['alər], gen. pl. of **All** (in comp. with the sup. = of all; with titles = most). **—dings**, adv. to be sure, of course, by all means. **—erst**, adj. & adv. first of all. **—hand**, **—lei**, indec. adj. of all sorts and kinds, diverse, sundry.

—**liebſt**, *adj.* dearest; charming.
—**meiſt**, I. *adj.* most of all. II. *adv.*
especially, chiefly. —**nächſt**, I. *adj.*
the very next. II. *adv.* close, hard by;
immediately. —**ſeelen**, *pl.* All Souls'
(Day). —**ſeits**, *adv.* on all sides; from
all parts; altogether.

Alliieren [alľiːrən], *v.a.* to ally, unite.

Almanach ['almanax], *m.* (—**s**, *pl.* —**e**)
almanac.

Almoſen ['almoːzən], *n.* (—**s**, *pl.* —)
alms.

Aloe ['aːloːe], *f.* (*pl.* —(e)**n**) aloe; aloes.

1 **Alp** [alp], *m.* (—**es**, *pl.* —**e**) nightmare.

2 **Alp** [alp], *f.* (*pl.* —**en**) mountain; hilly
tract of country; Alps. —**in**,
—**iniſch**, *adj.* alpine.

Alphabet [alfa'beːt], *n.* (—**s**, *pl.* —**e**)
alphabet. —**iſch**, *adj.* & *adv.* alpha-
betical, alphabetically.

Alraun [al'raun], *m.* (—**es**, *pl.* —**e**)
mandrake.

Als [als], *conj. in comparisons*, than, as;
demonstratively, as, in the capacity or
character of; *in an explanatory sense*,
als (*or* **als da ſind**) denotes as, such as,
for example; *as an expletive before
relatives*, — **welche**, which; *after a
negative*, but, except, other than;
noting past time, when, as, as soon as.
—**bald**, *adv.* as soon as; forthwith, at
once, immediately. —**dann**, *adv.*
then.

Alſo ['alzoː], I. *adv.* so, thus, so much,
so far. II. *conj.* therefore, consequently.

Alt [alt], *adj.* & *adv.* (*comp.* **älter**; *sup.*
älteſt) old; ancient, antique, long-
established; stale. —**bekannt**, *adj.*
long-known. —**klug**, *adj.* knowing,
precocious. —**modiſch**, *adj.* old-
fashioned. —**väterlich**, *adj.* ancestral,
primitive, old.

Alt [alt], *m.* (—(e)**s**, *pl.* —**e**) alto,
counter-tenor. —**iſtin**, *f.* contralto
singer.

Altan [al'taːn], *m.* (—**s**, *pl.* —**e**)
balcony; gallery.

Altar [al'taːr], *m.* (—**s**, *pl.* —**e** &
Altäre) altar. —**diener**, *m.* acolyte.

Alt—**e** ['eltə], *f.* oldness (*obs.*). —**lich**,
adj. & *adv.* elderly, oldish.

Alter ['altər], *n.* (—**s**) age, old age;
antiquity; epoch, age. —**tum**, *n.*
(—**tums**, *pl.* —**tümer**) antiquity.
—**s**=**genoß**, *m.*, —**s**=**genoſſin**, *f.* person
of the same age; contemporary.

—**tums**=**kunde**, *f.*, —**tums**=**wiſſenſchaft**,
archæology.

Am [am] (=**an dem**), *see* **An**. *It forms
the superlative of the adverb.* — **beſten**,
best; — **eheſten**, soonest.

Amboß ['ambɔs], *m.* (—**ſſes**, *pl.* —**ſſe**)
anvil.

Ameiſe ['amaːzə], *f.* (*pl.* —**n**) ant,
emmet. —**n**=**haufen**, *m.* ant-hill.

Amme ['amə], *f.* (*pl.* —**n**) nurse.

Ammoniak [amoni'aːk], *n.* (—**s**) ammonia.

Amneſtie [amnɛs'tiː], *f.* (*pl.* —**n**)
amnesty.

Ampel ['ampəl], *f.* (*pl.* —**n**) hanging
lamp.

Amphibie [am'fiːbiə], *f.* (*pl.* —**n**)
amphibious animal. —**n**=**haft**, *adj.* &
adv. amphibious.

Amſel ['amzəl], *f.* (*pl.* —**n**) blackbird.

Amt [amt], *n.* (—**es**, *pl.* **Ämter**) any responsible situation, office, place, employment; administration; jurisdiction; domain, sphere of duty; place of
public business; **ein öffentliches** —
bekleiden *or* **inne haben**, to fill a public
office; **kraft meines** —**es**, by virtue of
my office. —**lich**, *adj.* & *adv.* official,
ministerial. —**los**, *adj.* & *adv.* out of
office. —**mann**, *m.* magistrate. —**s**=
bericht, *m.* official report. —**s**=**beſcheid**,
m. sentence, decree. —**s**=**bezirk**, *m.*
extent of jurisdiction. —**s**=**blatt**, *n.*
official gazette. —**s**=**bruder**, *m.* colleague. —**s**=**diener**, *m.* serjeant,
beadle, usher. —**s**=**eid**, *m.* oath of
office. —**s**=**führung**, *f.* administration.
—**s**=**gebühr**, *f.* (*usually in the pl.*) fees
due to an official. —**s**=**genoß**, *m.* colleague. —**s**=**gericht**, *n.* lower court,
police court. —**s**=**kleidung**, *f.* official
costume. —**s**=**kreis**, *m.* district. —**s**=
mäßig, *adj.* official, professional. —**s**=
richter, *m.* district-judge. —(**s**)=**ſtube**,
f. court-house. —**s**=**tag**, court-day.
—**s**=**vertreter**, *m.* deputy in office.
—**s**=**verwalter**, *m.* substitute. —**s**=
vogt, *m.* bailiff.

Amüſant [amy'zant], *adj.* & *adv.*
amusing.

Amüſieren [amy'ziːrən], *v.a.* & *refl.* to
amuse; to enjoy (*oneself*).

An [an], I. *prep.* at; at *or* to the edge
of; by, close by; against; along; to;
towards, near; near to, not far from;
as far as, up to; till; on, upon, with;
in (*very often with verbs, e.g.* **glauben**

— eine Sache); of; about; by means of; in respect to, in the way of; by reason of. *Used with dat.* 1. *when signifying rest or motion within a place (in answer to the question* wo? where?); 2. *when denoting a point of time (in answer to* wann? when?); 3. *after verbs expressive of delight, want, doubt, recognition, anger, etc.;* 4. *after such adjs. as* arm, poor; reich, rich; krant, sick; ähnlich, like; ftart, strong; fchwach, weak, etc.; 5. *in answer to* woran, on, in, of what, *etc.;* 6. *in answer to* an wem? to whom, whose? *Used with acc. signifying* 1. *progression or motion towards a place or thing (in answer to* wohin? whereto?); 2. *expressing duration of time (in answer to* bis wann? to what time, *etc.?);* 3. *after verbs of believing and remembering;* 4. *in answer to the question* an wen? an was? to whom? to what? II. *adv.* on, onward; along; up, along upward; close to, adjoining; oben —, up above; unten —, below, at the end; berg—, uphill; neben—, close by. III. *Separable prefix, meaning* at, to, on, *etc.*

Ananas ['a:nanas], *f.* pineapple.

Anarch—ie [anar'çi:], *f.* (*pl.* —ieen) anarchy. —ist ['çıst], *m.* (—iften, *pl.* —iften) anarchist.

Anatom—ie [anato:'mi:], *f.* anatomy. —iter [—'tomikər], *m.* (—iters, *pl.* —iter) anatomist. —ieren, *v.a.* to dissect. —ifch, *adj.* anatomical.

Anbahnen ['anba:nən], *v.a.* to open, break a way for.

Anbau ['anbau], *m.* (—s, *pl.* Anbauten) cultivation, culture; addition (*to a building*); outhouse. —bar, —lich, *adj.* cultivable.

Anbau—en ['anbauən], *v.a.* to cultivate; to add to by building; fich —en, to settle. —er, *m.* (—ers, *pl.* —er) cultivator; settler.

Anbefehlen ['anbəfe:lən], *ir.v.a.* to enjoin.

Anbeginn ['anbəgɪn], *m.* earliest beginning, origin.

Anbei [an'baɪ], *adv.* annexed, enclosed.

Anbelangen ['anbəlaŋən], *v.a.* to concern.

Anbet—en ['anbe:tən], *v.a.* to adore, worship, idolize. —er, *m.* (—ers, *pl.* —er) adorer, lover. —ung, *f.* adoration.

Anbetreffen ['anbətrefən], *ir.v.a.* to concern, refer to. —d, *p. & adj.* concerning, as for.

Anbiet—en ['anbi:tən], *ir.v.a.* to offer, proffer, propose; angeboten ['angə-bo:tən], *p.p. & adj.* offered. —ung, *f.* offer.

Anblid ['anblɪk], *m.* (—s) look; view; aspect; beim erften —, at first sight.

Anbliden ['anblɪkən], *v.a.* to look at, view.

Anbrennen ['anbrenən], *ir.v.* I. a. to kindle, set fire to. II. n. (aux. f.) to catch fire; to kindle.

Anbringen ['anbrɪŋən], *ir.v.a.* to bring about, in *or* on; to apply; to construct; to dispose of; Geld —, to invest money; wohl angebracht, seasonable, apt; das ift bei ihm nicht angebracht, that won't do with him.

Anbruch ['anbrux], *m.* (—(e)s, *pl.* Anbrüche) break, beginning; opening. Anbrüchig ['anbryçıç], *adj. & adv.* rotten, spoilt.

Andacht ['andaxt], *f.* (*pl.* —en) devotion. —s=los, irreverent, undevout. —s=voll, *adj.* devotional, devout.

Andächtig ['andeçtɪç], *adj. & adv.* devout.

Andauern ['andauərn], *v.n.* to continue, to last.

Andenten ['andeŋkən], *n.* (—s, *pl.* —) remembrance; keepsake; memory.

Ander ['andər], *adj.* other, else, different; second, next; *used substantively or as pron.* anyone else, anything else, someone else; unter —en, among other things; das ift etwas —es, that alters the case. —lei, *indec. adj.* of another kind. —n=falls, *adv.* otherwise, else, in the contrary case. —n=teils, *adv.* on the other hand. —feits, *adv.* on the other side. —wärts, *adv.* elsewhere. —weit, *adv.* in another place; at another time; otherwise. —weitig, *adj.* from another quarter; done in another way *or* at another time; further, furthermore.

Ander—n ['andərn], *v.a.* to alter, change; fich —n, to alter, vary, reform. —bar, *adj. & adv.* alterable. —ung, *f.* change, alteration, variation.

Anders ['andərs], *adv.* otherwise; else; differently; under other circumstances. —wo, *adv.* elsewhere.

Anderthalb ['andəthalp], *adj.* one and a half; — Pfund, a pound and a half.

Andeut—en ['andɔytən], *v.a.* to signify, point out, indicate; to intimate. **—ung,** *f.* intimation; signification; suggestion.

Andrang ['andraŋ], *m.* (**—es**) pressure; congestion (*Med.*); crowd, press.

Andring—en ['andrɪŋən], *ir.v.a.* & *n.* (*aux.* ſ.) to press on *or* against; to push *or* urge forward; to rush upon (**gegen**); to charge (*Mil.*). **—end,** *p.* & *adj.* urgent, pressing; pathetic.

Aneignen ['an?aɪgnən], *v.r.* to appropriate; to adapt; to assimilate.

Aneinander [an?aɪ'nandər], *adv.* together; to *or* against one another.

Anekdote [anɛk'do:tə], *f.* (*pl.* **—n**) anecdote.

Anerbiet—en ['an?ɛrbi:tən], *ir.v.a.* to offer. **—ung,** *f.* offer, proffer.

Anerkenn—en ['an?ɛrkɛnən], *ir.v.a.* to recognize, appreciate; to acknowledge. **—tnis,** *f.* & *n.* acknowledgment; clear perception (*of a truth, etc.*). **—ung,** *f.* acknowledgment; recognition.

Anfachen ['anfaxən], *v.a.* to blow into a flame; to kindle.

Anfahr—en ['anfa:rən], *ir.v.* I. *n.* (*aux.* ſ.) to drive up to; to arrive; to put in (*at a port*). II. *a.* to carry *or* bring near, up *or* to; to land; to address angrily, rudely. **—t,** *f.* (*pl.* **—ten**) approach, arrival; place of arrival.

Anfall ['anfal], *m.* (**—s,** *pl.* **Anfälle**) onset, attack, assault; fit; fall against, on.

Anfallen ['anfalən], *ir.v.a.* to fall on, assail.

Anfang ['anfaŋ], *m.* (**—s,** *pl.* **Anfänge**) commencement; beginning. **—s,** *adv.* in the beginning.

Anfangen ['anfaŋnə], *ir.v.* I. *a.* to begin, commence; to set about, take up. II. *n.* (*aux.* ħ.) to begin, originate.

Anfäng—er ['anfɛŋər], *m.* (**—ers,** *pl.* **—er**), **—erin,** *f.* beginner, tyro.

Anfassen ['anfasən], *v.a.* to take hold of, to seize.

Anfecht—en ['anfɛçtən], *ir.v.a.* to attack, to assail; to trouble; to contest; **was ficht dich an?** what is the matter with you? **—ung,** *f.* attack; opposition; vexation.

Anfertig—en ['anfɛrtɪçən], *v.a.* to make, manufacture. **—ung,** *f.* making, preparation.

Anfleh—en ['anfle:ən], *v.a.* to implore. **—ung,** *f.* supplication.

Anforder—(e)n ['anfɔrdər(ə)n], *v.a.* to demand as due, to claim. **—ung,** *f.* claim, demand; pretension.

Anfrage ['anfra:gə], *f.* (*pl.* **—n**) enquiry; demand.

Anfragen ['anfra:gən], *reg.* (& *ir.*) *v.n.* (*aux.* ħ.) to ask in passing.

Anfügen ['anfy:gən], *v.a.* to join to; to add to.

Anführ—en ['anfy:rən], *v.a.* to lead on; to bring up to *or* near; to lead; to guide; to quote. **—er,** *m.* (**—ers,** *pl.* **—er**) leader, general. **—ung,** *f.* command; quotation; allegation; deception; training. **—ungs=zeichen,** *n.* quotation mark, inverted comma.

Anfüllen ['anfylən], *v.a.* to fill; **neu —,** to replenish.

Angabe ['anga:bə], *f.* (*pl.* **—n**) declaration; account.

Angeb—en ['ange:bən], *ir.v.* I. *a.* to make a statement, give an account of; to mention; to estimate; to denounce; to instance; to give in part payment; to suggest; to sketch, plan; **den Ton —en,** to lead the fashion; **Gründe —en,** to specify reasons; **Waren —en,** to enter goods at the custom-house. II. *n.* (*aux.* ħ.) to deal first (*at cards*); to follow suit. **—er,** *m.* (**—ers,** *pl.* **—er**) declarer; informer; tale-bearer; author. **—lich,** *adj.* & *adv.* alleged; pretended, nominal.

Angeboren ['angəbo:rən], *adj.* inborn, innate.

Angebot ['angəbo:t], *n.* (**—es,** *pl.* **—e**) (first) offer; first bid; **— und Nachfrage,** supply and demand.

Angehen ['ange:hən], *ir.v.* I. *a.* to approach; to solicit; to concern, be related to; **was geht's mich an?** what's that to me? II. *n.* (*aux.* ſ.) to begin, commence; to grow; to catch fire; to be practicable; to be endurable. **—d,** I. *adj.* beginning. II. *prep.* concerning, as for; **mich —d,** as for me. **—ds,** *adv.* at first; in the beginning.

Angehör—en ['angəhø:rən], *v.a.* (*aux.*) ſ.) to belong to, appertain to. **—ig,** *adj.* & *adv.* belonging to; related to; **feine —igen,** *pl.* his relations.

Angeklagt—e(r) ['angəkla:ktə(r)], *m.* (**—en,** *pl.* **—en**) person accused, defendant.

Angel ['aŋəl], *m.* (**—s,** *pl.* **—n**) hinge; fishing-rod; pivot. **—förmig,** *adj.* barbed, hooked. **—hafen,** *m.* fishing-

hook. —**ſchnur**, *f.* fishing-line.
—**zeug**, *n.* fishing-tackle.

Angelegen ['angələ:gən], *p.p. & adj.*
adjacent; important; **ſich** (*dat.*) — **ſein
laſſen**, to interest oneself in. —**heit**,
f. (*pl.* —**heiten**) concern, affair, business; transaction. —**t=lich**, *adj. &
adv.* pressing, urgent.

Angeln ['aŋəln], *v.a.* to angle, to fish
(**nach**, for).

Angeloben ['angəlo:bən], *v.a.* to vow.

Angemeſſen ['angəmɛsən], *p.p. of
anmeſſen & adj.* adapted to, in keeping
with; proper; suitable, conformable.
—**heit**, *f.* propriety; suitableness,
fitness.

Angenehm ['angəne:m], *adj. & adv.*
acceptable, agreeable, pleasing.

Anger ['aŋər], *m.* (—**s**, *pl.* —) grassy
place, green.

Angeſehen ['angəze:n], *p.p. of anſehen
& adj.* respected; esteemed; distinguished.

Angeſeſſen ['angəzɛsən], *adj.* settled;
resident.

Angeſicht ['angəzɪçt], *n.* (—**s**, *pl.* —**er**)
face; countenance. —**s**, *prep.* (*gen.*)
in view of, considering; immediately
on (*receiving, seeing, etc.*).

Angetan ['angəta:n], *p.p. & adj.* clad,
attired.

Angewöhn—en ['angəvø:nən], *v.a.*
(**einem etwas**) to accustom, inure to.
—**ung**, *f.* accustoming or inuring to.

Angewohnheit ['angəvo:nhaɪt], *f.* (*pl.*
—**en**) custom, use, habit; **aus** —,
from habit.

Anglotzen ['anglotsən], *v.a.* to stare,
glare at.

Angreifbar ['angraɪfba:r], *adj.* assailable; open to criticism.

Angreif—en ['angraɪfən], *ir.v.* I. *a.* to
handle, touch; to feel; to undertake;
to attack; to exhaust. II. *r.* to exert
oneself. —**end**, *adj.* offensive, aggressive; tiring, exhausting. —**er**, *m.*
(—**ers**, *pl.* —**er**) aggressor, assailant.
—**lich**, *adj.* touchable; tangible;
assailable.

Angrenzen ['angrɛntsən], *v.a.* (*aux.* ſ.)
to border upon, adjoin. —**d**, *p. & adj.*
adjacent.

Angriff ['angrɪf], *m.* (—**s**, *pl.* —**e**)
attack, assault; handling; handle;
etwas in — **nehmen**, to undertake
something.

Angſt [aŋst], *f.* (*pl.* **Angſte**), anguish;
anxiety, fear. —**geſchrei**, *n.* cry of
terror or anguish. —**voll**, *adj.* fearful;
painful. —**ſchweiß**, *m.* cold sweat.

Angſt—igen ['ɛŋstɪgən], *v.a.* to alarm,
distress; to worry; **ſich** —**igen** (**über
eine Sache**), to fret, be uneasy or
alarmed (about something). —**lich**,
adj. & adv. anxious; nervous, timid;
scrupulous. —**lichkeit**, *f.* anxiety;
nervousness.

Anhaben ['anha:bən], *ir.v.a.* to have
or be dressed in; **einem etwas** —,
to harm one.

Anhalt ['anhalt], *m.* (—**es**, *pl.* —**e**)
stopping, pause, stay; hold, support.
—**ſam**, *adj.* persevering; uninterrupted. —**ſamkeit**, *f.* perseverance.
—**(e)punkt**, *m.* stopping-place; station; important point or fact.

Anhalt—en ['anhaltən], I. *ir.v.a.* to
check, stop, pull up; to seize. II.
ir.v.n. (*aux.* h.) to stop, halt, draw up;
to continue, persevere; to persist in;
—**en um**, to sue for. III. *subst.n.*
stopping; stoppage; clinging to; solicitation, *etc.* —**end**, *p. & adj.* continuous, lasting; persevering.

Anhang ['anhaŋ], *m.* (—**es**, *pl.* **An=
hänge**) appendix; appendage; postscript; followers, party.

Anhangen ['anhaŋən], *ir.v.n.* (*aux.* ſ.)
to hang on or upon; to adhere to;
(*aux.* h.) to stick to; to hold by.

Anhäng—en ['anhɛŋən], *v.a.* to hang
on or fasten to; to attach, append,
affix; to add; to bestow. —**er**, *m.*
(—**ers**, *pl.* —**er**) partisan, adherent;
hanger-on. —**ig**, *adj. & adv.* adherent;
cleaving to; importunate. —**lich**, *adj.*
attached to; faithful. —**lichkeit**, *f.*
adherence; attachment, constancy.

Anhauchen ['anhauxən], *v.a.* to breathe
upon.

Anhäufen ['anhɔyfən], *v.a.* to heap
up; to accumulate.

Anheb—en ['anhe:bən], *ir.v.* I. *a.* to
heave up or towards; to commence.
II. *n.* (*aux.* h.) to begin. —**er**, *m.*
(—**ers**, *pl.* —**er**) beginner, author,
instigator.

Anheim [an'haɪm], *adv.* at home; —
fallen, to devolve on; — **geben**,
— **ſtellen**, to place in the keeping of.

Anhetz—en ['anhɛtsən], *v.a.* to incite,
stimulate. —**er**, *m.* (—**ers**, *pl.* —**er**),
—**erin**, *f.* (*pl.* —**erinnen**) inciter,
instigator.

Anhör—en ['anhøːrən], *v.a.* to listen to. **—ung,** *f.* audience, hearing.

Anilin [ani'liːn], *n.* (**—s**) aniline.

Ankauf ['ankauf], *m.* (**—s,** *pl.* **Ankäufe**) purchase; buying.

Ankaufen ['ankaufən], *v.a.* to purchase, buy up.

Anker ['ankər], *m.* (**—s,** *pl.* **—**) anchor; **den** *or* **die — lichten,** to weigh anchor; **vor — liegen,** to ride at anchor.

Ankern ['ankərn], *v.a. & n.* to anchor.

Anketten ['ankɛtən], *v.a.* to chain.

Anklag—bar ['ankla:kbaːr], *adj. & adv.* indictable. **—e,** *f.* (*pl.* **—en**) accusation. **—ebank,** *f.* prisoner's bench, dock.

Anklagen ['ankla:gən], *v.a.* to accuse.

Ankläger ['ankle:gər], *m.* (**—s,** *pl.* **—**), **—in,** *f.* (*pl.* **—innen**) accuser; plaintiff.

Anklammern ['anklamərn], *v.r.* **sich an eine Sache —,** to cling to a thing.

Anklang ['anklaŋ], *m.* (**—s,** *pl.* **Anklänge**) accord, harmony; approbation.

Ankleben ['ankle:bən], *v.* I. *n.* to stick to. II. *a.* to glue *or* paste on, up, *or* to. **—d,** *p. & adj.* adhesive.

Ankleid—en ['anklaɪdən], *v.* I. *a.* to attire. II. *r.* to dress (oneself). **—ezimmer,** *n.* dressing-room.

Anklingeln ['anklɪŋəln], *v.n.* to ring the bell; **jemand —,** to ring up someone on the telephone.

Anklingen ['anklɪŋən], *ir.v.* I. *n.* (*aux.* **h.**) to accord in sound. II. *a.* to clink (*glasses*).

Anklopfen ['anklɔpfən], *v.n.* to knock at.

Anknüpfen ['anknypfən], *v.a.* to tie; to begin; **ein Gespräch wieder —,** to resume a conversation.

Ankommen ['ankɔmən], *ir.v.* I. *a.* to befall, come upon. II. *n.* (*aux.* **ſ.**) to approach; to arrive; to depend on; to concern.

Ankömm—ling ['ankœmlɪŋ], *m.* (**—lings,** *pl.* **—linge**) new-comer.

Ankünd—en ['ankyndən], **—igen** ['ankyndɪgən], *v.a.* to announce. **—iger,** *m.* (**—igers,** *pl.* **—iger**) announcer. **—igung,** *f.* proclamation.

Ankunft ['ankʊnft], *f.* arrival.

Anlächeln ['anlɛçəln], *v.a.* to smile at.

Anlage ['anla:gə], *f.* (*pl.* **—n**) laying out; plan; pleasure-ground, park; talent; **er hat — zur Musik,** he has a talent for music.

Anlangen ['anlaŋən], *v.* I. *n.* (*aux.* **ſ.**) to arrive at, reach. II. *a.* to concern, relate to. **—d,** *p. used as prep.* concerning.

Anlaß ['anlas], *m.* (**—ſſes,** *pl.* **Anläſſe**) cause, occasion, motive.

Anläßlich ['anlɛslɪç], *prep.* (*gen.*) à propos of; on the occasion of.

Anlaſſen ['anlasən], *ir.v.* I. *a.* to leave on; to let loose. II. *r.* to appear; to promise.

Anlauf ['anlauf], *m.* (**—(e)s,** *pl.* **Anläufe**) start, run; rise; attack.

Anlaufen ['anlaufən], *ir.v.n.* (*aux.* **ſ.**) to rush against; to rise, swell.

Anleg—en ['anle:gən], I. *v.a.* to apply; to lay out, plan; to sketch; **Geld —,** to invest money. II. *r.* to lean against; to adhere to. **—ung,** *f.* planning; investment.

Anlehnen ['anle:nən], *v.a. & r.* to lean against.

Anleihe ['anlaɪə], *f.* (*pl.* **—n**) loan.

Anleit—en ['anlaɪtən], *v.a.* to guide to; to train. **—ung,** *f.* guidance; introduction.

Anliegen ['anli:gən], I. *ir.v.n.* to lie close to; to fit well; to concern; **einem —,** to urge *or* solicit a person. II. *subst.n.* concern.

Anlock—en ['anlɔkən], *v.a.* to allure, entice. **—end,** *p. & adj.* attractive, alluring. **—ung,** *f.* enticement.

Anmarſch ['anmarʃ], *m.* (**—es,** *pl.* **Anmärſche**) advance (*of an army*).

Anmaß—en ['anma:sən], *v.r.* to pretend to; to presume. **—end,** *p. & adj.* arrogant. **—lich,** *adj. & adv.* presumptive. **—ung,** *f.* presumption; arrogance.

Anmelden ['anmɛldən], *v.a.* to announce; to report; **ſich — laſſen,** to send in one's name.

Anmerk—en ['anmɛrkən], *v.a.* to notice; to note. **—er,** *m.* (**—ers,** *pl.* **—er**) observer; annotator. **—ung,** *f.* remark; note.

Anmeſſen ['anmɛsən], *ir.v.a.* to measure, take the measure for. **angemeſſen,** *p.p. & adj.* suitable, proper.

Anmut ['anmuːt], *f.* charm, grace. **—ig,** *adj.* pleasant; graceful; gracious.

Annäher—n ['anne:ərn], *v.* I. *a.* to approximate. II. *r.* to approach. III. *n.* (*aux.* **ſ.**) to approach, draw near. **—ung,** *f.* approximation; approach.

Annahme ['anna:mə], f. (pl. —n) taking; assumption.

Annalen [a'na:lən], pl. annals.

Annehmbar ['anne:mba:r], adj. acceptable, admissible.

Annehm—**en** ['anne:mən], ir.v.a. to take; to close with; to admit; to employ; to suppose; to undertake; **Vernunft** —**en**, to listen to reason; **sich einer Sache** —**en**, to interest oneself in a thing. —**er**, m. (—**ers**, pl. —**er**) accepter. —**lich**, adj. & adv. acceptable; agreeable. —**lichkeit**, f. acceptableness.

Anonym [ano'ni:m], adj. & adv. anonymous.

Anordn—**en** ['an'ɔrdnən], v.a. to order; to regulate. —**er**, m. (—**ers**, pl. —**er**) arranger; director. —**ung**, f. arrangement; regulation.

Anpacken ['anpakən], v.a. to grasp; to attack.

Anpass—**en** ['anpasən], v. I. n. (aux. f.) to fit, suit. II. a. to adapt. —**d**, p. & adj. fit, suitable to.

Anprall ['anpral], m. (—**s**) impact; shock.

Anputz ['anputs], m. (—**es**) dress, finery. —**en**, v.a. to dress out, bedizen.

Anrechnen ['anrɛçnən], v.a. to reckon; **einem etwas** —, to charge something to someone; **hoch** —, to value greatly.

Anrede ['anre:də], f. (pl. —n) address.

Anreden ['anre:dən], v.a. to speak to.

Anreg—**en** ['anre:gən], v.a. to stir up; to incite. —**end**, stimulating, interesting. —**ung**, f. stimulation; hint.

Anreiz—**en** ['anraitsən], v.a. to incite, induce (**zu**, to). —**end**, p. & adv. attractive. —**ung**, f. instigation; incentive.

Anricht—**en** ['anrıçtən], v.a. to prepare; to produce; to serve up (a meal). —**ung**, f. preparation, etc.

Anritt ['anrıt], m. (—**es**) cavalry charge.

Anrücken ['anrykən], v. I. n. (aux. f.) to approach; to advance. II. a. to move or bring near to.

Anruf ['anru:f], m. (—**s**) appeal; summons.

Anruf—**en** ['anru:fən], ir.v.a. to call to; to challenge; to appeal to. —**er**, m. (—**ers**, pl. —**er**) appellant. —**ung**, f. appeal; invocation. —**ungs-gericht**, n. court of appeal.

Anrühren ['anry:rən], v.a. to touch; to touch upon.

Ans [ans], abbr. of **an das**.

Ansag—**en** ['anza:gən], v.a. to announce, notify; to summon. —**ung**, f. notification.

Ansammeln ['anzaməln], v.a. to collect, accumulate.

Ansammlung ['anzamluŋ], f. accumulation.

Ansässig ['anzɛsıç], adj. settled in a place, domiciled.

Ansatz ['anzats], m. (—**es**, pl. **Ansätze**) putting to or upon; deposit, crust; onset; assessment, tax.

Anschaff—**en** ['anʃafən], v.a. to provide; to procure; to furnish with. —**er**, m. (—**ers**, pl. —**er**) provider; remitter. —**ung**, f. procuring, etc.; provision.

Anschau—**en** ['anʃauən], I. v.a. to look at. II. subst.n. aspect. —**lich**, adj. & adv. intuitive. —**ung**, f. view; perception. —**ungs-begriff**, m. intuitive idea.

Anschein ['anʃain], m. (—**s**) appearance; **sich den** — **geben**, to assume the appearance.

Anschicken ['anʃıkən], v.r. to get ready; **sich zu etwas** —, to prepare for.

Anschlag ['anʃla:k], m. (—**s**, pl. **Anschläge**) stroke; striking (of a clock); placard, poster.

Anschlagen ['anʃla:gən], ir.v.a. to strike against; to estimate, value; **der Hund schlägt an**, the dog barks.

Anschließen ['anʃli:sən], ir.v. I. a. to annex, enclose. II. r. to join, attach oneself to.

Anschluß ['anʃlus], m. (—**sses**, pl. **Anschlüsse**) joining, addition; connection (Railw.). —**bahn**, f. branch line.

Anschmiegen ['anʃmi:gən], v. I. a. to bend or press to; to adapt. II. r. to cling to; to conform to.

Anschnallen ['anʃnalən], v.a. to buckle on.

Anschreiben ['anʃraibən], ir.v.a. to write on; to note; to enter, charge to.

Anschreien ['anʃraiən], ir.v.a. to hail; to talk angrily at.

Anschrift ['anʃrıft], f. (pl. —en) address.

Anschüren ['anʃy:rən], v.a. to stir up; to excite.

Anschwärzen ['anʃvɛrtsən], v.a. to blacken; (fig.) to slander, backbite.

Anschwellen ['anʃvɛlən], reg. & ir. v.a.

& n. (aux. f.) to swell. —d, p. adj. &
adv. crescendo (Mus.).

Anseh—en ['anze:ən], I. ir.v.a. to look
at; to see; to regard; to respect. II.
subst.n. aspect; authority, consequence; respect. —n=lich, adj. & adv.
important; stately; eminent.

Ansetzen ['anzɛtsən], v.a. to join; to
apply; die Feder —, to put pen to
paper.

Ansicht ['anziçt], f. (pl. —en) sight,
prospect; opinion. —s=postkarte, f.
picture postcard.

Ansied—eln ['anzi:dəln], v. I. a. to
settle, colonize. II. r. to settle. —ler,
m. (—lers, pl. —ler) settler, colonist.

Anspannen ['anʃpanən], v.a. to yoke
to; to stretch.

Anspiel—en ['anʃpi:lən], v.n. (aux. h.)
to begin to play; to allude to. —ung,
f. allusion (auf eine S., to a thing).

Anspornen ['anʃpornən], v.a. to spur;
to incite.

Ansprache ['anʃpra:xə], f. (pl. —n)
address.

Ansprechen ['anʃprɛçən], ir.v. I. n. (aux.
h.) to sound, emit a sound. II. a. to
address; to appeal to; to claim. —d,
part. prepossessing; plausible.

Ansprengen ['anʃprɛŋən], v. I. a. to
besprinkle. II. n. (aux. f.) to gallop
up or on.

Anspritzen ['anʃpritsən], v.a. to besprinkle.

Anspruch ['anʃprux], m. (—s, pl.
Ansprüche) claim, title, pretension.
— haben auf, to be entitled to. —s=
los, adj. & adv. unassuming, modest.
—s=losigkeit, f. modesty. —s=voll,
adj. presumptuous.

Anstalt ['anʃtalt], f. (pl. —en) preparation, arrangement; institution; school.

Anstand ['anʃtant], m. (—es, pl. An-
stände) delay, pause; demeanour; de-
corum; grace; — nehmen, to hesitate,
doubt, pause; ohne —, unhesitatingly.
— s=besuch, m. (—es, pl. —e), formal
call. —s=gefühl, n. tact. —s=halber,
adv. for decency's sake. —s=los,
adj. unhesitating.

Anständig ['anʃtɛndiç], adj. & adv.
proper, decorous. —keit, f. (pl.
—keiten) propriety.

Anstarren ['anʃtarən], v.a. to stare at.

Anstatt [an'ʃtat], prep. (gen.) instead
of, in the place of.

Ansteck—en ['anʃtɛkən], v.a. to stick

on; to infect, taint. —end, p. &
adj. contagious; infectious. —ung, f.
kindling; infection; contagion.

Ansteigen ['anʃtaigən], ir.v.n. (aux. f.)
to mount, ascend.

Anstell—en ['anʃtɛlən], v. I. a. to place,
to post; to appoint, employ; to arrange. II. r. to behave; to feign. —er,
m. (—ers, pl. —er) employer; instigator. —ig, adj. & adv. handy, able,
adroit. —ung, f. act of appointing, etc.

Anstift—en ['anʃtiftən], v. I. a. to set
on foot; to plot. II. subst.n. (—ens),
—ung, f. instigation. —er, m. (—ers,
pl. —er) instigator.

Anstimm—en ['anʃtimən], v.a. to strike
up; to tune (fiddle). —ung, f. intona-
tion; tuning.

Anstoß ['anʃto:s], m. (—es, pl. Anstöße)
striking against, shock; impulse;
scandal, offence.

Anstoß—en ['anʃto:sən], ir.v. I. a. to
strike, push, knock against; to clink
(glasses); to give offence. II. n. (aux.
h.) to run, dash against; to border on.
—end, p. & adj. contiguous, adjoining.

Anstößig ['anʃto:siç], adj. & adv. offensive, shocking.

Anstreng—en ['anʃtrɛŋən], v. I. a. to
strain; to stretch; —end für die
Augen, trying to the eyes. II. r. to
exert oneself. —ung, f. exertion, effort.

Anstrich ['anʃtriç], m. (— s, pl. —e)
coat of paint; colour.

Anströmen ['anʃtrø:mən], v.n. (aux. f.)
to flow towards; to crowd towards.

Ansturm ['anʃturm], m. (—s, pl.
Anstürme) attack, charge, assault.

Anstürmen ['anʃtyrmən], v.n. (aux. f.)
to storm, assail.

Ansturz ['anʃturts], m. (—es, pl.
Anstürze) violent onset.

Anstürzen ['anʃtyrtsən], v. I. a. to
throw up against. II. n. (aux. f.) to
rush against.

Antasten ['antastən], v.a. to touch; to
attack.

Anteil ['antail], m. (—s, pl. —e) portion; sympathy, interest; — nehmen
an (dat.), to sympathize with. —los,
adj. & adv. unsympathetic. —mäßig,
adj. & adv. proportionate.

Antenne [an'tɛnə], f. (pl. —n) aerial,
antenna (Radio). —n=abstimmittel, n.
aerial-tuner. —n=anlage, f. aerial-
plant. —n=kreis, m. aerial-circuit,
—n=mast, m. antenna-pole. —n=

ſchalter, *m.* aerial-switch. —n=
ſchwingung, *f.* aerial oscillation.

Anti—pathie [antipa'ti:], *f.* (*pl.* —pa=
thieen) antipathy.

Antiq—uar [anti'kva:r], *m.* (—uars,
pl. —uare) antiquary; dealer in
antiques.

Antitheſe [anti'te:sə], *f.* (*pl.* —n)
antithesis.

Antlitz ['antlɪts], *n.* (—es, *pl.* —e)
countenance; face.

Antrag ['antra:k], *m.* (—s, *pl.* Anträge)
offer; proposition. —ſteller, *m.* mover
(*of a resolution*).

Antragen ['antra:gən], *ir.v.a.* to carry,
bring near to, up to; to propose, offer.

Antrauen ['antrauən], *v.a.* to unite in
marriage.

Antreffen ['antrɛfən], *ir.v.* I. *a.* to meet;
to concern. II. *n.* to strike against.

Antreiben ['antraibən], *ir.v.a.* to drive,
push on; to urge on, incite.

Antreten ['antre:tən], *ir.v.* I. *a.* to tread
on; to enter upon; to begin. II. *n.*
(*aux.* ſ.) to begin; to fall in (*Mil.*);
angetreten! fall in!

Antrieb ['antri:p], *m.* (—s, *pl.* —e)
impulse.

Antritt ['antrɪt], *m.* (—s, *pl.* —e)
entrance on; start; commencement.

Antun ['antu:n], *ir.v.a.* to put on; to
inflict something on someone.

Antwort ['antvɔrt], *f.* (*pl.* —en)
answer, reply.

Antworten ['antvɔrtən], *v.a. & n.* to
answer.

Anvertrau—en ['anfɛrtrauən], *v.a.* to
confide, entrust to. —t, *p.p. & adj.*
entrusted to.

Anverwandt ['anfɛrvant], *adj.* related,
akin.

Anwalt ['anvalt], *m.* (—es, *pl.* —e, *also*
Anwälte) lawyer, solicitor. —ſchaft,
f. agency, attorneyship.

Anwand—eln ['anvandəln], *v.* I. *n.*
(*aux.* ſ.) to approach slowly. II. *a.*
imp. to befall; to attack (*of illness,*
etc.). —lung, *f.* seizure; fit, paroxysm.

Anwart—en ['anvartən], *v.n.* (*aux.* h.)
(*with* auf eine S.) to wait for. —ſchaft,
f. reversion.

Anweiſ—en ['anvaizən], *ir.v.a.* to assign, allot; to show; to instruct; to
admonish. —er, *m.* (—ers, *pl.* —er)
instructor; adviser. —ung, *f.* assignment; injunction; cheque; bill of
exchange; advice; method, course.

Anwendbar ['anventba:r], *adj. & adv.*
applicable; practicable; available.
—keit, *f.* applicability; availability.

Anwend—en ['anvendən], *reg. & ir.v.a.*
to employ, use, make use of. —ung, *f.*
application; practice; employment.

Anweſen—d ['anve:zond], *p. & adj.*
present. —heit, *f.* presence.

Anwuchs ['anvʊks], *m.* (—(ſ)es, *pl.*
Anwüchſe) growth; increase.

Anzahl ['antsa:l], *f.* number, quantity.

Anzeichnen ['antsaiçnən], *v.a.* to mark,
note.

Anzeige ['antsaigə], *f.* (*pl.* —n) notice,
intimation; advertisement; indication.
—blatt, *n.* advertisement journal.
—brief, *m.* circular.

Anzeig—en ['antsaigən], *v.a.* to announce, to notify; to advertise; to
point out; to indicate. angezeigt, *p.p.*
& adj. advisable, necessary. —er, *m.*
(—ers, *pl.* —er) advertiser; informer.

Anzieh—en ['antsi:ən], *ir.v.* I. *a.* to
draw tight; put on clothes, dress; to
attract; to quote, cite. II. *n.* (*aux.* h.)
to draw; to hold fast; to take effect;
(*aux.* ſ.) to draw near, to approach.
—end, *p. & adj.* attractive; interesting. —ung, *f.* attraction. —ungs=
kraft, *f.* force of attraction. —ungs=
punkt, *m.* centre of attraction.

Anzug ['antsu:k], *m.* (—s, *pl.* Anzüge)
approach; dressing; clothes; accoutre-
ments. der Winter iſt im —, winter
is approaching.

Anzüglich ['antsy:klɪç], *adj. & adv.*
severe; offensive. —keit, *f.* sarcasm,
invective; offensiveness.

Anzünd—en ['antsyndən], *v.a.* to
kindle, ignite. —er, *m.* (—ers, *pl.*
—er) incendiary; lighter. —ung, *f.*
ignition.

Apfel ['apfəl], *m.* (—s, *pl.* Äpfel) *n.*
apple. —garten, *m.* orchard. —torte,
f. apple tart. —wein, *m.* cider.

Apfelſine [apfəl'zi:nə], *f.* (*pl.* —n)
orange.

Apoſtel [a'pɔstəl], *m.* (—s, *pl.* —)
apostle.

Apoſtoliſch [apɔs'to:lɪʃ], *adj. & adv.*
apostolic.

Apothek—e [apo'te:kə], *f.* (*pl.* —en)
chemist's shop. —er, *m.* (—ers, *pl.*
—er) chemist, apothecary.

Apparat [apa'ra:t], *m.* (—s, *pl.* —e)
apparatus.

Appetit [ape'ti:t], *m.* (—s) appetite.

—lich, adj. dainty; appetizing. —los, adj. devoid of appetite.

Aprikose [apri'ko:zə], f. (pl. —n) apricot.

April [a'prɪl], m. (—s) April.

Arbeit ['arbaɪt], f. (pl. —en) work, labour, toil. —sam, adj. & adv. laborious, industrious. —samkeit, f. industry, diligence. —s=scheu, I. adj. idle, lazy. II. f. laziness. —s= fähig, adj. able-bodied.

Arbeit—en ['arbaɪtən], v. I. a. to work. II. n. (aux. h.) to toil, labour. —er, m. (—ers, pl. —er), —erin, f. (—erinnen) worker. —erschaft, f. working class. —erverein, m. workmen's union.

Archäo—log [arçɛ:o'lo:k], m. (—logen, pl. —logen) archæologist. —logisch, adj. archæological.

Arche ['arçə], f. (pl. —n) ark.

Archi—[arçi] (in comp.)—tekt [—'tɛkt], m. (—tekten, pl. —tekten) architect. —tektur [—tɛk'tu:r], f. (pl. —tekturen) architecture.

Archiv [ar'çi:f], n. (—es, pl. —e) archives. —ar [arçi'va:r], m. (—ars, pl. —are) keeper of the archives.

Arg [ark], adj. & adv. (ärger, ärgst) bad, wicked; hard, sad. —heit, f. wickedness, malice. —list, f. craftiness, deceit. —listig, adj. & adv. cunning, crafty, deceitful. —los, adj. & adv. innocent, guileless. —losigkeit, f. harmlessness; guilelessness. —s= wohn, m. (no pl.) mistrust, suspicion. —wöhnisch, adj. & adv. suspicious.

Ärger ['ɛrgər], m. (—s) vexation; anger. —lich, adj. & adv. annoying; easily annoyed; vexed.

Ärger—n ['ɛrgərn], v.a. to annoy; to offend. —nis, n. (—nisses, pl. —nisse) scandal; offence.

Arie ['a:rɪə], f. (pl. —n) tune, air, song.

Aristokrat [arɪsto'kra:t], m. (—en, pl. —en) aristocrat. —isch, adj. aristocratic.

Arithmet—ik [arɪtme'ti:k], f. arithmetic. —iker [—'me:tɪkər], m. (—ikers, pl. —iker) arithmetician. —isch [—'me:tɪʃ], adj. & adv. arithmetical.

Arktisch ['arktɪʃ], adj. & adv. arctic.

Arm [arm] (ärmer, ärmst), adj. & adv. poor. —selig, adj. & adv. poor; wretched. —seligkeit, f. wretchedness, misery; paltriness. —ut, f. indigence, poverty. —en=anstalt, f. almshouse. —en=haus, n. almshouse, poor-house. —en=kasse, f. poor-box. —en=pflege, f. charity organization.

Arm [arm], m. (—es, pl. —e) arm. —band, n. bracelet. —höhle, f. armpit. —leuchter, m. chandelier. —los, adj. without arms.

Armee [ar'me:], f. (pl. —en) army.

Ärmel ['ɛrməl], m. (—s, pl. —) sleeve.

Ärm—lich ['ɛrmlɪç], adj. & adv. poor, miserable. —lichkeit, f. poverty, scantiness.

Arrest [a'rɛst], m. (—es, pl. —e) arrest.

Arretieren [are'ti:rən], v.a. (see festnehmen, verhaften) to arrest.

Arsenik [ar'ze:nɪk], n. (—s) arsenic.

Art [a:rt], f. (pl. —en) kind, species, sort; method, way. —ig, adj. good, well-behaved; civil, kind; nice. Suffix: -like, resembling (as gut—ig, goodnatured; bös—ig, malicious). —igkeit, f. good behaviour; politeness.

Artikel [ar'tikəl], m. (—s, pl. —) article.

Artiller—ie [artɪlə'ri:], f. artillery. —ist [—'rɪst], m. (—isten, pl. —isten) artilleryman.

Artischocke [arti'ʃɔkə], f. (pl. —n) artichoke.

Arznei [arts'naɪ], f. (pl. —en) medicine, physic. —lich, adj. & adv. medicinal.

Arzt [a:rtst], m. (—es, pl. Ärzte) doctor.

As, Aß [as], n. (—sses, pl. —sse) ace.

Asbest [as'bɛst], m. (—(e)s, pl.—e) asbestos.

Asch—e ['aʃə], f. ashes. —ig, adj. ashy. —en=becher, m. ash-tray. —en= brödel, n. (& f.) slut; Cinderella. —en=fall, m. ash-pit. —en=farbig, adj. ashy.

Assekuranz [aseku'rants], f. (pl. —en) assurance, insurance.

Assessor [a'sɛsɔr], m. (—s, pl. —en [—'o:rən]) assessor.

Ast [ast], m. (—es, pl. Äste) bough, branch.

Astro—log [astro'lo:k], m. (—logen, pl. —logen) astrologer. —logie [—lo'gi:], f. astrology. —nom [—'no:m], m. (—nomen, pl. —nomen) astronomer. —nomie [—no'mi:], f. astronomy. —nomisch, adj. astronomical.

Atem ['a:təm], m. (—s) breath. —los, adj. breathless. —zug, m. breath, respiration.

Atlas ['atlas], *m.* (—(ſſ)es, *pl.* —(ſſ)e *and* Atlanten) atlas; satin.

Atm—en ['a:tmən], I. *v.a. & n.* to breathe. II. *subst.n.* act of breathing. —ung, *f.* respiration.

Atmoſphär—e [atmɔs'fɛ:rə], *f.* (*pl.* —en) atmosphere. —iſch, *adj.* atmospheric.

Atom [a'to:m], *n.* (—s, *pl.* —e) atom.

Atz—en ['ɛtsən], *v.a.* to etch. —ung, *f.* cauterizing; etching.

Auch [aux], *conj. & adv.* also, too; even; likewise; *after* wer, was, welcher, wie, = ever, soever.

Audienz [audɪ'ɛnts], *f.* (*pl.* —en) audience.

Aue ['auə], *f.* (*pl.* —n) meadow; pasture.

Auer—hahn ['auərha:n], *m.*, —huhn [—hu:n], *n.* capercailzie.

Auf [auf], I. *prep. With dat. signifying rest, or limited motion in a place*; on, upon; in; of; at; by. — dem nächſten Wege, by the nearest way. *With acc. when signifying motion to a place, or change; or when used not locally, but metaphorically*; on; in; of; immediately after; at; by; to, for; all but, up to; towards; up. II. *adv.* up, upwards, open, awake; — oder ab, up or down, more or less; — und nieder, up and down. Berg —, uphill. III. *interj.* —, up! arise! Auf = *before many verbs:* up, on, upon; un−; open; afresh, anew. *It is a separable prefix, e.g.* aufbieten, ich biete auf, aufgeboten. *In case a possible compound is not given in the following lists see under the simple word.*

Aufatmen ['auf⁹a:tmən], *v.n.* (*aux.* h.) to breathe again.

Aufbauen ['aufbauən], *v.a.* to erect; to rebuild.

Aufbäumen ['aufbɔymən], *v.a.* to wind up; ſich —, to rear up.

Aufbewahr—en ['aufbəva:rən], *v.a.* to store up; to reserve. —ung, *f.* storage.

Aufbieten ['aufbi:tən], *ir.v.a.* to summon; to call up for service; to give notice of.

Aufblähen ['aufblɛ:ən], *v.a.* to swell; to inflate.

Aufbleiben ['aufblaɪbən], *ir.v.n.* (*aux.* ſ.) to remain open; to sit up, remain up.

Aufblick ['aufblɪk], *m.* upward glance.

Aufblicken ['aufblɪkən], *v.n.* (*aux.* h.) to look upwards.

Aufbrauchen ['aufbrauxən], *v.a.* to use up, waste, consume.

Aufbrechen ['aufbrɛçən], I. *ir.v.a.* to break open, up. II. *v.n.* (*aux.* ſ.) to decamp, depart.

Aufbringen ['aufbrɪŋən], *ir.v.a.* to raise; to bring up; to produce; to enrage.

Aufbruch ['aufbrux], *m.* (—s, *pl.* Aufbrüche) departure; decampment.

Aufdecken ['aufdɛkən], *v.a.* to uncover; to disclose, expose.

Aufdring—en ['aufdrɪŋən], *ir.v.a.* to press upon, urge on; to obtrude; ſich —en, to intrude. —lich, *adj. & adv.* importunate; obtrusive. —lich-keit, *f.* (*pl.* —lichkeiten) importunity, obtrusiveness. —ung, *f.* obtrusion, intrusion.

Aufdruck ['aufdruk], *m.* (—(e)s, *pl.* Aufdrücke) surcharge.

Aufdrucken ['aufdrukən], *v.a.* to impress, imprint.

Aufdrücken ['aufdrykən], *v.a.* to press open; to stamp on.

Aufeinander [auf⁹aɪ'nandər], *adv.* one upon another, one after another.

Aufenthalt ['aufɛnthalt], *m.* (—s, *pl.* —e) stay; sojourn. —s-ort, *m.* dwelling.

Auferlegen ['auf⁹ɛrle:gən], *v.a.;* einem etwas —, to enjoin something on a person; to impose (*taxes*).

Auferſteh—en ['auf⁹ɛrſte:ən], *ir.v.n.* (*aux.* ſ.) to rise up; to rise from the dead. —ung, *f.* resurrection.

Auferwecken ['auf⁹ɛrvɛkən], *v.a.* to wake. —ung, *f.* resuscitation.

Auffahr—en ['auffa:rən], *ir.v.n.* (*aux.* ſ.) to ascend; to mount; to start up; to get into a passion. —end, *p.*, —eriſch, *adj.* passionate, vehement; irritable. —t, *f.* (*pl.* —ten) ascent; driving up.

Auffallen ['auffalən], *ir.v.n.* (*aux.* ſ.) to fall upon; einem —, to astonish, to shock. —d, *p.*, auffällig, *adj. & adv.* striking; shocking.

Auffangen ['auffaŋən], *ir.v.a.* to snap, snatch up; to intercept.

Auffaſſ—en ['auffasən], *v.a.* to collect; to comprehend, take in. —ung, *f.* comprehension.

Aufflammen ['aufflamən], *v.n.* (*aux.* ſ.) to flame up; to blaze.

Auffliegen ['auffli:gən], *ir.v.a.* (*aux.* ſ.) to fly upwards; to ascend.

Aufforderer ['aʊffɔrdərər], *m.* (—s, *pl.* —) summoner; challenger.

Auffforder—n ['aʊffɔrdərn], *v.a.* to summon; to challenge; to invite, ask. —**ung,** *f.* invitation; challenge.

Aufführ—en ['aʊffy:rən], *v.a.* to represent, perform; to erect. —**ung,** *f.* representation; erection; conduct.

Aufgabe ['aʊfga:bə], *f.* (*pl.* —n) problem; statement; task, lesson; giving up.

Aufgang ['aʊfgaŋ], *m.* (—es, *pl.* Aufgänge) rise, ascension.

Aufgeben ['aʊfge:bən], *ir.v.a.* to give up; to abandon, relinquish; einem etwas —, to set one a task.

Aufgeblasen ['aʊfgəbla:zən], *p.p.* & *adj.* puffed up; haughty.

Aufgebot ['aʊfgəbo:t], *n.* (—es, *pl.* —e) publication (*of banns*); calling out (*of troops*).

Aufgedunsen ['aʊfgədʊnzən], *p.p.* & *adj.* inflated, puffed up.

Aufgehen ['aʊfge:hən], *ir.v.n.* (*aux.* ſ.) to rise; to evaporate; to open, expand.

Aufgeklärt ['aʊfgəkle:rt], *p.p.* & *adj.* enlightened; civilized; liberal-minded.

Aufgelegt ['aʊfgəle:kt], *p.p.* & *adj.* disposed; inclined.

Aufgeräumt ['aʊfgərɔʏmt], *p.p.* & *adj.* in high spirits. —heit, *f.* cheerfulness, gaiety.

Aufgewedt ['aʊfgəvɛkt], *p.p.* & *adj.* intelligent, bright; lively.

Aufgießen ['aʊfgi:sən], *ir.v.a.* to pour upon.

Aufhalt—en ['aʊfhaltən], *ir.v.a.* to stop, arrest; to keep open; to detain, delay; ſich —en, to stop (*in a place*); ſich über etwas —en, to find fault with. —ung, *f.* hindrance, delay.

Aufheb—en ['aʊfhe:bən], I. *ir.v.a.* to lift; to pick up; to arrest; to keep, preserve; to repeal. II. *subst.n.* lifting (up). —ung, *f.* the lifting *or* taking up; abrogation; suppression.

Aufheiter—n ['aʊfhaɪtərn], *v.a.* to brighten; to cheer up, enliven. —ung, *f.* cheering up; clearing up.

Aufhelfen ['aʊfhɛlfən], *ir.v.a.*; einem —, to help someone up; to succour.

Aufhell—en ['aʊfhɛlən], *v.a.* to clear, brighten up. —ung, *f.* elucidation, explanation.

Aufhetz—en ['aʊfhɛtsən], *v.a.* to rouse; to stir up. —er, *m.* (—ers, *pl.* —er) instigator.

Aufhören ['aʊfhø:rən], I. *v.n.* (*aux.* h.) to cease, stop, end. II. *subst.n.* cessation.

Aufklär—en ['aʊfkle:rən], **Aufklär—en** ['aʊfkla:rən], *v.a.* to clear up; to elucidate. —er, *m.* (—ers, *pl.* —er) instructor, enlightener. —ung, *f.* clearing up; explanation.

Aufknüpfen ['aʊfknypfən], *v.a.* to untie, undo a knot.

Aufkommen ['aʊfkɔmən], I. *ir.v.n.* (*aux.* ſ.) to rise, get up; to come up; to come into fashion; to prosper. II. *subst.n.* recovery; introduction (*of a fashion*); rise in the world.

Auffömmling ['aʊfkœmlɪŋ], *m.* (—s, *pl.* —e) upstart.

Aufkünd—en ['aʊfkyndən], —igen [—igən], *v.a.*; einem etwas —en, to give notice, warning; to retract. —igung, —ung, *f.* warning notice (*of removal, withdrawal, etc.*).

Auflachen ['aʊflaxən], *v.n.* (*aux.* h.) to burst into laughter.

Auflad—en ['aʊfla:dən], *ir.v.a.* to load, put on a load. —er, *m.* (—ers, *pl.* —er) packer, loader.

Auflage ['aʊfla:gə], *f.* (*pl.* —n) edition; tax, duty.

Auflauern ['aʊflaʊərn], *v.n.* (*aux.* h.) to lie in wait (einem, for one).

Auflaufen ['aʊflaʊfən], *ir.v.n.* (*aux.* ſ.) to rise, run up, swell.

Aufleben ['aʊfle:bən], *v.n.* (*aux.* ſ.) to be revived.

Aufleg—en ['aʊfle:gən], *v.a.* to lay on, apply; to impose, inflict (*a fine, a tax, etc.*); to publish, issue. —ung, *f.* application; imposition; infliction.

Auflesen ['aʊfle:zən], *ir.v.a.* to glean; to pick up.

Aufleuchten ['aʊflɔʏçtən], *v.n.* (*aux.* h.) to flash, shine.

Auflodern ['aʊflo:dərn], *v.n.* (*aux.* ſ.) to flash, flare up.

Auflösbar ['aʊfløsba:r], *adj.* & *adv.* soluble. —feit, *f.* solubility.

Auflös—en ['aʊflø:zən], *v.* I. *a.* to dissolve; to loosen; to solve; to decompose; to analyse; to break up (*an assembly*); to disband. II. *r.* to get loose; to melt, dissolve; to die. —end, *p.* & *adj.* solvent. —ung, *f.* loosening; decomposition; solution; analysis; elucidation; death.

Aufmachen ['aʊfmaxən], *v.a.* to open; to undo.

Aufmarſch ['aʊfmarʃ], *m.* (—es, *pl.* Aufmärſche) marching up.

Aufmerk—en ['aʊfmɛrkən], *v.* I. *a.* to note. II. *n.* (*aux.* ɧ.) to attend, give heed to. —ſam, *adj.* & *adv.* attentive, observant. —ſamkeit. *f.* attention.

Aufmunter—n ['aʊfmʊntərn], *v.a.* to encourage, inspirit. —nd, *p.* & *adj.* rousing, encouraging. —ung, *f.* encouragement.

Aufnahme ['aʊfna:mə], *f.* taking up; borrowing; reception; admission; survey; taking of a photograph.

Aufnehmen ['aʊfne:mən], *ir.v.a.* to take up; to shelter; to take possession of; to admit.

Aufnötigen ['aʊfnø:tɪgən], *v.a.*; einem etwas —, to force something on one.

Aufopfer—n ['aʊfˀɔpfərn], *v.a.* to offer up, sacrifice. —nd, *adj.* sacrificing; devoted. —ung, *f.* sacrifice.

Aufpacken ['aʊfpakən], *v.a.* to pack.

Aufpaſſen ['aʊfpasən], *v.* I. *a.* to adapt, fit on. II. *n.* (*aux.* ſ.) to fit; (*aux.* ɧ.) to pay attention; aufgepaßt! attention!

Aufpflanzen ['aʊfpflantsən], *v.a.* to set up, erect.

Aufräum—en ['aʊfrɔʏmən], *v.a.* to arrange, put in order; to clear, take away. —ung, *f.* arranging, making tidy.

Aufrechn—en ['aʊfrɛçnənʲ], *v.a.* to reckon up; to put to one's account. —ung, *f.* balancing of accounts.

Aufrecht ['aʊfrɛçt], *adj.* & *adv.* upright, erect; straight. —erhaltung, *f.* maintenance, preservation. —halter, *m.* supporter.

Aufreg—en ['aʊfre:gən], *v.a.* to stir up; to excite; to enrage. —end, *p.* & *adj.* exciting; seditious. —er, *m.* (—ers, *pl.* —er) agitator. —ung, *f.* agitation; tumult.

Aufreiz—en ['aʊfraɪtsən], *v.a.* to incite, provoke. —ung, *f.* provocation.

Aufricht—en ['aʊfrɪçtən], *v.a.* to set up, erect; to found, establish. —ig, *adj.* & *adv.* sincere, candid.

Aufriegeln ['aʊfri:gəln], *v.a.* to unbolt, unbar.

Aufriß ['aʊfrɪs], *m.* (—ſſes, *pl.* —ſſe) sketch, draft.

Aufrücken ['aʊfrʏkən], *v.* I. *n.* (*aux.* ſ.) to advance upwards, rise (*in rank*). II. *a.* to push, move up.

Aufruf ['aʊfru:f], *m.* (—s, *pl.* —e) calling up, summons; appeal.

Aufrufen ['aʊfru:fən], *ir.v.a.* to summon, call up.

Aufruhr ['aʊfru:r], *m.* (—s) tumult, riot.

Aufrühren ['aʊfry:rən], *v.a.* to stir up; to provoke (*a tumult*).

Aufs [aʊfs] (Auf's), *abbr. of* auf das.

Aufſagen ['aʊfza:gən], *v.a.* to repeat; to recant.

Aufſammeln ['aʊfzaməln], *v.a.* to collect.

Aufſäſſig ['aʊfzɛsɪç], Aufſäßig [—zɛt-sɪç], *adj.* hostile.

Aufſatz ['aʊfzats], *m.* (—es, *pl.* Aufſätze) anything placed on another (*as ornament, etc.*); essay, composition.

Aufſchieben ['aʊfʃi:bən], *ir.v.a.* to shove; to postpone; to delay.

Aufſchlag ['aʊfʃla:k], *m.* (—es, *pl.* Aufſchläge) impact; cuff; facings (*on coat*); advance (*in price*).

Aufſchließen ['aʊfʃli:sən], *ir.* I. *a.* to unlock; to disclose. II. *r.* to open.

Aufſchlitzen ['aʊfʃlɪtsən], *v.a.* to rip, slit up.

Aufſchluß ['aʊfʃlʊs], *m.* (—ſſes, *pl.* Aufſchlüſſe) opening up; disclosure.

Aufſchnappen ['aʊfʃnapən], *v.a.* to snap up.

Aufſchnitt ['aʊfʃnɪt], *m.* (—es, *pl.* —e) cut, slit, incision; slice (*meat*).

Aufſchnüren ['aʊfʃny:rən], *v.a.* to unlace, untie.

Aufſchrauben ['aʊfʃraʊbən], *reg.* & *ir. v.a.* to screw on; to unscrew.

Aufſchrecken ['aʊfʃrɛkən], I. *v.a.* to startle; to rouse. II. *ir.v.n.* (*aux.* ſ.) to start up.

Aufſchrei ['aʊfʃraɪ], *m.* (—es, *pl.* —e) outcry, shriek, scream.

Aufſchreiben ['aʊfʃraɪbən], *ir.v.a.* to write down.

Aufſchreien ['aʊfʃraɪən], *ir.v.n.* (*aux.* ɧ.) to cry out.

Aufſchrift ['aʊfʃrɪft], *f.* (*pl.* —en) address, direction; epitaph.

Aufſchub ['aʊfʃʊp], *m.* (—s) postponement; adjournment.

Aufſchürzen ['aʊfʃʏrtsən], *v.a.* to tuck up (*a skirt, etc.*).

Aufſchwellen ['aʊfʃvɛlən], I. *v.a.* to puff out; to encourage. II. *ir.v.n.* (*aux.* ſ.) to swell; to rise; to surge up.

Aufſchwingen ['aʊfʃvɪŋən], *ir.v.a.* to brandish; ſich —, to soar upwards.

Aufſchwung ['aʊfʃvʊŋ], *m.* (—es) swing; soaring; rapture.

Aufſeh—en [ˈaʊfzeːən], I. *ir.v.a.* (*aux. h.*) to look up, upon. II. *subst.n.* observation; stir, sensation. —**er,** *m.* (—**ers,** *pl.* —**er**) overseer, inspector.

Aufſetzen [ˈaʊfzɛtsən], *v.a.* to set on *or* up; to put *or* pile up; to put down. **eine Rechnung —,** to cast up an account.

Aufſicht [ˈaʊfzɪçt], *f.* inspection; care, charge; control; custody.

Aufſitz [ˈaʊfzɪts], *m.* (—**es**) mounting (*on horseback*).

Aufſitzen [ˈaʊfzɪtsən], *ir.v.n.* (*aux. h.*) to sit, rest on; to take horse.

Aufſpannen [ˈaʊfʃpanən], *v.a.* to stretch, strain; to cock (*a gun*).

Aufſparen [ˈaʊfʃpaːrən], *v.a.* to save, lay by.

Aufſpeiſen [ˈaʊfʃpaɪzən], *v.a.* to eat up, consume.

Aufſperren [ˈaʊfʃpɛrən], *v.a.* to open wide.

Aufſprengen [ˈaʊfʃprɛŋən], *v.a.* to burst *or* blow open; to blow up.

Aufſpringen [ˈaʊfʃprɪŋən], *ir.v.n.* (*aux. f.*) to leap up, bound; to fly open.

Aufſprung [ˈaʊfʃprʊŋ], *m.* (—**es,** *pl.* **Aufſprünge**) bound, leap.

Aufſpüren [ˈaʊfʃpyːrən], *v.a.* to spy *or* trace out, track.

Aufſtand [ˈaʊfʃtant], *m.* (—**es,** *pl.* **Aufſtände**) commotion; revolt.

Aufſteden [ˈaʊfʃtɛkən], *v.a.* to set up, fix.

Aufſtehen [ˈaʊfʃteːhən], *ir.v.n.* (*aux. f.*) to stand up; to rise, get up; to rise, revolt.

Aufſteigen [ˈaʊfʃtaɪgən], I. *ir.v.n.* (*aux. f.*) to ascend, rise, mount. II. *subst.n.* mounting (*a horse, etc.*); ascent.

Aufſtell—en [ˈaʊfʃtɛlən], *v.* I. *a.* to set up; to range, draw up. II. *r.* to draw up (*in battle-array, etc.*). —**ung,** *f.* disposition; assertion, statement.

Aufſtreb—en [ˈaʊfʃtreːbən], *v.n.* (*aux. f.*) to aspire, soar up. —**end,** *p. & adj.* aspiring. —**ung,** *f.* aspiring; exertion.

Aufſtreichen [ˈaʊfʃtraɪçən], *ir.v.* I. *a.* to lay on; to spread.

Aufſtülpen [ˈaʊfʃtʏlpən], *v.a.* to cock (*a hat, etc.*); **eine aufgeſtülpte Naſe,** a turned-up nose.

Aufſuch—en [ˈaʊfzuːxən], *v.a.* to go in quest of. —**ung,** *f.* search.

Auftauchen [ˈaʊftaʊxən], *v.n.* (*aux. f.*) to emerge.

Auftauen [ˈaʊftaʊən], *v.n.* (*aux. f.*) to thaw; (*fig.*) to become lively.

Auftrag [ˈaʊftraːk], *m.* (—**es,** *pl.* **Aufträge**) commission; errand, message.

Auftragen [ˈaʊftraːgən], *ir.v.a.* to carry up, serve up; to commission; to charge one with (*a duty*).

Auftreten [ˈaʊftreːtən], *ir.v.* I. *a.* to open by treading on, crush open. II. *n.* (*aux. f.*) to step up *or* on; to appear.

Auftritt [ˈaʊftrɪt], *m.* (—**s,** *pl.* —**e**) treading on; step, doorstep; appearance; scene (*in a play*).

Auftun [ˈaʊftuːn], *ir.v.a.* to open.

Auftürmen [ˈaʊftʏrmən], *v.a.* to raise, to heap. **aufgetürmt,** *p.p. & adj.* high-heaped, towering.

Aufwachen [ˈaʊfvaxən], *v.n.* (*aux. f.*) to awake, wake up.

Aufwachſen [ˈaʊfvaksən], *ir.v.n.* (*aux. f.*) to grow, shoot up.

Aufwall—en [ˈaʊfvalən], *v.n.* (*aux. f.*) to boil up; to roll, foam up. —**ung,** *f.* ebullition; effervescence.

Aufwand [ˈaʊfvant], *m.* (—**es**) expense; expenditure; display.

Aufwart—en [ˈaʊfvartən], *v.n.* (*aux. h.*) (*einem*) to wait upon, attend on; to call on. —**ung,** *f.* attendance; visit.

Aufwärter [ˈaʊfvɛrtər], *m.* (—**s,** *pl.* —) attendant, waiter. —**in,** *f.* waiting-maid.

Aufwärts [ˈaʊfvɛrts], *adv.* upwards.

Aufwaſchen [ˈaʊfvaʃən], *ir.v.a.* to wash up, away *or* off.

Aufweden [ˈaʊfvɛkən], *v.a.* to rouse, awake; to animate.

Aufwenden [ˈaʊfvɛndən], *reg. & ir.v.a.* to spend, expend.

Aufwerfen [ˈaʊfvɛrfən], *ir.v.a.* to cast up; to dig; to throw open.

Aufwideln [ˈaʊfvɪkəln], *v.a.* to wind; to loosen (*hair*); to unfurl.

Aufwiegen [ˈaʊfviːgən], *ir.v.a.* to outweigh; to counterbalance.

Aufwiegler [ˈaʊfviːglər], *m.* (—**s,** *pl.* —), —**in,** *f.* (*pl.* —**innen**) mutineer, agitator.

Aufzählen [ˈaʊftsɛːlən], *v.a.* to reckon up.

Aufzehr—en [ˈaʊftseːrən], *v.a.* to consume; to waste. —**ung,** *f.* consumption, expenditure.

Aufzeichn—en [ˈaʊftsaɪçnən], *v.a.* to note down, take a note of; to record. —**er,** *m.* (—**ers,** *pl.* —**er**) designer. —**ung,** *f.* note; account; inventory.

Aufziehen [ˈaʊftsiːən], *ir.v.* I. *a.* to draw up, raise; to bring up (*children*);

to rear, breed; to wind up (*a watch*); to undo (*a knot*). II. *n.* (*aux.* ſ.) to mount guard; to march up.

Aufzug [ˈauftsuːk], *m.* (—s, *pl.* **Aufzüge**) act of drawing up; warp; procession; lift; act (*of a play*); equipment; suite; pomp.

Aufzwingen [ˈauftsvɪŋən], *ir.v.a.*; **einem** —, to force on one.

Auge [ˈaugə], *n.* (—s, *pl.* —n) eye; **im** — **behalten**, to keep one's eye on; **große —n machen**, to be much surprised, thunderstruck; **unter vier —n**, tête-à-tête; private.

Augen— [ˈaugən] (*Comp.*) **—arzt**, *m.* oculist. **—blid**, *m.* moment, instant. **—blidlich** [—ˈblɪklɪç], I. *adj.* momentary, instantaneous. II. *adv.* instantly, forthwith. **—bogen**, *m.* iris. **—braue**, *f.* eye-brow. **—fällig**, *adj.* evident, obvious. **—höhle**, *f.* socket (*of the eye*). **—kreis**, *m.* orbit. **—lid**, *n.* (*pl.* —**lider**) eyelid. **—los**, *adj.* blind; eyeless. **—nerv**, *m.* optic nerve. **—paar**, *n.* pair of eyes. **—schein**, *m.* inspection; appearance; **in —schein nehmen**, to inspect. **—scheinlich** [—ˈʃaɪnlɪç], *adj.* self-evident, apparent. **—scheinlichkeit**, *f.* obviousness. **—weide**, *f.* delight of the eyes. **—wimper**, *f.* eyelash. **—zahn**, *m.* eye-tooth. **—zeuge**, *m.* eye-witness. **—zeugnis**, *n.* ocular proof.

August [auˈgust], *m.* (—s) August.

Aus [aus], I. *prep. With dat.* out of; from; of; by, for; on, upon, on account of; in; — **Mangel an**, for want of. II. *adv. & sep. prefix*, over; out, forth; forward, in front; ended, past.

Aus— [aus] (*separable*) *prefix, denoting* out; thoroughly, sufficiently; stop, cease. *For compounds not found in the following lists, see the simple verbs.*

Ausarbeit—en [ˈausˀarbaɪtən], *v.a.* to work out; to elaborate. **—ung**, *f.* carrying out (*of a plan*); elaboration.

Ausart—en [ˈausˀaːrtən], *v.n.* (*aux.* ſ.) to degenerate. **—ung**, *f.* degenerating; deterioration.

Ausatmen [ˈausˀaːtmən], *v.* I. *a.* to breathe out *or* forth. II. *n.* (*aux.* h.) to expire.

Ausbauen [ˈausbauən], *v.a.* to finish a building; to improve, cultivate.

Ausbeding—en [ˈausbedɪŋən], *ir.v.a.* to stipulate; **sich** (*dat.*) **—en**, to reserve to oneself by stipulation. **—ung**, *f.* reservation; stipulation.

Ausbesser—n [ˈausbesərn], *v.a.* to mend; to repair. **—ung**, *f.* repair, mending.

Ausbeute [ˈausbɔʏtə], *f.* gain; profit.

Ausbieten [ˈausbiːtən], *ir.v.a.* to offer for sale; to outbid.

Ausbild—en [ˈausbɪldən], *v.a.* to form, develop; to mature. **—ung**, *f.* development; culture.

Ausbitten [ˈausbɪtən], *ir.v.a.* to beg for, ask for; to require; **das bitte ich mir aus**, I must insist on this; **darf ich mir —?** may I trouble you for?

Ausblasen [ˈausblaːzən], *ir.v.a.* to blow out (*a light, etc.*).

Ausbleiben [ˈausblaɪbən], I. *ir.v.a.* (*aux.* ſ.) to stay away, fail to appear; to be wanting. II. *subst.n.* absence.

Ausblick [ˈausblɪk], *m.* (—s) outlook, prospect, view.

Ausbrechen [ˈausbreçən], *ir.v.* I. *a.* to break out; to vomit; to quarry. II. *n.* (*aux.* ſ.) to break out (*as fire, etc.*); to break forth, burst out.

Ausbreit—en [ˈausbraɪtən], *v.a.* to spread, stretch; to divulge, circulate. **—ung**, *f.* spreading; propagation.

Ausbrennen [ˈausbrenən], *ir.v.* I. *a.* to burn out. II. *n.* (*aux.* h.) to cease burning.

Ausbruch [ˈausbrux], *m.* (—(e)s, *pl.* **Ausbrüche**) outbreak, eruption.

Ausbrüten [ˈausbryːtən], *v.a.* to hatch; to brood over, plot.

Ausbund [ˈausbunt], *m.* (—s, *pl.* **Ausbünde**) paragon.

Ausdampfen [ˈausdampfən], *v.n.* (*aux.* ſ.) to evaporate.

Ausdauer [ˈausdauər], *f.* perseverance; persistence; endurance.

Ausdauern [ˈausdauərn], *v.* I. *a.* to endure; to hold out. II. *n.* (*aux.* h.) to persevere, to be steadfast. **—d**, *p. & adj.* persevering, steadfast; perennial.

Ausdehnbar [ˈausdeːnbaːr], *adj.* expansible; diffusible; ductile. **—keit**, *f.* expansibility.

Ausdehn—en [ˈausdeːnən], *v.a.* to extend, enlarge, expand; to spread out. **—end**, *p. & adj.* expansive. **—ung**, *f.* expansion.

Ausdenken [ˈausdɛŋkən], *ir.v.a.* to contrive, devise; to think out.

Ausdeut—en [ˈausdɔʏtən], *v.a.* to interpret; to decipher. **—ung**, *f.* interpretation.

Ausdruck [ˈausdrʊk], *m.* (—s, *pl.*

Ausdrücke) expression; phrase. **—s=leer, —s=los,** adj. expressionless. **—s=voll,** adj. & adv. expressive.

Ausdrucken ['aʊsdrʊkən], v.a. to print in full.

Ausdrück—en ['aʊsdrykən], v.a. to press, to squeeze out; to express, utter. **—lich,** adj. & adv. express(ly). **—lichkeit,** f. expressness, explicitness.

Ausduft—en ['aʊsdʊftən], v.n. (aux. f.) to exhale. **—ung,** f. exhalation.

Ausdulden ['aʊsdʊldən], v.a. to endure.

Ausdunsten ['aʊsdʊnstən], v.n. (aux. f.) to evaporate.

Auseinander [aʊs²aɪ'nandər], adv. asunder, apart; separated.

Auserkoren ['aʊs²ɛrkoːrən], adj. chosen, elect, selected.

Auserlesen ['aʊs²ɛrleːzən], I. ir.v.a. to choose, select. II. p.p. & adj. choice, picked, select.

Auserwähl—en ['aʊs-ɛrvɛːlən], v.a. to select, choose out; **die —ten,** the elect.

Ausfahr—en ['aʊsfaːrən], ir.v. I. a. to deepen; to take out for a drive. II. n. (aux. f.) to drive out (in a carriage, etc.). **—t,** f. drive; excursion.

Ausfall ['aʊsfal], m. (—(e)s, pl. **Ausfälle**) falling out; sally, sortie; thrust.

Ausfall—en ['aʊsfalən], ir.v.n. (aux. f.) to fall out; to make a sortie; to turn out, result. **—end,** adj. aggressive, insulting.

Ausfertig—en ['aʊsfɛrtɪgən], v.a. to execute (an order); to fit out. **—ung,** f. despatch (of business); equipment.

Ausflucht ['aʊsflʊxt], f. (pl. **Ausflüchte**) flight; evasion, subterfuge.

Ausflug ['aʊsfluːk], m. (—s, pl. **Ausflüge**) flight; ramble, excursion.

Ausfluß ['aʊsflʊs], m. (—(ſſ)es, pl. **Ausflüsse**) flowing out; outlet.

Ausforderer ['aʊsfordərər], m.(—s, pl. —) challenger.

Ausforder—n ['aʊsfordərn], (usually **herausfordern**), v.a. to call out for a duel. **—ung,** f. challenge.

Ausforsch—en ['aʊsfɔrʃən], v.a. to enquire after; to search, hunt out. **—ung,** f. investigation.

Ausfuhr ['aʊsfuːr], f. exportation; export trade. **—handel,** m. export trade. **—zoll,** m. export duty.

Ausführ—en ['aʊsfyːrən], v.a. to export; to carry into effect. **—er,** m. (—ers, pl. **—er**) exporter. **—lich**

[aʊs'fyːrlɪç] I. adj. detailed, circumstantial. II. adv. in detail, circumstantially. **—lichkeit,** f. prolixity. **—ung,** f. carrying on, out; exportation; realization; completion.

Ausfüll—en ['aʊsfylən], v.a. to fill out; to stuff. **—ung,** f. filling up, out, padding.

Ausgabe ['aʊsgaːbə], f. (pl. —n) delivery (of letters, etc.); edition (of a book); expenditure; announcement.

Ausgang ['aʊsgaŋ], m. (—(e)s, pl. **Ausgänge**) act of going out, exit; outlet; result.

Ausgeb—en ['aʊsgeːbən], ir.v. I. a. to give out; to distribute (orders, money, etc.). II. n. (aux. h.) to bear, yield, bring in. **—er,** m. (—ers, pl. **—er**) distributor; drawer (of a bill, etc.).

Ausgehen ['aʊsgeːhən], ir.v.n. (aux. f.) to go out; to proceed; to fail, be exhausted; to result, end in.

Ausgelassen ['aʊsgəlasən], p.p. & adj. wild, unruly. **—heit,** f. boisterousness; wildness.

Ausgemacht ['aʊsgəmaxt], p.p. & adj. settled; decided.

Ausgenommen ['aʊsgənɔmən], p.p. & prep. except, with the exception of.

Ausgezeichnet ['aʊsgətsaɪçnət], p.p. & adj. excellent; distinguished, illustrious.

Ausgiebig ['aʊsgiːbɪç], adj. plentiful, abundant, rich.

Ausgießen ['aʊsgiːsən], ir.v.a. to pour out.

Ausgleich ['aʊsglaɪç], m. (—es) settlement, agreement; compromise.

Ausgleich—en ['aʊsglaɪçən], ir.v.a. to make even; to equalize; to level; to balance (accounts). **—end,** p. & adj. compensatory. **—ung,** f. adjustment; balance; settlement.

Ausgraben ['aʊsgraːbən], ir.v.a. to dig up, out.

Ausguß ['aʊsgʊs], m. (—(ſſ)es, pl. **Ausgüsse**) outpouring; sink; gutter.

Aushalten ['aʊshaltən], ir.v. I. a. to hold out, endure. II. n. (aux. h.) to endure; to persevere.

Aushang ['aʊshaŋ], m. (—s) placard.

Aushangen ['aʊshaŋən], ir.v.n. (aux. h.) to hang out, be suspended.

Aushängen ['aʊshɛŋən], v.a. to hang out (a sign, a flag, etc.).

Ausharren ['aʊsharən], v.n. (aux. h.) to endure to the end, hold out.

Ausheben ['aʊshe:bən], *ir.v.a.* to lift out *or* up; to take off the hinges.

Ausheilen ['aʊshaɪlən], *v.* I. *a.* to cure perfectly. II. *n.* to be healed, heal up.

Aushelf—en ['aʊshɛlfən], *ir.v.n.* (*aux.* h.) to help out; to aid. **—er**, *m.* (**—ers**, *pl.* **—er**), **—in**, *f.* (*pl.* **—innen**) help, helper.

Aushilf—e ['aʊshɪlfə], *f.* aid, assistance; stop-gap. **—s=weise**, *adv.* as a makeshift, temporarily.

Aushöhl—en ['aʊshø:lən], *v.a.* to hollow out; to excavate. **—ung,** *f.* excavation.

Aushören ['aʊshø:rən], *v.a.* to hear to the end.

Auskaufen ['aʊskaʊfən], *v.a.* to buy out.

Auskehr—en ['aʊske:rən], *v.a.* to sweep out. **—icht**, *n.* (**—s**) sweepings.

Auskleiden ['aʊsklaɪdən], *v.a.* to undress.

Ausklingen ['aʊsklɪŋən], *ir.v.n.* (*aux.* h.) to cease to sound.

Auskommen ['aʊskɔmən], I. *ir.v.n.* (*aux.* f.) to come, go out; to become public; to hold good, answer the purpose; to agree, live peaceably with; to make do. II. *subst.n.* act of getting out; competence; peaceable intercourse.

Auskunft ['aʊskʊnft], *f.* (*pl.* **Auskünfte**) means of subsistence; intelligence, information; expedient, resource. **—s=bureau**, *n.* inquiry office. **—s=mittel**, *n.* resource, expedient.

Auslachen ['aʊslaxən], *v.a.* to laugh at; to deride; **sich —**, to laugh one's fill.

Auslad—en ['aʊsla:dən], *ir.v.a.* to unload, discharge. **—ung,** *f.* unloading.

Auslage ['aʊsla:gə], *f.* (*pl.* **—n**) disbursement; expenses.

Ausland ['aʊslant], *n.* (**—es**) foreign country; **im —e**, abroad.

Ausländ—er ['aʊslɛndər], *m.* (**—ers**, *pl.* **—er**) foreigner, alien. **—isch,** *adj.* foreign.

Auslangen ['aʊslaŋən], *v.n.* (*aux.* h.) to be sufficient, suffice, do.

Auslass—en ['aʊslasən], *ir.v.a.* to let out, let go; to let off; to leave out, omit. **—ung,** *f.* letting out; omission; utterance.

Ausleer—en ['aʊsle:rən], *v.a.* to empty; to drain. **—ung,** *f.* evacuation.

Ausleg—en ['aʊsle:gən], *v.a.* to lay, spread out; to explain, expound.

—ung, *f.* exposition; explanation; laying out (*of money*).

Ausleihen ['aʊslaɪhən], *ir.v.a.* to lend out; to hire out.

Auslernen ['aʊslɛrnən], *v.n.* (*aux.* h.) to finish learning. **—ausgelernt,** *p.p.* & *adj.* experienced, practised.

Auslese ['aʊsle:zə], *f.* (*pl.* **—n**) selection; assortment; the pick.

Auslesen ['aʊsle:zən], *ir.v.a.* to select, pick out.

Auslieser—n ['aʊsli:fərn], *v.a.* to hand over, deliver up. **—ung,** *f.* surrender; delivery.

Auslöschen ['aʊsløʃən], *v.a.* to put out, extinguish; to efface; to pay off (*a debt*).

Auslosen ['aʊslo:zən], *v.a.* to draw lots for; to raffle.

Auslös—en ['aʊslø:zən], *v.a.* loosen, release; to redeem, ransom. **—ung,** *f.* redeeming; ransom.

Ausmachen ['aʊsmaxən], *v.a.* to make up; to take out; to settle (*a dispute*); **ausgemacht!** agreed! **es macht nichts aus,** it does not matter.

Ausmarsch ['aʊsmarʃ], *m.* (**—es,** *pl.* **Ausmärsche**) marching out, departure (*of troops*).

Ausmess—en ['aʊsmesən], *ir.v.a.* to measure out; to survey. **—ung,** *f.* measurement; survey.

Ausmustern ['aʊsmʊstərn], *v.a.* to discharge (*soldiers*).

Ausnahm—e ['aʊsna:mə], *f.* (*pl.* **—en**) exception; **ohne —e,** without exception. **—s=weise,** *adv.* by way of exception.

Ausnehmen ['aʊsne:mən], *ir.v.a.* to take out; to select; to except, exempt; **ausgenommen,** *p.p.* & *adj.* except.

Auspacken ['aʊspakən], *v.a.* to unpack.

Ausprägen ['aʊsprɛ:gən], *v.a.* to stamp, impress; to coin.

Auspressen ['aʊspresən], *v.a.* to squeeze out; to extort from.

Ausräumen ['aʊsrɔymən], *v.a.* to clear out, away, off.

Ausrechn—en ['aʊsreçnən], *v.a.* to calculate, compute. **—ung,** *f.* computation.

Ausrede ['aʊsre:də], *f.* (*pl.* **—n**) excuse, pretence.

Ausreden ['aʊsre:dən], *v.* I. *n.* (*aux.* h.) to finish speaking. II. *a.* **einem etwas —**, to dissuade from doing a thing. III. *r.* to excuse oneself from.

Ausregnen ['aʊsreːgnən], *v.r.* (*aux.* h.) to cease raining.

Ausreiß—en ['aʊsraɪsən], *ir.v.* I. *a.* to pluck, tear out. II. *n.* (*aux.* ſ.) to run away, decamp; to desert. —er, *m.* (—ers, *pl.* —er) deserter.

Ausreiten ['aʊsraɪtən], *ir.v.a.* & *n.* (*aux.* h.) to ride out, take a ride.

Ausrichten ['aʊsrɪçtən], *v.a.* to make straight *or* level; to execute (*an order*); to deliver (*a message*); to accomplish (*a purpose*); nichts —, to labour in vain.

Ausritt ['aʊsrɪt], *m.* (—es, *pl.* —e) ride.

Ausrot—ten ['aʊsrɔtən], *v.a.* to extirpate, exterminate. —ung, *f.* extirpation.

Ausrücken ['aʊsrykən], *v.n.* (*aux.* ſ.) to march out.

Ausruf ['aʊsruːf], *m.* (—(e)s, *pl.* —e) proclamation; exclamation.

Ausruf—en ['aʊsruːfən], *ir.v.* I. *a.* to proclaim. II. *n.* (*aux.* h.) to cry out, exclaim. —er, *m.* (—ers, *pl.* —er) crier, hawker. —ungs=zeichen, *n.* mark of exclamation.

Ausruhen ['aʊsruːhən], *v.n.* & *r.* to rest.

Ausrüst—en ['aʊsrystən], *v.a.* to equip, fit out. —er, *m.* (—ers, *pl.* —er) outfitter, preparer. —ung, *f.* outfitting; preparation; equipment.

Ausſaat ['aʊszaːt], *f.* (*pl.* —en) sowing; seed; seed-corn.

Ausſäen ['aʊszeːən], *v.a.* to sow.

Ausſage ['aʊszaːgə], *f.* (*pl.* —n) declaration, statement; deposition.

Ausſagen ['aʊszaːgən], *v.a.* to state, declare, assert.

Ausſatz ['aʊszats], *m.* (—es) leprosy.

Ausſätzig ['aʊszetsɪç], *adj.* leprous. —e(r), *m.* leper.

Ausſchauen ['aʊsʃaʊən], *v.* I. *a.* (*aux.* h.) to look out (nach einem, for one). II. *n.* to look, to have an appearance.

Ausſcheiden ['aʊsʃaɪdən], I. *ir.v.a.* to separate. II. *ir.v.n.* (*aux.* ſ.) to secede, withdraw from.

Ausſchenken ['aʊsʃɛŋkən], *v.a.* to pour, fill out.

Ausſchiffen ['aʊsʃɪfən], *v.* I. *a.* to disembark. II. *n.* (*aux.* ſ.) to put to sea.

Ausſchlafen ['aʊsʃlaːfən], *ir.v.n.* (*aux.* h.) to sleep one's fill *or* enough.

Ausſchlag ['aʊsʃlaːk], *m.* (—es, *pl.* Ausſchläge) budding, sprouting (*of trees, etc.*); rash; result, end. —gebend, *adj.* decisive.

Ausſchlag—en ['aʊsʃlaːgən], I. *ir.v.a.* to strike out, beat out; to trim; to refuse (*an invitation, etc.*). II. *ir.v.n.* (*aux.* h.) to lash out (*as horses*); to sprout, bud. III. *subst.n.* refusal; renunciation; eruption, etc. —end, *p.* & *adj.* deciding, decisive.

Ausſchließ—en ['aʊsʃliːsən], *ir.v.a.* to lock out; to exclude. —lich, I. *adj.* & *adv.* exclusive; exceptional. II. *prep.* exclusive of. —lichkeit, *f.* exclusiveness. —ung, *f.* exclusion; exemption.

Ausſchluß ['aʊsʃlʊs], *m.* (—(ſſ)es) exception; exemption.

Ausſchmücken ['aʊsʃmykən], *v.a.* to deck out, adorn.

Ausſchneiden ['aʊsʃnaɪdən], *ir.v.a.* to cut out.

Ausſchnitt ['aʊsʃnɪt], *m.* (—(e)s, *pl.* —e) notch; cut. —handel, *m.* retail business. —waren, *pl.* dry goods.

Ausſchöpfen ['aʊsʃœpfən], *v.a.* to scoop, bale out; to drain off; to exhaust.

Ausſchreib—en ['aʊsʃraɪbən], *ir.v.a.* to write out; to copy; to plagiarise. —er, *m.* (—ers, *pl.* —er) copyist; plagiarist. —erei, *f.* plagiarism.

Ausſchreiten ['aʊsʃraɪtən], *ir.v.* I. *a.* to pace, step out (*a distance*). II. *n.* (*aux.* ſ.) to step out; to overstep (*reasonable limits*).

Ausſchuß ['aʊsʃʊs], *m.* (—(ſſ)es, *pl.* Ausſchüſſe) selection; dross, refuse; choice *or* best part; committee.

Ausſchütten ['aʊsʃʏtən], *v.a.* to pour out; to shower down.

Ausſchweif—en ['aʊsʃvaɪfən], *v.* I. *a.* to slope. II. *n.* (*aux.* h.) to roam about; to be prolix. —end, *p.* & *adj.* extravagant; eccentric; dissolute. —ung, *f.* excess, intemperance.

Ausſehen ['aʊszeːən], I. *ir.v.a.* to see to the end (*play, etc.*). II. *ir.v.n.* (*aux.* h.) to look (nach einem, for one); to look, appear. III. *subst.n.* exterior; appearance.

Außen ['aʊsən], *adv.* out, without; outside; abroad; nach —, outwards.

Ausſenden ['aʊszɛndən], *ir.v.a.* to send out; to emit.

Außer ['aʊsər], I. *prep.* *With dat.* out of, outside of; without; besides; except; — Dienſt, retired from active service. *With acc.* (*after an active verb of placing*), out of. II. *conj.* except, unless, save, but. — dem, *adv.* be-

sides, moreover. —**halb**, I. *prep.*
With gen. outside, beyond. II. *adv.*
on the outside, externally. — **ordent=**
lich, *adj. & adv.* extraordinary; unusual.

Außer ['ɔysər], *attrib. adj.* outer, exterior, external. —**(e)s**, *n.* outward
appearance; exterior; foreign affairs.
—**lich**, *adj. & adv.* external, outward.
—**ſt**, I. *adv.* extremely. II. *adj.* extreme, utmost. —**ung**, *f.* utterance,
assertion, expression.

Außern ['ɔysərn], *v.a.* to utter, express, give utterance to.

Ausſetzen ['aʊsʦetsən], *v.* I. *a.* to set
out, put out; to set (*a task*); to defer.
II. *n.* (*aux.* h.) to pause, stop, intermit.

Ausſicht ['aʊszɪçt], *f.* (*pl.* —**en**) prospect, view.

Ausſinnen ['aʊszɪnən], *ir.v.a.* to ex-
cogitate; to invent.

Ausſöhn=en ['aʊszøːnən], *v.a.* to expiate; to reconcile. —**ung**, *f.* atonement; reconciliation.

Ausſpähen ['aʊsʃpɛːən], *v.a.* to spy out.

Ausſpann=en ['aʊsʃpanən], *v.a.* to
unharness, unyoke; to expand, stretch
out. —**ung**, *f.* relaxation.

Ausſperren ['aʊsʃpɛrən], *v.a.* to shut
out, exclude.

Ausſpielen ['aʊsʃpiːlən], *v.a.* to play
out; to lead; to raffle.

Ausſprache ['aʊsʃpraːxə], *f.* (*pl.* —**en**)
pronunciation, enunciation, accent.

Ausſprechen ['aʊsʃprɛçən], *ir.v.* I. *a.*
to pronounce, articulate; to utter.
II. *r.* to speak out one's mind.
ausgeſprochen, *p.p. & adj.* avowed,
strongly marked.

Ausſpruch ['aʊsʃprʊx], *m.* (—**(e)s**, *pl.*
Ausſprüche) declaration of opinion;
decision, verdict.

Ausſpüren ['aʊsʃpyːrən], *v.a.* to track
out, trace.

Ausſtaffierung ['aʊsʃtafiːrʊŋ], *f.* outfit,
equipment.

Ausſtand ['aʊsʃtant], *m.* (—**es**, *pl.*
Ausſtände) strike (*of workers*); out-
standing debt.

Ausſtatt—en ['aʊsʃtatən], *v.a.* to provide with; to endow; to equip. —**ung**,
f. outfit, portion; wedding trousseau.

Ausſtehen ['aʊsʃteːən], *ir.v.* I. *n.* (*aux.*
h. *and* ſ.) to stand out. II. *a.* to
endure, undergo, bear.

Ausſteigen ['aʊsʃtaɪgən], *ir.v.n.* (*aux.*
ſ.) to alight; to disembark.

Ausſtell—en ['aʊsʃtɛlən], *v.a.* to expose,
set out; to exhibit; to blame, find
fault with; to draw (*a bill of exchange*).
—**er**, *m.* (—**ers**, *pl.* —**er**) exhibitor;
drawer (*of a bill*). —**ung**, *f.* exhibition; blame, censure.

Ausſterben ['aʊsʃtɛrbən], *ir.v.n.* (*aux.*
ſ.) to die out; to become extinct.

Ausſteuer ['aʊsʃtɔyər], *f.* dowry;
trousseau; endowment.

Ausſtopfen ['aʊsʃtopfən], *v.a.* to stuff.

Ausſtoßen ['aʊsʃtoːsən], *ir.v.a.* to
thrust out, knock out; to expel.

Ausſtrahlen ['aʊsʃtraːlən], *v.a. & n.*
(*aux.* h.) to radiate, shine forth.

Ausſtrecken ['aʊsʃtrɛkən], *v.a.* to reach
out, extend.

Ausſtreichen ['aʊsʃtraɪçən], *ir.v.* I. *a.*
to smooth; to erase, strike out. II.
n. (*aux.* ſ.) to roam, rove about.

Ausſtrömen ['aʊsʃtrøːmən], *v.* I. *a.* to
pour forth. II. *n.* (*aux.* ſ.) to issue
forth; to emanate.

Ausſtudieren ['aʊsʃtuˈdiːrən], *v.* I. *n.*
(*aux.* h.) to finish one's studies. II.
a. to study thoroughly. **ausſtudiert**
[—ʃtuˈdiːrt], *p.p. & adj.* learned.

Ausſuchen ['aʊszuːxən], *v.a.* to seek
out; to select.

Austausch ['aʊstaʊʃ], *m.* (—**es**) barter;
exchange. —**en**, *v.a.* to barter, exchange.

Austeil—en ['aʊstaɪlən], *v.a.* to distribute (**unter**, among); to dispense.
—**ung**, *f.* distribution.

Auster ['aʊstər], *f.* (*pl.* —**n**) oyster.
— **bank**, *f.* oyster-bed.

Austilgen ['aʊstɪlgən], *v.a.* to exterminate; to eradicate.

Austrag ['aʊstraːk], *m.* (—**(e)s**, *pl.*
Austräge) end, issue; decision.

Austragen ['aʊstraːgən], *ir.v.a.* to
carry out; to amount to.

Austreiben ['aʊstraɪbən], *ir.v.a.* to
drive out; to eject.

Austritt ['aʊstrɪt], *m.* (—**s**, *pl.* —**e**)
stepping out; retirement (*from an
office, etc.*).

Ausüb—en ['aʊsʔyːbən], *v.a.* to practise (*law, etc.*); to exercise (*authority,
etc.*); to execute, carry out. —**ung**, *f.*
practice; exercise; execution.

Ausverkauf ['aʊsfɛrkaʊf], *m.* (—**s**) a
selling off, clearance sale.

Ausverkaufen ['aʊsfɛrkaʊfən], *v.a.* to
sell off.

Auswachſen ['aʊsvaksən], *ir.v.n.* (*aux.*

f.) to grow out, sprout; to attain full growth.

Auswägen ['ausvɛːgən], *reg. & ir.v.a.* to weigh out.

Auswahl ['ausvaːl], *f.* choice, selection.

Auswählen ['ausvɛːlən], *v.a.* to choose out, select. **ausgewählt**, *p.p. & adj.* selected, choice.

Auswanderer ['ausvandərər], *m.* (—s, *pl.* —) emigrant.

Auswander—n ['ausvandərn], *v.a.* (*aux.* f.) to emigrate. —**ung,** *f.* emigration.

Auswärt—ig ['ausvɛrtɪç], *adj.* foreign; abroad; outward; **das —ige Amt,** Foreign Office. —**s,** *adv.* outward; outwards; abroad.

Auswechseln ['ausvɛksəln], *v.a.* (**gegen eine S.**), to exchange.

Ausweg ['ausveːk], *m.* (—es, *pl.* —e) way out, issue; shift, evasion.

Ausweich—en ['ausvaiçən], *ir.v.n.* (*aux.* f.) to turn aside; to give place to; to yield; to shirk. —**end,** *p. & adj.* evasive. —**ung,** *f.* evasion, avoidance, shirking, *etc.*

Ausweinen ['ausvainən], *v.a.* to weep; **sich —,** to have a good cry.

Ausweis ['ausvais], *m.* (—(f)es, *pl.* —(f)e) statement, purport; evidence; certificate, voucher.

Ausweis—en ['ausvaizən], *ir.v.a.* to banish, expel; to show, prove, decide. —**ung,** *f.* banishment, expulsion.

Auswendig ['ausvendɪç], *adj. & adv.* outside, outward; —**lernen,** to learn by heart.

Auswickeln ['ausvɪkəln], *v.a.* to unwrap.

Auswirken ['ausvɪrkən], *v.a.* to work out; to contrive.

Auswuchs ['ausvuːks], *m.* (—(f)es, *pl.* **Auswüchse**) excrescence; sprout.

Auswurf ['ausvurf], *m.* (—s, *pl.* **Auswürfe**) ejection; excrement.

Auswürf—ling ['ausvyrflɪŋ], *m.* (—lings, *pl.* —linge) outcast.

Auszahl—en ['austsaːlən], *v.a.* to pay out. —**ung,** *f.* payment.

Auszählen ['austsɛːlən], *v.* I. *a.* to count out. II. *n.* (*aux.* h.) to count to the end.

Auszehren ['austseːrən], *v.* I. *a.* to consume. II. *n.* (*aux.* f.) & *r.* to waste away. —**ung,** *f.* consumption.

Auszeichn—en ['austsaiçnən], *v.a.* to mark out; to distinguish. **ausgezeich=**

net, *p.p. & adj.* distinguished, excellent. —**ung,** *f.* distinction.

Ausziehen ['austsiːən], *ir.v.* I. *a.* to draw out, extract; to draw, take off. II. *n.* (*aux.* f.) to remove (*from a house, etc.*).

Auszug ['austsuːk], *m.* (—s, *pl.* **Aus= züge**) marching, going out *or* off; departure; removal; procession; extract; abstract, epitome.

Authentisch [au'tentɪʃ], *adj.* (*see* **glaub= würdig, zuverlässig**) authentic.

Auto ['autoː], *n.* (—s, *pl.* —s) motor-car. —**mat,** *m.* (—maten, *pl.* —maten) automaton, automatic machine. —**matisch,** *adj.* automatic. —**mobil,** *n.* (—s, *pl.* —e) motor-car.

Autor ['autor], *m.* (—s, *pl.* —en [—'toːrən]) (*see* **Verfasser, Schrift= steller**) author. —**ität** [—i'tɛːt], *f.* authority.

Aviat—ik [avl'aːtɪk], *f.* aviation. —**iker,** *m.* aviator.

Axt [akst], *f.* (*pl.* **Äxte**) axe, hatchet.

Azur [a'tsuːr], *m.* (—(e)s) azure.

B

B, b [beː], B, b.

Bach [bax], *m.* (—es, *pl.* **Bäche,** *dim.* **Bächlein**) brook.

Backbord ['bakbort], *m.* larboard, port (*Naut.*).

Back—e ['bakə], *f.* (*pl.* —en), —**en,** *m.* (—ens, *pl.* —en) cheek. —**en=bart,** *m.* whiskers. —**en=zahn,** *m.* molar tooth. —**feige,** *f.* box on the ear. —**fisch,** *m.* fish for frying; girl in her teens, flapper (*sl.*). —**ofen,** *m.* baker's oven. —**trog,** *m.* kneading trough. —**werk,** *n.* pastry.

Back—en ['bakən], *reg. & ir.* I. *n.* (*aux.* h.) to bake. II. *a.* to bake.

Bäcker ['bɛkər], *m.* (—s, *pl.* —) baker. —**ei** [—'rai], *f.* (*pl.* —eien) bakery; bakehouse. —**in,** *f.* baker's wife.

Bad [baːt], *n.* (—es, *pl.* **Bäder**) bath; watering-place. —**e=anstalt,** *f.* baths, bathing establishment. —**e=gast,** *m.* visitor at a watering-place. —**e=kur,** *f.* course of mineral waters. —**e=reise,** *f.* journey to a watering-place. —**e= wanne,** *f.* (*pl.* —en) bath-tub, bath. —**e=zimmer,** *n.* (—s, *pl.* —er) bathroom.

Bad—en ['baːdən], *v.a. & r.* to bathe. —**er,** *m.* (—ers, *pl.* —er) bathkeeper; bather.

Bagage [ba'ga:ʒə], *f.* (*see* **Gepäck**) baggage.

Bagger ['bagər], *m.* (—s, *pl.* —) dredger.

Bahn [ba:n], *f.* (*pl.* —en) path, road; railroad; course. —**brecher**, *m.* (—s, *pl.* —) pioneer. —**brücke**, *f.* railway bridge. —**fahrt**, *f.* railway journey. —**hof**, *m.* railway station. —**los**, *adj.* pathless, trackless. —**steig**, *m.* platform (*at railway stations*).

Bahnen ['ba:nən], *v.a.* to make a pathway; to pioneer; **sich einen Weg** —, to force one's way.

Bahre ['ba:rə], *f.* (*pl.* —n) bier, litter.

Bai [baɪ], *f.* (*pl.* —en) bay, cove.

Bajonett [bajo'nɛt], *n.* (—s, *pl.* —e) bayonet.

Bakterie [bak'te:rɪə], *f.* (*pl.* —n) bacterium.

Bald [balt], *adv.* (**eher; am ehesten**) soon, shortly, directly; almost, nearly; quickly; easily. —**igst**, *adv.* as soon as possible; — **so**, — **so**, now one way, now another.

Balg [balk], *m.* (—es, *pl.* **Bälge**) bag; skin; bellows; brat, urchin.

Balken ['balkən], *m.* (—s, *pl.* —) beam, rafter.

Balkon [bal'kõ:], *m.* (—s, *pl.* —e) balcony.

¹**Ball** [bal], *m.* (—es, *pl.* **Bälle**) ball; globe, sphere. —**hof**, *m.* tennis-court.

²**Ball** [bal], *m.* (—s, *pl.* **Bälle**) dance. —**kleid**, *n.* ball-dress.

Ballade [ba'la:də], *f.* (*pl.* —n) ballad.

Ballen ['balən], *m.* (—s, *pl.* —) bundle, bale, package.

Ballen ['balən], *v.a.* to form into a ball; to clench (*a fist*).

Ballett [ba'lɛt], *n.* (—s, *pl.* —e) ballet.

Ballon [ba'lõ:], *m.* (—s, *pl.* —s) balloon. —**halle**, *f.* hangar.

Balsam ['balzam], *m.* (—s, *pl.* —e) balsam, balm. —**isch**, *adj.* balmy; fragrant.

Bambus ['bambʊs], *m.* (—(ss)es, *pl.* —(ss)e), —**rohr**, *n.* bamboo, bamboo-cane.

Band [bant], I. *n.* (—es, *pl.* **Bänder** *dim.* **Bändchen,** narrow ribbon) band; ribbon; hoop. II. *n.* (—es, *pl.* —e) tie, bond; (*pl.*) fetters. III. *m.* (—es, *pl.* **Bände**) volume, tome.

Bande ['bandə], *f.* (*pl.* —n) band; set, gang.

Bändig ['bɛndɪç], *adj.* (*in compounds*) in . . . volumes.

Bändig—**en** ['bɛndɪgən], *v.a.* to restrain; to break in (*a horse*). —**ung,** *f.* taming, subduing.

Bang [baŋ], —**e** (**banger, bänger; bangst, bängst**), *adj. & adv.* afraid; anxious. —**igkeit**, *f.* fear, uneasiness.

¹**Bank** [baŋk], *f.* (*pl.* **Bänke**) bench; seat; **auf die lange** — **schieben,** to delay, put off.

²**Bank** [baŋk], *f.* (*pl.* —en), bank, banking establishment. —**aktie**, *f.* bankstock. —**anweisung**, *f.* cheque, bankbill. —**bruch**, *m.* bankruptcy. —**konto**, *n.* banking account. —**note,** *f.* bank-note. —**wesen**, *n.* banking. —**zettel**, *m.* bank-note; cheque. —**zettelbuch**, *n.* cheque-book.

Bank(e)rott [baŋkə'rɔt], I. *m.* bankruptcy. II. *adj. & adv.* bankrupt.

Bankier [baŋki'e:], *m.* (—s, *pl.* —s) banker.

Bann [ban], *m.* (—es) proscription; curse; ban; excommunication; **in den** — **tun,** to excommunicate.

Bannen ['banən], *v.a.* to banish; to enchant.

Banner ['banər], *n.* (—s, *pl.* —) banner.

Bar [ba:r], *adj. & adv.* bare, naked; ready (*of money*); —**e Zahlung,** cash payment; —**er Unsinn,** sheer nonsense. —**schaft**, *f.* ready money.

Bar [ba:r], *f.* (*pl.* —s) bar (*for refreshments*); low dancing-room.

Bär [bɛ:r], *m.* (—en, *pl.* —en) bear; **jemandem einen** — **anbinden,** to hoax someone. —**in**, *f.* (*pl.* —innen) she-bear.

Barbar [bar'ba:r], *m.* (—en, *pl.* —en) barbarian. —**ei** [—'raɪ], *f.* barbarity; vandalism.

Barbier [bar'bi:r], *m.* (—s, *pl.* —e) barber.

Barbieren [bar'bi:rən], *v.a.* to shave.

Barchent ['barçənt], *m.* (—s, *pl.* —e) fustian.

Bard—**e** ['bardə], *m.* (—en, *pl.* —en) bard; minstrel. —**isch**, *adj.* bardic.

Bariton ['ba:riton], *m.* (—s, *pl.* —e) barytone.

Barke ['barkə], *f.* (*pl.* —n) bark; barge.

Barmherzig ['barmhɛrtsɪç], *adj. & adv.* compassionate; charitable. —**keit,** *f.* compassion, charity, mercy.

Baromet—**er** [baro'me:tər], *n.* (*also m.*) (—ers, *pl.* —er) barometer.

Baron [ba'ro:n], *m.* —s, *pl.* —e)

baron. —**in**, *f.* (*pl.* —**innen**), —**eſſe**, *f.*
(*pl.* —**eſſen**) baroness.

Barſch [barʃ], *adj. & adv.* rough; rude.

Bart [baːrt], *m.* (—**es**, *pl.* **Bärte**, *dim.*
Bärtchen) beard; comb (*of a cock*);
wards (*of a key*); **Schnurr—**, moustache; **Baden—**, whiskers. —**los**,
adj. beardless.

Bärtig [ˈbɛːrtɪç], *adj.* bearded.

Baſe [ˈbaːzə], *f.* (*pl.* —**n**) female cousin.

Baß [bas], *m.* (—(ſſ)**es**, *pl.* **Bäſſe**) bass.
—(ſſ)**iſt** [—ˈsɪst], *m.* (—(ſſ)**iſten**, *pl.*
—(ſſ)**iſten**) bass-singer. —**geige**, *f.*
bass-viol.

Baſtei [baˈstaɪ], **Baſtion** [bastiˈoːn], *f.*
(*pl.* —**en**) bastion, bulwark.

Bataill—on [batalˈjoːn], *n.* (—**ons**, *pl.*
—**one**) battalion.

Batiſt [baˈtɪst], *m.* (—**es**, *pl.* —**e**)
cambric.

Batterie [batəˈriː], *f.* (*pl.* —**n**) battery.

Bau [bau], *m.* (—**es**, *pl.* —**e**, —**ten**)
building, erection; build, frame, form;
cultivation, agriculture (*especially as
suffix*); **Ader—**, agriculture. **Berg—**,
mining. —**art**, *f.* style of architecture. —**fälligkeit**, *f.* dilapidation.
—**gerüſt**, *n.* scaffolding. —**kunſt**, *f.*
architecture, engineering. —**leute**, *pl.*
workmen employed on a building.
—**meiſter**, *m.* architect; master-
builder. —**riß**, *m.* plan, architect's
drawing. —**ſtätte**, —**ſtelle**, *f.* building-
ground; site. —**werk**, *n.* edifice,
building.

Bauch [baux], *m.* (—**es**, *pl.* **Bäuche**)
belly; paunch. —**ig**, *adj.* bulgy,
bellied. —**redner**, *m.* ventriloquist.
—**rednerei**, *f.* ventriloquism.

Bauen [ˈbauən], *v.* I. *a.* to build; to
construct; to till, cultivate; to work
(*a mine*). II. *n.* (*aux.* **h.**) to count
upon, rely on.

¹**Bauer** [ˈbauər], *m.* (—**s**, *pl.* —)
builder, constructor (*especially as the
second part of compound*), *e.g.* **Orgel-
bauer**, **Schiffsbauer**.

²**Bauer** [ˈbauər], *m.* (—**s &** —**n**, *pl.* —**n**)
husbandman, peasant; pawn (*Chess*).
—**n=gut**, *n.* farm. —**n=hof**, *m.* farm-
buildings. —**n=ſtand**, *m.* peasant
class, peasantry.

³**Bauer** [ˈbauər], *n.* (*rarely m.*) (—**s**, *pl.*
—) (*bird-*)cage.

Bäu(e)r—in [ˈbɔy(ə)rm], *f.* (*pl.* —**innen**)
female peasant.

Baum [baum], *m.* (—**es**, *pl.* **Bäume**,

dim. **Bäumchen**, **Bäumlein**) tree;
beam. —**garten**, *m.* orchard; tree-
nursery. —**öl**, *n.* olive oil, sweet oil.
—**ſchule**, *f.* tree-nursery. —**wolle**, *f.*
cotton. —**wollen**, *adj.* made of
cotton.

Bäumen [ˈbɔymən], *v.a. & refl.* to rear,
prance.

Baus— [baus], *also* **Paus—**. —**bad**,
m. chubby face. —**bädig**, *adj.*
chubby-faced.

Bauſch [bauʃ], *m.* (—**es**, *pl.* **Bäuſche**)
pad, bolster; **in — und Bogen**, in the
lump.

Be [beː], *inseparable prefix. It is joined
with verbs, and changes an intransitive
into a transitive verb or changes the
object of the action of a transitive verb;
it is also used to form transitive verbs
from substantives and adjectives.*

Beabſichtigen [bəˈʔapzɪçtɪgən], *v.a.* to
aim at, intend.

Beacht—en [bəˈʔaxtən], *v.a.* to take
heed to, pay attention to; to take into
consideration. —**ens=wert**, —**ungs=
wert**, *adj.* worthy of notice, noticeable.

Beamt—e(r) [bəˈʔamtə(r)], *m.* (—**en**, *pl.*
—**en**) functionary; official. —**en=
verein**, *m.* (—**es**, *pl.* —**e**) civil-service
association.

Beängſt—igen [bəˈʔɛŋstɪgən], *v.a.* to
make anxious. —**ung**, *f.* anxiety,
uneasiness, alarm.

Beanſpruchen [bəˈʔanʃpruxən], *v.a.* to
claim, lay claim to.

Beanſtanden [bəˈʔanʃtandən], *v.a.* to
object to.

Beantragen [bəˈʔantraːgən], *v.a.* to
move, to propose.

Beantwort—en [bəˈʔantvɔrtən], *v.a.*
to answer, reply to. —**lich**, *adj.*
answerable. —**ung**, *f.* answering;
answer.

Bearbeit—en [bəˈʔarbaɪtən], *v.a.* to
till, cultivate (*land*); to treat, work up
(*a subject*); to arrange, adapt; to revise, re-write. —**er**, *m.* (—**ers**, *pl.*
—**er**) compiler; author; reviser.
—**ung**, *f.* treatment (*of a subject*);
compilation (*of a book*); revision.

Beauffichtig—en [bəˈʔaufzɪçtɪgən], *r.a.*
to inspect, superintend. —**ung**, *f.*
superintendence.

Beauftragen [bəˈʔauftraːgən], *v.a.* to
commission, delegate, empower.

Bebauen [bəˈbauən], *v.a.* to build on:
to cultivate, till.

Beben ['be:bən], I. v.n. (aux. h.) to shiver, quake. II. subst.n. trembling; tremor; thrill. —b, p. & adj. tremulous; shivering.

Becher ['bɛçər], m. (—s, pl. —) beaker, cup, chalice, goblet.

Becken ['bɛkən], n. (—s, pl. —) basin; cymbal (Mus.).

Bedacht [bə'daxt], I. m. (—es) consideration; deliberation. II. adj. intent (on), thoughtful (of). —fam, adj. considerate. —los, adj. & adv. inconsiderate.

Bedächtig [bə'dɛçtıç], adj. & adv. circumspect, discreet, prudent. —feit, f. prudence.

Bedanken [bə'daŋkən], v.r. to return thanks for; to refuse.

Bedarf [bə'darf], m. (—(e)s) requirements, requisites.

Bedauerlich [bə'dauərlıç], adj. regrettable, deplorable.

Bedauer—n [bə'dauərn], I. v.a. to pity (einen wegen, one for); to deplore; to commiserate. II. subst.n. sorrow, regret; pity. —ns-würdig, adj. deplorable, unfortunate.

Bedeck—en [bə'dɛkən], v.a. to cover; to shelter, protect; to hide from view; sich—en, to put on one's hat. —ung, f. covering; escort, convoy; breastwork.

Bedenk—en [bə'dɛŋkən], I. ir.v.a. to consider, reflect on; to heed; to care for, bear in mind. II. subst.n. reflection, consideration; scruple, doubt. —lich, adj. doubtful; critical; serious; delicate. —lichfeit, f. scrupulousness, nicety; hesitation; timidity.

Bedeut—en [bə'dɔytən], v.a. to inform; to signify, mean, imply; to portend; to be of importance; was soll das —en? what does this mean? —end, p. adj. & adv. considerable; important; significant. —fam, adj. significant. —famfeit, f. significance; importance. —ung, f. signification, meaning; importance.

Bedien—en [bə'di:nən], v. I. a. to serve, wait on; to do the duty of (an office). II. r. to help oneself. —te(r), m. servant, footman. —tenhaft, adj. servile. —ung, f. service, attendance; servants.

Beding—en [bə'dıŋən], reg. & ir.v.a. to stipulate, bargain, agree on or for. —t, p.p. & adj. conditional, qualified;

hypothetical. —ung, f. stipulation, condition, terms. —ungs-los, adj. & adv. unconditional(ly). —ungs-weise, adv. conditionally.

Bedräng—en [bə'drɛŋən], v.a. to oppress, grieve, afflict. —er, m. (—ers, pl. —er) oppressor. —t, p.p. & adj. in distress, in difficulties. —nis, f. (pl. —ni(ff)e), —ung, f. oppression; distress.

Bedroh—en [bə'dro:ən], v.a. to threaten, menace. —lich, adj. & adv. threatening. —ung, f. menacing; threat.

Bedrück—en [bə'drykən], v.a. to oppress, harass. —er, m. (—ers, pl. —er) oppressor. —ung, f. oppression.

Bedürf—en [bə'dyrfən], ir.v.n. (aux. h.) & imp. (gen.) to be in want of, need, require. —nis, n. (—ni(ff)es, pl. —ni(ff)e) necessity, requirement; Lebensbedürfnisse, necessaries of life. —tig, adj. poor, needy.

Beehren [bə'ʔe:rən], v.a. to confer an honour on; to honour; ich beehre mich zu . . ., I have the honour to . . .

Beeidig—en [bə'ʔaɪdɪgən], Beeiden [bə'ʔaɪdən], v.a. to confirm by oath. —ung, f. swearing.

Beeifern [bə'ʔaɪfərn], v.r. to exert oneself for; to be zealous about.

Beeilen [bə'ʔaɪlən], v.a. & r. to hurry, hasten.

Beeinflussen [bə'ʔaɪnflusən], v.a. to influence.

Beeinträchtig—en [bə'ʔaɪntrɛçtɪgən], v.a. to injure, wrong; to encroach upon (another's rights). —end, p. & adj. prejudicial. —ung, f. prejudice; injury.

Beendig—en [bə'ʔɛndɪgən], Beenden [bə'ʔɛndən], v.a. to terminate, conclude. —ung, f. termination, finish.

Beengen [bə'ʔɛŋən], v.a. to cramp; to constrain.

Beerben [bə'ʔɛrbən], v.a.; einen —, to be a person's heir, inherit from one.

Beerdig—en [bə'ʔɛrdɪgən], v.a. to bury (only of human beings). —ung, f. interment, burial. —ungs-feier, f. funeral obsequies.

Beer—e ['be:rə], f. (pl. —en) berry. —en-ähnlich, —en-artig, —en-förmig, adj. berry-like.

Beet [be:t], n. (—s, pl. —e) border, bed.

Beete ['be:tə], f. (pl. —n) beet, beetroot.

Befähig—en [bə'fɛ:ɪgən], v.a. to

qualify. —ung, f. qualification; authorization.

Befahren [bə'fa:rən], *ir.v.a.* to travel over; to navigate; **ein sehr —er Weg**, a much-frequented road.

Befallen [bə'falən], *ir.v.a. & imp.* to befall; to attack.

Befangen [bə'faŋən], *p.p. & adj.* embarrassed; partial; prejudiced; preoccupied (with), engrossed (in). —**heit**, *f.* embarrassment; prejudice, bias.

Befassen [bə'fasən], *v.a.* to touch, handle; to comprehend; **sich mit etwas —**, to occupy oneself with, to engage in.

Befehl [bə'fe:l], *m.* —**s**, *pl.* —**e**) command, order; **ich stehe Ihnen zu —**, I am at your service; **Ober—**, supreme command (*Mil.*). —**erisch**, *adj. & adv.* haughty, overbearing. —**shaber**, *m.* commanding officer; chief. —**swidrig**, *adj. & adv.* contrary to orders. —**swort**, *n.* word of command.

Befehl—en [bə'fe:lən], *ir.v.a.* to order, command; to commit to, commend to the care of. —**end**, *p. & adj.* imperative, dictatorial.

Befestig—en [bə'fɛstɪgən], **Befesten** [bə'fɛstən], *v.a.* to fasten; to fortify; to strengthen. —**ung**, *f.* fastening; fortification.

Befeuchten [bə'fɔyçtən], *v.a.* to dampen, moisten.

Befind—en [bə'fɪndən], I. *ir.v.a.* to find, deem, consider. II. *ir.v.r.* to be, fare, feel; **wie —en Sie sich?** how are you? III. *subst.n.* state of health; condition; **nach —en**, as you may think fit. —**lich**, *adj. & adv.* to be found; existing.

Beflecken [bə'flɛkən], *v.a.* to defile, pollute; to patch. —**ung**, *f.* contamination, pollution.

Beflissen [bə'flɪsən], *adj. & adv.* studious (**einer Sache**); diligent; intent (upon), devoted (to). —**heit**, *f.* assiduity. —**tlich**, *adv.* sedulously.

Beflügel—n [bə'fly:gəln], *v.a.* to accelerate, urge on. —**t**, *p.p. & adj.* winged.

Beförder—er [bə'fœrdərər], *m.* (—**ers**, *pl.* —**er**) forwarding agent; promoter; patron. —**lich**, *adj.* favourable, conducive, furthering.

Beförder—n [bə'fœrdərn], *v.a.* to forward (*letters, goods, etc.*); to despatch (*business*); to further, promote, advance; to prefer (*to an office*). —**ung**, *f.* forwarding (*of goods, etc.*); furthering (*of plans*); promotion; advancement; encouragement.

Befracht—en [bə'fraxtən], *v.a.* to freight (*a vessel*). —**er**, *m.* (—**ers**, *pl.* —**er**) charterer; shipper. —**ung**, *f.* freighting.

Befragen [bə'fra:gən], *reg. & ir.v.a.* to interrogate, question.

Befrei—en [bə'fraiən], *v.a.* to free; to rescue. —**er**, *m.* (—**ers**, *pl.* —**er**) liberator. —**te(r)**, *m.* (—**ten**, *pl.* —**ten**) one who is exempt or free. —**ung**, *f.* liberation; exemption, *etc.*

Befremd—en [bə'frɛmdən], I. *v.a. & imp.* to appear strange, astonish, surprise. II. *subst.n.* surprise. —**end**, *p. & adj.*, —**lich**, *adj.* surprising.

Befreund—en [bə'frɔyndən], *v.a.* to befriend, favour; **sich —en mit**, to make friends with. —**et**, I. *p.p. & adj.* friendly; allied, akin. II. *adv.* on terms of friendship.

Befriedig—en [bə'fri:dɪgən], *v.a.* to satisfy; to appease. —**end**, *p. & adj.* satisfactory. —**ung**, *f.* satisfaction; gratification.

Befug—en [bə'fu:gən], *v.a.* to empower, authorize. —**nis**, *f.* (*pl.* —**ni(ss)e**) authorization; authority; warrant. —**t**, *p.p. & adj.* authorized.

Befühlen [bə'fy:lən], *v.a.* to feel.

Befürchten [bə'fyrçtən], *v.a.* to fear, apprehend; to suspect.

Begab—en [bə'ga:bən], *v.a.* to endow; to bestow upon. —**t**, *p.p. & adj.* gifted, talented. —**ung**, *f.* endowment; (*pl.*) talents.

Begaffen [bə'gafən], *v.a.* to stare at, gape at.

Begängnis [bə'gɛŋnɪs], *n.* (—(**ss**)**es**, *pl.* —(**ss**)**e**) celebration, solemnization.

Begatt—en [bə'gatən], *v.r.* to pair; to couple. —**ung**, *f.* pairing; copulation.

Begeb—en [bə'ge:bən], *ir.v.* I. *a.* to negotiate, transfer. II. *r.* to betake (*oneself*); to set about (*business, etc.*); **es begab sich, daß**, it fell out, chanced that; **sich auf die Flucht —en**, to take to flight. —**enheit**, *f.*, —**nis**, *n.* event, occurrence.

Begegn—en [bə'ge:gnən], *v.n.* (*aux.* **f.**) (*dat.*) to meet, encounter; to befall, happen. —**is**, *n.* (—(**ss**)**es**, *pl.* —(**ss**)**e**) occurrence, event. —**ung**, *f.* meeting, encounter.

Begeh—en [bə'ge:ən], *ir.v.a.* to traverse; to frequent (*a road*); to celebrate; to commit (*an error, etc.*). —ung, *f.* celebration, solemnization; perpetration.

Begehr [bə'ge:r], *m. & n.* (—s) desire.

Begehr—en [bə'ge:rən], I. *v.a.* to desire, want; to crave. II. *subst.n.* desire, demand, request. —lich, *adj. & adv.* covetous. —lichkeit, *f.* covetousness; inordinate desire. —ens= würdig, *adj.* desirable.

Begeister—n [bə'gaɪstərn], *v.a.* to inspire; to animate, fill with enthusiasm. —ung, *f.* inspiration; rapture; enthusiasm.

Begier [bə'gi:r], *f.,* —de, *f.* (*pl.* —den) eager desire; appetite, lust. —ig, *adj. & adv.* eager (nach, for); covetous; greedy; lustful. —igkeit, *f.* avidity.

Begießen [bə'gi:sən], *ir.v.a.* to water (*plants, etc.*); to sprinkle.

Beginn [bə'gɪn], *m.* (—(e)s) beginning, origin.

Beginnen [bə'gɪnən], *ir.v.a.* to begin, commence.

Beglaubig—en [bə'glaubɪgən], *v.a.* to attest, certify; to accredit; to confirm. —er, *m.* certifier; notary. —ung, attestation, verification. —ungs=brief, *m.,* —ungs=schreiben, *n.* credentials. —ungs=schein, *m.* certificate.

Begleichen [bə'glaɪçən], *v.a.* to balance, pay, settle (*a bill*).

Begleit—en [bə'glaɪtən], *v.a.* to accompany. —er, *m.* (—ers, *pl.* —er) attendant, escort. —ung, *f.* accompanying; escort, convoy; accompaniment. —schein, *m.* way-bill; permit.

Beglück—en [bə'glʏkən], *v.a.* to make happy, bless. —wünschen, *v.a.* to congratulate, felicitate. —wünschung, *f.* congratulation.

Begnad—en [bə'gna:dən], —igen [—ɪgən], *v.a.* to pardon; to grant favours to. —igung, *f.* pardoning; pardon; favour.

Begnügen [bə'gny:gən], *v.r.; sich* — (lassen) an einer S., to content oneself with a thing; to acquiesce (in).

Begraben [bə'gra:bən], *ir.v.a.* to bury.

Begräbnis [bə'grɛ:pnɪs], *n.* (—(ss)es, *pl.* —(ss)e) burial; funeral.

Begreif—en [bə'graɪfən], *ir.v.* I. *a.* to include; to comprehend, understand, conceive; begriffen sein, to be engaged in, to be about a thing. II. *r.* recollect

oneself; to be easy of comprehension; das —t sich leicht, that is easily understood. —lich, *adj. & adv.* comprehensible, conceivable.

Begrenz—en [bə'grɛntsən], *v.a.* to bound (*countries, etc.*); to limit, circumscribe. —t, *p.p. & adj.* bounded; narrow; limited. —ung, *f.* limitation; bounds.

Begriff [bə'grɪf], *m.* (—s, *pl.* —e) conception; idea, notion; concept; extent; contents; im —(e) sein, to be on the point of, in the act of; ich war im — zu gehen, I was about to go; schwer von — sein, to be slow (*in the uptake*).

Begründ—en [bə'grʏndən], *v.a.* to base, found; to prove, make good (*an assertion, etc.*); to confirm. —er, *m.* (—ers, *pl.* —er) founder. —ung, *f.* establishment; confirmation; proof.

Begrüß—en [bə'gry:sən], *v.a.* to greet, salute. —ung, *f.* greeting, salutation.

Begünstig—en [bə'gʏnstɪgən], *v.a.* to favour, befriend. —ung, *f.* encouragement, patronage.

Begutacht—en [bə'gu:tʔaxtən], *v.a.* to give an opinion on. —ung, *f.* formal opinion, expert opinion.

Begütert [bə'gy:tərt], *adj.* opulent, rich.

Begütigen [bə'gy:tɪgən], *v.a.* to appease. —d, *adv.* soothingly.

Behäbig [bə'hɛ:bɪç], *adj. & adv.* in easy circumstances; comfortable.

Behag—en [bə'ha:gən], I. *v.n.* (*aux.* h.) (*dat.*) to please, suit. II. *subst.n.* comfort, ease; enjoyment. —lich, *adj. & adv.* comfortable. —lichkeit, *f.* comfort, ease; sociability.

Behalt—en [bə'haltən], *ir.v.a.* to retain; to maintain; to remember. —sam, *adj.* retentive (*of memory*); lasting. →samkeit, *f.* retentiveness.

Behält—er [bə'hɛltər], *m.* (—ers, *pl.* —er) reservoir; receptacle.

Behand—eln [bə'handəln], *v.a.* to handle (*an object, a subject*); to treat; to manipulate, manage; to bargain for; Wunden —eln, to dress wounds. —lung, *f.* treatment; manipulation.

Beharr—en [bə'harən], I. *v.n.* (*aux.* h.) to persevere; to remain steadfast. II. *subst.n.* perseverance, persistence. —lich, *adj. & adv.* persevering; unyielding, firm. —lichkeit, *f.* perseverance, persistence.

Behaupt—en [bə'hauptən], *v.* I. *a.* to

assert; to affirm; to keep, maintain (*one's station, opinion, etc.*). II. *r.* to hold one's ground. —**ung**, *f.* assertion, statement.

Behausung [bə'hauzʊŋ], *f.* house, home.

Behelf [bə'hɛlf], *m.* (—**s**, *pl.* —**e**) expedient, shift.

Behelfen [bə'hɛlfən], *ir.v.r.* to manage, contrive; to have recourse to.

Behend—**e** [bə'hɛndə], *adj. & adv.* handy, agile; adroit. —**igkeit**, *f.* agility, activity.

Beherbergen [bə'hɛrbɛrgən], *v.a.* to lodge, shelter.

Beherrsch—**en** [bə'hɛrʃən], *v.a.* to rule over, govern; **sich** —**en**, to keep one's temper. —**er**, *m.* (—**ers**, *pl.* —**er**), —**erin**, *f.* ruler, master, sovereign. —**ung**, *f.* sway, control; domination.

Beherz—**igen** [bə'hɛrtsɪgən], *v.a.* to take to heart. —**t**, *p.p. & adj.* brave, courageous. —**t**=**heit**, *f.* spirit, intrepidity.

Behexen [bə'hɛksən], *v.a.* to bewitch.

Behilflich [bə'hɪlflɪç], *adj.* useful, serviceable, helpful.

Behorchen [bə'hɔrçən], *v.a.* to overhear; to eavesdrop.

Behörde [bə'hø:rdə], *f.* (*pl.* —**n**) magistracy, authority; the authorities.

Behuf [bə'hu:f], *m.* (—**s**) behalf, behoof. —**s**, *prep.* (*with gen.*) for the purpose of, in order to.

Behuft [bə'hu:ft], *p.p. & adj.* hoofed.

Behüt—**en** [bə'hy:tən], *v.a.* to guard (*vor*, against), to preserve (*from*); to defend, protect; —**e Gott!** God forbid!

Behutsam [bə'hu:tza:m], *adj. & adv.* prudent; careful. —**keit**, *f.* caution.

Bei [baɪ], I. *prep.* (*with dat.*) about; amidst, among(st); at; with; in possession of; by (*as instrument*); by, upon (*in oaths*); at the house of; during; for; by; near, by, at the side of; to; on, in case of; along with. II. *adv.* almost, nearly, about. III. *adv. or sep. prefix*, near, near by; beside, in addition.

Beibehalten ['baɪbəhaltən], *ir.v.a.* to retain (*in office*); to keep, preserve.

Beiblatt ['baɪblat], *n.* (—**s**, *pl.* **Beiblätter**) supplement (*to newspaper, etc.*).

Beibringen ['baɪbrɪŋən], *ir.v.a.* to bring forward; to cite (*authorities*); to deal (*blows*); **Kenntnis** —, to teach, instruct.

Beicht—**e** ['baɪçtə], *f.* (*pl.* —**en**) confession. —**kind**, *n.* penitent. —**stuhl**, *m.* confessional. —**vater**, *m.* father confessor.

Beichten ['baɪçtən], *v.a. & n.* to confess.

Beid—**e** ['baɪdə], *num. adj.* both; **alle** —**e**, both of them. —**erlei**, *indec. adj.* of both sorts, of either sort. —**erseitig**, *adj.* on both sides, mutual, reciprocal. —**erseits**, *adv.* reciprocally, mutually.

Beieinander [baɪ⁹aɪ'nandər], *adv.* together.

Beifall ['baɪfal], *m.* (—**s**) approbation; applause.

Beifällig ['baɪfɛlɪç], *adj.* incidental; assenting, approving.

Beifolgend ['baɪfɔlgənd], *adj.* enclosed, subjoined.

Beifüg—**en** ['baɪfy:gən], *v.a.* to add, enclose. —**ung**, *f.* addition.

Beigeben ['baɪge:bən], *ir.v.a.* to add, join to; **klein** —, (*coll.*) to come down a peg.

Beigehen ['baɪge:hən], *ir.v.n.* (*aux.* f.) to go with; to occur to.

Beigenannt ['baɪgənant], *p.p. & adj.* surnamed.

Beigeschmack ['baɪgəʃmak], *m.* (—**s**) flavour, savour.

Beigesellen ['baɪgəzɛlən], *v.a.* to associate.

Beihilf—**e** ['baɪhɪlfə], *f.* assistance, aid, succour. —**lich**, *adj.* helping; subsidiary.

Beikommen ['baɪkɔmən], *ir.v.n.* (*aux.* f.) to come at, get at.

Beil [baɪl], *n.* (—**s**, *pl.* —**e**) hatchet.

Beilage ['baɪla:gə], *f.* (*pl.* —**n**) something added; enclosure; appendix; **Fleisch mit** —, meat with vegetables.

Beiläufig ['baɪlɔyfɪç], I. *adj.* incidental. II. *adv.* incidentally, by the way; nearly, about.

Beileg—**en** ['baɪle:gən], *v.a.* to add; to enclose; to attribute, ascribe to; to settle (*dispute*). —**ung**, *f.* addition; attribution; settlement.

Beileibe nicht! [baɪ'laɪbə nɪçt] *interj.* not for the world! by no means!

Beileid ['baɪlaɪt], *n.* (—**es**) condolence.

Beiliegen ['baɪli:gən], *ir.v.n.* (*aux.* h.) to lie with; to be enclosed (*letter*).

Beim [baɪm], *short for* **bei dem**.

Beimisch—**en** ['baɪmɪʃən], *v.a.* to mix with. —**ung**, *f.* admixture.

Bein [baɪn], n. (—s, pl. —e) leg; bone; **er ist gut auf den —en**, he is a good walker; **einem auf die —e helfen**, to give a person a lift (help him); **sich auf die —e machen**, to start, to be off. **—ig**, adj. (suffix)=legged, as **krumm-beinig**, bandy-legged. **—kleider**, pl. trousers.

Beinah(e) ['baɪna:(ə)], adv. almost, nearly.

Beiname ['baɪna:mə], m. (—ns, pl. —n) surname, epithet.

Beiordnen ['baɪʔɔrdnən], v.a. to appoint as assistant; **beigeordnet**, p.p. & adj. adjunct.

Beipflicht—en ['baɪpflɪçtən], v.n. (aux. h.); **einem —en**, to agree with one in opinion. **—ung**, f. consent; approval.

Beirren [bə'ʔɪrən], v.a. to mislead, confuse.

Beisammen [baɪ'zamən], adv. together.

Beisatz ['baɪzats], m. (—es, pl. **Beisätze**) addition; **ohne —**, unalloyed.

Beischlaf ['baɪʃla:f], m. (—es) cohabitation.

Beischlafen ['baɪʃla:fən], ir.v.n. (aux. h.) to sleep with.

Beischluß ['baɪʃlʊs], m. (—sses, pl. **Beischlüsse**) enclosure.

Beisein ['baɪzaɪn], n. (—s) presence.

Beiseite [baɪ'zaɪtə], adv. aside, apart.

Beisetzen ['baɪzetsən], v.a. to lay aside; to bury.

Beisitz—en ['baɪzɪtsən], ir.v.n. (aux. h.) to sit by. **—er**, m. (—ers, pl. —er) assessor.

Beispiel ['baɪʃpi:l], n. (—s, pl. —e) example, precedent; **zum —** (abbrev. z. B.) for example. **—los**, adj. unexampled, unprecedented.

Beispringen ['baɪʃprɪŋən], ir.v.n. (aux. f.); **einem —**, to help someone.

Beiß—en ['baɪsən], ir.v.a.,& n. (aux. h.) to bite; to prick, sting; to smart; **ins Gras —en**, to bite the dust, die. **—end**, p. & adj. stinging; acrid, caustic. **—ig**, (obs.; now usually **bissig**) adj. & adv. snappish.

Beistand ['baɪstant], m. (—es) support, assistance.

Beisteh—en ['baɪʃte:hən], ir.v.n. (aux. h.) (einem) to aid, succour, help; **die —enden**, the bystanders, those present. **—er**, m. (—ers, pl. —er) assistant; second.

Beisteuer ['baɪʃtɔyər], f. (pl. —n) contribution, subsidy.

Beisteuern ['baɪʃtɔyərn], v.a. to contribute.

Beistimm—en ['baɪʃtɪmən], v.n. (aux. h. dat.) to assent to, agree with. **—ung**, f. assent, acquiescence.

Beistrich ['baɪʃtrɪç], m. (—s, pl. —e) comma.

Beitrag ['baɪtra:k], m. (—s, pl. **Beiträge**) contribution; share.

Beitragen ['baɪtra:gən], ir.v.a. to contribute; to bear a share; to help (zu).

Beitreten ['baɪtre:tən], ir.v.n. (aux. f. dat.) to agree to, assent to; **einem als Teilhaber im Geschäft —**, to enter into partnership with someone.

Beitritt ['baɪtrɪt], m. (—s) accession to (zu), taking part in; joining (a society).

Beiweg ['baɪve:k], m. (—s, pl. —e) by-way, by-road.

Beiwohn—en ['baɪvo:nən], v.n. (aux. h. dat.) to be present at, attend; to be inherent in. **—ung**, f. presence.

Beiwort ['baɪvɔrt], n. (—s, pl. —e) adjective; epithet.

Beizählen ['baɪtsɛ:lən], v.a. to number with, count among.

Beizeiten [baɪ'tsaɪtən], adv. betimes, early.

Bejah—en [bə'ja:hən], v.a. to answer in the affirmative. **—ung**, f. affirmative answer.

Bejahrt [bə'ja:rt], adj. aged, stricken in years.

Bejammern [bə'jamərn], v.a. to bewail, deplore.

Bekämpfen [bə'kɛmfən], v.a. to combat; to attack, oppose.

Bekannt [bə'kant], p.p. & adj. known; **allgemein —**, notorious. **—er**, m., **—e**, **—in**, f. acquaintance. **—lich**, (**—ermaßen**[—'masən]), adv. as is well known, as you know. **—schaft**, f. (pl. **—schaften**) acquaintance; knowledge. **—machung**, f. notification; public notice.

Bekehrbar [bə'ke:rba:r], adj. convertible.

Bekehr—en [bə'ke:rən], v.a. to convert; **sich —en**, to become converted. **—er**, m. (—ers, pl. —er) proselytizer, converter. **—te(r)**, m., **—te**, f. convert, proselyte. **—ung**, f. conversion.

Bekenn—en [bə'kɛnən], ir.v.a. to confess; **sich** (acc.) **zu einer Tat —en**, to acknowledge having done something; **Farbe —en**, to follow suit (cards);

fich zu einer Religion —en, to profess
a religion. —er, *m*. (—ers, *pl.* —er)
one who confesses *or* professes (*a religion*); follower. —tnis, *n*. (—tniffes,
pl. —tniffe) confession, avowal.

Beklag—en [bə'kla:gən], *v.a.* to lament,
bewail, deplore; fich —en, to complain
(über eine S., of a thing; bei einem, to
a person). —te(r), *m*., —te, *f*. defendant. —ens=wert, —ens=würdig, *adj.*
lamentable, deplorable.

Bekleben [bə'kle:bən], *v.a.* to paste on;
to line (*with paper*); to label.

Bekleid—en [bə'klardən], *v.a.* to
clothe; to paper (*a room*); to invest
(*with authority*); to occupy (*a post*).
—ung, *f*. clothes; drapery; hang-
ings; administration, exercise (*of an
office*).

Beklemm—en [bə'klɛmən], *v.a.* (*p.p.
often* beklommen, *which see*) to oppress
(*the heart, etc.*). —ung, *f*. anxiety;
anguish.

Beklommen [bə'klɔmən], *p.p. & adj.*
anxious, uneasy; depressed. —heit,
f. depression; anxiety.

Bekommen [bə'kɔmən], *ir.v.* I. *a.* to
get, gain, obtain, have. II. *n.* (*aux.
f.*) to agree with one, suit one; wohl
bekomm' es Ihnen! much good may
it do you! ift es Ihnen gut —? has
it done you good? es wird ihm
fchlecht —, he will suffer for it.

Bekömmlich [bə'kœmlɪç], *adj.* salu-
brious.

Beköstig—en [bə'kœstɪgən], *v.a.* to provide with food, to board. —ung, *f*.
boarding, catering.

Bekräftig—en [bə'krɛftɪgən], *v.a.* to
strengthen; to aver, corroborate.
—ung, *f*. corroboration, confirmation;
affirmation.

Bekränzen [bə'krɛntsən], *v.a.* to
wreathe, crown with a garland.

Bekreuzen [bə'krɔʏtsən], **Bekreuzigen**
[bə'krɔʏtsɪgən], *v.a.* to make the sign
of the cross upon; fich —, to cross
oneself.

Bekriegen [bə'kri:gən], *v.a.*; einen —,
to fight someone.

Bekümmer—n [bə'kymərn], *v.* I. *a.* to
grieve, afflict, distress, trouble. II.
r. to concern oneself about. —nis, *n*.
(—niffes, *pl.* —niffe), solicitude; grief,
affliction. —t, *p.p. & adj.* grieved,
afflicted.

Belachen [bə'laxən], *v.a.* to laugh at,

ridicule. —s=wert, —s=würdig, *adj.
& adv.* ridiculous.

Belad—en [bə'la:dən], *ir.v.a.* to load;
to burden. —ung, *f*. act of loading.

Belag [bə'la:k], *m*. (—s, *pl.* **Beläge**)
anything laid on or upon; meat, *etc.*,
laid on bread.

Belager—n [bə'la:gərn], *v.a.* to besiege.
—er (—ers, *pl.* —er) besieger. —ung,
f. siege. —ungs=zuftand, *m*. state of
siege.

Belang [bə'laŋ], *m*. (—s) amount; importance; von keinem —, of no importance.

Belang—en [bə'laŋən], *v.a.* to concern,
belong to. —end, *p. & adj.* touching,
concerning.

Belaft—en [bə'lastən], *v.a.* to load,
lade, freight; to burden, encumber;
to charge to one's account, debit
with. —ung, *f*. charge; load, burden;
debit. —ungs=zeuge, *m*. witness for
the prosecution.

Beläftig—en [bə'lɛstɪgən], *v.a.* to
burden; to trouble, molest. —ung, *f*.
burden; molestation.

Belauf [bə'lauf], *m*. (—s) amount,
sum.

Belauf—en [bə'laufən], *ir.v.a.* to walk,
go over; fich —en auf, to amount to.

Belaufch—en [bə'lauʃən], *v.a.* to listen
to; to play the spy on. —er, *m*.
(—ers, *pl.* —er) eavesdropper.

Beleb—en [bə'le:bən], *v.a.* to enliven;
to animate, invigorate; to cheer.
—end, *p. & adj.* enlivening; animat-
ing. —t, *p.p. & adj.* lively; bustling.
—theit, *f*. animation; liveliness.

Beleg [bə'le:k], *m*. (—es, *pl.* —e) document serving as voucher; receipt;
proof. —fchein, *m*., —ftück, *n*. voucher.

Beleg—en [bə'le:gən], I. *v.a.* to cover,
overlay; to shoe (*a wheel*); to show
proof of, verify; to secure, retain (*a
place*). II. *adj.* situated. —tes
Brot, sandwich; —te Zunge, furred
tongue.

Belehn—en [bə'le:nən], *v.a.* to enfeoff.
—te(r), *m*. (—ten, *pl.* —ten) vassal.
—ung, *f*. enfeoffment.

Belehr—en [bə'le:rən], *v.a.* to instruct;
to advise. —ung, *f*. instruction;
information.

Beleibt [bə'laɪpt], *adj.* stout, fat.

Beleidig—en [bə'laɪdɪgən], *v.a.* to
offend; to insult; to wrong. —end,
p. & adj. offensive; insulting. —er,

m. (—ers, *pl.* —er) offender; insulter.
—te(r), *m.*, —te, *f.* person insulted.
—ung, *f.* insult; affront.

Belesen [bə'le:zən], *adj.* well-read.
—heit, *f.* extensive reading.

Beleucht—en [bə'lɔyçtən], *v.a.* to illuminate; to illustrate. —ung, *f.* lighting (*of streets, etc.*); elucidation, illustration (*of a subject*).

Belfern ['bɛlfərn], *v.n.* (*aux.* h.) to snarl, yelp.

Belieb—en [bə'li:bən], I. *v.a.* to like; to think proper, resolve. II. *v.n. & imp.* (*aux.* h., *dat.*) to please; was —t Ihnen? what do you wish? III. *subst.n.* will, pleasure; nach —en, at will. —ig, *adj. & adv.* agreeable, to your liking. —t, *p.p. & adj.* favourite; popular.

Bellen ['bɛlən], *v.n.* (*aux.* h.) to bark, bay.

Belob—en [bə'lo:bən], *v.a.* to praise, commend. —ung, *f.* commendation.

Belohn—en [bə'lo:nən], *v.a.* to reward; to recompense. —ung, *f.* reward, recompense.

Belügen [bə'ly:gən], *ir.v.a.* to deceive by lying.

Belustig—en [bə'lʊstɪgən], *v.a.* to amuse, entertain. —end, *p. & adj.* amusing, diverting. —ung, *f.* amusement.

Bemächtig—en [bə'mɛçtɪgən], *v.r.*(*gen.*) to take possession of, seize. —ung, *f.* (*act of*) obtaining possession of; seizure.

Bemeistern [bə'maɪstərn], *v.a.* (& *r.* with *gen.*) to gain the mastery over; to overcome (*difficulties, etc.*).

Bemerkbar [bə'mɛrkba:r], *adj.* perceptible; sensible, noticeable. —keit, *f.* perceptibility.

Bemerk—en [bə'mɛrkən], *v.a.* to observe, perceive; to note; to remark. —ung, *f.* observation, remark; note. —ens=wert, —ens=würdig, *adj.* noteworthy.

Bemitleiden [bə'mɪtlaɪdən], *v.a.* to pity.

Bemittelt [bə'mɪtəlt], *adj.* well off, well-to-do.

Bemüh—en [bə'my:ən], I. *v.a.* to trouble, give trouble; darf ich Sie darum —en? may I trouble you for it? II. *v.r.* to take trouble, pains; to strive, endeavour. III. *subst.n.* —ung, *f.* trouble, pains, effort.

Benachbart [bə'naxba:rt], *adj.* neighbouring, adjoining, adjacent.

Benachrichtig—en [bə'naxrɪçtɪgən], *v.a.*; einen von etwas —en, to acquaint, apprise, warn someone of something. —ung, *f.* notification; intimation; advice.

Benachteiligen [bə'naxtaɪlɪgən], *v.a.* to prejudice, injure.

Benagen [bə'na:gən], *v.a.* to gnaw.

Benähen [bə'nɛ:hən], *v.a.* to sew upon; to patch.

Benebel—n [bə'ne:bəln], *v.a.* to wrap in mist; fich —n, to get slightly tipsy. —t, *p.p. & adj.* clouded over.

Benedeien [bene'daɪən], *v.a.* (*p.p.* (ge)benedeit) to bless.

Benefiz [bene'fi:ts], *n.* (—es, *pl.* —e) benefit; (*pl.* —ien) benefice, living.

Benehmen [bə'ne:mən], I. *ir.v.a.* to take away. II. *ir.v.r.* to behave, demean oneself; to act. III. *subst.n.* conduct, behaviour.

Beneiden [bə'naɪdən], *v.a.* (einen, einen um eine S., *or* wegen einer S., einem etwas) to envy. —s=wert, *adj.* enviable.

Benenn—en [bə'nɛnən], *ir.v.a.* to name. —ung, *f.* naming, designation.

Benetzen [bə'nɛtsən], *v.a.* to wet, moisten.

Bengel ['bɛŋəl], *m.* (—s, *pl.* —) rough fellow. —haft, *adj.* clownish, boorish, rude.

Benötigen [bə'nø:tɪgən], *v.a.* to require, need; einer S. benötigt sein, to stand in need of a thing.

Benutzbar [bə'nʊtsba:r], *adj.* usable.

Benutzen [bə'nʊtsən], Benützen [bə'nytsən], *v.a.* to make use of, utilize.

Benzin [bɛn'tsi:n], *n.* (—s) benzine; petrol (*Motor.*).

Beobacht—en [bə'ʔo:baxtən], *v.a.* to observe; to watch. —er, *m.* (—ers, *pl.* —er) observer. —ung, *f.* observation.

Bepflanzen [bə'pflantsən], *v.a.* to plant.

Bepflügen [bə'pfly:gən], *v.a.* to plough.

Bequem [bə'kve:m], *adj.* convenient, commodious, comfortable; proper; fond of ease; indolent.

Bequemen [bə'kve:mən], *v.* I. *a.* to accommodate, suit. II. *r.* to accommodate oneself, conform, put up with; to comply with.

Berat—en [bə'ra:tən], *ir.v.* I. *a.* to

furnish with what is necessary; to counsel, advise. II. *r.* to take counsel together, deliberate. —**er,** *m.* (—**ers,** *pl.* —**er**) adviser, counsellor.

Beratschlag—**en** [bə'ra:tʃla:gən], *v.n. & refl. (aux. h.)* to deliberate. —**ung,** *f.* consultation, deliberation; counsel.

Berauben [bə'raubən], *v.a.* (einen einer Sache) to rob (a person of a thing).

Berauschen [bə'rauʃən], *v.a.* to intoxicate.

Berechn—**en** [bə'rɛçnən], *v.a.* to compute, calculate; to cast up (*an account*); to estimate (auf, at). —**er,** *m.* (—**ers,** *pl.* —**er**) calculator, computer. —**ung,** *f.* calculation, computation.

Berechtig—**en** [bə'rɛçtigən], *v.a.* to entitle (one) to; to authorize, empower. —**ung,** *f.* title, right; qualification.

Bered—**en** [bə're:dən], *v.a.*; einen zu etwas —**en,** to persuade someone to a thing. —**sam,** *adj.* eloquent. —**samkeit,** *f.* eloquence; rhetoric. —**t,** *p.p., adj. & adv.* eloquent; talkative.

Bereich [bə'raiç], *m. & n.* (—**s,** *pl.* —**e**) scope; sphere; province.

Bereichern [bə'raiçərn], *v.a.* to enrich.

Bereisen [bə'raizən], *v.a.* to travel over *or* through a country.

Bereit [bə'rait], *adj.* ready, prepared; — halten, to keep, hold in readiness. —**s,** *adv.* already. —**schaft,** *f.* readiness, preparation. —**willig,** *adj. & adv.* ready, willing; willingly.

1**Bereiten** [bə'raitən], *v.a.* to prepare, make ready.

2**Bereiten** [bə'raitən], *ir.v.a.* to ride over; to train, break in (a horse); **beritten,** mounted (*Mil.*); broken in.

Berennen [bə'rɛnən], *ir.v.a.* to invest, blockade; to attack, assault.

Bereu—**en** [bə'rɔyən], *v.a.* to repent, regret. —**ung,** *f.* repentance, regret.

Berg [bɛrk], *m.* (—**es,** *pl.* —**e**) mountain, hill; die Haare standen mir zu —**e,** my hair stood on end; wir sind noch nicht über den —, we are not yet out of the wood. —**ig,** *adj.* mountainous, hilly. —'**ab,** *adv.* downhill. —'**an** *or* —'**auf,** *adv.* uphill. —**arbeit,** *f.* mining (industry). —**bau,** *m.* mining; working of mines. —**baukunst,** *f.* science of mining; metallurgy. —**fried,** *m.* watch-tower. —**herr,** *m.* mine-owner. —**kette,** *f.* mountain chain, ridge of mountains.

—**land,** *n.* hilly country. —**leute,** *pl.* miners; mountaineers. —**mann,** *m.* miner. —**öl,** *n.* petroleum. —**schotten,** *pl.* Scotch Highlanders. —**werk,** *n.* mine; pit; ein —**werk bauen,** to sink, work a mine. —**wesen,** *n.* mining affairs.

Bergen ['bɛrgən], *ir.v.a.* to save, secure; to conceal. —**egeld,** *n.* salvage-money.

Bericht [bə'rɪçt], *m.* (—**s,** *pl.* —**e**) report, statement; intelligence; — erstatten, to present *or* hand in a report. —**erstatter,** *m.* reporter, relater. —**erstattung,** *f.* reporting; report.

Berichten [bə'rɪçtən], *v.a.* to inform; to report.

Berichtig—**en** [bə'rɪçtigən], *v.a.* to set right, rectify; to correct (*errors; proofs, etc.*). —**ung,** *f.* correction; emendation.

Beritten [bə'rɪtən], *adj.* mounted, on horseback.

Berlin—**e** [bɛr'li:nə], *f.* (*pl.* —**en**) a sort of carriage. —**erblau,** *n.* prussian blue.

Berlocke [bɛr'lɔkə], *f.* (*pl.* —**n**) trinket, charm.

Bernstein ['bɛrnstain], *m.* (—**s**) amber.

Bersten ['bɛrstən], *ir.v.n. (aux. f.)* to burst, crack.

Berüchtig—**en** [bə'rʏçtigən], *v.a.* to defame. —**t,** *p.p. & adj.* infamous, notorious.

Berücken [bə'rʏkən], *v.a.* to ensnare; to take in, cheat. —**b,** *p. & adj.* ensnaring, fascinating, charming.

Berücksichtig—**en** [bə'rʏkzɪçtigən], *v.a.* to respect; to take into consideration. —**ung,** *f.* consideration, regard.

Beruf [bə'ru:f], *m.* (—**s,** *pl.* —**e**) calling; vocation; profession; faculty. —**smäßig,** *adj. & adv.* professional.

Beruf—**en** [bə'ru:fən], *ir.v.a.* to call; to call together; sich auf einen —**en,** to appeal to a person; unberufen! let the devil rest! —**ung,** *f.,* —**ungs-,** (*in comp.*) act of summoning *or* of appealing; vocation; appeal. —**ungsgericht,** *n.* court of appeal.

Beruhen [bə'ru:ən], *v.a. (aux. h.)* to rest; etwas —**lassen,** to leave a thing alone.

Beruhig—**en** [bə'ru:igən], *v.a.* to tranquillize, pacify. —**end,** *p. & adj.* sedative. —**ung,** *f.* quieting, calming; pacification.

Berühm—**en** [bə'ry:mən], *v.r.*; sich

einer Sache —en, to boast or brag of a thing. —t, p.p. & adj. famous, celebrated. —theit, f. celebrity, distinction; person of fame.

Berühr-en [bə'ry:rən], v.a. to touch; to touch upon, allude to; to meddle with. —end, p. & adj. contiguous; touching; tangent. —ung, f. contact; contiguity; collision; reference to (a subject).

Beryll [be'ryl], m. (—s, pl. —e) beryl.

Besäen [bə'zɛ:ən], v.a. to sow.

Besag-en [bə'za:gən], v.a. to purport. —end, p. & adj. to the effect, etc. —t, p.p. & adj. aforesaid.

Besan [be'za:n], m. (—s, pl. —e) mizzen.

Besänftig-en [bə'zɛnftɪgən], v.a. to assuage; to appease. —end, adj. calming. —ung, f. allayment; appeasing.

Besatz [bə'zats], m. (—es, pl. Besätze) trimming. —ung, f. garrison.

Beschädig-en [bə'ʃɛ:dɪgən], v.a. to damage. —t, p.p. & adj. damaged.

Beschaffen [bə'ʃafən], I. ir.v.a. to create. II. p.p. & adj. constituted; die Sache ist so —, the matter stands thus. —heit, f. nature, kind; disposition.

Beschäftig-en [bə'ʃɛftɪgən], v.a. to occupy, employ. —t, p.p. & adj. busy. —ung, f. occupation, business.

Beschatten [bə'ʃatən], v.a. to shade.

Beschau-en [bə'ʃauən], v.a. to behold; to inspect, to gaze upon. —er, m. (—ers, pl. —er) looker-on, spectator. —lich, adj. & adv. perceptible. —ung, f. examination; inspection.

Bescheid [bə'ʃart], m. (—es, pl. —e) knowledge; instructions; answer; award; decision, decree; ich weiß hier nicht —, I am a stranger here.

Bescheid-en [bə'ʃaidən], I. ir.v.a. to allot; to order. II. adj. & adv. modest; discreet. —enheit, f. modesty; diffidence; moderation.

Bescheinig-en [bə'ʃaɪnɪgən], v.a. to attest; to vouch for. —ung, f. certificate; voucher.

Beschenken [bə'ʃɛnkən], v.a. to present with.

Bescheren [bə'ʃe:rən], reg.v.a. (einem etwas) to give, bestow upon.

Beschießen [bə'ʃi:sən], ir.v.a. to bombard.

Beschimpf-en [bə'ʃɪmpfən], v.a. to insult, revile. —end, p. & adj.

defamatory; libellous. —ung, f. affront, insult.

Beschirm-en [bə'ʃɪrmən], v.a. to screen; to protect. —ung, f. defence, safeguard.

Beschlag [bə'ʃla:k], m. (—s, pl. Beschläge) anything attached to an article; embargo; distraint. —nahme, f. distraint, seizure, sequestration.

Beschlagen [bə'ʃla:gən], ir.v.a. to hammer; to sheathe; to shoe (a horse); to drape.

Beschleunig-en [bə'ʃlɔynɪgən], v.a. to hasten, expedite. —end, p. & adj. accelerating. —ung, f. acceleration; despatch; speed.

Beschließen [bə'ʃli:sən], ir.v.a. to conclude; to resolve, decide. beschlossen [—'ʃlɔsən], p.p. & adj. resolved.

Beschluß [bə'ʃlus], m. (—(ß)es, pl. Beschlüsse) conclusion; resolve, resolution. —nahme, f. determination; decree.

Beschränk-en [bə'ʃrɛŋkən], v.a. to limit, circumscribe; to restrict. —t, p.p. & adj. limited; circumscribed. —theit, f. narrowness; dullness, stupidity. —ung, f. restraint; limitation.

Beschreib-en [bə'ʃraibən], ir.v.a. to describe. —end, p. & adj. descriptive. —ung, f. description.

Beschuldig-en [bə'ʃuldɪgən], v.a. (einen einer Sache) to accuse of. —er, m. (—ers, pl. —er) accuser; plaintiff. —t, p.p. & adj. accused; der —te, person accused, defendant. —ung, f. accusation.

Beschütz-en [bə'ʃytsən], v.a. to protect, guard, defend. —er, m. (—ers, pl. —er), —erin, f. protector; guardian; patron, patroness. —ung, f. protection.

Beschwer [bə'ʃve:r], f. (no pl.) & n. (—s, no pl.), —de [bə'ʃve:rdə], f. (pl. —den) trouble, difficulty; hardship; grievance; complaint. —lich, adj. painful; difficult, hard. —lichkeit, f. troublesomeness; hardship; inconvenience; difficulty.

Beschweren [bə'ʃve:rən], v.a. to burden; to be troublesome to; sich —, to complain (bei einem über, to someone of).

Beschwichtig-en [bə'ʃvɪçtɪgən], v.a. to soothe; to allay. —ung, f. appeasing; hushing up.

Beschwindeln [bə'ʃvɪndəln], v.a. to cheat.

Beſchwör—en [bəˈʃvøːrən], *ir.v.a.* to testify on oath; to conjure; to exorcise. —er, *m.* (—ers, *pl.* —er) exorcist, magician. —ung, *f.* exorcism.

Beſehen [bəˈzeːən], *ir.v.a.* to look on or at; to inspect.

Beſeitigen [bəˈzaɪtɪgən], *v.a.* to put aside; to put an end to.

Beſen [ˈbeːzən], *m.* (—s, *pl.* —) besom, broom. —binder, *m.* broom-maker.

Beſeſſen [bəˈzɛsən], *p.p.* (*of* beſitzen) & *adj.* possessed; der —e, demoniac. —heit, *f.* demoniacal possession.

Beſetz—en [bəˈzɛtsən], *v.a.* to put, lay on; to trim; to garrison; to fill (*an office*); to engage (*a place*). —ung, *f.* trimming; the taking possession of, occupation.

Beſicht—igen [bəˈzɪçtɪgən], *v.a.* to inspect; to survey. —igung, *f.* inspection, survey.

Beſiedeln [bəˈziːdəln], *v.a.* to colonize.

Beſiegen [bəˈziːgən], *v.a.* to vanquish.

Beſinn—en [bəˈzɪnən], I. *ir.v.r.*; ſich (auf eine S.) —en, to recollect, remember, think of. II. *subst.n.* reflection. —ung, *f.* recollection; consideration; consciousness; wieder zur —ung kommen, to recover consciousness; jemanden zur —ung bringen, to bring someone to his senses.

Beſitz [bəˈzɪts], *m.* (—es) possession; property. —tum, *n.* (—tums, *pl.* Beſitztümer) possession, property.

Beſitz—en [bəˈzɪtsən], *ir.v.a.* to possess. —er, *m.* (—ers, *pl.* —er) —erin, *f.* possessor; master; owner; occupier; Grund—er, land-owner.

Beſolden [bəˈzɔldən], *v.a.* to pay.

Beſonder [bəˈzɔndər], *adj.* particular, peculiar; separate, distinct, especial; odd, strange. —heit, *f.* specialty; peculiarity; strangeness; individuality. —s, *adv.* especially, in particular; separately; peculiarly; extraordinarily.

Beſonnen [bəˈzɔnən], *p.p.* (*of* beſinnen) & *adj.* prudent, circumspect. —heit, *f.* prudence; self-possession.

Beſorg—en [bəˈzɔrgən], *v.* I. *a.* to take care of; to provide for; to do, effect. II. *n.* (*aux.* ſ.) to be anxious about. —nis, *f.* (*pl.* —niſſe) care; anxiety. —ung, *f.* care, management; commission; —ungen ausrichten, to go on errands.

Beſprech—en [bəˈʃprɛçən], *ir.v.a.* to discuss (*a subject*). —ung, *f.* discussion; conference, parlːy.

Beſſer [ˈbɛsər], *adj.* & *adv.* (*comparative of* gut) better; je mehr deſto —, the more the better.

Beſſer—n [ˈbɛsərn], *v.a.* to better, improve upon. —ung, *f.* improvement, amendment.

Beſt [bɛst], *adj.* & *adv.* (*superlative of* gut) best; der erſte —e, the first that comes; jemanden zum —en haben, to make fun of, to hoax someone. —ens, *adv.* in the best way; Danke —ens, many thanks.

Beſtand [bəˈʃtant], *m.* (—es, *pl.* Beſtände) continuance; certitude; stability, firmness; amount, value. —geld, *n.* balance in cash. —gut, *n.* farm let on lease. —los, *adj.* inconsistent, unstable. —teil, *m.* constituent part; ingredient.

Beſtänd—ig [bəˈʃtɛndɪç], *adj.* & *adv.* continual; constant, steady, unchanging, steadfast. —igkeit, *f.* continuance; permanence; constancy; steadfastness.

Beſtärk—en [bəˈʃtɛrkən], *v.a.* to confirm, corroborate. —ung, *f.* confirmation, strengthening.

Beſtätig—en [bəˈʃtɛːtɪgən], *v.a.* to confirm, corroborate, verify. —ung, *f.* confirmation; ratification; sanction.

Beſtatt—en [bəˈʃtatən], *v.a.* to bury. —ung, *f.* burial.

Beſtech—en [bəˈʃtɛçən], *ir.v.a.* to bribe, corrupt. —ung, *f.* bribery; bribe.

Beſtehen [bəˈʃteːən], *ir.v.a.* to undergo, endure; to stand (*a test*).

Beſtell—en [bəˈʃtɛlən], *v.a.* to order; to bespeak; to arrange; to appoint, constitute; to execute (*a commission*); es iſt ſchlecht mit ihm —t, he is in a sad plight. —ung, *f.* bespeaking; order, commission; appointment.

Beſtie [ˈbɛstiə], *f.* (*pl.* —n) beast, brute.

Beſtimm—en [bəˈʃtɪmən], *v.a.* to decide; to determine; to settle; to define. —end, *p.* & *adj.* determining, deciding. —t, *p.p.*, *adj.* & *adv.* fixed, settled.

Beſtrafen [bəˈʃtraːfən], *v.a.* to punish.

Beſtreb—en [bəˈʃtreːbən], I. *v.r.* to exert oneself, strive. II. *subst.n.*, —ung, *f.* effort, endeavour, exertion.

Beſtreit—en [bəˈʃtraɪtən], *ir.v.a.* to attack; to oppose; to pay for. —ung, *f.* combating; defrayal (*of cost*).

Beſtreuen [bəˈʃtrɔyən], *v.a.* to bestrew, sprinkle over.

Bestürz—en [bə'ʃtyrtsən], *v.a.* (*also* **bestürzt machen**) to startle, surprise; to throw into confusion; to dismay. **—t**, *p.p. & adj.* confounded, dismayed.

Besuch [bə'zu:x], *m.* (**—es**, *pl.* **—e**) visit; visitors, company; **wir haben —**, we have a visitor. **—skarte**, *f.* visiting-card.

Besuchen [bə'zu:xən], *v.a.* to visit.

Betätig—en [bə'tɛ:tɪgən], *v.a.* to manifest, practise, put into practice. **—ung**, *f.* practical proof, application, practice.

Betäub—en [bə'tɔʏbən], *v.a.* to stun, deafen; to bewilder, confuse. **—end**, *p. & adj.* deafening. **—ung**, *f.* deafening; bewilderment; state of insensibility. **—ungs=mittel**, *n.* narcotic.

Bete ['be:tə], *f.* (*pl.* **—n**) beet.

Beteilig—en [bə'taɪlɪgən], *v.a.* to assign a share. **—ung**, *f.* share, interest in an undertaking.

Bet—en ['be:tən], *n.* (*aux.* **h.**) to pray. **—bruder**, *m.* devotee, bigot.

Beteuer—n [bə'tɔʏərn], *v.a.* to assert, protest, asseverate. **—ung**, *f.* asseveration, protestation.

Beton [bə'to:n], *m.* (**—s**) concrete.

Beton—en [bə'to:nən], *v.a.* to stress, accentuate; to emphasize. **—ung**, *f.* accentuation; emphasis; stress.

Betracht [bə'traxt], *m.* (**—s**) respect; consideration.

Betracht—en [bə'traxtən], *v.a.* to view; to contemplate; to regard, reflect upon. **—ung**, *f.* contemplation; consideration.

Betrag [bə'tra:k], *m.* (**—es**, *pl.* **Beträge**) amount; sum total.

Betragen [bə'tra:gən], I. *ir.v.a.* to come to, amount to. II. *ir.v.r.* to conduct oneself, to behave. III. *subst.n.* behaviour.

Betreff [bə'trɛf], *m.* (**—s**) reference, regard; **in —** (**einer Sache**), with regard to. **—s**, *adv.* concerning.

Betreff—en [bə'trɛfən], *ir.v.a.* to befall; to concern, affect. **—end**, *p., adj. & adv.* concerning; with reference to.

Betreib—en [bə'traɪbən], *ir.v.a.* to manage, carry on, exercise; to cultivate. **—ung**, *f.* carrying on, management; exercise (*of a profession*).

Betreten [bə'tre:tən], I. *ir.v.a.* to set foot on *or* in. II. *p.p. & adj.* startled, surprised; trodden.

Betrieb [bə'tri:p], *m.* (**—es**, *pl.* **—e**)

trade, profession; impulse; working. **—sam**, *adj.* active, industrious. **—samkeit**, *f.* activity; industry.

Betroffen [bə'trɔfən], *p.p.* (*of* **betreffen**) *& adj.* struck with surprise, confounded, perplexed. **—heit**, *f.* perplexity, surprise.

Betrüb—en [bə'try:bən], *v.a.* to grieve, afflict. **—nis**, *f.* (*pl.* **—nisse**), *n.* (**—nisses**, *pl.* **—nisse**) sorrow, grief. **—t**, *p.p. & adj.* sad.

Betrug [bə'tru:k], *m.* (**—s**, *no plur.*; **Betrügereien**) fraud, deception.

Betrüg—en [bə'try:gən], *ir.v.a.* to cheat, deceive. **—er**, *m.* (**—ers**, *pl.* **—er**) swindler, cheat. **—erisch**, *adj. & adv.* deceitful; fraudulent, knavish.

Bett [bɛt], *n.* (*dimin.* **Bettchen**, **Bettlein** *n.*) (**—es**, *pl.* **—en**) bed; **sich ins — legen**, go to bed. **—decke**, *f.* counterpane. **—laken**, *n.* sheet. **—stelle**, *f.* bedstead. **—tuch**, *n.* sheet.

Bettel ['bɛtəl], *m.* (**—s**) act of begging. **—arm**, *adj.* very poor. **—haft**, *adj.* beggarly.

Bettel—n ['bɛtəln], *v.n.* (*aux.* **h.**) to beg.

Bettler ['bɛtlər], *m.* (**—s**, *pl.* **—**), **—in**, *f.* (*pl.* **—innen**) beggar.

Beuge ['bɔʏgə], *f.* bow, bend; curve.

Beug—en [bɔʏgən], *v.* I. *a.* to bend, curve; to humble; to afflict. II. *r.* to bend, bow down; to humble oneself. **—sam**, *adj. & adv.* pliant, flexible. **—samkeit**, *f.* pliability. **—ung**, *f.* bending.

Beul—e ['bɔʏlə], *f.* (*pl.* **—en**) swelling; boil; dint. **—en=pest**, *f.* bubonic plague.

Beurlauben [bə'ʔu:rlaʊbən], *v.a.* to give leave of absence to.

Beurteil—en [bə'ʔʊrtaɪlən], *v.a.* to judge; to criticize. **—ung**, *f.* judgment; review.

Beute ['bɔʏtə], *f.* booty, loot, plunder.

Beut—el ['bɔʏtəl], *m.* (**—els**, *pl.* **—el**) bag; pouch; **Geld—**, purse, money-bag.

Bevölker—n [bə'fœlkərn], *v.a.* to people, populate. **—ung**, *f.* population.

Bevollmächtigen [bə'fɔlmɛçtɪgən], *v.a.* to invest with full powers.

Bevor [bə'fo:r], *adv. & sep. prefix*, before, beforehand.

Bevorstehen [bə'fo:rʃte:ən], *ir.v.n.* (*aux.* **h.** *dat.*) (*sep.*) to be at hand.

Bevorzug—en [bə'fo:rtsu:gən], *v.a.* (*insep.*) to favour; to privilege. **—t**, p.p. & adj. privileged; specially favoured.

Bewachen [bə'vaxən], v.a. to watch, guard.

Bewaffnen [bə'vafnən], v.a. to arm.

Bewahren [bə'va:rən], v.a. to keep, preserve; **Gott bewahre!** God forbid! not at all!

Bewahrheit—en [bə'va:rhartən], v.a. to verify. —ung, f. verification; zur —ung dessen, in faith whereof (Law).

Bewähr—en [bə'vɛ:rən], v. I. a. to prove, verify. II. r. to prove true. —ung, f. proof; trial.

Bewältigen [bə'vɛltɪgən], v.a. to overcome.

Bewandert [bə'vandərt], p.p. & adj. skilled, experienced.

Bewandt [bə'vant], p.p. & adj. circumstanced, conditioned. —nis, f. condition, state (of affairs).

Beweg—en [bə've:gən], I. v.a. to stir; to move. II. ir.v.a. to induce, persuade. —lich, adj. & adv. movable; changeable. —barkeit, f., —lichkeit, f. mobility; nimbleness. —ung, f. movement; motion; agitation. —= ungs=grund, m. reason (for action), motive.

Beweinen [bə'vaɪnən], v.a. to weep for, lament.

Beweis [bə'vaɪs], m. (—(f)es, pl. —(f)e) proof, demonstration. —bar, —lich, adj. demonstrable.

Beweisen [bə'vaɪzən], ir.v.a. to prove.

Bewerb—en [bə'vɛrbən], ir.v.r. (um eine S.) to seek to obtain something. —er, m. (—ers, pl. —er) suitor; candidate (for). —ung, f. application; candidature; courtship, wooing.

Bewillig—en [bə'vɪlɪgən], v.a. to grant, concede. —ung, f. grant; permission.

Bewillkommnen [bə'vɪlkəmən], v.a. to welcome.

Bewirten [bə'vɪrtən], v.a. to entertain (guests).

Bewirtschaften [bə'vɪrtʃaftən], v.a. to manage; to carry on, conduct.

Bewohn—en [bə'vo:nən], v.a. to inhabit, to dwell, live in. —er, m. (—ers, pl. —er) inhabitant; tenant; resident.

Bewunder—n [bə'vundərn], v.a. to admire; to wonder at. —er, m. (—ers, pl. —er) admirer. —ung, f. admiration; wonder.

Bewußt [bə'vʊst], adj. known; conscious; die —e Sache, the matter in question. —heit, f. knowledge; consciousness. —los, adj. unconscious, senseless. —fein, n. (—feins) consciousness; conviction.

Bezahlbar [bə'tsa:lba:r], adj. payable, to be paid.

Bezahl—en [bə'tsa:lən], v.a. to pay. —ung, f. payment; pay.

Bezauber—n [bə'tsaʊbərn], v.a. to bewitch, enchant; to fascinate. —ung, f. fascination, charm; spell.

Bezeichn—en [bə'tsaɪçnən], v.a. to mark, denote; to designate; to define. —end, p. & adj. characteristic; significant, expressive. —ung, f. mark, accentuation.

Bezeigen [bə'tsaɪgən], v.a. (einem etwas) to show.

Bezeug—en [bə'tsɔʏgən], v.a. to attest, certify. —ung, f. attestation; testimony.

Bezieh—en [bə'tsi:ən], ir.v. I. a. to cover; to resort to, frequent a place; to occupy; to get, gain possession of; to receive (payment); to procure. II. r. to refer, relate, make allusion, appeal (auf, to). —er, m. (—ers, pl. —er) drawer (of a bill). —ung, f. reference (to a subject); relation, connection; bearing.

Bezirk [bə'tsɪrk], m. (—s, pl. —e) circuit; precinct; district; sphere; department. —e, pl. confines; frontiers. —=amt, n. jurisdiction of a district. —=gericht, n. county-court. —= weise, adv. by districts.

Bezug [bə'tsu:k], m. (—es, pl. Bezüge) covering; case; relation, reference; in — auf (eine S.), with regard to, in relation to, as to; — nehmen auf (eine S.), to refer to. —nahme, f. reference. —=bedingungen, f. pl. terms of delivery. —=quelle, f. source of supply.

Bezüglich [bə'tsy:lɪç], adj. & adv. relative (auf eine S., to a thing).

Bezwecken [bə'tsvɛkən], v.a. to aim at, purpose; was will er damit —? what is he aiming at?

Bezweifeln [bə'tsvaɪfəln], v.a. to doubt; nicht zu —, indubitable, unquestionable.

Bezwingen [bə'tsvɪŋən], ir.v.a. to overcome, conquer.

Bibel ['bi:bəl], f. (pl. —n) Bible. —fest, adj. versed in the scriptures;

true as gospel. —**kunde,** f. biblical knowledge. —**spruch,** m. biblical phrase. —**stelle,** f. scriptural passage or sentence. —**stunde,** f. Bible class.

Biber ['bi:bər], m. (—**s,** pl. —) beaver, castor.

Biblio—thek [biblio'te:k], f. (pl. —**s theken**) (see **Bücherei**) library. — **thekar** [bibliote:'ka:r], m. (—**thekars,** pl. —**thekare**) librarian.

Biblisch ['bi:blɪʃ], adj. biblical, scriptural.

Bieder ['bi:dər], adj. upright, honest; staunch, loyal. —**keit,** f. loyalty, true-heartedness; probity. —**mann,** m. man of integrity; man of honour.

Bieg—e ['bi:gə], f. (pl. —**en**) curve, bend. **Bieg—en** ['bi:gən], ir.v.a. to bend, curve; to bow. —**sam,** adj. & adv. flexible; yielding; supple. —**samkeit,** f. pliancy; suppleness, flexibility. —**ung,** f. curve; bend; declension.

Biene ['bi:nə], f. (pl. —**n**) bee. —**n= korb,** n. hive. —**n=stock,** m. bee-hive. —**n=vater,** m. bee-farmer. —**n=zucht,** f. bee-keeping.

Bier [bi:r], n. (—**es,** pl. —**e**) beer. —**bank,** f. alehouse-bench. —**faß,** m. beer-cask. —**garten,** m. popular restaurant. —**krug,** m. jug, mug, pot. —**schenke,** f. beer-house. —**seidel,** n. beer-glass, beer-mug.

Bieten ['bi:tən], ir.v.a. to offer, proffer, present (the hand; aid, etc.); **das läßt er sich nicht —,** he won't stand that.

Bigam—ie [biga'mi:], f. bigamy. —**isch** [—'ga:mɪʃ], adj. bigamous.

Bilanz [bi'lants], f. (pl. —**en**) balance. —**conto,** n., —**rechnung,** f. balance-account.

Bild [bɪlt], n. (—**es,** pl. —**er**) image, figure, picture; idea; metaphor.

Bild—en ['bɪldən], v.a. to fashion, to shape; to compose; to train. —**end,** p. & adj. educational, instructive. —**lich,** adj. & adv. figurative. —**ner,** m. (—**ners,** pl. —**ner**) sculptor; artist; moulder. —**ne'rei,** f. plastic art, sculpture. —**nerisch,** adj. relating to sculpture; creative. —**nis,** n. (—**nisses,** pl. —**nisse**) portrait; effigy; parable. —**sam,** adj. plastic, ductile. —**samkeit,** f. flexibility, adaptiveness, plasticity. —**ung,** f. formation; form; organization, constitution; education, culture; civilization. —**e=kunst,** f. plastic art. —**er=bogen,** m. picture-

sheet. —**er=schrift,** f. hieroglyphics. —**er=sprache,** f. metaphorical language. —**er=stürmer,** m. image-breaker, iconoclast. —**hauer,** m. sculptor. —**hübsch,** —**schön,** adj. extremely pretty. —(**rund**)**funk,** m. television. —**säule,** f. statue.

Billard ['bɪljart], n. (—**s,** pl. —**s**) billiards.

Billett [bɪl'jet], n. (—(**e**)**s,** pl. —**e &** —**s**) (see **Fahrkarte**) ticket; note. —**abgabe,** f. giving up of ticket. —**schalter,** m. ticket-office, booking-office. !

Billig ['bɪlɪç], adj. & adv. reasonable, just; moderate, cheap.

Billig—en ['bɪlɪgən], v.a. to sanction; to approve of. —**ung,** f. approval, sanction.

Billion [bɪl'o:n], f. (pl. —**en**) billion.

Bims=stein ['bɪmʃtaɪn], m. (—**s**) pumice-stone.

Bind—e ['bɪndə], f. (pl. —**en**) bandage; band. —**e=mittel,** n. cement. —**e=strich,** m. hyphen.

Bind—en ['bɪndən], ir.v.a. to bind, tie. —**end,** p. & adj. binding, obligatory (on). —**ung,** f. tying, binding, etc.; connection.

Binnen ['bɪnən], I. prep. with gen. & dat. within. II. adv. within, in the interior; (in comp.=) inner, internal, inland. III. adv. inwards.

Bins—e ['bɪnzə], f. (pl. —**en**) rush (Bot.). —**ig,** adj. sedgy, rush-grown.

Bio— [bio] (in comp.). —**graphie** [—gra'fi:], f. biography. —**logie** [—lo'gi:], f. biology.

Biplan ['bi:pla:n], m. (—**s,** pl. —**e**) biplane.

Birke ['bɪrkə], f. (pl. —**n**) birch-tree.

Birn—e ['bɪrnə], f. (pl. —**en**) pear. —**enbaum,** m. pear-tree.

Bis [bɪs], I. prep. or particle joined with a preposition to give it a special or additional force; as far as to; up to; down to; to; till, until; even to. II. conj. till. —**her,** adv. as far as here, hitherto, up to now, till now. —**weilen,** adv. sometimes, now and then, occasionally.

Bisam ['bi:zam], m. (—**s**) musk.

Bischen, Bißchen ['bɪsçən], n. (—**s,** pl. —) little bit, morsel; a little.

Bischof ['bɪʃo:f], m. (—**s,** pl. **Bischöfe**) bishop. —**s=amt,** n. episcopate. —**s=stab,** m. crosier.

Bismut ['bɪsmuːt], *m.* & *n.* (*pl.* —e) bismuth.

Bison ['biːzɔn], *m.* (—s, *pl.* —s) bison.

Biß [bɪs], *m.* (—(ſſ)es, *pl.* —(ſſ)e) bite; sting. —(ſſ)ig, *adj.* biting; snappish, cutting.

Bistum ['bɪstuːm], *n.* (—s, *pl.* **Bistü-mer**) bishopric.

Bitte ['bɪtə], *f.* (*pl.* —n) request, petition; ich habe eine — an Sie, I have a favour to ask you.

Bitt—en ['bɪtən], *ir.v.a.* to ask, request; to entreat; to invite; —e, don't mention it (*in answer to thanks*); I beg your pardon; please.

Bitter ['bɪtər], *adj.* & *adv.* bitter; severe. —**keit**, *f.* bitterness. —**lich**, I. *adj.* bitterish. II. *adv.* bitterly.

Bizarr [bi'tsar], *adj.* & *adv.* strange, odd. —**erie** [—ə'riː], *f.* (*pl.* —**erieen**) strangeness, oddity.

Blähen ['blɛːən], *v.a.* to inflate, swell.

Blam—age [bla'maːʒə], *f.* shame, disgrace, failure. —**ieren** [—'miːrən], *v.a.* to expose to ridicule; bring into disrepute; sich —**ieren**, to make a fool of oneself; to disgrace oneself.

Blank [blaŋk], *adj.* & *adv.* blank; bright; clean.

Bläschen ['blɛːsçən], *n.* (—s, *pl.* —) pimple; little bubble.

Blas—e ['blaːzə], *f.* (*pl.* —en) bubble; blister; bladder.

Blasen ['blaːzən], *ir.v.a.* & *n.* (*aux.* h.) to blow.

Blaß [blas] (*compar.* blasser & blässer; *superl.* blassest & blässest) *adj.* & *adv.* pale, pallid.

Blässe ['blɛsə], *f.* paleness, pallor.

Blatt [blat], *n.* (—es, *pl.* **Blätter**) leaf; newspaper; sheet (*of paper*); kein — vor den Mund nehmen, to be plain-spoken.

Blättchen ['blɛtçən], *n.* (—s, *pl.* —) leaflet.

Blatter ['blatər], *f.* (*pl.* —n) pustule, pimple; die —n, small-pox. —**ig**, *adj.* pustular. —**n-impfung**, *f.* vaccination.

Blättern ['blɛtərn], *v.n.* (*aux.* h.) to turn over the leaves.

Blau [blau], I. *adj.* blue. II. *n.* (—es), das —(e), blue (*colour*), blueness; the sky. —**äugig**, *adj.* blue-eyed. —**säure**, *f.* prussic acid.

Blech [blɛç], *n.* (—es, *pl.* —e) thin plate of metal; tin.

Blech—e(r)n ['blɛçə(r)n], *adj.* of sheet-metal *or* tin. —**ner**, *m.* tinman, tinker. —**geschirr**, *n.* tin (*can, etc.*).

Blei [blai], *n.* (—es) lead. —**ern**, *adj.* leaden. —**stift**, *m.* (—stift(e)s, *pl.* —stifte) lead-pencil.

Bleiben ['blaibən], I. *ir.v.n.* (*aux.* ſ.) remain, stay; to last, endure; to stay away; to be left, remain. II. *subst.n.* abode, stay. —**d**, *p.* & *adj.* permanent, abiding.

Bleich [blaiç], *adj.* pale, wan, pallid. —**e**, *f.* pallor, paleness; bleaching.

Bleich—en ['blaiçən], I. *v.a.* to bleach. II. *ir.v.n.* (*aux.* h. & ſ.) to grow, turn pale; to fade. III. *subst.n.* bleaching. —**er**, *m.* (—ers, *pl.* —er) bleacher. —**erin**, *f.* laundress.

Blende ['blɛndə], *f.* (*pl.* —n) blind.

Blend—en ['blɛndən], *v.a.* to blind; to dazzle; to deceive. —**end**, *p.* & *adj.* dazzling; delusive.

Bleß—ieren [blɛ'siːrən], *v.a.* to wound. —**ur** [—'suːr], *f.* (*pl.* —**uren**) wound.

Blick [blɪk], *m.* (—es, *pl.* —e) look; glance; view, prospect; glimpse.

Blicken ['blɪkən], *v.n.* (*aux.* h.) to glance, look; sich —**lassen**, to appear, let oneself be seen.

Blind [blɪnt], *adj.* & *adv.* blind; false, sham; dull; blank; — laden, to load with blank cartridge. —**heit**, *f.* blindness. —**lings**, *adv.* blindly, blindfold. —**darm**, *m.* appendix (*Anat.*). —**ekuh**, *f.* blindman's buff.

Blinz—en ['blɪntsən], —**eln** [—əln], *v.n.* (*aux.* h.) to blink, wink, twinkle.

Blitz [blɪts], *m.* (—es, *pl.* —e) flash (*of lightning*); lightning. —**ableiter**, *m.* lightning-conductor. —**blank**, *adj.* resplendent. —**licht**, *n.* flash-light.

Blitzen ['blɪtsən], *v.* I. *imp.* & *n.* to lighten. II. *a.* to flash, sparkle.

Block [blɔk], *m.* (—(e)s, *pl.* **Blöcke**) block, log; boulder.

Blöd—e ['bløːdə], *adj.* bashful, shy; stupid. —**igkeit**, *f.* imbecility; bashfulness, coyness, timidity. —**sichtig**, *adj.* weak-sighted; idiotic. —**sinn**, *m.* imbecility; nonsense. —**sinnig**, *adj.* silly.

Blöken ['bløːkən], *v.n.* (*aux.* h.) to bleat.

Blond [blɔnt], *adj.* blond, fair.

Bloß [bloːs], I. *adj.* bare, naked; destitute; pure, mere. II. *adv.* barely; merely, only.

Blöße ['blø:sə], *f.* (*pl.* —n), bareness; nakedness.

Blüh—en ['bly:ən], *v.n.* (*aux.* h.) to bloom, blossom. **—end**, *p.* & *adj.* blooming.

Blüm—chen ['bly:mçən], **—lein** [—laɪn], *n.* (—chens, —leins, *pl.* —chen, —lein) floweret.

Blum—e ['blu:mə], *f.* (*pl.* —en) flower, blossom; **durch die —e sprechen**, to speak in metaphors. **—en=beet**, *n.* flower-bed. **—en=fohl**, *m.* cauliflower. **—en=topf**, *m.* flower-pot. **—en= zwiebel**, *f.* flower-bulb.

Bluse ['blu:zə], *f.* (*pl.* —n) blouse, smock-frock; tunic.

Blut [blu:t], *n.* (—es) blood; race, lineage; sap; juice (*of plants, etc.*); **ein junges —**, a young thing. **—ig**, *adj.* & *adv.* bloody, cruel. **—arm**, *adj.* poor as a church-mouse. **—bad**, *n.* massacre, butchery. **—egel**, *m.* (—= igel) leech. **—gier**, *f.* bloodthirstiness. **—gierig**, *adj.* sanguinary, blood-thirsty. **—jung**, *adj.* very young. **—schuld**, *f.* blood-guiltiness; capital crime. **—s=verwandt**, *adj.* related by blood (**mit**, to). **—s=verwandt= schaft**, *f.* consanguinity.

Blüte ['bly:tə], *f.* (*pl.* —n) blossom; bud.

Bluten ['blu:tən], *v.n.* (*aux.* h.) to bleed.

Bö [bø:], *f.* (*pl.* —en) sudden squall of wind.

¹Bock [bɔk], *m.* (—s, *pl.* **Böcke**) ram; he-goat. **—leder**, *n.* buckskin. **—sprung**, *m.* caper, gambol.

²Bock [bɔk], *m.* (—es) (—bier, *n.*) strong beer.

Boden ['bo:dən], *m.* (—s, *pl.* — or **Böden**) ground; soil; floor; garret. **—kammer**, *f.* garret. **—los**, *adj.* bottomless. **—zins**, *m.* ground-rent.

Bogen ['bo:gən], *m.* (—s, *pl.* —, or **Bögen**) bow; arc; arch, vault; sheet (*of paper*). **—förmig**, *adj.* arched.

Bohle ['bo:lə], *f.* (*pl.* —n) plank.

Bohne ['bo:nə], *f.* (*pl.* —n) bean.

Bohr—en ['bo:rən], *v.a.* to pierce, bore, drill. **—er**, *m.* (—ers, *pl.* —er) gimlet.

Boje ['bo:jə], *f.* (*pl.* —n) buoy.

Bollwerk ['bɔlverk], *n.* (—(e)s, *pl.* —e) bulwark.

Bolz [bɔlts], *m.* (—es, *pl.* —e), —en, *m.* (—ens, *pl.* —en) bolt.

Bombe ['bɔmbə], *f.* (*pl.* —n) bomb.

Boot [bo:t], *n.* (—es, *pl.* —e) boat.

Bord [bɔrt], *m.* (—es, *pl.* —e) ship-board; border, rim; shore; **an —**, aboard of.

Borg [bɔrk], *m.* (—es, *pl.* —e) borrowing. **—(s)=weise**, *adv.* on credit.

Borg—en ['bɔrgən], *v.a.* to borrow; to take on credit; to lend. **geborgt**, *p.p.* & *adj.* borrowed; fictitious, false. **—er**, *m.* (—ers, *pl.* —er) borrower.

Börse ['bœrzə], *f.* (*pl.* —n) purse; exchange; **auf der —**, on 'change. **—n=kurs**, *m.* rate of exchange. **—n= makler**, *m.* stock-broker.

Borst—e ['bɔrstə], *f.* (*pl.* —en) bristle. **—ig**, *adj.* bristly.

Bös ['bø:s], **Bös—e** ['bø:zə], *adj.* & *adv.* bad; ill; evil; wicked; angry; sore; cross. **—artig**, *adj.* malicious; virulent; wild, vicious. **—e=wicht**, *m.* (—ewichts, *pl.* —ewichte, —ewichter) scoundrel. **—haft**, *adj.* & *adv.* malicious; angry. **—haftigkeit**, *f.* malice. **—heit**, *f.* ill-nature; crossness.

Botan—ik [bo'ta:nɪk], *f.* botany. **—iker**, *m.* (—ikers, *pl.* —iker) botanist.

Bot—e ['bo:tə], *m.* (—en, *pl.* —en) messenger. **—schaft**, *f.* (*pl.* —schaften) message. **—schafter**, *m.* (—schafters, *pl.* —schafter) ambassador.

Bött(i)cher ['bøt(ɪ)çər], *m.* (—s, *pl.* —) cooper.

Bottich ['bɔtɪç], *m.* (—es, *pl.* —e) tub, vat.

Bowle ['bo:lə], *f.* (*pl.* —n) spiced wine, cup.

Brach [bra:x], *adj.* & *adv.* fallow, untilled. **—e**, *f.* fallow ground.

Brand [brant], *m.* (—es, *pl.* **Brände**) burning; fire, conflagration. **—ig**, *adj.* blasted, blighted; gangrenous. **—mal**, **—mark**, *n.* stigma. **—stätte**, **—stelle**, *f.* scene of a conflagration. **—stifter**, *m.* incendiary. **—stiftung**, *f.* arson.

Brand—en ['brandən], *v.n.* to break, surge. **—ung**, *f.* breakers; surf.

Branntwein ['brantvaɪn], *m.* (—s, *pl.* —e) brandy.

Brat—en ['bra:tən], I. *reg.* & *ir.v.a.* & *n.* (*aux.* h.) to roast. II. *subst.n.* roasting, *etc.* III. *m.* (—ens, *pl.* —en) roast meat, joint.

Bratsche ['bra:tʃə], *f.* (*pl.* —n) viola.

Brau [brau], *m.* & *n.* (—es, *pl.* —e) brew. **—haus**, *n.* brewery.

Brauch [braux], *m.* (—(e)s, *pl.* **Bräuche**)

use; usage, custom. —**bar**, *adj. &
adv.* of use, useful; serviceable.
—**barkeit**, *f.* utility, usefulness.

Brauch—**en** ['brauxən], *v.* I. *a.* to use,
make use of; to want, require. II. *v.
imp. (gen.)* to need; **es** —**t keines
Beweises**, no proof is required.

Braue ['brauə], *f.* (*pl.* —**n**) brow, eye-
brow.

Brau—**en** ['brauən], *v.a.* to brew.
—**er**, *m.* (—**ers**, *pl.* —**er**) brewer.
—**e'rei**, *f.* (*pl.* —**ereien**) brewery.

Braun [braun], *adj.* brown.

Braus [braus], *m.* (—**(f)es**) tumult; **in
Saus und** — **leben**, to live riotously.

Brausen ['brauzən], *v.n.* (*aux.* **h.**) to
storm, rage.

Braut [braut], *f.* (*pl.* **Bräute**) be-
trothed, affianced bride; fiancée.
—**jungfer**, *f.* bridesmaid. —**führer**,
m. best man.

Bräutigam ['brɔytıgam], *m.* (—**s**, *pl.*
—**e**) husband elect; fiancé, intended;
bridegroom.

Brav [bra:f], I. *adj. & adv.* honest, upright; worthy; brave; — **gemacht!**
well done! II. *int.* bravo!

Brech—**en** ['breçən], I. *ir.v.a.* to break;
to break up *or* asunder; to gather.
II. *ir.v.r.* to break (*as waves*); to
vomit. III. *ir.v.n.* (*aux.* **f.**) to dawn;
to appear. IV. *subst.n.* violation;
breach; breaking. —**mittel**, *n.*
emetic. —**ung**, *f.* breaking.

Brei [brai], *m.* (—**es**) pap; pulp; broth.

Breit [brait], *adj. & adv.* broad; wide.
—**e**, *f.* (*pl.* —**en**) breadth, width.
—**beinig**, *adj. & adv.* straddle-legged.

1Bremse ['brɛmzə], *f.* (*pl.* —**n**) horse-
fly, gadfly.

2Bremse ['brɛmzə], *f.* (*pl.* —**n**) barnacle;
brake, drag-wheel.

Brems—**en** ['brɛmzən], *v.a.* to put on
the brake. —**er**, *m.* brakesman.

Brennbar ['brɛnba:r], *adj.* combustible;
inflammable. —**keit**, *f.* inflammability.

Brenn—**en** ['brɛnən], *ir.v.* I. *a.* to
burn; to distil (*spirits*). II. *n.* (*aux.* **h.**)
to burn; to smart. —**end**, *p. & adj.*
burning; smarting; ardent; eager.
—**er**, *m.* (—**ers**, *pl.* —**er**) distiller;
brickmaker. —**e'rei**, *f.* distillery.

Bresche ['brɛʃə], *f.* (*pl.* —**n**) breach.

Brett [brɛt], *n.* (—**es**, *pl.* —**er**) board;
plank; table; shelf; tray. —**chen**, *n.*
(—**chens**, *pl.* —**chen**) a little board.
—**ern**, *adj.* made of boards, boarded.

—**spiel**, *n.* backgammon; draughts,
etc. —**stein**, *m.* man at draughts.

Breviar—**ium** [brevi'a:rıum], *n.* (—**s,
iums**, *pl.* —**ien**), **Brevier** [bre'vi:r],
n. (—**s**, *pl.* —**e**) breviary.

Brezel ['bre:tsəl], *f.* (*pl.* —**n**) cracknel.

Brief [bri:f], *m.* (—**es**, *pl.* —**e**) letter;
written document; charter; **Wech-
sel**—, draft (*C.L.*); **eingeschriebener**
—, registered letter. —**lich**, *adj. &
adv.* epistolary. —**abgabe**, *f.* delivery
of letters. —**aufgabe**, *f.* posting a
letter. —**aufgabestempel**, *m.* post-
mark. —**aufschrift**, *f.* address of a
letter. —**bogen**, *m.* sheet of note-
paper. —**kasten**, *m.* letter-box. —
mappe, *f.* writing-case. —**marke**, *f.*
postage-stamp. —**porto**, *n.* postage.
—**tasche**, *f.* pocket-book, portfolio.
—**taube**, *f.* carrier pigeon. —**träger**,
m. postman. —**umschlag**, *m.* envelope. —**wechsel**, *m.* correspondence.

Brigad—**e** [bri'ga:də], *f.* (*pl.* —**en**)
brigade. —**ier** [—di'e:], *m.* (—**iers**,
pl. —**iere**) brigadier-general.

Brillant [brıl'jant], I. *adj.* brilliant.
II. *m.* (—**en**, *pl.* —**en**) brilliant,
diamond.

Brille ['brılə], *f.* (*pl.* —**n**) (pair of)
spectacles; glasses.

Bringen ['brıŋən], *ir.v.a.* to bring,
fetch.

Brise ['bri:zə], *f.* (*pl.* —**n**) breeze, light
wind.

Bröckel—**n** ['brøkəln], *v.a., r. & n.* (*aux.*
h.) to crumble. —**ig**, (**Bröcklig**), *adj.*
crumbly; fragile; crisp.

Brocken ['brɔkən], *m.* (—**s**, *pl.* —)
crumb, fragment; (*pl.*) scraps.

Brodeln ['bro:dəln], *v.n.* (*aux.* **h.**) to
bubble, to boil up.

Brodem ['bro:dəm], *m.* (—**s**) steam,
vapour.

Brodieren [bro'di:rən] *v.a. & n.* (*see
sticken*), to embroider.

Brokat [bro'ka:t], *m.* (—**(e)s**, *pl.* —**e**)
brocade.

Brom [bro:m], *n.* (—**s**) bromine.

Brombeere ['brombe:rə], *f.* (*pl.* —**n**)
blackberry.

Bromid [bro'mi:t], *n.* (—**s**) bromide.

Bronz—**e** ['brõ:sə], *f.* bronze, brass.
—**en**, *adj.* made of bronze. —**ieren**,
v.a. to bronze.

Brosam ['bro:za:m], *m. & n.* (—**(e)s,
pl.* —**e**); —**e**, *f.* (—**e**, *pl.* —**en**) crumb.

Brosche ['brɔʃə], *f.* (*pl.* —**n**) brooch.

Broſch—ieren [brɔ'ʃiːren], v.a. to stitch together (as a pamphlet). —iert, p.p. & adj. in pamphlet form. —üre [—ʃuːrə], f. (pl. —üren) pamphlet.

Brot [broːt], n. (—es, pl. —e) bread; loaf. —beutel, m. haversack. —er= werb, m. bread-winning. —forb, m. bread-basket. —los, adj. without bread. —neid, m. trade jealousy. —ſchnitte, f. slice of bread. —ſchrant, m. pantry; bread-cupboard.

Brötchen ['brøːtçən], n. (—s, pl. —) small roll of bread; Schinken—, ham-sandwich.

Bruch [brux], I. m. (—es, pl. Brüche) breach; breakage; fracture; rupture; gewöhnlicher —, vulgar fraction; Stein—, stone quarry. II. m. & n. [bruːx], gen. —es, pl. Brüche, Brücher) bog, fen, swamp, marsh. —ig, adj. foggy, marshy —ſtein, m. quarry stone; ashlar.

Brüchig ['brɣçɪç], adj. full of flaws; brittle.

Brüde ['brʏkə], f. (pl. —n) bridge.

Bruder ['bruːdər], m. (—s, pl. Brüder) brother.

Brüder—lich ['brʏːdərlɪç], adj. & adv. fraternal. —lichkeit, f. brotherliness, fraternity. —ſchaft, f. brotherhood, fellowship.

Brüh—e ['brʏːə], f. (pl. —n) soup; sauce; broth. —heiß, adj. scalding hot.

Brühen ['brʏːən], v.a. to scald.

Brüllen ['brʏlən], v.a. & n. (aux. h.) to roar, bellow.

Brumm—en ['brumən], v. I. n. (aux. h.) to growl; to snarl; to low; to buzz. II. a.; ein Lied —en, to hum an air. —bär, —bart, m. grumbler, growler. —eiſen, n. jew's-harp. —fliege, f. blue-bottle fly.

Brummig ['brumɪç], adj. grumbling, unfriendly.

Brunnen ['brunən], m. (—s, pl. —) spring; well; fountain. —becken, n. basin of a fountain.

Brunſt [brunst], f. (pl. Brünſte) ardour, passion.

Brünſtig ['brʏnstɪç], adj. & adv. burning; ardent; sensual. —feit, f. ardour; heat.

Bruſt [brust], f. (pl. Brüſte) breast; bosom; chest. —bild, n. half-length portrait. —entzündung, f. inflammation of the chest. —wehr, f. breast-work, rampart.

Brüſten ['brʏstən], v.r. to give oneself airs; to brag.

Brut [bruːt], f. (pl. —en) brood; fry, spawn.

Brüt—en ['brʏːtən], v.a. & n. (aux. h.) to sit (on eggs). —ofen, m. incubator.

Brutto ['bruto:], adv. gross, in gross (weight, etc.).

Bube ['buːbə], m. (—n, pl. —n) boy, lad; scamp. —n=ſtreich, m. knavish trick.

Buch [buːx], n. (—es, pl. Bücher) book. —druf, m. printing of books. — druder, m. printer. —druckerei [—'rai], f. printing; printing-office. —haltung, f. book-keeping. —händ= ler, m. bookseller. —handlung, f. bookseller's shop, book-shop.

Buch—e ['buːxə], f. (pl. —en) beech-tree. —eder, m. beech-nut. —= weizen, m. buckwheat.

Bücherei [byːçə'rai], f. (pl. —en) library.

Buchsbaum ['buksbaum], m. box-tree.

Büchſe ['bʏksə], f. (pl. —n) box; case; pot, jar; tube; rifle, carbine. —n= lauf, m., —n=rohr, m. rifle-barrel.

Buchſtab ['buːxʃtaːp], m. (—en, pl. —en), —e, (—ens, pl. —en) letter, written character. —ieren [—'biːrən], v.a. to spell. —ierung, f. spelling.

Buchſtäblich ['buːxʃtɛplɪç], adj. literal, verbal.

Bucht [buxt], f. (pl. —en) inlet; bay.

Budel ['bukəl], I. m. (—s, pl. —) hump; hump-back. II. f. (pl. —n) boss, knob; buckle. —ig, adj. & adv. hump-backed, humpy.

Büd—en ['bʏkən], v.r. to bow. —ling, m. (—lings, pl. —linge) bow, obeisance.

Büd(l)ing ['bʏk(l)ɪŋ], m. (—s, pl. —e) smoked herring.

Bude ['buːdə], f. (pl. —n) stall, booth; room.

Büfett [by'fɛt], n. (—s, pl. —s, Büfette) sideboard.

Büffel ['bʏfəl], m. (—s, pl. —) buffalo; buff (leather).

Bug [buːk], m. (—(e)s, pl. Büge) bend, bow; bow (of a ship). —ſpriet, n. (—ſpriet(e)s, pl. —ſpriete) bowsprit.

Bügel ['byːgəl], m. (—s, pl. —) bent piece of wood or metal; ring; hoop; stirrup. —eiſen, n. flat-iron. —los, adj. without stirrups. —riemen, m. stirrup-leather.

Büg—eln ['by:gəln], v.a. to smooth, iron. —lerin, f. ironing woman.

Buhl—e ['bu:lə], m. (—en, pl. —en) & f. (pl. —en), —in, f. lover; sweetheart; lady-love.

Buhl—en ['bu:lən], v.n. (aux. h.) to woo, make love to. —erin, f. courtesan. —erisch, adj. amorous; unchaste.

Bühn—e ['by:nə], f. (pl. —en) stage, boards (of a theatre). —en=anweisung, f. stage direction. —en=behör, n. stage properties. —en=bekleidung, f. stage-decoration, scenery.

1Bulle ['bulə], m. (—n, pl. —n) bull, bullock.

2Bulle ['bulə], f. (pl. —n) seal (on a deed); papal bull.

Bumm—el ['buməl], m. stroll; einen —el machen, to go for a stroll. —eln, v.n. (aux. h.) to loaf about; to dawdle. —ler, m. (—lers, pl. —ler) idler, loafer. —elzug, m. slow train.

Bund [bunt], I. n. (—es, pl. usually —e) bundle; bunch. II. m. (—es, pl. Bünde) band, tie; league, alliance, confederacy. —es=genoß, m. confederate. —es=rat, m. Federal Council. —es=tag, m. Federal Diet. —holz, n. faggots.

Bunt [bunt], adj. & adv. gay-coloured; bright, glaring; variegated; disorderly. —heit, f. gayness (of colours).

Bürde ['byrdə], f. (pl. —n) burden; load.

Büreau [by'ro:], n. (—s, pl. —s) (see Büro) bureau, office. —krat [—'kra:t], m. (—kraten, pl. —kraten) red-tapist. —kratie [—kra'ti:], f. red-tapism, officialdom.

Burg [burk], f. (pl. —en) castle; citadel; stronghold. —graben, m. castle-moat. —graf, m. burgrave, lord of a feudal castle.

Bürg—e ['byrgə], m. (—en, pl. —en) surety, bail; —en stellen, to find bail. —schaft, f. security, bail.

Bürger ['byrgər], m. (—s, pl. —) citizen, townsman, burgher. —lich, adj. & adv. citizen-like; simple, homely. —schaft, f. townspeople, corporation. —meister, m. mayor, burgomaster. —stand, m. citizen class. —steig, m. pavement, sidewalk.

Büro [by'ro:], n. (—s, pl. —s) bureau, office. —krat, m. (—kraten, pl.

—kraten) red-tapist. —kratie, f. red-tapism, officialdom.

Bursch [burʃ], m. (—en, pl. —en); —e, m. (—en, pl. —en) young man, boy.

Bürste ['byrstə], f. (pl. —n) brush, whisk.

Bürsten ['byrstən], v.a. to brush.

Busch [buʃ], m. (—es, pl. Büsche) bush; thicket, copse.

Büschel ['byʃəl], m. (—s, pl. —) tuft, bunch. —ig, adj. & adv. tufted. —artig, adj. tufty.

Busen ['bu:zən], m. (—s, pl. —) breast, bosom; (Meer)— gulf, bay.

Buße ['bu:sə], f. amends; fine; penance; repentance.

Büß—en ['by:sən], v. I. a. to make amends for, atone; to expiate. II. n. (aux. h.) to do penance, atone for (für). —er, m. (—ers, pl. —er) penitent. —ung, f. penance, atonement.

Büste ['bystə], f. (pl. —n) bust.

Bütt—e ['bytə], Butt—e ['butə], f. (pl. —en) tub.

Butter ['butər], f. butter; —schlagen, to churn. —ig, adj. buttery. —brot, n. (slice of) bread and butter; belegtes —brot, sandwich.

Buttern ['butərn], v.t. to churn.

C

[Words not given under C in the latest German spelling should be looked for under K, Sch, or Z.]

C, c [tse:], n. C, c; C=Do (Mus.); C=Dur (Moll), (the key of) C major (minor).

Café [ka'fe:], n. (—s, pl. —s) café.

Cello ['tsɛlo], n. (—s, pl. —s or —i) violoncello.

Ces [tsɛs], n. C flat (Mus.).

Champagner [ʃam'panjər], m. (—s) champagne.

Cha—os ['ka:ɔs], n. (gen. —os) chaos. —ötisch [ka'o:tıʃ], adj. & adv. chaotic.

Charakter [ka'raktər], m. (—s, pl. —e [—'te:rə]) character, mental constitution, disposition.

Charge ['ʃarʒə], f. (pl. —n) appointment, rank, post, position.

Charpie [ʃar'pi:], f. (pl. —(e)n) lint.

Chaussee [ʃo'se:], f. (pl. —n) high road. —bau, m. road-making.

Cheď, Scheď [ʃɛk], m. (—s, pl. —s) cheque.

Chef [ʃef], *m.* (—s, *pl.* —s) chief, chief commander. —**redakteur**, *m.* chief editor.

Chem—ie [çɛ'miː], *f.* chemistry. —**italien** [—'kaliən], *pl.* chemicals.

Chem—iker ['çɛːmɪkər], *m.* (—**ikers**, *pl.* —**iker**) scientific *or* analytical chemist. —**isch**, *adj.* chemical.

Chiffre ['ʃɪfər], *f.* (*pl.* —n) cipher.

Chin—arinde ['çiːnarɪndə], *f.*, —**in** [çi'niːn], *n.* (—s) *f.* quinine.

Chirurg [çi'rʊrk], *m.* (—en, *pl.* —en) surgeon.

Chlor [kloːr], *n.* (—s) chlorine. —'**al**, *n.* (—s) chloral. —'**id**, *n.* (—(e)s, *pl.* —e) chloride.

Cholera ['koːləraː], *f.* cholera.

Chor [koːr], *m.* & *n.* (—(e)s, *pl.* **Chöre**) choir. —**gang**, *m.* aisle. —**gesang**, *m.* singing in chorus; choral song. —**hemd**, *n.* surplice. —**herr**, *m.* canon.

Choral [ko'raːl], *m.* (—s, *pl.* **Choräle**) hymn, anthem.

Christ [krɪst], I. *m.* Christ (*the usual form is now* **Christus**). II. *m.* (—en, *pl.* —en) Christian. —**in**, *f.* female Christian. —**en-tum**, *n.* Christianity; Christendom. —**lich**, *adj.* Christian; *adv.* Christian-like; kindly. —**us**, *m.* (—i, *Dat.* —o, *Acc.* —um, *Voc.* —e) Christ. —**abend**, *m.* Christmas-eve. —**baum**, *m.* Christmas-tree. —**nacht**, *f.* night of Christmas eve. —**tag**, *m.* Christmas day.

Chronik ['kroːnɪk], *f.* (*pl.* —en) chronicle.

Cis [tsɪs], *n.* (—) C sharp (*Mus.*).

Coulant [kuˈlant], **Kulant**, *adj.* fluent, easy (*style*).

Couplet [kuˈpleː], *n.* (—s, *pl.* —s) comic song.

Cour [kuːr], *f.* court; courtship.

Courage [kuˈraːʒə], *f.* courage.

Courant [kuˈrant], *adj.* current.

D

D, d [deː], *n.* D, d; Re, D (*Mus.*); **d dur**, D major; **D moll**, D minor.

Da [daː], I. *adv.* (*a*) there. (*b*) then, at that time. II. *in compds. with preps. for a dat. or acc. sing. & plur. of* **der, die, das,** *or of* **er, sie, es,** *used with regard to things, not persons;* **ich muß Sie —ran erinnern,** I must remind you of it. III. *interj.;* —! there!

IV. *conj.* then, under these circumstances, since, because; inasmuch as; while, whilst; although.

Dabei [daˈbaɪ], *adv.* thereby, thereat, therewith, by that, by it; at that place, near, close by; with it, with them; at the same time; in doing so; moreover; considering; nevertheless; with that.

Dach [dax], *n.* (—s, *pl.* **Dächer**) roof; shelter, cover. —**kammer**, —**stube**, *f.* garret, attic.

Dachen ['daxən], *v.a.* to roof.

Dachs [daks], *m.* (—(f)es, *pl.* —(f)e) badger. —**hund**, *m.* badger-dog.

Dächsel ['dɛksəl], *m.* badger-dog.

Dadurch [daˈdʊrç], *adv.* thereby; through that, through it; by this means; in that way.

Dafür [daˈfyːr], *adv.* for that, for it, for them; on behalf of it; in return for, instead of it; **ich kann nichts —,** I can't help it. —**halten**, *subst.n.* opinion; **nach meinem —halten,** in my opinion.

Dagegen [daˈgeːgən], I. *adv.* against it, that, them; in comparison with, over against it; in return, exchange, for it; on the contrary; on the other hand; **ich habe nichts —,** I have no objection. II. *conj.* against that, in objection to that, on the contrary, on the other hand; but then.

Daheim [daˈhaɪm], *adv.* at home; in one's own country.

Daher [daˈheːr], I. *adv.* thence, from that place, from that, (*also conj.*) hence, for that reason, therefore; — **kommt es, daß,** hence it happens that. II. *sep. prefix with verbs of motion=* along; away, as; —**schlendern,** to stroll along.

Daherum ['daːhɛrʊm], *adv.* thereabouts.

Dahin [daˈhɪn], *adv.* thither; to that place, time, state; thitherwards; (*used with verbs as sep. prefix=*) away, along, gone, past. —**ab**, *adv.* down there. —**aus**, *adv.* out thither.

Dahinten [daˈhɪntən], *adv.* behind, behind there.

Dahinter [daˈhɪntər], *adv.* behind that *or* it; there behind, *etc.*

Damal—ig ['daːmaːlɪç], *adj.* & *adv.* then being, of that time. —**s**, *adv.* then; at that time.

Damast [daˈmast], *m.* (—s, *pl.* —e) damask.

Dame ['da:mə], *f.* (*pl.* —n) lady; dame; queen (*at cards*); draughts. —n= brett (*also* **Dambrett**), *n.* draughts-board.

Damit [da'mɪt], I. *adv.* therewith, with it, with that; by it *or* this. II. *conj.* in order to, that, so that, to; — nicht, lest.

Damm [dam], *m.* (—es, *pl.* Dämme) dam; dyke; auf dem — sein, to be very well, in good form.

Dämmen ['dɛmən], *v.a.* to dam in; (*fig.*) to restrain.

Dämmer—n ['dɛmərn], *v.n.* (*aux.* h.) to dawn; to grow dusk. —ung, *f.* twilight, dawn.

Dämon ['dɛ:mɔn], *m.* (—s, *pl.* —en [—'mo:nən]) demon. —isch, *adj.* de-moniacal.

Dampf [dampf], *m.* (—es, *pl.* Dämpfe) vapour, steam; mist; smoke. —kessel, *m.* boiler. —maschine, *f.* steam-en-gine. —schiff, *n.* steamboat, steamer.

Dampf—en ['dampfən], *v.n.* (*aux.* h.) to smoke, to send forth steam. —er, *m.* (—ers, *pl.* —er) steamer.

Dämpf—en ['dɛmpfən], *v.a.* to suffo-cate; to extinguish; to deaden (*sound*); Speisen —, to stew food.

Danach [da'na:x], *adv.* after that, afterwards, thereafter; accordingly, according to that; towards, to that; upon that; for that *or* it; er sieht ganz — aus, he looks very much like it.

Daneben [da'ne:bən], *adv.* near it, next to it, by the side of it; close by, beside; (*also conj.*) moreover, besides, at the same time, also.

Dank [daŋk], *m.* (—es) thanks; grati-tude. —bar, *adj.* grateful, obliged. —barkeit, *f.* gratitude. —opfer, *n.* thank-offering. —sagung, *f.* returning thanks. —schreiben, *n.* letter of thanks *or* acknowledgment.

Danken ['daŋkən], *v.a.* & *n.* (*aux.* h. *dat.*) to return thanks; to decline an offer; wollen Sie etwas trinken? (ich) danke, will you drink anything? No, thank you.

Dann [dan], *adv.* then, at that time; thereupon; — und wann, now and then.

Daran [da'ran], **Dran** [dran], *adv.* thereon, thereat, thereby; at *or* on it, that, them; to it *or* that; about, near it *or* that; in regard to it *or* that; was liegt —? what does it matter?

Darauf [da'rauf], **Drauf** [drauf], *adv.* thereon, thereupon; upon it, that *or* them; to that; after that; afterwards; then, next; in addition.

Daraus [da'raus], **Draus** [draus], *adv.* thereout, therefrom; thence; from out of it, this, that, them; forth from it; by reason of it *or* that.

Darben ['darbən], *v.n.* (*aux.* h.) to starve, famish.

Darbiet—en ['da:rbi:tən], *ir.v.a.* to offer, tender. —ung, *f.* offering; ex-planation.

Darbringen ['da:rbrɪŋən], *ir.v.a.* to bring; to offer.

Darein [da'rain], **Drein** [drain], *adv.* thereto, thereinto; into it *or* that; to it *or* that; in addition, over and above; on, along, into *or* against it, that, *etc.*

Darin [da'rɪn], **Drin** [drɪn], *adv.* there-in, in there; in, within, at it. —nen (*usually* drinnen), *adv.* there within, inside.

Darleg—en ['da:rle:gən], *v.a.* to lay down; to demonstrate. —ung, *f.* statement, exposition.

Darleh(e)n ['da:rle:ən], *n.*(—s, *pl.* — *or* —e) loan.

Darleihe ['da:rlaiə], *f.* (*pl.* —n) loan.

Darm [darm], *m.* (—(e)s, *pl.* Därme) intestine, bowel. —saite, *f.* catgut-string.

Darnach [da:r'na:x], *see* **Danach**.

Da(r)nieder [da(r)'ni:dər], *adv.* on the ground; down.

Darob [da'rɔp], *adv.* on account of it, that, them; at it, that, them.

Darstell—en ['da:rʃtɛlən], *v.a.* to place, bring before; to exhibit; to state; to represent. —er, *m.* (—ers, *pl.* —er) representer, actor. —ung, *f.* exhibi-tion; representation; performance.

Darüben [da'ry:bən], **Drüben** ['dry:bən], *adv.* over there, over yonder, beyond, yonder, opposite.

Darüber [da'ry:bər], **Drüber** ['dry:ber], *adv.* over that *or* it; thereon, about that; concerning it *or* that; of it *or* that; on that point; over and above; besides; in the meantime, before that; across it *or* that; wir werden — sterben, we shall die before that.

Darum [da'rum], **Drum** [drum], *adv.* thereabout, around it *or* that; for it *or* that; respecting it, that, them; therefore; on that account; about

that; **es ift mir nur — zu tun**, my
only object is.

Darunten [da'runtən], **Drunten** ['drun-
tən], *adv.* below, down there, beneath.

Darunter [da'runtər], **Drunter** ['drun-
tər], *adv.* under that, it, them, there;
beneath it, that, them; among them;
less; **alles geht drunter und drüber**,
everything is topsy-turvy.

Das [das], *nom. & acc. of the neut. sing.
of* **der**. I. *def. art.* the. II. *rel. pron.*
which, that. III. *dem. adj.* that, it.
IV. *dem. pron.* that one, it.

Dajein ['da:zaın], I. *ir.v.n.* (*aux.* f.) to
be there present; to exist. II. *subst.n.*
presence; existence; life.

Dajelbft [da'zɛlpst], *adv.* there, in that
very place.

Daß [das], *conj.* that.

Datieren [da'ti:rən], *v.a.* to date.

Dat—iv [da'ti:f], *m.* (—ivs, *pl.* —ive)
dative (*case*). —o, *adv.* of the date.

Dattel ['datəl], *f.* (*pl.* —n) date (*fruit*).

Datum ['da:tum], *n.* (—s, *pl.* Data *or*
Daten) date (*of month, etc.*).

Dauer ['dauər], *f.* duration, continuance; length; **auf die —**, for long; in
the long run. —**haft**, *adj.* durable,
permanent. —**haftigkeit**, *f.* durability.

¹**Dauern** ['dauərn], *v.n.* (*aux.* h.) to
last; to hold out; to keep (*of meat*).

²**Dauern** ['dauərn], *v.a. & imp.* to
regret, to grieve.

Daumen ['daumən], *m.* (—s, *pl.* —)
thumb.

Däumling ['dɔymlıŋ], *m.* (—s, *pl.* —e)
thumb-stall; **der kleine —**, Tom
Thumb.

Daun—e ['daunə], *f.* (*pl.*—en) down.
—**icht**, —**ig**, *adj.* downy.

Davon [da'fɔn], *adv.* therefrom, there-
of, thereby; of, by, respecting it, that
or them; thence; hence; away; off.

Davor [da'fo:r], *adv.* before it, that *or*
them; for, because of, from it, that *or*
them; against it, that *or* them.

Dawider [da'vi:dər], *adv.* against it,
that *or* them; to the contrary.

Dazu [da'tsu:], *adv.* thereto; to, for, at
it, that *or* them; for that purpose, to
that end; moreover, besides, in addition; **ich komme nie —**, I can never
find time to. —**mal** ['da:tsuma:l],
adv. then, at that time.

Dazwischen [da'tsvıʃən], *adv.* between,
amongst them, in between, in the

midst of it, that *or* them; there
between.

Debatte [de'batə], *f.* (—*pl.* n) debate.

Dechant [dɛ'çant], *m.* (—en, *pl.* —en)
dean.

Deck [dɛk], *n.* (—es, *pl.* —e) deck.
—**e**, *f.* (*pl.* —en) cover, coverlet, quilt;
veil; rug, cover; case; ceiling; roof.
—**el**, *m.* (—els, *pl.* —el) lid, cover.

Deck—en ['dɛkən], *v.a.* to cover (*also
Mil.*); to protect, to conceal; **für vier
Perjonen —en**, to lay covers for four
persons. —**ung**, *f.* covering, protecting, *etc.*; protection.

Defekt [de'fɛkt], I. *m.* (—es, *pl.* —e)
defect. II. *adj.* defective; damaged.

Degen ['de:gən], *m.* (—s, *pl.* —) sword.

Dehn—bar ['de:nba:r], *adj.* extensible,
ductile, malleable. —**barkeit**, *f.*
extensibility; ductility.

Dehnen ['de:nən], *v.a.* to stretch, extend; **gedehnte Silbe**, long syllable.
—**ung**, *f.* extension.

Deich [daıç], *m.* (—es, *pl.* —e) dike,
dam; embankment.

Deich—en ['daıçən], *v.a.* to dike. —**er**,
m. ditcher, navvy.

Deichjel ['daıksəl], *f.* (*pl.* —n) pole (*of
a carriage*).

Dein [daın] (—, —e, —) *poss. adj.* thy,
thine. —**ige**, (**der, die, das** —**ige**)
poss. pron. thine. —**erjeits**, *adv.* on
thy side; for thy part, as concerns
thee; in thy turn. —**ethalben**, —**et-
wegen**, —**etwillen**, *adv.* on thy
account, for thy sake, as far as thou
art concerned. —**esgleichen**, *indec.
adj. & pron.* the like of you, such as
thou, of thy kind.

Dekalog [deka'lo:k], *m.* (—s) Deca-
logue.

Dekret [de'kre:t], *n.* (—es, *pl.* —e)
decree. —**ale** ['ta:lə], *f.* (*pl.* —alien)
decretal.

Delegat [dele'ga:t], *m.* (—en, *pl.* —en)
delegate.

Delikat [deli'ka:t], *adj.* delicate, fine,
nice, dainty; delicious. —**esse**
[—'tɛsə], *f.* (*pl.* —essen) dainty.

Delphin [dɛl'fi:n], *m.* (—s, *pl.* —e)
dolphin.

Delta ['dɛlta:], *n.* (—s, *pl.* —s) delta.

Dem [dɛːm, dɛm, dəm], *dat. sing. of*
der, das; **wie — auch jei**, however that
may be. —**gemäß**, *adv.* accordingly,
according to that. —**nächst**, *adv.*
thereupon, after this; shortly, soon

after. —**ohngeachtet,** —**ungeachtet,** *conj.* notwithstanding, nevertheless, in spite of that.

Demagog [dema'go:k], *m.* (—**en,** *pl.* —**en**) demagogue.

Demokrat [demo'kra:t], *m.* (—**en,** *pl.* —**en**) democrat.

Demut ['de:mu:t], *f.* humility, lowliness.

Demütig ['de:my:tıç], *adj.* & *adv.* humble, submissive.

Demütig—**en** ['de:my:tɪgən], *v.a.* to humble; to subdue. —**ung,** *f.* humiliation; depression.

Denk—**bar** ['dɛŋkba:r], *adj.* imaginable, conceivable. —**barkeit,** *f.* conceivability. —**lich,** *(in compounds) adj.* thinkable. —**art,** *f.* way of thinking; mentality, disposition. —**mal,** *n.* monument, memorial. —**münze,** *f.* commemorative medal. —**säule,** *f.* memorial column. —**schrift,** *f.* record; memorial. —**spruch,** *m.* motto, sentence; maxim; device. —**würdig,** *adj.* memorable, notable. —**würdigkeit,** *f.* memorable occurrence. —**zettel,** *m.* memorandum; punishment; **jemandem einen ' —zettel geben,** to punish someone.

Denk—**en** ['dɛŋkən], I. *ir.v.a.* & *n.* (*aux.* **h.**) to think (**an eine Sache**); **sich** (*dat.*) —**en,** to form an idea of. II. *subst.n.* philosophical speculation; meditation. —**er,** *m.* (—**ers,** *pl.* —**er**) thinker.

Denn [dɛn], I. *conj.* then; for. II. *adv.* in that case; unless, or else (*obs.*); **er bezahle mich** —, unless he pay me.

Dennoch ['dɛnɔx], *conj.* yet, nevertheless, for all that, however.

Depesche [de'pɛʃə], *f.* (*pl.* —**n**) despatch; telegram.

Deputierte(r) [depu'ti:rtə(r)], *m.* (—**en,** *pl.* —**e(n)**) deputy, member of a deputation.

Der[de:r, der, dər], **Die** [di:], **Das** [das], I. *nom. sing. of def. art.* the; **zweimal des Tages,** twice a day. II. *nom. sing. of dem. adj.* & *pron.* that, this, he, it; that one. III. *nom. sing. of rel. pron.* who, which, that; **unser Vater,** — **Du bist im Himmel,** our Father who art in Heaven.

Derb [dɛrp], *adj.* & *adv.* firm, solid; smart, severe; hearty; blunt; rough, uncouth. **heit,** *f.* firmness; sturdiness; bluntness.

Der—**einst** [dɛr'aınst], *adv.* at some future time. —**gestalt,** *adv.* in such manner; to such a degree. —**gleichen,** *indec. adj.* of such kind, the like. —**lei,** *indec. adj.* of that sort *or* kind. —**maßen,** *adv.* to that degree; in such a manner; so much. —**o,** *gen. pl. of* **der, die,** your; his; —**o Gnaden,** your Grace. —**'weile,** —**'weilen,** *adv.* meanwhile. —**zeit,** *adv.* at that time, at present.

Deren ['de:rən], *gen. sing. f.* & *gen. pl. m. f.* & *b.* of **der, die, das, dem.** & *rel. pron.*; —**thalben,** —**twegen, (um)** —**twillen,** *adv.* for her sake, on her account, on their account, on whose account.

Derer ['de:rər], *gen. pl. of* **der, die, das,** *dem. pron.*; **das Geschlecht** —**er von Bismarck,** the race of the Bismarcks.

Derjenige ['de:rje:nıgə], **Diejenige** ['di:—], **Dasjenige** ['das—], *pl.* **Diejenigen,** *dem. adj.* & *pron.* those; such; he, she, it (*before a rel. pron.*).

Derselbe [de:r'zɛlbə], **Dieselbe** [di:—], **Dasselbe** [das—], *pl.* **Dieselben, Derselbige,** *dem. adj.* & *pron.* the same, the self-same.

Derwisch ['dɛrvıʃ], *m.* (—(e)s, *pl.* —**e**) dervish.

¹**Des** [dɛs], *n.* D flat (*Mus.*); —**sDur,** D flat major; —**sMoll,** D flat minor.

²**Des** [dɛs, dəs], *gen. sing.* (*Arch.* & *Poet.*) *of dem. pron.* **der, das.** —**gleichen,** I. *indec. adj.* similar, such-like. II. *adv.* in like manner, after the same fashion, likewise. III. *conj.* as also. —**halb,** *adv.* & *conj.* on this account, therefore. —**wegen,** *adv.* on that account, for that reason.

Dessen ['dɛsən], *gen. sing. of the dem.* & *rel. prons.* **der, das,** whose, of whom, of which, of that; whereof. —**ungeachtet,** *conj.* notwithstanding that, in spite of that.

Desto ['dɛsto:], *adv.* (*used before comparatives*); the, so much; **je mehr,** — **besser,** the more, the better; — **besser,** so much the better; **nichts** — **weniger,** nevertheless.

Detail [de'ta:j], *n.* (—**s,** *pl.* —**s**) detail, particular. —**handlung,** *f.* retail business. —**list,** *m.* (—**listen,** *pl.* —**listen**) retailer.

Deut—**en** ['dɔytən], *v.* I. *a.* to explain, expound, interpret. II. *n.* (*aux.* **h.**) (**auf**) to make a sign, point (to); to signify. —**lich,** *adj.* & *adv.* distinct, clear. —**lichkeit,** *f.* distinctness, clearness. —ung, f. meaning, signification; application.

Deutſch [dɔʏtʃ], adj. & adv. German. —land, n. Germany. —tum, n. German nationality; German customs and manners; German patriotism. —tümlich, adj. thoroughly German.

Deviſe [de'vi:zə], f. (pl. —n) device, motto; bill of exchange.

Dezember [de'tsɛmbər], m. (—s, pl. —), December.

Dezimal [detsi'ma:l], adj. & n. decimal.

Diakon [dai'ko:n], m. (—s, & —en, pl. —en) deacon. —at [—ko'na:t], n. (—(e)s, pl. —e) diaconate. —iſſin, f. deaconess.

Dialekt [dia'lɛkt], m. (—s, pl. —e) dialect. —iſch, adj. dialectal. —ik [—'lɛktɪk], f. dialectics.

Dialog [dia'lo:k], m. (—s, pl. —e) dialogue.

Diamant [dia'mant], m. (—en, pl. —en) diamond.

Diät [di'ɛ:t], f. diet; (obs.) diet, legislative assembly. —en, pl. day's salary.

Dich [dɪç], acc. of Du.

Dicht [dɪçt], adj. & adv. close (in texture, etc.); thick, dense, compact; —neben, close by.

Dicht—en ['dɪçtən], I. v.a. & n. (aux. h.) to compose; to make verses, write poetry. II. subst.n. composition of poetry. —er, m. (—ers, pl. —er) poet. —erin, f. poetess. —eriſch, adj. & adv. poetic. —ung, f. poetry, poesy; poem; fiction.

Dick [dɪk], adj. & adv. thick; fat, stout; voluminous; ſich — tun, to brag, talk big. —e, f. thickness; density. —häuter, m. (—s, pl. —) pachyderm. —icht, n. (—ichts, pl. —ichte) thicket.

Die [di:], f. sing. nom. & acc. of I. def. art. II. dem. pron. III. rel. pron. IV. nom. & acc. pl. of der, die, das.

Dieb [di:p], m. (—es, pl. —e) thief. —erei [—ə'raɪ], f. theft. —in, f. female thief. —iſch, adj. & adv. thievish; by theft. —ſtahl, m. theft, robbery

Diele ['di:lə], f. (pl. —n) board, plank; floor; saloon-bar, small wine-restaurant.

Dielen ['di:lən], v.a. to floor; to board, plank.

Dien—en ['di:nən], v.n. (aux. h.) to serve; to assist; to be good for, useful to. —er, m. (—ers, pl. —er) (man)

servant, attendant; einen —er machen, to make a bow. —erin, f. maid servant. —erſchaft, f. the domestics. —lich, adj. & adv. serviceable. —lichkeit, f. serviceableness. —ertracht, f. livery.

Dienſt [di:nst], m. (—es, pl. —e) service; worship; employment; zum — (abbr. z. D.), in active service (Mil.); außer — (abbr. a. D.), retired (Mil.). —bar, adj. serviceable. —barkeit, f. servitude, bondage, subjection. —lich, adj. & adv. official. —bote, m. domestic servant. —eifer, m. zeal of office. —fähig, adj. fit for service. —fertig, adj. officious; obliging. —kleid, n. uniform, livery. —lohn, m. servant's wages. —pflicht, f. liability to service; duty of office. —untauglich, adj. unfit for military service. —vorſchrift, f. rule of the service, instruction.

Dienstag ['di:nsta:k], m. (—s, pl. —e) Tuesday.

Dies [di:s], abbr. of Dieses. —bezüglich, adj. referring to this. —jährig, adj. of this year. —mal, adv. this time, now. —seits, adv. & prep. with gen. on this side.

Dieser ['di:zər], m., Diese ['di:zə], f., Dieses ['di:zəs], or Dies, n. (pl. dieſe) dem. adj. & pron. this, that, these, the latter, this one, etc.

Dieweil [di'vaɪl], adv. & conj. as long as; because.

Ding [dɪŋ], n. (—es, pl. —e or —er) (das Dings, coll.) thing; matter; guter —e ſein, to be in good spirits.

Dingbar ['dɪŋba:r], adj. hireable.

Dingen ['dɪŋən], reg. & ir.v.a. & n. to bargain for; to hire; to engage.

Dingfeſt [dɪŋfɛst], adj. confirmed by law; jemanden — machen, to arrest a person.

Diplom [di'plo:m], n. (—s, pl. —e) diploma, patent. —at [—'ma:t], m. (—aten, pl. —aten). —atier [—'ma:tɪkər], m. (—atifers, pl. —atier) diplomatist, schemer. —atiſch, adj. diplomatic.

Dir [di:r], dat. of Du.

Direkt [di'rɛkt], adj. & adv. direct; eine —e Fahrkarte, a through-ticket. —ion [—tsi'o:n], f. management; board of directors. —or, m. (—ors, pl. —oren) director; manager.

Dirigieren [diri'gi:rən], v.a. to direct, manage.

Dirne ['di:rnə], f. (pl. —n) (obs.) maid, girl; (now) hussy.

Distant [dɪs'kant], m. (—s, pl. —e) treble, soprano.

Diskont[dɪs'kɔnt],Diskonto[dɪs'kɔnto:], m. discount; rebate. —ieren[—'ti:rən], v.a. to discount.

Diskurs [dɪs'kʊrs], m. (—(ſ)es, pl. —(ſ)e) discourse.

Distel ['dɪstəl], f. (pl. —n) thistle. —fink, m. goldfinch.

Diwan ['di:van], m. (—s, pl. —s & —e) council; divan, sofa.

Doch [dɔx], adv. & conj.; part. yet, still, however, nevertheless; for all that; but; at least; though; surely.

Docht [dɔxt], m. (—es, pl. —e) wick.

Dock—e ['dɔkə], f. dock. —en, v.a. to dock (ships).

Dogge ['dɔgə], f. (pl. —n) bulldog, mastiff.

Dogma ['dɔgma:], n. (—s, pl. Dogmen) dogma. —tiker [—'ma:tɪkər], m. (—tikers, pl. —tiker) dogmatist. —tiſch, adj. dogmatic.

Dohle ['do:lə], f. (pl. —n) jackdaw.

Doktor ['dɔktər], m. (—s, pl. —en [—'to:rən]) doctor; physician, surgeon. —at [—'ra:t], n. (—at(e)s, pl. —ate), —würde, f. doctorate, doctor's degree. —in, f. doctor's wife; woman doctor.

Dolch [dɔlç], m. (—es, pl. —e) dagger.

Dolmetſch—en ['dɔlmɛtʃən], v.a. to interpret. —er, m. (—ers, pl. —er) interpreter.

Dom [do:m], m. (—(e)s, pl. —e) cathedral; dome. —chor, m. choir of a cathedral. —herr, m. prebendary, canon.

Domäne [do'mɛ:nə], f. (pl. —n), Domanialgut [doma:ni'algu:t], n. domain, demesne.

Domino ['do:mino:], I. m. (—s, pl. —s) domino (cloak). II. n. (—s, pl. —s) game of dominoes; —steine, pl. dominoes.

Donner ['dɔnər], m. (—s, pl. —) thunder. —keil, m. thunder-bolt. —ſchlag, m. thunder-clap. —s=tag, m. Thursday. —wetter, I. n. thunderstorm. II. int. zounds! hang it!

Donnern ['dɔnərn], v.n. (aux. h.) to thunder.

Doppel—heit ['dɔpəlhaɪt], f. doubleness, duplicity. —gänger, m. double,

wraith. —geſpann, n. four-in-hand. —n, v.a. & n. to double. —punkt, m. colon.

Dorf [dɔrf], n. (—es, pl. Dörfer) village. —gemeinde, f. rural parish.

Dörf—chen ['dɔrfçən], (—chens, pl. —chen), —lein, n. (—leins, pl. —lein) little village, hamlet.

Dorn [dɔrn], m. (es, pl. —en) thorn. —ig, adj. & adv. thorny. —röschen, n. Sleeping Beauty.

Dorren ['dɔrən], v.n. (aux. ſ.) to become dry; to wither.

Dörren ['dɔrən], v.a. to dry, bake.

Dorſch [dɔrʃ], m. (—es, pl. —e) codfish.

Dort [dɔrt], Dorten (obs.) adv. there, yonder. —her, adv. from yonder, thence. —hin, adv. to that place, thither.

Dose ['do:zə], f. (pl. —n; dim. Döschen) box, snuff-box.

Döſig ['dø:zɪç], adj. stupid, dull.

Dosis ['do:zɪs], f. (pl. Doſen) dose.

Dotter ['dɔtər], n. (—s, pl. —) yolk of an egg.

Dozent [do'tsɛnt], m. (—en, pl. —en) university teacher, professor, lecturer.

Drache ['draxə], m. (—n, pl. —n), (less good) —n, m. (—ns, pl. —n) dragon.

Dragoner [dra'go:nər], m. (—s, pl. —) dragoon.

Draht [dra:t], m. (—es, pl. Drähte) thread; wire. —en, adj. (made) of wire, wiry. —los, adj. wireless; —loſe Telegraphie, wireless telegraphy.

Drall [dral], adj. & adv. tight; strong, robust; smart; active.

Drama ['dra:ma:], n. (—s, pl. Dramen) drama. —tiker [—'ma:tɪkər], m. (—tikers, pl. —tiker) dramatist. —tiſch [—'ma:tɪʃ], adj. dramatic. —tiſieren [—ti'zi:rən], v.a. to dramatize. —turgie [—tu:r'gi:], f. dramatic theory.

Drang [draŋ], m. (—(e)s) throng; pressure, urgency; hurry; violence. —ſal, n. (—ſals, pl. —ſale) & f. (pl. —ſalen) oppression; hardship.

Drängen ['drɛŋən], v.a. to press, crowd; to afflict. gedrängt, p.p. & adj. crowded close.

Draußen ['draʊsən], adv. outside, out of doors.

Drechseln ['drɛksəln], v.a. & n. (aux. h.) to turn (on a lathe). gedrechſelt, p.p. & adj. elaborate; affected.

Drechsler ['drɛkslər], *m.* (—**s**, *pl.* —) turner. —**ei** [—'raɪ], *f.* turner's workshop.

Dreck [drɛk], *m.* (*fam. & dial.*) (—**es**) dirt, filth; dung. —**ig**, *adj.* muddy, dirty; nasty.

Dreh—**bar** ['drɛːbaːr], *adj. & adv.* revolving. —**bank**, *f.* turning-lathe.

Dreh—**en** ['dreːən], I. *v.a.* to turn; to twist; to distort. II. *v.n.* (*aux. h.*) to turn; to veer. III. *subst.n.* turning; turn, rotation. —**end**, *p. & adj.* turning; rotary.

Drei [draɪ], I. *num. adj.* three. II. *f.* three. —**heit**, *f.* triad. —**ßig**, *num. adj.* thirty. —**ßigst**, *num. adj.* thirtieth. —**achtel**, *pl.* three-eighths. —**bund**, *m.* Triple Alliance. —**eck**, *n.* triangle. —**edig**, *adj.* triangular, three-cornered. —**einheit**, *f.* triad; trinity. —**einig**, *adj. & adv.* triune. —**erlei**, *indec. adj.* of three kinds, three-fold. —**fach**, *adj. & adv.* three-fold; triple. —**faltig**, *adj. & adv.* threefold. —**faltigkeit**, *f.* Trinity. —**fuß**, *m.* tripod. —**gesang**, *m.* trio. —**gespann**, *n.* team of three horses. —**mal**, *adv.* three times, thrice. —**malig**, *adj.* done three times, repeated three times. —**rad**, *n.* tricycle. —**zehn**, *adj.* thirteen. —**zehnte**, *n.* thirteenth. —**zehntel**, *n.* thirteenth part.

Dreist [draɪst], *adj. & adv.* bold; courageous, confident. —**igkeit**, *f.* boldness; audacity; confidence; courage.

Drell [drɛl], *m.* (—**s**, *pl.* —**e**) diaper; strong ticking.

Dresch—**e** ['drɛʃə], *f.* thrashing. —**en**, *ir.v.a.* to thrash. —**er**, *m.* (—**ers**, *pl.* —**er**) thrasher. —**flegel**, *m.* flail. —**tenne**, *f.* thrashing-floor.

Dress—**ieren** [drɛ'siːrən], *v.a.* to train; to drill. —**ur** [—'suːr], *f.* training.

1Drill—**en** ['drɪlən], *v.a.* to turn round; to drill (*soldiers*). —**er**, *m.* driller, trainer. —**meister**, *m.* drill-sergeant.

2Drillen ['drɪlən], *v.a.* to drill, bore; to harass, torment.

Drilling ['drɪlɪŋ], *m.* (—**s**, *pl.* —**e**) one of three produced at a birth, triplet.

Dring—**en** ['drɪŋən], *ir.v.* I. *n.* (*aux. h. & f.*) to press forward; to throng, crowd; to penetrate, pierce. II. *a.* **drängen**, to urge, force, compel. —**end**, *p. & adj.* pressing, urgent.

—**lich**, *adj. & adv.* urgent, pressing. —**lichkeit**, *f.* urgency.

Drinnen ['drɪnən], *adv.* within.

Dritt—**e** ['drɪtə], *num. adj.* third. —**ens**, *num. adv.* thirdly. —**letzt**, *adj.* last but two.

Droben ['droːbən], *adv.* there above, on high.

Droge ['droːgə], *f.* (*pl.* —**n**) drug. —**nhändler**, *m.* druggist. —**rie** [—'riː], *f.* druggist's shop.

Drogist [dro'gɪst], *m.* (—**en**, *pl.* —**en**) druggist, chemist.

Droh—**en** ['droːən], *v.a. & n.* (**einem mit etwas** *or* **einem etwas**) to threaten, menace with. —**ung**, *f.* threat.

Drohne ['droːnə], *f.* (*pl.* —**n**) drone.

Drollig ['drɔlɪç], *adj.* droll, funny; odd.

Dromedar [drome'daːr], *m.* (—**s**, *pl.* —**e**) dromedary.

Droschke ['drɔʃkə], *f.* (*pl.* —**n**) cab, hackney carriage. —**nkutscher**, *m.* (—**s**, *pl.* —) cab-driver.

1Drossel ['drɔsəl], *f.* (*pl.* —**n**) thrush. —**beere**, *f.* mountain ash.

2Drossel ['drɔsəl], *f.* (*pl.* —**n**) throttle, throat. —**ader**, *f.* jugular vein. —**bein**, *n.* throttle; collar-bone.

Drosseln ['drɔsəln], *v.a.* to throttle.

Druck [druk], *m.* (—**es**, *pl.* —**e**) pressure; impulse; spring; print; printing; proof, impression; stamp; type; oppression, burden; grievance, hardship. —**bar**, *adj.* that may be pressed *or* printed. —**bogen**, *m.* proof-sheet, proof. —**buchstaben**, *pl.* type. —**er arbeit**, *f.* presswork. —**erschwärze**, *f.* printer's ink. —**fehler**, *m.* misprint, erratum. —**form**, *f.* forme (*Typ.*); printing-block. —**knopf**, *m.* (—**es**, *pl.* —**knöpfe**) patent fastener, press-button. —**sache**, *f.* printed matter, printed papers. —**schrift**, *f.* type; publication. —**waren**, *pl.* (cotton) prints.

Druck—**en** ['drukən], *v.a.* to press, impress; to stamp; to print. —**er**, *m.* printer. —**erei** [—ə'raɪ], *f.* press, printing press.

Drück—**en** ['drykən], *v.* I. *a.* to press, clasp; to pinch; to annoy, afflict. **wo** —**t der Schuh?** what is the matter? what is troubling you? II. *n.* (*aux. h.*) to gravitate; to draw; to oppress. —**eberger**, *m.* shirker. —**end**, *adj.* heavy, oppressive. —**er**, *m.* (—**ers**, *pl.* —**er**) handle.

Drud—e ['dru:də], f. witch; nightmare.
—en=fuß, m. pentagram.

Druid—e [dru'i:də], m. (—en, pl. —en)
Druid. —ijch, adj. Druidical.

Drunten ['drʊntən], adv. below (there).

Druj—e ['dru:zə], f. (pl. —en) decayed
ore; glanders. —icht, adj. decayed.

Drüj—e ['dry:zə], f. (pl. —en) gland.
—ig, adj. adj. & adv. glandular.

Dschungel ['dzʊŋəl], f. (pl. —n) jungle.

Du [du:], I. pers. pron. thou; mit jemand
auf — und — stehen, to be on intimate terms with a person. II. n. dein
anderes —, thine other self.

Duden ['dʊkən], v.a. & n. (aux. h.) to
bow; to stoop.

Duckmäuser ['dʊkmɔyzər], m. (—s, pl.
—) sneak, hypocrite.

Dudel—n ['du:dəln], v.n. (aux. h.) to
play on the bagpipe. —kasten, m.
barrel-organ. —jack, m. bagpipe.

Duell [du'ɛl], n. (—s, pl. —e) duel.
—ant [—'lant], m. (—anten, pl.
—anten) duellist. —ieren [—'li:rən],
v.r. to fight a duel.

Duett [du'ɛt], n. (—s, pl. —e) duet,
duetto.

Duft [dʊft], m. (—es, pl. Düfte) scent,
fragrance, exhalation. —ig, adj.
misty; fragrant, odoriferous.

Duft—en ['dʊftən], v. I. n. (aux. h. &
j.) to exhale fragrance, scent, be
odoriferous. II. a. to smell; to perfume. —end, adj. scented.

Dukaten [du'ka:tən], m. (—s, pl. —)
ducat.

Duld—en ['dʊldən], I. v.a. to suffer,
endure. II. subst.n. sufferance, endurance. —er, m. (ers, pl. —er), —erin,
f. sufferer. —ung, f. endurance;
toleration.

Duldjam ['dʊltza:m], adj. enduring,
patient, tolerant. —keit, f. toleration,
spirit of toleration.

Dumm [dʊm], adj. & adv. dull, stupid;
—es Zeug, (stuff and) nonsense.
—dreist, adj. & adv. foolhardy, impudent. —heit, f. stupidity, folly;
nonsense. —kopf, —er=ja(h)n, m.
blockhead, simpleton.

Dumpf [dʊmpf], adj. & adv. damp,
moist; dull; gloomy; stifling; dull in
sound, muffled. —heit, f. dullness,
hollowness; gloominess; stupor, torpor.
—ig, adj. & adv. moist; fusty, musty.
—igkeit, f. dampness, mustiness. —=
finn, m. dull-mindedness, stupefaction.

Düne ['dy:nə], f. (pl. —n) sandhill.

Düng—en ['dyŋən], v.a. to manure.
—er, m. (—ers) manure.

Dünkel ['dyŋkəl], m. (—s) self-conceit;
arrogance. —haft, adj. self-con-
ceited; arrogant.

Dunkel ['dʊŋkəl], I. adj. & adv. dark,
obscure; cloudy; dim; mystical. II.
subst.n. (—s) obscurity; ambiguity.
—heit, f. darkness; obscurity. —=
kammer, f. dark-room (Phot.); camera
obscura.

Dunkeln ['dʊŋkəln], v.n. (aux. h.) to
grow dark or dim.

Dünken ['dyŋkən], ir.v. I. n. (aux. h.)
& imp. to seem, look, appear. II.
r. to imagine oneself, fancy.

Dünn [dyn], adj. thin, fine.

Dunst [dʊnst], m. (—es, pl. Dünste)
vapour; fume; steam. —ig, adj. &
adv. misty; foggy; damp. —bild, n.
phantasm. —kreis, m. atmosphere.

Dur [du:r], adj. major, sharp (Mus.).

Durch [dʊrç], I. prep. with acc. through;
by; by means of; across; throughout,
during; owing to. II. adv. throughout; thoroughly; through; — und
—, completely, thoroughly. III.
sep. & insep. prefix. Verbs compounded with durch when separable
have the principal accent on durch;
when inseparable, on the root of the
verb. (The meaning of durch in such
compounds is as a rule through or
thoroughly (or one after another), and,
in a number of inseparable compounds:
to pass time in.) —aus [dʊrç'aʊs],
adv. throughout, thoroughly, quite;
absolutely, positively, by all means;
—aus nicht, by no means. —einander
[—aɪ'nandər], adv. in confusion,
promiscuously.

Durchbeben [dʊrç'be:bən], v.a. (insep.)
to shake, agitate thoroughly.

Durchblättern ['dʊrçblɛtərn], v.a. (sep.
& insep.) to turn over the leaves (of a
book).

Durchblicken ['dʊrçblɪkən], v. I. n.
(aux. h.) (sep.) to look, peep, appear
through. II. a. (insep. & sep.) to penetrate, see through.

Durchbraten ['dʊrçbra:tən], ir.v.a.
(sep.) to roast well or thoroughly.
durchgebraten, p.p. & adj. well done.

Durchbringen ['dʊrçbrɪŋən], ir.v.a.
(sep.) to bring through; to squander,
dissipate; to bring up, rear.

Durchbruch ['dʊrçbrʊx], *m.* (—es, *pl.* Durchbrüche) breach.

Durchdring—en ['dʊrçdrɪŋən], *ir.v.* I. *n.* (*aux.* f.) (*sep.*) to press, crowd through; to penetrate; to permeate; to prevail. II. *a.* (*insep.*) to permeate; to pervade. —end, *p. & adj.* penetrating; shrill; acute, keen, sharp. —lich, *adj. & adv.* penetrable, permeable. —lichkeit, *f.* penetrability. —ung, *f.* penetration.

Durchfallen ['dʊrçfalən], *ir.v.n.* (*aux.* f.) (*sep.*) to fall through; to fail.

Durchfinden ['dʊrçfɪndən], *ir.v.r.* (*sep.*) to find one's way through; to master (*a problem*).

Durchflechten [dʊrç'flɛçtən], *v.a.* (*insep.*) to interweave.

Durchforschen [dʊrç'fɔrʃən], *v.a.* (*insep.*) to examine thoroughly; to investigate.

Durchfuhr ['dʊrçfu:r], *f.* (*pl.* —en) passage, transit.

Durchführ—en ['dʊrçfy:rən], *v.a.* (*sep.*) to convey *or* lead through; to bring to an issue. —ung, *f.* the carrying through; accomplishment; execution, performance.

Durchgang ['dʊrçgaŋ], *m.* (—(e)s, *pl.* Durchgänge) thoroughfare; passage; — verboten! no thoroughfare! —s= handel, *m.* transit-trade. —s=zug, *m.* through train; corridor-train.

Durchgehen ['dʊrçge:ən], *ir.v.* I. *n.* (*aux.* f.) (*sep.*) to go, pass through; to escape, elope; to pass, be approved; to stampede, bolt. II. *a.* (*sep.*) to walk, go through *or* over; to look over, to retouch; to peruse; to wear out. —d, *p. & adj.* pervading.

Durchgießen ['dʊrçgi:sən], *v.a.* to filter; to pour through.

Durchgreifen ['dʊrçgraɪfən], *ir.v.n.* (*sep.*) (*aux.* h.) to act decidedly; to prevail. —d, *p. & adv.* energetic, thorough.

Durchguß ['dʊrçgʊs], *m.* (—(ss)es, *pl.* Durchgüsse) strainer, colander; sink.

Durchhauen ['dʊrçhaʊən], *ir.v.a.* (*sep. & insep.*) to hew *or* cut through; einen —, (*sep.*) to give someone a thrashing; sich —, to cut one's way through.

Durchkauen ['dʊrçkaʊən], *v.a.* (*sep. & insep.*) to chew thoroughly; (*coll.*) to ruminate on.

Durchkommen ['dʊrçkɔmən], *ir.v.n.* (*aux.* f.) (*sep.*) to come, get through; to come off; to recover; to pass (*examinations*); mit seiner Einnahme —, to make both ends meet.

Durchlaß—en ['dʊrçlasən], I. *ir.v.a.* (*sep.*) to let through; to filter; to transmit (*light, etc.*). —end, *p. & adj.* pervious; nicht —end, impermeable (*by water, etc.*). II. *subst.n.*, —ung, *f.* transmission.

Durchlaucht ['dʊrçlaʊxt], *f.* (*pl.* —en) Highness, Serene Highness; Ew. (= Euer) —, your Highness. —igkeit, *f.* Serene Highness (*obs.*).

Durchlesen ['dʊrçle:zən], *v.a.* to peruse, read through.

Durchleuchten ['dʊrçlɔʏçtən], *v.* I. *n.* (*sep.*) to shine through. II. *a.* (*insep.*) to illuminate; to irradiate; to subject to X-rays (*Med.*).

Durchlöchern [dʊrç'lœcərn], *v.a.* to perforate, pierce.

Durchmachen ['dʊrçmaxən], *v.a.* (*sep.*) to finish, accomplish; to experience, suffer.

Durchmesser ['dʊrçmɛsər], *m.* (—s, *pl.* —) diameter.

Durchmuster—n ['dʊrçmʊstərn], *v.a.* (*sep. & insep.*) to pass in review; to examine, scrutinize. —ung, *f.* examination, inspection, scrutiny.

Durchreise ['dʊrçraɪzə], *f.* passing through, passage.

Durchreisen ['dʊrçraɪzən], *v.* I. *n.* (*aux.* f.) (*sep.*) to travel through; to traverse. II. *a.* (*insep.*) to travel over. —de(r), *m.* traveller, passer-through.

Durchschauen ['dʊrçʃaʊən], *v.* I. *n.* (*aux.* h.) (*sep.*) to see through. II. *a.* (*insep.*) to look through, penetrate; to see into the heart of someone.

Durchscheinen ['dʊrçʃaɪnən], *ir.v.n.* (*aux.* h.) (*sep.*) to shine through. —d, *p.p. & adj.* transparent; translucent.

Durchschlagen ['dʊrçʃla:gən], *ir.v.* (*sep.*) I. *a.* to pierce; to open; to strain, filter; to beat soundly. II. *r.* to cut one's way through (*an enemy*); to struggle through life. III. *n.* (*aux.* h.) to penetrate; to wet through; to blot; to have effect.

Durchschlingen ['dʊrçʃlɪŋən], *ir.v.a.* (*sep. & insep.*) to interlace, entwine.

Durchschlüpfen ['dʊrçʃlʏpfən], *v.* I. *a.* (*sep. & insep.*) to slip *or* creep through. II. *n.* (*aux.* f.) (*sep.*) to slip through; to escape.

Durchschneiden ['dʊrçʃnaɪdən], *ir.v.a.*

(*sep.* & *insep.*) to cut through; to intersect; to traverse.

Durchschnitt ['durçʃnıt], *m.* (—s, *pl.* —e) a cutting through; section; average. —lich, *adj.* & *adv.* average, on an average. —s=linie, *f.* line of intersection; diameter. —s=punkt, *m.* point of intersection.

Durchschuß ['durçʃus], *m.* weft.

Durchschütteln ['durçʃytəln], *v.a.* (*sep.*) to shake thoroughly.

Durchschwitzen ['durçʃvıtsən], *v.n.* (*aux.* ʃ.) (*sep.* & *insep.*) to perspire greatly.

Durchsehen ['durçze:ən], *ir.v.* I. *n.* (*aux.* h.) (*sep.*) to see *or* look through. II. *a.* (*sep.*) to look over; to revise; (*insep.*) to scrutinize; to penetrate.

Durchsein ['durçzaın], *ir.v.n.* (*sep.*) to have finished with a person *or* a thing.

Durchsetzen ['durçzetsən], *v.* (*sep.*) I. *n.* (*aux.* h.) to break, burst through. II. *a.* to accomplish, carry (*anything*) through; to succeed.

Durchsicht ['durçzıçt], *f.* perusal; revision; looking through; vista. —ig, *adj.* transparent. —igkeit, *f.* transparency.

Durchstechen ['durçʃteçən], *ir.v.* I. *n.* (*aux.* ʃ.) (*sep.*) to pierce through; to stab; to gore. II. *a.* (*sep.*) to cut *or* dig through.

Durchstich ['durçʃtıç], *m.* cut; aperture.

Durchstöbern ['durçʃtø:bərn], *v.a.* (*sep.* & *insep.*) to ransack.

Durchstrahlen ['durçʃtra:lən], *v.* I. *n.* (*aux.* h.) (*sep.*) to shine through. II. *a.* (*insep.*) to irradiate.

Durchstreichen ['durçʃtraıçən], *ir.v.a.* (*sep.*) to strike out, erase, cancel; (*insep.*) to roam through.

Durchstrich ['durçʃtrıç], *m.* erasure.

Durchsuch—en ['durçzu:xən], *v.a.* (*sep.* & *insep.*) to search thoroughly; to search all over. —ung, *f.* search.

Durchtönen ['durçtø:nən], *v.* I. *n.* (*aux.* h.) (*sep.*), to sound through. II. *a.* (*insep.*) to resound, ring with.

Durchtreten ['durçtre:tən], *ir.v.a.* (*sep.*) to tread thoroughly; to work by treading.

Durchweben [durç've:bən], *v.a.* (*insep.*) to interweave; to intermix.

1Durchweg ['durçve:k], *m.* (—es, *pl.* —e) thoroughfare, passage.

2Durchweg [durç'vɛk], *adv.* throughout, altogether.

Durchwehen ['durçve:ən], *v.* I. *n.* (*aux.*

h.) (*sep.*). II. *a.* (*insep.*) to blow through, breathe through.

Durchziehen ['durçtsi:ən], *ir.v.* I. *a.* (*sep.*) to draw, pull through; to censure; (*insep.*) to interweave. II. *n.* (*aux.* ʃ.) (*sep.*) to go *or* march through.

Durchzug ['durçtsu:k], *m.* (—s, *pl.* Durchzüge) passing through; passage (*of birds; an army, etc.*).

Dürf—en ['dyrfən], *ir.v.n.* (*aux.* h.) to be permitted; to need, want; to be able; to feel authorized. —tig, *adj.* needy, poor; paltry; shabby; insufficient. —igkeit, *f.* poverty, neediness; meanness; insufficiency.

Dürr [dyr], *adj.* dry; arid; barren, withered. —e, *f.* aridity, dryness, drought; leanness.

Durst [durst], *m.* (—es) thirst.

Durst—en ['durstən], (*obs.*) Dürst—en, *v.n.* (*aux.* h.) to be thirsty, to thirst. —ig, *adj.* thirsty, athirst.

Dusel ['du:zəl], *m.* (—s) stupor; giddiness, dizziness; sleepiness. —ig, *adj.* giddy, dizzy; sleepy.

Düster ['dy:stər], *adj.* & *adv.* dark; gloomy; sad, mournful; dismal. —heit, —keit, *f.* gloom; gloominess. —rot, *adj.* dusky red, lurid.

Düt—chen ['dy:tçən], *n.* (—chens, *pl.* —chen), Dute ['du:tə], Düt—e ['dy:tə], *f.* (*pl.* —en) paper bag.

Dutzend ['dutsənt], *n.* (—s, *pl.* —e) dozen. —weise, *adv.* by the dozen.

Duzen ['du:tsən], *v.a.* & *r.* to address one another as thou.

E

E, e [e:], *n.* E, e; E, mi (*Mus.*).

Ebbe ['ɛbə], *f.* (*pl.* —n) ebb, ebbtide.

Ebben ['ɛbən], *v.n.* (*aux.* h. & ʃ.) to ebb.

Eben ['e:bən], I. *adj.* even, level, plain, smooth. II. *adv.* & *part.* evenly, *etc.*; just; precisely; quite; certainly; — deswegen, for that very reason; — so viel, just as much. —heit, *f.* evenness, smoothness. —bild, *n.* image, exact likeness. —bürtig, *adj.* of equal birth, equal in rank. —da selbst, *adv.* in *or* at the very same place. —falls, *adv.* likewise. —maß, *n.* symmetry, proportion. —mäßig, *adj.* symmetrical. —nächtig, *adj.* equinoctial. —zeitig, *adj.* contemporary.

Ebene ['e:bənə], *f.* (*pl.* —n) level tract of country; plain; plane.

Eb(e)nen ['e:b(ə)nən], *v.a.* to make even, level.

Eben—baum ['e:bənbaum], *m.* ebony tree. —**holz,** *n.* ebony.

Eber ['e:bər], *m.* (—s, *pl.* —) wild boar; boar. —**esche,** *f.* mountain-ash.

Echt [eçt], *adj.* genuine; real; authentic; true. —**heit,** *f.* genuineness; authenticity.

Eck [ek], *n.* (—s, *pl.* —e) edge; corner; angle; **Drei**—, triangle; **Vier**—, quadrangle; **Acht**—, octagon; **Viel**—, polygon. —**e,** *f.* (*pl.* —en) edge; corner; angle, nook; **an allen —en und Enden,** everywhere. —**ig,** *adj.* edged; angular. —**igkeit,** *f.* angularity; awkwardness. —**zahn,** *m.* (—**zahnes,** *pl.* —**zähne**) eye-tooth.

Edel ['e:dəl], *adj. & adv.* high-born; noble; precious. —**dame,** —**frau,** *f.* gentlewoman, noblewoman. —**knabe,** *m.* page. —**mann,** *m.* nobleman. —**mut,** *m.* high-mindedness, generosity, magnanimity. —**mütig,** *adj.* noble-minded, magnanimous. —**stein,** *m.* precious stone, gem, jewel. —**weiß,** *n.* edelweiss. —**wild,** *n.* deer.

Edikt [e'dıkt], *n.* (—es, *pl.* —e) edict.

Edle(**r**) ['e:dlər], *m.* (—en, *pl.* —e(n)) nobleman.

Efeu ['e:fɔy], *m.* (—s) ivy.

Effekt [e'fɛkt], *m.* (—es, *pl.* —e) effect. —**en,** *pl.* effects; securities, stocks. —**iv** [—'ti:f], *adj.* effective, in specie, ready money.

Egal [e'ga:l], *adj. & adv.* equal; all one, the same.

Egel ['e:gəl], *m.* (—s, *pl.* —) leech.

Egg—e ['ɛgə], *f.* (*pl.* —en) harrow; selvage. —**en,** *v.a.* to harrow.

Ego—ismus [ego'ısmus], *m.* (—, *pl.* **Egoismen**) egotism, selfishness. —**ist,** *m.* (—**isten,** *pl.* —**isten**) egotist. —**istisch,** *adj.* selfish, egotistic.

¹Eh—e ['e:ə], I. *adv.* sooner, earlier; before; formerly. II. *conj.* before. —**er,** *adv.* (*compar. of* **ehe**) sooner; rather; formerly; earlier; **je —er, je lieber,** the sooner the better. —**est,** *adj. & adv.* (*sup. of* **ehe**) earliest; first; next; speediest; soonest; **am —esten = am leichtesten,** most easily, sooner than anywhere else. —**estens,** *adv.* as soon as possible. —**edem** *adv.* before this time, heretofore. —**emals,** *adv.* formerly, of old. —**malig,** *adj.* former, late, old.

²Ehe ['e:ə], *f.* (*pl.* —n) marriage; wedlock. —**lich,** *adj. & adv.* matrimonial, conjugal; legitimate. —**band,** *n.* conjugal tie. —**bett,** *n.* nuptial bed. —**brechen,** *ir.v.n.* to commit adultery. —**brecher,** *m.* adulterer. —**brecherin,** *f.* adulteress. —**bruch,** *m.* adultery. —**bund,** *m.,* —**bündnis,** *n.* matrimony. —**frau,** *f.* lawful spouse, wife. —**gatte,** *m.,* —**gattin,** *f.* lawful spouse, husband, wife. —**gemahl,** *m.,* —**gemahlin,** *f.* lawful husband, lawful spouse. —**leute,** *pl.* married people. —**mann,** *m.* (*pl.* —**männer**) husband. —**scheidung,** *f.* divorce. —**stand,** *m.* married state, wedlock. —**stifter,** *m.,* —**stifterin,** *f.* matchmaker.

Ehern [e'ɛːrn], *adj.* brazen, of brass, of bronze.

Ehrbar ['e:rba:r], *adj. & adv.* honourable; respectable; honest. —**keit,** *f.* honesty; respectability.

Ehr—e ['e:rə], *f.* (*pl.* —en) honour; reputation; glory; praise; credit. —**enhaft,** *adj.* honourable. —**enhaftigkeit,** *f.* honour, uprightness. —**lich,** *adj. & adv.* just, honest; honourable. —**lichkeit,** *f.* honesty; honourable dealing. —**begierde,** *f.* ambition. —**begierig,** *adj. & adv.* ambitious. —**enamt,** *n.* post of honour. —**enbahn,** *f.* career of honour. —**enfall,** *m.* point of honour. —**engericht,** *n.* court of honour. —**enkreuz,** *n.* decoration (*for bravery, etc.*). —**enmann,** *m.* man of honour, gentleman. —**enmünze,** *f.* medal. —**enrede,** *f.* panegyric —**ensache,** *f.* affair of honour; duel. —**ensäule,** *f.* monument. —**ensold,** *m.* honorarium. —**enstand,** *m.* honourable condition, dignity. —**enstelle,** *f.* dignity, post of honour. —**entitel,** *m.* honorary title; title of honour. —**envoll,** *adj. & adv.* honourable, creditable. —**enwort,** *n.* parole; word of honour. —**erbietig,** *adj. & adv.* reverential, respectful. —**furcht,** *f.* respect, awe. —**furchtslos,** *adj.* disrespectful, irreverent. —**gefühl,** *n.* sense of honour. —**geiz,** *m.* ambition. —**geizig,** *adj.* ambitious. —**gier,** *f.* inordinate ambition. —**los,** *adj.* dishonourable. —**losigkeit,** *f.* infamy. —**süchtig,** *adj.* greedy of honour. —**würdig,** *adj.* venerable; sacred, reverend. —**würdigkeit,** *f.* venerableness.

Ehren ['e:rən], *v.a.* to honour, esteem, revere.

¹Ei [aɪ], *int.* indeed! ay! why!

²Ei [aɪ], *n.* (—(e)s, *pl.* —er) egg. —dotter, *m.* (& *n.*) yolk of egg. —er= becher, *m.* egg-cup. —er=schale, *f.* egg-shell. —förmig, *adj.* oval, oblong. —gelb, *n.* yolk. —weiß, *n.* albumen.

Eia ['aɪa:], *interj.* hey! heyday! —= popeia, *interj.* & *n.* lullaby, hush-a-by.

Eibe ['aɪbə], *f.* (*pl.* —n) yew tree.

Eich—e ['aɪçə], *f.* (*pl.* —en) oak. —el, *f.* (*pl.* —eln) acorn. —en, *adj.* & *adv.* oaken.

Eichhorn ['aɪçhɔrn], *n.* (—s, *pl.* Eichhörner) squirrel.

Eid [aɪt], *m.* (—es, *pl.* —e) oath; einen — auf etwas ablegen, to take an oath upon a thing. —lich, *adj.* & *adv.* sworn, by *or* upon oath. —bruch, *m.* perjury. —es=formel, *f.* form of oath. —es=leistung, *f.* affidavit. —genoß, *m.* confederate.

Eidam ['aɪdam], *m.* (—s, *pl.* —e) son-in-law.

Eidechse ['aɪdɛksə], *f.* (*pl.* —n) lizard.

Eider ['aɪdər], *m.* (—s, *pl.* —), —ente, *f.*, —vogel, *m.* eider-duck, eider-goose. —daunen, —dunen, *f. pl.* eider-down.

Eifer ['aɪfər], *m.* (—s) zeal; ardour, fervour. —sucht, *f.* jealousy. —= süchtig, *adj.* & *adv.* jealous, envious.

Eifer—n ['aɪfərn], *v.n.* (*aux.* h.) to be zealous; to vie, emulate, rival; to declaim passionately against (gegen); to be envious; to grow angry at (über eine Sache). —er, *m.* (—ers, *pl.* —er) zealot.

Eifrig ['aɪfrɪç], *adj.* & *adv.* zealous; passionate; emulous. —keit, *f.* zeal; officiousness.

Eigen ['aɪgən], *adj.* & *adv.* proper, own; peculiar, special; strange, curious; exact; difficult, ticklish; specific; real; aus —em Antriebe, spontaneously. —heit, *f.* peculiarity; oddity. —schaft, *f.* attribute; characteristic quality; character; peculiarity. — tlich, I. *adj.* proper; true, real; intrinsic. II. *adv.* properly speaking; in actuality. —art, *f.* originality, individuality. —artig, *adj.* of a peculiar kind, peculiar. —dünkel, *m.* self-sufficiency, conceitedness. —händig, *adj.* & *adv.* autographic. —liebe, *f.* self-love. —lob, *n.* self-praise.

—mächtig, *adj.* & *adv.* arbitrary, despotic. —name, *m.* proper name. —nutz, *m.* self-interest. —nützig, *adj.* selfish. —nützigkeit, *f.* selfishness. —sinn, *m.* self-will; obstinacy. —= sinnig, *adj.* & *adv.* self-willed; head-strong, obstinate. —sucht, *f.* egotism; selfishness. —süchtig, *adj.* selfish. —wille, *m.* wilfulness. —tum, *n.* (—tums, *pl.* —tümer) property; ownership. —tümlich, *adj.* & *adv.* belonging exclusively to, proper; peculiar, queer, odd. —tümlichkeit, *f.* peculiarity; singularity; characteristic.

Eignen ['aɪgnən], *v.* I. *r.* to be adapted *or* suited (zu, for). II. *n.* (*aux.* h.) to be one's own; to suit, befit.

Eiland ['aɪlant], *n.* (—s, *pl.* —e) island.

Eil—e ['aɪlə], *f.* haste, speed. —ig, *adj.* & *adv.* hasty, quick, speedy, hurried. —bote, *m.* express messenger. —fer= tig, *adj.* hasty, precipitate. —fertig= keit, *f.* overhaste; hastiness. —zug, *m.* (—es, *pl.* —züge) fast train, express train.

Eil—en ['aɪlən], *v.* I. *a.* to hasten. II. *r.* to make haste. —ends, *adv.* hastily.

Eimer ['aɪmər], *m.* (—s, *pl.* —) pail, bucket.

Ein [aɪn], I. (Eine, Ein), *ind. art.* a, an; was für —, what sort of, what (*used as an adj.*). II. *num. adj.* one. III. *pron.* (—er, —e, —(e)s) one, a person, they, people; the one for us, our; noch —, further; so —er, such a one; unser —er, one of us. —ig, I. *adj.* & *adv.* one, united, accordant, agreed, peaceful. II. *adj.* & *adv.* any, some; (*pl.*) some, sundry, a few; —ige zehn Jahre, some ten years; —ige, some people. —igkeit, *f.* unity; harmony; unanimity; concord. —s, I. *adv.* of one mind, at one; once, only; wir sind —s, we are at one. II. *f.* (*the number*) one; ace. III. *indec. adj.* one; immaterial; indifferent.

Ein [aɪn], *adv.* & *sep. prefix* in, into. [*Words beginning with* Ein *not found in this paragraph should be looked for alphabetically.*] —ander [aɪ'nandər], *indec. pron.* one another, each other. —deutig, *adj.* & *adv.* having but one meaning, unequivocal. —er=seits, *adv.* on the one hand. —igermaßen, *adv.* in some measure, somewhat,

rather. —**jährig**, *adj. & adv.* lasting
a year; one year old. —**mal**, *adv. &
part.* once, one time; once upon a
time; once for all; just, only, for once;
auf —mal, all at once, suddenly;
noch —mal, once more. —**maleins**,
n. multiplication-table. —**feitig**, *adj.
& adv.* one-sided; biased. —**feitigfeit**,
f. partiality, narrow-mindedness. —**=
filbig**, *adj. & adv.* monosyllabic,
taciturn, laconic. —**ftödig**, *adj.* one-
storied (*house*).

Einatmen ['aɪnʔaːtmən], *v.a.* to inhale.
Einballen ['aɪnbalən], *v.a.* to pack.
Einband ['aɪnbant], *m.* (—**s**, *pl.*
Einbände) binding, cover of a book.
Einbegreifen ['aɪnbəgraɪfən], *ir.v.a.* to
include, contain; **mit einbegriffen**,
included, implied.
Einberufen ['aɪnbəruːfən], *ir.v.a.* to
convene; to call in *or* out.
Einbezieh—en ['aɪnbətsiːən], *v.a.* to
include. —**ung**, *f.* inclusion.
Einbieg—en ['aɪnbiːgən], *ir.v.a.* to
bend inwards, downwards *or* back; to
inflect. **eingebogen**, *p.p. & adj.*
inflected; sinuous. —**ung**, *f.* the
bending inwards; inflection; recess.
Einbild—en ['aɪnbɪldən], *v.a.* (*with
dat. of refl. pron.*) to fancy, imagine;
to take into one's head; to be conceited. —**ung**, *f.* imagination; fancy.
—**ungs=kraft**, *f.*(power of)imagination.
Einblick ['aɪnblɪk], *m.* (—**es**, *pl.* —**e**)
glance into; insight.
Einbrech—en ['aɪnbrɛçən], *ir.v.* I. *a.*
to pull down; to break open. II. *n.*
(*aux.* ſ.) to break in, give way; to
begin, draw on, approach; to set in
(*as winter, etc.*). **bei —ender Nacht**,
at nightfall. —**er**, *m.* (—**ers**, *pl.* —**er**)
burglar.
Einbringen ['aɪnbrɪŋən], *ir.v.a.* to
bring in as profit; to fetch a price; to
bring with.
Einbroden ['aɪnbrɔkən], *v.a.* to crumble
into; **fich etwas —**, to get into trouble.
Einbruch ['aɪnbrux], *m.* (—**s**, *pl.*
Einbrüche) burglary; invasion, inroad.
Einbürger—n ['aɪnbyrgərn], *v.a.* to
naturalize. —**ung**, *f.* naturalization.
Einbuße ['aɪnbuːsə], *f.* loss, damage.
Einbüßen ['aɪnbyːsən], *v.a.* to suffer
loss from.
Eindämmen ['aɪndɛmən], *v.a.* to dam in.
Eindecker ['aɪndɛkər], *m.* (—**s**, *pl.* —)
monoplane.

Eindrängen ['aɪndrɛŋən], *v.* I. *a.* to
squeeze into, to force into. II. *r.* to
crowd in; to intrude oneself into.
Eindring—en ['aɪndrɪŋən], *ir.v.n.* (*aux.*
ſ.) (**in etwas**) to enter (into) by force;
to break in; to press upon; to pierce;
to soak; to search into (*a matter*).
—**lich**, *adj.* penetrating; affecting,
impressive, forcible; intrusive, forward; urgent. —**lichkeit**, *f.* impres-
siveness. —**ling**, *m.* (—**lings**, *pl.*
—**linge**) intruder.
Eindruck ['aɪndruk], *m.* (—**es**, *pl.*
Eindrücke) impression, mark, stamp.
—**en**, *v.a.* to imprint. —**s=voll**, *adj.
& adv.* impressive.
Einerlei ['aɪnər'laɪ], *indec. adj.* of the
same kind; **es ist mir —**, it is all the
same to me.
Einfach ['aɪnfax], *adj. & adv.* simple,
single; indivisible; plain, homely.
—**heit**, *f.* simplicity.
Einfahr—en ['aɪnfaːrən], *ir.v.* I. *a.* to
bring, carry in (*on wheels*); to run,
drive into. II. *n.* (*aux.* ſ.) to drive
in, enter. —**t**, *f.* (*pl.* —**ten**) entry,
entrance.
Einfall ['aɪnfal], *m.* (—**es**, *pl.* **Einfälle**)
falling in; invasion; downfall; ruin;
sudden idea; fancy, notion; sally.
Einfallen ['aɪnfalən], *ir.v.n.* (*aux.* ſ.)
to fall in; to invade; to break in; to
fall to ruin; to occur (*to one's mind*).
—**d**, *p. & adj.* incident.
Einfällig ['aɪnfɛlɪç], *adj. & adv.*
ruinous.
Ein—falt ['aɪnfalt], *f.* simplicity, silliness. —**fältig**, *adj. & adv.* simple,
plain; silly. —**fältigfeit**, *f.* simplicity; silliness.
Einfangen ['aɪnfaŋən], *ir.v.* I. *a.* to
take and shut in. II. *n.* (*aux.* ħ.) to
catch.
Einfass—en ['aɪnfasən], *v.a.* to frame;
to border, edge; to enclose. —**ung**,
f. enclosing; enclosure; setting;
border; trimming; framing; embankment.
Einfinden ['aɪnfɪndən], *ir.v.r.* to appear; to come and be present, arrive.
Einflößen ['aɪnfløsən], *v.a.* (**einem
etwas**) to cause to flow in; to instil,
inspire with, to suggest.
Einfluß ['aɪnflus], *m.* (—(ſſ)**es**, *pl.*
Einflüſſe) influx; influence, power.
—**reich**, *adj.* influential.
Einflüster—n ['aɪnflystərn], *v.a.* to

insinuate. —ung, f. insinuation, innuendo.

Einförmig ['aɪnførmɪç], adj. uniform; monotonous. —keit, f. uniformity; monotony.

Einfried—(ig)en ['aɪnfri:d(ɪg)ən], v.a. to enclose, fence in. —igung, f. enclosure.

Einfrieren ['aɪnfri:rən], ir.v.n. (aux. f.) to freeze in; to be ice-bound. eingefroren, p.p. & adj. frost-bound.

Einfüg—en ['aɪnfy:gən], v.a. to fit in, insert; to dovetail. —ung, f. fitting in; insertion; dovetailing.

Einfuhr ['aɪnfu:r], f. (pl. —en) import, importation. —handel, m. import trade. —zoll, m. (—es, pl. —zölle) import-duty.

Einführ—en ['aɪnfy:rən], v.a. to bring in; to import; to introduce; to set up, establish. —ung, f. introduction.

Eingabe['aɪnga:bə], f. (pl.—n)petition, memorial.

Eingang ['aɪngaŋ], m. (—(e)s, pl. Eingänge) entry; arrival; place of entrance; doorway, hall; introduction; access; verbotener —, no admission.

Eingeb—en ['aɪnge:bən], ir.v.a. to give in; to insert; to suggest, inspire. —ung, f. administration; inspiration, suggestion.

Eingeboren ['aɪngəbo:rən], p.p. & adj. native, indigenous.

Eingedenk ['aɪngədɛŋk], adj. mindful of, remembering.

Eingehen ['aɪnge:ən], ir.v.n. (aux. f.) to go in, enter; to penetrate; to cease, come to an end; to understand, conceive; to shrink; to come to hand; auf eine S. —, to acquiesce in, agree to a thing; in eine S. —, to look into a thing. —d, adj. & adv. searching, exhaustive, in detail.

Eingemacht ['aɪngəmaxt], p.p. & adj. preserved. —e(s), n. preserves; pickles.

Eingenommen ['aɪngənɔmən], p.p. & adj. von einem —, prepossessed in favour of. —heit, f. predilection; prepossession.

Eingeschränktheit ['aɪngəʃrɛnkthaɪt], f. narrowness; frugality; narrow-mindedness.

Eingeschrieben ['aɪngəʃri:bən], p.p. & adj. registered.

Eingesessen ['aɪngəzɛsən], p.p. & adj. settled, established.

Eingeständnis ['aɪngəʃtɛntnɪs], n. (—s (ſſ)es, pl. —(ſſ)e) avowal, confession.

Eingestehen ['aɪngəʃte:ən], ir.v.a. to confess; to allow.

Eingeweide ['aɪngəvaɪdə], n. (—s, pl. —) bowels, intestines.

Eingeweiht—e(r) ['aɪngəvaɪtər], m. (—en, pl. —e(n)) initiated man, adept.

Eingewöhnen ['aɪngəvø:nən], v. I. a. to accustom to. II. r. to get used to; to settle down.

Eingewurzelt ['aɪngəvʊrtsəlt], p.p. & adj. deep-rooted; inveterate.

Eingezogen ['aɪngətso:gən], p.p. & adj. retired, secluded. —heit, f. retirement; solitary life.

Eingraben ['aɪngra:bən], ir.v. I. a. to dig in, bury. II. r. intrench oneself

Eingreifen ['aɪngraɪfən], ir.v.a. (aux. h.) to interfere with, intrench upon.

Eingriff ['aɪngrɪf], m. (—s, pl. —e) seizure; encroachment; infringement, interference; invasion; usurpation.

Einhalt ['aɪnhalt], m. (—s) stop, check; prohibition; — tun, to check.

Einhalten ['aɪnhaltən], ir.v. I. a. to check, restrain; die Zeit —, to be punctual. II. n. (aux. h.) to stop, leave off; to pause; to desist.

Einhauchen ['aɪnhauxən], v.a. to inspire; to inculcate, instil.

Einhauen ['aɪnhauən], ir.v. I. a. to hew, cut into; to break open. II. n. (aux. h.) to charge (Mil.).

Einheb—en ['aɪnhe:bən], ir.v.a. to lift into; to collect. —ung, f. collection (of taxes).

Einheften ['aɪnhɛftən], v.a. to stitch in; to file (papers).

Einhegen ['aɪnhe:gən], v.a. to fence in, enclose.

Einheimisch ['aɪnhaɪmɪʃ], adj. native; indigenous.

Einheit ['aɪnhaɪt], f. unity; unit. —lich, adj. & adv. uniform.

Einhellig ['aɪnhɛlɪç], adj. unanimous. —keit, f. unanimity.

Einher [aɪn'he:r], adv. & sep. prefix, along, forth. — gehen, ir.v.n. to move along; to pace.

Einholen ['aɪnho:lən], v.a. to bring in; to overtake.

Einhorn ['aɪnhɔrn], n. (—(e)s, pl. Einhörner) unicorn.

Einhüllen ['aɪnhʏlən], v.a. to wrap up or in.

Einig—en ['aɪnɪgən], v.a. to unite,

cause to agree. —**keit,** *f.* unity, harmony.

Einimpf—en [ˈaɪmɪmpfən], *v.a.* to inoculate, vaccinate. —**ung,** *f.* inoculation; vaccination.

Einkauf [ˈaɪnkauf], *m.* (—(e)s, *pl.* **Einkäufe**) purchase, marketing.

Einkaufen [ˈaɪnkaufən], *v.a.* to purchase.

Einkäufer [ˈaɪnkɔʏfər], *m.* (—s, *pl.* —) purchaser.

Einkehren [ˈaɪnke:rən], *v.n.* (*aux.* f.) to enter.

Einklang [ˈaɪnklaŋ], *m.* (—(e)s) unison, harmony.

Einkleiden [ˈaɪnklaɪdən], *v.a.* to clothe; to invest with.

Einkommen [ˈaɪnkɔmən], I. *ir.v.n.* (*aux.* f.) to come in; to petition; to interpose, intervene. II. *subst.n.* income, revenue. —**steuer,** *f.* income tax.

Einkreisen [ˈaɪnkraɪzən], *v.a.* to encircle, to isolate.

Einkunft [ˈaɪnkʊnft], *f.* (*pl.* **Einkünfte**) coming in, arrival; (*pl.*) income, revenues.

¹**Einlad—en** [ˈaɪnla:dən], *ir.v.a.* to invite. —**ung,** *f.* invitation, summons.

²**Einladen** [ˈaɪnla:dən], *ir.v.a.* to lade, freight.

Einlage [ˈaɪnla:gə], *f.* (*pl.* —n) laying in; enclosure (*in a letter, etc.*).

Einlagern [ˈaɪnla:gərn], *v.a.* to lodge; to billet; to store.

Einlaß [ˈaɪnlas], *m.* (—(ſſ)es, *pl.* **Einläſſe**) letting in; admission; inlet. —**geld,** *n.* entrance money. —**karte,** *f.* card of admission.

Einlassen [ˈaɪnlasən], *ir.v.* I. *a.* to let in, admit. II. *r.* (*with* auf eine S. *or* in eine S. *or* mit einer S.) to engage in; to venture on; to meddle with.

Einleben [ˈaɪnle:bən], *v.r.* to grow or get accustomed to.

Einleg—en [ˈaɪnle:gən], *v.a.* to lay, put in; to store up; to deposit; **Früchte** —**en,** to preserve fruit. —**ung,** *f.* laying; enclosing; preservation.

Einleit—en [ˈaɪnlaɪtən], *v.a.* to introduce; to bring about; to usher in. —**end,** *p.* & *adj.* introductory, preliminary. —**ung,** *f.* introduction; exordium.

Einlenken [ˈaɪnlɛŋkən], *v.* I. *a.* to set (*a limb*); to lead into a certain channel (*of conversation, etc.*) II. *n.* (*aux.* h.) to bend, turn in; to resume.

Einlösbar [ˈaɪnlø:sba:r], *adj.* redeemable.

Einlös—en [ˈaɪnlø:zən], *v.a.* to ransom, redeem. —**ung,** *f.* redemption; taking up of a bill.

Einmachen [ˈaɪnmaxən], *v.a.* to preserve, pickle.

Einmarsch [ˈaɪnmarʃ], *m.* (—es, *pl.* **Einmärsche**) marching in, entry. —**ieren,** *v.n.* (*aux.* f.) to enter.

Einmauern [ˈaɪnmauərn], *v.a.* to immure, imprison.

Einmischen [ˈaɪnmɪʃən], *v.a.* to intermix, mingle; **sich** —, to meddle with; to interfere.

Ein—mut [ˈaɪnmu:t], *m.* (—(e)s) unanimity, concord, agreement. —**mütig,** *adj.* & *adv.* unanimous. —**mütigkeit,** *f.* unanimity.

Einnahme [ˈaɪnna:mə], *f.* (*pl.* —n) revenue; taking (*possession of*); capture; — **und Ausgabe,** receipts and expenditure.

Einnehm—en [ˈaɪnne:mən], *ir.v.a.* to take in; to capture; to charm, fascinate. —**end,** *p.* & *adj.* captivating, charming, engaging. —**er,** *m.* (—**ers,** *pl.* —**er**) receiver, collector. —**ung,** *f.* occupation; capture.

Einordnen [ˈaɪnˀɔrdnən], *v.a.* to arrange; to classify.

Einpack—en [ˈaɪnpakən], *v.* I. *a.* to pack up in. II. *n.* (*aux.* h.) to pack up; to become silent. —**ung,** *f.* packing up.

Einpassen [ˈaɪnpasən], *v.a.* & *n.* to fit (in).

Einpflanzen [ˈaɪnpflantsən], *v.a.* to plant; to implant. **eingepflanzt,** *p.p* & *adj.* innate.

Einpökeln [ˈaɪnpø:kəln], *v.a.* to salt, to pickle; **eingepökeltes Fleisch,** corned meat.

Einprägen [ˈaɪnprɛ:gən], *v.a.* to imprint.

Einräum—en [ˈaɪnrɔʏmən], *v.a.* to give up (*a room, a house*); to clear, put away, (einem etwas) —**en,** to concede, allow, grant; (einem) **seinen Platz** —**en,** to give up one's place to. —**ung,** *f.* concession, granting.

Einrede [ˈaɪnre:də], *f.* (*pl.* —n) objection, exception.

Einreden [ˈaɪnre:dən], *v.* I. *a.* to persuade one to; **jemandem Mut** —, to encourage. II. *n.* (*aux.* h.) to interrupt; to contradict; to object, oppose.

Einreih—en ['aınraɪən], *v.a.* to range in a row; to enrol (*Mil.*). —ig, *adj.* of one row; single-breasted (*coat*).

Einricht—en ['aınrıçtən], *v.a.* to arrange, order; to adapt; to organize; eine Wohnung —en, to furnish a flat. —ung, *f.* adjustment; arrangement; furnishing, household establishment, fittings.

Einrücken ['aınrʏkən], *v.* I. *n.* (*aux.* ſ.) to march into. II. *a.* to enter, insert, put in.

Einrufen ['aınru:fən], *ir.v.a.* to call in; to recall.

Einſalzen ['aınzaltsən], *ir.v.a.* to salt, to pickle; Eingeſalzene(ṡ), salt provisions.

Einſam ['aınza:m], *adj. & adv.* lonely; alone; retired. —keit, *f.* loneliness; solitude.

Einſaṫ ['aınzats], *m.* (—es, *pl.* Einſäṫe) putting in; deposit; share, stock; stake; insertion; paragraph.

Einſchalt—en ['aınſaltən], *v.a.* to insert, put in, intercalate; to switch on (*elec.*); to put in (*gear*) (*motor*). —ung, *f.* insertion; interpolation. —ungsẕeichen, *n.* caret (∧).

Einſchenken ['aınſɛnkən], *v.a.* to pour in; to fill.

Einſchiff—en ['aınſıfən], *v.a.* to embark, ship; to entrain. —ung, *f.* embarkation.

Einſchirren ['aınſırən], *v.a.* to harness.

Einſchlafen ['aınſla:fən], *ir.v.n.* (*aux.* ſ.) to fall asleep.

Einſchlag ['aınſla:k], *m.* (—s, *pl.* Einſchläge) act of driving, beating, striking in; thing beaten in; wrapper; woof, weft.

Einſchlagen ['aınſla:gən], *ir.v.* I. *a.* to drive, knock in; to wrap up (*in paper*); to take (*a road*); to enclose. II. *n.* (*aux.* h.) to shake hands; to succeed; to concern.

Einſchließ- -en ['aınſli:sən], *ir.v.a.* to lock in or up; to enclose; to comprise. —lich, *adj. & adv.* included, inclusive. —ung, *f.* locking in, up; inclusion; enclosure.

Einſchlingen ['aınſlɪŋən], *ir.v.a.* to swallow (*down*); to interlace.

Einſchluß ['aınſlus], *m.* (—(ſ)es, *pl.* Einſchlüſſe) enclosure.

Einſchmelzen ['aınſmɛltsən], *irreg. & reg. v.a.* to melt down.

Einſchnitt ['aınſnıt], *m.* (—(e)s, *pl.* —e)

incision; cut; notch, indentation; segment.

Einſchränk—en ['aınſrɛŋkən], *v.a.* to circumscribe; to narrow. ſich —en, to limit one's expenses. —end, *p. & adj.* restrictive. —ung, *f.* restriction; restraint; reservation.

Einſchreib—en ['aınſraıbən], *ir.v.a.* to write in or down; to inscribe; to register. —ung, *f.* inscription; registration; entry (*of a name*). —e-brief, *m.* registered letter. —e-gebühr, *f.* fee for registration.

Einſchuß ['aınſus], *m.* (—(ſ)es, *pl.* Einſchüſſe) capital advanced; share; contribution.

Einſegn—en ['aınze:gnən], *v.a.* to consecrate. —ung, *f.* consecration; benediction.

Einſehen ['aınze:ən], I. *ir.v.a.* to see into; to perceive, comprehend; to examine. II. *ir.v.n.* (*aux.* h.) to look into.

Einſeṫ—en ['aınzetsən], *v.a.* to put, set in; to intercalate; to switch in; to deposit. —er, *m.* (—ers, *pl.* —er) one who puts in, inserts, *etc.*; institutor. —ung, *f.* setting or putting in; pledging; installation; constitution; institution; appointment.

Einſicht ['aınzıçt], *f.* (*pl.* —en) insight; intelligence. —ig, *adj.* intelligent, sensible.

Einſied—elei [aınzi:də'laı], *f.* hermitage. —ler, *m.* (—lers, *pl.* —ler) hermit.

Einſiṫen ['aınzıtsən], *ir.v.n.* (*aux.* h.) to stay at home. eingeſeſſen, *p.p. & adj.* settled, resident, domiciled.

Einſpannen ['aınſpanən], *v.a.* to harness up; to yoke.

Einſperr—en ['aınſpɛrən], *v.a.* to shut or lock up. —ung, *f.* imprisonment.

Einſprache ['aınſpra:xə], *f.* (*pl.* —n) objection; protest.

Einſprechen ['aınſprɛçən], *ir.v.* I. *a.* (einem etwas) to inculcate, instil; Mut —, to encourage; Troſt —, to comfort. II. *n.* (*aux.* h.) to protest (against, gegen).

Einſpriṫen ['aınſprıtsən], *v.a.* to inject, syringe.

Einſpruch ['aınſprux]. *m.* (—s, *pl.* Einſprüche) prohibition, objection; —erheben, to protest.

Einſt [aınst], *adv.* one time, once, one day. —ig, *adj.* future, to come sometime. —weilen, adv. in the meantime; for the present, just now; for a while; temporarily. —weilig, adj. & adv. temporary, provisional.

Einstand ['aɪnʃtant], m. deuce (tennis).

Einsteig—en ['aɪnʃtaɪgən], ir.v.n. (aux. ſ.) to mount, step into. —estelle, ſ. departure platform.

Einstell—en ['aɪnʃtɛlən], v. I. a. to put in; to discontinue; to suspend (payment); to strike (work). II. r. to appear; to set in. —ung, ſ. recruiting; cessation.

Einstimm—en ['aɪnʃtɪmən], v.a. to agree, consent. —ig, adj. & adv. unanimous. —igkeit, ſ. unanimity.

Einstudieren ['aɪnʃtudi:rən], v.a. to con; to rehearse.

Einstürzen ['aɪnʃtʏrtsən], v.n. to fall down, fall to pieces.

Eintausch ['aɪntauʃ], m. (—es, pl. —e) exchange.

Eintausch—en ['aɪntauʃən], v.a. to exchange. —ung, ſ. exchange.

Einteil—en ['aɪntaɪlən], v.a. to divide; to classify. —ung, ſ. distribution; division; classification.

Eintönig ['aɪntø:nɪç], adj. & adv. monotonous. —keit, ſ. monotony.

Ein—tracht ['aɪntraxt], ſ. concord, union; agreement. —trächtig, adj. & adv. harmonious, united, accordant.

Eintrag ['aɪntra:k], m. (—es, pl. Einträge) woof, weft; prejudice, damage.

Eintrag—en ['aɪntra:gən], I. ir.v.a. to carry in; to yield, bring in; to register. II. subst.n., —ung, ſ. entering, registering.

Einträg—er ['aɪntrɛ:gər], m. (—ers, pl. —er) registrar; bookkeeper. —lich, adj. & adv. lucrative; profitable. —lichkeit, ſ. profitableness.

Eintreffen ['aɪntrɛfən], ir.v.n. (aux. ſ.) to fit in, coincide; to happen; to arrive.

Eintreten ['aɪntre:tən], ir.v.n. (aux. ſ.) to enter; für jemand —, to intercede for a person.

Eintritt ['aɪntrɪt], m. (—s, pl. —e) entry, entrance. —sgeld, n. admission-fee.

Einüben ['aɪn'y:bən], v.a. to practise; to drill.

Einverleib—en ['aɪnfɛrlaɪbən], v.a. to incorporate, embody. —ung, ſ. incorporation.

Einverstanden ['aɪnfɛ:rʃtandən], interj. agreed! — sein, to be agreed.

Einwand ['aɪnvant], m. (—es, pl. Einwände) objection; pretext. —frei, adj. & adv. without objection; nicht —frei, objectionable.

Einwander—n ['aɪnvandərn], v.n.(aux. ſ.) to immigrate. —ung, ſ. immigration.

Einwärts ['aɪnvɛrts], adv. inward(s).

Einweih—en ['aɪnvaɪən], v.a. to initiate; to consecrate. —ung, ſ. consecration; initiation.

Einwend—en ['aɪnvɛndən], reg. & ir.v.a. to object, take exception to. —ung, ſ. objection, exception.

Einwerfen ['aɪnvɛrfən], ir.v.a. to throw in; to object.

Einwickeln ['aɪnvɪkəln], v.a. to envelop, wrap up.

Einwiegen ['aɪnvi:gən], v.a. to rock asleep.

Einwillig—en ['aɪnvɪlɪgən], v.n. (aux. h.) to consent to. —ung, ſ. consent, assent.

Einwirk—en ['aɪnvɪrkən], v.n. (aux. h.) to influence; to operate. —end, p. & adj. influential, effective. —ung, ſ. influence.

Einwohn—en ['aɪnvo:nən], v.n. to inhabit. —end, p. & adj. inhabiting; inherent. —er, m. (—ers, pl. —er) inhabitant. —erschaft, ſ. inhabitants, population.

Einwurf ['aɪnvurf], m. (—s, pl. Einwürfe) objection; opening in pillar-box.

Einwurzeln ['aɪnvurtsəln], v.n. (aux. ſ.) to take root.

Einzelheit ['aɪntsəlhaɪt], ſ. (pl. —en) singleness, individuality; (pl.) details, particulars.

Einzeln ['aɪntsəln], adj. & adv. single, sole, individual; isolated, detached.

Einzieh—en ['aɪntsi:ən], ir.v. I. a. to draw, pull in; to collect. II. r. to shrink; to retrench. III. n. (aux. ſ.) to enter, march in. —ung, ſ. drawing in; collection; confiscation.

Einzig ['aɪntsɪç], adj. & adv. only, single, sole, unique.

Einzug ['aɪntsu:k], m. (—s, pl. Einzüge) entry.

Eis [aɪs], n. (—(ſ)es) ice. —(ſ)ig, adj. icy. —bär, m. (—en, pl. —en) polar bear. —flöße, pl. ice-floes. —meer, n. polar sea. —scholle, ſ. floe. —zapfen, m. icicle.

Eisen ['aɪzən], n. (—s, pl. —) iron. —bahn, f. railway. —bahn=damm, m. embankment. --bahn=hof, m. (railway) station. —blech, n. (—es) sheet-iron. —erz, n. iron-ore. —= farbe, f. iron-grey. —fest, adj. inflexible. —gießerei [—'raɪ], f. ironfoundry. —hütte, f. iron-works, forge. —schlacke, f. iron-dross.

Eisern ['aɪzərn], adj. & adv. iron, of iron.

Eitel ['aɪtəl], adj. & adv. vain; frivolous; nothing but, mere. —keit, f. vanity; nothingness.

Eiter ['aɪtər], m. & n. (—s) matter, pus. —ig, adj. & adv. purulent. —n, v.n. (aux. h.) to suppurate, fester. —ung, f. suppuration, festering.

Ekel ['e:kəl], m. (—s, pl. —) nausea; loathsomeness; disgust, aversion. —= haft, adj. & adv. nauseous; loathsome, disgusting. —haftigkeit, f. loathsomeness. —ig (Eklig), adj. & adv. disagreeable.

Ekeln ['e:kəln], v.n. (aux. h.) to disgust, sicken.

Eklip=se [ɛ'klɪpsə], f. (pl. —sen) eclipse. —tik, f. ecliptic. —tisch, adj. ecliptic.

Elast—izität [elastitsi'te:t], f. elasticity. —isch [e'lastɪʃ], adj. elastic.

Elefant [eleˈfant], m. (—en, pl. —en) elephant. —en=rüssel, m. elephant's trunk. —en=zahn, m. tusk.

Elegan—t [eleˈgant], adj. & adv. elegant. —z, f. elegance, refinement.

Elegie [eleˈgi:], f. (pl. —n) elegy.

Elektrisch [elɛkˈtrɪʃ], adj. electric.

Elektrizität [elɛktritsiˈte:t], f. electricity.

Elektro= [eˈlɛktro], adj. (in compounds) electro-. —techniker, m. (—s, —) electrical engineer.

Element [eleˈment], n. (—s, pl. —e) element; principle. —ar [—ˈta:r], prefix (in comp.) elementary; rudimentary. —ar=klasse, f. junior form. —ar=lehrer, m. primary teacher.

Elend ['e:lent], I. n. (—s) misery, distress. II. adj. & adv. miserable; wretched. —iglich, adv. miserably, wretchedly.

Elentier ['e:lɛnti:r], n. (—s, pl. —e) elk, moose.

1Elf [ɛlf], m. (—en, pl. —en), —e, f. (pl. —en) elf; fairy; goblin.

2Elf [ɛlf], num. adj. eleven. —te, num. adj. eleventh. —tel, n. (—tels, pl. —tel) the eleventh part. —tens, adv. in the eleventh place. —mal, adv. eleven times.

Elfenbein ['ɛlfənbaɪn], n. (—s) ivory.

Elle ['ɛlə], f. (pl. —n) yard, ell.

Ell(en)bogen ['ɛl(ən)bo:gən], m. (—s, pl. —) elbow.

Ellipse [ɛˈlɪpsə], f. ellipse; ellipsis.

Elster ['ɛlstər], f. (pl. —n) magpie.

Elter—lich ['ɛltərlɪç], adj. & adv. parental. —n, pl. parents.

Eminenz [emiˈnɛnts], f. (pl. —en) eminence (title).

Empfang [ɛmˈpfan], m. (—s, pl. Empfänge) reception, receipt. —= nahme, f. receipt. —nehmung, f. reception. —s=schein, m. receipt.

Empfangen [ɛmˈpfaŋən], ir.v.a. to take, receive; to welcome.

Empfäng—er [ɛmˈpfɛŋər], m. (—ers, pl. —er) receiver; acceptor (of a bill). —lich, adj. susceptible. —lichkeit, f. susceptibility. —nis, f. (pl. —nisse) conception.

Empfehl—en [ɛmˈpfe:lən], ir.v. I. a. to commend, entrust; to recommend. II. r. to bid farewell; to present one's compliments. —ens=wert, adj. commendable. —ung, f. pl. recommendation; introduction; compliments.

Empfind—bar [ɛmˈpfɪntba:r], adj. sensitive; perceptible. —lich, adj. & adv. sharp; grievous; sensitive; tender; touchy. —lichkeit, f. sensibility; sensitiveness; irritability. —sam, adj. & adv. sensible; feeling; susceptible. —samkeit, f. susceptibility; sentimentality. —ung, f. sensation; feeling; perception. —ungs=kraft, f. power of perception. —ungs=los, adj. unfeeling; callous.

Empfind—en [ɛmˈpfɪndən], ir.v.a. to feel; to perceive. —end, p. & adj. sensible, sensitive.

Empor [ɛmˈpo:r], I. adv. & sep. prefix, up, upwards, on high, aloft. —kom= men, ir.v.n. (aux. ʃ.) to rise in the world, to thrive. —kömmling, m. (—kömmlings, pl. —kömmlinge) upstart. —ragen, v.a. to tower (über, above).

Empör—en [ɛmˈpø:rən], v. I. a. to excite; to enrage. —t, p.p. & adj. indignant. II. r. to revolt, rebel; to grow furious. —end, p. & adj. revolting, shocking. —er, m. (—ers, pl.

—er) insurgent. **—erifch,** *adj. & adv.* mutinous. **—ung,** *f.* rebellion, revolt.

Emfig ['ɛmzɪç], *adj. & adv.* busy, active; industrious.

End—e ['ɛndə], *n.* (**—es,** *pl.* **—en**) end. **—lich,** I. *adj.* final, concluding, last. II. *adv.* at last. **—gültig,** *adj. & adv.* final, definitive, conclusive. **—los,** *adj.* endless, boundless, infinite. **—lofigfeit,** *f.* endlessness, infinity. **—punft,** *m.* end; terminus. **—zweck,** *m.* ultimate object.

End—(ig)en ['ɛnd(ɪg)ən], *v.a.* to finish. **—ung,** *f.* termination.

Energ—ie [enɛr'giː], *f.* energy. **—ifch** [e'nɛrgɪʃ], *adj. & adv.* energetic.

Eng [ɛŋ], **Enge** ['ɛŋə], *adj. & adv.* narrow; tight; strict; confined. **—e,** *f.* (*pl.* **—en**) narrowness; narrow place. **—heit,** *f.* narrowness; crowded state.

Engel ['ɛŋəl], *m.* (**—s,** *pl.* **—**) angel. **—chen,** *n.* (**—chens,** *pl.* **—chen**) little angel. **—haft,** *adj. & adv.* angelic; angelically. **—fchar,** *f.* angelic host.

Eng—en ['ɛŋən], *v.a.* to make narrow. **—ern,** *v.a.* to make narrower.

¹Englifch ['ɛŋlɪʃ], I. *adj.* English. II. *adv.* in the English fashion.

²Englifch ['ɛŋlɪʃ], *adj. & adv.* angelic.

¹Enfel ['ɛŋkəl], *m.* (**—s,** *pl.* **—**) ankle.

²Enfel ['ɛŋkəl], *m.* (**—s,** *pl.* **—**) grandson; descendant. **—in,** *f.* granddaughter.

Ent [ɛnt], *insep. and unaccented prefix; in composition with other words generally =* forth, from, out, away, dis-; *also has a sense of deprivation, negation or separation.*

Entart—en [ɛnt'ʔaːrtən], *v.n. (aux.* ſ.) to degenerate. **—ung,** *f.* degeneration; deterioration.

Entäußer—n [ɛnt'ʔɔysərn], *v.r. (einer* Sache) to dispose of. **—ung,** *f.* renunciation; parting with.

Entbehr—en [ɛnt'beːrən], *v.a. (gen.* (now *obs.) & acc.*) to do without. **—lich,** *adj.* dispensable, unnecessary. **—lichfeit,** *f.* superfluousness. **—ung,** *f.* abstinence; renunciation; self-denial.

Entbieten [ɛnt'biːtən], *ir.v.a.* to bid; to present, offer.

Entbind—en [ɛnt'bɪndən], *ir.v.a.* to unbind; to release. **—ung,** *f.* releasing; unbinding; delivery. **—ungs=anftalt,** *f.* maternity hospital.

Entblöß—en [ɛnt'bløːsən], *v.a.* to strip. **—t,** *p.p. & adj.* bare.

Entdeck—en [ɛnt'dɛkən], *v.a.* to discover. **—ung,** *f.* discovery; detection; disclosure.

Ent—e ['ɛntə], *f.* (*pl.* **—en**) duck. **—erich,** *m.* (**—erichs,** *pl.* **—eriche**) drake. **—chen,** *n.* (**—chen,** *pl.* **—chen**), **—lein,** *n.* (**—leins,** *pl.* **—lein**) duckling.

Entehr—en [ɛnt'ʔeːrən], *v.a.* to dishonour. **—end,** *adj.* dishonourable, disgraceful. **—er,** *m.* (**—ers,** *pl.* **—er**) dishonourer. **—ung,** *f.* dishonouring; ravishing.

Enterb—en [ɛnt'ʔɛrbən], *v.a.* to disinherit. **—ung,** *f.* disinheriting.

Entfalten [ɛnt'faltən], *v.a.* to unfold.

Entfärben [ɛnt'fɛrbən], *v.* I. *a.* to discolour. II. *r.* to change colour; to grow pale.

Entfern—en [ɛnt'fɛrnən], *v.* I. *a.* to remove. II. *r.* to absent oneself; to withdraw, retire. **—t,** *p.p. & adj.* distant, remote. **—ung,** *f.* separation; distance.

Entfremd—en [ɛnt'frɛmdən], *v.a.* (einem etwas, etwas von einem) to estrange; to alienate. **—ung,** *f.* estrangement.

Entführ—en [ɛnt'fyːrən], *v.a.* to abduct; to elope with; to kidnap. **—er,** *m.* (**—ers,** *pl.* **—er**) abductor. **—ung,** *f.* abduction.

Entgegen [ɛnt'geːgən], I. *prep. (with preceding dat.)* against, in face of; opposed to; towards. II. *adv. & sep. prefix,* counter; in opposition. **—eilen,** *v.n. (aux.* ſ., *dat.)* to hasten to meet. **—gehen,** *ir.v.n. (aux.* ſ., *dat.)* to go to meet. **—gefetzt,** *p.p. & adj.* contrary, opposite. **—halten,** *ir.v.a.* to oppose, object. **—kommen,** *ir.v.n. (aux.* ſ., *dat.)* to advance to meet. **—fetzen,** *v.a. (dat. & acc.)* to oppose. **—fetzung,** *f.* opposing; comparison; antithesis.

Entgegn—en [ɛnt'geːgnən], *v.a.* (einem etwas) to rejoin; to retort. **—ung,** *f.* reply.

Entgelt—en [ɛnt'gɛltən], *ir.v.a.* (einem etwas) to make someone suffer for. **—ung,** *f.* recompense; atonement.

Enthalt—en [ɛnt'haltən], *ir.v.* I. *a.* to hold, contain; to comprise. II. *r.* to abstain, forbear. **—fam,** *adj. & adv.* abstinent; temperate. **—famfeit,** *f.* abstemiousness.

Enthaupt—en [ɛnt'haʊptən], *v.a.* to behead. **—ung**, *f.* beheading, decapitation.

Entheiligen [ɛnt'haɪlɪgən], *v.a.* to profane, desecrate.

Enthüll—en [ɛnt'hʏlən], *v.a.* to unveil; to reveal. **—ung**, *f.* revealing; disclosure.

Enthülsen [ɛnt'hʏlzən], *v.a.* to shell (*peas, etc.*).

Entkleiden [ɛnt'klaɪdən], *v.a. & r.* to unclothe.

Entkommen [ɛnt'kɔmən], *ir.v.n.* (*aux.* f., *dat.*) to get off *or* away.

Entkräft(ig)—en [ɛnt'krɛft(ɪg)ən], *v.a.* to fatigue, enervate. **—ung**, *f.* exhaustion.

Entladen [ɛnt'la:dən], *ir.v.a.* to unload; to exonerate.

Entlass—en [ɛnt'lasən], *ir.v.a.* to permit to leave; to dismiss, discharge. **—ung**, *f.* dismissal; discharge; release.

Entlasten [ɛnt'lastən], *v.a.* to unburden; to relieve of.

Entledigen [ɛnt'le:dɪgən], *v.a.* to set free; to exempt (from, *gen.*).

Entlegen [ɛnt'le:gən], *adj.* remote, distant. **—heit**, *f.* remoteness, distance.

Entnehmen [ɛnt'ne:mən], *ir.v.a.* to take away; to learn; to gather.

Enträtseln [ɛnt'rɛ:tsəln], *v.a.* to unriddle; to guess.

Entreißen [ɛnt'raɪsən], *ir.v.a.* to tear away.

Entrinnen [ɛnt'rɪnən], *ir.v.n.* (*aux.* f., *dat.*) to escape from.

Entrüst—en [ɛnt'rʏstən], *v.* I. *a.* to provoke, make angry. II. *r.* to become angry; to fly into a passion. **—ung**, *f.* indignation, anger, wrath.

Entsag—en [ɛnt'za:gən], *v.r. & n.* (*aux.* h., *dat.*) to renounce; to abdicate. **—ung**, *f.* (**auf** & *acc.*) renunciation, resignation; abdication.

Entsatz [ɛnt'zats], *m.* (**—es**) relief, succour.

Entschädig—en [ɛnt'ʃɛ:dɪgən], *v.a.* to indemnify, compensate. **—ung**, *f.* indemnity.

Entscheid—en [ɛnt'ʃaɪdən], *ir.v.a.* to decide; give judgment. **—end**, *p. & adj.* decisive. **—ung**, *f.* decision; crisis.

Entschieden [ɛnt'ʃi:dən], *p.p. & adj. or adv.*, *see* **Entscheiden**, decided. **—heit**, *f.* firmness; determination.

Entschließ—en [ɛnt'ʃli:sən], *ir.v.* I. *a.* to unlock. II. *v.r.* to determine (zu, upon); to decide (für, on *or* in favour of); to make up one's mind. **—ung**, *f.* resolution; fixed purpose.

Entschlossen [ɛnt'ʃlɔsən], *p.p. & adj.* resolved; resolute; determined. **—heit**, *f.* determination, fixity of purpose.

Entschlüpfen [ɛnt'ʃlʏpfən], *v.n.* (*aux.* f.) to slip from; to escape.

Entschluß [ɛnt'ʃlus], *m.* (**—(ß)es**, *pl.* **Entschlüsse**) resolve.

Entschuldig—en [ɛnt'ʃʊldɪgən], *v.a.* to excuse, exculpate; to justify; **sich —en**, to apologize (bei, gegen, to; wegen, for). **—ung**, *f.* excuse, apology.

Entschwinden [ɛnt'svɪndən], *ir.v.n.* (*aux.* f., *dat.*) to vanish, disappear.

Entsetz—en [ɛnt'zɛtsən], I. *v.a.* to displace; to dismiss; to depose; to relieve. II. *v.r.* to be terrified, amazed, shocked. III. *subst.n.* terror, fright, horror. **—lich**, *adj.* terrific, frightful, horrible. **—lichkeit**, *f.* (*pl.* **—lichkeiten**) frightfulness, terribleness. **—ung**, *f.* dismissal.

Entsiegeln [ɛnt'zi:gəln], *v.a.* to unseal.

Entsinnen [ɛnt'zɪnən], *ir.v.r.* (**sich einer Sache**) to recollect.

Entsprech—en [ɛnt'ʃprɛçən], *ir.v.n.* (*aux.* f., *dat.*) to answer, suit; to respond to; to meet (*a demand*). **—end**, *adj.* suitable; corresponding.

Entspringen [ɛnt'ʃprɪŋən], *ir.v.n.* (*aux.* f.) to escape; to arise, originate from.

Entstehen [ɛnt'ʃte:ən], I. *ir.v.n.* (*aux.* f.) to begin, originate (aus, in). II. *subst.n.* beginning, arising, origin.

Entstell—en [ɛnt'ʃtelən], *v.a.* to deform, distort. **—t**, *p.p. & adj.* disfigured, deformed. **—ung**, *f.* distortion, misrepresentation.

Enttäusch—en [ɛnt'tɔʏʃən], *v.a.* to undeceive. **—ung**, *f.* disabusing; disillusion.

Entvölker—n [ɛnt'fœlkərn], *v.a.* to depopulate. **—t**, *adj. & p.p.* depopulated. **—ung**, *f.* depopulation.

Entwaffnen [ɛnt'vafnən], *v.a.* to disarm.

Entwässern [ɛnt'vesərn], *v.a.* to drain.

Entweder [ɛnt've:dər], *conj.* either; **— dies oder das**, either this or that.

Entweich—en [ɛnt'vaɪçən], *ir.v.n.* (*aux.* f.) to give way; to escape. **—ung**, *f.* escape; absconding; disappearance.

Entweih—en [ɛnt'vaiən], *v.a.* to profane. **—ung** *f.* profanation ; sacrilege.

Entwend—en [ɛnt'vɛndən], *reg. & ir.v.a.* to steal; to embezzle. **—ung**, *f.* theft, embezzlement.

Entwerfen [ɛnt'vɛrfən], *ir.v.a.* to sketch; to project; to plan, design.

Entwert—en [ɛnt'vɛrtən], *v.a.* to depreciate. **—ung**, *f.* depreciation.

Entwickel—n [ɛnt'vɪkəln], *v.* I. *a.* to develop. II. *r.* to expand; to evolve. **—ung**, *f.* development; evolution.

Entwirren [ɛnt'vɪrən], *v.a.* to disentangle, unravel.

Entwischen [ɛnt'vɪʃən], *v.n.* (*aux.* ſ., *dat.*) to give the slip to, steal away.

Entwöhnen [ɛnt'vøːnən], *v.a.* (einen einer Sache, einen von einer Sache) to disaccustom.

Entwürdig—en [ɛnt'vʏrdɪgən], *v.a.* to degrade; to profane. **—ung**, *f.* degradation.

Entwurf [ɛnt'vurf], *m.* (—(e)s, *pl.* **Entwürfe**) draft (*of a document*); sketch, outline; project, plan.

Entzieh—en [ɛnt'tsiːən], *ir.v.* I. *a.* (einem etwas) to take away, remove; to withdraw. II. *r.* to avoid; to forsake. **—ung**, *f.* withdrawal; removal.

Entziffer—bar [ɛnt'tsɪfərbaːr], *adj.* explicable; decipherable. **—er**, *m.* (—ers, *pl.* **—er**) decipherer. **—n**, *v.a.* to decipher. **—ung**, *f.* deciphering.

Entzück—en [ɛnt'tsykən], I. *v.a.* to charm, delight, overjoy. II. *subst.n.*, **—ung**, *f.* rapture, delight. **—end**, *p. & adj.* delightful, charming. **—t**, *p.p. & adj.* charmed, enraptured, overjoyed.

Entzünd—bar [ɛnt'tsʏntbaːr], *adj.* inflammable. **—barkeit**, *f.* inflammability. **—en**, *v.* I. *a.* to kindle. II. *r.* to catch fire. **—ung**, *f.* ignition; inflammation.

Entzwei [ɛnt'tsvai], *adv. & sep. prefix*, in two; asunder, apart. **—brechen**, *ir.v.a. & n.* (*aux.* ſ.) to break in two, asunder.

Enzian ['ɛntsiaːn], *m.* (—s, *pl.* —e) gentian.

Enzyklopä—die [ɛntsyklopɛ'diː], *f.* (*pl.* —n) encyclopedia. **—disch** [—'pɛːdɪʃ], *adj.* encyclopedic.

Ep—if ['eːpɪk], *f.* epic poetry. **—iker**, *m.* (—ikers, *pl.* —iker) epic poet. **—isch**, *adj. & adv.* epic.

¹Er [eːr, ɛr, ər], *pers. pron.* **he.**

²Er [ɛr], *compounded with verbs is insep. and unaccented; the p.p. loses the* **ge**, *as* **erachtet**, *deemed; it usually gives to verbs the idea of beginning, or of attainment by the action of the verb; it often equals* **auf**, *e.g.* **erstehen**, *etc.*

Erachten [ɛr'ʔaxtən], I. *v.a.* to think, deem, be of opinion. II. *subst.n.* opinion, judgment.

Erbarm—en [ɛr'barmən], I. *v.a.* to move to pity; **daß Gott —e!** God help us! II. *v.r.* (*with gen. or* **über** *with acc.*) to pity, commiserate, show mercy to. III. *subst.n.* pity, compassion. **—end**, *p. & adj.* compassionate. **—ung**, *f.* pity. **—ens-wert**, **—ens-würdig**, *adj. & adv.* pitiable. **—ungs-los**, *adj.* pitiless, merciless. **—ungs-voll**, *adj.* compassionate.

Erbärmlich [ɛr'bermlɪç], *adj. & adv.* pitiable, miserable, wretched. **—keit**, *f.* misery, wretchedness.

Erbau—en [ɛr'bauən], *v.a.* to build up; to cultivate; to edify. **—er**, *m.* (—ers, *pl.* **—er**) builder; founder; edifier. **—lich**, *adj. & adv.* edifying; improving. **—ung**, *f.* building up; construction; edification.

Erb— [ɛrp], *in compounds usually =* hereditary. **—bar**, *adj.* inheritable.

Erb—e ['ɛrbə], I. *m.* (—n, *pl.* —n) heir. II. *n.* (—es, *pl.* **—schaften** *or* **—güter**) heritage, inheritance. **—in**, *f.* female heir, heiress. **—lich**, *adj. & adv.* hereditary, inheritable. **—schaft**, *f.* heritage, inheritance. **—adel**, *m.* hereditary nobility. **—begräbnis**, *n.* family vault. **—feind**, *m.* hereditary enemy. **—folge**, *f.* succession by inheritance. **—folger**, *m.* heir, successor. **—gut**, *n.* patrimonial estate; heirloom. **—sünde**, *f.* original sin. **—teil**, *n.* portion, inheritance.

Erben ['ɛrbən], *v.* I. *a.* to inherit. II. *n.* (*aux.* ſ.) **—auf**, to descend to, devolve on.

Erbeuten [ɛr'bɔytən], *v.a.* to gain *or* take as booty.

Erbiet—en [ɛr'biːtən], I. *ir.v.r.* to offer; to volunteer. II. *subst.n.* offer. **—ung**, *f.* offer, proffer.

Erbitt—en [ɛr'bɪtən], *ir.v.a.* to beg, request; to obtain by entreaty. **—lich**, *adj. & adv.* yielding to entreaty.

Erbitterung [ɛr'bɪtəruŋ], *f.* exasperation; bitter anger.

Erblassen ['ɛr'blasən], *v.n. (aux.* ʃ.) to grow pale.

Erblicken [ɛr'blıkən], *v.a.* to catch sight of.

Erblinden [ɛr'blındən], *v.n. (aux.* ʃ.) to grow blind.

Erbse ['ɛrpsə], *f. (pl.* —n) pea. —n=ſchote, *f.* pea-pod.

Erd—e ['e:rdə], *f. (old gen. & dat. sing.* —en, *now* —e; —en *survives in many compounds; pl.* —en) earth, ground; the earth, the world. —en, *(first part of comp.=)* earthly, terrestrial. —ig, *adj.* earthy. —achse, *f. (pl.* —n) axis of the earth. —bahn, *f.* orbit of the earth. —ball, *m.* globe, world. —bau, *m.* earthwork; crypt, vault. —beben, *n.* earthquake. —beere, *f.* strawberry. —boden, *m.* the earth, ground. —enge, *f.* isthmus. —en=kind, *n.,* —en=ſohn, *m.* mortal. —forſcher, *m.* geologist. —forſchung, *f.* geology. —kreis, *m.* globe; sphere of the earth. —kreis=linie, *f.* horizon (line). —kunde, *f.* geography; geology. —leitung, *f.* earth-wire (*Radio*). —öl, *n.* petroleum. —pech, *n.* bitumen. —reich, *n.* earth, ground; the world at large. —ſtrich, *m.* zone. —ſturz, *m.* landslip. —teil, *m.* part of the world; continent.

Erdenk—en [ɛr'dɛŋkən], *ir.v.a.* to invent; to imagine. —bar, —lich, *adj.* imaginable, conceivable. —ung, *f.* invention.

Erdicht—en [ɛr'dıçtən], *v.a.* to devise; to imagine. —et, *p.p. & adj.* feigned; fictitious. —ung, *f.* fabrication; fiction.

Erdreiſten [ɛr'draıstən], *v.r.* to dare, presume.

Erdroſſeln [ɛr'drɔsəln], *v.a.* to strangle.

Erduld—en [ɛr'dʊldən], *v.a.* to endure, suffer; to put up with. —ung, *f.* endurance; submission (to); toleration (of).

Ereifern [ɛr'ʔaıfərn], *v.r.* to grow warm, fly into a passion; — Sie ſich nicht, keep your temper.

Ereig—nen [ɛr'ʔaıgnən], *v.r. imp.* to come to pass; to happen. —nis, *n.* (—(ſ)es, *pl.* —(ſ)e) event, occurrence.

Ereilen [ɛr'ʔaılən], *v.a.* to hasten up to; to overtake.

Eremit [ere'mi:t], *m.* (—en, *pl.* —en) hermit.

Ererben [ɛr'ʔɛrbən], *v.a.* to inherit.

Erfahr—en [ɛr'fa:rən], I. *ir.v.a.* to learn, be told; to experience. II. *p.p. & adj.* experienced, expert, skilful. —enheit, *f.* experience, practice, skill. —ung, *f.* experience, practice.

Erfassen [ɛr'fasən], *v.a.* to lay hold of, seize; to comprehend.

Erfind—bar [ɛr'fıntba:r], *adj.* discoverable, devisable. —ſam, *adj.* inventive. —ſamkeit, *f.* inventiveness, ingenuity.

Erfind—en [ɛr'fındən], *ir.v.a.* to find (out); to contrive, invent. —er, *m.* (—ers, *pl.* —er) designer, inventor. —eriſch, *adj. & adv.* inventive. —ung, *f.* invention; device. —ungs=gabe, *f.* inventive faculty.

Erfolg [ɛr'fɔlk], *m.* (—es, *pl.* —e) success. —los, I. *adj.* unsuccessful, unavailing. II. *adv.* vainly, in vain. —reich, *adj.* successful.

Erfolgen [ɛr'fɔlgən], *v.n. (aux.* ʃ.) to ensue, result.

Erforder—lich [ɛr'fɔrdərlıç], *adj.* requisite, necessary. —nis, *n.* (—(ſſ)es, *pl.* —(ſſ)e) requisite.

Erfordern [ɛr'fɔrdərn], *v.a.* to require; to demand.

Erforſch—en [ɛr'fɔrʃən], *v.a.* to search into, investigate; to discover. —er, *m.* (—ers, *pl.* —er) investigator; discoverer. —ung, *f.* investigation; exploration.

Erfragen [ɛr'fra:gən], *reg. & ir.v.a.* to find out by asking; zu — bei, inquire at (*for information*).

Erfreu—en [ɛr'frɔyən], *v.a.* to rejoice, gladden; to cheer, comfort. —lich, *adj.* delightful, pleasing, satisfactory.

Erfrieren [ɛr'fri:rən], *ir.v.n. (aux.* ʃ.) to freeze; to suffer cold; to perish with cold. erfroren, *p.p. & adj.* frozen, benumbed with cold.

Erfriſch—en [ɛr'frıʃən], *v.a.* to freshen, refresh. —end, *p. & adj.* refreshing, cooling. —ung, *f.* recreation, refreshment.

Erfüll—en [ɛr'fʏlən], *v.a.* to fulfil, perform; ein Verſprechen—en, to keep a promise. —ung, *f.* fulfilment, accomplishment.

Ergänz—en [ɛr'gɛntsən], *v.a.* to complete, perfect. —end, *p. & adj.* supplementary. —ung, *f.* completion; supplement.

Ergeb—en [ɛr'ge:bən], I. *v.a.* to deliver

up, yield to; to show, prove. II. *v.r.* to surrender; to acquiesce (in); to devote oneself to; to become addicted to; to come to pass, happen. III. *p p.* & *adj.* devoted; submissive, humble. **—enſt**, (*sup.*) *adj.* & *adv.* most devoted; most humble. **—en=heit**, *f.* fidelity, loyalty, devotion, resignation. **—nis**, *n.* (**—ni(ſſ)es**, *pl.* **—ni(ſſ)e**) result, consequence. **—ung**, *f.* submission, resignation; surrender.

Ergiebig [ɛr'giːbɩç], *adj.* productive. **—feit**, *f.* productiveness; fertility.

Ergießen [ɛr'giːsən], *ir.v.a.* to pour out *or* forth.

Erglänzen [ɛr'glɛntsən], *v.n.* (*aux.* ɧ.) to sparkle, shine forth.

Ergötz—en [ɛr'gøtsən], *v.a.* to delight, please. **—end**, *p.* & *adj.* amusing. **—lich**, *adj.* amusing; delightful. **—ung**, *f.* delight; pleasure.

Ergreifen [ɛr'graɩfən], *ir.v.a.* to lay hold of, seize; **die Flucht —**, to take to flight.

Ergrimmen [ɛr'grɩmən], *v.n.* (*aux.* ſ.) to grow angry.

Ergründ—en [ɛr'grʏndən], *v.a.* to fathom, investigate. **—lich**, *adj.* & *adv.* penetrable. **—ung**, *f.* research; exploration.

Erhaben [ɛr'haːbən], *adj.* & *adv.* raised; exalted, noble; sublime; stately.

Erhalt—en [ɛr'haltən], *ir.v.a.* to keep up; to preserve; to maintain, support; to get, to receive. **—er**, *m.* (**—ers**, *pl.* **—er**) preserver; supporter; upholder. **—ung**, *f.* obtaining; receipt; maintenance, *etc.*

Erharren [ɛr'harən], *v.a.* to expect; to wait for.

Erhaſchen [ɛr'haʃən], *v.a.* to seize, catch up; to overtake.

Erheb—en [ɛr'heːbən], *ir.v.a.* to raise up; to exalt, elevate; to extol; to collect, gather; to bring (*an action against*). **—er**, *m.* (ers, *pl.* **—er**) raiser; promoter; collector. **—lich**, *adj.* & *adv.* important; considerable. **—lichfeit**, *f.* importance, consequence; weight. **—ung**, *f.* elevation; promotion; exaltation; levy, collecting.

Erheiter—n [ɛr'haɩtərn], *v.a.* to cheer; to enliven, exhilarate. **—ung**, *f.* amusement, fun.

Erhitz—en [ɛr'hɩtsən], *v.a.* to heat; to warm; to inflame. **—end**, *p.* & *adj.* inflammatory. **—t**, *p.p.* & *adj.* heated.

Erhöh—en [ɛr'høːən], *v.a.* to heighten; to raise, increase. **—t**, *p.p.* & *adj.* elevated; additional (*of taxes*). **—ung**, *f.* raising; exaltation; elevation.

Erhol—en [ɛr'hoːlən], *v.r.* to recover; to rest; to recreate. **—ung**, *f.* recovery.

Erinner—n [ɛr'ʔɩnərn], *v.* I. *a.* (**einen an eine S.**) to remind, call to mind; to draw attention to. II. *r.* (*with gen. or an & acc.*) to recall, remember. **—ung**, *f.* reminiscence; recollection; reminder. **—ungs=vermögen**, *n.* memory. **—ungs=zeichen**, *n.* keepsake.

Erfalten [ɛr'kaltən], *v.n.* (*aux.* ſ.) to grow cold.

Erfält—en [ɛr'kɛltən], *v.* I. *a.* to cool. II. *r.* to catch cold. **—ung**, *f.* catching cold; cold.

Erfaufen [ɛr'kaufən], *v.a.* to buy, purchase.

Erfennbar [ɛr'kɛntbaːr], *adj.* perceptible, discernible.

Erfenn—en [ɛr'kɛnən], *ir.v.a.* to know, perceive; to recognize (**an**, by); **ſich zu —en geben**, to make oneself known. **—tlich**, *adj.* grateful; discernible. **—tlichfeit**, *f.* readiness to acknowledge (*a favour*); gratitude. **—tnis**, I. *f.* (*pl.* **—tniſſe**) knowledge; perception; acknowledgment. II. *n.* (**—tniſſes**, *pl.* **—tniſſe**) verdict, sentence, judgment. **—ung**, *f.* recognition; perception; knowledge.

Erflär—en [ɛr'klɛːrən], *v.* I. *a.* to explain; to expound; to declare. II. *r.* to explain oneself. **—t**, *p.p.* & *adj.* professed, declared. **—ung**, *f.* declaration; explanation.

Erflingen [ɛr'klɩŋən], *ir.v.n.* (*aux.* ſ.) to resound.

Erforen [ɛr'koːrən], *adj.* select, chosen; **die —en**, *pl.* the elect.

Erfranfen [ɛr'kraŋkən], *v.n.* (*aux.* ſ.) to fall sick or ill.

Erfundig—en [ɛr'kʊndɩgən], *v.r.* to inquire, make inquiries (**bei einem nach einer S.**, of a person, for a thing; **wegen einer S.**, about *or* concerning a thing). **—ung**, *f.* inquiry, search.

Erlahmen [ɛr'laːmən], *v.n.* (*aux.* ſ.) to grow lame; (*fig.*) to become weak.

Erlangen [ɛr'laŋən], *v.a.* to attain, acquire.

Erlaß [ɛr'las], *m.* (**—(ſſ)es**, *pl.* **—(ſſ)e**) deduction, abatement; remission, pardon; dispensation, exemption; edict, decree.

Erlaff—en [ɛr'lasən], *ir.v.a.* to let go, release; to remit; to let off from; to proclaim; to abate *(price)*. **—ung,** *f.* remission; dispensation; release.

Erläßlich [ɛr'lɛslɪç], *adj. & adv.* pardonable, venial.

Erlaub—en [ɛr'laubən], *v.a.* **(einem etwas)** to allow, permit. **—nis,** *f.* *(pl.* **—ni(ff)e)** leave, permission. **—t,** *p.p. & adj.* allowable; lawful.

Erlaucht [ɛr'lauxt], I, *adj.* illustrious, noble. II. *f.* **Ew.** *or* **Eure —,** Your Highness.

Erläuter—n [ɛr'lɔytərn], *v.a.* to explain, illustrate. **—er,** *m.* commentator. **—ung,** *f.* explanation, elucidation, comment.

Erle ['ɛrlə], *f.* *(pl.* **—n)** alder. **—n,** *adj.* (made of) alder.

Erleb—en [ɛr'le:bən], *v.a.* to experience. **—nis,** *n.* (**—ni(ff)es,** *pl.* **—ni(ff)e)** experience; occurrence, event.

Erledig—en [ɛr'le:dɪgən], *v.a.* to release, to acquit, discharge (from, *gen. or* **von)** to despatch *(business)*; to vacate *(an office).* **—t,** *p.p. & adj.* settled. **—ung,** *f.* release; discharge; settlement.

Erleichter—n [ɛr'laɪçtərn], *v.a.* to ease, lighten; to alleviate. **—ung,** *f.* relief; alleviation.

Erleiden [ɛr'laɪdən], *ir.v.a.* to suffer, endure, undergo.

Erl(en)tönig ['ɛrl(ən)kø:nɪç], *m.* (**—es,** *pl.* **—e)** fairy king, erl-king.

Erlesen [ɛr'le:zən], I. *ir.v.a.* to select, choose. II. *p.p. & adj.* select; selected.

Erleucht—en [ɛr'lɔyçtən], *v.a.* to enlighten. **—ung,** *f.* enlightenment; illumination.

Erliegen [ɛr'li:gən], *ir.v.n.* *(aux.* **h.** & **f.,** *dat. or* **unter)** to succumb.

Erlogen [ɛr'lo:gən], *p.p.* *(of* **erlügen)** & *adj.* false, untruthful.

Erlöschen [ɛr'lɔʃən], *p.p.* *(of* **erlöschen)** & *adj.* extinguished, extinct, dead.

Erlösch—en [ɛr'løʃən], *ir.v.* I. *n.* *(aux.* **f.)** to be extinguished; to die out. II. *v.a.* *(aux.* **h.)** to extinguish, put out. **—ung,** *f.* extinction; expiration.

Erlös—en [ɛr'lø:zən], *v.a.* to ransom; to rescue; to redeem; to get *(as proceeds from a sale).* **—er,** *m.* (**—ers,** *pl.* **—er)** redeemer, deliverer; Saviour.

—ung, *f.* release; redemption; salvation.

Erlügen [ɛr'ly:gən], *ir.v.a.* to obtain by lying; to invent *(a lie).*

Ermächtig—en [ɛr'mɛçtɪgən], *v.a.* to empower, authorize. **—ung,** *f.* authorization.

Ermahn—en [ɛr'ma:nən], *v.a.* to admonish, warn, remind. **—ung,** *f.* admonition, exhortation.

Ermangel—n [ɛr'maŋəln], *v.n.* *(aux.* **h.)** to fail, want, to lack, be in want of. **—ung,** *f.* want, deficiency.

Ermannen [ɛr'manən], *v.r.* to take courage, pull oneself together.

Ermässigen [ɛr'mɛ:sɪgən], *v.a.* to abate, lessen.

Ermatt—en [ɛr'matən], *v.* I. *a.* to weary, weaken. II. *n.* *(aux.* **f.)** to grow faint *or* weary. **—ung,** *f.* exhaustion.

Ermessen [ɛr'mɛsən], I. *ir.v.a.* to measure; to weigh. II. *subst.n.* judgment, estimation, opinion.

Ermittel—n [ɛr'mɪtəln], *v.a.* to ascertain, find out. **—ung,** *f.* inquiry, research.

Ermöglichen [ɛr'mø:klɪçən], *v.a.* to render possible *or* feasible.

Ermutig—en [ɛr'mu:tɪgən], *v.* I. *a.* to animate, encourage. II. *r.* to take courage. **—igung,** *f.* encouragement.

Ernähr—en [ɛr'nɛ:rən], *v.* I. *a.* to nourish; to support. II. *r.* to earn one's livelihood. **—end,** *p. & adj.* nutritive. **—er,** *m.* (**—ers,** *pl.* **—er)** nourisher, supporter. **—ung,** *f.* support, maintenance, nutrition.

Ernenn—en [ɛr'nɛnən], *ir.v.a.* to nominate, appoint. **—ung,** *f.* nomination, appointment.

Erneu—ern [ɛr'nɔyərn], *v.a.* to renew, renovate, repair. **—(e)rung,** *f.* renewal; renovation.

Erniedrig—en [ɛr'ni:drɪgən], *v.a.* to humble, degrade, humiliate. **—ung,** *f.* humiliation, degradation, abasement.

Ernst [ɛrnst], I. *m.* (**—es)** earnestness, seriousness, gravity; sternness. II. *adj. & adv.* **—haft,** *adj.* earnest. **—haftigkeit,** *f.* earnestness. **—lich,** *adj. & adv.* earnest.

Ernte ['ɛrntə], *f.* *(pl.* **—n)** harvest.

Ernt—en ['ɛrntən], *v.a.* to harvest; to reap. **—er,** *m.* (**—ers,** *pl.* **—er)** harvester, reaper.

Ernüchtern [ɛr'nʏçtərn], v. I. a. to sober; to disenchant. II. r. to become sober; to be disenchanted.

Eroberer [ɛr'ʔoːbərər], m. (—s, pl. —) conqueror.

Erober—n [ɛr'ʔoːbərn], v.a. to conquer. —ung, f. conquest.

Eröffn—en [ɛr'ʔøfnən], v.a. to open, unclose. —ung, f. opening.

Erörter—en [ɛr'ʔørtərn], v.a. to discuss fully or in detail; to debate. —ung, f. discussion, debate.

Erpreß—en [ɛr'prɛsən], v.a. to extort, exact. —er, m. (—ers, pl. —er) extortioner. —ung, f. extortion; blackmail.

Erprob—en [ɛr'proːbən], v.a. to try, prove. —t, p.p. & adj. tried, approved.

Erquick—en [ɛr'kvɪkən], v.a. to revive, refresh. —end, p. & adj. refreshing. —lich, adj. refreshing, reviving. —ung, f. refreshment.

Erraten [ɛr'raːtən], ir.v.a. to guess.

Erregbar [ɛr're:kba:r], adj. excitable; irritable. —keit, f. excitability; irritability.

Erreg—en [ɛr're:gən], v.a. to excite, stir up, agitate. —end, p. & adj. exciting. —er, m. (—ers, pl. —er) agitator. —t, p.p. & adj. excited. —theit, f. agitation; irritability; animation. —ung, f. stirring up; excitement.

Erreichbar [ɛr'raɪçbaːr], adj. attainable.

Erreich—en [ɛr'raɪçən], v.a. to reach; to attain. —ung, f. attainment.

Erricht—en [ɛr'rɪçtən], v.a. to erect, raise. —ung, f. erection; establishment.

Erröt—en [ɛr'røːtən], I. v.n. (aux. ſ.) to redden; to blush. II. subst.n., —ung, f. reddening, blush.

Errungenſchaft [ɛr'rʊŋənʃaft], f. (pl. —en) acquisition, gain.

Erſatz [ɛr'zats], m. (—es) amends, compensation, reparation; equivalent; substitution. —ſtück, n. duplicate. —truppen, pl. reserve forces.

Erſchaff—en [ɛr'ʃafən], ir.v.a. to produce, create. —er, m. (—ers, pl. —er) creator. —ung, f. creation.

Erſchallen [ɛr'ʃalən], reg. & ir.v.n. (aux. ſ.) to resound.

Erſchein—en [ɛr'ʃaɪnən], I. ir.v.n. (aux. ſ.) to appear. II. subst.n. appearance.

—ung, f. apparition; phenomenon; outward appearance, aspect, mien; bearing; eine glänzende —ung ſein, to make a splendid appearance.

Erſchießen [ɛr'ʃiːsən], ir.v.a. to shoot.

Erſchlaff—en [ɛr'ʃlafən], v. I. n. (aux. ſ.) to grow slack. —ung, f. relaxation; flagging; debility, enervation.

Erſchlagen [ɛr'ʃlaːgən], ir.v.a. to slay, to strike dead.

Erſchmeicheln [ɛr'ʃmaɪçəln], v.a. to obtain by flattery.

Erſchöpf—en [ɛr'ʃøpfən], v.a. to drain; to exhaust. —end, p. & adj. exhaustive; exhausting. —t, p.p. & adj. spent, exhausted. —ung, f. exhaustion.

Erſchreck—en [ɛr'ʃrekən], ir.v.n. (aux. ſ.) to be alarmed or startled (über eine S., at, by a thing); to start (vor, at). —lich, adj. & adv. terrific, terrible, dreadful.

Erſchütter—n [ɛr'ʃʏtərn], v. I. a. to convulse; to affect deeply. II. n. (aux. ſ.) to shake, quake. —ung, f. shock; convulsion; strong emotion.

Erſchwing—en [ɛr'ʃvɪŋən], ir.v.a. to attain with difficulty. —lich, adj. attainable.

Erſehnen [ɛr'zeːnən], v.a. to long for, desire greatly.

Erſetzbar [ɛr'zɛtsbaːr], adj. reparable.

Erſetz—en [ɛr'zɛtsən], v.a. to repair, compensate; to make good; to reimburse; to restore; etwas —t bekommen, to recover damages. —lich, adj. & adv. reparable; replaceable. —ung, f. indemnification, reimbursement; see Erſatz.

Erſinn—en [ɛr'zɪnən], ir.v.a. to think out. erſonnen, p.p. & adj. devised, invented. —lich, adj. imaginable.

Erſpar—en [ɛr'ʃpaːrən], v.a. to save; to spare. —nis, f. (pl. —ni(ſſ)e), n. (—ni(ſſ)es, pl. —ni(ſſ)e) savings.

Erſt [e:rst, ɛrst], I. adj. first (in number); first, foremost, prime. II. adv. firstly; at first; for the first time; not till; only; but just; es wurde — heute fertig, it was only ready to-day. —ens, adv. firstly, in the first place.

Erſtarr—en [ɛr'ʃtarən], v. I. n. (aux. ſ.) to be benumbed. II. a. to stiffen; to freeze, chill. —t, p.p. & adj. benumbed, torpid. —ung, f. numbness, stiffness; chill.

Erſtatten [ɛr'ʃtatən], v.a. to compensate, restore; **Bericht —**, to report, render an account.

Erſtaun—en [ɛrˈʃtaunən], I. *v.n.* (*aux.* ſ.) to be astonished (**über eine S.**, at a thing). II. *subst.n.* astonishment, amazement. **—end**, *p.* & *adj.* astonishing. **—lich**, *adj.* & *adv.* astonishing, amazing, marvellous.

Erſteh—en [ɛrˈʃteːən], *ir.v.* I. *n.* (*aux.* ſ.) to arise, rise. II. *a.* to pick up, buy; to suffer, endure. **—ung**, *f.* resurrection.

Erſteig—en [ɛrˈʃtaigən], *ir.v.a.* to ascend, mount. **—ung**, *f.* escalade (*Mil.*).

Erſterben [ɛrˈʃtɛrbən], *ir.v.n.* (*aux.* ſ.) to die; to become extinct.

Erſtick—en [ɛrˈʃtikən], I. *v.a.* to stifle, suffocate. II. *v.n.* (*aux.* ſ.) to choke, be choked. III. *subst.n.*, **—ung**, *f.* suffocation.

Erſtreb—en [ɛrˈʃtreːbən], *v.a.* to strive for *or* after; to obtain by endeavour. **—ung**, *f.* pursuit (*of an object*).

Erſuch—en [ɛrˈzuːxən], I. *v.a.* to beseech, implore (**um**, for). II. *subst.n.* entreaty, solicitation. **—ung**, *f.* petition.

Ertappen [ɛrˈtapən], *v.a.* to catch, seize.

Erteil—en [ɛrˈtailən], *v.a.* (**einem etwas**) to impart, give. **—er**, *m.* (**—ers**, *pl.* **—er**) bestower. **—ung**, *f.* bestowal.

Ertönen [ɛrˈtøːnən], *v.n.* (*aux.* ſ.) to resound.

Ertrag [ɛrˈtraːk], *m.* (**—es**, *pl.* **Erträge**) produce; proceeds; revenue.

Ertragen [ɛrˈtraːgən], *ir.v.a.* to bear, suffer, endure.

Erträglich [ɛrˈtrɛːklɪç], *adj.* supportable; tolerable.

Ertrinken [ɛrˈtrɪŋkən], *ir.v.n.* (*aux.* ſ.) to drown.

Erwachen [ɛrˈvaxən], I. *v.n.* (*aux.* ſ.) to awaken. II. *subst.n.* awakening.

Erwachſen [ɛrˈvaksən], I. *ir.v.n.* (*aux.* ſ.) to grow (**aus**, out of, from); to grow up. II. *p.p.* & *adj.* grown up.

Erwäg—en [ɛrˈvɛːgən], *ir.v.a.* to ponder; to consider; to discuss. **—ung**, *f.* consideration; deliberation.

Erwähl—en [ɛrˈvɛːlən], *v.a.* to choose, to elect.

Erwähn—en [ɛrˈvɛːnən], *v.a.* (& *n.* (*aux.* h., *acc.*)) to mention. **—ung**, *f.* mention.

Erwart—en [ɛrˈvartən], *v.a.* to expect;

to await. **—et**, *p.p.* & *adj.* expected. **—ung**, *f.* expectation; anticipation.

Erweck—en [ɛrˈvɛkən], *v.a.* to rouse, awaken. **—ung**, *f.* awaking.

Erweich—en [ɛrˈvaiçən], *v.a.* to soften. **—end**, *p.* & *adj.* softening. **—ung**, *f.* softening.

Erweis [ɛrˈvais], *m.* (**—(ſ)es**, *pl.* **—(ſ)e**) proof, demonstration. **—(ſ)en**, *ir.v.a.* to prove; to show, render (*mercy, honour, favour, etc.*).

Erwerb [ɛrˈvɛrp], *m.* (**—es**) gain; earnings; business.

Erwerb—en [ɛrˈvɛrbən], *ir.v.a.* to gain, obtain; to earn; to win. **—er**, *m.* (**—ers**, *pl.* **—er**) acquirer. **—nis**, *n.* (**—ni(ſſ)es**, *pl.* **—ni(ſſ)e**) acquisition, gain; earnings. **—ſam**, *adj.* & *adv.* industrious. **—ſamkeit**, *f.* diligence, industry. **—ung**, *f.* acquisition, gain; acquiring. **—s-fähig**, *adj.* capable of earning one's living. **—s-mittel**, *n.* means of living.

Erwider—n [ɛrˈviːdərn], *v.a.* to render in return; to requite; to retaliate; to reply. **—ung**, *f.* return; retaliation; reply.

Erwieſen [ɛrˈviːzən], *p.p.* (*of* **Erweiſen**) & *adj.* proved.

¹**Erz** [eːrts], *n.* (**—es**, *pl.* **—e**) ore; metal; brass, bronze. **—en**, *adj.* brazen. **—ader**, *f.* vein of ore. **—bild**, *n.* bronze statue. **—bruch**, *m.* mine. **—gießer**, *m.* brass-founder. **—gießerei**, *f.* brass-foundry. **—grube**, *f.* pit, mine. **—hütte**, *f.* smelting house.

²**Erz—** [ɛrts], (*in comp.* =) principal; arch-, chief; excellent; very; extremely; high. **—biſchof**, *m.* archbishop. **—engel**, *m.* archangel. **—feind**, *m.* arch-enemy. **—herzog**, *m.* archduke. **—herzogin**, *f.* archduchess. **—vater**, *m.* patriarch. **—väterlich**, *adj.* patriarchal.

Erzähl—en [ɛrˈtseːlən], *v.a.* to tell, relate. **—er**, *m.* (**—ers**, *pl.* **—er**) narrator. **—ung**, *f.* narration; account, report; narrative, tale, story.

Erzeigen [ɛrˈtsaigən], *v.a.* (**einem etwas**) to show, do (*kindness*).

Erzeugbar [ɛrˈtsɔykbaːr], *adj.* that may be generated; producible.

Erzeug—en [ɛrˈtsɔygən], *v.a.* to raise, produce, breed. **—er**, *m.* (**—ers**, *pl.* **—er**) begetter; father; raiser, grower. **—erin**, *f.* parent, mother. **—nis**, *n.* (**—ni(ſſ)es**, *pl.* **—ni(ſſ)e**) offspring, product; production. —**ung**, *f.* begetting; production.

Erzieh—en [ɛr'tsi:ən], *ir.v.a.* to train; to educate; to rear. —**er**, *m.* (—**ers**, *pl.* —**er**) teacher; tutor. —**erin**, *f.* lady teacher, governess. —**ung**, *f.* rearing, bringing up; education.

Erzielen [ɛr'tsi:lən], *v.a.* to aim at; to strive after.

Erzürnen [ɛr'tsʏrnən], *v.* I. *a.* to irritate. II. *r.* & *n.* (*aux.* ʃ.) to grow angry.

Erzwingen [ɛr'tsvɪŋən], *ir.v.a.* to force, enforce; to extort from.

Es [ɛs,‿ əs], *pers. pron.* I. (*nom. acc. of 3rd sing. neut.*) it. II. *used as a subject of imp. verbs sometimes* = there; — **giebt Leute**, there are people. III. *used demonstratively* = he, she, it, they; — **sind Männer von Ansehen**, they are men of position, of consequence. IV. *used as completion of predicate* = so, it; **ich bin —**, it is I; **er sagt —**, he says so; **es lebe der König!** long live the King!

Esche ['ɛʃə], *f.* (*pl.* —**n**) (—**n=baum**, *m.*) ash, ash-tree. —**n**, *adj.* ashen.

Esel ['e:zəl], *m.* (—**s**, *pl.* —) ass. —**ei** [—'laɪ], *f.* (*pl.* —**eien**) asinine behaviour. —**haft**, *adj.* & *adv.* stupid. —**in**, *f.* she-ass. —**s=ohr**, *n.* dog's ear (*in a book*).

Eskadron [ɛska'dro:n], *f.* (*pl.* —**en**) squadron.

Espe ['ɛspə], *f.* (*pl.* —**n**) aspen-tree. —**n**, *adj.* aspen. —**n=laub**, *n.* foliage of aspen; **zittern wie** —**nlaub**, to tremble like an aspen leaf.

Eß—bar ['ɛsba:r], *adj.* & *adv.* eatable. —**barkeit**, *f.* (*pl.* —**barkeiten**) eatableness; (*pl.*) eatables. —**begier**, *f.* craving for food, appetite; gluttony. —**gierig**, *adj.* & *adv.* ravenous. —**waren**, *pl.* eatables, provisions. —**zimmer**, *n.* dining-room.

Eß—en ['ɛsən], I. *ir.v.a.* & *n.* (*aux.* ḥ.) to eat. II. *subst.n.* eating; food, meal. —**er**, *m.* eater.

Essenz [ɛ'sɛnts], *f.* (*pl.* —**en**) essence.

Essig ['ɛsɪç], *m.* (—**s**, *pl.* —**e**) vinegar. —**gurke**, *f.* pickled cucumber.

Estrich ['ɛstrɪç], *m.* (—**s**, *pl.* —**e**) flooring; floor.

Etat [e'ta:], *m.* (—**s**, *pl.* —**s**) establishment; list (*of officers, etc.*).

Eth—ik ['e:tɪk], *f.* ethics. —**iker**, *m.* (—**ikers**, *pl.* —**iker**) moral philosopher. —**isch**, *adj.* ethical.

Etlich ['ɛtlɪç], *pron.* & *adj.*, —**e**, *pl. of* **etlich**, some, several; a few; any.

Etwa ['ɛtva], I. *adv.* perhaps, perchance; possible; indeed, forsooth; nearly, about; somewhere; at any time; in some way. II. *part.*; **er wird doch nicht** — **glauben**, he will not believe, I hope. —**ig** [ɛt'va:ɪç], *adj.* & *adv.* possible, eventual.

Etwas ['ɛtvas], I. *ind. pron.* (*indec.*) something, somewhat, some. II. *adj.* some, any. III. *adv.* somewhat; a little; rather.

Euch [ɔʏç], *pers. pron.* (*acc.* & *dat. pl. of* **Du**) you, to you, yourselves, one another, each other.

Euer ['ɔʏər] (*abbrev.* **Ew.**). I. *gen. pl. of* **Du**, of you, your. II. *poss. adj.* your, your own. III. *poss. pron.* (**der, die, das** —**e**, *or* —**er**, —**e**, —**es**) yours, your own. —(**er)seits**, *adv.* on your side; for your part; as concerns you; in your turn. —**s=gleichen**, *indec. adj. or pron.* of your kind; like you. (**um**) —**t=halben**, —**t=wegen**, —**t=willen**, *adv.* on your account; for your sake; as far as you are concerned.

Euter ['ɔʏtər], *n.* (—**s**, *pl.* —) udder.

Evangel—isch [evaŋ'ge:lɪʃ], *adj.* & *adv.* evangelical; Protestant. —**ium**, *n.* (—**iums**, *pl.* **Evangelien**) gospel.

Ewig ['e:vɪç], *adj.* & *adv.* everlasting; eternal; perpetual, for ever; **der** —**e Jude**, the wandering Jew. —**keit**, *f.* eternity; perpetuity.

Exam—en [ɛk'sa:mən], *n.* (—**ens**, *pl.* **Examina**) (*see* **Prüfung**) examination. —**inieren** [—'ni:rən], *v.a.* to examine.

Exemp—el [ɛk'sɛmpəl], *n.* (—**els**, *pl.* —**el**) example. —**lar** [—'pla:r], *n.* (—**lars**, *pl.* —**lare**) model. —**larisch** [—'pla:rɪʃ], *adj.* & *adv.* exemplary; excellent.

Exerzier—en [ɛksɛr'tsi:rən], I. *v.a.* to exercise; to drill. II. *subst.n.* drill. —**meister**, *m.* drill-sergeant.

Exist—enz [ɛksɪs'tɛnts], *f.* (*pl.* —**enzen**) existence; being. —**ieren** [—'ti:rən], *v.n.* (*aux.* ḥ.) to exist.

Export [ɛks'pɔrt], *m.* (—**s**, *pl.* —**en**) export. —**geschäft**, *n.* (*pl.* —**e**) export house. —**handel**, *m.* export trade.

Extra ['ɛkstra:], *adj.* extra, additional; special. —**blatt**, *n.* special edition (*of a newspaper*). —**zug**, *m.* special train, excursion train.

Exzellenz [ɛkstsɛ'lɛnts], f. (pl. —en) excellence; Excellency (title).

F

F, f [ɛf], n. F, f; F or Fa (Mus.).

Fabel ['fa:bəl], f. (pl. —n) fable, tale. —haft, adj. fabulous, mythical; incredible.

Fabrik [fa'bri:k], f. (pl. —en) factory, manufactory. —ant [—'kant], m. (—anten, pl. —anten) manufacturer. —at [—'ka:t], n. (—ates, pl. —ate) manufacture. —zeichen, n. trademark.

Fabrizieren [fabri'tsi:rən], v.a. to fabricate, manufacture.

Fabulist [fabu'lɪst], m. (—en, pl. —en) fable-writer.

Fach [fax], I. n. (—(e)s, pl. Fächer) compartment, division; department; shelf; special subject; special branch (of a trade or profession). II. suff. (in comp.=) -fold; hundert—, hundredfold. —kundig, adj. competent. —mann, m. expert.

Fäch—eln ['fɛçəln], —ern ['fɛçərn], v.a. & n. (aux. h.) to fan gently. —er, m. (—ers, pl. —er) fan.

Fackel ['fakəl], f. (pl. —n) torch. —zug, m. torchlight procession.

Fädchen ['fɛ:tçən], n. (—s, pl. —) little thread, dim. of Faden.

Fädeln ['fɛ:dəln], v. I. a. to thread (a needle); to string. II. r. to untwist, ravel out.

Faden ['fa:dən], m. (—s, pl. Fäden) thread; cord. —nudeln, f. pl. vermicelli. —scheinig, adj. threadbare.

Fähig ['fɛ:ɪç], adj. & adv. (with gen.) able, capable. —keit, f. capacity, ability.

Fahl [fa:l], adj. & adv. fallow; fawn-coloured; faded.

Fahne ['fa:nə], f. (pl. —n) flag; vane, weather-cock. —neid, m. military oath. —nflucht, f. desertion (of the colours).

Fahr—bar ['fa:rba:r], adj. & adv. practicable; passable; navigable. —barkeit, f. practicableness; navigableness. —betrieb, m. traffic. —geld, n. fare. —karte, f. ticket (Railw.). —lässig, adj. negligent; careless. —lässigkeit, f. negligence, carelessness. —rad, n. (bi)cycle, (tri)cycle. —schein, m. ticket. —stuhl, m. lift.

Fähre ['fɛ:rə], f. (pl. —n) ferry; ferryboat.

Fahr—en ['fa:rən], ir.v. I. n. (aux. f.) to go (in any sort of conveyance); to travel; to drive; to go in a boat, row, sail; hinauf, herauf —en, to ascend; hinab, herab —en, to descend; —e wohl! farewell. II. a. to drive; to navigate; to convey. —end, p. & adj. going, travelling; vagrant. —er, m. (—ers, pl. —er) driver.

Fahrt [fa:rt], f. (pl. —en) ride, drive, row, passage, journey. —ballast, m. (—ballastes, pl. —ballaste) ballast (for aircraft). —höhe, f. flight-altitude (Av.).

Fakultät [fakul'tɛ:t], f. (pl. —en) faculty, Board of Studies.

Falb [falp], adj. fallow, pale yellow, pale. —e, m. & f.; ein —er, a cream or dun-coloured horse.

Falke ['falkə], m. (—n, pl. —n) falcon, hawk. —njagd, f. hawking.

Fall [fal], m. (—(e)s, pl. Fälle) fall; decay, ruin, downfall; failure; case, event; condition, situation; auf keinen —, on no account. —s, adv. in case, if, supposing that; andern—s, otherwise. —brücke, f. drawbridge. —schirm, m. parachute. —sucht, f. epilepsy.

Falle ['falə], f. (pl. —n) pitfall; trap, snare.

Fallen ['falən], I. ir.v.n. (aux. f.) to fall, tumble; — auf (with acc.), to hit, light on, turn upon; es fällt mir schwer, it is difficult for me; jemandem in die Rede —, to interrupt a person. II. subst.n. subsidence; fall; decay; diminution.

Fall—ieren [fa'li:rən], v.n. (aux. h.) to fail; to become bankrupt. —it [fa'li:t], m. (—iten, pl. —iten) bankrupt.

Fällen ['fɛlən], v.a. to fell or lay low; to bring down.

Fällig ['fɛlɪç], adj. due, payable.

Falsch ['falʃ], adj. & adv. false, untrue; meine Uhr geht —, my watch is wrong. —heit, f. falsity, untruth; deceit.

Fälsch—en ['fɛlʃən], v.a. to falsify. —er, m. (—ers, pl. —er) falsifier, forger. —ung, f. falsification.

Fält—chen ['fɛltçən], n. (—chens, pl. —chen) crease, wrinkle.

Falt—e ['faltə], f. (pl. —en) fold, plait;

crease; wrinkle. **—ig,** *adj. & adv.*
wrinkled; (*in comp.*=) -fold, as **vier-**
—ig, fourfold. **—en,** *v.a.* to fold;
to wrinkle.

Familie [fa'mi:liǝ], *f.* (*pl.* **—n**) family.
—n=ähnlichkeit, *f.* family likeness.
—n=angelegenheiten, *pl.* family affairs.
—n=glück, *n.* domestic happiness.

Famos [fa'mo:s], *adj. & adv.* famous;
excellent, splendid; **—er Kerl,** capital
fellow.

Fanat—iker [fa'na:tıkǝr], *m.* (**—ikers,**
pl. **—iker**) fanatic. **—ismus** [—'tıs-
mus], *m.* fanaticism. **—isch,** *adj.*
& adv. fanatic(al).

Fang [faŋ], *m.* (**—es,** *pl.* **Fänge**)
catching, capture. **—brief,** *m.*
warrant of arrest. **—eisen,** *n.* iron trap.

Fangen ['faŋǝn], *ir.v.* I. *a.* to catch,
seize. II. *r.* to be caught, become
entangled; to catch, take hold.

Farb—e ['farbǝ], *f.* (*pl.* **—en**) colour,
tint, hue; dye. **—en,** *adj.* (*in compds.*)
coloured. **—en=blind,** *adj.* colour-
blind. **—ig,** *adj.* coloured; stained.
—los, *adj.* colourless. **—losigkeit,** *f.*
pallor.

Färb—en ['ferbǝn], *v.* I. *a.* to colour,
to dye, to stain. II. *r.* to blush.
—er, *m.* (**—ers,** *pl.* **—er**) dyer.
—erei [—'raı], *f.* dyer's trade; dyeing;
dye-house *or* works. **—ung,** *f.* colour-
ing.

Farn [farn], *m.* (**—es,** *pl.* **—e**) fern.
—gebüsch, *n.* brake. **—kraut,** *n.* fern.

Farre ['farǝ], *m.* (**—en,** *pl.* **—(e)n**)
bullock.

Färse ['ferzǝ], *f.* (*pl.* **—n**) heifer, young
cow.

Fasan [fa'za:n], *m.* (**—s, —en,** *pl.* **—en**)
pheasant.

Fasel—n ['fa:zǝln], *v.* I. *a.* to separate
the threads *or* fibres; **sich —n,** to ravel
out. II. *n.* (*aux.* h.) to act *or* talk
foolishly; to dote; to drivel. **—er,** *m.*
(**—ers,** *pl.* **—er**) silly, blundering
fellow. **—ig, —haft,** *adj. & adv.*
fickle, flighty, silly.

Faser ['fa:zǝr], *f.* (*pl.* **—n**) thread,
fibre. **—ig,** *adj.* fibrous.

Faß [fas], *n.* (**—(ss)es,** *pl.* **Fässer**) vat,
tub; cask; **frisch vom —,** drawn from
the wood.

Fass—en ['fasǝn], *v.* I. *a.* to hold, contain; to grasp, seize. II. *r.* to collect
oneself; **sich kurz —en,** to be brief.
gefaßt, *p.p. & adj.* collected, com-

posed. III. *n.* to catch. **—(ß)lich,**
adj. & adv. comprehensible. **—ung,** *f.*
grasp; frame; comprehension; self-
command; style; valve-holder (*Radio,
Elect.*).

Fast [fast], *adv.* almost, nearly.

Fast—en ['fastǝn], I. *v.n.* to fast. II.
subst.n. fasting. III. *pl.* fast; Lent.
—(en)=abend, *m.* Shrove-Tuesday.
—en=mäßig, *adj.* Lenten. **—nacht,** *f.*
Shrove-Tuesday; shrovetide; carnival;
—nacht halten, to keep carnival.

Faul [faul], *adj. & adv.* decayed,
rotten; lazy; **—e Witze,** poor jokes.
—en, *v.n.* (*aux.* f.) to rot, putrefy.
—heit, *f.* slothfulness; idleness.

Faulenz—en ['faulɛntsǝn], *v.n.* (*aux.*
h.) to idle, lounge about. **—er,** *m.*
sluggard, idler.

Faust [faust], *f.* (*pl.* **Fäuste**) fist; **die
geballte —,** clenched fist; **auf eigene
—,** on one's own account.

Februar ['fe:brua:r], *m.* (**—s,** *pl.* **—e**)
February.

Fecht—en ['fɛçtǝn], *ir.v.n.* (*aux.* h.) to
fight; to fence. **—er,** *m.* (**—ers,** *pl.*
—er) fighter; fencer. **—boden,** *m.*
fencing school.

Feder ['fe:dǝr], *f.* (*pl.* **—n**), feather;
pen; spring (*of a machine*). **—busch,**
m. plume; crest. **—messer,** *n.* pen-
knife. **—zeichnung,** *f.* pen-and-ink-
drawing.

Fee [fe:], *f.* (*pl.* **—n**) fairy. **—n=haft,**
adj. fairy-like, magical.

Feg—en ['fe:gǝn], *v.* I. *a.* to cleanse,
scour, sweep; to scold. II. *n.* (*aux.* h.
& f.) to scamper. **—er,** *m.* (**—ers,** *pl.*
—er) sweeper. **—ung,** *f.* cleansing,
sweeping. **—(e)=feuer,** *n.* purgatory.

Fehde ['fe:dǝ], *f.* (*pl.* **—n**) feud. **—brief,**
m. (written) challenge.

Fehl [fe:l], *adv. & sep. prefix,* wrong,
amiss. **—bar,** *adj.* fallible. **—barkeit,**
f. fallibility. **—druck,** *m.* misprint.
—tritt, *m.* stumble, false step.

Fehl—en ['fe:lǝn], *v.* I. *a.* to miss. II.
n. (*aux.* h.) to be absent; to be wanting, deficient; to ail. **—end,** *p. &
adj.* wanting, deficient.

Fehler ['fe:lǝr], *m.* (**—ers,** *pl.* **—er**) fault,
defect; want; error. **—frei,** *or* **—los,**
adj. faultless. **—haft,** *adj.* faulty,
defective. **—haftigkeit,** *f.* faultiness.

Feier ['faıǝr], *f.* (*pl.* **—n**) holiday;
celebration; festival. **—lich,** *adj. &
adv.* solemn; festive. **—lichkeit,** *f.*

solemnity; pomp, ceremony. **—abend,** *m.* eve of a holiday. **—tag,** *m.* holiday.

Feiern ['faɪərn], *v.* I. *n.* (*aux.* **h.**) to make holiday. II. *a.* to celebrate.

1**Feig—e** ['faɪgə], *adj.* cowardly. **—heit,** *f.* cowardice.

2**Feig—e** ['faɪgə], *f.* (*pl.* **—en**) fig.

Feil [faɪl], *adj.* & *adv.* to be sold; venal; mercenary. **—heit,** *f.* venality.

Feil—e ['faɪlə], *f.* (*pl.* **—en**) file. **—bogen,** *m.* steel-saw. **—en,** *v.a.* to file, polish. **gefeilt,** *p.p.* & *adj.* filed, polished, elaborate.

Feilsch—en ['faɪlʃən], *v.a.* & *n.* (*aux.* **h.**) to bargain; to cheapen. **—er,** *m.* (**—ers,** *pl.* **—er**) haggler, bargainer.

Fein [faɪn], *adj.* & *adv.* fine; delicate; nice; beautiful; polite; elegant; fashionable; sly, artful. **—bäckerei,** *f.* fancy bakery. **—heit,** *f.* fineness; refinement; politeness; elegance; cunning. **—gefühl,** *n.* refinement of feeling, tact. **—schmecker,** *m.* (**—s, —**) gourmet.

Feind [faɪnt], I. *adj.* hostile. II. *m.* (**—es,** *pl.* **—e**) enemy, foe. **—in,** *f.* foe, enemy. **—lich,** *adj.* & *adv.* hostile, inimical. **—lichkeit,** *f.* hostility. **—schaft,** *f.* enmity, hatred, hostility. **—schaftlich,** *adj.* & *adv.* hostile. **—selig,** *adj.* & *adv.* hostile; malignant.

Feist [faɪst], *adj.* fat.

Feld [fɛlt], *n.* (**—es,** *pl.* **—er**) field, open land, plain. **—arzt,** *m.* military surgeon. **—bau,** *m.* agriculture, tillage. **—ein** [—'daɪn], **—einwärts** [—'daɪnvɛrts], *adv.* across country. **—gericht,** *n.* court martial. **—herr,** *m.* commander-in-chief; general. **—lazarett,** *n.* ambulance. **—prediger,** *m.* army chaplain. **—wache, —wacht,** *f.* outpost. **—webel,** *m.* sergeant-major. **—zug,** *m.* campaign, expedition.

Felge ['fɛlgə], *f.* (*pl.* **—n**) felloe (*of a wheel*).

Fell [fɛl], *n.* (**—es,** *pl.* **—e**) skin, hide; **ein dickes — haben,** to be thick-skinned.

Felleisen ['fɛlˀaɪzən], *n.* (**—s,** *pl.* **—**) knapsack.

Fels [fɛls], *m.* **—(s)en,** *m.* (**—(s)ens,** *pl.* **—(s)en**) rock, cliff. **—ig,** *adj.* rocky.

Felsen ['fɛlzən] (*in comp.*) **—insel,** *f.* rocky island. **—klippe,** *f.* cliff. **—kluft,** *f.* chasm. **—riß,** *m.* reef of rocks. **—schlucht,** *f.* rocky gorge. **—schicht,** *f.* layer of rock. **—steg,** *m.* rocky path.

Fenn [fɛn], *n.* (**—s,** *pl.* **—e**) fen, swamp.

Fenster ['fɛnstər], *n.* (**—s,** *pl.* **—**) window. **—futter,** *n.* sash. **—laden,** *m.* window-shutter. **—nische,** *f.* embrasure. **—rahmen,** *m.* window-frame. **—scheibe,** *f.* pane of glass.

Ferien ['fe:rɪən], *pl.* vacation, holidays. **—kolonie,** *f.* holiday camp.

Ferkel ['fɛrkəl], *n.* (**—s,** *pl.* **—**) young pig; (*fig.*) dirty fellow.

Fern [fɛrn], *adj.* & *adv.* far, distant. **—e,** *f.* (*pl.* **—en**) remoteness, distance. **—er,** *adj.* & *adv.* farther; moreover. **—rohr,** *n.* telescope. **—schalter,** *m.* distant control (*Radio*). **—sehen,** *n.* television (*Radio*). **—sprecher,** *m.* telephone.

Ferse ['fɛrzə], *f.* (*pl.* **—n**) heel; **—ngeld geben,** to take to one's heels.

Fertig ['fɛrtɪç], *adj.* & *adv.* ready, prepared; complete, perfect; skilful, dexterous. **—keit,** *f.* skill; fluency; completeness.

Fertig—en ['fɛrtɪgən], *v.a.* to make, get ready, finish. **—er,** *m.* (**—ers,** *pl.* **—er**) maker. **—ung,** *f.* making, fabrication.

Fesch [fɛʃ], *adj.* stylish; smart.

Fessel ['fɛsəl], *f.* (*pl.* **—n**) fetter. **—ballon,** *m.* captive balloon. **—bein,** *n.* pastern.

Fesseln ['fɛsəln], *v.a.* to fetter, chain; (*fig.*) to captivate.

1**Fest** [fɛst], I. *adj.*, *adv.* & *sep. prefix,* firm, stable; solid, hard; fixed; permanent. II. *suff.* (*in comp.*); **sattel—,** firm in the saddle. **—gebannt,** *adj.* spell-bound. **—nehmen,** *ir.v.a.* to seize, arrest. **—setzen,** *v.a.* to fix (*a day, etc.*); to settle. **—stellen,** *v.a.* to fix, settle.

2**Fest** [fɛst], *n.* (**—es,** *pl.* **—e**) festival; holiday; feast; **ein — begehen,** to celebrate a festival. **—lich,** *adj.* & *adv.* festive. **—lichkeit,** *f.* festivity, solemnity. **—abend,** *m.* eve of a holiday. **—essen,** *n.* banquet. **—geber,** *m.* host. **—mahl,** *n.*, **—schmaus,** *m.* banquet, feast. **—spiel,** festival play. **—tag,** *m.* holiday.

Fest—igen ['fɛstɪgən], *v.a.* to make fast *or* firm. **—igkeit,** *f.* firmness, fixedness; steadiness; constancy. **—ung,**

f. fortress; stronghold. **—ungs=arrest,** *m.* imprisonment in a fortress.

Fetisch ['fe:tɪʃ], *m.* (—(e)s, *pl.* —e) fetish.

Fett [fɛt], I. *n.* (—es) fat; grease. II. *adj.* & *adv.* fat. **—ig,** *adj.* & *adv.* fatty, greasy.

Fetzen ['fɛtsən], *m.* (—s, *pl.* —) rag, tatter, shred.

Feucht [fɔʏçt], *adj.* moist, damp. **—heit,** *f.* humidity, damp. **—igkeit,** *f.* moisture. **—igkeits=messer,** *m.* hygrometer.

Feuer ['fɔʏər], *n.* (—s, *pl.* —) fire; ardour, passion. **—ig, feurig,** *adj.* fiery; ardent. **—berg,** *m.* volcano. **—glocke,** *f.* alarm-bell. **—lösch= apparat,** *m.* fire-extinguisher. **—rad,** *n.* Catherine-wheel. **—rot,** *adj.* red as fire. **—s=brunst,** *f.* fire, conflagration. **—schaden,** *m.* damage caused by fire. **—stein,** *m.* flint. **—ung,** *f.* firing; fuel. **—versicherung,** *f.* fire-insurance. **—=versicherungs=police,** *f.* fire-policy. **—wehr,** *f.* fire-brigade. **—werk,** *n.* firework.

Feuern ['fɔʏərn], *v.* I. *a.* to fire; to kindle. II. *n.* to burn, glow.

Fibel ['fi:bəl], *f.* (*pl.* —n) spelling-book, primer.

Fiber ['fi:bər], *f.* (*pl.* —n) fibre.

Ficht—e ['fɪçtə], *f.* (*pl.* —en) common spruce. **—en,** *adj.* pine. **—en=harz,** *m.* common resin. **—en=holz,** *n.* pine-wood. **—en=zapfen,** *m.* pine-cone.

Fideikommiß [fi:deiko'mɪs], *m.* (—(ß)es, *pl.* —(ß)e) entail.

Fidel [fi'de:l], *adj.* & *adv.* merry, jolly.

Fieber ['fi:bər], *n.* (—s, *pl.* —) fever. **—haft,** *adj.* & *adv.* feverish. **—haftig= keit,** *f.* feverishness. **—isch,** *adj.* & *adv.* feverish. **—n,** *v.n.* (*aux.* h.) to have a fever. **—rinde,** *f.* quinine. **—traum,** *m.* feverish dream.

Fiedel ['fi:dəl], *f.* (*pl.* —n) fiddle. **—er, (Fiedler,)** *m.* (—ers, *pl.* —er) fiddler. **—n,** *v.a.* (*aux.* h.) to fiddle. **—bogen,** *m.* fiddle-bow, bow.

Figur [fi'gu:r], *f.* (*pl.* —en) figure; trope.

Filet [fi'le:], *n.* (—s, *pl.* —s, —en) netting, net-work; fillet (*of meat*).

Filiale [fili'a:lə], *f.* (*pl.* —n) branch establishment or office.

Film [fɪlm], *m.* (—s, *pl.* —e) film (*Phot.*).

Filz [fɪlts], *m.* (—es, *pl.* —e) felt. **—er,**

m. (—ers, *pl.* —er) miser, niggard. **—ig,** *adj.* of felt; stingy; sordid.

Finanz [fi'nants], *f.* (*usually in the pl.* **Finanzen**) finances. **—kammer,** *f.* treasury board.

Findel ['fɪndəl], *pref.* (*in comp.*=) foundling. **—kind,** *n.* foundling.

Find—en ['fɪndən], *ir.v.* I. *a.* to find; to think, consider. II. *r.* to find oneself; to submit to, comply with. **—er,** *m.* (—ers, *pl.* —er) finder, discoverer. **—ig,** *adj.* resourceful; ingenious. **—igkeit,** *f.* resourcefulness; sharpness, shrewdness, ingenuity. **—ung,** *f.* finding; discovery.

Finger ['fɪŋər], *m.* (—s, *pl.* —) finger. **—brett,** *n.* keys (*of a piano*). **—hut,** *m.* thimble. **—n,** *v.a.* & *n.* (*aux.* h.) to finger.

Fingier—en [fɪŋ'gi:rən], *v.a.* to feign, forge, invent. **—t,** *p.p.* & *adj.* assumed, fictitious.

Fink [fɪŋk], **Fink—e,** *m.* (—en, *pl.* —en) finch.

Finne ['fɪnə], *f.* (*pl.* —n) fin.

Finster ['fɪnstər], *adj.* & *adv.* dark; gloomy. **—nis,** *f.* darkness.

Firma ['fɪrma], *f.* (*pl.* **Firmen**) firm, business.

Firnis ['fɪrnɪs], *m.* (—(ß)es, *pl.* —(ß)e) varnish. **—(ß)en,** *v.a.* to varnish.

Fisch [fɪʃ], *m.* (—es, *pl.* —e) fish. **—= artig,** *adj.* fishlike. **—er,** *m.* (—ers, *pl.* —er) fisher, fisherman. **—er=boot,** *n.* fishing boat. **—er=dorf,** *n.* fishing village. **—erei** [—'rai], *f.* fishery; fishing. **—erin,** *f.* fisherwoman, fisherman's wife *or* daughter. **—er=hütte,** *f.* fisherman's hut. **—n,** *v.a.* & *n.* (*aux.* h.) to fish. **—fang,** *m.* fishing; fishery. **—gräte,** *f.* bone of a fish. **—hälter,** *m.* fish-pond. **—töder,** *m.* bait for fishes. **—laich,** *m.* spawn.

Fitt—ich ['fɪtɪç] (—ichs, *pl.* —iche), **—ig,** *m.* (—igs, *pl.* —ige) wing, pinion.

¹**Fix** [fɪks], *adj.* & *adv.* quick, nimble; **— und fertig,** quite ready.

²**Fix** [fɪks], *adj.* & *adv.* firm, fixed.

Flach [flax], *adj.* & *adv.* flat, plain, level. **—heit,** *f.* flatness; insipidity. **—en,** *v.a.* to flatten. **—ung,** *f.* levelling.

Fläche ['flɛçə], *f.* (*pl.* --en) flatness; plane surface. **—n=inhalt,** *m.* area. **—n=lautsprecher,** *m.* cabinet-speaker (*Radio*).

Flachs [flaks], *m.* (—(ſ)es, *pl.* —(ſ)e) flax. —**ähnlich,** *adj.* flaxen. —**ſamen,** *m.* linseed.

Flackern [ˈflakərn], *v.n.* (*aux.* h.) to flare, flicker.

Flagge [ˈflagə], *f.* (*pl.* —n) flag.

Flamme [ˈflamə], *f.* (*pl.* —n) flame. —n, *v.n.* (*aux.* h.) to flame, blaze.

Flanell [flaˈnɛl], *m.* (—s, *pl.* —e) flannel.

Flanke [ˈflankə], *f.* (*pl.* —n) flank, side.

Flasche [ˈflaʃə], *f.* (*pl.* —n); *dim.* **Fläsch=chen,** *n.* flask, phial, bottle.

Flatter=er [ˈflatərər], *m.* (—ers, *pl.* —er) inconstant person. —**haft,** *adj.* & *adv.* fickle. —**haftigkeit,** *f.* inconstancy. —**geiſt,** —**ſinn,** *m.* inconstancy. —n, *v.n.* (*aux.* h. & ſ.) to flutter; to be unsteady.

Flau [flau], *adj.* & *adv.* feeble; insipid. —**heit,** —**igkeit,** *f.* flatness; dullness, deadness (*of trade*).

Flaum [flaum], *m.* (—es, *pl.* —e, —en) down. —**ig,** *adj.* & *adv.* downy. —**bart,** *m.* stripling. —**feder,** *f.* down.

Flaus [flaus], *m.* (—(ſ)es, *pl.* —(ſ)e) pilot cloth.

Flecht=e [ˈflɛçtə], *f.* (*pl.* —en) twist, braid; plait; basket-work. —**en,** *ir.v.a.* to plait; to wreathe, twine together. —**korb,** *m.* wicker basket. —**rohr,** *n.* cane-plaiting.

Fleck [flɛk], *m.* (—(e)s, *pl.* —e) piece (*of ground*); plot; flaw; blot; patch; **wir kommen nicht vom** —, we don't get along. —**chen,** *n.* (—chens, *pl.* —chen) speckle. —**en,** *v.a.* to spot, stain; to patch.

Fleder=n [ˈfledərn], *v.a.* to dust with a feather-brush. —**maus,** *f.* bat. —**wiſch,** *m.* feather-broom.

Flegel [ˈfleːgəl], *m.* (—s, *pl.* —) flail. —**ei** [—ˈlaɪ], *f.* rudeness, coarseness; insolence. —**haft,** *adj.* & *adv.* clownish, rude. —**jahre,** *pl.* years of indiscretion, hobbledehoyhood.

Flehen [ˈfleːən], I. *v.a.* & *n.* (*aux.* h.) to implore. II. *subst.n.* prayers; supplication. —**d,** *p.* & *adj.* suppliant, imploring. —**tlich,** *adj.* & *adv.* suppliant, imploring.

Fleiſch [flaɪʃ], *n.* (—es) flesh; pulp (*of fruit*). —**ig,** *adj.* & *adv.* fleshy. —**igkeit,** *f.* fleshiness. —**lich,** *adj.* & *adv.* fleshly, carnal, sensual. —**lich=keit,** *f.* sensuality. —**bank,** *f.* butcher's stall, shambles. —**brühe,** *f.* broth,

gravy. —**freſſend,** *adj.* carnivorous. —**halle,** *f.* meat-market.

Fleiß [flaɪs], *m.* (—es) diligence, industry. —**ig,** *adj.* & *adv.* industrious.

Flick—en [ˈflɪkən], I. *v.a.* to patch, mend. II. *m.* (—ens, *pl.* —er) patch.

Flieder [ˈfliːdər], *m.* (—s) elder.

Flieg—e [ˈfliːgə], *f.* (*pl.* —en) fly. —**en,** I. *ir.v.n.* (*aux.* ſ. & h.) to fly. II. *subst.n.* flight. —**end,** *p.* & *adj.* flying. —**en=ſchrank,** *m.* meat-safe, larder. —**er,** *m.* (—ers, *pl.* —er) flyer, aviator. —**er=angriff,** *m.* aerial attack. —**erin,** *f.* airwoman. —**er=kampf,** *m.* aerial combat.

Fliehen [ˈfliːən], *ir.v.* I. *n.* (*aux.* ſ.) to flee. II. *a.* to shun, avoid.

Flieſe [ˈfliːzə], *f.* (*pl.* —n) paving tile.

Fließ [fliːs], *also* **Blies,** *n.* (—es, *pl.* —e) fleece.

Fließ—en [ˈfliːsər], *ir.v.n.* (*aux.* h. & ſ.) to flow. —**end,** *p.* *adj.* & *adv.* flowing; fluent.

Flimmern [ˈflɪmərn], *v.n.* (*aux.* h.) to glitter, glisten.

Flink [flɪnk], *adj.* & *adv.* brisk, agile; lively. —**heit,** *f.* nimbleness.

Flint—e [ˈflɪntə], *f.* (*pl.* —en) gun, musket, rifle. —**en=kolben,** *m.* butt-end of a gun.

Flitter [ˈflɪtər], *m.* (—s, *pl.* —) tinsel. —**haft,** —**ig,** *adj.* & *adv.* tinsel; showy. —**wochen,** *pl.* honeymoon.

Flock—e [ˈflɔkə], *f.* (*pl.* —en) flake (*of snow*); flock (*of wool, hair, etc.*). —**ig,** *adj.* & *adv.* flaky.

Floh [floː], *m.* (—s, *pl.* **Flöhe**) flea.

Flor [floːr], I. *m.* (—s, *pl.* —e) gauze; crape; veil. II. *m.* (—s) & *f.* blossoming; bloom.

Floskel [ˈflɔskəl], *f.* (*pl.* —n) rhetorical flourish.

Floß [floːs], *n.* & *m.* (—(ß)es, *pl.* **Flöße**) raft. —**graben,** *m.* canal. —**holz,** *n.* floated timber.

Flöße—n [ˈfløːsən], *v.a.* to float. —**r,** *m.* (—rs, *pl.* —r) raftsman.

Flöte [ˈfløːtə], *f.* (*pl.* —n) flute. —**n,** *v.a.* & *n.* (*aux.* h.) to play on the flute.

Flott [flɔt], I. *adj.* & *adv.* buoyant; gay, jolly; —**leben,** to lead a gay life. II. *adv.* afloat.

Flott—e [ˈflɔtə], *f.* (*pl.* —en) fleet, navy. —**ille** [—ˈtɪljə], *f.* (*pl.* —illen) flotilla, squadron.

Fluch [fluːx], *m.* (—es, *pl.* **Flüche**)

curse. —en, v. I. n. (aux. h.) to curse, swear. II. a. to curse, execrate.

Flucht [fluxt], f. (pl. —en) escape; flight (of birds).

Flücht—en ['flyçtən], v.r. & n. (aux. f.) to flee. —ig, adj. & adv. flying, fugitive, runaway; (Chem.) volatile; ein —iger Mensch, a hasty, inconstant person. —ling, m. (lings, pl. —linge) fugitive; deserter.

Flug [flu:k], m: (—es, pl. Flüge) flying; flight, soaring. —boot, n. flying-boat. —gast, m. air-passenger. —hafen, m. aerodrome. —halle, f. hangar. —platz, m. aerodrome. —schrift, f. pamphlet. —zeug, n. aeroplane. —zeug=führer, m. air-pilot. —zeug=rumpf, m. body of aeroplane.

Flügel ['fly:gəl], m. (—s, pl. —) wing. —ig, adj. & adv. winged.

Flugs [flu:ks], adv. hastily, quickly, at once.

Flunder ['flundər], m. (—s, pl. —) flounder.

Flur [flu:r], I. f. (pl. —en) fields, meadows; common. II. m. (—es, pl. —e, Flüre) paved floor; entrance-hall.

Fluß [flus], m. (—(ss)es, pl. Flüsse) river.

Flüssig ['flysiç], adj. & adv. fluid. —keit, f. fluidity.

Flüster—er ['flystərər], m. (—ers, pl. —er) whisperer. —n, v.a. & n. (aux. h.) to whisper.

Flut [flu:t], f. (pl. —en) flood; waves; flood-tide; die Sündflut, the Flood. —en, v.n. (aux. h.) to flood. —zeit, f. high water.

Fock—e ['fokə], f. (pl. —en) fore-sail. —mast, m. fore-mast.

Fohl—e ['fo:lə], f. (pl. —en) filly. —en, n. (—ens, pl. —en) foal.

Föhre ['fø:rə], f. (pl. —n) pine, Scots fir.

Folg—e ['folgə], f. (pl. —en) succession; consequence; continuation; retinue. —lich, I. adv. & conj. consequently, therefore, accordingly, then. II. adj. future, subsequent. III. adv. afterwards, subsequently. —sam, adj. & adv. obedient, tractable, docile. —samkeit, f. obedience. —en, v.n. (aux. f., dat.) to follow, wait on. —end, p. & adj. subsequent, next. —endermaßen, adv. as follows, in the following manner. —erung, f. inference, deduction. —ezeit, f. time to come; posterity.

Folter ['foltər], f. (pl. —n) rack; torture; auf die — legen, to put to the rack. —kammer, f. torture chamber. —n, v.a. to put to the rack, torture. —ung, f. torture.

Förder—er ['fordərər], m. (—ers, pl. —er), —erin, f. furtherer, promoter. —lich, adj. & adv. furthering; promotive (of); conducive (to). —n, v.a. to further, promote, advance. —ung, f. furtherance, help.

Forder—n ['fordərn], v.a. to demand, ask; to challenge; zu viel —n, to overcharge. —ung, f. demand; claim; challenge.

Forelle [fo'rɛlə], f. (pl. —n) trout.

Forke ['forkə], f. (pl. —n) pitchfork, large fork.

Form [form], f. (pl. —en) form; figure; make, fashion. —al [—'ma:l], adj. & adv. formal. —alien [—'ma:liən], pl. formalities. —alist [—'lɪst], m. (—alisten, pl. —alisten) formalist. —alität [—i'tɛt], f. (pl. —alitäten) formality. —el, f. (pl. —eln) formula. —en, v.a. to form, mould. —enwesen, n. formality; ceremoniousness. —los, adj. shapeless; informal.

Förm—ig ['formiç], suff. (in comp.=) -formed, -shaped. —lich, adj. & adv. formal, ceremonious. —lichkeit, f. formality.

Formulieren [formu'li:rən], v.a. to formulate.

Forsch—en ['forʃən], I. v.a. & n. (aux. h.) to search out, search; to inquire; to investigate. —er, m. (—ers, pl. —er) searcher; investigator. —ung, f. investigation, inquiry; research.

Forst [forst], m. (—es, pl. —e) forest. —akademie, f. school of forestry.

Förster ['forstər], m. (—s, pl. —) forest-keeper; ranger.

Fort [fort], adv. & sep. prefix, away, off, gone; forward, onward; continuously. —an [fort'?an], adv. onward; henceforth. —bilden, v.r. to continue one's studies. —dauernd, p. & adj. lasting, permanent. —fahren, ir.v.n. (aux. f.) to drive off or away, depart; (aux. h.) (mit or in einer S. —) to continue, proceed, go on. —führen, v.a. (eine S.) to carry or lead on, extend. —führung, f. continuation; conveyance. —rücken, I. v.a. & n. (aux. f.) to advance. II. subst.n. advancement. —rückend, p. & adj. progressive.

—schaffen, v.a. to get out of the way. —schaffung, f. removal. —schreitend, p. & adj. progressive. —schritt, m. progress; advance. —setzen, v.a. to continue; to pursue. —setzung, f. continuation. —während, p., adj. & adv. lasting, continuous, permanent.

Fossil [fɔ'si:l], n. (—s, pl. —ien) fossil.

Fracht [fraxt], f. (pl. —en) freight, cargo. —bar, adj. & adv. transportable. —brief, —zettel, m. bill of lading; way-bill. —en, v.a. & n. (aux. h.) to freight, load. —frei, adj. & adv. carriage-free.

Frack [frak], m. (—es, pl. —s and Fräde) dress-coat.

Frage ['fra:gə], f. (pl. —n) question; eine — stellen, to ask a question.

Frag—en ['fra:gən], reg. & (less good) irreg. v.a. & n. (aux. h.) to ask, inquire. —end, p.adj. & adv. interrogative; interrogatory. —er, m. (—ers, pl. —er) questioner. —lich, adj. & adv. questionable; doubtful. —lichkeit, f. questionableness. —(e)=zeichen, n. mark of interrogation.

Frakt—ion [fraktsɪ'o:n], f. (pl. —ionen) fraction. —ur=schrift [—'tur-ʃrıft], f. German or Old English type.

Frank [frank], adj. & adv. free; frank, open. —ieren [—'ki:rən], v.a. to send post-paid. —o, adv. post-paid; carriage-paid. —o=brief, m. post-paid letter. —o=spesen, pl. free of cost, no charges.

Franz—ose [fran'tso:zə], m. (—osen, pl. —osen) Frenchman. —ösin [—'tsø:zın], f. Frenchwoman. —ösisch [—tsø:zıʃ], adj. French.

Fratze [fratsə], f. (pl. —n) grimace; caricature; whim.

Frau [frau], f. (pl. —en) woman; wife. —en=haft, adj. & adv. woman-like, womanly. —en=bewegung, f. feminist movement. —en=stand, m. wifehood; womanhood. —en=zimmer, n. female, woman.

Fräulein ['frɔylaın], n. (—s, pl. —) young lady; Miss.

Frech [freç], adj. & adv. shameless, bold, insolent. —heit, f. insolence, impudence, shamelessness.

Fregatte [fre'gatə], f. (pl. —n) frigate.

Frei [fraı], adj. & adv. free (von, of); — ins Haus, free delivery; —e Künste, liberal arts. —e, n. the open air; open space. —heit, f. freedom.

—lich, adv. to be sure, certainly, truly, by all means. —ballon, m. balloon (without motor). —gebig, adj. liberal, generous. —gebigkeit, f. liberality, generosity. —geist, m. freethinker. —herr, m. baron. —=herrin, f. baroness. —mut, m. frankness. —mütig, adj. & adv. candid, frank. —mütigkeit, f. ingenuousness. —schütz(e), m. marksman who uses charmed bullets. —sinn, m. liberality of mind. —sinnig, adj. enlightened. —sprechen, ir.v.a. (sep.) to acquit, absolve. —willig, adj. voluntary. —willige(r), m. volunteer.

Frei—en ['fraıən], v.a. to woo, court. —er, m. (—ers, pl. —er) wooer, suitor.

Freitag ['fraıta:k], m. (—s, pl. —e) Friday.

Fremd [fremt], adj. & adv. strange, foreign; ich bin hier —, I am a stranger in this place. —e, f. foreign country. —e(r), m. foreigner; stranger. —heit, f. foreignness, strangeness. —ling, m. (—linges, pl. —linge) stranger, foreigner, alien. —artig, adj. strange. —artigkeit, f. oddness. —herrschaft, f. foreign rule.

Fressen ['fresən], I. ir.v.a. & n. (aux. h.) to eat (of beasts). II. subst.n. act of feeding; food (for beasts).

Freud—e ['frɔydə], f. (pl. —en) joy, gladness; delight. —en=botschaft, f. glad tidings. —ig, adj. & adv. joyful. —igkeit, f. joyousness.

Freu—en ['frɔyən], I. v.a. & (usually) imp. to make glad or give pleasure to; es —t mich (daß), I am glad (that). II. v.r. to rejoice, be glad (über eine S., at a thing).

Freund [frɔynt], m. (—es, pl. —e) friend. —in, f. female friend; lady-love. —lich, adj. friendly, kind; affable. —lichkeit, f. kindness; pleasantness; affability. —schaft, f. friendship. —schaftlich, adj. friendly. —los, adj. friendless.

Frevel ['fre:fəl], m. (—s, pl. —thaten) misdeed. —haft, adj. & adv. wicked; mischievous; malicious. —haftigkeit, f. wickedness; wantonness. —tat, f. outrage.

Fried—e ['fri:də], m. (—ens, pl. —ens=schlüsse) peace; tranquillity. —lich, adj. & adv. peaceable, peaceful. —lichkeit, f. peacefulness. —ens=

ſtifter, *m.* peacemaker. **—ens=ſtörer,** *m.* disturber of the peace; rioter. **—ens=vertrag,** *m.* (**—ens=vertrages,** *pl.* **—ens=verträge**) peace-treaty. **—= fertig,** *adj.* peaceable.

Friedhof ['fri:dho:f], *m.* (**—(e)s,** *pl.* **Friedhöfe**) churchyard, cemetery.

Frieren ['fri:rən], I. *ir.v.n.* (*aux.* h. & ſ.) to freeze. II. *ir.v.a.* & *imp.* to freeze, to chill. III. *subst.n.* freezing.

Friſch [frɪʃ], *adj.* & *adv.* fresh; cool. **auf —er Tat,** in the very act. **—e,** *f.,* **—heit,** *f.* freshness.

Friſt [frɪst], *f.* (*pl.* **—en**) space of time; period.

Froh [fro:], *adj.* & *adv.* glad, joyous, joyful; gay, mirthful. **—locken,** I. *v.n.* (*aux.* h.) to exult. II. *subst.n.* exultation, triumph. **—mut,** *m.,* **—ſinn,** *m.* cheerfulness, happy disposition. **—mütig,** **—ſinnig,** *adj.* & *adv.* cheerful, joyful, happy.

Fröhlich ['frø:lɪç], *adj.* & *adv.* joyous, joyful; gay. **—keit,** *f.* joyousness; gaiety; gladness.

Fromm [frɔm], *adj.* & *adv.* honest, excellent, worthy; devout. **—en,** *v.n.* (*aux.* h., *dat.*) to advantage, avail, profit; **was, wozu —t es dir?** what does it profit you?

Frömmigkeit ['frœmɪçkaɪt], *f.* piety, devoutness; kindness.

Front—(e) ['frɔnt(ə)], *f.* (*pl.* **—en**) front.

Froſch [frɔʃ], *m.* (**—es,** *pl.* **Fröſche**) frog; handle of the violin-bow.

Froſt [frɔst], *m.* (**—es,** *pl.* **Fröſte**) frost; feverish shivering. **—ig,** *adj.* & *adv.* frosty. **—igkeit,** *f.* frigidity. **—beule,** *f.* chilblain. **—fieber,** *n.* fever and ague.

Fröſteln ['frœstəln], I. *v.a.* & *imp.* to make chilly. II. *v.n.* & *imp.* to shiver (*with cold*).

Frucht [frʊxt], *f.* (*pl.* **Früchte**) fruit; crop. **—bar,** *adj.* & *adv.* fruitful, fertile; prolific. **—barkeit,** *f.* fruitfulness, fertility; fecundity. **—los,** *adj.* fruitless; barren; useless. **—loſigkeit,** *f.* fruitlessness.

Früh, Frühe ['fry:(ə)], *adj.* & *adv.* early; **heute —,** this morning; **— reif,** precocious. **—er,** *adj.* & *adv.* (*comp. of* früh) earlier, sooner; prior; former; formerly. **—ling,** *m.* (**—lings,** *pl.* **—linge**) spring. **—ſtück,** *n.* breakfast. **—ſtücken,** *v.a.* & *n.* to breakfast.

—zeitig, *adj.* & *adv.* early; in good time.

Fuchs [fʊks], *m.* (**—(ſ)es,** *pl.* **Füchſe**) fox; chestnut horse; freshman (*stud. slang*).

Fuchtel ['fʊxtəl], *f.* (*pl.* **—n**) rod, ferule.

Fuder ['fu:dər], *n.* (**—s,** *pl.* **—**) load; large measure (*for wine, grain, etc.*).

Fug [fu:k], *m.* (**—es**) suitableness, convenience; reason; right. **—e** ['fu:gə], *f.* (*Mus.*) fugue.

Füg—en ['fy:gən], *v.* I. *a.* to fit together, join, unite. II. *r.* to accommodate oneself to. III. *r.* & *imp.* to come to pass, happen; coincide. **—ig,** *adj.* & *adv.* fit, suitable. **—lich,** *adj.* & *adv.* fit, suitable, convenient. **—ſam,** *adj.* & *adv.* adaptive; pliant, yielding. **—ſamkeit,** *f.* pliancy; submission. **—ung,** *f.* fitting together, joining; arrangement; submission, resignation. **—e=wort,** *n.* conjunction.

Fühlbar ['fy:lba:r], *adj.* & *adv.* sensible; perceptible. **—keit,** *f.* sensibility, susceptibility; perceptibility.

Fühl—en ['fy:lən], *v.a.* & *n.* (*aux.* h.) to feel, perceive by the organs of sensation. **—end,** *p.* & *adj.* sensitive; feeling; susceptible. **—er,** *m.* (**—ers,** *pl.* **—er**) feeler.

Fuhr—e ['fu:rə], *f.* carrying, conveyance; vehicle. **—lohn,** *n.* freight, fare. **—mann,** *m.* driver, coachman. **—= ſtraße,** *f.,* **—weg,** *m.* highway, carriage-road. **—wagen,** *m.* freightwaggon. **—werk,** *n.* vehicle, carriage.

Führ—en ['fy:rən], *v.a.* to carry, convey; to conduct, guide; to manage. **—er,** *m.* (**—ers,** *pl.* **—er**) leader, conductor; driver; pilot. **—er=gondel,** *f.* (*pl.* **—n**) control-cabin (*aircraft*). **—er=ſitz,** *m.* pilot's cockpit. **—ung,** *f.* leading, conducting; behaviour; guidance; management.

Füll—e ['fylə], *f.* fullness, abundance. **—en,** *v.a.* to fill. **—horn,** *n.* horn of plenty. **—ung,** *f.* filling (up); contents.

Füllen ['fylən], *n.* (**—s,** *pl.* **—**) foal.

Fund [fʊnt], *m.* (**—es,** *pl.* **—e**) finding; discovery, invention.

Fünf [fynf], *num. adj.* five. **—tens,** *adv.* fifthly, in the fifth place. **—zig,** *num. adj.* fifty. **—zehn,** *num. adj.* fifteen. **—ed,** *n.* pentagon.

Funk—e ['fʊŋkə], *m.* (**—en,** *pl.* **—en**), **—en,** *m.* (**—ens,** *pl.* **—en**) spark; flash.

—el=neu, adj., —el=nagelneu, adj. brand-new, spick and span. —= empfang, m. wireless reception. —en= telegrafie, f. wireless telegraphy. —er, m. radio-operator. —röhre, f. wireless valve. —fender, m. broadcaster. —fpruch, m. wireless message. —station, f. wireless station. —wefen, n. broadcasting in general.

Funkeln ['fuŋkəln], I. v.n. (aux. h.) to sparkle, glitter. II. subst.n. sparkling.

Für [fy:r, fyr], prep. (with acc.) for; instead of; in favour of; Tag — Tag, day after day; ich — meine Perfon, as for me; an und — fich, in itself. —bitte, f. intercession. —lieb, adv.; —lieb nehmen, to be content with, put up with.

Furch=e ['furçə], f. (pl. —en) furrow; wrinkle. —ig, adj. & adv. furrowed.

Furcht [furçt], f. (no pl.) fear, terror. —bar, adj. & adv. frightful, dreadful. —barkeit, f. terribleness. —fam, adj. & adv. timid, faint-hearted. —famkeit, f. timidity.

Fürcht=en ['fyrçtən], v.r. to be afraid; to stand in fear (vor, of). —erlich, adj. & adv. fearful, frightful, horrible.

Fürder ['fyrdər], I. adj. further, onwards. II. adv. henceforward; further.

Fürst [fyrst], m. (—en, pl. —en) prince, sovereign. —en=tum, n. (—entums, pl. Fürstentümer) principality. —in, f. princess. —lich, adj. & adv. princely.

Fürwort ['fy:rvɔrt], n. (—(e)s, pl. Fürwörter) pronoun.

Füfilier [fyzi'li:r], m. (—s, pl. —e) fusilier. —en, v.a.; einen —en, to shoot a person (Mil.).

Fuß [fu:s], m. (—es, pl. Füße) foot; auf grossem —e leben, to live in grand style; auf freien — fetzen, to set at liberty. —boden, m. floor; ground; flooring. —dede, f. carpet. —tritt, m. kick; step.

¹Futter ['futər], n. (—s) fodder, provender. —n, v.a. to feed. —ung, f. fodder; food.

²Futter ['futər], n. (—s, pl. —) case; sheath; lining. —n, v.a. to line. —ung, f. lining. —al [futə'ra:l], n. (—als, pl. —ale) case; box; sheath.

Futur=ifch [fu'tu:rif], adj. future. —um, n. (—ums, pl. Futura) future tense.

G

G, g [ge:], n. G, g; G, sol (Mus.); der — Schlüffel, the treble clef; — Dur, G major; — moll, G minor.

Gabe ['ga:bə], f. (pl. —n) gift. —= fpender, m. almsgiver.

Gabel ['ga:bəl], f. (pl. —n) fork. —frühftüd, n. light luncheon. —ig, adj. & adv. forked.

Gad—eln ['gakəln], —ern [—ərn], —fen [—sən], I. v.n. (aux. h.) to cackle. II. subst.n. cackling.

Gaff—en ['gafən], v.n. (aux. h.) to gape, stare. —er, m. (—ers, pl. —er). —erin, f. starer, gaper.

Gähn—en ['gɛ:nən], I. v.n. (aux. h.) to yawn. II. subst.n. yawning. —er, m. (—ers, pl. —er) yawner.

Galanterie [galantə'ri:], f. (pl. —n) gallantry, courtesy. —waren, pl. fancy goods.

Galeere [ga'le:rə], f. (pl. —n) galley.

Galgen ['galgən], m. (—s, pl. —) gallows. —frift, f. short delay, respite. —humor, m. grim humour.

Gall—e ['galə], f. (pl. —en) gall; rancour, spite. —ig, adj. & adv. bilious; choleric; bitter. —apfel, m. gallnut. —(en)=fucht, f. jaundice.

Galopp [ga'lɔp], m. (—s, pl. —e & —s) gallop. —ieren, v.n. (aux. h.) to gallop.

Galvan—ifch [gal'va:nif], adj. galvanic. —ifieren [—'zi:erən], v.a. to galvanize. —ifierung, f. galvanization. —ismus [—'nismus], m. galvanism.

Gamafchen [ga'mafən], pl. gaiters. —dienft, m. pedantry (as to uniform, etc.) in military matters.

Gang [gaŋ], m. (—es, pl. Gänge) going; progress; carriage; gait; walk, alley, avenue; in — bringen, to set in motion. —bar, adj. customary; current.

Gans [gans], f. (pl. Gänfe) goose. Gänschen, n. (—s, pl. —) gosling.

Gänfe— ['gɛnzə] (in compounds) —= haft, adj. & adv. stupid. —rich, m. (—richs, pl. —riche) gander. —marfch, m. goose-step. —schmalz, n. goose-dripping. —wein, m. Adam's ale, water.

Ganz [gants], I. adj. whole, entire; all; complete; excellent. II. adv. quite; wholly, altogether; perfectly. — und gar nicht, not at all; im —en, on the whole.

Gänzlich ['gɛntslɪç], *adj. & adv.* complete.

Gar [ga:r], I. *adj. (indec.)* finished, complete, ready. II. *adv. & part.* quite, entirely, fully, absolutely; very, even; at all; perhaps; I hope; — **keiner**, nobody at all; — **nicht**, not at all, by no means; — **nichts**, nothing at all. —**aus**, I. *adj.* completely finished. II. *m. (& n.) (indec.)* utter ruin; end; death.

Garbe ['garbə], *f. (pl.* —**n**) sheaf.

Gard—**e** ['gardə], *f. (pl.* —**en**) guard; guards. —**ist** [—'dɪst], *m.* (—**iften**, *pl.* —**iften**) guardsman.

Garderobe [gardə'ro:bə], *f.* wardrobe.

Gardine [gar'di:nə], *f. (pl.* —**n**) curtain.

Gär—**en** ['gɛːrən], *ir.v.* I. *n. (aux. h. & f.)* to ferment. —**ung**, *f.* fermentation.

Garn [garn], *n.* (—**s**, *pl.* —**e**) yarn; thread; net; snare. —**en**, *adj.* of thread. —**knäuel**, *m.* ball of thread.

Garnifon [garni'zo:n], *f. (pl.* —**en**) garrison.

Garftig ['garstɪç], *adj. & adv.* filthy, foul. —**keit**, *f.* filthiness; nastiness.

Garten ['gartən], *m.* (—**s**, *pl.* **Gärten**) garden. —**bau**, *m.* horticulture. —**haus**, *n.* summer-house.

Gärtner ['gɛrtnər], *m.* (—**s**, *pl.* —) gardener. —**in**, *f.* gardener's wife; female gardener. —**ifch**, *adj. & adv.* horticultural. —**n**, *v.n. (aux. h.)* to garden.

Gas [ga:s], *n.* (—(*f*)**es**, *pl.* —(*f*)**e**) gas. —**artig**, *adj.* gaseous. —**beleuchtung**, *f.* lighting by gas. —**brenner**, *m.* burner. —**messer**, *m.* (gas-) meter.

Gasse ['gasə], *f. (pl.* —**n**) street; lane. —**nbube**, —**njunge**, *m.* street-arab. —**nhauer**, *m.* street song.

Gaft [gast], *m.* (—**es**, *pl.* **Gäfte**) guest, visitor; **jemanden zu** —**e bitten**, to invite someone. —**freund**, *m.* intimate friend; guest; host. —**freund(schaft)- lich**, *adj.* hospitable. —**freundlichkeit**, *f.* hospitality. —**freundschaft**, *f.* hospitality. —**haus**, *n.* restaurant; inn; tavern. —**hof**, *m.* hotel; inn; —**hof- besitzer**, innkeeper. —**mahl**, *n.* entertainment, banquet. —**wirt**, *m.* innkeeper. —**wirtin**, *f.* hostess. —**wirt- schaft**, *f.* inn.

Gatt—**e** ['gatə], *m.* (—**en**, *pl.* —**en**) husband; consort; (*pl.*) married people. —**en**, *v.a.* to match. —**in**, *f.* spouse, wife.

Gatter ['gatər], *n.* (—**s**, *pl.* —) grating, lattice.

Gattung ['gatʊŋ], *f.* kind, class; species; race, breed; gender; style.

Gau [gau], *m. (& n.)* (—**es**, *pl.* —**e**) district; country (*as opp. to city*).

Gauch [gaux], *m.* (—**es**, *pl.* —**e & Gäuche**) fool.

Gaukel—**ei** [gaukə'lai], *f. (pl.* —**eien**) juggling; trick, imposture. —**haft**, —**ig**, *adj. & adv.* juggling; delusive. —**bild**, *n.* illusion.

Gaukler ['gauklər], *m.* (—**s**, *pl.* —) buffoon; juggler.

Gaul [gaul], *m.* (—(**e**)**s**, *pl.* **Gäule**) horse, nag.

Gaum [gaum], —**en**, *m.* (—**ens**, *pl.* —**en**) palate.

Gauner ['gaunər], *m.* (—**s**, *pl.* —) rogue, sharper; cheat.

Gazelle [ga'tsɛlə], *f. (pl.* —**n**) gazelle.

Ge— [gə], *an unaccented prefix, is used especially to form:* (1) Collective nouns *derived from substantives, nearly all of the neuter gender, the root vowel of the substantives being, if possible, modified; e.g.* **Gestein, Gewölf, Geſträuch**. (2) Verbal nouns *denoting repetition or continuation of the action of the verb, all of the neuter gender and without plural; e.g.* **Geheul, Gerede**. (3) Past participles; *e.g.* **geachtet** (esteemed), **geboren** (born).

Geäder [gə'ʔɛ:dər], *n.* (—**s**) veins. —**t, Geädert**, *adj.* veined.

Geartet [gə'ʔa:rtət], *suff. (in comp.=)* natured, disposed.

Gebäck [gə'bɛk], *n.* (—**es**, *pl.* —**e**) pastry.

Gebackene(s) [gə'bakənə(s)], *n.* anything baked.

Gebärde [gə'bɛːrdə], *f. (pl.* —**n**) bearing, gesture. —**nspiel**, *n.* dumb-show, pantomime.

Gebaren [gə'ba:rən], I. *v.r.* to seem, appear; to conduct oneself. II. *subst.n.* conduct.

Gebären [gə'bɛːrən], *ir.v.a.* to give birth to.

Gebäude [gə'bɔydə], *n.* (—**s**, *pl.* —) building.

Gebell [gə'bɛl], *n.* (—**s**) continual barking.

Geben [ge:bən], *v.* I. *ir.a.* to give. **sein Wort** —, to pledge one's word; **sich zu erkennen** —, to make oneself known. II. *r.* to yield. III. *a. imp.*:

es gibt, there is, there are; **was gibt's?** what is the matter? IV. *subst.n.* giving.

Geber ['ge:bər], *m.* (**—s,** *pl.* **—**), **—in,** *f.* giver, donor.

Gebet [gə'be:t], *n.* (**—es,** *pl.* **—e**) prayer.

Gebiet [gə'bi:t], *n.* (**—(e)s,** *pl.* **—e**) jurisdiction; district; sphere. **—en,** *ir.v.a.* (einem etwas) to command. **—end,** *p. & adj.* commanding; imperious. **—er,** *m.* (**—ers,** *pl.* **—er**) lord; master, commander. **—erin,** *f.* mistress. **—erisch,** *adj.* domineering.

Gebildet [gə'bɪldət], *p.p. & adj.* shaped; accomplished; well-bred; refined.

Gebirg [gə'bɪrk], *n.* (**—(e)s,** *pl.* **—e**), **—e,** *n.* (**—es,** *pl.* **—e**) mountain; mountain-chain. **—s=kamm,** *m.* mountain-ridge.

Gebogen [gə'bo:gən], *p.p. of* **biegen;** *adj.* bent, curved; hooked; arched.

Geboren [gə'bo:rən], *p.p. of* **gebären;** *adj.* (*abbreviated* **geb.**) born.

Gebot [gə'bo:t], *n.* (**—es,** *pl.* **—e**) command.

Gebrauch [gə'braux], *m.* (**—s,** *pl.* **Gebräuche**) use; usage; custom. **—en,** *v.a.* to use, make use of; need, want. **—s=anweisung,** *f.* directions for use.

Gebräuchlich [gə'brɔyçlıç], *adj. & adv.* usual, customary.

Gebrechlich [gə'breçlıç], *adj.* defective; infirm.

Gebrüder [gə'bry:dər], (*abbr.* **Gbr.**) *pl.* brothers.

Gebrüll [gə'bryl], *n.* (**—es**) roaring.

Gebrumme [gə'brumə], *n.* (**—s**) growling.

Gebühr [gə'by:r], *f.* (*pl.* **—en**) duty; propriety, seemliness; fee, money due; moderation; **über die —en,** immoderately. **—en,** *v.* I. *n.* (*aux.* **h.**) to be due, belong of right to. II. *r. & imp.* to be fit, proper, becoming. **—end,** *p. & adj.* due, fit, meet, befitting. **—lich,** *adj. & adv.* fitting; decent; becoming. **—lichkeit,** *f.* fitness, propriety.

Gebunden [gə'bundən], *p.p. of* **binden;** *adj.* bound, obliged.

Geburt [gə'bu:rt], *f.* (*pl.* **—en**) birth; production; origin; extraction. **—s=stadt,** *f.* native town. **—s=tag,** *m.* birthday.

Gebürtig [gə'byrtıç], *adj. & adv.* native (of, **aus**), born in.

Gebüsch [gə'byʃ], *n.* (**—es,** *pl.* **—e**) thicket, underwood.

Geck [gɛk], *m.* (**—en,** *pl.* **—en**) fool, fop.

Gedächtnis [gə'dɛçtnıs], *n.* (**—(ff)es,** *pl.* **—(ff)e**) memory; memorial, monument. **—feier,** *f.* commemoration.

Gedanke [gə'daŋkə], *m.* (**—ns,** *pl.* **—n**) thought, idea; **in —n sein,** to be absorbed in thought. **—n=austausch,** *m.* interchange of ideas. **—n=lauf,** *m.* train of thoughts. **—n=leer,** *adj.* void of ideas. **—n=los,** *adj.* thoughtless. **—n=losigkeit,** *f.* thoughtlessness. **—n=reich,** *adv.* fertile in ideas. **—n=strich,** *m.* dash. **—n=voll,** *adj.* thoughtful, pensive.

Gedärm [gə'dɛrm], *n.* (**—(e)s,** *pl.* **—e**) entrails, bowels.

Gedeih—en [gə'daɪən], I. *ir.v.n.* (*aux.* **f.**) to thrive, get on well. II. *subst.n.* thriving, prosperity, success. **—lich,** *adj. & adv.* prosperous; salutary; nutritive.

Gedenken [gə'dɛŋkən], *ir.v.n.* (*aux.* **h.**) (an & *accus.*) to bear in mind, remember; to mention; to intend.

Gedicht [gə'dıçt], *n.* (**—es,** *pl.* **—e**) poem. **—sammlung,** *f.* anthology.

Gediegen [gə'di:gən], *p.p., adj. & adv.* solid; genuine, true. **—heit,** *f.* solidity; genuineness; pithiness.

Gedräng—e [gə'drɛŋə], *n.* (**—es**) crowd, throng; distress; difficulty. **—t,** *adj. & adv.* crowded.

Gedruckte(s) [gə'drukta(s)], *n.* printed matter.

Geduld [gə'dult], *f.* patience. **—en,** *v.r.* to have patience. **—ig,** *adj. & adv.* patient.

Geeignet [gə'ʔaɪgnət], *p.p. of* **eignen;** *adj. & adv.* fit, meet.

Gefahr [gə'fa:r], *f.* (*pl.* **—en**) danger. **—los,** *adj.* safe, without risk. **—losigkeit,** *f.* safety, security.

Gefähr—den [gə'fɛ:rdən], *v.a.* to endanger, imperil. **—lich,** *adj. & adv.* dangerous.

Gefährt—e [gə'fɛ:rtə], *m.* (**—en,** *pl.* **—en**), **—in,** *f.* travelling companion, comrade.

Gefall—e [gə'falə], *m.* (**—ens**), **—en,** *m.* (**—ens,** *pl.* **—en**) pleasure; **jemandem einen —en tun,** to do someone a favour. **—en,** *ir.v.n.* (*aux.* **h.**, *dat.*) to suit, please; **wie es Ihnen gefällt,** as you please.

Gefällig [gə'fɛlɪç], *adj. & adv.* pleasing; obliging; kind. **—keit,** *f.* (*pl.* **—keiten**) courtesy; obligingness; favour; (*pl.*) good offices. **—st,** *adv.* if you please.

Gefangen [gə'faŋən], *p.p. & adj.* captive; imprisoned. **—e(r),** *m.* captive, prisoner. **—schaft,** *f.* captivity, imprisonment.

Gefäng—nis [gə'fɛŋnɪs], *n.* (**—ni(ss)es,** *pl.* **—ni(ss)e**) prison, jail. **—nisstrafe,** *f.* (penalty of) imprisonment.

Gefäß [gə'fɛːs], *n.* (**—es,** *pl.* **—e**) vessel.

Gefaßt [gə'fast], *p.p. & adj.* ready, prepared; calm.

Gefecht [gə'fɛçt], *n.* (**—es,** *pl.* **—e**) combat.

Gefieder [gə'fiːdər], *n.* (**—s**) plumage; fowl; feathered tribe.

Gefilde [gə'fɪldə], *n.* (**—s**) fields, open country.

Geflissen [gə'flɪsən], *adj. & adv.* diligent, industrious. **—heit,** *f.* diligence. **—tlich,** I. *adj. & adv.* wilful, intentional. II. *adv.* with malice aforethought (*Law*).

Geflügel [gə'flyːgəl], *n.* (**—s**) poultry. **—t,** *p.p. & adj.* winged.

Geflüster [gə'flʏstər], *n.* (**—s**) whisper.

Gefolge [gə'fɔlgə], *n.* (**—s**) retinue.

Gefreit—e(r) [gə'fraitər], *m.* (**—en,** *pl.* **—e(n)**) lance corporal.

Gefrieren [gə'friːrən], *ir.v.n.* (*aux.* f.) to freeze, congeal; **auf dem Gefrierpunkt stehen,** to be at zero (*thermometer*). **Gefrorene(s),** *n.* ices, ice cream.

Gefüg—e [gə'fyːgə], *n.* (**—es**) joining, fitting together. **—ig,** *adj. & adv.* pliant; adaptable.

Gefühl [gə'fyːl], *n.* (**—s,** *pl.* **—e**) feeling; sensation; sentiment. **—los,** *adj. & adv.* unfeeling, hard. **—losigkeit,** *f.* heartlessness; apathy.

Gegen ['geːgən], I. *prep.* (*with acc.; in older German with dat.*) towards, to, in the direction of; about, somewhere near; against, opposed to; over against; opposite to; compared with; in presence of; before; in exchange, in return for; for, to; **— bar,** for cash; **— Empfang,** on receipt. II. *adv. & in comp.*=contrary, opposing, counter, *etc.* **—antwort,** *f.* rejoinder. **—besuch,** *m.* return visit; **einen**

—besuch machen, to return a call. **—bild,** *n.* contrast; counterpart. **—gewicht,** *n.* counterpoise. **—gift,** *n.* antidote. **—satz,** *m.* antithesis; contrast; opposition; rejoinder. **—sätzlich,** *adj.* contrary, adverse, opposite. **—seitig,** *adj.* reciprocal, mutual. **—sinn,** *m.* contrary sense. **—stand,** *m.* subject; object. **—tausch,** *m.* exchange; interchange. **—teil,** *n.* contrary, reverse. **—über** [ge:gən'y:bər], I. *adv.* opposite. II. *prep.* (*with preceding dat.*) opposite (to) over against; opposed to; in presence of; in relation to, as concerns. **—wart,** *f.* presence; present time. **—wärtig,** *adj. & adv.* present, actual, extant; at present, just now. **—wehr,** *f.* resistance, defence. **—wert,** *adj.* equivalent.

Gegend ['geːgənt], *f.* (*pl.* **—en**) region; neighbourhood; **er wohnt ganz in unserer —,** he lives quite near us.

Gegliedert [gə'gliːdərt], *adj.* having members; jointed; organized.

Gegner ['geːgnər], *m.* (**—s,** *pl.* **—**), **—in,** *f.* opponent; adversary. **—isch,** *adj. & adv.* antagonistic.

Gehader [gə'haːdər], *n.* (**—s**) brawling.

Gehalt [gə'halt], I. *m.* (**—s,** *pl.* **—e**) contents; capacity. II. *n.* (**—s,** *pl.* **Gehälter**) salary; pay. **—reich,** *adj.* of great value.

Geharnischt [gə'harnɪʃt], *adj.* armoured; **eine —e Antwort geben,** to answer in angry tones.

Geheim [gə'haim], *adj.* secret. **—nis,** *n.* (**—ni(ss)es,** *pl.* **—ni(ss)e**) secret; mystery. **—(e)rat,** *m.* privy councillor. **—schreiber,** *m.* private secretary. **—schrift,** *f.* cipher-writing.

Gehen ['geːən], I. *ir.v.n.* (*aux.* f.) to go, move, walk, proceed; **zugrunde —,** to go to ruin. II. *subst.n.* going; walking.

Gehilf—e [gə'hilfə], *m.* (**—en,** *pl.* **—en**), **—in,** *f.* helpmate; assistant.

Gehirn [gə'hirn], *n.* (**—s,** *pl.* **—e**) brain, brains.

Gehölz [gə'hœlts], *n.* (**—es,** *pl.* **—e**) wood, copse.

Gehör [gə'høːr], *n.* (**—s**) hearing; audience.

Gehör—en [gə'høːrən], *v.* I. *n.* (*aux.* h., *dat.*) to belong to. II. *r. & imp.* to be suitable *or* proper; **das —t sich nicht,** that is not proper. **—ig,** *adj. & adv.* belonging; fitting, suitable.

Gehorchen [gə'hɔrçən], *v.n.* (*aux.* ḥ., *dat.*) to obey.

Gehorsam [gə'ho:rza:m], I. *adj. & adv.* obedient. II. *m.* (—s) obedience. —ft, *adj. & adv.* (*sup.*) most obedient.

Geier ['gaɪər], *m.* (—s, *pl.* —) vulture.

Geifer ['gaɪfər], *m.* (—s) slaver; venom. —ig, *adj. & adv.* drivelling. —n, *v.n.* (*aux.* ḥ.) to slaver; to vent one's anger. —er, *m.* (—ers, *pl.* —er) slanderer.

Geige ['gaɪgə], *f.* (*pl.* —n) violin.

Geil [gaɪl], *adj.* fat; proud; obscene.

Geisel [gaɪsəl], *m.* (—s, *pl.* —(n)) hostage.

Geiser ['gaɪzər], *m.* (—s, *pl.* —) geyser.

Geiß [gaɪs], *f.* (*pl.* —en) goat.

Geißel ['gaɪsəl], *f.* (*pl.* —n) scourge. —n, *v.a.* to scourge.

Geist [gaɪst], *m.* (—es, *pl.* —er) spirit; soul, mind, intellect; genius; **den —aufgeben,** to give up the ghost. —erhaft, *adj. & adv.* supernatural; ghostly; ghostlike. —ig, *adj. & adv.* spiritual, mental, intellectual; witty; spiritual, immaterial; —ige Getränke, alcoholic drinks. —igkeit, *f.* spirituality; spirituousness. —lich, *adj. & adv.* spiritual, religious; clerical. —liche(r), *m.* clergyman. —lichkeit, *f.* priesthood, clergy. —er=banner, *f.* —er=beschwörer, *m.* necromancer; exorcist. —ermüdend, *adj.* fatiguing to the mind. —erquickend, *adj.* refreshing to the mind. —er=reich, *n.*, —er=welt, *f.* the realm of spirits. —er=seher, *m.* visionary, ghost-seer. —es=abwesend, *adj.* absent-minded. —es=gegenwart, *f.* presence of mind. —los, *adj.* unintellectual. —losigkeit, *f.* mental dullness. —reich, *adj.*, —voll, *adj.* gifted, ingenious, witty.

Geiz [gaɪts], *m.* (—es) avarice; greediness. —en, *v.n.* (*aux.* ḥ.) to covet. —ig, *adj. & adv.* avaricious, covetous; niggardly; eager. —hals, —hammel, —kragen, *m.* miser.

Gekläff [gə'klɛf], *n.* (—s) continual yelping.

Gekrächz [gə'krɛçts], *n.* (—es) croaking.

Gelächter [gə'lɛçtər], *n.* (—s) laughter; **er wird zum — der Stadt,** he is becoming the laughing-stock of the town.

Gelag(e) [gə'la:k, —'la:gə], *n.* (—s) banquet; revel.

Gelähmt [gə'lɛmt], *p.p. & adj.* paralysed.

Gelände [gə'lɛndə], *n.* (—s) arable land; region; tract of country.

Geländer [gə'lɛndər], *n.* (—s, *pl.* —) balustrade; parapet.

Gelangen [gə'laŋən], *v.n.* (*aux.* ʃ.) to reach; arrive at.

Gelassen [gə'lasən], *p.p.* of lassen; *adj. & adv.* calm; cool; deliberate. —heit, *f.* self-possession; moderation; calmness; patience.

Geläufig [gə'lɔyfɪç], *adj. & adv.* fluent; easy; **mir ist die englische Sprache —,** I am familiar with the English language.

Gelaunt [gə'launt], *adj.* disposed; **ich bin gut —,** I am in a good humour.

Geläut(e) [gə'lɔyt(ə)], *n.* (—(e)s) chime, peal of bells.

Gelb [gɛlp], *adj. & adv.* yellow. —e, I. *n.* yellow colour. II. *f.* yellowness; jaundice. —heit, *f.* yellowness. —lich, *adj. & adv.* yellowish. —sucht, *f.* jaundice.

Geld [gɛlt], *n.* (—es, *pl.* —er) coin; money; cash; **bares — or Bar—,** ready money. —anleihe, *f.* loan (of money). —anweisung, *f.* postalorder, cheque. —mangel, *m.* scarcity of money. —strafe, *f.* fine.

Gelegen [gə'le:gən], *p.p.* of liegen; *adj.* situated; convenient; opportune; **es ist mir nichts daran —,** it is of no importance to me. —heit, *f.* occasion; opportunity. —tlich, I. *adj.* occasional, incidental; opportune. II. *adv.* on an occasion, incidentally.

Gelehr—samkeit [gə'le:rza:mkaɪt], *f.* learning, erudition. —t, *adj.* learned. —te(r), *m.*, —te, *f.* scholar.

Geleise [gə'laɪzə], *n.* (—s, *pl.* —) usually **Gleis,** *n.* (—(s)es, *pl.* —(s)e) track; line of rails.

Geleit [gə'laɪt], *n.* (—(e)s, *pl.* —e) conducting, accompanying; retinue; escort. —en, *v.a.* to accompany. —er, *m.* (—ers, *pl.* —er) guide, conductor. —(s)=stern, *m.* satellite.

Gelenk [gə'lɛŋk], I. *adj. & adv.* pliant, supple; limber; nimble. II. *n.* (—(e)s, *pl.* —e) joint.

Geliebt—e(r) [gə'li:ptə(r)], *m.* (—en, *pl.* —e(n)) lover; sweetheart. —e, *f.* sweetheart, ladylove, mistress.

Gelind [gə'lɪnt], —e, *adj. & adv.* smooth, soft; gentle; tender. —igkeit, —heit, *f.* mildness, lenity, indulgence.

Gelingen [gə'lɪŋən], I. *ir.v.n.* (*aux.* ʃ.)

(einem) to succeed, to prosper.
II. *subst.n.* success.

Gellen ['gɛlən], *v.n.* (*aux.* h.) to yell.
—d, *p. & adj.* shrill, piercing.

Gelob—en [gə'lo:bən], *v.a.* to promise
solemnly, vow; das —te Land, the
land of promise.

Gelöbnis [gə'lø:pnɪs], *n.* (—(ſſ)es, *pl.*
—(ſſ)e) solemn promise, vow.

Gelt [gɛlt], *interj.* is it not so? do you
not think so? truly!

Gelt—en [gɛltən], *ir.v.n.* (*aux.* h.) to be
worth, have value (for); to be valid
or of force; to have influence, be in
favour (with); to prove effectual,
prevail; to pass current; to be esteemed; to be permitted; to be real
or true; to concern. es gilt unſer
Leben, our life is at stake; —end
machen, to make good, to urge, assert,
vindicate; to set off, show to advantage; to plead (*as excuse*). —ung, *f.*
value, worth; acceptation (*of a word*);
ſich (*dat.*) —ung verſchaffen, to make
oneself felt *or* respected.

Gelübde [gə'lʏpdə], *n.* (—s, *pl.* —) vow.

Gelüſten [gə'lʏstən], *v.a. & n.* (*aux.* h.)
& *usually imp.* to desire, long for.

Gemach [gə'ma:x], I. *adj.* comfortable.
II. *adv.* softly, gently. III. *n.* (—(e)s,
pl. Gemächer) chamber, room.

Gemächlichkeit [gə'mɛçlɪçkaɪt], *f.* convenience, comfort, ease.

Gemahl [gə'ma:l], *m.* (—s, *pl.* —e)
consort, husband. —in, *f.* consort,
wife.

Gemälde [gə'mɛ:ldə], *n.* (—s, *pl.* —)
picture. —ausſtellung, *f.* picture-
exhibition.

Gemäß [gə'mɛ:s], I. *adj. & adv.* pro-
portionable. II. *prep.* (*with preceding
or following dat.*) conformably to,
according to.

Gemein [gə'maɪn], *adj. & adv.* common; general; familiar; vulgar; —er
Soldat, private (soldier). —heit, *f.*
vileness; meanness, vulgarity. —s
iglich, *adv.* usually, generally. —s
nützig, *adj.* of public utility. —ſam,
adj & adv. joint, combined, mutual.
—ſchaft, *f.* common possession *or* interest; partnership. —ſchaftlich, *adj.
& adv.* common, mutual; joint.

Gemeinde [gə'maɪndə], *f.* (*pl.* —n)
municipality; community; parish.
—bezirk, *m.* municipality. —ſchule,
f. board school.

Gemenge [gə'mɛŋə], *n.* (—s) mixture;
medley.

Gemeſſen [gə'mɛsən], *p.p.* of meſſen,
& *adj.* measured. —heit, *f.* precision.

Gemiſch [gə'mɪʃ], *n.* (—es, *pl.* —e)
mixture.

Gemme ['gɛmə], *f.* (*pl.* —n) gem.

Gemſe ['gɛmzə], *f.* (*pl.* —n) chamois.

Gemurmel [gə'mʊrməl], *n.* (—s)
murmuring.

Gemüſe [gə'my:zə], *n.* (—s, *pl.* —)
vegetables.

Gemüt [gə'my:t], *n.* (—es, *pl.* —er)
mind; disposition; spirit; temper.
—lich, *adj. & adv.* good-natured;
comfortable, cosy. —lichkeit, *f.* (the
quality of) good-natured, sanguine, easy-going disposition. —s=
krankheit, *f.* disorder of the mind,
melancholy.

Genannt [gə'nant], *p.p.* of nennen,
called, surnamed.

Genau [gə'nau], *adj. & adv.* exact, precise. —igkeit, *f.* accuracy, precision.

Genehm [gə'ne:m], *adj.* acceptable,
agreeable. —igen, *v.a.* to approve.
—igung, *f.* acceptance; approbation.

Geneigt [gə'naɪçt], *p.p.* of neigen, &
adj.; — zu, inclined, disposed to.

General [genə'ra:l], I. *adj. & adv.*
general. II. *m.* (—s, *pl.* —e) general,
(supreme) commander. —kommando,
n. corps headquarters. —leutnant
[—'lɔytnant], *m.* lieutenant-general.
—major [—ma'jo:r], *m.* major-general.
—nenner, *m.* common denominator.
—ſtab, *m.* staff. —ſtäbler, *m.* staff-
officer. —ſtabsarzt, *m.* surgeon-general.

Geneſ—en [gə'ne:zən], *ir.v.n.* (*aux.* ſ.)
to grow well; to recover. —ung, *f.*
recovery.

Genick [gə'nɪk], *n.* (—(e)s, *pl.* —e)
nape, neck.

Genie [ʒe'ni:], *n.* (—s) genius, talent;
engineering. —korps, *n.* Royal
Engineers.

Genieren [ʒe'ni:rən], *v.a.* to embarrass,
make uneasy, inconvenience; to bore;
ſich —, to feel awkward; — Sie ſich
nicht, make yourself at home.

Genießbar [gə'ni:sba:r], *adj. & adv.*
enjoyable, eatable; der Salat iſt
einfach un—, the salad simply cannot
be eaten; Karl iſt heute un—, Karl is
in very bad mood to-day.

Genießen [gə'ni:sən], *ir.v.a.* to eat *or*
drink; to enjoy.

Genoff—e [gə'nɔsə], **Genoß,** *m.* (—(ff)= en, *pl.*—(ff)en), —in, [*f.* (*pl.* —innen) comrade. —enfchaft, *f.* company, association; confederacy.

Genug [gə'nu:k], *indec. adj.* (*with gen.*) & *adv.* enough, sufficient. —tuend, *adj.* giving satisfaction. —tuung, *f.* satisfaction, compensation; amends, atonement.

Genüg—e[gə'ny:gə], *f.* & *n.* sufficiency. —lich, *adj.* & *adv.* sufficient. —fam, *adj.* & *adv.* contented; moderate; frugal. —famfeit, *f.* moderation. —en, *v.* I. *a.* (*aux.* h.) to be enough, to suffice; (*with dat.*) to satisfy. II. *subst.n.* satisfaction; competency. —end, *p.* & *adj.* sufficient.

Genuß [gə'nus], *m.* (—(ff)es, *pl.* Genüffe) enjoyment. —mittel, *n.* (*usually pl.*) luxury. —reich, *adj.* enjoyable. —fucht, *f.* sensuality. —füchtig, *adj.* pleasure-seeking, epicurean.

Geo—graph [geo'gra:f], *m.* (—graphen, *pl.* —graphen) geographer. — graphifch, *adj.* & *adv.* geographical. —meter [—'me:tər], *m.* (—meters, *pl.* —meter) geometrician. —metrie [—me'tri:], *f.* geometry. —metrifch [—'me:trɪʃ], *adj.* & *adv.* geometrical.

Gepäck [gə'pɛk], *n.* (—(e)s, *pl.* —e) luggage, baggage. —träger, *m.* porter. —wagen, *m.* luggage-van.

Gepflogen [gə'pflo:gən], *p.p.* of pflegen. —heit, *f.* custom, habit.

Geplauder [gə'plaudər], *n.* (—s) small-talk; chat.

Gepräge [gə'prɛ:gə], *n.* (—s) stamp, impression.

Ge(e)rad—e [g(ə)'ra:də], I. *adj.* straight, direct; erect; straightforward, honest; even. II. *adv.* quite; just; — an dem Abend, that very evening; er ift — fortgegangen, he has just gone away. III. —e, *f.* straightness. —e=aus [—'aus], *n.* straight on, right ahead. —e=hin [—'hɪn], *adv.* straight in, rashly; unceremoniously. —(e)=zu [—'tsu:], *adv.* straight on.

Gerate—n [gə'ra:tən], I. *ir.v.n.* (*aux.* f.) to get, fall *or* come into, to *or* upon; to prove; to prosper; in Vergeffenheit —n, to fall into oblivion. II. *p.p.* & *adj.* successful; advisable. —wohl, *n.* haphazard, chance; aufs —wohl, at random.

Gerät [gə'rɛ:t], *n.* (—es, *pl.* —e) imple-

ments; utensils; effects. —fammer, *f.* lumber-room.

Geräumig [gə'rɔymɪç], *adj.* & *adv.* roomy. —feit, *f.* roominess, spaciousness.

Geräufch [gə'rɔyʃ], *n.* (—es, *pl.* —e) noise. —los, *adj.* noiseless. —voll, *adj.* noisy.

Gerb—en ['gɛrbən], *v.a.* to tan. —er, *m.* (—ers, *pl.* —er) tanner. —erei [—ə'rai], *f.* tannery.

Gerecht [gə'rɛçt], *adj.* & *adv.* just, righteous; upright. —igfeit, *f.* righteousness; justice; right. —fam, *adj.* & *adv.* rightful.

Gerede [gə're:də], *n.* (—s) talk, report.

Gereizt [gə'raitst], *p.p.* of reizen, & *adj.* irritated; vexed. —heit, *f.* irritation.

Gericht [gə'rɪçt], *n.* (—s, *pl.* —e) court of justice; dish, course. —lich, I. *adj.* judicial; legal. II. *adv.* judicially. —s=banf, *f.* tribunal. —s=beamte(r), *m.* magistrate, justiciary. —s=bezirf, *m.* circuit, jurisdiction. —s=halter, *m.* justiciary. —s=handel, *m.* law-suit. —s=hof, *m.* court of justice, tribunal. —s=foften, *pl.* law expenses. —s=rat, *m.* counsellor. —s=fchreiber, *m.* clerk of the court.

Gering [gə'rɪŋ], *adj.* & *adv.* small, little, petty; unimportant; nicht im —ften, not in the least. —heit, *f.* smallness; meanness. —achtung, *f.* contempt, disdain. —fügig, *adj.* insignificant. —fchätzig, *adj.* depreciatory; disdainful; contemptible.

Gerippe [gə'rɪpə], *n.* (—s, *pl.* —) skeleton; framework.

Gern(e) ['gɛrn(ə)], *adv.* (*comp.* lieber; *sup.* am liebften) with pleasure, willingly.

Gerfte ['gɛrstə], *f.* (*pl.* —n) barley. —n, *adj.* (of) barley.

Gerte ['gɛrtə], *f.* (*pl.* —n) whip.

Geruch [gə'rux], *m.* (—(e)s, *pl.* Gerüche) smell. —los, *adj.* scentless, odourless.

Gerücht [gə'rʏçt], *n.* (—(e)s, *pl.* —e) rumour, report. —lich, *adj.* & *adv.* according to report.

Gerümpel [gə'rʏmpəl], *n.* (—s) lumber, rubbish.

Gerüft [gə'rʏst], *n.* (—es, *pl.* —e) scaffold(ing).

Gefamt [gə'zamt] (*older spelling:* Gefammt), *adj.* & *adv.* whole; all;

united; total, collective. —e(s), *n.* the whole, the (sum) total. —heit, *f.* the whole; all. —betrag, *m.* sum-total. —ertrag, *m.* entire proceeds. —zahl, *f.* total number.

Gesandt [gə'zant], *p.p. of* senden. —e(r), *m.* (—en, *pl.* —e(n)) ambassador. —in, *f.* ambassador's wife, ambassadress. —schaft, *f.* embassy, legation.

Gesang [gə'zaŋ], *m.* (—es, *pl.* Gesänge) song, melody. —verein, *m.* choral society.

Geschäft [gə'ʃɛft], *n.* (—es, *pl.* —e) business; Engros—, wholesale business; Detail—, retail business. —ig, *adj. & adv.* busy. —igkeit, *f.* activity; zeal; industry. —lich, *adj. & adv.* relating to business, commercial. —s=freund, *m.* customer. —s=führer, *m.* manager. —s=inhaber, *m.* owner of a firm, principal. —s=mann, *m.* (*pl.* —s=leute) man of business, tradesman, trader. —s=mäßig, *adj. & adv.* businesslike. —s=personal [—'na:l], *n.* (—s, *pl.* —e) staff of a firm. —s=reisende(r), *m.* commercial traveller. —s=teilhaber, *m.* partner. —s=träger, *m.* representative, agent (*of a firm*); chargé d'affaires.

Geschehen [gə'ʃe:ən], *ir.v.n.* (*aux.* ſ.) to come to pass; to happen; das geschieht Ihnen recht, that serves you right. —e(s), *n.* what is done.

Gescheit [gə'ʃait], *adj.* shrewd. —heit, *f.* prudence, discretion; cleverness; er ist nicht recht —, he is a bit dotty.

Geschenk [gə'ʃɛŋk], *n.* (—es, *pl.* —e) present.

Geschicht=e [gə'ʃɪçtə], *f.* (*pl.* —en) history; story; event. —lich, *adj. & adv.* historical. —en=buch, *n.* storybook. —s=buch, *n.* history-book. —s=forscher, *m.* historian. —s=forschung, *f.* historical research. —s=mäßig, *adj.* historical. —(s)=schreiber, *m.* historian.

Geschick [gə'ʃɪk], *n.* (—es, *pl.* —e) knack, skill, aptitude; fate, destiny. —lichkeit, *f.* skill, cleverness, dexterity. —t, *p.p. & adj.* fit; able, dexterous.

Geschirr [gə'ʃɪr], *n.* (—es, *pl.* —e) implements; harness; apparatus.

Geschlecht [gə'ʃlɛçt], *n.* (—es, *pl.* —er) genus; sex; race. —s=alter, *n.* generation.

Geschliffen [gə'ʃlɪfən], *p.p. of* schleifen, & *adj.* polished, polite.

Geschmack [gə'ʃmak], *m.* (—es, *pl.* Geschmäcke) taste. —los, *adj.* tasteless, insipid; in bad taste. —losigkeit, *f.* want of taste, bad taste. —s=sache, *f.*; das ist —s=sache, that is a matter of taste. —voll, *adj.* tasteful; stylish, elegant. —widrig, *adj.* tasteless, inelegant.

Geschmeid=e [gə'ʃmaidə], *n.* (—es, *pl.* —e) jewels, trinkets. —ig, *adj. & adv.* supple, flexible. —igkeit, *f.* suppleness, flexibility.

Geschöpf [gə'ʃœpf], *n.* (—es, *pl.* —e) creature.

Geschoß [gə'ʃos], *n.* (—(ſſ)es, *pl.* —(ſſ)e) projectile; story, floor.

Geschrei [gə'ʃrai], *n.* (—s, *pl.* —e) cry; clamour, outcry.

Geschütz [gə'ʃʏts], *n.* (—es, *pl.* —e) gun, cannon.

Geschwader [gə'ʃva:dər], *n.* (—s, *pl.* —) squadron.

Geschwätz [gə'ʃvɛts], *n.* (—es, *pl.* —e) babble; tittle-tattle, gossiping. —ig, *adj. & adv.* talkative. —igkeit, *f.* talkativeness.

Geschweige [gə'ʃvaigə], *adv.* not to mention; much less; far from.

Geschwind [gə'ʃvɪnt], *adj. & adv.* quick. —igkeit, *f.* quickness.

Geschwister [gə'ʃvɪstər], *n.* (obs.), now usually *pl.* sisters, brothers, brothers and sisters; ſie ſind —, they are brother and sister.

Geschwor=(e)ne(r) [gə'ʃvo:r(ə)nə(r)], *m.* juror. —(e)nen, *pl.* jury.

Geschwür [gə'ʃvy:r], *n.* (—(e)s, *pl.* —e) ulcer, abscess. —ig, *adj.* ulcerous.

Gesell=(e) [gə'zɛl(ə)], *m.* (—en, *pl.* —en) companion. —en, *v.a.* to join, associate. —ig, *adj. & adv.* sociable; companionable. —schaft, *f.* society; association; company; fellowship; club. —schaftlich, *adj.* social. —schafts=spiel, *n.* drawing-room game.

Gesetz [gə'zɛts], *n.* (es, *pl.* —e) law. —lich, *adj. & adv.* lawful, legal; statutory. —lichkeit, *f.* legality, lawfulness. —buch, *n.* law-book; code. —gebend, *adj.* legislative. —geber, *m.* legislator, lawgiver. —gebung, *f.* legislation. —gültig, —kräftig, *adj.* legally sanctioned, having the force of law. —kundig, *adj.* versed in law. —los, *adj. & adv.* lawless; anarchical. —losigkeit, *f.* lawlessness, illegality; anarchy. —mäßig, *adj. & adv.* lawful, legitimate, legal. —**widrig**, *adj.* & *adv.* illegal, contrary to law.

Gesetz [gə'zɛtst], *p.p.* & *adj.* fixed; steady; *used with a case absolute or as conj.* supposing, in case; **von —em Alter**, of mature age; —**essei wahr,** supposing it is true.

Gesicht [gə'zɪçt], *n.* —(e)s, *pl.* —**er** sight; visage, countenance; —**er schneiden,** to make grimaces. —**s=farbe,** *f.* complexion. —**s=freis,** *m.* field of vision. —**s=punkt,** *m.* point of view.

Gesims [gə'zɪms], *n.* —(s)es, *pl.* —(s)e cornice; moulding; shelf.

Gesind=e [gə'zɪndə], *n.* —es domestic servants. —**el,** *n.* —els rabble; vagabonds.

Gesinn=t [gə'zɪnt], *adj.* minded, disposed. —**ung,** *f.* sentiment; conviction; intention.

Gesittet [gə'zɪtət], *adj.* mannered.

Gespalten [gə'ʃpaltən], *adj.* cleft.

Gespann [gə'ʃpan], *n.* —(e)s, *pl.* —**e** team; couple.

Gespannt [gə'ʃpant], *p.p. of* **spannen,** *adj.* & *adv.* intent, eager; stretched; — **sein auf,** to look forward eagerly; to be curious, anxious. —**heit,** *f.* tension; intentness; anxiety; estrangement.

Gespenst [gə'ʃpɛnst], *n.* —es, *pl.* —**er** ghost. —**erhaft,** —**ig,** —**isch,** *adj.* & *adv.* ghostly; ghostlike.

Gespiele [gə'ʃpiːlə], *m.* —n, *pl.* —n), —**in,** *f.* playmate.

Gespräch [gə'ʃprɛːç], *n.* —(e)s, *pl.* —**e** conversation, talk. —**ig,** *adj.* & *adv.* talkative. —**igkeit,** *f.* talkativeness; affability.

Gespreizt [gə'ʃpraitst], *adj.* spread out.

Gestalt [gə'ʃtalt], *f.* (*pl.* —**en**) form; shape, figure; stature; aspect, manner. —**los,** *adj.* & *adv.* shapeless. —**en,** *v.* I. *a.* to form, fashion. II. *r.* to take shape.

Gestank [gə'ʃtaŋk], *m.* —es, *pl.* **Gestänke** stench.

Gestatt=**en** [gə'ʃtatən], *v.a.* to permit, allow, grant. —**ung,** *f.* permission, consent.

Geste ['gɛstə], *f.* (*pl.* —n) gesture.

Gestehen [gə'ʃteːən], *ir.v.a.* to own, confess.

Gestein [gə'ʃtain], *n.* —s, *pl.* —**e** stone, rock.

Gestell [gə'ʃtɛl], *n.* —(e)s, *pl.* —**e** stand; frame; trestle.

Gester=**ig** ['gɛstərɪç], **Gestrig,** *adj.* & *adv.* of yesterday. —**n,** I. *adv.* yesterday. II. *n.* yesterday.

Gestiefelt [gə'ʃtiːfəlt], *p.p.* & *adj.* booted.

Gestielt [gə'ʃtiːlt], *adj.* helved; stemmed (*Bot.*).

Gestirn [gə'ʃtɪrn], *n.* —es, *pl.* —**e** star; constellation.

Gestöber [gə'ʃtøːbər], *n.* —s) drift (*of dust or snow*); storm.

Gesträuch [gə'ʃtrɔyç], *n.* —(e)s, *pl.* —**e**) shrubs, bushes.

Gestrüpp(e) [gə'ʃtryp(ə)], *n.* —(e)s underwood.

Gestüt [gə'ʃtyːt], *n.* —es, *pl.* —**e** stud. —**hengst,** *m.* stallion. —**stute,** *f.* brood-mare.

Gesuch [gə'zuːx], *n.* —(e)s, *pl.* —**e** petition, request. —**t,** *adj.* choice.

Gesumme [gə'zumə], *n.* —s) humming, buzzing.

Gesund [gə'zunt], *adj.* & *adv.* sound, healthy. —**heit,** *f.* health; wholesomeness.

Getose [gə'toːzə], **Getöse** [gə'tøːzə], *n.* —s) deafening noise, din, uproar.

Getränk [gə'trɛŋk], *n.* —es, *pl.* —**e** drink.

Getreide [gə'traidə], *n.* —s) corn, grain. —**speicher,** *m.* granary.

Getreu [gə'trɔy], *adj.* & *adv.* faithful, true. —**lich,** *adv.* faithfully, truly, loyally.

Getriebe [gə'triːbə], *n.* —s) driving, drift; motion; motive power.

Getrost [gə'troːst], I. (*orig. a p.p of* **trösten**) *adj.* & *adv.* comforted. II. *int.* cheer up!

Getümmel [gə'tyməl], *n.* —s) tumult.

Geübtheit [gə'ʔyːpthait], *f.* skill, dexterity, practice.

Gevatter [gə'fatər], *m* —s, *pl.* —**n**), —**in,** *f.* godfather, godmother, sponsor.

Gewächs [gə'vɛks], *n.* —(f)es, *pl.* —(f)e growth; sprout, excrescence.

Gewahr [gə'vaːr], *adj.*; **etwas** *or* **einer Sache** (*becoming obs.*) — **werden,** to perceive, become aware of.

Gewähr [gə'vɛːr], *f.* (*pl.* —**en**) safekeeping; guarantee. —**en,** *v.* I. *a.* to be surety for. II. *n.* (*aux.* **h.**) to last, continue. —**leistung,** *f.* guarantee.

Gewalt [gə'valt], *f.* (*pl.* —**en**) might, power; violence. —**ig,** *adj.* & *adv.* powerful. —**sam,** *adj.* & *adv.* forcible, violent. —**samkeit,** *f.* violence.

—haber, m. autocrat, dictator. —=
haberei [—'raı], f. despotism. —=
herrschaft, f. despotism. —herrscher,
m. despot. —tätig, adj. & adv.
violent, outrageous.

Gewand [gə'vant], n. (—(e)s, pl.
Gewänder) garment, dress.

Gewandt [gə'vant], p.p. of wenden.
adj. active, nimble; adroit; skilled.
—heit, f. adroitness, dexterity;
cleverness.

Gewärtig [gə'vɛrtıç], adj. & adv.
awaiting, expectant. —en, v.a., r. &
n. to expect.

Gewehr [gə've:r], n. (—es, pl. —e)
weapon.

Geweih [gə'vaı], n. (—es, pl. —e)
horns, antlers.

Gewellt[gə'vɛlt], p.p. & adj. corrugated
(iron).

Gewerb—e [gə'vɛrbə], n. (—(e)s)
trade, business. —lich, adj. & adv.
industrial; professional. —sam, adj.
industrious. —samkeit, f. industry.
—s=leute, f. tradespeople, tradesmen.
—s=mäßig, adj. professional. —tätig,
adj. industrial.

Gewicht [gə'vıçt], n. (—es, pl. —e)
weight; gravity; weightiness. —ig,
adj. & adv. weighty.

Gewimmel [gə'vıməl], n. (—s) crowd,
swarm.

Gewimmer [gə'vımər], n. (—s) whining, wailing.

Gewinn [gə'vın], m. (—es, pl. —e)
earnings, gain, profit. —bar, adj. &
adv. obtainable, gainable. —bringend,
adj. profitable, lucrative. —los, adj.
& adv. profitless. —en, ir.v. I. a. to
win; to earn. II. n. (aux. h.) to improve; jemanden lieb —en, to become
fond of a person.

Gewiß [gə'vıs], I. adj. & adv. sure,
certain. II. adv. certainly. —heit,
f. certainty.

Gewissen [gə'vısən], n. (—s) conscience. —haft, adj. & adv. conscien-
tious; scrupulous. —haftigkeit, f.
conscientiousness. —los, adj. unprincipled, unscrupulous. —losigkeit, f.
unscrupulousness.

Gewitter [gə'vıtər], n. (—s, pl. —)
thunderstorm.

Gewogen [gə'vo:gən], adj. (einem)
kind, favourable; friendly; affectionate. —heit, f. attachment, affection.

Gewohn—t [gə'vo:nt], p.p. & adj.

accustomed. —heit, f. (pl. —heiten)
habit; custom.

Gewöhn—en [gə'vø:nən], v.a. & r. to
accustom, habituate. —t, p.p. & adj.
habituated, trained. —lich, adj. &
adv. usual, ordinary, customary.

Gewölbe [gə'vølbə], n. (—s, pl. —)
vault, arch. —bogen, m. arch of a
vault.

Gewühl [gə'vy:l], n. (—es) tumult,
bustle.

Gewürz [gə'vyrts], n. (—es, pl. —e)
spice. —haft, —ig, adj. & adv. spicy,
aromatic.

Gezänt(e) [gə'tsɛŋk(ə)], n. (—(e)s)
continual quarrelling, wrangling.

Geziem—en [gə'tsi:mən], v.r. & n.
(aux. h.) imp. to be suitable, fit.
—end, —lich, adj. proper.

Gezücht [gə'tsxçt], n. (—(e)s) breed;
set, crew (contempt).

Gezweige [gə'tsvarkə], n. (—s, pl. —)
branches (of a tree).

Gezwungen [gə'tsvuŋən], adj. & adv.
forced, unnatural, affected. —heit,
f. constraint.

Gicht [gıçt], f. gout.

Giebel ['gi:bəl], m. (—s, pl. —) gable.
—ig, adj. & adv. gabled.

Gier [gi:r] (obs.: —de), f. eagerness,
greediness. —ig, adj. & adv. eager,
greedy, covetous (nach, for, of).
—igkeit, f. eagerness, greediness.

Gieß—en ['gi:sən], ir.v.a. to pour
forth; to shed; to water(flowers). —er,
m. (—ers, pl. —er) founder. —erei
[—'raı], f. foundry; casting, founding.
—form, f. mould. —kanne, f. ewer;
watering-can.

Gift [gıft], n. (—s, pl. —e) poison.
—ig, adj. & adv. poisonous.

Gilde ['gıldə], f. (pl. —n) guild.

Gimpel ['gımpəl], m. (—s, pl. —)
bullfinch; simpleton.

Gipfel ['gıpfəl], m. (—s, pl. —) summit, top.

Gips [gırps], m. (—(f)es, pl. —(f)e)
plaster of paris, stucco.

Giraffe [gi'rafə], f. (pl. —n) giraffe.

Gisch—en ['gıʃən], v.n. to foam, froth.
—t, m. foam.

Gitter ['gıtər], n. (—s, pl. —) trellis;
grating. —tür, f. grated door.
—werf, n. trellis-work; grating.
—zaun, m. fence of trellis-work.

Glanz [glants], m. (—es) lustre;
gleam.

Glänz-en ['glɛntsən], v. I. n. (aux. h.) to shine, glitter. II. a. to burnish; to glaze. —end, p., adj. & adv. brilliant; splendid.

Glas [glaːs], n. (—(ſ)es, pl. Gläſer) glass; drinking-glass. —haus, n. hot-house. —(ſ)ig, adj. glassy.

Gläſern ['glɛːzərn], adj. of glass; glassy.

Glatt [glat] (comp. —er, sup. —eſt) I. adj. smooth, even; polished. II. adv. smoothly; quite, entirely; plainly; —heraus ſagen, to speak frankly. —eis, n. slippery frost; jemanden aufs —eis führen, to get a person into trouble. —raſiert, adj. clean-shaven.

Glätt-e ['glɛtə], f. smoothness; polish; politeness. —eiſen, n. smoothing-iron.

Glatz-e ['glatsə], f. bald spot. —töpſig, adj. & adv. bald-pated, bald.

Glaub-e ['glaubə], m. (—ens) faith; belief; auf Treu und —en, in good faith. —haft, —haftig, adj. & adv. credible; true. —haftigkeit, f. credibility; authenticity. —lich, adj. & adv. credible, likely. —ensbekenntnis, n. confession of faith, creed; apoſtoliſches —ensbekenntnis, the Apostles' creed. —würdig, adj. & adv. worthy of belief, credible, authentic. —würdigkeit, f. credibility; authenticity.

Glauben ['glaubən], v.a. & n. (aux. h.) to believe.

Gläubig ['glɔybɪç], adj. believing; devout; credulous. —e(r), m., —e, f. believer. —er, m. (—ers, pl. —er) creditor.

Gleich [glaɪç], I. adj. & adv. even, level; straight; equal, equivalent; like, resembling. II. adv. alike, equally, exactly; immediately, instantly, directly, presently. III. conj. although. —en, ir.v. I. n. (aux. h., dat.) to equal; to resemble. II. reg.v.a. to equalize. —heit, f. equality, identity; likeness, similarity; evenness. —nis, n. (—ni(ſſ)es, pl. —ni(ſſ)e) simile, comparison; parable. —ſam, adv. as if, as it were, as though; almost. —ergeſtalt, —ermaßen, —erweiſe, adv. in like manner, likewise. —falls, adv. & conj. likewise, also, even, in like case. —geltend, adj. (dat.) equivalent (to), tantamount (to). —geſinnt, adj. like-minded. —geſtaltet, adj. of the same shape. —geſtimmt, adj.

congenial. —gewicht, n. equilibrium, equipoise. —gewichts=punkt, m. centre of gravity. —gültig, adj. indifferent (gegen, to). —gültigkeit, f. indifference. —mäßig, adj. & adv. uniform; similar; symmetrical; equal. —maß, n. symmetry; proportion; uniformity. —mut, m. equanimity. —mütig, adj. even-tempered, calm. —ſam, adv. as it were. —viel, adv. no matter, all the same; it's all one. —wert, m. equivalent. —wie, conj. & adv. as, just as, even as. —wohl, conj. & adv. nevertheless, notwithstanding. —zeitig, I. adj. contemporary; simultaneous. II. adv. together, at the same time. —zu, adv. straightway; without ceremony.

Gleis [glaɪs], n. see Geleiſe.

Gleisner ['glaɪsnər], m. (—s, pl. —), —in, f. hypocrite.

Gleit-en ['glaɪtən], (reg. &) ir.v.n. (aux. ſ. & h.) to glide. —flugzeug, n. glider (aeroplane).

Gletſcher ['glɛtʃər], m. (—s, pl. —) glacier.

Glied [gliːt], n. (—es, pl. —er) limb, member. —erig, adj. & adv. limbed, jointed. —erbau, m. formation; frame.

Glimm-en ['glɪmən], (reg. &) ir.v.n. (aux. h.) to glimmer, glow. —er, m. (—ers) faint glow, glimmering. —erig, adj. glimmering. —ern, v.n. to glimmer.

Glimpf [glɪmpf], m. (—es) indulgence. —lich, adj. forbearing, indulgent.

Glocke ['glɔkə], f. (pl. —n) bell; etwas an die große — hängen, to make a great fuss about a thing.

Glotzen ['glɔtsən], v.n. (aux. h.) to gape; to stare.

Glück [glyk], n. (—es, no pl.) luck; fortune; good luck; success. auf gut —, at a venture; da können wir von — reden, we can call ourselves lucky. —lich, adj. & adv. fortunate, lucky; happy. —licherweiſe, adv. by good fortune, fortunately. —ſelig, adj. blissful, very happy. —ſeligkeit, f. blissfulness, rapture. —s=fall, m. (—s=fälle, pl. is often used as pl. of Glück q.v.) lucky chance, piece of good luck. —s=pilz, m. lucky fellow. —s=ritter, m. adventurer. —wunſch, m. congratulation.

Glücken ['glykən], v.n. (aux. h. & ſ.) imp. (einem) to prosper, to succeed.

Glüh—e ['gly:ə], **—ung**, *f.* state of being red-hot. **—en**, *v.* I. *a.* to make red-hot. 'I. *n.* (*aux.* h.) to glow; to burn. **—d**, *p. & adj.* glowing, ardent. **—feuer**, *n.* glowing fire. **—hitze**, *f.* red heat. **—lampe**, *f.* incandescent lamp. **—wein**, *m.* mulled wine.

Glut [glu:t], *f.* (*pl.* **—en**) heat; glow; ardour.

Gnad—e ['gna:də], *f.* (*pl.* **—n**) favour; grace; pardon. **—en-alt**, *m.* act of grace. **—en-brief**, *m.* letter of pardon. **—en-wahl**, *f.* predestination.

Gnädig ['gnɛ:dɪç], *adj. & adv.* merciful, kind; favourable, gracious; **—e Frau**, madam.

Gnom [gno:m], *m.* (**—en**, *pl.* **—en**) gnome.

Gockel ['gɔkəl], *m.* (**—s**), **Gockel-hahn**, *m.* rooster, cock.

Gold [gɔlt], *n.* (**—es**) gold. **—en**, *adj.* golden. **—ig**, *adj.* golden. **—arbeiter**, *m.* goldsmith; jeweller. **—artig**, *adj.* golden. **—barren**, *m.* ingot of gold. **—bergwerf**, *n.* gold-mine. **—blatt**, **—blättchen**, *n.* leaf-gold. **—blume**, *f.* marigold. **—draht**, *m.* gold-wire. **—lack**, *m.* gold-varnish; wall-flower. **—macher**, *m.* alchemist. **—münze**, *f.* gold coin; gold medal. **—regen**, *m.* laburnum. **—schnitt**, *m.* gilt edges of a book. **—tresse**, *f.* gold lace. **—wage**, *f.* scales for gold; **alles auf die —wage legen**, to be very particular.

Golf [gɔlf], I. *m.* (**—(e)s**, *pl.* **—e**) gulf. II. *n.* (**—s**) golf.

Gondel ['gɔndəl], *f.* (*pl.* **—n**) gondola; car of a balloon.

Gönn—en ['gœnən], *v.a.* to favour; to wish well to; to bestow; to grant; to permit; **ich —e es Ihnen von Herzen,** I wish you every joy with it. **—er,** *m.* (**—ers,** *pl.* **—er**) well-wisher; patron, protector. **—erhaft,** *adj.* favouring; patronizing. **—erin,** *f.* patroness.

Gott [gɔt], *m.* (**—es**, *pl.* **Götter**) God; god. **—heit,** *f.* deity; divinity; God-head. **—ähnlich,** *adj.* godlike, divine. **—ergeben,** *adj.* devout. **—es-acker,** *m.* churchyard. **—es-dienst,** *m.* divine service. **—es-gelehrtheit,** *f.* divinity, theology. **—es-gelehrsamfeit,** *f.* divinity, theology. **—es-gelehrte(r),** *m.* divine, theologian. **—es-lästerer,** *m.* blasphemer. **—es-lästerlich,** *adj.* blasphemous. **—es-leugner,** *m.* atheist. **—es-leugnerisch,**

adj. atheistical. **—es-leugnung,** **—es-leugnerei** [—ə'raɪ], *f.* atheism. **—lob** [—'lo:p], *int.* thank God! God be praised! **—los,** *adj.* irreligious, ungodly; impious. **—seibeiuns,** *m.* (*euphemism for*) the devil. **—selig,** *adj.* godly, pious; blessed. **—selig-feit,** *f.* godliness, piety, devotion.

Gött—erhaft ['gœtərhaft], *adj.* godlike. **—erschaft,** *f.,* **—ertum,** *n.* the gods (*coll.*); divine nature. **—in,** *f.* goddess. **—lich,** *adj.* godlike, divine. **—lichfeit,** *f.* divinity; godliness. **—er-däm-merung,** *f.* twilight of the gods. **—er-lehre,** *f.* mythology. **—er-sage,** *f.* myth.

Götze ['gœtsə], *m.* (**—n,** *pl.* **—n**) idol. **—ntum,** *n.* idolatry. **—n-bild,** *n.* idol.

Grab [gra:p], *n.* (**—es,** *pl.* **Gräber**) grave. **—gesang,** *m.* dirge. **—schrift,** *f.* epitaph. **—tuch,** *n.* winding-sheet, shroud.

Graben ['gra:bən], I. *ir.v.a.* to dig. II. *m.* (**—s,** *pl.* **Gräben**) ditch; trench.

Grad [gra:t], *m.* (**—es,** *pl.* **—e**) step; degree. **—weise,** *adj. & adv.* gradual. **—uiren** [—du'i:rən], *v.a. & n.* (*aux.* h.) to graduate, take a degree. **—uierte(r),** *m.* graduate.

Graf [gra:f], *m.* (**—en,** *pl.* **—en**) earl, count. **—schaft,** *f.* county, earldom.

Gräf—in ['grɛ:fɪn], *f.* countess. **—lich,** *adj.* like a count *or* earl.

Gram [gra:m], *m.* (**—(e)s**) grief, sorrow.

Gräm—en ['grɛ:mən], I. *v.a.* to grieve. II. *v.r.* to grieve (for); **sich zu Tode —en,** to die with grief. **—lich,** *adj.* peevish, morose, sullen.

Gramm [gram], *n.* (**—s**) gramme (15·438 *grains troy*); *abbr.* **G.**

Grammat—ik [gra'matɪk], *f.* (*pl.* **—ifen**) grammar. **—isch,** **—ifalisch** [—'ka:lɪʃ], *adj.* grammatical.

Granat [gra'na:t], *m.* (**—(e)s,** *pl.* **—e**) garnet. **—apfel,** *m.* pomegranate. **—stein,** *m.* garnet.

Granat—e [gra'na:tə], *f.* (*pl.* **—en**) grenade; shell (*Mil.*). **—en-splitter,** *pl.,* **—en-stücke,** *pl.* splinters of shell. **—tartätschen,** *pl.* shrapnel. **—fugel,** *f.* shell.

Granit [gra'ni:t], *m.* (**—(e)s,** *pl.* **—e**) granite. **—en,** *adj.* granitic.

Gras [gra:s], *n.* (**—(f)es,** *pl.* **Gräser**) grass. **—(f)ig,** *adj.* grassy. **—halm,**

m. blade of grass. —**müde**, *f.* hedge-sparrow.

Gräßlich ['grɛslɪç], *adj.* terrible, shocking. —**feit**, *f.* atrocity.

Grat [graːt], *m.* (—**es**, *pl.* —**e**) point; edge, ridge.

Gräte ['grɛːtə], *f.* (*pl.* —**n**) fish-bone.

Grat—ulieren [gratuˈliːrən], *v.a.* (einem) to congratulate (a person).

Grau [grau], I. *adj.* grey. II. *subst.n.* grey colour. —**heit**, *f.* greyness. —**lich**, *adj.* & *adv.* grizzly, greyish. —**haarig**, *adj.* grizzled, grey-haired.

Grau—en ['grauən], I. *v.n.* (*aux.* h.) to grow grey; to dawn. II. *v.n.* & *imp.* (einem) to have a horror of. III. *subst.n.* horror, dread. —**enhaft**, *adj.* & *adv.* horrible; uncanny; dreadful. —**envoll**, *adj.* awful, horrible. —**lich**, *adj.* horrible.

Graupe ['graupə], *f.* (*pl.* —**n**) peeled barley, groat. —**n=grütze**, *f.* barley-groats. —**n=suppe**, *f.* barley broth.

Graus [graus], *m.* (—**(f)es**) horror, dread; dreadful thing.

Grausam [grauzaːm], *adj.* & *adv.* cruel, inhuman, fierce. —**feit**, *f.* cruelty, ferocity.

Grav—ieren [graˈviːrən], *v.a.* to engrave. —**ierer**, *m.* engraver. —**üre** [—ˈvyːrə], *f.* engraving.

Greif [graif], *m.* (—**(e)s**, *pl.* —**e**) griffin.

Greifen ['graifən], *ir.v.a.* & *n.* (*aux.* h.) to grasp; man kann es mit Händen —, it is quite evident.

Greinen ['grainən], *v.n.* (*aux.* h.) to cry.

Greis [grais], I. *adj.* hoary. II. *m.* (—**(f)es**, *pl.* —**(f)e**) old man. —**=(f)enhaft**, *adj.* senile, oldish. —**(f)in**, *f.* old woman. —**(f)en=alter**, *n.* old age, senility.

Grell [grɛl], *adj.* dazzling; glaring. —**heit**, *f.* harshness; glaringness.

Grenadier [grenaˈdiːr], *m.* (—**s**, *pl.* —**e**) grenadier.

Grenz—e ['grɛntsə], *f.* (*pl.* —**en**) frontier; boundary. —**en**, *v.n.* (*aux.* h.) to border (on, an *with acc.*); to adjoin. —**en=los**, *adj.* boundless, unlimited. —**mal**, *n.* landmark.

Greuel ['grɔyəl], *m.* (—**s**, *pl.* —) abomination; outrage. —**=tat**, *f.* atrocity, deed of horror.

Gries [griːs], *m.* (—**(f)es**) gravel. —**(f)ig**, *adj.* & *adv.* gritty, gravelly. —**gram**, *m.* ill-humour; grumbler. —**grämig**, —**grämlich**, *adj.* morose.

Griff [grɪf], *m.* (—**es**, *pl.* —**e**) grip, grasp; handle; hilt.

Grill—e ['grɪlə], *f.* (*pl.* —**en**) cricket (*Ent.*); whim. —**enhaft**, —**ig**, *adj.* & *adv.* whimsical, capricious. —**en=fänger**, *m.* whimsical fellow. —**en=haftigfeit**, *f.* fancifulness, capriciousness.

Grimasse [griˈmasə], (*pl.* —**n**) grimace.

Grimm [grɪm], *m.* (—**(e)s**) fury, rage. —**ig**, *adj.* & *adv.* enraged; fierce, grim; violent. —**igfeit**, *f.* fury, grimness.

Grinsen ['grɪnzən], I. *v.n.* (*aux.* h.) to grin; to sneer. II. *subst.n.* grin, sneer.

Grippe ['grɪpə], *f.* (*pl.* —**n**) influenza.

Grob [groːp], *adj.* & *adv.* (*comp.* **gröber**, *sup.* **gröbst**) coarse; rude, uncivil. —**=heit**, *f.* coarseness; insolence. —**ian**, *m.* (—**ians**, *pl.* —**iane**) rude fellow.

Gröblich ['grøːplɪç], *adj.* & *adv.* somewhat coarse *or* gross.

Groll [grɔl], *m.* (—**(e)s**) ill-will; resentment. —**en**, *v.n.* (*aux.* h.) (*usually dat. but also with* auf (*acc.*), gegen, *or* mit) be angry with; to roar; to rumble (*of thunder*).

Gros [groː], *n.* gross; en —, wholesale.

Groschen ['grɔʃən], *m.* (—**s**, *pl.* —) small obsolete silver coin.

Groß [groːs] (*comp.* **größer**, *sup.* **größ=(ef)t**), *adj.* & *adv.* tall; high; large; big, vast; huge; important; im —en und ganzen, on the whole. —**heit**, *f.* greatness. —**artig**, *adj.* & *adv.* grand, noble, magnificent. —**artigfeit**, *f.* grandeur. —**eltern**, *pl.* grandparents. —**enfel**, *m.* great-grandson. —**enfelin**, *f.* great-granddaughter. —**en=teils**, *adv.* mainly, to a large extent. —**fürst**, *m.* grand-duke. —**handel**, *m.* wholesale trade. —**händler**, *m.* wholesale dealer *or* merchant. —**handlung**, *f.* wholesale warehouse *or* firm. —**herzog**, *m.* grand-duke. —**herzogin**, *f.* grand-duchess. —**her=zoglich**, *adj.* grand-ducal. —**herzog=tum**, *n.* grand-duchy. —**mächte**, *pl.* the great powers (*of Europe*). —**mächtig**, I. *adj.* high and mighty. II. *adv.* enormously. —**mut**, *f.* magnanimity; generosity. —**mütig**, *adj.* magnanimous; generous. —**mutter**, *f.* grandmother. —**sprecherisch**, *adj.* boastful; swaggering. —**spurig**, *adj.* arrogant, conceited. —**vater**, *m.* grandfather. —**vater=stuhl**, *m.* arm-chair, easy-chair. —zügig, *adj.* on a grand scale.

Größe ['grø:sə], *f.* (*pl.* —n) height; size; bulk; magnitude.

Grotte ['grotə], *f.* (*pl.* —n) grotto.

Grube ['gru:bə], *f.* (*pl.* —n) pit; hole; mine.

Grüb—chen ['gry:pçən], *n.* (—s, *pl.* —) dimple. —eln, *v.n.* (*aux.* h.) to brood.

Gruft [gruft], *f.* (*pl.* Grüfte) vault; cave.

Grün [gry:n], I. *adj. & adv.* green; —er Junge, greenhorn. II. *n.* green colour, verdure. —e, *f.* greenness. —lich, *adj. & adv.* greenish. —span, *m.* (—span(e)s, *pl.* —spane) verdigris.

Grund [grunt], *m.* (—es, *pl.* Gründe) ground, earth, soil; bottom; valley; basis, groundwork; reason, cause, motive; argument. —besitz, *m.* landed property. —besitzer, *m.* landed proprietor. —falsch, *adj.* fundamentally wrong. —legung, *f.* laying the foundation. —los, *adj. & adv.* bottomless; unfathomable; unfounded. —satz, *m.* principle; rule of conduct; axiom. —text, *m.* (—es, *pl.* —e) original text.

Gründ—en ['gryndən], I. *v.a.* to establish. II. *n.* (*aux.* h.) to sound the depth. —er, *m.* (—ers) founder; establisher. —lich, *adj. & adv.* thorough. —lichkeit, *f.* thoroughness. —ung, *f.* foundation, establishment.

Grunzen ['gryntsən], I. *v.n.* (*aux.* h.) to grunt. II. *subst.n.* grunt.

Grupp—e ['grupə], *f.* (*pl.* —en) group. —ieren [—'pi:rən], *v.a.* to group. —ierung, *f.* arrangement; organization. —enweise, *adv.* in groups or clusters.

Gruß [gru:s], *m.* (—es, *pl.* Grüße) salute; greeting.

Grüßen ['gry:sən], *v.a.* to greet; to salute; — lassen, to send one's kind regards.

Grütze ['grytsə], *f.* (*pl.* —n) peeled grain, groats.

Guck [guk], *m.* (—s) look, peep. —en, *v.n.* (*aux.* h.) to look, to peep. —er, *m.* (—ers, *pl.* —er) peeper; spy-glass; Opern—er, opera glass.

Gulden ['guldən], *m.* (—s, *pl.* —) florin, guilder.

Gült—ig ['gyltɪç], *adj. & adv.* valid, legal; binding; current; admissible;

applicable; available. —igkeit, *f.* validity.

Gummi ['gumi:], *n.* (—s) rubber; gum. —artig, *adj.* gummy. —artikel, *pl.* indiarubber goods or articles. —band, *n.* elastic band. —schuhe, *pl.* goloshes.

Gunst [gunst], *f.* (*pl.* —bezeugungen) favour, grace.

Günst—ig ['gynstɪç], *adj. & adv.* favourable, gracious. —ling, *m.* (—lings, *pl.* —linge) favourite.

Gurgel ['gurgəl], *f.* (*pl.* —n) gullet, throat. —n, *v.n.* (*aux.* h.) to utter a gurgling sound; to gargle.

Gurke ['gurkə], *f.* (*pl.* —n) cucumber.

Gurren ['gurən], *v.n.* (*aux.* h.) to coo.

Gurt [gurt], *m.* (—es, *pl.* —e), —e, *f.* (*pl.* —en) girth.

Gürtel ['gyrtəl], *m.* (—s, *pl.* —) girdle. —tier, *n.* (—es, *pl.* —e) armadillo.

Gürten ['gyrtən], *v.a.* to gird.

Guß ['gus], *m.* (—(ss)es, *pl.* Güsse) gush; downpour; spout.

Gut [gu:t], (*comp.* besser, *sup.* best) I. *adj. & adv.* good; —er Dinge sein, to be of good cheer; kurz und —, in short; etwas wieder — machen, to repair; to compensate; er hat es —, he is well off, lucky. II. *n.* (—es, *pl.* Güter) good thing, blessing; property; estate; farm. —achten, *n.* opinion. —befinden, *n.* discretion; approval. —haben, *n.* credit, balance in one's favour. —heißung, *f.* approbation, consent. —herzig, *adj.* good-hearted; kind. —mütig, *adj.* good-natured. —s= besitzer, —s=herr, *m.* landowner. —willig, *adj.* voluntary; obliging. —willigkeit, *f.* willingness.

Güt—e ['gy:tə], *f.* kindness; goodness; excellence. haben Sie die —e, be so kind as to. —ig, *adj. & adv.* good, kind; gracious; benevolent. —ig= keit, *f.* goodness, kindness. —lich, *adj. & adv.* amicable.

Gymnas—iast [gymnazɪ'ast], *m.* (—s iasten, *pl.* —iasten) grammar-school boy. —ium [gym'na:zɪəm], *n.* (—iums, *pl.* Gymnasien) grammar-school.

H

H, h, *n.* H, h.

Haar [ha:r], *n.* (—es, *pl.* —e) hair. um ein —, within a hair's breadth. —ig, *adj.* hairy. —klein, *adj. & adv.*

to a hair, to a nicety. —los, *adj.*
hairless. —nadel, *f.* hair-pin. —=
scharf, *adj. & adv.* very sharp.
—sträubend, *adj.* shocking, atrocious.
Habe ['ha:bə], *f.* property; Hab' und
Gut, goods and chattels.
Haben ['ha:bən], I. *ir.v.a.* to have;
gern —, to like. II. *subst.n.* credit;
Soll und —, debit and credit.
Hab=gier ['ha:pgi:r], *f.,* —sucht
[—suxt], *f.* covetousness, avarice,
greediness. —gierig, —süchtig, *adj.*
avaricious, covetous, greedy.
Habicht [ha:bɪçt], *m.* (—s, *pl.* —e)
hawk.
Hack [hak], *m.* (—es, *pl.* —e) hack.
—en, *v.a.* to chop, hack. —fleisch,
n. minced meat.
¹Hacke ['hakə], *f.* (*pl.* —n) pickaxe.
²Hacke ['hakə], *f.* (*pl.* —n), —n, *m.*
(—ns, *pl.* —n) heel (*of a shoe*).
Häderling ['hɛkərlɪŋ], *m.*(—s) chopped
straw.
Hader ['ha:dər], *m.* (—s) quarrel,
brawl, strife. —er (—ers, *pl.* —er)
wrangler, brawler. —süchtig, *adj.*
quarrelsome.
Hadern ['ha:dərn], *v.n.* (*aux.* h.) to
quarrel, dispute.
Hafen ['ha:fən], *m.* (—s, *pl.* Häfen)
harbour; refuge. —stadt, *f.* seaport.
Hafer ['ha:fər], *m.* (—s) oats.
Haft [haft], I. *m.* (—es, *pl.* —e) hold,
keeping hold. II.*f.*(*pl.*—en) custody;
prison. III. *suff.* (*second part of
comp.=*) possessing; causing; giving;
like. —befehl, —brief, *m.* warrant of
arrest. —en, *v.r.* (*aux.* h.) to cling to.
—ung, *f.* security, bail; mit beschränk=
ter —ung, limited (liability) (*C.L.*).
Hag [ha:k], *m.* (—es, *pl.* —e) hedge.
—e=buche, *f.* hornbeam. —e=butte, *f.*
hip, haw. —e=dorn, *m.* hawthorn.
—e=stolz, *m.* (—estolzen, *pl.* —estolzen)
(old) bachelor.
Hagel ['ha:gəl], *m.* (—s) hail. —dicht,
adj. thick as hail. —wetter, *n.* hail-
storm.
Hager ['ha:gər], *adj.* thin, lean. —keit,
f. leanness, meagreness.
Häher ['hɛ:ər], *m.* (—s, *pl.* —) jay.
Hahn [ha:n], *m.* (—(e)s, *pl.* Hähne,
dim. Hähnchen, cockerel) cock. —en=
kamm, *m.* cock's comb. —en=ruf,
—en=schrei, *m.* cock-crowing.
Hai [hai], —fisch,) *m.* (—s, *pl.* —e)
shark.

Hain [hain], *m.* (—es, *pl.* —e) grove,
wood, thicket.
Hät=chen ['hɛkçən], *n.* (—chens, *pl.*
—chen) little hook, crochet. —elei
[—'lai], *f.* crochet-work. —el=arbeit,
f. crochet-work. —el=hafen, *m.,* —el=
nadel, *f.* crochet-needle.
Hak=en ['ha:kən], I. *m.*(ens, *pl.* —en)
hook. II. *v.a.* to hook; to grapple.
—ig, *adj. & adv.* hooked. —en=kreuz,
n. swastika.
Halb [halp], I. *adj.* half. II. *adv.* by
halves, half. III. *n.* half; *as a suffix=*
account, reason, because [*as* deshalb,
on this, that account] *or=*side [*as*
außer—, outside]. IV. *pref.* (*in comp.*)
*generally=*semi, demi, half. —e(s), *n.*
half, moiety. —en (—er), *prep.* (*with
preceding gen.*) for, on account of, on
behalf of, because of, for the sake of.
—gott, *m.* demigod. —insel, *f.* peninsula. —insel=förmig, *adj.* peninsular.
—jährlich, *adj.* occurring every six
months, half-yearly. —kreis, *m.* semi-
circle. —kreis=förmig, *adj.* semi-
circular. —kugel, *f.* hemisphere.
—laut, *adj. & adv.* in an undertone.
—mond, *m.* crescent, half-moon.
—wegs, *adv.* half-way; tolerably(*coll.*).
Hälfte ['hɛlftə], *f.* (*pl.* —n) half.
Halfter ['halftər], *f.* (*pl.* —n), *sometimes m. & n.* (—s, *pl.* —) halter.
Halle ['halə], *f.* (*pl.* —n) hall.
Hallen ['halən], *v.n.* (*aux.* h.) to sound,
resound.
Halm [halm], *m.* (—(e)s, *pl.* —e)
blade; stalk.
Hals [hals], *m.* (—(f)es, *pl.* Hälse)
neck; throat; — über Kopf, head over
heels; aus vollem —e lachen, to
laugh heartily. —band, *n.* collar;
necklace. —bein, *n.* collar-bone. —=
binde, *f.* cravat; necktie. —bräune,
f. quinsy. —brechend, dangerous.
—tragen, *m.* cape, collar.
Halt [halt], I. *m.* (—(e)s, *pl.* —e) hold.
II. *int.* halt! hold! stop! —bar, *adj.
& adv.* tenable, defensible; durable.
—barkeit, *f.* defensibility; durability,
firmness, strength. —los, *adj.* unsteady; vain; unprincipled. —losigkeit,
f. instability, unsteadiness. —en, I.
ir.v.a. to hold; to keep; to maintain;
to deem, consider; eine Rede —en,
to deliver a speech; große Stücke —en
auf, to have a high opinion of. II.
n. (*aux.* h.) to hold out, endure. III.

r. to behave; to last, keep good.
—er, *m.* (—ers, *pl.* —er) holder;
keeper. —ung, *f.* holding; keeping.
Hämisch ['hɛːmɪʃ], *adj.* malicious;
spiteful.
Hammel ['haməl], *m.* (—s, *pl.* Hämmel)
wether. —braten, *m.* roast mutton.
—fleisch, *n.* mutton.
Hammer ['hamər], *m.* (—s, *pl.* Häm=
mer) hammer.
Hämmern ['hɛmərn], *v.a. & n. (aux. h.)*
to hammer.
Hand [hant], *f. (pl.* Hände; *in some
phrases* Handen, *e.g.* vorhanden) hand;
jemandem die — drüden, to shake
hands with a person; aus bester —,
from the best source; eine — wäscht
die andere, one good turn deserves
another. —haft, *adj. & adv.* actual,
in the act. —lich, *adj. & adv.* easily
managed. —lung, *f.* action, deed;
business, trade, commerce; shop,
warehouse; firm. —arbeit, *f.* manual
labour. —arbeiter, *m.* workman;
labourer. —ballen, *m.* ball of the
thumb. —buch, *n.* handbook. —=
fertig, *adj.* skilful with one's hands.
—fertigkeit, *f.* manual skill. —greif=
lich, *adj.* palpable, obvious. —griff,
m. handle; handrail. —haben,
ir.v.a. (*insep.*) to handle; to manage.
—fuß, *m.* kissing of the hand.
—schlag, *m.* shaking hands; blow.
schrift, *f.* manuscript. —schriftlich,
adj. & adv. in manuscript. —schuh,
m. glove. —tuch, *n.* towel. —voll,
f. handful. —weiser, *m.* finger-post.
—werf, *n.* handicraft. —werker,
workman. —werker=stand, *m.* artisans.
—werker=verein, *m.* trade-union. —=
werks=innung, *f.* guild. —wörterbuch,
n. pocket dictionary.
Händ=ig ['hɛndɪç], *suff.* (*in comp.*=)
-handed. —ler, *m.* (—lers, *pl.* —ler)
dealer. —e=drud, *m.* shake of the
hand, hand-shaking. —e=klatschen, *n.*
clapping of hands, applause.
Handel ['handəl], *m.* (—s, *pl.* Händel)
transaction, business; trade, com=
merce; bargain (*pl.*); dispute. —schaft,
f. trade, commerce. —schaftlich, *adj.
& adv.* mercantile. *Comp.* —s, *as the
first part of numerous compounds=*
commercial, mercantile, trade-; *of*
commerce or trade, business. —s=
brauch, *m.* trade-custom. —s=einig,
adj.; —seinig werden, to come to an

agreement. —s=freund, *m.* business-
friend, correspondent. —s=genoß, *m.*
partner. —s=genossenschaft, *f.* partnership; trading company. —s=
gesellschaft, *f.* trading company; partnership in trade. —s=gesetz, *n.* commercial law. —s=hochschule, *f.* commercial academy. —s=kammer, *f.*
chamber of commerce. —s=konjunk=
tur, *f.* course of the market. —s=
leute, *pl.* tradespeople; merchants.
—s=mann, *m.* merchant; man of business, tradesman. —s=reisende(r), *m.*
commercial traveller. —s=stand, *m.*
trading class; the merchants; the
commercial world. —s=vorrat, *m.*
stock-in-trade. —s=wesen, *n.* anything relating to commerce *or* trade,
business. —s=zeichen, *n.* trade-mark.
—treibend, *adj.* trading, commercial.
Handel—n ['handəln], *v.n. (aux. h.)* to
behave, act; to bargain; to deal,
trade; es —t sich um, the question
is.
Hanf [hanf], *m.* (—es) hemp. —en,
adj. hempen.
Hang [haŋ], *m.* (—es) slope; inclination, propensity. —en, *ir.v.n. (aux.
h. & s.)* to hang.
Häng—en ['hɛŋən], *v.a.* to cause to
hang, hang. —e=brüde, *f.* suspension-
bridge. —er, *m.* (—ers, *pl.* —er)
pendant. —e=matte, *f.* hammock.
Hantier—en [han'tiːrən], *v.* I. *a.* to
handle. II. *n. (aux. h.)* to do business.
—er, *m.* (—ers, *pl.* —er) tradesman.
—ung, *f.* business; trade; management.
Happ—en ['hapən], *m.* (—s, *pl.* —)
morsel, mouthful. —ig, *adj.* greedy.
Harf—e ['harfə], *f. (pl.* —en) harp.
—en, *n. (aux. h.)* to play the harp.
—enist, *m.* (—enisten, *pl.* —enisten),
—ner, *m.* (—ners, *pl.* —ner) harper,
harpist. —en=saite, *f.* harp-string.
Häring ['hɛːrɪŋ], *m.* (—s, *pl.* —e)
herring.
Harm [harm], *m.* (—s) grief. —los,
adj. harmless; without sorrow.
Harmonie [harmo'niː], *f. (pl.* —n)
harmony.
Harn [harn], *m.* (—s) urine.
Harpune [har'puːnə], *f. (pl.* —n)
harpoon.
Harren ['harən], *v.n. (aux. h.)* to wait
in expectation.
Hart [hart], *adj. & adv.* (härter,

härteft) hard; harsh. —nädig, adj. obstinate.

Härt—e ['hɛrtə], f. (pl. —en) harshness. —en, v.a. to harden; to temper.

Harz [harts], n. (—es, pl. —e) resin, rosin. —ig, adj. resinous.

Hafchen ['haʃən], I. v.a. to catch, to seize. II. v.n. (aux. h.); — nach, to snatch at; to aim at.

Hafe [ha:zə], m. (—n, pl. —n) hare. —n=fuß, m. coward. —n=haft, adj. & adv. faint-hearted, timid. —n= hetze, f. coursing.

Hafel ['ha:zəl], f. (pl. —en) hazel-bush.

Hafpe ['haspə], Häfpe ['hɛspə], f. (pl. —en) hasp, hinge.

Hafpel ['haspəl], m. (—s) reel; wind-lass. —n, v.a. & n. (aux. h.) to wind.

Haß [has], m. (—(ß)es) hate. —(ß)en, v.a. to hate, detest. —(ß)er, m. (—(ß)ers, pl. —(ß)er) hater; enemy.

Häßlich ['hɛslɪç], adj. odious; base; loathsome; ugly. —feit, f. ugliness; badness; loathsomeness.

Haft [hast], f. haste. —en, v. I. a. to hasten. II. n. (aux. h.) & imp. to haste. —ig, adj. & adv. hasty, rash; passionate. —igfeit, f. hastiness; rashness.

Hau [hau], m. (—es, pl. —e) stroke. —bar, adj. & adv. fit for felling.

Haube ['haubə], f. (pl. —n) cap, coif; hood; unter die — bringen, to find a husband for a girl.

Haubitze [hau'brtsə], f. howitzer.

Hauch [haux], m. (—es) breath. —en, v. I. n. (aux. h.) to breathe, respire. II. a. to breathe out, exhale. —laut, m. aspirate.

Haue ['hauə], f. (pl. —n) hoe.

Hauen ['hauən], ir.v.a. to hew.

Hauf—en ['haufən], m. (—ens, pl. —en) heap; troop; swarm; über den —en fallen, to tumble down.

Häuf—en ['hɔyfən], v.a. to accumulate; to heap up. —ung, f. heaping.

Häufig ['hɔyfɪç], I. adj. copious, abundant; frequent. II. adv. often; abundantly. —feit, f. frequency.

Haupt [haupt], n. (—es, pl. Häupter) head. In compounds: main, principal. —begriff, m. leading idea. —betrag, m. sum total. —beweis, m. main proof. —mann, m. (—mannes, pl. —leute) captain (Mil.). —punkt, m. cardinal point; chief feature. —quartier, n. headquarters. —fache, f.

chief matter, main point; (pl.) essentials. —fächlich, I. adj. essential, principal, main, of chief importance. II. adv. essentially, chiefly, particularly, above all. —ftadt, f. metropolis, capital. —ftädtisch, adj. metropolitan.

Haus [haus], n. (—fes, pl. Häuser) house; zu —(ß)e, at home; nach —(ß)e, homeward; von —(ß)e, from home. —arzt, m. family doctor. —besitzer, m. proprietor of a house. —flur, f. vestibule. —frau, f. mistress of a house. —freund, m. family friend. —friede, m. domestic peace, domestic security. —halt, m. housekeeping; house, household. —halten, I. ir.v.a. to keep house; to economize. II. subst.n. housekeeping; management. —hälter, —halter, m. householder; good manager, economist. —hälterin, f. housekeeper. —hälterisch, adj. economical. —lehrer, m. private tutor. —wesen, n. domestic concerns, household. —wirt, m. landlord; host. —wirtin, f. landlady; hostess. —= wirtschaft, f. housekeeping; domestic economy.

Häus—chen ['hɔysçən], n. (—chens, pl. —chen) small house, cottage. —lich, adj. domestic; household.

Hauf—en ['hauzən], v.n. (aux. h.) to lodge. —ieren [—'zi:rən], v.n. (aux. h.) to go about peddling. —ierer, m. (—ierers, pl. —ierer) pedlar.

Haut [haut], f. (pl. Häute) hide; skin; bis auf die — durchnäßt, drenched to the skin; arme —, poor creature! —pflege, f. cosmetics.

Heb—e ['he:bə], f. (pl. —en) —el, m. (—els, pl. —el) lever. —eln, v.a. & n. (aux. h.) to move with a lever. —en, ir.v. I. a. to lift, raise; aus dem Sattel —en, to unhorse. II. r. to rise. —er, m. (—ers, pl. —er) lifter, raiser; crane. —lich, adj. & adv. that may be raised. —ung, f. raising. —amme, f. midwife. —eeisen, n. crowbar. —elfraft, f. leverage (-power).

Hech—el [hɛçəl], f. (pl. —eln) hackle, flax-comb. —eln, v.a. to hackle.

Hecht [hɛçt], m. (—es, pl. —e) pike.

Heck [hɛk], n. (—(e)s, pl. —e) lattice-work fence; stern. —e, f. (pl. —en) hedge.

Heer [he:r], n. (—es, pl. —e) army; host. —führer, m. general, commander-in-chief. —schau, f. military review. —ſtraße, f. military road; highway. —zug, m. march of an army; army on the march; campaign.

Hefe ['he:fə], f. (pl. —n) yeast; dregs.

Heft [heft], n. (—es, pl. —e) handle, hilt; number, or part, of a work; copybook. —en, v.a. to fasten; to stitch; to pin. —pflaſter, n. (—s, pl. —) adhesive-plaster. —ung, f. fastening. —weiſe, adv. in numbers, in parts.

Heft=ig ['heftɪç], adj. & adv. forcible, violent. —igkeit, f. vehemence, violence, impetuosity.

Hegen ['he:gən], v.a. to enclose; to protect, preserve.

Hehl [he:l], n. (—(e)s) concealment; er macht kein — daraus, he makes no secret of it. —en, v.a. to conceal. —er, m. (—ers, pl. —er) concealer; receiver (of stolen goods).

Hehr [he:r], adj. & adv. exalted, majestic.

Heida [haɪ'da:], Heiſa, int. huzza!

[1] Heid—e [haɪdə], f. (pl. —en) heath. —ig, adj. & adv. heathy. —e=kraut, n. heather. —el=beere, f. bilberry.

[2] Heid—e ['haɪdə], m. (—en, pl. —en), —in, f. heathen. —angſt, f. great fear; ich habe eine —enangſt, I am in mortal terror. —en=bild, n. idol. —en=tum, n. heathendom. —niſch, adj. & adv. heathenish, pagan.

Heil [haɪl], I. adj. & adv. sound, whole; healed. II. n. (—(e)s) prosperity; salvation, redemption. —and, m. (—ands, pl. —ande) Saviour. —bar, adj. & adv. curable. —barkeit, f. curableness. III. —! int. hail! —en, v. I. a. to heal, cure. II. n. (aux. ſ.) to grow well; to heal. —er, m. (—ers, pl. —er) healer. —los, adj. & adv. wicked. —ſam, adj. & adv. healing; wholesome. —ſamkeit, f. wholesomeness. —ung, f. healing; cure. —anſtalt, f. hospital. —mittel, n. remedy. —s=armee, f. Salvation Army.

Heilig ['haɪlɪç], I. adj. & adv. holy; —ſprechen, to canonize. —e(r), m., —e, f. saint. —keit, f. holiness. —tum, n. (—tums, pl. —tümer) sanctuary; relic. —abend, m. Christmas Eve. —en, v.a. to sanctify. —ung, f. sanctification; consecration.

Heim [haɪm], I. adv. home, homeward. II. n. (—s, pl. —e) home. —at, f. (pl. —aten) home, native place or country. —chen, n. (Entom.) cricket. —iſch, adj.

& adv. home-bred; domestic. —lich, adj. & adv. secret; stealthy. —lichkeit, f. secrecy. —atlos, adj. homeless. —fehr, —kunft, f. return home. —tücke, f. malice. —tückiſch, adj. malicious, mischievous. —wärts, adv. homeward. —weh, n. home-sickness.

Heirat ['haɪra:t], f. (pl. —en) marriage. —en, v.a. & n. (aux. h.) to marry.

Heiſer ['haɪzər], adj. & adv. hoarse. —keit, f. hoarseness.

Heiß [haɪs], adj. & adv. hot.

Heiß—en ['haɪsən], ir.v. I. a. to command; to name; willkommen —en, to bid welcome. II. n. (aux. h.) to be called, to bear a name; to mean; das —t, that is to say.

Heiter ['haɪtər], adj. & adv. happy, cheerful; calm, unruffled. —keit, f. serenity, brightness; cheerfulness.

Heiz—en ['haɪtsən], v.a. to heat. —er, m. (—ers, pl. —er) stoker; heating-apparatus. —ung, f. heating, steam.

Hektar [hɛk'ta:r], m. & n. (—s, pl. —e) hectare.

Hekto— ['hɛkto], (in comp.) —gramm, n. hectogramme. —liter, n. & m. hectolitre.

Held [hɛlt], m. (—en, pl. —en) hero. —en=gedicht, n. epic. —enhaft, adj. & adv. heroic. —entum, n. heroism. —en=alter, n. heroic age. —en=mütig, adj. & adv. heroic. —en=mut, m. heroism. —in, f. heroine.

Helf—en ['hɛlfən], ir.v.n. (aux. h., dat.) to help; es hilft nichts, it is of no use. —er, m. (—ers, pl. —er) helper.

Hell [hɛl], adj. & adv. clear, bright. —en, v.a. to make clear or bright. —igkeit, f. clearness; brightness.

Heller ['hɛlər], m. (—s, pl. —) small copper coin, farthing.

Helm [hɛlm], m. (—es, pl. —e) helmet. —buſch, m. plume of a helmet.

Hemd—(e) [hɛmt, 'hɛmdə], n. (—(e)s, pl. —(e)n) shirt; chemise.

Hemiſphäre [hɛmɪs'fɛ:rə], f. (pl. —n) hemisphere.

Hemm—en ['hɛmən], v.a. to check, stop; to hinder. —nis, n. (—ni(ſſ)es, pl. —ni(ſſ)e) check, clog. —ung, f. arrest, restraint; prohibition.

Hengſt [hɛŋst], m. (—es, pl. —e) stallion.

Henkel ['hɛŋkəl], m. (—s, pl. —) handle.

Henker ['hɛŋkər], m. (—s, pl. —)

hangman. —s=knecht, *m.* hangman's assistant. —s=mahl, *n.* last meal before execution; farewell dinner.

Henne ['hɛnə], *f.* (*pl.* —n) hen.

Her [he:r], *adv.* hither, here, this way; near (*of place*); since, ago (*of time*); **hin und —**, to and fro; **es ist nicht weit — damit**, it is of little value. **—=bringen**, *ir.v.a.* to bring hither, in *or* up; to establish; to transmit; **—=gebracht**, handed down (to our own times), customary, established. **—=kommen**, I. *ir.v.n.* (*aux.* **s.**) to approach, advance; to be derived *or* descended (*from*). II. *subst.n.* origin, descent; traditional custom, usage. **—kömmlich**, *adj.* & *adv.* traditional, customary, usual. **—kunft**, *f.* arrival; origin, extraction. **—nach** [—'nax], *adv.* afterwards, hereafter; (*with preceding acc.*) **den Tag —nach**, the day after. **—nehmen**, *ir.v.a.* to take, *or* get, from (*somewhere*); to deduce, derive. **—nieder** [—'ni:dər], *adv.* & *sep. prefix*, down (*hither*). **—recken**, *v.a.* to stretch forth. **—reichen**, *v.a.* to reach, hand (to). **—über** [—'ry:bər], *adv.* & *sep. prefix*, over hither, to this side, across. **—zu** [—'tsu:], *adv.* & *sep. prefix*, hither.

Herab [hɛ'rap], *adv.* & *sep. prefix*, down (*hither*), down here; down from; downward; (*with preceding acc.*) **den Berg —**, down (*from*) the mountain. **—kommen**, *ir.v.n.* (*aux.* **s.**) to come down; to be brought low. **—lassen**, *ir.v.* I. *a.* to lower, to let down. II. *r.* to condescend; to stoop; **—lassend**, *adj.* condescending, affable. **—lassung**, *f.* condescension. **—sehen**, *ir.v.n.* (*aux.* **h.**) to look down (**auf einen** *or* **etwas**, upon a person *or* a thing), to despise. **—setzen**, *v.a.* to lower, degrade.

Heraldisch [he'raldɪʃ], *adj.* heraldic.

Heran [hɛ'ran], *adv.* & *sep. prefix*, on (*hither*), near, along; up along, upwards, from away; (*with preceding acc. signifies* motion towards the speaker); **nur —!** come on! **—kommen**, *ir.v.n.* (*aux.* **s.**) to approach. **—kunft**, *f.* approach. **—rücken**, *v.n.* (*aux.* **s.**) to push onward, advance; to draw near. **—wachsen**, *v.n.* to grow up.

Herauf [hɛ'rauf], *adv.* & *sep. prefix*, up (*hither*); upwards, from below (*towards the speaker*).

Heraus [hɛ'raus], *adv.* & *sep. prefix*, out (*hither*); from within, forth, from among (*towards the speaker*); **— damit!** out with it, speak up! **—=fordern**, *v.a.* to challenge; to defy. **—gabe**, *f.* edition; publication. **—=geben**, *ir.v.a.* to give forth, hand out; to publish; to edit. **—geber**, *m.* editor; publisher. **—rücken**, *v.n.* (*aux.* **s.**) to march out, come forth.

Herb [hɛrp], *adj.* & *adv.* acid, sharp; harsh; bitter; sullen. **—e**, **—heit**, *f.* bitterness, harshness.

Herbei [hɛr'baɪ], *adv.* & *sep. prefix*, hither, near, on, this way, into the vicinity of (*the speaker or point contemplated*).

Herberg—e ['hɛrbɛrgə], *f.* (*pl.* **—en**) shelter, quarters; hostel. **—en**, *v.a.* & *n.* (*aux.* **h.**) to shelter, lodge.

Herbst [hɛrbst], *m.* (**—es**, *pl.* **—e**) autumn. **—lich**, *adj.* & *adv.* autumnal.

Herd [he:rt], *m.* (**—es**, *pl.* **—e**) hearth.

Herde ['he:rdə], *f.* (*pl.* **—n**) herd.

Herein [hɛ'raɪn], *adv.* & *sep. prefix*, in hither, in here; inward; **—!** come in! **—lassen**, *ir.v.a.* to admit.

Hermelin [hɛrmə'li:n], *n.* & *m.* (**—s**, *pl.* **—e**) ermine.

Herold ['he:rɔlt], *m.* (**—(e)s**, *pl.* **—e**) herald.

Herr [hɛr], *m.* (**—(e)n**, *pl.* **—en**) master; lord; gentleman; sir (*in address*); Mr. (*before proper names*). **—in**, *f.* lady; mistress. **—isch**, *adj.* & *adv.* domineering; imperious. **—lich**, *adj.* & *adv.* lordly; magnificent; glorious; capital; excellent. **—lichkeit**, *f.* lordliness; excellence; splendour. **—schaft**, *f.* lordship; dominion; mastery; **meine —schaften**, ladies and gentlemen! **—en=haus**, *n.* manor (house); mansion. **—en=los**, *adj.* ownerless. **—gott**, *m.* Lord God. **—n=huter**, *m.* Moravian (brother).

Herrsch—en ['hɛrʃən], *v.n.* (*aux.* **h.**) to rule, govern; to domineer. **—end**, *p.* & *adj.* ruling; predominant, prevailing. **—er**, *m.* (**—ers**, *pl.* **—er**) ruler. **—begier**, **—begierde**, *f.* lust of power.

Herum [hɛ'rʊm], *adv.* & *sep. prefix*, round about, around, right round, about; **rings —**, **rund —**, all round. **—schweifend**, *p.* & *adj.* wandering; vagrant.

Herunter [hɛ'rʊntər], *adv.* & *sep. prefix*, down; downward (*towards the speaker or point contemplated*). **—bringen**,

ir.v.a. to get down; to lower, reduce.
—**kommen**, *ir.v.n.* *(aux.* ſ.) to come
down; to alight; to decline, decay.
Hervor [her'fo:r], *adv. & sep. prefix,*
forth; forward, out; — **mit euch**!
come out! —**bringen**, *ir.v.a.* to bring
forth, produce; to utter; to elicit.
—**heben**, *ir.v.a.* to bring into prominence; to call special attention to.
—**leuchten**, *v.n.(aux.* ḥ.) to shine forth;
to be conspicuous. —**ragen**, *v.n.*
(aux. h.) to project; to rise above; to
exceed, surpass. —**ragend**, *p. & adj.*
prominent; distinguished; salient.
—**rufen**, *ir.v.a.* to call forth.
Herz [herts], *n.* (—**ens**, *pl.* —**en**) heart;
ſich etwas zu —**en nehmen**, to take a
thing to heart. —**haft**, *adj. & adv.*
courageous, brave. —**haftigkeit**, *f.*
courage, bravery. —**ig**, *adj. & adv.*
charming, sweet; *(in comp.=)* -heart-
ed. —**igkeit**, *f.* heartiness; loveliness;
(in comp.=) -heartedness. —**lich**, *adj.*
& adv. hearty, cordial, affectionate;
—**lich gern**, with all my heart. —**lich-**
keit, *f.* heartiness, cordiality, sincere
affection. —**allerliebſt** [—'li:pst], *adj.*
best beloved. —**blatt**, *n.* diaphragm.
—**erhebend**, *adj.* heart-stirring. —**-**
erſchütternd, *adj.* appalling. —**innig**,
adj. & adv. hearty, heart-felt. —**lieb**,
adj. & adv. very dear, dearly beloved.
—**liebchen**, *n.* sweetheart. —**zer-**
reiſſend, *adj.* heart-rending.
Herzen [hertsən], *v.a.* to caress, fondle;
to embrace.
Herzog ['hertso:k], *m.* (—**s**, *pl.* **Herzöge**)
duke. —**in**, *f.* duchess. —**lich**, *adj.*
& adv. ducal. —**tum**, *n.* (—**tums**, *pl.*
—**tümer**) duchy, dukedom.
Herzu [her'tsu:], *adv. & sep. prefix,*
up, towards a place.
Hetze ['hetsə], *f.* (*pl.* —**n**) chase, hunt.
—**n**, *v.a.* to hunt. —**r**, *m.* (—**rs**, *pl.*
—**r**) baiter; inciter. —**rei** [—'rai], *f.*
baiting; harassing.
Heu [hoy], *n.* (—**es**) hay.
Heuchelei [hoyçə'lai], *f.* hypocrisy.
Heuch—**eln** ['hoyçəln], *v.a.* to feign,
affect, simulate. —**ler**, *m.* (—**lers**, *pl.*
—**ler**), —**lerin**, *f.* hypocrite, dissembler. —**leriſch**, *adj. & adv.*
hypocritical.
Heulen ['hoylən], *v.n.(aux.* ḥ.) to howl.
Heut—**e** ['hoytə], *adv.* to-day; **von —e**
an, from this day forward; —**e vor**
acht Tagen, a week ago; —**e über**

vierzehn Tage, this day fortnight;
—**e früh**, this morning; —**e abend**,
to-night. —**zutage**, *adv.* nowadays.
—**ig**, *adj. & adv.* of to-day.
Hex—**e** ['heksə], *f.* (*pl.* —**en**) witch,
sorceress; hag. —**en**, *v.* I. *a.* to conjure up; to bewitch. II. *n.* (*aux.* ḥ.)
to conjure, to practise sorcery. —**en-**
meiſter, *m.* wizard. —**en-ſchuß**, *m.* lum-
bago.—**erei** [—ə'rai], *f.* witchcraft.
Hieb [hi:p], *m.* (—**es**, *pl.* —**e**) blow.
Hier [hi:r], *adv.* here; present; in this
place; in this ʾpoint or matter; *in
comp. with a prep.=the prep. with a
case of the dem. pron.* —**'ab**, *adv.*
herefrom, from this, *etc.* —**'an**, *adv.*
hereon, on, at *or* by this. —**'auf**, *adv.*
hereupon, upon this, at this; up here;
after that, afterwards, then. —**aus**,
adv. out of this, from here, from this,
hence, hereby, by this. —**'außen**,
adv. out here. —**bei**, *adv.* hereby, by,
at, in *or* with this; enclosed. —**durch**,
adv. through this place, through here;
by this means; by this, hereby.
—**ein**, *adv.* in(to) this place, in(to)
this. —**für**, *adv.* for this, for it,
instead of this. —**gegen** (ŋiegegen)
adv. against this *or* it; in return for
this. —**her**, *adv.* to this place, this
way, hither; **bis —her**, hitherto, till
now, so far. —**he'rum**, *adv.* here-
abouts, in this neighbourhood. —**hin**,
adv. in this direction, this way. —**in**,
adv. herein; in this. —**mit**, *adv.* here-
with, (along) with this; saying, doing
this. —**nach**, *adv.* after this; hereupon;
according to this. —**nächſt**, *adv.* next
to this, after this; close by. —**neben**,
adv. close by; besides. —**ſein**, *n.*
being here, sojourn here; presence.
—**ſelbſt**, *adv.* here, in this very place;
local *(in addresses)*. —**über**, *adv.* over
here; concerning this; hereat; on this
account. —**um**, *adv.* about *or* round
this place; about *or* concerning this.
—**unten**, *adv.* down here, here below.
—**'unter**, *adv.* hereunder; under this
or it; in, by this; among these.
—**von**, *adv.* hereof, of *or* from this.
—**wider**, *adv.* against this. —**zu**,
adv. to this; add to this; moreover;
to it; for it. —**'zwiſchen**, *adv.* between;
between these things.
Hilf—**e** ['hilfə], *f.* (*pl.* —**en**) help, aid;
—**e leiſten**, to help, assist. —**reich**,
adj. helpful. —**los**, *adj.* helpless.

—s=mittel, *n.* remedy. —s=zeitwort, *n.* auxiliary verb.

Himbeere ['hɪmbe:rə], *f.* (*pl.* —n) raspberry.

Himmel ['hɪməl], *m.* (—s, *pl.* —) heaven; heavens, sky; unter freiem —, in the open air. —an, —auf, *adv.* heavenwards. —fahrt, *f.* ascension. —hoch, *adj.* high as heaven, very high. —reich, *n.* kingdom of heaven; bliss. —s=gegend, *f.* quarter of the heavens; die vier —sgegenden, the four points of the compass. —weit, *adj. & adv.* very distant.

Himmlisch ['hɪmlɪʃ], *adj. & adv.* heavenly, celestial.

Hin [hɪn], *adv. & sep. prefix expressing motion from the speaker or point contemplated,* hence, that way, thither, towards that place; *used in regard to time to come or expressing duration of time,* towards, on, along; *sometimes implying simply motion with no distinct reference to direction,* along; gone, lost; spent; undone; er weiß weder — noch her, he is at his wits' end; — ist —, gone is gone, lost is lost. (*In comp. with verbs* hin *is sep. and has the accent; with preps. & advs. is insep. and the accent is on the prep. or adv.*) —arbeiten, *v.* I. *n.* (*aux.* h.) (auf eine S.) to aim at, struggle towards. II. *r.* to work one's way towards, attain with difficulty. —bannen, *v.a.* to conjure; —gebannt, spellbound. —begeben, *ir.v.r.* to betake oneself, repair (zu, to). —blic, *m.* prospect; im —blic auf, with regard to. —blicken, *v.a.* (*aux.* h.) to look towards. —blühen, *v.n.* (*aux.* ſ.) to fade away. —deuten, *v.n.* (*aux.* h.) to show the way. —deutung, *f.* (auf eine S.) hint. —eilen, *v.n.* (*aux.* ſ.) to hasten (away) to. —fort, *adv.* henceforth, in future. —führung, *f.* guiding, leading to *or* on. —gebung, *f.* resignation; devotion. —langen, *v.* I. *a.* (einem etwas) to hand, reach over. II. *n.* (*aux.* h.) to be adequate, suffice. —länglich, *adj.* sufficient, adequate. —legen, *v.* I. *a.* to lay down; to put away. II. *r.* to lie down. —reichend, *p. & adj.,* —reichlich, *adj.* sufficient, adequate, enough. —richten, *v.a.* to execute (*a malefactor*). —richtung, *f.* execution. —sichtlich, —sichts, *prep.* (*with gen.*) with regard to, as to, touching.

—streben, *v.n.* (*aux.* h.) (nach etwas) to tend towards; to strive after.

Hinab [hɪ'nap], *adv. & sep. prefix,* down (*thither*), downwards; — mit ihm! down with him!

Hinan [hɪ'nan], *adv. & sep. prefix,* up to (*a place*), towards, up (*away from the speaker or point contemplated*).

Hinauf [hɪ'nauf], *adv. & sep. prefix,* up (*thither*), up (*thence*), upwards; up to.

Hinaus [hɪ'naus], *adv. & sep. prefix,* out (*hence*), out (*thither*), forth, away out; beyond; vorn —, in the front; hinten —, at the back part *or* in the back (*of a house, etc.*); — mit ihm! turn him out! hoch —wollen, to aim high; wo wollen Sie —? what are you driving at?

Hinder—bar ['hɪndərba:r], *adj. & adv.* preventable. —lich, *adj.* (*with dat.*) & *adv.* hindering, embarrassing. —n, *v.a.* to hinder. —nis, *n.* (—ni(ſſ)es, *pl.* —ni(ſſ)e) hindrance. —nisrennen, *n.* steeplechase.

Hindurch [hɪn'durç], *adv. & sep. prefix,* through.

Hinein [hɪ'naɪn], *adv. & sep. prefix,* in (*thither*), into, from out here.

Hingegen [hɪn'ge:gən], *adv. & conj.* on the contrary, on the other hand.

Hinken ['hɪŋkən], *v.n.* (*aux.* h. & ſ.) to hobble, limp.

Hinnen ['hɪnən], *adv.* from hence.

Hinten ['hɪntən], *adv.* behind; in the rear; at the end, aft. —=drein, —=nach, *adv.* after, afterwards, after the event; last. —=vorn, *adv.* in an inverted state.

Hinter ['hɪntər], I. *adj. & insep. prefix,* hind, hinder. II. *adj. & insep. prefix,* behind, back; backwards. III. *prep.* behind; after; back of, in rear of; (*with acc. when implying motion to a place; with dat. when implying rest or limited motion in a place*); — her, after, behind. —e, *m.* posterior. —bringen, *ir.v.a.* (*insep.*) (einem etwas) to inform (*a person of a thing*). —bringer, *m.* informer; spy; telltale. —drein, *adv.* afterwards. —gehen, *ir.v.a.* (*insep.*) to deceive. —grund, *m.* background. —halt, *m.* ambush; reserve. —land, *n.* inland province, hinterland. —liſt, *f.* fraud. —liſtig, *adj. & adv.* cunning, artful, wily. —wärts, *adv.* backwards, behind.

Hinüber [hɪn'y:bər], *adv. & sep. prefix,* over there, thither, across.

Hinunter [hɪn'ʊntər], *adv. & sep. prefix,* down (*hence*), downward, from up here.

Hinweg [hɪn'vɛk], *adv. & sep. prefix,* away forth from here, off; let us go! —**nahme,** *f.* taking away.

Hinzu [hɪn'tsu:], *adv. & sep. prefix,* to, toward; near; to it, in addition. —**fügen,** *v.a.* to add to. —**kommen,** *ir.v.n. (aux.* ſ.) to approach.

Hirn [hɪrn], *n.* (—(e)s, *pl.* —e) brain, brains. —**gespinst,** *n.* phantom, illusion. —**verbrannt,** *adj.* insane.

Hirsch [hɪrʃ], *m.* (—es, *pl.* —e) stag. —**leder,** *n.* buckskin. —**ledern,** *adj.* made of buckskin.

Hirse ['hɪrzə], *f.* (*pl.* —n) millet.

Hirt [hɪrt], *m.* (—en, *pl.* —en), —e, *m.* (—en, *pl.* —en) herdsman, shepherd. —**en=mädchen,** *n.* shepherdess. —**en=volk,** *n.* nomadic tribe.

Histor—ie [hɪs'to:rɪə], *f.* (*pl.* —ien) history. —**iker,** *m.* (—ikers, *pl.* —iker) historian. —**isch,** *adj. & adv.* historical.

Hitz—e ['hɪtsə], *f.* heat. —**ig,** *adj. & adv.* hot. —**schlag,** *m.* sunstroke.

Hobel ['ho:bəl], *m.* (—s, *pl.* —) plane. —**n,** *v.a.* to plane.

Hoch [ho:x], I. *adj. & adv. (when followed by* e *of the inflected cases* ch *becomes* h, *as:* hoher, hohe, hohes, *or* der, die, das hohe; *comp.* höher; *sup.* höchst) high; — lebe der Kaiser! long live the Kaiser! das ist mir zu —, that is beyond my reach (*of comprehension*). II. *n.* (—s) cheer; toast. —**achtung,** *f.* esteem, regard. —**achtungs=voll,** *adj. & adv.* most respectful. —**deutsch,** *adj. & adv.* High-German. —**land,** *n.* highland, upland. —**länder,** *m.* highlander. —**mut,** *m.* haughtiness, pride, arrogance. —**mütig,** *adj.* of great courage. —**mütig,** *adj.* haughty, proud, arrogant. —**ofen,** *m.* blast-furnace. —**schule,** *f.* university. —**verrat,** *m.* high treason. —**verräter,** *m.* person guilty of high treason.

Höch—lich ['hø:çlɪç], *adv.* highly. —**st,** I. *adj.* (*see* Hoch) highest, extreme. II. *adv.* most, at the most, very, in the highest degree; (*in comp. generally=*) all, most.

Hochzeit ['hoxtsaɪt], *f.* (*pl.* —en) wedding, marriage. —**(s)feier,** *f.,* —**(s)fest,** *n.* wedding-feast.

Hocke ['hɔkə], *f.* (*pl.* —n) heap of sheaves.

Hocken ['hɔkən], *v.n. (aux.* h.) to crouch, cower.

Hof [ho:f], *m.* (—es, *pl.* Höfe) yard; farm; court; am, bei —e, at court; einem den — machen, to pay court to one. —**bauer,** *m.* peasant proprietor, farmer. —**beamte(r),** *m.* court-official. —**fähig,** *adj.* having the right to appear at court. —**gut,** *n.* domain, demesne. —**hund,** *m.* watch-dog. —**rat,** *m.* aulic council; aulic councillor; title of honour. —**zeitung,** *f.* court-gazette.

Hof—fart ['hofa:rt], *f.* arrogance, pride. —**färtig,** *adj. & adv.* haughty.

Hoff—en ['hɔfən], I. *v.a. & n. (aux.* h.) to hope. II. *subst.n.* hoping. —**entlich,** *adv.* it is to be hoped. —**nung,** *f.* hope.

Höf—isch ['hø:fɪʃ], *adj. & adv.* courtly. —**lich,** *adj. & adv.* polite, courteous. —**lichkeit,** *f.* politeness, courtesy. —**ling,** *m.* (—lings, *pl.* —linge) courtier.

Höhe ['hø:ə], *f.* (*pl.* —n) height; auf der — sein, to be up to date. —**punkt,** *m.* culminating point, zenith.

Hoheit ['ho:haɪt], *f.* highness, loftiness; majesty.

Hohl [ho:l], *adj. & adv.* empty; hollow. **Höhl—e** ['hø:lə], *f.* (*pl.* —en) hollow; cave.

Hohn [ho:n], *m.* (—(e)s) scorn; ihr zum —, in defiance of her. —**gelächter,** *n.* scornful laughter.

Höhn—en ['hø:nən], *v.a.* to scoff, jeer, laugh at. —**er,** *m.* (—ers, *pl.* —er) mocker. —**isch,** *adj.* scornful, sneering.

Hold [hɔlt], *adj. & adv.* favourable; friendly; charming, lovely. —**selig,** *adj.* most gracious. —**seligkeit,** *f.* sweetness, loveliness; graciousness.

Holen ['ho:lən], *v.a.* to (go and) fetch; to take; sich bei jemand Rat —, to consult a person; Atem —, to draw breath.

Höll—e ['hølə], *f.* (*pl.* —en) hell. —**isch,** *adj. & adv.* infernal. —**en= angst,** *f.* mortal terror. —**en=maschine,** *f.* infernal machine. —**en=pein,** *f.* excruciating pain.

Holperig ['hɔlpərɪç], *adj.* rough, uneven.

Holunder [ho'lʊndər], *m.* (—s, *pl.* —) elder. —**beere,** *f.* elderberry.

Holz [hɔlts], *n.* (**—es,** *pl.* **—e, Hölzer**) wood. **—apfel,** *m.* wild apple. **—hader,** *m.* wood-cutter. **—handel,** *m.* timber-trade. **—händler,** *m.* timber-merchant. **—hauer,** *m.* wood-cutter. **—schnitt,** *m.* woodcut. **—späne,** *pl.* shavings.

Hölzern ['hœltsərn], *adj.* wooden; awkward.

Honig ['ho:nɪç], *m.* (**—s**) honey. **—tuchen,** *m.* ginger-bread. **—scheibe,** *f.* honeycomb.

Honorar [hono'ra:r], *n.* (**—s,** *pl.* **—e**) fee.

Hopfen ['hɔpfən], *m.* (**—s,** *pl.* **—**) hop; hops; **an ihm ift — und Malz verloren,** he is no good (*hopeless*).

Hörbar ['hø:rba:r], *adj. & adv.* audible.

Horch—en ['hɔrçən], *v.n.* (*aux.* **h.**) (*with dat. or* **auf** *& acc.*) to hearken, listen; to obey. **—er,** *m.* (**—ers,** *pl.* **—er**) listener; eavesdropper.

Horde ['hɔrdə], *f.* (*pl.* **—n**) horde.

Hör—en ['hø:rən], *v.a. & n.* (*aux.* **h.**) to hear; to listen. **—enfagen,** *n.* hearsay, rumour. **—er,** *m.* (**—ers,** *pl.* **—er**) hearer. **—erschaft,** *f.* audience. **—rohr,** *n.,* **—trichter,** *m.* ear-trumpet; stethoscope. **—faal,** *m.* lecture-room. **—weite,** *f.* within hearing.

Horizont [hori'tsɔnt], *m.* (**—(e)s,** *pl.* **—e**) horizon. **—al** [—'ta:l], *adj. & adv.* horizontal. **—ale,** *f.* horizontal line.

Horn [hɔrn], *n.* (**—es,** *pl.* **Hörner**) horn. **—ig,** *adj. & adv.* horny; callous.

Hörnchen ['hœrnçən], *n.* (**—s,** *pl.* **—**) small horn; crescent roll.

Hornis [hɔrnɪʃ], *f.* (*pl.* **—(ſſ)e**), **—ſſe,** *f.* (*pl.* **—ſſen**) hornet.

Horst [hɔrst], *m.* (**—es,** *pl.* **—e**) eyrie.

Hort [hɔrt], *m.* (**—es,** *pl.* **—e**) hoard, treasure.

Hof—e ['ho:zə], *f.* (*pl.* **—en**) (pair of) trousers (*mostly* **—en,** *pl.*). **—en=band,** *n.* garter. **—en=träger,** *m.* braces.

Hoſp—ital [hɔspi'ta:l], *n.* (**—itals,** *pl.* **—itäler**) hospital.

Hoſtie ['hɔstlə], *f.* (*pl.* **—n**) the consecrated wafer, the Host.

Hotel [ho'tɛl], *n.* (**—s,** *pl.* **—s**) hotel.

Hüben ['hy:bən], *adv.* on this side; **und drüben,** on this side and on the other side, on either side.

Hübſch [hypʃ], *adj. & adv.* handsome, pretty; fine; nice; **das iſt nicht —,** that is not fair.

Huf [hu:f], *m.* (**—(e)s,** *pl.* **—e**) hoof. **—ig,** *adj. & adv.* (*suffix in comp.=*) -hoofed. **—eifen,** *n.* horse-shoe. **—ſchlag,** *m.* horse-shoeing; horse's kick.

Hüft—e ['hyftə], *f.* (*pl.* **—en**) hip. **—gelenf,** *n.* hip-joint.

Hügel ['hy:gəl], *m.* (**—s,** *pl.* **—**) hill. **—ig,** *adj.* hilly; hill-like.

Huhn [hu:n], *n.* (**—es,** *pl.* **Hühner**) (*dim.* **Hühnchen,** *n.*) hen.

Hühner ['hy:nər], *see* Huhn (*in comp. generally=*chicken, hen). **—auge,** *n.* corn (*on the foot*). **—braten,** *m.* roast fowl. **—ei,** *n.* hen's egg. **—hof,** *m.* poultry-yard. **—ftall,** *m.* fowl-house. **—ftange,** *f.* hen-roost. **—vieh,** *n.* poultry. **—zucht,** *f.* poultry-rearing.

Huld [hʊlt], *f.* grace, favour, affection. **—reich, —voll,** *adj. & adv.* gracious, benevolent, favourable. **—reiz,** *m.* irresistible charm.

Huldig—en ['hʊldɪgən], *v.n.* (*aux.* **h.**) (einem) to swear allegiance; to pay homage. **—ung,** *f.* homage; admiration, respect.

Hüll—e ['hylə], *f.* (*pl.* **—en**) cover, covering; **in — und Fülle,** in abundance. **—en,** *v.a.* to wrap up, cover; to hide.

Hülf—e ['hylzə], *f.* (*pl.* **—en**) hull, shell, husk. **—en=artig,** *adj.* leguminous. **—en=frucht,** *f.* pod, legume.

Hummel ['huməl], *f.* (*pl.* **—n**) humble-bee.

Hummer ['humər], *m.* (**—s,** *pl.* **—**) lobster.

Humor [hu'mo:r], *m.* (**—s**) humour.

Hund [hʊnt], *m.* (**—(e)s,** *pl.* **—e**) dog. **—e=bellen,** *n.* barking of dogs. **—e=leben,** *n.* wretched life. **—e=elend,** *adj.* very miserable, wretched.

Hundert ['hʊndərt], **I.** *num. adj.* hundred; (*in comp.=*) having *or* with a hundred. **II.** *subst.n.* (**—s,** *pl.* **—e**) hundred. **—er,** *m.* (**—ers,** *pl.* **—er**) hundred; figure indicating the hundreds. **—ft,** *adj.* hundredth. **—fach, —fältig,** *adj.* hundredfold, centuple. **—fuß, —füßler,** *m.* centipede. **—jährig,** *adj.* centenary, centenarian. **—mal,** *adv.* a hundred times.

Hünd—in ['hyndɪn], *f.* she dog, bitch. **—iſch,** *adj.* doggish.

Hunger ['hʊŋər], *m.* (**—s**) hunger. **—ig, hungrig,** *adj. & adv.* hungry, starving. **—jahr,** *n.* year of famine.

—s=not, f. famine. —tuch, n.; am
—tuche nagen, to be starving.
Hunger—n ['huŋərn], v. I. n. (aux. h.)
to hunger. II. a. imp.; mich —t, es
—t mich, I am hungry.
Hupf [hupf], m. (—es, pl. —e) hop,
jump.
Hüpfen ['hypfən], v.n. (aux. h. & f.)
to hop; to frisk about.
Hurra [hu'ra], int. hurra(h)!
Hurtig ['hurtiç], adj. & adv. quick,
swift, agile. —keit, f. swiftness,
agility.
Husar [hu'za:r], m. (—en, pl. —en)
hussar.
Husten ['hu:stən], I. v.n. (aux. h.) to
cough; to have a cough. II. m. (—s)
cough. —anfall, m. fit of coughing.
1 Hut [hu:t], m. (—es, pl. Hüte) hat.
2 Hut [hu:t], f. (pl. —en) shelter; guard,
charge. auf der — sein, to be on
one's guard.
Hüt—en ['hy:tən], v. I. a. to watch, to
guard; er muß das Bett —en, he is
confined to bed. II. r. to be on one's
guard. —er, m. (—ers, pl. —er)
guardian; herdsman.
Hütte ['hytə], f. (pl. —n) cottage, hut.
—n=arbeiter, m. workman in a foundry. —n=bau, m. smelting business
attached to a mine. —n=werk, n.
foundry, smelting-house.
Hyäne [hy'ɛ:nə], f. (pl. —n) hyena.
Hymne ['hymnə], f. (pl. —n) hymn.
Hypothek [hypo'te:k], f. (pl. —en)
mortgage.

J

J, i [i:], n. I, i; as abbr. J.=Ihre,
your; their; i wo! certainly not!
whatever next!
Ich [iç], I. pers. pron. I; — selbst, I
myself. II. n. self; ego.
Ideal [ide'a:l], I. n. (—s, pl. —e) ideal.
II. adj. & adv. ideal. —ismus
[—'lismus], m. idealism. —ität
[—'tɛ:t], f. ideality.
Idee [i'de:], f. (pl. —en) idea.
Identifizieren [idɛntifi'tsi:rən], v.a. to
identify.
Idiomatisch [idio'ma:tiʃ], adj. idio-
matic.
Idyll—e [i'dylə], f. (pl. —en) idyll.
—enhaft, —isch, adj. & adv. idyllic,
pastoral.
Igel ['i:gəl], m. (—s, pl. —) hedgehog.

Ihm [i:m], pers. pron. (dat. sing. of
er, es) (to) him, (to) it.
Ihn [i:n], pers. pron. (acc. sing. of er)
him; it.
Ihnen ['i:nən], (dat. of sie, pl.) (to)
them;(and with cap.,dat.of Sie)(to) you.
Ihr [i:r], I. pers. pron. 1. (nom. pl. of
du) ye, you; 2. (dat. of sie, f. sing.) to
her, to it. II. poss. adj. (orig. gen. of
pers. pron.) ihr, ihre, ihr) her; its;
their; (with cap.) your. III. poss.
pr. (orig. gen. of pers. pron.) hers, its,
theirs; (with cap.) yours. IV. I.
pers. pron. 1. (gen. of sie, 3 pers. f.)
of her, of it; 2. (gen. of sie, 3 pers.
pl.) of them; (with cap.) of you. II.
poss. adj. (gen. & dat. sing. & gen. pl.
of ihr) of her, to her; of their; (with
cap.) of your. —ige (der, die, das
—ige; pl. die —igen), poss. pron. hers,
its, theirs; (with cap.) yours. —o, old
gen. pl. of ihr. —er=seits, adv. in her,
its, their turn; for her, its, their part;
as far as she, it, they are concerned;
(with cap.) for your part, in your turn.
—es=gleichen, indec. adj. & adv. of
her, its, their kind; like her, it, them;
(with cap.) of your kind; like you.
—et=halben, —et=wegen, —et=will-
en, adv. on her, its, their account or
behalf; for her, its, their sake; so
far as she, it, they are concerned;
(with cap.) on your account, etc.
Iliade ['lli'a:də], Ilias ['ili:as], f. Iliad.
Illustriert [ilus'tri:rt], adj. illustrated.
Iltis ['iltis], m. (—(ss)es, pl. —ss)e)
polecat, fitchet.
Im [im], contr. for in dem, in the.
Imbiß ['imbis], m. (—(ss)es, pl. —(ss)e)
light meal.
Immer ['imər], adv. always; ever.
—dar, adv. always, ever. —fort,
adv. continually. —hin, I. adv. &
part. always, all the time; in spite of
everything; no matter; after all; I
care not; still, yet. II. int. well and
good! —mehr, adv. more and more;
ever more. —zu, adv. & int. always.
Impf—en ['impfən], v.a. to inoculate;
to vaccinate. —er, m. vaccinator.
—ung, f. inoculation, vaccination.
Imponieren [impo'ni:rən], v.n. (aux.
h.) (einem) to impress forcibly. —d,
part. adj. imposing, impressive.
Imposant [impo'zant], adj. imposing.
Imstande [im'ʃtandə], adv. capable
(of); — sein, to be able.

Jn [ɪn], *prep. expressing rest or (limited or circular) motion in a place (with dat.); implying motion to or towards (with acc.),* in, at, into, to, within.

Inbegriff ['ɪnbəgrɪf], *m.* (—(e)s, *pl.* —e) contents, purport; summary, epitome; sum total. **—en,** *adv.* inclusively, including.

Inbrunst ['ɪnbrʊnst], *f.* ardour, fervour.

Inbrünstig ['ɪnbrʏnstɪç], *adj. & adv.* ardent, fervent.

Indem [ɪn'de:m], I. *adj.* just now, this moment. II. *conj.* during the time that, whilst, while, as; in that; since, because, as.

Indes, Indeß ['ɪndɛs], **Indessen** [—'dɛsən], I. *adv.* meantime, meanwhile. II. *conj.* whilst, while; however, nevertheless.

Individu—um [ɪndi'vi:duʊm], *n.* (*pl.* —en) individual.

Indoss—ant [ɪndɔ'sant], *m.* (—en, *pl.* —en) indorser. **—at,** *m.* (—en, *pl.* —en) indorsee.

Industri—e [ɪndʊs'tri:], *f.* (*pl.* —en) industry. **—ell** [—'ɛl], *adj.* industrial, manufacturing. **—elle(r),** *m.* (—en, *pl.* —e(n)) manufacturer, tradesman. **—egesellschaft,** *f.* trade-union.

Ineinander [ɪn'aɪ'nandər], *adv. & sep. prefix,* into one another; confusedly.

Infam [ɪn'fa:m], *adj. & adv.* infamous. **—ie** [—a'mi:] *f.* infamy.

Infanter—ie [ɪnfantə'ri:], *f.* infantry. **—ist,** *m.* (—isten, *pl.* —isten) foot-soldier.

Ingenieur [ɪnʒenɪ'ø:r], *m.* (—s, *pl.* —e) engineer.

Ingrimm ['ɪngrɪm], *m.* (—s) concealed *or* sullen rage; violent anger. **—ig,** *adj. & adv.* fiercely angry.

Ingwer ['ɪnvər], *m.* (—s) ginger.

Inhab—en ['ɪnha:bən], *ir.v.a.* to have in one's possession, possess. **—er,** *m.* (—ers, *pl.* —er) possessor.

Inhalt ['ɪnhalt], *m.* (—s) contents; tenor, purport. **—reich,** —**schwer,** **—voll,** *adj.* rich in, full of meaning, significant. **—s=maß,** *n.* measure of capacity, cubic measure. **—s=verzeichnis,** *n.* index, table of contents.

Inland ['ɪnlant], *n.* (—(e)s) inland.

Inländ—er ['ɪnlɛndər], *m.* (—ers, *pl.* —er), **—erin,** *f.* inlander; native. **—isch,** *adj. & adv.* inland; indigenous; native.

Inmitten [ɪn'mɪtən], *adv. & prep.* (*with gen.*) in the midst.

Inn—e ['ɪnə], *adv. & sep. prefix,* within. **—en,** *adv.* within. **—ig,** *adj. & adv.* heartfelt, sincere. **—igteit,** *f.* cordiality; intimacy. **—iglich,** *adv.* intimately, heartily, fervently. **—e haben,** *ir.v.a.* to occupy; to possess.

Inner ['ɪnər], *adj.* interior; internal; **Ministerium des Innern,** Home Office, Ministry of Home Affairs. **—lich,** *adj. & adv.* interior, inner, inward. **—lichteit,** *f.* inwardness; subjectivity. **—st,** *adj. & adv.* (*sup. of* **inner**) inmost.

Innung ['ɪnʊn], *f.* (*pl.* —en) guild.

Ins— [ɪns] (*in comp.*) **—be'sondere,** *adv.* especially, in particular. **—s ge'heim,** *adv.* secretly, privily. **—s ge'mein,** *adv.* in common; usually. **—ge'samt,** *adv.* all together, in a body.

Inschrift ['ɪnʃrɪft], *f.* (*pl.* —en) inscription.

Insett [ɪn'zɛkt], *n.* (—s, *pl.* —en) insect.

Insel ['ɪnzəl], *f.* (*pl.* —n) island. **—meer,** *n.* archipelago. **—stadt,** *f.* insular town.

Inser—ant [ɪnzɛ'rant], *m.* (—anten, *pl.* —anten) advertiser. **—at** [—'ra:t], *n.* (—ates, *pl.* —ate) advertisement in a paper.

Inso—fern [ɪn'zo:fərn], **—weit** [vart], *adv. & conj.* in as far as, inasmuch as; according as.

Inständig ['ɪnʃtendɪç], *adj. & adv.* instant, urgent.

Intelligenz [ɪntɛli'gɛnts], *f.* intelligence, cleverness; sharpness. **—blatt,** *n.* advertiser (*newspaper*). **—bureau,** *n.* intelligence department.

Intendant [ɪntɛn'dant], *m.* (—en, *pl.* —en) steward, superintendent.

Interess—ant [ɪntərɛ'sant], *adj.* interesting. **—e,** *n.* (—es, *pl.* —en) interest. **—ieren** [—'si:rən], *v.a. & r.* to interest; to take an interest. **—iert,** *p.p. & adj.* interested; selfish, self-interested.

Intim [ɪn'ti:m], *adj. & adv.* intimate.

Invalid [ɪnva'li:t], *adj.* weak, invalid. **—e,** *m.* (—en, *pl.* —en) invalid; disabled soldier. **—en=haus,** —**en=heim,** *n.* hospital for disabled soldiers. **—en=sold,** *m.* old-age pension.

Inventar [ɪnvɛn'ta:r], *n.* (—s, *pl.* —e, —ien) inventory.

Inwärt—ig ['ɪnvɛrtɪç], *adj. & adv.* internal, inward. —s, *adv.* inwards, internally.

Inwendig ['ɪnvɛndɪç], *adj. & adv.* interior, inside, inward.

Inwohn—en ['ɪnvo:nən], *v.n. (aux. h.)* to dwell in; to be inherent. —end, *p. & adj.* inherent. —er, *m.* (—ers, *pl.* —er) lodger, inhabitant.

Inzwischen [ɪn'tsvɪʃən], *adv. & conj.* in the meantime, meanwhile.

Ird—en ['ɪrdən], *adj.* earthen. —isch, *adj. & adv.* earthly.

Irgend ['ɪrgənt], *adv.* any; some; perhaps; ever, at any time; about, nearly; in any way, anywhere; *before a pron., adj. or pronominal adverb often=*soever, at all, ever, etc. —wo, *adv.* anywhere, at any place whatever; somewhere. —wo'her, *adv.* from some place or another. —wo'hin, *adv.* to some place or another.

Ironi—e [iro'ni:], *f.* irony. —sch [i'ro:nɪʃ], *adj.* ironical.

Irr—e ['ɪrə], I. *adj. & adv.* in error, astray; —e machen, to bewilder; to divert from. II. *f.* wandering; mistaken course. —en, *v.i. n. (aux. h. & ſ.)* to go astray. II. *a.* to mislead. III. *r.* to be mistaken. —garten, *m.* labyrinth. —ig, *adj. & adv.* false; wrong. —licht, *n.* will-o'-the-wisp. —ſinn, *m.* insanity; delirium. —ſtern, *m.* comet; wandering star. —tum, *m.* (—tums, *pl.* —tümer) error, mistake. —tümlich, *adj. & adv.* erroneous. —wahn, *m.* delusion.

J

J, j [jɔt], *n.* J, j.

Ja [ja:]. I. *adv. & part.* yes (*used to add force to another particle or to the verb; e.g.* nimm dich — in Acht, be sure to take care); da ſind Sie —! well, there you are. II. *n.* (—s, *pl.* —s) yes; aye. —wohl, *adv.* yes, indeed. —wort, *n.* affirmation.

Jacht [jaxt], *f. (pl.* —en) yacht.

Jacke ['jakə], *f. (pl.* —n) jacket.

Jagd [ja:kt], *f. (pl.* —en) chase, hunt. —anzug, *m.* hunting-suit. —bezirk, *m.* hunting-ground. —freund, *m.* sportsman. —geſetz, *n.* game-law.

Jagen ['ja:gən], *v.i. n. (aux. h. & ſ.)*

to hunt, chase; to race, gallop. II. *a.* to chase away, drive off.

Jäger ['jɛ:gər], *m.* (—s, *pl.* —) hunter; gamekeeper; rifleman.

Jäh—(e) ['jɛ:(ə)], *adj.* rapid, sudden; steep, precipitous. —e, —igkeit, *f.* haste; steepness. —lings, *adv.* precipitously; abruptly; suddenly, in violent haste. —zorn, *m.* sudden anger; irritability. —zornig, *adj.* hasty; irritable, passionate.

Jahr [ja:r], *n.* (—(e)s, *pl.* —e) year. —es=viertel, *n.* quarter of a year. —es=wechſel, *m.* new year. —es=zahl, *f.* date of the year. —es=zeit, *f.* season, date of the year. —hundert, *n.* century, age. —lang, *adv.* year after year. —markt, *m.* annual fair. —tauſend, *n.* millennium.

Jähr—lich ['jɛ:rlɪç], *adj. & adv.* yearly, annual. —ling, *m.* yearling.

Jammer ['jamər], *m.* (—s) lamentation; misery; es iſt —ſchade, it is a thousand pities. —n, *v.i. n. (aux. h.)* to lament. II. *a. & imp.* to move to pity.

Jämmer—lich ['jɛmərlɪç], *adj. & adv.* deplorable, pitiable, wretched. —lichkeit, *f.* wretchedness; pitiableness.

Januar ['janua:r], *m.* (—s, *pl.* —e) January.

Jasmin [jas'mi:n], *m.* (—s, *pl.* —e) jasmine, jessamine.

Jauchzen ['jauxtsən], *v.n. (aux. h.)* to shout with joy.

1Je [je:], I. *adv.* ever, at any time, at every time; in any case; at a time; each, apiece; (*before comparatives=*) the; von — her, at all times. II. *int.* well! ah! why! —doch, *adv.* however, notwithstanding, nevertheless, yet. —=länger=je=lieber, *n.* honeysuckle, woodbine. —mals, *adv.* ever, at any time. —mand, *indef. pron.* (*gen.* —mandes; *dat.* —mand; *acc.* —mand) somebody, someone, anybody, anyone; ſonſt —mand=(—mand anders), somebody, anybody else; irgend —mand, anyone.

2Je [je:] (*abbr. of* Jeſus), *int.* heavens! gracious!

Jed—er ['je:dər], —e, —es, I. *adj.* each, every, either. II. *pron.* (ein —er, eine —e, ein —es) each, every, either; everyone, everybody; Alle und —e, one and all. —en=falls, *adv.* at all events. —er=lei, *indec. adj.* of every or any kind. —er=mann, pron. every man, everyone, everybody. —er=zeit, adv. at any time, always, ever. —es=mal, adv. each time, always. —es=malig, adj. existing, actual. —weder, —wede, —wedes, pron. every, each, every one.

Jeglich—er ['je:klıçər], —e, —es, adj. & pron. every, each.

Jen—er ['je:nər], —e, —es, I. dem. adj. yon, that, yonder. II. dem. pron. that one, that person; the former (opp. to dieser, etc.). —ig, pron. (suff. in comp. as, derjenige, etc.) that. —seits, adv. on the other side.

Jesuit [jezu'i:t], m. (—en, pl. —en) Jesuit.

Jetz—ig ['jɛtsıç], adj. present, actual, modern. —t [jɛtst], adv. at the present time, now.

Joch [jɔx], n. (—es, pl. —, —e) yoke.

Jod [jo:t], n., —ine [jo'di:nə], f. iodine.

Johannis [jo'hanıs] (in comp. for Johannes), —beere, f. currant. —kraut, n. St. John's wort. —nacht, f. St. John's eve (night of June 24). —tag, m. Midsummer Day. —wurm, m. glow-worm.

Joppe [jɔpə], f. (pl. —n) shooting-jacket.

Journal [zur'na:l], n. (—s, pl. —e) journal, newspaper. —ist [—'lıst], m. (—isten, pl. —isten) journalist. —istik, f. journalism.

Jubel ['ju:bəl], m. (—s) exultation, jubilation. —ei [—'laɪ], f. public rejoicing, merry-making. —feier, f., —fest, n. jubilee. —gesang, m. song of rejoicing. —geschrei, n. shout of exultation. —jahr, n. year of jubilee. —n, v.n. (aux. h.) to rejoice. —ton, m. joyous sound.

Jubil—äum [jubi'lɛum], n. (—äums, pl. —äen) jubilee.

Juch—he [jux'he:], —hei(sa) [—'haɪ(za:)], int. hurrah! huzza!

Jucken ['jukən], v.n. (aux. h.) to itch.

Jude—he ['ju:də], m. (—n, pl. —n) Jew; der ewige —, the wandering Jew. —ntum, n. Judaism. —nsland, n. Judea; Palestine.

Jüd—in ['jy:dın], f. Jewess. —isch, adj. & adv. Jewish.

Jugend ['ju:gənt], f. youth. —lich, adj. & adv. youthful, juvenile. —lichkeit, f. youthfulness. —alter, n. (days of) youth. —blüte, f. bloom of

youth. —schriften, pl. books for the young. —zeit, f. time of youth, youth.

Juli ['ju:li:], m. (—s), Julius ['ju:lıus], m. July.

Jung [jʊŋ], adj. & adv. (comp. jünger, sup. jüngst) young; —er Wein, new wine. —e, m. (—en, pl. —en or —ens (dial. & coll.)) boy. —frau, f. young woman, maid, maiden. —gesell, m. bachelor.

Jüng—er ['jyŋər], I. adj. (comp. of jung) younger. II. m. (—ers, pl. —er), —erin, f. disciple. —erhaft, adj. & adv. in the manner of a disciple. —ling, m. (—lings, pl. —linge) young man. —ft, I. adj. (sup. of jung) youngest; latest, last; das —fte Gericht, der —fte Tag, day of judgment, the last day, doomsday. II. adv. lately, recently, the other day.

Jungfer ['jʊŋfər], f. (pl. —n) young girl; alte —, old maid. —n=kranz, m. bridal wreath. —n=schaft, f. virginity. —n=stand, m. spinster-condition.

Juni ['ju:ni:], m. (—s) June.

Junker ['jʊŋkər], m. (—s, pl. —) squire; young noble; pl. Junkers. —tum, n. petty feudal nobles; squirearchy; haughtiness of the petty feudal nobility.

Jur—a ['ju:ra:], pl. law. —ist [—'rıst], m. (—isten, pl. —isten) lawyer; law-student. —istisch, adj. & adv. relating to the law.

Just [jʊst], adv. just, exactly. —iz [jʊs'tɪts], f. justice; administration of the law. —iz=kammer, —iz=stelle, f. court or chamber of justice. —iz=minister, m. minister of justice. —iz=rat, m. councillor of justice. —iz=wesen, n. justiciary system.

Jute ['ju:tə], f. (pl. —n) jute.

Juwel [ju've:l], m. (& n.) (—s, pl. —e & —en) jewel. —ier [—'li:r], m. (—iers, pl. —iere) jeweller, goldsmith. —en=schmuck, m. set of jewels.

K

K, k [ka:], n. K, k, as abbr. K. or k. = kaiserlich, königlich, imperial, royal.

Kabal—e [ka'ba:lə], f. (pl. —en) cabal, intrigue. —istisch [—'lıstıʃ], adj. cabalistic.

Rabel ['ka:bəl], n. (—s, pl. —) cable.
—feil, n., —tau, n. cable.

Rabeljau ['ka:bəljau], m. (—s, p. —s
& —e) codfish.

Rabinett [kabi'nɛt], n. (—s, pl. —e)
cabinet. —befehl, m. royal or imperial order.

Rachel ['kaxəl], f. (pl. —n) glazed tile.
—ofen, m. stove made of tiles.

Rabaver [ka'da:vər], m. (—s, pl. —)
carrion, carcase; corpse.

Rabett [ka'dɛt], m. (—en, pl. —en)
cadet. —en=corps, n. cadet corps.
—en=schule, j. military academy.

Räfer ['kɛ:fər], m. (—s, pl. —) beetle.

Raffee ['kafe:], m.(—s) coffee. —brett,
n. coffee-tray. —tanne, f. coffee-pot.
—flatsch, m. ladies' coffee-party.
—schale, f., —schälchen, n. coffee-cup.
—wirt, m. keeper of a coffee-house.
—trichter, m. coffee-strainer.

Räfig ['kɛ:fɪç], m. (& n.) (—s, pl. —e)
cage.

Rahl [ka:l], adj. & adv. bald.

Rahn [ka:n], m. (—s, pl. Rähne) boat,
skiff.

Rai [kaɪ], m. (—s, pl. —e) quay.

Raiser ['kaɪzər], m. (—s, pl. —)
emperor. —in, f. empress. —lich,
adj. & adv. imperial.

Rajüte [ka'jy:tə], f. (pl. —n) cabin.

Rakadu ['kakadu:], m. (—s, pl. —s &
—e) cockatoo.

Rakao [ka'ka:o:], m. (—s) cocoa.

Raktus ['kaktus], m. (— or —(ff)es, pl.
Rakteen or —(ff)e) cactus.

Ralb [kalp], n.(—(e)s, pl. Rälber) calf.
—e, f. (pl. —en) heifer. —fleisch, n.
veal. —s=braten, m. roast veal.

Ralender [ka'lɛndər], m. (—s, pl. —)
calendar, almanac.

Ralesche [ka'lɛʃə], f. (pl. —n) light
carriage.

Rali ['ka:li:], n. (—s) potash.

Raliber [ka'li:bər], m. (—s, pl. —)
calibre.

Ralif [ka'li:f], m. (—en, pl. —en)
caliph.

Ralk [kalk], m. (—(e)s, pl. —e) lime.
—ig, adj. & adv. chalky. —artig, adj.
calcareous. —brennerei [—'raɪ], f.
lime-kiln. —bruch, m. limestone
quarry.

Ralomel ['ka:lomɛl], n. (—s) calomel.

Ralt [kalt], adj. & adv. (fälter, fältest)
cold. —blütigfeit, f. cold-bloodedness;
composure.

Rälte ['kɛltə], f. cold, coldness; indifference. —n, v.a. to make cold. —grad,
m. degree of cold.

Ramee [ka'me:], Rameo [—'me:o:], m.
(—s, pl. Rameen) cameo.

Ramel [ka'me:l], n. (—s, pl. —e)
camel; blockhead. —garn, n. mohair.

Ramelie [ka'me:lIə], f. (pl. —n)
camellia.

Ramerad [kamə'ra:t], m. (—en, pl.
—en) comrade. —schaftlich, adj. &
adv. comrade-like, companionable.
—schaft, f. comradeship, fellowship.

Ramille [ka'mIlə], f. (pl. —n) camomile.

Ramin [ka'mi:n], m. & n. (—s, pl.
—e) chimney; fireplace, fireside.
—ede, f., —winkel, m. chimney-
corner. —feger, m. (chimney-)sweep.
—feuer, n. open fireplace. —gerät, n.
fire-irons. —sims, m. mantelpiece.
—rost, m. grate.

Ramm [kam], m. (—(e)s, pl. Rämme)
comb; cog-tooth (of a wheel). —rad,
n. cog-wheel.

Rämm—en ['kɛmən], v.a. to comb; to
card. —er, m. (—ers, pl. —er)
comber, carder. —erei [—'raɪ], f.
wool-combing.

Rammer ['kamər], f. (pl. —n) room.
—amt, n. office of the exchequer.
—beamte(r), m. clerk to the exchequer. —dame, f. lady of the
bed-chamber. —diener, m. valet. —=
frau, f. waiting-woman. —fräulein, n.
maid of honour. —gericht, n. supreme
court of judicature. —gut, n. crown
land; public revenue. —herr, m.
chamberlain. —fonzert, n. concert
without orchestra. —rat, m. councillor of the exchequer.

Rämmer—chen ['kɛmərçən], (—chens,
pl. —chen), —lein, n. (—leins, pl.
—lein) closet, small chamber.

Rampf [kampf], m.(—(e)s, pl. Rämpfe)
combat, fight; der — ums Dasein,
struggle for existence. —erprobt,
adj. veteran, tried in battle. —fähig,
adj. effective (Mil.). —fertig, adj.
ready for action. —flugzeug, n.
battle-plane (Av.). —geschrei, n. war-
cry. —hahn, m. game-cock; quarrelsome fellow. —ordnung, f. order of
battle. —platz, m. field of battle;
arena. —richter, m. umpire. —spiel,
n. tournament. —unfähig, adj. disabled.

Kämpfen ['kɛmpfən], *v.n. (aux. h.)* to fight.

Kampfer ['kampfər], *m.* (—s) camphor.

Kanal [ka'na:l], *m.* (—s, *pl.* Kanäle) canal (*artificial*); channel (*natural*); der englische —, the English Channel.

Kanarien— [ka'na:rɪən], (*in comp.* =) canary.

Kandelaber [kande'la:bər], *m.* (—s, *pl.* —) chandelier.

Kandid—at [kandi'da:t], *m.* (—aten, *pl.* —aten) *abbr.* Kand., Cand., candidate; probationer.

Känguruh [kɛngu'ru:], *n.* (—s, *pl.* —s) kangaroo.

Kaninchen [ka'ni:nçən], *n.* (—s, *pl.* —) rabbit.

Kanne ['kanə], *f.* (*pl.* —n, *dim.* Kännchen) can, tankard, mug.

Kanevas ['kanəvas], *m.* (—(f)fes, *pl.* —(f)fe) canvas.

Kannibalisch [kani'ba:lɪʃ], *adj.* cannibal.

Kanon—ade [kano'na:də], *f.* cannonade. —e [ka'no:nə], *f.* (*pl.* —en) cannon. —ier [—'ni:r], *m.* gunner. —ieren, *v.a.* & *n.* to cannonade. —en=futter, *n.* food for powder. —en=schuß, *m.* cannon-shot. —en=schuß=weite, *f.* cannon-shot range.

Kanon—itus [ka'no:nikus], *m.* (*pl.* —iter) prebendary, canon.

Kant—e ['kantə], *f.* (*pl.* —en) edge. —ig, *adj.* & *adv.* edged, cornered, angular.

Kantine [kan'ti:nə], *f.* (*pl.* —n) canteen.

Kanton [kan'to:n], *m.* (—s, *pl.* —e) canton. —ieren [—'ti:rən], *v.n.* to be in cantonment. —ierung, *f.* cantonment.

Kantor ['kantər], *m.* (—s, *pl.* Kantoren) precentor.

Kanzel ['kantsəl], *f.* (*pl.* —n) pulpit.

Kanz—lei [kants'lai], *f.* (*pl.* —leien) government office. —ler ['kantslər], *m.* (—lers, *pl.* —ler) chancellor.

Kap [kap]. *n.* (—s, *pl.* —s) cape (*Geog.*).

Kapell—e [ka'pɛlə], *f.* (*pl.* —en) chapel; band *or* choir. —meister, *m.* bandmaster, conductor of a choir.

Kapital [kapi'ta:l], I. *n.* (—s, *pl.* —ien) capital; — und Zinsen, principal and interest. II. *n.* (*pl.* Kapitäler) capital (*Arch.*). III. *adj.* capital. —ist [—'lɪst], *m.* (—isten, *pl.* —isten) capitalist. —konto, *n.*, —rechnung,

f. stock account. —kräftig, *adj.* wealthy, substantial. —s=abgabe, *f.* capital levy. —steuer, *f.* property tax. —verbrechen, *n.* capital crime.

Kapitän [kapi'tɛ:n], *m.* (—s, *pl.* —e) captain (*of a ship*).

Kapitel [ka'pɪtəl], *n.* (—s, *pl.* —) head, chapter.

Kaplan [ka'pla:n], *m.* (—(e)s, *pl.* Kapläne) chaplain.

Kapp—e ['kapə], *f.* (*pl.* —en) cap; hood.

Kapsel ['kapsəl], *f.* (*pl.* —n) cover; box; capsule. —ig, *adj.* capsular.

Kaputt [ka'put], *adj.* spoilt, broken.

Kapuz—e [ka'pu:tsə], *f.* (*pl.* —en) cowl. —iner [—'tsi:nər], *m.* (—iners, *pl.* —iner) Capuchin monk.

Kar— [ka:r] (*in comp.*; *older spelling* Char—, *originally meaning ' sorrow,' ' care '*) —freitag, *m.* Good Friday. —woche, *f.* Passion week.

Karabin—er [kara'bi:nər], *m.* (—ers, *pl.* —er) carbine, rifle. —ier [— binl'e:], *m.* (—iers, *pl.* —iere) carbineer.

Karaffe [ka'rafə], *f.* (*pl.* —n) carafe.

Karawan—e [kara'va:nə], *f.* (*pl.* —en) caravan. —serei [—zə'rai], *f.* (*pl.* —sereien) caravanserai.

Karbatsche [kar'ba:tʃə], *f.* (*pl.* —n) leather scourge. —n, *v.a.* to whip, flog soundly.

Karbolsäure [kar'bo:lzɔyrə], *f.* carbolic acid.

Karbonade [karbo'na:də], *f.* (*pl.* —n) chop, cutlet.

Karbonsäure [kar'bo:nzɔyrə], *f.* carbonic acid.

Kardätsche ['kar'dɛːtʃə], *f.* (*pl.* —n) carding-comb; curry-comb. —n, *v.a.* to card wool; to curry. —r, *m.* carder; one who curries (*a horse*).

Kardinal [kardi'na:l], I. *m.* (—s, *pl.* Kardinäle) cardinal. II. *adj.* cardinal. —at [—'la:t], *n.* cardinalate.

Karfunkel [kar'fuŋkəl], *m.* (—s, *pl.* —s) carbuncle (*gem*).

Karg [kark], *adj.* & *adv.* (*comp.* kärger, *sup.* kärg(e)st), miserly. —heit, *f.* parsimony, stinginess.

Kärglich ['kɛrklɪç], *adj.* & *adv.* scanty, poor.

Karmeliter [karme'li:tər], *m.* (—s, *pl.* —) & *adj.* Carmelite.

Karmesin [karme'zi:n], *adj.* crimson.

Karmin [kar'mi:n], *m.* (—s) carmine.

Karneol [karne'o:l], Karniol, m. (—s, pl. —e) cornelian.

Karneval ['karnəval], m. (& obs. n). (—s, pl. —s & —e) carnival.

Karo ['ka:ro:], n. (—s, pl. —s) diamonds (cards); square; check.

Karosse [ka'rosə], f. (pl. —n) state coach.

Karotte [ka'rotə], f. (pl. —n) carrot.

Karpfen ['karpfən], m. (—s, pl. —) carp.

Karre ['karə], f. (pl. —n) wheelbarrow.

Karren ['karən], m. (—s, pl. —) car; dray. —baum, m. shaft of a cart. —führer, m. drayman, carter. —gabel, f. cart-shafts. —gaul, m. cart-horse.

Karik—atur [karika'tu:r], f. (pl. —aturen) caricature.

Kartätsche [kar'tɛ:tʃə], f. (pl. —n) grape-shot, shrapnel.

Kart—ause [kar'tauzə], f., older Karth—ause, (pl. —ausen) Carthusian monastery. —äuser, m. (—äusers, pl. —äuser) Carthusian friar.

Karte ['kartə], f. (pl. —n) visiting or playing card; map, chart; bill of fare; programme. —n=brief, n. lettercard. —n=kunststück, n. card-trick. —n=spiel, n. game at cards; pack of cards.

Kartoffel [kar'tofəl], f. (pl. —n) potato. —brei, m. mashed potatoes.

Karussell [karu'sɛl], n. (—s, pl. —s) merry-go-round.

Karzer ['kartsər], m. & n. (—s, pl. —) lock-up.

Käs—e ['kɛ:zə] (South German: Käs), m. (—es, pl. —e) cheese. —ig, adj. cheesy. —en, v.n. to curdle.

Kaserne [ka'zɛrnə], f. (pl. —n) barracks.

Kass—a ['kasa:], —e ['kasə], f. (pl. —(e)n) money-chest; till; office-counter (in a bank). —ier [—'si:r] (—iers, pl. —iere), —ierer, m. (—ierers, pl. —ierer), cashier, treasurer. —ieren, v.a. to collect in cash. —en=anweisung, f. treasury bill; paper money. —en=beamter, m. cashier; revenue clerk. —en=bestand, —en=betrag, m. balance in hand. —en=buch, —a=buch, n. cash-book. —en=dieb, m. embezzler. —en=schein, m. treasury note; banknote. —en=sturz, m. audit. —en=tisch, m. counter.

—en=übersicht, f. balance-sheet. —en=verwalter, m. treasurer.

Kassation [kasatsi'o:n], f. cashiering.

Kastanie [kas'ta:niə], f. (pl. —n) chestnut. —n=baum, m. chestnut tree.

Kästchen ['kɛstçən], n. (—s, pl. —) casket.

Kaste ['kastə], f. (pl. —n) caste.

Kastei—en [kas'taiən], v.a. to chastise. —ung, f. chastisement.

Kastell [kas'tɛl], n. (—(e)s, pl. —e) small fort or castle.

Kasten ['kastən], m. (—s, pl. —) box, chest.

Kata—kombe [kata'kombə], f. (pl. —komben) catacomb. —lepsie [—lɛp'si:], f. catalepsy. —log [—'lo:g], m. (—logs, pl. —loge) catalogue, list.

Katech—etisch [kate'çe:tɪʃ], adj. & adv. catechetical. —isieren [—i'zi:rən], v.a. to catechize. —ismus, m. (pl. —ismen) catechism.

Kategor—ie [katego'ri:], f. (pl. —ieen) category. —isch, adj. & adv. categorical; positive.

Kater ['ka:tər], m. (—s, pl. —) tom-cat; einen — haben, to feel ill after a carouse.

Kathed—er [ka'te:dər], m. & n. (—ers, pl. —er) professor's lecturing desk. —rale [—'dra:lə], f. (pl. —ralen) cathedral.

Kathol—ik [kato'li:k], m. (—iken, pl. —iken) Catholic. —isch [ka'to:lɪʃ], adj. catholic.

Kattun [ka'tu:n], m. (—s, pl. —e) cotton, calico. —en, adj. made of calico or cotton.

Katz—e ['katsə], f. (pl. —en) cat. —en=artig, adj. catlike, feline. —en=buckel, m. humped back. —en=kopf, m. box on the ear. —en=steg, —en=steig, m. narrow path.

Kauderwelsch ['kaudərvɛlʃ], n. (—es) argot; gibberish.

Kau—en ['kauən], I. v.a. to chew. II. subst.n. mastication, chewing. —tabak, m. plug-tobacco. —zahn, m. grinder, molar tooth.

Kauern ['kauərn], v.n. (aux. f.) & r. to squat. —ð, p. & adj. squat.

Kauf [kauf], m. (—es, pl. Käufe) buying, purchase; das müssen Sie mit in — nehmen, you must put up with that. —bar, adj. & adv. purchasable. —brief, m. bill of sale. —geld, n.

purchase-money. —leute, *pl.* merchants.

Kaufen ['kaufən], *v.a. & n. (aux.* h.) to buy.

Käuf—er ['kɔyfər], *m.* (—ers, *pl.* —er) purchaser.

Kaufmann ['kaufman], *m.* (—s, *pl.* Kaufleute) merchant; tradesman, shopkeeper; — im Großen, wholesale merchant; — im Kleinen, retailer, shopkeeper. —schaft, *f.* mercantile class; commerce.

Kaum [kaum], *adv.* with difficulty, hardly, scarcely.

Kaution [kautsi'o:n], *f.* security, bail.

Kauz [kauts], *m.* (—es, *pl.* Käuze) screech-owl; (*fig.*) strange fellow.

Kavalier—ie [kavalə'ri:], *f.* cavalry. —ist [—'rist], *m.* (—isten, *pl.* —isten) horseman.

Keck [kɛk], *adj. & adv.* sprightly, lively.

Kegel ['ke:gəl], *m.* (—s, *pl.* —) skittle; ninepin; — schieben, to play ninepins. —ig, *adj. & adv.* conical. —ähnlich, *adj.* conical, conoidal. —bahn, *f.* skittle-alley. —schnitt, *m.* conic section.

Kehl—e ['ke:lə], *f.* (*pl.* —en) throat. —kopf, *m.* larynx.

¹Kehr—en ['ke:rən], *v.a.* to turn; sich an etwas —en, to heed a thing. —aus, *m.* clearance; end. —reim, *m.* refrain. —seite, *f.* reverse side.

²Kehr—en ['ke:rən], *v.a.* to sweep. —icht, *n.* (—ichts) sweepings. —ichtkasten, *m.* dust-bin, rubbish-box.

Keif—en ['kaifən], *ir.v.a. (aux.* h.) to bark; to scold. —er, *m.* (—ers, *pl.* —er) scolder; brawler. —erin, *f.* shrew.

Keil [kail], *m.* (—es, *pl.* —e) wedge. —ähnlich, —artig, —förmig, *adj.* wedge-shaped, cuneiform.

Keim [kaim], *m.* (—(e)s, *pl.* —e) germ. —en, *v.n. (aux.* h. & f.) to germinate. —frei, *adj.* sterile, sterilized.

Kein [kain], *adj.* not any, no, not a, not one. —er, —e, —es, *pron.* no one, not any one, none. —erlei, *indec. adj.* of no sort, not any; auf —erlei Weise, by no means, in no way. —erseits, *adv.* on neither side. —es-weg(e)s, *adv.* in no wise, by no means, not at all. —mal, *adv.* not once, never.

Kek [ke:k], *m.* (kes, *pl.* —ke) biscuit.

Kelch [kɛlç], *m.* (—es, *pl.* —e) cup, goblet.

Kell—er ['kɛlər], *m.* (—ers, *pl.* —er) cellar. —ner, *m.* (—ners, *pl.* —ner) waiter. —nerin, *f.* female waitress; barmaid. —er-geschoß, *n.* basement.

Kelter ['kɛltər], *f.* (*pl.* —n) wine-press. —n, *v.a.* to tread or press (grapes).

Kennbar ['kɛnba:r], *adj. & adv.* recognizable.

Kenn—en ['kɛnən], *ir.v.a.* to know; to be acquainted with. —tlich, *adj. & adv.* knowable, distinguishable.

Kenner ['kɛnər], *m.* (—s, *pl.* —) connoisseur.

Kenntnis ['kɛntnis], *f.* (*pl.* —(ss)e) knowledge; — nehmen von, to take note of.

Kentern ['kɛntərn], *v.a.* to capsize, cant.

Kerbe ['kɛrbə], *f.* (*pl.* —n) notch.

Kerker ['kɛrkər], *m.* (—s, *pl.* —) prison.

Kerl [kɛrl], *m.* (—s, *pl.* —e) fellow; ein ganzer —, a fine fellow.

Kern [kɛrn], *m.* (—s, *pl.* —e) kernel. —gesund, thoroughly healthy. —haft, *adj. & adv.* substantial. —frucht, *f.* stone fruit. —truppen, *pl.* choice troops, picked men.

Kerze ['kɛrtsə], *f.* (*pl.* —n) candle. —ngerade, *adj.* straight as a dart.

Kessel ['kɛsəl], *m.* (—s, *pl.* —) kettle; caldron; boiler.

Kette ['kɛtə], *f.* (*pl.* —n) chain. —n, *v.a.* to chain, to fetter. —n-brücke, *f.* suspension-bridge. —n-hund, *m.* watchdog.

Ketzer ['kɛtsər], *m.* (—s, *pl.* —), —in, *f.* heretic. —ei [—'rai], *f.* heresy. —haft, —isch, *adj. & adv.* heretical, heterodox. —schaft, *f.*, —tum, *n.* heresy; body of heretics.

Keuch—en ['kɔyçən], *v.n. (aux.* h.) to pant, gasp. —husten, *m.* whooping-cough.

Keule ['kɔylə], *f.* (*pl.* —n) club; leg (of meat).

Keusch [kɔyʃ], *adj. & adv.* chaste, pure; modest. —heit, *f.* chastity.

Kichern ['kiçərn], *v.n. (aux.* h.) to giggle, titter.

Kiebitz ['ki:bits], *m.* (—es, *pl.* —e) peewit.

Kiefer ['ki:fər], I. *m.* (—s, *pl.* —) jaw. II. *f.* (*pl.* —n) (Scots) fir. —n, *adj.* made of fir, fir. —gehölz, *n.* pine-grove. —holz, *n.* pine-wood, red deal. —zapfen, *m.* fir-cone.

Kiel [ki:l], *m.* (—s, *pl.* —e) quill; haulm, straw; keel.

Kieme ['ki:mə], *f.* (*pl.* —n) gill of a fish.

Kien [ki:n], *m.* (—(e)s, *pl.* —e) pine-wood; pine-resin. —fackel, *f.* pine-torch. —harz, *n.* resin of pine trees. —holz, *n.* resinous wood.

Kies [ki:s], *m.* (—(ſ)es, *pl.* —(ſ)e) gravel. —(ſ)ig, *adj.* gravelly; gritty.

Kiesel ['ki:zəl], *m.* (—s, *pl.* —) pebble. —ig, *adj.* pebbly. —glas, *n.* flint-glass. —stein, *m.* pebble.

Kikeriki [ki:kəri'ki:], *int.* cock-a-doodle-doo.

Kilo—gramm [kilo'gram], *n.* - (—s gramms, *pl.* —gramme) kilogramme. —meter [—'me:tər], *n.* (—meters, *pl.* —meter) kilometre.

Kind [kint], *n.* (—es, *pl.* —er) child; Annahme an —es-statt, adoption. —chen (—chens, *pl.* —chen) (*also* —erchen), —lein, *n.* (—leins, *pl.* —lein) (*also* —erlein) baby, infant, little child. —haft, *adj.* & *adv.* child-like, childish. —heit, *f.* childhood, infancy. —iſch, *adj.* & *adv.* childish. —lich, *adj.* & *adv.* childlike; filial.

Kinder ['kɪndər], *pl. see* Kind. —ei [—'raɪ], *f.* childishness; trifle. —s-garten, *m.* kindergarten; infant-school. —märchen, *n.* nursery tale. —ſpiel, *n.* children's game; child's play, easy matter; trifle; es iſt kein —ſpiel, it is not easy, no joke. —ſpielwaren, *pl.*, —ſpielzeug, *n.* toys, playthings. —wagen, *m.* perambulator. —wäſche, *f.* baby-linen.

Kinn [kɪn], *n.* (—es, *pl.* —e) chin. —bart, *m.* imperial.

Kippen ['kɪpən], *v.a.* to tilt, tip over; to upset.

Kirch—e ['kɪrçə], *f.* (*pl.* —en) church. —lich, *adj.* & *adv.* ecclesiastical. —ner, *m.* (—ners, *pl.* —ner) sexton. —fahne, *f.* vane on a church. —hof, *m.* churchyard, graveyard. —meſſe, *f.* fair. —ſpiel, *n.* parish. —turm, *m.* steeple.

Kirchen ['kɪrçən], *pl. see* Kirche. —haft, *adj.* & *adv.* church-like. —tum, *n.* church affairs generally. —bann, *n.* excommunication.

Kirmes ['kɪrməs], *f.* (*pl.*—(ſſ)en) church fair; *see* Kirchmeſſe.

Kirren ['kɪrən], *v.n.* (*aux.* h.) to coo.

Kirſch—e ['kɪrſə], *f.* (*pl.* —en) cherry. —kern, *m.* cherry-stone. —kuchen,

m. cherry-tart. —waſſer, *n.* cherry brandy.

Kiſſen ['kɪsən], *n.* (—s, *pl.* —, *dim.* Kißchen, Kißlein, *n.*) cushion, pillow.

Kiſt—e ['kɪstə], *f.* (*pl.* —en) box, chest, coffer. —ler, *m.* (—lers, *pl.* —ler), —ner —ners, *pl.* —ner) *m.* chest-or trunk-maker.

Kitt [kɪt], *m.* (—es, *pl.* —e) cement; putty. —en, *v.a.* to cement; to putty.

Kittel ['kɪtəl], *m.* (—s, *pl.* —) smock-frock; blouse.

Kitzel ['kɪtsəl], *m.* (—s) itching. —ig, *adj.* & *adv.* ticklish; delicate, difficult. —n, *v.a.* to tickle; es —t mich, I feel tempted, I am itching to.

Klaff [klaf], *m.* (—(e)s) bark. —en, *v.n.* (*aux.* h. & ſ.) to bark, yelp; to gape, yawn. —end, *p.* & *adj.* gaping, yawning; ajar.

Klafter ['klaftər], *f.* (*pl.* —n) fathom; cord (*of wood*).

Klag—bar ['kla:kba:r], *adj.* & *adv.* actionable. —e, *f.* (*pl.* —en) complaint, lament; eine —e führen, to complain. —en, *v.* I. *a.* bewail. II. *n.* (*aux.* h.) to complain, lament (über, um, for); to sue (*at law*). —end, *p.* & *adj.* complaining; plaintive; der —ende, the plaintiff.

Kläg—er ['klɛ:gər], *m.* (—ers, *pl.* —er) plaintiff, complainant. —eriſch, *adj.* & *adv.* litigious. —lich, *adj.* & *adv.* lamentable, deplorable.

Klamm [klam], I. *adj.* & *adv.* tight, close. II. *n.* (—es) spasm, cramp. III. *f.* (*pl.* —en) ravine. —er, *f.* (*pl.* —ern) clamp. —ern, *v.a.* to clasp, clamp, rivet; ſich ans Leben —ern, to cling to life.

Klampe ['klampə], *f.* (*pl.* —n) clamp.

Klang [klaŋ], *m.* (—(e)s, *pl.* Klänge) sound; ringing (*of bells*); clang.

Klapp [klap], I. *m.* (—es, *pl.* —e) slap. II. *int.* bang! clack! —e, *f.* (*pl.* —en) flap; lid. —ig, *adj.* valvular. —hut, *m.* opera-hat. —kragen, *m.* turn-down collar. —ſtuhl, *m.* camp-stool. —tiſch, *m.* folding table. —tür, *f.* trap-door.

Klappen ['klapən], *v.* I. *a.* to flap, strike together rapidly. II. *n.* (*aux.* h.) to clap, flap; to clatter; wenn es zum — kommt, if things come to a head.

Klapper ['klapər], *f.* (*pl.* —n) rattle. — dürr ['dyr], *adj.* lean as a rake.

—n, *v.n.* (*aux.* h.) to clatter, rattle; mit den Zähnen —n, to chatter one's teeth. —schlange, *f.* rattlesnake.

Rlar [kla:r], *adj. & adv.* clear; serene; distinct. —heit, *f.* clearness; brightness. —äugig, *adj.* clear-eyed; clearsighted. —stellen, *v.a.* to elucidate; eine Sache —stellen, to clear up a matter.

Rlären ['klɛːrən], *v.a.* to clear.

Rlarinett—e [klari'nɛtə], *f.* (*pl.* —en) clarionet. —ist [—'tɪst], *m.* (—isten, *pl.* —isten) clarionet-player.

Rlaff—e ['klasə], *f.* (*pl.* —n) class, rank. —ifizieren [—i'tsiːrən], *v.a.* to classify. —ifer, *m.* (—ifers, *pl.* —ifer) classical author. —ifch, *adj. & adv.* classical.

Rlatfch [klatʃ], *m.* (—es, *pl.* —e) slap, smack; gossip. —en, *v.* I. *a.* to clap; to blab, tell tales; Beifall —en, to applaud. II. *n.* (*aux.* h.) to crack; to babble (*vulg.*); in die Hände —en, to clap the hands. —er, *m.* (—ers, *pl.* —er) clapper, applauder.

Rlau—e ['klauə], *f.* (*pl.* —en) claw. —en, *v.a.* to claw, to clutch. —ig, *adj.* having claws, *etc.* —en-hieb, *m.* stroke, blow (*of a paw or talon*).

Rlauf—el ['klauzəl], *f.* (*pl.* —eln) clause. —(s)ner, *m.* (—(e)ners, *pl.* —(e)ner), —(s)nerin, *f.* hermit, recluse.

Rlavier [kla'viːr], *n.* (—s, *pl.* —e) pianoforte. —ftunde, *f.* piano-lesson.

Rleb—en ['kleːbən], *v.* I. *a.* to paste, glue. II. *n.* (*aux.* h.) to cleave, stick, adhere (an, to). —(e)rig, *adj. & adv.* sticky, viscous.

Rlecf—s [klɛks], *m.* (—(s)es, *pl.* —(s)e) blot. —(s)en, *v.n.* (*aux.* h.) to blot. —fer, *m.* scribbler; dauber.

Rlee [kleː], *m.* (—s) clover.

Rlei [klaɪ], *m.* (—(e)s, *pl.* —e) clay. —ig, *adj.* clayey.

Rleid [klaɪt], *n.* (—(e)s, *pl.* —er) garment; garb; dress. —en, *v.* I. *a.* to clothe, dress. II. *r.* to dress oneself. III. *n.* (*aux.* h., *dat.*) to fit, suit, *or* be becoming to. —fam, *adj. & adv.* fitting well, becoming. —famfeit, *f.* becomingness. —ung, *f.* clothing, dress. —ungs-ftüd, *n.* article of clothing *or* dress.

Rlei—e ['klaɪə], *f.* (*pl.* —en) bran. —ig, *adj.* branny.

Rlein [klaɪn], I. *n.* (—s) giblets. II. *adj. & adv.* little, small; von — auf, from one's infancy. —heit, *f.*

smallness; pettiness. —lich, *adj.* rather small; mean, paltry, petty, trivial. —bauer, *m.* small farmer *or* freeholder. —bild, *n.* miniature. —geld, *n.* small change. —= handel, *m.* retail trade. —händler, *m.* shopkeeper, retailer. —herzig, *adj.* faint-hearted. —laut, *adj. & adv.* low-spirited, dejected, meek. —mütig, *adj.* faint-hearted; dejected. —finnig, *adj.* petty, small-minded. —städter, *m.* inhabitant of a small provincial town. —städtifch, *adj.* provincial, countrified. —vieh, *n.* small cattle, *viz.*, sheep, goats, pigs. —ware, *f.* hardware; trinkets.

Rleinigfeit ['klaɪnɪçkaɪt], *f.* (*pl.* —en) trifle.

Rleinod ['klaɪnoːt], *n.* (—s, *pl.* —e *or* Rleinodien) jewel.

Rleifter ['klaɪstər], *m.* (—s) paste, stickfast. —ig, *adj.* pasty, sticky. —n, *v.a.* to paste.

Rlemm—e ['klɛmə], *f.* (*pl.* —en) clip, holdfast; straits; distress, difficulty; in der —e fein, to be in a fix. —en, *reg. & ir.v.a.* to squeeze, pinch, cramp. —er, *m.* pince-nez.

Rlempner ['klɛmpnər], *m.* (—s, *pl.* —) tinman, tinker. —ei [—'raɪ], *f.* tinman's trade.

Rlepper ['klɛpər], *m.* (—s, *pl.* —) nag, hack.

Rlettern ['klɛtərn], *v.n.* (*aux.* h. & f.) to climb, clamber.

Rlima ['kliːma:], *n.* (—s, *pl.* —ta *or* —te) climate.

Rlimmen ['klɪmən], *reg. & (usually) ir.v.n.* (*aux.* h. & f.) to climb (auf eine S.); to aspire to (nach einer S.).

Rlinge ['klɪŋə], *f.* (*pl.* —n) blade; sword; über die — fpringen laffen, put to the sword.

Rlingel ['klɪŋəl], *f.* (*pl.* —n) small bell, handbell. —n, *v.n.* (*aux.* h.) to ring the bell. —fchnur, *f.* bell-rope. —zieher, *m.* bell-pull.

Rling—en ['klɪŋən], *ir.v.n.* (*aux.* h.) to tinkle, clink, ring. —end, *p. & adj.* resonant, sonorous.

Rlinfe ['klɪŋkə], *f.* (*pl.* —n) latch.

Rlipp—e ['klɪpə], *f.* (*pl.* —en) cliff, crag, steep rock. —ig, *adj.* rocky, craggy. —en-wand, *f.* rocky wall.

Rlirren ['klɪrən], *v.n.* (*aux.* h. & f.) to clink.

Rlopf—en ['klɔpfən], *v.* I. *a.* to knock.

II. *n. (aux.* h.) to beat, knock. —er,
m. (—ers, *pl.* —er) beetle; knocker.
Rloß [klo:s], *m.* (—es, *pl.* Rlöße) meat-
ball; dumpling; blockhead. —ig,
adj. & adv. clod-like; doughy.
Rloster ['klo:stər], *n.* (—s, *pl.* Rlöster)
monastery, convent, abbey. —gang,
m. cloister(s). —gemeinde, *f.* fraternity, sisterhood.
Rlösterlich ['kløstərlıç], *adj. & adv.*
monastic, conventual.
Rloß [klots], *m.* (—es, *pl.* Rlöße) block.
Rluft [kluft], *f.* (*pl.* Rlüfte) cleft;
chasm.
Rlug [klu:k], *adj. & adv. (comp.* flüger;
sup. flügst) wise, sagacious; prudent.
—heit, *f.* prudence, good sense.
Rlüglich ['kly:klıç], *adv.* prudently,
wisely, discreetly, shrewdly.
Rlump [klump], *m.* (—s, *pl.* —en),
(*usually*) —en, *m.* (—ens, *pl.* —en)
mass, clod; cluster; heap.
Rlüver ['kly:vər], *n.* (—s, *pl.* —) jib
(*Naut.*). —baum, *m.* jib-boom.
Rnabe ['kna:bə], *m.* (—n, *pl.* —n; *dim.*
Rnäbchen, Rnäblein) boy. —nhaft,
adj. & adv. boyish. —nhaftigkeit, *f.*
boyishness. —n=alter, *n.* boyhood.
—n=streich, *m.* boyish trick. —n=zeit,
f. youth, boyhood.
Rnack [knak], I. *m.* (—es, *pl.* —e)
crack, split, snap. II. *int.* crack!
snap! —en, *v.a. & n. (aux.* h.) to
crack. —er, *m.* (—ers, *pl.* —er)
cracker. —ern, *v.n. (aux.* h.) to
crackle. —erig, *adj. & adv.* crackling,
crisp. —wurst, *f.* saveloy.
Rnall [knal], *m.* (—es, *pl.* —e) sharp
report, crack; detonation; —und
Fall, suddenly. —en, *v.* I. *n. (aux.* h.)
to burst, explode. II. *a.* to crack,
smack; to explode.
Rnapp [knap], *adj. & adv.* close-
fitting; neat. —heit, *f.* scantiness,
scarcity; tightness.
Rnappe ['knapə], *m.* (—n, *pl.* —n)
youth; squire, shield-bearer.
Rnarren ['knarən], *v.a. & n. (aux.* h.)
to creak, squeak; to rattle.
Rnaster ['knastər], *m.* (—s, *pl.* —)
canister tobacco.
Rnattern ['knatərn], *v.n. (aux.* h.) to
rattle, crackle.
Rnäuel ['knɔyəl], *m. & (usually) n.*
(—s, *pl.* —) ball, hank, skein.
Rnauser ['knauzər], *m.* (—s, *pl.* —)
niggard. —ig, *adj. & adv.* niggardly.

Rnebel ['kne:bəl], *m.* (—s, *pl.* —) cudgel;
gag. —bart, *m.* turned-up moustache.
Rnecht [kneçt], *m.* (—(e)s, *pl.* —e) servant; thrall; vassal. —schaft, *f.*
servitude, slavery.
Rneif—en ['knaifən], *ir.v.a.* to pinch.
—er, *m.* (—ers, *pl.* —er) pince-nez.
Rneipe ['knaipə], *f.* (*pl.* —n) instrument for pinching; pinch; public-
house. —n, I. *reg. & ir.v.a.* to pinch.
II. *reg. v.n. (aux.* h.) to tipple.
Rnet—en ['kne:tən], I. *v.a.* to knead.
II. *subst.n.* kneading; massage. —=
trog, *m.* kneading-trough.
Rnid—en ['knıkən], *v.* I. *a.* to crack;
to break. II. *n. (aux.* h. & f.) to crack;
to break; ein geknidter Mann, a bent
(broken-down) man. —s, *m.* (—(s)es,
pl. —(s)e) bow, courtesy, reverence;
einen —s machen, to curtsey.
Rnie [kni:], *n.* (—(e)s, *pl.* —e) knee.
—en, *v.n. (aux.* h.) to kneel; (*aux.* f.)
to go down on one's knees. —nd, *p.,
adj. & adv.* kneeling, on one's knees.
—hose, *f.* breeches.
Rniff [knıf], *m.* (—(e)s, *pl.* —e) pinch;
trick, dodge.
Rnirps [knırps], *m.* (—(f)es, *pl.* —(f)e)
pigmy. —(f)ig, *adj.* stunted, dwarfish.
Rnirschen ['knırʃən], *v.a. & n. (aux.* h.)
to gnash.
Rnister—ig ['knıst(ə)rıç], *adj.* crack-
ing, crisp. —n, *v.n. (aux.* h.) to
crackle.
Rnoblauch ['kno:plaux], *m.* (—s)
garlic.
Rnöchel ['knœçəl], *m.* (—s, *pl.* —)
knuckle; joint.
Rnochen ['knɔxən], *m.* (—s, *pl.* —)
bone. —gelenk, *n.* joint. —gerippe,
—gerüst, *n.* skeleton.
Rnoll—e ['knɔlə], *f.* (*pl.* —en), —en, *m.*
(—ens, *pl.* —en; *dim.* Rnöllchen)
clod, lump; bulb, tuber. —ig, *adj.*
knotty, knobby.
Rnopf [knɔpf], *m.* (—es, *pl.* Rnöpfe)
button; knob. —loch, *n.* button-hole.
Rnöpf—chen ['knøpfçən], *n. dim. of*
Rnopf. —en, *v.a.* to button. —er,
m. button-hook.
Rnorpel ['knɔrpəl], *m.* (—s, *pl.* —)
cartilage, gristle.
Rnorr—en ['knɔrən], *m.* (—ens, *pl.*
—en) knotty excrescence. —ig, *adj.*
knotty, knobbed, gnarled.
Rnosp—e ['knɔspə], *f.* (*pl.* —en, *dim.*
Rnöspchen) bud.

Knot—en ['kno:tən], I. m. (ens, pl. —en) knot. II. v.a. & n. (aux. h.) to knot. —en=haft, —ig, adj. & adv. knotty. —en=punkt, m. junction.

Knüpf—en ['knʏpfən], I. v.a. to fasten together, join. II. subst.n., —ung, f. uniting, tying.

Knüppel ['knʏpəl], m. (—s, pl. —) cudgel; roll of bread.

Knurr—en ['knurən], I. v.n. (aux. h.) to growl, snarl. II. subst.n. purring; snarling. —ig, adj. & adv. growling, snarling.

Knute ['knu:tə], f. (pl. —n) knout.

Knüttel ['knʏtəl], m. (—s, pl. —) cudgel.

Kobold ['ko:bɔlt], m. (—(e)s, pl. —e) hobgoblin.

Koch [kɔx], m. (—es, pl. Köche) cook. —en, v. I. n. (aux. h.) to cook; to boil. II. a. to cook; to boil. —gefäß, —gerät, —geschirr, n. cooking vessel or utensil.

Köcher ['kœçər], m. (—s, pl. —) quiver.

Köchin ['kœçɪn], f. (pl. —nen) female cook.

Köder ['kø:dər], m. (—s, pl. —) bait. —n, v.a. to bait, lure, decoy.

Koffer ['kɔfər], m. (—s, pl. —) trunk, portmanteau; box. —deckel, m. box-lid. —riemen, m. trunk-strap. —=träger, m. porter.

Kohl [ko:l], m. (—s, pl. —e) cabbage.

Kohl—e ['ko:lə], f. (pl. —en) charcoal; (Stein=) coal; carbon; abgeschwefelte —e, coke; glühende —en, red-hot or live coals. —en, v.a. & n. (aux. h.) to char; to carbonize. —en=arbeiter, m. coal-miner, collier. —en=bant, f. coal-bed. —en=bergwert, n. coal-mine, colliery. —en=brenner, m. charcoal-burner. —en=dampf, m. coal-gas, smoke of burning coals. —en=gestübe, n. coal-dust; slack. —en=grus, m. slack. —en=händler, m. coal-merchant. —en=riß, m. charcoal sketch. —en=säure, f. carbonic acid. —en=schlade, f. coal-cinder. —en=schütte, f. coal-scuttle.

Köhler ['kø:lər], m. (—s, pl. —) charcoal-burner; collier.

Kokett [ko'kɛt], adj. coquettish. —e, f. (pl. —en) flirt, coquette.

Kokos— ['ko:kɔs] (in comp.) —baum, m., —palme, f. coco-nut palm. —nuß, f. coco-nut.

Koks [ko:ks], m. (—(f)es, pl. —(f)e) coke.

Kolben ['kɔlbən], m. (—s, pl. —) club; butt-end; mallet.

Kolleg [kɔ'le:k], n. (—s, pl. —ien & —ia) University lecture. —e [kɔ'le:gə], m. (—en, pl. —en) colleague.

Koller ['kɔlər], n. & m. (—s, pl. —) collar; doublet; rage; er hat einen —, he is in a frenzy.

Kolon—ial [koloni'a:l], adj. colonial. —ie [—'ni:], f. (pl. —ieen) colony. —isieren [—z'i:rən], v.a. to colonize. —ist [—'nɪst], m. colonist.

Koloß [ko'lɔs], m. (—(ff)es, pl. —(ff)e) colossus. —(ff)al [—'sa:l], adj. & adv. colossal; very, extremely.

Kolumne [ko'lumnə], f. (pl. —n) column. —n=titel, m. heading. —n=weise, adj. in columns.

Kombinieren [kɔmbi'ni:rən], v.a. to combine.

Komet [ko'me:t], m. (—en, pl. —en) comet. —en=bahn, f. orbit of a comet. —en=schweif, m. tail of a comet.

Komi—k ['ko:mɪk], f. comicality. —ter, m. (—ters, pl. —ter) comic writer; comedian. —sch, adj. funny, droll; peculiar; strange.

Komitee [komi'te:], n. (—s, pl. —s) committee.

Komma ['kɔma:], n. (—s, pl. —s, —ta) comma.

Kommand—ant [kɔman'dant], m. (—=anten, pl. —anten) commander. —=ieren [—'di:rən], v.a. to command. —o [—'mando:], n. (—os, pl. —os) command.

Kommen ['kɔmən], I. ir.v.n. (aux. ſ.) to come; etwas — sehen, to foresee a thing; auf seine Kosten —, to recover one's expenses; in Verlegenheit —, to get into trouble; zu Fall —, to be ruined. II. subst.n. coming, arrival. —d, p. & adj. der, die, das —de, the coming; the comer; —de und Gehende, comers and goers; —de Woche, next week.

Komment [kɔ'mãː], m. (—s) student law or code. —ar [—mɛn'ta:r], m. (—ars, pl. —are) commentary, comment. —ieren [—'ti:rən], v.a. to comment on.

Kommers [kɔ'mɛrs], m. (—(ſ)es, pl. —(ſ)e) (students' slang) drinking-bout. —buch, n. book of drinking songs.

Kommerzienrat [kɔ'mɛrtsiənra:t], m. councillor of commerce.

Rommis [kɔ'mi:], m. (—, pl. —) clerk.

Rommiß [kɔ'mɪs], n. (m.) (—(ſſ)es, pl. —) uniform (sl.). —brot, n. regimental bread.

Rommiſſär [kɔmɪ'sa:r], m. (—s, pl. —e) commissary, commissioner.

Rommode [kɔ'mo:də], subst.f. (pl. —n) chest of drawers.

Rommun—iſmus [kɔmu'nɪsmu:s], m. communism. —iſt, m. (—iſten, pl. —iſten) communist.

Romöb—iant [komødi'ant], m. (—ianten, pl. —ianten) comedian; actor. —ie [ko'mø:diə], f. (pl. —ien) comedy; play.

Rompanie [kɔmpa'ni:], f. (pl. —en) company (Mil.). —chef, m. captain.

Rompaß ['kɔmpas], m. (—(ſſ)es, pl. —(ſſ)e) compass. —häuschen, n. binnacle. —roſe, f. compass-card.

Rompliment [kɔmpli'mɛnt], n. (—s, pl. —e) compliment; keine —e! no ceremony! —ieren [—'ti:rən], v.a. to compliment.

Romplot(t) [kɔm'plɔt], n. (—(e)s, pl. —e) plot.

Romponieren [kɔmpo'ni:rən], v.a. & n. to compose (Mus.). —iſt [—'nɪst], m. (—iſten, pl. —iſten), —iſtin, f. composer.

Romtur [kɔm'tu:r], m. (—s, pl. —e) commander of an order. —ei [—'raɪ], f. commandery.

Ronditor [kɔn'di:tɔr], m. (—s, pl. —en) confectioner. —ei [—'raɪ], f. confectioner's shop.

Ronfekt [kɔn'fɛkt], n. (—(e)s, pl. —e) sweetmeats.

Ronferenz [kɔnfe'rɛnts], f. (pl. —en) conference.

Ronfus [kɔn'fu:s], adj. puzzled, confused.

Rönig ['kø:nɪç], m. (—s, pl. —e) king. —in, f. queen. —lich, adj. royal. —tum, n. (—tums, pl. —tümer) kingship. —reich, n. kingdom, realm. —swürde, f. royal dignity; kingship.

Ronkurr—ent [kɔnku'rɛnt], m. (—enten, pl. enten) competitor. —enz [—'rɛnts], f. (pl. —enzen) competition. —ieren [—'ri:rən], v.n. (aux. h.) to compete; to concur.

Ronkurs [kɔn'kurs], m. (—(ſ)es, pl. —(ſ)e) bankruptcy, failure. —erklärung, f. declaration of insolvency. —gericht, n. court of bankruptcy. —maſſe, f. estate of a bankrupt.

Rönnen ['kønən], ir.v. I. a. to know, understand (how to do a thing); to have skill in; to have power, be able to; er kann nichts, he knows nothing, he can do nothing. [Rönnen is used for gekonnt when accompanying an inf. in compound tenses; as, er hätte es tun —, he might have done it.] II. n. (aux. h.) to be able; to be permitted; es kann ſein, it may be; ich kann mich irren, I may be mistaken; was kann ich dafür? how can I help it?

Ronſiſtor—ium [kɔnzɪs'to:rɪum], m. (—iums, pl. —ien, —ia) consistory.

Ronſonant [kɔnzo'nant], m. (—en, pl. —en) consonant.

Ronſul [kɔn'zul], m. (—s, pl. —n) consul. —ariſch [—'la:rɪʃ], adj. & adv. consular. —at [—'la:t], m. (—ats, pl. —ate) consulate.

Ronterfei ['kɔntərfaɪ], n. (—(e)s, pl. —e) portrait, likeness; counterfeit.

Ronto ['kɔnto:], n. (—s, pl. —s, Ronti) account, credit. —korrent, m. & n. (—korrent(e)s, pl. —korrente) current account. —ſaldo, n. balance account.

Rontor [kɔn'to:r], n. (—s, pl. —e) counting-house; office.

Rontra ['kɔntra], (in comp.=) counter; contra. —baß, m. double-bass.

Rontrolle [kɔn'trɔlə], f. (pl. —n) control; army-list.

Ronvent [kɔn'vɛnt], m. (—(e)s, pl. —e) convention.

Ronzert [kɔn'tsɛrt], n. (—s, pl. —e) concert.

Ropf [kɔpf], m. (—es, pl. Röpfe) head; aus dem —, by heart; Hals über —, head over heels; vor den — ſtoßen, to offend. —haut, f. scalp. —hörer, m.pl. earphones (Radio). —kiſſen, n. pillow. —längs, adv. headlong. —los, adj. heedless; silly, stupid. —niden, n. nod. —puß, m. coiffure. —ſchüttelnd, adj. & adv. shaking the head. —weh, n. headache. —zerbrechen, n. perplexity; ohne viel —zerbrechen, without much pondering.

Rop—ie [ko'pi:], f. (pl. —ieen) copy. —ieren, v.a. to copy.

Röpfen ['køpfən], v.a. to behead.

Roppel ['kɔpəl], f. (pl. —n) leash. —n, v.a. to couple, leash.

Rorall—e [ko'ralə], f. (pl. —en) coral. —en, adj. coralline. —enriff, n. coral-reef. —enſchnur, f. coral necklace.

Rorb [kɔrp], *m.* (**—es**, *pl.* **Rörbe**, *dim.* **Rörbchen**) basket; hamper. **—=antenne,** *f.* cage-aerial (*Radio*).

Rorde ['kɔrdə], *f.* (*pl.* **—n**) string. **—l,** *f.* (*pl.* **—ln**) cord; strong thread.

Rorinthe [ko'rɪntə], *f.* (*pl.* **—n**) dried currant.

Rorf [kɔrk], *m.* (**—es**, *pl.* **—e** *and* **Rörfe**) cork. **—en,** I. *adj.* of cork, corky. II. *v.a.* to cork. **—zieher,** *m.* corkscrew.

Rorn [kɔrn], *n.* (**—s**, *pl.* **Rörner**) grain; corn (*in general*). **—ähre,** *f.* ear of corn. **—bau,** *m.* cultivation of cereals. **—blau,** *adj.* blue like the cornflower. **—blume,** *f.* cornflower. **—boden,** *m.* granary. **—börse,** *f.* corn-exchange. **—brand,** *m.* blight in corn. **—fege,** *f.* winnowing machine. **—flur,** *f.* corn-fields. **—garbe,** *f.* sheaf of corn. **—lade,** *f.* corn-bin. **—rade,** *f.* corn-cockle.

Rörn—chen ['kørnçən], *n.* (**—chens,** *pl.* **—chen**) grain, granule. **—el=ung,** *f.* granulation. **—ig,** *adj.* granular; pithy, nervous.

Rornett [kɔr'nɛt], *n.* (**—s**, *pl.* **—e**) cornet (*Mus.*). **—bläser,** *m.* cornet-player.

Rörper ['kørpər], *m.* (**—s**, *pl.* **—**) body. **—haft,** *adj.* corporeal. **—lich,** *adj.* & *adv.* bodily; corporeal. **—schaft,** *f.* corporate body, corporation. **—schaftlich,** *adj.* of a corporation. **—bau,** *m.* frame; build, make. **—bildung,** *f.* bodily structure, physique. **—fülle,** *f.* corpulence, plumpness. **—größe,** *f.* stature; tallness. **—traft,** *f.* physical power. **—los,** *adj.* immaterial, incorporeal. **—stimmung,** *f.* temperament, constitution. **—übung,** *f.* bodily exercise, athletics, gymnastics.

Rorps [kɔːr], *n.* (**—,** *pl.* **—**) army corps; a special kind of students' club.

Rorreft [kɔ'rɛkt], *adj.* correct. **—heit,** *f.* correctness. **—ur=bogen,** *m.* proof-sheet.

Rorrespond—ent [kɔrɛspɔn'dɛnt], *m.* (**—enten,** *pl.* **enten**) correspondent. **—enz** [—'dɛnts], *f.* correspondence. **—ieren** [—'diːrən], *v.n.* to correspond.

Rose—n ['koːzən], *v.a.* to caress. **—name,** *m.* pet-name.

Rost [kɔst], *f.* food; **freie —,** free board.

Rostbar ['kɔstbaːr], *adj.* & *adv.* expensive; precious; valuable. **—feit,** *f.*

(*pl.* **—feiten**) costliness; preciousness; jewel, valuable.

¹Rost—en ['kɔstən], *pl.* cost(s), expense(s), expenditure. **—en=anschlag,** *m.* estimate (of cost). **—en=aufwand,** *m.* expenditure. **—en=frei, —en=los,** *adj.* free of charge *or* expense. **—en=preis,** *m.* cost-price. **—spielig,** *adj.* expensive, costly.

²Rosten ['kɔstən], I. *v.a.* to taste; to try, make trial of. II. *subst.n.* tasting.

³Rost—en ['kɔstən], *v.a.* (einen etwas) to cost; **es —et viel Zeit,** it requires much time.

Röstlich ['kœstlɪç], *adj.* & *adv.* costly; precious; delicious. **—feit,** *f.* delicacy; costliness; excellence.

Rostüm [kɔs'tyːm], *n.* (**—s**, *pl.* **—e**) costume.

Rot [koːt], *m.* (**—(e)s**) dirt, filth. **—ig,** *adj.* & *adv.* dirty, muddy, filthy.

Rotelett [kɔt(ə)lɛt], *n.* (**—en,** *pl.* **—en**) cutlet.

Röter ['køːtər], *m.* (**—s**, *pl.* **—**) watch-dog; cur.

Rrabbe ['krabə], *f.* (*pl.* **—n**) crab.

Rrach [krax], *m.* (**—es**, *pl.* **—e**) crack, crash; quarrel; bankruptcy.

Rrachen ['kraxən], I. *v.n.* (*aux.* h. & f.) to crack; to crash. II. *v.a.* to crack (*nuts, etc.*). III. *subst.n.* crack, crash, roar.

Rrächzen ['krɛçtsən], *v.* I. *a.* to croak out. II. *n.* (*aux.* h.) to croak; to caw.

Rraft [kraft], I. *f.* (*pl.* **Rräfte**) strength; vigour; power; in **— treten,** to come into force. II. *prep.* (*with gen.*) in virtue of, on the strength of, by authority of. **—aufwand,** *m.* effort, expenditure of force *or* energy. **—ausdruck,** *m.* pithy expression. **—fahrzeug,** *n.* motor vehicle. **—los,** *adj.* impotent, powerless. **—probe,** *f.* trial of strength. **—sammler,** *m.* accumulator. **—verlust,** *m.* loss of power. **—verstärker,** *m.* power-amplifier (*Radio*). **—voll,** *adj.* full of strength, vigorous, powerful. **—wagen,** *m.* motor vehicle.

Rräftig ['krɛftɪç], *adj.* & *adv.* strong, powerful. **—feit,** *f.* robustness; energy. **—en,** *v.a.* to strengthen. **—ung,** *f.* strengthening, invigoration.

Rragen ['kraːgən], *m.* (**—s**, *pl.* **—**) collar.

Rräh—e ['krɛːə], *f.* (*pl.* **—en**) crow. **—en,** *v.n.* (*aux.* h.) to crow.

Rrall—e ['kralə], *f.* (*pl.* **—en**) claw.

—en, *v.a.* & *n.* (*aux.* h.) to claw; to clutch. —ig, *adj.* clawed.

Rram [kra:m], *m.* (—(e)s, *pl.* Rräme) retail trade; small wares; stuff, rubbish. —en, *v.n.* (*aux.* h.) to retail (*goods*); to keep a small shop. —=handel, *m.* retail trade. —laden, *m.*, —bude, *f.* small shop, retail shop, stall. —kammer, *f.* lumber-room.

Rrämer ['krɛ:mər], *m.* (—s, *pl.* —) shopkeeper. —ei [—'rai], *f.* shopkeeping, retailing; trading.

Rrampe ['krampə], *f.* (*pl.* —n) cramp-iron; staple. —n, *v.a.* to cramp, to fasten.

Rrampf [krampf], *m.* (—es, *pl.* Rrämpfe) cramp, spasm; convulsion; fit. —en, *v.a.* & *r.* to contract convulsively; to clasp convulsively. —=haft, *adj.* & *adv.* convulsive; spasmodic. —ader, *f.* varicose vein.

Rran [kra:n], *m.* (—(e)s, *pl.* Rräne) crane (*Mach.*).

Rranich ['kra:nɪç], *m.* (—s, *pl.* —e) crane (*bird*).

Rrank [kraŋk], *adj.* & *adv.* (*comp.* kränker, *sup.* kränk(e)st) ill; — werden, to fall ill. —e(r), *m.*, —e, *f.* invalid. —haft, *adj.* & *adv.* diseased, morbid. —=haftigkeit, *f.* morbidity. —=bett, *n.* sick-bed. —en=kost, *f.* invalid diet. —en=wärter, *m.*, —en=wärterin, *f.* sick-attendant, sick-nurse.

Rränk—en ['krɛŋkən], *v.a.* to vex; to insult; to injure, wrong. —lich, *adj.* & *adv.* sickly. —lichkeit, *f.* sickliness. —ung, *f.* offending; outrage; mortification.

Rrankheit ['kraŋkhart], *f.* (*pl.* —en) illness.

Rranz [krants], *m.* (—es, *pl.* Rränze) garland, wreath.

Rränz—chen ['krɛntscən], *n.* (—chens, *pl.* —chen) little garland; girls' club. —en, *v.a.* to crown, to wreathe.

Rratz [krats], *m.* (—es, *pl.* —e) scratch; scar. —bürste, *f.* scrubbing-brush; cross, irritable person. —en, *v.a.* & *n.* (*aux.* h.) to scratch. —er, *m.* (—ers, *pl.* —er) person *or* thing that scrapes. —fuß, *m.* awkward bow.

Rrätz—e ['krɛtsə], *f.* (*pl.* —en) itch; mange. —ig, *adj.* & *adv.* itchy; scabby; rough.

Rraus [kraus], *adj.* & *adv.* crisp, curly; die Stirn — ziehen, to frown. —kopf, *m.* curly-head.

Rräuseln ['krɔyzəln], *v.a.* to curl.

Rraut [kraut], *n.* (—es, *pl.* Rräuter) herb; plant.

Rräuter ['krɔytər], —artig, *adj.* herbaceous. —buch, *n.* herbal.

Rravatte [kra'vatə], *f.* (*pl.* —n) cravat; tie, scarf.

Rrawall [kra'val], *m.* (—s, *pl.* —e) uproar, riot.

Rrebs [krɛps], *m.* (—(s)es, *pl.* —(s)e) crayfish, cancer (*Med.*). —kreis, *m.*, —linie, *f.*, —wendekreis, *m.* Tropic of Cancer.

Rredit [kre'di:t], *m.* (—es) credit. —fähig, *adj.* solvent, sound.

Rreid—e ['kraidə], *f.* (*pl.* —en) chalk. —ig, *adj.* chalky. —eweiß, *adj.* as white as a sheet.

Rreis [krais], *m.* (—(s)es, *pl.* —(s)e) circle; district. —beamte(r), *m.* district civil officer. —lauf, *m.* rotation, revolution. —linie, *f.* circumference. —viertel, *n.* quadrant.

Rreischen ['kraisən], *ir.v.n.* (*aux.* h.) to shriek.

Rreisen ['kraizən], *v.* I. *n.* (*aux.* h.) to move in a circle. II. *a.* to surround.

Rrepp [krɛp], *m.* (—s, *pl.* —e) crape.

Rresse ['krɛsə], *f.* (*pl.* —n) cress.

Rreuz [krɔyts], *n.* (—es, *pl.* —e) cross, crucifix; — und quer, zigzag, in all directions. —band, *n.* cross-beam; postal wrapper; unter —band schiden, to send by book-post. —bild, *n.* crucifix. —fidel, *adj.* as happy as can be. —verhör, *n.* cross-examination. —ritter, *m.* crusader. —zug, *m.* crusade.

Rreuz—en ['krɔytsən], *v.* I. *a.* to mark with a cross; to thwart; to cross (breeds). II. *r.* to make the sign of the cross; to intersect. III. *n.* (*aux.* h.) to cross; to cruise. —er, *m.* (—ers, *pl.* —er) a small coin; cruiser. —er=flotte, *f.*, —er=geschwader, *n.* squadron of cruisers. —igen, *v.a.* to crucify. —igung, *f.* crucifixion. —ung, *f.* cross-breeding.

Rriech—en ['kri:çən], *ir.v.n.* (*aux.* h. & f.) to creep. —erei [—'rai], *f.* servility. —erisch, *adj.* fawning, cringing.

Rrieg [kri:k], *m.* (—(e)s, *pl.* —e) war. —en, *v.* I. *n.* (*aux.* h.) to wage war. II. *a.* to get; to obtain, gain. —er [—gər], *m.* (—ers, *pl.* —er) warrior, soldier. —erisch, *adj.* & *adv.* warlike; martial. —er=stand, *m.* profession of arms. —er=verein, m. association of veterans.

Kriegs [kri:ks] (in comp.) —adel, m. military nobility. —amt, n. war office. —anleihe, f. war loan. —auf= gebot, —aufruf, m. call to arms. —behörde, f. war office. —dienst, m. active military service; duty. —= entschädigung, f. war indemnity. —erklärung, f. declaration of war. —gefangene(r), m. prisoner of war. —gericht, n. court martial. —kasse, f. military chest. —marine, f. navy. —not, f. stress of war. —rat, m. council of war. —schauplatz, m. seat of war. —schiff, n. man-of-war, battleship (Naut.). —schule, f. military academy. —schüler, m. cadet, military pupil. —zustand, —stand, m. state of war.

Krippe ['krɪpə], f. (pl. —n) crib, manger.

Krise ['kri:zə], Krisis [—zɪs], f. (pl. Krisen) crisis.

Kristall [krɪs'tal], m. (—s, pl. —e) crystal. —en, adj. of crystal; crystal-line. —isieren [—i'si:rən], v.a. to crystallize. —isierung, —isation [—zatsl'o:n], f. crystallization.

Kritik [kri'ti:k], f. (pl. —en) criticism. —er ['kri:tɪkər], m. (—ers, pl. —er) (—en=schreiber, m.) critic, reviewer.

Kritt—el ['krɪtəl], m. (—els, pl. —el) captiousness. —lich, adj. fault-find-ing, captious.

Kritz [krɪts], m. (—es, pl. —e) scratch, scrawl. —eln, v. I. a. to scratch. II. n. (aux. h.) to splutter (as pens). —ler, m. (—lers, pl. —ler) scribbler.

Krokodil [kroko'di:l], n. (—s, pl. —e) crocodile.

Kron—e ['kro:nə], f. (pl. —en) crown. —leuchter, m. chandelier. —prinz, m. crown-prince. —prinzessin, f. crown-princess, princess-royal. —= prinzlich, adj. relating or belonging to the crown-prince; das —prinzliche Paar, the crown-prince and the crown-princess. —rat, m. privy council. —räuber, m. usurper. —= rede, f. speech from the throne. —= zeuge, m. witness for the crown.

Krön—en ['krø:nən], v.a. to crown. —ung, f. coronation.

Kronsbeere ['kro:nsbe:rə], f. (pl. —n) cranberry.

Kropf [krɔpf], m. (—es, pl. Kröpfe) crop, craw. —ader, f. varicose vein. —artig, adj. wen-like, goitrous. —eisen, n. crowbar. —gans, f. common pelican.

Kröte ['krø:tə], f. (pl. —n) toad.

Krücke ['krʏkə], f. (pl. —n) crutch.

Krug [kru:k], m. (—es, pl. Krüge) pitcher, jug; public-house.

Krume ['kru:mə], f. (pl. —n) the crumb (of bread).

Krumm [krum], adj. & adv. (comp. krummer, sup. krummst less good; krümmer, krümmst), crooked, bent, curved. —beinig, adj. bandy-legged.

Krümmen ['krʏmən], v. I. a. to bend. II. r. to grow crooked; to wriggle.

Krüppel ['krʏpəl], m. (—s, pl. —) cripple.

Krust—e ['krustə], f. (pl. —en, dim. Krüstchen) crust. —ig, adj. crusty. —entiere, pl. crustacea.

Kübel ['ky:bəl], m. (—s, pl. —) bucket.

Kubik— [ku'bi:k], pref. (in comp.=) cube, cubic. —fuß, m. cubic foot. —inhalt, m., —maß, n. cubic con-tents. —wurzel, f. cube-root.

Kubisch ['ku:bɪʃ], adj. cubic.

Kubus ['ku:bus], m. (pl. Kuben) cube.

Küche ['kʏçə], f. (pl. —n) kitchen; kalte —, cold meat.

Kuchen ['ku:xən], m. (—s, pl. —) (dim. Küchelchen) cake; tart.

Kuckuck [kukuk], m. (—s, pl. —e) cuckoo.

Kufe ['ku:fə], f. (pl. —n) vat, tub.

Küfer ['ky:for], m. (—s, pl. —) cooper.

Kugel ['ku:gəl], f. (pl. —n) ball; sphere; bullet. —ig, adj. spherical, globular. —bahn, f. bowling-green.

Kuguar ['ku:gua:r], m. (—s, pl. —) puma (Zool.).

Kuh [ku:], f. (pl. Kühe) cow; blinde —, blind man's buff. —hürde, f., —stall, m. cow-stall.

Kühl [ky:l], adj. & adv. cool; fresh. —e, f. coolness; coldness; freshness. —apparat, m. refrigerator. —en, v. I. a. to cool. II. r. & n. (aux. h.) to grow cool. —end, p. & adj. cooling.

Kühn [ky:n], adj. & adv. bold, daring. —heit, f. courage, boldness.

Kult [kult], m. (—(e)s, pl. —e), Kultus, m. (—) church ceremonies. —ivieren [—i'vi:rən], v.a. to cultivate. —ur [—'tu:r], f. cultivation; culture; civi-lization.

Kümmel ['kʏməl], m. (—s, pl. —) caraway-seed.

Kummer ['kumər], *m.* (—s) grief, sorrow; trouble. —**frei**, —**los**, *adj.* untroubled, without care, careless. —**voll**, *adj.* sorrowful, painful, doleful.

Kümmerlich ['kymərlıç], I. *adj.* & *adv.* sorrowful; miserable. II. *adv.* scarcely, barely, with great trouble.

Kümmer—n ['kymərn], *v.* I. *a.* to grieve, afflict; to concern; **was —t mich das?** what is that to me? II. *r.* to care about (**um einen** *or* **eine S.**); to grieve for (**über eine S.**). III. *n.* (*aux.* h. & f.) to fret. —**nis**, *f.* (*pl.* —**ni(ff)e**) annoyance; affliction.

Kund [kunt], *indec. adj.* (*only used as predicate*) known; **die Sache ift —**, it is generally known. —**bar**, *adj.* notorious, well-known. —**barkeit**, *f.* notoriety, publicity. —**e**, *f.* (*pl.* —**en**) *see* **Kenntnis**; information, notice; (*as the second part of compounds*) science. —**ig**, *adj.* & *adv.* knowing, skilful, learned. —**gebung**, *f.* demonstration (*political, etc.*). —**schaft**, *f.* custom; customers; goodwill (*C.L.*); practice; notice, information. —**schaften**, *v.* I. *n.* (*aux.* h.) to scout, spy, reconnoitre. II. *a.* to find out. —**schafter**, *m.* (—**schafters**, *pl.* —**schafter**) spy, emissary, scout.

Künd—igen ['kyndıgən], *v.a.* to give notice *or* warning; to publish, make known. —**igung**, *f.* notice, warning; **halbjährliche —igung**, six months' notice.

Künftig ['kynftıç], I. *adj.* future; coming, next. II. *adv.* for the future, henceforth.

Kunst [kunst], *f.* (*pl.* **Künste**) art; skill; trade, profession; **freie Künste**, liberal arts; **schöne Künste**, fine arts. —**arbeit**, *f.* work of art; artificial work. —**ausdruck**, *m.* technical term. —**ausstellung**, *f.* exhibition of works of art, art gallery. —**butter**, *f.* margarine. —**seide**, *f.* artificial silk. —**griff**, *m.* dexterity, knack. —**halle**, *f.* art museum. —**händler**, *m.* dealer in works of art. —**stück**, *m.* work of art. —**trieb**, *m.* artistic instinct. —**verein**, *m.* art union. —**voll**, *adj.* ingenious, artistic.

Künst—ler ['kynstlər], *m.* (—**lers**, *pl.* —**ler**), —**lerin**, *f.* artist; artiste. —**lerisch**, *adj.* artistic, artist-like. —**lich**, *adj.* artificial.

Küp—e ['ky:pə], *f.* (*pl.* —**en**) large tub.

—**er**, *n.* (—**ers**, *pl.* —**er**) cooper, cellarman.

Kupfer ['kupfər], *n.* (—**s**, *pl.* —) copper. —**ig**, *adj.* coppery. —**n**, *adj.* of copper. —**blatt**, *n.* copperplate print. —**blech**, *n.* sheet copper. —**druck**, *m.* copperplate print. —**münze**, *f.* copper coin. —**stich**, *m.* copperplate engraving *or* print.

Kupp—el ['kupəl], *f.* (*pl.* —**eln**) cupola, dome. —**ig**, *adj.* peaked, topped. —**eln**, *v.a.* to make a match. —**elung**, *f.* joint; coupling.

1**Kur** [ku:r], (*older* **Cur**,) *f.* (*pl.* —**en**) cure. —**ieren**, *v.a.* to cure. —**gast**, *m.* patient at a health resort. —**haus**, *n.* pump-room, casino. —**ort**, *m.* health resort. —**saal**, *m.* casino.

2**Kur**, **Kür** [ky:r] (*obs.*), *f.* election; electoral dignity. —**fürst**, *m.* elector (*in the old German Empire*). —**pfalz**, *f.* the Palatinate.

Küraß ['ky:ras], *m.* (—(f)fes), *pl.* —(f)fe) cuirass. —**ffier** [—'si:r], *m.* (—(ff)iers, *pl.* —(ff)iere) cuirassier.

Kurb—e ['kyrbə], —**el**, *f.* (*pl.* —**en**, —**eln**) crank. —**e(l)n**, *v.n.* (*aux.* h.) to turn the winch.

Kürbis ['kyrbıs], *m.* (—(f)fes, *pl.* —(f)fe) gourd.

Kurios [kurı'o:s], *adj.* curious. —**s** (f)**ität** [—i'tɛ:t], *f.* (*pl.* —(f)itäten) curiosity; rarity.

Kurs [kurs], *m.* (—(f)es, *pl.* —(f)e) (rate of) exchange. —**buch**, *n.* time-table.

Kürschner ['kyrſnər], *m.* (—**s**, *pl.* —) furrier.

Kurz [kurts] (*comp.* **kürzer**, *sup.* **kürz(e)ft**), I. *adj.* short, brief. II. *adv.* in short, in a word; **über — oder lang**, sooner or later; **zu — kommen**, to be the loser. —**ab**, *adv.* briefly, abruptly. —**schreiber**, *m.* shorthand writer. —**schrift**, *f.* shorthand writing. —**schluß**, *m.* short circuit (*Elec.*). —**sichtig**, *adj.* near-sighted. —**um**, *adv.* in short, to sum up. —**waren**, *f. pl.* small wares; hardware. —**weg**, *adv.* simply, plainly; off-hand; curtly; only. —**weil**, *f.* pastime. —**weilig**, *adj.* amusing, pleasant. —**welle**, *f.* short wave (*Radio*).

Kürz—e ['kyrtsə], *f.* shortness, brevity. —**en**, *v.a.* to shorten. —**lich**, *adv.* lately, not long ago; shortly; soon; briefly.

Ruß [kus], _m._ (—(f)es, _pl._ **Küsse**) kiss.
Küssen ['kʏsən], _v.a._ to kiss.
Küste ['kʏstə], _f._ (_pl._ —n) coast. —n= **land**, _n._ maritime country.
Küster ['kʏstər], _m._ (—s, _pl._ —) sacristan, sexton.
Kutsch—e ['kutʃə], _f._ (_pl._ —en) carriage; coach. —er, _m._ (—ers, _pl._ —er) coachman, driver. —ieren [—'ʃi:rən], _v.n._ (_aux._ h. & f.) to drive in a carriage. —(en)=**ſchlag**, _m._ carriage-door. —er= **bod**, _m._ box.
Kutte ['kutə], _f._ (_pl._ —n) cowl.
Kuvert [ku'vɛrt], _n._ (—s, _pl._ —e) cover; envelope.

L

L, l [ɛl], _n._ L, l.
Lab—e ['la:bə], _f._ (_pl._ —en) refreshment; comfort. —en, _v.a._ to refresh. —ſal, _n._ (—ſals, _pl._ —ſale) refreshment.
¹**Lache** ['laxə], _f._ (_pl._ —n) laugh, laughter.
²**Lach**—e ['laxə], _f._ (_pl._ —en) pool. —ig, _adj._ marshy.
Läch—eln ['lɛçəln], I. _v.n._ (_aux._ h.) to smile (**über einen** or **eine S.**, at a person _or_ a thing); **einem** —**eln**, to smile upon _or_ at a person; **höhniſch** —**eln**, to sneer. II. _v.a._ to smile (_applause, etc._). III. _subst.n._ smile. —**erlich**, _adj._ & _adv._ laughable; ridiculous. —**erlichkeit**, _f._ absurdity.
Lach—en ['laxən], I. _v.n._ (_aux._ h.) to laugh; **über** (**einen** or **eine S.**) —**en**, to laugh at. II. _subst.n._ laughter, laugh. —**end**, _p._ & _adj._ laughing; pleasant; glad.
Lachs [laks], _m._ (—(f)es, _pl._ —(f)e) salmon. —**ſchinken**, _m._ fillet of smoked ham.
Lack [lak], _m._ (—(e)s, _pl._ —e) varnish, lacquer. —**draht**, _m._ japanned insulated wire (_Radio_). —**ieren** [—'ki:rən], _v.a._ to lacquer, varnish. —**leder**, _n._ patent leather.
Lade ['la:də], _f._ (_pl._ —n) box, chest, case.
¹**Lad**—en ['la:dən], _ir.v.a._ to load, lade. —e=**dauer**, _f._ length of charge-period (_Radio_). —e=**ſchein**, _m._ bill of lading. —**ung**, _f._ loading, lading; freight.
²**Lad**—en ['la:dən], _ir._ (& _obs. reg._) _v.a._ to invite. —**ung**, _f._ invitation.

³**Laden**, _m._ (—s), I. (_pl._ —) shutter. II. (_pl._ **Läden**) shop.
Lage ['la:gə], _f._ (_pl._ —n) situation, position; attitude, posture; state, condition. —r, _n._ (—rs, _pl._ —r or (_dial._) **Läger**) couch, bed; camp; stock, supply; storehouse.
Lager— ['la:gər] (_in comp._) —**bier**, _n._ beer brewed for keeping, lager (beer). —**geld**, _n._, —**zins**, _m._, —**miete**, _f._, —**gebühren**, _pl._ storage, warehouse rent. —**gerät**, _n._ camp-furniture. —**meiſter**, _m._ quarter-master. —**raum**, _m._ storeroom.
Lagern ['la:gərn], _v.n._ (_aux._ h. & f.) & _r._ to lie down, rest; to encamp.
Lagune [la'gu:nə], _f._ (_pl._ —n) lagoon.
Lahm [la:m], _adj._ & _adv._ lame. —**heit**, _f._ lameness.
Lähm—en ['lɛ:mən], _v.a._ to lame. —**ung**, _f._ laming, maiming.
Laib [laip], _m._ (—es, _pl._ —e) loaf.
Laich [laiç], _m._ & _n._ (—es) spawn. —e, _f._ spawning-time. —en, _v.n._ (_aux._ h.) to spawn.
Laie ['laiə], _m._ (—n, _pl._ —n) layman. —n=**haft**, _adj._ belonging to the laity. —n=**bruder**, _m._ lay-brother. —n= **ſtand**, _m._ laity.
Lakai [la'kai], _m._ (—s _and_ —en, _pl._ —en) lackey.
Lake ['la:kə], _f._ (_pl._ —n) brine, pickle.
Laken ['la:kən], _n._ (—s, _pl._ —) sheet.
Lakoniſch [la'ko:nɪʃ], _adj._ & _adv._ laconic.
Lakritze [la'krɪtsə], _f._ (_pl._ —n) licorice.
Lallen ['lalən], _v.a._ & _n._ (_aux._ h.) to stammer.
Lamm [lam], _n._ (—s, _pl._ **Lämmer**) lamb.
Lämm—**chen** ['lɛmçən] (—**chens**, _pl._ —**chens**), —**lein** (—**leins**, _pl._ —**lein**) _n._ lambkin.
Lampe ['lampə], _f._ (_pl._ —n) lamp. —n=**fieber**, _n._ stage-fright. —n= **ſockel**, _m._ valve-holder (_Radio_).
Land [lant], _n._ (—(e)s) land (_as opp. to water_); country (_as opp. to town_); (_pl._ **Länder**) piece of ground, country, region; **ans** —, ashore. —**adel**, _m._ landed gentry. —**amt**, _n._ land-office; land-court. —**beſitzer**, _m._ landed proprietor. —**en**, _v.a._ & _n._ (_aux._ h. & f.) to land. —**enge**, _f._ isthmus. —**gericht**, _n._ county court. —**graf**, _m._ landgrave. —**gräfin**, _f._ landgravine. —**grenze**, _f._ landmark; boundary.

—**gut**, *n.* country estate. —**läufer**, *m.*, —**läuferin**, *f.* vagabond, tramp. —**meſſer**, *m.* land-surveyor. —**rat**, *m.* sub-prefect. —**s=knecht**, *m.* hired trooper, mercenary. —**s=leute**, *pl.* countrymen, compatriots. —**s=mann**, *m.*, —**s=männin**, *f.* compatriot. —**s ſteuer**, *f.* land-tax. —**ſtraße**, *f.* high-road, highway. —**ſtreicher**, *m.*, —**ſtreicherin**, *f.* tramp. —**ſturm**, *m.* local militia. —**tag**, *m.* diet. —**tagen**, *v.n.* to hold a diet (*insep.*). —**tags= abgeordnete(r)**, *m.* deputy to the diet. —**ung**, *f.* landing, disembarkation. —**s wehr**, *f.* militia, yeomanry. —**wirt**, *m.* farmer. —**wirtſchaft**, *f.* farming, husbandry. —**wirtſchaftlich**, *adj.* agricultural.

Ländes— ['landəs] (*in comp.*) —**adel**, *m.* nobility of a country. —**brauch**, *m.* custom of a country. —**verrat**, *m.* high treason. —**verräter**, *m.* traitor to his country. —**verwalter**, *m.* viceroy. —**verweiſung**, *f.* banishment; exile.

Ländlich ['lɛntlɪç], *adj.* rural, country-like.

Landſchaft ['lantʃaft], *f.* (*pl.* —**en**) province, district; landscape, scenery. —**s=maler**, *m.* landscape-painter. —**s= malerei** [—'raɪ], *f.* landscape painting.

Lang [laŋ], I. *adj. & adv.* (*comp.* **länger**, *sup.* **längſt**) long. II. *adv. & prep.* preceded by acc., long; during; **Jahre** —, for years; **mir wird die Zeit** —, time hangs heavy on my hands. III. —**e**, *adv.* (*comp.* **länger**; *sup.* **am längſten, längſt**) a long while, long; by far; **von** —**e her**, of long standing. **ich bin noch** —**e nicht fertig**, I am not nearly ready. —**en**, *v.n.* (*aux.* **h.**) to stretch, reach, extend; to reach after. —**erwünſcht**, *adj.* long wished for. —**e=weile**, —**weile**, *f.* (*gen. & dat., if preceded by the article* —**en=weile**, *if not preceded by the article* —**er=weile**) tediousness, boredom, ennui. —**finger**, *m.* thief. —**s jährig**, *adj.* of long standing. —**mut**, —**mütig**, *adj.* forbearing, patient. —**mütigkeit**, *f.* forbearance. —**ſam**, *adj. & adv.* slow; tardy. —**ſamkeit**, *f.* slowness, tardiness. —**ſtreckenflug**, *m.* long-distance flight. —**weilig**, *adj.* tedious, irksome. —**wierig**, *adj.* lasting; lengthy; chronic.

Läng—**e** ['lɛŋə], *f.* (*pl.* —**en**) length; length of time; **der** —**e nach**, length-

wise. —**s**, *adv. & prep.* (*with gen. or dat.*) along. —**s=durchſchnitt**, *m.* longitudinal section. —**ſt**, *adv.* long ago, long since. —**ſtens**, *adv.* at the furthest or at the most; at the latest.

Lanze ['lantsə], *f.* (*pl.* —**n**) lance, spear.

Lanzette [lan'tsɛtə], *f.* (—**n**) lancet.

Lapp—**en** ['lapən], I. *m.* (—**ens**, —**en**) flap (*of the ear*); lobe; patch; rag; duster. II. *v.a.* to patch, mend.

Läppiſch ['lɛpɪʃ], *adj.* silly, trifling.

Lärche ['lɛrçə], *f.* (*pl.* —**n**) larch.

Lärm [lɛrm], *m.* (—**(e)s**), —**en**, *m.* (*obs.*) (—**s**) noise; — **ſchlagen**, to give the alarm. —**en**, *v.n.* (*aux.* **h.**) to make a noise. —**er**, *m.* (—**ers**, *pl.* —**er**) noisy person; blusterer.

Larve ['larfə], *f.* (*pl.* —**n**, *dim.* **Lärv= chen**) mask.

Laſſen ['lasən], I. *ir.v.n.* (*aux.* **h.**) to let appear, to appear; to become, suit. II. *ir.v.a.* to let alone, refrain from doing; to relinquish, let go. *When governing another verb in the inf. (to which it frequently gives a passive sense) often* = to cause, make, effect, get done; to order, command; to permit, suffer; to let; **er hat ſich einen Zahn ausziehen** —, he has had a tooth drawn; (*etwas*) **bleiben** or **ſein** —, to leave alone, not to do; **laß das Schreien!** stop screaming! **laß mich zufrieden**, let me alone; **das läßt ſich denken**, that may easily be imagined; **das läßt ſich hören**, that is quite plausible. *As forming the imper.* = let; **laßt uns gehen**, let us go. III. *subst.n.* letting, leaving, permitting.

Läſſ—**ig** ['lɛsɪç], *adj. & adv.* inactive, sluggish, lazy. —**igkeit**, *f.* laziness, etc. —**(h)=lich**, *adj. & adv.* venial. —**(h)=lichkeit**, *f.* veniality; indulgence.

Laſt [last], *f.* (*pl.* —**en**) load, charge, burden, weight. —**tier**, *n.* beast of burden.

Laſten ['lastən], *v.* I. *n.* (*aux.* **h.**) to press heavy upon; to oppress. II. *a.* to burden, load, lade.

Laſter ['lastər], *n.* (—**s**, *pl.* —) vice; depravity. —**haft**, *adj.* vicious, wicked, abandoned. —**haftigkeit**, *f.* viciousness, wickedness. —**frei**, *adj.* free from vice. —**tat**, *f.* heinous deed, crime. —**voll**, *adj.* profligate.

Läſter—**er** ['lɛstərər], *m.* (—**ers**, *pl.* —**er**) slanderer, calumniator. —**haft**, *adj.* vicious, wicked. —**lich**, *adj. &*

adv. shameful, disgraceful. —**n**, *v.a.*
to blaspheme. —**ung**, *f.* reviling;
abuse, slander; blasphemy.

Lästig ['lɛstɪç], *adj.* burdensome,
troublesome.

Lasur [la'zu:r], *m.* (—**s**) lapis lazuli.

Latein [la'taɪn], *n.* (—**s**) Latin language. —**er**, *m.* (—**ers**, *pl.* —**er**)
Latin scholar. —**isch**, *adj.* Latin.

Laterne [la'tɛrnə], *f.* (*pl.* —**n**) lantern.

Latte ['latə], *f.* (*pl.* —**n**) lath.

Lattich ['latɪç], *m.* (—(e)**s**, *pl.* —**e**)
lettuce.

Latz [lats], *m.* (—**es**, *pl.* **Lätze**; *dim.*
Lätzchen) bib.

Lau [laʊ], *adj. & adv.* lukewarm. —**heit**,
—**igkeit**, *f.* lukewarmness; indifference.
—**warm**, *adj.* tepid; indifferent.

Laub [laʊp], *n.* (—(e)**s**, —**e and
Läuber**; *dim.* **Läubchen**) foliage,
leaves. —**e**, *f.* (*pl.* —**en**) bower,
arbour. —**ig**, *adj.* leafy, leaflike.
—**gitter**, *n.* trellis. —**säge**, *f.* fret-saw.

Lauch [laʊx], *m.* (—(e)**s**, *pl.* —**e**) leek.

Lauer ['laʊər], *f.* ambush; lying-in-
wait. —**er**, *m.* (—**ers**, *pl.* —**er**) spy,
lurker. —**n**, *v.n.* (*aux.* **h.**) to watch;
to lurk, lie in wait for.

Lauf [laʊf], *m.* (—(e)**s**, *pl.* **Läufe**) course,
run. —**bahn**, *f.* career; racecourse.
—**bohne**, *f.* scarlet-runner. —**bursche**,
m. messenger-boy. —**brief**, *m.* circular.
—**graben**, *m.* communication-trench.

Laufen ['laʊfən], I. *ir.v.n.* (*aux.* **h. & f.**)
to run; **der Kessel läuft**, the kettle
leaks. II. *ir.v.a.* to contract by
running; to run; **sich müde —**, to tire
oneself with running. III. *subst.n.*
running, run.

Läufer ['lɔyfər], *m.* (—**s**, *pl.* —)
runner; racer; sand-glass; bishop (*in
Chess*).

Lauge ['laʊgə] (*pl.* —**en**) lye. —**en-
artig**, *adj.* like lye; alkaline. —**en-
asche**, *f.* alkaline ashes, potash.

Laune ['laʊnə], *f.* (*pl.* —**en**) humour,
temper, mood; whim, caprice. —**en**,
v.n. (*aux.* **h.**) to have whims, be in a
certain mood (*only used in the past
part.*); **gelaunt**, disposed. —**enhaft**,
adj. fanciful, whimsical, capricious.
—**ig**, *adj.* humorous. —**isch**, *adj.* ill-
humoured.

Laus [laʊs], *f.* (*pl.* **Läuse**) louse.

Lausch—e ['laʊʃə], *f.* lurking, eaves-
dropping. —**er**, *m.* (—**ers**, *pl.* —**er**)
—**erin**, *f.*) eavesdropper, listener.

—**ig**, *adj.* prying; snug; pleasant; **eine
—ige Ecke**, a snug corner.

Laut [laʊt], I. *adj. & adv.* loud; noisy;
aloud. II. *m.* (—(e)**s**, *pl.* —**e**) sound,
tone; purport, tenor. III. *prep.*
(*with gen.*) according to, by the tenor
or terms of; in consequence of; in
virtue of; — **Verfügung**, as directed.
—**bar**, *adj. & adv.* audible; notorious,
public. —**heit**, *f.* sonorousness;
loudness. —**los**, *adj.* silent, mute.
—**sprecher**, *m.* loud-speaker (*Radio*).
—**stärke**, *f.* volume of sound (*Radio*).

Laute ['laʊtə], *f.* (*pl.* —**n**) lute. —**n-
schläger**, *m.* (—**s**, *pl.* —) lute-player.

Lauten ['laʊtən], *v.n.* (*aux.* **h.**) to
sound; to purport.

Läut—en ['lɔytən], I. *v.a. & n.* (*aux.*
h.) to ring, peal, toll. II. *subst.n.*
ringing, tolling. —**er**, *m.* (—**ers**, *pl.*
—**er**) bell-ringer.

Lauter ['laʊtər], I. *adj.* clear, pure;
genuine. II. *adv.* (*used as indec. adj.*)
downright, mere, nothing but; **vor —
Freude**, out of sheer joy. —**keit**, *f.*
purity; sincerity.

Läuter—n ['lɔytərn], *v.a.* to purify.
—**ung**, *f.* purification; refining.

Lavendel [la'vɛndəl], *m.* (—**s**) lavender.

Lawine [la'vi:nə], *f.* (*pl.* —**n**) avalanche.

Lazarett [latsa'rɛt], *n.* (—**s**, *pl.* —**e**)
hospital.

Leb—en ['le:bən], I. *v.n.* (*aux.* **h.**) to
live. —(**e**) **wohl!** —**en Sie wohl!**
farewell! **jemand hoch —en lassen**,
to drink a person's health. II. *v.a.*
to live (a life); **hier —t es sich gut**, it
is pleasant living here. III. *subst.n.*
(—**ens**, *pl.* —**en**) life; **am —en, bei
—en sein**, to be alive; **bei meinem
—en**, as long as I live; **ums —en
kommen**, to perish. —**end**, *p. & adj.*
living, alive. —**haft**, *adj. & adv.*
lively. —**haftigkeit**, *f.* liveliness,
vivacity. —**ig**, *suff.* (*in comp.=*)
-lived. —**emann**, *m.* man of the
world. —**e(n)slang**, *n.* whole life,
lifetime. —**los**, *adj.* lifeless; inanimate.

Lebendig [le'bɛndɪç], *adj. & adv.*
living, alive. —**keit**, *f.* being alive;
liveliness, vivacity.

Lebens— ['le:bəns] (*in comp.*) —**alter**,
n. age. —**anschauung** *f.* conception
of life. —**art**, *f.* way, mode of living.
—**bahn**, *f.* course, career. —**bedürf-
nisse**, *pl.* necessaries of life. —**blüte**,

f. prime of life. —**dauer**, *f.* duration of life. —**gang**, *m.* career, fate, life. —**gefahr**, *f.* danger of one's life. —**lang**, *adv.* lifelong. —**lauf**, *m.* course of life. —**mittel**, *n.* food; provisions. —**wandel**, *m.* conduct. —**weife**, *f.* mode of life, habits. —**zeit**, *f.* time of life, age; lifetime.

Leber ['le:bər], *f.* (*pl.* —n) liver. —**tran**, *m.* cod-liver oil. —**wurft**, *f.* liver-sausage.

Lebkuchen ['le:pku:xən], *m.* (—s, *pl.* —) spice-cake.

Lechzen ['lɛçtsən], *v.n.* (*aux.* h.) to be parched with thirst; nach einer S. —, to languish, long for something.

Led [lɛk], I. *adj.* leaky. II. *m. & n.* (—(e)s, *pl.* —e) leak.

Leden ['lɛkən], *v.a.* to lick. —**er**, *m.* (—ers, *pl.* —er) I. dainty person. II. *adj.* delicate, dainty. —**erei** [—ə'raɪ], *f.* daintiness; dainty. —**erhaft**, *adj.* dainty.

Leder ['le:dər], *n.* (—s, *pl.* —) leather. —**n**, *adj.* leathern.

Ledig ['le:dɪç], *adj. & adv.* empty; unmarried. —**lich**, *adv.* only, quite, entirely. —**laffung**, *f.* release. —**fprechung**, *f.* acquittal.

Leer [le:r], *adj. & adv.* empty. —**e**, *f.* (*pl.* —en) void, emptiness. —**en**, *v.a.* to empty.

Legat [le'ga:t], I. *m.* (—en, *pl.* —en) legate. II. *n.* (—s, *pl.* —e) legacy. —**ion** [—tsi'o:n], *f.* (*pl.* —ionen) legation, embassy. —**ions**z**rat**, *m.* counsellor to a legation. —**ions**s**fekretär**, *m.* secretary of legation.

Legen ['le:gən], *v.* I. *a.* to lay, put, place. **Karten** —, to tell the fortune by cards; sich ins Mittel —, to interpose; vor Anker —, to cast anchor. II. *r.* to lie down; to subside, abate.

Legende [le'gɛndə], *f.* (*pl.* —n) legend.

Leh(e)n ['le:(ə)n], *n.* (—(e)s, *pl* —) fief, fee. —**bar**, *adj.* feudal. —**dienft**, *m.* feudal service, vassalage. —(s)z**herr**, *m.* liege lord. —(s)z**mann**, *m.* vassal.

Lehm [le:m], *m.* (—(e)s, *pl.* —e) loam, clay. —**boden**, *m.* clay-floor.

Lehne ['le:nə], *f.* (*pl.* —n) hand-rail; arm *or* back of a chair.

Lehn—**en** ['le:nən], *v.a. & n.* (*aux.* h. & f.) to lean, incline, recline. —**feffel**, —**ftuhl**, *m.* easy-chair, arm-chair.

Lehrbar ['le:rba:r], *adj.* teachable.

Lehr—**e** ['le:rə], *f.* (*pl.* —en) doctrine, tenet; science; rule, precept; system of instruction; apprenticeship; in der —e fein, to serve an apprenticeship; das foll Ihnen eine —e fein, let that be a warning to you. —**en**, *v.a.* (einen or (obs.) einem etwas) to teach, instruct. —**end**, *p. & adj.* instructive, etc. —**er**, *m.* (—ers, *pl.* —er) teacher. —**erin**, *f.* mistress; governess. —**haft**, *adj.* instructive. —**ling**, *m.* (—lings, *pl.* —linge) pupil, scholar; apprentice. —**famkeit**, *f.* docility. —**amt**, *n.* office of a teacher. —**anftalt**, *f.* school. —**buch**, *n.* text-book. —**burfche**, *m.* apprentice. —**er**z**ftand**, *m.* scholastic profession; body of teachers. —**jahre**, *pl.* years of apprenticeship. —**junge**, *m.* apprentice. —**mittel**, *n.* means of instruction. —**reich**, *adj.* instructive. —**faal**, *m.* lecture-room; class-room.

Lei [laɪ] *as the second part of compounds* = of . . . kind, of . . . sorts, *e.g.* aller—, of all kinds; keiner—, of no kind.

Leib [laɪp], *m.* (—(e)s, *pl.* —er) body. bei lebendigem —e, alive. —**chen**, *n.* (—chens, *pl.* —chen) bodice; corset. —**haft**, —**haftig**, *adj. & adv.* corporal, bodily. —**lich**, *adj.* bodily. —**arzt**, *m.* physician in ordinary (*to the king, etc.*). —**eigen** [laɪb'aɪgən], *adj.* bond, in thraldom; ein —eigener, serf, bondman. —**garde**, *f.* bodyguard, lifeguard. —**gardift** [—'dɪst], *m.* lifeguardsman. —**kompagnie**, *f.* first company of a regiment.

Leibes— ['laɪbəs] (*in comp.*) —**bau**, *m.* build of body, form. —**ftrafe**, *f.* corporal punishment. —**übung**, *f.* bodily exercise.

Leich—**e** ['laɪçə], *f.* (*pl.* —en) dead body, corpse. —**enhaft**, *adj.* corpselike. —**en**z**fchau**, *f.* inquest on a dead body. —**nam**, *m.* (—nams, *pl.* —name) body; dead body.

Leichen—**artig** ['laɪçənartɪç], *adj.* cadaverous. —**begleiter**, *m.* mourner. —**blaß**, *adj.* pale as death. —**bläffe**, *f.* ghastliness. —**gefang**, *m.* dirge. —**gewand**, —**hemd**, *n.* winding-sheet, shroud. —**wagen**, *m.* hearse. —**zug**, *m.* funeral procession.

Leicht [laɪçt], *adj. & adv.* light; easy, not difficult. —**heit**, —**igkeit**, *f.* lightness; agility; facility; ease, readiness. —**beweglich**, *adj.* quick; changeable, mobile. —**fertig**, *adj.* frivolous; volatile; wanton. —**fertigkeit**, *f.* frivolity; light-mindedness. —**gläubig**, *adj.* credulous. —**herzig**, *adj.* cheerful. —**hin** [—'hın], *adv.* lightly, superficially. —**finn**, *m.*, —**finnigkeit**, *f.* levity, frivolity. —**finnig**, *adj.* frivolous.

Leid [laıt], *n.* (—es) harm, hurt, injury, wrong; pain; sorrow, grief; es tut mir —, I regret, I am sorry; es tut mir um die Frau —, I am sorry for the woman.

Leid—en ['laıdən], I. *ir.v.a.* to suffer, bear, endure. II. *ir.v.n.* (aux. h.) to suffer; to be in pain. III. *subst.n.* suffering. —**en(s)=voll**, *adj.* full of sorrow *or* suffering. —**er**, *adv.* & *int.* I am sorry to say; alas! —**er Gottes**! most unfortunately! —**lich**, *adj.* & *adv.* tolerable; middling, passable. —**lichkeit**, *f.* tolerableness.

Leidenschaft ['laıdənʃaft], *f.* (pl. —en) violent emotion *or* desire; passion; rage. —**lich**, *adj.* passionate. —**lichkeit**, *f.* passionateness. —**s=frei**, *adj.* dispassionate. —**s=los**, *adj.* apathetic, calm. —**s=losigkeit**, *f.* apathy.

Leier ['laıər], *f.* (pl. —n) lyre; die alte —, always the same old story. —**mann**, *m.* organ-grinder.

Leih—en ['laıən], *ir.v.a.* to lend. —**er**, *m.* (—ers, pl. —er) lender; borrower; hirer. —**bibliothek**, *f.* circulating library. —**haus**, *n.* loan-office, pawnbroker's shop. —**kaffe**, *f.* loan-office.

Leim [laım], *m.* (—es) adhesive substance; glue; auf den — gehen, to fall into the trap. —**en**, *v.a.* to glue. —**ig**, *adj.* gluey.

Lein [laın], *m.* (—(e)s, pl. —e) flax. —**e**, *f.* (pl. —en) cord. —**en**, I. *adj.* linen. II. *n.* (—ens, pl. —en) linen; linen goods. —**bau**, *m.* cultivation of flax. —**en=zwirn**, *m.* thread. —**kuchen**, *m.* oil-cake; —**öl**, *n.* linseed-oil.

Leinwand ['laınvant], *f.* (pl. —arten) linen, linen cloth.

Leife ['laızə], *adj.* & *adv.* low, soft; gentle.

¹**Leist**—en ['laıstən], *v.a.* to perform, accomplish; das kann ich mir nicht —en, I cannot afford that. —**ung**, *f.* act of doing, rendering *or* performing; performance, execution; payment. —**ungs=fähigkeit**, *f.* capacity for work; mechanical power (*of a machine*).

²**Leisten**, *m.* (—s, pl. —) shoemaker's last.

Leitbar ['laıtba:r], *adj.* manageable, that may be led.

Leit—en ['laıtən], *v.a.* to lead, conduct; to train. —**er**, *m.* (—ers, pl. —er) leader; manager; conductor (*Elec.*). —**ung**, *f.* leading, guidance, direction. —**faden**, *m.* clue; guide. —**motiv**, *n.* motif recurring throughout a whole composition. —**riemen**, *m.* driving-rein. —**ungs=draht**, *m.* conducting-wire.

Leiter ['laıtər], *f.* (pl. —n) ladder.

Lektion [lɛktsi'o:n], *f.* (pl. —en) lesson.

Lende ['lɛndə], *f.* (pl. —n) loin.

Lenk—bar ['lɛŋkba:r], *adj.* capable of being steered; —**bares Luftschiff**, dirigible airship. —**en**, *v.a.* to bend, turn; to guide, direct. —**er**, *m.* (—ers, pl. —er) ruler; guide. —**sam**, *adj.* tractable, manageable, docile; flexible. —**samkeit**, *f.* docility. —**ung**, *f.* directing, ruling; management; steering.

Lenz [lɛnts], *m.* (—es, pl. —e) spring.

Leopard [leo'part], *m.* (—en, pl. —en) leopard.

Lerche ['lɛrçə], *f.* (pl. —n) lark.

Lernen ['lɛrnən], I. *v.a.* to learn; to study; kennen —, to become acquainted with. II. *subst.n.* learning.

Les—bar ['le:sba:r], *adj.* legible. —**barkeit**, *f.* legibility. —**art**, *f.* manner of reading; reading; nach der gewöhnlichen —**art**, according to the ordinary version.

Les—e ['le:zə], *f.* (pl. —n) gleaning; harvest. —**en**, I. *ir.v.a.* to gather, collect, glean; (*also used intransitively with aux. h.*) to read. II. *subst.n.* gathering; reading. —**e=buch**, *n.* reading-book, reader. —**ens=wert**, worth reading. —**er**, *m.* (—ers, pl. —er), —**erin**, *f.* gatherer; gleaner; reader. —**ung**, *f.* reading. —**er=kreis**, *m.* the reading public. —**e=saal**, *m.* reading-room; lecture-room. —**e=welt**, *f.* reading public. —**e=zeichen**, *n.* bookmark. —**e=zeit**, *f.* time for reading; vintage-time.

Letzt [lɛtst], I. *adj.* & *adv.* last; latest; final. II. *adv.* lately, of late, in the last place; zu guter —, finally. —**ens**, *adv.* lastly; in the last place; lately, of late, recently; finally. —**erer**, *m.*, —**ere**, *f.*, —**eres**, *n.* (der, die, das

—ere) the latter. —**lich**, adv. lastly, at last; finally; to conclude; lately, the other day. —**erwähnt**, —**genannt**, adj. last-named. —**jährig**, adj. last-year's, of last year. —**verstorben**, adj. late.

Leucht—**e** ['lɔʏçtə], f. (pl. —**en**) any object giving light. —**en**, I. v.n. (aux. h.) to shine. II. subst.n. shining, burning; glare; coruscation; glimmer; **Meeres**—**en**, phosphorescence (of the sea); **Wetter**—**en**, sheet lightning. —**end**, p. & adj. shining, bright; lucid. —**er**, m. (—**ers**, pl. —**er**) candlestick. —**turm**, m. lighthouse.

Leugn—**en** ['lɔʏgnən], v.a. to deny; to disown. **das ist nicht zu** —**en**, that is undeniable. —**er**, m. (—**ers**, pl. —**er**) denier, disclaimer. —**ung**, f. disavowal.

Leumund ['lɔʏmʊnt], m. (—**es**) rumour; reputation.

Leute ['lɔʏtə], pl. people; men.

Leutnant ['lɔʏtnant], m. (—**s**, pl. —**s**) lieutenant.

Leutselig ['lɔʏtze:liç], adj. affable, pleasant. —**keit**, f. kindness; affability.

Libell [li'bɛl], n. (—**s**, pl. —**e**) libel. —**ist** [—'lɪst], m. (—**isten**, pl. —**isten**) libeller, lampooner.

Libelle [li'bɛlə], f. (pl. —**n**) dragon-fly.

Licht [lɪçt], I. adj. & adv. light; bright; lucid; clear; thin, open; —**er Tag**, broad daylight. II. n. (—(**e**)**s**, pl. —**er**, lights; —**e**, candles) light; luminary; **bei** —**e besehen**, to examine closely. —**antenne**, f. mains aerial (Radio). —**chen**, —**lein** (—**s**, **leins**, pl. —**lein**) small light or taper. —**anlage**, f. lighting-plant. —**bild**, n. photograph. —**druck**, m. phototype. —**er=loh** [—'lo:], I. adj. blazing. II. adv. ablaze. —**farb(en)**, —**farbig**, adj. light-coloured. —**hell**, adj. lighted up; very bright.

¹**Licht**—**en** ['lɪçtən], v.a. to light, light up; to clear (a wood). —**ung**, f. clearing; thinning; glade.

²**Lichten**, v.a. to lift up, heave up.

³**Lichte**—**n**, v.a. to lighten, unload. —**r**, m. (—**rs**, pl. —**r**) lighter, barge.

Lid [li:t], n. (—**es**, pl. —**er**) eye-lid.

Lieb [li:p], adj. & adv. dear, beloved. —**chen**, n. (—**chens**, pl. —**chen**) love, sweetheart. —**den**, f. (word of address used amongst sovereigns; exclusively in the form **Ew. Liebden = Euer Liebden**); **Ew.** —**den**, my dear prince. —**elei** [li:bə'laɪ], f. flirtation. —**eln**, v.n. (aux. h.) to flirt, to dally. —**er**, I. adj. comp. of **lieb**, q.v. II. adv. comp. of **gern & lieb**; rather, sooner, more willingly; **es ist mir** —**er**, I prefer. III. m. **mein** —**er**, my dear fellow. —**lich**, adj. & adv. lovely; charming. —**lichkeit**, f. charm, loveliness, sweetness, pleasantness. —**ling**, m. (—**lings**, pl. —**linge**) darling. —**lings**, in comp.=favourite. —**schaft**, f. love; love-affair. —**st**, sup. of **lieb** and **gern; der, die** —**ste**, dearest, love, sweetheart. —**äugeln**, v.n. (aux. h.) to ogle. —**haber**, m., —**haberin**, f. lover; fancier; amateur. —**haberei** [—'raɪ], f. inclination, fondness; partiality; hobby. —**kosen** (sep. & insep.) v.a. to caress, fondle, hug. —**kosung**, f. caressing; blandishment. —**kosungs=wort**, n. word of endearment, pet word. —**lings=idee** [—i'de:], f. favourite idea.

Liebe ['li:bə], f. love; affection. —**bang**, adj. anxious with love. —**trunken**, adj. intoxicated with love.

Lieben ['li:bən], v. I. a. to love. II. n. (aux. h.) to be in love. —**d**, p. & adj. loving. —**s=würdig**, adj. kind, amiable; **das ist sehr** —**s=würdig von ihm**, that is very kind of him.

Liebes— ['li:bəs] (in comp.) —**abenteuer**, n. love-adventure. —**andenken**, n. love-token. —**angelegenheiten**, pl. love-affairs. —**erklärung**, f. love-suit, proposal. —**gabe**, f. charitable gift. —**glück**, n. good luck in love. —**glut**, f. amorous flame or rapture. —**gunst**, f. favours. —**handel**, m. love intrigue. —**kind**, n. il legitimate child. —**mahl**, n. love-feast; banquet. —**pfand**, n. love-token. —**rausch**, m. transport of love.

Lied [li:t], n. (—**es**, pl. —**er**) song. —**chen**, n. (—**chens**, pl. —**chen**) ditty. —**er=buch**, n. book of songs. —**er=tafel**, f. choral society.

Liederlich ['li:dərlɪç], adj. & adv. disorderly; dissolute. —**keit**, f. disorderliness; debauchery; negligence.

Liefer—**ant** [li:fə'rant], m. (—**anten**, pl. —**anten**) —**er** ['li:fərər], m. (—**ers**, pl. —**er**) purveyor. —**bar**, adj. deliverable; to be delivered.

Liefer—**n** ['li:fərn], v.a. to deliver. —**ung**, f. delivery; supply.

Lieg—en ['li:gən], *ir.v.n.* (*aux.* h. & f.) to lie; to be situated; **jemand links —en laſſen**, to disregard a person; **es —t nichts daran**, it does not matter. **—end**, *p.* & *adj.* recumbent; horizontal; situated.

Liga ['li:ga:], *f.* (*pl.* **—s**) league; **— für Völkerbund**, Covenant of the League of Nations.

Likör [li'kø:r], *m.* (**—s**, *pl.* **—e**) liqueur.

Lila ['li:la:], *adj.* lilac (*coloured*).

Lilie ['li:liə], *f.* (*pl.* **—n**) lily.

Lim—onade [limo'na:də], *f.* lemonade. **—one** ['—'mo:nə], *f.* (*pl.* **—onen**) lemon.

¹**Linde** ['lɪndə], *f.* (*pl.* **—n**) linden, lime-tree.

²**Linde** ['lɪndə], *adj.* & *adv.* soft, gentle.

Linder—n ['lɪndərn], *v.* I. *a.* to mitigate; to soothe, allay. II. *r.* to be soothed; to abate. **—nd**, *p.* & *adj.* soothing. **—ung**, *f.* alleviation, mitigation.

Lindwurm ['lɪntvurm], *m.* (**—s**, *pl.* **Lindwürmer**) winged dragon.

Linea—l [line'a:l], I. *n.* (**—ls**, *pl.* **—le**) ruler. II. *adj.* lineal. **—r** [—'a:r], **—riſch**, *adj.* linear.

Linie ['li:niə], *f.* (*pl.* **—n**) line.

Link [lɪŋk], *adj.* & *adv.* left. **—e**, *f.* left hand, left. **—heit**, *f.* awkwardness. **—iſch**, *adj.* & *adv.* awkward; wrong. **—s**, *adv.* to the left; **— um kehrt!** left about turn! **—hand**, *f.* left-handed person.

Linſe ['lɪnzə], *f.* (*pl.* **—n**) lentil; lens.

Lipp—e ['lɪpə], *f.* (*pl.* **—en**) lip. **—ig**, *adj.* lipped.

Liſt [lɪst], *f.* (*pl.* **—en**) cunning. **—ig**, *adj.* & *adv.* crafty, cunning, deceitful. **—igkeit**, *f.* craftiness.

Liſte ['lɪstə], *f.* (*pl.* **—n**) list.

Litanei [lita'naɪ], *f.* (*pl.* **—en**) litany.

Liter ['li:tər], *m.* & *n.* (**—s**, *pl.* **—**) litre.

Liter—ariſch [li:tə'ra:rɪʃ], *adj.* literary. **—at** [—'ra:t], *m.* (**—aten**, *pl.* **—aten**), **—ator** [—ra'to:r], *m.* (**—ators**, *pl.* **—atoren**) man of letters. **—atur** [—a'tu:r], *f.* literature.

Litz—e ['lɪtsə], *f.* (*pl.* **—en**) braid. **—ung**, *f.* lace-trimming.

Livree [li'vre:], *f.* (*pl.* **—en**) livery.

Lob [lo:p], *n.* (**—(e)s**) praise; **Gottlob!** Thank God!

Lob—en ['lo:bən], *v.a.* to praise; **gelobt ſei Gott!** God be praised! **—er**, *m.* (**—ers**, *pl.* **—er**) praiser, extoller. (*obs.*) **—eſam**, *adj.* honourable, worthy. **—ens=wert**, **—ens=würdig**, *adj.* praiseworthy. **—preiſen**, *insep. v.a.* to praise, extol. **—rede**, *f.* panegyric.

Loch [lɔx], *n.* (**—es**, *pl.* **Löcher**) hole. **—maſchine**, *f.* punching-machine.

Lock—e ['lɔkə], *f.* (*pl.* **—en**) lock (*of hair, etc.*). **—ig**, *adj.* curly. **—en= haar**, *n.* curly hair. **—en=kopf**, *m.* curly-headed person.

Lock—en ['lɔkən], *v.a.* & *n.* (*aux.* h.) to decoy; to allure. **—ung**, *f.* enticing; allurement.

Locker ['lɔkər], *adj.* & *adv.* loose, slack; lax; wild; **ein —er Vogel**, a loose fellow. **—heit**, *f.* looseness; lightness; libertinism; laxity.

Loden ['lo:dən], *m.* (**—s**, *pl.* **—**) coarse woollen cloth. **—mantel**, *m.* water-proof cape.

Lodern ['lo:dərn], *v.n.* (*aux.* h.) to blaze, flame up.

Löffel ['lœfəl], *m.* (**—s**, *pl.* **—**) spoon. **—weiſe**, *adv.* by spoonfuls.

Löffeln ['lœfəln], *v.a.* & *n.* (*aux.* h.) to ladle out.

Log—e ['lo:ʒə], *f.* (*pl.* **—en**) box (*in a theatre*); Freemasons' lodge. **—en= bruder**, *m.* Freemason. **—en=ſchlieſſer**, *m.* box-keeper (*Theat.*). **—ieren** [—'ʒi:rən], *v.n.* (*aux.* h.) to lodge, dwell.

Logi—k ['lo:gɪk], *f.* (*pl.* **—ken**) logic. **—ter**, *m.* (**—ters**, *pl.* **—ter**) logician. **—ſch**, *adj.* logical.

¹**Loh—e** ['lo:ə], *f.* (*pl.* **—en**) blaze, flame.

²**Loh—e**, *f.* (*pl.* **—en**) tanning-bark, tan.

Lohn [lo:n], *m.* (**—(e)s**, *pl.* **Löhne**) reward; (*also n.*) payment; wages. **—en**, *v.a.* & *n.* (*aux.* h.) (**einem für eine Sache**) to reward; to pay. **—end**, *p.* & *adj.* remunerative. **—arbeit**, *f.* hired labour. **—arbeiter**, *m.* labourer. **—kutſcher**, *m.* keeper of livery stables. **—tag**, *m.* pay-day.

Löhn—en ['lø:nən], *v.a.* to pay (*wages, etc.*). **—ung**, *f.* pay.

Lokal [lo'ka:l], I. *adj.* local. II. *n.* (**—(e)s**, *pl.* **—e**) locality, place; public-house.

Lokomotive [lokomo'ti:və], *f.* (*pl.* **—n**) locomotive, engine.

Lorbeer ['lɔrbe:r], *m.* (**—s**, *pl.* **—(e)n**) laurel. **—e**, *f.* (*pl.* **—en**) laurel-berry. **—baum**, *m.* laurel *or* bay-tree.

—**hain**, *m.* laurel-grove. —**franz**, *m.* laurel-wreath.

Lorgnette [lɔrn'jetə], *f.* (*pl.* —n) eye-glasses.

¹**Los** [lo:s], *n.* (—(f)es, *pl.* —(f)e) lot, lottery ticket *or* prize; fate; **das grosse —**, the first prize (*in a lottery*, *etc.*). —(f)ung, *f.* drawing lots.

²**Los**,]. *adj. & adv.* (*not often used attributively*): loose; **was ist los?** what is the matter? **ein —er Mund**, a bad (*wicked*) tongue. II. *suffix=* less; **hoffnungs—**, without hope. III. *adv. & sep. prefix*, on, forward, up to, off; away; *giving to verbs with which it is compounded the idea*: 1. *of* loose, free; 2. *of unrestrained, violent action or motion*; *and* 3. *of commencement;* **es geht —**, it commences, it breaks out; **frisch drauf —!** at him! **go on!** (let us) go at it with a will! **nun geht das Weinen —**, now they fall a-crying, begin to cry. —(f)e, *adj. & adv.* loose; not firm *or* fixed; unsteady.

Los (*in comp.*) —**binden**, *ir.v.a.* to untie. —**brennen**, *ir.v.a.* to discharge, to fire (off). —**drücken**, *v.a. & n.* (*aux. h.*) to fire off (*a gun*). —**geben**, *ir.v.a.* to set free. —**gebung**, *f.* release. —**kaufen**, *v.a.* to redeem, ransom. —**käuflich**, *adj.* redeemable. —**kommen**, *ir.v.n.* (*aux. f.*) to get rid of; to get free. —**lassen**, *ir.v.a.* to let loose, let go; to release, set free. —**lassung**, *f.* setting free, *etc.*; release. —**machen**, *v.* I. *a.* to loosen, make loose. II. *r.* to get away; to get rid (of). —**reißen**, *ir. v.* I. *a.* to pull *or* tear off *or* away; to separate by violence. II. *r.* to break loose; to tear oneself away (**von**, from; **aus**, out of). —**sagung**, *f.* renunciation, withdrawal. —**sprechen**, *ir.v.a.* to declare free, release; to acquit, absolve. —**ziehen**, *ir.v.n.* (*aux. f.*) to set out; **über jemand —ziehen**, to run down a person.

Lösbar ['løːsbaːr], *adj.* soluble.

Lösch—en ['løʃən], *ir.v.* I. *n.* (*aux. f.*) to go out, be extinguished. II. *a.* to extinguish, quench; **eine Schuld —en**, to wipe out a debt; **Durst —en**, to quench thirst. —**er**, *m.* (—ers, *pl.* —er) extinguisher, *etc.* —**ung**, *f.* quenching; extinguishing. —**mannschaft**, *f.* fire-brigade. —**papier**, *n.* blotting paper.

¹**Los—en** ['loːzən], I. *v.n.* (*aux. h.*) to draw lots (**um**, for). II. *s.f.* drawing lots. —**ung**, *f.* drawing lots.

²**Los—en**, *v.n.* (*prov.*) to listen. —**ung**, *f.* watchword. —**ungs=wort**, *n.* watchword.

Lös—en ['løːzən], *v.a.* to loosen; to untie. —**ung**, *f.* loosening; solution, explanation. —**e=geld**, *n.* ransom.

Lot [loːt], *n.* (—(e)s, *pl.* —e) plummet. —**en**, *v.a. & n.* (*aux. h.*) to take soundings.

Löt—e ['løːtə], *f.* soldering; solder. —**en**, *v.a.* to solder. —**er**, *m.* (—ers, *pl.* —er) solderer.

Lotse ['loːtsə], *m.* (—n, *pl.* —n), **Lotsmann**, *m.* pilot. —**n**, *v.a.* to pilot.

Lotterie [lɔtə'riː], *f.* (*pl.* —en) lottery.

Löw—e ['løːvə], *m.* (—en, *pl.* —en) lion. —**enhaft**, *adj.* lion-like, leonine. —**in**, *f.* lioness. —**en=zahn**, *m.* dandelion (*Bot.*).

Luchs [luks], *m.* (—(f)es, *pl.* —(f)e) lynx. —**äugig**, *adj.* lynx-eyed.

Lücke ['lykə], *f.* (*pl.* —n) gap, chasm. —**n=haft**, *adj.* defective, incomplete. —**n=haftigkeit**, *f.* incompleteness.

Luft [luft], *f.* (*pl.* **Lüfte**) air; breeze. —**abwehr**, *f.* anti-aircraft defence. —**angriff**, *m.* air raid. —**ballon**, *m.* balloon. —**dicht**, *adj.* air-tight. —**druck**, *m.* atmospheric pressure. —**fahrwesen**, *n.* aviation. —**fahrzeug**, *n.* aircraft. —**hafen**, *m.* airport. —**kreis**, *m.* atmosphere. —**reifen**, *m.* pneumatic tire. —**schiff**, *n.* airship. —**schiffer**, *m.* aeronaut.

Lüften ['lyftən], *v.a.* to ventilate; **den Hut —**, to raise one's hat.

Lüg—e ['lyːgə], *f.* (*pl.* —en) lie. —**en**, I. *ir.v.a. & n.* (*aux. h.*) to lie; **jemanden —en strafen**, to give a person the lie. II. *subst.n.* lying, *etc.* —**enhaft(ig)**, *adj. & adv.* lying, false. —**enhaftigkeit**, *f.* lying disposition, mendacity; falseness. —**ner**, *m.* (—ners, *pl.* —ner), —**nerin**, *f.* liar.

Lump [lump], *m.* (—s, —en, *pl.* —e(n)) ragamuffin; scoundrel. —**en**, *m.* (—ens, *pl.* —en) rag, tatter. —**ig**, *adj.* ragged, tattered. —**en=gesindel**, —**en=pack**, —**en=volk**, *n.* riff-raff, rabble. —**en=händler**, *m.* dealer in rags. —**en=hund**, —**en=kerl**, *m.* scamp.

Lunge ['luŋə], *f.* (*pl.* —n) lung(s).

Lunte ['luntə], *f.* (*pl.* —n) slow-match (*Artil.*); — **riechen**, to smell a rat.

Lupe ['lu:pə], f. (pl. —n) magnifying glass.

Lust [lʊst], f. (pl. Lüste) pleasure, joy, delight; desire, wish, longing. —barkeit, f. amusement. —ig, adj. & adv. merry; sich —ig machen über, to make fun of. —igkeit, f. gaiety; jollity; drollness. —spiel, n. comedy. —wäldchen, n. grove. —wandeln, v.n. to stroll about.

Lüst—en ['lʏstən], v. I. a. imp.; es —et mich (nach einer S., for a thing), I desire, wish, long (nach, for). II. n. (aux. h.) to wish, long (nach, for). —ern, adj. (nach einer S. or auf eine S.) greedy (for); desirous, covetous (of).

Luv [lu:f], f. luff, weather side (Naut.).

Luxus ['lʊksʊs], m. (—, no pl.) luxury. —artikel, m. article of luxury. —zug, m. saloon train.

Lyr—ik ['ly:rɪk], f. lyric poetry. —iker, m. (—ikers, pl. —iker) lyric poet. —isch, adj. lyric(al).

Lyzeum [ly'tse:ʊm], n. (—s, pl. Lyzeen) secondary school for girls; college.

M

M, m [ɛm], n. M, m; in abbr. M.=1. Mark, mark; 2. Monat, month (C.L.); 3. Meile, mile.

Maat [ma:t], m. (—s, pl. —e) mate (Naut.).

Mach—en ['maxən], v.a. to make; ich — mich nichts daraus, I don't care about it; das —t nichts, that is of no consequence; was —t die Rechnung? how much does the bill come to? —er, m. (—ers, pl. —er), —erin, f. maker. —erlohn, m. cost of making.

Macht [maxt], f. (pl. Mächte) might, strength, force. —gebot, n. strict order. —haber, m. lord, ruler. —haberisch, adj. dictatorial, despotic. —herr, —herrscher, m. despot. —los, adj. powerless; weak. —losigkeit, f. impotence. —voll, adj. mighty.

Mächtig ['mɛçtɪç], I. adj. & adv. mighty, powerful. II. adv. much, in a great degree, enormously.

Mädchen ['mɛdçən], n. (—s, pl. —) girl; maiden. —haft, adj. & adv. girlish; maidenly. —haftigkeit, f. girlishness; maidenliness. —name, m. maiden name.

Made ['ma:də], f. (pl. —n) maggot.

Madonnen— [ma'dɔnən] (in comp.) —bild, n. image or picture of the Blessed Virgin Mary.

Magazin [maga'tsi:n], n. (—s, pl. —e) warehouse.

Magd [ma:kt], f. (pl. Mägde) maid; maidservant.

Magen ['ma:gən], m. (—s, pl. —) stomach.

Mager ['ma:gər], adj. & adv. lean; thin. —keit, f. leanness; poorness, etc. —milch, f. skim-milk.

Magie [ma'gi:], f. magic.

Magi—er ['ma:gJər], m. (—ers, pl. —er) magician; (pl.) magi. —ter, m. (—ters, pl. —ter) magician. —sch, adj. magic(al).

Magist—er [ma'gɪstər], m. (—ers, pl. —er) schoolmaster. —erhaft, adj. pedantic, didactic. —rat [—'tra:t], m. (—rats, pl. —rate) magistrate; municipal council. —ratur [—ra'tu:r], f. magistracy.

Magnet [ma'gne:t], m. (—s, —en, pl. —e) magnet, loadstone. —isch, adj. magnetic. —isieren [—'zi:rən], I. v.a. to magnetize. II. subst.n. magnetization. —ismus [—'tɪsmʊs], m. magnetism. —nadel, f. magnetic needle.

Mahagoni [maha'go:ni], n. (—s) mahogany.

Mahd [ma:t], f. (pl. —en) mowing.

Mäh—en ['mɛ:ən], v.a. & n. (aux. h.) to mow. —er, m. (—ers, pl. —er), —erin, f. mower, reaper. —er=lohn, m. reaper's wages. —(e)=zeit, f. mowing time. —maschine, f. reaping machine, mower.

Mahl [ma:l], n. (—es, pl. —e, Mähler) meal, repast; banquet. —zeit, f. mealtime, meal; ich wünsche Ihnen eine gesegnete —zeit! may your meal be blessed; Prost —zeit! you are much mistaken!

Mahl—en ['ma:lən], reg. & ir.v.a. & n. (aux. h.) to grind. —stein, m. millstone.

Mahlstrom ['ma:lʃtro:m], m. (—s) maelstrom, whirlpool.

Mähn—e ['mɛ:nə], f. (pl. —en) mane. —ig, adj. maned.

Mahn—en ['ma:nən], v.a. to remind; to warn. —er, m. (—ers, pl. —er) admonisher; dun. —ung, f. admonition. —brief, m., —schreiben, n. dunning letter. —ruf, m. warning cry. —zettel, m. reminder; demand note.

Mähre ['mɛ:rə], f. (pl. —n) mare.
Mai [maɪ], m. (—s, pl. —e) May.
—baum, m. may-pole; —glöckchen, n.
lily-of-the-valley. —käfer, m. cockchafer.
Majestät [majes'tɛ:t], f. (pl. —en)
majesty; Majesty. —isch, adj. majestic. —s=beleidigung, f. crime of
lese-majesty.
Major [ma'jo:r], m. (—s, pl. —e, obs.
—s) major (Mil.). —at [—'ra:t], n.
(—ats, pl. —ate) right of primogeni-
ture; entail. —enn [—'rɛn], adj. of
(full) age. —in, f. major's wife. —ität
[—i'tɛ:t], f. (pl. —itäten) majority.
—atsgut, n. property entailed on the
eldest child.
Makel ['ma:kəl], m. (—s, pl. —) stain;
defect, fault. —ig, adj. spotted,
stained. —los, adj. spotless, immaculate. —losigkeit, f. spotlessness.
Mäk=elig ['mɛ:kəlıç], adj. censorious;
fastidious. —eln, v. I. n. (aux. h.) to
act as a broker. II. a. & n. (aux. h.)
to carp at. —eler, Makler, m.
(—(e)lers, pl. —(e)ler) broker; Mäkler,
fault-finder.
Makrele [ma'kre:lə], f. (pl. —n)
mackerel.
Makulatur [makʊla'tu:r], f. (pl. —en)
waste paper.
Mal [ma:l], I. n. (—(e)s, pl. —e and
Mäler) sign, mark, token; mole;
point of time, time. II. adv. & part.
(shortened from einmal and always
unaccented)=once, etc.; es war — ein
König, there was once a king. —ig,
adj. & adv. of so many times (as
dreimalig, happening three times).
Mal—en ['ma:lən], v.a. to paint.
—kasten, m. paint-box.
Maler ['ma:lər], m. (—s, pl. —), —in,
f. painter, artist. —ei [—'raɪ], f.
painting. —isch, adj. & adv. pic-
turesque, graphic. — stock, m. mahl-
stick.
Malve ['malvə], f. (pl. —n) mallow.
Malz [malts], n. (—es, pl. —e) malt.
—en, v.a. & n. (aux. h.) to malt.
Mälzer ['mɛltsər], m. (—s, pl. —)
maltster.
Mama [ma'ma], f. (pl. —s) mamma.
Mammut ['mamu:t], n. (—(e)s, pl. —s
& —e) mammoth.
Man [man], indef. pron. (only used in
the nom. sing.; in other cases of the
singular an oblique case of einer is

used) people, one, they, we, you, a
person; — sagt, it is said, they say.
Manch [manç] (—er, —e, —es), indef.
adj. & pron. many a, many a one;
— einer, many a man, many a one.
—erlei [—ər'laɪ], indec. adj. of several
sorts, various, sundry, divers. —mal,
adv. often.
Mandat [man'da:t], n. (—(e)s, pl. —e)
authorization, mandate.
1Mandel ['mandəl], f. (pl. —n) almond;
(Anat.) tonsil. —entzündung, f.
mumps.
2Mandel, f. (pl. —n) number of fifteen.
Mangan [man'ga:n], n. (—s) man-
ganese.
Mang=e (pl. —en), —el ['manə(l)], f.
(pl. —eln) mangle. —eln, —en, v.a.
to mangle, calender.
Mangel ['manəl], m. (—s, pl. Mängel)
want; defect, blemish; dearth; aus —
an, for want of, in default of. —haft,
adj. defective. —haftigkeit, f. imper-
fection; faultiness. —n, v.n. (aux. h.)
& imp. to want, lack.
Manie [ma'ni:], f. (pl. —n) mania,
madness.
Manier [ma'ni:r], f. (pl. —en) manner,
way; (pl.) manners. —lich, adj. civil,
polite. —lichkeit, f. politeness. —t,
adj. affected.
Mann [man], m. (—es, pl. Männer)
man; male; husband; (pl. —en) re-
tainer, vassal; (pl. —) soldier, man;
der gemeine —, common people.
—haft, adj. & adv. manly. —haftig=
keit, f. manliness; bravery. —heit, f.
manhood; virility. —schaft, f. body
of picked men; forces, crew. —es=
alter, n. manhood. —es=würde, f.
dignity of a man. —s=bild, n. man,
male person (coll.). —schaftsrolle, f.
muster-roll.
Männ—chen ['mɛnçən], n. (—chens, pl.
—chen) little man; male (of birds, etc.).
—in, f. virago. —isch, adj. mannish,
unwomanly. —lich, adj. manly.
—lichkeit, f. masculinity. —er=mor=
dend, adj. homicidal.
Mannig ['manıç], —fach, —faltig,
adj. various, manifold.
Manöv—er [ma'nø:vər], n. (—ers, pl.
—er) review, manœuvres. —rieren
[—'vri:rən], v.n. (aux. h.) to manœuvre; to hold a review.
Mansarde [man'zardə], f. (pl. —n)
attic.

Manſchette [man'ʃɛtə], f. (pl. —n) cuff;
—n haben vor jemand, to be afraid
of a person.
Mantel ['mantəl], m. (—s, pl. Mäntel;
dim. Mäntelchen) cloak. —ſad, m.
portmanteau.
Manufaktur [manufak'tuːr], f. (pl.
—en) manufacture. —iſt [—tu'rıst],
m. (—iſten, pl. —iſten) manufacturer.
Mappe ['mapə], f. (pl. —n) portfolio,
case.
Märchen ['mɛrçən], n. (—s, pl. —)
fairy-tale, fable, legend. —haft, adj.
fabulous, fictitious. —haftigkeit, f.
fabulousness.
Marder ['mardər], m. (—s, pl. —)
marten.
Marien [ma'riːən] (in comp.) —bild,
n. image of the Virgin Mary. —blume,
f. daisy. —feſt, n. Lady Day. —glas,
n. isinglass. —käfer, m. lady-bird.
Marine [ma'riːnə], f. (pl. —n) navy.
—amt, n. Admiralty. —weſen, n.
naval affairs.
Marinieren [mari'niːrən], v.a. to pickle.
Marionette [mario'nɛtə], f. (pl. —n)
puppet; —n=theater, n. puppet-show.
¹Mark [mark], f. (pl. —en) boundary,
limit; border-country. —graf, m.
margrave, count of the marches.
—gräfin, f. margravine.
²Mark, f. (pl. —) (abbrev. M., Mk.)
mark (a modern German coin).
—ſchein, m. note; 100 —ſchein, 100-
mark note. —ſtüd, n. mark-piece.
³Mark, n. (—es) marrow; das geht mir
durch — und Bein, that cuts me
to the quick. —ig, adj. marrowy;
pithy. —los, adj. marrowless.
Marke ['markə], f. (pl. —n) mark,
token; postage-stamp; stamp.
Mark—en ['markən], v.a. to settle a
boundary. —ung, f. demarcation;
boundary.
Marketender [marke'tɛndər], m. (—s,
pl. —) sutler. —in, f. canteen-
woman.
Markt [markt], m. (—es, pl. Märkte)
market; market-place; bargain, business; Jahr—, (yearly) fair. —fleden,
m. borough, market-town. —gängig,
adj. current. —halle, m. covered
market. —ſchreier, m. quack,
mountebank. —zoll, m. duty on
goods brought to market.
Marmelade [marmə'laːdə], f. (pl. —n)
jam.

Marmor ['marmor], m. (—s, pl. —e)
marble. —iert [—'riːrt], p.p. & adj.
marbled, mottled. —n, adj. marble.
—bild, n. marble statue. —bruch,
m., —grube, f. marble quarry.
—platte, f. marble slab.
Marod—e [ma'roːdə], adj. weary.
—eur [—'dør], m. (—eurs, pl. —eure
& —eurs) marauder, pillager. —ieren
[—'diːrən], v.n. (aux. h.) to pillage.
Marone [ma'roːnə], f. (pl. —n) edible
chestnut.
Mars [mars], m. (—, pl. —(ſ)en) top
(Naut.). —ſegel, n. topsail.
¹Marſch [marʃ], f. (pl. —en) marsh.
—ig, adj. marshy.
²Marſch [marʃ], m. (—es, pl. Märſche)
march. —ieren [mar'ʃiːrən], v.n.
(aux. h. & ſ.) to march.
Marſchall ['marʃal], m. (—s, pl. Mar-
ſchälle) marshal. —in, f. marshal's
wife. —s=ſtab, m. marshal's baton.
Marter ['martər], f. (pl. —n) rack,
torture; martyrdom. —er, m. (—ers,
pl. —er) torturer, tormenter. —n,
v.a. to torture.
Märtyrer ['mɛrtyrər], m. (—s, pl. —),
—in, f. martyr. —tum, (Märtyrtum,)
n. (—s) martyrdom.
März [mɛrts], m. (—es, older and in
some comps. —en) March. —lich,
adj. March-like.
Maſch—e ['maʃə], f. (pl. —en) mesh.
—en=werk, n. net-work.
Maſchin—e [ma'ʃiːnə], f. (pl. —en)
machine. —erie, f. machinery. —iſt
[—'nıst], m. (—iſten, pl. —iſten)
machinist; engineer. —en=bau, m.
machine-making. —en=garn, n.
machine-spun yarn. —en=raum, m.
engine-room; engine-shed. —en=
ſchacht, m. engine-shaft. —en=
ſchmierer, m. lubricator, greaser.
—en=ſchreiber, m. typewriter, typist.
Maſ—er ['maːzər], f. (pl. —ern), also
m. (—ers, pl. —er) speck, spot.
—erig, adj. mottled, speckled. —ern,
pl. measles.
Maſt—e ['maskə], f. (pl. —en; dim.
Mäskchen) mask. —erade [—'raːdə],
f. (pl. —eraden) masquerade. —ieren
[—'riːrən], v.a. to mask. —en=ball,
m. masquerade.
Maß [mas], n. (—es, pl. —e) measure
(for a coat, etc.); moderation; limit;
degree. —e, f. (pl. —en) measure;
proportion, just measure; mode,

manner, way; über alle —en, beyond measure; (*generally used in the plural and in comp. with another word*). —gabe, f. measure, proportion. —gebend, *adj.* decisive; standard. —gebung, f. measure, proportion, limitation. —los, *adj.* boundless, exorbitant. —nahme, —nehmung, f. measuring; measure; mode of acting. —regel, f. measure. —stab, *m.* measure; standard; scale.

Masse ['masə], f. (*pl.* —en) mass. —enhaft, *adj.* in a mass; bulky; enormous. —ig, *adj.* large. —iv, *adj.* massive.

Mäßig ['mɛ:sɪç], *adj. & adv.* moderate; frugal. —keit, f. moderation, temperance. —en, *v.a.* to moderate; gemäßigte Zone, temperate zone. —keit, f. moderation, temperance. —ung, f. diminution; moderation; mitigation.

1Mast [mast], *m.* (—es, *pl.* —en) mast. —er (—ers, *pl.* —er) *suffix in comp.* -master, of so many masts; *as:* Drei—er, three-master. —korb, *m.* crow's nest (*Naut.*).

2Mast, f. mast, acorns, beech-nuts, *etc.* —schwein, *n.* fat pig. —vieh, *n.* fattened cattle.

Mäst—en ['mɛstən], *v.a.* to fatten, cram. —ung, f. fattening.

Material [materi'a:l], I. *n.* (—s, *pl.* —ien) material. II. *adj.* material. —ismus [—'lɪsmʊs], *m.* materialism. —ist [—'lɪst], *m.* (—isten, *pl.* —isten) materialist. —istisch, *adj.* materialistic. —(waren)=geschäft, *n.*, (waren)=handlung, f. grocery stores. —waren, *pl.* groceries.

Materi—e [ma'te:rɪə], f. (*pl.* —en) matter, stuff. —ell [—ri'ɛl], *adj.* material, real.

Mathematik [matema'ti:k], f. mathematics.

Mathemati—ker [mate'ma:tɪkər], *m.* (—kers, *pl.* —ker) mathematician. —sch, *adj.* mathematical.

Matratze [ma'tratsə], f. (*pl.* —n) mattress.

Matrose [ma'tro:zə], *m.* (—n, *pl.* —n) sailor.

Matt [mat], I. *adj.* faint, feeble; — geschliffenes Glas, frosted glass. II. *n.* (—s) mate (*Chess*); Schach (und) —, checkmate. —heit, f. faintness. —igkeit, f. exhaustion, fatigue.

Matte ['matə], f. (*pl.* —n) mat.

Mauer ['mauər], f. (*pl.* —n) wall. —n, *v.* I. *n.* to build with stone *or* brick; to make a wall. II. *a.* to wall up. —werk, *n.* masonry, stonework. —ziegel, *m.* brick.

1Maul [maul], *n.* (—s, *pl.* Mäuler), —esel, *m.*, —pferd, —tier, *n.* mule.

2Maul, *n.* (—s, *pl.* Mäuler) mouth. —affe, *m.* silly person; —affen feil haben, to stand gaping. —korb, *m.* muzzle. —schelle, f. slap on the face. —sperre, f. lock-jaw.

Maulbeere ['maulbe:rə], f. (*pl.* —n) mulberry.

Maulen ['maulən], *v.n.* to sulk, pout.

Maulwurf ['maulvurf], *m.* (—s, *pl.* Maulwürfe) mole. —s=haufen, —s=hügel, *m.* mole-hill.

Maur—e ['maurə], *m.* (—en, *pl.* —en), —in, f. Moor. —isch, *adj.* Moorish.

Maur—er ['maurər], *m.* (—ers, *pl.* —er) mason, builder; (Frei—)er, free-mason. —erei [—ə'rai], f. masonry. —erisch, *adj.* masonic. —er=gesell, *m.* journeyman mason. —er=kelle, f. mason's trowel. —er=meister, *m.* master-mason.

Maus [maus], f. (*pl.* Mäuse) mouse. —(s)en, I. *v.n.* (*aux.* h.) to catch mice; (*aux.* h. & f.) to steal noiselessly about. II. *v.a.* to pilfer, purloin. III. *subst.n.* mousing, mouse-hunting. —(s)e=falle, f. mouse-trap. —(s)e=still, *adj. & adv.* still as a mouse. —(s)e=tot, *adj.* as dead as mutton. —ig, *adj.* pert; sich —ig machen, to give oneself airs.

Mäuschen ['mɔysçən], *n.* (—s, *pl.* —) little mouse; my pet! duckie!

Mechan—ik [me'ça:nɪk], f. (*pl.* —iken) mechanics; mechanism. —iker, *m.* (—ikers, *pl.* —iker), *m.* (—s) mechanician. —isch, *adj. & adv.* mechanical. —ismus [—'nɪsmʊs], *m.* mechanism.

Meckern ['mɛkərn], *v.n.* (*aux.* h.) to bleat.

Medaill—e [me'daljə], f. (*pl.* —en) medal.

Medizin [medi'tsi:n], f. (*pl.* —en) medicine. —al [—'na:l], *adj. & adv.* medicinal. —er, *m.* (—ers, *pl.* —er) medical man. —isch, *adj.* medical; medicinal. —al=behörde, f. board of health.

Meer [me:r], *n.* (—es, *pl.* —e) sea.

—boden, —es=boden, m. bottom of the sea. —busen, m. gulf, bay. —enge, f. straits, channel. —es=arm, m. inlet. —es=spiegel, m. sea-level. —es=strom, m., —es=strömung, f. ocean-current. —gras, n. seaweed. —katze, f. long-tailed monkey. —rettich, m. horse-radish. —schaum, m. sea-froth, sea-foam; meerschaum. —schwein, n. porpoise. —schwein= chen, n. guinea-pig. —tang, m. sea-weed. —weib, n. mermaid.

Mehl [me:l], n. (—s, pl. —e) meal. —ig, adj. mealy, farinaceous. —= zucker, m. caster-sugar.

Mehr [me:r], I. ind. num. adj. (generally indec. but pl. —e, now usually —ere= more than one) more; (pl.) several, sundry, divers. II. adv. more; above, upwards; past; further; besides; longer; rather; kein Wort —! not an-other word! —aufwand, m. additional expenditure. —betrag, m. surplus. —deutig, adj. ambiguous. —deutig= keit, f. ambiguity. —ere=mal, adv. several times. —er'lei, indec. adj. of more than one kind, various, diverse. —fach, adj. & adv. manifold; several times, more than once. —forderung, f. increased demand, higher claim. —gebot, n. outbidding. —genannt, adj. aforesaid. —gewicht, n. surplus-weight. —heit, f. majority. —heits= beschluß, m. decision by a majority. —malig, adj. repeated, reiterated. —mals, adv. again and again; more than once, several times. —seitig, adj. polygonal. —silbig, adj. poly-syllabic. —wert, m. surplus of value. —zahl, f. majority; plural (Gram.); überwiegende —zahl, vast majority.

Mehren ['me:rən], v.a. & r. to increase.

Meid—en ['maidən], ir.v.a. to avoid, shun. —lich, adj. (in comp.) avoid-able.

Meier ['maiər], m. (—s, pl. —) tenant of a farm. —ei [—'rai], f. (dairy-) farm; farm-house.

Meile ['mailə], f. (pl. —n) mile. —n= zeiger, m. mile-stone.

¹**Mein** [main] (—, —e, —), I. poss. adj. my, mine; —es teils, for my part, as for me. II. poss. pron. (orig. gen.) mine; dieses Haus ist —, this house is mine. III. old gen. sing. of ich; gedenke —, think of me. IV. n. my own, my property; das — und Dein, what is

mine and what is thine; die —en, my family. —e, (der, die, das —e,) —er, —e, —es, —ige, (der, die, das —ige,) poss. pron. mine. —er=seits, adv. for my part; in my turn. —es= gleichen, indec. adj. or pron. my equals, such as I. —et=halben, —et= wegen, —et=willen, adv. for my sake; so far as I am concerned; for aught I care.

²**Mein**, (in comp.=) false; mean. —eid, m. perjury. —eidig, adj. perjured. —eidigkeit, f. perjury.

Mein—en ['mainən], v.a. & n. (aux. h.) to be of opinion, think, suppose. —ung, f. thought; opinion, notion; meaning, signification; intention. —= ungs=austausch, m. interchange of ideas. —ungs=äußerung, f. expression of opinion. —ungs=verschiedenheit, f. diversity of opinion.

Meise ['maizə], f. (pl. —n) titmouse, tomtit.

Meist [maist], I. adj. (sup. of mehr) most. II. adv. am —en, most of all, for the most part, mostly; die —en, most people. —ens, —enteils, adv. generally, usually —gebot, n. best offer, highest bid.

Meister ['maistər], m. (—s, pl. —) master. —haft, I. adj. masterly; skilful. II. adv. in a masterly manner. —haftigkeit, f. mastery; masterliness. —in, f. mistress, master's wife. —n, v.a. to master; to rule. —schaft, f. mastery; championship (sport). —= stück, n. masterpiece.

Meißel ['maisəl], m. (—s, pl. —) chisel. —n, v.a. to chisel.

Melancho—lie [melaŋko'li:], f. melan-choly. —liker [—'ko:lkər], m. (—likers, pl. —liker) melancholy per-son. —lisch [—'ko:liʃ], adj. melan-choly.

Meld—en ['meldən], v. I. a. to an-nounce. II. r. to report oneself (Mil.); sich zum Examen —en, to enter for an examination; sich —en lassen, to send in one's name. —er, m. (—ers, pl. —er) announcer, informer. —ung, f. notification; announcement; report. —e=amt, n. information office; regis-tration office. —e=brief, m. letter of advice. —e=zettel, m. registration form.

Melf [melk], adj. milch. —en, reg. & ir.v. I. a. to milk. II. n. (aux. h.) to give milk. **—er,** *m.* (**—ers,** *pl.* **—er**) milker. **—erei** [—'raɪ], *f.* milking; dairy. **—ſchemel,** *m.* milking-stool.

Melod—ie [melo'di:], *f.* (*pl.* **—n** [—'di:ən]) melody, tune, air. **—iſch** [—'lo:dɪʃ], *adj.* melodious.

Melone [me'lo:nə], *f.* (*pl.* **—n**) melon; bowler hat.

Membrane [mɛm'bra:nə], *f.* (*pl.* **—n**) diaphragm (*Phone*).

Memme ['mɛmə], *f.* (*pl.* **—n**) coward, poltroon.

Menge ['mɛŋə], *f.* (*pl.* **—n**) great quantity *or* number; multitude, crowd; mass; **eine — Geld,** plenty of money.

Meng—en ['mɛŋən], *v.a.* to mix; **ſich —en in,** to meddle with. **—er,** *m.* (**—ers,** *pl.* **—er**) mixer. **—ſel,** *n.* (**—ſels**) medley.

Menſch [mɛnʃ], *m.* (**—en,** *pl.* **—en**) human being. **—heit,** *f.* human nature, humanity. **—lein,** *n.* (**—leins,** *pl.* **—lein**) little (bit of a) man. **—lich,** *adj. & adv.* human. **—lichkeit,** *f.* humanity, human nature. **—en= ähnlich,** *adj.* like man. **—en=alter,** *n.* generation, age. **—en=feind,** *m.* misanthropist. **—en=feindlich,** *adj.* misanthropic. **—en=freſſer,** *m.* cannibal. **—en=freund,** *m.* philanthropist. **—en=kenner,** *m.* one who knows mankind. **—en=kind,** *n.* human being. **—en=möglich,** *adj.* within human power. **—en=ſchen,** *adj.* unsociable, misanthropic. **—en=ſeele,** *f.* human soul ; **keine —en=ſeele,** not a living soul.

Menſur [mɛn'zu:r], *f.* (*pl.* **—en**) measure; fencing ground.

Menuett [menu'ɛt], *n.* (**—s,** *pl.* **—s &** **—e**) & (*obs.*) *f.* (*pl.* **—en**) minuet.

Mergel ['mɛrgəl], *m.* (**—s**) marl. **—ig,** *adj.* marly.

Merkbar ['mɛrkba:r], *adj. & adv.* noticeable.

Merk—en ['mɛrkən], *v.a. & n.* (*aux.* **h.**) to mark, note, observe; **das werde ich mir —en,** I shall bear that in mind; **ſich nichts —en laſſen,** to seem to know nothing of a thing, take no notice. **—er,** *m.* (**—ers,** *pl.* **—er**) marker, noter. **—mal,** *n.* sign, mark. **—würdig,** *adj. & adv.* remarkable; noticeable, noteworthy. **—würdigkeit,** *f.* remarkableness.

Merkur [mɛr'ku:r], *m.* (**—s**) mercury; Mercury.

Merle ['mɛrlə], *f.* (*pl.* **—n**) blackbird.

Meſſe ['mɛsə], *f.* (*pl.* **—n**) Mass; fair.

Meß— [mɛs] (*from* **Meſſe** *in both senses*; *in comp.*) **—bar,** *adj.* measurable. **—barkeit,** *f.* measurability. **—buch,** *n.* missal. **—woche,** *f.* fair-week. **—zeit,** *f.* fair-time.

Meſſ—en ['mɛsən], I. *ir.v.n.* (*aux.* **h.**) to measure; to hold, contain. II. *ir.v.a.* to measure; to scan. III. *subst.n.* measuring; mensuration.

Meſſer ['mɛsər], I. *n.* (**—s,** *pl.* **—**) knife. II. *m.* measurer; meter.

Meſſing ['mɛsɪŋ], *n.* (**—s,** *pl.* **—e**) brass. **—en,** *adj.* brazen.

Metall [me'tal], *n.* (**—(e)s,** *pl.* **—e**) metal. **—en,** *adj.* metal. **—iſch,** *adj.* metallic.

Meter ['me:tər], *n.* (*also m.*) (**—s,** *pl.* **—**) metre. **—maß,** *n.* metric system

Method—e [me'to:də], *f.* (*pl.* **—en**) method. **—iſch,** *adj.* methodical.

Metr—ik ['me:trɪk], *f.* versification. **—iſch,** *adj. & adv.* metrical.

Meß—ge ['mɛtsgə], *f.* shambles. **—ger,** *m.* (**—gers,** *pl.* **—ger**) butcher (*dial.*).

Meuch—elei [mɔʏçə'laɪ], *f.* (*pl.*—**eleien**) plot, conspiracy. **—eln** [—'mɔʏçəln], *v.a.* to plot. **—ler,** *m.* (**—lers,** *pl.* **—ler**) conspirer; assassin. **—leriſch,** *adj.* treacherous. **—lings,** *adv.* treacherously. **—el=mord,** *m* assassination. **—el=mörder,** *m.* assassin.

Meute ['mɔʏtə], *f.* (*pl.* **—n**) pack of hounds.

Meuter—ei [mɔʏtə'raɪ], *f.* (*pl.* **—en**) mutiny. **—er** ['mɔʏtərər], *m.* (**—ers,** *pl.* **—er**) mutineer. **—iſch,** *adj.* mutinous. **—n,** *v.a.* to mutiny.

Miauen [mi'aʊən], *v.n.* (*aux.* **h.**) to mew; to caterwaul.

Mich [mɪç], *acc. of* **ich,** me; **— ſelbſt,** myself.

Mieder ['mi:dər], *n.* (**—s,** *pl.* **—**) bodice.

Miene ['mi:nə], *f.* (*pl.* **—n**) mien, expression.

Miesmuſchel ['mi:smʊʃəl], *f.* (*pl.* **—n**) edible mussel.

Miet—e ['mi:tə], *f.* (*pl.* **—n**) rent. **—en,** *v.a.* to hire; to rent. **—er,** *m.* (**—ers,** *pl.* **—er**) hirer; tenant, lodger. **—(s)=bedingung,** *f.* terms of hire *or* lease. **—(s)=leute,** *pl.* lodgers. **—(s)= lohn,** *m.* hire; servants' wages. **—ung,** *f.* hiring, renting.

Mikro—phon [mikro'fo:n], n. (—phons, pl. —phone) microphone (Radio). —ſkop [—'sko:p], n. (—ſkops, pl. —ſkope) microscope. —ſkopiſch, adj. microscopic.

Milch [mɪlç], f. milk; milt, soft roe. —en, v.n. (aux. h.) to give milk. —bruder, m. foster-brother. —kur, f. milk diet. —ſtraſſe, f. Milky Way.

Mild [mɪlt], —e, adj. & adv. mild. —e, f. mildness.

Mild—ern ['mɪldərn], v.a. to soften; to modify. —erung, f. mitigation, alleviation.

Militär [mili'tɛːr], I. m. (—s, pl. —s) soldier. II. n. (—s) the military. —iſch, adj. & adv. military, soldierly.

Miliz [mi'liːts], f. (pl. —en) militia.

Mill—ion [mɪli'oːn], f. (pl. —ionen) million. —ionär [—'nɛːr], m. (—s ionärs, pl. —ionäre) millionaire.

Milz [mɪlts], f. spleen. —füchtig, adj. splenetic, hypochondriac.

Mim—e ['miːmə], m. (—en, pl. —en) mime. —en, v.a. to act. —ik, f. mimicry. —iker, m. (—ikers, pl. —iker) mimic. —iſch, adj. mimic.

Mimoſe [mi'moːzə], f. (pl. —n) mimosa.

Minder ['mɪndər], adj. & adv. less; nicht mehr, nicht —, neither more nor less. —heit, f. minority; inferiority. —jährig, under age, minor. —jährig= keit, f. minority. —wertig, adj. inferior, of poor quality. —zahl, f. minority.

Minder—n ['mɪndərn], v.a. to diminish. —ung, f. decrease, diminution.

Mindeſt ['mɪndɛst], adj. & adv. least; nicht im —en, not in the least, not at all, by no means. —ens, adv. at least.

Mine ['miːnə], f. (pl. —n) mine. —n=gräber, m. miner.

Mineral [mine'raːl], n. (—s, pl. —e, —ien) mineral. —iſch, adj. mineral.

Miniſter [mi'nɪstər], m. (—s, pl. —) minister. —ial [—terl'aːl], adj., —iell [—'ɛl], adj. & adv. ministerial. —ium, n. (—iums, pl. —ien) ministry. —ial=rat, m. councillor in the ministry. —präſident, m. prime minister. —rat, m. cabinet council.

Minn—e ['mɪnə], f. love. —ig(lich), adj. & adv. lovely, charming. —e= ſänger, —e=ſinger, m. minnesinger (German lyric poet of the 12th or 13th century).

Minorenn [mino'rɛn], adj. under (full) age, minor.

Minute [mi'nuːtə], f. (pl. —n) minute. —n=weiſer, —n=zeiger, m. minute-hand.

Minze ['mɪntsə], f. mint (Bot.).

Mir [miːr], dat. of ich, me, to me.

Mirakel [mi'raːkəl], n. (—s, pl. —) miracle.

Miſch—en ['mɪʃən], v. I. a. to mix; Karten —, to shuffle cards. II. r. to interfere, meddle with. —ling, m. (—s, pl. —) mongrel. —ung, f. mixture; medley.

Miſpel ['mɪspəl], f. (pl. —n) medlar; medlar-tree.

Miß [mɪs], adv. & (properly) inſep. prefix (some verbs in comp. with miß have the inf. & p.p. sep. as well as insep.; such verbs are marked below sep. & insep.)=mis-, dis-, amiss; false, etc. —lich, Mislich, adj. & adv. doubtful, precarious, uncertain. —achten, v.a. (sep. & insep.) to disregard. —behagen, subst.n. displeasure, discontent. —behaglich, adj. & adv. disagreeable. —billigen, v.a. (sep. & insep.) to disapprove. —billigung, f. disapprobation, disapproval. —brauch, m. misuse; abuse. —brau= chen, v.a. (rarely and obsol. with gen.) (sep. & insep.) to misuse; to abuse. —erfolg, m. failure, ill-success. —fallen, I. ir.v.n. (aux. h., dat.) to displease, to be disagreeable to; es —fällt mir, I dislike it. II. subst.n. displeasure, dissatisfaction. —geſchick, n. misfortune. —glücken, v.n. (aux. ſ.) to fail, miscarry. —gönnen, v.a. (einem etwas) to begrudge. —griff, m. blunder, mistake. —gunſt, f. envy, ill-will. —günſtig, adj. envious, jealous. —handeln, v. I. n. (aux. h.) (sep.) to do wrong. II. a. (insep.) to abuse, ill-treat. —hand= lung, f. ill-usage; misdeed. —heirat, f. misalliance. —hellig, adj. dissonant; disagreeing. —klang, m. dissonance, discord. —lingen, I. ir.v.n. (aux. ſ.) & imp. (with dat.) to turn out ill, prove unsuccessful. II. subst.n. failure; disappointment. —mutig, adj. dejected; discouraged. —ſtim= mung, f. discord; dissension; ill-humour. —tönen, v.n. (aux. h.) (sep.) to be out of tune. —trauen, I. v.n. (aux. h., dat.) to mistrust. II. subst.n.

suspicion, mistrust. —**trauisch**, *adj.* distrustful; suspicious. —**verständnis**, *n.* misunderstanding. —**verstehen**, *ir.v.a.* to misunderstand, mistake.

Missen ['mɪsən], *v.a.* to lack; to feel the want of.

Misse—tat ['mɪsəta:t], *f.* (*pl.* —**taten**) misdeed, crime. —**täter** (—**täters**, *pl.* —**täter**) *m.* evil-doer, criminal.

Mission [mɪsɪ'o:n], *f.* (*pl.* —**en**) mission. —**ar** [—'na:r], *m.* (—**ars**, *pl.* —**are**) missionary.

Mist [mɪst], *m.* (—**es**) dung. —**beet**, *n.* hot-bed.

Mistel ['mɪstəl], *f.* (*pl.* —**n**) mistletoe.

Mit [mɪt], I. *adv. & sep. prefix,* along, along with, together *or* in company with; in unison; likewise, also; simultaneously; (*in comp. with nouns and pronouns generally =*) fellow-, joint-, co-, sym-, *etc.*; (*in comp. with verbs generally =*) along, in common with, with, simultaneously, co-, *etc.* II. *prep.* (*with dat.*) with; along with, at the same time with, in company with; by; composed of; possessed of, *etc.*; — 5 **Jahren,** at the age of five; — **einem Wort,** in a word; — **der Zeit,** in time.

Mitarbeite—n ['mɪt'arbaɪtən], *v.a.* to assist; to co-operate. —**r,** *m.* (—**rs,** *pl.* —**r**) fellow-labourer.

Mitbringen ['mɪtbrɪŋən], *ir.v.a.* to bring along with (one).

Mitbürger ['mɪtbyrgər], *m.* (—**s,** *pl.* —) fellow-citizen. —**in,** *f.* (*pl.* —**innen**) female neighbour.

Miteinander ['mɪt'aɪnandər], *adv.* with one another, together, jointly.

Mitführen ['mɪtfy:rən], *v.a.* to bring along with.

Mitgefühl ['mɪtgəfu:l], *n.* (—**s**) compassion, sympathy.

Mitgehen ['mɪtge:ən], *ir.v.n.* (*aux.* f.) to accompany.

Mitgift ['mɪtgɪft], *f.* (*pl.* —**en**) dowry.

Mitglied ['mɪtgli:t], *n.* member.

Mithin [mɪt'hɪn], *adj. & conj.* consequently, therefore.

Mitlaut ['mɪtlaʊt], *m.* (—**s,** *pl.* —**e**) consonant.

Mitleid ['mɪtlaɪt], *n.* (—**s**) pity, compassion. —**s=los,** *adj.* pitiless, unfeeling.

Mitleid—en ['mɪtlaɪdən], *ir.v.n.* (*aux.* h.) to pity; to sympathize. —**ig,** *adj.* compassionate.

Mitmachen ['mɪtmaxən], *v.a.* to join, take part in; **die Mode** —, to follow the fashion.

Mitrechnen ['mɪtrɛçnən], *v.* I. *a.* to include in the reckoning. II. *n.* (*aux.* h.) to be reckoned in; **das rechnet nicht mit,** that does not count.

Mitreden ['mɪtre:dən], *v.n.* (*aux.* h.) to join in the conversation.

Mitschuld ['mɪtʃʊlt], *f.* complicity. —**ig,** *adj.* participating in guilt. —**ige(r),** *m.* accomplice.

Mitschüler ['mɪtʃy:lər], *m.,* —**in,** *f.* schoolfellow.

Mittag ['mɪta:k], *m.* (—**s,** *pl.* —**e**) midday, noon. —**s=essen,** *n.* mid-day meal, lunch. —**s=freis,** *m.* meridian. —**s=volf,** *n.* southern people.

Mitt—e ['mɪtə], *f.* (*pl.* —**en**) middle, midst. —**schiffs,** *adv.* amidships. —**sommer,** *m.* midsummer. —**woch,** *m.* (—**s**) Wednesday.

Mitteil—en ['mɪttaɪlən], *v.a.* (**einem etwas**) to communicate. —**end,** *p. & adj.* —**sam,** *adj.* communicative. —**ung,** *f.* communication; intelligence.

Mittel ['mɪtəl], *n.* (—**s,** *pl.* —) middle, midst; expedient; means; average; medium; **sich ins** — **legen,** to interpose, to interfere. —**s,** —**st,** *adv. & prep.* (*with gen.*) by means of, by the help of, through. —**st,** *adj. sup. of* **Mittel,** midmost, middlemost. —**alter,** *n.* Middle Ages. —**alter= lich,** *adj.* mediæval. —**freis,** *m.* equator. —**ländisch,** *adj.* inland; **das** —**ländische Meer,** the Mediterranean (Sea). —**maß,** *n.* average; middling size; mediocrity. —**mäßig,** *adj.* middling, indifferent, ordinary. —**s mäßigkeit,** *f.* mediocrity. —**mast,** *m.* main-mast (*Naut.*). —**schule,** *f.* intermediate school. —**stand,** *m.* middle class(es). —**straße,** *f.* middle road; **die goldene—straße,** the happy mean.

Mitten ['mɪtən], *adv.* (*used with a prep. following*) midway; — **in,** — **auf,** in the midst, middle of; — **entzwei,** in two, broken in the middle.

Mitter ['mɪtər] (*in comp.*) —**nacht,** *f.* midnight; north. —**nachts,** *adv.* at midnight.

Mittler ['mɪtlər], *m.* (—**s,** *pl.* —) mediator.

Mittlerweile [mɪtlər'vaɪlə], *adv.* meanwhile, in the meantime.

Mitunter [mɪt'ʊntər], *adv.* among

other things; occasionally, now and then. —schreiben, —zeichnen, v.a. & n. (aux. h.) to countersign. —schrift, f. joint signature.

Mitwelt ['mɪtvɛlt], f. the age we live in.

Mitwirk—en ['mɪtvɪrkən], v.n. (aux. h.) to co-operate. —end, p. & adj. co-operative. —ung, f. co-operation, assistance.

Mitwisse—n ['mɪtvɪsən], I. ir.v.n. (aux. h.); um etwas —n, to know of a thing. II. subst.n. cognizance; ohne mein —n, without my knowing.

Möbel ['møːbəl], n. (—s, pl. —, better than —n) piece of furniture; (pl.) furniture.

Mobil [moˈbiːl], I. adj. mobile (Mil.); — machen, to put in motion; to mobilize (troops). II. n. (—s, pl. —e) motive power. —ien, pl. goods and chattels, furniture. —isieren [—biˈliːziːrən], v.a. to mobilize.

Möb—lieren [møˈbliːrən], v.a. to furnish. —lierer, m. (—lierers, pl. —lierer) upholsterer.

Mod—e ['moːdə], f. (pl. —en) fashion, mode. —isch, adj. fashionable.

Moder ['moːdər], m. (—s) mould, decay. —ig, adj. mouldy, musty. —n, v.n. (aux. f. & h.) to putrefy, rot.

Modern [moˈdɛrn], adj. modern.

Modus ['moːdʊs], m. (—, pl. Modi) mood (Gram.).

Mög—en ['møːgən], ir.v.a. & n. (aux. h.) to be willing; to like; to desire, have a mind to; to be able; to be permitted or at liberty to do; to be possible; (used as modal auxiliary = may, might, let;) ich möchte gern mit Ihnen sprechen, I should like to speak to you; ich möchte, daß sie kämen, I wish they would come; mag er tun, was er will, let him do what he likes; ich mag das nicht, I do not like that. —lich, adj. & adv. possible. —lichkeit, f. possibility. —lichst, adv. as much as, etc., possible; —lichst bald, as soon as possible. —lichenfalls, adv. if possible; possibly; —licher=weise, adv. as far as possible; possibly; perhaps.

Mohn [moːn], m. (—s, pl. —e) poppy.

Mohr [moːr], m. (—en, pl. —en) Moor. —in, f. negress. —isch, adj. Moorish.

Möhre ['møːrə] (Mohr=rübe), f. (pl. —n) carrot.

Molch [mɔlç], m. (—es, pl. —e) salamander; monster.

Molk—e ['mɔlkə], f. (pl. —en) whey. —erei [—ˈraɪ], f. dairy. —ig, adj. whey-like, containing whey.

Moll [mɔl], adj. & n. (—s) minor (Mus.). —ig, adj. soft; comfortable.

Moment [moˈmɛnt], I. m. (—s, pl. —e) moment. II. n. momentum. —an [—ˈtaːn], adj. momentary.

Monarch [moˈnarç], m. (—en, pl. —en) monarch. —ie [—ˈçiː], f. (pl. —ieen) monarchy. —isch, adj. monarchical.

Monat ['moːnat], m. (—s, pl. —e) month; vor anderthalb —en, a month and a half ago. —lich, adj. monthly. —s=schrift, f. monthly magazine. —s=tag, m. day of the month, date.

Mönch [mønç], m. (—es, pl. —e) monk.

Mond [moːnt], m. (—es (obs. —en surviving in compds.), pl. —e) moon. —(en)=schein, m. moonshine. —fin=sternis, f. lunar eclipse. —scheibe, f. disk of the moon. —sucht, f somnambulism; lunacy. —süchtig, adj. lunatic; moonstruck.

Montag ['moːntaːk], m. Monday; des —s, every Monday.

Mont—eur [mɔ̃ˈtøːr], m. (—eurs, pl. —eure) engine-fitter, mechanic. —ieren [—ˈtiːrən], v.a. to mount (machines); to equip (soldiers). —ierung, f. adjusting, erection (of an engine); equipment (Mil.). —ur [—ˈtuːr], f. uniform, regimentals.

Moor [moːr], n. (—s, pl. —e) bog, swamp. —ig, adj. marshy. —bad, n. mud-bath.

Moos [moːs], n. (—(f)es, pl. —(f)e) moss.

Mops [mɔps], m. (—fes, pl. Möpfe) pug.

Moral [moˈraːl], f. morals, ethics. —isch, adj. & adv. moral.

Moraft [moˈrast], m. (—s, pl. Moräfte) morass. —ig, adj. marshy.

Mord [mɔrt], m. (—es, pl. —e) murder. —begierig, —süchtig, adj. bloodthirsty. —brand, m. arson. —brenner, m. incendiary. —geschrei, n. cries of murder. —s=kerl, m. devil of a fellow. —tat, f. murder, murderous deed.

Morden ['mɔrdən], v.a. to murder.

Mörder ['mørdər], m. (—s, pl. —) murderer. —in, f. murderess. —isch, adj. murderous, bloody.

Morgen ['mɔrgən], I. adv. to-morrow; — früh, to-morrow morning; über—, the day after to-morrow; —

über 8 Tage, to-morrow week. II.
n. (—s, pl. —) the next day. III. m.
(—s, pl. —) morning; east. IV. m.
(—s, pl. —) measure of land, acre.
—s, adv. in the morning. —däm=
merung, f. day-break, dawn. —land,
n. the east; the Orient. —ländiſch, adj.
eastern, oriental. —röte, f. dawn.

Morſch [morſ], adj. decaying, rotten.
—heit, f. rottenness.

Mörſer ['mørzər], m. (—s, pl. —)
mortar (also Artil.).

Mörtel ['mørtəl], m. (—s, pl. —)
mortar; plaster.

Moſaik [moza'i:k], f. mosaic. —fuß=
boden, m. tessellated pavement.

Moſchee [mo'ʃe:], f. (pl. —en) mosque.

Moſchus ['moʃus], m. (—)musk.

Moſt [most], m. (—es, pl. —e) new
wine. —kelter, —preſſe, f. wine-press.

Motor [mo'to:r], m. (—s, pl. —en)
motor. —rad, n. motor-bicycle.

Mott—e ['motə], f. (pl. —en) moth.
—ig, adj. moth-eaten.

Möwe ['mø:və], f. (pl. —n) sea-gull.

Müce ['mykə], f. (pl. —n) gnat,
midge; —n haben, to have whims, be
capricious.

Müd—e ['my:də], adj. & adv. weary,
tired. —igkeit, f. weariness, fatigue.

Muff [muf], m. (—es, pl. Müffe), —e,
f. (pl. —en) muff. —ig, adj. stuffy,
musty.

Müh—e ['my:ə], f. (pl. —en) trouble,
pains; nicht der —e wert, not worth
while; ſich —e geben, to take pains.
—ſal, n. (—ſals, pl. —ſale), f. (pl.
—ſale) toil; distress. —ſam, adj.
& adv. toilsome. —ſamkeit, f. difficulty; laboriousness; trouble. —
ſelig, adj. & adv. toilsome; wretched;
weary. —ſeligkeit, f. hardship. Comp.
—(e)=los, adj. without toil or trouble.
—(e)=loſigkeit, f. ease, easiness, facility. —(e)=voll, adj. laborious,
troublesome, irksome.

Mühle ['mu:lə], f. (pl. —n) mill.
—teich, m. mill-pond.

Muhme ['mu:mə], f. (pl. —n, dim.
Mühmchen) aunt.

Mulatt—e [mu'latə], m. (—en, pl.
—en), —in, f. mulatto.

Müller ['mylər], m. (—s, pl. —) miller.
—in, f. miller's wife; miller's daughter.

Mumie ['mu:miə], f. (pl. —en)
mummy. —enhaft, adj. mummy-like.

Mumm—e ['mumə], f. (pl. —en) mask;

masker. —en, v.a. to mask, disguise.
—er, m. (—ers, pl. —er) masker,
mummer. —erei [—ə'raɪ], f. mum-
mery; buffoonery. —en=ſpiel, n.
masquerade.

Mund [munt], m. (—es, pl. —e and
Münder) mouth; reinen — halten, to
keep a secret; kein Blatt vor den —
nehmen, to speak frankly; den —
halten, to hold one's tongue. —art,
f. idiom, dialect. —artlich, adj.
dialectic. —ſperre, f. lock-jaw.

Münd—lich ['myntlɪç], adj. & adv.
oral, verbal, by word of mouth.

Münd—el ['myndəl], m. (—els, pl.
—el) ward; minor. —ig, adj. of age.
—igkeit, f. majority.

Munden ['mundən], v.n. (aux. h.) to
be appetizing.

Mundung ['mundʊŋ], f. mouth (of a
river).

Munition [munitsi'o:n], f. (pl. —en)
military or naval stores.

Münſter ['mynstər], m. & n. (—s, pl.
—) cathedral, minster.

Munter ['muntər], adj. lively; merry;
vigorous. —keit, f. liveliness, spright-
liness.

Münz—e ['myntsə], f. (pl. —n) coin;
medal. —en, v.a. & n. (aux. h.) to
coin; das iſt auf ihn gemünzt, that is
meant for him. —einheit, f. standard
of currency. —er, m. (—ers, pl. —er)
coiner. —fälſcher, m. utterer of base
coin. —fälſchung, f. forging of coin.

Mürbe ['myrbə], adj. decayed, brittle;
— werden, to give in.

Murmel—n ['murməln], v.a. & n. (aux.
h.) to murmur. —tier, n. marmot.

Murren ['murən], v.a. & n. (aux. h.)
to murmur, grumble.

Mürriſch ['myrɪʃ], adj. surly, morose.

Mus [mu:s], n. (—(ſ)es, pl. —(ſ)e)
pap; stewed fruit, etc.

Muſchel ['muʃəl], f. (pl. —n) mussel.

Muſ—e ['mu:zə], f. (pl. —en) muse.
—eum [—'ze:ʊm], n. (—eums, pl.
—een) museum.

Muſik [mu'zi:k], f. music. —aliſch,
adj. & adv. musical. —ant, m.
(—anten, pl. —anten) musician. —er
['mu:zɪkər], m. (—ers, pl. —er)
musician; composer. —us ['mu:zɪkus],
m. (—, pl. Muſici) musician; member
of an orchestra. —alien=handlung, f.
music shop. —ſtunde, f. music lesson.
—verein, m. musical society.

Musizieren [mu:zi'tsi:rən], *v.n.* (*aux. h.*) to perform or practise music.

Muskat [mʊs'ka:t], *m.* (—s, *pl.* —e), —e, *f.* (*pl.* —en) nutmeg. —eller [—'telər], *m.* (—ellers) muscatel.

Muskel ['mʊskəl], *m.* (—s, *pl.* —n), *f.* (*pl.* —n) muscle. —ig, **Muskulös**, *adj.* muscular. —anstrengung, *f.* muscular exertion.

Musket—e [mʊs'ke:tə], *f.* (*pl.* —en) musket. —ier [—'ti:r], *m.* (—iers, *pl.* —iere) musketeer.

Muße ['mu:sə], *f.* leisure, spare *or* idle time; mit —, at one's leisure.

Musselin [mʊsə'li:n], *m.* (—s, *pl.* —e) muslin. —en, *adj.* muslin.

Müssen ['mʏsən], *ir.v.n. aux.* of mood, to be obliged, have to, must; to be bound by duty, *etc.*; (*preceded by the inf. of another verb*, **müssen** *is used for p.p.* gemußt).

Müßig ['my:sɪç], *adj. & adv.* idle. —gang, *m.* idleness.

Muster ['mʊstər], *n.* (—s, *pl.* —) model; pattern; paragon. —haft, *adj. & adv.* exemplary; standard. —haftigkeit, *f.* exemplariness. —n, *v.a.* to muster; examine critically. —ung, *f.* mustering, review. —bild, *n.* paragon; ideal. —leistung, *f.* splendid achievement, record.

Mut [mu:t], *m.* (—es) disposition, courage; mood, humour; guten —es sein, to be of good cheer; — fassen, to take courage; den — sinken lassen, to lose heart. —ig, *adj. & adv.* courageous. —beseelt, —erfüllt, —voll, *adj.* full of courage, high-spirited. —los, *adj.* without vigour; despondent. —losigkeit, *f.* despondency, dejection. —maßen, *v.a.* (*insep.*) to have an idea of; to suppose, surmise, guess. —maßer, *m.* conjecturer. —maßlich, *adj. & adv.* conjectural, presumable; probable. —maßlichkeit, *f.* probability. —maßung, *f.* surmise. —wille, *m.* wantonness. —willig, *adj. & adv.* wanton, mischievous.

Mutter ['mʊtər], *f.* (*pl.* Mütter; *used without art. sometimes gen.* —s; *dat.* —n (*coll.*)) mother. —schaft, *f.* maternity, motherhood. —seele, *f.* human being; —seelen-allein, quite alone; abandoned. —söhnchen, *n.* spoilt child. —sprache, *f.* mother-tongue.

Mütter—chen ['mʏtərçən], *n.* mamsie,

granny. —lich, *adj. & adv.* motherly; on the mother's side. —lichkeit, *f.* motherliness.

Mütze ['mʏtsə], *f.* (*pl.* —n) cap.

Myrte ['mɪrtə], *f.* (*pl.* —n) myrtle.

Mysteriös [mɪste:ri'ø:s], *adj. & adv.* mysterious.

Myth—e ['my:tə], *f.* (*pl.* —en) myth, fable. —isch, *adj.* mythical. —ologie [—lo'gi:], *f.* mythology. —us, *m.* (*pl.* —en) myth.

N

N, n [ɛn], *n.* N, n.

Na [na:], *int.* well! come now!

Nabe ['na:bə], *f.* (*pl.* —n) nave.

Nabel ['na:bəl], *m.* (—s, *pl.* —) navel.

Nach [na:x], I. *adv. & sep. prefix*, after, behind; afterwards; conformably; — und —, little by little; — wie vor, as usual, now as before. II. *prep.* (*with dat.*) after, behind, following; after, later; towards, to; in conformity with, according to, agreeably to; in imitation of, after the manner of; on the authority of; by; at; in; for, considering; like to; — Süden, towards the south; ich gehe — Hause, I am going home; ein Viertel — fünf, a quarter past five; einer — dem anderen, one by one; — der Reihe, in turn.

Nachahm—en ['na:xʔa:mən], *v.a. & n.* (*aux. h.*, *dat.*) to imitate. —ens-wert, *adj.* worthy of imitation. —er, *m.* (—ers, *pl.* —er) imitator, copier; counterfeiter. —ung, *f.* imitation; counterfeiting.

Nachbar ['na:xba:r], *m.* (—s, —n, *pl.* —n), —in, *f.* neighbour. —lich, *adj.* neighbouring; neighbourly. —schaft, *f.* neighbourhood.

Nachbild ['na:xbɪlt], *n.* copy, imitation, counterfeit. —en, *v.a.* to copy. —ung, *f.* copy.

Nachbleibe—n ['na:xblaɪbən], *ir.v.n.* (*aux. s.*) to be left behind; to be kept in at school (*as punishment*). —nd, *p. & adj.* residuary.

Nachdem [na:x'de:m], I. *adv.* afterwards; je —, accordingly; that depends. II. *conj.* after the time that; according as, according to the way that.

Nachdenk—en ['na:xdɛŋkən], I. *ir.v.n.* (*aux. h.*); über eine S. —en, to reflect, consider. II. *subst.n.* reflection, meditation, consideration. —**end**, *p.* & *adj.* reflecting, thoughtful, pensive. —**lich**, *adj.* critical (*rare*).

Nachdruck ['na:xdruk]. *m.* reprint; energy, vigour. —**s=voll**, *adj.* emphatic(al), forcible.

Nachdrück—en ['na:xdrykən], *v.a.* to urge forward, push. —**lich**, *adj.* & *adv.* energetic, vigorous, emphatic. —**lichkeit**, *f.* explicitness; energy.

Nacheifer ['na:x⁹aɪfər], *m.* (—**s**) emulation. —**er**, *m.* (—**ers**, *pl.* —**er**) rival; emulator. —**n**, *v.n.* (*aux.* ḥ.) (*dat.*) to follow eagerly, emulate. —**ung**, *f.* emulation.

Nacheilen ['na:x⁹aɪlən], *v.n.* (*aux.* ſ.) to hasten after, pursue.

Nacheinander [na:x⁹aɪ'nandər], *adv.* one after another, by *or* in turns. —**folgend**, *adj.* successive, subsequent.

Nachen ['na:xən], *m.* (—**s**, *pl.* —) boat, skiff.

Nacherzählen ['na:x⁹ɛrtsɛ:lən], *v.a.* to repeat; **dem Spanischen nacherzählt**, adapted from the Spanish.

Nachfolge ['na:xfolgə], *f.* succession (*in office*, etc.). —**n**, *v.n.* (*aux.* ſ.) (**einem**) to follow; to imitate, to succeed. —**nd**, *p.* & *adj.* subsequent. —**r**, *m.* (—**rs**, *pl.* —**r**) successor; imitator.

Nachfrage ['na:xfra:gə], *f.* (*pl.* —**n**) inquiry; demand. —**n**, *reg.* & *ir.v.* (*aux.* ḥ., *dat.*) to inquire about; **ich frage nichts danach**, I care nothing about it.

Nachgeben ['na:xge:bən], *ir.v.* I. *a.* to give up, yield; to grant. II. *n.* (*aux.* ḥ.) to give way, slacken.

Nachgiebig ['na:xgi:bɪç], *adj.* flexible; yielding; obliging. —**keit**, *f.* complaisance; indulgence.

Nachgrübeln ['na:xgry:bəln], *v.n.* (*aux.* ḥ., *dat.*) to search minutely into.

Nachhall ['na:xhal], *m.* (—**s**), resonance. —**en**, *v.n.* (*aux.* ḥ.) to resound.

Nachher [na:x'he:r], *adv.* afterwards, after that; later in the day; subsequently.

Nachholen ['na:xho:lən], *v.a.* to retrieve, recover; to overtake.

Nachhut ['na:xhu:t], *f.* (*pl.* —**en**) rearguard (*Mil.*).

Nachklang ['na:xklaŋ], *m.* echo, reverberation; after-effect.

Nachkomme ['na:xkomə], *m.* (—**n**, *pl.* —**n**) descendant.

Nachkommen ['na:xkomən], *ir.v.n.* (*aux.* ſ., *dat.*) to come after, follow; to execute, fulfil. —**schaft**, *f.* posterity.

Nachlaß ['na:xlas], *m.* (—(ſſ)**es**, *pl.* **Nachlässe**) legacy; literary remains; estate of one deceased; discount, remission. —(ſſ)**en**, I. *ir.v.a.* to leave behind; to transmit; to slacken, relax. II. *ir.v.n.* (*aux.* ḥ.) to subside, abate; to diminish; to cease. III. *subst.n.* relaxation; abatement, reduction. —**end**, *p.* & *adj.* intermittent.

Nachlässig ['na:xlɛsɪç], *adj.* & *adv.* negligent, careless. —**keit**, *f.* negligence, carelessness.

Nachlese ['na:xle:zə], *f.* gleanings; supplement. —**n**, *ir.v.a.* & *n.* (*aux.* ḥ.) to glean.

Nachmachen ['na:xmaxən], *v.a.* to copy, imitate.

Nachmal—ig ['na:xma:lɪç], *adj.* subsequent. —**s**, *adv.* afterwards.

Nachmittag ['na:xmɪta:k], *m.* afternoon. —**s**, *adv.* in the afternoon.

Nach—nahme ['na:xna:mə], *f.* reimbursement. —**nehmen**, *ir.v.a.* to collect charges; to reimburse oneself for charges. —**nahme=betrag**, *m.* amount to be collected on delivery. —**nahme=sendung**, *f.* C.O.D. parcel.

Nachordnen ['na:x⁹ordnən], *v.a.* to class next after.

Nachporto ['na:xporto:], *n.* (—**s**, *pl.* —**s**) surcharge (*on letters*, etc.).

Nachrede ['na:xre:də], *f.* epilogue; rejoinder; calumny.

Nachricht ['na:xrɪçt], *f.* (*pl.* —**en**) news. —**lich**, *adj.* & *adv.* by way of information.

Nachruf ['na:xru:f], *m.* (—(**e**)**s**, *pl.* —**e**) obituary notice, *etc.*

Nachsagen ['na:xza:gən], *v.a.* to repeat.

Nach—schreiben ['na:xʃraɪbən], *ir.v.a.* & *n.* (*aux.* ḥ.) to write from dictation. —**schreiber**, *m.* transcriber; one who takes notes. —**schrift**, *f.* postscript; transcript.

Nachsicht ['na:xzɪçt], *f.* indulgence; forbearance.

Nächst [nɛ:çst], I. *sup. adj.*, see **Nah**; next, nearest, closest. II. *adv.* next; soon; lately; **am** —**en**, nearest. III. *prep.* (*with dat.*) next to, after. —**beste(e)**, *m.* second best. —**ens**, *adv.* shortly, very soon; by and by. —**en=liebe**, *f.* Christian charity. —**folgend**, *adj.* immediately following.

Nachſteuer ['na:xſtoyər], *f.* (*pl.* —n) additional tax.

Nachſtreben ['na:xſtre:bən], *v.n.* (*aux.* h., *dat.*) to strive after, aspire to; to emulate.

Nachſuchen ['na:xzu:xən], *v.a.* & *n.* (*aux.* h.) to search for.

Nacht [naxt], *f.* (*pl.* Nächte) night. —s, *adv.* by night, at night. —falter, *m.* night moth; (*coll.*) night-bird. —hemd, *n.* night-shirt; night-dress. —quartier, *n.* quarters for the night. —wächter, *m.* watchman. —wandeln, I. *v.n.* (*aux.* h.) (*insep.*) to walk in one's sleep. II. *subst.n.* somnambulism. —wandler, *m.*, —wandlerin, *f.* somnambulist.

Nachteil ['na:xtaɪl], *m.* (—s, *pl.* —e) disadvantage. —ig, *adj.* disadvantageous, prejudicial.

Nachtigall ['naxtɪgal], *f.* (*pl.* —en) nightingale.

Nachtiſch ['na:xtɪʃ], *m.* (—es, *pl.* —e) dessert.

Nachtrag ['na:xtra:k], *m.* (—(e)s, *pl.* Nachträge) addendum.

Nachträglich ['na:xtrɛklɪç], I. *adj.* supplementary, additional. II. *adv.* by way of appendix *or* supplement; subsequently.

Nachtrete—n ['na:xtre:tən], *ir.v.n.*(*aux.* ſ., *dat.*) to follow after; to follow closely. —r, *m.* (—rs, *pl.* —r) follower, adherent.

Nachweis ['na:xvaɪs], *m.* (—(ſ)es, *pl.* —(ſ)e) information; citation. —bar, —lich, *adj.* authenticated, assignable (*as a reason*). —(ſ)en, I. *ir.v.a.* (einem etwas) to point out, show, indicate; to prove; to establish (*a claim*). II. *subst.n.*, —(ſ)ung, *f.* proof, demonstration; direction; information; reference.

Nachwelt ['na:xvɛlt], *f.* posterity.

Nachwirk—en ['na:xvɪrkən], *v.a.* & *n.* (*aux.* h.) to operate *or* take effect afterwards. —ung, *f.* after-effect; consequences, result.

Nachwort ['na:xvɔrt], *n.* epilogue.

Nachzug ['na:xtsu:k], *m.* train, suite; rearguard (*Mil.*).

Nacken ['nakən], *m.* (—s, *pl.* —) neck.

Nackt [nakt], **Nackend** ['nakənd], *adj.* naked, bare. —heit, *f.* nakedness.

Nadel ['na:dəl], *f.* (*pl.* —n) (Näh—) needle; (Steck—) pin. —futteral, *n.*

needle-case. —holz, *n.* conifers. —öhr, *n.* eye of a needle.

Nagel ['na:gəl], *m.* (—s, *pl.* Nägel) nail (*on fingers, toes*); nail, tack. —n, *v.a.* to nail. —feſt, *adj.* nailed, immovable. —neu, *adj.* quite new, brand-new.

Nage—n ['na:gən], *v.a.* & *n.* (*aux.* h.) to gnaw, nibble. —r, *m.* (—rs, *pl.* —r) gnawer; rodent. —tiere, *pl.* rodents.

Nah(e) ['na:(ə)], *adj.* & *adv.* (*comp.* näher ['nɛ:ər], *sup.* nächſt) near, close, neighbouring; imminent; closely related *or* attached, kindred; almost. —e=hin, —e=zu, *adv.* nearly, almost.

Nähe ['nɛ:ə], *f.* nearness, proximity; neighbourhood; environs.

Nah—en ['na:ən], *v.r.* & *n.* (*aux.* ſ., *dat.*) to approach. —bar, *adj.* approachable, accessible.

Näh—en ['nɛ:ən], I. *v.a.* & *n.* (*aux.* h.) to sew. II. *subst.n.*, —ung, *f.* sewing. —erei [—'raɪ], *f.* sewing; needlework. —erin, *f.* needle-woman, seamstress. —garn, *n.* sewing-cotton. —korb, *m.* work-þasket.

Näher—n ['nɛ:ərn], *v.* I. *a.* & *n.* (*aux.* h.) to bring near; to approximate. II. *r.* to approach, draw near. —ung, *f.* approach; approximation.

Nähr—en ['nɛ:rən], *v.* I. *a.* to nourish. II. *r.* to gain a livelihood. III. *n.* (*aux.* h.) to be nourishing. —end, *p.* & *adj.* nutritious. —er, *m.* (—ers, *pl.* —er), —erin, *f.* supporter, nourisher. —ung, *f.* nourishment, nutrition; bringing up. —boden, *m.* fertile soil. —geld, *n.* money allowed for maintenance. —mittel, *n.* (*usually pl.*) articles of food. —mutter, *f.* foster-mother. —wert, *m.* nutritive quality.

Nahr—haft ['na:rhaft], *adj.* nutritive. —haftigkeit, *f.* nutritiousness. —ung, *f.* food; livelihood; profession. —ungs=mittel, *n.pl.* victuals.

Naht [na:t], *f.* (*pl.* Nähte) seam. —los, *adj.* seamless; jointless.

Nam—e ['na:mə], *m.* (—ens, *pl.* —en) name; —ens A, named *or* called A; ich kenne ihn dem —en nach, I know him by name. —entlich, I. *adj.* by name, nominal. II. *adv.* particularly, especially. —haft, *adj.* & *adv.* named, specified; renowned. —en-los, *adj.* & *adv.* nameless; anonymous.

Nämlich ['nɛ:mlɪç], I. *adj.*; der, die,

das —e, the (self-)same. **II.** *adv.* namely, to wit, that is to say.

Napf [napf], *m.* **(—es,** *pl.* **Näpfe)** dish, bowl.

Narb—e ['narbə], *f.* **(***pl.* **—n;** *dim.* **Närbchen)** scar. **—en,** *v.a.* to scar, mark. **—ig,** *adj.* scarred.

Narr [nar], *m.* **(—en,** *pl.* **—en), Närrin,** *f.* fool; **zum —en haben,** to make a fool of. **—heit,** *f.* folly. **—en(s)=poffe,** *f.* (*usually plur.*) foolery, nonsense. **—en=streich,** *m.* foolish trick.

Narziffe [nar'tsɪsə], *f.* (*pl.* **—n**) narcissus; **gelbe —,** daffodil.

Nafch—en ['naʃən], *v.a.* & *n.* (*aux.* **h.**) to eat dainties; to nibble secretly. **—fatze,** *f.* sweet-tooth, greedy person.

Näfch—er ['nɛʃər], *m.* **(—ers,** *pl.* **—er), —erin,** *f.* sweet-tooth.

Nafe ['na:zə], *f.* (*pl.* **—n**) nose; **die Tür vor der — zumachen,** to shut the door in a person's face. **—n=flügel,** *m.* side of the nose. **—n=rücken,** *m.* bridge of the nose. **—n=rümpfen,** *n.* turning up one's nose; sneer. **—weis,** *adj.* & *adv.* pert, saucy. **—weisheit,** *f.* pertness.

Nashorn ['na:shɔrn], *n.* **(—s,** *pl.* **—e** & **Nashörner)** rhinoceros.

Naß [nas], **I.** *adj.* & *adv.* (*comp.* **naffer,** *sup.* **naffeft,** & **näffer, näffeft**) wet. **II.** *n.* **(—(ff)es)** humidity, wetness. **—falt,** *adj.* damp and cold.

Näffe ['nɛsə], *f.* wet, wetness, humidity.

Nation [natsi'o:n], *f.* (*pl.* **—en**) nation. **—al** [—'na:l], *adj.* national. **—alität** [—'tɛːt], *f.* nationality. **al=fozia`lift** (*abbrev.* **Nazi**), *m.* National Socialist.

Natter ['natər], *f.* (*pl.* **—n**) adder.

Natur [na'tu:r], *f.* (*pl.* **—en**) nature; **nach der — zeichnen,** to draw from nature. **—ell** [—'rɛl], *n.* **(—ells,** *pl.* **—elle)** nature, disposition. **—begebenheit,** *f.* phenomenon. **befchreiber,** *m.* naturalist. **—erfcheinung,** *f.* natural phenomenon. **—forfcher,** *m.* student of natural science. **—forfchung,** *f.* natural science. **—gemäß,** *adj.* & *adv.* conformable to nature, natural. **—funde,** *f.* natural philosophy, physics. **—fpiel,** *n.* freak of nature. **—trieb,** *m.* instinct. **—widrig,** *adj.* unnatural. **—wiffenfchaft,** *f.* natural science.

Natürlich [na'ty:rlɪç], **I.** *adj.* & *adv.* natural. **II.** *adv.* of course, certainly, naturally.

Nazi ['natsi:], *see* **National=fozialift.**

Nebel ['ne:bəl], *m.* **(—s,** *pl.* **—)** mist. **—haft,** *adj.* foggy. **—bank,** *f.* fog-bank. **—n,** *v.n.*(*aux.* **h.**) to be or grow misty or foggy; **es —t,** there is a fog.

Neben ['ne:bən], **I.** *adv.* beside. **II.** *prep.* with acc. when expressing motion absolutely; with dat. when expressing rest or limited motion; near, next to, by the side of, close to; with; besides. *Comp.* (*in comp.*=accessory, secondary, collateral, incidental, opposed to **Haupt—,** chief . . .). **—an** [—'na:n], *adv.* close by; next door. **—arbeit,** *f.* work of secondary importance; extra work. **—bei** [—'baɪ], *adv.* close by; along with something else; by the way; incidentally; besides, by the by. **—beweis,** *m.* additional or collateral proof. **—blatt,** *n.* supplement. **—buhler,** *m.*, **—buhlerin,** *f.* rival. **—ding,** *n.* accessory; secondary matter. **—einander=liegen,** *n.* contiguity. **—einander=ftehen,** *n.*, **—einander=ftellung,** *f.* juxtaposition. **—rolle,** *f.* subordinate rôle or part. **—fache,** *f.* matter of secondary importance; accessory; incident; **als —fache,** accidental, non-essential. **—fat,** *m.* subordinate sentence. **—ftraße,** *f.* side-street.

Nebft [nɛːpst], *prep.* (*with dat.*) with, together or along with, in addition to, besides.

Neck—en ['nɛkən], *v.a.* to tease. **—er,** *m.* **(—ers,** *pl.* **—er)** banterer. **—erei** [—'raɪ], *f.* raillery, chaff. **—ifch,** *adj.* & *adv.* teasing.

Neffe ['nɛfə], *m.* **(—n,** *pl.* **—n)** nephew.

Neger ['ne:gər], *m.* **(—s,** *pl.* **—)** negro. **—in,** *f.* negress.

Nehmen ['ne:mən], *ir.v.a.* to take; **ein Ende —,** to come to an end; **Partei für,** to side with; **ftreng genommen,** strictly speaking.

Neid [naɪt], *m.* **(—es)** envy. **—en,** *v.a.* & *n.* (*aux.* **h.**) to envy; **einem etwas —en,** to envy a person something. **—er,** *m.* **(—ers,** *pl.* **—er)** envier, grudger. **—ifch,** *adj.* envious; jealous (**auf einen,** of a person).

Neig—e ['naɪgə], *f.* (*pl.* **—en**) bow, courtesy; slope, incline. **—en,** *v.* I. *a.* to incline, bend, bow. II. *r.* & *n.* (*aux.* **h.**) to make a reverence, bow; to slope; `to decline, wane. **—ung,** *f.* inclination, disposition, tendency;

affection; gradient, incline. **—ungs= winkel**, *m.* angle of inclination.

Nein [naɪn], *adv.* no.

Nelke ['nɛlkə], *f. (pl. —n)* carnation. **—n=baum**, *m.* clove-tree. **—n=öl**, *n.* oil of cloves. **—n=pfeffer**, *n.* allspice, Jamaica pepper.

Nennbar ['nɛnbaːr], *adj.* nameable.

Nenn—en ['nɛnən], *ir.v.a.* to name. **—er**, *m. (—ers, pl. —er)* namer; denominator. **—ung**, *f.* naming; nomination. **—ens=wert**, *adj. & adv.* especially worth mentioning; notable. **—fall**, *m.* nominative case. **—wert**, *m.* nominal value. **—wort**, *n.* noun, substantive.

Nerv [nɛrf], *m. (—(e)s & —en, pl. —en), —e, f. (pl. —en) (obs.)* nerve. **—ig**, *adj.* sinewy. **—ös** [nɛrˈvøːs], *adj.* nervous; forcible.

Nerven ['nɛrfən] *(in comp.)* **—auf= regung**, *f.* nervous excitement. **— frank**, *adj.* nervous, suffering from the nerves. **—frankheit**, *f.* nervous affec- tion. **—leiden**, *n.* nervous complaint or affection. **—los**, *adj.* nerveless.

Nerz [nɛrts], *m. (—es, pl. —e)* mink *(Zool.).*

Nessel ['nɛsəl], *f. (pl. —n)* nettle. **—fieber**, *n.* nettle-rash. **—tuch**, *n.* muslin.

Nest [nɛst], *n. (—es, pl. —er)* nest. **—ling**, *m. (—lings, pl. —linge)* nestling.

Nett [nɛt], *adj. & adv.* neat, spruce, trim; nice; pretty. **—igfeit**, *f.* neat- ness, spruceness; prettiness.

Netto ['nɛtoː], *adv. (abbr. n°)* net. **—betrag**, *m.* net amount. **—ein= nahme**, *f.* net profits. **—ertrag**, *m.* net proceeds. **—gewicht**, *n.* net weight. **—preis**, *m.* net price.

Netz [nɛts], *n. (—es, pl. —e)* net.

Netzen ['nɛtsən], *v.a.* to wet, moisten.

Neu [nɔy], *adj. & adv.* new. **—er**, *comp.* of **neu**; newer; modern; **von —em**, anew, afresh; **—ere Sprachen**, modern languages. **—ern**, *v.n. (aux. h.)* to innovate. **—heit**, *f. (pl. —heiten)* newness; novelty. **—ig= feit**, *f. (pl. —igfeiten)* piece of news; novelty. **—lich**, I. *adj.* late, recent. II. *adv.* the other day, quite recently. **—ling**, *m. (—lings, pl. —linge)* novice, neophyte. **—er=dings**, *adv.* recently. **—erfunden**, *adj.* newly- invented. **—gier(de)**, *f.* curiosity,

inquisitiveness. **—jahr**, *n.* New Year. **—jahrs=abend**, *m.* New Year's eve.

Neun [nɔyn], I. *num. adj.* nine. II. *f. (pl. —en)* nine. **—t**, *num. adj.* ninth; **der —te Januar**, the ninth of January. **—tel**, *n. (—tels, pl. —tel)* ninth part. **—tens**, *adv.* ninthly, in the ninth place. **—zig**, *num. adj. & f.* ninety. **—auge**, *n.* river-lamprey. **—ed**, *n.* nonagon. **—erlei** [—ərˈlaɪ], *indec. adj.* of nine different sorts. **—fach, —fältig**, *adj.* ninefold. **—mal**, *adv.* nine times. **—teilig**, *adj.* of nine parts. **—zehn**, *num. adj.* nineteen. **—zehntel**, *n.* nineteenth part.

Neutr—um ['nɔytrʊm], *n. (—ums, pl. —a)* neuter.

Nicht [nɪçt], *adv.* not; no; **durchaus —**, not at all; by no means; **noch —**, not yet; **— wahr?** is it not so? isn't that so? **—ig**, *adj. & adv.* null, void; invalid. **—igfeit**, *f.* nullity. **—achtung**, *f.* want of esteem, disrespect. **—= leiter**, *m.* non-conductor *(Phys.).*

Nichte ['nɪçtə], *f. (pl. —n)* niece.

Nichts [nɪçts], I. *ind. & indec. pron.* naught, nothing; *adverbially:* **in nothing**, nowise; **not at all; — als**, nothing but, nothing short of; **— der Art**, nothing of the kind, no such thing; **— dergleichen**, no such thing; **— destoweniger**, nevertheless, notwithstanding, however. II. *n.* nothingness; **soviel wie —**, next to nothing. **—nutz(ig), —nützig**, *adj.* useless, worthless. **—nutzigfeit**, *f.* futility; worthlessness. **—tuer**, *m.* idler. **—tuerei** [—ˈraɪ], *f.*, **—tun**, *n.* idling, inaction. **—würdig**, I. *adj.* worthless. II. *adv.* on no account. **—würdigfeit**, *f.* worthlessness; base- ness.

Nick [nɪk], *m. (—es, pl. —e)* nod. **—en**, *v.n. (aux. h.)* to nod.

Nickel ['nɪkəl], *(in comp.=)* nickel *(metal).*

Nie [niː], **Niemals** ['niːmals], *adv.* never (before), at no time, never; **nie wieder**, never again.

Nieder ['niːdər], I. *adj.* nether, under, beneath; low; subordinate; inferior. II. *adv. & sep. prefix*, down; low. **—fall**, *m.,* **—fallen**, *n.* downfall; prostration. **—gang**, *m.* setting *(of the sun);* descent. **—gehen**, *ir.v.n. (aux. ſ.)* to descend. **—geschlagen**, *adj.* dejected. **—land**, *n.* low-lying land; **die —lande**, the Netherlands or Low Countries. **—länder,** *m.* dweller in a low-lying country. **—spannung,** *f.* low-tension (*Radio*). **—trächtig,** *adj.* low, mean.

Riedlich ['ni:tlıç], *adj. & adv.* pretty, nice. **—keit,** *f.* prettiness, niceness.

Riedrig ['ni:drıç], *adj. & adv.* low; lowly; base. **—keit,** *f.* lowness; lowliness.

Riemand ['ni:mant], *ind. pron.* (—(e)s, *dat.* —, *acc.* —) nobody, no one.

Riere ['ni:rə], *f.* (*pl.* —n) kidney. **—nsbraten,** *m.* roast loin of mutton.

Riesen ['ni:zən], I. *v.n.* (*aux.* h.) to sneeze. II. *subst.n.* sneeze; sneezing.

Riet [ni:t], *n.* (—(e)s, *pl.* —e) rivet. **—en,** *v.a.* to rivet, clinch. **—nagel,** *m.* rivet.

Ril=pferd ['ni:lpfert], *n.* (—(e)s, *pl.* —e) hippopotamus.

Rimmer ['nımər], *adv.* never(more); at no time. **—mehr,** *adv.* never more; never; not at all; not likely! **—satt,** *adj.* insatiable. **—wiedersehen,** *n.*; **auf —wiedersehen,** farewell for ever.

Ripp [nıp], *m.* (—(e)s, *pl.* —e) nip, sip. **—en,** *v.a. & n.* (*aux.* h.) to sip, nip.

Rirgend(s) ['nırgent(s)], (—wo), *adv.* nowhere.

Rische ['ni:ʃə], *f.* (*pl.* —n) niche.

Rist=e(l)n ['nıstə(l)n], *v.n.* (*aux.* h.) to nestle; to build a nest.

Ritrat [ni'tra:t], *n.* (—(e)s, *pl.* —e) nitrate.

Rix [nıks], *m.* (—es, *pl.* —e) water-sprite, merman. **—e,** *f.* (*pl.* —en) water-nymph, mermaid.

Robel ['no:bəl], *adj.* (*comp.* nobler) noble; grand.

¹**Roch** [nox], *adv. & part.* in addition; besides; further; still, yet, as yet. **—mal,** *adv.* once again; twice. **—malig,** *adj.* repeated. **—mals,** *adv.* once more, again.

²**Roch,** *conj.* nor; weder M. — R., neither M. nor N.

Ronne ['nonə], *f.* (*pl.* —n; *dim.* Nönnchen ['nønçən], **Rönnlein**) nun. **—kloster,** *n.* nunnery. **—nweihe,** *f.* taking of the veil.

Rord [nort], *m.* (—es) north. **—en,** *m.* (—ens, *pl.* —en) north. **—isch,** *adj.* northern. **—meer,** *n.* Arctic Ocean. **—pol,** *m.* North Pole. **—see,** *f.* North Sea, German Ocean. **—stern,** *m.* polar-star. **—wärts,** *adv.* northward.

Nördlich ['nørtlıç], *adj. & adv.* northern, Arctic; **das —e Eismeer,** the Arctic Ocean.

Rorm [norm], *f.* (*pl.* —en) standard. **—al** [—'ma:l], *adj.* normal, regular. **—al=uhr,** *f.* standard clock.

Rot [no:t], I. *f.* (*pl.* Nöte) need, want; necessity, compulsion; trouble; danger; misery; — **leiden,** to suffer want; **mit — entkommen,** to have a narrow escape; **zur —,** at the worst. II. *adj.* needful, necessary; wanting; — **tun,** to be necessary. **—ausgang,** *m.* emergency exit. **—dringend,** *adj.* pressing, urgent. **—durft,** *f.* necessaries of life; necessity. **dürftig,** *adj.* scanty; needy. **—dürftigkeit,** *f.* indigence; want. **—fall,** *m.* case of necessity. **—lüge,** *f.* white lie, fib. **—sache,** *f.* case of necessity, urgent case. **—stand,** *m.* state of distress, critical state. **—stands=gesetz,** *n.* emergency bill. **—wehr,** *f.* self-defence. **—wendig,** *adj.* necessary. **—wendigkeit,** *f.* urgency; necessity. **—werk,** *n.* work of necessity. **—zwang,** *m.* the compulsion of necessity, the force of circumstances.

Rotar [no'ta:r], *m.* (—s, *pl.* —e) notary.

Rote ['no:tə], *f.* (*pl.* —n) note; banknote. **—nblatt,** *n.* sheet of music. **—nbuch,** *n.* music-book.

Rötig ['nø:tıç], *adj. & adv.* needful, necessary.

Rötig=en ['nø:tıgən], *v.a.* to necessitate; **sich —en lassen,** to stand upon ceremony. **—ung,** *f.* urgency; constraint.

Rotiz [no'ti:ts], *f.* (*pl.* —en) notice; memorandum.

Rotorisch [no'to:rıʃ], *adj.* notorious.

Rovelle [no'velə], *f.* (*pl.* —n) short novel.

Rovember [no'vembər], *m.* (—s) November.

Ru [nu:], I. *int.* well! well now! II. *m. & n.* instant; **im —,** in a trice.

Rüchtern ['nʏçtərn], *adj. & adv.* fasting; sober; calm; insipid. **—heit,** *f.* temperance; sobriety.

Rudel ['nu:dəl], *f.* (*pl.* —n) macaroni.

Rull [nul], I. *indec. adj.* nil, null; — **und nichtig,** null and void. II. *f.* (*pl.* —en) naught, cipher.

Rumerisch [nu'me:rıʃ], *adj. & adv.* numerical.

Nummer ['numər], f. (pl. —n) number. —folge, f. numerical order.

Nun [nu:n], I. adv. now, at present; under present circumstances; (also part.) now, well; — und nimmermehr! never! von — an, henceforth. II. conj. indeed, then; now. III. int. well! —mehrig [—'me:rɪç], adj. present, actual, now existing.

Nur [nu:r], adv. & part. only, merely; scarcely; a little while ago, a moment ago, but just; after wer, was, wie, wo= ever, soever, possibly, in any way; alle, — ich nicht, all except me.

Nuß [nus], f. (pl. Nüsse) nut (also Mech.); welsche —, walnut. —baum, m. nut-tree. —kern, m. kernel of a nut. —knacker, m. nut-cracker. —schale, f. nut-shell.

Nüster ['ny:stər], f. (pl. —n) (pl.) nostrils (of horses).

Nutz [nuts], —e, I. adj. useful, profitable; zu nichts — sein, to be good for nothing. II. m. (—es) use, profit. — anwendung, f. practical application. —bar, adj. useful. —barkeit, f. usefulness. —en I. v.a. to make use of. II. v.n. (aux. h., dat.) to be of use or profitable. —los, adj. useless, unprofitable. —losigkeit, f. uselessness.

Nützen ['nytsən], v.n. to be of use. —lich, adj. & adv. useful. —lichkeit, f. utility, usefulness.

O

O, o [o:], n. O, o.

Oase [o'a:zə], f. (pl. —n) oasis.

1Ob [ɔp], conj. if, whether; na —, of course. —gleich, —schon, —wohl, —zwar, conj. (in older German often separable) although, albeit, notwithstanding.

2Ob, prep. (with dat.) over; above, on, upon; (with gen.) on account of; beyond. —acht, f. superintendence; care. —dach, n. shelter. —herrschaft, f. supremacy. —hut, f. guard. — liegen, ir.v.n. (sep.) (aux. f.) to prevail (B.); (aux. h., dat.) to be incumbent on. —liegend, p. & adj. incumbent. —liegenheit, f. duty.

Oben ['o:bən], adv. above, aloft, on high; at the top; jemand von — herab behandeln, to treat someone haughtily. —an [—'na:n], adv. at the head; in the first place. —auf [—'nauf], adv. above, atop; uppermost. —drein [—'dram], —ein [—'nam], adv. over and above, into the bargain. —erwähnt, —gesagt, adj. aforesaid, above-mentioned. —hin [—'hɪn], adv. along the surface; slightly.

Ober ['o:bər], I. prep. (with dat.) over, above. II. adj. situated above, upper, higher, superior; chief, principal. —aufsicht, f. superintendence. —baumeister, m. chief architect, director of works. —befehl, m. supreme command. —befehlshaber, m. commander-in-chief. —fläche, f. surface. —flächlich, adj. & adv. superficial. —leutnant, m. first lieutenant.

Oberst ['o:bərst], I. sup. adj. see **Ober**; top; supreme; highest. II. m. (—en, pl. —en) colonel (Mil.). —leutnant, m. lieutenant-colonel.

Obig ['o:bɪç], adj. above, foregoing, above-mentioned.

Objekt [ɔp'jɛkt], n. (—s, pl. —e) object. —iv, I. adj. objective, impartial, dispassionate. II. n. (—s) objective case.

Obrigkeit ['o:brɪçkart], f. (pl. —en) magistrates, authorities.

Obst [o:pst], n. (—es; pl. —e, —arten) fruit. —garten, m. orchard. —händler, m. fruiterer.

Ochs [ɔks], m. (—(s)en, pl. —(s)en), **Ochse**, m. (—n, pl. —n) ox.

Ode ['o:də], f. (pl. —n) ode.

Öde ['ø:də]. I. adj. waste, desert. II. f. (pl. —n) desert.

Odem ['o:dəm], m. (—s) breath.

Oder ['o:dər], conj. or; otherwise.

Ofen ['o:fən], m. (—s, pl. Öfen) oven, stove. —kachel, f. Dutch tile. —vorsetzer, m. fender.

Offen ['ɔfən], adj. & adv. open; candid; —er Wechsel, blank cheque. —bar, adj. & adv. manifest. —baren [—'ba:rən], v.a. to reveal, discover; to disclose. —bart, adj. disclosed, revealed. —barung, f. manifestation; revealing. —herzig, adj. candid, sincere. —herzigkeit, f. frankness, candour.

Öffentlich ['øfəntlɪç], adj. & adv. public, open.

Offiz—ial [ɔfɪtsɪ'a:l], m. (—ials, pl. —iale) official. —iell [—tsi'ɛl], adj. & adv. official. —ier [—'tsi:r], m.

(—iers, pl. —iere) (military) officer.
—in [—'tsi:n], f. (pl. —innen) laboratory. —iös [—tsi'ø:s], adj. officious.

Öff=nen ['œfnən], v.a. & r. to open.
—nend, p. & adj. opening. —nung,
aperture, gap.

..Xt [ɔft], adv. (comp. öfter, sup. öftest)
often, frequently. —mals, adv. oftentimes, often, frequently. —malig, adj.
frequent, repeated.

Öfter ['œftər], see Oft, I. adv. more frequently. II. adj. more frequent.

Oheim ['o:harm], Ohm [o:m], m. (—s,
pl. —e) uncle.

Ohm [o:m], m. & n. (—es, pl. —e), —e,
f. (pl. —en) liquid measure (=about
40 gallons).

Ohne ['o:nə], prep. (with acc.) without,
apart from; but for, not to speak of;
except, save. —dem [—'de:m],
—dies [—'di:s], —hin [—'hm], adv.
apart from this, besides; all the
same; moreover; likewise. —gleichen
[—'glaɪçən], adj. unequalled.

Ohn=macht ['o:nmaxt], f. fainting fit,
swoon; in —macht fallen, to swoon.
—mächtig, adj. swooning, faint.

Ohr [o:r], n. (—(e)s, pl. —en) ear.
—(en)=brausen, n. singing in the ears.
—en=beichte, f. auricular confession.
—feige, f. box on the ear. —feigen,
v.a. (insep.) to box a person's ears.
—gehänge, —ring, m. ear-ring.
—zeuge, m. ear-witness.

Ökonom [øko'no:m], m. (—en, pl. —en)
economical person; farmer. —ie
[—'mi:], f. economy; agriculture;
domestic economy. —isch, adj.
economical.

Oktober [ok'to:bər], m. (—s) October.

Okulieren [oku'li:rən], v.a. to graft,
inoculate.

Öl [ø:l], n. (—s, pl. —e) oil. —en, v.a.
to oil; to anoint. —ig, adj. oily;
unctuous. —ung, f. oiling; lubrication; anointing; die letzte —ung,
extreme unction. —baum, m. olive-tree. —beere, f. olive. —berg, m.
Mount of Olives. —n, oil-painting. —gemälde, n. oil-painting.
—same(n), m. linseed. —zweig, m.
olive branch.

Olive [o'li:və], f. (pl. —n) olive.

Onkel ['ɔŋkəl], m. (—s, pl. —) uncle.

Oper ['o:pər], f. (pl. —n) opera; opera-house. —n=dichter, m. libretto-writer.
—n=glas, n., —n=gucker, m. opera-

glass. —n=sänger, m., —n=sängerin,
f. opera-singer.

Opfer ['ɔpfər], n. (—s, pl. —) offering,
sacrifice; victim. —er, m. (—ers,
pl. —er) sacrificer. —kasten, m.
poor-box. —n, v.a. & n. (aux. h.) to
sacrifice. —ung, f. offering, sacrifice.

Opt=ik ['ɔptɪk], f. optics. —iker, m.
(—ikers, pl. —iker), m. optician.
—isch, adj. optic(al).

Orakel [o'ra:kəl], n. (—s, pl. —)
oracle. —spruch, m. oracle, oracular
sentence.

Orange [o'rã:ʒə], f. (pl. —n) orange.
—n, adj. orange.

Orden ['ɔrdən], m. (—s, pl. —) order;
decoration. —tlich, adj. & adv.
orderly, regular; proper. —tlichkeit,
f. regularity, orderliness. —s=band,
n. ribbon of an order. —s=bruder,
m. member of an order.

Ordinär [ɔrdi'nɛ:r], adj. common,
ordinary, vulgar.

Ordn=en ['ɔrdnən], v.a. to arrange,
set in order. —er, m. (—ers, pl. —er)
regulator, arranger; director. —ung,
f. arrangement; order. —ungs=
gemäß, —ungs=mäßig, adj. & adv.
orderly, regular, according to order.
—ungs=los, adj. disorderly. —ungs=
widrig, adj. irregular. —ungs=zahl,
f. ordinal number.

Ordonnanz [ɔrdo'nants], f. (pl. —en)
order, general order; orderly. —reiter,
m. mounted orderly.

Organ [ɔr'ga:n], n. (—s, pl. —e) organ.
—isch, adj. organic.

Orgel ['ɔrgəl], f. (pl. —n) organ (Mus.).
—chor, m. organ-loft. —kasten, m.
organ-case. —pfeife, f. organ-pipe.
—spieler, m. organist. —stimme, f.
organ-stop. —treter, m. bellows-blower. —zug, m. organ-stop; row of
organ-pipes.

Orient—alisch [oriɛn'ta:lɪʃ], adj. oriental, eastern. —ieren [—'ti:rən], v. I.
a. to turn towards the east. II. r. to
learn how the land lies; ich kann mich
nicht —ieren, I have lost my bearings.
—ierung, f. orientation (of a church);
survey.

Orkan [ɔr'ka:n], m. (—s, pl. —e)
hurricane.

Ort [ɔrt], m. (—(e)s, pl. —e) place;
locality. —schaft, f. (inhabited) place;
district. —s=sender, m. local transmitter (Radio).

Örtlich ['örtlıç], adj. local.

Öse ['ö:zə], f. (pl. —n) shank of a button; eye (of needles, etc.).

Ost [ost], m. (—es) east. —en, m. (—ens) east, the east, orient. —wärts, adv. eastwards.

Oster ['o:stər], —n ['o:stərn], n. & f. pl. Easter. —abend, m. Easter eve. —ei, n. Easter egg.

Otter ['otər], f. (pl. —n) otter.

Ozean ['o:tsea:n], m. (—s, pl. —e) ocean.

P

P, p [pe:], n. P, p.

Paar [pa:r], I. adj. even; matching; used with ein as an ind. & indec. num. adj. ein being also indec., some, a few; man trifft dort immer ein — Leute, one always meets a few people there; ein — mal, several times. II. n. (—s, pl. —e) pair, couple. —weise, adv. by pairs, in couples. —en, v.a. to pair.

Pacht [paxt], f. (pl. —en), m. (—es, pl. —e), tenure, lease. —en, v.a. to take a lease of, to farm, rent. —lich, adj. & adv. on lease. —ung, f. taking on lease, farming. —bauer, m. tenant-farmer. —besitz, m. tenure on lease. —brief, —kontrakt, —vertrag, m. lease. —gut, n., —hof, m. farm, leasehold estate. —herr, m. landlord.

Pächter ['pεçtər], m. (—s, pl. —) farmer, tenant, lessee.

Pack [pak], I. m. (—e)s, pl. —e, Päcke; dim. Päckchen) packet, parcel; mit Sack und —, with all one's belongings. II. n. (—(e)s) rabble, pack. —en, m. (—ens, pl. —en) bale. —esel, m. pack-ass; (fig.) drudge, fag.

Pack—en ['pakən], v. I. a. to pack (up); to seize, grasp. II. r.; —' dich ! begone ! get away ! —end, adj. thrilling. —garn, n. pack-thread. —papier, n. wrapping paper. —träger, m. porter.

Paff [paf], m. (—s, pl. —e) bang, pop; ich bin ganz —, I am astounded.

Palast [pa'last], m. (—es, pl. Paläste) palace.

Palme ['palmə], f. (pl. —n) palm (-tree).

Panier [pa'ni:r], n. (—s, pl. —e) banner, standard.

Panne ['panə], f. (pl. —n) break-down (Motor.).

Panther ['pantər], m. (—s, pl. —) panther.

Pantoffel [pan'tofəl], m. (—s, pl. —) slipper.

Panzer ['pantsər], m. (—s, pl. —) coat of mail. —hemd, n. mail-shirt. —kreuzer, m. armoured cruiser. —zug, m. armoured train.

Päonie [pe'o:niə], f. (pl. —n) peony.

Papagei [papa'gaı], m. (—s, —en, pl. —en) parrot.

Papier [pa'pi:r], n. (—s, pl. —e) paper. —en, adj. made of paper. —blatt, n., —bogen, m. sheet of paper. —geld, n. paper money. —händler, m. stationer.

Papp [pap], m. (—es, pl. —e), —e, f. paste; (geleimte) pasteboard. —arbeit, f. cardboard work. —band, n. (binding in) boards. —bogen, m. sheet of cardboard. —(en)=deckel, m. paste-board, millboard. —dose, f., —kasten, m., —schachtel, f. band-box; paste-board box. —en=stiel, m. trifle.

Pappel ['papəl], f. (pl. —n) poplar.

Papst [pa:pst], m. (—es, pl. Päpste) pope. —tum, n. (—tums) papacy.

Päpstlich ['pε:pstlıç], adj. papal.

Parad—e [pa'ra:də], f. (pl. —en) parade. —ieren [—'di:rən], v.n. (aux. h.) to parade. —e=anzug, m. full dress, review order. —e=aufzug, m. review. —e=marsch, m. march past. —schritt, m. drill step.

Paradies [para'di:s], n. (—(f)es, pl. —(f)e) paradise. —(f)isch, adj. heavenly; delightful.

Pardon [par'dõ], m. (—s, pl. —s) pardon; quarter.

Parfüm [par'fy:m], n. (—(e)s, pl. —e) perfume. —ieren [—'mi:rən], v.a. to perfume, scent.

Parier—en [pa'ri:rən], v.a. & n. (aux. h.) to parry. —ung, f. parrying.

Park [park], m. (—(e)s, pl. —e) park. —anlagen, pl. pleasure-grounds.

Parkett [par'kεt], n. (—(e)s, pl. —e) inlaid floor; stalls (theatre).

Parlament [parla'mεnt], n. (—(e)s, pl. —e) parliament. —arisch, adj. parliamentary.

Parodie [paro'di:], f. (pl. —n) parody.

Parole [pa'ro:lə], f. (pl. —n) parole; watchword.

Partei [par'taı], f. (pl. —en) party. —isch, —lich, adj. partial, biased.

—lichteit, f. partiality, bias. **—los,** adj. impartial.

Parterre [par'tɛrə], n. (**—s,** pl. **—s**) ground-floor; pit (theatre).

Partie [par'ti:], f. (pl. **—en**) parcel, lot; game (of whist, etc.); **eine glänzende — machen,** to make a brilliant match or marriage.

Partitur [parti'tu:r], f. (pl. **—en**) score (Mus.).

Parzelle [par'tsɛlə], f. (pl. **—n**) allotment.

Pascha ['paʃa:], m. (**—,** **—s,** pl. **—s**) pasha, pacha.

Paß [pas], m. (**—(f)es,** pl. **Päffe**) pace; pass, defile; passport. **—lich,** adj. & adv. fit, suitable, proper. **—brief,** m. passport; permit.

Passagier [pasa'ʒi:r], m. (**—s,** pl. **—e**) passenger.

Passatwind [pa'sa:tvɪnt], m. (**—s,** pl. **—e**) trade-wind.

Passen ['pasən], v. I. n. (aux. h.) to watch, wait for; to fit; to suit. II. r. to be fit, proper, suitable, convenient; **das paßt sich nicht,** that is not becoming; that is not done. III. a. to adapt; to fit on. **—d,** p. & adj. fit, fitting, suitable.

Passieren [pa'si:rən], v.n. (aux. f.) to pass.

Past—e ['pastə], f. (pl. **—en**) paste. **—etchen,** n. patty, little pasty. **—ete** [—'te:tə], f. (pl. **—eten**) pie.

Pastor [pas'to:r], m. (**—s,** pl. **—en**) pastor, clergyman. **—at** [—'ra:t], n. (**—ats,** pl. **—ate**) incumbency. **—in,** f. clergyman's wife.

Pat—e ['pa:tə], m. (**—en,** pl. **—en**), **—e, —in,** f. godparent. **—enkind,** n. godchild.

Patent [pa'tɛnt], n. (**—s,** pl. **—e**) letters patent. **—amt,** n. patent office.

Patri—archalisch [patrɪar'ça:lɪʃ], adj. patriarchal. **—ot** [patrɪ'o:t], m. (**—oten,** pl. **—oten**) patriot. **—otisch,** adj. & adv. patriotic.

Patrone [pa'tro:nə], f. (pl. **—n**) cartridge.

Patsch—en ['patʃən], v.n. (aux. h. & f.) to slap, smack; to splash. **—füßig,** adj. web-footed.

Patzig ['patsɪç], adj. insolent, pert, saucy.

Pauke ['paukə], f. (pl. **—n**) kettledrum.

Paus—e ['pauzə], f. (pl. **—en**) pause.

—ieren [—'zi:rən], v.n. (aux. h.) to pause. **—papier,** n. tracing-paper.

Pavian ['pa:via:n], m. (**—s,** pl. **—e**) baboon.

Pech [pɛç], n. (**—es**) pitch; **er hat —,** he has bad luck. **—draht,** m. cobbler's thread, waxed end. **—finster,** adj. pitch-dark.

Pedant [pe'dant], m. (**—en,** pl. **—en**) pedant. **—isch,** adj. pedantic.

Peil—en ['parlən], v.a. to gauge, measure; to take bearings (Naut.). **—er,** m. direction-finder (Radio).

Pein [parn], f. pain, agony, torture. **—igen,** v.a. to torture. **—iger,** m. (**—igers,** pl. **—iger**) torturer. **—igung,** f. tormenting; torment. **—lich,** adj. painful, distressing. **—lichteit,** f. painfulness; minute exactness.

Peitsche ['partʃə], f. (pl. **—n**) whip. **—n,** v.a. to (horse)whip. **—nhieb,** m. lash with a whip.

Pelikan ['pe:lika:n], m. (**—s,** pl. **—e**) pelican.

Pell—e ['pɛlə], f. (pl. **—n**) skin, peel. **—kartoffeln,** f. pl. potatoes in their jackets.

Pelz [pɛlts], m. (**—es,** pl. **—e**) pelt, fur. **—en,** adj. furred, fur. **—ig,** adj. furry. **—futter,** n. fur lining. **—mantel,** m. fur coat.

Pendel ['pɛndəl], n. & m. (**—s,** pl. **—**) pendulum.

Pension [pãsɪ'o:n], f. (pl. **—en**) boarding-house. **—är** [—'nɛ:r], m. (**—ärs,** pl. **—äre**) pensioner; boarder. **—at** [—'na:t], n. (**—ats,** pl. **—ate**) boarding-school. **—ieren** [—'ni:rən], v.a. to put on half-pay, pension (off). **—ierte(r),** m. pensioner. **—ierung,** f. pensioning off, superannuation.

Pensum ['pɛnzum], n. (**—s,** pl. **Pensa**) task, lesson.

Perfekt [per'fɛkt], I. adj. perfect. II. n. (**—s,** pl. **—e**), **—um,** n. (**—ums,** pl. **—a**) perfect tense.

Pergament [pɛrga'mɛnt], n. (**—(e)s,** pl. **—e**) parchment.

Period—e [peri'o:də], f. (pl. **—en**) period. **—isch,** adj. & adv. periodic(al).

Perl—chen ['pɛrlçən], n. (**—chens,** pl. **—chen**) little pearl or bubble. **—e,** f. (pl. **—en**) pearl. **—en,** v.n. (aux. h.) to sparkle, glisten. **—en, —ig,** adj. of pearl, pearly. **—enschnur,** f. string of pearls. **—huhn,** n. guinea-fowl. **—mutter,** f. mother-of-pearl.

Person [per'zo:n], f. (pl. —en) person. **—al** [—'na:l], n. (—s) staff, employees. **—alien**, f. personalities.
Persönlich [per'zø:nlıç], I. adj. personal. II. adv. in person, personally. **—keit**, f. personality.
Perücke [pe'rʏkə], f. (pl. —n) wig.
Pest [pɛst], f. (pl. —en) plague; **daß dich die** —! plague on you! **—ilenz** [—i'lɛnts], f. (pl. —ilenzen) pestilence.
Petersilie [pe:tər'zi:liə], f. parsley.
Petroleum [pe'tro:leum], n. (—s) petroleum.
Petschaft ['pɛtʃaft], n. (—s, pl. —e) seal, signet.
Pfad [pfa:t], m. (—es, pl. —e) path. **—finder**, m. pathfinder, boy scout.
Pfaff [pfaf], m. (—en, pl. —en), **—e**, m. (—en, pl. —en) priest; parson. **—entum**, n. clericalism.
Pfahl [pfa:l], m. (—s, Pfähle) stake, post. **—bau**, m. pile-work. **—bauten**, m.pl. lake-dwellings.
Pfalz [pfalts], f. Palatinate. **—graf**, m. Count-Palatine, Palsgrave. **—gräfin**, f. Palsgravine.
Pfand [pfant], n. (—es, pl. Pfänder) pledge; pawn. **—bar**, adj. that can be pledged. **—belastung**, f. mortgage. **—brief**, m. (deed of) mortgage. **—gläubiger**, m. mortgagee. **—gut**, n. lands given in mortgage. **—leiher**, m. pawnbroker. **—schein**, m. pawnticket.
Pfänd—en ['pfɛndən], v.a.; **einen um eine S. —en**, to seize, distrain something from someone; **eine S. —en**, to take in pledge. **—erspiel**, n. game of forfeits. **—lich**, adj. & adv. as a pledge. **—ung**, f. distraint.
Pfann—e ['pfanə], f. (pl. —en) pan. **—kuchen**, m. pancake.
Pfarr—e ['pfarə], f. (pl. —en) pastorate; living; parsonage. **—er**, m. (—ers, —er) clergyman. **—erin**, f. parson's wife. **—amt**, n. incumbency, pastorate. **—haus**, n. rectory, vicarage.
Pfau [pfau], m. (—(e)s, —en, pl. —en) peacock.
Pfeffer ['pfɛfər], m. (—s, pl. —) pepper. **—büchse**, f. pepper-caster. **—gurke**, f. gherkin. **—kuchen**, m. ginger-bread; spice-cake. **—minz(e)**, f. peppermint. **—minz-küchelchen**, n. peppermint (lozenge). **—n**, v.a. to pepper.

Pfeif—e ['pfaifə], f. (pl. —n) pipe, tube; (Quer—) fife; whistle. **—en**, ir.r.a. & n. (aux. h.) to pipe; to whistle. **—er**, m. (—ers, pl. —er) piper, fife-player; whistler.
Pfeil [pfail], m. (—s, pl. —e) arrow. **—eisen**, n. arrow-head. **—feder**, f. feather of an arrow. **—förmig**, adj. arrow-shaped. **—gerade**, adj. straight as a bolt. **—geschwind**, I. adj. (as) swift as an arrow. II. adv. rapidly. **—köcher**, m. quiver.
Pfeiler ['pfailər], m. (—s, pl. —) pillar.
Pfennig ['pfɛnıç], m. (—s, pl. —e, —) the one-hundredth part of a mark.
Pferd [pfert], n. (—es, pl. —e) horse. **—chen**, n. (—chens, pl. —chen) pony. **—earzt**, m. veterinary surgeon. **—ebahn**, f. tramway. **—ebeschlag**, m. horse-shoeing; horse-shoes. **—efuß**, m. club-foot; (fig.) cloven hoof. **—egeschirr**, n. harness. **—egurt**, m. horse-girth. **—ekraft**, f. horsepower. **—erennen**, n. horse-race; horse-racing. **—estall**, m. stable. **—ezucht**, f. breeding of horses.
Pfiff [pfıf], m. (—es, pl. —e) whistle. **—ig**, adj. & adv. sly. **—igkeit**, f. artfulness, craftiness.
Pfingst—en ['pfıŋstən], n. (—ens, —en) Whitsuntide.
Pfirsich ['pfırzıç], m. (—s, pl. —e) & f. (pl. —e), —e, f. peach.
Pflanz—e ['pflantsə], f. (pl. —en) plant. **—lich**, adj. vegetable. **—enkost**, f. vegetarian diet. **—enlehre**, f. botany. **—enwelt**, f. vegetable kingdom, flora. **—en**, v.a. to plant. **—er**, m. (—ers, pl. —er) planter. **—ung**, f. plantation.
Pflaster ['pflastər], n. (—s, pl. —) plaster; pavement. **—stein**, m. paving-stone.
Pflaume ['pflaumə], f. (pl. —n) plum.
Pfleg—e ['pfle:gə], f. care; rearing. **—en**, reg. & ir. v. I. a. (pflegte, gepflegt) (aux. h.; gen. & acc.) to tend, nurse, take care of. II. n. (pflegte, gepflegt) to be accustomed to, to be wont. **—er**, m. (—ers, pl. —er), **—erin**, f. nurse; benefactor; guardian. **—eamt**, n. guardianship. **—ebruder**, m. foster-brother. **—eeltern**, pl. foster-parents. **—ehaus**, n. hospital. **—ekind**, n. foster-child. **—emutter**, f. foster-mother; nurse.

—e=ſchweſter, f. foster-sister. —e=
vater, m. foster-father.

Pflicht [pflɪçt], f. (pl. —en) duty.
—frei, adj. free from obligation.
—gefühl, n. sense of duty. —gemäß,
adj. & adv. as in duty bound. —=
vergeſſen, adj. disloyal. —leiſtung,
f. performance of duty.

Pflücken ['pflʏkən], v.a. to pluck.

Pflug [pfluːk], m. (—es, pl. Pflüge)
plough.

Pflügen ['pflyːgən], v.a. & n. (aux. h.)
to plough.

Pfört—chen ['pfœrtçɔn], n. (—chens,
pl. —chen) little door; wicket-gate.
—ner, m. (—ners, pl. —ner) porter.

Pfort—e ['pfɔrtə], f. (pl. —en) gate,
door.

Pfoſte ['pfɔstə], f. (pl. —n), —n, m.
(—ns, pl. —n) post.

Pfote ['pfoːtə], f. (pl. —n; dim.
Pfötchen n.) paw.

Pfriem [pfriːm], m. (—s, pl. —e),
f. (pl. —en), —en, m. (—ens, pl. —en)
awl. —en, v.a. to punch; to bore.

Pfropf [pfrɔpf], m., —en, m. (—ens,
—en) cork; bung. —en, v.a. to
cork; to plug. —(en)=zieher, m. corkscrew.

Pfründ—e ['pfrʏndə], f. (pl. —en)
benefice. —ner, m. (—ners, pl. —ner)
beneficiary. —gut, n. glebe lands.
—haus, n. parsonage, rectory.

Pfuhl [pfuːl], m. (—s, pl. —e) pool.

Pfühl [pfyːl], m. (& n.) (—s, pl. —e)
pillow.

Pfui! [pfui], int. fie! shame!

Pfund [pfʊnt], n. (—(e)s, pl. —e)
pound (weight); pound (sterling).
—weiſe, adj. by the pound.

Pfütze ['pfʏtsə], f. (pl. —n) puddle.

Phänomen [fɛno'meːn], n. (—s, pl. —e)
phenomenon.

Phant—aſie [fanta'ziː], f. (pl. —aſieen)
imagination. —aſt [—'tast], m.
(—aſten, pl. —aſten) visionary. —=
aſtiſch, adj. fanciful; fantastic.

Phariſä—er [farı'zɛːər], m. (—s, pl.
—) Pharisee. —iſch, adj. Pharisaical.

Philiſter [fi'lɪstər], m. (—s, pl. —)
Philistine; vulgarian.

Philolog [filo'loːk], m. (—en, pl. —en)
philologist.

Philoſoph [filo'zoːf], m. (—en, pl. —en)
philosopher. —ie [—zo'fiː], f. philosophy. —iſch, adj. philosophical.

Phiole [fi'oːlə], f. (pl. —n) phial.

Phosphor ['fɔsfɔr], m. (—s) phos-
phorus.

Photograph [foto'graːf], m. (—en, pl.
—en) photographer. —ie [—'fiː], f.
(pl. —ieen) photograph. —ieren
[—'fiːrən], v.a. to photograph. —iſch,
adj. photographic.

Phraſe ['fraːzə], f. (pl. —n) phrase.

Pick [pɪk], m. (—es, pl. —e) puncture.
—e, f. (pl. —en) pickaxe, pick. —en,
v.a. & n. (aux. h.) to peck; to pick.
—hacke, f. pickaxe.

Pickel ['pɪkəl], m. (—s, pl. —) pickaxe,
ice-axe; pimple. —flöte, f. piccolo.
—haube, f. spiked helmet.

Piep! [piːp], int. chirp! tweet! —(ſ)en,
v.n. (aux. h.) to peep, chirp,
cheep.

Piet—ät [pie'tɛːt], f. piety, reverence.
—iſt [—'tɪst], m. (—iſten, pl. —iſten)
pietist. —iſtiſch, adj. & adv. sancti-
monious.

Pik [piːk], m. (—s, pl. —s) pique;
spades (Cards); er hat einen — auf ſie,
he bears her a grudge. —ant [—'kant],
adj. piquant. —ieren [—'kiːrən],
v.a. to pique, annoy.

Pike ['piːkə], f. (pl. —n) pike.

Pilger ['pɪlgər], m. (—s, pl. —), —in,
f. pilgrim. —n, v.n. (aux. h. & ſ.) to
go on or make a pilgrimage; to
wander. —fahrt, f. pilgrimage.
—ſchar, f. troop of pilgrims. —taſche,
f. pilgrim's scrip.

Pille ['pɪlə], f. (pl. —n) pill.

Pilz [pɪlts], m. (—es, pl. —e) mushroom. —haft, —ig, adj. fungous.

Pinſcher ['pɪnʃər], m. (—s, pl. —)
English fox-terrier.

Pinſel ['pɪnzəl], m. (—s, pl. —) paint-
brush. —haft, —ig, adj. silly, stupid.
—n, v.a. & n. (aux. h.) to paint; to
daub.

Pirſch [pɪrʃ], f. hunting, deer-stalking.

Piſtole [pɪs'toːlə], f. (pl. —n) pistol.

Plack [plak], m. (—es, pl. —e), —en,
m. (—ens, pl. —en) patch, piece.

Plag—e ['plaːgə], f. (pl. —en) plague,
torment. —en, v.a. to vex, annoy.
—er, m. (—ers, pl. —er) vexer,
tormentor.

Plakat [pla'kaːt], n. (—es, pl. —e)
bill, placard.

Plan [plaːn], I. adj. & adv. plain. II.
m. (—s, pl. —e, Pläne) plane; plain;
plan, design. —los, adj. & adv.
planless, purposeless. —loſigkeit, f.

want of design *or* purpose. —**mäßig**, *adj.* systematical.

Planet [pla'ne:t], *m.* (—en, *pl.* —en) planet. —**arisch** [—'ta:rıʃ], *adj.* planetary. —**enbahn**, *f.* orbit of a planet. —**ensystem**, *n.* planetary system.

Plank—e ['plaŋkə], *f.* (*pl.* —en) plank, board. —**en**, *v.a.* to plank.

Plapper—haft ['plapərhaft], *adj.* talkative, babbling. —**maul**, *n.* chatterbox. —**n**, *v.a. & n.* (*aux.* h.) to babble.

Platsch [platʃ] *int.* splash! —**en**, *v.n.* (*aux.* h.) to splash.

Platt [plat], *adj. & adv.* flat, level; dull; vulgar; downright. —**heit**, *f.* flatness; insipidity. —**deutsch**, *adj. & n.* Low German.

Platte ['platə], *f.* (*pl.* —n) plate; disk; bald head. —**ndruck**, *m.* stereotyping.

¹**Platz** [plats], *m.* (—es, *pl.* **Plätze**) place; — **nehmen**, to take a seat; — **da!** make way there!

²**Platz**, *int.* smash, crack. —**regen**, *m.* sudden downpour of rain.

Platzen ['platsən], *v.n.* (*aux.* h.) to fall with a crash; (*aux.* f.) to burst, explode.

Plauder—er ['plaudərər], *m.* (—ers, *pl.* —er) gossip. —**haft**, *adj.* talkative, gossiping. —**haftigkeit**, *f.* loquacity. —**n**, *v.n.* (*aux.* h.) to babble, chatter; to gossip.

Pleb—ejer [ple'be:jər], *m.* (—ejers, *pl.* —ejer), —**ejerin**, *f.* plebeian.

Plombe ['plombə], *f.* (*pl.* —n) lead; filling (*for a tooth*).

Plötzlich ['plœtslıç], I. *adj.* sudden, abrupt. II. *adv.* all at once. —**keit**, *f.* suddenness, abruptness.

Pluderhosen ['plu:dərho:zən], *pl.* wide trousers, plus fours.

Plump [plump], I. *adj.* coarse; rude. II. *m.* (—es, *pl.* —e) heavy fall. —**heit**, *f.* coarseness, clumsiness; bluntness.

Plunder ['plundər], *m.* (—s) lumber, trash, rubbish. —**kammer**, *f.* lumberroom. —**kram**, *m.* litter, lumber. —**mann**, *m.* rag-man. —**markt**, *m.* rag-fair. —**wagen**, *m.* baggagewaggon.

Plünderer ['plyndərər], *m.* (—s, *pl.* —) plunderer.

Plünder—n ['plyndərn], *v.a.* to plunder, pillage. —**ung**, *f.* plundering.

Plüsch [ply:ʃ], *m.* (—es, *pl.* —e) plush.

Pöbel ['pø:bəl], *m.* (—s, *pl.* —) mob, rabble. —**haft**, *adj.* vulgar, plebeian.

Poch—en ['poxən], *v.a. & n.* (*aux.* h.) to knock; er —t auf sein Geld, he boasts of his money. —**er**, *m.* (—ers, *pl.* —er) knocker.

Pock—e ['pokə], *f.* (*pl.* —en) pock; die —en, small-pox.

Poesie [poe'zi:], *f.* (*pl.* —n) poetry.

Poet [po'e:t], *m.* (—en, *pl.* —en) poet. —**isch**, *adj.* poetic.

Pokal [po'ka:l], *m.* (—s, *pl.* —e) goblet.

Pökel ['pø:kəl], *m.* (—s) brine, pickle. —**n**, *v.a.* to pickle. —**fleisch**, *n.* corned beef. —**hering**, *m.* pickled herring.

Pol [po:l], *m.* (—s, *pl.* —e) pole. —**ar** [—'la:r], *adj.* polar. —(**ar**)=**kreis**, *m.* polar circle. —**ar=meer**, *n.* Arctic Ocean; südliches —**ar=meer**, Antarctic Ocean. —**ar=zone**, *f.* frigid zone. —**höhe**, *f.* latitude.

Polier—en [po'li:rən], *v.a.* to polish. —**er**, *m.* (—ers, *pl.* —er) polisher.

Politik [poli'ti:k], *f.* politics.

Polit—iker [po'li:tıkər], *m.* (—ikers, *pl.* —iker) politician. —**isch**, *adj. & adv.* political; politic.

Polizei [poli'tsaı], *f.* (*pl.* —en) police. —**lich**, *adj. & adv.* police. —**amt**, —**büro**, *n.* police-station. —**beamte(r)**, *m.* police-officer. —**behörde**, *f.* police (authorities). —**diener**, *m.* policeman. —**stunde**, *f.* closing hour for public-houses.

Polka ['polka], *f.* (*pl.* —s) polka.

Polster ['polstər], *n.* (—s, *pl.* —) cushion; bolster. —**n**, *v.a.* to stuff, pad.

Polter—er ['poltərər], *m.* (—ers, *pl.* —er) bully. —**n**, *v.n.* (*aux.* h. & f.) to make a noise by knocking things about. —**abend**, *m.* nuptial eve. —**geist**, *m.* hobgoblin. —**kammer**, *f.* lumber-room.

Pomp [pomp], *m.* (—s, *pl.* —e) pomp. —**haft**, *adj.* pompous, stately. —**ös** [—'pø:s], *adj.* splendid, magnificent.

Popul—är [popu'lɛ:r], *adj. & adv.* popular. —**arität** [—i'tɛ:t], *f.* popularity.

Porree ['pore:], *m.* (—s, *pl.* —s) leek.

Portion [portsi'o:n], *f.* (*pl.* —en) portion; zwei —en Tee, tea for two.

Porto ['porto:], *n.* (—s) postage; carriage. —**frei**, *adj.* post-free. —**frei=**

heit, f. exemption from postage.
—pflichtig, adj. subject to postage.
—fatz, m. rate of postage.
Porzellan [pɔrtsɛˈlaːn], n. (—s, pl. —e)
porcelain. —en, adj. porcelain,
china.
Pofaune [poˈzaʊnə], f. (pl. —n) trumpet.
Pose [ˈpoːzə], f. (pl. —n) pose.
Poff—e [ˈpɔsə], f. (pl. —en) jest.
—en=haft, adj. droll. —en=reitzer, m.
buffoon, jester. —en=spiel, —en=stüd,
n. farce. —ierlich [—siːrlɪç], adj. odd.
—ierlichkeit, f. comicalness.
Post [pɔst], f. (pl. —en) post-office;
post, mail; news. —en, m. (—ens,
pl. —en) post; picket. —amt, n.
post-office. —anweisung, f. money
order. —beförderung, f. postal
service. —bote, m. postman, letter-
carrier. —frei, adj. post-paid.
—gebühr, f. postal charge. —karte,
f. post-card; Ansichts —karte, pictorial post-card. —kasten, m. letter-
box. —lagernd, adj. poste restante.
—marke, f. postage stamp. —=
wendend, adv. by return of post.
Post—ament [pɔstaˈmɛnt], n. (—=
aments, pl. —amente) pedestal,
base. —ieren [ˈtiːrən], v.a. to post,
place. —illion [—ɪlˈjoːn], m. (—=
illions, pl. —illione) postilion.
Pottasche [poˈtaʃə], f. potash.
Pracht [praxt], f. pomp; splendour.
—ausgabe, f. luxury edition. —kerl,
m. splendid fellow. —liebend, adj.
fond of show. —los, adj. unostenta-
tious. —stüd, n. fine specimen.
—voll, adj. gorgeous, magnificent.
Prächtig [ˈprɛçtɪç], adj. & adv. magnificent, splendid.
Präg—en [ˈprɛːgən], v.a. to coin.
—er, m. (—ers, pl. —er) coiner,
stamper. —ung, f. stamping, coining.
Prahl—en [ˈpraːlən], v.n. (aux. h.) to
boast. —er, m. (—ers, pl. —er)
boaster. —erei [—əˈraɪ], f. brag,
boasting. —erisch, adj. boastful.
Prakt—isch [ˈpraktɪʃ], adj. & adv.
practical. —izieren [—tɪˈtsiːrən], v.a.
& n. (aux. h.) to practise.
Prälat [prɛˈlaːt], m. (—en, pl. —en)
prelate.
Prall [pral], I. adj. tight; chubby.
II. m. (—s, pl. —e) bounce. —en,
v.n. (aux. h. & f.) to rebound. —heit,
f. elasticity. —kraft, f. elasticity.

Prämie [ˈprɛmiə], f. (pl. —n) premium,
prize. —n=schein, m. premium bond.
Prangen [ˈpraŋən], v.n. (aux. h.) to
make a show.
Pranger [ˈpraŋər], m. (—s, pl. —)
pillory.
Präfident [prɛziˈdɛnt], m. (—en, pl.
—en) president, chairman.
Praffeln [ˈprasəln], v.n. (aux. h. & f.)
to crackle; —der Regen, pattering
rain.
Praffen [ˈprasən], v.n. (aux. h.) to live
in luxury; to feast.
Praxis [ˈpraksɪs], f. practice (Med.,
etc.).
Predig—en [ˈpreːdɪgən], v.a. & n.
(aux. h.) to preach. —er, m. (—ers,
pl. —er) preacher. —erin, (—er(s)=
frau,) f. pastor's wife. —t, f. (pl.
—ten) sermon.
Preis [praɪs], m. (—(f)es, pl. —(f)e)
price, cost, charge; reward, prize;
praise, glory; um keinen —, not for all
the world. —(f)en, ir.(& obs. reg.) v.a.
to praise, extol. —(f)er, m. (—(f)ers,
pl. —(f)er) praiser. —geben, ir.v.a. to
deliver up, abandon. —gebung, f.
surrender. —liste, f. priced catalogue.
—bewerber, m. competitor. —würdig, adj. praiseworthy.
Prell—en [ˈprɛlən], v.a. to cheat,
swindle. —er, m. (—ers, pl. —er)
cheat. —erei [—əˈraɪ], f. cheating.
Preß [prɛs], adj. & adv. tight, close-
fitting. —bar, adj. compressible.
Preff—e [ˈprɛsə], f. (pl. —en) press;
pressure; the Press. —freiheit, f.
liberty of the Press. —zwang, m.
suppression of the freedom of the
Press.
Preff—en [ˈprɛsən], v.a. to press;
to oppress. —ung, f. pressure,
pressing.
Prid—e [ˈprɪkə], f. (pl. —en) prick.
—el, m. (—els, pl. —el) prickle;
prickling. —elig, adj. prickly. —eln,
v.a. & n. (aux. h.) to prick; to sting.
—elnd, p. & adj. prickling; piquant.
Priefter [ˈpriːstər], m. (—s, pl. —)
priest. —in, f. priestess. —lich, adj.
sacerdotal, priestly. —tum, n.
priesthood.
Prim—a [ˈpriːmaː], f. (pl. —en) the
highest class of a school for boys.
—aner [—ˈmaːnər], m. (—aners, pl.
—aner) sixth-form boy.
Prinz [prɪnts], m. (—en, pl. —en)

prince. —**effin** [—'tsɛsɪn], f. princess. —**lich**, adj. & adv. princely.

Prinzip [prɪn'tsiːp], n. (—**s**, pl. —**e**, —**ien**) principle. —**al** [—'paːl], m. (—**als**, pl. —**ale**) principal, chief.

Priv—**at** [pri'vaːt], adj. & adv. private. —**at=dozent**, m. (—**at=dozenten**, pl. —**at=dozenten**) unsalaried lecturer. —**at=mann**, m. private person. —**at= recht**, n. civil law.

Prob—**e** ['proːbə], f. (pl. —**en**) trial, experiment; proof, test. —**e=abzug**, m. proof. —**e=blatt**, n., —**e=bogen**, m. proof-sheet.

Proben [proːbən], v.a. to mark; to rehearse.

Probieren [pro'biːrən], v.a. to try, test.

Problematisch [proble'maːtɪʃ], adj. problematic.

Produkt [pro'dʊkt], n. (—(e)**s**, pl. —**e**) produce; product. —**en=handel**, m. trade in home produce.

Profess—**or** [pro'fɛsɔr], m. (—**ors**, pl. —**oren**) professor. —**orin**, f. (Frau —) wife of a professor. —**ur** [—'suːr], f. professorship.

Profil [pro'fiːl], n. (—**s**, pl. —**e**) profile.

Profos [pro'foːs], m. (—(f)**es** or —(f)**en**, pl. —(f)**se** or —(f)**sen**) provost.

Programm [pro'gram], n. (—**s**, pl. —**e**) programme. —**mäßig**, adj. & adv. according to programme.

Prolog [pro'loːk], m. (—**s**, pl. —**e**) prologue.

Promenade [promə'naːdə], f. promenade.

Promovieren [promo'viːrən], v.a. to promote; to confer a doctor's degree on.

Proph—**et** [pro'feːt], m. (—**eten**, pl. —**eten**) prophet. —**etisch**, adj. prophetic. —**ezeien** [—e'tsaɪən], v.a. to prophesy. —**ezeiung**, f. prophecy.

Prosa ['proːzaː], f. prose.

Prosit! ['proːzɪt] **Prost!** int. your health! — **Neujahr!** a Happy New Year to you.

Protest [pro'tɛst], m. (—**es**, pl. —**e**) protest. —**ant** [—'tant], m. (—**anten**, pl. —**anten**) —**antin**, f. Protestant. —**antisch**, adj. Protestant. —**antismus** [—'tɪsmʊs], m. Protestantism. — **ieren** [—'tiːrən], v. I. n. (aux. h.) (gegen etwas) to protest, declare. II. a. to protest (a bill, etc.); einen **Wechsel** —**ieren lassen**, to have a bill protested.

Protokoll [proto'kɔl], n. (—**s**, pl. —**e**) record, minutes; zu — nehmen, to record.

Protz—**e** ['prɔtsə], f. (pl. —**en**) limber (Artil.). —**kasten**, m. ammunition-box.

Proviant [provi'ant], m. (—**s**) provisions. —**ieren** [—'tiːrən], v.a. to provision, victual. —**amt**, n. store-office, commissariat.

Provinz [pro'vɪnts], f. (pl. —**en**) province.

Prozent [pro'tsɛnt], n. (—**s**, pl. —**e**) per cent., percentage. —**ig**, adj. of or yielding a certain percentage.

Prozeß [pro'tsɛs], m. (—(ſſ)**es**, pl. —(ſſ)**e**) process, operation; proceedings; lawsuit; kurzen — machen mit, to make short work of.

Prüf—**en** ['pryːfən], v.a. to try, examine, prove. —**ung**, f. examination; proof; test.

Prügel ['pryːgəl], m. (—**s**, pl. —) cudgel, stick; thrashing. —**ei** [—'laɪ], f. beating; fight, row. —**n**, v.a. to cudgel, thrash.

Prunk [prʊnk], m. (—(e)**s**) pomp.

Prusten ['pruːstən], v.n. (aux. h.) to snort.

Psalm [psalm], m. (—(e)**s**, pl. —**en**) psalm.

Publik [pu'bliːk], adj. public.

Publikum ['puːblikʊm], n. (—**s**, pl. —**s**) the public.

Pudel ['puːdəl], m. (—**s**, pl. —) poodle. —**närrisch**, adj. playful; droll, funny. —**naß**, adj. drenched.

Puder ['puːdər], m. (—**s**, pl. —) powder (for the face).

Puff [pʊf], I. int. puff! bang! II. m. (—(e)**s**, pl. —**e**, **Püffe**) cuff, thump. —**er**, buffer (Railw.). —**spiel**, n. backgammon.

Puls [pʊls], m. (—(ſ)**es**, pl. —(ſ)**e**) pulse. —(ſ)**ieren** [—'ziːrən], v.n.(aux. h.) to pulsate. —**ader**, f. artery.

Pult [pʊlt], n. (—(e)**s**, pl. —**e**) desk.

Pulver ['pʊlvər], n. (—**s**, pl. —) powder; gunpowder. —**ig**, adj. powdery. —**n**, v.a. to pulverize.

Pump [pʊmp], I. int. bump! bounce! II. m. (—(e)**s**, pl. **Pümpe**) hollow sound; thump. —**e**, f. (pl. —**en**) pump. —**en**, v.a. & n. (aux. h.) to take on credit (sl.); to pump. —**er**, m.(—**ers**, pl. —**er**) pumper; borrower. —**er=nidel**, m. rye-bread.

Punkt [pʊnkt], m. (—(e)**s**, pl. —**e**)

point; — 2 Uhr, on the stroke of two. —um, n. (—ums, pl. —a) full stop; end.

Pünkt—lich ['pynktlıç], adj. punctual, precise, accurate. —lichkeit, f. punctuality.

Punsch [punʃ], m. (—es, pl. —e) punch. —napf, m., f. punch-bowl.

Pupille [pu'pılə], f. (pl. —n) ward; pupil (of the eye).

Pupp—e ['pupə], f. (pl. —en) doll. —enspiel, n. puppet-show.

Pur [pu:r], adj. pure, genuine; sheer (curiosity, etc.).

Purpur ['purpur], m. (—s) purple. —n, I. adj. purple. II. v.a. to dye purple.

Purzel—n ['purtsəln], v.n. (aux. ſ.) to fall (head over heels). —baum, m. somersault.

Pute ['pu:tə], f. (pl. —n) turkey-hen. —r, m. (—rs, pl. —r) turkey-cock. —(r)shahn, m. turkey-cock.

Putsch [putʃ], m. (—es, pl. —e) riot; unsuccessful insurrection.

Putz [puts], m. (—es) attire, dress; ornaments. —en, v.a. to clean; to adorn; ſich die Naſe —en, to wipe one's nose. —er, m. (—ers, pl. —er) cleaner; polisher. —händlerin, f. milliner. —käſtchen, n. dressing-case. —ſucht, f. passion for dress.

Pygmä—e [pyg'mɛ:ə], m. (—en, pl. —en pigmy. —iſch, adj. pigmy.

Pyramide [pyra'mi:də], f. (pl. —n) pyramid.

Q

Q, q [ku:], n. Q, q.

Quad—ſalber ['kvakzalbər], m. (—s ſalbers, pl. —ſalber) quack. —ſalberei [—ə'raı], f. quackery.

Quad—er ['kva:dər], m. (—ers, pl. —er) & f. (pl. —ern) hewn stone. —rat [—'dra:t], n. (—rats, pl. —rate) square. —ratiſch, adj. square, quadratic. —ratwurzel, f. square root. —rille [ka'drıljə], f. (pl. —rillen) quadrille.

Quak [kva:k], m. (—(e)s) croak; quack. —en, v.n. (aux. h.) to croak.

Qual [kva:l], f. (pl. —en) torment, torture. —voll, adj. full of anguish, distressing.

Quäl—en ['kvɛ:lən], v.a. to torture. —er, m. (—ers, pl. —er) tormentor.

—erei [—ə'raı], f. tormenting; vexation; persecution. —geiſt, m. tormentor, bore.

Qualm [kvalm], m. (—s) thick smoke; mist. —en, v. I. n. (aux. h.) to steam; to smoke. II. a. to puff out smoke. —ig, adj. steaming; smoky.

Quant—ität [kvanti'tɛ:t], f. (pl. —s itäten) quantity. —um ['kvantum], n. (—ums, pl. —a) quantity; portion.

Quarantäne [karã'tɛ:nə], f. quarantine.

Quark [kvark], m. (—(e)s) curds; trash, rubbish. —ig, adj. containing curds; dirty. —käſe, m. whey-cheese.

Quart—al [kvar'ta:l], n. (—s, pl. —e) quarter-day. —aner [—'ta:nər], m. (—aners, pl. —aner) third-form boy. —band, m. (—s, pl. —bände) quarto volume. —ett [—'tɛt], n. (—ett(e)s, pl. —ette) quartette.

Quartier [kvar'ti:r], n. (—s, pl. —e) quarters, lodging. —en, v.a. to quarter, billet. —meiſter, m. quartermaster.

Quarz [kva:rts], m. (—es, pl. —e) quartz.

Quaſt [kvast], m. (—es, pl. —e), —e, f. (pl. —en) tassel. —ig, adj. tasselled.

Quatember [kva'tɛmbər], m. (—s, pl. —) ember day.

Quatſch [kvatʃ], adj. silly, stupid. —en, v. I. n. (aux. h. & ſ.) to splash, flop; (aux. h.) to talk trash, bosh. II. a. to crush, squash. —topf, m. twaddler.

Quecke ['kvɛkə], f. (pl. —n) couch-grass. Queckſilber ['kvɛkzılbər], n. (—s) quicksilver, mercury. —n, adj. mercurial.

Quell—e ['kvɛlə], f. (pl. —en) spring; source. —en, ir.v.n. (aux. ſ. & h.) to spring, gush up; to issue, flow. —brunnen, m. fountain, well, spring.

Quer [kve:r], I. adj. transverse, oblique, diagonal. II. adv. athwart, across; crosswise; perversely; —durch, across; —über, over against. —e, f. diagonal; jemanden in die —e kommen, to thwart a person's design; geh' mir aus der —e! get out of my way! —flöte, f. German flute. —topf, m. odd fellow. —köpfig, adj. odd, cross-grained. —linie, f. diagonal. —ſattel, m. side-saddle.

Quetſch—en ['kvɛtʃən], v.a. to crush. —kartoffeln, pl. mashed potatoes.

Quiet [kvi:k], int. & m. (—es, pl. —e)

squeak. —en, —fen (coll.), v.n. (aux. h.) to squeak.

Quint—a ['kvɪnta], f. (pl. —en) fifth form in a school. —aner [—'ta:nər], m. (—aners, pl. —aner) scholar of the fifth class. —effenz, f. quintessence.

Quirl [kvɪrl], m. (—s, pl. —e) twirling-stick, whisk. —en, v.a. to twirl; to whisk.

Quitt [kvɪt], adj. (only used as predicate with gen.) quits, even; rid, free. —ieren [—'ti:rən], v.a. to receipt (an account); to quit, abandon. —ung, f. receipt.

Quitte ['kvɪtə], f. (pl. —n) quince. —nbrei, m. stewed quinces.

Quot—e ['kvo:tə], f. (pl. —en) quota, share. —ient [kvotsi'ɛnt], m. (—ienten, pl. —ienten) quotient. —ieren [—'ti:rən], v.a. to quote (prices).

R

R, r [ɛr], n. R, r.

Rabatt [ra'bat], m. (—(e)s) discount.

Rabbi ['rabi:], m. (—s, pl. —s), —ner [ra'bi:nər], m. (—s, pl. —) rabbi. —nifch, adj. rabbinical.

Rabe ['ra:bə], m. (—n, pl. —n) raven; weiffer —, rare bird. —neltern, pl. unnatural parents. —nftein, m. place of execution.

Rach—e ['raxə], f. revenge. —begier, —begierde, f., —durft, m., —luft, —fucht, f. revengefulness; vindictiveness.

Rachen ['raxən], m. (—s, pl. —) jaws (of beasts).

Räch—en ['rɛçən] (rarely ir.), v.a. to avenge, revenge. —er, m. (—ers, pl. —er) avenger. —erifch, adj. revengeful.

Racker ['rakər], m. (—s, pl. —) rogue.

Rad [ra:t], n. (—s, pl. Räder) wheel. —achfe, f. axle-tree. —arm, m. spoke of a wheel. —ebrechen, v.a. (insep.) to speak a language badly. —fahren, v.a. to cycle. —fahrer, m., —fahrerin, f. cyclist. —reif, m. tyre. —fchuh, m. brake. —fpeiche, f. spoke.

Radau [ra'dau], m. (—s) noise, row.

Rädelsführer ['rɛ:dəlsfy:rər], m. ring-leader.

Radier—en [ra'di:rən], v.a. to etch; to erase. —ung, f. etching.

Rad—ies [ra'di:s], n. (—iefes, pl. —iefe), —ieschen, n. radish.

Radikal [radi'ka:l], adj. & adv. radical.

Radio ['ra:dio:], n. (—s, pl. —s) wireless, radio.

Raff—en ['rafən], v. I. a. to snatch away, gather up. II. n. (aux. h.) to snatch at (nach).

Raffin—ade [rafi'na:də], f. refined sugar. —ieren [—'ni:rən], v.a. (aux. h.) to refine. —iert, adj. refined; cunning (fig.).

1Rahm [ra:m], m. (—s) cream. —en, v.a. to skim.

2Rahm, m. (—s) soot, dirt.

Rahmen ['ra:mən], I. m. (—s, pl. —) frame (picture-, window-, embroidery-, etc.). II. v.a. to frame.

Rain [rain], m. (—s, pl. —e) ridge (between two fields); limit. —weide, f. privet.

Rakete [ra'ke:tə], f. (pl. n) rocket.

Rakett [ra'kɛt], n. (—s, pl. —s) racket.

Ramm—eln ['raməln], v.a. to ram in. —er, m. (—ers, pl. —er) rammer.

Rampe ['rampə], f. perron; ascent. —nlichter, pl. footlights (Theat.).

Ramfch [ramʃ], m. (—es, pl. —e) job goods; (pl.) refuse; im — kaufen, to buy in the lump or in lots.

Rand [rant], m. (—es, pl. Ränder) edge, brink; am — des Verderbens, on the verge of ruin.

Rang [raŋ], m. (—(e)s, pl. Ränge) row, tier; grade; rank; erfter —, dress circle (Theat.). —mäßig, adj. & adv. according to rank. —ordnung, f. order of precedence.

Rangieren [rã'ʒi:rən], v.a. to arrange.

Rant [raŋk], I. adj. winding; slender. II. m. (—es, usually in the pl. Ränke) crookedness; trick, wile. —e, f. (pl. —en) tendril. —en, v.r. & n. (aux. h. & f.) to creep, to climb. —ig, adj. having tendrils. —engewächs, n. creeper, climber.

Ranzen ['rantsən], m. (—s, pl. —), Ränzel ['rɛntsəl], or Ränzlein, n. (—s, pl. —) knapsack.

Rappe ['rapə], m. (—n, pl. —n) black horse.

Rappel ['rapəl], m. (—s, pl. —) fit of madness; crazy idea.

Raps [raps], m. (—(f)es, pl. —(f)e) rape-seed.

Rar [ra:r], adj. rare, scarce. —ität [—i'tɛ:t], f. rarity; curiosity.

Rasch [raʃ], adj. quick, swift. —eln, v.n. (aux. h.) to rustle. —heit, f. quickness.

1Rasen [ˈraːzən], v. I. n. (aux. h.) to rave, rage; to be mad. II. a. to do or say in fury. —end, adj. & adv. raving. —erei [—əˈraɪ], f. rage, frenzy.

2Rasen, m. (—ens, pl. —en) turf, sward. —ig, adj. grassy.

Rasieren [raˈziːrən], v.a. to shave. —messer, n. razor.

Raspel [ˈraspəl], f. (pl. —n) rasp.

Rasse [ˈrasə], f. (pl. —n) race, breed.

Rast [rast], f. (pl. —en) rest. —en, v.a. & n. (aux. h.) to rest. —los, adj. restless.

Rat [raːt], m. (—(e)s, pl. Ratschläge; Beratschlagungen) counsel, advice; (pl. Ratsversammlungen) senate, council; (pl. Räte) councillor, counsellor; (pl. Ratsherrn, rarely Räte) alderman, senator; — schaffen, to devise means.

Raten [ˈraːtən], ir.v.a. & n. (aux. h.) to counsel, advise; to guess, conjecture. —sam, adj. & adv. advisable, expedient. —samkeit, f. expediency. —geber, m. adviser. —haus, n. townhall, guildhall. —los, adj. unadvised; perplexed. —schlag, m. advice. —schlagen, v.n. (aux. h.) (insep.) to deliberate. —schluß, m. resolution.

Rätin [ˈrɛːtɪn], f. counsellor's wife.

Ration [ratsɪˈoːn], f. (pl. —en) ration, portion.

Rational [ratsɪoˈnaːl], adj. rational. —ismus [—ˈnɪsmus], m. rationalism. —istisch [—ˈlɪstɪʃ], adj. rationalistic.

Rätsel [ˈrɛːtsəl], n. (—s, pl. —) riddle. —haft, adj. & adv. enigmatical.

Ratte [ˈratə], f. (pl. —n) rat. —enfänger, m. rat-catcher.

Raub [raʊp], m. (—(e)s) robbery; booty. —en, v.a. to rob, steal. —begierig, adj. rapacious. —ritter, m. robber-knight. —sucht, f. rapacity. —süchtig, adj. rapacious. —tier, n. beast of prey. —vogel, m. bird of prey.

Räuber [ˈrɔybər], m. (—s, pl. —) robber. —haft, —isch, adj. & adv. thievish; rapacious.

Rauch [raʊx], m. (—(e)s) smoke. —en, v.n. (aux. h.) to smoke. —er, m. (—ers, pl. —er) smoker. —fang, m. chimney, flue.

Räucher—n [ˈrɔyçərn], I. v.a. to fumigate; to smoke-dry; geräucherte Heringe, smoked herrings, bloaters. II. v.n. (aux. h.) to burn incense. III. subst.n. curing; burning of incense. —ung, f. fumigation; smoking.

Räud—e [ˈrɔydə], f. scab, mange. —ig, adj. scabby; mangy.

Rauf—en [ˈraʊfən], v.a. to pluck, tear out. —er, m. (—ers, pl. —er) brawler. —erei [—əˈraɪ], f. scuffle. —bold, m. (—bold(e)s, pl. bolde) bully.

Rauh [raʊ], adj. & adv. rough. —(h)eit, f. roughness; rudeness.

Raum [raʊm], m. (—s, pl. Räume) room, space. —lehre, f. geometry.

Räum—en [ˈrɔymən], v.a. to clear away; to evacuate. —ig, adj. spacious. —ung, f. removing, removal.

Raunen [ˈraʊnən], v.a. & n. (aux. h.) to whisper.

Raupe [ˈraʊpə], f. (pl. —n) caterpillar.

Rausch [raʊʃ], m. (—es, pl. Räusche) intoxication. —en, v.n. (aux. h.) to rush; to rustle. —end, p. & adj. rustling. —gold, n. tinsel.

Räuspern [ˈrɔyspərn], v.r. & (rarely) n. (aux. h.) to clear the throat.

Raute [ˈraʊtə], f. rue (Bot.).

Real [reˈaːl], I. adj. real, substantial. II. n. (—s, pl. —e) reality. —schule, f. non-classical secondary school.

Reb—e [ˈreːbə], f. (pl. —en) vine. —en=stock, m. vine. —huhn, n. partridge.

Rechen [ˈrɛçən], I. m. (—s, pl. —) rake. II. v.a. to rake.

Rechen—fehler [ˈrɛçənfɛːlər], m. miscalculation. —schaft [—ʃaft], f. reckoning, account.

Rechn—en [ˈrɛçnən], v.a. & n. (aux. h.) to count. —er, m. (—ers, pl. —er) reckoner, arithmetician.

Rechnung [ˈrɛçnʊŋ], f. calculation; account; bill; eine — ausgleichen, to strike a balance. —s=art, f. method of calculation. —s=artikel, m. item. —s=betrag, m. sum total of an account. —s=prüfer, m. auditor, controller.

Recht [rɛçt], I. adj. & adv. right; mir ist es —, I don't mind, it suits me; —e Seite, right side. II. n. (—es, pl. —e) right; law; justice; taxes, duties. —e, f. the right hand; right side. —lich, adj. & adv. just. —lich= keit, f. legality. —s, on the right hand; to the right. —**ecfig**, *adj.* rectangular. —**fertigung**, *f.* justification. —**gläubig**, *adj.* orthodox. —**gläubigkeit**, *f.* orthodoxy. —**linig**, *adj.* rectilinear. —**mäßig**, *adj.* legal, legitimate; just. —**mäßigkeit**, *f.* legality; legitimacy. —**fchaffen**, *adj.* upright, honest. —**zeitig**, *adj.* & *adv.* opportune, seasonable.

Rechts [rɛçts] (*in comp.*) —**amt**, *n.* court of justice. —**anwalt**, *m.* counsel, solicitor. —**fähig**, *adj.* competent. —**fähigkeit**, *f.* competence. —**gelehrte(r)**, *m.* lawyer, jurist. —**gemäß**, *adv.* according to law. —**weg**, *m.* course of law; **von —wegen**, by right.

Recf [rɛk], *n.* (—(e)s, *pl.* —e) horizontal bar (*Gymn.*).

Recfe [ˈrɛkə], *m.* (—n, *pl.* —n) renowned warrior.

Recfen [ˈrɛkən], *v.a.* to stretch.

Redaft—eur [redakˈtøːr], *m.* (—eurs, *pl.* —eure, —eurs) editor (*of a journal*). —**ion** [—tsiˈoːn], *f.* (*pl.* —ionen) editorship.

Red—e [ˈreːdə], *f.* (*pl.* —n) speech; **jemandem in die —e fallen**, to interrupt someone. —**en**, I. *v.a.* & *n.* (*aux.* h.) to speak. II. *subst.n.* talking; speech. —**end**, *p.* & *adj.* speaking; expressive. —**lich**, *adj.* & *adv.* honest; upright. —**lichkeit**, *f.* honesty. —**ebild**, *n.* figure of speech. —**efertig**, *adj.* of ready speech, of glib tongue. —**ensart**, *f.* expression, phrase; idiom. —**eweife**, *f.* manner of speech. —**felig**, *adj.* talkative. —**feligkeit**, *f.* loquacity.

Redner [ˈreːdnər], *m.* (—s, *pl.* —) orator; speaker. —**ifch**, *adj.* oratorical.

Reede [ˈreːdə], *f.* (*pl.* —n) roadstead.

Reed—en [ˈreːdən], *v.a.* to fit out ships. —**er**, *m.* (—ers, *pl.* —er) owner (*of a ship*).

Reform—ation [reformatsiˈoːn], *f.* (*pl.* —ationen) reformation. —**ierte(r)** [—ˈmiːrtə(r)], *m.* (—ierten, *pl.* —ierten)) member of the Reformed Church.

Rege [ˈreːgə], *adj.* astir; animated.

Regel [ˈreːgəl], *f.* (*pl.* —n) rule. —**n**, *v.a.* to regulate. —**los**, *adj.* without rule. —**losigkeit**, *f.* irregularity. —**mäßig**, *adj.* regular. —**mäßigkeit**, *f.* regularity. —**recht**, *adj.* normal; orderly; correct. —**widrig**, *adj.* irregular.

Reg—en [ˈreːgən], *v.a.* to move, stir. —**fam**, *adj.* & *adv.* active, nimble, brisk. —**famkeit**, *f.* agility, activity. —**ung**, *f.* motion.

Regen [ˈreːgən], *m.* (—s) rain. —**bogen**, *m.* rainbow. —**bogenhaut**, *f.* iris (*Anat.*). —**mantel**, *m.* mackintosh. —**fchirm**, *m.* umbrella.

Reg—ent [reˈgɛnt], *m.* (—enten, *pl.* —enten) ruler; sovereign. —**ieren** [—ˈgiːrən], *v.* I. *a.* to govern, rule. II. *n.* (*aux.* h.) to reign. —**ierung**, *f.* government.

Regiment [regiˈmɛnt], *n.* (—s, *pl.* —er) regiment (*of soldiers*). —**stapelle**, —**smufif**, *f.* regimental band.

Regn—en [ˈreːgnən], *v.a.* & *n.* (*aux.* h.) & *imp.* to rain. —**erifch**, *adj.* rainy.

Regulierung [reguˈliːruŋ], *f.* adjustment (*Radio*).

Reh [reː], *n.* (—s, *pl.* —e) roe. —**bock**, *m.* roebuck.

Reib—en [ˈraɪbən], *ir.v.a.* to rub, to grate. —**eifen**, *n.* grater. —**ung**, *f.* rubbing; friction.

Reich [raɪç], I. *adj.* & *adv.* rich. II. *n.* (—(e)s, *pl.* —e) empire. —**lich**, *adj.* & *adv.* ample, copious, plentiful. —**lichkeit**, *f.* plentifulness, abundance. —**tum**, *m.* (—tums, *pl.* —tümer) riches, wealth.

Reich—en [ˈraɪçən], *v.* I. *a.* to reach. II. *n.* (*aux.* h.) to extend to; to suffice. —**weite**, *f.* range (*Radio*).

Reichs—banf [ˈraɪçsbaŋk], *f.* imperial bank. —**behörden**, *f.pl.* imperial authorities. —**folge**, *f.* imperial succession. —**land**, *n.* territory of the German Empire. —**tag**, *m.* Imperial Diet. —**verfaffung**, *f.* constitution of the empire.

¹**Reif** [raɪf], *adj.* ripe, mature. —**e**, *f.* maturity. —**en**, *v.n.* (*aux.* f.) to mature, ripen.

²**Reif**, *m.* (—(e)s, *pl.* —e) ring, circle.

Reigen [ˈraɪgən], *m.* (—s, *pl.* —) round dance.

Reih—e [ˈraɪə], *f.* (*pl.* —en) row, rank; **ich bin an der —e**, it is my turn; **in —' und Glied**, in rank and file. —**en**, *v.a.* to put in a row; to rank; to arrange. —**enfolge**, *f.* sequence. —**entanz**, *m.* round dance.

Reiher [ˈraɪər], *m.* (—s, *pl.* —) heron.

Reim [raɪm], *m.* (—s, *pl.* —e) rhyme. —**en**, *v.a.r.* & *n.* (*aux.* h.) to rhyme. —**er**, *m.* (—ers, *pl.* —er) rhymer, versifier. —**art**, f. kind of rhyme or verse.

Rein [raɪn], I. adj. clean, pure; —**er Gewinn**, net profit; **ins —e bringen**, to clear up; to settle; **ins —e ſchreiben**, to make a fair copy of. II. adv. quite, entirely. —**heit**, f. purity. —**lich**, adj. clean, cleanly; neat. —**lichkeit**, f. neatness, etc.

Reinig—en [ˈraɪnɪgən], v.a. to clean, cleanse. —**er**, m. (—**ers**, pl. —**er**) cleanser; refiner. —**ung**, f. purification.

¹**Reis** [raɪs], n. (—(ſ)**es**, pl. —(ſ)**er**) twig, sprig. —(ſ)**ig**, n. (—(ſ)**igs**) brushwood.

²**Reis**, m. (—(ſ)**es**) rice.

Reiſ—e [ˈraɪzə], f. (pl. —**en**) journey. —**en**, v.n. (aux. h. & ſ.) to travel, journey; **wir —en über**, we go via. —**end**, p. & adj. itinerant. —**e-empfänger**, m. (—**s**, pl. —) portable set (Radio).

Reiß—en [ˈraɪsən], I. ir.v.a. to tear, rend; to sketch; **Poſſen —en**, to play the fool. II. ir.v.n. (aux. ſ.) to burst, split. III. subst.n. bursting, rending. —**aus** [—ˈsaʊs], n. (—**es**) flight; **das —aus nehmen**, to take to flight. —**end**, p., adj. & adv. rapid; impetuous; acute.

Reit—en [ˈraɪtən], ir.v. I. n. (aux. h. & ſ.) to ride. II. a. to ride. III. subst.n. riding. —**end**, p. & adj. mounted. —**er**, m. (—**ers**, pl. —**er**) rider, horseman. —**erei** [—əˈraɪ], f. cavalry. —**erin**, f. horsewoman. —**lings**, adv. astride. —**anzug**, m. riding-habit or dress. —**bahn**, f. riding-school. —**gerte**, f. riding-whip. —**knecht**, m. groom. —**kunſt**, f. horsemanship.

Reiz [raɪts], m. (—**es**, pl. —**e**) charm, grace; attractiveness. —**bar**, adj. sensitive, susceptible. —**barkeit**, f. susceptibility; irritability.

Reiz—en [ˈraɪtsən], v.a. to excite; to charm. —**end**, p. & adj. charming; tempting; stimulative. —**ung**, f. irritation; provocation. —**fähigkeit**, f. susceptibility. —**los**, adj. unattractive. —**loſigkeit**, f. unattractiveness. —**mittel**, n. stimulant; stimulus. —**voll**, adj. charming, attractive.

Reklam—e [reˈklaːmə], f. (pl. —**en**) advertisement. —**ieren** [—ˈmiːrən], v.a. to claim.

Rekrut [reˈkruːt], m. (—**en**, pl. —**en**) recruit. —**ieren** [—ˈtiːrən], v.a. & n. (aux. h.) to recruit. —**ierung**, f. recruiting.

Rekt—or [ˈrektor], m. (—**ors**, pl. —**oren** [—ˈtoːrən]) rector (of a university).

Relig—ion [reliɡiˈoːn], f. (pl. —**ionen**) religion. —**iös** [—ˈiˈøːs], adj. religious.

Reliquie [reˈliːkviə], f. (pl. —**n**) relic.

Rendant [renˈdant], m. (—**en**, pl. —**en**) accountant.

Renegat [reneˈɡaːt], m. (—**en**, pl. —**en**) renegade.

Renken [ˈrɛŋkən], v.a. to twist, wrench.

Renn—en [ˈrɛnən], I. ir.v.n. (aux. h. & ſ.) to run; to race; **um die Wette —en**, to run a race. II. subst.n. race. —**bahn**, f. race-course.

Renntier [ˈrɛntiːr], n. (—(**e**)**s**, pl.—**e**) reindeer.

Renomm—ieren [renoˈmiːrən], v.n. (aux. h.) to boast; to swagger. —**iert**, p.p. & adj. renowned.

Rent—abel [renˈtaːbəl], adj. profitable, lucrative. —**abilität** [—ˈtɛːt], f. profitableness. —**bar**, adj. yielding rent or revenue. —**e**, f. (pl. —**en**) rent; income. —**en**, —**ieren** [—ˈtiːrən], v.n. (aux. h.) to yield a revenue. —**ner**, m. (—**ners**, pl. —**ner**), —**nerin**, f. capitalist. —**enhaber**, m. annuitant. —**kammer**, f. board of revenue.

Repet—ieren [repeˈtiːrən], v.a. & n. (aux. h.) to repeat. —**ieruhr**, f. repeater (watch, etc.).

Represſalien [reprɛˈsaːliən], pl. reprisals.

Reps [rɛps], m. (—(ſ)**es**, pl. —(ſ)**e**), (—**kohl**, m.) rape (Bot.).

Reptil [repˈtiːl], n. (—**s**, pl. —**e** or —**ien**) reptile.

Republik [repuˈbliːk], f. (pl. —**en**) republic. —**aner** [—ˈkaːnər], m. (—**aners**, pl. —**aner**) republican. —**aniſch**, adj. republican.

Reſeda [reˈzeːda], **Reſede**, f. (pl. **Reſeden**) mignonette.

Reſerv—e [reˈzɛrvə], f. (pl. —**en**) reserve. —**ieren** [—ˈviːrən], v.a. to reserve. —**iſt** [—ˈvɪst], m. (—**iſten**, pl. —**iſten**) reservist.

Reſid—ent [reziˈdɛnt], m. (—**enten**, pl. —**enten**) resident. —**enz** [—ˈdɛnts], f. (pl. —**enzen**) seat of the court, capital. —**enzſtadt**, f. capital town.

—ieren [—'di:rən], v.n. (aux. h.) to reside.

Respekt [re'spɛkt], m. (—s) respect. —widrig, adj. disrespectful.

Ressort [rɛ'so:r], n. (—s, pl. —s) department.

Rest [rɛst], m. (—es, pl. —e) residue, remainder. —ant [—'tant], m. (—anten, pl. —anten) defaulter; (pl.) arrears. —bestand, m. remainder, remains, remnant. —los, I. adj. without a rest. II. adv. absolutely.

Result—ante [rezʊl'tantə], f. resultant. —at [—'ta:t], n. (—ats, pl. —ate) result.

Retraite [rə'trɛːtə], f. retreat; tattoo.

Rett—en ['rɛtən], v.a. to save, rescue. —er, m. (—ers, pl. —er) deliverer; saviour. —ung, f. saving; deliverance, rescue. —ungs=boot, n. lifeboat. —ungs=gürtel, m. life-belt. —ungs=los, adj. & adv. irremediable.

Rettich ['rɛtɪç], m. (—s, pl. —e) radish.

Reu—e ['rɔyə], f. repentance; regret; remorse. —en, v.a. & n. (aux. h.) & imp. to regret; to repent. —e=voll, —ig, adj. repentant.

Reverenz [reve'rɛnts], f. (pl. —en) reverence; bow.

Revier [re'vi:r], n. (—s, pl. —e) district.

Rezens—ent [retsɛn'zɛnt], m. (—enten, pl. —enten) critic.

Rezept [re'tsɛpt], n. (—s, pl. —e) receipt; recipe.

Rhabarber [ra'barbər], f. & m. (—s, pl. —) rhubarb.

Rheumat—isch [rɔy'ma:tɪʃ], adj. rheumatic. —ismus [—'tɪsmʊs], m. (pl. —ismen) rheumatism.

Rhinozeros [ri'no:tsərɔs], n. (—, pl. —(ſ)ſe) rhinoceros.

Rhythm—isch ['rytmɪʃ], adj. rhythmical. —us, m. (pl. —en) rhythm.

Richt—e ['rɪçtə], f. direction. —en, v. I. a. to set right, adjust, arrange; sich —en nach, to conform with. II. a. & n. (aux. h.) to judge. —er, m. (—ers, pl. —er) judge. —ung, f. direction; course; tendency. —= antenne, f. directive aerial (Radio). —saal, m. judgment-hall; court (of justice). —schnur, f. level; plumb-line. —wage, f. level.

Richtig ['rɪçtɪç], I. adj. & adv. right, accurate. II. int. & part. truly; right;

certainly, etc. —keit, f. correctness; accuracy.

Riech—en ['ri:çən], ir.v.a. & n. (aux. h.) to smell. —end, p. & adj. redolent.

Riegel ['ri:gəl], m. (—s, pl. —) bolt. —n, v.a. to bar, bolt.

Riemen ['ri:mən], m. (—s, pl. —) strap.

Riemer ['ri:mər], m. (—s, pl. —) saddler.

Ries—e ['ri:zə], m. (—en, pl. —en) giant. —in, f. giantess. —enhaft, —ig, adj. & adv. gigantic. —en= schlange, f. boa constrictor.

Riesel ['ri:zəl], m. (—s, pl. —) rippling; drizzling. —n, v.n. (aux. h. & ſ.) to ripple; to trickle; to drizzle.

Riff [rɪf], n. (—(e)s, pl. —e) reef, ridge.

Riffel ['rɪfəl], f. (pl. —n) flax-comb.

Rille ['rɪlə], f. (pl. —n) rill.

Rind [rɪnt], n. (—es, pl. —er) bullock. —er=braten, m. roast beef. —vieh, n. horned cattle.

Rinde ['rɪndə], f. (pl. —n) rind; bark of a tree; bread-crust.

Ring [rɪŋ], m. (—(e)s, pl. —e) ring. —el, m. (—els, pl. —el) ringlet, curl. —elig, adj. annular. —bahn, f. circular railway.

Ringeln ['rɪŋəln], v.a. to curl.

Ring—en ['rɪŋən], ir.v. I. n. (aux. h.) to struggle; to wrestle. II. a. to wring (one's hands, etc.). —er, m. (—ers, pl. —er) wrestler. —platz, m. wrestling-ground.

Rings [rɪŋs], adv. around, in a circle.

Rinn—e ['rɪnə], f. (pl. —en) gutter. —sal, n. (—sals, pl. —sale) channel. —stein, m. gutter; sink; sewer.

Rinnen ['rɪnən], ir.v.n. (aux. ſ.) to run, flow.

Ripp—e ['rɪpə], f. (pl. —en) rib. —ig, adj. ribbed. —en=fell=entzündung, f. pleurisy.

Ris—iko ['ri:ziko], n. (—itos, pl. —itos) risk. —(s)tieren [—'ki:rən], v.a. to risk.

Riß [rɪs], m. (—(ſ)es, pl. —(ſ)e) tearing; chink; gap; design, drawing. —(ſ)ig, adj. torn, rent.

Ritt [rɪt], m. (—(e)s, pl. —e) ride. —lings, adv. astride. —meister, m. cavalry captain.

Ritter ['rɪtər], m. (—s, pl. —) knight; zum — schlagen, to create a person a knight. —lich, adj. & adv. knightly, chivalrous; valiant. —lichkeit, f. gallantry, chivalry. —schaft, f.

knighthood; chivalry. —**gut,** *n.* estate, manor. —**kampf,** *m.* tournament. —**orden,** *m.* knightly order. —**sitte,** *f.* knightly custom. —**spiel,** *n.* tournament.

Ritus ['ri:tus], *m.* (—, *pl.* **Riten**) rite.

Ritz [rɪts], *m.* (—**es,** *pl.* —**e**), —**e,** *f.* (*pl.* —**en**) cleft. —**ig,** *adj.* cracked.

Ritz—en ['rɪtsən], *v.a.* to scratch. —**ung,** *f.* scratching; scratch.

Rizinusöl ['ri:tsinus'ø:l], *n.* (—**s,** *pl.* —**e**) castor-oil.

Robbe ['rɔbə], *f.* (*pl.* —**n**) seal. —**n= fell,** *n.* seal-skin.

¹**Roche** ['rɔxə], *m.* (—**n,** *pl.* —**n**), —**n,** *m.* (—**ns,** *pl.* —**n**) ray, thorn-back.

²**Roch—e,** *m.* (—**en,** *pl.* —**en**) castle, rook (*at chess*). —**en,** —**ieren** [—'ʃi:- rən], *v.n.* (*aux.* **h.**) to castle.

Röcheln ['rœçəln], I. *v.n.* (*aux.* **h.**) to have a rattling in the throat. II. *subst.n.* death-rattle.

Rod [rɔk], *m.* (—**(e)s.** *pl.* **Röde**) coat; skirt.

Roden ['rɔkən], *m.* (—**s,** *pl.* —) distaff.

Rodeln ['ro:dəln], *v.n.* to toboggan.

Roden ['ro:dən], *v.a.* & *n.* (*aux.* **h.**) to root out.

Rogen ['ro:gən], *m.* (—**s**) (hard) roe, spawn.

Roggen ['rɔgən], *m.* (—**s**) rye.

Roh [ro:], *adj.* & *adv.* raw; rough; rude. —**heit,** *f.* rawness; roughness; rudeness. —**material,** *n.,* —**stoff,** *m.,* raw material.

Rohr [ro:r], *n.* (—**s,** *pl.* —**e**) reed, cane; tube, pipe. —**ig,** *adj.* reedy. —**flöte,** *f.* reed pipe. —**huhn,** *n.* moor-hen, coot. —**post,** *f.* pneumatic post. —**stock,** *m.* cane; bamboo.

Röhr—e ['rø:rə], *f.* (*pl.* —**en**) pipe, tube. —**en=förmig,** *adj.* tubular.

Roll—e ['rɔlə], *f.* (*pl.* —**en**) roll; cylinder; part, rôle (*Theat.*); roller. —**baum,** *m.* windlass. —**brett,** *n.* mangling-board. —**en=welle,** *f.* roller. —**fuhrwerk,** *n.* truck; cart. —**wagen,** *m.* truck; go-cart.

Rollen ['rɔlən], *v.a.* & *n.* (*aux.* **h.** & **ſ.**) to roll; to revolve.

Roman [ro'ma:n], *m.* (—**s,** *pl.* —**e**) novel, work of fiction. —**haft,** *adj.* romantic. —**isch,** *adj.* Romance; Romanesque. —**tik,** *f.* romanticism. —**tiker,** *m.* (—**tikers,** *pl.* —**tiker**) romantic author. —**tisch,** *adj.* romantic. —**ze,** *f.* (*pl.* —**zen**) romance; ballad.

—**dichter,** —**schreiber,** *m.,* —**dichterin, schreiberin,** *f.* novelist.

Römer ['rø:mər], *m.* (—**s,** *pl.* —) Roman; drinking glass (*obs.*).

Ros—a ['ro:za:], *adj.* rose-coloured. —**e,** *f.* (*pl.* —**en;** *dim.* **Röschen**) rose. —**ig,** *adj.* rosy. —**en=busch,** *m.* rosebush, rose-tree. —**en=duft,** *m.* scent *or* fragrance of roses. —**en=farbig,** *adj.* rose-coloured. —**en=holder,** *m.* guelder-rose. —**en=holz,** *n.* rosewood. —**en=knospe,** *f.* rosebud. —**en=kranz,** *m.* garland of roses; rosary. —**en= kreuzer,** *m.* Rosicrucian. —**en= strauch,** *m.* rose-bush. —**en=strauß,** *m.* bunch of roses.

Rosine [ro'zi:nə], *f.* (*pl.* —**n**) raisin.

Rosmarin [rɔsma'ri:n], *m.* (—**s**) rosemary.

Roß [rɔs], *n.* (—**(ſſ)es,** *pl.* —**(ſſ)e**) steed, horse.

¹**Rost** [rɔst], *m.* (—**es,** *pl.* —**e**) gridiron.

²**Rost,** *m.* (—**es**) rust; blight. —**ig,** *adj.* rusty, rusted. —**en,** *v.n.* (*aux.* **h.** & **ſ.**) to rust.

Röst—en ['rɔstən], *v.a.* to roast; to toast (*bread*). —**ung,** *f.* roasting; frying.

Rot [ro:t], I.(*comp.* **röter,** *sup.* **rötest**), *adj.* red. II. *n.* (—**(e)s**) red; redness; rouge. —**auge,** *n.* roach (*Icht.*). —**äugig,** *adj.* red-eyed. —**bädig,** *adj.* ruddy. —**= bart,** *m.* red-beard; **Kaiser —bart,** Frederick Barbarossa (†*1190*). —**= blond,** *adj.* auburn. —**braun,** *adj.* bay (*horse*). —**fink,** *m.* chaffinch; bullfinch. —**gelb,** *adj.* orange. —**glühend,** *adj.* red-hot. —**haarig,** *adj.* red-haired. —**haut,** *f.* red-skin, red Indian. —**käppchen,** *n.* Little Red-Riding-Hood. —**kehlchen,** *n.* robin red-breast. —**kohl,** *m.,* —**kraut,** *n.* red cabbage. —**schimmel,** *m.* roan horse. —**Röt—e** ['rø:tə], *f.* redness; flush. —**lich,** *adj.* reddish. —**lich=blau,** *adj.* lilac. —**lich=gelb,** *adj.* buff. —**eln,** *f.pl.* German measles.

Rotte ['rɔtə], *f.* (*pl.* —**n**) troop, band. —**n,** *v.a.* & *r.* to troop, assemble together.

Rüb—e ['ry:bə], *f.* (*pl.* —**en**) rape; (**weiße**) turnip; **gelbe —e,** carrot; **rote —e,** beetroot. —**en=zucker,** *m.* beetroot-sugar.

Rubin [ru:'bi:n], *m.* (—**s,** *pl.* —**e**) ruby.

Ruchbar ['ru:xba:r], *adj.* notorious. —**keit,** *f.* notoriety.

Ruchlos ['ru:xlo:s], *adj.* impious, wicked; infamous. —(ſ)igkeit, *f.* infamy.

Ruck [ruk], *m.* (—(e)s, *pl.* —e) jolt, jerk. —weiſe, *adv.* by fits and starts.

Rück [ryk], *in compounds* = back. —lings, *adv.* from behind; backwards. —bewegung, *f.* retrograde movement. —bleibſel, *n.* residue, remainder. —blick, *m.* backward glance. —gang, *m.* back stroke (*C.L.*) decline. —gängig, *adj.* retrograde, retrogressive. —halt, *m.* restraint, reserve; support, prop. —halten, *v.a.* to keep back, reserve. —kehr, —kunft, *f.* return. —kehrend, *adj.* returning; homeward-bound (*ship*). —klang, *m.* reverberation, echo. —ſchlag, *m.* back stroke; recoil, rebound; reaction. —ſchritt, *m.* retrogression; relapse. —ſicht, *f.* consideration; notice; discretion. —ſichtlich, *adv. & prep.* (*with gen. or* auf) with regard to, considering. —ſichtnahme, *f.* respect, consideration. —ſichts, *adv. & prep.* (*with gen.*) with regard to. —ſichts=los, *adj.* regardless, inconsiderate. —ſichts=loſigkeit, *f.* want of consideration. —ſichts=voll, *adj.* considerate, thoughtful. —ſiß, *m.* back seat. —ſprache, *f.* conference. —ſprung, *m.* rebound. —ſtand, *m.* arrears. —ſtändig, *adj.* in arrears. —tritt, *m.* retreat; resignation (*of a post*). —wand, *f.* back wall. —wärts, *adv.* backward(s), back.

1Rücken ['rykən], *m.* (—s, *pl.* —) back. —mark, *m.* spinal marrow.

2Rücken, *v.* I. *a. & n.* to jerk, pull. II. *n.* (*aux.* h. & ſ.) to move, go along.

Rückgrat ['rykgra:t], *n.* (& *m.*) (—(e)s, *pl.* —e) backbone, spine. —s=tiere, *pl.* vertebrate animals.

Rucksack ['ruksak], *m.* (—s, *pl.* Rucksäcke) wallet, knapsack.

Ruder ['ru:dər], *n.* (—s, *pl.* —) oar; rudder. —er, *m.* (—ers, *pl.* —er) rower, sculler. —ig, *adj.* (*in comp.*=) -oared. —bank, *f.* thwart. —gat, *n.* rowlock. —griff, *m.* oar-handle. —pinne, *f.* tiller. —platte, *f.* blade of an oar. —rad=dampfſchiff, *n.* paddlesteamer. —rad=gehäuſe, *n.* paddlebox. —ſchiff, *n.* galley. —ſchlag, *m.* stroke of the oar. —ſklave, *m.* galley-slave.

Rudern ['ru:dərn], I. *v.a. & n.* (*aux.* h. & ſ.) to row. II. *subst.n.* rowing.

Ruf [ru:f], *m.* (—(e)s, *pl.* —e) call; repute, reputation. —en, *ir.v.a. & n.* (*aux.* h.) to call; —en laſſen, to send for. —er, *m.* (—ers, *pl.* —er) crier; caller.

Ruh—e ['ru:ə], *f.* rest, repose; laſſen Sie mich in —e, let me alone! —en, *v.n.* (*aux.* h.) to rest. —end, *p. & adj.* resting. —ig, *adj. & adv.* quiet, tranquil, still. —e=bett, *n.* sofa, couch. —e=gehalt, *n.* pension. —e=los, *adj.* restless; changeable. —e=loſigkeit, *f.* restlessness. —e=punkt, *m.* centre of gravity. —e=ſtand, *m.* state of rest; retired list. —e=ſtörung, *f.* breach of the peace, riot. —e=voll, *adj.* tranquil, peaceful. —e=zeit, *f.* rest, leisure time.

Ruhm [ru:m], *m.*(—(e)s) glory; honour; renown. —los, *adj.* inglorious, without fame. —reich, *adj.* glorious. —voll, *adj.* famous, glorious.

Rühm—en ['ry:mən], *v.a.* to praise, extol; ſich einer Sache —en, to boast of a thing. —lich, *adj. & adv.* laudable, praiseworthy.

Ruhr [ru:r], *f.* diarrhœa.

Rühr—en ['ry:rən], I. *v.n.*; —en an (*acc.*) to touch. II. *v.a.* to stir, move; to touch; —t Euch! stand at ease! (*Mil.*). III. *v.r.* to bestir oneself, be active. —end, *p. & adj.* stirring, *etc.*; affecting, pathetic. —ig, *adj. & adv.* stirring; active. —igkeit, *f.* activity; agility. —ung, *f.* feeling, emotion; sympathy. —ei, *n.* scrambled egg. —faß, *n.* churn. —kartoffeln, *pl.* mashed potatoes. —kelle, *f.* potladle. —milch, *f.* buttermilk.

Ruin—e [ru'i:nə], *f.* (*pl.* —en) ruins, a ruin. —en=haft, *adj.* dilapidated. —ieren [—'ni:rən], *v.a.* to ruin, destroy.

Rummel ['ruməl], *m.* (—s) uproar; den —kennen, to know what's what. —n, *v.n.* (*aux.* ſ.) to rumble.

Rumor [ru'mo:r], *m.* (—s, *pl.* —e) rumour; noise, uproar.

Rumpel—n ['rumpəln], *v.a.* to jolt; Alles durcheinander —n, to turn everything topsy-turvy. —kammer, *f.* lumber-room; (*fig.*) rattletrap old car or carriage.

Rumpf [rumpf], *m.*(—(e)s, *pl.* Rümpfe) trunk (*of a tree, etc.*); body (*of a man, etc.*); hull (*of a ship*).

Rümpfen ['rʏmpfən], v.a. to wrinkle.

Rund [rʊnt], I. adj. & adv. round. II.
n. (—(e)s, pl. —e) round object; globe,
orb. —e, f. round, circle. —lich,
adj. roundish; plump; arched. —⸗
lichkeit, f. rotundity. —flug, m.
circuitous flight (aeroplane). —funk,
m. radio, broadcasting. —funken,
v.a. to broadcast. —funkstelle, f.
broadcasting station. —gang, m.
rotation. —gesang, m. glee; catch.
—hohl, adj. concave. —höhlung, f.
concavity. —reim, m. refrain.
—reise, f. circular tour; circuit.
—schau, m. panorama. —schreiben,
n. circular. —um, adv. round about.
—weg, adv. flatly, plainly.

Ründe ['rʏndə], f. roundness.

Runge ['rʊŋə], f. rung (of a ladder).

Runkelrübe ['rʊŋkəlry:bə], f. beetroot.

Runzel ['rʊntsəl], f. (pl. —n) wrinkle.
—ig, adj. wrinkled. —n, v.a. & n.
(aux. h.) to wrinkle.

Rupfen ['rʊpfən], v.a. to pluck, pull.

Ruß [rʊs], m. (—es, pl. —e) soot.
—ig, adj. sooty. —braun, n., —farbe,
f. bistre. —farbe, f. soot-colour.
—schwarz, n. lamp-black.

Rüssel ['rʏsəl], m. (—s, pl. —) snout.
—ig, adj. proboscis-like; snouted.

Rüst⸗en ['rʏstən], v. I. a. to prepare;
to fit out, equip. II. n. (aux. h.) to
make preparations, get ready. —ig,
adj. & adv. strong, vigorous, robust,
active. —igkeit, f. vigour, activity.
—ung, f. preparations (for war, a
feast, etc.); equipment; armour, armament; implements, apparatus; scaffolding. —haus, n. arsenal. —⸗
kammer, f. armoury; arsenal. —⸗
woche, f. Holy Week.

Rute ['ru:tə], f. (pl. —n) rod; switch;
die — geben, to whip.

Rutsch [rʊtʃ], m. (—es, pl. —e) push,
shove. —en, v.n. (aux. h. & ſ.) to
slide, slip. —bahn, f. slide.

Rütteln ['rʏtəln], v.a. & n. (aux. h.) to
shake.

S

S, ſ [ʔɛs], n. S, s; 's=1. das, as, ins
Haus gehen, to go into the house;
2. es, as, geht's nicht? won't it do?

Saal [za:l], m. (—(e)s, pl. Säle, dimin.
Sälchen) hall, room.

Saat [za:t], f. (pl. —en) seed; standing
corn. —kartoffel, f. seed-potato.
—korn, n. seed(-corn), corn for sowing.
—krähe, f. rook. —lerche, f. skylark.
—reihe, f. drill (for seed).

Sabbat ['zabat], m. (—(e)s, pl. —e)
Sabbath; Sunday.

Säbel ['zɛ:bəl], m. (—s, pl. —) sabre.
—n, v.a. to sabre. —hieb, m. sword-
cut. —klinge, f. sabre-blade. —⸗
scheide, f. scabbard. —tasche, f.
sabretache.

Sach⸗e ['zaxə], f. (pl. —en) thing;
cause; action, case; matter, affair,
business, concern; event; fact; circumstance; (pl.) goods. —lich, adj.
& adv. real, essential; pertinent; to
the point. —lichkeit, f. reality, essen-
tiality. —erfahren, adj. expert.
—lage, f. state of affairs. —verständig, adv. versed, expert. —walter, m.
counsel, legal adviser. —waltung, f.
management.

Sacht(e) ['zaxt(ə)], I. adj. & adv. soft,
gentle. II. adv. by degrees; cauti-
ously; gently.

Sack [zak], m. (—(e)s, pl. —, Säcke) sack,
bag; mit — und Pack, with bag and
baggage. —gasse, f. blind-alley.

Sä⸗en ['zɛ:ən], v.a. & n. (aux. h.) to
sow. —er, m. (—ers, pl. —er) sower.
—mann, m. sower.

Saffian ['zafla:n], m. (—s) morocco
(leather).

Saft [zaft], m. (—(e)s, pl. Säfte) juice.
—ig, adj. juicy. —reich, adj. juicy,
succulent.

Sage ['za:gə], f. (pl. —n) saying; tale;
fable.

Säge ['zɛ:gə], f. (pl. —n) saw. —n,
v.a. & n. (aux. h.) to saw. —grube, f.
saw-pit. —späne, pl. sawdust.

Sagen ['za:gən], I. v.a. to say, tell;
laß dir das gesagt sein, let it be a
warning to you. II. subst.n. saying,
etc. —haft, adj. legendary, mythical.

Sago ['za:go:], m. (—s) sago, tapioca.

Sahn⸗e ['za:nə], f. cream. —ig, adj.
creamy.

Sait⸗e ['zaitə], f. (pl. —en) string (of
a violin, etc.). —ig, adj. stringed.
—en⸗brett, n. sounding-board. —en⸗
draht, m. piano-wire. —en⸗klang,
m. music of strings. —en⸗spiel,
n. string music. —en⸗spieler, m.

player on a string instrument;
lute-player.

Sakrament [zakra'mɛnt], *n.* (—(e)s, *pl.*
—e) sacrament.

Sakrist—an [zakrɪs'ta:n], *m.* (—ans,
pl. —ane) sexton. —**ei** [—'taɪ], *f.*
vestry.

Salat [za'la:t], *m.* (—(e)s, *pl.* —e) salad.

Salb—e ['zalbə], *f.* (*pl.* —en) ointment.
—**en,** *v.a.* to anoint. —**ung,** *f.*
anointing; unction.

Salbei ['zalbaɪ], *m.* (—s, *pl.* —e), *f.*
(*pl.* —en) sage (*Bot.*).

Sald—ieren [zal'di:rən], *v.a.* to strike
a balance. —**ierung,** *f.* balancing,
settlement. —**o** ['zaldo:], *n.* (—os, *pl.*
—os) balance of an account.

Salm [zalm], *m.* (—s, *pl.* —e) salmon.

Salpeter [zal'pe:tər], *m.* (—s, *pl.* —)
nitre, saltpetre.

Salz [zalts], *n.* (—es, *pl.* —e) salt.
—**ig,** *adj.* salty, salt. —**grube,** *f.*
salt-mine. —**gurke,** *f.* pickled
cucumber.

Salzen ['zaltsən], *irreg. & reg. v.a.* to
salt; to pickle.

Sam—e ['za:mə], *m.* (—en, *pl.* —en),
—**en,** *m.* (—ens, *pl.* —en) seed ;
spawn; posterity. —**en=korn,** *n.* grain
of seed.

Samm—eln ['zaməln], *v.* I. *a.* to
gather, collect. II. *r.* to assemble,
flock together ; to collect one's
thoughts. —**ler,** *m.* (—lers, *pl.*
—ler) collector. —**lung,** *f.* collection.
—**el=name,** *m.* collective noun.

Sammet ['zamət], **Samt,** *m.* (—(e)s, *pl.*
—e) velvet. —**en,** *adj.* velvety.
—**band,** *n.* velvet ribbon.

Samstag ['zamsta:k], *m.* (—s, *pl.* —e)
Saturday.

Samt [zamt], I. *adv.*; — **und sonders,**
alle —, collectively and individually,
one and all. II. *prep.* (*with dat.*) with,
together with, along with ; **mit—,**
together with.

Sämtlich ['zɛmtlɪç], I. *adj.* all, all
together; complete, entire; collective.
II. *adv.* collectively, in a body.

Samum ['za:mum], *m.* (—s, *pl.* —s,
—e) simoom, simoon.

Sand [zant], *m.* (—(e)s) sand. —**ig,**
adj. sandy, gravelly. —**dünen,** *pl.*
sand-hills, downs. —**korn,** *n.* grain
of sand. —**kuchen,** *m.* sponge-cake.
—**torte,** *f.* madeira cake. —**uhr,** *f.*
hour-glass.

Sandel ['zandəl], *m.* (—s, *pl.* —),
(—holz, *n.*) sandalwood.

Sanft [zanft], *adj. & adv.* soft; gentle.
—**heit,** *f.* softness; mildness, gentle-
ness. —**mütig,** *adj.* tender-hearted.
—**mut,** *f.* good cheerful temper.

Sänft—e ['zɛnftə], *f.* (*pl.* —en) sedan
chair. —**igen,** *v.a.* to mitigate,
appease.

Sang [zaŋ], *m.* (—(e)s, *pl.* Sänge) song.

Sänger ['zɛŋər], *m.* (—s, *pl.* —) singer;
minstrel, bard. —**in,** *f.* songstress,
singer. —**bund,** *m.* choral society.
—**fest,** *n.* choral festival.

Sanität [zani'tɛ:t], *f.* hygiene. —**lich,**
adj. relating to health. —**s=beamte(r),**
m. health officer. —**s=wagen,** *m.*
ambulance.

Sankt [zaŋkt], *indec. adj.* (*abbr.* S.,
St.) saint.

Saphir ['zafɪr], *m.* (—s, *pl.* —e
[za'fi:rə]) sapphire. —**en,** *adj.* sapphire.

Sapp—e ['zapə], *f.* (*pl.* —en) sap (*in
sieges*). —**en,** *v.a.* to undermine.
—**eur** [—'pø:r], *m.* (—eurs, *pl.*
—eure, —eurs) sapper.

Sard—elle [zar'dɛlə], *f.* (*pl.* —ellen)
anchovy. —**ine** [—'di:nə], *f.* sardine.

Sarg [zark], *m.* (—(e)s, *pl.* Särge)
coffin.

Satanisch [za'ta:nɪʃ], *adj.* Satanic.

Satir—e [za'ti:rə], *f.* (*pl.* —en) satire.
—**iker,** *m.* (—ikers, *pl.* —iker) satirist.
—**isch,** *adj.* satirical.

Satt [zat], *adj. & adv.* satiated; **eine**
Sache — bekommen, to get tired *or*
sick of a thing. —**heit,** *f.* satiety.
—**sam,** *adj. & adv.* sufficiently.

Satt—ler ['zatlər], *m.* (—lers, *pl.* —ler)
saddler. —**lerei** [—'raɪ], *f.* saddlery.

Sattel ['zatəl], *m.* (—s, *pl.* Sättel)
saddle. —**baum,** —**bogen,** *m.* saddle-
bow. —**n,** I. *v.a.* to saddle. II.
subst.n. saddling.

Sättigen ['zɛtɪgən], *v.a.* to satisfy.

Satyr ['za:tyr], *m.* (—s, *pl.* —s,
—e(n)) Satyr.

Satz [zats], *m.* (—es, *pl.* Sätze) setting,
putting, laying; leap, bound; heap,
pile; dregs; deposit; sentence, passage.
—**lehre,** *f.* syntax. —**ung,** *f.* statute,
law.

Sau [zau], *f.* (*pl.* —en, Säue) sow.
—**bohne,** *f.* broad bean. —**hatz,**
—**hetze,** *f.* boar-hunting. —**hirt,** *m.*
swineherd. —**stall,** *m.* pigsty. —**trog,**
m. pig's trough.

Sauber ['zaubər], *adj.* clean. —keit, *f.* cleanness.

Säuberlich ['zɔybərlıç], *adj. & adv.* clean.

Sauer [zauər], *adj. & adv.* (*comp.* saurer, *sup.* sauerst) (*when inflected generally* saur) sour, acid. —ampfer, *m.* sorrel. —kraut, *n.* pickled cabbage. —stoff, *m.* oxygen.

Saufen ['zaufən], *ir.v.a. & n.* (*aux.* h.) to drink (*of beasts*); to drink to excess.

Säufer ['zɔyfər], *m.* (—s, *pl.* —) drunkard, toper.

Säug—en ['zɔygən], *v.a.* to suckle, nurse. —er, *m.* (—ers, *pl.* —er) sucking animal. —ling, *m.* (—lings, *pl.* —linge) infant. —amme, *f.* wet-nurse. —etier, *n.* mammal. —ezahn, *m.* milk-tooth.

Saugen ['zaugən], *ir.v.a. & n.* (*aux.* h.) to suck.

Säul—e ['zɔylə], *f.* (*pl.* —en) column; pillar. —engang, *m.* colonnade, arcade.

¹Saum [zaum], *m.* (—s, *pl.* Säume) hem, seam.

²Saum, *m.* (—s, *pl.* Säume) burden.

Säum—en ['zɔymən], *v.n.* (*aux.* h.) to delay, linger, tarry. —ig, *adj. & adv.* tardy, slow; negligent. —igkeit, *f.* slowness; negligence. —nis, *f.* (*pl.* —nisse) & *n.* (—nisses, *pl.* —nisse) delay; obstacle.

Säure ['zɔyrə], *f.* (*pl.* —n) acid; sourness, acidity.

Saus [zaus], *m.* (—(s)es) rush, storm; in — und Braus leben, to lead a riotous life.

Sausen ['zauzən], *v.n.* (*aux.* h. & s.) to bluster, howl (*wind*); to hum (*ears*).

Säuseln ['zɔyzəln], *v.a. & n.* (*aux.* h.) to rustle.

Schab—e ['ʃa:bə], *f.* (*pl.* —en) cockroach. —en, *v.a.* to scrape. —sel, *n.* (—sels, *pl.* —sel) scrapings, parings. —efleisch, *n.* minced meat.

Schabernack ['ʃa:bərnak], *m.* (—s, *pl.* —e) mischievous trick, hoax.

Schäbig ['ʃɛ:bıç], *adj.* mangy; shabby.

Schablon—e [ʃa'blo:nə], *f.* (*pl.* —en) stencil. —enmäßig, *adj. & adv.* stereotyped, mechanical.

Schach [ʃax], *n.* (—(e)s) chess. —brett, *n.* chess-board.

Schacher—er ['ʃaxərər], *m.* (—ers, *pl.* —er) petty dealer. —n, *v.n.* (*aux.* h.) to chaffer, higgle.

Schacht [ʃaxt], *m.* (—(e)s, *pl.* Schächte) shaft, pit (*Min.*).

Schachtel ['ʃaxtəl], *f.* (*pl.* —n) box; alte —, old maid.

Schad—e ['ʃa:də], *m.* (—en, *pl.* —en), —en, *m.* (—ens, *pl.* Schäden) damage, loss; injury. —haft, *adj.* damaged, injured. —haftigkeit, *f.* unsoundness. —enfreude, *f.* malicious joy. —enfroh, *adj.* mischief-loving, malicious. —los, *adj.* harmless; indemnified; —los halten, to indemnify.

Schädel ['ʃɛ:dəl], *m.* (—s, *pl.* —) skull.

Schaden ['ʃa:dən], *v.n.* (*aux.* h., *dat.*) to harm; das schadet nichts, that doesn't matter.

Schäd—igung ['ʃɛ:dıguŋ], *f.* wrong; hurt. —lich, *adj.* prejudicial, destructive. —lichkeit, *f.* harmfulness.

Schaf [ʃa:f], *n.* (—(e)s, *pl.* —e) sheep; (*fig.*) simpleton.

Schäf—chen ['ʃɛ:fçən], *n.* (—chens, *pl.* —chen), —lein, *n.* (—leins, *pl.* —lein) little sheep; sein —chen ins Trockene bringen, to feather one's nest. —er, *m.* (—ers, *pl.* —er) shepherd. —erin, *f.* shepherdess. —ertum, *n.* shepherd's life. —erstab, *m.* shepherd's crook. —erstunde, *f.* lovers' hour.

Schaff—en ['ʃafən], I. *ir.v.a. & n.* (*aux.* h.) to create; to produce. II. *reg.v.a.* to do, make, work; to procure, provide. III. *reg.v.n.* (*aux.* h.) to work, be busy; er ist für diese Stellung wie geschaffen, he is the very man for this post. IV. *subst.n.* creating, creation. —end, *p. & adj.* creative. —ensdrang, *m.* creative impulse. —enskraft, *f.* creative power, genius.

Schaffner ['ʃafnər], *m.* (—s, *pl.* —) manager; guard (*Railw.*).

Schafott [ʃa'fɔt], *n.* (—s, *pl.* —e) scaffold.

¹Schaft [ʃaft], *m.* (—(e)s, *pl.* Schäfte) shaft.

²Schaft, *suffix in comp.* = -ship.

Schakal ['ʃa:kal], *m.* (—s, *pl.* —e) jackal.

Schäker ['ʃɛ:kər], *m.* (—s, *pl.* —) jester. —haft, *adj.* playful, waggish. —n, *v.n.* (*aux.* h.) to jest.

Schal [ʃa:l], *adj.* stale, flat. —heit, *f.*, —sein, *n.* insipidity.

Schäl—en ['ʃɛ:lən], *v.a.* to peel; to shell. —ung, *f.* peeling.

Schal—e ['ʃa:lə], *f.* (*pl.* —en) shell;

peel, rind. —**ig**, *adj.* scaly. —**en=förmig**, *adj.* cup-shaped. —**tier**, *n.* crustacean. —**wage**, *f.* scales.

Schalk [ʃalk], *m.* —(e)s, *pl.* —e) wag; rogue. —**haft**, *adj.* roguish. —**haftig=keit**, —**heit**, *f.* roguishness. —**s=narr**, *m.* buffoon.

Schall [ʃal], *m.* —(e)s) sound; ring. —**en**, *reg. & ir.v.n. (aux. h. & f.)* to sound, resound. —**beden**, *n.* cymbal. —**boden**, *m.* sounding-board.

Schalotte [ʃa'lotə], *f. (pl.* —n) shallot.

Schalt=en ['ʃaltən], *v.n. (aux. h.)* to direct, govern. —**er**, *m.* (—ers, *pl.* —er) ruler; wall letter-box; booking-office. —**brett**, *n.* switch-board. —**jahr**, *n.* leap-year. —**tag**, *m.* inter-calary day.

Scham [ʃa:m], *f.* shame; modesty. —**haft**, *adj.* modest. —**haftigkeit**, *f.* modesty. —**los**, *adj.* shameless, impudent. —**losigkeit**, *f.* shamelessness; impudence.

Schämen ['ʃɛːmən], *v.r.* to be ashamed (*über eine S., wegen einer S., also with gen.*).

Schand—barkeit ['ʃantbaːrkart], *f.* in-famy. —**e**, *f. (pl.* —en) shame, dis-grace; **zu** —**en gehen**, to go to ruin. —**mal**, *n.* brand of infamy. —**maul**, *n.* slanderer. —**schrift**, *f.* lampoon. —**tat**, *f.* infamous action.

Schänd=en ['ʃɛndən], *v.a.* to damage; to violate, profane. —**er**, *m.* (—ers, *pl.* —er) despoiler. —**lich**, *adj. & adv.* infamous, dishonourable. —**ung**, *f.* spoiling; profanation.

Schank [ʃank], *m.* (—(e)s) public-house.

Schanz=e ['ʃantsə], *f. (pl.* —en) bul-wark. —**en**, *v.a.* to throw up as an entrenchment.

Schar [ʃaːr], *f. (pl.* —en) (plough)share; troop, band. —**en**, *v.* I. *a.* to collect. II. *r.* to congregate. —**führer**, *m.* leader, captain of a band. —**en=weise**, *adv.* in bands *or* troops.

Scharf [ʃarf], *adj. & adv. (comp. schärfer, sup. schärfst)* sharp; **ein** —**es Ohr**, a quick ear. —**richter**, *m.* executioner. —**schießen**, *n.* shooting with ball cart-=idge. —**sichtig**, *adj.* sharp-sighted. —**sinn**, *m.* sagacity, acuteness. —**sinnig**, *adj.* sagacious; ingenious. —**sinnigkeit**, *f.* sagacity.

Schärf=e ['ʃɛrfə], *f. (pl.* —en) edge; sharpness. —**en**, *v.a.* to whet, sharpen.

Scharlach ['ʃarlax], *m.* (—s) scarlet.

—**en**, *adj.* scarlet. —**fieber**, *n.* scarlet fever.

Schärpe ['ʃɛrpə], *f. (pl.* —n) scarf, sash.

Scharpie, **Charpie** [ʃar'piː], *f.* (—, *pl.* —(e)n) lint.

Scharr=e ['ʃarə], *f. (pl.* —n) rake; scraper. —**en**, *v.a. & v.n. (aux. h.)* to scrape. —**er**, *m.* (—ers, *pl.* —er) scraper.

Schart=e ['ʃartə], *f. (pl.* —en) notch; loophole; **eine** —**e ausweten**, to make amends, repair damage.

Schatt=en ['ʃatən], *m.* (—ens, *pl.* —en) shadow. —**en=haft**, *adj.* shadowy. —**ig**, *adj.* shady. —**en=bild**, *n.* sil-houette. —**en=los**, *adj.* shadowless. —**en=reich**, I. *adj.* umbrageous, shady. II. *n.* Hades.

Schatz [ʃats], *m.* (—es, *pl.* **Schätze**) treasure; sweetheart. —**amt**, *n.* treasury, exchequer. —**anweisung**, *f.* exchequer-bill. —**gräber**, *m.* treasure-digger. —**kammer**, *f.* treasury.

Schätzbar ['ʃɛtsbaːr], *adj.* valuable; estimable. —**keit**, *f.* preciousness.

Schätz=en ['ʃɛtsən], *v.a.* to value; to esteem; to consider. —**ung**, *f.* esti-mation; **Gering—ung**, disdain. —**ens=wert**, —**ens=würdig**, *adj.* estimable, precious.

Schau [ʃau], *f. (pl.* —en) show, view; **zur** —**stellen**, to exhibit. —**en**, *v.* I. *a.* to look at. II. *n. (aux. h.)* to look, gaze, see; **auf etwas** (*acc.*) —**en**, to have regard to. —**er**, *m.* (—ers, *pl.* —er) spectator. —**begierig**, *adj.* eager to see. —**bühne**, *f.* stage. —**fenster**, *n.* shop window. —**platz**, *m.* theatre, scene; **Kriegs—platz**, seat of war.

Schauder ['ʃaudər], *m.* (—s, *pl.* —) shudder, horror. —**haft**, *adj.* horrible. —**n**, *v.n. (aux. h. & f.) & imp.* to shudder, shiver; to feel dread of *or* awed. —**gefühl**, *n.* feeling of dread. —**szenen**, *pl.* ghastly scenes.

Schauer ['ʃauər], *m.* (—s, *pl.* —) shower (*of rain, etc.*); chill. —**gefühl**, *n.* feeling of horror.

Schaufel ['ʃaufəl], *f. (pl.* —n) shovel. —**kasten**, *m.* paddle-box. —**rad** *n.*, paddle-wheel.

Schauk=el ['ʃaukəl], *f. (pl.* —eln) swing. —**eln**, *v.* I. *n. (aux. h.)* to balance. II. *a.* to swing. —**el=brett**, *n.* see-saw. —**el=pferd**, *n.* rocking-horse. —**el=stuhl**, *m.* rocking-chair.

Schaum [ʃaum], m. (—(e)s, pl. Schäume)
foam. —bedeckt, adj. covered with
foam. —kelle, f. skimming ladle.
—wein, m. sparkling wine.

Schäumen ['ʃɔymən], v.n. (aux. h.) to
foam, froth.

Schauspiel ['ʃauʃpiːl], n. (—s, pl. —e)
spectacle, play, drama; ins — gehen,
to go to the theatre. —er, m. (—ers,
pl. —er) player, actor. —erin, f.
actress. —haus, n. theatre. —kunst,
f. dramatic art. —schreiber, m.
playwright.

¹Scheck [ʃɛk], m. (—en, pl. —en), —e,
f. (pl. —en) piebald horse. —ig, adj.
piebald.

²Scheck, m. (—s, pl. —s) cheque.

Scheel [ʃeːl], adj. oblique; squint-eyed.
—auge, n. squinting eye, evil eye.
—äugig, adj. squinting; jealous.
—sucht, f. envy. —süchtig, adj.
envious, jealous.

Scheffel ['ʃɛfəl], m. (—s, pl. —) bushel.

Scheib—e ['ʃaɪbə], f. (pl. —en) disk;
slice; target; pane (of glass). —en-
honig, m. honey in the comb. —en-
schießen, n. target-practice (Mil.).

Scheid—bar ['ʃaɪtbaːr], adj. separable.
—e, f. (pl. —en) sheath; scabbard.
—en, I. ir.v.r. & n. (aux. ſ.) to separate; to depart. II. ir.v.a. to separate,
divide, part; to analyse; to divorce.
III. subst.n. parting, separation.
—e-brief, m. farewell letter; bill of
divorce. —e-weg, m. cross-road.

Schein ['ʃaɪn], m. (—s, pl. —e) shine;
light (of the lamp, sun, moon, etc.);
splendour; show; semblance; receipt;
bond, bill. —bar, adj. apparent,
seeming. —barkeit, f. likelihood,
plausibility. Comp. (generally = pretended, sham). —bild, n. illusion;
phantom. —fromm, adj. hypocritical.
—grund, m. apparent reason; pretence. —s-halber, adv. to save ap-
pearances. —tod, m. apparent death,
trance. —werfer, m. reflector;
search-light.

Scheinen ['ʃaɪnən], ir.v.n. (aux. h.) to
shine; to seem.

Scheit [ʃaɪt], n. (—(e)s, pl. —e, —er)
log. —er-haufen, m. pyre. —holz, n.
log(s).

Scheitel ['ʃaɪtəl], m. (—s, pl. —)
summit; crown of the head. —linie,
f. vertical line. —recht, adj. & adv.
vertical; perpendicular.

Scheitern ['ʃaɪtərn], v.n. (aux. h. & ſ.)
to become a wreck; (fig.) to miscarry.

Schelle ['ʃɛlə], f. (pl. —n) bell. —n-
kappe, f. fool's cap and bells, coxcomb.

Schellen ['ʃɛlən], v.a. & n. (aux. h.) to
ring the bell.

Schellfisch ['ʃɛlfɪʃ], m. (—es, pl. —e)
haddock.

Schelm [ʃɛlm], m. (—(e)s, —en, pl. —e,
—en) rogue, rascal. —erei [—ə'raɪ] f.
roguery; villainy. —isch, adj. knavish.

Schelt—bar ['ʃɛltbaːr], adj. blamable.
—e, f. (pl. —en) rebuke, reprimand.
—en, ir.v.a. & n. (aux. h.) to blame;
to scold. —er, m. (—ers, pl. —er)
scolder. —wort, n. invective.

Schema ['ʃeːma], n. (—s, pl. Schemata)
scheme. —tisch, adj. in accordance
with plan.

Schemel ['ʃeːməl], m. (—s, pl. —) foot-
stool.

Schenk [ʃɛŋk], m. (—en, pl. —en) butler.
—e, f. (pl. —en) tavern, public-house.

Schenkel ['ʃɛŋkəl], m. (—s, pl. —) leg;
thigh; side of an angle. —bein, n.
thigh-bone.

Schenk—en ['ʃɛŋkən], v.a. to pour out;
to present, bestow. —er, m. (—ers,
pl. —er) donor, giver. —ung, f.
donation; gift. —mamsell, f. barmaid. —stube, f. taproom. —wirt,
m. publican, landlord. —wirtin, f.
landlady.

Scher—e ['ʃeːrə], f. (pl. —en) scissors;
shears; claw (of lobster). —en, ir.v.a.
to shear; sich um etwas —en, to
trouble about a thing. —er, m. (—ers,
pl. —er) shearer. —becken, n. shav-
ing-basin.

Scherbe ['ʃɛrbə], f. (pl. —n), —l, —n,
m. (—ns, pl. —n) potsherd; débris.

Scherf [ʃɛrf], m. (—(e)s, pl. —e), —lein,
n. (—leins, pl. —lein) mite, farthing.

Scherge ['ʃɛrgə], m. (—n, pl. —n)
beadle; constable.

Scherz [ʃɛrts], m. (—es, pl. —e) jest,
joke. —haft, adj. jesting. —haftigkeit, f. jocularity. —wort, n. word
spoken in jest.

Scherzen ['ʃɛrtsən], v.n. (aux. h.) to
jest, joke.

Scheu [ʃɔy], I. adj. shy, timid; —
machen, to frighten. II. f. shyness;
timidity.

Scheuche ['ʃɔyçə], f. pl. —n) scarecrow.
—n, v.a. to scare.

Scheu—en ['ʃɔyən], v. I. a. to fear; to shrink from; sich —en vor, to be afraid of. II. n. (aux. h.) to be frightened; to shy. —heit, f. shyness.

Scheuer—n ['ʃɔyərn], v.a. to scour, scrub. —er, Scheurer, m. (—ers, pl. —er), scourer. —bürste, f. scrubbing-brush. —frau, f. charwoman. —lappen, m. dish-cloth. —stein, m. holystone (Naut.).

Scheune ['ʃɔynə], f. (pl. —n) barn.

Scheusal ['ʃɔyza:l], n. (—s, pl. —e) monster, horrible object.

Scheußlich ['ʃɔyslɪç], adj. horrible, frightful, abominable. —keit, f. hideousness; atrocity.

Schicht [ʃɪçt], f. (pl. —en), —e, f. (pl. —en) layer; (fig.) class, rank. —arbeiter, m. day-labourer. —ordnung, f. stratification.

Schick [ʃɪk], m. (—(e)s) fitness; tact.

Schick—en ['ʃɪkən], v. I. a. to send; nach einem —en, to send for a person; einen in den April —en, to make an April fool of a person. II. r. to come to pass, to happen; to prepare (for); to suit, be fit (zu, for). —lich, adj. & adv. proper; becoming. —lichkeit, f. propriety; fitness. —sal, n. (—sals, pl. —sale) destiny, fate.

Schieb—en ['ʃi:bən], ir.v. I. a. & n. (aux. h. & ʃ.) to shove, push. II. r. to move off; to slide. —er, m. (—ers, pl. —er) pusher; profiteer. —(e)karren, m. (wheel-)barrow, hand-barrow.

Schieds— ['ʃi:ts] (in comp.) —gericht, n. court of arbitration, of equity. —mann, —richter, m. arbitrator, umpire. —spruch, m. award.

Schief [ʃi:f], I. adj. & adv. crooked; sloping; wry; —e Ebene, inclined plane; auf die —e Ebene geraten, to go to the dogs. II. adv. awry; cross-wise; ill; — gehen, to go all wrong. —e, —heit, f. obliqueness, crookedness; slope; wrongness.

Schiefer ['ʃi:fər], m. (—s, pl. —) slate. —dach, n. slated roof.

Schiel—en ['ʃi:lən], v.n. (aux. h.) to squint; —en nach, to leer at. —end, p. & adj. squint-eyed. —er, m. (—ers, pl. —er), —erin, f. squinting person. —äugig, adj. squint-eyed.

Schien—e ['ʃi:nə], f. (pl. —en) splint; rail. —bein, n. shin-bone.

1Schier [ʃi:r], adj. & adv. plain; sheer.

2Schier, adv. almost, all but; quite, totally.

Schierling ['ʃi:rlɪŋ], m. (—s, pl. —e) hemlock.

Schieß—en ['ʃi:sən], ir.v. I. n. (aux. ʃ.) to shoot (as stars). II. a. & n. (aux. h.) to shoot; to discharge (a gun, an arrow, etc.); einen Bock —en, to make a bad mistake. —er, m. (—ers, pl. —er) shooter. —hund, m. pointer, sporting-dog.

Schiff [ʃɪf], n. (—(e)s, pl. —e) ship, vessel. —bar, adj. navigable. —barkeit, f. navigableness. —chen, n. (—chens, pl. —chen) little vessel, skiff. —bruch, m. shipwreck. —brüchig, adj. shipwrecked. —fahrer, m. navigator. —fahrt, f. navigation; voyage. —(s)grund, m. hold (of a ship).

Schiff—en ['ʃɪfən], v. I. a. to ship (goods, etc.). II. a. & n. (aux. ʃ.) to navigate, sail (on). —er, m. (—ers, pl. —er) seaman, sailor.

Schiffs— ['ʃɪfs] (in comp.) —gerät, n. ship's rigging. —junge, m. cabin-boy. —leute, pl. crew. —luken, pl. hatches. —patron, m. ship-master. —raum, m. hold. —reeder, m. ship-owner. —rose, f. mariner's compass. —rüstung, f. naval equipment. —werft, f. dockyard.

Schikane [ʃi'ka:nə], f. (pl. —n) chicanery, trickery.

Schild [ʃɪlt], I. m. (—es, pl. —e) shield. II. n. (—es, pl. —er) signboard. —erhaus, n. sentry-box. —knappe, —knecht, m. shield-bearer, squire. —kröte, f. tortoise, turtle. —krötenschale, f. tortoise-shell. —wache, f. sentinel.

Schilder—n ['ʃɪldərn], v. I. a. to depict, describe. II. n. (aux. h.) to stand sentry. —ung, f. picture; portrayal; description. —er, m. portrayer, describer.

Schilf [ʃɪlf], n. (—(e)s, pl. —e) reed; rush. —ig, adj. reedy, sedgy. —dach, n. reed-thatch. —decke, f. rush-mat. —meer, n. Red Sea (B.).

Schiller—n ['ʃɪlərn], v.n. (aux. h.) to change in colour. —nd, adj. iridescent. —seide, f. shot silk.

Schilling ['ʃɪlɪŋ], m. (—s, pl. —e) shilling.

Schimmel ['ʃɪməl], m. (—s, pl. —) mildew; white horse.

Schimmer ['ʃɪmər], *m.* (—s, *pl.* —) shimmer; glimmer. —n, *v.n.* (*aux.* h.) to twinkle, glimmer. —nd, *p. & adj.* glistening; lustrous.

Schimpf [ʃɪmpf], *m.* (—(e)s, *pl.* —e) affront; insult; abuse. —lich, *adj.* insulting; infamous. —lichkeit, *f.* disgracefulness. —lied, *n.* lampoon.

Schimpfen ['ʃɪmpfən], *v.a. & n.* (*aux.* h.) to affront, insult.

Schindel ['ʃɪndəl], *f.* (*pl.* —n) shingle. —dach, *n.* shingle-roof.

Schind-en ['ʃɪndən], *ir.v.a. & n.* (*aux.* h.) to skin, flay. —er, *m.* (—ers, *pl.* —er) flayer; hangman (*in curses, etc.*). —erei [—ərai], *f.* knacker's yard; extortion. —er=mäßig, *adj.* cruel, harsh.

Schinken ['ʃɪŋkən], *m.* (—s, *pl.* —) ham. —brötchen, —butterbrot, *n.* ham-sandwich.

Schirm [ʃɪrm], *m.* (—(e)s, *pl.* —e) screen; umbrella. —dach, *n.* awning; shed. —futter, *n.* umbrella-case. —gestell, *n.* umbrella-frame. —herr, *m.* protector, patron.

Schirm-en ['ʃɪrmən], *v.a.* to screen, protect. —r, *m.* (—rs, *pl.* —r) protector.

Schirren ['ʃɪrən], *v.a.* to harness.

Schlacht [ʃlaxt], *f.* (*pl.* —en) battle; — liefern, to give battle. —feld, *n.* field of battle. —fertig, *adj.* ready for battle. —ruf, *m.* battle-cry.

Schlacht-en ['ʃlaxtən], *v.* I. *a.* to slaughter; to slay. II. *n.* (*aux.* h.). —er, *m.* (—ers, *pl.* —er) butcher. —bant, *f.* shambles. —haus, *n.* slaughter-house.

Schlacke ['ʃlakə], *f.* dross of metals.

Schlaf [ʃlaːf], *m.* (—(e)s) sleep.

Schläf-chen ['ʃlɛːfçən], *n.* (—chens, *pl.* —chen) doze. —er, *m.* (—ers, *pl.* —er), —erin, *f.* sleeper. —(e)rig, *adj.* sleepy.

Schläfe ['ʃlɛːfə], *f.* (*pl.* —n) temple. —n=ader, *f.* temporal vein.

Schlaf-en ['ʃlaːfən], *ir.v.n.* (*aux.* h.) to sleep. —anzug, *m.* pyjamas. —end, *p. & adj.* sleeping. —gemach, *n.*, —=stube, *f.* bedroom. —genoß, —gesell, *m.* bedfellow. —kammer, *f.* (*small*) bedroom. —los, *adj.* sleepless, restless. —mütze, *f.* nightcap; (*fig.*) dreamy person. —rod, *m.* dressing-gown. —saal, *m.* dormitory. —sucht, *f.* somnolence, stupor, lethargy. —=

süchtig, *adj.* somnolent. —trunken, *adj.* very drowsy.

Schlaff [ʃlaf], *adj.* slack, loose. —heit, *f.* slackness.

Schlag [ʃlaːk], *m.* (—es, *pl.* Schläge) blow; stroke; stroke, fit of apoplexy; carriage door. —sahne, *f.* whipped cream.

Schlag-en ['ʃlaːgən], I. *ir.v.a.* to beat, strike; Alarm —en, to sound the alarm; an's Kreuz —en, to crucify; ein Kreuz —en, to make the sign of the cross; aus der Art —en, to degenerate. II. *ir.v.r.* to fight. III. *ir.v.n.* (*aux.* h.) to beat; to rap; to strike (*of clocks*). IV. *subst.n.* striking, beating. —ader, *f.* artery. —anfall, *m.* apoplectic attack. —baum, *m.* turnpike. —brüde, *f.* drawbridge. —fertig, *adj.* ready (*to fight*); sharp, quick-witted. —fertigkeit, *f.* readiness for battle; ready wit.

Schläger ['ʃlɛːgər], *m.* (—s, *pl.* —) success, draw, hit (*play, song, etc.*).

Schlamm [ʃlam], *m.* (—(e)s) mud. —ig, *adj.* muddy.

Schlange ['ʃlaŋə], *f.* (*pl.* —n) snake.

Schlängel-n ['ʃlɛŋəln], *v.a.* (*aux.* h.) & *r.* to twist. —nd, *p. & adj.* meandering, winding.

Schlank [ʃlaŋk], *adj.* slim, slender. —heit, *f.* slenderness. —weg, *adv.* easily, without obstacles.

Schlappe ['ʃlapə], *f.* (*pl.* —n) slap.

Schlaraffe [ʃla'rafə], *m.* (—n, *pl.* —n) sluggard. —n=land, *n.* lotus land.

Schlau [ʃlau], *adj.* sly, cunning. —heit, —igkeit, *f.* slyness. —berger, *m.* artful dodger, clever fellow.

Schlauch [ʃlaux], *m.* (—(e)s, *pl.* Schläuche) leathern bottle *or* skin; hose (*of fire-engines*).

Schlecht [ʃlɛçt], I. *adj. & adv.* bad, wicked; mir ist —, I feel ill; —e Zeiten, hard times. II. *adv.* ill; poorly. —igkeit, *f.* baseness; wickedness. —er=dings, *adv.* utterly; absolutely. —hin, *adv.* simply. —weg, *adv.* plainly, without ceremony.

Schlegel ['ʃleːgəl], *m.* (—s, *pl.* —el) mallet.

Schlehe ['ʃleːə], *f.* (*pl.* —n) sloe.

Schleich-en ['ʃlaiçən], *ir.v.* I. *r. & n.* (*aux.* h.) to slink; to crawl, creep. II. *a.* to smuggle; to slip into. —end, *p. & adj.* sneaking; furtive. —er, *m.* (—ers, *pl.* —er) person who walks

stealthily. —**erei** [—'rai], *f.* sneaking;
underhand dealing. —**handel**, *m.*
smuggling trade. —**händler**, *m.*
smuggler. —**ware**, *f.* contraband
goods.

Schlei(e) ['ʃlaiə], *f.* (*pl.* —n) tench.

Schleier ['ʃlaiər], *m.* (—s, *pl.* —) veil.
—n, *v.a.* to veil.

1**Schleifen** ['ʃlaifən], *v.* I. *n.* (*aux.* h. &
ʃ.) to slide. II. *a.* to drag.

2**Schleif**—en, *ir.v.a.* to grind, polish.
—er, *m.* (—ers, *pl.* —er) grinder.

Schleim [ʃlaim], *m.* (—s, *pl.*—e) slime;
mucus. —ig, *adj.* slimy.

Schleißen ['ʃlaisən], *ir.v.a.* to split.

Schlemmen ['ʃlemən], *v.n.* (*aux.* h.) to
carouse.

Schlend—erer ['ʃlendərər], *m.* (—erers,
pl. —erer) lounger. —ern, *v.n.* (*aux.*
h. & ʃ.) to dawdle, lounge.

Schleppe ['ʃlepə], *f.* (*pl.* —n) train (*of a
dress*).

Schlepp—en ['ʃlepən], *v.* I. *a.* to drag,
trail. II. *r.* to move slowly. —end,
p. & adj. tedious; drawling. —er, *m.*
(—ers, *pl.* —er) one who drags;
tow-rope. —en=träger, *m.* train-
bearer. —boot, *n.* tug, tow-boat.

Schleuder—n ['ʃlɔydərn], *v.* I. *a.* to
sling. II. *n.* to shake; to skid (*Motor.*).
—honig, *m.* strained honey. —preis,
m. low price; zu—preisen, dirt-cheap.

Schleunig ['ʃlɔyniç], *adj. & adv.* quick,
speedy.

Schleuse ['ʃlɔyzə], *f.* (*pl.* —n) sluice,
lock. —n=kammer, *f.* lock-chamber.
—n=meister, *m.* sluice-keeper. —n=
tür, *f.*, —n=tor, *n.* lock-gate.

Schlicht [ʃliçt], *adj. & adv.* plain,
simple. —en, *v.a.* to make straight or
plain; einen Streit —en, to settle a
quarrel. —heit, *f.* plainness, smoothness; simplicity. —ig, *adj.* sleek;
even.

Schließ—en ['ʃliːsən], *ir.v.* I. *a.* to shut;
to lock; to join; to close (*a discussion,
etc.*); der Schlüssel —t nicht, the key
doesn't fit the lock. II. *r.* to close,
shut. III. *n.* (*aux.* h.) to end, conclude; to fit well or close. —lich, I.
adj. final, definitive. II. *adv.* finally,
in conclusion. —ung, *f.* closing.

Schlimm [ʃlim], *adj. & adv.* bad, ill.

Schlinge ['ʃliŋə], *f.* (*pl.* —n) noose,
loop. —l, *m.* (—ls, *pl.* —l) rascal.
—lhaft, *adj.* rascally.

Schlingen ['ʃliŋən], I. *ir.v.a.* to wind;

to swallow, devour. II. *ir.v.n.* (*aux.*
ʃ.) to glide; to creep.

Schlitte—n ['ʃlitən], *m.* (—ns, *pl.* —n)
sledge, sleigh. —rn, I. *v.n.* (*aux.* h. &
ʃ.) to slide. II. *subst.n.* slide. —n=
fahrt, *f.* sledge-drive. —r=bahn, *f.*
slide.

Schlittschuh ['ʃlitʃuː], *m.* skate; —laufen,
to skate. —laufen, *n.* skating.
—läufer, *m.*, —läuferin, *f.* skater.

Schlitz [ʃlits], *m.* (—es, *pl.* —e) slit.
—auge, *n.* Mongolian eye, slit eye.

Schloß [ʃlɔs], *n.* (—(ʃ)es, *pl.* Schlö(ʃ)er)
castle; lock (*of firearms, doors, etc.*).
—feder, *f.* spring of a lock.

Schlosser ['ʃlɔsər], *m.* (—s, *pl.* —) locksmith. —gesell, *m.* journeyman-
locksmith.

Schlot [ʃlot], *m.* (—(e)s, *pl.* —e, Schlöte)
chimney, flue.

Schlotterig ['ʃlɔtəriç], *adj. & adv.*
flabby; slovenly.

Schlottern ['ʃlɔtərn], *v.n.* (*aux.* h.) to
shake; to slouch.

Schlucht [ʃluxt], *f.* (*pl.* —en) ravine,
glen, gorge.

Schluchzen ['ʃluxtsən], I. *v.n.* (*aux.* h.)
to sob. II. *subst.n.* sobbing.

Schluck [ʃluk], *m.* (—(e)s, *pl.* —e,
Schlücke) sip, gulp. —en, *v.a.* to
swallow, gulp. —er, *m.* hiccup;
starveling; armer —er, poor wretch.

Schlummer ['ʃlumər], *m.* (—s, *pl.* —)
slumber. —n, *v.n.* (*aux.* h.) to slumber. —nd, *p. & adj.* slumbering.
—gott, *m.* Morpheus.

Schlund [ʃlunt], *m.* (—(e)s, *pl.*
Schlünde) gullet; gorge; abyss.

Schlupf [ʃlupf], *m.* (—es, *pl.* Schlüpfe)
slipping; running knot. —loch, *n.*
loophole (*for escape*). —winkel, *m.*
hiding-place.

Schlüpf—en ['ʃlypfən], *v.n.* (*aux.* ʃ.) to
slip, slide, glide. —(e)rig, *adj.* slippery;
delicate; unreliable; (*fig.*) obscene.

Schlürfen ['ʃlyrfən], *v.* I. *a.* to sip, lap.
II. *n.* (*aux.* h. & ʃ.) to shuffle in
walking.

Schluß [ʃlus], *m.* (—(ʃ)es, *pl.* Schlüsse)
shutting, closing; end, conclusion;
consequence; inference. —bein, *n.*
hip-bone. —folge, *f.* conclusion; result. —punkt, *m.* full-stop, period.
—rechnung, *f.* annual balance.

Schlüssel ['ʃlysəl], *m.* (—s, *pl.* —) key.
—bein, *n.* collar-bone. —blume, *f.*
cowslip.

Schmach [ʃmaːx], f. disgrace. —voll, adj. disgraceful.

Schmachten ['ʃmaxtən], v.n. (aux. h.) to languish.

Schmächtig ['ʃmeçtɪç], adj. slender, slim, delicate-looking.

Schmachhaft ['ʃmakhaft], adj. tasty.

Schmähen ['ʃmeːər], v.a. & n. (aux. h.) to revile, abuse.

Schmal [ʃmaːl], adj. (comp. —er, sup. —st) small. —heit, f. narrowness.

Schmälen ['ʃmeːlən], v.a. & n. (aux. h.) to scold.

Schmalz [ʃmalts], n. (—es) dripping; (Schweine—) lard. —ig, adj. greasy.

Schmaroß—en [ʃma'rotsən], v.n. to sponge (bei, upon). —er, m. (—s, pl. —) sponger, parasite.

Schmaus [ʃmaus], m. (—(f)es, pl. Schmäuse) feast.

Schmeden ['ʃmɛkən], v. I. a. to taste. II. n. (aux. h.) to taste (bitter, sweet); to be pleasant to the taste; die Limonade schmedt mir, I like the lemonade.

Schmeich—elei [ʃmaɪçə'laɪ], f. flattery. —elhaft, adj. flattering. —lerisch, adj. adulatory, fawning.

Schmeich—eln ['ʃmaɪçəln], v.n. (aux. h., dat.) to flatter. —ler, m. (—lers, pl. —ler), —lerin, f. flatterer. —elkaße, f. wheedler. —elrede, f., —elwort, n. flattering word or speech.

Schmelz ['ʃmɛlts], m. (—es) enamel. —bar, adj. fusible. —barfeit, f. fusibility. —e, f. melting; smelting. —en, I. ir.v.n. (aux. f.) to melt. II. reg. & ir.v.a. to melt, dissolve. —end, p. & adj. melting; languishing, melodious. —er, m. (—ers, pl. —er) smelter. —ung, f. melting, fusion. —arbeit, f. smelting. —eisen, n. cast iron. —hütte, f. smelting-house, foundry. —ofen, m. furnace; forge.

Schmer [ʃmeːr], n. (—(e)s) fat, grease, suet.

Schmerz [ʃmɛrts], m. (—es, (—ens) (acc. also —en) pl. —en) pain, ache. —en, v. I. a. to pain. II. n. (aux. h.) to be painful, smart, ache. —haft, —lich, adj. & adv. painful; grievous. —ens-kind, n. child of sorrow. —ens-reich, adj. deeply afflicted. —los, adj. painless. —voll, adj. painful.

Schmetterling ['ʃmɛtərlɪŋ], m. (—s, pl. —e) butterfly.

Schmettern ['ʃmɛtərn], v. I. n. (aux. h.

& f.) to crash; to resound (as a trumpet). II. a. to dash, throw down violently.

Schmied [ʃmiːt], m. (—(e)s, pl. —e) smith. —bar, adj. malleable. —barfeit, f. malleability. —e, f. (pl. —en) smithy, forge.

Schmieden ['ʃmiːdən], v.a. to forge.

Schmieg—en ['ʃmiːgən], v.a. to bend, incline. —sam, adj. pliant. —samfeit, f. pliancy.

Schmier—e ['ʃmiːrə], f. (pl. —n) grease. —en, v.a. to smear, grease; to scrawl, scribble. —ig, adj. greasy, dirty. —finf, m. dirty fellow. —öl, n. lubricating oil. —seife, f. soft soap.

Schmint—e ['ʃmɪnkə], f. (pl. —n) paint, rouge. —en, v.a. to paint. —mittel, n. cosmetic.

Schmirgel ['ʃmɪrgəl], m. (—s) emery.

Schmöfer ['ʃmøːkər], m. (—s, pl. —) old tattered book.

Schmollen ['ʃmolən], v.n. (aux. h.) to pout, be sulky.

Schmoren [ʃmoːrən], v.a. to stew; to bake (meat).

Schmud [ʃmuk], I. m. (—(e)s) jewels, ornaments; finery. II. adj. spruce, neat, smart. —heit, f. smartness, elegance. —händler, m. jeweller. —fachen, pl. jewels, ornaments.

Schmüden ['ʃmykən], v.a. to attire, dress; to decorate.

Schmugg—el ['ʃmugəl], m. (—els, pl. —el), —elei [—'laɪ], f. smuggling. —eln, v.a. & n. (aux. h.) to smuggle. —ler, m. (—lers, pl. —ler) smuggler.

Schmunzeln ['ʃmuntsəln], v.n. (aux. h.) to smirk.

Schmutz [ʃmuts], m. (—es) filthiness; dirt. —ig, adj. dirty; muddy.

Schnabel ['ʃnaːbəl], m. (—s, pl. Schnäbel) bill, beak.

Schnalle ['ʃnalə], f. (pl. —n) buckle. —n, v.a. to buckle.

Schnalzen ['ʃnaltsən], v.n. (aux. h.) to crack, click.

Schnappen ['ʃnapən], v.n. (aux. h. & f.) to snap; to snatch; nach Luft —, to gasp for breath.

Schnaps [ʃnaps], m. (—(f)es, pl. Schnäpse) brandy, gin.

Schnarch—en ['ʃnarçən], v.n. (aux. h.) to snore. —er, m. (—ers, pl. —er) snorer.

Schnarren ['ʃnarən], v.n. (aux. h.) to rattle.

Schnatter—er ['ʃnatərər], m. (—ers, pl. —er) chatterer.

Schnattern ['ʃnatərn], v.n. (aux. h.) to chatter, gabble.

Schnauben ['ʃnaubən], reg. & ir.v.a. & n. (aux. h. & f.) to pant; to snort.

Schnauz—e ['ʃnautsə], f. (pl. —en) snout.

Schnecke ['ʃnɛkə], f. (pl. —n) snail. —n=haus, n. snail-shell. —n=linie, f. spiral line.

Schnee [ʃne:], m. (—s) snow. —ig, adj. snowy. —blume, f. snowdrop. —flocke, f. snowflake. —trift, f. snow-drift. —wehe, f. snow-drift. —s wetter, n. snow-storm.

Schneid—e ['ʃnaidə], f. (pl. —n) edge (of a knife, etc.). —ig, adj. adj. & cutting; energetic, spirited. —igkeit, f. energy, smartness. —en, ir.v.a. & n. (aux. h.) to cut. II. a. to cut up to chop. —end, p. & adj. cutting, sharp; sarcastic. —er, m. (—ers, pl. —er) tailor. —erei [—ə'rai], f. tailoring. —erin, f. dressmaker; tailor's wife. —e=bohnen, f. pl. French beans.

Schneien ['ʃnaiən], v.n. (aux. h. & f.) to snow.

Schnell [ʃnɛl], adj. & adv. rapid; swift, quick. —igkeit, —heit, f. velocity; swiftness, speed. —kraft, f. elasticity. —schreibe=kunst, f. shorthand, stenography. —schreibe=maschine, f. typewriter. —schreiber, m. (—schreibers, pl. schreiber) shorthand writer. —s schrift, f. shorthand.

Schnepfe ['ʃnɛpsə], f. (pl. —n) snipe.

Schnipp [ʃnip], int. snap! —chen, n. (—chens, pl. —chen) snap (with the fingers); jemandem ein —chen schla=gen, to snap one's fingers at a person. —sel, m. (—sels, pl. —sel) snip, shred. —isch, adj. snappish, pert.

Schnitt [ʃnit], m. (—(e)s, pl. —e) cut; section; slice (of bread, meat, etc.); pattern, model. —e, f. (pl. —en) cut, slice (of bread, etc.). —er, m. (—ers, pl. —er) reaper, mower. —lauch, m. chive. —waren, f.pl. drapery trade.

Schnitz [ʃnits], m. (—es, pl. —e) slice, cut. —el, n. (—els, pl. —el) cutlet; (pl.) parings, shavings. —eln, v.a. & n. (aux. h.) to carve. —en, v.a. & n. (aux. h.) to carve, cut. —er, m. (—ers, pl. —er) carver, cutter. —arbeit, f. wood-carving.

Schnöde ['ʃnø:də], adj. base, mean.

Schnörkel ['ʃnœrkəl], m. (—s, pl. —) spiral or twisted ornament; flourish (in writing).

Schnüffeln ['ʃnyfəln], v.n. (aux. h.) to snuff, sniff; to act the spy.

Schnupf—en ['ʃnupfən], I. m. (—ens, pl. —en) cold in the head; den —en bekommen, to catch cold. II. v.a. & n. (aux. h.) to take snuff. —er, m. (—ers, pl. —er) snuff-taker.

Schnur [ʃnu:r], f. (pl. Schnüre) string, cord. —g(e)rade, —gerecht, adj. & adv. straight as a line.

Schnür—en ['ʃny:rən], v.a. to lace; to tie. —band, n. stay-lace. —stiefel, m. laced-boot.

Schnurr—e ['ʃnurə], f. (pl. —en) anything humming; rattle. —en, v.n. (aux. h. & f.) to hum, buzz. —ig, adj. droll, funny. —bart, m. moustache.

Schober ['ʃo:bər], m. (—s, pl. —) stack, rick.

Schock [ʃok], n. (—s, pl. —e, —) heap; three-score.

Schokolade [ʃoko'la:də], f. (pl. —n) chocolate.

Schol—ar [ʃo'la:r], m. (pl. —aren) scholar, pupil. —astisch [—'lastiʃ], adj. scholastic.

1Scholl—e ['ʃolə], f. (pl. —en) clod. —ig, adj. cloddy.

2Scholle, f. (pl. —n) sole; plaice.

Schon [ʃo:n], adv. & part. already, yet; besides; only, alone; certainly, indeed, no doubt; after all; wenn —, ob—, though, although. — gut! all right! — der Gedanke, the very thought.

Schön [ʃø:n], adj. & adv. beautiful, handsome; fine. —e, n. the beautiful. —heit, f. beauty. —dank, int. many thanks! —geist, m. wit. —s geistig, adj. æsthetic. —heits= gefühl, n. feeling for beauty, taste.

Schon—en ['ʃo:nən], v.a. seldom n. (aux. h. gen.) to be sparing of; to save, spare. —ung, f. sparing; consideration, forbearance.

Schopf [ʃopf], m. (—(e)s, pl. Schöpfe) top of the head.

Schöpf—en ['ʃøpfən], v.a. to draw (water, etc.); Mut —en, to take courage; Verdacht —en, to get suspicious. —erisch, adj. creative; productive. —ung, f. creation; the universe. —er=geist, —er=sinn, m.

creative genius. —**er=kraft**, f. creative power or energy.

Schoppen ['ʃɔpən], m. (—s, pl. —) liquid measure.

Schornstein ['ʃɔrnʃtarn], m. (—s, pl. —e) chimney. —**feger**, m. chimney-sweep.

¹**Schoß** [ʃos], m. (—(ſſ)es, pl. —(ſſ)e and **Schöſſe**) sprig; story (Arch.).

²**Schoß** [ʃo:s], m. (—es, pl. **Schöße**) lap; flap, skirt (of a coat). —**hund**, m. lap-dog.

Schote ['ʃo:tə], f. (pl. —n, dim. **Schötchen**) pod, husk. —**n**, f. pl. green peas.

Schräg [ʃrɛ:k], adj. oblique; slanting. —**e**, f. (pl. —en) obliquity.

Schramm=e [ʃramə], f. (pl. —en) scratch. —**en**, v.a. to scratch. —**ig**, adj. scarred; scratched.

Schrank [ʃraŋk], m. (—(e)s, pl. **Schränke**) cupboard. —**e**, f. (pl. —en) barrier. —**en=los**, adj. boundless; unrestrained. —**en=loſigkeit**, f. boundlessness; licence.

Schranz(e) ['ʃrantsə], m. (—en, pl. —en) parasite.

Schraube ['ʃraubə], f. (pl. —n) screw (also Naut.).

Schraub=en ['ʃraubən], reg. & ir.v.a. to screw. —**en=ſchlüſſel**, m. spanner. —**en=welle**, f. propeller shaft. —**en=winde**, f. screw-jack. —**ſtock**, m. vice.

Schreck=bar ['ʃrɛkba:r], adj. timid. —**haft**, adj. fearsome. —**lich**, adj. & adv. frightful, terrible. —**lichkeit**, f. frightfulness.

Schreck=en ['ʃrɛkən], I. v.a. to frighten, alarm. II. m. (—s) fright; fear, horror. —**ens=herrſchaft**, f. reign of terror. —**ens=jahr**, n. terrible year.

Schrei [ʃrai], m. (—(e)s, pl. —e) cry, scream.

Schreib=en ['ʃraibən], I. ir.v.a. & n. (aux. h.) to write. II. subst.n. writing. —**er**, m. (—ers, pl. —er) writer; clerk. —(e)=**brief**, m. epistle. —**maſchine**, f. typewriter. —(e)=**pult**, n. writing-desk.

Schrei=en ['ʃraiən], ir.v.a. & n. (aux. h.) to cry, shriek. —**end**, p. & adj. crying, etc.

Schrein [ʃrain], m. (—s, pl. —e) cupboard; chest. —**er**, m. (—ers, pl. —er) joiner.

Schreiten ['ʃraitən], ir.v.n. (aux. ſ.) to stride, step.

Schrift [ʃrift], f. (pl. —en) letters; script; text; writing; periodical; pamphlet. —**lich**, adj. & adv. written, in writing. —**kürzung**, f. abbreviation. —**leiter**, m. editor. —**leitung**, f. editorship. —**mäßig**, adj. scriptural, biblical. —**ſetzer**, m. compositor. —**ſteller**, m. author; writer. —**ſtellerin**, f. authoress. —**ſtelleriſch**, adj. literary. —**verfälſchung**, f. forgery. —**wechſel**, m. correspondence.

Schrill [ʃril], adj. shrill. —**en**, v.n. (aux. h.) to chirp.

Schrippe ['ʃripə], f. (pl. —n) french roll.

Schritt [ʃrit], m. (—(e)s, pl. —e) step; pace. —**lings**, adv. pacing; astride.

Schroff [ʃrɔf], adj. & adv. rough, rugged. —**heit**, f. roughness, rudeness.

Schrot [ʃro:t], m. & n. (—s, pl. —e) chips, clippings; **von altem —** Korn, a chip of the old block. —**korn**, n. groats.

Schub [ʃu:p], m. (—(e)s, pl. **Schübe**) shove, push. —**fach**, n. drawer. —**fenſter**, n. sash-window. —**karren**, m. wheelbarrow. —**lade**, f. drawer; set of drawers.

Schüchtern ['ʃʏçtərn], adj. shy, timid. —**heit**, f. shyness, bashfulness.

Schuft [ʃuft], m. (—(e)s) scamp, rascal.

Schuh [ʃu:], m. (—(e)s, pl. —e, as measure —) shoe. —**abſatz**, m. heel of a shoe. —**anzieher**, m. shoeing-horn. —**band**, n. boot-lace. —**leiſten**, m. last. —**macher**, m. shoemaker. —**riemen**, m. shoe-lace. —**wichſe**, f. boot-polish, blacking.

Schuld [ʃult], f. (pl. —en) debt; fault; blame; sin; crime; guilt; **er iſt — daran**, he is to blame for it. —**ig**, adj. due, indebted; guilty, culpable; bound; **etwas —ig ſein**, to owe something. —**iger**, m. (—igers, pl. —igere) culprit; debtor. —**igkeit**, f. duty, obligation; due. —**igſt**, adv. most duly. —**ner**, m. (—ners, pl. —ner) debtor. —**bewußt**, adj. conscious of guilt. —**brief**, m. bond, promissory note. —**buch**, n. journal, ledger. —**en=laſt**, f. burden of debt. —**los**, adj. guiltless, innocent. —**opfer**, n. expiatory sacrifice. —**ſchein**, m. debenture; promissory note. —**voll**, adj. guilty.

Schul=e ['ʃu:lə], f. (pl. —en) school; **die — ſchwänzen**, to play truant. —**en**, v.a. to teach. —**bank**, f. school bench. —**direktor**, m. headmaster.

—lehrer, *m.* schoolmaster. —zwang, *m.* compulsory attendance at school.

Schüler ['ʃyːlər], *m.* (—s, *pl.* —), —in, *f.* school-boy, school-girl.

Schulter ['ʃultər], *f.* (*pl.* —n) shoulder. —ig, *adj.* (*in comp.* =) shouldered.

Schultheiß ['ʃulthaɪs], *m.* (—en, *pl.* —en), Schulze, *m.* (—n, *pl.* —n) village-mayor.

Schupp—e ['ʃupə], *f.* (*pl.* —en) scale; scurf. —ig, *adj.* scaly, scaled.

Schüppe ['ʃypə], *f.* shovel.

Schuppen ['ʃupən], *m.* (—s, *pl.* —) shed.

Schür—en ['ʃyːrən], *v.a.* to poke, rake (*the fire*); to trim (*a lamp*). —er, *m.* (—ers, *pl.* —er) stoker. —eisen, *n.* poker.

Schurke ['ʃurkə], *m.* (—n, *pl.* —n) scoundrel.

Schürze ['ʃyrtsə], *f.* (*pl.* —n) apron.

Schürzen ['ʃyrtsən], *v.a.* to tuck, pin up.

Schuß [ʃus], *m.* (—(ss)es, *pl.* Schüsse, *as measure* —) rush (*of water, etc.*); shoot, sprout; shot; gun-shot wound. —fest, *adj.* bullet-proof; invulnerable. —weite, *f.* range.

Schüssel ['ʃysəl], *f.* (*pl.* —n) dish. —brett, *n.* kitchen-dresser.

Schuster ['ʃuːstər], *m.* (—s, *pl.* —) cobbler.

Schutt [ʃut], *m.* (—(e)s) rubbish.

Schüttel—n ['ʃytəln], *v.a.* to shake. —ung, *f.* shaking; jerk.

Schütten ['ʃytən], *v.a.* to spill; to pour out.

Schutz [ʃuts], *m.* (—es) defence, refuge, protection. —amt, *n.* protectorship, guardianship. —blech, *n.* mud-guard. —brief, *m.* safe-conduct. —herr, *m.* patron, protector. —leistung, *f.* protection. —los, *adj.* defenceless. —mann, *m.* policeman.

Schütz [ʃyts], —e, *m.* (—en, *pl.* —en), —in, *f.* marksman, markswoman. —en=graben, *m.* rifle-pit.

Schütz—en ['ʃytsən], *v.a.* to protect, guard. —er, *m.* (—ers, *pl.* —er) protector. —ling, *m.* (—lings, *pl.* —linge) protégé(e).

Schwabe ['ʃvaːbə], *f.* (*pl.* —n) cockroach.

Schwach [ʃvax], *adj. & adv.* (*comp.* schwächer, *sup.* schwächst) weak, feeble. —heit, *f.* weakness. —sinn, *m.* feeble-mindedness; imbecility.

Schwäche ['ʃvɛçə], *f.* (*pl.* —n) weakness; debility.

Schwäch—en ['ʃvɛçən], *v.a.* to weaken. —lich, *adj.* feeble, weakly; sickly. —lichkeit, *f.* infirmity; delicacy. —ling, *m.* (—lings, *pl.* —linge) feeble person.

Schwadron [ʃvaˈdroːn], *f.* (*pl.* —en) squadron. —ieren [—ˈniːrən], *v.n.* (*aux.* h.) to brag, bluster.

Schwager ['ʃvaːgər], *m.* (—s, *pl.* Schwäger) brother-in-law; postilion.

Schwägerin ['ʃvɛːgərin], *f.* sister-in-law.

Schwalbe ['ʃvalbə], *f.* (*pl.* —n) swallow.

Schwamm [ʃvam], *m.* (—(e)s, *pl.* Schwämme) sponge; mushroom. —ig, *adj.* spongy, fungous. —igkeit, *f.* sponginess.

Schwan [ʃvaːn], *m.* (—(e)s (*obs.* —en), *pl.* Schwäne) swan. —en=gesang, *m.* swan-song.

Schwanger ['ʃvaŋər], *adj.* pregnant.

Schwank [ʃvaŋk], *adj.* pliable, supple.

Schwanken ['ʃvaŋkən], I. *v.n.* (*aux.* h.) to totter, tremble. II. *subst.n.* rocking; staggering.

Schwanz [ʃvants], *m.* (—es, *pl.* Schwänze) tail.

Schwären ['ʃvɛːrən], *ir.v.n.* (*aux.* h. & f.) to suppurate, fester.

Schwarm [ʃvarm], *m.* (—(e)s, *pl.* Schwärme) swarm.

Schwärm—en ['ʃvɛrmən], *v.n.* (*aux.* h. & f.) to swarm; to dream, muse; to rave, be enthusiastic (für, about). II. *subst.n.* swarming; rioting; enthusiasm. —er, *m.* (—ers, *pl.* —er), —erin, *f.* enthusiast, dreamer; noisy reveller. —erei [—əˈraɪ], *f.* enthusiasm; fanaticism; ecstasy. —erisch, *adj. & adv.* enthusiastic; fanciful.

Schwarz [ʃvarts], I. *adj. & adv.* (*comp.* schwärzer, *sup.* schwärzest) black; —auf weiß, in black and white. II. *n. indec.* black colour, blackness. —e, I. *m.* (—en, *pl.* —en) negro. II. *n.* bull's-eye (*of a target*). —blech, *n.* sheet-iron. —brot, *n.* brown bread. —kunst, *f.* black art. —künstler, *m.* necromancer, magician. —wald, *m.* Black Forest.

Schwatzen ['ʃvatsən], *v.a. & n.* (*aux.* h.) to chatter.

Schweben ['ʃveːbən], *v.n.* (*aux.* h.) to soar; to hover; in Gefahr —, to be in danger.

Schwefel ['ʃveːfəl], *m.* (—s) sulphur. —ig, *adj.* sulphurous. —säure, *f.* sulphuric acid.

Schweif [ʃvaif], m. (—(e)s, pl. —e) tail; train (of dresses).

Schweig—en ['ʃvaigən], I. ir.v.n. (aux. h.) to be silent. II. subst.n. silence. —sam, adj. taciturn; secretive. —samkeit, f. taciturnity. —e=geld, n. hush-money.

Schwein [ʃvain], n. (—s, pl. —e) hog, pig. —erei [—ə'rai], f. filthiness. —isch, adj. swinish. —s=braten, m. roast pork. —s=fleisch, n. pork. —e=hirt, m. swineherd. —e=hund, m. swineherd's dog; filthy fellow (vulg.). —e=schmalz, n. hog's lard. —s=stall, m. pigsty. —e=zucht, f. pig-breeding. —igel, m. hedgehog.

Schweiß [ʃvais], m. (—es, pl. —e) sweat. —en, v. I. n. (aux. h. & f.) to sweat. II. a. to weld. —er, m. (—ers, pl. —er) welder. —ung, f. welding.

Schweizer ['ʃvaisər], m. (—s, pl. —) doorkeeper, porter; Switzer.

Schweigen ['ʃvaigən], v.n. (aux. h.) to feast, carouse.

Schwelle ['ʃvelə], f. (pl. —n) threshold.

Schwell—en ['ʃvelən], ir.v.n. (aux. f.) to swell. —ung, f. swelling.

Schwemme ['ʃvemə], f. (pl. —n) horse-pond.

Schwemmen ['ʃvemən], v.a. to float (wood, etc.).

Schwenk—en ['ʃveŋkən], v. I. a. to swing. II. r. & n. (aux. h.) to turn, wheel about. —ung, f. swinging, whirling; rinsing; change of mind; evolution.

Schwer [ʃveːr], adj. & adv. heavy, weighty; difficult, hard; grievous; —er Atem, short of breath; es fällt mir —, I find it hard. —e, f. (pl. —en) burdensomeness, weight. —=lich, adv. hardly, scarcely. —atmig, adj. asthmatic. —blütig, adj. melancholic. —e=mittelpunkt, m. centre of gravity. —fällig, adj. heavy; slow, sluggish; awkward; unwieldy; dull. —fälligkeit, f. heaviness, clumsiness, etc. —gläubig, adj. incredulous. —hörig, adj. hard of hearing. —kraft, f. gravitation, (force of) gravity. —leibig, adj. corpulent. —mut, f. melancholy, sadness, depression. —mütig, adj. dejected, sad. —punkt, m. centre of gravity. —verständlich, adj. difficult to understand.

Schwert [ʃveːrt], n. (—(e)s, pl. —er) sword. —fisch, m. sword-fish. —hieb, m. sword-cut. —lilie, f. iris.

Schwester ['ʃvestər], f. (pl. —n) sister. —chen, n. (—chens, pl. —chen) (dear) little sister. —lich, adj. & adv. sisterly.

Schwieger—eltern ['ʃviːgər=eltərn], pl. parents-in-law. —kind, n. son- or daughter-in-law. —mutter, f. mother-in-law. —sohn, m. son-in-law. —tochter, f. daughter-in-law. —vater, m. father-in-law.

Schwiel—e ['ʃviːlə], f. (pl. —en) weal. —ig, adj. callous.

Schwierig ['ʃviːrɪç adj. & adv. hard, difficult. —keit, f. difficulty.

Schwimm—en ['ʃvimən], ir.v.n. (aux. h. & f.) to swim; to float. —er, m. (—ers, pl. —er) swimmer. —gürtel, m. life-belt.

Schwind—el ['ʃvindəl], m. (—els, pl. —el) giddiness, vertigo; fraud, cheat. —elhaft, —(e)lig, adj. dizzy; fraudulent, cheating. —eln, v.n. (aux. h., dat.) & imp. to be giddy; to swindle, cheat. —el=anfall, m. attack of giddiness. —ler, m. (—lers, pl.—ler) swindler; charlatan. —lerhaft, —lerisch, adj. fraudulent, cheating.

Schwind—en ['ʃvindən], ir.v.n. (aux. f.) to waste away; to vanish, disappear. —sucht, f. consumption, phthisis. —süchtig, adj. consumptive.

Schwing—en ['ʃviŋən], ir.v. I. a. to swing, whirl round. II. r. to vault, leap; to ascend. III. n. (aux. h.) to oscillate, vibrate. —ung, f. swinging; oscillation. —seil, n. slack-rope; swing. —stock, m. flail.

Schwirren ['ʃviran], v.n. (aux. h. & f.) & imp. to whiz, whir.

Schwitze ['ʃvitsə], f. sweating. —n, v.n. (aux. h.) to sweat.

Schwören ['ʃvøːrən], ir.v.a. & n. (aux. h.) to swear.

Schwül ['ʃvyːl], adj. sultry, close.

Schwülstig ['ʃvylstɪç], adj. swollen.

Schwung ['ʃvuŋ], m. (—(e)s, pl. Schwünge) swing; bound, spring; flight (of fancy); energy, impetus; im —e sein, to be in vogue. —haft, adj. spirited, emphatic; lofty, soaring. —gewicht, n. pendulum. —kraft, f. buoyancy; centrifugal power.

Schwur ['ʃvuːr], m. (—s, pl. Schwüre) swearing; oath; vow. —gericht, n. jury; court of assizes. —zeuge, m. sworn witness.

Sechs [zɛks], I. *num. adj.* six; halb —, half-past five; drei viertel —, a quarter to six. II. *f. (pl.* —(f)en), —(f)e, *f. (pl.* —(f)en) the number six. —t, *num. adj.* (der, die, das —te) the sixth. —tel, *n.* (—tels, *pl.* —tel) sixth part, sixth. —tens, *adv.* sixthly, in the sixth place.

Sechzehn ['zɛçtse:n], I. *num. adj.* sixteen. II. *f.* the number sixteen. —t (der, die, das —te), *num. adj.* sixteenth. —tel=note, *f.* semi-quaver.

Sechzig ['zɛçtsɪç], I. *num. adj.* sixty. II. *f. (pl.* —e) the number sixty.

See [ze:], I. *m.* (—s, *pl.* —(e)n) lake. II. *f. (pl.* —(e)n) sea. —fahrend, *adj.* seafaring. —fahrer, *m.* sailor; seafarer. —handel, *m.* maritime trade. —hund, *m.*, —kalb, *n.* seal (*Icht.*). —krankheit, *f.* sea-sickness. —mann, *m.* sailor. —räuber, *m.* pirate. —weg, *m.* sea route; auf dem —wege, by sea.

Seel—e ['ze:lə], *f. (pl.* —en) soul. —(en)=amt, *n.* office for the dead. —en=angst, *f.* mental agony. —en= freund, *m.* bosom friend. —en=froh, *adj.* enraptured. —en=größe, *f.* greatness of soul. —en=heil, *n.* spiritual welfare. —en=tag, *m.*; aller —entag, All Souls' Day. —entzückend, *adj.* soul-entrancing. —en=verwandt, *adj.* congenial (*in mind*), sympathetic. —sorger, *m.* clergyman, minister.

Segel ['ze:gəl], *n.* (—s, *pl.* —) sail; unter — gehen, to set sail. —flugzeug, *n.* glider (*Av.*).

Segeln ['ze:gəln], *v.a. & n. (aux.* h. & f.) to sail.

Segen ['ze:gən], *m.* (—s, *pl.* —) blessing. —los, *adj.* unblessed. —sprechen, *n.* benediction. —(s)reich, *adj.* prosperous, blessed.

Segge ['zɛgə], *f. (pl.* —n) sedge, rush.

Segler ['ze:glər], *m.* (—s, *pl.* —) sailor; sailer, ship.

Segn—en ['ze:gnən], *v.a.* to bless. —er, *m.* (—ers, *pl.* —er) blesser; charmer. —ung, *f.* blessing; exorcism.

Seh—en ['ze:(ə)n], *ir.v.a. & n. (aux.* h.) to see; to perceive; to appear; ich —e gut, my eyesight is good. —er, *m.* (—ers, *pl.* —er) one who sees; seer, prophet. —erin, *f.* prophetess. —= ens=wert, —ens=würdig, *adj.* worth seeing. —ens=würdigkeit, *f.* object of interest. —kraft, *f.* eyesight; strength of vision.

Sehn—e ['ze:nə], *f. (pl.* —en) sinew, tendon. —ig, *adj.* sinewy.

Sehn—en ['ze:nən], *v.r.* to long, yearn (for). —sucht, *f.* longing, ardent desire. —süchtig, *adj.* longing, yearning.

Sehr [ze:r], *adv.* very, much, greatly.

Seide ['zaɪdə], *f.* silk. —n, *adj.* silken; silky. —n=papier, *n.* tissue-paper. —n=raupe, *f.* silkworm.

Seidel ['zaɪdəl], *n.* (*sometimes m.*) (—s, *pl.* —) liquid measure (*generally a little more than a pint*); beer-tankard.

Seif—e ['zaɪfə], *f.* soap. —en, *v.a.* to soap. —ig, *adj.* soapy. —en=blase, *f.* soap-bubble.

Seih—e ['zaɪə], *f. (pl.* —en) strainer; filter. —en, *v.a.* to strain, to filter.

Seil [zaɪl], *n.* (—(e)s, *pl.* —e) rope. —brücke, *f.* suspension-bridge made of ropes. —draht, *m.* wire-rope.

¹Sein [zaɪn], I. (—e, —) *poss. adj.* his, its, her; one's. II. *poss. pron.* (for —es, das —e), his. —e, (der, die, das —e), —er, —e, —es, —ige, (der, die, das —ige,) *poss. pron.* his; das —ige, his property, his part *or* duty; jedem das —e, to every one his due; die —igen, his own family *or* people. —er=seits, *adv.* on his side; for his part. —er=zeit, *adv.* (*gen.*) in due time. —es=gleichen, *indec. adj. & pron.* of his kind, such as he. (um) —et= halben, —et=wegen, —et=willen, *adv.* on his account; for aught he cares.

²Sein, I. *ir.v.n. (aux.* f.) to be; to exist; (*as aux.=*) to be, to have. II. *subst.n.* being; existence; essence.

Seit [zaɪt], I. *prep. (with dat.)* since; for; zwei Tagen, for the last two days. II. *conj.* since. —dem, I. *adv.* since, since that time, ever since. II. *conj.* since. —her, *adv.* since then, from that time; hitherto.

Seit—e ['zaɪtə], *f. (pl.* —en) side; page. —ens, *prep. (with gen.)* on *or* from the side (*of*); on the part of. —ig, *suffix (in comp.=*) -sided. —lich, *adj.* lateral. —s, *suffix (in comp.)*; mütter= licher—s, on the mother's side. —ab, *adv.* aside, apart. —en=blick, *m.* sideglance; sneer. —en=gewehr, *n.* sidearms. —en=sprung, *m.* side-leap; (*fig.*) evasion. —wärts, *adv.* aside; sideways; on one side.

Sekret—är [zekre'tɛ:r], *m.* (—ärs, *pl.* —äre) secretary.

Sekt [zɛkt], *m.* (—es) champagne.

Sekt—e ['zɛktə], f. (pl. —en) sect. —ion [—tsɪ'oːn], f. (pl. —ionen) section.

Sekund—a [ze'kʊndaː], f. (pl. —s, —en) fifth form. —aner [—'daːnər], m. (—aners, pl. —aner) fifth-form boy. —e, f.(pl. —en) second (Chron.).

Selb [zɛlp], —e, —ige ['zɛlbɪgə] (der, die, das —e, —ige), —iger, —ige, —iges, adi. & pron. the same, the selfsame; zur —igen Stunde, at the same hour. —ander, pronominal adj.; I and another, we two. —dritt, pronominal adj. myself with two others. —ständig, adj. self-support-ing; independent; separate. —ständigkeit, f. independence.

Selbst [zɛlpst], I. indec. adj. or pron. (generally used in apposition to a pre-ceding noun or pron.) self; myself, himself, yourself, etc.; ich —, I myself. II. n. (indec.); sein ganzes —, his whole being. III. adv. even; very; —seine Freunde or seine Freunde —, even his friends, his very friends. —heit, f. individuality; egoism; self-fishness. —ling, m. (—lings, pl. —linge) egotist. —achtung, f. self-esteem. —aufopferung, f. self-sacri-fice. —beherrschung, f. self-possession; self-restraint. —bewußt, adj. self-conscious; conceited. —bewußtsein, n. self-consciousness. —laut, m. vowel. —mord, m. suicide. —mörder, m., —mörderin, f. suicide. —mörder-isch, adj. suicidal. —redend, adj. self-evident. —schöpferisch, adj. original. —sucht, f. egotism; selfishness. —süchtig, adj. egotistic; selfish. —tätig, adj. self-acting; spontaneous. —vergessen, adj. unselfish. —ver-ständlich, adj. & adv. of course! —vertrauen, n. self-confidence.

Selig ['zeːlɪç], adj. & adv. blessed; deceased, late; (coll.) tipsy. —keit, f. happiness, bliss. —sprechen, v.a. to beatify.

Sellerie ['zɛləriː], m. (—s) & f. celery.

Selt—en ['zɛltən], I. adj. rare, unusual; scarce. II. adv. seldom. —enheit, f. rarity, scarcity. —sam, adj. & adv. strange, unusual. —samkeit, f. strangeness; oddness.

Semester [ze'mɛstər], n. (—s, pl. —) (term of) six months, half-year.

Seminar [zemi'naːr], n.(—s, pl. —e and —ien) seminary.

Semmel ['zɛməl], f. (pl. —n) roll (of wheaten flour).

Senat [ze'naːt], m. (—s, pl. —e) senate. —or, m. (—ors, pl. —oren [—'toːrən]) senator.

Send—en ['zɛndən], reg. & (usually) ir.v.a. to send, despatch; to broad-cast (Radio). —er, m. transmitter (Radio). —ung, f. sending; expedition; consignment. —bote, m. messenger. —brief, m., —schreiben, n. despatch. —eanordnung, f. transmitting device (Radio).

Senf [zɛnf], m. (—(e)s) mustard.

Sengen ['zɛŋən], v. I. a. to singe, scorch. II. n. (aux. h.) to burn, be singed.

Senk—en ['zɛŋkən], v. I. a. to sink (a shaft, etc.); to let down, lower. II. r. to settle; to sink. —ung, f. sinking; depression; dip. —blei, n. plummet, sounding lead. —recht, adj. perpen-dicular, vertical.

Sense ['zɛnzə], f. (pl. —n) scythe. —eisen, n. blade of a scythe. —mann, m. mower, reaper; Death.

Sentenz [zɛn'tɛnts], f. (pl. —en) sentence; maxim. —enhaft, adj. sententious.

Sentimental [zɛntimɛn'taːl], adj. senti-mental. —ität [—i'tɛːt], f. senti-mentalism.

Separat [zepa'raːt], adj. separate, special.

September [zɛp'tɛmbər], m. (—s, pl. —) September.

Serie ['zeːriə], f.(pl. —n) series.

Serv—iette [zɛrvi'ɛtə], f. (pl. —ietten) table-napkin. —ieren [—'viːrən], v.a. & n. (aux. h.) to serve, wait (at table).

Sessel ['zɛsəl], m. (—s, pl. —) seat; arm-chair.

Setz—en ['zɛtsən], I. v.a. to place, set, put, fix. II. v.r. to seat oneself, take a seat. III. v.n. (aux. h. & f.) to run, spring, leap; to attack; an die Luft —en, to turn a person out; auf's Spiel —en, to venture, risk.

Seuche ['zɔyçə], f. (pl. —n) epidemic; pestilence; illness.

Seufze—n ['zɔyftsən], I. v.n. (aux. h.) to sigh; to groan. II. subst.n. sighing, groaning. —r, m. (—rs, pl. —r) sigh, groan.

Sext—a ['zɛkstaː], f.(pl. —en) first form.

Sezieren [ze'tsiːrən], v.a. to dissect.

Sich [zɪç] (3 sing. or pl. dat. & acc. m.,

f. & n. of) refl. pron. himself, herself, itself, themselves; one another.

Sichel ['zɪçəl], *f. (pl.* —n) sickle.

Sicher ['zɪçər], *adj. & adv.* secure, safe; sure, certain. —**heit**, *f.* certainty; security, safety. —**heits-nadel**, *f.* safety-pin. —**lich**, *adv.* surely, certainly, undoubtedly. —**n**, *v.a.* to ensure, make sure. —**ung**, *f.* securing, ensuring; guarantee; safety-fuse (*Radio*).

Sicht [zɪçt], *f.* sight; auf —, at sight. —**bar**, *adj. & adv.* visible. —**barkeit**, *f.* visibleness. —**lich**, *adj. & adv.* visible, apparent; obvious.

Sie [zi:], I. *pers. pron.* 1. (*3 sing. f. nom. & acc.*) she, her, (it). 2. (*3 pl. m., f. & n. nom. & acc.*) they; them; (Sie) you (*in addressing*). II. *f.* she, female.

Sieb [zi:p], *n.* (—es, *pl.* —e) sieve.

Sieben ['zi:bən], I. *num. adj.* seven; halb —, half-past six; meine — Sachen, my goods and chattels. II. *f.* number seven. —t, *num. adj.* (der, die, das —te) seventh.

Siebzehn ['zi:ptse:n], *num. adj.* seventeen. —er, *m.* (—ers, *pl.* —er) the figure seventeen. —t, *num. adj.* (der, die, das —te) seventeenth. —tens, *adv.* seventeenthly. —tel, *n.* (—tels, *pl.* —tel) a seventeenth part (¹⁄₁₇).

Siebzig ['zi:ptsɪç], *num. adj.* seventy. —st, (der, die, das —ste,) *num. adj.* seventieth.

Siech [zi:ç], *adj. & adv.* sickly; infirm. —heit, *f.*, —tum, *n.* (—tums) sickliness. —enhaus, *n.* hospital for incurables.

Siede ['zi:də], *f.* boiling. —n, *reg. & ir.v.a. & n.* (*aux.* h.) to boil. —grad, *m.* boiling-point.

Sieg [zi:k], *m.* (—(e)s, *pl.* —e) victory. —es-gewiß, *adj.* confident of victory. —es-lauf, *m.* triumphal progress. —reich, *adj.* victorious; triumphant.

Siegel ['zi:gəl], *n.* (—s, *pl.* —) seal. —brief, *m.* letters patent. —lack, —wachs, *n.* sealing-wax. —n, *v.a.* to seal. —ring, *m.* signet ring. —ung, *f.* sealing.

Siege—n ['zi:gən], *v.n.* (*aux.* h.) to be victorious. —r, *m.* (—rs, *pl.* —r) conqueror, victor.

Signal [zɪ'gna:l], *n.* (—s, *pl.* —e) signal.

Silbe ['zɪlbə], *f.* (*pl.* —n) syllable.

Silber ['zɪlbər], *n.* (—s) silver. —n, *adj.* (of) silver.

Silvesterabend, [zɪl'vɛstərʔabənt] *m.* New Year's Eve.

Sims [zɪms], *m.* (& *n.*) (—(f)es, *pl.* —(f)e) cornice, moulding; shelf.

Simulieren [zimu'li:rən], *v.a. & n.* (*aux.* h.) to feign, simulate.

Sing—en ['zɪŋən], *ir.v.a. & n.* (*aux.* h.) to sing. —spiel, *n.* musical comedy. —spielhalle, *f.* music-hall.

Singular [zɪŋgu'la:r], *m.* singular (number) (*Gram.*).

Singulär [zɪŋgu'lɛ:r], *adj.* strange, peculiar, odd.

Sinken ['zɪŋkən], *ir.v.* I. *a.* to sink (a shaft). II. *n.* (*aux.* f.) to sink, give way; die Stimme — lassen, to lower one's voice.

Sinn [zɪn], *m.* (—(e)s, *pl.* —e) sense; intellect, mind, intelligence; disposition; tendency; character; temper; import, meaning, signification; von —en sein, to be out of one's mind; viele Köpfe, viele —e, many men, many minds. —ig, *adj. & adv.* sensible, judicious; reflective; ingenious; (*in comp.=*) -minded. —igkeit, *f.* judgment, sense; thoughtfulness, ingenuity. —lich, *adj.* affecting the senses; material. —lichkeit, *f.* perceptive faculty; material nature; sensuality. —bild, *n.* symbol, type; allegory. —bildlich, *adj.* symbolic, emblematic. —enwelt, *f.* material world. —es-art, *f.* character, disposition. —es-kraft, *f.* power of the senses; thinking faculty. —es-organ, *n.* organ of sense. —es-täuschung, *f.* illusion; hallucination. —gedicht, *n.* epigram. —leer, *adj.* unmeaning. —los, *adj.* mad; foolish, unmeaning. —losigkeit, *f.* senselessness; absurdity. —reich, *adj.* sensible; clever, witty. —spruch, *m.* device, motto. —widrig, *adj.* contrary to sense, nonsensical.

Sinnen ['zɪnən], I. *ir.v.n.* (*aux.* h. & f.) to think, meditate, reflect; to speculate (über (*acc.*), upon); — auf (*acc.*), to study, to contrive, devise. —d, *pres.p.* musing, pensive. II. *ir.v.a.* to cogitate, think out. III. *subst.n.* thinking, planning; thoughts, aspirations.

Sintflut ['zɪntflu:t], *f.* flood, deluge (*B.*).

Sipp—e ['zɪpə], *f.* (*pl.* —en) kin,

kindred, relations. **—ſchaft,** f. kindred; clique.

Sirene [zi′re:nə], f. (pl. **—n**) siren (*Myth.*).

Sirup [′zi:rup], m. (**—s,** pl. **—e**) syrup.

Sitt—e [′zɪtə], f. (pl. **—en**) custom; habit; etiquette; (*pl.*) manners; (*pl.*) morals. **—ig,** adj. & adv. moral; polite; well-bred. **—lich,** adj. & adv. customary; moral, ethical. **—lichkeit,** f. morality. **—ſam,** adj. modest; virtuous; proper. **—ſamkeit,** f. modesty, decency, bashfulness. **—en=geſetz,** n. moral code. **—en=lehre,** f. moral philosophy, ethics. **—en=los,** adj. immoral, profligate. **—en=loſig= keit,** f. immorality.

Sitz [′zɪts], m. (**—es,** pl. **—e**) sitting; seat (*in all its senses*); residence. **—en,** ir.v.n. (*aux.* h.) to sit. **—end,** p. & adj. seated. **—ung,** f. sitting, session. **—bad,** n. hip-bath. **—fleiſch,** n. assiduity, steadiness; **ich habe kein —fleiſch,** I can't sit still; I do not persevere.

Skandal [skan′da:l], m. (**—s,** pl. **—e**) scandal; row.

Skat [ska:t], m. (**—s,** pl. **—e**) skat (*a German game at cards*).

Skelett [ske′lɛt], n. (**—(e)s,** pl. **—e**) skeleton.

Skep—ſis [′skɛpsɪs], f. doubt. **—tik,** f. doubt, scepticism. **—tiker,** m. (**—tikers,** pl. **—tiker**) sceptic. **—tiſch,** adj. & adv. sceptical.

Skizz—e [′skɪtsə], f. (pl. **—en**) sketch. **—en=haft,** adj. sketchy. **—ieren** [skɪ′tsi:rən], v.a. to sketch. **—en= buch,** n. sketch-book.

Sklav—e [′skla:və], m. (**—en,** pl. **—en**), **—in,** f. slave. **—en=ſchaft,** f., **—en= tum,** n., **—erei** [—ə′raɪ], f. slavery. **—iſch,** adj. enslaved, slavish.

Skrup—el [′skru:pəl], m. (**—els,** pl. **—el**) scruple (*also weight*). **—ulös** [—u′lø:s], adj. scrupulous.

Skurril [sku′ri:l], adj ludicrous.

Smaragd [sma′rakt], m. (**—(e)s,** pl. **—e**) emerald. **—en,** adj. emerald.

Smoking [′smo:kɪŋ], m. (**—s,** pl. **—s**) dinner-jacket.

So [zo:], I. adv. so, thus, in this or in such a manner or degree; as; so (*poetical use*); — **etwas,** that sort of thing; —? indeed? really? **ſein Betragen war —, daß,** his conduct was such as (to); **er ſpricht bald —,**

bald —, he says now this, now that; — **viel,** so or as much, so or as many; — **viel ich weiß,** as far as I know. II. adv. & conj.; **Ihr Freund war nicht zu Hauſe,** — **war mein Gang vergebens,** your friend was not at home, so I had my walk for nothing. III. *part.*; — **hören Sie doch!** do listen! do but hear! IV. int. indeed! well, well! really! V. conj. if, in case; — **Gott will,** if it please God. **—′bald,** I. adv. so soon. II. conj. as soon as. **—= ′dann,** adv. & conj. then, in that case. **—′daß,** conj. so that. **—′eben,** adv. just, but just. **—′fern,** I. adv. so far. II. conj. as far as; if; **in —fern,** inasmuch as. **—′fort,** adv. immediately, forthwith, at once. **—′gar,** adv. or part. even. **—genannt,** adj. so-called; pretended; would-be. **—= ′gleich,** see **—fort.** **—′hin, —′mit, —′nach,** adv. consequently, accordingly, then. **—′ſo,** adv. tolerably well, middling. **—′wie,** conj. so as, according as, as also, as well as. **—′wohl,** adv. so much; as well.

Sockel [′zɔkəl], m. (**—s,** pl. **—**) pedestal.

Sodbrennen [′zo:tbrɛnən], n. (**—s**) heart-burn.

Soda [′zo:da:], f. (carbonate of) soda (*Chem.*).

Sofa [′zo:fa:], n. (**—s,** pl. **—s**) sofa.

Sohle [′zo:lə], f. (pl. **—n**) sole (*of a foot, etc.*).

Sohn [zo:n], m. (**—(e)s,** pl. **Söhne,** dim. **Söhnchen**) son; **der verlorene —,** the prodigal son.

Solch [zɔlç], I. adj. & dem. pron. (**—er, —e, —es**) such; **ein —er Menſch,** — **ein Menſch,** a man like him, such a man. II. adv. **ein —,** or — **ein häßliches Kind,** such an ugly child. **—en=falls,** adv. in this case, in such a case. **—er=geſtalt,** adv. in such a way, so; thus. **—erlei** [ər′laɪ], indec. adj. of such kind,such; such-like.

Sold [zɔlt], m. (**—(e)s**) pay; salary, wages.

Soldat [zɔl′da:t], m. (**—en,** pl. **—en**) soldier. **—en=haft, —iſch,** adj. soldier-like, soldierly; martial.

Sole [′zo:lə], f. brine.

Solid [zo′li:t], **Solid—e,** adj. solid; settled, respectable.

Soll [zɔl], n. (**—s,** pl. **—s**) command; debit; debtor's side (*of the ledger*).

Soll—en ['zɔlən], ir.v. I. a. to owe. II. n. (aux. h.) to be obliged or bound in duty; to be or have to; to be in debt; to mean; to be of use for, be intended for; to be allowed, to be granted; to be said; to be believed; to pass for; (as aux.=) shall, should, owe, ought, must; du —ſt nicht töten, thou shalt not kill; was — ich? what am I to do? was —en dieſe Tor= heiten? what is the meaning of these tomfooleries? er — gelehrt ſein, he is said to be a scholar.

Söller ['zœlər], m. (—s, pl. —) balcony; loft.

Solo ['zo:lo:], I. adv. alone. II. n. (—s, pl. —s, Soli) solo.

Sommer ['zɔmər], m. (—s, pl. —) summer. —haft, —lich, adj. summer-like; (of) summer. —fäden, pl. gossamer. —friſchler, m. holiday-maker. —ſproſſe, f. freckle.

Sonate [zo'na:tə], f. (pl. —n) sonata.

Sonder ['zɔndər], I. adj. separate, special, peculiar. II. prep. (with acc.) without; — Zweifel, without doubt. —bar, adj. & adv. singular, peculiar. —barkeit, f. peculiarity, oddity, strangeness. —heit, f. peculiarity; speciality; in —heit, in particular. —lich, adj. & adv. special, peculiar. —ling, m. (—lings, pl. —linge) odd person. —ausgabe, special edition. —gleichen, adj. unequalled, matchless.

¹Sondern ['zɔndərn], conj. but.

²Sonder—n ['zɔndərn], v.a. to separate. —ung, f. separation, division.

Sonett [zo'nɛt], n. (—(e)s, pl. —e) sonnet.

Sonn—e ['zɔnə], f. (pl. —en; old gen. sing. —en) sun, sunshine. —enhaft, adj. radiant; sun-like. —ig, adj. sunny. —abend, m. Saturday. —abends, adv. on Saturdays; on a Saturday. —enaufgang, m. sunrise; the east. —en=bahn, f. ecliptic. —en= blume, f. sunflower. —en=klar, adj. clear, evident; bright. —en=kreis, m. zodiac. —en=los, adj. sunless. —en= reich, adj. sunny. —en=ſchirm, m. sunshade, parasol. —en=ſtich, m. sunstroke. —en=ſtillſtand, m. solstice. —en=ſyſtem, n. solar system. —en= uhr, f. sun-dial. —en=untergang, m. sunset. —en=verbrannt, adj. sun-burnt. —en=wende, f. solstice. —en= wendepunkt, m. solstitial point.

Sonnen ['zɔnən], v.a. & r. to sun, air.

Sonntag ['zɔnta:k], m. (—(e)s, pl. —e) Sunday; auf (den) —, on Sunday; —s, on Sundays. —s=kind, n. very lucky person.

Sonſt [zɔnst], I. adv. else, otherwise; besides; in other respects; independently of that; moreover; formerly, of yore; — niemand, no one else. II. n. das — und das Jetzt, the past and present. —ig, adj. other, existing besides; former.

Sopran [zo'pra:n], m. (—s, pl. —e) soprano.

Sorg—e ['zɔrgə], f. (pl. —en) care; trouble, concern; laſſen Sie das meine —e ſein, leave that to me. —lich, adj. & adv. careful, anxious; sad. —los, adj. thoughtless, reckless, careless. —ſam, adj. careful, anxious. —ſamkeit, f. carefulness. —en=frei, adj. free from care. —falt, f. carefulness, heedfulness. —fältig, adj. anxious; careful.

Sorge—n ['zɔrgən], I. v.n. (aux. h.) to fear, be afraid; to be anxious; to attend to, look after. II. v.r. ſich um eine S. —en, to trouble oneself about a thing.

Sort—e ['zɔrtə], f. (pl. —en) kind, sort. —ieren [—'ti:rən], v.a. to assort.

Soße ['zo:sə], f. (pl. —n) sauce.

Souverän [suvə'rɛ:n], I. m. (—s, pl. —s, —e) sovereign. II. adj. sovereign. —ität [—i'tɛ:t], f. sovereignty.

Sozial [zotsi'a:l], adj. social. —ismus [—'lɪsmʊs], m. Socialism. —iſtiſch [—'lɪstɪʃ], adj. socialist(ic). —demo= krat, m. Social-Democrat. —demo= kratie, f. Democratic Socialism.

Soz—ietät [zotsie'tɛ:t], f. society; partnership. —ius ['zotsiʊs], m. (—ius, pl. —ii) partner.

Spähe—n ['ʃpɛ:ən], v. I. n. (aux. h.) to pry into, watch. II. a. to search, explore; to spy out. —r, m. (—rs, pl. —r) spy. —r=blick, m. searching glance.

Spalt [ʃpalt], m. (—(e)s, pl. —e) cleft, chink, slit. —fuß, m. cloven-foot. —holz, n. split wood, firewood.

Spalt—en ['ʃpaltən] (p.p. geſpalten and geſpaltet). I. v.a. to split; cleave. II. v.r. & n. (aux. ſ.) to split; to gape, open. —er, m. (—ers, pl. —er) cleaver. —ig, adj. split, fissured.

Span [ʃpa:n], m. (—s, pl. Späne) chip,

shaving; wedge (*Carp.*). —**ferkel**, *n.* sucking pig. —**holz**, *n.* chips.

Spange ['ʃpaŋə], *f.* (*pl.* —**n**) clasp, bracelet, buckle.

Spann—**en** ['ʃpanən], *v.* I. *a.* to span; to strain, brace; to tighten, make tense; to brace (*the nerves, etc.*); to excite, intensify (*hopes, fears, interest*); to bend (*a bow*); to cock (*a gun*); to harness (*horses*). II. *n.* (*aux.* h.) to be exciting *or* interesting. —**er**, *m.* (—**ers**, *pl.* —**er**) bender, *etc.*; trigger; span; **Einspänner**, one-horse vehicle. —**ung**, *f.* stretching, *etc.*; voltage (*Radio*). —**ungs-abfall**, *m.* drop of voltage (*Radio*). —**aber**, *f.* sinew; nerve. —**balken**, *m.* tie-beam. —**feder**, *f.* spring. —**kraft**, *f.* elasticity.

Spar—**en** ['ʃpa:rən], I. *v.a.* to spare, save, economize. II. *v.n.* (*aux.* h.) to be thrifty, economical. III. *subst.n.* saving, thrift. —**er**, *m.* (—**ers**, *pl.* —**er**) economical person, saver. —**sam**, *adj.* economical, saving. —**samkeit**, *f.* economy; parsimony. —**kasse**, *f.* savings-bank. —**sucht**, *f.* parsimony.

Spargel ['ʃpargəl], *m.* (—**s**) asparagus.

Spärlich ['ʃpɛ:rlɪç], *adj.* scanty; meagre.

Sparren ['ʃparən], *m.* (—**s**, *pl.* —) spar, rafter.

Spaß [ʃpa:s], *m.* (—**es**, *pl.* **Späße**) jest; joke.

Spaß—**en** ['ʃpa:sən], *v.n.* (*aux.* h.) to joke, jest. —**macher**, *m.* (—**ers**, *pl.* —**er**) wag, joker.

Spät [ʃpɛ:t], *adj. & adv.* late; backward, behindhand. —**e**, *f.* advanced hour; lateness. —**er**, *comp. of* **spät**; subsequent, after, later. —**estens**, (**aufs** —**este**) *adv.* at the latest, at the farthest.

Spat [ʃpa:t], *m.* (—(**e**)**s**, *pl.* —**e**) spar (*Min.*).

Spaten ['ʃpa:tən], *m.* (—**s**, *pl.* —) spade.

Spatz [ʃpats], *m.* (—**es**, —**en**, *pl.* —**en**) sparrow (*coll.*).

Spazier—**en** [ʃpa'tsi:rən], *v.n.* (*aux.* f.); —**en** *or* —**en gehen** (**laufen**), to take a walk; —**en fahren**, to take a drive; to go (out) in a boat; —**en reiten**, to go for a ride. —**fahrt**, *f.* drive; sail. —**gang**, *m.* promenade; walk; **einen** —**gang machen**, to take a walk. —**gänger**, *m.*, —**gängerin**, *f.* walker.

Specht [ʃpɛçt], *m.* (—(**e**)**s**, *pl.*—**e**) woodpecker.

Sped [ʃpɛk], *m.* (—(**e**)**s**) bacon.

Sped—**ieren** [ʃpe'di:rən], *v.a.* to forward. —**iteur** [—i'tø:r], *m.* (—**iteurs**, *pl.* —**iteure**) forwarding agent. —**ition** [—tsi'o:n], *f.* despatch.

Speer [ʃpe:r], *m.* (—(**e**)**s**, *pl.* —**e**) lance, spear.

Speiche ['ʃpaɪçə], *f.* (*pl.* —**n**) spoke (*of a wheel*).

Speichel ['ʃpaɪçəl], *m.* (—**s**, *pl.* —) spittle, saliva.

Speicher ['ʃpaɪçər], *m.* (—**s**, *pl.* —) granary. —**n**, *v.a.* to store.

Speien ['ʃpaɪən], *ir.v.a.* & *n.* (*aux.* h.) to spit.

Speise ['ʃpaɪzə], *f.* (*pl.* —**n**) food. —**öl**, *n.* salad oil. —**en**, *v.* I. *a.* to feed. II. *n.* (*aux.* h.) to eat. —**ung**, *f.* eating; meal; food. —**kammer**, *f.* larder; pantry. —**karte**, *f.* bill of fare, menu. —**saal**, *m.* dining-room.

Spektakel [ʃpɛk'ta:kəl], *m.* (—**s**, *pl.* —) noise, row (*coll.*).

Spekulant [ʃpeku'lant], *m.* (—**en**, *pl.* —**en**) speculator.

Spende ['ʃpɛndə], *f.* (*pl.* —**n**) alms, charity; bounty. —**en**, *v.a.* to dispense; to bestow. —**er**, *m.* (—**ers**, *pl.* —**er**) dispenser; benefactor.

Sperling ['ʃpɛrlɪŋ], *m.* (—**s**, *pl.* —**e**) sparrow.

Sperr—**e** ['ʃpɛrə], *f.* (*pl.* —**en**) blockade; obstruction. —**en**, *v.* I. *a.* to spread open; to close; to barricade, obstruct; to blockade. II. *r.* to resist, oppose. —**ung**, *f.* spreading out; barricade; stoppage, prohibition. —**baum**, *m.* turnpike. —**beinig**, *adj.* straddling. —**feuer**, *n.* barrage (*Artil.*). —**hahn**, *m.* stop-cock. —**holz**, *n.* gag. —**kette**, *f.* door-chain. —**klappe**, *f.* organ-valve. —**rad**, *n.* cog-wheel. —**sitz**, *m.* stall, reserved seat (*Theat.*).

Spesen ['ʃpe:zən], *pl.* charges, costs. —**frei**, *adj.* all expenses paid. —**nachnahme**, *f.* reimbursement for charges.

Spezerei [ʃpetsə'raɪ], *f.* (*usually in the pl.* —**en**) spices.

Spezial [ʃpetsi'a:l], *adj.* special.

Spe—**zies** ['ʃpe:tsies], *f.* (*pl.* —**zies**) species. **die 4** —**zies**, the 4 first rules of arithmetic. —**zimen**, *n.* (—**zimens**, *pl.* —**zimina** [—'tsrmina]) specimen.

Sphär—**e** ['sfɛ:rə], *f.* (*pl.* —**en**) sphere; globe. —**isch**, *adj.* spherical.

Spick—en ['ʃpɪkən], *v.a.* to lard. **—aal**, *m.* smoked eel. **—gans**, *f.* smoked goose(-breast).

Spiegel ['ʃpi:gəl], *m.* (—s, *pl.* —) looking-glass, mirror. **—bild**, *n.* reflected image; mirage. **—ei**, *n.* poached egg. **—fechter**, *m.* dissembler; juggler. **—fechterei** [—'raɪ], *f.* sham-fight; pretence. **—fenster**, *n.* plate-glass window. **—glas**, *n.* plate-glass. **—glatt**, *adj.* as smooth as a mirror.

Spiegel—n ['ʃpi:gəln], *v.* I. *n.* (*aux.* h.) to be bright; to sparkle. II. *a.* to reflect. III. *r.* to look at oneself in a glass. **—ung**, *f.* reflection; mirage.

Spiel [ʃpi:l], *n.* (—(e)s, *pl.* —e) play, game, sport; auf's **—** setzen, to stake. **—en**, *v.a.* & *n.* (*aux.* h.) to play, sport; to gamble; to act, perform (*Theat.*); to play (*Mus.*). **—end**, I. *p.* & *adj.* playing, opalescent. II. *adv.* easily. **—er**, *m.* (—ers, *pl.* —er) player; actor; performer; gambler. **—erei** [—ə'raɪ], *f.* play, sport; trifle. **—erin**, *f.* actress. **—art**, *f.* variety (*of plants*). **—karte**, *f.* playing-card. **—mann**, *m.* musician. **—platz**, *m.* playground. **—ratte**, *f.* gambler. **—raum**, *m.* (free) play, scope; elbow-room. **—sache**, *f.* plaything, toy. **—schule**, *f.* kindergarten.

Spieß [ʃpi:s], *m.* (—es, *pl.* —e) spit; spear. **—bürger**, *m.* commonplace fellow, philistine. **—bürgerlich**, *adj.* vulgar.

Spinat [ʃpi'na:t], *m.* (—(e)s, *pl.* —e) spinach.

Spindel ['ʃpɪndəl], *f.* (*pl.* —n) spindle; distaff.

Spinett [ʃpi'nɛt], *n.* (—(e)s, *pl.* —e) spinet (*Mus.*).

Spinne ['ʃpɪnə], *f.* (*pl.* —n) spider.

Spinn—en ['ʃpɪnən], *ir.v.a.* & *n.* (*aux.* h.) to spin; to purr. **—er**, *m.* (—ers, *pl.* —er) spinner. **—erei** [—ə'raɪ], *f.* spinning; spinning-mill. **—erin**, *f.* spinner, spinster. **—(en)gewebe**, **—ennetz**, **—ennest**, *n.*, **—e(n)=webe**, *f.* cobweb. **—maschine**, *f.* spinning-jenny. **—rad**, *n.* spinning-wheel. **—rocken**, *m.* distaff.

Spion [ʃpi'o:n], *m.* (—s, *pl.* —e) spy. **—age** [—'na:ʒə], *f.*, **—entum**, *n.*(—entums) spying. **—ieren** [—'ni:rən], *v.n.* (*aux.* h.) to play the spy.

Spiral [ʃpi'ra:l], *adj.* spiral. **—antenne**, *f.* spiral aerial (*Radio*).

Spiritu—alismus [ʃpiritua'lɪsmʊs], *m.* spiritualism. **—ell** [—tu'ɛl], *adj.* spiritual. **—osen**[—tu'o:zən], *pl.* spirituous liquors. **—s**, *m.* spirit, alcohol.

Spitz [ʃpɪts], I. *adj.* & *adv.* pointed; sharp. II. *m.* (—es, *pl.* —e) Pomeranian dog. **—chen**, *n.* (—chens, *pl.* —chen) little point; lace. **—e**, *f.* (*pl.* —en) point; top, peak; head; (*pl.*) lace. **—bart**, *m.* pointed beard. **—berg**, *m.* peak. **—bub(e)**, *m.* rascal, rogue. **—bubenstreich**, *m.* knavish trick. **—findig**, *adj.* sharp; crafty; ingenious; subtle. **—findigkeit**, *f.* subtlety. **—name**, *m.* nickname.

Spitz—en ['ʃpɪtsən], *v.a.* to point; **die Ohren —en**, to prick up one's ears. **—ig**, *adj.* pointed; sharp; sarcastic. **—igkeit**, *f.* sharpness; piquancy; sarcasm.

Splitter ['ʃplɪtər], *m.* (—s, *pl.* —) splinter, chip. **—holz**, *n.* chips of wood. **—nackt**, *adj.* stark naked.

Splittern ['ʃplɪtərn], *v.* I. *a.* to shatter. II. *n.* (*aux.* j.) to splinter.

Sporn [ʃpɔrn], *m.* (—(e)s, *pl.* **Sporen**) spur. **—en**, *v.a.* to spur.

Spott [ʃpɔt], *m.* (—es) mockery, ridicule. **—billig**, *adj.* extremely cheap (*in price*). **—gedicht**, *n.* satirical poem.

Spött—er ['ʃpøtər], *m.* (—ers, *pl.* —er) mocker. **—isch**, I. *adj.* mocking. II. *adv.* in mockery.

Spotten ['ʃpɔtən], *v.n.* (*aux.* h. *gen.* or *über with acc.*) to mock, jeer at.

Sprach—e ['ʃpra:xə], *f.* (*pl.* —en) speech; language; idiom; **heraus mit der —e!** out with it! speak out! **—lich**, *adj.* linguistic; grammatical. **—armut**, *f.* poverty of expression. **—art**, *f.* idiom, dialect. **—fehler**, *m.* error in speech. **—fertig**, *adj.* fluent, voluble. **—fertigkeit**, *f.* fluency of speech.

Sprech—en ['ʃprɛçən], *ir.v.a.* & *n.* (*aux.* h.) to speak, say; to talk; to declare, pronounce (*judgment*); **er ist nicht zu —en**, he is not at home, not to be seen. **—end**, *p.* & *adj.* speaking. **—er**, *m.* (—ers, *pl.* —er) speaker; spokesman. **—art**, *f.* manner of speaking, diction. **—maschine**, *f.* phonograph. **—stunde**, *f.* consultation-hour.

Spreiten ['ʃpraɪtən], *v.a.* to spread out, extend.

Spreng—en ['ʃprɛŋən], *v.* I. *a.* to

sprinkle, strew; to water; to blow up, blast. II. *n.* (*aux.* f.) to gallop, ride at full speed. —**er**, *m.* (—**ers**, *pl.* —**er**) sprinkler. —**ung**, *f.* springing, blasting, *etc.*

Spreu [ʃprɔʏ], *f.* chaff; husks. —**regen**, *m.* drizzling rain.

Sprich— [ʃpriç] (*in comp.*) —**wort**, *n.* proverb. —**wörtlich**, *adj.* proverbial.

Sprießen ['ʃpriːsən], *ir.v.n.* (*aux.* f.) to sprout.

Spring [ʃpriŋ], *m.* (—(e)s, *pl.* —e) spring, source (*of water*).

Spring—en ['ʃpriŋən], *ir.v.n.* (*aux.* h. & f.) to leap, spring, jump; to gush, spout; to burst, fall in pieces. —**er**, *m.* (—**ers**, *pl.* —**er**) jumper; knight (*Chess*). —**brunnen**, *m.* fountain. —**flut**, *f.* spring-tide. —**kraft**, *f.* elasticity.

Spritze ['ʃpritsə], *f.* (*pl.* —n) syringe.

Spritzen ['ʃpritsən], *v.* I. *n.* (*aux.* h. & f.) to gush forth. II. *a.* to squirt, spurt.

Spröd—e ['ʃpröːdə], I. *adj.* & *adv.* brittle; coy; shy. II. *f.* (*pl.* —en) prude. —**heit**, —**igkeit**, *f.* demureness, coyness; prudery.

Sproß [ʃprɔs], *m.* (—(ff)es, *pl.* —(ff)en) shoot, sprig.

¹**Sprosse** ['ʃprɔsə], *f.* (*pl.* —n) point, prong.

²**Sprosse**, *f.* (*pl.* —n) rung.

Sprossen ['ʃprɔsən], *v.n.* (*aux.* h. & f.) to sprout.

Sprotte ['ʃprɔtə], *f.* (*pl.* —n) sprat.

Spruch [ʃprʊx], *m.* (—(e)s, *pl.* **Sprüche**) sentence, decree; verdict; saying; maxim, motto. —**haft**, *adj.* sententious.

Sprudel ['ʃpruːdəl], *m.* (—s, *pl.* —) bubbling spring; hot spring. —**n**, *v.* I. *n.* (*aux.* f.) to bubble, effervesce. II. *a.* to spurt forth.

Sprüh—en ['ʃpryːən], *v.* I. *a.* to sprinkle; to scatter. II. *n.* (*aux.* h.) to sparkle, scintillate. —**regen**, *m.* drizzling rain.

Sprung [ʃprʊŋ], *m.* (—es, *pl.* **Sprünge**) crack, fissure; spring, leap.

Spuck—e ['ʃpukə], *f.* spittle, saliva. —**en**, *v.a.* & *n.* (*aux.* h.) to spit.

Spuken ['ʃpuːkən], *v.n.* (*aux.* h.) & *imp.* to haunt (*a place*); **es spukt im Hause**, the house is haunted.

Spul—e ['ʃpuːlə], *f.* (*pl.* —en) spool, bobbin; coil (*Radio*). —**en**, *v.a.* to

wind upon a reel. —**er**, *m.* (—**ers**, *pl.* —**er**) winder.

Spülen ['ʃpyːlən], *v.* I. *a.* to wash, clean, scour. II. *n.* (*aux.* h.) to wash against, lap. —**wasser**, *n.* slops, dish-water.

Spund [ʃpʊnt], *m.* (& *n.*) (—es, *pl.* **Spünde**) bung.

Spur [ʃpuːr], *f.* (*pl.* —en) trace, track. —**los**, *adj.* trackless; without leaving a trace.

Spür—en ['ʃpyːrən], *v.* I. *a.* & *n.* (*aux.* h.) to trace, track. II. *a.* to perceive; to discover. —**hund**, *m.* dog that hunts by scent. —**nase**, *f.* inquisitive person.

Staat [ʃtaːt], *m.* (—s, *pl.* —en) state, parade, pomp; state, country; government; condition. —**en-bund**, *m.* confederation. —**licher-seits**, *adv.* on the part of the state. —**s-akten**, *pl.* state papers; state records. —**s-aktien**, *pl.* government bonds *or* securities. —**s-amt**, *n.* public office; civil service. —**s-angehörige(r)**, *m.* subject of a state. —**s-anwalt**, *m.* public prosecutor. —**s-anweisung**, *f.* bond, exchequer-bill. —**s-anzeiger**, *m.* official advertiser *or* gazette. —**s-behörde**, *f.* government authorities. —**s-grund-satz**, *m.* political maxim. —**s-mann**, *m.* (*pl.* —**männer**) statesman, politician —**s-minister**, *m.* secretary of state. —**s-rat**, *m.* council of state; councillor of state. —**s-rätin**, *f.* wife of a councillor of state. —**s-verfassung**, *f.* political constitution. —**s-verwaltung**, *f.* administration of a state; government. —**s-wirtschaft**, *f.* political economy.

Stab [ʃtaːp], *m.* (—s, *pl.* **Stäbe**, *as measure* —) staff; stick. —**s-offizier**, *m.* staff-officer.

Stachel ['ʃtaxəl], *m.* (—s, *pl.* —n) prickle; thorn; sting. —**ig**, (**stachlig**,) *adj.* prickly, thorny; stinging, poignant. —**beere**, *f.* gooseberry. —**draht**, *m.* barbed wire. —**draht-zaun**, *m.* barbed-wire fence. —**rede**, *f.* satirical speech. —**schwein**, *n.* porcupine.

Stacheln ['ʃtaxəln] *v.a.* to prick, sting.

Stadt [ʃtat], *f.* (*pl.* **Städte**) town. —**abgeordnete(r)**, *m.* town-councillor. —**bewohner**, *m.* townsman, dweller in a town. —**bezirk**, *m.* ward. —**gemeinde**, *f.* city corporation, municipality. —graben, m. town-moat. —haus, n. town-hall. —schreiber, m. town-clerk.

Staffel ['ʃtafəl], f. (& m. dial.) (pl. —n) step, round (of a ladder). —ei [—'lai], f. easel (Paint.).

Stahl [ʃta:l], m. (—s, pl. —e and Stähle) steel. —blech, n. steel plate, sheet-steel. —brunnen, m. chalybeate spring. —feder, f. steel pen; steel spring. —härtung, f. tempering of steel. —stich, m. steel engraving, print.

Stall [ʃtal], m. (—es, pl. Ställe) stall, stable. —knecht, m. ostler, groom. —meister, m. master of the horse; riding-master.

Stamm [ʃtam], m. (—es, pl. Stämme) stem, trunk; family; race, stock, breed. —en, v.n. (aux. ʃ.) to be descended, sprung (from). —baum, m. genealogical tree. —folge, f. line of descent. —gast, m. habitué, constant visitor (at an inn, etc.). —halter, m. son and heir. —mutter, f. ancestress. —verwandt, f. kinship.

Stamm—ein ['ʃtaməln], v.a. & n. (aux. h.) to stammer. —ler, m. (—lers, pl. —ler) stammerer.

Stämm—ig ['ʃtɛmɪç], adj. & adv. with a stem; strong, sturdy. —igkeit, f. strength, sturdiness.

Stampfen ['ʃtampfən], v. I. a. & n. (aux. h.) to stamp. II. a. to pound, crush.

Stand [ʃtant], m. (—es, pl. Stände) act of standing; position; station; profession; stand, stall; state, rate (of exchange, etc.); (pl.) estates of the realm; ein Mann von —e, a man of rank. —haft(ig), adj. steady, constant. —haftigkeit, f. constancy; resoluteness. —bild, n. statue. —es=amt, n. registrar's office. —es=gebühr, f. honour due to rank. —es=gemäß, —es=mäßig, adj. in accordance with one's rank. —punkt, m. point of view, standpoint.

Standarte [ʃtan'dartə], f. (pl. —n) standard, ensign.

Ständ—chen ['ʃtɛntçən], n. (—chens, pl. —chen) serenade. —ig, adj. fixed; permanent, settled.

Stange ['ʃtaŋə], f. (pl. —n) pole. —n= besen, m. long-handled broom. —n= bohne, f. climbing bean.

Stanze ['ʃtantsə], f. (pl. —n) stanza.

Stapel ['ʃta:pəl], m. (—s, pl. —) beam; pile; scaffolding. —n, v. I. a. to pile up. II. n. (aux. ʃ.) to stride, stalk. —gut, n. staple commodity. —holz, n. piled wood. —lauf, m. launching, launch. —ort, —platz, m. staple market.

¹Star [ʃta:r], m. (—(e)s & —(e)n, pl. —e & —en) starling.

²Star, m. (—(e)s, pl. —e); (grauer —) cataract. —blind, adj. blind from a cataract.

Stark [ʃtark], adj. & adv.(comp. stärker, sup. stärkst) strong; —er Esser, a hearty eater. —strom, m. high-power current (Radio).

Stärke ['ʃtɛrkə], f. strength, force; starch.

Stärk—en['ʃtɛrkən], v.a. to strengthen; to starch. —ung, f. strengthening, fortifying; starching. —ungs=mittel, n. restorative, tonic.

Starr [ʃtar], adj. stiff, motionless. —en, v.n. (aux. h.) to stiffen, be benumbed or rigid. —heit, f. stiffness, rigidity; obstinacy. —äugig, adj. & adv. staring, with fixed eyes. —kopf, m. stubborn person. —köpfig, adj. headstrong.

Statt [ʃtat], I. f. place. II. prep. (with gen.) instead of (of), in lieu (of), in the place (of); an meiner —, meiner —, instead of me, in my place. —lich, adj. & adv. stately. —lichkeit, f. elegance; magnificence. —halter, m. viceroy; governor; Stadtholder (in Holland).

Statue ['ʃta:tuə], f. (pl. —n) statue.

Stat—ur [ʃta'tu:r], f. (pl. —uren) height. —ut [—'tu:t], n. (—(e)s, pl. —uten) statute, law.

Staub [ʃtaup], m.—(e)s) dust; sich aus dem —e machen, to abscond. —ig, adj. dusty. —igkeit, f. dustiness. —regen, m. fine rain; spray. —fame, m. pollen. —wolke, f. cloud of dust.

Staud—e ['ʃtaudə], f. (pl. —en; dim. Stäudchen, Stäudlein, n.) shrub; bush. —ig, adj. shrub-like. —en= gebüsch, n. copse.

Staunen ['ʃtaunən], I. v.n. (aux. h.) to be astonished. II. subst.n. astonishment. —s=wert, —s=würdig, adj. astonishing.

Stech—en ['ʃtɛçən], ir.v.a. & n. (aux. h.) to prick; to pierce; to sting; to stab; to engrave; in See —en, to put to sea.

—**palme,** *f.* holly. —**feide,** *f.* embroidery-silk.

Sted—en ['ʃtɛkən], I. *reg. & (sometimes) ir.v.a.* to stick; to put, place; **in Brand —en,** to set on fire. II. *reg. & ir.v.n.* (*aux.* ɥ.) to stick fast, be fixed. III. *subst.n.* setting, putting, *etc.* —**brief,** *m.* warrant of arrest. —**en= pferd,** *n.* hobby; fad, whim. —**ꜱ fontaft,** *m.* wall-plug (*Radio*). —**ꜱ nadel,** *f.* pin. —**rübe,** *f.* turnip.

Steg [ʃteːk], *m.* (—(e)s, *pl.* —e) foot-path, narrow path. —**reif,** *m.* stirrup; **aus dem —reif(e) reden,** to speak extempore.

Steh—en ['ʃteːən], I. *ir.v.n.* (*aux.* ɥ. & f.) to stand. II. *v.a.* **feinen Mann —en,** to hold one's own against, be a match for another; **Rede und Antwort —en,** to answer questions. III. *subst.n.* standing, *etc.* —**end,** *p. & adj.* standing; stationary; upright.

Stehlen ['ʃteːlən], *ir.v.a. & n.* (*aux.* ɥ.) to steal.

Steif [ʃtaif], *adj. & adv.* stiff; inflexible; obstinate. —**heit,** *f.* stiffness; rigidity; awkwardness. —**halfig,** *adj.* stiff-necked.

Steig [ʃtark], *m.* (—(e)s, *pl.* —e) steep *or* narrow way.

Steig—en ['ʃtargən], I. *ir.v.n.* (*aux.* ɥ. & f.) to mount; **in den Kopf —en,** to go to one's head. II. *subst.n.* rise; advance; increase. —**erer,** *m.* (—ꜱ **erers,** *pl.* —**erer**) auctioneer. —**ern,** *v.a.* to raise, enhance; to outbid; to buy at an auction. —**erung,** *f.* raising, enhancing; auction. —**bügel,** *m.* stirrup.

Steil [ʃtail], *adj.* steep. —**heit,** *f.* steepness.

Stein [ʃtain], *m.* (—(e)s, *pl.* —e) stone. —**e(r)n,** *adj.* stone. —**icht,** *adj.* stone-like, stony. —**ig,** *adj.* stony. —**bild,** *n.* statue. —**brecher,** *m.* quarryman. —**bruch,** *m.* quarry. —**butt,** *m.,* —**butte,** *f.* turbot. —**drud,** *m.* litho-graphy. —**meß,** *m.* stone-cutter, stone-mason. —**öl,** *n.* petroleum, rock-oil. —**werf,** *n.* masonry. —**zeit,** *f.* stone age.

Stelle ['ʃtɛlə], *f.* (*pl.* —n) place; **auf der —e,** on the spot, immediately.

Stell—en ['ʃtɛlən], *v.* I. *a.* to put, place; **eine Frage —en,** to put a question; **eine Uhr —en,** to regulate a watch. II. *r.* to place *or* post one something,

take one's stand; to feign, pretend. —**er,** *m.* (—**ers,** *pl.* —**er**) one that sets, places, *etc.* —**ung,** *f.* putting, placing; arrangement; disposition; posture, attitude; position; station. —**ꜱ dichein,** *n.* meeting, rendezvous. —**vertretend,** *adj.* vicarious, represen-tative. —**vertreter,** *m.* deputy; proxy. —**vertretung,** *f.* representation; de-putyship.

Stelz—e ['ʃtɛltsə], *f.* (*pl.* —**en**) stilt. —**bein,** *n.* wooden leg.

Stemmen ['ʃtɛmən], *v.a.* to fell; to stand firm against; to stem (*water, etc.*).

Stempel ['ʃtɛmpəl], *m.* (—ꜱ, *pl.* —) stamp; die. —**gebühr,** *f.,* —**geld,** *n.* stamp-duty.

Stempel—n ['ʃtɛmpəln], I. *v.a.* to stamp. II. *subst.n.,* —**ung,** *f.* stamp-ing; coining.

Stempler ['ʃtɛmplər], *m.* (—ꜱ, *pl.* —) stamper.

Stenge ['ʃtɛŋə], *f.* (*pl.* —**n**) topmast. —**l,** *m.* (—ꜱ, *pl.* —**l**) stalk, stem. —**l=glas,** *n.* wine-glass (*with stem*).

Steppdede ['ʃtɛpdɛkə], *f.* (*pl.* —**n**) quilt.

Sterb—en ['ʃtɛrbən], I. *ir.v.n.* (*aux.* f.) to die. II. *subst.n.* dying; death; **im —en liegen,** to be dying. —**lich,** *adj. & adv.* mortal. —**lichkeit,** *f.* mortality. —**e=gewand,** *n.* winding-sheet, shroud.

Steril [steˈriːl], *adj.* unproductive, barren.

Sterlet ['ʃtɛrlɛt], *m.* (—ꜱ, *pl.* —e) small sturgeon.

Stern [ʃtɛrn], *m.* (—(e)s, *pl.* —e) star. —**chen,** *n.* (—**chens,** *pl.* —**chen**) little star; asterisk. —**funde,** —**lehre,** *f.* astronomy. —**schnuppe,** *f.,* —**schuß,** *m.* shooting star. —**deuterei** [—ˈrai], *f.* astrology. —**warte,** *f.* observatory.

Stets [ʃteːts], *adv.* steadily, continu-ally, always.

1**Steuer** [ˈʃtɔyər], *n.* (—ꜱ, *pl.* —) rudder, helm. —**bord,** *n.* starboard. —**mann,** *m.* helmsman.

2**Steuer,** *f.* (*pl.* —**n**) tax. —**amt,** *n.* customs-office. —**anlage,** —**auflage,** *f.* imposition of a tax. —**anschlag,** *m.* assessment. —**beamte(r),** *m.* revenue-officer; tax-collector. —**ꜱ einnehmer,** *m.* tax-collector. —**ꜱ einschätzung,** *f.* assessment. —**erhe= bung,** *f.* collecting *or* levying of taxes. —**frei,** *adj.* free of duty.

¹Steuer—n ['ʃtɔyərn], v. I. a. to steer. II. n. (aux. h. & ſ.) to steer; to stand for (Naut.).

²Steuern, v.a. & n. (aux h.) to pay taxes.

Stich [ʃtɪç], m. (—(e)s, pl. —e) prick, puncture; sting; im — laſſen, to leave in the lurch. —eln, v.a. & n. (aux. h.) to taunt, jeer. —ler, m. (—lers, pl. —ler) giber, taunter. —wort, n. catchword, cue (Theat.).

Stick—en ['ʃtɪkən], v. I. a. & n. (aux. ſ.) to suffocate, choke. II. a. to embroider. —er, m., —erin, f. embroiderer. —erei [—ə'raɪ], f. embroidery. —garn, n. embroidery cotton. —häkchen, n. crochet needle. —huſten, m. whooping cough. —ſeide, f. crewel-silk. —ſtoff, n. nitrogen.

Stieben ['ʃti:bən], ir.v. I. a. to start, set suddenly in motion; auseinander —, to disperse. II. n. (aux. h. & ſ.) to rise like dust.

Stief [ʃti:f], prefix (in comp. generally =) step. —bruder, m. step-brother. —mütterchen, n. pansy.

Stiefel ['ʃti:fəl], m. (—s, pl. —) boot. —knecht, m. boot-jack. —leiſten, m. boot-last. —putzer, m. shoeblack.

Stiege ['ʃti:gə], f. (pl. —n) staircase, (flight of) stairs.

Stieglitz ['ʃti:glɪts], m. (—es, pl. —e) goldfinch.

Stiel [ʃti:l], m. (—(e)s, pl. —e) haft, handle.

¹Stier [ʃti:r], adj. fixed, staring.

²Stier, m. (—(e)s, pl. —e) bull, steer. —kampf, m. bull-fight.

¹Stift [ʃtɪft], m. (—(e)s, pl. —e) brad, pin, peg, rivet. —farbe, f. pastel. —gemälde, n. crayon drawing.

²Stift, n. (—(e)s, pl. —e and —er) convent, monastery.

Stift—en ['ʃtɪftən], v.a. to found, establish, institute. —er, m. (—ers, pl. —er), —erin, f. founder; author, originator. —ung, f. founding; establishment; institution. —s-dame, —s-frau, f., —s-fräulein, n. canoness. —s-gebäude, n. chapter-house. —s-gemeinde, f. congregation of a cathedral. —s-herr, m. canon, prebendary.

Stil [ʃti:l], m. (—s, pl. —e) style.

Still [ʃtɪl], —e, adj. & adv. still, silent; quiet; der — Ozean, Pacific Ocean. —e, f. calm, stillness, silence. —halten, n. stop, pause, halt. —s

ſchweigen, n. silence. —ſchweigend, adj. & adv. silent; tacit, implied. —ſtand, m. stand-still, stop. —ſtehen, n. stop. —ſtehend, adj. stationary.

Still—en ['ʃtɪlən], v.a. to quiet, appease; den Durſt —en, to quench thirst. —end, p. & adj. soothing, sedative. —ung, f. stilling; appeasing. —amme, f. wet-nurse.

Stimm—e ['ʃtɪmə], f. (pl. —en) voice; vote; stop (of an organ); opinion; entſcheidende —e, casting vote. —s en-einheit, -en-einhelligkeit, f. unanimity. —en-mehrheit, f. majority. —en-minderheit, f. minority. —s gabel, f. tuning-fork. —pfeife, f. tuning-pipe, pitch-pipe. —recht, n. right of voting, franchise. —wechſel, m. breaking of the voice. —zettel, m. voting paper.

Stimm—en ['ʃtɪmən], v. I. a. to tune; to dispose, incline; to determine, induce. II. n. (aux. h.) to agree; to accord; to harmonize; to vote. —er, m. (—ers, pl. —er) tuner. —ung, f. tuning; tune, pitch. —ungs-voll, adj. & adv. in high spirits.

Stink—en ['ʃtɪŋkən], ir.v.n. (aux. h.) to stink. —end, p. & adj., —ig, adj. stinking. —tier, n. skunk.

Stipendium [ʃtipɛndi'u:m], m. (—s, pl. Stipendien) scholarship.

Stirn [ʃtɪrn], —e, f. (pl. —en) forehead; brow. —runzeln, n. frowning.

Stock [ʃtɔk], I. m. (—(e)s, pl. Stöcke) stick; cane; über — und Stein, up hill and down dale. II. m. (pl. —) floor, story (of a house). —blind, adj. stone-blind. —dunkel, —finſter, adj. pitch-dark. —dürr, adj. dry as a bone. —fiſch, m. stockfish. —ſtill, adj. stock-still. —taub, adj. stonedeaf. —werk, n. story, floor.

Stöck—chen ['ʃtœkçən], n. (—chens, pl. —chen) cane. —ig, suffix (in comp. =) -storied; zwei—iges Haus, two-storied house. —iſch, adj. obstinate, stiff.

Stock—en ['ʃtɔkən], I. v.a. to prop, stake. II. v.n. (aux. h. & ſ.) to stop; to be dull, to stagnate. III. subst.n. stopping, cessation; stagnation. —ig, adj. mildewed, fusty.

Stoff [ʃtɔf], m. (—(e)s, pl. —e) matter; substance.

Stöhnen ['ʃtø:nən], v.n. (aux. h.) to groan (über eine S., over, at a thing).

Sto—iker ['ʃtoːɪkər], m. (—ikers, pl. —iker) Stoic. —ism, adj. Stoic.

Stollen ['ʃtolən], m. (—s, pl. —) prop, post; cake or bun.

Stolper ['ʃtolpər], m. (—s, pl. —), —ei [—ə'raɪ], f. stumble; blunder. —er, m. (—ers, pl. —er) stumbler, blunderer. —ig, adj. stumbling; uneven, rough (as a road).

Stolpern ['ʃtolpərn], I. v.n. (aux. ḥ. & ʃ.) to stumble; to blunder. II. subst.n. stumble; blunder.

Stolz [ʃtolts], I. adj. & adv. proud. II. m. (—s) pride.

Stopf—en ['ʃtopfən], v. I. a. to stuff; to darn, mend; gestopft voll, crammed full. II. r. to gorge. —er, m. (—ers, pl. —er) stuffer, filler, stopper. —fled, m. patch, darn. —garn, n. darning-cotton. —nadel, f. darning-needle. —naht, f. darn.

Stopp—el ['ʃtopəl], f. (pl. —eln) stubble. —el=haft, —elig, adj. stubbly, like stubble. —el=rübe, f. turnip. —el=werk, n. (literary) patchwork.

Stör [ʃtøːr], m. (—s, pl. —e) sturgeon. —ei, n., —rogen, m. caviare.

Storch [ʃtorç], m. (—(e)s, pl. Störche) stork.

Störch—in ['ʃtørçɪn], f. (pl. —innen) female stork. —ling, m. (—lings, pl. —linge) young stork.

Stör—en ['ʃtøːrən], v. I. a. to disturb; to interrupt. II. n. (aux. ḥ.) to stir, poke (im Feuer, the fire). —er, m. (—ers, pl. —er) disturber. —ung, f. disturbance; trouble. —befreier, m. interference-eliminator (Radio). —en= fried, m. mischief-maker.

Störr—ig ['ʃtorɪç], —isch, adj. stubborn; peevish. —igkeit, f. stubbornness.

Stoß [ʃtoːs], m. (—es, pl. Stöße) push, shove, thrust.

Stoßen ['ʃtoːsən], I. ir.v.a. to push, shove; to strike, hit; to kick; to stab. II. ir.v.r. to hit, strike (an, against). III. ir.v.n. (aux. ḥ. & ʃ.) to thrust, push, knock, strike (an, auf, gegen, against); to blow (in ein Horn, a horn). IV. subst.n. pushing, thrusting.

Stotter—er ['ʃtotərər], m. (—ers, pl. —er) stutterer, stammerer. —ig, adj. stuttering. —n, v.n. (aux. ḥ.) to stammer, stutter.

Strafbar ['ʃtraːfbaːr], adj. punishable;

criminal. —keit, f. punishableness; culpability.

Strafe ['ʃtraːfə], f. (pl. —n) punishment.

Straf—en ['ʃtraːfən], v.a. to punish. —end, p. & adj. punishing, punitive. —er, m. (—ers, pl. —er) punisher, chastiser. —befehl, m. order to inflict a punishment. —erlaß, m. remission of punishment. —fall, m. penal case. —geld, n. fine. —gericht, n. criminal court. —gesetz, n. penal law. —= gesetzbuch, n. penal code. —los, adj. & adv. unpunished; exempt from punishment, guiltless. —losigkeit, f. impunity. —predigt, f. severe sermon or lecture. —vollziehung, —= vollstreckung, f., —vollzug, m. infliction of punishment. —würdig, adj. deserving punishment; punishable, penal.

Straff [ʃtraf], adj. & adv. stretched, tight; erect; close; austere. —heit, f. tightness, tension. —seil, n. tightrope. —ziehen, n. tension.

Sträf—lich ['ʃtrɛːflɪç], adj. punishable, criminal. —ling, m. culprit; convict.

Strahl [ʃtraːl], m. (—(e)s, pl. —en) ray, beam. —en, v. I. n. (aux. ḥ.) to beam, radiate. II. a. to beam, shed forth. —end, p. & adj. radiant; beaming. —ig, adj. radiant. —ung, f. radiance; radiation (Radio).

Stramm [ʃtram], adj. & adv. vigorous; buxom.

Strand [ʃtrant], m. (—(e)s, pl. —e) strand, beach.

Strang [ʃtraŋ], m. (—es, pl. Stränge) rope, cord. —leder, n. trace-leather.

Straße ['ʃtraːsə], f. (pl. —n) street; road. —=bahn, f. tramway. —n= damm, m. causeway. —n=dieb, m. highwayman; pickpocket. —n=feger, m. scavenger. —n=junge, m. street-arab. —n=kleid, n. walking dress.

Strateg—e [ʃtra'teːgə], m. (—en, pl. —en) strategist. —ie [—e'giː], f. strategy. —isch, adj. strategic.

Sträuben ['ʃtroybən], v. I. a. to ruffle up. II. r. to stand, bristle up; (fig.) to struggle against.

Strauch [ʃtraux], m. (—(e)s, pl. Sträuche, Sträucher) shrub, bush. —ig, adj. bushy.

1Strauß [ʃtraus], m. (—es, pl. Sträuße) top-knot; nosegay, bouquet.

2Strauß, m. (—es, pl. —e) ostrich.

Streb—en ['ʃtreːbən], I. v.n. (aux. h.) to strive, struggle. II. subst.n. striving, endeavour. —er, m. (—es, pl. —er) pushing fellow. —fam, adj. assiduous; aspiring. —famkeit, f. assiduity, perseverance.

Streck—bar ['ʃtrɛkbaːr], adj. extensible. —barkeit, f. extensibility; ductility. —e, f. (pl. —en) tract, stretch; distance.

Strecken ['ʃtrɛkən], v. I. a. to stretch, extend, spread. II. r. to stretch oneself. —weife, adv. here and there.

Streich [ʃtraɪç], m. (—(e)s, pl. —e) stroke, trick, prank, joke; dummer —, foolish action. —eln, v.a. to stroke; to caress. —en, I. ir.v.n. (aux. h. & f.) to stretch, extend (towards, etc.); to run, fly, sweep over. II. ir.v.a. to touch; to spread; to scrape. —er, m. (—ers, pl. —er) rover, rambler; whet-stone. —hölzchen, pl. (lucifer-)matches. —instrument, n. stringed instrument. —vogel, m. bird of passage.

Streif [ʃtraɪf], m.(—(e)s,pl.—e), —chen, n. (—chens, pl. —chen) strip. —en, m. (—ens, pl. —en) stripe, streak; slip, scrap (of paper).

Streif—en ['ʃtraɪfən], I. v.a. to streak, stripe. II. v.n. (aux. h. & f.) to ramble, rove. —er, m. (—ers, pl. —er) scout; rambler. —ig, adj. striped. —band, n. postal wrapper. —blick, m. glance. —efel, m. zebra. —fchuß, m. grazing shot. —wache, f. patrol. —wunde, f. scratch, slight wound.

Streik [ʃtraɪk], m. (—(e)s, pl. —e and —s), strike, suspension of work.

Streit [ʃtraɪt], m. (—(e)s, pl. —e (obs.), —igkeiten) dispute, quarrel. —bar, adj. fit for fighting, effective. —barkeit, f. warlike spirit or character.

Streit—en ['ʃtraɪtən], ir.v.n. (aux. h.) to fight. —er, m. (—ers, pl. —er) combatant. —ig, adj. contending. —igkeit, f. dispute, controversy. —handel, m. lawsuit. —fache, f. matter in dispute. —fchlichter, m. peacemaker; arbitrator. —fchrift, f. polemic treatise. —fucht, f. quarrelsomeness.

Streng [ʃtrɛŋ], —e, adj. & adv. severe, stern. —e, f. (pl. —en) sternness, austerity. —gläubig, adj. strictly orthodox.

Streu [ʃtrɔʏ], f. (pl. —en) litter.

Streu—en ['ʃtrɔʏən], v.a. to strew. —ung, f. strewing, scattering. —büchfe, f. caster (for pepper, sugar, etc.). —stroh, n. litter-straw. —zucker, m. caster-sugar.

Strich [ʃtrɪç], m. (—es, pl. —e) stroke, line, dash; gegen den —, against the grain; einen — durch die Rechnung machen, to upset a person's plans. —punkt, m. semicolon.

Strick [ʃtrɪk], m. (—(e)s, pl. —e) cord, rope.

Strick—en ['ʃtrɪkən], v.a. to knit; to net; to ensnare. —er, m. (—ers, pl. —ers), —erin, f. knitter. —erei [—ə'raɪ], f. knitting. —garn, n. knitting-yarn. —nadel, f. knitting-needle.

Striegel ['ʃtriːgəl], m. (—s, pl. —) curry-comb. —n, v.a. to curry.

Striem—e ['ʃtriːmə], f. (pl. —en), —en, m. (—ens, pl. —en) stripe; streak; mark or weal.

Stroh [ʃtroː], n. (—s) straw. —ig, adj. strawy. —witwe, f. grass-widow.

Strolch [ʃtrɔlç], m. (—es, pl. —e(r)) vagabond.

Strom [ʃtroːm], m. (—(e)s, pl. Ströme) large river; stream. —'ab, —'ab-wärts, adv. down-stream. —'auf, —'aufwärts, adv. up the river.

Ström—en ['ʃtrøːmən], v.n. (aux. h. & f.) to stream, flow. —ung, f. streaming; current.

Strotzen ['ʃtrɔtsən], v.n. (aux. h.) to be puffed up. —d, p. & adj. swollen, distended.

Strudel ['ʃtruːdəl], m. (—s, pl. —) whirlpool.

Strumpf [ʃtrʊmpf], m. (—(e)s, pl. Strümpfe) stocking. —band, n. garter.

Struppig ['ʃtrʊpɪç], adj. rough, bristly.

Stube ['ʃtuːbə], f. (pl. —n) room. —n-hoder, m. stay-at-home. —n-mäd-chen, n. housemaid.

Stück [ʃtʏk], n. (—(e)s, pl. —e, as measure —) piece; aus freien —en, of one's own free will.

Student [ʃtu'dɛnt], m. (—en, pl. —en) student. —enhaft, —ifch, adj. & adv. student-like. —entum, n. (—s) student life or habits. —in, f. (woman) student.

Stud—ie ['ʃtuːdiə], f. (pl. —ien) study (of a painter), (pl.) studies. —ieren [—'diːrən], I. v.a. & n. (aux.

h.) to study. II. *subst.n.* studying.
—ierende(r), *m.* student. —iert,
p.p. & *adj.* studied.

Stufe [ʃtu:fə], *f.* (*pl.* —n) step, stair;
degree, rank. —n=ſchalter, *m.* step-
switch (*Radio*).

Stuhl [ʃtu:l], *m.* (—(e)s, *pl.* Stühle) seat;
chair.

Stülp—en [ʃtylpən], *v.a.* to turn upside
down *or* inside out; to turn up.
—naſe, *f.* turned-up nose.

Stumm [ʃtʊm], *adj.* dumb, mute.

Stümper [ʃtympər], *m.* (—s, *pl.* —)
bungler.

Stumpf [ʃtʊmpf], I. *adj.* & *adv.*
stumpy; blunt, dull. II. *m.* (—(e)s, *pl.*
Stümpfe) stump. —fuß, *m.* club-
foot. —näschen, *n.* little turn-up
nose. —ſinn, *m.* stupidity. —=
ſinnig, *adj.* dull, stupid.

Stunde [ʃtʊndə], *f.* (*pl.* —n) hour.
—n=lang, *adj.* & *adv.* for hours.

Stündlich [ʃtyntlɪç], I. *adj.* hourly.
II. *adv.* from hour to hour.

Sturm [ʃtʊrm], *m.* (—(e)s, *pl.* Stürme)
storm; tumult. —feſt, *adj.* tempest-
proof. —flut, *f.* high tide raised by a
storm. —glocke, *f.* tocsin. —laufen,
n. assault. —läufer, *m.* stormer.
—leiter, *f.* scaling-ladder.

Stürm—en [ʃtyrmən], *v.* I. *a.* to storm;
to take by storm. II. *n.* (*aux.* h.) to
storm, be violent. —end, *p.* & *adj.*
attacking; violent. —iſch, *adj.* &
adv. stormy; impetuous.

Sturz [ʃtʊrts], *m.* (—es, *pl.* Stürze)
sudden fall, crash; cataract; downfall,
ruin. —bach, *m.* torrent, rapid stream.

Stürzen [ʃtyrtsən], I. *v.a.* to hurl,
throw, plunge; to overturn. II. *v.r.*
& *n.* (*aux.* ſ.) to sink, be precipitous;
to rush. III. *v.n.* (*aux.* ſ.) to fall
(*suddenly and violently*).

Stute [ʃtu:tə], *f.* (*pl.* —n) mare.

Stüß—e [ʃtytsə], *f.* (*pl.* —en) prop, stay.
—en, *v.a.* to sustain, support; to
lean (*one's arm, etc.*).

Stutz—en [ʃtʊtsən], I. *v.n.* (*aux.* h.)
to stop short; to hesitate; to be
startled. II. *v.a.* to cut short. III.
subst.n. cropping, *etc.*; hesitation,
stopping short. —er, *m.* (—ers, *pl.*
—er) fop, dandy. —erhaft, *adj.*
foppish. —ig, *adj.* surprised.

Subjekt [zʊp'jɛkt], *n.* (—s, *pl.* —e)
subject (*Gram., Log.*). —iv [—'ti:f],
adj. subjective.

Substanz [zʊp'stants], *f.* (*pl.* —en)
substance, matter, stuff.

Suche [ˈzu:çə], *f.* (*pl.* —n) search, quest.
—en, *v.a.* & *n.* (*aux.* h.) to seek,
search. —er, *m.* (—ers, *pl.* —er)
seeker.

Sucht [zʊxt], *f.* (*pl. rare* Süchte)
sickness, disease.

Süchtig [ˈzʏçtɪç], *adj.* sickly.

Sud [zu:t], *m.* (—(e)s, *pl.* —e) boiling;
brewing. —el, *m.* (—els, *pl.* —el)
puddle. —elhaft, —elig, *adj.* dirty,
filthy.

Süd [zy:t], *m.* (—es) (*poet.* & *in
compds.*) —en, *m.* —ens, *abbr.* S.)
south; (*in comp.=*) south. —lich,
adj. & *adv.* south, southern. —breite,
f. south latitude (*Geog.*). —früchte,
pl. tropical fruit. —pol, *m.* Antarctic
pole. —ſee, *f.* Pacific Ocean.

Sühn—e [ˈzy:nə], *f.* atonement, expiation. —en, *v.a.* to conciliate; to atone
for. —er, *m.* (—ers, *pl.* —er) atoner.
—ung, *f.* reconciliation; atonement.

Sulz—e [ˈzʊltsə], Sülz—e [ˈzʏltsə], *f.*
pickle, brine. —en, *v.a.* to pickle,
corn.

Summ—a [ˈzʊma:], *f.* (*pl.* —en) sum;
in —a, in short. —e, *f.* (*pl.* —en) sum;
amount. —en, —ieren [—'mi:rən],
v.a. to sum up.

Summen [ˈzʊmən], Sumſen, *v.* I. *a.*
& *n.* (*aux.* h.) to hum. II. *n.* (*aux.* h.)
to buzz.

Sumpf [zʊmpf], *m.* (—(e)s, *pl.* Sümpfe)
swamp. —ig, *adj.* marshy. —huhn,
n. moor-hen; (*fig.*) debauchee.

Sund [zʊnt], *m.* (—(e)s, *pl.* —e) sound,
strait.

Sünd—e [ˈzʏndə], *f.* (*pl.* —en) sin;
offence. —er, *m.* (—ers, *pl.* —er)
sinner. —haft, —ig, *adj.* sinful.
—haftigkeit, *f.* sinfulness. —igen, *v.a.*
& *n.* (*aux.* h.) to (commit a) sin. —lich,
adj. sinful; criminal. —lichkeit, *f.*
iniquity. —en=bahn, *f.* road to perdition. —en=bock, *m.* scapegoat. —en=
erlaß, *m.* absolution. —en=fall, *m.*
fall (*of man*). —en=frei, *adj.* free from
sin. —flut, *f.* the Flood.

Suppe [ˈzʊpə], *f.* (*pl.* —n) soup, broth.
—n=kraut, *n.* pot-herb.

Süß [zy:s], *adj.* & *adv.* sweet. —chen,
n. (—chens, *pl.* —chen) sweetheart,
darling. —e, *f.* sweetness. —en, *v.a.*
to sweeten. —igkeit, *f.* (*pl.* —igkeiten)
sweetness. —lich, *adj.* sweetish;

mawkish. —lichkeit, f. sweetishness.
—ling, m. (—lings, pl. —linge)
flatterer; fop. —wasser, n. fresh
water.

Sylph—e ['zylfə], f. (pl. —en, —iden)
sylph.

Symbol—if [zym'bo:lɪk], f. symbolism.
—isch, adj. symbolical.

Symmet—rie [zymɛ'tri:], f. symmetry.
—risch [—me:trɪʃ], adj. symmetrical.

Sympath—etisch [zympa'te:tɪʃ], adj.
& adv. sympathetic. —ie [—'ti:], f.
sympathy.

T

T, t [te:], n. T, t.

Tabak ['ta:bak], m. (—s, pl. —e)
tobacco. —s=dose, f. snuff-box.

Tabelle [ta'bɛlə], f. (pl. —n) table,
index.

Tablett [ta'blɛt], n. (—s, pl. —e) tray.

Tadel ['ta:dəl], m. (—s) blame. —haft,
adj. blameable. —haftigkeit, f.
blameableness. —frei, —los, adj.
irreproachable. —n, v.a. to blame.
—ns=wert, adj. blameable.

Tadler ['ta:dlər], m. (—s, pl. —), —in,
f. fault-finder.

Tafel ['ta:fəl], f. (pl. —n) table;
tablet; cake (of chocolate, etc.). —arbeit,
f. panelling. —werk, n. wainscoting.
—zeug, n. table-linen; plate.

Taffet, Taft ['tafɛt, taft], m. (—(e)s, pl.
—e) taffeta. —en, adj. of taffeta.

Tag [ta:k], m. (—(e)s, pl. —e) day; daylight; open air; es ist (heller) —, it is
broad day(light); der jüngste —, the
Last Day, Doomsday; in den —
hineinleben, to live from hand to
mouth, at random. —(c)=arbeiter, m.
day-labourer. —(e)=arbeiterin, f.
charwoman. —(e)=blatt, daily paper.
—(e)=buch, n. diary. —'aus, —'ein,
adv. every day of the week, daily.
—(e)=lohn, m. day's wages. —(e)=
löhner, m. workman. —(e)=löhnerin,
f. charwoman. —täglich, adj. daily.
— =und = 'Nacht=gleiche, f. equinox.

Tages— ['ta:gəs] (in comp.) —'anbruch,
m. break of day, daybreak. —arbeit,
f. day's work. —bericht, m. daily
report. —grauen, n. dawn. —helle,
f. light of day. —licht, n. daylight.
—zeit, f. time of day.

Täg—ig ['tɛ:gɪç], suff. (in comp.);
drei —ig, lasting three days. —lich,
adj. & adv. daily; every day.

Takel ['ta:kəl], n. (—s, pl. —) tackle
(Naut.). —meister, m. rigger; boat-
swain. —wert, n. rigging, tackle.

Takt [takt], m. (—(e)s, pl. —e) time,
measure (Mus.); tact; — halten, to
keep time. —los, adj. tactless.
—losigkeit, f. want of tact. —mäßig,
adj. in good time, well-timed; regular.
—voll, adj. tactful, discreet.

Taktik ['taktɪk], f. (pl. —en) tactics.
—er, m. (—ers, pl. —er) tactician.

Tal [ta:l], n. (—s, pl. Täler, dim.
Tälchen) valley. —abwärts, adv.
down-stream; down-hill.

Talent [ta'lɛnt], n. (—(e)s, pl. —e)
talent, natural gift. —los, adj. without talent. —voll, adj. talented.

Taler ['ta:lər], m. (—s, pl. —) dollar.

Talg [talk], m. (—(e)s) tallow. —ig,
adj. tallowy.

Tambour ['tambu:r], m. (—s, pl. —e)
drummer; drum. —in [—u'ri:n], n.
(—ins, pl. —ine) tambourine. —
major, m. drum-major.

Tändel—ei [tɛndə'laɪ], f. dallying.
—er, Tändler ['tɛndlər], m. (—ers, pl.
—er) trifler; dawdler. —haft, —ig,
adj. trifling. —n, v.n. (aux. h.) to
trifle; to flirt.

Tang [taŋ], m. (—(e)s, pl. —e) sea-weed.

Tann—e ['tanə], f. (pl. —n) (silver)
fir. —en, adj. fir. —ig, adj. planted
with firs; fir. —en=baum, m. fir-tree.

Tante ['tantə], f. (pl. —n, dim. Tant=
chen, n.) aunt.

Tantieme [tantɪ'ɛ:mə], f. (pl. —n) share
in profits, royalty.

Tanz [tants], m. (—es, pl. Tänze)
dance. —en, v.a. & n. (aux. h. & f.)
to dance. —boden, m. public ball-
room. —karte, f. programme.

Tänz—er ['tɛntsər], m. (—ers, pl. —er),
—erin, f. dancer.

Tapet [ta'pe:t], n. (—(e)s) carpet; auf's
— bringen, to broach a subject.
—e, f. (pl. —en) wall-paper.

Tapezier [tapə'tsi:r], m. (—s, pl. —e),
—er, m. (—ers, pl. —er) upholsterer;
paper-hanger. —en, v.a. to (hang
with) paper. —ung, f. papering (of
walls, rooms).

Tapfer ['tapfər], adj. & adv. brave.
—keit, f. bravery, valour.

Tapir ['ta:pɪr], m. (—s, pl. —e) tapir.

Tapisserie [tapɪsə'riː], f. (pl. —en) tapestry-work.

Tapp [tap], int. tap! —e, f. (pl. —en) claw; footstep. —en, v.n. (aux. h. & f.) to grope one's way.

Täppisch ['tɛpɪʃ], adj. awkward, clumsy.

Tarn [tarn] (in comp.) —haut, —kappe, f. cloak of invisibility.

Tasche ['taʃə], f. (pl. —n) pocket. —n=dieb, m. pickpocket. —n=dieb= stahl, m. pocket-picking. —n=geld, n. pocket-money. —n=spieler, m. juggler, conjurer. —n=tuch. n. pocket-handkerchief.

Tasse ['tasə], f. (pl. —n, dim. Täßchen, n.) cup; Ober— und Unter—, cup and saucer.

Tastatur [tasta'tuːr], f. (pl. —en) keyboard (of a piano).

Tast—e ['tastə], f. (pl. —en) key (of a piano, etc.).

Tasten ['tastən], I. v.a. & n. (aux. h.) to touch, feel; to grope, fumble. II. subst.n. feeling, touching; groping.

Tat [taːt], f. (pl. —en), deed, action; auf frischer —, in the very act; in der —, indeed, in fact. —bestand, m. matter of fact. —kraft, f. energy. —sache, f. fact.

Täter ['tɛːtər], m. (—s, pl. —), —in, f. doer, culprit; author.

Tätig ['tɛːtɪç], adj. active; effective.

Tät(t)owieren [tɛto'viːrən], v.a. to tattoo.

Tatze ['tatsə], f. (pl. —n) paw; claw.

¹Tau [tau], n. (—(e)s, pl. —e) rope, cable. —en, v.a. to tow (a ship, etc.). —werk, n. cordage; rigging.

²Tau, m. (—(e)s) dew. —en, v.n. (aux. h. & f.) & imp. to thaw. —ig, adj. dewy. —regen, m. mild rain. —wetter, n. thaw. —wind, m. mild breeze.

Taub [taup], adj. deaf. —heit, f. deafness. —stumm, adj. deaf and dumb. —stummheit, f. deaf-and-dumbness.

Taube ['taubə], f. (pl. —n) pigeon; dove. —n=haft, adj. pigeon-like, dove-like. —n=post, f. pigeon post. —n=schlag, m. dovecot.

Tauch—en ['tauxən], v. I. r. & n. (aux. h. & f.) to dive. II. a. to dip; to duck, plunge. —er, m. (—ers, pl. —er) diver; diving-bird. —er=anzug, m. diver's dress. —er=glocke, f. diving-bell.

Tauf—e ['taufə], f. (pl. —en) baptism; christening. —en, v.a. to baptize, christen. —becken, n. (christening) font. —name, m. Christian name. —schein, m. certificate of baptism.

Täuf—er ['tɔyfər], m. (—ers, pl. —er) baptizer; see Wieder—er; Johannes der —er, John the Baptist. —ling, m. (—lings, pl. —linge) infant receiving baptism.

Taug—en ['taugən], v.n. (aux. h.) to be of use; to serve, to be good or fit for. —lich, adj. qualified, fit, useful; available. —e=nichts, m. ne'er-do-well.

Taumel ['taumǝl], m. (—s) giddiness. —ig, Taumlig, adj. reeling; giddy. —n, v.n. (aux. h. & f.) to reel, stagger; to be giddy.

Tausch [tauʃ], m. (—es, pl. —e) barter; im — gegen, in exchange for. —bar, adj. exchangeable.

Tausch—en ['tauʃən], v.a. & n. (aux. h.) to exchange; to barter. —handel, m. barter; exchange trade.

Täusch—en ['tɔyʃən], v.a. to deceive, delude; to cheat; sich —en lassen, to let oneself be deceived. —er, m. (—ers, pl. —er) deceiver, cheat. —ung, f. deception, fraud; illusion; disappointment.

Tausend ['tauzent], I. num. adj. thousand; — und aber —, thousands and thousands. II. n. (—s, pl. —e) thousand. III. int. (ei,) der —! Potz —! the deuce! —st, num. adj. thousandth. —erlei [—'lai], indec. adj. & adv. of a thousand kinds. —fach, —fältig, I. adj. a thousand times, thousand-fold. II. adv. in a thousand ways. —künstler, m. conjurer; jack-of-all-trades. —mal, a thousand times. —schön, n. daisy. —weise, adv. by thousands.

Taxameter [taksa'meːtər], m. (—s, pl. —) taximeter. —=droschke, f. taxi-cab.

Tax—e ['taksə], f. (pl. —en) tax, duty. —ieren [—'ksiːrən], v.a. to tax.

Techn—ik ['tɛçnɪk], f. technical art. —iker, m. —ikers, pl. —iker) one skilled in an art. —isch, adj. & adv. technical.

Tedel ['tɛkəl], m. (—s, pl. —) dachshund.

Tee [teː], m. (—s, pl. —s) tea. —brett, n. tea-tray. —büchse, f. tea-caddy. —kanne, f. teapot. —löffel, m. teaspoon. —rose, f. tea-rose.

Teer [te:r], m. & n. (—s) (Steinkohlen=) (coal-)tar. —en, v.a. to tar. —icht, adj. tarry. —ig, adj. tarry; tarred.

Teich [taɪç], m. (—(e)s, pl. —e) pond, pool.

Teig [taɪk], I. m. (—(e)s, pl. —e) dough, paste. II. adj. mellow; over-ripe. —ig, adj. doughy.

Teil [taɪl], m. & n. (—s, pl. —e) part, share; beide —e, both parties; ich für meinen —, I for my part. —chen, m. (—chens, pl. —chen) particle. —=haft(ig), adj. (with gen.) partaking of, sharing in. —s, adv. partly, in part. —haber, m. sharer; joint-owner; partner. —nahme, f. participation, share; sympathy; interest. —s nahmlos, adj. unfeeling, indifferent. —nahmlosigkeit, f. indifference. —s nehmend, adj. sharing; sympathetic. —nehmer, m. participator; accomplice. —weise, adj. & adv. partial.

Teilbar ['taɪlba:r], adj. divisible.

Teil—en ['taɪlən], v.a. to divide; to share. —er, m. (—ers, pl. —er) divider; sharer; divisor (Arith.). —ung, f. division. —ungs=zeichen, n. hyphen; mark of division.

Tele—gramm [tele'gram], n. (—s gramms, pl. —gramme) telegram. —graph [—'graf], m. (—graphen, pl. —graphen) telegraph. —graphie [—gra'fi:], f. telegraphy; drahtlose —graphie, wireless telegraphy. —s graphieren, v.a. & n. (aux. h.) to telegraph. —'graphisch, adj. telegraphic. —phon [—'fo:n], n. (—s phons, pl. —phons) telephone. —s phonieren [—fo'ni:rən], v.a. & n. (aux. h.) to telephone.

Teller ['tɛlər], m. (—s, pl. —) plate.

Tempel ['tɛmpəl], m. (—s, pl. —) temple; sanctuary. —herr, (Templer,) m. (Knight-)Templar. —orden, m. order of the Templars. —raub, m. sacrilege.

Temper—ament [tɛmpəra'mɛnt], n. (—(e)s, pl. —e) temperament. —atur [—a'tu:r], f. temperature.

Tempo ['tɛmpo:], n. (—s, pl. —s) time, pace.

Tend—enz [tɛn'dɛnts], f. (pl. —enzen) tendency. —enz=roman, m. (—enz= stück, n.) novel (drama) written with a purpose.

Tenne ['tɛnə], f. (pl. —n) threshing-floor.

Tennis ['tɛnɪs], n. (—) lawn-tennis.

Tenor [te'no:r], m. (—s, pl. —e) tenor. —ist [—'rɪst], m. (—isten, pl. —isten) tenor-singer.

Teppich ['tɛpɪç], m. (—s, pl. —e) carpet.

Termin [tɛr'mi:n], m. (—s, pl. —e) time, term; fixed day; in vier —en zahlbar, payable in 4 instalments.

Terpentin [tɛrpɛn'ti:n], m. (—s, pl. —e) turpentine.

Terr—ain [tɛ'rɛ:ŋ], n. (—ains, pl. —ains) ground; country (Mil., etc.). —asse [—'rasə], f. (pl. —assen) terrace. —ine [—'ri:nə], f. (pl. —inen) tureen.

Tert—ia ['tɛrtsia:], f. (—ia, pl. —ien) third form. —ianer [—tsi'a:nər], m. (—ianers, pl. —) third-form boy.

Testament [tɛsta'mɛnt], n. (—(e)s, pl. —e) testament, will. —lich, —arisch [—'ta:rɪʃ], adj. testamentary, by will.

Teuer ['tɔyər], adj. & adv. dear, costly; wie — ist es? what does it cost? —ung, Teurung, f. dearth, famine; dearness.

Teufel ['tɔyfəl], m. (—s, pl. —) devil.

Teuflisch ['tɔyflɪʃ], adj. devilish, diabolical.

Text [tɛkst], m. (—es, pl. —e) text; letter-press. —buch, n. libretto.

Textil [tɛks'ti:l], adj. textile.

Textur [tɛks'tu:r], f. (pl. —en) texture.

Th . . .; words not found under Th—should be looked for under T—.

Theat—er [te'a:tər], n. (—ers, pl. —er) theatre. —ralisch [—'tra:lɪʃ], adj. theatrical. —er=kasse, f. box-office. —er=stück, n. play.

Them—a ['te:ma:], n. (—as, pl. —as, —ata, —en) theme.

Theo—log [teo'lo:k], m. (—logen, pl. —logen) theologian. —logie [—lo'gi:], f. theology. —logisch [—'lo:gɪʃ], adj. theological.

Theor—em [teo're:m], n. (—ems, pl. —eme) theorem. —etiker [—'re:tɪkər], m. (—etikers, pl. —etiker) theorist. —etisch, adj. & adv. theoretic(al). —ie [—'ri:], f. (pl. —ieen) theory.

Thermometer [tɛrmo'me:tər], n. (& m.) thermometer.

Thes—e ['te:zə], f. (pl. —en), —is, f. (pl. —en) thesis.

Thron [tro:n], m. (—(e)s, pl. —e) throne. —besteigung, f. accession to the crown. —bewerber, m. aspirant to the throne. —erbe, m. heir-apparent.

—folge, f. succession to the throne. —himmel, m. canopy.

Thunfisch ['tu:nfɪʃ], m. (—es, pl. —e) tunny.

Tief [ti:f], adj. & adv. deep; —es Rot, dark red; im —ften Winter, in the depth of winter. —e, f. (pl. —en) depth. —finn, m., —finnigkeit, f. profoundness; thoughtfulness. —finnig, adj. thoughtful; pensive; serious.

Tier [ti:r], n. (—(e)s, pl. —e) animal; beast. —chen, n. (—chens, pl. —chen) little beast; animalcule. —isch, adj. animal; brutish, beastly. —art, f. species of animals. —arzt, m. veterinary surgeon. —garten, m. zoological gardens. —haus, n. menagerie. —heilkunde, f. veterinary science. —hetze, f. chase. —kenner, —kundige(r), m. zoologist. —freis, m. zodiac (Astr.). —kunde, —lehre, f. zoology. —wärter, m. keeper.

Tiger ['ti:gər], m. (—s, pl. —) tiger. —in, f. tigress. —n, v.a. to spot, to speckle; getigert, speckled. —dede, —haut, f., —fell, n. tiger-skin (rug).

Tilg—en ['tɪlgən], v.a. to extinguish; to erase, blot out; to eradicate, destroy. —er, m. (—ers, pl. —er) destroyer, exterminator. —ung, f. extermination; cancelling; liquidation.

Tint—e ['tɪntə], f. (pl. —en) ink; in der —e sitzen, to be in a bad scrape. —ig, adj. inky. —en=faß, n. inkstand. —en=fleck, m. blot, ink-stain. —en= fleds, m. ink-stain or blot.

Tisch [tɪʃ], m. (—(e)s, pl. —e) table. —chen, —lein, n. (—leins, pl. —lein) small table. —gebet, n. grace. —rüden, n. table-turning. —tuch, n. table-cloth. —zeit, f. meal-time.

Tischler ['tɪʃlər], m. (—s, pl. —) joiner, carpenter; cabinet-maker. —ei [—'rai], f. cabinet-making.

Titan—e [ti'ta:nə], m. (—en, pl. —en) Titan. —enhaft, —isch, adj. Titanic.

Titel ['ti:təl], m. (—s, pl. —) title.

Tob—en ['to:bən], v.n. (aux. h.) to storm, rage, bluster. —fucht, f. frenzy, delirium.

Tochter ['tɔxtər], f. (pl. Töchter) daughter.

Töchter—chen ['tœçtərçən], n. (—chens, pl. —chen) little daughter. —lich, adj. daughterly, filial.

Tod [to:t], m. (—(e)s, pl. —e, often Todesfälle) death. —bange, adj. frightened to death. —bringend, adj. fatal; mortal. —es=angst, f. mortal terror. —es=fall, m. death; casualty (in war); (pl.) deaths (used as a pl. of Tod). —es=feier, f. funeral solemnity. —es=gefahr, f. deadly peril. —es=kampf, m. throes of death; mortal combat. —es=pein, f. pangs of death. —es=strafe, f. capital punishment. —matt, —müde, adj. dead tired. —fünde, f. deadly sin.

Toilette [toa'lɛtə], f. (pl. —n) toilet; dress.

Toler—ant [tole'rant], adj. tolerant (gegen, of). —anz, f. toleration. —ieren [—'ri:rən], v.a. to tolerate.

Toll [tɔl], adj. & adv. mad. —en, v.n. (aux. h. & f.) to be boisterous or rollicking; to fool about. —heit, f. madness, frenzy; rage, fury; eccentricity. —haus, n. lunatic asylum. —kühn, adj. foolhardy, rash. —kühn= heit, f. foolhardiness, rashness. —sucht, f. madness. —wut, f. raving (madness); frenzy; hydrophobia (of dogs).

Tölp—el ['tœlpəl], m. (—els, pl. —el), Tolpatsch, m. (—es, pl. —e) blockhead; booby; lout; gannet (Orn.); dodo (Orn.). —elhaft, —isch, adj. clumsy; doltish; stupid; loutish.

Tomate [to'ma:tə], f. (pl. —n) tomato.

1Ton [to:n], m. (—(e)s, pl. —e) clay. —ig, adj. clayey. —pfeife, f. clay pipe.

2Ton, m. (—(e)s, pl. Töne) sound; note (Mus.). —angeber, m. leader of fashion. —art, f. key, mode; tone. —kunft, f. music, musical art. —leiter, —reihe, f. gamut, scale. —los, adj. soundless; unaccented. —losig= keit, f. absence of sound; absence of stress. —welle, f. sound-wave. —zeichen, n. accent; note (Mus.).

Tönen ['tø:nən], v.n. (aux. h.) to sound, resound.

Tönern ['tø:nərn], adj. (of) clay, earthen.

Tonne ['tɔnə], f. (pl. —n, dim. Tönn=chen) tun, butt; cask, barrel; ton.

Tonsur [tɔn'zu:r], f. (pl. —en) tonsure.

Topf [tɔpf], m. (—es, pl. Töpfe) pot. —dedel, m. pot-lid.

Töpf—chen ['tœpfçən], n. (—chens, pl. —chen) small pot or jar. —er, m.

(—ers, *pl.* —er) potter. —er=geſchirr, —er=gut, *n.* earthenware, pottery, crockery.

Topp [tɔp], *int.* done! agreed! all right!

¹Tor [to:r], *n.* (—s, *pl.* —e) gate; gateway. —flügel, *m.* wing of a gate. —hüter, *m.* gate-keeper, porter. —pfoſten, *pl.* docr-posts.

²Tor, *m.* (—en, *pl.* —en) fool. —heit, *f.* folly.

Torf [tɔrf], *m.* (—(e)s, *pl.* —e, Törfe) peat. —boden, *m.* peat-bog. —land, *n.* moor.

Tör=icht ['tø:rɪçt], *adj.* foolish, silly. —in, *f.* foolish woman.

Torniſter [tɔr'nɪstər], *m.* (—s, *pl.* —) haversack.

Torpedoboot [tɔr'pe:do:ʔbo:t], *n.* torpedo-boat.

Torte ['tɔrtə], *f.* (*pl.* —n, *dim.* Törtchen) fancy cake.

Toſen ['to:zən], *v.n.* (*aux.* h. & ſ.) to rage, storm.

Tot [to:t], *adj.* dead; —es Kapital, unemployed capital. —e(r), *m.*, —e, *f.* dead person; die —en, the dead. —enhaft, *adj.* deathlike. —lachen, *n.*; es iſt zum —lachen, it is enough to make one die with laughing.

Total [to'ta:l], *adj.* & *adv.* total, whole.

Toten—amt ['to:tənʔamt], *n.* burial-service. —beſchwörer, *m.* necromancer. —bett, *n.* death-bed. —blaß, *adj.* pale as death. —feier, *f.* funeral rites. —geleit, *n.* funeral train. —geſang, *m.* funeral dirge. —gewand, *n.* shroud. —glocke, *f.* funeral bell; knell. —gräber, *m.* gravedigger. —hemd, *n.* shroud. —kopf, *m.* death's head. —ſchein, *m.* certificate of death. —ſtill, *adj.* as still as death. —ſtille, *f.* dead silence or calm. —verbrennung, *f.* cremation.

Töt—en ['tø:tən], I. *v.a.* to kill. II. *subst.n.* killing. —er, *m.* (—ers, *pl.* —er) killer. —lich, *adj.* fatal; deadly; mortal. —lichkeit, *f.* deadliness, fatal nature.

Tour [tu:r], *f.* (*pl.* —en) tour. —iſt [—'rɪst], *m.*(—iſten,*pl.* —iſten) tourist.

Trab [tra:p], *m.* (—(e)s) trot.

Tracht [traxt], *f.* (*pl.* —en) dress, costume; eine — Prügel, a sound thrashing.

Trachten ['traxtən], *v.n.* (*aux.* h.) to endeavour, strive; einem nach dem Leben —, to seek a person's life.

Träg—e ['trɛ:gə], *adj.* slow; lazy. —heit, *f.* laziness, indolence.

Trag—en ['tra:gən], I. *ir.v.a.* to bear, carry; to yield, produce. II. *subst.n.* bearing; carriage. —bahre, *f.* stretcher, litter. —ſtuhl, *m.* sedanchair.

Träger ['trɛ:gər], *m.* (—s, *pl.* —) carrier, porter.

Trag—iſch ['tra:gɪʃ], *adj.* & *adv.* tragic(al). —ödie [tra'gø:dlə], *f.* tragedy.

Trakt—at [trak'ta:t], *m.* (—ats, *pl.* —ate) treatise. —ieren [—'ti:rən], *v.a.* & *n.* (*aux.* h.) to treat; to entertain.

Trällern ['trɛlərn], *v.n.* (*aux.* h.) to hum, trill (*a tune*).

Tram— ['tram] (*in comp.*) —bahn, *f.* tram-line. —wagen, *m.* tram-car.

Trampel ['trampəl], *m.* (—s, *pl.* —), *f.* clumsy person. —n, (Trampſen,) *v.n.* (*aux.* h.) to trample; to stamp. —tier, *n.* dromedary.

Tran [tra:n], *m.* (—s) train-oil. —ig, *adj.* containing train-oil. —ſeife, *f.* soft soap. —ſpeck, *m.* blubber.

Träne ['trɛ:nə], *f.* (*pl.* —n) tear. —nlos, *adj.* tearless, dry-eyed. —nvoll, *adj.* tearful.

Trank [traŋk], *m.* (—(e)s, *pl.* Tränke) drink, beverage.

Tratte ['tratə], *f.* (*pl.* —n) bill of exchange.

Traub—e ['traubə], *f.* (*pl.* —en) bunch of grapes. —ig, *adj.* clustered; grapelike. —en=leſe, *f.* vintage. —en=ſaft, *m.* juice of the grape; wine. —en= zeit, *f.* time when the grapes are ripe, time of vintage.

Trau—en ['trauən], *v.* I. *n.* (*aux.* h.); einem —en, to trust, have confidence in, rely on a person. II. *a.* to unite in marriage. —lich, *adj.* familiar; homely; snug, cosy. —lichkeit, *f.* familiarity, intimacy; comfort. —ung, *f.* marriage-ceremony. —ring, *m.* wedding-ring. —ſchein, *m.* certificate of marriage; marriage-licence.

Trauer ['trauər], *f.* grief, affliction; mourning. —kleid, *n.*, —kleidung, *f.* mourning dress; weeds. —marſch, *m.* funeral march. —ſpiel, *n.* tragedy. —weide, *f.* weeping willow.

Trauern ['trauərn], *v.n.* (*aux.* h.) to mourn, lament.

Trauf—e ['traufə], *f.* (*pl.* —en) drip;

gutter; eaves; **vom Regen in die —e,** from bad to worse.

Träufeln ['trɔyfəln], v. ᵀ n. (aux. h. & f.) to trickle. II. a. to drop.

Traum [traum], m. (—(e)s, pl. **Träume**) dream. **—haft,** adj. dreamlike. **—bild,** n. vision. **—zustand,** m. (hypnotic) trance.

Träum—en ['trɔymən], v.a. & n. (aux. h.) & imp. to dream. **—er,** m. (—ers, pl. **—er**) dreamer; visionary. **—erei** [—ə'raɪ], f. dreaming; fancy; reverie. **—erisch,** adj. dreaming.

Traun! [traun], int. (for **in Treuen**) indeed! faith!

Traurig ['trauriç], adj. sad, melancholy. **—keit,** f. sadness; melancholy; grief.

Traut [traut], adj. dear, beloved.

Treff [tref], m. (—(e)s, pl. **—e**) club (at cards).

Treff—en ['trefən], I. ir.v.a. & n. (aux. h.) to hit, strike; to affect; to befall; to guess; to fall in with; **das trifft sich gut,** that's lucky; **sich getroffen fühlen,** to feel hurt. II. subst.n. encounter; battle; striking. **—end,** p. & adj. striking; pertinent; suitable. **—er,** m. (—ers, pl. **—er**) home-thrust, good shot; hit, lucky chance. **—lich,** adj. & adv. excellent, choice; first-rate; admirable. **—lichkeit,** f. excellence, perfection.

Treib—en ['traɪbən], I. ir.v.a. to drive, push; to put in motion; to occupy oneself with. II. ir.v.n. (aux. h. & f.) to drive, drift. III. subst.n. driving, etc.; germination; impulse; doings; movement; study. **—er,** m. (—ers, pl. **—er**) driver; instigator; driving-wheel, propeller. **—baum,** m. driving-axle. **—(e)=beet,** n. hotbed. **—haus,** n. hothouse, greenhouse. **—kraft,** f. motive power. **—rad,** n. driving-wheel. **—riemen,** m. driving-belt (of machines). **—stange,** f. connecting-rod. **—welle,** f. main shaft (of a machine). **—werk,** n. engine, machine.

Trennbar ['trenba:r], adj. separable, divisible. **—keit,** f. separableness, divisibility.

Trenn—en ['trenən], v.a. to separate, divide. **—ung,** f. separation; dissolution.

Trepp—e ['trepə], f. (pl. **—en**) stair-case; **—auf, —ab,** upstairs and down-

stairs. **—'ab,** adv. coming downstairs. **—'auf,** adv. going upstairs. **—en=absatz,** m. landing (of a staircase). **—en=geländer,** n. railing, balustrade. **—en=läufer,** m. stair-carpet. **—en=stufe,** f. step of a staircase.

Tresse ['tresə], f. (pl. **—n**) lace; braid (of hair).

Tret—en ['tre:tən], ir.v. I. n. (aux. h. & f.) to step, walk; **zu nahe —en,** to offend. II. a. to walk upon, trample; to kick. **—er,** m. (—ers, pl. **—er**) treader.

Treu [trɔy], adj. & adv. faithful; true; sincere; loyal. **—e,** f. fidelity, faithfulness. **—lich,** adv. truly, faithfully; conscientiously. **—bruch,** m. perfidy; disloyalty. **—brüchig,** adj. faithless, perfidious; disloyal. **—gesinnt,** adj. loyal. **—herzig,** adj. sincere, true, loyal; candid. **—liebchen,** n. true-love. **—los,** adj. faithless, perfidious. **—losigkeit,** f. faithlessness, perfidy; treachery.

Tribüne [tri'by:nə], f. (pl. **—n**) platform.

Tribut [tri'bu:t], m. (—(e)s, pl. **—e**) tribute.

Trichter ['trɪçtər], m. (—s, pl. **—**) funnel; shell-hole (Mil.).

Trieb [tri:p], m. (—(e)s, pl. **—e**) movement; moving force; impetus; instinct, impulse; inclination; liking. **—feder,** f. spring; mainspring; motive. **—kraft,** f. impetus; motive power. **—rad,** n. driving-wheel. **—sand,** m. quicksand. **—welle,** f. driving-shaft (Locom.). **—werk,** n. machinery, mechanism.

Trief—en ['tri:fən], ir.v.n. (aux. h. & f.) to droop, drip. **—end,** p. & adj., **—ig,** adj. dropping, dripping. **—äugig,** adj. blear-eyed.

Trift [trɪft], f. (pl. **—en**) pasture, common. **—ig,** adj. drifting, adrift.

Trikot [tri'ko:], n. (—s, pl. **—s**) stockinet; (pl.) tights.

Triller ['trɪlər], m. (—s, pl. **—**) trill, shake (Mus.). **—n,** v. I. a. to trill. II. a. & n. (aux. h.) to warble (as birds); to hum (a song).

Trinität [trini'tɛ:tl], f. Trinity.

Trinkbar ['trɪŋkba:r], adj. drinkable.

Trink—en ['trɪŋkən], I. ir.v.a. & n. (aux. h.) to drink. II. subst.n. drink; drinking; drunkenness. **—er,** m. (—ers, pl. **—er**) drinker; drunkard.

—geld, n. tip (coll.). —geschirr, n. drinking-vessel. —spruch, m. toast.

Trippeln ['trɪpəln], v.n. (aux. h.) to trip.

Tritt [trɪt], m. (—(e)s, pl. —e) step; pace. —brett, n. treadle; pedal. —leiter, f. (pair of) steps.

Trock—en ['trɔkən], adj. & adv. dry; arid. —enheit, f. dryness; aridity; barrenness. —ne, f. dryness; dry land; auf dem —enen sitzen, to be without money. —nen, v. I. n. (aux. f.) to dry, become dry. II. v.a. to dry; to air. III. subst.n., —nung, f. drying; desication.

Tröd—el ['trø:dəl], m. (—els, pl. —el) rubbish; lumber. —ler, m., —lerin, f. dealer in old clothes, etc.

Trog [tro:k], m.(—(e)s, pl. Tröge) trough.

Trommel ['trɔməl], f. (pl. —n) drum. —n, v.a. & n. (aux. h.) to drum, to beat the drum. —fell, n. drum-skin. —flöppel, —schlägel, m. drumstick. —schlag, m. beat of the drum. —stod, m. drumstick. —wirbel, m. roll of the drum.

Trommler ['trɔmlər], m. (—s, pl. —) drummer.

Trompete [trɔm'pe:tə], f. (pl. —n) trumpet. —r, m. (—rs, pl. —r) trumpeter. —n-schall, m. sound of the trumpet. —n-stoß, m. flourish of the trumpet. —n-tusch, m. flourish of trumpets.

Trop—e ['tro:pə], f. (pl. —en) (pl.) the tropics. —isch, adj. tropical; metaphorical, figurative.

Tropf [trɔpf], m. (—(e)s, pl. Tröpfe) booby, simpleton. —en, m. (—ens, pl. —en) drop. —stein, m. stalactite.

Tröpf—chen ['trœpfçən], n. (—chens, pl. —chen) little drop. —eln, v. I. n. (aux. h. & f.) to drip, trickle. II. v. to drop.

Trophäe [tro'fɛ:ə], f. (pl. —n) trophy.

Troß [trɔs], I. m. (—(ß)es, pl. —(ß)e) baggage (Mil.); baggage-train; crowd; followers. II. n. (—(ß)es, pl. —(ß)e) & f. hawser (Naut.). —pferd, n. baggage-horse. —wagen, m. baggage-waggon.

Trost [tro:st], m. (—es) comfort, consolation. —brief, m. letter of condolence. —bringend, adj. comforting, consolatory. —bringer, —geber, m. comforter. —los, adj. comfortless; inconsolable. —reich, adj. consoling, comforting.

Tröst—en ['trø:stən], v.a. to comfort, console. —er, m. (—ers, pl. —er) comforter, consoler. —lich, adj. consoling, comforting; pleasant. —ung, f. consolation, comfort.

Trott [trɔt], m. (—(e)s, pl. —e) trot. —oir [trɔto'a:r], n. (—oirs, pl. —oirs) pavement.

Troß [trɔts], I. m. (—es) boldness, intrepidity; obstinacy; insolence; disdain; defiance. II. prep. (with dat. or gen.) in spite of; despite; notwithstanding; — alledem, for all that.

Troß—en ['trɔtsən], v.n. (aux. h.) to bid defiance to, to defy. —er, m. (—ers, pl. —er) defiant, haughty or insolent person. —ig, adj. & adv. haughty, proud, overbearing; insolent; defiant. —kopf, m. stubborn or pig-headed person. —wort, n. defiant word, disdainful expression.

Trüb, Trüb—e, ['try:b(ə)], I. adj. & adv. troubled, muddy, turbid; opaque; dull, gloomy. II. f. (pl. —en) muddy, turbid state; dimness; opaqueness; gloom. —en, v.a. to darken, dim; to tarnish. —sal, f. (pl. —sale) (& n. —sals, pl. —sale) affliction; trouble; distress; —sal blasen, to be in the dumps. —selig, adj. troubled. —sinn, m. melancholy, dejection. —sinnig, adj. low-spirited; sad.

Truchseß ['truxzes], m. (—(ss)en, pl. —(ss)en) Lord High Steward (of a royal household).

Trüffel ['tryfəl], f. (pl. —n) truffle.

Trug [tru:k], m. (—(e)s) deceit; imposture. —bild, n. phantom. —schluß, m. false conclusion.

Trüg—en ['try:gən], ir.v.a. & n. (aux. h.) to deceive. —erisch, —lich, adj. deceptive.

Truhe ['tru:ə], f. (pl. —n) trunk, chest.

Trümmer ['trymər], pl. fragments; wreckage. —haft, adj. ruinous, decayed. —haufe(n), m. heap of ruins.

Trumpf [trumpf], m. (—(e)s, pl. Trümpfe) trump (Cards); was ist —? what are trumps? —en, v.a. & n. (aux. h.) to trump.

Trunk [trunk], m. (—(e)s, pl. Trünke) drink, liquor; draught. —en-heit, f. drunkenness. —en-bold, m. drunkard.

Trupp [trup], m. (—s, pl. —s) troop; band. —e, f. (pl. —en) troop (of soldiers); troupe (of actors). —en-übung, f. manœuvres (Mil.).

Trut— [tru:t] (*in comp.*) —hahn, *m.* turkey(-cock). —henne, *f.*, —huhn, *n.* turkey(-hen).

Tuch [tu:x], *n.* (—(e)s, *pl.* Tücher, *after numerals* —) cloth; piece of cloth. —en, *adj.* cloth.

Tüchtig ['tʏçtɪç], *adj. & adv.* fit, able, qualified; sound, hearty, good; thorough; clever; excellent; efficient. —=keit, *f.* ability, fitness; solidity, soundness; excellence; proficiency.

Tück—e ['tʏkə], *f.* (*pl.* —en) prank, trick. —(i)sch, *adj.* malicious, spiteful.

Tugend ['tu:gɛnt], *f.* (*pl.* —en) virtue; chastity. —haft, *adj.* virtuous. —haftigkeit, *f.* virtue.

Tulpe ['tʊlpə], *f.* (*pl.* —n) tulip. —=zwiebel, *f.* tulip-bulb.

Tummeln ['tʊməln], *v.* I. *a.* to turn round. II. *r.* to move, bustle about.

Tumult [tu 'mʊlt], *m.* (—(e)s, *pl.* —e) row, riot.

Tun [tu:n], I. *ir.v.a.* to do, perform, make; to put; weh —, to grieve, to hurt. II. *ir.v.n.* (*aux.* h.) to act, to do; to pretend, to affect; to behave; zu — haben, to be busy. III. *ir.v.r.* sich — lassen, to be practicable, feasible; das läßt sich —, that can be done. IV. *subst.n.* doing; doings, conduct, action. —lich, *adj.* feasible, practicable. —lichst, *adv.* as far as possible *or* practicable. —lichkeit, *f.* feasibleness.

Tünch—e ['tʏnçə], *f.* whitewash; plastering. —en, *v.a.* to whitewash; to plaster; to roughcast. —er, *m.* (—ers, *pl.* —er) whitewasher; plasterer.

Tunk—e ['tʊŋkə], *f.* (*pl.* —en) sauce. —näpfchen, *n.*, —schale, *f.* sauce-boat.

Tunnel ['tʊnəl], *m.* (—s, *pl.* —s) tunnel.

Tür [ty:r], —e, *f.* (*pl.* —en) door. —angel, *f.* hinge of a door. —griff, *m.* door-handle.

Turm [tʊrm], *m.* (—(e)s, *pl.* Türme) tower; rook, castle (*Chess*).

Turn—en ['tʊrnən], I. *v.n.* (*aux.* h.) to do *or* practise gymnastics. II. *subst.n.* gymnastics. —er, *m.* (—ers, *pl.* —er) gymnast. —erei [—ə'raɪ], *f.* gymnastic exercises. —erisch, *adj.* gymnastic. —ier [—'ni:r], *n.* (—iers, *pl.* —iere) tournament. —halle, *f.* gymnasium. —kunst, *f.* gymnastics.

—lehrer, *m.* teacher of gymnastics. —platz, *m.* athletic grounds. —verein, *m.* gymnastic or athletic club.

Turteltaube ['tʊrtəltaʊbə], *f.* (*pl.* —n) turtle-dove.

Tusch—e ['tʊʃə], *f.* (*pl.* —en) Indian ink. —en, *v.a.* to draw in Indian ink. —farbe, *f.* water-colour. —kasten, *m.* paint-box.

Tütchen ['ty:tçən], *n.* (—s, *pl.* —) small paper bag.

Tute, Tüte ['tu:tə, ty:tə], *f.* (*pl.* —n) paper bag; (paper) screw.

Tutel [tu'te:l], *f.* (*pl.* —en) guardianship.

Typ [ty:p], *m.* (—(e)s, *pl.* —e(n), —us, *m.* (—us, *pl.* —en) type. —en=haft, —isch, *adj.* typical.

Type ['ty:pə], *f.* (*pl.* —n) type, character (*for printing*).

Tyrann [ty'ran], *m.* (—en, *pl.* —en) tyrant. —ei [—'naɪ], *f.* tyranny; despotism. —isch, *adj.* tyrannical; despotic. —isieren [—ni'zi:rən], *v.* I. *a.* to tyrannize over. II. *n.* to act the tyrant. —en=joch, *n.* yoke of despotism.

U

U, u [u:], *n.* U, u.

Übel ['y:bəl], I. *adj. & adv.* (übler, üble, übles; *comp.* übler) evil, ill; das ist nicht —, not bad, rather nice; — nehmen, to be offended at. II. *n.* (—s, *pl.* —) evil. —sein, *n.* indisposition. —tat, *f.* misdeed. —täter, *m.*, —täterin, *f.* evil-doer. —tätig, *adj.* mischievous, doing evil. —tun, *n.* wrong-doing. —wollen, *n.* ill-will. —wollend, *adj.* malevolent.

Üb—en ['y:bən], *v.a.* to exercise, practise; to use; to drill; Geduld —en, to have patience; Rache —en, to take vengeance. —lich, *adj.* usual, customary. —lichkeit, *f.* usage; customariness. —ung, *f.* exercise, practice. —ungs=fähigkeit, *f.* capacity for exercise.

Über ['y:bər], I. *prep.* (*with acc. & dat.*) *with dat. when implying rest or a limited or circula·r motion*, over, above, superior to; in the process of, during, while. *With acc. when signifying transfer or motion to, over or past*, across, from one side to another; beyond, on the further side of; after;

by way of, viâ; *or, when used without any reference to motion, signifying* with regard to, as for, concerning, about; alone, over; **heute —s Jahr,** a year from to-day; — **furz ober lang,** sooner or later. II. *adv. & sep. or (mostly) insep. pref. (when sep.* **über** *has the accent)* over, above, too much, in excess.

Überall [y:bər'?al], *adv.* everywhere; all over, throughout; at all times; positively.

Überarbeiten ['y:bər?arbaitən], *v.a.* *(sep.)* to work in excess.

Überbleib—en ['y:bərblaibən], *ir.v.n.* *(aux.* **f.**) *(sep.)* to remain (over). **—fel,** *n.* **(—fels,** *pl.* **—fel)** remainder, residue.

Überblick ['y:bərblik], *m.* survey, view; summary. **—en,** *v.a. (insep.)* to glance at, survey.

Überbreiten [y:bərbraitən], *v.a. (sep. & insep.)* to spread, cover over.

Überded—e ['y:bərdɛkə], *f.* upper cover, coverlet. **—en,** *v.a. (sep.)* to stretch over; *(insep.)* to cover with. **—ung,** *f.* cover.

Überdenken [y:bər'dɛŋkən], *ir.v.a. (insep.)* to reflect, meditate.

Überdies [y:bər'di:s], *adv.* in addition to this, besides, moreover.

Über—druß ['y:bərdrus], *m.* **(—druffes)** weariness, ennui; disgust. **—drüffig,** *adj. & adv. (with gen.)* tired; satiated; disgusted.

Übereil—e ['y:bər'ailə], *f.* precipitation. **—en** *(insep.), v.* I. *a.* to overtake. II. *r.* to hurry too much; to act precipitately. **—t,** *p.p. & adj.* precipitate, rash. **—ung,** *f.* precipitation; rashness.

Überein [y:bər'?ain], *adv. & sep. pref.* in accordance; conformably, alike, agreeably (to). **—kommen,** *ir.v.n. (aux.* **f.**) to agree (with); to come to terms with. **—kunft,** *f.* agreement. **—stimmen,** *v.n. (aux.* **h.**) to accord; to coincide, suit. **—stimmung,** *f.* accord; agreement.

Übereinander [y:bər'ai'nandər], *adv.* one upon another.

Überfahr—en ['y:bərfa:rən], *ir.v.n. (aux.* **f.**) *(sep.)* to pass *(drive, sail, etc.)* over. **—t,** *f.* passage, crossing.

Überfall ['y:bərfal], *m.* unexpected attack. **—en,** *ir.v.* I. *a. (insep.)* to fall upon suddenly, surprise. II. *n. (aux.*

f.) *(sep.)* to fall over. III. *imp. fig.* to imagine.

Überfliegen [y:bərfli:gən], I. *v.n. (aux.* **f.**) *(sep.)* to fly over. II. *a. (insep.)* to fly across; *(fig.)* to glance over.

Überfließen ['y:bərfli:sən], *ir.v.* I. *n. (aux.* **f.**) *(sep.)* to flow over. II. *a. (insep.)* to overspread, flow over.

Über—fluß ['y:bərflus], *m.* **(—fluffes)** overflow; superabundance. **—flüffig,** *adj. & adv.* abundant, profuse; superfluous.

Überfracht ['y:bərfraxt], *f.* overfreight.

Überfülle ['y:bərfylə], *f.* superabundance.

Übergabe ['y:bərga:bə], *f.* delivery; surrender.

Übergang ['y:bərgaŋ], *m.* passage, crossing; desertion.

Übergeben [y:bərge:bən], *ir.v.* I. *a. (insep.)* to deliver to; to surrender. II. *r.* to vomit.

Übergehen [y:bərge:ən], *ir.v.* I. *n. (aux.* **f.**) *(sep.)* to overflow; to cross, pass over; to change sides. II. *a. (insep.)* to skip, to pass over; to glance at; to overlook.

Übergenug ['y:bərgənu:k], *adv.* more than enough.

Übergewicht ['y:bərgəviçt], *n.* overweight; preponderance, ascendancy.

Übergießen ['y:bərgi:sən], *ir.v.a. (sep.)* to pour over; to spill; *(insep.)* to pour on; to sprinkle.

Über—greifen ['y:bərgraifən], *ir.v.n. (aux.* **h.**) *(sep.)* to overlap; to encroach. **—griff,** *m.* **(—(e)s,** *pl.* **—e)** encroachment.

Überhand—nahme [y:bər'hantna:mə], *f.* rapid growth. **— nehmen,** *v.n.* to prevail, spread, increase.

Überhang ['y:bərhaŋ], *m.* projection (*Arch.*); canopy. **—en,** *ir.v.n. (aux.* **h.**) *(sep.)* to hang over.

Überhaupt [y:bər'haupt], *adv.* in general, generally; upon the whole; at all; — **nicht,** not at all.

Überhoch ['y:bərho:x], *adj.* too high; exceedingly high.

Überholen [y:bərho:lən], *v.a. (sep.)* to overhaul; *(insep.)* to overtake.

Überhören [y:bər'hø:rən], *v.a. (insep.)* not to hear *(through inattention, etc.)*.

Überirdisch ['y:bər'ırdiʃ], *adj.* above the earth; supernatural; unearthly.

Überklug ['y:bərklu:k], *adj.* over-wise.

—**heit**, f. too great sharpness or cleverness.

Überkraft ['y:bərkraft], f. superior power.

Überland— [y:bər'lant] (in comp.) —**eisenbahn**, f. transcontinental railway. —**reise**, f. overland route.

Überlang ['y:bərlaŋ], adj. too long. —**e**, adv. too or ever so long.

Überlass—**en** ['y:bərlasən], ir.v. I. a. (sep.) to let pass; to leave (remaining); (insep.) to leave (to someone else); to give up, relinquish. —**ung**, f. leaving; yielding up, cession.

Überlast ['y:bərlast], f. overweight; trouble. —**en**, v.a. (insep.) to overload.

Überlästig ['y:bərlɛstɪç], adj. burdensome.

Überlaufen [y:bərlaufən], ir.v. I. a. (sep.) to run over or down; (insep.) to spread over, overrun; to pester, annoy. II. n. (aux. f.) (sep.) to run over, overflow.

Überläufer ['y:bərlɔyfər], m. (—**s**, pl. —) deserter (Mil.).

Überleben [y:bər'le:bən], v.a. (insep.) to outlive, survive; **das hat sich überlebt**, that has had its day.

1**Überlegen** [y:bər'le:gən], adj. superior. —**heit**, f. superiority.

2**Überleg**—**en** ['y:bərle:gən], v.a. (sep.) to lay over or upon; to lean, bend over; (insep.) to cover all over; to overburden; to reflect on, ponder over. —**t**, p.p. & adj. well weighed, deliberate. —**ung**, f. reflection, deliberation.

Überliefer—**n** [y:bər'li:fərn], v.a. (insep.) to deliver, hand over. —**ung**, f. delivery; surrender.

Überlisten [y:bər'lɪstən], v.a. (insep.) to outwit.

Übermach—**en** [y:bər'maxən], v.a. (insep.) (einem etwas) to make or hand over; to transmit; to consign. —**ung**, f. consignment, remittance.

Übermacht ['y:bərmaxt], f. superior force; preponderance.

Übermächtig ['y:bərmɛçtɪç], adj. superior.

Übermannen [y:bər'manən], v.a. (insep.) to overcome, master.

Über—**maß** ['y:bərmas], n. (—**es**) excess; abundance. —**mäßig**, adj. & adv. extravagant; excessive. —**mäßigkeit**, f. excess; exorbitancy.

Übermensch ['y:bərmɛnʃ], m. superhuman being, demigod. —**lich**, adj. superhuman.

Übermittel—**n** [y:bər'mɪtəln], v.a. (insep.) to convey; to hand over, transmit. —**ung**, f. conveyance; delivery, transmission.

Übermorgen ['y:bərmorgən], adv. & n. the day after to-morrow.

Über—**mut** ['y:bərmu:t], m. wild spirits; wantonness; arrogance, haughtiness; bravado. —**mütig**, adj. in high spirits; haughty, supercilious; insolent.

Übernahme ['y:bərna:mə], f. the taking possession of; taking upon oneself; assumption.

Übernatürlich ['y:bərnaty:rlɪç], adj. supernatural. —**keit**, f. supernaturalism, miraculousness.

Übernehm—**en** [y:bərne:mən], ir.v. I. a. (sep.) to take over or across; (insep.) to take possession of; to receive; to undertake; to seize. II. r. (insep.) to undertake too much. —**er**, m. (—**ers**, pl. —**er**) receiver.

Überragen [y:bər'ra:gən], v.a. (insep.) to overtop, rise or tower above; to extend beyond; to overlook; to command (a town, etc., Fort.); to hang over; to crown; to surpass, to excel.

Überrasch—**en** [y:bər'raʃən], v.a. (insep.) to surprise. —**ung**, f. surprise.

Überred—**en** [y:bər're:dən], v.a. (insep.) to persuade. —**end**, p. & adj. persuasive. —**ung**, f. persuasion. —**ungskraft**, f. power of persuasion.

Überreich—**en** [y:bərraiçən], v. I. n. (aux. h.) (sep.) to extend over or beyond. II. a. (sep.) to stretch over or above; (insep.) to hand, reach over; to present. —**ung**, f. handing over; presentation.

Überreif ['y:bərraif], adj. over-ripe. —**e**, f. over-ripeness.

Überreiz—**en** [y:bər'raitsən], v.a. (insep.) to over-excite. —**theit**, —**ung**, f. over-excitement; excess of irritation.

Überrest ['y:bərrɛst], m. (—(e)s, pl.—**e**) remains, remnant; residue.

Überrock ['y:bərrɔk], m. frock-coat (of men); skirt (of women); overcoat.

Überschätzen [y:bər'ʃɛtsən], v.a. (insep.) to over-rate.

Überschicken [y:bər'ʃɪkən], v.a. (insep.) to transmit.

Überschlag ['y:bərʃla:k], *m.* tumbling over; bias, inclination; cuff; rough calculation, estimate. **—en**, *ir.v.* I. *a.* (*sep.*) to throw over; (*insep.*) to overlook; to skip, miss; to calculate (*roughly*); to consider, think over. II. *n.* (*aux.* ſ.) (*sep.*) to turn over; to tumble over, fall down; to fall, descend to.

Überschreib—en [y:bərʃraibən], *ir.v.a.* (*sep.*) to transcribe; (*insep.*) to superscribe, inscribe; to direct, address. **—ung**, *f.* superscription; transcription; transfer.

Überschreiten [y:bərʃraitən], *ir.v.* I. *a.* (*insep.*) to step *or* stride over; to overstep; to exceed; to transgress; **sein Guthaben —**, to overdraw one's balance *or* account. II. *n.* (*aux.* ſ.) (*sep.*) to step over.

Überschrift ['y:bərʃrıft], *f.* heading, title.

Über—schuß ['y:bərʃus], *m.* surplus. **—schüssig**, *adj.* projecting; surplus, remaining.

Überschwemm—en [y:bər'ʃvɛmən], *v.a.* (*insep.*) to overflow. **—ung**, *f.* inundation, flood.

Überschwenglich ['y:bərʃvɛnlıç], *adj.* superabundant. **—keit**, *f.* excess, exuberance.

Übersehen [y:bərze:ən], *ir.v.* I. *a.* (*insep.*) to perceive; to overlook, survey; to run the eye over; to overlook, not see; to take no notice of. II. *n.* (*aux.* h.) (*sep.*) to look over.

Übersend—en [y:bərzɛndən], *ir.v.a.* (*sep.*) to send over *or* across; (*insep.*) to send, transmit. **—er**, *m.* (**—ers**, *pl.* **—er**) sender, remitter; forwarding agent. **—ung**, *f.* transmission.

Übersetz—en [y:bərzɛtsən], *v.* I. *n.* (*aux.* ſ.) (*sep.*) to leap, bound over; to cross, pass over (*in a boat, etc.*). II. *a.* (*insep.*) to translate. **—er**, *m.* (**—ers**, *pl.* **—er**), **—erin**, *f.* translator. **—ung**, *f.* translation.

Übersicht ['y:bərzıçt], *f.* view; review; abstract. **—lich**, *adj.* clear, distinct.

Übersiedel—n [y:bərzi:dəln] (*sep.* & *insep.*), *v.* I. *n.* (*aux.* ſ.) to emigrate (**nach**, to). II. (*insep.*) *a.* to transplant, take to another country. **—ung**, *f.* emigration; removal.

Überspann—en [y:bərʃpanən], *v.a.* (*sep.*) to stretch over; (*insep.*) to overstrain, overexert. **—t**, *p.p.* & *adj.* over-

strained; exaggerated. **—theit**, *f.* excitement; extravagance, exaggeration. **—ung**, *f.* over-tension.

Überstehen [y:bərʃte:ən], *ir.v.* I. *a.* (*insep.*) to endure, overcome. II. *n.* (*aux.* h.) (*sep.*) to project, hang over; to stand, lie over.

Übersteigen [y:bərʃtaigən], *ir.v.* I. *a.* (*insep.*) to step, get over; to surmount, overcome; to exceed, surpass. II. *n.* (*aux.* ſ.) (*sep.*) to step over *or* across; to overflow.

Überstimmen [y:bər'ʃtımən], *v.a.* (*insep.*) to outvote.

Überstürz—en [y:bərʃtyrtsən], *v.* I. *a.* (*sep.*) to put on; (*insep.*) to overturn, upset. II. *n.* (*aux.* ſ.) (*sep.*) to capsize, upset; to dash across *or* over. III. *r.* (*insep.*) to act rashly. **—ung**, *f.* precipitation.

Übertrag—en [y:bərtra:gən], *ir.v.a.* (*sep.*) to carry over, transport; (*insep.*) to transfer, transmit. **—bar**, *adj.* transferable, catching (*disease*). **—ung**, *f.* transfer, transference.

Übertreffen [y:bər'trɛfən], *ir.v.a.* (*insep.*) to surpass, excel, outdo.

Übertreib—en [y:bərtraibən], *ir.v.a.* (*sep.*) to drive over; to force over; (*insep.*) to overdrive; to exaggerate. **—ung**, *f.* exaggeration.

Übertret—en [y:bərtre:tən], *ir.v.* I. *a.* (*sep.*) to tread down at heel; (*insep.*) to overstep; to transgress. II. *n.* (*aux.* ſ.) (*sep.*) to step, pass over; **zum Katholizismus —en**, to turn Roman Catholic. **—er**, *m.* (**—ers**, *pl.* **—er**) trespasser, transgressor. **—ung**, *f.* transgression.

Überwältig—en [y:bər'vɛltıgən], *v.a.* (*insep.*) to overcome. **—er**, *m.* (**—ers**, *pl.* **—er**) conqueror.

Überweis—en [y:bər'vaizən], *ir.v.a.* (*insep.*) to convince; to convict; to assign. **—end**, *p.* & *adj.* convincing. **—ung**, *f.* conviction; assignment, cession. **—ungs-grund**, *m.* convincing argument.

Überwiegen [y:bər'vi:gən], *ir.v.a.* (*insep.*) to outweigh. **—d**, *adj.* predominant, paramount.

Überwind—en [y:bərvındən], *ir.v.a.* (*sep.*) to wind round; (*insep.*) to overcome, prevail over. **—er**, *m.* (**—ers**, *pl.* **—er**) conqueror. **—ung**, *f.* overcoming; victory.

Überwintern [y:bər'vıntərn], *v.n.* (*aux.*

h.) (*insep.*) to hibernate; to pass the winter.

überwölken [y:bər'vəlkən], *v.r.* (*insep.*) to cloud over.

Überzahl ['y:bərtsa:l], *f.* surplus; superior numbers.

überzeug—**en** [y:bər'tsɔygən], *v.a.* (*insep.*) to convince. —**ung**, *f.* persuasion; conviction.

überzieh—**en** [y:bərtsi:ən], *ir.v.a.* (*sep.*) to put on; to cover; (*insep.*) to cover over with. —**er**, *m.* overcoat.

üblich ['yplıç] *see* **Üben**.

übrig ['y:brıç], *adj. & adv.* left over, remaining; superfluous; **die** —**en**, the others. —**ens**, *adv.* as for the rest, moreover; besides.

Ufer ['u:fər], *n.* (—**s**, *pl.* —) sea-coast, beach; bank (*of a river, etc.*).

Uhr [u:r], *f.* (*pl.* —**en**) clock; time of the day, hour; **wie viel** — **ist's?** what o'clock is it? —**zeiger**, *m.* hand of a watch *or* clock.

Uhu ['u:hu:], *m.* (—**s**, *pl.* —**s**) great horned owl.

Ulan [u'la:n], *m.* (—**en**, *pl.* —**en**) uhlan, lancer.

Ulk [ʊlk], *m.* (—(e)**s**, *pl.* —**e**) trick, frolic.

Ulme ['ʊlmə], *f.* (*pl.* —**n**) elm. —**n**, *adj.* elm.

Um [ʊm], I. *prep.* (*with acc.*) about; — . . . **herum**, about, round, around; round about; about, near, towards; about, with regard to, concerning; for, because of; for (to buy *or* sell a thing); for, in exchange for; by (*signifying the amount of difference*); at; alternately with, after; — **so besser**, all the better. II. *conj.* — **zu** (*with infin.*), so as, in order to; to; — **Ihnen zu beweisen**, in order to prove to you. III. *adv. & sep. prefix* (*or insep. indicating complete surrounding*) (*verbs compounded with* um *when sep. have the accent on* um, *when insep. on the root of the verb*) about; past, out, ended, over; over, upset; around, enclosing, surrounding; round about *or* over; (*in comp. with verbs, substantives & adverbs* um *signifies change, alteration, doing over again, turning, bringing to an end, completion, etc.*).

Umarm—**en** [ʊm'ʔarmən], *v.a.* (*insep.*) to embrace. —**ung**, *f.* embrace, hug.

Umbau ['ʊmbau], *m.* rebuilding.

Umbild—**en** ['ʊmbıldən], *v.a.* (*sep.*) to remould. —**ung**, *f.* remodelling.

Umblick ['ʊmblık], *m.* survey. —**en**, *v.r. & n.* (*aux.* h.) (*sep.*) to look round.

Umbringen ['ʊmbrıŋən], *ir.v.a.* (*sep.*) to make away with, slay, kill.

Umdreh—**en** ['ʊmdre:ən], *v.a.* (*sep.*) to turn, twist round. —**ung**, *f.* rotation; revolution.

Umfahr—**en** [ʊmfa:rən], *ir.v.a.* (*sep.*) to run down, drive over; (*insep.*) to drive, go round; to (sail) round. —**ung**, *f.* circumnavigation.

Umfang ['ʊmfaŋ], *m.* circumference, circuit; extent. —**en** [ʊm'faŋən], *ir.v.a.* (*insep.*) to surround, encircle, encompass; to embrace, to clasp. —**reich**, *adj.* wide, broad, extensive.

Umfass—**en** [ʊm'fasən], *v.a.* (*insep.*) to clasp round, enclose; to include, comprise. —**end**, *p. & adj.* far-reaching; extensive; comprehensive. —**ung**, *f.* enclosure.

Umfließen [ʊm'fli:sən], *ir.v.a.* (*insep.*) to flow (a)round.

Umformer ['ʊmfɔrmər], *m.* (—**s**, *pl.* —) converter (*Radio*).

Umfrage ['ʊmfra:gə], *f.* (*pl.* —**n**) general inquiry.

Umgang ['ʊmgaŋ], *m.* round, circuit; procession; rotation, revolution; intercourse, familiar acquaintance; connection. —**ssprache**, *f.* colloquial language.

Umgänglich ['ʊmgɛŋlıç], *adj.* sociable; affable. —**keit**, *f.* sociability.

Umgebung [ʊm'ge:bʊŋ], *f.* surroundings; environment.

Umgegend ['ʊmge:gənt], *f.* environs, neighbourhood.

Umgeh—**en** [ʊmge:ən], *ir.v.* I. *n.* (*aux.* f.) (*sep.*) to go round; to revolve; to associate, have intercourse with. II. *a.* (*insep.*) to walk round. —**end**, *p. & adj.* going about; alternate; **mit** —**ender Post**, by return of post.

Umher [ʊm'he:r], *adv. & sep. prefix*, about, up and down; all round; this way and that way; here and there. —**gehen**, *ir.v.n.* (*aux.* f.) to go, walk, stroll about. —**ziehend**, *p. & adj.* itinerant.

Umhin [ʊm'hın], *adv.*; **ich kann nicht** —, **zu**, I cannot refrain from.

Umhüll—**en** [ʊmhylən], *v.a.*; (*sep.*) **sich** (*dat.*) **ein Tuch** —**en**, to wrap oneself up in a shawl; (*insep.*) to envelop, cover. **—ung,** *f.* envelopment; cover.

Umkehr ['ʊmkeːr], *f.* turning back, return. **—en,** (*sep.*) *v.* I. *n.* (*aux.* ſ.) to turn back; to turn round; to return. II. *a.* to turn (round *or* about, inside out, etc.); to turn over *or* up; to overturn; to throw into disorder.

Umkleiden ['ʊmklaɪdən], *v.a.* (*sep.*) to change the dress of; (*insep.*) to clothe.

Umkommen ['ʊmkɔmən], *ir.v.n.* (*aux.* ſ.) (*sep.*) to perish.

Umkreis ['ʊmkraɪs], *m.* circuit.

Umlagern [ʊmˈlaːgərn], *v.a.* (*insep.*) to enclose; to besiege.

Umlauf ['ʊmlaʊf], *m.* turn, revolution; circulation. **—en,** (*sep.*) *ir.v.* I. *a.* to run over; **wir ſind eine Meile umgelaufen,** we have gone one mile out of our way. II. *n.* (*aux.* ſ.) to revolve; to circulate.

Umlaut ['ʊmlaʊt], *m.* modification of a vowel (*as* a, o, u, *to* ä *or* e, ö, ü).

Umlegen [ʊmˈleːgən], *v.a.* (*insep.*) to surround (with).

Umliegen [ʊmˈliːgən], *ir.v.n.* (*aux.* ſ.) (*sep.*) to lie around; **—d,** neighbouring; circumjacent.

Umnebeln [ʊmˈneːbəln], *v.a.* (*insep.*) to wrap in fog; to cloud.

Umringen [ʊmˈrɪŋən], *ir.v.a.* (*insep.*) to close in, beset.

Umriß ['ʊmrɪs], *m.* **(—ſſ)es,** *pl.* **—(ſſ)e** outline; sketch; ground-plan.

Umſatteln ['ʊmzatəln], *v.* I. *a.* (*sep.*) to resaddle (*a horse*). II. *n.* (*aux.* h.) to change one's profession or political creed.

Umſchalter ['ʊmʃaltər], *m.* **(—s,** *pl.* **—)** change-over switch (*Radio*).

Umſchatten [ʊmˈʃatən], *v.a.* (*insep.*) to shade, overshadow.

Umſchau ['ʊmʃaʊ], *f.* looking round. **—en,** *v.r.* & *n.* (*aux.* h.) (*sep.*) to look about, around.

Umſchlag ['ʊmʃlaːk], *m.* **(—e)s,** *pl.* **Umſchläge)** turning up *or* over; alteration; wrapper; envelope; cuff; turned-up brim; rim. **—en,** (*sep.*) I. *ir.v.a.* to knock down *or* over; to wrap round, wrap up. II. *ir.v.n.* (*aux.* ſ.) to capsize, upset. II. to turn, change suddenly; to degenerate. III. *subst.n.* sudden overthrow; overturning; change, crisis; wrapping up.

Umſchreiben [ʊmˈʃraɪbən], *ir.v.a.* (*sep.*) to re-write; (*insep.*) to paraphrase;

einen Wechſel —, to re-indorse a bill of exchange.

Umſchrift ['ʊmʃrɪft], *f.* (*pl.* **—en**) legend (*on a coin*); transcript.

Umſchweif ['ʊmʃvaɪf], *m.* **(—s,** *pl.* **—e)** roundabout way, circumlocution.

Umſchwung ['ʊmʃvʊŋ], *m.* **(—s)** rotation; revolution; revulsion (*of feeling, etc.*).

Umſehen ['ʊmzeː(ə)n], *ir.v.r.* (*sep.*) to look back, look round; to look about one; **im —,** in a twinkling.

Umſein ['ʊmzaɪn], *ir.v.n.* (*sep.*) to expire (*of a term*); to be over.

Umſetz—bar ['ʊmzɛtsbaːr], *adj.* convertible. **—barkeit,** *f.* convertibility. **—en,** I. *v.a.* (*sep.*) to transpose; to exchange; to convert into cash. II. *subst.n.,* **—ung,** *f.* change of place; transposition.

Umſicht ['ʊmzɪçt], *f.* looking about; circumspection; prudence. **—ig,** *adj.* circumspect; prudent. **—ige(r),** *m.* prudent, far-seeing person.

Umſonſt [ʊmˈzɔnst], *adv.* for nothing, gratuitously, gratis; aimlessly; to no purpose, in vain.

Umſtand ['ʊmʃtant], *m.* **(—(e)s,** *pl.* **Umſtände)** circumstance; consideration; condition, situation; (*pl.*) formalities, ceremonies; **ohne Umſtände,** without ceremony. **—s-wort,** *n.* adverb.

Umſtändlich ['ʊmʃtɛntlɪç], *adj.* & *adv.* circumstantial; minute, detailed; ceremonious.

Umſtehen [ʊmˈʃteː(ə)n], *ir.v.* I. *a.* (*insep.*) to stand round *or* about, surround. II. *n.* (*aux.* h.) (*sep.*) to stand about; **wie —d,** as stated overleaf.

Umſteigen ['ʊmʃtaɪgən], *ir.v.n.* (*aux.* ſ.) (*sep.*) to change carriages; **nach Hannover —!** change for Hanover!

Umſtellen ['ʊmʃtɛlən], *v.a.* (*sep.*) to transpose; to invert. **—ung,** *f.* change of position.

Umſtrahlen [ʊmˈʃtraːlən], *v.a.* (*insep.*) to shine round.

Umſturz ['ʊmʃtʊrts], *m.* falling down, fall; overthrow; revolution; ruin. **—partei,** *f.* revolutionary party.

Umſtürzen ['ʊmʃtʏrtsən], (*sep.*) *v.* I. *a.* to overthrow, upset. II. *n.* (*aux.* ſ.) to fall down, tumble.

Umtrieb ['ʊmtriːp], *m.* constant movement; activity; (*pl.*) intrigues, plots.

Umwälzen ['umvɛltsən], *v.a.* (*sep.*) to roll, whirl round; to overturn.

Umwandeln ['umvandəln], *v.* I. *a.* (*sep.*) to change, turn. II. *n.* (*insep.*) to walk slowly round. **Umwandlung,** *f.* change, transformation.

Umwenden ['umvɛndən], *reg. & ir.v.a.* (*sep.*) to reverse; to invert.

Umwerfen ['umvɛrfən], *ir.v.a.* (*sep.*) to overturn, upset.

Umwickeln [umvɪkəln], *v.a.* (*sep.*) to wrap round; (*insep.*) **mit etwas —,** to wrap up in.

Umwohn—en [um'voːnən], *v.a.* (*insep.*) to live, dwell around. **—er,** *pl.* the neighbours.

Umzäun—en [um'tsɔynən], I. *v.a.* (*insep.*) to fence in. II. *subst.n.,* **—ung,** *f.* enclosure, hedge, fence.

Umziehen ['umtsiːən], *ir.v.* I. *a.* (*sep.*) to pull down; to put on. II. *n.* (*aux. f.*) (*sep.*) to remove, change one's dwelling. III. *r.* (*sep.*) to change; **der Himmel hat sich umzogen,** the sky has become overcast.

Umzug ['umtsuːk], *m.* wandering about; removal; procession.

Un [un], *negative particle used as prefix* (*in comp. with subst.s, adj.s, adv.s and past participles=*) un-, in-, im-, dis-, ir-, not, non-. *The principal meanings of* **un=** *are:* (1) *absolute negation; e.g.* **Unglück;** (2) *a bad sort of; e.g.* **Unmensch;** (3) *excessive amount; e.g.* **Unmenge.** *Only the most important of the numberless compounds with* **un=** *can be given here. The meaning of others will be obvious when un-, in-, or not is prefixed to the equivalent of the second part of the compound. If the second word is a participle, see the verb to which it belongs. In case it is a derivative in =bar, =lich, or =sam look up the verb from which it is derived.*

Unabänderlich [un'ap'?ɛndərlıç], *adj.* invariable.

Unabgemacht ['un'?apgəmaxt], *adj.* unsettled.

Unabhängig ['un'aphɛnıç], *adj. & adv.* independent. **—keit,** *f.* independence.

Unabkömmlich ['un'?apkœmlıç], *adj.* indispensable. **—keit,** *f.* indispensableness.

Unablässig [un'?ap'lɛsıç], **Unabläßlich,** *adj. & adv.* incessant.

Unähnlich ['un'?ɛːnlıç], *adj.* unlike, dissimilar. **—keit,** *f.* unlikeness, dissimilarity.

Unangenehm ['un'?angəneːm], *adj.* unpleasant.

Unangesehen ['un'?angəzeːən], I. *adj.* undistinguished. II. *prep.* (*with gen.*) regardless of.

Unannehmlichkeit ['un'?anneːmlıçkaɪt], *f.* disagreeableness.

Unanständig ['un'?anʃtɛndıç], *adj.* improper.

Unantastbar [un'?an'tastbaːr], *adj.* inviolable.

Unart ['un'?aːrt], I. *f.* bad conduct; rudeness. II. *m.* (**—s,** *pl.* **—e**) rude person. **—ig,** *adj.* naughty; ill-bred.

Unaufhalt—bar [un'?auf'haltbaːr], **—sam,** *adj.* irresistible.

Unaufhörlich [un'?auf'høːrlıç], *adj.* incessant.

Unauslösch—bar [un'?aus'løʃbaːr], **—lich,** *adj. & adv.* inextinguishable; indelible.

Unausstehlich [un'?aus'ʃteːlıç], *adj. & adv.* insupportable.

Unbändig ['unbɛndıç], *adj.* unruly, intractable.

Unbeabsichtigt ['unbə'apzıçtıçt], *adj.* unintentional, undesigned.

Unbeachtet ['unbə'axtət], *adj.* disregarded.

Unbebaut [unbə'baut], *adj.* uncultivated.

Unbedeutend ['unbədɔytənt], *adj.* insignificant. **Unbedeutenheit,** *f.* insignificance.

Unbedingt ['unbədıŋt], *adj.* unconditional, unqualified, absolute.

Unbefangen ['unbəfaŋən], *adj. & adv.* unprejudiced; impartial. **—heit,** *f.* impartiality.

Unbefriedig—end ['unbəfriːdıgənt], *adj.* unsatisfactory; insufficient. **—t,** *adj.* unsatisfied.

Unbefugt ['unbəfuːkt], *adj.* unauthorized.

Unbegreiflich ['unbəgraɪflıç], *adj.* inconceivable. **—keit,** *f.* incomprehensibility.

Unbegrenzt ['unbəgrɛntst], *adj.* boundless. **—heit,** *f.* boundlessness.

Unbegriffen ['unbəgrɪfən], *adj.* not comprehended *or* understood.

Unbegründet ['unbəgryndət], *adj.* unfounded.

Unbehag—en ['unbəhaːgən], *n.* (**—ens**)

discomfort. —lid, *adj.* & *adv.*
uncomfortable, uneasy.

Unbeholfen ['ʊnbəhɔlfən], *adj.* clumsy,
awkward.

Unbekannt ['ʊnbəkant], *adj.* unknown.

Unbeliebt ['ʊnbəli:pt], *adj.* disliked.
—heit, *f.* unpopularity.

Unberufen ['ʊnbəru:fən], *adj.* unbidden, uncalled for; —! (*lit. without
invoking ill-luck*); may no evil
ensue!

Unbeschränkt ['ʊnbəʃrɛŋkt], *adj.*
boundless, unlimited. —heit, *f.*
limitlessness; absoluteness.

Unbeschreiblich [ʊnbə'ʃraɪplɪç], I. *adj.*
& *adv.* indescribable. II. *adv.* inex-
pressibly.

Unbesetzt ['ʊnbəzɛtst], *adj.* unoccupied;
free.

Unbesonnen ['ʊnbəzɔnən], *adj.* thoughtless, inconsiderate. —heit, *f.* im-
prudence, thoughtlessness.

Unbesorgt ['ʊnbəzɔrkt], *adj.* easy, not
worried; sei deswegen —, make your
mind easy about that.

Unbestimmt [ʊnbə'ʃtɪmt], *adj.* inde-
terminate; vague. —heit, *f.* indecision; vagueness.

Unbeweg—lich ['ʊnbə've:klɪç], *adj.*
immovable. —lichkeit, *f.* immovable-
ness; inflexibility. —t, *adj.* unmoved;
motionless.

Unbeweint ['ʊnbəvaɪnt], *adj.* unwept
(for), unlamented.

Unbewußt ['ʊnbəvʊst], *adj.* unknown;
unconscious.

Unbiegsam ['ʊnbi:kza:m], *adj.* inflexible; stubborn.

Unbill ['ʊnbɪl], *f.* (*pl.* Unbilden)
iniquity; insult. —ig, *adj.* unfair,
unjust.

Unbrauchbar ['ʊnbrauxba:r], *adj.* useless; good for nothing. —keit, *f.*
uselessness; incompetence.

Und [ʊnt], *conj.* and.

Undank ['ʊndaŋk], *m.* ingratitude.
—bar, *adj.* ungrateful. —barkeit, *f.*
ingratitude.

Undenk—bar [ʊn'dɛŋkba:r], *adj.* inconceivable, unimaginable. —lich,
adj. immemorial; seit—licher Zeit,
from time immemorial.

Unduldsam ['ʊndʊltza:m], *adj.* intolerant. —keit, *f.* intolerance.

Undurchdringlich [ʊndʊrç'drɪŋlɪç], *adj.*
impenetrable.

Uneben ['ʊn'e:bən], *adj.* uneven.

—heit, *f.* unevenness; inequality;
ruggedness.

Unecht ['ʊn'ɛçt], *adj.* not genuine;
false; artificial; —e Farben, not fast
colours.

Unehelich ['ʊn'e:əlɪç], *adj.* illegitimate.

Uneingedenk ['ʊn'aɪŋgədɛŋk], *adj.*
(*with gen.*) forgetful of; regardless
of.

Uneingenommen['ʊn'aɪŋgənɔmən],*adj.*
unprejudiced.

Uneingeschränkt ['ʊn'aɪŋgəʃrɛŋkt], *adj.*
unlimited, unrestrained.

Uneinig ['ʊn'aɪnɪç], *adj.* disunited; at
variance. —keit, *f.* disunion; discord.

Unempfänglich ['ʊn'ɛmpfɛŋlɪç], *adj.*
not susceptible (für, to), unimpres-
sionable.

Unempfindlich ['ʊn'ɛmpfɪndlɪç], *adj.*
insensible; cold. —keit, *f.* coldness;
insensibility.

Unendlich [ʊn'ʔɛntlɪç], *adj.* & *adv.*
endless.

Unentgeltlich [ʊn'ʔɛnt'gɛltlɪç], *adj.* &
adv. free (of charge).

Unergründ—et ['ʊn'ʔɛrgrʏndət], *adj.*
unfathomed. —lich, *adj.* impenetrable,
profound.

Unerhört [ʊn'ʔɛr'hø:rt], *adj.* unheard,
not granted; unheard of; fabulous.

Unerlaubt ['ʊn'ʔɛrlaʊpt], *adj.* unlawful,
illicit.

Unerschütter—lich [ʊn'ʔɛr'ʃʏtərlɪç], *adj.*
immovable; firm, steady. —t, *adj.*
unshaken, steadfast.

Unerwartet ['ʊn'ʔɛrvartət], *adj.* unexpected; sudden.

Unfähig ['ʊnfɛ:ɪç], *adj.* incapable (of),
unfit (for); incompetent.

Unfall ['ʊnfal], *m.* accident; di...ster.

Unfern ['ʊnfɛrn], I. *adj.* & *adv.* near.
II. *prep.* (*with gen., dat.* or von)
near, not far from.

Unfertig ['ʊnfɛrtɪç], *adj.* unfinished;
unprepared.

Unförm—ig ['ʊnfœrmɪç], —lich, *adj.*
misshapen.

Unfried—e ['ʊnfri:də], *m.* (—ens) discord, disunion. —lich, *adj.* discordant; quarrelsome.

Unfug ['ʊnfu:k], *m.* (—(e)s) wrong;
disorder.

Unfügsam ['ʊnfy:kza:m], *adj.* unyielding; intractable.

Ungeachtet ['ʊngə'axtət], I. *adj.* disregarded, not esteemed. II. *prep.*
(*with preceding or following gen.* or

dat.) notwithstanding, in spite of; **dessen** —, in spite of, for all that. III. *conj.* though, although.

Ungeahndet ['ʊngəʔa:ndət], *adj.* unpunished, unrevenged.

Ungeahnt ['ʊngəʔa:nt], *adj.* unthought of, unsuspected; unexpected.

Ungebärdig ['ʊngəbɛːrdɪç], *adj.* unruly.

Ungebeten ['ʊngəbe:tən], *adj.* uninvited; —**er Gast**, intruder.

Ungebräuchlich ['ʊngəbrɔʏçlɪç], *adj.* unusual; unused.

Ungebühr ['ʊngəby:r], *f.* abuse; impropriety; excess. —**end**, —**lich**, *adj.* undue, excessive.

Ungebunden ['ʊngəbʊndən], *adj.* unrestrained; unbridled; licentious.

Ungeeignet ['ʊngəʔaɪgnət], *adj.* unsuitable, unfit.

Ungefähr ['ʊngəfɛːr], I. *adj. & adv.* casual, accidental; approximate. II. *adv.* casually, by chance; about, near, almost. III. *n.* (—**s**) chance.

Ungefüg—e ['ʊngəfy:gə], —**ig**, *adj.* unpliant, unyielding.

Ungehalten ['ʊngəhaltən], *adj.* unkept, unfulfilled; angry.

Ungeheuer ['ʊngəhɔʏər], I. *adj.* monstrous; huge; atrocious; frightful. II. *n.* (—**s**, *pl.* —) monster. —**lich**, *adj.* monstrous.

Ungeleg—en ['ʊngəle:gən], *adj.* inconvenient; inopportune. —**enheit**, *f.* inconvenience.

Ungelenk ['ʊngəlɛŋk], *adj.* stiff; clumsy. —**heit**, *f.* awkwardness.

Ungemächlich ['ʊngəmɛçlɪç], *adj.* toilsome; troublesome. —**keit**, *f.* discomfort.

Ungemein ['ʊngəmaɪn], *adj.* extraordinary; uncommon.

Ungemessen ['ʊngəmesən], *adj.* unmeasured; immense; immoderate. —**heit**, *f.* (*pl.* —**heiten**) excess; boundlessness.

Ungeniert ['ʊnʒeni:rt], *adj.* unembarrassed, free and easy. —**heit**, *f.* unconstraint.

Ungenießbar ['ʊngəni:sba:r], *adj.* unpalatable; uneatable.

¹**Ungeraten** ['ʊngəra:tən], *adj.* stunted; that has failed, unsuccessful; spoiled; —**e Kinder**, spoiled children.

²**Ungeraten**, *adj.* not guessed, unsolved.

Ungerecht ['ʊngəreçt], *adj.* unjust. —**igkeit**, *f.* injustice.

Ungereimt ['ʊngəraɪmt], *adj.* unrhymed; absurd.

Ungern ['ʊngɛrn], *adv.* unwillingly.

Ungesäumt ['ʊngəzɔʏmt], I. *adj.* prompt, immediate. II. *adv.* without delay.

Ungeschickt ['ʊngəʃɪkt], *adj.* awkward.

Ungeschoren ['ʊngəʃo:rən], *adj.* unshorn; unmolested.

Ungestalt ['ʊngəʃtalt], I. *adj.* shapeless; misshapen. II. *f.* deformity.

Ungestört ['ʊngəʃtøːrt], *adj. & adv.* untroubled. —**heit**, *f.* tranquillity.

Ungestraft ['ʊngəʃtraft], *adj.* not punished. *adv.* with impunity. —**heit**, *f.* impunity.

Ungestüm ['ʊngəʃty:m], I. *adj.* stormy; blustering. II. *n.* impetuosity, violence.

Ungesund ['ʊngəzʊnt], *adj.* unhealthy, unwholesome.

Ungewandt ['ʊngəvant], *adj.* awkward, slow.

Ungewiß ['ʊngəvɪs], *adj.* uncertain, doubtful. —**heit**, *f.* doubt, uncertainty.

Ungewitter ['ʊngəvɪtər], *n.* (—**s**, *pl.* —) violent storm.

Ungewöhnlich ['ʊngəvøː:nlɪç], *adj.* unusual.

Ungeziefer ['ʊngətsi:fər], *n.* (—**s**, *pl.* —) vermin.

Ungezogen ['ʊngətso:gən], *adj.* illbred; rude.

Unglaub—e ['ʊnglaʊbə], *n.* (—**ens**) incredulity; unbelief. —**lich**, *adj.* incredible. —**lichkeit**, *f.* incredibility.

Ungläubig ['ʊnglɔʏbɪç], *adj.* incredulous, sceptical. —**e(r)**, *m.* (—**en**, *pl.* —**e(n)**) unbeliever; sceptic.

Ungleich ['ʊnglaɪç], I. *adj.* unequal; dissimilar; uneven; disproportionate; changeable; incompatible. II. *adv.* incomparably, much. —**heit**, *f.* inequality; difference.

Unglück ['ʊnglyk], *n.* (—**(e)s**, *pl.* **Unglücksfälle**) mishap; ill-luck. —**lich**, *adj. & adv.* unhappy; unlucky. —**selig**, *adj.* unfortunate, disastrous. —**sfall**, *m.* misfortune; casualty. —**srabe**, *m.* bird of ill omen.

Ungnade ['ʊngna:də], *f.* displeasure.

Ungnädig ['ʊngnɛ:dɪç], *adj. & adv.* ungracious.

Ungültig ['ʊngʏltɪç], *adj.* not current; invalid.

Ungünstig [ˈʊngʏnstɪç], *adj.* unfavourable.

Ungut [ˈʊnguːt], *adj.*; für — nehmen, to take amiss; nichts für —, no harm meant! no offence!

Unheil [ˈʊnhaɪl], *n.* (—s) harm; disaster; evil.

Unheilig [ˈʊnhaɪlɪç], *adj.* unholy; profane.

Unheim—isch [ˈʊnhaɪmɪʃ], *adj.* foreign, exotic. —lich, *adj.* uneasy; gloomy; sinister; very (*coll.*).

Unhöflich [ˈʊnhøːflɪç], *adj.* impolite, uncivil.

Unhold [ˈʊnholt], I. *adj.* ungracious; unfriendly. II. *m.* (—(e)s, *pl.* —e) monster; demon.

Unhörbar [ˈʊnhøːrbaːr], *adj.* inaudible, imperceptible.

Uni—form [uniˈfɔrm], *adj. & f.* (*pl.* —formen) uniform. —versal [—verˈzaːl], —versell [—verˈzɛl], *adj.* universal.

Universität [univerziˈtɛːt], *f.* (*pl.* —en) university.

Unke [ˈʊŋkə], *f.* (*pl.* —n) toad.

Unkosten [ˈʊnkostən], *pl.* expense(s); costs.

Unkraut [ˈʊnkraʊt], *n.* weed, weeds.

Unkund—e [ˈʊnkʊndə], *f.* ignorance. —ig, *adj.* (*with gen.*) ignorant of.

Unlängst [ˈʊnlɛŋst], *adv.* of late; recently, the other day.

Unleserlich [ˈʊnleːzərlɪç], **Unlesbar** [ʊnˈleːsbaːr], *adj.* illegible; unreadable. —keit, *f.* illegibility.

Unmanier—lich [ˈʊnmaniːrlɪç], *adj. & adv.* unmannerly. —lichkeit, *f.* unmannerliness; awkwardness.

Unmäßig [ˈʊnmɛsɪç], *adj.* immoderate; intemperate. —keit, *f.* excess; intemperance, *etc.*

Unmensch [ˈʊnmɛnʃ], *m.* inhuman person; monster. —lich, *adj.* inhuman; superhuman. —lichkeit, *f.* inhumanity.

Unmittelbar [ˈʊnmɪtəlbaːr], *adj.* immediate, direct. —keit, *f.* directness.

Unmöglich [ˈʊnmøːklɪç], *adj. & adv.* impossible. —keit, *f.* impossibility.

Unmündig [ˈʊnmʏndɪç], *adj.* minor, not of age.

Unnütz [ˈʊnnʏts], *adj. & adv.* useless, unprofitable. —lich, *adj.* useless; idle. —lichkeit, *f.* uselessness.

Unpaar [ˈʊnpaːr], *adj.* uneven. —igkeit, *f.* inequality.

Unpartei—isch [ˈʊnpartaɪʃ], —lich, *adj.* impartial. —lichkeit, *f.* impartiality.

Unpassend [ˈʊnpasənt], *adj.* unsuitable.

Unpünktlich [ˈʊnpʏŋktlɪç], *adj.* unpunctual.

Unrat [ˈʊnraːt], *m.* rubbish, refuse.

Unrätlich [ˈʊnrɛːtlɪç], **Unratsam** [ˈʊnratzaːm], *adj.* inexpedient; unsuitable.

Unrecht [ˈʊnrɛçt], I. *adj. & adv.* wrong; unjust. II. *n.* (—(e)s) wrong; injustice; error; einem — tun, to wrong a person; im — sein, to be wrong; einem — geben, to decide against someone. —lich, *adj.* unjust, wrongful; illegal. —lichkeit, *f.* injustice, dishonesty. —mäßig, *adj.* illegal. —mäßigkeit, *f.* illegality.

Unregelmäßig [ˈʊnreːgəlmɛsɪç], *adj.* irregular. —keit, *f.* irregularity; anomaly.

Unreif [ˈʊnraɪf], *adj.* unripe. —e, —heit, *f.* unripeness; immaturity.

Unrein [ˈʊnraɪn], *adj.* unclean, impure. —heit, *f.* uncleanness; impurity. —lich, *adj.* unclean; dirty.

Unrichtig [ˈʊnrɪçtɪç], *adj.* false; incorrect. —keit, *f.* injustice; incorrectness.

Unruh—e [ˈʊnruːə], *f.* (*pl.* —en) unrest; anxiety. —ig, *adj.* unquiet, restless.

Uns [ʊns], *pers. pron.* (*acc. & dat. of* wir) us; to us; ourselves; to ourselves.

Unsanft [ˈʊnzanft], *adj.* ungentle, harsh, rough.

Unschädlich [ˈʊnʃɛːtlɪç], *adj.* innocuous, harmless; ein Gift — machen, to neutralize a poison.

Unschicklich [ˈʊnʃɪklɪç], *adj.* unbecoming, unseemly. —keit, *f.* impropriety.

Unschlüssig [ˈʊnʃlʏsɪç], *adj.* wavering; irresolute. —keit, *f.* indecision.

Unschön [ˈʊnʃøːn], *adj.* unlovely.

Unschuld [ˈʊnʃʊlt], *f.* innocence. —ig, *adj.* innocent, guiltless.

Unser [ˈʊnzər], I. *pers. pron.* (*gen. of* wir) of us; —eins, —einer, one of us. II. *poss. adj.* (unser, uns(e)re, unser) our. III. — *or* Uns(e)rer, Uns(e)re, Uns(e)res, (der, die, das —e *or* —ige,) *poss. pron.* ours. —thalben, —twegen, (um) —twillen, *adv.* for our sake, on account of us.

Unsicher [ˈʊnzɪçər], *adj.* uncertain; insecure. —heit, *f.* insecurity; uncertainty.

Unsinn [ˈʊnzɪn], *m.* nonsense; folly; madness. —ig, *adj.* nonsensical, absurd, foolish; mad. **—igfeit,** *f.* absurdity.

Unsinnlich ['ʊnzɪnlɪç], *adj.* spiritual.

Unsitt—e ['ʊnzɪtə], *f.* bad habit *or* custom. **—lich,** *adj.* immoral. **—=** **lichfeit,** *f.* immorality.

Unsterblich [ʊn'ʃtɛrplɪç], *adj.* immortal. **—feit,** *f.* immortality.

Unstet ['ʊnʃte:t], *adj.* inconstant. **—=** **igfeit,** *f.* inconstancy.

Unstreitig ['ʊnʃtraɪtɪç], I. *adj.* incontestable, unquestionable. II. *adv.* no doubt, doubtless.

Untadel—haft [ʊn'ta:dəlhaft], **—ig,** *adj.* irreproachable.

Untat ['ʊnta:t], *f.* (*pl.* **—en**) outrage, atrocity.

Untätig ['ʊntɛ:tɪç], *adj.* inactive; idle. **—feit,** *f.* inaction.

Untauglich ['ʊntaʊklɪç], *adj.* unfit; unserviceable; useless. **—feit,** *f.* uselessness.

Unteilbar [ʊn'taɪlba:r], *adj.* indivisible. **—feit,** *f.* indivisibility.

Unten ['ʊntən], *adv.* below, beneath, underneath; at the end; downstairs. **—'an,** *adv.* at the foot *or* bottom, at the end. **—'hin,** *adv.* downwards, near the bottom.

Unter ['ʊntər], I. *prep.* (*with acc. or dat.*) 1. *with dat. implying rest or being in a place, or in answer to* wo? *where?* under, below, beneath, underneath, among, amongst, during; by; under, on; — **vier Augen,** tête-à-tête. 2. *with acc. signifying motion towards or in answer to* wohin? *whither?* under; beneath; underneath; among. II. *adj.* (*sup.* **—st**) under; underneath; lower; low; **—st,** the lowest, the last. III. *sep. & insep. pref.* below, beneath, under; among; amid. **—bleiben,** I. *ir.v.a.* (*insep.*) to be left undone; to discontinue. II. *ir.v.n.* (*aux.* f.) (*sep.*) to remain below. III. *subst.n.* cessation, discontinuance. **—brechen,** I. *ir.v.a.* (*insep.*) to interrupt; to discontinue. II. *subst.n.,* **—brechung,** *f.* interruption; cessation, stop. **—=** **brecher,** *m.* interrupter. **—breiten,** *v.a.* (*sep.*) to spread under; (*insep.*) to present, lay before. **—bringen,** *ir.v.a.* (*sep.*) to shelter; to provide (*a place*) for. **—'des, —'dessen,** *adv. & conj.* meanwhile, in the meantime. **—=** **drücken,** *v.a.* (*sep.*) to push under; (*insep.*) to repress, restrain; to crush,

quell. **—'drücker,** *m.* oppressor, tyrant. **—'drückung,** *f.* oppression; suppression. **—einander,** *adv.* mutually, reciprocally; confusedly; together. **—fangen,** *ir.v.r.* (*insep.*) (*gen.*) to attempt, undertake. **—flechten,** *ir.v.a.* (*sep.*) to entwine; to interweave; (*insep.*) to interlace; to mix, mingle. **—gang,** *m.* setting, sinking; the west; ruin. **—geben,** *ir.v.a.* (*sep.*) to put out, provide for; (*insep.*) to commit, entrust to; to subordinate. **—'gebe=** **ne(r),** *m.* subaltern; subordinate. **—'gebenheit,** *f.* subordination; inferiority (*in office*). **—gehen,** *ir.v.n.* (*aux.* f.) (*sep.*) to sink; to go to ruin; to perish; to set (*of the sun*). **—geord=** **net,** *p.p. & adj.* subordinate. **—=** **geordnete(r),** *m.* inferior. **—graben,** *ir.v.a.* (*insep.*) to undermine, sap; to destroy. **—grund,** *m.* subsoil; underground. **—halt,** *m.* maintenance, livelihood. **—halten,** I. *ir.v.a.* (*sep.*) to hold under; (*insep.*) to support, stay up; to maintain, sustain; to entertain, amuse. II. *subst.n.,* **—=** **'haltung,** *f.* maintenance; conversation. **—'handeln,** *v.a. & n.* (*aux.* h.) (*insep.*) to negotiate (*a peace, etc.*); to parley. **—'handlung,** *f.* negotiation, transaction. **—irdisch,** *adj.* underground. **—kommen,** *ir.v.n.* (*aux.* f.) (*sep.*) to find shelter *or* accommodation; to find employment, to be taken in. **—törper,** *m.* lower part of the body. **—funft,** *f.* shelter; lodging; situation. **—lage,** *f.* anything laid underneath to support some other thing; prop, support; bracket; trestle; base, foundation. **—laß,** *m.;* **ohne** **—laß,** without intermission. **—lassen,** *ir.v.a.* (*insep.*) to discontinue; to fail, omit to do; to forbear; to abstain (*from doing*). **—lassung,** *f.* omission, cessation. **legen,** *v.a.* (*sep., rarely insep.*) to lay, put under *or* to; to attribute (*to a person*) motives *or* words. **—leib,** *m.* abdomen. **—liegen,** *ir.v.n.* (*aux.* f.) (*insep.*) to succumb; to be defeated. **—nehmen,** *ir.v.a.* (*insep.*) to undertake; to attempt. **—nehmend,** *p. & adj.* enterprising, bold. **—'nehmer,** *m.* person engaged in an enterprise; contractor. **—=** **'nehmung,** *f.* enterprise. **—nehmungs=** **geist,** *m.* enterprising spirit. **—offizier,** *m.* non-commissioned officer. **—=**

ordnen, *v.a.* (*sep.*) to subordinate. —**pfand**, *n.* pledge; security. —'reden, *v.r.* (*insep.*) to converse, confer (with, mit). —'redung, *f.* conversation. —richt, *m.* (—(e)s) instruction, lessons. —'richten, *v.a.* (*insep.*) to teach, instruct. —richter, *m.* instructor. —fagen, *v.a.* (*insep.*) to forbid, prohibit. —faß, *m.* (—(ff)en, *pl.* —(ff)en) vassal. —faß, *m.* support; stand. —schätzen, *v.a.* (*insep.*) to undervalue. —schätzung, *f.* undervaluation. —'scheidbar, *adj.* distinguishable. —'scheiden, *ir.v.a.* (*insep.*) to distinguish; to discriminate. —='scheidend, *p.* & *adj.* distinctive. —'scheidung, *f.* distinction; discrimination. —'scheidungs=gabe, —'scheidungs=kraft, *f.*, —'scheidungs=vermögen, *n.* power of discrimination, discernment. —schied, *m.* (—s, *pl.* —e) distinction, difference. —'schieden, *p.p.* & *adj.* different; distinct. —='schreiben, *ir.v.a.* (*sep.*) to write under; (*insep.*) to sign. —schrift, *f.* signature. —see=boot, *n.* submarine boat. —'seeisch, *adj.* submarine. —stehen, *ir.v.* I. *n.* (*aux.* f.) (*sep.*) to stand under; to shelter under. II. *r.* (*insep.*) to dare, presume. —stützen, *v.a.* (*sep.*) to underprop, shore up; (*insep.*) to support; to protect, patronize. —'stützung, *f.* propping; support; assistance —suchen, *v.a.* (*insep.*) to inquire, search into; to examine. —sucher, *m.* examiner; investigator; explorer. —suchung, *f.* examination; investigation; research. —tan, I. *p.p.* & *adj.* subject (to); dependent. II. *m.* (—tans, —tanen, *pl.* —tanen) subject. —tänig, *adj.* submissive; dutiful. —tasse, *f.* saucer. —teil, *m.* (& *n.*) lower part; base. —wärts, I. *adv.* downwards, underneath. II. *prep.* (*with gen.*) on the lower side of. —'weg(e)s, *adv.* on the way. —'weisen, *ir.v.a.* (*insep.*) to instruct, teach. —'weiser, *m.* instructor. —'weisung, *f.* instruction. —welt, *f.* the nether world, lower regions. —werfen, *ir.v.a.* (*sep.*) to throw under; (*insep.*) to subjugate. —werfung, *f.* subjection; submission; acquiescence (*in*). —'würsig, *adj.* submissive; obsequious. —'würsigkeit, *f.* subjection; servility. —'zeichnen, *v.a.* (*sep.*) to draw underneath; (*insep.*) to sign.

—'zeichne(te)r, *m.* signer; subscriber. —'zeichnung, *f.* signature; ratification. **Untier** ['ʊntiːr], *n.* monster; brute. **Untilgbar** [ʊn'tɪlkbaːr], *adj.* indestructible. **Untreu** ['ʊntrɔy], *adj.* unfaithful, faithless. **Untüchtig** ['ʊntʏçtɪç], *adj.* incapable; incompetent; inefficient. —keit, *f.* incapacity, incompetence. **Untunlich** ['ʊntuːnlɪç], *adj.* impracticable, impossible. —keit, *f.* impossibility. **Unumgänglich** [ʊn⁹ʊm'gɛnlɪç], *adj.* unsociable; inevitable. —keit, *f.* unsociableness; inevitableness. **Unumschränkt** ['ʊn⁹ʊmʃrɛŋkt], *adj.* unlimited. **Ununterbrochen** ['ʊn⁹ʊntərbrɔxən], *adj.* & *adv.* uninterrupted. **Unveränder—lich** [ʊnfɛr'ɛndərlɪç], *adj.* unchangeable; invariable. —lichkeit, *f.* immutability, etc. —t, *adj.* unchanged. **Unverantwortlich** [ʊnfɛr'⁹antvɔrtlɪç], *adj.* irresponsible; unjustifiable, inexcusable. —keit, *f.* irresponsibility; inexcusableness. **Unverbesserlich** [ʊnfɛr'bɛsərlɪç], *adj.* incorrigible; perfect. —keit, *f.* incorrigibility; perfection. **Unverdau—lich** ['ʊnfɛrdaʊlɪç], *adj.* indigestible. —t, *adj.* not digested; crude. **Unverderblich** ['ʊnfɛrdɛrplɪç], *adj.* incorruptible. —keit, *f.* incorruptibility. **Unverdient** ['ʊnfɛrdiːnt], *adj.* unmerited. **Unverdorben** ['ʊnfɛrdɔrbən], *adj.* unspoiled. —heit, *f.* unspoiled condition, uprightness. **Unverdrossen** ['ʊnfɛrdrɔsən], *adj.* unwearied; assiduous; cheerful. —heit, *f.* assiduity; cheerfulness. **Unverehelicht** ['ʊnfɛr'⁹eːəlɪçt], *adj.* unmarried. **Unvereinbar** ['ʊnfɛr'⁹aɪnbaːr], *adj.* incompatible. —keit, *f.* incompatibility. **Unverfälscht** ['ʊnfɛrfɛlʃt], *adj.* unadulterated. —heit, *f.* genuineness. **Unvergänglich** ['ʊnfɛrgɛnlɪç], *adj.* imperishable. —keit, *f.* immortality. **Unvergessen** ['ʊnfɛrgɛsən], *adj.* unforgotten; unforgetting. **Unvergeßlich** [ʊnfɛr'gɛslɪç], *adj.* not to be forgotten. —keit, *f.* memorableness.

Unvergleich—bar [unfer'glaiçba:r], —⸗ lich, adj. matchless; unique. —lich⸗ keit, f. incomparableness.

Unvergolten ['unfɛrgɔltən], adj. unrewarded, unrecompensed.

Unverhältnismäßig ['unfɛrhɛltnɪsmɛ⸗ sɪç], adj. disproportionate. —keit, f. disproportion.

Unverhofft ['unfɛrhɔft], adj. unhoped (for); unexpected.

Unverletz—bar [unfɛr'lɛtsba:r], —lich, adj. invulnerable. —barkeit, —lich⸗ keit, f. invulnerability; inviolability. —t, adj. unhurt, uninjured.

Unvermeid—bar [unfɛr'maitba:r]. —⸗ lich, adj. inevitable.

Unvermögen ['unfɛrmø:gən], n. powerlessness, incapacity. —d, adj. incapable; impotent; poor. —s⸗fall, m.; im —s⸗falle, in case of insolvency.

Unvermutet ['unfɛrmu:tət], adj. unthought-of, unexpected.

Unvernehm—bar [unfɛr'ne:mba:r], —⸗ lich, adj. indistinct. —barkeit, —lich⸗ keit, f. inaudibleness, indistinctness.

Unvernunft ['unfɛrnunft], f. unreasonableness.

Unvernünftig ['unfɛrnynftɪç], adj. irrational; unreasonable, absurd.

Unverrichtet ['unfɛrrɪçtət], adj. unperformed.

Unverschämt ['unfɛrʃɛ:mt], adj. shameless, impudent. —heit, f. impudence; effrontery.

Unversehen [unfɛr'ze:ən], adj. unexpected, unforeseen. —s, adv. unexpectedly.

Unversehr—t [unfɛr'ze:rt], adj. uninjured; intact. —theit, f. entirety.

Unversöhnlich [unfɛr'zø:nlɪç], adj. irreconcilable.

Unverstand ['unfɛrʃtant], m. want of understanding or judgment. —en, adj. not understood; misunderstood.

Unverständ—ig ['unfɛrʃtɛndɪç], adj. imprudent; unwise. —lich, adj. unintelligible. —lichkeit, f. unintelligibility, incomprehensibility.

Unverwandt ['unfɛrvant], adj. unmoved; unrelated (mit, with).

Unverzagt ['unfɛrtsa:kt], adj. undaunted, undismayed. —heit, f. intrepidity; boldness, courage.

Unverzeihlich [unfɛr'tsailɪç], adj. unpardonable.

Unverzüglich [unfɛr'tsy:klɪç], I. adj. immediate, instant. II. adv. without delay, forthwith.

Unvorsichtig ['unfo:rzɪçtɪç], adj. improvident; incautious. —keit, f. want of foresight.

Unvorteilhaft ['unfo:rtailhaft], adj. disadvantageous.

Unwahr ['unva:r], adj. false, untrue. —haft, adj. untrue. —haftigkeit, f. inaccuracy; falseness. —heit, f. falsehood; inaccuracy.

Unwahrscheinlich ['unva:rʃamlɪç], adj. improbable.

Unwandelbar [un'vandəlba:r], adj. immutable, unchangeable.

Unweigerlich [un'vaigərlɪç], adj. unresisting, unhesitating.

Unweit ['unvait], adv. & prep. (with gen.) not far off or from, near, close by.

Unwert ['unvɛ:rt], I. adj. unworthy; worthless. II. m. worthlessness; futility.

Unwesen ['unve:zən], n. disorder; abuse.

Unwesentlich ['unve:zəntlɪç], adj. unessential.

Unwichtig ['unvɪçtɪç], adj. unimportant. —keit, f. insignificance.

Unwiderleg—bar [unvi:dər'le:kba:r], —lich, adj. unanswerable, irrefutable. —barkeit, —lichkeit, f. unanswerableness.

Unwiderruflich [unvi:dər'ru:flɪç], adj. irrevocable.

Unwiderstehlich [unvi:dər'ʃte:lɪç], adj. & adv. irresistible.

Unwill—e(n) ['unvilə(n)], m. indignation; vexation; reluctance. —ig, adj. indignant; reluctant, unwilling. —fährig, adj. disobliging or uncomplying. —fährigkeit, f. want of compliance. —kommen, adj. unwelcome. —kürlich, adj. involuntary. —kürlich⸗ keit, f. involuntariness.

Unwirk—lich ['unvirklɪç], adj. not real or existing. —sam, adj. ineffectual; inoperative; null, void. —samkeit, f. inefficacy; inefficiency.

Unwirsch ['unvirʃ], adj. cross; morose. —heit, f. bad temper; brusqueness.

Unwissen—d ['unvisənt], adj. ignorant. —heit, f. ignorance. —schaftlich, adj. unscientific.

Unwohl ['unvo:l], adj. unwell, indisposed.

Unwürdig ['unvy:rdɪç], adj. unworthy.

Unzähl—bar [ʊn'tsɛːlbaːr], —ig, adj. innumerable, numberless.

Unzart ['ʊntsaːrt], adj. not tender; rude; devoid of tact. —heit, f. rudeness; want of delicacy or tenderness.

1Unze ['ʊntsə], f. (—n) ounce.

2Unze, f. (—n) ounce (Zool.).

Unzeit ['ʊntsaɪt], f. wrong time. —ig, adj. untimely.

Unzerstör—bar [ʊntsɛr'ʃtøːrbaːr], —lich, adj. indestructible; imperishable. —barkeit, f. indestructibleness.

Unziem—end ['ʊntsiːmənt], —lich, adj. unbecoming.

Unzier ['ʊntsiːr], —de, f. blemish. —lich, adj. inelegant, ungraceful.

Unzucht ['ʊntsʊxt], f. unchastity.

Unzüchtig ['ʊntsʏçtɪç], adj. unchaste. —keit, f. immodesty.

Unzufrieden ['ʊntsufriːdən], adj. dissatisfied.

Unzugänglich ['ʊntsugɛnlɪç], adj. inaccessible; not affable. —keit, f. inaccessibility.

Unzulänglich ['ʊntsulɛnlɪç], adj. insufficient. —keit, f. insufficiency.

Unzulässig ['ʊntsulɛsɪç], adj. inadmissible. —keit, f. inadmissibility.

Unzuverlässig ['ʊntsuferlɛsɪç], adj. unreliable. —keit, f. untrustworthiness.

Unzweifelhaft ['ʊntsvaɪfəlhaft], adj. undoubted, indubitable.

Üppig ['ʏpɪç], adj. luxuriant, rank; sensual; overbearing; in high spirits. —keit, f. exuberance; richness; luxury; voluptuousness.

1Ur [uːr], m. (—(e)s, pl. —e) species of wild ox. —ochs, m. aurochs.

2Ur, prefix of nouns & adjs. generally implying primitiveness, origin or extreme antiquity; sometimes it merely adds an intensive force.

Urahn ['uːrʔaːn], m. (—en, pl. —en), —e, f. (pl. —en) (—herr, m., —frau, f.), great-grandfather, great-grandmother; ancestor, ancestress.

Uralt ['uːrʔalt], adj. extremely old.

Uranfänglich ['uːrʔanfɛnlɪç], adj. primeval.

Urbar ['uːrbaːr], adj. arable; —s machen, to cultivate (land).

Urbewohner ['uːrbəvoːnər], m. original inhabitant; (pl.) aborigines.

Urbild ['uːrbɪlt], n. original; archetype. —lich, adj. original; ideal.

Ureltern ['uːrʔɛltərn], pl. ancestors; first parents.

Urenkel ['uːrʔɛnkəl], m., —in, f. great-grandchild.

Urgroß— ['uːrgroːs] (in comp.) —s eltern, pl. great-grandparents. —s mutter, f. great-grandmother. —s vater, m. great-grandfather.

Urheber ['uːrheːbər], m., —in, f. author, originator. —schaft, f. authorship, parentage. —recht, n. copyright (an Werken der Litteratur, of literary productions).

Urkomisch ['uːrkoːmɪʃ], adj. extremely comical.

Ur—kraft ['uːrkraft], f. original force. —kräftig, adj. very or most powerful; of original force.

Urkund—e ['uːrkʊndə], f. (pl. —en) deed, document; record; attestation. —lich, adj. documentary; authentic.

Urlaub ['uːrlaʊp], m. (—s) leave of absence, furlough. —er, m. (—ers, pl. —er) soldier on furlough; ticket-of-leave man.

Urmensch ['uːrmɛnʃ], m. (—en, pl. —en) primitive man.

Urne ['ʊrnə], f. (pl. —n) urn.

Urplötzlich ['uːrpløtslɪç], adv. all of a sudden.

Urquell ['uːrkvɛl], m. (—s, pl. —e), —e, f. (pl. —en) fountain-head.

Ursache ['uːrzaxə], f. (first) cause, (original) motive, ground, occasion.

Urschrift ['uːrʃrɪft], f. original text; autograph. —lich, adj. autographic.

Ursprung ['uːrʃprʊn], m. (first) source; origin.

Ursprünglich ['uːrʃprʏnlɪç], adj. primitive; primary; original.

Urteil ['ʊrtaɪl], n. (—s, pl. —e) judgment, decision; judicial sentence. —s kraft, f. (power of) judgment, discernment.

Urteilen ['ʊrtaɪlən], v.n. (aux. h.) to judge.

Urtext ['uːrtɛkst], m. original text.

Urvater ['uːrfaːtər], m. first parent, forefather.

Urväter—lich ['uːrfɛːtərlɪç], adj. primitive; ancestral. —zeit, f. olden times, days of yore.

Urvorfahr ['uːrfoːrfaːr], m. (first) ancestor, forefather.

Urwald ['uːrvalt], m. primeval or virgin forest.

Urwelt ['uːrvɛlt], f. primeval world. —lich, adj. primitive; antediluvian.

Uzen ['uːtsən], v.a. to mock, tease, chaff.

B

B, v [fau], n. V, v.

Baluta [va'lu:ta:], f. value, currency; **beständige —,** standard.

Banille [va'nɪljə], f. vanilla.

Basall [va'zal], m. (—en, pl. —en), —in, f. vassal.

Base ['va:zə], f. (pl. —n) vase.

Bater ['fa:tər], m. (—s, pl. Bäter) father. —haus, n. the paternal roof. —land, n. native country. —ländisch, adj. national. —lands=liebe, f. patriotism. —mord, m. parricide. —mörder, m. parricide. —stadt, f. native town. — unser, n. the Lord's Prayer.

Bäter=chen ['fɛ:tərçən], n. (—chens, pl. —chen) papa; daddie. —lich, adj. paternal.

Beilchen ['faɪlçən], n. (—s, pl. —) violet (Bot.).

Bene ['ve:nə], f. (pl. —n) vein.

Bentil [vɛn'ti:l], n. (—s, pl. —e) valve.

Ber— [fɛr], insep. prefix added to verbs and to the nouns and adjectives derived from them, with the idea of removal, loss, untoward action, using up, change, reversal, etc. But frequently it is used to form verbs from nouns, adjectives and other verbs, sometimes to denote change and sometimes without modifying the meaning, e.g. **ver=ursachen,** to cause; **ver=edeln,** to ennoble.

Berabfolg—en [fɛr'ʔapfɔlgən], v.a. to deliver. —ung, f. delivery; remitting.

Berabreden [fɛr'ʔapre:dən], v.a. to concert, agree upon.

Berabsäumen [fɛr'ʔapzɔymən], v.a. to neglect.

Berabscheuen [fɛr'ʔapʃɔyən], v.a. to abhor.

Berabschieden [fɛr'ʔapʃi:dən], v.a. to dismiss, discharge; sich —, to take leave.

Beracht—en [fɛr'ʔaxtən], v.a. to despise. —ung, f. disdain, contempt.

Berächtlich [fɛr'ʔɛçtlɪç], adj. contemptuous, disdainful.

Beralt—en [fɛr'ʔaltən], v.n. (aux. f.) to grow old. —et, p.p. & adj. old; obsolete.

Beränder—lich [fɛr'ʔɛndərlɪç], adj. changeable; unsteady, fickle. —lich= keit, f. variability. —n, v.a. to change.

Beranlass—en [fɛr'ʔanlasən], v.a. to

cause, occasion. —er, m. (—ers, pl. —er), —erin, f. author, cause. —ung, f. cause, motive.

Beranstalt—en [fɛr'ʔanstaltən], v.a. to prepare; to contrive. —er, m. (—ers, pl. —er) arranger, organizer. —ung, f. preparation; arrangement.

Berantwort—en [fɛr'ʔantvɔrtən], v.a. to answer for, account for. —lich, adj. responsible for. —lichkeit, f. responsibility. —ung, f. responsibility; auf seine —ung, at his own peril.

Berarbeit—en [fɛr'ʔarbaɪtən], v.a. to work, to manufacture; im Geiste —en, to ponder over. —ung, f. manufacturing; working up.

Berargen [fɛr'ʔargən], v.a. to take amiss, misconstrue.

Beräußer—n [fɛr'ʔɔysərn], v.a. to alienate, to sell. —ung, f. alienation; sale.

Berb [vɛrp], n. (—s, pl. —en) verb.

Berband [fɛr'bant], m. (—(e)s, pl. Berbände) binding, joining; bond; joint; union; club.

Berbann—en [fɛr'banən], v.a. to banish. —te(r), m. exile. —ung, f. banishment, exile.

Berbeißen [fɛr'baɪsən], ir.v.a. to stifle, suppress; sich in etwas —, to stick obstinately to a thing.

Berbergen [fɛr'bɛrgən], ir.v.a. to hide, conceal.

Berbesser—er [fɛr'bəsərər], m. (—ers, pl. —er), —in, f. improver; reformer. —lich, adj. improvable. —n, v.a. to improve. —ung, f. improvement.

Berbeug—en [fɛr'bɔygən], v.r. to bow. —ung, f. bow.

Berbieten [fɛr'bi:tən], ir.v.a. to forbid.

Berbind—en [fɛr'bɪndən], ir.v.a. to bind; to unite; ich bin ihm sehr verbunden, I am much obliged to him. —lich, adj. binding, obligatory; obliging, courteous. —lichkeit, f. binding force or power; obligation; liability; obligingness. —ung, f. binding, joining; union; league, alliance; connection; engagement; bandaging, dressing (Surg.). —ungs=linie, f., —ungs= weg, m. line of communication. —ungs=wort, n. conjunction.

Berbissen [fɛr'bɪsən], p.p. & adj. sullen, crabbed. —heit, f. sullenness.

Berbitten [fɛr'bɪtən], ir.v.a.; sich (dat.) etwas von einem —, to beg to decline, to beg a person not to do a thing; **das verbitte ich mir,** don't do that again.

Verbleiben [fɛr'blaɪbən], *ir.v.n.* (*aux.* f.) to remain in a certain condition.

Verbleichen [fɛr'blaɪçən], *ir.v.n.* (*aux.* f.) to grow (deadly) pale.

Verblend—en [fɛr'blɛndən], *v.a.* to blind, dazzle. **—ung,** *f.* blinding, dazzling; infatuation, fascination.

Verblüff—en [fɛr'blʊfən], *v.a.* to disconcert, confuse. **—end,** *adj.* startling; stupendous. **—t,** abashed, dumbfounded. **—theit,** *f.* stupefaction.

Verblühen [fɛr'blyːən], *v.n.* (*aux.* h. & f.) to fade, to wither.

Verblut—en [fɛr'bluːtən], *v.r.* & *n.* (*aux.* f.) to bleed profusely; to bleed to death. **—ung,** *f.* hæmorrhage; bleeding to death.

¹**Verborgen** [fɛr'bɔrgən], *v.a.* to lend out.

²**Verborgen,** *p.p.* (*of* verbergen) & *adj.* hidden, secret. **—heit,** *f.* concealment; retirement; secrecy.

Verbot [fɛr'boːt], *n.* (—(e)s, *pl.* —e) prohibition. **—en,** *p.p.* & *adj.* forbidden; illicit.

Verbräm—en [fɛr'brɛːmən], *v.a.* to trim; to embellish. **—ung,** *f.* border, trimming.

Verbrauch [fɛr'braux], *m.* (—s) consumption. **—en,** *v.a.* to use, consume.

Verbrech—en [fɛr'brɛçən], I. *ir.v.a.* to commit a crime. II. *subst.n.* crime; misdeed. **—er,** *m.* (—ers, *pl.* —er) criminal. **—erisch,** *adj.* criminal; sinful. **—erkolonie,** *f.* convict colony.

Verbreit—en [fɛr'braɪtən], *v.a.* to spread; to circulate. **—er,** *m.* (—ers, *pl.* —er) publisher; propagator. **—ung,** *f.* propagation; dissemination.

Verbrenn—en [fɛr'brɛnən], *ir.v.a.* to burn, consume by fire. **—ung,** *f.* burning; cremation (*of the dead*).

Verbrief—en [fɛr'briːfən], *v.a.* to furnish with documents. **—t,** *p.p.* & *adj.* chartered, documented.

Verbringen [fɛr'brɪŋən], *ir.v.a.* to spend, pass (*time*); to squander, waste.

Verbum ['vɛrbʊm], *n.* (—s, *pl.* Verba) verb.

Verbürg—en [fɛr'byrgən], *v.a.* & *r.* to guarantee. **—t,** *p.p.* & *adj.* authentic(ated).

Verbüßen [fɛr'byːsən], *v.a.* to atone for.

Verdacht [fɛr'daxt], *m.* (—(e)s) suspicion; **in — haben,** to suspect.

Verdächtig [fɛr'dɛçtɪç], *adj.* suspected, suspicious.

Verdamm—en [fɛr'damən], *v.a.* to condemn. **—nis,** *f.* (*pl.* —nisse) damnation; perdition. **—ung,** *f.* condemnation. **—enswert, —enswürdig,** *adj.* damnable; criminal. **—ungsurteil,** *n.* sentence of condemnation.

Verdampf—en [fɛr'dampfən], *v.* I. *a.* to cause to evaporate. II. *n.* (*aux.* f.) to evaporate. **—ung,** *f.* evaporation.

Verdanken [fɛr'daŋkən], *v.a.* (**einem etwas**) to owe (something to a person); to be obliged (to a person for a thing).

Verdau—en [fɛr'dauən], *v.a.* to digest. **—lich,** *adj.* digestible. **—lichkeit,** *f.* digestibleness. **—ung,** *f.* digestion.

Verdeck [fɛr'dɛk], *n.* (—(e)s, *pl.* —e) covering; deck (*Naut.*). **—en,** *v.a.* to cover; to hide. **—t,** *p.p.* & *adj.* covered; covert. **—ung,** *f.* covering; concealing.

Verdenken [fɛr'dɛŋkən], *v.a.* to blame, take amiss.

Verderb [fɛr'dɛrp], *m.* (—(e)s) ruin; destruction.

Verderb—en [fɛr'dɛrbən], I. *reg.* & *ir.v.a.* to spoil; to destroy; **es mit jemand —en,** to incur a person's displeasure. II. *ir.v.n.* (*aux.* f.) to spoil; to perish. **—er,** *m.* (—ers, *pl.* —er) destroyer, corrupter. **—lich,** *adj.* corruptible; perishable; ruinous; fatal. **—lichkeit,** *f.* corruptibility; ruinousness. **—nis,** *f.* (*pl.* —nisse) & *n.* (—nisses, *pl.* —nisse) corruption; depravity, perversion. **—t,** *p.p.* & *adj.* perverse, depraved, vicious. **—theit,** *f.* corruptness; depravity.

Verdien—en [fɛr'diːnən], *v.a.* to earn; to get, win; to merit. **—st,** *m.* & *n.* (—stes, *pl.* —ste) (*generally m.*) gain, profit; merit; deserts. **—stlich,** *adj.* & *adv.* meritorious. **—stlichkeit,** *f.* meritoriousness. **—stlos,** *adj.* undeserving; unprofitable. **—stvoll,** *adj.* meritorious.

Verdikt [vɛr'dɪkt], *n.* (—(e)s, *pl.* —e) verdict.

Verding—en [fɛr'dɪŋən], *reg.* & *ir.v.a.* to hire out. **—ung,** *f.* hiring, contract.

Verdoppeln [fɛr'dɔpəln], *v.a.* to double.

Verdorben [fɛr'dɔrbən], *p.p.* & *adj.* unsound; spoilt, rotten. **—heit,** *f.* spoiled condition; rottenness; depravity.

Verdrängen [fɛr'drɛŋən], *reg. & ir.v.a.* to crowd out; to supplant.

Verdreh—en [fɛr'dre:ən], *v.a.* to twist, wrench; to warp, pervert; **die Augen —en**, to roll one's eyes. **—t**, *p.p. & adj.* distorted. **—theit**, *f.* distortedness; craziness. **—ung**, *f.* twisting, distortion; sprain.

Verdrieß—en [fɛr'dri:sən], *ir.v.a.* to grieve, vex, annoy. **—lich**, *adj.* vexed, annoyed; peevish; vexatious. **—lichkeit**, *f.* bad temper; annoyance.

Verdroffen [fɛr'drosən], *p.p. & I. adj.* cross, peevish. **II.** *adv.* unwillingly.

Verdruß [fɛr'drus], *m.* **(—(ff)es)** ill-humour; discontent; disgust; annoyance.

Verdunkel—n [fɛr'duŋkəln], *v.a.* to darken; to obscure. **—ung**, *f.* darkening.

Verdunst—en [fɛr'dunstən], *v.n. (aux. f.)* to evaporate. **—ung**, *f.* evaporation.

Verdüster—n [fɛr'dy:stərn], *v.* **I.** *a.* to darken. **II.** *r. & n. (aux. f.)* to grow dark *or* gloomy. **—ung**, *f.* darkening, gloom.

Verdutz—en [fɛr'dutsən], *v.a.* to bewilder; **—t machen**, to disconcert, abash.

Vered—eln [fɛr'?e:dəln], *v.a.* to ennoble. **—elung, —lung**, *f.* ennobling; improvement.

Verehelichen [fɛr'?e:əlıçən], *v.a. & r.* to marry.

Verehr—en [fɛr'?e:rən], *v.a.* to venerate, respect. **—er**, *m.* **(—ers, pl. —er)** devoted admirer, lover. **—lich**, *adj.* venerable. **—ung**, *f.* respect, veneration.

Vereid(ig)en [fɛr'?aɪd(ıg)ən], *v.a.*; **einen —**, to put a person to *or* on his oath.

Verein [fɛr'?aɪn], *m.* **(—s, pl. —e)** union; confederation; club; partnership. **—bar**, *adj.* combinable; consistent. **—baren**, *v.a.* to unite, connect; to reconcile. **—barkeit**, *f.* compatibility. **—barung**, *f.* agreement. **—igen**, *v.a.* to unite, join; to associate; to reconcile. **—s=leitung**, *f.* management of a society.

Vereinfach—en [fɛr'?aɪnfaxən], *v.a.* to simplify. **—ung**, *f.* simplification.

Vereinigung [fɛr'?aɪnɪguŋ], *f.* (*pl.* **—en**) union; meeting; combination; alliance; confederation; reconciliation; agreement. **—s=ort**, *m.* place of assembly.

Vereinzel—n [fɛr'?aɪntsəln], *v.a.* to isolate; to separate. **—ung**, *f.* isolation; separation.

Vereitel—n [fɛr'?aɪtəln], *v.a.* to make vain or fruitless; to frustrate, baffle. **—ung**, *f.* frustration.

Verenge(r)n [fɛr'?ɛŋə(r)n], *v.a.* to narrow, contract.

Vererb—en [fɛr'?ɛrbən], *v.* **I.** *a.* **(einem etwas** *or* **etwas auf einen)** to leave, bequeath. **II.** *r. & n. (aux. f.)* to devolve (on, **auf**); to be hereditary. **—lich**, *adj.* inheritable; hereditary. **—t**, *p.p. & adj.* hereditary.

Verewigen [fɛr'?e:vɪgən], *v.a.* to perpetuate; to immortalize.

Verfahr—en [fɛr'fa:rən], **I.** *ir.v.n. (aux. h. & f.)* to act, behave, proceed. **II.** *ir.v.a.* to convey, transport; to elude. **III.** *ir.v.r.* to lose one's way. **IV.** *subst.n.* proceeding; procedure, behaviour. **—ung**, *f.* transport, conveyance; exportation.

Verfall [fɛr'fal], *m.* **(—s)** decay, dilapidation; decline. **—frift**, *f.*, **—tag, —termin**, *m.*, **—zeit**, *f.* day on which a bill becomes due.

Verfallen [fɛr'falən], *ir.v.n. (aux. f.)* to fall due; to lapse; **in eine Geldstrafe —**, to incur a fine; **—e Gesichtszüge**, worn features.

Verfälsch—en [fɛr'fɛlʃən], *v.a.* to falsify. **—er**, *m.* **(—ers, pl. —er)** forger. **—ung**, *f.* falsification; forging.

Verfaff—en [fɛr'fasən], *reg. & ir.v.a.* to compose. **—er**, *m.* **(—ers, pl. —er)**, **—erin**, *f.* author. **—erschaft**, *f.* authorship. **—ung**, *f.* composition; condition; situation, state; constitution; organization. **—ungs=bruch**, *m.* violation of the constitution. **—ungs=los**, *adj.* without a constitution.

Verfehlen [fɛr'fe:lən], *v.a.* to fail; to miss.

Verfeinden [fɛr'faɪndən], *v.a.* to make an enemy of.

Verfeinern [fɛr'faɪnərn], *v.a.* to refine.

Verfertig—en [fɛr'fɛrtɪgən], *v.a.* to manufacture; to prepare. **—er**, *m.* **(—ers, pl. —er)** manufacturer; maker. **—ung**, *f.* making; fabrication; manufacture.

Verflecht—en [fɛr'flɛçtən], *ir.v.a.* to entwine, interlace. **—ung**, *f.* interlacing, interweaving.

Verfluch—en [fɛr'flu:xən], *v.a.* to curse. **—t**, *p.p., adj. & adv.* accursed.

Verfolg [fɛr'fɔlk], *m.* (—(e)s) course, progress.

Verfolg—en [fɛr'fɔlgən], *v.a.* to pursue; to persecute; to prosecute. **—er,** *m.* (—ers, *pl.* —er) pursuer; persecutor. **—ung,** *f.* pursuit; persecution; result, sequel. **—ungs=geist,** *m.* spirit of persecution.

Verfüg—en [fɛr'fy:gən], I. *a.* to dispose, arrange; to decree; to provide. II. *r.*; **sich (nach einem Orte** *or* **zu einem Menschen) —en,** to betake oneself to a person *or* a place. III. *n.* (aux. h.) **über (eine S.) —en,** to dispose of. **—er,** *m.* (—ers, *pl.* —er) disposer, arranger. **—ung,** *f.* disposal, disposition.

Verführ—en [fɛr'fy:rən], *v.a.* to lead astray, mislead. **—er,** *m.* (—ers, *pl.* —er) tempter, seducer. **—erisch,** *adj.* seductive; tempting. **—ung,** *f.* transportation, exportation.

Vergangen [fɛr'gaŋən], *p.p. & adj.* past, gone; **im —en Monat,** last month.

Vergänglich [fɛr'gɛŋlıç], *adj.* fleeting, transitory.

Vergeb—en [fɛr'ge:bən], *ir.v.a.* to give away; to forgive, pardon; **sich etwas —en,** to compromise one's dignity. **—ens,** *adv.* in vain. **—lich,** *adj. & adv.* vain, idle. **—ung,** *f.* forgiveness.

Vergeh—en [fɛr'ge:ən], I. *ir.v.n.* (aux. s.) to vanish, disappear; **vor Gram —en,** to pine away; **mir ist der Appetit vergangen,** I have lost my appetite. II. *ir.v.r.* to go astray. III. *subst.n.* disappearance; offence, crime. **—ung,** *f.* fault, offence.

Vergelten [fɛr'gɛltən], *v.a.* (einem etwas) to requite, repay; **Gott vergelte es Ihnen,** may God reward you for it. **—ung,** *f.* requital, reward, recompense.

Vergess—en [fɛr'gɛsən], I. *ir.v.a.* to forget. II. *subst.n.* forgetting, oblivion. **—en=heit,** *f.* forgetfulness; neglect. **—lich,** *adj.* forgetful; easily forgotten. **—lichkeit,** *f.* forgetfulness; negligence. **—en=sein,** *n.* oblivion.

Vergeud—en [fɛr'gɔydən], *v.a.* to squander (away). **—er,** *m.* (—ers, *pl.* —er) squanderer, spendthrift. **—ung,** *f.* a squandering.

Vergift—en [fɛr'gıftən], *v.a.* to poison. **—er,** *m.* (—ers, *pl.* —er), **—erin,** *f.* poisoner. **—ung,** *f.* poisoning.

Vergißmeinnicht [fɛr'gısmaınnıçt], *n.* forget-me-not (*Bot.*).

Vergleich [fɛr'glaıç]. *m.* (—(e)s, *pl.*—e) agreement; contract; arrangement; comparison; parallel. **—bar,** *adj.* comparable (**mit,** *to*). **—barkeit,** *f.* comparableness.

Vergleich—en [fɛr'glaıçən], *ir.v.* I. *a.* to make equal *or* even; to adjust; to settle (*disputes*); to compensate; to compare; to draw a comparison (*between or with*). II. *r.* to compound; to become reconciled. **—ung,** *f.* adjustment, equalization; comparison, parallel.

Verglimmen [fɛr'glımən], *ir.v.* (*r.*) & *n.* (aux. s.) to be slowly extinguished.

Verglühen [fɛr'gly:ən], *v.n.* (aux. s.) to cease glowing.

Vergnüg—en [fɛr'gny:gən], I. *v.a.* to please, gratify. II. *subst.n.* pleasure, delight; amusement. **—lich,** *adj. & adv.* contented; pleasant; amusing. **—lichkeit,** *f.* contentment, satisfaction. **—t,** *p.p. & adj.* pleased; joyous. **—ung,** *f.* amusement; recreation. **—ungs=reisender,** *m.* tourist.

Vergönnen [fɛr'gœnən], *v.a.* to grant, permit, allow.

Vergötter—n [fɛr'gœtərn], *v.a.* to deify; to idolize. **—ung,** *f.* deification.

Vergreif—en [fɛr'graıfən], *ir.v.* I. *a.* to seize *or* touch wrongly; to seize upon, buy up; **die Waren sind vergriffen,** the goods are sold out; **sich am Gesetz —en,** to violate the law. II. *r.* to seize wrongly.**—ung,** *f.* wronging ; profanation.

Vergrößer—n [fɛr'grø:sərn], *v.* I. *a.* to enlarge; to exaggerate. II. *r.* to aggrandize oneself. **—ung,** *f.* enlargement; increase; aggrandizement. **—ungs=glas,** *n.* magnifying glass. **—ungs=kraft,** *f.* magnifying power.

Vergüt—en [fɛr'gy:tən], *v.a.* to make amends. **—ung,** *f.* compensation, amends.

Verhaft [fɛr'haft], *m.* (—(e)s) arrest. **—en,** *v.a.* to arrest. **—ung,** *f.* arrest; imprisonment. **—s=befehl,** **—s=brief,** *m.* warrant, writ of arrest.

Verhallen [fɛr'halən], *v.n.* (aux. s.) to die *or* fade away (*of sound*).

Verhalt—en [fɛr'haltən], I. *ir.v.a.* to keep back; to hide, dissimulate. II. *ir.v.r. & n.* (aux. s.) to stop, remain. III. *ir.v.r.* to be circumstanced, situated; to have a certain relation to; to conduct, comport oneself; **ſich ruhig —en**, to keep quiet; **es verhält ſich ſo**, such is the case. IV. *subst.n.* conduct, behaviour. **—ung**, *f.* suppression; concealment.

Verhältnis [fɛr'hɛltnɪs], *n.* (—(ſſ)es, *pl.* —(ſſ)e) relation, bearing; (*generally pl.*) situation, circumstances; love-affair. **—los**, *adj.* having no relation *or* proportion. **—mäßig**, I. *adj.* proportionate, proportional. II. *adv.* in proportion; comparatively (speaking). **—mäßigkeit**, *f.* proportion(-ateness). **—regel**, *f.* rule of three (*Arith.*). **—widrig**, *adj.* disproportioned, disproportionate. **—wort**, *n.* preposition.

Verhand—eln [fɛr'handəln], *v.* I. *a.* & *n.* (*aux.* h.) to treat; to deliberate upon; to negotiate. II. *a.* to sell; to lose in speculation. **—lung**, *f.* discussion; negotiation; proceeding.

Verhäng—en [fɛr'hɛŋən], *v.a.* to decree, ordain. **—nis**, *n.* (—niſſes, *pl.* —niſſe) fate, destiny. **—nis=voll**, *adj.* fatal, disastrous, fateful.

Verharren [fɛr'harən], *v.n.* (*aux.* h. & ſ.) to remain unchanged; to persevere.

Verhärt—en [fɛr'hɛrtən], *v.a.* to harden. **—et**, *adj.* (*fig.*) obdurate, callous. **—ung**, *f.* hardening; obduracy.

Verhaßt [fɛr'hast], *adj.* odious, hateful.

Verheer—en [fɛr'he:rən], *v.a.* to ravage, devastate. **—er**, *m.* (—ers, *pl.* —er) devastator. **—ung**, *f.* devastation.

Verhehl—en [fɛr'he:lən], *v.a.* to hide; to receive (*stolen goods*). **—ung**, *f.* concealing; dissimulation; receiving (*of stolen goods*).

Verheimlich—en [fɛr'haɪmlɪçən], *v.a.* to conceal. **—ung**, *f.* concealment.

Verheiraten [fɛr'haɪra:tən], *v.* I. *a.* to marry. II. *r.* to marry.

Verheiß—en [fɛr'haɪsən], *ir.v.a.* to promise; **das —ene Land**, the Promised Land. **—ung**, *f.* promise.

Verhinder—n [fɛr'hɪndərn], *v.a.* to hinder, prevent. **—ung**, *f.* obstacle, impediment.

Verhohlen [fɛr'ho:lən], *adj.* secretive; clandestine.

Verhöhn—en [fɛr'hø:nən], *v.a.* to deride. **—er**, *m.* (—ers, *pl.* —er) scorner, derider. **—ung**, *f.* derision, mockery; insult.

Verhör [fɛr'hø:r], *n.* (—(e)s, *pl.* —e) judicial examination; trial. **—en**, *v.a.* to hear, examine, try; **ſich —en**, to misunderstand.

Verhüll—en [fɛr'hylən], I. *v.a.* to cover, veil, wrap up. II. *subst.n.*, **—ung**, *f.* covering, disguise.

Verhungern [fɛr'huŋərn], *v.n.* (*aux.* ſ.) to die of hunger.

Verhüt—en [fɛr'hy:tən], *v.a.* to avert; to prevent; **das —e Gott!** God forbid! **—ung**, *f.* prevention.

Verirr—en [fɛr'ʔɪrən], *v.r.* & *n.* (*aux.* ſ.) to err, go astray. **—ung**, *f.* aberration; wandering; error.

Verjag—en [fɛr'ja:gən], *v.a.* to drive away. **—ung**, *f.* expulsion; dislodgment.

Verjähr—en [fɛr'jɛ:rən], *v.n.* (*aux.* ſ.) to grow old. **—t**, *p.p.* & *adj.* inveterate, deep-rooted; obsolete. **—ung**, *f.* superannuation.

Verjüng—en [fɛr'jyŋən], *v.* I. *a.* to rejuvenate. II. *r.* to grow young again. **—ung**, *f.* rejuvenescence.

Verkapp—en [fɛr'kapən], *v.a.* to muffle up; to mask, disguise. **—t**, *p.p.* & *adj.* disguised.

Verkauf [fɛr'kauf], *m.* (—(e)s, *pl.* **Verkäufe**) sale. **—en**, *v.a.* to sell.

Verkäuf—er [fɛr'kɔyfər], *m.* (—ers, *pl.* —er), **—erin**, *f.* seller, vendor. **—lich**, I. *adj.* for sale; mercenary. II. *adv.* by sale. **—lichkeit**, *f.* venality.

Verkehr [fɛr'ke:r], *m.* (—(e)s) traffic; intercourse; commerce, trade; communication. **—s=störung**, *f.* interruption of communication.

Verkehr—en [fɛr'ke:rən], *v.* I. *a.* to turn the wrong way; to turn, change, convert into; to overturn, overthrow. II. *r.* to change (*into*). III. *n.* (*aux.* h.) to frequent; to have intercourse (with); to trade. **—t**, *p.p.* & *adj* & *adv.* turned the wrong way; wrong; perverse; absurd, preposterous. **—t= heit**, *f.* perversity, absurdity. **—ung**, *f.* overturning; perversion.

Verkenn—en [fɛr'kɛnən], *ir.v.a.* to mistake; **verkanntes Genie**, misunderstood genius. **—ung**, *f.* mistaking; want of appreciation.

Verklag—en [fɛr'kla:gən], *v.a.* to accuse, impeach; to inform against. **—te(r)**, *m.*, **—te**, *f.* accused, defendant. **—ung**, *f.* accusation; prosecution.

Verkläger [fɛrˈklɛːgər], m. (—s, pl. —)
accuser, plaintiff.

Verklär—en [fɛrˈklɛːrən], v.a. to make
bright or luminous. —ung, f. transfiguration.

Verkleid—en [fɛrˈklaɪdən], v.a. to disguise (by a change of dress). —ung,
f. covering; panelling; disguise.

Verkleiner—n [fɛrˈklaɪnərn], v.a. to
diminish, reduce; to disparage. —ung,
f. diminution; detraction.

Verklingen [fɛrˈklɪŋən], ir.v.n. (aux. ʃ.)
to fade away (of sounds).

Verknüpf—en [fɛrˈknypfən], v.a. to
knot, tie, bind. —ung, f. knotting;
uniting; bond.

Verkommen [fɛrˈkɔmən], I. ir.v.n. (aux.
ʃ.) to decay. II. p.p. & adj. decayed;
degenerate. —heit, f. depravity,
demoralization.

Verkörper—n [fɛrˈkœrpərn], v.a. to
embody. —ung, f. embodiment,
personification.

Verkümmer—n [fɛrˈkymərn], v. I. a.
to stunt; to spoil. II. n. (aux. ʃ.) to
pine or wear away; to languish.
—ung, f. deprivation, degeneration.

Verkünd—en [fɛrˈkyndən], —igen, v.a.
to announce; to make known.
—(ig)er, m. (—(ig)ers, pl. —(ig)er),
—(ig)erin, f. announcer; prophet;
proclaimer. —igung, f. announcement; proclamation.

Verkünstel—n [fɛrˈkynstəln], v.a. to
over-refine. —t, p.p. & adj. affected.

Verkürz—en [fɛrˈkyrtsən], v.a. to
shorten; to lessen, diminish; to
prejudice. —ung, f. abridgment;
abbreviation; wrong, injury.

Verlad—en [fɛrˈlaːdən], ir.v.a. to load,
lade, ship. —er, m. (—ers, pl. —er)
shipping-agent. —ung, f. lading;
shipment.

Verlag [fɛrˈlaːk], m. (—s) publication
(of a book); firm of publishers; stocks
of books, publications. —s=buch=
handel, m. publishing business.
—s=buchhändler, m. publisher.
—s=(buch)handlung, f. publishing
house. —s=recht, n. copyright.

Verlangen [fɛrˈlaŋən], v. I. a. to
demand; to require; to desire. II.
n. (aux. h.) to desire; wish, long for.

Verlänger—n [fɛrˈlɛŋərn], v.a. to
lengthen; to prolong. —ung, f.
lengthening; prolongation.

Verlaß [fɛrˈlas], m. (—(ff)es, pl.

—(ff)e) reliance, trust; es ist kein —
auf ihn, there is no relying on him.

Verlassen [fɛrˈlasən], I. ir.v.a. to leave,
quit; to forsake, desert. II. p.p. &
adj. deserted, forsaken. —heit, f.
abandonment; destitution. —schaft,
f. bequest, legacy.

Verlaub [fɛrˈlaup], m. (—(e)s) permission; mit —, by your leave; excuse me.

Verlauf [fɛrˈlauf], m. (—(e)s) lapse;
einen schlimmen — nehmen, to take
a bad turn.

Verlaufen [fɛrˈlaufən], ir.v. I. a. to
spend in running. II. r. (aux. h.) & n.
(aux. ʃ.) to lose one's way, go astray.

Verlautbaren [fɛrˈlautbaːrən], v. I. a.
to divulge. II. n. (aux. h. & ʃ.) to
transpire.

Verleb—en [fɛrˈleːbən], v.a. to waste,
wear out (one's constitution). —t,
p.p. & adj. worn out, broken down.

¹**Verleg**—en [fɛrˈleːgən], v.a. to misplace; to bar, cut off (the way); to
delay, postpone; to publish. —er, m.
(—ers, pl. —er) publisher (of a book).
—ung, f. removal; transportation;
barricading; publication (of a book).

²**Verlegen**, p.p. & adj. embarrassed,
confused. —heit, f. embarrassment;
dilemma; in —heit sein, to be in a
scrape.

Verleiden [fɛrˈlaɪdən], v.a. to spoil; to
disgust.

Verleih—en [fɛrˈlaɪən], ir.v.a. to lend;
to give, grant. —er, m. (—ers, pl.
—er), —erin, f. lender; patron.
—ung, f. loan; grant; bestowal.

Verleit—en [fɛrˈlaɪtən], v.a. to lead
astray. —ung, f. temptation; seduction.

Verletz—bar [fɛrˈlɛtsbaːr], —lich, adj.
vulnerable. —barkeit, —lichkeit, f.
vulnerability.

Verletz—en [fɛrˈlɛtsən], v.a. to wound;
to damage, injure. —ung, f. injury,
damage; wrong; insult.

Verleugn—en [fɛrˈlɔygnən], v.a. to
deny; to disavow. —er, m. (—ers,
pl. —er) disowner, denier. —ung,
f. denial; disavowal.

Verleumd—en [fɛrˈlɔymdən], v.a. to
calumniate, slander. —er, m. (—ers,
pl. —er), —erin, f. slanderer; libeller;
backbiter. —erisch, adj. slanderous,
defamatory. —ung, f. calumny,
slander.

Verlieb—en [fɛrˈliːbən], v.r.; sich in

einen —en, to fall in love with a person. —t, *p.p. & adj.* in love (with). —theit, *f.* amorousness (*of disposition*).

Verlier—en [fɛr'liːrən], *ir.v.a.* to lose; die Fassung —en, to lose one's self-control. —er, *m.* (—ers, *pl.* —er), —erin, *f.* loser.

Verließ [fɛr'liːs], *n.* (—es, *pl.* —e) dungeon.

Verlob—en [fɛr'loːbən], *v.a.* to engage, betroth. —ung, *f.* betrothal.

Verlock—en [fɛr'lɔkən], *v.a.* to entice away. —ung, *f.* allurement; seduction.

Verlogen [fɛr'loːgən], *p.p. & adj.* untruthful. —heit, *f.* untruthfulness.

Verlohnen [fɛr'loːnən], *v.a. imp.*; es verlohnt sich der Mühe, it is worth the trouble, it is worth while.

Verloren [fɛr'loːrən], *p.p. & adj.* lost; —e Eier, poached eggs; der —e Sohn, the prodigal son. —heit, *f.* lost condition. —gehen, *n.* loss, miscarriage (*of letters, etc.*).

Verlösch—en [fɛr'løʃən], I. *v.a.* to extinguish; to obliterate, efface. II. *ir.v.n.* (*aux.* f.) to be extinguished. —ung, *f.* extinction.

Verlos—en [fɛr'loːzən], *v.a.* to raffle. —ung, *f.* raffling.

Verlust [fɛr'lʊst], *m.* (—es, *pl.* —e) loss; damage; bei — von, with forfeiture of; under pain of.

Vermächtnis [fɛr'mɛçtnɪs], *n.* (—(ff)es, *pl.* —(ff)e) testament; legacy.

Vermähl—en [fɛr'mɛːlən], *v.* I. *a.* to marry. II. *r.* to espouse, wed. —ung, *f.* wedding.

Vermaledeien [fɛrmale'daɪən], *v.a.* to curse, to execrate.

Vermehr—en [fɛr'meːrən], *v.a.* to increase, augment. —ung, *f.* increase.

Vermeid—en [fɛr'maɪdən], *ir.v.a.* to avoid, evade. —ung, *f.* avoidance.

Vermein—en [fɛr'maɪnən], *v.a.* to think, believe. —tlich, *adj.* supposed, presumed.

Vermeff—en [fɛr'mɛsən], I. *ir.v.a.* to measure; to deal out, distribute. II. *r.* to presume, have the audacity (to); to boast. III. *p.p. & adj.* daring, presumptuous; rash; arrogant. —enheit, *f.* boldness; arrogance; insolence. —ung, *f.* measurement; survey.

Vermieten [fɛr'miːtən], *v.a.* to let, to hire out.

Verminder—n [fɛr'mɪndərn], *v.a.* to lessen, diminish. —t, *p.p. & adj.* lessened, reduced. —ung, *f.* diminution, decrease.

Vermisch—en [fɛr'mɪʃən], *v.a.* to mix. —ung, *f.* mixture.

Vermissen [fɛr'mɪsən], *v.a.* to miss; to regret.

Vermitt—eln [fɛr'mɪtəln], *v.a.* to mediate; to adjust, arrange (*a difference, etc.*); den Handel —eln, to carry on trade. —(e)lung, *f.* mediation. —ler, *m.* (—lers, *pl.* —ler), —lerin, *f.* mediator, mediatrix. —(e)lungs-geschäft, *n.* (commission-)agency.

Vermöge [fɛr'møːgə], *prep.* (*with gen.*) in pursuance of.

Vermög—en [fɛr'møːgən], I. *ir.v.a.* to be able. II. *subst.n.* ability; power; capacity; means; riches, property. —end, *p. & adj.*, —lich, *adj.* capable of, able; rich; well off.

Vermut—en [fɛr'muːtən], I. *v.a.* to conjecture, imagine; to expect; to suspect. II. *subst.n.* supposing, expectation. —lich, *adj.* presumable, probable, likely. —ung, *f.* supposition.

Vernachlässig—en [fɛr'naːxlɛsɪgən], *v.a.* to neglect. —ung, *f.* negligence.

Vernarr—en [fɛr'narən], *v.r.*; sich (in einen *or* etwas) —en, to become infatuated with. —theit, *f.* infatuation.

Vernehmbar [fɛr'neːmbaːr], *adj.* audible, perceptible. —keit, *f.* audibility.

Vernehm—en [fɛr'neːmən], I. *ir.v.a.* to hear; to perceive; to understand. II. *subst.n.* hearing; perceiving; intelligence. —lich, *adj.* audible; distinct, clear. —lichkeit, *f.* clearness, intelligibility. —ung, *f.* hearing; examination, trial.

Verneig—en [fɛr'naɪgən], *v.r.* to bow; to curtsy. —ung, *f.* bow; curtsy.

Vernein—en [fɛr'naɪnən], *v.a.* to deny; to contradict. —end, *p. & adj.* negative. —ung, *f.* denial, negation.

Vernicht—en [fɛr'nɪçtən], *v.a.* to annihilate; to annul. —end, *p. & adj.* destroying; annulling; injurious. —er, *m.* (—ers, *pl.* —er) destroyer. —ung, *f.* annihilation. —ungs-kampf, —ungs-krieg, *m.* war of extermination.

Vernunft [fɛr'nʊnft], *f.* reason; understanding; sense; intelligence; die gesunde —, common sense. —glaube, *m.* rationalism. —los, *adj.* senseless;

irrational; unreasoning. —**losigkeit**, f. want of reason; irrationality.

Vernünft—ig [fɛrˈnʏnftɪç], adj. reasonable, sensible. —**igkeit**, f. reasonableness; good sense.

Veröd—en [fɛrˈʔøːdən], v. I. a. to lay waste, devastate. II. n. (aux. ʃ.) to become waste. —**ung**, f. desolation; devastation.

Veröffentlich—en [fɛrˈʔøfəntlɪçən], v.a. to publish. —**ung**, f. promulgation.

Verordn—en [fɛrˈʔɔrdnən], v.a. to order; to decree, enact. —**ung**, f. order; precept, decree.

Verpacht—en [fɛrˈpaxtən], v.a. to let on lease. —**er**, **Verpächter**, m. (—**s**, pl. —) lessor. —**ung**, f. farming out, letting on lease.

Verpack—en [fɛrˈpakən], v.a. to pack up. —**er**, m. (—**ers**, pl. —**er**) packer.

Verpassen [fɛrˈpasən], v.a. to let slip, miss, lose.

Verpfänd—en [fɛrˈpfɛndən], v.a. to pledge; to pawn. —**ung**, f. pledging; pledge.

Verpfleg—en [fɛrˈpfleːgən], v.a. to take care of; to support. —**ung**, f. feeding; maintenance, support. —**ungs=amt**, n. poor-law board.

Verpflicht—en [fɛrˈpflɪçtən], v.a. to bind by obligation or duty; to oblige; **zu Dank —en**, to lay a person under obligation. —**ung**, f. obligation, duty.

Verrat [fɛrˈraːt], m. (—(e)s) treason; treachery. —**en**, ir.v.a. to betray.

Verräter [fɛrˈrɛːtər], m. (—**s**, pl. —), —**in**, f. traitor, traitress. —**ei** [—əˈraɪ], f. treason; treachery. —**isch**, adj. treacherous.

Verrechnen [fɛrˈrɛçnən], v. I. a. to reckon. II. r. to make a mistake in calculating.

Verrenk—en [fɛrˈrɛŋkən], v.a. to dislocate. —**ung**, f. dislocation, sprain.

Verricht—en [fɛrˈrɪçtən], v.a. to do, perform, execute. —**ung**, f. performance, execution.

Verringern [fɛrˈrɪŋərn], v.a. to diminish, lessen.

Verrucht [fɛrˈruːxt], adj. infamous. —**heit**, f. infamy.

Verrück—en [fɛrˈrʏkən], v.a. to derange, disturb, unsettle. —**t**, p.p. & adj. wrong; mad, crazy. —**theit**, f. madness.

Verruf [fɛrˈruːf], m. (—(e)s) obloquy; **in** — **kommen**, to get into disrepute. —**en**, I. ir.v.a. to cry down, condemn. II. p.p. & adj. notorious, infamous. —**ung**, f. defamation, depreciation.

Vers [fɛrs], m. (—(s)es, pl. —(s)e) verse. —**art**, f. metre.

Versag—en [fɛrˈzaːgən], I. v.a. to deny, refuse. II. v.n. (aux. h.) to fail (of the voice, strength, etc.). III. subst.n., —**ung**, f. refusal, denial.

Versamm—eln [fɛrˈzaməln], v. I. a. to assemble. II. r. to meet; to muster (Mil.). —**lung**, f. assembly; concourse, gathering.

Versand [fɛrˈzant], m.(—(e)s) despatch. —**bier**, n. beer for exportation.

Versäum—en [fɛrˈzɔymən], v. I. a. to let slip (an opportunity, etc.); to neglect. II. r. to neglect oneself. —**nis**, f. (pl. —**nisse**) & n. (—**nisses**, pl. —**nisse**) neglect, negligence. —**ung**, f. neglect.

Verschaff—en [fɛrˈʃafən], I. v.a. (einem etwas) to procure, supply with. II. subst.n., —**ung**, f. furnishing, providing.

Verschallen [fɛrˈʃalən], ir.v.n. (aux. ʃ.) to cease to sound, die away.

Verschämt [fɛrˈʃɛːmt], adj. ashamed. —**heit**, f. confusion; timidity.

Verschanz—en [fɛrˈʃantsən], v.a. to intrench. —**ung**, f. intrenchment.

Verscheiden [fɛrˈʃaɪdən], I. ir.v.n. (aux. ʃ.) to depart (this life); to die, expire. II. subst.n. death.

Verschieb—en [fɛrˈʃiːbən], I. ir.v.a. to displace; to disarrange; to postpone. II. subst.n., —**ung**, f. displacement, disarrangement; delay.

Verschieden [fɛrˈʃiːdən], adj. & adv. different. —**heit**, f. difference; variety. —**tlich**, I. adj. different. II. adv. differently.

Verschlafen [fɛrˈʃlaːfən], I. ir.v.a. to spend in sleeping. II. p.p. & adj. sleepy, drowsy. —**heit**, f. sleepiness, drowsiness.

Verschlag [fɛrˈʃlaːk], m. (—(e)s, pl. **Verschläge**) boarded partition.

Verschlagen [fɛrˈʃlaːgən], I. ir.v.a. to board off, partition off (a room); to send too far or wrong. II. ir.v.n. (aux. ʃ.) to become lukewarm. III. p.p. & adj. cunning. —**heit**, f. subtlety, cunning.

Verschlemmen [fɛrˈʃlɛmən], v.a. to waste in carousing.

Verschleuder—n [fɛr'ʃlɔydərn], v.a. to squander, dissipate. —ung, f. wasting.

Verschließen [fɛr'ʃliːsən], ir.v.a. to close, shut; to lock up or away.

Verschlimmern [fɛr'ʃlɪmərn], v. I. a. to make worse. II. r. & n. (aux. ʃ.) to deteriorate, grow worse.

¹Verschling—en [fɛr'ʃlɪŋən], ir.v.a. to gulp down (drinks); to devour (food). —er, m. (—ers, pl. —er) devourer. —ung, f. devouring.

²Verschling—en—en, ir.v.a. to interlace, (inter)twine. —ung, f. festoon; intricacy.

Verschlossen [fɛr'ʃlɔsən], p.p. & adj. uncommunicative; taciturn. —heit, f. taciturnity.

Verschlucken [fɛr'ʃlʊkən], v. I. a. to swallow. II. r. to swallow the wrong way.

Verschluß [fɛr'ʃlus], m. (—(ſ)es, pl. Verschlüsse) closure; lock; custody.

Verschmacht—en [fɛr'ʃmaxtən], v. I. a.; sein Leben —en, to drag on a lingering existence. II. n. (aux. ʃ.) to languish; to faint. —ung, f. languishing existence.

Verschmähen [fɛr'ʃmɛːən], v.a. to disdain.

Verschmelz—en [fɛr'ʃmɛltsən], reg. & ir.v. I. a. to melt away. II. n. (aux. ʃ.) to melt, blend. —ung, f. melting.

Verschon—en [fɛr'ʃoːnən], v.a.; einen or etwas —en, to spare a person or a thing. —ung, f. forbearance, exemption.

Verschön—en [fɛr'ʃøːnən], v. I. a. to beautify, adorn. II. r. to grow beautiful. —ern, v.a. to beautify. —erung, f. embellishment.

Verschuld—en [fɛr'ʃuldən], I. v.a. to involve in debt; to be guilty of; to incur (blame); to merit; to be the cause of. II. subst.n., —ung, f. involving in debt; fault, guilt.

Verschütten [fɛr'ʃytən], v.a. to block up; to overwhelm.

Verschweig—en [fɛr'ʃvaɪgən], ir.v.a. to keep secret, conceal. —ung, f. reticence.

Verschwend—en [fɛr'ʃvɛndən], v.a. to waste, squander. —er, m. (—ers, pl. —er) spendthrift. —erisch, adj. prodigal. —ung, f. prodigality.

Verschwiegen [fɛr'ʃviːgən], p.p. & adj. close; discreet; reserved; taciturn. —heit, f. silence; secrecy.

Verschwinden [fɛr'ʃvɪndən], ir.v.n. (aux. ʃ). to vanish, disappear.

Verschwör—en [fɛr'ʃvøːrən], ir.v. I. a. to curse; to forswear. II. r. to conspire; to bind oneself by an oath. —er, m. (—ers, pl. —er) conspirator. —ung, f. conspiracy.

Verschworene(r) [fɛr'ʃvoːrənə(r)], m. conspirator, plotter.

Versehen [fɛr'zeːən], I. ir.v.a. to provide, supply; to administer; to overlook, omit, miss; to make a mistake; es bei einem —, to incur a person's displeasure. II. r. to blunder, to commit an error. III. subst.n. oversight; mistake, blunder.

Versend—en [fɛr'zɛndən], ir.v.a. to send, despatch. —er, m. (—ers, pl. —er) carrier; exporter; consigner. —ung, f. consignment; transmission, transport.

Versengen [fɛr'zɛŋən], v.a. to singe.

Versenk—en [fɛr'zɛŋkən], v.a. to (cause to) sink; to submerge; to destroy. —ung, f. sinking; lowering.

Versetz—en [fɛr'zɛtsən], v. I. a. to change the place of; to misplace; to advance, promote; to obstruct; to pledge, pawn. II. r. to change one's place. III. a. & n. (aux. h.) to answer. —ung, f. displacing, removal; promotion; pledging; repartee.

Versicher—bar [fɛr'zɪçərbaːr], adj. that may be insured. —er, m. (—ers, pl. —er) insurer; underwriter. —n, v. I. a. to insure, assure; to aver, assert. II. r. to ascertain; to insure one's life. —ung, f. insurance; security; guarantee. —ungs=gesellschaft, f. insurance company. —ungs=prämie, f. premium of insurance. —ungs=schein, m. policy (of insurance).

Versinken [fɛr'zɪŋkən], ir.v.n. (aux. ʃ.) to sink; in Gedanken versunken sein, to be lost in thought.

Versöhn—en [fɛr'zøːnən], v.a. to conciliate, reconcile. —end, expiatory. —er, m. (—ers, pl. —er) reconciler, mediator. —lich, adj. forgiving. —lichkeit, f. forgiving or conciliatory spirit. —ung, f. reconciliation; atonement.

Versorg—en [fɛr'zɔrgən], v.a. to provide, supply; to provide for. —er, m. (—ers, pl. —er) —erin, f. maintainer, supporter. —ung, f. maintenance; provision. —ungs=anstalt, f.,

—ungs=haus, n. charitable institution.

Verspät—en [fɛr'ʃpɛːtən], v. I. a. to make late. II. r. to come too late. —ung, f. delay.

Versperr—en [fɛr'ʃpɛrən], v.a. to bar, barricade. —ung, f. barricade, obstruction; blockade (of a port).

Verspielen [fɛr'ʃpiːlən], v.a. to lose, gamble away; ich habe verspielt, I have lost the game.

Verspott—en [fɛr'ʃpɔtən], v.a. to scoff, ridicule. —er, m. (—ers, pl. —er) scoffer, mocker. —ung, f. scoffing; derision, ridicule.

Versprech—en [fɛr'ʃprɛçən], I. ir.v.a. to promise. II. ir.v.r. to promise; to become engaged. III. subst.n., —ung, f. promise; engagement.

Verstand [fɛr'ʃtant], m. (—(e)s) understanding, mind, intellect; intelligence; sense; signification, meaning. —es= begriff, m. (abstract) idea. —es=kraft, f. intellectual power. —es=mäßig, adj. reasonable. —es=mensch, m. matter-of-fact person. —es=schärfe, f. penetration, sagacity. —es=schwäche, f. imbecility. —es=störung, f. mental derangement. —es=wesen, n. intelligent being.

Verständ—ig [fɛr'ʃtɛndɪç], adj. sensible; intelligent; clever. —igen, v.a. (einen von etwas) to acquaint (someone) with. —igkeit, f. wisdom, good sense. —lich, adj. intelligible; distinct. —lichkeit, f. intelligibility. —nis, n. (—nisses, pl. —nisse) comprehension; agreement, understanding. —nis= innig, adj. of deep meaning; significant.

Verstärk—en [fɛr'ʃtɛrkən], v.a. to strengthen, fortify. —ung, f. strengthening, etc.; corroboration.

Versteck [fɛr'ʃtɛk], n. (& m.) (—(e)s, pl. —e) hiding-place; ambush; —spielen, to play hide-and-seek. —er, m. amplifier (Radio).

Verstecken [fɛr'ʃtɛkən], v.a. to hide.

Verstehen [fɛr'ʃteːən], ir.v. I. a. to understand; to mean; er versteht keinen Spaß, he cannot take a joke; versteht sich, of course! that's understood. II. r. to understand oneself; to understand one another.

Versteiger—er [fɛr'ʃtaɪɡərər], m. (—s, pl. —) auctioneer. —n, v.a. to (sell by) auction. —ung, f. auction.

Versteiner—n [fɛr'ʃtaɪnərn], v.a., r. & n. (aux. ſ.) to petrify. —ung, f. petrifaction; fossil.

Verstell—en [fɛr'ʃtɛlən], I. v.a. to remove, change the place of; to misplace; to disfigure, deform; to disguise; to pretend. II. v.r. to disguise oneself; to dissemble. III. subst.n., —ung, f. change of place, removal; disarrangement; dissimulation, pretence.

Verstimm—en [fɛr'ʃtɪmən], v.a. to put out of tune; to put into a bad temper. —theit, —ung, f. discord; ill-humour.

Verstock—en [fɛr'ʃtɔkən], v. I. a. to harden. II. n. (aux. ſ.) to grow musty, rot. III. r. & n. (aux. ſ.) to grow hard, impenitent. —theit, —ung, f. stubbornness, hardness of heart; callousness.

Verstohlen [fɛr'ʃtoːlən], adj. stealthy, furtive.

Verstopf—en [fɛr'ʃtɔpfən], v.a. to stop, plug up. —ung, f. stopping, obstructing.

Verstör—en [fɛr'ʃtøːrən], v.a. to trouble, disturb, disquiet. —theit, f. consternation.

Verstoß [fɛr'ʃtoːs], m. (—es, pl. Verstöße) offence; mistake.

Verstoß—en [fɛr'ʃtoːsən], ir.v. I. n. (aux. h.); gegen eine S. —en, to give offence to, offend in regard to. II. a. to push, turn away; to reject. —ung, f. expulsion; rejection.

Verstumm—en [fɛr'ʃtʊmən], v.n. (aux. ſ.) to hold one's tongue, be silent. —ung, f. loss of speech.

Versuch [fɛr'zuːx], m. (—(e)s, pl. —e) attempt, endeavour; experiment. —s= weise, adv. as an experiment.

Versuch—en [fɛr'zuːxən], v.a. to attempt; to tempt, entice. —er, m. (—ers, pl. —er) tempter. —ung, f. temptation.

Versündig—en [fɛr'zʏndɪɡən], v.r. to sin. —ung, f. sin.

Versunkenheit [fɛr'zʊŋkənhaɪt], f. stagnation, depression (of trade, etc.); absorption (in thought).

Vertag—en [fɛr'taːɡən], v.a. to adjourn. —ung, f. adjournment; prorogation.

Vertausch—en [fɛr'taʊʃən], v.a. to exchange, barter; to confound, mistake. —ung, f. exchange; barter; confounding one thing with another.

Verteidig—en [fɛr'taɪdɪgən], v.a. to defend. —er, m. (—ers, pl. —er) defender; advocate. —ung, f. defence; vindication. —ungs=los, adj. defenceless. —ungs=rede, f. apology; defence.

Verteil—en [fɛr'taɪlən], v.a. to distribute, divide. —ung, f. distribution.

Vertiefen [fɛr'ti:fən], v. I. a. to deepen; to sink. II. r. to become deeper.

Vertilg—en [fɛr'tɪlgən], v.a. to destroy; to extirpate. —ung, f. extermination.

Vertrag [fɛr'tra:k], m. (—(e)s, pl. Verträge) agreement; covenant, bargain.

Vertrag—en [fɛr'tra:gən], ir.v. I. a. to carry away; to wear out; to digest; to bear, suffer, endure; to make peace between; ich kann keinen Wein —en, wine doesn't agree with me. II. r. to live, get on (well or ill) together; to agree. —s=bruch, m. breach of a contract.

Verträglich [fɛr'trɛ:klɪç], adj. conciliatory. —keit, f. sociableness; easy temper.

Vertrau—en [fɛr'trauən], I. v.a. to confide, entrust. II. v.n. (aux. h.) (einem auf einen or etwas) to trust or confide in. III. subst.n. confidence, trust; reliance. —lich, adj. & adv. familiar; confidential. —lichkeit, f. intimacy; familiarity; confidence. —t, p.p. & adj. intimate; familiar. —te(r), m. intimate friend; confidant. —theit, f. intimacy, familiarity. —ens=bruch, m. breach of confidence.

Vertreib—en [fɛr'traɪbən], ir.v.a. to drive away, expel; to beguile (time). —ung, f. expulsion; banishment.

Vertret—en [fɛr'tre:tən], ir.v.a. to injure by treading on, over or down; to obstruct by stepping in the way; to supply the place of another, stand in his stead; einen —en, to represent a person. —er, m. (—ers, pl. —er) representative, substitute, proxy; deputy.

Vertrieb [fɛr'tri:p], m. (—s) sale.

Verübeln [fɛr'ʔy:bəln], v.a. to take amiss.

Verüb—en [fɛr'ʔy:bən], v.a. to commit, perpetrate. —er, m. (—ers, pl. —er) perpetrator, author. —ung, f. perpetration; commission (of a crime).

Verunglimpf—en [fɛr'ʔʊnglɪmpfən],
v.a. to disparage; to slander. —ung, f. defamation, calumny.

Verunglück—en [fɛr'ʔʊnglykən], v.n. (aux. f.) to meet with an accident or misfortune. —ung, f. failure, miscarriage.

Verursach—en [fɛr'ʔu:rzaxən], v.a. to cause, occasion. —er, m. (—ers, pl. —er) author. —ung, f. cause, occasion.

Verurteil—en [fɛr'ʔu:rtaɪlən], v.a. to condemn, sentence. —ung, f. condemnation, sentence.

Verviel—fachen [fɛr'fi:lfaxən], —fältigen, v.a. to multiply. —fältiger, m. (—fältigers, pl. —fältiger) multiplier. —fachung, —fältigung, f. multiplication; reproduction.

Verwachs—en [fɛr'vaksən], ir.v. I. a. to outgrow. II. n. (aux. f.) to be overgrown; to grow crooked; to grow too fast. —ung, f. cicatrization; defective growth.

Verwahr—en [fɛr'va:rən], v.a. to guard, secure; to keep. —er, m. (—ers, pl. —er) keeper; guardian. —ung, f. guarding, keeping; preservation; gegen etwas —ung einlegen, to protest against something. —losen, v.a. to neglect. —losung, f. neglect, negligence.

Verwais—en [fɛr'vaɪzən], v. I. a. to orphan. II. n. (aux. f.) to become an orphan. —t, p.p. & adj. orphan(ed). —ung, f. orphaned state.

Verwalt—en [fɛr'valtən], v.a. to administer, manage; to govern, rule. —er, m. (—ers, pl. —er) administrator; manager. —erin, f. administratrix. —ung, f. administration; management; government. —ungsrat, m. board of directors.

Verwand—eln [fɛr'vandəln], v.a. to change; to transform. —lung, f. change; transformation; metamorphosis.

Verwandt [fɛr'vant], adj. related; allied; congenial. —e(r), m., —e, —in, f. (male, female) relative; der nächste —e, the next of kin. —schaft, f. relationship; affinity; relations (coll.). —schaftlich, adj. kindred allied.

Verwechsel—n [fɛr'vɛksəln], I. v.a. to change, exchange; to change by mistake; wir haben unsere Bücher —t, we have exchanged books. II *subst.n.*, —**ung**, *f.* confusion (*of names*); exchange.

Verwegen [fɛr'veːgən], *adj.* bold, daring; presumptuous; insolent. —**heit**, *f.* audacity.

Verweiger—n [fɛr'vaɪgərn], *v.a.* (**einem etwas**) to refuse. —**ung**, *f.* denial, refusal.

Verweilen [fɛr'vaɪlən], *v.* I. *a.* to stop, delay. II. *n.* (*aux.* h.) to stay.

Verweis [fɛr'vaɪs], *m.* —(f)es, *pl.* —(f)e) reprimand, rebuke.

1**Verweif—en** [fɛr'vaɪzən], *ir.v.a.* to reprove, to rebuke.

2**Verweif—en**, *v.a.* to refer to; to banish to. —**ung**, *f.* reference (**auf**, **to**); banishment, exile.

Verwendbar [fɛr'vɛntbaːr], *adj.* applicable (to), suitable (for). —**keit**, *f.* applicability; suitability.

Verwend—en [fɛr'vɛndən], *reg.* & *ir.v.* I. *a.* to turn away *or* aside; to turn into; to apply to; to employ in *or* for. II. *r.* to use one's influence on behalf of. —**ung**, *f.* use, application, expenditure; converting; intercession.

Verwerf—en [fɛr'vɛrfən], *ir.v.* I. *a.* to throw, cast away; to reject; to disallow; to repudiate. II. *r.* to throw badly. —**lich**, *adj.* objectionable; reprehensible; bad. —**lichkeit**, *f.* objectionableness. —**ung**, *f.* rejection; refusal; reprobation.

Verwert—en [fɛr'vɛrtən], *v.a.* to convert into money; to make use of. —**ung**, *f.* realization; making profit by; **ich habe keine —ung dafür**, I have no use for it.

Verwef—en [fɛr'veːzən], *v.n.* (*aux.* f.) to decay, moulder, rot. —**ung**, *f.* decomposition; putrefaction.

Verweslich [fɛr'veːslɪç], *adj.* corruptible. —**keit**, *f.* corruptibility.

Verwickel—n [fɛr'vɪkəln], *v.a.* to entangle; to complicate. —**ung**, *f.* entanglement; complication; intricacy; embarrassment.

Verwilder—n [fɛr'vɪldərn], *v.r.* & *n.* (*aux.* f.) to grow wild *or* savage. —**t**, *p.p.* & *adj.* wild; savage; unruly. —**ung**, *f.* return to a wild *or* savage state; wildness; barbarism.

Verwirklich—en [fɛr'vɪrklɪçən], *v.* I. *a.* to realize. II. *r.* to be realized, to come true. —**ung**, *f.* realization.

Verwirr—en [fɛr'vɪrən], *ir.v.a.* to entangle (*thread, etc.*); to put into dis-

order; to embarrass, confuse. —**ung**, *f.* confusion, disorder; perplexity.

Verwisch—en [fɛr'vɪʃən], *v.a.* to efface, obliterate. —**ung**, *f.* effacement.

Verwittwen [fɛr'vɪtvən], *v.* I. *a.* to widow. II. *n.* (*aux.* f.) to become a widow(er). —**et**, *p.p.* & *adj.* widowed.

Verwöhn—en [fɛr'vøːnən], *v.a.* to spoil (*a child*). —**theit**, *f.* bad habits, spoiled condition.

Verworfen [fɛr'vɔrfən], *p.p.* & *adj.*, *see* **Verwerfen**; depraved, vile. —**heit**, *f.* depravity.

Verworren [fɛr'vɔrən], *p.p.* & *adj.* confused; intricate. —**heit**, *f.* confusion.

Verwund—en [fɛr'vundən], *v.a.* to wound. —**et**, *p.p.* wounded. —**ung**, *f.* wound.

Verwunder—n [fɛr'vundərn], I. *v.a.* to surprise. II. *subst.n.*, —**ung**, *f.* astonishment, surprise.

Verwünsch—en [fɛr'vynʃən], *v.a.* to curse; to bewitch. —**t**, *p.p.* & I. *adj.* cursed. II. *int.* —**t**! confound it! —**ung**, *f.* enchantment; curse.

Verwüst—en [fɛr'vuːstən], *v.a.* to lay waste, ruin. —**er**, *m.* (—**ers**, *pl.* —**er**) destroyer, devastator.

Verzag—en [fɛr'tsaːgən], I. *v.n.* (*aux.* f.) to despond, despair (**an einer S.**, of a thing). II. *subst.n.* despair, despondency (*B.*). —**t**, *p.p.* & *adj.* despondent, dejected. —**theit**, *f.* despair, despondency; cowardice.

Verzauber—n [fɛr'tsaubərn], *v.a.* to bewitch, enchant. —**ung**, *f.* enchantment.

Verzehr—en [fɛr'tseːrən], *v.a.* to consume; to waste. —**er**, *m.* (—**ers**, *pl.* —**er**) consumer. —**ung**, *f.* consumption (*also Med.*).

Verzeichn—en [fɛr'tsaɪçnən], *v.a.* to sketch, trace out; to note down, record. —**is**, *n.* (—**isses**, *pl.* —**isse**) list; inventory. —**ung**, *f.* incorrect drawing; sketch; memorandum.

Verzeih—en [fɛr'tsaɪən], *ir.v.a.* (**einem etwas**) to forgive. —**lich**, *adj.* pardonable. —**lichkeit**, *f.* veniality. —**ung**, *f.* pardon.

Verzerr—en [fɛr'tsɛrən], *v.a.* **to** distort. —**ung**, *f.* distortion.

Verzicht [fɛr'tsɪçt], *m.* —(e)s) renunciation. —**brief**, *m.* act *or* deed of renunciation. —**leistung**, *f.* renunciation.

Verzichten [fɛr'tsɪçtən], v.n. (aux. h.) (auf eine S.) to renounce, resign.

Verzieh—en [fɛr'tsi:ən], ir.v. I. a. to draw wrongly; to distort, twist (up); to train badly; to put off, delay; den Mund —en, to screw up one's mouth, make grimaces. II. r. to draw away; to withdraw; to be twisted. III. r. & n. (aux. f.) to move, remove. —ung, f. distortion; spoiling; change of residence; delay.

Verzier—en [fɛr'tsi:rən], v.a. to adorn, ornament. —er, m. (—ers, pl. —er) decorator. —ung, f. ornamentation.

Verzinf—en [fɛr'tsɪntsən], v.a. to pay interest on or for something; eine Summe zu 2% —en, to pay 2% on a sum. —ung, f. payment of interest.

Verzöger—n [fɛr'tsø:gərn] v. I. a. to delay; to procrastinate. II. r. to delay; to be protracted. —ung, f. delay; adjournment.

Verzollbar [fɛr'tsɔlba:r], adj. excisable.

Verzollen [fɛr'tsɔlən], v.a. to pay duty on; haben Sie etwas zu —? have you anything to declare?

Verzück—en [fɛr'tsʏkən], v.a. to fill with rapture. —t, p.p. & adj. enraptured. —ung, f. ecstasy, rapture.

Verzug [fɛr'tsu:k], m. (—(e)s, pl. Verzüge) delay.

Verzweif—eln [fɛr'tsvaɪfəln], I. v.n. (aux. h. & f.) to despair. II. subst.n., —(e)s[lung, f. despair.

Verzwick—en [fɛr'tsvɪkən], v.a. to pinch, nip off. —t, p.p. & adj. clipped; odd; confused; difficult; eine —te Sache, an intricate matter. —theit, f. oddness; difficulty.

Vestalin [vɛs'ta:lɪn], f. (pl. —nen) vestal (virgin).

Veteran [vete'ra:n], m. (—en, pl. —en) veteran.

Veterinär [veteri'nɛ:r], I. m. (—s, pl. —s, —e) veterinary surgeon. II. adj. veterinary.

Vettel ['fɛtəl], f. (pl. —n) slut.

Vetter ['fɛtər], m. (—s, pl. —n) male cousin. —lich, adj. cousinly. —schaft, f. cousinship.

Vexieren [vɛ'ksi:rən], v.a. to vex.

Vieh [fi:], n. (—(e)s) cattle. —handel, m. cattle trade. —händler, m. cattle-dealer. —seuche, f. cattle disease. —stall, m. cow-house. —zucht, f. cattle-breeding.

Viel [fi:l] (comp. mehr, sup. meist), adj.

& adv. much; (pl. —e) many; noch einmal so —, as much again; seine —en Geschäfte, his numerous affairs. —heit, f. multiplicity; multitude (in Comps. viel— often =many-, multi-, poly-). —bedeutend, adj. very significant. —deutig, adj. having many significations; ambiguous. —deutigkeit, f. ambiguity. —ed, n. polygon. —er'lei, indec. adj. of many sorts or kinds. —fach, I. adj. manifold; various; multitudinous. II. adv. often, frequently; in many ways. —förmig, adj. multiform. —leicht [fi'laɪçt], adv. perhaps. —malig, adj. often-repeated; frequent. —mal(s), adv. often. —'mehr, I. adv. rather, much more. II. conj. rather; on the contrary. —seitig, adj. many-sided. —seitigkeit, f. many-sidedness. —silbig, adj. polysyllabic. —versprechend, adj. very promising.

Vier [fi:r], I. num. adj. (nom. & acc. rarely —e; dat. —en, when used substantively) four; unter — Augen, tête-à-tête, confidentially. II. f. (pl. —en), —e, f. (pl. —en) the number four; auf allen —en, on all fours. —t, I. num. adj. (der, die, das —e) fourth. II. n. quart (measure). —tens, adv. fourthly, in the fourth place. —ed, n. square; quadrangle. —edig, adj. & adv. square. —fach, adj. quadruple. —fältig, adj. four-fold. —füßler, m. quadruped. —gesang, m. quartette. —mal, adv. four times. —malig, adj. repeated four times. —spännig, adj. four-in-hand (coach). —teilen, v.a. to divide into four parts.

Viertel ['fɪrtəl], I. n. (—s, pl. —) fourth part; quarter; district; ein — (auf) vier, a quarter past three; drei — vier, a quarter to four. II. adj.; eine — Elle, a quarter of an ell. —jährlich, adj. quarterly.

Vierzehn ['fɪrtse:n], I. num. adj. fourteen; heute über — Tage, this day fortnight; vor — Tagen, a fortnight ago. II. f. the number fourteen. —t, adj. (der, die, das —e) the fourteenth. —tel, n. (—tels, pl. —tel) fourteenth part. —tens, adv. in the fourteenth place.

Vierzig ['fɪrtsɪç], I. num. adj. forty. II. f. the number forty. —st, num. adj. (der, die, das —ste) fortieth. —stel, n. (—stels, pl. —stel) fortieth part. —stens, adv. in the fortieth place.

Vikar [vi'ka:r], m. (—s, pl. —e) curate.

Vill—a ['vɪla:], f. (pl. —en, —as) villa.

Viol—ine [vio'li:nə], f. (pl. —inen) violin. —inist [—'nɪst], m. (—inisten, pl. —inisten), —inistin, f. violinist. —oncell(o) [—'tʃɛl(o:)], n. (—oncells, pl. —oncells) violoncello.

Virtuos [vɪrtu'o:s], I. adj. masterly. II. m. (—(f)en, pl. —(f)en), —(f)in, f. virtuoso. —(f)ität [—i'tɛ:t], f. great perfection, mastery.

Visit—e [vi'zi:tə], f. (pl. —en) visit. —ieren [—i'ti:rən], v.a. to visit. —en=karte, f. visiting-card.

Vlies [fli:s], n. (—(f)es, pl. —(f)e), skin, hide; fleece.

Vogel ['fo:gəl], m. (—s, pl. Vögel) bird. —er, Vogler, m. (—s, pl. —) fowler, bird-snarer. —frei, adj. outlawed. —haus, n. aviary. —perspektive, f. bird's-eye view. —scheuche, f. scarecrow. —stange, f. perch (in a bird-cage).

Vögelchen ['fø:gəlçən], Vöglein ['fø:g-lain], n. (—s, pl. —) little bird.

Vogt [fo:kt], m. (—(e)s, pl. Vögte) bailiff; steward; policeman. —ei [—'tai], f. (pl. —eien) office, jurisdiction or residence of a vogt; prison (prov.).

Vokabel [vo'ka:bəl], f. (pl. —n) word, vocable.

Vokal [vo'ka:l], I. m. (—s, pl. —e) vowel. II. adj. vocal.

Volk [fɔlk], n. (—(e)s, pl. Völker) people; nation. —s=tum, n. (—s=tums, pl.—s=tümer) nationality. —s=tümlich, adj. popular; national. —s=buch, n. chap-book. —s=dichter, m. national poet. —s=feind, m. enemy of the people. —s=feindlich, adj. hostile to the people. —s=küche, f. public soup kitchen. —s=kunde, f. folklore. —s=lied, n. popular song, ballad. —s=schule, f. primary school. —s=sprache, f. vernacular; vulgar tongue. —s=stamm, m. tribe, race. —s=wirtschaft, f. political economy. —s=zählung, f. census.

Völk=chen ['fœlkçən], n. (—chens, pl. —chen) tribe. —er=kunde, —er=lehre, f. ethnology. —er=recht, n. international law. —er=stamm, m. race. —er=wanderung, f. migration of nations.

Voll [fɔl], I. adj. (usually followed by a gen. or von with dat.) full; filled; complete, whole, entire; aus —em Herzen, from the bottom of one's heart; mit —em Rechte, with perfect right; einen für — ansehen, to take a person seriously. II. insep. prefix signifying completion, accomplishment, etc.; also=full. —ends, adv. entirely, wholly. —er, I. indec. adj. (stereotyped nom. sing. masc.) in the sense of voll von; er (fie) ist —er Lift, he (she) is full of cunning. II. Comparative of voll. —heit, f. fullness, completeness. —'auf, adv. abundantly. —bürger, m. citizen possessing full civil and political rights. —gewalt, f. full power. —jährig, adj. of full age. —macht, f. full power or authority; warrant; proxy. —mond, m. full moon. —ständig, adj. complete, entire. —ständigkeit, f. completeness. —zählig, adj. complete.

Vollbring—en [fɔl'brɪŋən], ir.v.a. (insep.) to accomplish; to complete. —er, m. (—ers, pl. —er) one who accomplishes or achieves. —ung, f. achievement; execution.

Vollend—en [fɔ'lɛndən], v. I. a. (insep.) (aux. h.) to bring to a complete close. II. r. & n. (aux. h.) to die. —er, m. (—ers, pl. —er) achiever, finisher. —et, p.p. & adj. accomplished, achieved. —ung, f. completion.

Völlig ['fœliç], adj. & adv. full, complete.

Vollkommen [fɔl'kɔmən], adj. perfect. —heit, f. perfection; completeness.

Vollstreck—en [fɔl'ʃtrɛkən], v.a. (insep.) to put into effect, carry out. —er, m. (—ers, pl. —er) executor. —erin, f. executrix. —ung, f. execution.

Von [fɔn], prep. (with dat.) of; from; by; in; on, upon; concerning. Before family names von is a sign of nobility. I. von=of; 1. to denote possession or used for the genitive; ein Freund — mir, a friend of mine. 2. to express the partitive genitive; zwei — uns, two of us. 3. before numerals; eine Frau — vierzig Jahren, a woman of forty. 4. to denote quality or material; ein Mann — edelm Sinne, a man of noble mind. 5. before a proper name which is part of a title; Königin — England, Queen of England. 6. to *denote the worth or price;* — **gutem Schrot und Korne,** of due weight and alloy, of sterling worth. 7. *to denote the subject treated of;* — **wem sprechen Sie?** of whom are you speaking? II.=from; off: 1. *when used with an adv. or prep. following, as* **an, auf, aus, her, herab, ɾc.;** — **außen,** from without; — **oben,** from above. 2. *to denote motion from;* — **Berlin kommen,** to come from Berlin. 3. *with verbs signifying separation or privation;* **nehmen Sie das vom Tische weg,** take that away from the table. III. **von** *is variously translated in other cases, as in the following idioms:* — **Gottes Gnaden,** by the grace of God; — **Seiten jemandes,** on the part of someone; — **Sinnen kommen,** to lose consciousness; **was wollen Sie — mir?** what do you want with *or* from me? — **neuem,** anew, afresh. —**nöten,** *adv.;* —**nöten haben,** to stand in need of; —**nöten sein,** to be needful, necessary. — *wannen, adv.* from whence.

Vor [foːr], I. *prep. (with dat. implying rest or in answer to the question* **wo?** *with acc. implying motion or in answer to the question* **wohin?)** —'m=**vor dem;** —s=**vor das;** before *(in time or place),* in front of; in presence of; for; on account of, through, because of, with; from, against *(with verbs of protecting, warning, etc.);* in preference to, more than, above; *(denoting time=)* since, ago; — **Hunger sterben,** to die of hunger; — **Kälte zittern,** to tremble with cold; — **allen Dingen,** above all. II. *n.,* **das — und Nach,** the Before and After. III. *adv. & sep. prefix;* before; formerly; **nach wie —,** now as before. —**ig,** *adj.* former, last, preceding, previous; —**iges Jahr,** last year.

Vor—abend ['foːrʔaːbənt], *m.* eve; evening before. —**ahnen,** *v.a.* to have a presentiment of. —**ahnung,** *f.* presentiment.

Voran [fo'raːn], *adv. & sep. prefix,* before, on, onwards; at the head, in front, foremost, first. —**eilen,** *v.n. (aux.* ſ.), —**laufen,** *ir.v.n. (aux.* ſ.) to run, hasten on before. —**gehen,** *ir.v.n. (aux.* ſ.) to take the lead. —**schicken,** *v.a.* to send on before. —**schreitend,** *adj.* progressive.

Voraus [fo'raus], *adv. & sep. prefix,* in advance; in front, on ahead, before the rest; previously; in preference. —**bezahlung,** *f.* payment in advance. —**gehen,** *ir.v.n. (aux.* ſ.) to go before. —**nahme,** *f.* anticipation, forestalling. —**nehmen,** *ir.v.a.* to take in advance; to anticipate, forestall. —**setzen,** *v.a.* to suppose, presume. —**setzung,** *f.* supposition; hypothesis. —**sicht,** *f.* foresight, prudence. —**sichtlich,** *adj.* probable, presumable.

Vor—bedacht ['foːrbədaxt], *m.* forethought, premeditation. —**bedächtig,** *adj.* full of forethought; cautious. —**bedenken,** *ir.v.a.* to premeditate. —**bedeuten,** *v.a.* to forebode, presage. —**bedeutung,** *f.* foreboding, omen. —**behalt,** *m.* reservation. —**behalten,** *ir.v.a.* to keep back, withhold; to stipulate for.

Vorbei [foːr'bai], *adv. & sep. prefix,* along, by; past; passing before; past, over, done with. —**gehen,** I. *ir.v.n. (aux.* ſ.) (**an einem**) go by (a person). II. *subst.n.* passing; **im —gehen,** in passing. —**kommen,** *ir.v.n. (aux.* ſ.) to pass before, pass by. —**können,** *ir.v.n. (aux.* h.) to be able to pass. —**müssen,** *ir.v.n. (aux.* h.) to be obliged to pass.

Vor—bereiten ['foːrbəraitən], *v.a.* to prepare, get ready beforehand. —**s bereitung,** *f.* preparation. —**beugen,** *v.* I. *a.* to bend forward. II. *n. (aux.* h.) to hinder, prevent. —**beugend,** *p. & adj.* preventive. —**beugung,** *f.* bending forward; prevention. —**bild,** *n.* model, pattern; (beau) ideal. —**bilden,** *v.a.* to prepare; to typify; to represent. —**bildlich,** *adj.* typical; model, ideal. —**bildung,** *f.* preparation; training. —**bitte,** *f.* intercession (for). —**bote,** *m.* herald; presage; symptom.

Vorder ['fordər], *adj.* fore, forward, anterior, front; foremost. —**ansicht,** *f.* front view. —**glied,** *n.* fore-limb. —**grund,** *m.* foreground.

Vor—drängen ['foːrdrɛŋən], *v.a. & r.* to press *or* push forward. —**dringen,** *ir.v.n. (aux.* ſ.) to push on, advance. —**dringlich,** *adj.* forward; importunate. —**eilen,** *v.n. (aux.* ſ.) to hasten on before; to precede. —**eilig,** *adj.* hasty, precipitate. —**eiligkeit,** *f.* precipitation, rashness. —**eingenommen,**

adj. prejudiced, biased. —**eltern,** *pl.* ancestors, forefathers. —**empfinden,** *ir.v.a.* to anticipate, surmise. —**empfindung,** *f.* presentiment. —**enthalten,** *ir.v.a.* (einem etwas) to withhold, keep back. —**enthaltung,** *f.* withholding, retention. —**'erſt,** *adv.* first of all, before all. —**erwähnt,** *adj.* aforesaid. —**fahr,** *m.* (—s *and* —en, *pl.* —en) ancestor. —**fall,** *m.* occurrence; event. —**fallen,** *ir.v.n.* (*aux.* ſ.) to fall (*down*) before; to happen, occur. —**führen,** *v.a.* to bring forward. —**gang,** *m.* occurrence, incident, event. —**gänger,** *m.* leader; forerunner; predecessor. —**gängig,** *adj.* preliminary, preparatory. —**geben,** *ir.v.a.* to give an advantage, to give points (*at billiards, etc.*); to assert, allege; to plead. —**gebirge,** *n.* hills at the foot of a mountain-chain; promontory. —**geblich,** I. *adj.* pretended; ostensible. II. *adv.* ostensibly. —**gefühl,** *n.* presentiment; anticipation. —**gehen,** *ir.v.n.* (*aux.* ſ.) to go too fast (*of watches, etc.*); to go first, take the lead; to march (upon, auf); to jut out, stand out; to outstrip (einem, one); to take precedence of; to surpass, excel (einem, a person); to happen, take place. —**gemeldet,** —**genannt,** *adj.* aforementioned, before-mentioned. —**geſetzte(r),** *m.* chief; superior. —**geſtern,** *adv.* the day before yesterday. —**geſtrig,** *adj.* of the day before yesterday. —**greifen,** *ir.v.n.* (*aux.* h.) to anticipate, forestall; to encroach upon (einem, a person's rights). —**greiflich,** *adv.* in anticipation. —**greifung,** *f.* anticipation. —**haben,** I. *ir.v.a.* to have before one; to have in view; to purpose, intend. II. *subst.n.* intention, design. —**halt,** *m.* reproach. —**halten,** *ir.v.* I. *a.* (einem etwas) to hold before; to reproach with. II. *n.* (*aux.* h.) to hold out. —**'handen,** *adj.* & *adv.* at hand, ready, present. —**'handen-ſein,** *n.* existence, presence. —**hang,** *m.* curtain.

Vorher [fo:r'he:r], *adv.* & *sep.* prefix, beforehand, in advance; before, previously; on before, in front; am **Abend** —, (on) the previous evening; **kurz** —, a little while before. —**ig,** *adj.* previous, preceding, antecedent, former, last. —**beſtimmen,** *v.a.* to determine beforehand. —**beſtimmung,**

f. predestination. —**daſein,** *n.* pre-existence. —**empfinden,** *ir.v.a.* to have a presentiment (of). —**gehen,** *ir.v.n.* (*aux.* ſ.); einer Sache —**gehen,** to precede, happen before something.

Vor—**hin** [fo:r'hɪn], *adv.* before, heretofore; a short time ago. —**hof,** *m.* vestibule. —**jahr,** *n.* preceding year. —**jährig,** *adj.* of last year. —**lehr,** *f.* provision, precaution. —**fehren,** *v.a.* to sweep forth; to provide (*against* or *for*). —**fenntnis,** *f.* previous knowledge. —**fommen,** I. *ir.v.n.* (*aux.* ſ.) to come forth, out, on; to come forward, appear; to surpass, outstrip; to be admitted; to outrun; to be brought forward for discussion; to happen, occur; to seem; to present itself, fall in a person's way. II. *subst.n.* occurrence; presence. —**fommnis,** *n.* (—ſes, *pl.* —ſe) occurrence, event. —**ladung,** *f.* citation, summons. —**lage,** *f.* subject or matter (*brought forward for discussion, etc.*); bill (*Parl.*); text, copy. —**längſt,** *adv.* long ago, long since. —**laß,** *m.* admission, access. —**laſſen,** *ir.v.a.* to suffer to go or come forward. —**laſſung,** *f.* admission, admittance. —**läufer,** *m.*, —**läuferin,** *f.* forerunner. —**läufig,** I. *adj.* previous, preliminary. II. *adv.* previously; first of all; provisionally; in the meantime. —**legen,** *v.a.* to display, exhibit; to produce; to propose. —**legung,** *f.* laying before; exhibition; representation; proposition. —**leſen,** *ir.v.a.* to read aloud, read to; to gather the first ripe grapes. —**leſer,** *m.,* —**leſerin,** *f.* reader (*to others*). —**leſung,** *f.* reading aloud; lecture. —**leſungs-zimmer,** *n.* lecture room. —**letzt,** *adj.* last but one. —**lieb,** *adv.* —**lieb nehmen mit,** to put up with, to be satisfied with. —**liebe,** *f.* predilection, partiality. —**liegen,** *ir.v.n.* (*aux.* h.) to lie before; einem —**liegen,** to be submitted to someone; es liegt heute nichts —, there is nothing to be discussed to-day. —**malig,** *adj.* former. —**mals,** *adv.* formerly; once upon a time. —**marſch,** *m.* advance, march forward. —**marſchieren,** *v.n.* (*aux.* ſ.) to advance. —**maſt,** *m.* foremast.

Vormittag ['fo:rmɪta:k], *m.* (—s, *pl.* —e) morning, forenoon.

Vormittäg—**ig** ['fo:rmɪtɛ:gɪç], *adj.* in

the forenoon. —**lich,** *adj.* of every
morning.

Bormund ['foːrmʊnt], *m.* (—(e)s, *pl.*
Bormünder), —**münderin,** *f.* guardian; trustee. —**ſchaft,** *f.* guardianship; trusteeship.

Born—(e) ['forn(ə)], I. *adv.* in front;
in the forepart, before; **ganz —,** right
in front. II. *n.;* **das — und hinten,**
the front and back; **von — anfangen,**
to begin at the beginning.

Borname ['foːrnaːmə], *m.* (—ns, *pl.*
—n) first name; Christian name.

Bornehm ['foːrneːm], *adj.* refined, distinguished; eminent; aristocratic; **die**
—**e Welt,** the world of fashion. —**heit,**
f. (air of) distinction; superiority.
—**lich,** *adv.* particularly, above all.

Bornehmen ['foːrneːmən], I. *ir.v.a.* to
take in hand, take up, undertake. II.
subst.n. undertaking; project.

Bor—**neigung** ['foːrnaigʊŋ], *f.* inclination, bending forward; predilection.
—**poſten,** *m.* outpost. —**prüfung,** *f.*
preliminary examination. —**ragen,**
v.n. (*aux.* h.) to be prominent; to
overtop. —**ragend,** *adj.* prominent,
salient. —**rang,** *m.* pre-eminence,
superiority, precedence.

Borrat ['foːrraːt], *m.* (—(e)s, *pl.*
Borräte) store, provision, supply.
—**s-kammer,** *f.* storeroom.

Borrätig ['foːrreːtɪç], *adj.* on hand, in
stock.

Bor—**rechnen** ['foːrreçnən], *v.a.* to
enumerate. —**recht,** *n.* privilege, prerogative. —**rede,** *f.* prefatory discourse; preface. —**reden,** *v.a.* (**einem
etwas**) to tell (someone something); to
speak (a person) fair; to talk into *or*
over. —**richten,** *v.a.* to prepare, make
ready. —**richtung,** *f.* preparation,
arrangement. —**rücken,** *v.* I. *a.* to put,
push forward (*a chair; a watch, etc.*).
II. *n.* (*aux.* ſ.) to advance; to be pro-
moted. —**ſagen,** *v.a.* to say beforehand. —**ſager,** *m.* prompter. —**ſatz,**
m. design, project, plan. —**ſätzlich,**
adj. & adv. intentional, done design-
edly. —**ſchein,** *m.;* **zum —ſchein
kommen,** to appear. —**ſchießen,** *ir.v.*
I. *a.;* **einem eine Summe Geld —
ſchießen,** to lend *or* advance a person a
sum of money. II. *n.* (*aux.* ſ.) to
dart, rush forth; to surpass, excel.

Borſchlag ['foːrʃlaːk], *m.* (—(e)s, *pl.*
Borſchläge) proposition, proposal; offer.

Borſchlagen ['foːrʃlaːgən], I. *ir.v.a.* to
put forward, propose; to overrate; to
overcharge; to strike, beat, thrust,
throw forward. II. *ir.v.n.* (*aux.* ſ.) to
rush headlong forward.

Bor—**ſchreiben** ['foːrʃraibən], *ir.v.a.* to
set (**einem,** someone) a copy; (**einem
etwas**) —**ſchreiben,** to dictate, prescribe; to order, direct. —**ſchreiten,**
ir.v.n. (*aux.* ſ.) to step forth; to advance, march on. —**ſchrift,** *f.* writing-
copy; recipe; prescription; precept,
rule; order, instructions. —**ſchrifts-
mäßig,** *adj.* according to instructions.
—**ſchrifts-widrig,** *adj.* contrary to
directions. —**ſchritt,** *m.* step forward,
advance.

Borſchuß ['foːrʃʊs], *m.* (—(ſ)es, *pl.*
Borſchüſſe) (cash) advance. —**verein,**
m. loan-society. —**zahlung,** *f.* payment in advance.

Bor—**ſchweben** ['foːrʃveːbən], *v.n.* (*aux.*
h., & *now obs.,* ſ.) to hover before.
—**ſehen,** *ir.v.* I. *a.* to foresee; to provide for. II. *r.* to take care, be on
one's guard. —**ſehung,** *f.* providence.
—**ſein,** *ir.v.n.* to be in advance, on
before; to have the first chance; to
be discussed; to be tried.

Borſetzen ['foːrzetsən], *v.a.* to set before; place at the head of; to prefer;
ſich —, to purpose, intend.

Bor—**ſicht** ['foːrzɪçt], *f.* foresight; prudence, caution. —**ſichtig,** *adj.* cautious, prudent. —**ſichts-maßregeln,**
pl. precautionary measures. —**ſitz,** *m.*
presidency. —**ſitzen,** *ir.v.n.* (*aux.* h.)
to preside. —**ſitzer, ſitzende(r),** *m.*
president, chairman. —**ſorge,** *f.* foresight, care. —**ſorgen,** *v.n.* (*aux.* h.) to
take (*the necessary*) precautions; to
provide for. —**ſorglich,** *adj. & adv.*
provident, careful. —**ſpann,** *m.* relay,
fresh horses. —**ſpannen,** *v.a.* to put
horses to a carriage. —**ſpann-pferd,**
n. fresh horse. —**ſpiegelung,** *f.* illusion, sham; **ſpiegelung falſcher
Tatſachen,** false pretences. —**ſpiel,**
n. prelude (*Mus.*). —**ſprung,** *m.* projection; start; advantage. —**ſtadt,** *f.*
suburb. —**ſtädter,** *m.* resident in a
suburb. —**ſtädtiſch,** *adj.* suburban.
—**ſtand,** *m.* board of directors, execu-
tive committee. —**ſtandſchaft,** *f.*
directorship, directorate.

Borſteh—**en** ['foːrʃteːən], *ir.v.n.* (*aux.*
h.) to stand before (*a thing*); to pro-

ject, overhang; to precede; to manage, direct, administer. —**er,** *m.* (—**ers,** *pl.* —**er**), —**erin,** *f.* chief, principal; director, manager.

Vorstell—**en** ['fo:rʃtɛlən], *v.a.* to put in front of; to present, introduce; to represent, act; to personate; to remonstrate, protest. —**ung,** *f.* presentation (*at court, etc.*); performance; plea, remonstrance; expostulation; memorial; idea, notion, image. —**ungs=vermögen,** *n.* imaginative faculty.

Vor—**stoß** ['fo:rʃtɔs], *m.* push forward. —**stoßen,** *ir.v.* I. *a.* to push forward. II. *n.* (*aux.* ſ.) to push forward, march against. —**sündflutlich,** *adj.* antediluvian.

Vorteil ['fortail]. *m.* (—(e)s, *pl.* —e) advantage, profit, benefit. —**haft,** *adj.* advantageous; profitable.

Vortrab ['fo:rtra:p], *m.* (—(e)s, *pl.* —e) vanguard. —**en,** *v.n.* (*aux.* ſ.) to trot on in front.

Vortrag ['fo:rtra:k], *m.* (—(e)s, *pl.* **Vorträge**) diction, delivery; lecture, discourse; explanation, exposition; report; proposal.

Vortrag—**en** ['fo:rtra:gən], I. *ir.v.a.* to bring forward *or* before; to explain, expound; to propose; to deliver (*a speech, etc.*); **den Saldo** —**en,** to carry forward the balance. II. *subst.n.,* —**ung,** *f.* reporting; delivery; explanation, *etc.*

Vor—**trefflich** [fo:r'trɛflɪç], *adj.* excellent, admirable. —'**trefflichkeit,** *f.* excellence. —**treten,** *ir.v.n.* (*aux.* ſ.) to step before; to come forth, advance. —**tritt,** *m.* step forward; precedence. —**tun,** *ir.v.* I. *a.* to put before; to do beforehand; to show how to do; **es einem** —**tun,** to surpass someone in doing.

Vorüber [fo'ry:bər], *adv.* & *separable prefix,* before *or* in front; along by, past; gone by, over, finished. —**fliegen,** *ir.v.n.* (*aux.* ſ.) to fly past *or* across. —**fliehen,** *ir.v.n.* (*aux.* ſ.) to hurry past. —**gehen,** I. *ir.v.n.* (*aux.* ſ.) to pass. II. *subst.n.;* **im** —**gehen,** in passing; by the way. —**gehend,** *p.* & *adj.* passing; transitory. —**ziehen,** *ir.v.n.* (*aux.* ſ.) to pass (by).

Vorurteil ['fo:r⁹urtail], *n.* (—s, *pl.* —e) prejudice. —**s=frei,** —**s=los,** *adj.*

unprejudiced, unbiased. —**s=voll,** *adj.* prejudiced.

Vor—**vater** ['fo:rfa:tər], *m.* forefather, ancestor. —**vorgestern,** *adv.* three days ago. —**vorig,** *adj.* last but one. —**vorletzt,** *adj.* last but two. —**wand,** *m.* pretext, excuse.

Vorwärts ['fo:rvɛrts], *adv.* & *sep. prefix,* forward, onward.

Vor—**weg** [fo:r've:k], *adv.* before; from before; beforehand. —'**weg= nahme,** *f.* anticipation. —'**weg= nehmen,** *ir.v.a.* to anticipate (*a person in*). —**weisen,** *ir.v.a.* to exhibit, show (forth). —**welt,** *f.* former ages, antiquity. —**weltlich,** *adj.* of former ages; of a primitive world. —**wenden,** *reg.* & *ir.v.a.* to allege, pretend. —**werfen,** *ir.v.a.* to throw out; to cast before; **einem (etwas)** —**werfen,** to reproach a person with. —**wissen,** *n.* foreknowledge. —**witz,** *m.* curiosity; impertinence. —**witzig,** *adj.* inquisitive; forward, impertinent. —**wort,** *n.* preface; preamble. —**wurf,** *m.* reproach. —**wurfs=frei,** —**wurfs=los,** *adj.* irreproachable, blameless. —**wurfs= voll,** *adj.* reproachful. —**zeichen,** *n.* omen, prognostic. —**zeigung,** *f.* production, exhibition. —**zeit,** *f.* antiquity, days of yore. —'**zeiten,** *adv.* formerly. —**zeitig,** *adj.* premature. —**ziehen,** *ir.v.* I. *a.* to draw forward *or* forth; to draw before; to prefer, give the preference to. II. *n.* (*aux.* ſ.) to march before. —**zimmer,** *n.* ante-room. —**zug,** *m.* preference; excellence; superiority; privilege. —'**züglich,** *adj.* preferable; superior; excellent; remarkable. —'**züglichkeit,** *f.* superiority, excellence.

Vulkan [vul'ka:n], *m.* (—s, *pl.* —e) volcano; —**isch,** *adj.* volcanic.

W

W, w [ve:], *n.* W, w.

Waag—**e** ['va:gə], *f.* (*pl.* —en) balance, weighing machine; pendulum; equilibrium. —**e=recht,** *adj.* horizontal, level. —(e)**=schale,** *f.* balance-scale; (*pl.*) scales.

Wabe ['va:bə], *f.* (*pl.* —n) honeycomb.

Wach [vax], *adj.* awake. —**sam,** *adj.* vigilant, watchful. —**samkeit,** *f.* vigilance.

Wache ['vaxə], *f.* guard, watch; sentinel; **auf — ziehen,** to mount guard; **— ins Gewehr!** turn out, guard! **—en,** *v.n.* (*aux.* h.) to watch; to be awake.

Wacholder [va'xɔldər], *m.* (**—s,** *pl.* **—**) juniper.

Wachs [vaks], *n.* (**—(f)es,** *pl.* **—(f)e**) wax. **—bild,** *n.* wax figure. **—tuch,** *n.* oilcloth.

Wachsen ['vaksən], I. *ir.v.n.* (*aux.* f.) to grow; **jemandem gewachsen fein,** to be a match for a person. II. *subst.n.* growth; increase. **—d,** *p. & adj.* growing.

Wächse—n ['veksən], *v.a.* to wax. **—rn,** *adj.* waxen.

Wachstum ['vakstu:m], *n.* (**—s**) growth.

Wacht [vaxt], *f.* (*pl.* **—en**) watch (*Naut.*); guard (*Mil.*); watch-house. **—meister,** *m.* sergeant-major (of cavalry).

Wachtel ['vaxtəl], *f.* (*pl.* **—n**) quail. **—hund,** *m.* spaniel.

Wächter ['veçtər], *m.* (**—s,** *pl.* **—**) guard; caretaker.

Wack—elig ['vakəlıç], *adj. & adv.* shaky, tottering. **—eln,** I. *v.n.* (*aux.* h.) to shake; to totter. II. *subst.n.* shakiness. **—ler,** *m.* (**—lers,** *pl.* **—ler**), **—lerin,** *f.* waddler.

Wacker ['vakər], I. *adj.* valiant, brave. II. *adv.* bravely; well.

Wade ['va:də], *f.* (*pl.* **—n**) calf (*of the leg*).

Waff—e ['vafə], *f.* (*pl.* **—en**) weapon. **—nen,** *v.a.* to arm. **—enschmied,** *m.* armourer. **—enstillstand,** *m.* truce, armistice. **—enstreckung,** *f.* laying down of arms, surrender.

Wägelchen ['ve:gəlçən], *n.* (**—s,** *pl.* **—**) little carriage.

Wägen ['ve:gən], *ir.v.a.* to weigh; balance.

1Wag—en ['va:gən], *v.a.* to venture, risk; to dare, attempt. **—nis,** *n.* (**—nisses,** *pl.* **—nisse**) risky undertaking. **—(e)shals,** *m.* foolhardy person. **—estück,** *n.* daring deed.

2Wagen ['va:gən], *m.* (**—s,** *pl.* **—**) vehicle; waggon, cart; carriage. **—abteil,** *n.* compartment (of a railway carriage). **—führer,** *m.* waggoner; coachman.

Wahl [va:l], *f.* (*pl.* **—en**) choice; election (*of a member of parliament, etc.*); alternative. **—akt,** *m.* election. **—akten,** *pl.* election returns (*Parl.*).

—frei, *adj.* optional. **—fürst,** *m.* princely elector. **—recht,** *n.* right to vote, electoral franchise. **—spruch,** *m.* device, motto. **—urne,** *f.* ballot-box. **—verwandt,** *adj.* congenial; **—verwandte Seelen,** kindred spirits. **—verwandtschaft,** *f.* congeniality; elective affinity (*Chem.*).

Wähl—en ['ve:lən], *v.a.* to choose; to elect. **—er,** *m.* (**—ers,** *pl.* **—er**) chooser; elector. **—erisch,** *adj.* dainty.

Wahn [va:n], *m.* (**—s**) illusion; delusion; fancy; madness. **—bild,** *n.* vision, phantom. **—glaube,** *m.* superstition. **—finn,** *m.* insanity. **—finnig,** *adj.* insane.

Wähnen ['ve:nən], *v.a. & n.* (*aux.* h.) to think, fancy, suppose.

Wahr [va:r], *adj. & adv.* true; real; **so — ich lebe,** as sure as I live; **so — mir Gott helfe!** so help me God! **—haft,** *adj.* true, genuine. **—haftig,** *adv.* truly; really, indeed. **—haftigkeit,** *f.* veracity. **—heit,** *f.* truth. **—lich,** *adv.* truly. **—heits=gemäß,** *adj.* **—heits=getreu,** *adj.* faithful, in accordance with truth. **—nehmbar,** *adj.* perceptible. **—nehmen,** *ir.v.a.* (*sep.*) to notice; to profit by. **—nehmung,** *f.* perception; observation. **—zeichen,** *n.* mark, token.

Währ—en ['ve:rən], *v.n.* (*aux.* h.) to last, continue. **—end,** I. *p. & adj.* lasting; **ewig —end,** everlasting. II. *prep.* (*usually takes the gen.*) during, in the course of. III. *conj.* during the time that, whilst. **—ung,** *f.* duration.

Wahrsag—en ['va:rza:gən], *v.a. & n.* (*aux.* h.) (*insep.*) to prophesy. **—er,** *m.* (**—ers,** *pl.* **—er**) soothsayer. **—erin,** *f.* prophetess. **—erisch,** *adj.* soothsaying.

Wahrscheinlich [va:r'ʃaınlıç], *adj. & adv.* probable, likely. **—keit,** *f.* probability; likelihood; plausibility.

Waise ['vaızə], *f.* (*pl.* **—n**), *sometimes* (*in case of a boy*) *m.* (**—n,** *pl.* **—n**) orphan.

1Wal [va:l], *m.* (**—s,** *pl.* **—e**) (**—fisch,** *m.*) whale. **—fisch=bein,** *n.* whalebone. **—fisch=fett,** *n.* blubber. **—fisch=laich,** *m.* spermaceti. **—fisch=tran,** *m.* train-oil. **—rat,** *m. & n.,* **—rat=fett,** *n.* spermaceti. **—roß,** *n.* walrus.

2Wal, *n.* (*now only in compounds, often spelt* **Wahl—**). **—feld,** *n.,* **—platz,** *m.,* **—statt,** *f.* battle-field. **—halla,** *f.*

Valhalla. **—füre,** *f.* (**—füren**) Valkyrie.

Wald [valt], *m.* (**—(e)s,** *pl.* **Wälder**) wood, forest. **—ig,** *adj.* wooded. **—ung,** *f.* wood; woodland. **—'ein,** *adv.* into the forest. **—gott,** *m.* faun. **—teufel,** *m.* wood-demon.

Walf—en ['valkən], *v.a.* to full (*cloth*). **—er,** *m.* (**—ers,** *pl.* **—er**) fuller. **—(er)-erde,** *f.* fuller's earth.

¹**Wall** [val], *m.* (**—(e)s,** *pl.* **Wälle**) rampart; mound.

²**Wall,** *m.* (**—(e)s,** *pl.* **—e**) boiling.

¹**Wall—en** ['valən], *v.n.* (*aux.* **h.**) to undulate; to heave; to bubble, boil up. **—ung,** *f.* ebullition; undulation; agitation.

²**Wall—en,** *v.n.* (*aux.* **f.**) to wander about; to go on a pilgrimage. **—=fahrer,** *m.*, **—fahrerin,** *f.* pilgrim. **—fahrt,** *f.* pilgrimage.

Walnuß ['valnus], *f.* (*pl.* **Walnüsse**) walnut.

Walten ['valtən], I. *v.n.* (*aux.* **h.**) to rule, govern; **das walte Gott!** God grant it! Amen! II. *n.* rule, government.

Walz—e ['valtsə], *f.* (*pl.* **—en**) cylinder; roller. **—en,** *v.* I. *a.* to roll. II. *r.* & *n.* (*aux.* **h.**) to waltz. **—ende(r),** *m.* waltzer. **—er,** *m.* (**—ers,** *pl.* **—er**) waltz. **—blech,** *n.* rolled plate. **—blei,** *n.* sheet-lead. **—eisen,** *n.* rolled iron. **—en=förmig,** *adj.* cylindrical.

Wamme ['vamə], *f.* (*pl.* **—n**) paunch.

Wams [vams] (*dim.* **Wämschen,** *n.*), *n.* (& *m.*) (**—(f)es,** *pl.* **Wämser**) doublet, jerkin.

Wand [vant], *f.* (*pl.* **Wände**) wall.

Wandel ['vandəl], *m.* **—s**) walking, going; progress; change, mutation; conduct, behaviour; traffic; **Handel und —,** trade, commerce. **—bar,** *adj.* & *adv.* changeable, variable, fickle; current; practicable, passable; fragile, perishable; decayed. **—bar-keit,** *f.* changeableness; vicissitude. **—haft,** *adj.* changeable; fragile; disordered. **—halle,** *f.* corridor.

Wand—eln ['vandəln], I. *v.a.* & *r.* to change. II. *v.n.* (*aux.* **h.** & **f.**) to go, walk; to wander. **—ler,** *m.* (**—lers,** *pl.* **—ler**) wanderer. **—lung,** *f.* change, alteration.

Wander—er ['vandərər], *m.* (**—ers,** *pl.* **—er**), **—in,** *f.* wanderer. **—n,** *v.n.* (*aux.* **f.**) to travel (*on foot*), walk; to wander. **—nd,** *p.* & *adj.* strolling; nomadic. **—ung,** *f.* travelling; trip, tour. **—bursch,** **—gesell,** *m.* travelling journeyman. **—jahre,** *pl.* journeyman's years of travel (*following his* **Lehrjahre**). **—lust,** *f.* desire to travel. **—s=mann,** *m.* (*pl.* **s=leute**) traveller. **—vögel,** *pl.* birds of passage; hikers.

Wang—e ['vaŋə], *f.* (*pl.* **—en**) cheek. **—ig,** *suff.* (*in cpds.=*) -cheeked.

Wankel—haft ['vankəlhaft], *adj.* unstable, fickle. **—mut,** *m.* fickleness, inconstancy. **—mütig,** *adj.* fickle.

Wanken ['vaŋkən], *v.n.* (*aux.* **h.** & **f.**) to stagger.

Wann [van], I. *adv.* when; **dann und —,** now and then; **seit —?** since what time? II. *conj.* when.

Wanne ['vanə], *f.* (*pl.* **—n**) tub; pail.

Wanst [vanst], *m.* (**—es,** *pl.* **Wänste**) belly, paunch.

Wanze ['vantsə], *f.* (*pl.* **—n**) bug.

Wappen ['vapən], *n.* (**—s,** *pl.* **—**) (*coat of*) arms. **—bild,** *n.* heraldic figure. **—schild,** *m.* escutcheon.

Ware ['va:rə], *f.* (*pl.* **—n**) ware, merchandise. **—n=stempel,** *m.* trade-mark.

Warm [varm], *adj.* & *adv.* (*comp.* **wärmer,** *sup.* **wärmst**) warm; **mir ist —,** I am warm; **die Sonne scheint —,** the sun is hot.

Wärm—e ['vermə], *f.* warmth; heat. **—e=grad,** *m.* degree of heat. **—en,** *v.a.* to warm, heat. **—ung,** *f.* warming, heating.

Warn—en ['varnən], *v.a.* (**einen vor einem**) to warn *or* caution (a person against someone). **—er,** *m.* (**—ers,** *pl.* **—er**) admonisher. **—ung,** *f.* warning.

Wart—en ['vartən], I. *v.n.* (*aux.* **h.**) to wait, stay. II. *v.a.* to attend to, nurse. III. *subst.n.* waiting; tending. **—ung,** *f.* nursing; attendance. **—(e)-faal,** *m.* waiting-room (*Railw.*). **—e-turm,** *m.* watch-tower.

Wärter ['vertər], *m.* (**—s,** *pl.* **—**) attendant. **—in,** *f.* sick-nurse.

Wärts [verts], *adv.* towards; (*in comp.=*) -wards.

Warum [va'rum], *adv.* & *conj.* why, on what account.

Warze ['vartsə], *f.* (*pl.* **—n**) wart.

Was [vas], I. *inter. pron.* what; why; whatever; **— für ein?** what sort of? II. *rel. pron.* what; that which; whatever. III. *coll. for* **etwas.**

Wäsch—e ['veʃə], *f.* washing; wash.

—er, *m.* (—ers, *pl.* —er) washer,
washerman. —erin, *f.* washerwoman.
Waſch—en ['vaʃən], *ir.v.a. & n.* (*aux.*
h.) to wash. —ung, *f.* washing. —an=
ſtalt, *f.* public laundry. —echt, *adj.*
genuine (*fig.*). —leder, *n.*, —ledern,
adj. wash-leather.
Waſſer ['vasər], *n.* (—s, *pl.* —) water;
piece of water. —dicht, *adj.* water-
tight; water-proof. —fall, *m.* cascade.
—flugzeug, *n.* hydroplane. —kraft, *f.*
water *or* hydraulic power. —kreſſe, *f.*
water-cress. —leitung, *f.* water-
supply. —mangel, *m.* water-shortage.
—rinne, *f.* gutter. —ſtoff, *m.* hydro-
gen. —ſturz, *m.* waterfall. —ſucht, *f.*
dropsy.
Wäſſer—ig ['vɛsəriç], *adj.* watery.
—igkeit, *f.* wateriness; insipidity.
Wäſſern ['vɛsərn], *v.* I. *a.* to water,
irrigate. II. *n.* (*aux.* h.) to water.
Waten ['vaːtən], *v.n.* (*aux.* h. & ſ.) to
wade.
Web—en ['veːbən], I. *reg. & ir.v.a.* to
weave. II. *reg. v.n.* (*aux.* h.) to move.
—er, *m.* (—ers, *pl.* —er) spinner,
weaver. —erei [—ə'rai], *f.* weaving.
—erbaum, *m.* weaver's beam.
Wechſel ['vɛksəl], *m.* (—s, *pl.* —)
change; variation; changing; interchange; bill of exchange. —bar, *adj.*
changeable. —brief, *m.* bill of exchange. —geber, *m.* drawer (*of a bill*).
—gebühr, *f.* commission; discount.
—ſeitig, *adj.* reciprocal, mutual.
—ſtrom, *m.* A.C., alternating current
(*Radio*). —n, *v.* I. *a. & n.* (*aux.* h. &
ſ.) to change; to draw bills; (ſich) —n
mit, to replace, change places with.
II. *a.* to exchange; to interchange;
die Zähne —n, to get one's new teeth.
—geſang, *m.* alternate song. —=
geſpräch, *n.* dialogue. —makler, *m.*
bill-broker. —rede, *f.* dialogue; reply.
Wechsler ['vɛkslər], *m.* (—s, *pl.* —)
money-changer.
Wed—en ['vekən], I. *v.a.* to awake,
waken. II. *subst.n.* awaking, awakening. —er=uhr, *f.* (*pl.* —er=uhren)
alarm-clock.
Wedel ['veːdəl], *m.* (—s, *pl.* —) fly-
brush; duster.
Wedeln ['veːdəln], *v.a. & n.* (*aux* h.)
to wag the tail.
Weder ['veːdər], *conj.* neither; — er
noch ich, neither he nor I.
Weg [veːk], I. *m.* (—(e)s, *pl.* —e) way,

road ; auf gemütlichem —e, amicably;
verbotener —, no thoroughfare. II.
[vɛk], *adv., part. & sep. prefix,* away;
gone. III. *int.* — da! be off there!
look out! —ſam ['veːkzaːm], *adj.*
passable, practicable. —e=lag(e)rer,
m. highwayman, brigand. —e=
lagerung, *f.* highway robbery. —(e)=
los, *adj.* pathless, impracticable.
—fall, *m.* suppression; abolition.
—fallen, *ir.v.n.* (*aux.* ſ.) to fall away;
to be omitted. —führen, *v.a.* to lead
away, carry off. —geben, *ir.v.a.* to
give away. —nahme, *f.* taking away;
seizure. —nehmen, *ir.v.a.* to take
away. —räumen, *v.a.* to clear away;
to remove. —reiſen, *v.n.* (*aux.* ſ.) to
depart, set out. —ſchaffen, *v.a.* to
clear away; to get rid of. —weiſen,
ir.v.a. to send away; to direct to
another place. —weiſer, *m.* guide;
finger-post.
Wegen ['veːgən], *prep.* (*with preceding
or following gen., sometimes dat.*)
because of, on account of; for the
sake of, for; von Rechts —, by right.
Weh [veː], —e, I. *int.* alas! woe! II.
adj. & adv. painful, sore. III. *n.*
(—(e)s) misery; misfortune; woe;
pain; — tun, to pain, hurt, ache.
—klage, *f.* lamentation, wail. —=
klagen, *v.a. & n.* (*aux.* h.) (*insep.*) to
lament. —leidig, *adj.* woebegone.
—mut, *m.* pensive melancholy. —=
mütig, *adj.* sad, melancholy.
Wehe ['veːə], *f.* drift (*of snow*). —n,
v. I. *a.* to blow along, drift. II. *n.*
(*aux.* h.) to blow; to flutter, wave.
¹**Wehr** [veːr], *f.* (*pl.* —en) defence;
weapon; protection. —haft, *adj.*
valiant. —haftigkeit, *f.* valour.
—kraft, *f.* defensive force. —los,
adj. unarmed; defenceless. —pflicht,
f. obligation to serve in the army;
allgemeine —pflicht, universal con-
scription. —pflichtig, *adj.* liable to
military service. —ſtand, *m.* military
profession, the army.
²**Wehr**, *n.* (—(e)s, *pl.* —e) weir (*of a
mill*), dam.
Wehren ['veːrən], *v.* I. *a. & n.* (*aux.* h.)
to prevent; to oppose; to control.
II. *a.* (einem etwas) to hinder, prevent (*a person from*); to forbid (*someone to do a thing*). III. *r.* to defend
oneself; to resist.
Weib [vaip], *n.* (—(e)s, *pl.* —er) woman;

wife; zum —e nehmen, to marry.
—chen, n. (—chens, pl. —chen) little
wife or woman; female (of animals).
—erhaft, adj. womanlike; effeminate.
—isch, adj. womanish, effeminate.
—lich, adj. womanly; female. —lich=
keit, f. womanliness; feminine weakness. —ling, m. (—lings, pl. —linge)
milksop. —er=art, f. women's way.
—er=feind, m. misogynist. —er=held,
m. lady-killer. —s=bild, n. hussy,
wench.

Weich [vaiç], adj. & adv. soft; tender.
—heit, f. softness; tenderness. —=
lich, adj. & adv. somewhat soft, tender;
feeble. —lichkeit, f. softness, etc.;
delicacy; effeminacy. —ling, m.
(—lings, pl. —linge) effeminate man.
—tier, n. mollusc.

Weiche ['vaiçə], f. (pl. —n) siding.

1Weichen ['vaiçən], I. v.a. to soften,
soak. II. v.n. (aux. h. & f.) to become
soft.

2Weichen, I. ir.v.n. (aux. f.) to yield,
give way. II. subst.n. zum — bringen,
to push back, repel.

Weid [vait], f. hunt, chase. —mann, m.
huntsman; —manns Heil! hunter's
greeting. —männisch, adj. sportsman-
like. —werk, n. chase, sport.

1Weid=e ['vaidə], f. (pl.—n) pasture,
grazing; pasture-land. —lich,
I. adj. & adv. brave, strong. II. adv.
very much, thoroughly. —eland, n.
pasture-land.

2Weid=e ['vaidə], f. (pl. —en) willow,
osier. —en, adj. willow. —en=korb,
m. wicker-basket.

Weiden ['vaidən], v.a. to graze; feine
Augen — an, to feast one's eyes on.

Weiger=n ['vaigərn], v. I. a. (einem
etwas) to refuse, deny, object to.
II. r. to refuse. —ung, f. refusal.

Weih [vai], m. (—en, pl. —en), —e,
m. (—en, pl. —en) & f. (pl. —en) kite
(Orn.).

Weih=e ['vaiə], f. consecration. —en,
v.a. to consecrate. —nacht, f., —=
nachten, pl. (also sing. n.) Christmas.
—nachts=abend, m. Christmas-eve.
—nachts=feier, f. celebration of Christmas. —rauch, m. incense. —rauch=
faß, n. censer. —wasser, n. holy
water.

Weiher ['vaiər], m. (—s, pl. —)
fish-pond.

Weil [vail], conj. because, since.

—chen, n. (—chens, pl. —chen) little
while. —e, f. a while, a (space of)
time; leisure.

Weilen ['vailən], v.n. (aux. h.) to stay,
stop; to tarry.

Weiler ['vailər], m. (—s, pl. —)
hamlet.

Wein [vain], m. (—(e)s, pl. —e) wine;
vine. —haft, —ig, adj. vinous.
—bau, m. wine- or vine-growing.
—bauer, m. wine-grower. —beere,
f. grape. —berg, m. vineyard. —=
blatt, n. vine-leaf. —blume, f. bouquet (of wine). —ernte, f. vintage.
—faß, n. wine-cask. —garten, m.
vineyard. —geist, m. spirits of wine;
alcohol. —geländer, n. trellis for
vines. —gut, n. vineyard. —händler,
m. wine-merchant. —handlung, f.
wine-shop. —karte, f. wine-list.
—lese, f. vintage; —lese halten, to
gather in the grapes. —leser, m.,
—leserin, f. vintager. —stein, m.
tartar. —stein=säure, f. tartaric acid.
—stock, m. vine. —traube, f. bunch of
grapes. —treber, —trester, pl. skins
or husks of pressed grapes.

Wein=en ['vainən], I. v.a. & n. (aux.
h.) to weep. II. subst.n. weeping.
—erlich, adj. crying; tearful.

Weis=e ['vaizə], I. adj. wise; prudent.
II. f. (pl. —en) manner, mode, way;
melody, tune. —(s)heit, f. wisdom.
—(s)lich, adv. wisely, prudently.

Weis=en ['vaizən], ir.v.a. to show; to
direct; to reprove; von sich —en, to
reject; aus dem Lande —en, to
banish, to exile. —er, m. (—ers, pl.
—er) pointer; guide.

Weissag=en ['vaisza:gən], v.a. & n.
(insep.) to foretell, prophesy. —end,
p. & adj. prophetic. —er, m., —erin, f.
prophet(ess), fortune-teller. —ung,
f. prophecy, prediction.

Weiß [vais], I. adj. white. II. n. white.
—e, f. whiteness; whitewash. —en,
v.a. & n. (aux. f.) to whiten. —blech,
n. tin, white-metal. —dorn, m.
hawthorn. —fisch, m. whiting.
—waren, pl. linens, cottons, white
goods. —wein, m. white wine,
hock.

Weit [vait], adj. & adv. wide; broad;
far; far off; far on, advanced; bei —=
em, by far. —e, I. f.(pl. —en) distance;
width, breadth. II. n. open space;
das —e suchen, to run away. —er,

adj. (*comp. of* Weit) wider, more distant; und ſo —er, and so forth; —er nichts, nothing more. —'aus, *adv.* far off; by far, much. —aus=ſehend, *adj.* extensive. —'hin, —hi'naus, *adv.* far off. —'hergeholt, *adj.* far-fetched. —läuf(t)ig, *adj.* & *adv.* distant; copious; diffuse; long-winded. —läuf(t)igfeit, *f.* diffuseness, prolixity; copiousness; (*pl.*) cere-monies, difficulties. —ſichtig, *adj.* long-sighted.

Weit—en ['vaitən], *v.a.* to widen. —ern, *v.a.* to widen, enlarge. —erung, *f.* extension.

Weizen ['vaitsən], *m.* (—s) wheat.

Welch [vɛlç], I. *inter. adj.* which? what? II. (—er, —e, —es) *inter. pron.* which, what. III. *rel. pron.* (*gen. sing. m. & n.* deſſen; *f.* deren; *gen. pl.* deren) which, what, that, who. IV. *rel. adj.* —er=geſtalt, *adv.* in what form *or* manner; in consequence of which. —er=lei, *indec. adj.* & *adv.* of what kind *or* sort. —ermaßen, *adv.* in what form *or* manner.

Welt [vɛlk], *adj.* withered, faded. —en, *v.a.* & *n.* (*aux.* ſ.) to wither. —heit, *f.* withered state.

Well—e ['vɛlə], *f.* (*pl.* —en) wave; roller; cylinder. —blech, *n.* corrugated iron *or* plate. —en=förmig, *adj.* undulating. —ig, *adj.* wavy.

Welt [vɛlt], *f.* (*pl.* —en) world; alle —, all the world. —lich, *adj.* worldly; secular. —lichfeit, *f.* secular state; worldliness. —ling, *m.* (—lings, *pl.* —linge) worldling. —all, *n.* universe. —alter, *n.* age of the world; age. —ball, *m.* the globe. —bau, *m.* structure of the world; cosmic system, the universe; the world. —befannt, *adj.* generally known, notorious. —berühmt, *adj.* of world-wide fame. —bürger, *m.*, —bürgerin, *f.* citizen of the world, cosmopolitan. —bürgerlich, *adj.* cosmopolitan. —bürgerſinn, *m.*, —bürgertum, *n.* cosmopolitanism. —dame, *f.* woman of the world, fash-ionable lady. —erfahren, *adj.* ex-perienced in the (ways of the) world. —fund, *n.* worldling. —flug, *adj.* worldly-wise. —freis, *m.* world. —fugel, *f.* globe; world. —mann, *m.* man of the world. —männiſch, *adj.* well-bred, gentlemanly. —meer, *n.* ocean. —raum, *m.* space. —=

ſchmerz, *m.* (affected) weariness of life, pessimism.

Wem [ve:m], *dat. of* wer; to whom.

Wen [ve:n], *acc. of* wer; whom.

Wend—e ['vɛndə], *f.* (*pl.* —en) turning; turn. —en, *reg.* & *ir.v.a.* & *n.* (*aux.* h.) to turn; to change; Poſt —end, by return of post; ſich an jemand —en, to apply to a person. —ung, *f.* action of turning; turn; turning (*of a street, etc.*); turn (*of expression, etc.*); entſcheidende —ung, crisis, catas-trophe (*Dram.*). —e=freis, *m.* tropic (des Krebſes, of Cancer; des Stein-bods, of Capricorn). —el=baum, *m.* axle-tree, winch. —el=treppe, *f.* winding stairs. —e=punft, *m.* criti-cal moment, turning-point, crisis; solstitial point (*Astr.*).

Wenig ['ve:nɪç], *adj.* & *adv.* little, small; (*pl.*) few; mit —en Worten, in a few words; —er, less; nichts deſto —er, nevertheless, notwithstanding; am —ſten, least of all; zum —ſten, at least. —feit, *f.* the few; the little; trifle. —ſtens, *adv.* at least, at all events.

Wenn [vɛn], *conj.* when; if; in case, provided; though, although; — nicht, if not, unless; — gleich, although, even if; nevertheless; what of that, what does it matter?

Wer [ve:r], I. *inter. pron.* who? II. *rel. pron.* who; he who *or* that. — da, I. *int.* who goes there? II. *n.* sentinel's call *or* challenge.

Werb—en ['vɛrbən], *ir.v.a.* & *n.* (*aux.* h.) (um einen *or* etwas) —en, to sue for, to court; Refruten —en, to enlist recruits. —er, *m.* (—ers, *pl.* —er) recruiting officer; wooer. —ung, *f.* (*pl.* —en) wooing; solicitation; re-cruiting.

Werde—n ['ve:rdən], I. *ir.v.n.* (*the past part. is* geworden; *the older* worden *now only survives in the auxiliary and in obs. and poet. language*) (*aux.* ſ.) to become; to come to be, grow; to turn out, prove; to come into exist-ence, to be; böſe —n, to grow angry; was ſoll aus ihr —en? what shall become of her? große Dinge ſind im —n, great things are preparing. II. *As auxiliary:* 1. (*forming the future and conditional tenses*) ich — es ihm gleich ſagen, I shall tell him at once. 2. (*forming the passive voice, the p. part.*

being **worden**) ich —e geliebt, I am loved. III. *subst.n.* the state of growing *or* coming into existence; gradual development.

Werf—en ['vɛrfən], *ir.v.a. & n.* (*aux.* h.) to throw. 1—t, *m. & n.* (—t(e)s, *pl.* —te) woof, weft.

2**Werft** [vɛrft], *f.* (*pl.* —en), —e, *f.* (*pl.* —en) wharf; dockyard; dock. —**geld,** *n.* wharfage.

Werg [vɛrk], *n.* (—(e)s) tow; oakum.

Werk [vɛrk], *n.* (—(e)s, *pl.* —e) work, act, deed. —**bank,** *f.* work-bench. —**statt,** —**stätte,** —**stelle,** *f.* workshop. —**stuhl,** *m.* loom. —**täglich,** *adj. & adv.* work-a-day. —**tag,** *m.* working-day, week-day. —**tätigkeit,** *f.* activity, industry. —**zeug,** *n.* tool, implement; organ of the body.

Wermut ['veːrmuːt], *m.* (—s) worm-wood.

Wert [veːrt], I. *adj.* dear; honoured, worthy; worth; deserving; **nicht der Rede** —, not worth speaking of; **Ihr —es Schreiben,** your esteemed letter; **wie ist Ihr —er Name?** to whom have I the honour of speaking? II. *m.* (—(e)s) worth, value. —**en,** *v.a.* to value, appraise; to appreciate. —**ung,** *f.* valuing, appraising; valuation. —**betrag,** *m.* amount of value (*of a letter, etc.*). —**brief,** *m.* letter containing money. —**ersatz,** *m.* equivalent. —**herabsetzung,** *f.* depreciation. —**los,** *adj.* worthless; undeserving; futile. —**losigkeit,** *f.* worthlessness. —**papier,** *n.* bill; note; cheque; money-order. —**schätzung,** *f.* esteem, regard, value. —**voll,** *adj.* valuable, precious.

Wes [vɛs], *gen. sing.* of **wer, was** (*now usually replaced by*) **Wessen.** —**halb,** —**wegen,** *adv. & conj.* on account of which; wherefore, why; therefore, so.

Wesen ['veːzən], *n.* (—s, *pl.* —) being, existence; reality; nature, character; conduct; concerns (*coll.*); **ohne viel —s zu machen,** without much ado or fuss. —**haft,** *adj.* real. —**heit,** *f.* being, essence. —**los,** *adj.* unreal, shadowy, idle, vain. —**losigkeit,** *f.* unreality. —**(s)=gleich,** *adj.* identical. —**(s)=gleichheit,** *f.* identity. —**tlich,** *adj.* essential; real.

Wespe ['vɛspə], *f.* (*pl.* —n) wasp.

Wessen ['vɛsən], *gen. sing.* of **wer** and of **was,** whose.

West [vɛst], *m.* (—(e)s, *pl.* (*rare & poet.*)

—e) west. —**en,** *m.* (—ens *or* —en) the West; **nach** —en **zu, gegen** —en, westward, towards the west. —**lich,** *adj. & adv.* westerly.

Weste ['vɛstə], *f.* waistcoat; vest.

Wett—e ['vɛtə], *f.* (*pl.* —en) bet, wager; **was gilt die** —? what do you bet? —**en,** *v.a. & n.* (*aux.* h.) to bet. —**er,** *m.* —**erin,** *f.* better, wagerer. —**eifer,** *m.* emulation, rivalry. —**eiferer,** *m.* rival; competitor. —**eifern,** *v.n.* (*aux.* h.) (*insep.*) to emulate; to contend (with). —**fahren,** *ir.v.n.* (*aux.* f.) (*insep.*) to race (*in driving, etc.*). —**flug,** *m.* air-race. —**kampf,** *m.* contest, match. —**kämpfer,** *m.* prize-fighter. —**lauf,** *m.* (foot-)race, running-match. —**laufen,** *ir.v.n.* (*aux.* f.) (*insep.*) to race, run for a prize. —**läufer,** *m.* runner. —**rennen,** I. *ir.v.n.* (*aux.* f.) (*insep.*) to race, run. II. *subst.n.* racing (*of men, horses, etc.*); horse-racing; race.

Wetter ['vɛtər], *n.* (—s, *pl.* —) weather; storm; lightning; atmosphere; **alle** —! hang it all! —**bericht,** *m.* weather-forecast. —**hahn,** *m.* weather-cock. —**leuchten,** I. *v.n.* (*aux.* h.) *imp.* (*insep.*); **es —leuchtet,** it lightens, there is summer lightning. II. *subst.n.* sheet-lightning. —**wolke,** *f.* storm-cloud, thunder-cloud.

Wettern ['vɛtərn], *v.n.* (*aux.* h. & f.) & *imp.* to thunder and lighten.

Wetzen ['vɛtsən], *v.a.* to whet, sharpen.

Wichs—e ['vɪksə], *f.* (*pl.* —en) blacking, polish (*for shoes*). —**en,** *v.a.* to black, polish (*boots, etc.*).

Wicht [vɪçt], *m.* (—(e)s, *pl.* —e) wight, creature.

Wichtig ['vɪçtɪç], *adj.* weighty; important; — **tun,** to assume an important air. —**keit,** *f.* weight; importance.

Wicke ['vɪkə], *f.* (*pl.* —n) vetch.

Wick—el ['vɪkəl], *m.* (—els, *pl.* —el) roll; curl-paper. —**eln,** *v.a.* to roll, roll up, twist. —**el=band,** *n.* swaddling band.

Widder ['vɪdər], *m.* (—s, *pl.* —) ram.

Wider ['viːdər], I. *prep.* (*with acc.*) against, contrary to, in opposition to. II. *adv. & insep. pref.* against; in opposite direction; back again. —**lich,** *adj. & adv.* offensive, repugnant. —**lichkeit,** *f.* loathsomeness; repulsiveness. —'**fahren,** *ir.v.n.* (*aux.* f.)

(insep.) to happen. —**hafen**, m. barb,
barbed hook. —**hatig**, adj. barbed.
—**hall**, m. echo. —**hallen**, v.n. (aux.
h.) (sep. & insep.) to resound, re-echo.
—**halt**, m. support. —**haltig**, adj.
resisting. —'**legen**, v.a. (insep.) to
refute, disprove. —**rede**, f. contradiction. —**facher**, m. adversary, opponent. —**schein**, m. reflection. —**
spenstig**, adj. refractory. —**spenstig-
keit**, f. refractoriness; disobedience.
—**spiel**, n. opposition. —'**sprechen**,
ir.v.a. & n. (aux. h. dat.) (insep.) to
contradict; to oppose. —**spruch**, m.
contradiction; opposition. —**stand**,
m. opposition, resistance. —**wärtig**,
adj. & adv. disagreeable; perverse;
cross. —**wärtigkeit**, f. disagreeableness. —**wille**, m. repugnance.
—**willig**, adj. & adv. reluctant.
Widm—en ['vɪdmən], v.a. to dedicate;
to devote. —**er**, m. (—ers, pl. —er)
dedicator. —**ung**, f. dedication.
Widrig ['vi:drɪç], adj. & adv. adverse.
Wie [vi:], I. adv. how; in what way; in
what degree? — **geht's?** how are
you? — **dem auch sei**, be that as it
may. II. conj. how; as, like; as, for
instance, as if; such as; as, when,
when once. —**fern**, adv.; **in —fern?**
in what respect? —'**so**, adv.; —**so
weißt du das?** how is it that you
know that? —'**viel**, adv. how much.
den —vielten haben wir? what is
the date? —'**wohl**, conj. although.
Wieder ['vi:dər], I. adv. again, anew;
back again; in return. II. pref.
mostly sep., generally = once more,
again. —**abdruck**, m. reprint, reim-
pression. —**aufbau**, m. reconstruc-
tion. —**aufbringen**, ir.v.a. to revive
(a fashion, etc.). —**aufnahme**, f. resumption. —**aufnehmen**, ir.v.a. to
resume. —**auftreten**, ir.v.n. (aux. f.)
to reappear. —**erkennen**, ir.v.a. to
recognize. —**gabe**, f. restitution, return. —**geben**, ir.v.a. to give again;
to give back, return, restore. —**holen**,
I. v.a. (sep.) to bring, or carry back;
(insep.) to repeat; to rehearse (a
lesson); **kurz —holen**, to sum up, re-
capitulate; **sich —holen**, to repeat oneself. II. subst.n., —'**holung**, f. repetition; reiteration. —**kehren**, ir.v.n. (sep.)
(aux. f.) to return, come back. —**
kunft**, f. return. —**sehen**, I. ir.v.a. to
see again. II. subst.n.; **auf —sehen!**

till we meet again! au revoir! —**
taufe**, f. rebaptizing, second baptism.
—**täufer**, m. anabaptist.
Wiege ['vi:gə], f. (pl. —n) cradle.
—**n-fest**, n. birthday celebrations.
—**n-lied**, n. lullaby.
Wiegen ['vi:gən], I. ir.v.a. & n. (aux.
h.) to weigh. II. reg.v.a. to rock; to
chop into small pieces (food).
Wiehern ['vi:ərn], I. v.n. (aux. h.) to
neigh. II. subst.n. neighing, neigh.
Wiese ['vi:zə], f. (pl. —n) meadow.
Wiesel ['vi:zəl], n. (—s, pl. —) weasel.
Wiking ['vi:kɪŋ], m. (—s, pl. —er)
viking.
Wild [vɪlt], I. adj. & adv. wild, savage;
seid nicht so —, don't make so much
noise. II. n. (—es) wild animals;
game; a head of game. —**e(r)**, m.
savage. —**heit**, f. wildness, savagery.
—**nis**, f. wilderness; savage state.
—**bret**, —**pret**, n. (—s) game, venison.
—**dieb**, m. poacher. —**dieben**, v.n.
(aux. h.) (insep.) to poach. —**die-
be'rei**, f. poaching. —'**fremd**, adj.
quite strange or unknown. —**graf**, m.
Wildgrave. —**hüter**, m. game-keeper.
—**leder**, n. deerskin, buckskin. —**
schwein**, n. wild boar.
Will—e ['vɪlə], m. (—ens, pl. —en)
will; wish, inclination; **aus freiem
—en**, voluntarily; **mit —en**, on purpose. —**entlich**, adj. intentional.
—**ig**, adj. willing. —**igen**, v.n. (aux.
h.); **in eine S. —igen**, to consent to.
—**igkeit**, f. willingness. —**en-los**, adj.
weak-minded, characterless. —**en-
losigkeit**, f. want of will-power, indecision. —**fahren**, v.n. (aux. h.) (dat.) to
accede to, to comply with. —**fährig**,
adj. obliging. —**fährigkeit**, f. compliance; complaisance.
Willkommen [vɪl'kɔmən], I. adj. welcome. II. m. (—s, pl. —) welcome.
Willkür ['vɪlky:r], f. free will; caprice;
despotism. —**lich**, adj. arbitrary,
despotic.
Wimmeln ['vɪməln], v.n. (aux. h. & f.)
to swarm.
Wimmern ['vɪmərn], v.n. (aux. h.) to
whimper.
Wimpel ['vɪmpəl], m. (—s, pl. —)
pennon or pennant, streamer.
Wimper ['vɪmpər], f. (pl. —n) eye-lash.
Wind [vɪnt], m. (—(e)s, pl. —e) wind.
—**en**, v.n. (aux. h.) to catch the scent.
—**ig**, adj. windy, breezy; heedless;

unreliable; visionary. —**igfeit**, *f.* windiness. —**beutel**, *m.* pastry puff; (*fig.*) wind-bag. —**büchſe**, *f.* air-gun. —**fang**, *m.* ventilator. —**hunb**, *m.* greyhound. —**s=braut**, *f.* whirlwind, squall. —**ſchief**, *adj.* warped.

Winbe ['vɪndə], *f.* (*pl.* —**n**) bindweed; windlass; winch. —**I**, *f.* (*pl.* —**In**) swaddling clothes. —**In**, *v.a.* to swaddle.

Winb—en ['vɪndən], *ir.v.* I. *a.* to wind. II. *r.* to writhe; to wriggle. —**ung**, *f.* winding, twisting. —**e=baum**, *m.* beam (*of a windlass, etc.*).

Winf [vɪŋk], *m.* (—(e)s, *pl.* —e) sign; wink; **einem einen — geben**, to drop a person a hint.

Winfel ['vɪŋkəl], *m.* (—s, *pl.* —) angle; corner. **winflig**, *adj.* angular. —**recht**, I. *adj.* rectangular. II. *adv.* at right angles.

Winfen ['vɪŋkən], I. *v.a.* & *n.* (*aux.* h.) to wink; to sign; to beckon, nod, wave. II. *subst.n.* winking; sign.

Winſel—er ['vɪnzələr], *n.* (—ers, *pl.* —er) whiner. —**ig**, *adj.* whining. —**n**, *v.n.* (*aux.* h.) to whine.

Winter ['vɪntər], *m.* (—s, *pl.* —) winter. —**lich**, I. *adj.* winter, wintry. II. *adv.* as in winter. —**grün**, *n.* periwinkle (*Bot.*).

Winzig ['vɪntsɪç], *adj.* tiny.

Wipfel ['vɪpfəl], *m.* (—s, *pl.* —) (tree-)top.

Wir [viːr], *pers. pron.* (1*st pers. pl.*) we.

Wirbel ['vɪrbəl], *m.* (—s, *pl.* —) whirl; whirlpool; whirlwind; giddiness. —**haft**, —**ig**, *adj.* eddying, whirling. —**bein**, *n.* vertebra. —**los**, *adj.* invertebrate. —**ſäule**, *f.* spine. —**tiere**, *pl.* vertebrate animals. —**winb**, *m.* whirlwind.

Wirbel—n ['vɪrbəln], *v.a.* & *n.* (*aux.* h. & ſ.) to whirl, turn round; to warble; to trill (*a drum*).

Wirf—en ['vɪrkən], I. *v.a.* to effect; to work. II. *v.n.* (*aux.* h.) to work, operate (upon), act (upon); to affect. III. *subst.n.* acting, working; endeavour. —**enb**, *p.* & *adj.* operating; efficient, effective (*cause*). —**er**, *m.* (—ers, *pl.* —er) worker; maker; weaver. —**lich**, *adj.* & *adv.* real; true; genuine. —**lichfeit**, *f.* reality; actual fact. —**ſam**, *adj.* effective, efficacious. —**ſamfeit**, *f.* efficacy. —**ſtuhl**, *m.* loom. —**ung**, *f.* effect; operation, action.

—**ungs=freis**, *m.* sphere of activity. —**ungs=los**, *adj.* ineffectual, futile. —**ungs=voll**, *adj.* efficacious, effective.

Wirr [vɪr], *adj.* confused; entangled. —**e**, *f.* (*pl.* —en) tangle; (*pl.*) disturbances; complications. —**ſal**, *n.* (—ſals, *pl.* —ſale) confusion; perplexity. —**warr**, *m.* jumble.

Wirt [vɪrt], *m.* (—(e)s, *pl.* —e), —**in**, *f.* head of a house *or* family; host, hostess; **ein guter —**, a good manager. —**bar**, *adj.* hospitable; habitable. —**lich**, *adj.* frugal; thrifty. —**s=haus**, *n.* tavern, public-house. —**s=tafel**, *f.*, —**s=tiſch**, *m.* table d'hôte.

Wirtſchaft ['vɪrtʃaft], *f.* domestic economy; husbandry; innkeeping; public-house; doings; row, disturbance. —**en**, *v.n.* (*aux.* h.) to keep house; to keep an inn *or* public-house; to administer (*property*); to make a noise; **gut —en**, to economize. —**er**, *m.* (—ers, *pl.* —er) manager; economist. —**erin**, *f.*, *see* —**er**; manageress, steward's wife. —**lich**, *adj.* economical; orderly; domestic. —**lichfeit**, *f.* economy. —**s=gelb**, *n.* housekeeping-money. —**s=lehre**, *f.* economics.

Wiſchen ['vɪʃən], *v.a.* to wipe.

Wismut ['vɪsmuːt], *m.* & *n.* (—s) bismuth.

Wiſpern ['vɪspərn], *v.a.* & *n.* (*aux.* h.) to whisper.

Wiß—bar ['vɪsbaːr], *adj.* knowable. —**begier(be)**, *f.* thirst for knowledge; curiosity. —**begierig**, *adj.* inquisitive.

Wiſſen ['vɪsən], I. *ir.v.a.* to know; to understand; **ich weiß feinen Rat**, I don't know what to do; **weiß der Himmel!** Heaven knows! II. *subst.n.* knowledge, learning; **ohne mein —**, without my knowledge; **meines —s**, as far as I know. —**ſchaft**, *f.* science; learning; knowledge. —**ſchaft(l)er**, *m.* (—ſchaft(l)ers, *pl.* —ſchaft(l)er) man of science, learned man. —**ſchaftlich**, *adj.* scientific; scholarly. —**tlich**, *adj.* knowing, conscious.

Witter—n ['vɪtərn], *v.a.* & *n.* (*aux.* h.) to scent, smell, perceive. —**ung**, *f.* weather. —**ungs=bericht**, *m.* meteorological report.

Witwe ['vɪtvə], *f.* (*pl.* —**n**) widow. —**n=ſchaft**, *f.*, —**n=tum**, *n.* widow-

hood. —r, *m.* (—rs, *pl.* —r) widower.
—n=trauer, *f.* widow's weeds.

Wiß [vɪts], *m.* (—es, *pl.* —e) wit; joke.
—ig, *adj.* witty; clever; brilliant.
—ler, *m.* (—lers, *pl.* —ler) —ling,
m. (—lings, *pl.* —linge) would-be wit.
—blatt, *n.* comic journal. —bold,
m. witty fellow. —los, *adj.* stupid,
insipid. —wort, *n.* bon-mot, witty
remark.

Wo [vo:], I. *inter. adv.* where; in what
place. II. *rel. adv.* (=*a rel. pron. &
prep.*) where; in, on, at which (*place,
etc.*); at which (*time*), when, that; if,
in which case. —'bei, *inter. & rel.
adv.* (=*inter. or rel. pron. with prep.*)
whereby, whereat, near, at or in
connection with which or what (=
bei welchem, ꝛc.). —'durch, *inter. &
rel. adv.* (=*rel. pron. with prep.*)
whereby, through or by means of
which or what (=durch was, welches,
ꝛc.). —'fern, *conj.* if, in case of,
provided that, so far as. —'für,
inter. & rel. adv. (=*inter. or rel. pron.
with prep.*) wherefore; for which, for
what; (=für was, welches, ꝛc.).
—'gegen, *inter. & rel. adv.* (=*inter. or
rel. pron. with prep.*) against which,
what; in return or exchange for which
or what; (=gegen was, welches,
welche(n)). —'her, *inter. & rel. adv.*
(=*inter. or rel. pron. with prep.*)
whence, from whence, from which or
what place; how. —'hin, *inter. &
rel. adv.* (=*inter. or rel. pron. with
prep.*) whither, what way, to or toward
what place; —hin gehen Sie, or
(*more usually*) wo gehen Sie hin?
where are you going to? —hi'nab,
inter. & rel. adv. (=*inter. or rel. pron.
with prep.*) down which or what, at
the foot of which or what. —hin'aus,
inter. & rel. adv. (=*inter. or rel. pron.
with prep.*) to what place, which way;
out at what place. —'hinter, *inter.
& rel. adv.* (=*inter. or rel. pron. with
prep.*) behind or after what or which;
(=hinter was, welchem, ꝛc.). —'mit,
inter. & rel. adv. (=*inter. or rel. pron.
with prep.*) wherewith, with or by
which or what; (=mit welchem, ꝛc.).
—'nach, *inter. & rel. adv.* (=*inter. or
rel. pron. with prep.*) whereafter,
whereupon, after or towards or according to which or what (=nach
welchem, ꝛc.). —'selbst, *adv.* where.

—'von, *inter. & rel. adv.* (=*inter. or
rel. pron. with prep.*) whereof, of or
concerning which or what (=von
welchem, ꝛc.). —'vor, *inter. & rel. adv.*
(=*inter. or rel. pron. with prep.*) of,
from or before which or what (=vor
welchem, ꝛc.). —'zu, *inter. & rel. adv.*
(=*inter. or rel. pron. with prep.*)
whereto, to what purpose; why; to,
for, at or in addition to what or which
(=zu was, welchem, ꝛc.).

Woche ['vɔxə], *f.* (*pl.* —n) week;
künftige —, next week. —n=bett, *n.*
childbed. —n=tag, *m.* weekday.

Wöch—entlich ['vœçəntlɪç], *adj. & adv.*
weekly. —ig, *adj.* (*only in cpds.*);
vier—ig, lasting four weeks. —nerin,
f. woman in childbed.

Wog—e ['vo:gə], *f.* (*pl.* —en) wave,
billow. —en, *v.n.* (*aux.* h.) to surge.
—ig, *adj.* wavy, billowy; surging.

Wohl [vo:l], I. (*comp.* —er & besser,
sup. am —sten) *adv.* well; leben
Sie —, farewell; —bekomm's! much
good may it do you! II. *part.* (*without any stress*) indeed; to be sure;
forsooth; perhaps, probably. Sie irrt
sich —, she is probably wrong; ob er
— kommen wird? I wonder will he
come? III. *n.* (—s) weal, welfare.
—ig, *adj.* happy. —'an, I. *adv.*
boldly. II. *int.* come on! —'auf, I.
adv.; er ist —auf, he is well. II. *int.*
cheer up! come on! —bedacht, I. *adj.*
well considered, deliberate. II. *adv.*
deliberately, on purpose, consider-
ately. III. *n.*; mit —bedacht, after
mature reflection. —befinden, *n.* good
health; well-being. —behagen, *n.*
feeling of comfort or ease. —fahrt,
f. welfare. —feil, *adj.* cheap. —feilheit, *f.* cheapness. —gesinnt, *adj.* well
disposed. —gesittet, *adj.* well-man-
nered, well brought up. —habend, *adj.*
wealthy, well-to-do. —habenheit, *f.*
affluence. —flang, *m.* harmony,
melody. —flingend, *adj.* harmonious.
—lautend, *adj.* euphonious. —mei-
nend, *adj.* well-meaning, friendly.
—fein, *n.* good health. —stand, *m.*
well-being; comfort. —tat, *f.* benefit,
favour; good deed. —täter, *m.*,
—täterin, *f.* benefactor, benefactress.
—tätig, *adj.* beneficent; charitable.
—tätigkeit, *f.* charity, beneficence.
—tätigkeits=anstalt, *f.* charitable institution. —tuend, *adj.* salutary, com-

forting. —tun, *ir.v.n.* (*aux.* h.) (*sep.*) to benefit. —verdient, *adj.* just, well-merited. —weislich, *adv.* prudently. —wollen, I. *ir.v.n.* (*aux.* h.) (*sep.*) (einem) to wish a person well. II. *subst.n.* good-will. —wollend, *adj.* kind, benevolent.

Wohn—en ['vo:nən], *v.* I. *n.* (*aux.* h.) to dwell. —bar, *adj.* habitable. —barkeit, *f.* habitable condition. —haft, *adj.* dwelling, resident. —lich, *adj.* comfortable, commodious. —lich-keit, *f.* commodiousness (*of a house, etc.*). —ung, *f.* dwelling, residence. —gebäude, —haus, *n.* dwelling-house. —ort, *m.* place of residence. —fitz, *m.* residence; seat. —ftube, *f.*, —zimmer, *n.* sitting-room.

Wölben ['vølbən], *v.a.* to vault, arch.

Wolf [vølf], *m.* (—(e)s, *pl.* Wölfe) wolf. —s-falle, *f.* wolf-trap. —s-hunger, *m.* enormous appetite.

Wölf—chen ['vølfçən], *n.* (—chens, *pl.* —chen) wolf's cub. —in, *f.* she-wolf. —ifch, *adj.* wolfish.

Wölk—chen ['vølkçən], *n.* (—chens, *pl.* —chen) little cloud. —en, *v.a.* & *n.* (*aux.* h.) to cloud.

Wolk—e ['vølkə], *f.* (*pl.* —en) cloud. —en-haft, —ig, *adj.* clouded, cloudy. —en-bruch, *m.* cloud-burst. —en-leer, —en-los, *adj.* cloudless. —en-umgeben, *adj.* cloud-capped.

Wolle ['vølə], *f.* (*pl.* —en, *usually* Wollarten) wool.

Wollen ['vølən], I. *ir.v.a.* to wish; to will, be willing; fo Gott will! please God. II. *after an inf.* = *p.p.* gewollt; ich habe nur fcherzen —, I only intended to joke, I was only joking. III. *subst.n.* will, volition; inclination.

Woll—uft ['vøluʃt], *f.* (*pl.* —üfte) voluptuousness. —üftig, *adj.* volup-tuous.

Wonne ['vønə], *f.* (*pl.* —n) joy; rapture. —fam, wonnig, wonniglich, *adj.* de-lightful, delicious, blissful. —trunken, *adj.* intoxicated with bliss, enrap-tured.

Wor [vor], *see* Wo (*used as* wo *and in-stead of it in cmpds. with a prep. be-ginning with a vowel*). —'an, *inter.* & *rel. adv.* whereon, whereat, on, of, against *or* by which *or* what; —an denken Sie? what are you thinking of? —'auf, *inter.* & *rel. adv.* whereupon, upon, to *or* at which *or* what. —'aus,

inter. & *rel. adv.* by, out of *or* from which *or* what, whence. —'in, *inter.* & *rel. adv.* whereat, in which *or* what. —'über, *inter.* & *rel. adv.* wherein, whereof, of, at, over *or* upon which *or* what. —'um, *inter.* & *rel. adv.* for which. —'unter, *inter.* & *rel. adv.* in, under, among *or* betwixt which *or* what.

Worf—e(l)n ['vørfə(l)n], *v.a.* to fan, winnow. —ler, *m.* (—lers, *pl.* —ler) winnower. —tenne, *f.* winnowing-floor.

Wort [vørt], *n.* ((e)s, *pl. when signify-ing* single unconnected words *usually* Wörter; *in all other cases* Worte) word; ein Mann, ein —, word of honour! das große — führen, to swagger, to brag; kein — mehr! not another word! —bruch, *m.* breach of one's word. —brüchig, *adj.* false to one's word. —brüchigkeit, *f.* faith-lessness. —forfcher, *m.* philologist, etymologist. —forfchung, *f.* study of words, etymology. —fügung, *f.* syntax, structure of phrases. —fügungslehre, *f.* syntax. —führer, *m.* speaker. —karg, *adj.* laconic, taci-turn. —kargheit, *f.* taciturnity. —kunde, *f.* philology. —fpiel, *n.* pun. —wechfel, *m.* discussion; altercation, dispute.

Wört—chen ['vørtçən], *n.* (—chens, *pl.* —chen) little word. —lich, *adj.* literal, verbal, word for word. —lich-keit, *f.* literalness, literal character. —er-buch, *n.* dictionary.

Wrack [vrak], I. *adj.* cast off, waste. II. *n.* (—(e)s, *pl.* —e, —s) wreck. —fchiff, *n.* wrecked vessel.

Wringen ['vrɪŋən], *v.a.* to twist; to wring.

Wucher ['vu:xər], *m.* (—s, *pl.* —) usury; interest. —er, Wucherer, *m.* usurer. —haft, —ifch, wuchrifch, *adj.* usuri-ous. —zins, *m.*, —zinfen, *pl.* usurious interest.

Wuchern ['vu:xərn], *v.n.* (*aux.* h.) to grow luxuriantly.

Wuchs [vu:ks], *m.* (—(f)es, *pl.* Wüchfe) growth; von ftattlichem —, of a stately figure.

Wühlen ['vy:lən], *v.a.* & *n.* (*aux.* h.) to root, grub up; (*fig.*) to agitate, stir up.

Wulft [vulft], *m.* (—es, *pl.* Wülfte) & *f.* (*pl.* Wülfte) swelling.

Wund [vunt], *adj.* sore; wounded.

—e, f. (pl. —en) wound; sore. —∗
arᴣ(e)'neifunſt, f. surgery, surgical art.
—arᴣt, m. surgeon. —ärᴣtlich, adj.
surgical.

Wunder ['vʊndər], n. (—s, pl. —)
wonder; marvel; miracle. —bar, adj.
wonderful, amazing. —barfeit, f.
wonder, strange thing. —lich, adj.
strange, odd. —lichfeit, f. oddness.
—n, v.a. & n. (aux. h.) to wonder; es
—t mich, I am surprised. —ding, n.
marvel, prodigy. —find, n. prodigy
of a child. —mann, m. miracle-
worker. —reich, I. adj. wonderful,
full of wonders. II. n. land of wonders.
—ſchön, adj. wondrously beautiful,
exquisite.

Wunſch [vʊnʃ], m. (—es, pl. Wünſche)
wish, desire.

Wünſch—en ['vynʃən], v.a. to wish, to
desire; Glück —en, to wish joy; to
congratulate. —el∗hut, m., —el∗
hütlein, n. wishing-cap. —el∗rute, f.
wishing-wand, divining-rod. —ens∗
wert, —ens∗würdig, adj. to be desired.

Würd—e ['vyrdə], f. (pl. —en) dignity;
majesty; post (of honour); unter aller
—e, beneath contempt. —ig, adv.
worthy. —igfeit, f. merit; dignity.
—e∗voll, adj. grave, dignified.

Würdig—en ['vyrdɪgən], v.a. (acc. &
gen.) to deign, vouchsafe; to value,
rate. —ung, f. appreciation, estimation.

Wurf [vʊrf], m. (—es, pl. Würfe)
throw, cast (of balls, dice, a net).
—ſcheibe, f. quoit. —ſpeer, —ſpieß,
m. javelin, dart. —ſtein, m. stone
for throwing.

Würf—el ['vyrfəl], m. (—els, pl. —el)
die; cube; die —el ſind gefallen! the
die is cast. —el∗becher, m. dice-box.
—el∗brett, n. draught-board, back-
gammon-board. —el∗form, f. cubic
form. —el∗förmig, adj. cubical,
cube-shaped. —el∗inhalt, m. cubic
contents. —eln, v.n. (aux. h.) to play
at dice. —ier, m. (—iers, pl. —ier)
dice-player. —el∗ſpiel, n. dice-play-
ing. —el∗wurᴣel, f. cube-root. —el∗
ᴣahl, f. cube (of a number). —el∗ᴣoll,
m. cubic inch.

Würg—en ['vyrgən], I. v.n. (aux. h.)
& r. to choke. II. v.a. to choke; to
slaughter. III. subst.n., —ung, f.
choking; strangling. —er, m. (—ers,
pl. —er) strangler; destroyer; mur-

derer. —eriſch, adj. murderous,
slaughtering.

Wurm [vʊrm], m. (—(e)s, pl. Würmer;
Würme (obs. & poet.)) worm; little
child. —ig, adj. worm-eaten. —fräßig,
adj. worm-eaten.

Wurſt [vʊrst], f. (pl. Würſte) sausage.

Würſtchen ['vyrstçən], n. (—s, pl. —)
small sausage.

Wurᴣ [vʊrts], f. (pl. Würᴣe), —el, f.
(pl. —eln) root. —eln, v.n. (aux. h. &
f.) to take or strike root. —el∗ᴣeichen,
n. radical sign (Math.).

Würᴣ—e ['vyrtsə], f. (pl. —en) spice;
seasoning. —en, v.a. to spice. —haft,
—ig, adj. aromatic.

Wüſt [vy:st], adj. & adv. desert, waste.
—e, f. (pl. —en) desert, wilderness.
—ling, m. (—lings, pl. —linge) libertine.

Wut [vu:t], f. rage, fury; madness.
—anfall, m. fit of rage. —entbrannt,
adj. inflamed with rage, enraged.

Wüt—en ['vy:tən], v.n. (aux. h.) to
rage, be furious. —end, p. & adj.
enraged, furious. —erich, m. (—erichs,
pl. —eriche) frantic person. —ig,
adj. raging; mad, rabid.

ℨ

X, x [ɪks], n. X, x; jemandem ein X
für ein U machen, to throw dust in a
person's eyes; X∗Beine, turned-in
legs (bow-legs); X∗mal, ever so many
times; X∗Strahlen, Röntgen-rays,
X-rays.

Xenie ['kse:nlə], f. (pl. —n) epigram.

Xylograph [ksylo'gra:f], m. (—en, pl.
—en) wood-engraver.

ℨ

Ꝩ, y ['ypsilon], n. Z, z.

Ꝩſop ['i:zɔp], m. (—s, pl. —e or —s)
hyssop.

3

3, ᴣ [tsɛt], n. Z, z.

3ad—e ['tsakə], f. (pl. —en), —en, m.
(—ens, pl. —en) scallop. —ig, adj.
pointed; notched, indented.

3ag—en ['tsa:gən], v.n. (aux. h.) to
lack courage. —haft, adj. faint-
hearted, timorous. —haftigfeit, f.
timidity.

3äh(e) ['tsɛ:(ə)], adj. tough, tenacious.

Zahl [tsa:l], *f.* (*pl.* **—en**) number. **—bar**, *adj.* payable, due. **—(en)= größe**, *f.* number, numerical quantity. **—reich**, *adj.* numerous.

zahl—en ['tsa:lən], *v.a.* to pay. **—er**, *m.* (**—ers**, *pl.* **—er**) payer. **—ung**, *f.* payment. **—fähig**, *adj.* solvent. **—meister**, *m.* treasurer; paymaster.

zähl—bar ['tsɛ:lba:r], *adj.* computable, numerable. **—en**, *v.a.* & *n.* (*aux.* h.) to number, count. **—ung**, *f.* counting; calculation.

zahm [tsa:m], *adj.* tame. **—heit**, *f.* tameness.

zähm—bar ['tsɛ:mba:r], *adj.* tamable. **—barkeit**, *f.* tamableness. **—en**, *v.a.* to tame. **—ung**, *f.* taming. **—er**, *m.* (**—ers**, *pl.* **—er**) tamer; subduer.

Zahn [tsa:n], *m.* (**—s**, *pl.* **Zähne**) tooth. **—ig**, *adj.* toothed, indented; (*in comp.=*) with (*so many*) teeth. **—arm**, *adj.* having few teeth. **—artig**, *adj.* tooth-shaped, tooth-like. **—arzt**, *m.* dentist. **—rad**, *n.* cog-wheel. **—stocher**, *m.* tooth-pick. **—weh**, *n.* toothache.

Zange ['tsaŋə], *f.* (*pl.* **—n**) tongs; pincers. **—n=artig**, **—n=förmig**, *adj.* pincer-like.

Zank [tsaŋk], *m.* (**—(e)s**) quarrel; strife. **—haft**, *adj.* quarrelsome; irritable. **—apfel**, *m.* apple of discord, bone of contention.

zanken ['tsaŋkən], *v.r.* & *n.* (*aux.* h.) to quarrel.

Zapfe—n ['tsapfən], *m.* (**—ns**, *pl.* **—n**) peg; plug; cock, tap. **—n**, *v.a.* to tap (*a cask*). **—r**, *m.* (**—rs**, *pl.* **—r**) tapster, beer drawer. **—nloch**, *n.* bunghole. **—nstreich**, *m.* tattoo (*Mil.*).

zappeln ['tsapəln], *v.n.* (*aux.* h.) to sprawl, flounder, writhe.

Zar [tsa:r], *m.* (**—en**, **—s**, *pl.* **—en**, *also* **—e**) tsar. **—ewitsch**, *m.* tsarevich. **—ewna**, *f.* tsarevna. **—in**, *f.* tsarina, tsaritsa.

zart [tsa:rt] (*comp.* **—er**, *sup.* **—est**), *adj.* tender; soft, delicate. **—heit**, *f.* tenderness. **—fühlend**, *adj.* sensitive. **—gefühl**, *n.* delicacy of feeling.

zärtlich ['tsɛ:rtlɪç], *adj.* tender. **—keit**, *f.* tenderness.

Zauber ['tsaubər], *m.* (**—s**, *pl.* **—**) spell; charm; magic. **—ei** [**—'rai**], *f.* magic, sorcery. **—er**, *m.* (**—ers**, *pl.* **—er**) magician, sorcerer. **—haft**, **—isch**, *adj.* magical, enchanted.

zauber—n ['tsaubərn], *v.* I. *a.* to cast a spell on *or* over. II. *n.* (*aux.* h.) to conjure, to practise magic *or* witchcraft. **—bild**, *n.* magic image. **—flöte**, *f.* magic flute. **—formel**, *f.* incantation. **—ring**, *m.* magic ring. **—rute**, *f.* magic wand. **—trant**, *m.* magic potion.

Zauder—er ['tsaudərər], **Zaudrer**, *m.* (**—ers**, *pl.* **—er**), **—in**, **Zaudrerin**, *f.* dilatory person. **—haft**, *adj.* hesitating, irresolute. **—haftigkeit**, *f.* hesitation; dilatoriness. **—n**, I. *v.n.* (*aux.* h.) to hesitate; to delay. II. *subst.n.* procrastination; delay.

Zaum [tsaum], *m.* (**—(e)s**, *pl.* **Zäume**) bridle; rein; **im — halten**, to keep in check.

zäum—en ['tsɔymən], *v.a.* to bridle. **—ung**, *f.* bridling.

Zaun [tsaun], *m.* (**—(e)s**, *pl.* **Zäune**) hedge, fence. **—könig**, *m.* wren.

zäunen ['tsɔynən], *v.a.* to fence in.

zausen ['tsauzən], *v.a.* to pull (about), to tug.

Zebra ['tse:bra:], *n.* (**—s**, *pl.* **—s**) zebra.

Zech—e ['tsɛçə], *f.* (*pl.* **—en**) bill, banquet; mine. **—en**, *v.a.* & *n.* (*aux.* h.) to carouse. **—er**, *m.* (**—ers**, *pl.* **—er**) toper; reveller. **—erei** [**—ə'rai**], *f.* carousing. **—bruder**, *m.* boon companion, toper.

Zeder ['tse:dər], *f.* (*pl.* **—n**) cedar. **—n**, *adj.* of cedar.

Zeh [tse:], *m.* (**—(e)s**, **en**, *pl.* **—e(n)**), **—e**, *f.* (*pl.* **—en**) toe.

zehn [tse:n], I. *num. adj.* ten. II. *f.* (*pl.* **—en**) the figure ten; the number ten. III. *n.* ten, decade. **—t**, I. *num. adj.* (**der, die, das —te**) tenth. II. *n.* space of ten years, decennium. **—tel**, *n.* (**—tels**, *pl.* **—tel**) a tenth ($\frac{1}{10}$). **—tens**, *adv.* tenthly, in the tenth place. **—mal**, *adv.* ten times.

Zehnte ['tse:ntə] (**—n**, *pl.* **—n**), *m.* tithe; tenth.

zehr—en ['tse:rən], *v.n.* (*aux.* h.) to consume; to waste, become less. **—end**, *p.* & *adj.* eating and drinking; wasting. **—er**, *m.* (**—ers**, *pl.* **—er**) consumer, spender. **—ung**, *f.* living; waste.

Zeichen ['tsaiçən], *n.* (**—s**, *pl.* **—**) mark, token, sign. **—setzung**, *f.* punctuation.

zeich—nen ['tsaiçnən], I. *v.a.* & *n.* (*aux.* h.) to mark; to sign; to draw, sketch; **ich —ne hochachtungsvoll**, I remain yours respectfully. II. *subst.n.*

drawing. **—ner,** m. (—ners, pl. —ner), —nerin, f. drawer, designer. —nung, f. drawing. —en=ſchule, f. school of design.

Zeig—en ['tsaɪgən], v. I. a. to show, point out. II. r. to appear, emerge. —er, m. (—ers, pl. —er) one who shows; any instrument for pointing. —e=finger, m. forefinger, index.

Zeihen ['tsaɪən], ir.v.a. to accuse a person of (obs.).

Zeile ['tsaɪlə], f.(pl. —n) line (page, etc.).

Zeiſig ['tsaɪzɪç], m. (—s, pl. —e) siskin (Orn.); loderer —, loose fish (coll.).

Zeit [tsaɪt], f. (pl. —en) time (also Mus.); — Lebens, during lifetime; zu meiner —, in my time; auf —, on credit, on account; das hat —, there is plenty of time; mit der — fort= ſchreiten, to keep pace with the times. —ig, adj. early; opportune, season-able. —lich, adj. & adv. temporal. —alter, n. age; generation, era. —begebenheit, f. event of the time. —geiſt, m. spirit of the age. —gemäß, adj. seasonable; opportune. —genoß, —genoſſe, m., —genoſſin, f. contem-porary. —lauf, m. lapse of time, period. —punkt, m. moment. —raum, m. period, time. —ſchrift, f. periodical (publication), magazine. —verderb, m. waste of time. —verluſt, m. loss of time. —vertreib, m. pastime.

Zeitung ['tsaɪtʊŋ], f. (pl. —en) news-paper. —s=weſen, n. journalism.

Zell—e ['tsɛlə], f. (pl. —en) cell (of a nunnery or prison; of bees; Anat., etc.). —ig, adj. cellular.

Zelt [tsɛlt], n. (—(e)s, pl. —e) tent. —lager, n. camp.

Zenti—gramm [tsɛnti'gram], n. (—(e)s, pl. —e) centigramme. —meter, n. (—s, pl. —) centimetre.

Zentner ['tsɛntnər], m. (—s, pl. —) hundredweight, fifty kilogrammes.

Zentral [tsɛn'traːl], adj. central. —e, f. (pl. —n) control-station; chief office.

Zeppelin ['tsɛpəliːn], m. (—s, pl. —e) Zeppelin airship.

Zepter ['tsɛptər], n. & m. (—s, pl. —) sceptre.

Zer— [tsɛr], prefix (before verbs) usually denotes to pieces, away, asunder, etc., also to spoil by. For verbs not given in the following lists see the simple verbs.

Zerbrech—en [tsɛr'brɛçən], ir.v. I. a. & n. (aux. ſ.) to break in pieces; ſich den Kopf —en über, to rack one's brains over. II. a. to put out of joint. —lich, adj. brittle. —lichkeit, f. fragility.

Zerdrüden [tsɛr'drykən], v.a. to crush.

Zerfleiſch—en [tsɛr'flaɪʃən], v.a. to lacerate. —ung, f. laceration.

Zerglieder—er [tsɛr'gliːdərər], m. (—ers, pl. —er) anatomist. —n, v.a. to dissect; to analyse. —ung, f. dissec-tion, anatomy.

Zerhaden [tsɛr'hakən], v.a. to hack, mince.

Zerknirſch—en [tsɛr'knɪrʃən], v.a. to crush, crunch. —t, deeply contrite. —theit, —ung, f. broken-heartedness, contrition.

Zerleg—en [tsɛr'leːgən], v.a. to decom-pose; to dissect; to analyse. —er, m. (—ers, pl. —er) carver. —ung, f. taking to pieces, etc.; analysis.

Zerlumpt [tsɛr'lumpt], adj. ragged, tattered. —heit, f. ragged state.

Zermalm—en [tsɛr'malmən], I. v.a. to bruise, crush. II. subst.n., —ung, f. crushing.

Zerraufen [tsɛr'raufən], v.a. to tear or pull off.

Zerrbild [tsɛrbɪlt], n. (—es, —er) caricature.

Zerreib—en [tsɛr'raɪbən], ir.v.a. to rub away. —ung, f. grinding, tritura-tion.

Zerreiß—en [tsɛr'raɪsən], ir.v.a. to rend; das —t mir das Herz, that breaks my heart. —ung, f. rending.

Zerren ['tsɛrən], v.a. to pull, drag.

Zerrinnen [tsɛr'rɪnən], ir.v.n. (aux. ſ.) to melt.

Zerrütt—en [tsɛr'rytən], v.a. to dis-arrange. —ung, f. disorder.

Zerſchlagen [tsɛr'ʃlaːgən], I. ir.v.a. to batter; to bruise. II. ir.v.r. to break off; to be disappointed.

Zerſchmettern [tsɛr'ʃmɛtərn], v. I. a. to shatter, smash. II. n. (aux. ſ.) to be shattered.

Zerſchneiden [tsɛr'ʃnaɪdən], ir.v.a. to cut in pieces.

Zerſetz—en [tsɛr'zɛtsən], v.a. to decom-pose; to dissolve. —ung, f. decompo-sition.

Zerſpalten [tsɛr'ʃpaltən], v.a. & n. (aux. ſ.) to cleave.

Zerſplittern [tsɛr'ʃplɪtərn], v.a. to

split; to splinter; **feine Kräfte —**, to
have too many irons in the fire.
3erftörbar [tsɛr'ʃtøːrbaːr], *adj.* perishable. **—feit,** *f.* destructibility.
3erftör-en [tsɛr'ʃtøːrən], *v.a.* to
destroy; to disorganize. **—er,** *m.*
(**—ers,** *pl.* **—er**) destroyer, devastator.
—ung, *f.* destruction.
3erftreu-en [tsɛr'ʃtrɔyən], *v.* I. *a.* to
disperse. II. *r.* to break up; to amuse
oneself. **—t,** *p.p. & adj.* dispersed,
scattered; **—t fein,** to be absent-
minded. **—theit,** *f.* preoccupation
(*of mind*). **—ung,** *f.* dispersion;
distraction; diversion.
3erftüd—e(l)n [tsɛr'ʃtykə(l)n], *v.a.* to
cut into little pieces.
3erteil—en [tsɛr'tailən], *v.a.* to divide,
disjoin. **—ung,** *f.* division; dismem-
berment.
3ertrampeln [tsɛr'trampəln], *v.a.* to
trample under foot.
3ertrümmer—er [tsɛr'trymərər], *m.*
(**—ers,** *pl.* **—er**) destroyer. **—n,** *v.a.*
to destroy, shatter. **—ung,** *f.* ruin,
destruction.
¹3ettel ['tsɛtəl], *m.* (**—s,** *pl.* **—**) scrap
of paper; memorandum; ticket; bill.
—anfleber, *m.* bill-sticker.
²3ettel, *m.* (**—s,** *pl.* **—**) chain, warp
(*Weav.*).
3eug [tsɔyk], *n.* (*& dial. m.*)(**—(e)s,** *pl.*
—e) stuff, substance, matter; mate-
rial; implements, tools; apparatus;
albernes *or* **dummes —,** stuff and
nonsense. **—e,** *m.* (**—en,** *pl.* **—en**),
—in, *f.* witness. **—enfchaft,** *f.*
testimony. **—nis,** *n.* (**—(ff)es,** *pl.*
—(ff)e) testimony, evidence; testimonial. **—enbeweis,** *m.* evidence.
—haus, *n.* arsenal, armoury.
¹3eugen ['tsɔygən], *v.n.* to bear witness.
²3eug—en, *v.a.* to engender, beget.
—er, *m.* (**—ers,** *pl.* **—er**), **—erin,** *f.*
begetter, father, mother. **—ung,** *f.*
generation, begetting.
3idzad ['tsɪktsak], *m.* (**—s,** *pl.* **—e**) &
adv. zigzag.
3iege ['tsiːgə], *f.* (*pl.* **—n**) goat. **—n-**
leder, *n.* kid-leather. **—npeter,** *m.*
(**—s**) mumps.
3iegel ['tsiːgəl], *m.* (**—s,** *pl.* **—**) brick;
tile.
3iegler ['tsiːglər], *m.* (**—s,** *pl.* **—**) brickmaker.
3ieh—en ['tsiːən], I. *ir.v.a.* to draw (*a
carriage; the sword; water, etc.*); to

pull (*the bell*); to tow; to move (*at
draughts, etc.*); to obtain, bring; to
rear, nurture; to train; **einen Ver-**
gleich —, to make a comparison;
Nutzen —en, to derive profit; **den**
fürzeren —en, to get the worst of it;
zu Rate —en, to consult. II. *ir.v.r.*
to move, to draw (*towards*); to march
(*towards*); to stretch, extend. III.
ir.v.n. 1. (*aux.* h.) to draw, attract
the public; to swallow. 2. (*aux.* f.)
to advance slowly; to migrate. IV.
subst.n. drawing; pulling; cultivation;
rearing; migration; draught; removal;
attraction. **—er,** *m.* (**—ers,** *pl.* **—er**)
drawer; any instrument used for
drawing; siphon; trigger. **—ung,** *f.*
drawing (*of lots, etc.*). **—brunnen,**
m. draw-well. **—harmonifa,** *f.* accor-
dion. **—fraft,** *f.* power of drawing;
attraction. **—pferd,** *n.* draught-horse.
3iel [tsiːl], *n.* (**—s,** *pl.* **—e**) limit; end;
goal; aim, object. **—en,** *v.n.* (*aux.* h.)
to aim. **—er,** *m.* (**—ers,** *pl.* **—er**) one
who aims. **—bewußt,** *adj.* conscious
of one's aim. **—los,** *adj.* aimless.
—fcheibe, *f.* target.
3iem—en ['tsiːmən], *v.r. & n.* (*aux.* h.,
dat.) to beseem, become, to suit.
—lich, I. *adj.* fit, suitable, becoming;
tolerable; **eine —liche Anzahl,** a fair
number; **—lichfpät,** rather late. II.
adv. tolerably.
3ier [tsiːr], *f.* (*pl.* **—en**), **—at,** *m.* (**—ats,**
pl. **—ate**), **—de,** *f.* (*pl.* **—den**) ornament. **—en,** *v.* I. *a.* to ornament,
adorn. II. *r.* to be affected. **—lich,**
adj. decorative. **—lichfeit,** *f.* grace;
elegance.
3iffer ['tsɪfər], *f.* (*pl.* **—n**) figure,
numeral; cipher. **—n,** *v.a. & n.* (*aux.*
h.) to cipher. **—blatt,** *n.* face, dial-
plate (*of a clock*). **—brief,** *m.* letter
written in cipher. **—funft,** *f.* art of
writing in cipher.
3igarette [tsiga'rɛtə], *f.* (*pl.* **—n**)
cigarette. **—netui,** *n.* cigarette-case.
3igarre [tsi'garə], *f.* (*pl.* **—n**) cigar.
—nfpitze, *f.* cigar-holder. **—n-**
tafche, *f.* cigar-case.
3igeuner [tsi'gɔynər], *m.* (**—s,** *pl.* **—**)
gipsy. **—in,** *f.* female gipsy. **—haft,**
—ifch, *adj.* gipsylike, gipsy.
3imbel ['tsɪmbəl], *f.* (*pl.* **—n**) cymbal
(*Mus.*).
3immer ['tsɪmər], *n.* (**—s,** *pl.* **—**) room.
—antenne, *f.* indoor aerial (*Radio*).

—dede, f. ceiling. —jungfer, f., —mädchen, n. chambermaid, housemaid. —reihe, f. suite of rooms.

zimmer—n ['tsɪmərn], v.a. & n. (aux. h.) to carpenter; to fabricate. —ung, f. carpentering; timber-work. —arbeit, f. carpenter's work; timberwork. —gefell, m. journeyman-carpenter. —holz, n. timber, wood for building. —mann, m. (pl. —leute) carpenter. —meister, m. master-builder.

zimper—lich ['tsɪmpərlɪç], adj. prim, prudish. —lichkeit, f. affectation.

Zimt [tsɪmt], m. (—(e)s) cinnamon. —en, adj. cinnamon.

Zink [tsɪŋk], m. & n. (—(e)s) zinc.

Zinn [tsɪn], n. (—(e)s) tin. —e(r)n, adj. tin, pewter. —erz, n. tin-ore. —geschirr, n. pewter or tin vessel.

Zinne ['tsɪnə], f. (pl. —n) pinnacle.

Zinnober [tsɪ'no:bər], m. (—s) cinnabar.

Zins [tsɪns], m. (—(f)es, pl. —(f)e) rent; (pl. —(f)en) interest. —barkeit, f. liability to rent or tribute. —eszins, m. compound interest. —frei, adj. rent-free. —schein, m. dividend-warrant.

Zipfel ['tsɪpfəl], m. (—s, pl. —) tip, point.

Zirkel ['tsɪrkəl], m. (—s, pl. —) circle (Geom.). —bogen, m. arc.

Zirpe ['tsɪrpə], f. (pl. —n) cricket; grasshopper. —n, v.n. (aux. h.) to chirp.

Zisch [tsɪʃ], m. (—es, pl. —e) hiss, whiz. —elei [—ə'laɪ], f. whispering. —eln, v.a. & n. (aux. h.) to whisper.

Zit—at [tsi'ta:t], n. (—at(e)s, pl. —ate) quotation. —ieren [—'ti:rən] to summon; to quote.

Zither ['tsɪtər], f. (pl. —n) zither.

Zitrone [tsi'tro:nə], f. (—n) lemon. —nwasser, n. lemonade.

Zittern ['tsɪtərn], v.n. (aux. h.) to tremble.

zivil [tsi'vi:l], I. adj. civil; moderate. II. n. civilians. —anzug, m. plain clothes, mufti. —isation [—zatsi'o:n], f. civilization. —isieren [—'zi:rən], v.a. to civilize, refine. —ist [—'lɪst], m. (—iften, pl. —iften) civilian. —ehe, f. civil marriage. —stand, m. citizenship.

Zobel ['tso:bəl], m. (—s, pl. —) sable.

Zofe ['tso:fə], f. (pl. —n) lady's maid.

Zög—ern ['tsø:gərn], v.n. (aux. h.) to linger, loiter; to hesitate. —ernd, p. & adj. hesitating; slow. —erung, f. delay; hesitation.

Zögling ['tsø:klɪŋ], m. (—s, pl. —e) pupil.

¹Zoll [tsɔl], m. (—(e)s, pl. —, —e) inch.

²Zoll, m.(—(e)s, pl. Zölle) toll, custom. —bar, adj. liable to duty. —barkeit, f. liability to duty. —amt, n. custom-house. —beamte(r), m. (—beamten, pl. —beamte(n)) custom-house officer. —frei, adj. free of duty. —pflichtig, adj. liable to duty. —schein, m. customs receipt. —verein, m. customs union.

Zöllner ['tsɔlnər], m. (—s, pl. —) publican (B.).

Zone ['tso:nə], f. (pl. —n) zone.

Zoo—log [tsoo'lo:k], m. (—logen, pl. —logen) zoologist. —logisch, adj. zoological.

Zopf [tsɔpf], m.(—(e)s, pl. Zöpfe) tress; pigtail. —mensch, m. pedant. —zeit, f. age of pigtails; Georgian era.

Zorn [tsɔrn], m. (—(e)s) anger. —ig, adj. angry. —anfall, —ausbruch, m. fit of anger, passion. —(es)=blick, m. angry look or glance. —entbrannt, —glühend, adj. furious.

Zote ['tso:tə], f. (—n) obscenity; indecent expression.

Zott—e ['tsotə], f. (pl. —en) lock, tuft. —elig, adj. in tufts. —el=bär, m. shaggy bear.

zu [tsu:], I. prep. (with dat.) to, unto; in addition to, along with; at; in; at the rate of; on; by; for, in order to; for; —m Beispiel (z. B.), for instance ; — Hause, at home ; — Fuß, on foot; —Wasser werden, to come to nothing, to be frustrated; Tür —! shut the door! nur immer —! go on! II. adv. & sep. prefix, to; towards; together; closed; (preceding an adj. or adv.) too; overmuch.

zubehalten ['tsu:bəhaltən], ir.v.a. to keep shut or closed.

Zubehör ['tsu:bəhø:r], n. (m.) (—s) belongings; appurtenances.

zubereit—en ['tsu:bəraɪtən], v.a. to prepare; to adjust. —er, m. (—ers, pl. —er) preparer, dresser. —ung, f. preparation.

zubinden ['tsu:bɪndən], ir.v.a. to bind or tie up.

zubringen ['tsu:brɪŋən], ir.v.a. to bring, carry to; to pass, spend.

Zucht [tsʊxt], f. (pl. —en) breeding, rearing (of cattle, etc.); breed; race; young stock; education; discipline; chastisement, correction; propriety; modesty. —haus, n. house of correction. —haus=strafe, f. penal servitude. —los, adj. insubordinate; undisciplined. —losigkeit, f. disorderly ways. —meister, m. taskmaster.

Zücht=en ['tsʏçtən], v.a. to breed. —er, m. (—ers, pl. —er) breeder, cultivator. —ig, adj. modest; proper, discreet. —igen, v.a. to chastise. —iger, m. (—igers, pl. —iger) chastiser. —igkeit, f. modesty; propriety. —igung, f. chastisement, correction. —ung, f. breeding.

Zuck [tsʊk], m. (—(e)s, pl. —e) twitch; start. —en, v.n. (aux. h.) to jerk, to start; die Achseln —en, to shrug one's shoulders. —end, p. & adj. jerky; convulsive. —ung, f. jerk.

Zücken ['tsʏkən], v.a. to draw quickly.

Zucker ['tsʊkər], m. (—s) sugar. —ig, Zuckrig, adj. sugar. —n, f. v.a. to sugar, sweeten. II. adj. of sugar. —bäder, m. confectioner. —bäderei [—ə'raɪ], f. confectioner's shop. —büchse, —dose, f. sugar-basin. —dicksaft, m. molasses. —erbse, f. edible sweet pea. —guß, m. sugaricing. —krank, adj. diabetic. —rohr, n. sugar-cane. —rübe, f. beetroot.

Zudecken ['tsu:dɛkən], v.a. to cover up.

Zudem [tsu'de:m], adv. besides, moreover, in addition.

Zudenken ['tsu:dɛŋkən], ir.v.a. to destine, intend for.

Zudrang ['tsu:draŋ], m. (—(e)s) crowd, throng pressing towards.

Zudrängen ['tsu:drɛŋən], v.r. to throng or crowd to.

Zudrehen ['tsu:dre:ən], v.a. to turn off (by a cock, etc.); jemandem den Rücken —, to turn one's back on a person.

Zudringlich ['tsu:drɪŋlɪç], adj. & adv. importunate, obtrusive. —keit, f. importunity.

Zueign=en ['tsu:ʔaɪɡnən], v.a. (einem etwas) to attribute, ascribe; to dedicate (a book). —ung, f. dedication.

Zuerkenn=en ['tsu:ʔɛrkɛnən], ir.v.a. to adjudge, award; to acknowledge. —ung, f. award.

Zuerst [tsu'ʔe:rst], adv. firstly, in the first place, at first; first of all; above all, especially; foremost.

Zufahren ['tsu:fa:rən], ir.v.n. (aux. h. & f.) to drive or sail on; to drive fast; to approach.

Zufall ['tsu:fal], m. (—(e)s, pl. Zufälle) chance.

Zufallen ['tsu:falən], ir.v.n. (aux. f.) to fall towards; to fall to one's lot, devolve on.

Zufällig ['tsu:fɛlɪç], adj. & adv. accidental, fortuitous. —keit, f. chance; accident, incident.

Zuflucht ['tsu:flʊxt], f. refuge, shelter; recourse; zu etwas seine — nehmen, to have recourse to. —s=ort, m., —s=stätte, f. place of refuge.

Zufluß ['tsu:flʊs], m. (Zuflusses, pl. Zuflüsse) flowing in; concourse (of people); die Zuflüsse des Rheins, the tributaries of the Rhine; Abfluß und — des Meeres, ebb and flow of the tide; — von Waren, supply of goods.

Zufolge [tsu'fɔlɡə], prep. (with dat. when following, with gen. when preceding the case governed) in consequence of; according to.

Zufrieden [tsu'fri:dən], adj. content, pleased, satisfied. —heit, f. contentment, satisfaction.

Zufuhr ['tsu:fu:r], f. (pl. —en) conveying; conveyance; import.

Zuführ=en ['tsu:fy:rən], v.a. to conduct, lead, bring to; to convey, transport; to import. —er, m. (—ers, pl. —er) one that brings or conveys; procurer. —ung, f. conveyance; importation; supplying.

Zug [tsu:k], m. (—es, pl. Züge) drawing, pulling; pull; march; progress; expedition; current (of water); draught, strong current (of air); train, retinue, procession; troop; railway-train; line; touch; feature, lineament; move (at chess, etc.); bias; impulse; characteristic; draught (in drinking). —ig, adj. draughty. —brücke, f. drawbridge. —brunnen, m. draw-well. —kraft, f. force of attraction. —kräftig, adj. in vogue, attractive. —leine, f. towing-rope. —pferd, n. draught-horse. —vogel, m. bird of passage.

Zugabe ['tsu:ga:bə], f. (pl. —n) overweight; supplement.

Zugang ['tsu:gaŋ], m. access; approach.

Zugänglich ['tsu:gɛnlɪç], adj. accessible, approachable. —keit, f. accessibility; affability.

Zugeben ['tsu:ge:bən], *ir.v.a.* to add; to grant, concede, admit.

Zugegen [tsu'ge:gən], *indec. adv.* present.

Zugehen ['tsu:ge:ən], *ir.v.n. (aux. ſ.)* to close; to move towards; to go on faster; to take place, happen; — laſſen, to forward.

Zugehörig ['tsu:gəhø:rɪç], *adj.* appertaining, belonging to.

Zügel ['tsy:gəl], *m.* (—s, *pl.* —) rein, reins; bridle. —n, *v.a.* to bridle, curb, check. —los, *adj.* unbridled; unrestrained.

Zugeſtändnis ['tsu:gəʃtɛntnɪs], *n.* (—(ſſ)es, *pl.* —(ſſ)e) admission.

Zugetan ['tsu:gəta:n], *p.p.* & *adj.* fond of.

Zugleich [tsu'glaɪç], *adv.* at the same time, together, along (with).

Zugreifen ['tsu:graɪfən], *ir.v.n.* (*aux. ħ.*) to lay hold of; to bear a hand; to help oneself at table.

Zugrunde— [tsu'grundə] (*in comp.*) —gehen, *n.* destruction, ruin, loss. —richten, *n.* destruction, demolition.

Zuhalten ['tsu:haltən], *ir.v.a.* to keep shut.

Zuhanden [tsu'handən], *adv.* close at hand, ready.

Zuhöre—n ['tsu:hø:rən], *v.n. (aux. ħ., dat.)* to listen (to). —r, *m.* (—rs, *pl.* —r) listener. rſchaft, *f.* audience.

Zuknöpfen ['tsu:knœpfən], *v.a.* to button up.

Zukommen [tsu:kɔmən], *ir.v.n. (aux. ſ.)* to approach, arrive; to come to hand; to belong to (einem, a person).

Zukunft ['tsu:kunft], *f.* future.

Zukünftig ['tsu:kynftɪç], I. *adj.* future. II. *adv.* in future, for the future.

Zulage ['tsu:la:gə], *f.* (*pl.* —n) addition; extra pay; allowance.

Zulangen ['tsu:laŋən], *v.* I. *a.*; einem etwas —, to reach, hand something to a person. II. *n. (aux. ħ.)* to stretch out for; to suffice, be sufficient; to reach.

Zulänglich ['tsu:lɛŋlɪç], *adj.* sufficient. —keit, *f.* sufficiency.

Zulaß ['tsu:las], *m.* (—(ſſ)es, *pl.* Zuläſſe) admission; permission. —(ſſ)en, I. *ir.v.a.* to leave closed; to grant, permit. II. *subst.n.*, —(ſſ)ung, *f.* admission; permission, concession.

Zuläſſig ['tsu:lɛsɪç], *adj.* admissible, permissible. —keit, *f.* admissibility.

Zulauf 'tsu:lauf], *m.* crowd, influx,

throng; — haben, to be much run after.

Zuletzt [tsu'lɛtst], *adv.* finally.

Zumachen ['tsu:maxən], *v.* I. *a.* to close. II. *n. (aux. ħ.)* to make haste; mach zu! be quick!

Zumeiſt [tsu'maɪst], *adv.* mostly, for the most part.

Zumeſſen ['tsu:mɛsən], *ir.v.a.* to measure; to ascribe, impute to; to assign.

Zumut—en ['tsu:mu:tən], *v.a.* to demand, exact, require. —ung, *f.* demand, expectation; imputation; presumption.

Zunächſt [tsu'nɛ:çst], I. *adv.* next; first of all, chiefly. II. *prep. (with dat. or gen.)* next to.

Zunahme ['tsu:na:mə], *f.* (*pl.* —n) increase; progress.

Zuname(n) ['tsu:na:mə(n)], *m.* (—ns, *pl.* —n) surname, family name.

Zündbar ['tsyntba:r], *adj.* inflammable. —keit, *f.* inflammability.

Zünd—en ['tsyndən], *v.* I. *n. (aux. ħ.)* to take fire; to kindle, ignite. II. *a.* to kindle; to inflame, stir up. —end, *adj.* inflammable; rousing. —holz, —hölzchen, *n.* match. —ſtoff, *m.* inflammable matter.

Zunder ['tsundər], *m.* (—s, *pl.* —) tinder. —büchſe, *f.* tinder-box. —holz, *n.* touchwood.

Zunehmen ['tsu:ne:mən], I. *ir.v.a.* to take in addition, take more; to increase (*the number of stitches in knitting*). II. *ir.v.n. (aux. ħ.)* to increase, augment, grow larger.

Zuneig—en ['tsu:naɪgən], *v.a.* & *n.* to lean, incline towards. —ung, *f.* affection, attachment; partiality.

Zunft [tsunft], *f.* (*pl.* Zünfte) body, company, society; guild, corporation. —genoſſe, *m.* member of a guild or corporation. —meiſter, *m.* master of a guild.

Zung—e ['tsuŋə], *f.* (*pl.* —en) tongue, language; es lag mir auf der —e, I had it on the tip of my tongue; eine feine —e haben, to have a delicate palate. —en=fehler, *m.* lapsus linguæ. —en=fertig, *adj.* voluble. —en=fertigkeit, *f.* volubility. —en=ſpitze, *f.* tip of the tongue.

Zunichte [tsu'nɪçtə], *adv.* ruined destroyed.

Zuniden ['tsu:nɪkən], *v.a.* & *n.* (*aux ħ.*) (einem) to nod (*to a person*).

Zuordn—en ['tsu:ʔɔrdnən], *v.a.* to adjoin, associate with. **—ung,** *f.* coordination.

Zupfen ['tsʊpfən], *v.a.* to pull, tug.

Zuraten ['tsu:ra:tən], *ir.v.a. & n.* to advise, counsel.

Zurechn—en ['tsu:rɛçnən], *v.a.* to add (*in an account*); to ascribe, attribute to. **—ung,** *f.* imputation. **—ungs= fähig,** *adj.* accountable, responsible (*for one's actions*), of sound mind.

Zurecht [tsu'rɛçt], *adv. & sep. prefix,* in order; to rights; in the right place; as it ought to be. **—helfen,** *ir.v.n.* (einem) to come to a person's help. **—weisen,** *ir.v.a.* to set someone right; to rebuke, reprimand. **—weisung,** *f.* guidance, instruction; reprimand.

Zureden ['tsu:re:dən], I. *v.n.* (aux. h.) (einem) to exhort. II. *subst.n.* persuasion; entreaties.

Zureichen ['tsu:raiçən], *v.* I. *n.* (aux. h.) to suffice. II. *a.* (einem etwas) to reach, hand (something) over to (a person).

Zuricht—en ['tsu:rɪçtən], *v.a.* to turn towards; to prepare, make ready; **übel —en,** to use badly. **—er,** *m.* (—ers, *pl.* **—er**) one who prepares. **—ung,** *f.* preparation.

Zürnen ['tsʏrnən], *v.n.* (aux. h.) über or um eine S., wegen einer Sache —, to be irritated, angry at something; (mit) einem, auf einen —, to be angry with a person.

Zurück [tsu'rʏk], *adv. & sep. prefix,* back, backward(s), behindhand, in the rear, in arrears. **—behalten,** *ir.v.a.* to keep back, detain. **—bekommen,** *ir.v.a.* to get back; to recover. **— bleiben,** *ir.v.n.* (aux. ſ.) to remain behind. **—bliden,** *v.* I. *n.* (aux. h.) to look back. II. *a.* to recall, review (*the past, etc.*); **— blidend,** retrospective. **—fahrt,** *f.* return, return-journey. **—fallen,** I. *ir.v.n.* (aux. ſ.) to fall back; to be reflected; to relapse. II. *subst.n.* relapse; reversion. **—fordern,** *v.a.* to demand back; to reclaim. **— forderung,** *f.* reclamation. **—führung,** *f.* leading back; reduction (*Arith.*). **—gabe,** *f.* returning, giving back; restoration. **—geben,** *ir.v.a.* to return, restore. **—gehen,** *ir.v.n.* (aux. ſ.) to return; to go back, retrograde. **— gezogen,** *adj. & adv.* retired, secluded. **—halten,** I. *ir.v.a.* to hold back, to detain, delay; to curb, hold in; to suppress (*cries, etc.*). II. *ir.v.n.* (aux. h.); mit einer S. **—halten,** to keep back, to conceal, reserve. III. *subst.n.* repression; reserve. **—haltend,** *p. & adj.* reserved, cautious. **—haltung,** *f.* retention; detention; reserve; cautiousness. **—legen,** *v.a.* to place behind; to lay by (*money*); to travel, go over. **—müssen,** *ir.v.n.* (aux. h.) to be obliged to return. **—nahme,** *f.* the taking back, resumption; recantation; revocation. **—nehmen,** *ir.v.a.* to take back; to recall, retract; to revoke. **—rufen,** I. *ir.v.a.* to call back; to recall. II. *subst.n.,* **—rufung,** *f.* recall. **—schlagen,** *ir.v.* I. *a.* to strike, drive back; to repel, repulse. II. *n.* (aux. ſ.) to fall violently backward. **—= sehnen,** *v.r.;* er sehnt sich —, he wishes himself back, he longs to return. **—sein,** *ir.v.n.* to be behind; to be back, to have come back; to be behindhand. **—setzen,** *v.a.* to set, place back *or* behind; to replace; to neglect, slight; to degrade (*in office*); to reduce (*in circumstances*). **—stoßen,** *ir.v.a.* to repel, repulse; to retort. **—stoßend,** *p. & adj.* repulsive, repellent. **— stoßung,** *f.* pushing back, *etc.*; repulsion (*Phys., etc.*). **—strahlen,** *ir.v.* I. *n.* (aux. ſ.) to be reflected, shine back. II. *a.* to cause to reflect *or* reverberate. **—treten,** *ir.v.n.* (aux. ſ.) to step back; to recede; to subside. **—weichen,** I. *ir.v.n.* (aux. ſ.) to give way, retreat. II. *subst.n.* recoil (*of a gun*); retreat; ebb (*of the sea*). **—weisen,** *ir.v.a.* to send (*a person*) back; to refuse; to repulse. **—ziehen,** *ir.v.* I. *a.* to withdraw; to retract, recant. II. *n.* (aux. ſ.) to return, retire to; to retreat. **—ziehung,** *f.* retreat (*Mil.*).

Zuruf ['tsu:ru:f], *m.* (—(e)s, *pl.* **—e**) shout; cheer. **—en,** *ir.v.a. & n.;* einem etwas **—en,** to call something to a person; einem Beifall **—en,** to cheer, applaud a person.

Zurüst—en ['tsu:rʏstən], *v.a.* to fit out, equip. **—ung,** *f.* equipment; preparation.

Zusage ['tsu:za:gə], *f.* (*pl.* **—n**) promise, pledge; assent. **—n,** *v.* I. *a.* (einem etwas) to promise. II. *n.* (aux. h.) to meet, suit a person's wishes; die Speise sagt mir nicht zu, the food doesn't agree with me.

Zusammen [tsu'zamən], *adv. & sep.*

prefix, together, all together. —**arbeiten**, *v.* I. *a.* to work together. II. *n.* (*aux.* ↄ.) to work together, to co-operate. —**beſtehen**, *ir.v.n.* (*aux.* ↄ.) to be consistent. —**brechen**, *ir.v.n.* (*aux.* ſ.) to break (*in pieces*); to break down. —**bringen**, *ir.v.a.* to bring together; to collect. —**drücken**, *v.a.* to compress. —**fahren**, *ir.v.n.* (*aux.* ſ.) to drive, travel together; to come into collision; to shrink up. —**faſſen**, *v.a.* to grasp, seize; **kurz —faſſen**, to sum up, to abridge. —**finden**, *ir.v.r.* to meet (*together*). —**fluß**, *m.* confluence. —**fügen**, *v.a.* to join together. —**gehören**, *v.n.* (*aux.* ↄ.) to belong to one another; to match. —**gehörig**, *adj.* belonging to one another; homogeneous. —**geſetzt**, *p.p. & adj.* compound, complex. —**halt**, *m.* holding together; cohesion; union. —**halten**, *ir.v.* I. *a.* to compare. II. *n.* (*aux.* ↄ.) to hold together; to cohere. —**hang**, *m.* coherence, connection. —**hangen**, *ir.v.n.* (*aux.* ↄ.) to be connected. —**klang**, *m.* accord, consonance. —**kunft**, *f.* meeting; assembly, convention. —**laufen**, *ir.v.n.* (*aux.* ↄ.) to run together; to converge. —**laut**, *m.* consonance, harmony. —**nehmen**, *ir.v.a.* to take together; **ſich —nehmen**, to summon up all one's strength, pluck up courage. —**paſſen**, *v.* I. *n.* (*aux.* ↄ.) to suit together; to match; to agree. II. *a.* to adjust, match. —**raffen**, *v.* I. *a.* to snatch up. II. *r.* to collect *or* rouse oneself. —**ſchlagen**, *ir.v.* I. *n.* (*aux.* ſ.) to close with a bang *or* crash. II. *a.* to strike together. —**ſetzen**, I. *v.a.* to put together. II. *subst.n.*, —**ſetzung**, *f.* composition; combination; construction. —**ſetzer**, *m.* one who makes up, compounder; fitter. —**ſinken**, *ir.v.n.* (*aux.* ſ.) to sink down; to sink into ruin. —**ſtellen**, *v.a.* to place together; to compare. —**ſtimmen**, *v.n.* (*aux.* ↄ.) to accord, harmonize. —**ſtoß**, *m.* shock; collision (*on a railway*). —**treffen**, I. *ir.v.n.* (*aux.* ſ.) to meet, encounter; to coincide. II. *subst.n.* meeting, encounter; coincidence. —**wirken**, I. *v.n.* (*aux.* ↄ.) to act, work together; to co-operate; —**wirkend**, co-operation. —**ziehen**, *ir.v.* I. *a.* to draw together; to tighten. II. *r.* to collect; to contract; to gather.

Zuſatz ['tsu:zats], *m.* (—**es**, *pl.* **Zuſätze**) addition; appendix.

Zuſchaue—**n** ['tsu:ʃaʊən], *v.n.* (*aux.* ↄ., *dat.*) to look on at. —**r**, *m.* (—**rs**, *pl.* —**r**), —**rin**, *f.* spectator. —**rſchaft**, *f.* spectators; the public.

Zuſchicken ['tsu:ʃɪkən], *v.a.* (**einem etwas**) to send to, transmit to.

Zuſchlag ['tsu:ʃla:k], *m.* (—**es**, *pl.* **Zuſchläge**) the knocking down to a bidder (*at auctions*); extra charge.

Zuſchlag—**en** ['tsu:ʃla:gən], I. *ir.v.a.* to slam; to nail up *or* down; to knock down to (*a bidder*); to close; to strike a bargain. II. *ir.v.n.* (*aux.* ↄ.) to strike, hit hard; to agree with. III. *subst.n.*, —**ung**, *f.* striking towards, *etc.*; blows.

Zuſchließen ['tsu:ʃli:sən], *ir.v.a.* to lock up, shut up, close.

Zuſchneide—**n** ['tsu:ʃnaɪdən], *ir.v.a.* to cut up; to cut out (*a dress, etc.*). —**r**, *m.* (—**rs**, *pl.* —**r**), —**rin**, *f.* cutter-out.

Zuſchnitt ['tsu:ʃnɪt], *m.* (—**es**, *pl.* —**e**) cut (*of a dress, etc.*); style.

Zuſchnüren ['tsu:ʃny:rən], *v.a.* to lace up; **einem die Kehle —**, to strangle a person.

Zuſchreiben ['tsu:ʃraɪbən], *ir.v.a.* to write; to dedicate; to assign, attribute, impute to; **einem eine Summe —**, to place money to a person's credit.

Zuſchrift ['tsu:ʃrɪft], *f.* (*pl.* —**en**) letter; address. —**lich**, *adv.* by letter.

Zuſchuß ['tsu:ʃus], *m.* (—(**ſ**)**es**, *pl.* **Zuſchüſſe**) contribution, additional supply; subsidy.

Zuſehen ['tsu:ze:ən], I. *ir.v.n.* (*aux.* ↄ.) to look on at, watch; to witness; to oversee; to wait, delay; to connive *or* wink at; to take heed. II. *subst.n.* view, looking on. —**d(s)**, *adv.* visibly.

Zuſprechen ['tsu:ʃpreçən], *ir.v.* I. *a.* (**einem etwas**) to impart by speaking; to award, adjudge. II. *n.* (*aux.* ↄ.) (*dat.*) to address, accost; to exhort, encourage; to suit, agree with.

Zuſpruch ['tsu:ʃprux], *m.* (—**es**, *pl.* **Zuſprüche**) exhortation; encouragement.

Zuſtand ['tsu:ʃtant], *m.* (—**es**, *pl.* **Zuſtände**) condition.

Zuſtande— [tsu'ʃtandə], *in cmpds. see* **Stand**. —**bringen**, *n.* bringing about, accomplishment. —**kommen**, *n.* taking place.

Zuſtänd—ig ['tsu:ʃtɛndɪç], *adj.* belonging to, appertaining; duly qualified. **—igkeit**, *f.* competence. **—lich**, *adj.* neuter, not active.

Zuſtehen ['tsu:ʃteːən], *ir.v.n. (aux. h.)* (einem) to belong to; to be incumbent upon; to become, suit.

¹**Zuſteuern** ['tsu:ʃtɔʏərn], *v.a.* to contribute.

²**Zuſteuern**, *v.n. (aux. ſ.);* auf eine Sache —, to steer or make for a thing.

Zuſtimm—en ['tsu:ʃtɪmən], *v.n. (aux. h.)* to assent. **—ung**, *f.* assent.

Zuſtopfen ['tsu:ʃtɔpfən], *v.a.* to stop up.

Zuſtreben ['tsu:ʃtreːbən], *v.n. (aux. h.);* (einem Ziele) —, to strive for.

Zuteilen ['tsu:taɪlən], *v.a.* (einem etwas) to assign, allot.

Zuträg—er ['tsu:trɛːgər], *m.* (**—ers**, *pl.* **-er**), **—erin**, *f.* reporter; informer. **—lich**, *adj.* productive (of); beneficial. **—lichkeit**, *f.* advantageousness.

Zutrau—en ['tsu:traʊən], *v.a.;* einem etwas **—en**, to give a person credit for, expect from someone; einem **—en**, to trust, confide in. **—lich**, *adj.* & *adv.* confiding; familiar. **—lichkeit**, *f.* trust, confidence.

Zutreffen ['tsu:trɛfən], *ir.v.n. (aux. h.)* to fit, tally, agree with; to happen, take place. **—d**, *p.p.* & *adj.* apt, just, to the point.

Zutritt ['tsu:trɪt], *m.* (**—(e)s**, *pl.* **—e**) access; admission.

Zutulich ['tsu:tu:lɪç], *adj.* obliging. **—keit**, *f.* complaisance.

Zutun ['tsu:tu:n], *ir.v.a.* I. to add to; to close, shut. II. *subst.n.* assistance, co-operation.

Zuverläſſig ['tsu:fɛrlɛsɪç], *adj.* reliable. **—keit**, *f.* reliability; trustworthiness.

Zuverſicht ['tsu:fɛrzɪçt], *f.* confidence (auf eine S., in a thing). **—lich**, *adj.* confident. **—lichkeit**, *f.* trust.

Zuviel [tsu'fi:l], *adv.* = zu viel.

Zuvor [tsu'fo:r], *adv.* before, previously; once; beforehand; formerly. **—kommen**, *ir.v.n. (aux. ſ.)* to get in front of (a person); to take the lead. **—kommend**, *p.* & *adj.* anticipatory; obliging; civil. **—kommenheit**, *f.* obligingness; civility.

Zuvorderſt [tsu'fɔrdərst], *adv.* in the front rank, foremost.

Zuwachs ['tsu:vaks], *m.* (**—(ſ)es**) growth; increase.

Zuwachſen ['tsu:vaksən], *ir.v.n. (aux. h.)* to accrue (einem, to someone).

Zuwandern ['tsu:vandərn], *v.n. (aux. ſ.)* to wander or migrate towards.

Zuwege [tsu'veːgə], *adv.;* — bringen, to bring about.

Zuweilen [tsu'vaɪlən], *adv.* sometimes, at times.

Zuweiſen ['tsu:vaɪzən], *ir.v.a.;* (einem etwas) to assign or allot (something to someone).

Zuwider [tsu'viːdər], *adv.* & *prep.* (with dat.) contrary to, against; offensive; — ſein, to displease.

Zuwinken ['tsu:vɪŋkən], *v.n. (aux. h.);* einem —, to make signs to a person.

Zuzieh—en ['tsu:tsiːən], *ir.v.* I. *a.* to draw together, draw tight; to tie; to drag towards or to, to admit, to invite, call in; to cause; to incur. II. *n. (aux. ſ.)* to move towards; (aux. h.) to pull on; ſich eine Krankheit **—en**, to catch a disease. **—ung**, *f.* drawing together; tying; incurring; aid, assistance.

Zwacken ['tsvakən], *v.a.* to pinch; to tease.

Zwang [tsvaŋ], *m.* (**—(e)s**) coercion; constraint; restraint. **—los**, *adj.* unconstrained, free. **—loſigkeit**, *f.* freedom, unconstraint; ease. **—sanleihe**, *f.* forced loan. **—sarbeit**, *f.* compulsory labour. **—smaßregel**, *f.* coercive measure. **—smittel**, *n.* violent means. **—sweiſe**, *adv.* compulsory.

Zwanzig ['tsvantsɪç], I. *num. adj.* twenty. II. *f.* (*pl.* **—en**) (number) twenty. **—ſt**, *num. adj.* (der, die, das **—ſte**) twentieth.

Zwar [tsva:r], *adv.* indeed, truly, certainly; of course.

Zweck [tsvɛk], *m.* (**—(e)s**, *pl.* **—e**) aim, end, object. **—entſprechend**, *adj.* answering its purpose. **—los**, I. *adj.* aimless, objectless; purposeless, useless. II. *adv.* to no purpose, at random. **—loſigkeit**, *f.* aimlessness; uselessness. **—mäßig**, *adj.* practical; useful; fit. **—mäßigkeit**, *f.* appropriateness; fitness. **—widrig**, *adj.* inappropriate.

Zwei [tsvaɪ], I. *num. adj.* (gen. **—er**, when no subst. follows or before a subst. not preceded by an art. or adj. showing the case; dat. **—en**, when no subst. follows) two. II. *f.* (*pl.* **—en**) two. III. *n.* pair, couple. **—heit**, *f.*

duality, dualism. **—deutig,** *adj.* & *adv.* ambiguous. **—deutigfeit,** *f.* ambiguity. **—erlei** [—ər'laɪ], *indec. adj.* of two kinds; twofold. **—fach,** *adj.* double. **—fältig,** *adj.* twofold. **—füßig,** *adj.* with two feet, biped. **—füß(l)er,** *m.* biped. **—gejang,** *m.* duet. **—gejpann,** *n.* carriage with two horses. **—hufer,** *m.* cloven-footed animal. **—hufig,** *adv.* cloven-footed. **—fampf,** *m.* duel. **—mal,** *adv.* twice. **—malig,** *adj.* done *or* repeated twice. **—rad,** *n.* bicycle; **—rad für Wett-fahrten,** racer. **—räderig,** *adj.* two-wheeled.

Zweifel ['tsvaɪfəl], *m.* (**—s,** *pl.* **—**) doubt. **—haft,** *adj.* undecided, irresolute; questionable; suspicious. **—los,** *adj.* certain. **—mut,** *m.* irresolution; uncertainty. **—mütig,** *adj.* irresolute, wavering. **—s-ohne,** *adv.* doubtless, without doubt.

Zweifeln ['tsvaɪfəln], *v.n.* (*aux.* h.) to doubt, to suspect.

Zweifler ['tsvaɪflər], *m.* (**—s,** *pl.* **—**) doubter, sceptic.

Zweig [tsvark], *m.* (**—(e)s,** *pl.* **—e**) branch, bough. **—lein,** *n.* (**—leins,** *pl.* **—lein**) sprig, little twig. **—bahn,** *f.* branch line (*Railw.*).

Zweit [tsvaɪt], *num. adj.* (**der, die, das —e**) second; next. **—el,** *n.* (**—els,** *pl.* **—el**) second part, half. **—ens** (**zum —en**), *adv.* secondly, in the second place.

Zwerch [tsvɛrç], *adj.* athwart, across. **—fell,** *n.* diaphragm, midriff.

Zwerg [tsvɛrk], *m.* (**—(e)s,** *pl.* **—e**), **—in,** *f.* dwarf. **—haftigfeit,** **—heit,** *f.* dwarfishness. **—artig,** *adj.* dwarfish.

Zwid—en ['tsvɪkən], *v.a.* to pinch. **—er,** *m.* (**—ers,** *pl.* **—er**) one that pinches; eye-glasses, pince-nez. **—s-zange,** *f.* pincers, tweezers.

Zwie [tsvi:] (*in compds.=*) twice, double. **—bad,** *m.* rusk; biscuit. **—fach,** *adj.* twofold, double. **—fältig,** *adj.* twofold, double. **—gejpräch,** *n.* dialogue, private talk. **—laut,** *m.* diphthong. **—licht,** *n.* twilight. **—fpalt,** *m.* disunion, dissension; schism. **—fpaltig,** **—fpältig,** *adj.* divided. **—tracht,** *f.* discord, dissension. **—trächtig,** *adj.* discordant, at variance. **—trachts-stifter,** *m.* maker of mischief.

Zwiebel ['tsvi:bəl], *f.* (*pl.* **—n**) onion; bulb.

Zwil—lich ['tsvɪlɪç], *m.* (**—lichs,** *pl.* **—liche**), **—ch,** *m.* (**—ches,** *pl.* **—che**) ticking.

Zwilling ['tsvɪlɪŋ], *m.* (**—s,** *pl.* **—e**) (**—s-fnabe,** *m.,* **—s-mädchen,** *n.*) twin (boy or girl).

Zwing—en ['tsvɪŋən], *ir.v.a.* to constrain, compel; to master. **—end,** *p.* & *adj.* forcing; compulsory. **—er,** *m.* (**—ers,** *pl.* **—er**) one who forces *or* constrains; cage; kennel; dungeon, tower. **—burg,** *f.* citadel, fortress. **—herr,** *m.* despot, tyrant. **—herr-schaft,** *f.* despotism, tyranny.

Zwinte(r)n ['tsvɪŋkə(r)n], *v.n.* (*aux.* h.) to wink; to blink.

Zwirbeln ['tsvɪrbəln], *v.a.* to twirl.

Zwirn [tsvɪrn], *m.* (**—(e)s,** *pl.* **—e**) (*linen*) thread; twine. **—en,** I. *adj.* of thread. II. *v.a.* to twist (*wool or cotton*).

Zwischen ['tsvɪʃən], *prep.* (*with dat.* in answer to **wo?** where? *with acc.* in answer to **wohin?** whither, where to?) between, betwixt; among, amongst. **—ded,** *n.* between-decks, steerage. **—fall,** *m.* incident, episode. **—fre-quenz,** *f.* intermediate frequency (*Radio*). **—handel,** *m.* commission business. **—'her,** *adv.* in the interval, in the meantime, meanwhile. **—'hin,** *adv.* right into the *or* their midst. **—funft,** *f.* intervention. **—liegend,** *adj.* intermediate. **—pajjagier,** *m.* steerage passenger. **—raum,** *m.* intermediate space; interval. **—rede,** *f.* interruption; digression. **—redner,** *m.* interlocutor. **—regierung,** *f.* interregnum. **—steder,** *m.* adapter plug (*Radio*). **—ftüd,** *n.* interlude (*Theat.*). **—zustand,** *m.* intermediate state.

Zwift [tsvɪst], *m.* (**—es,** *pl.* **—e**) dissension. **—ig,** *adj.* discordant, disagreeing; in dispute. **—igfeit,** *f.* dissension, quarrel.

Zwitschern ['tsvɪʃərn], *v.a.* & *n.* (*aux.* h.) to twitter.

Zwitter ['tsvɪtər], *m.* (**—s,** *pl.* **—**) mongrel. **—haft,** **—ig,** *adj.* hybrid; mongrel.

Zwölf [tsvœlf], *num. adj.* (*nom.* & *acc.* **—e**) twelve. **—t,** *num. adj.* (**der, die, das —e**) twelfth.

Zyflon [tsy'klo:n], *m.* (**—s,** *pl.* **—e**) cyclone. **—e,** *f.* depression (*weather*).

Zylinder [tsi'lɪndər], *m.* (**—s,** *pl.* **—**) cylinder; lamp-chimney; (*coll.*) top-hat.

Zypreſſe [tsy'prɛsə], *f.* (*pl.* **—n**) cypress.

INDEX OF NAMES.

GEOGRAPHICAL AND PROPER NAMES.

In the subjoined list of Geographical and Proper Names the following classes of words have, as a rule, been *omitted*:—

1. Those in which the German and English forms correspond exactly; *e.g.* **Alfred**, Alfred; **Richard**, Richard; **London**, London; **Hamburg**, Hamburg, etc., etc.

2. Those names of countries in which the German terminations =ien, =ita, correspond to the English -ia, -ica; *e.g.* **Asien**, Asia; **Skandinavien**, Scandinavia, etc., etc.

It should also be noticed that where the difference between the English and German forms is very slight, the names usually occur in the English-German part only. Names of *rivers* which are the same in both languages appear in the English-German part, where the German gender is shown.

A

Aachen ['a:xən], *n.* Aix-la-Chapelle.

Abendland ['a:bəntlant], *n.* West, Occident. —**ländisch**, *adj.* Western.

Achill [a'xɪl], *m.* Achilles.

Adele [a'de:lə], *f.* Adela.

Adolf ['a:dɔlf], *m.* Adolphus.

Adriatisches Meer [a:dri'a:tɪʃəs me:r], *n.* Adriatic (Sea).

Afrikan—er [afri'ka:nər], *m.*, —**erin**, *f.*, —**isch**, *adj.* African.

Agathe [a'ga:tə], *f.* Agatha.

Ägypten [ε'gɪptən], *n.* Egypt.

Alarich ['a:larɪç], *m.* Alaric.

Alban—er [al'ba:nər], —**ese** [—'ba-ne:zə], *m.*, —**erin**, *m.*, —**esin**, *f.* Albanian. —**ien**, *n.* Albania.

Albrecht ['albrεçt], *m.* Albert.

Alpen ['alpən] (**die**), *pl.* the Alps.

Alpinisch [al'pi:nɪʃ], *adj.* Alpine.

Amalie [a'ma:liə], *f.* Amelia.

Amerikan—er [ameri'ka:nər], *m.* inhabitant of the United States of America. —**isch**, *adj.* American.

Anden ['andən], *pl.* Andes.

Andreas [an'dre:as], **Andres** ['andre:s], *m.* Andrew.

Anton ['anto:n], *m.* Anthony, Antony.

Antwerpen [ant'vεrpən], *n.* Antwerp.

Äquator [ε'kva:tər], *m.* (the) Equator.

Araber ['a:rabər], *m.*, —**erin**, *f.* Arab. **Arabisch**, *adj.* Arabian, Arab.

Ardennerwald [ar'dɛnərvalt], *m.* Forest of Ardennes.

Argonnerwald [ar'gɔnərvalt], *m.* Forest of Argonne.

Arier ['a:riər], *m.* (—**s**, *pl.* —) Aryan. —**paragraph**, *m.* clause excluding non-Aryans from public positions.

Aristoteles [arɪs'to:teləs], *m.* Aristotle.

Ärmelmeer ['ermelme:r], *n.* English Channel.

Aschen—brödel ['aʃənbrø:dəl], —**puttel**, *n.* Cinderella.

Asiat—e [azi'a:tə], *m.*, —**isch**, *adj.* Asiatic.

Athen [a'te:n], *n.* Athens.

Atlantisches Meer [at'lantɪʃəs me:r], the Atlantic (Ocean).

B

Balkanhalbinsel ['balkanhalpᵊmzəl], *f.* Balkan peninsula.

Balte ['baltə], *m.* inhabitant of the Baltic provinces.

Barbaden [bar'ba:dən] (**die**), *pl.* Barbados.

Basel ['ba:zəl], *n.* Basle, Bâle.

Bask—e ['baskə], *m.*, —**isch**, *adj.* Basque.

Bay—er ['baɪər], m., —erin, f., —(e)risch, adj. Bavarian. —ern, n., Bavaria.

Beduin—e [bedu'i:nə], m., —isch, adj. Bedouin.

Belg—ien ['bɛlgiən], n. Belgium. —(i)er, m., —isch, adj. Belgian.

Bergschotte ['bɛrkʃotə], m. (Scotch) Highlander.

Bern [bɛrn], n. Bern(e); Verona (poet.); Dietrich von —, Theodoric of Verona. —er, m., —erin, f., (—er)isch, adj. Bernese; —er Oberland, Bernese Alps, Highlands.

Binnenafrika ['bɪnən°afrɪka], n. Central Africa.

Biskaya [bɪs'ka:ja:], n. Biscay.

Blindheim ['blɪnthaɪm], n. Blenheim.

Blocksberg ['blɔksbɛrk], m. the Brocken.

Bodensee ['bo:dənze:], m. Lake Constance.

Böhm—en ['bø:mən], n. Bohemia. —er=brüder, —ische Brüder, pl. Bohemian Brethren, Moravians. —er=wald, m. Bohemian Forest.

Bolschew—ismus [bolʃe'vɪsmʊs], m. Bolshevism. —ist [—'vɪst], m. (—isten, pl. —isten) Bolshevik.

Borusse [bo'rʊsə], m. Prussian (archaic form); member of the students' club ' Borussia.'

Braunschweig ['braʊnʃvaɪç], n. Brunswick.

Britannien [brɪ'taniən], n. Britain. Brit(t)e, m., Brit(t)in, f.; Englishman, Englishwoman.

Brügge ['brygə], n. Bruges.

Brüssel ['brysəl], n. Brussels.

Buren ['bu:rən], pl. Boers.

Burgund [bʊr'gʊnt], n. Burgundy.

C

See also under K, Z.

Calvin [kal'vɪn], m. Calvin. —ismus [—nɪsmʊs], m. Calvinism. —istisch, adj. Calvinistic(al).

Cäsar ['tse:zar], m. (—s, pl. —en) Cæsar.

Chin—a ['çi:na:], n. China. —ese [—'ne:zə], m. Chinaman, Chinese. —esisch, adj. Chinese.

Christ [krɪst], m., —in, f. Christian; Christ (obs.). —lich, adj. Christian. —us (gen. —i, dat. —o, acc. —um, or

all cases in —us), Christ; vor (nach) —i Geburt, before (after) Christ (B.C., A.D.); —i Himmelfahrt, the Ascension; Ascension Day. —woche, f. Christmas week.

Christoph ['krɪstɔf], m. Christopher.

Comersee ['ko:mərze:], m. Lake Como.

D

Dän—e ['dɛ:nə], m., —in, f. Dane. —e=mark, n. Denmark. —isch, adj. Danish.

Däum(er)ling ['dɔym(ər)lɪŋ], m.; der kleine —, Tom Thumb.

Derwisch ['dɛrvɪʃ], m. Dervish.

Deutsch [dɔytʃ], adj. German; Teuton. —er, m., —e, f. German. —land, n. Germany.

Dietrich ['di:trɪç], m. Theodoric.

Donau ['do:naʊ], f. R. Danube.

Dornröschen ['dɔrnrøsçən], n. The Sleeping Beauty.

Dreikäsehoch [draɪ'kɛ:zəho:x], m. Tom Thumb (coll.).

Dummerjan ['dʊmərja:n], Dummrian, m. Simple Simon.

E

Eismeer ['aɪsme:r], n. Polar Sea; Nördliches —, Arctic Ocean; Süd=liches —, Antarctic Ocean.

Elia(s) [e'li:a(s)], m. Elias, Elijah (B.).

Elisa [e'li:za:], m. Elisha (B.).

Elisabeth [e'li:zabet], f. Eliza(beth).

Elsaß ['ɛlzas], n. Alsace. —=Lothrin=gen, n. Alsace and Lorraine.

Elsäss—er [el'zesər], m., —erin, f., —isch, adj. Alsatian.

Enak ['e:nak], m. Anak. —s=kind, n., —s=sohn, m., —s=tochter, f. child of Anak, giant.

Engländer ['ɛŋlɛndər], m. Englishman. —in, f. Englishwoman.

Englisch ['ɛŋlɪʃ], adj. English.

Erlkönig ['ɛrlkø:nɪç], m. the Elf-king, fairy-king.

Ernst [ɛrnst], m. Ernest.

Esaias [e'za:ias], m. Isaiah.

Est—land ['e:stlant], n. Esthonia. —nisch, adj. Esthonian.

Etzel ['etsɛl], m. poet. for Attila (King of the Huns).

Eugen [ɔy'ge:n], m. Eugene. —ie, f. Eugenia.

Europ—a [ɔɣˈroːpa], n. Europe. —äer [—ˈpɛːər], m., —äiſch, adj. European.

Ev—a [ˈeːfa], —e, f. Eve, Eva. —astind, n. human being, mortal.

F

Faſch—iſmus [faˈʃɪsmʊs], m. (—) Fascism. —iſt [—ˈʃɪst], m. (—iſten, pl. —iſten) Fascist.

Felſengebirge [ˈfɛlzəngəbɪrgə], n. Rocky Mountains.

Fernambuf [fɛrnamˈbuːk], n. Pernambuco. —holz, n. Brazil-wood.

Feuerland [ˈfɔɣərlant], n. Tierra del Fuego.

Fidſchi [ˈfɪdʒi], n. Fiji (Islands).

Flam—länder [ˈflaːmlɛndər], m. —s länderin, f. Fleming, Flamand. —iſch, adj. Flemish, boorish.

Fland—ern [ˈflandərn], n. Flanders. —riſch, adj. Flemish, from Flanders.

Florenz [floˈrɛnts], n. Florence (town).

Frant—e [ˈfraŋkə], m. Frank, Franconian. —en(land), n. Franconia.

Frankfurt [ˈfraŋkfʊrt], n. Frankfort; Frankfurt a / M or a / O, Frankfort on the Main or on the Oder.

Fräntiſch [ˈfrɛŋkɪʃ], adj. Frankish, Franconian.

Franz [frants], m. Francis.

Franz—oſe [franˈtsoːzə], m. Frenchman. —öſin, f. Frenchwoman. —öſiſch, adj. French. —ösling, m. aper of French manners.

Friedrich [ˈfriːdrɪç], m. Frederick.

Frieſ—e [ˈfriːzə], m. Frieslander, Frisian. —iſch, adj. Frisian. —s (s)land, n. Friesland, Frisia.

Fritz [frɪts], m., —chen, n. (dim. of Friedrich) Fred; der alte —, Frederick the Great.

G

Galilä—a [galiˈlɛːa], n. Galilee. —er, m., —iſch, adj. Galilean.

Galizien [gaˈliːtsɪən], n. Galicia.

Generalſtaaten [genəˈraːlʃtaːtən], pl. States-General of Holland.

Genf [gɛnf], n. Geneva. —er, m. Genevan. —er See, m. Lake of Geneva. —eriſch, adj. Genevan.

Gent [gɛnt], n. Ghent.

Genu—a [ˈgeːnua], n. Genoa. —eſe(r), m., —eſiſch, adj. Genoese.

Georg [geˈɔrk], m. George.

German—e [gɛrˈmaːnə], m. Teuton. —iſch, adj. Germanic, Teutonic.

Got—e [ˈgoːtə], m. Goth. —iſch, adj. Gothic. —iſche Schrift, f. black-letter type.

Gottſeibeiuns [gɔtzaɪˈbaɪʔʊns], m. the Evil One, the Devil.

Gret—e [ˈgreːtə], f., —el, —chen, —elchen, n. (dim. of Margarethe) Madge, Peggy.

Griech—e [ˈgriːçə], m., —in, f., —iſch, adj. Greek, Grecian, Hellenic. —enland, n. Greece.

Grönland [ˈgrøːnlant], n. Greenland.

Großbritannien [groːsbriˈtaːnɪən], n. Great Britain.

Großer Ozean [ˈgroːsər ˈoːtseaːn], m. Pacific (Ocean).

Grünes Vorgebirge [ˈgryːnəs ˈfoːrgəbɪrgə], n. Cape Verde.

Guſtav [ˈgʊstaf], m. Gustavus.

H

Haag [haːk] (der), m. The Hague.

Habichtsinſeln [ˈhaːbɪçtsʔɪnzəln], pl. the Azores.

Hall—enſer [haˈlɛnzər], m., —iſch, adj. of Halle.

Hannover [haˈnoːvər], n. Hanover. —aner, m., Hannoverſch, Hannöverſch, adj. Hanoverian.

Hans [hans], m. (pl. Hanſen or Hänſe) (dim. for Johann) Jack. —wurſt, m. clown.

Hanſ—a [ˈhanza], —e, f., —abund, m. Hansa, Hanse, Hanseatic Union or League. —eſtadt, f. Hanse-town. —iſch or —eatiſch, adj. Hanseatic.

Hebrä—er [heˈbrɛːər], m., —iſch, adj. Hebrew.

Heiduf [haɪˈdʊk], m. Heyduk, Hungarian foot-soldier.

Hein [haɪn], m.; Freund —, Death (coll.).

Hein—rich [ˈhaɪnrɪç], m. (dim. —e, —i, —z) Henry.

Helgoland [ˈhɛlgolant], n. Heligoland.

Helſingör [hɛlzɪŋˈøːr], n. Elsinore.

Herman(n) [ˈhɛrman], m. Herman; Arminius.

Herodes [heˈroːdəs], m. Herod.

Herrnhuter [hɛrnˈhuːtər], m., —iſch, adj. Moravian.

Hess—e ['hɛsə], m. Hessian. —en, n. Hesse. —isch, adj. Hessian.

Hiob ['hi:ɔp], m. Job. —s=bote, m. bringer of bad news.

Holländ—er ['hɔlɛndər], m., —erin, f., Dutchman, Dutchwoman. —isch, adj. Dutch.

Horatius [ho'ra:tsɪʊs], Horaz [ho'ra:ts], m. Horace. Horazisch, Horatian.

J

Ind—er ['ɪndər], m. (Asiatic) Indian, Hindoo. —ianer [—dɪ'a:nər], m. (American) Red Indian. —ien, n. India; the Indies.

Ir—e ['i:rə], —länder, m. Irishman. —in, f., — länderin, f. Irishwoman. —land, n. Ireland. —isch, —ländisch, adj. Irish; Erse (language).

Ischarioth [ɪ'ʃa:rɪɔt], m. Iscariot.

Is—land ['ɪslant], n. Iceland. —s länder, m. Icelander.

Ital—ien [i'ta:lɪən], n. Italy. [—s li'e:nər], m., —ienerin, f., —ienisch, adj. Italian.

J

Japan ['ja:pan], n., —er, —ese [—'ne:zə], m. Japanese. —(es)isch, adj. Japanese.

Jeremias [jere'mi:as], m. Jeremiah.

Jesaia(s) [je'za:ja(s)], m. Isaiah.

Jesuit [jezu'i:t], m. (—en, pl. —en) Jesuit.

Jesus ['je:zʊs], m. Jesus.

Johann [jo'han], m. John.

Jona(s) ['jo:na(s)], m. Jonah.

Jos—ef ['jo:zɛf], —eph, m. Joseph.

Juda ['ju:da], m. Judah. —ismus, m. Judaism.

Judäa [ju'dɛ:a], n. Judæa.

Jude ['ju:de], m. (—en, pl. —en) Jew. Jüdin ['jy:dɪn], f. Jewess.

Jugoslaw—e [ju:go'sla:və], m. (—en, pl. —en) Jugoslav. —ien, n. Jugoslavia.

K

Kain ['ka:ɪn], m. Cain.

Kalifornien [kali'fɔrnɪən], n. California.

Kamerun [kamə'ru:n], n. the Cameroons.

Kanaan ['ka:naʔan], n. Canaan.

Kanad—ier [ka'na:dɪər], m., —isch, adj. Canadian.

Kanal [ka'na:l], m. the (English) Channel.

Karl [karl], m., —chen, n. Charles.

Kärnt—en ['kɛrntən], n. Carinthia. —ner, m., —nerisch, adj. Carinthian.

Karpathen [kar'pa:tən] (die), pl. Carpathian Mountains.

Kart(h)äuser [kar'tɔyzər], m. Carthusian friar.

Kastilien [kas'ti:lɪən], n. Castile.

Klara ['kla:ra], f., dim. Klärchen, n., Kläre, f. Clara.

Kleinasien [klaɪnʔ'a:zɪən], n. Asia Minor.

Kleve ['kle:və], n. Cleves.

Knut [knu:t], m. Canute.

Köln [køln], Cöln [køln], n. Cologne.

Konfutse [kɔn'fu:tsə], m. Confucius.

Konrad ['kɔnra:t], m. Conrad.

Konstanz ['kɔnstants], n. Constance (town).

Konstanze [kɔn'stantsə], f. Constance.

Kors—e ['kɔrzə], m. Corsican. —ika, n. Corsica.

Kosak [ko'zak], m., —isch, adj. Cossack.

Krain [kraɪn], n. Carniola.

Krakau ['kra:kaʊ], n. Cracow.

Kreml ['krɛm(ə)l], m. the Kremlin.

Kreta ['kre:ta], n. Crete, Candia.

Krim [krɪm] (die), f. Crimea.

Kroate [kro'a:tə], m. (—n, pl. —n) Croat.

Kunz [kʊnts], m. (dim. of Konrad) Conrad.

Kur—bayern ['ku:rbaɪərn], n. Electorate of Bavaria. —hessen, n. Electorate of Hesse. —land, n. Courland. —pfalz, f. the Palatinate. —sachsen, n. Electorate of Saxony.

Kurt [kʊrt], m. (dim. of Konrad) Conrad.

L

Latein(isch) [la'taɪn(ɪʃ)], adj. Latin.

Lausitz ['laʊzɪts] (die), f. Lusatia.

Lea ['le:a], f. Leah.

Lenore [le'no:rə], Leonore, f. Leonora.

Lett—e ['lɛtə], m. Lett. —isch, adj. Lettic.

Levit [le'vi:t], m. Levite. —isch, adj. Levitical.

Libanon ['li:banɔn], m. Mount Lebanon.

Libysch ['li:byʃ], adj. Libyan.

Lili(i) ['lɪli], f. Lil(y).

Lissabon ['lɪsabɔn], n. Lisbon.

Litauen ['lɪtaʊən], n. Lithuania.

Livland [ˈliːflaŋt], *n.* Livonia.
Livorno [liˈvorno], *n.* Leghorn.
Lofoten [loˈfoːtən], *pl.* Lofoden Islands.
Lombard—e [lɔmˈbardə], *m.* Lombard.
—ei [—ˈdaɪ], *f.* Lombardy.
Lorelei [ˈloːrəlaɪ], *f.* Lorelei (*a siren who haunted a rock on the bank of the Rhine, between Bingen and Coblenz*).
Lorenz [ˈloːrɛnts], Laurence.
Lothringen [ˈloːtriŋən], *n.* Lorraine.
Lott—chen [ˈlɔtçən], *n.*, —e, *f.* (*dim. of* **Charlotte**) Lottie.
Löwen [ˈløːvən], *n.* Louvain.
Ludwig [ˈluːtvɪç], *m.* Lewis, Louis.
Luganersee [luˈgaːnərzeː], *m.* Lake Lugano.
Luise [luˈiːzə], *f.* Louisa.
Lukas [ˈluːkas], *m.* Luke.
Lutheraner [lutəˈraːnər], *m.* Lutheran.
Lutherisch [luˈteːrɪʃ], *adj.* Lutheran.
Lüttich [ˈlʏtɪç], *n.* Liège.
Luzern [luˈtsɛrn], *n.* Lucerne.

M

Maas [maːs], *f.* R. Meuse.
Mahlstrom [ˈmaːlʃtroːm], *m.* Maelstrom.
Mähr—e [ˈmɛːrə], *m.* Moravian. —en, *n.* Moravia. —isch, *adj.* Moravian.
Mailand [ˈmaɪlant], *n.* Milan.
Mainz [maɪnts], *n.* Mayence.
Makkabäer [makaˈbɛːər] (**die**), *pl.* the Maccabees.
Mameluck [maməˈlʊk], *m.* Mameluke.
Margarete [margaˈreːtə], *f.* Margaret.
Marie [maˈriə, —ˈriː], *f.*, —chen, *n.* Mary.
Mark [mark] (**die**), *f.* the March; — **Brandenburg**, (March of) Brandenburg.
Märk—er [ˈmerkər], *m.* inhabitants of the mark Brandenburg. —isch, *adj.* belonging to the electorate of Brandenburg.
Markus [ˈmarkʊs], *m.* Mark.
Marokkan—er [maroˈkaːnər], *m.* Moor (of Morocco). —isch, *adj.* Moorish.
Marokko [maˈroko], *n.* Morocco.
Mastricht [ˈmaːstrɪçt], *n.* Maestricht.
Matth—äus [maˈtɛːʊs], —ias, *m.* Matthew.
Maur—e [ˈmaʊrə], *m.*, —isch, *adj.* Moor(ish).
Mecheln [ˈmɛçəln], *n.* Mechlin, Malines.
Messias [meˈsiːas], *m.* Messiah.

Michael [ˈmɪçaɛl], **Michel**, *m.* Michael; **der deutsche —**, plain honest German.
Mittelländisches Meer [ˈmɪtəllɛndɪʃəs meːr], *n.* Mediterranean (Sea).
Mohr [moːr], *m.* Moor. —in, *f.* Moorish woman, negress.
Moldau [ˈmɔldaʊ] (**die**), *f.* Moldavia.
Morgenland [ˈmɔrgənlant], *n.* East, Orient.
Moritz [ˈmoːrɪts], *m.* Maurice.
Mosel [ˈmoːzəl], *f.* Moselle.
Mosk—au [ˈmɔskaʊ], *n.* Moscow. —owit(er) [—oˈviːt(ər)], *m.*, —owitisch, *adj.* Muscovite.
Muhamed [ˈmuːhamɛt], *m.* Mahomet, Mohammed. —aner [—ˈdaːnər], *m.*, —anisch, *adj.* Mahometan, Mohammedan.
München [ˈmʏnçən], *n.* Munich.

N

Nathanael [naˈtaːnaɛl], *m.* Nathaniel.
Nazar—äer [natsaˈrɛːər], *m.*, —enisch, *adj.* Nazarene.
Neapel [neˈaːpəl], *n.* Naples.
Neuenburg [ˈnoʏənburk], *n.* Neuchâtel.
Neu—fundland [nɔʏˈfuntlant], *n.* Newfoundland. —seeland [—ˈzeːlant], *n.* New Zealand. —schottland, *n.* Nova Scotia. —südwales, *n.* New South Wales.
Nibelunge [ˈniːbəluŋə], *pl.* the Nibelungs. —n-hort, *m.* Nibelung treasure. —en-lied, *n.* Lay of the Nibelungs.
Nieder—deutsch [ˈniːdərdɔʏtʃ], *n.* Low German. —deutschland, *n.* Lower *or* North Germany. —lande, *pl.* Netherlands; Low Countries. —länder, *m.* Dutchman. —rhein, *m.* Lower Rhine.
Nikola(u)s [ˈniːkolas, —laʊs], *m.* Nicholas; **der heilige —**, Santa Claus.
Nil [niːl], *m.* R. Nile. —pferd, *n.* hippopotamus.
Nimwegen [ˈnɪmveːgən], *n.* Nimeguen.
Nizza [ˈnɪtsa], *n.* Nice.
Nord—isch [ˈnordɪʃ], *adj.* Norse, Northern. —mann (*poet.*), *m.* Norseman.
Nordkap [ˈnortkap], *n.* North Cape. —see, *f.* North Sea, German Ocean.
Norne [ˈnornə], *f.* (*pl.* —n) old German goddess of Fate.
Norweg—en [ˈnorveːgən], *n.* Norway. —er, *m.*, —isch, *adj.* Norwegian.
Nürnberg [ˈnʏrnberk], *n.* Nuremberg.

O

Ober—ägypten ['o:bər'ɛgɪptən], n. Upper Egypt. —bayern, n. Upper Bavaria. —deutschland, n. Upper Germany (mountainous part, south of the Main).

Ofen ['o:fən], n. Buda; Ofen=Pesth, Budapest.

Ölberg ['ø:lbɛrk], m. Mount of Olives.

Olymp [o'lymp], m. Mt. Olympus.

Oranien [o'ra:nlən], m. Orange.

Oranje=Freistaat [o'ranjəfraɪʃta:t], m. Orange Free State.

Osman—e [ɔs'ma:nə], m., —isch, adj. Ottoman.

Österreich ['ø:stəraɪç], n. Austria. —er, m., —isch, adj. Austrian. —= Ungarn, n. Austria-Hungary. —isch= ungarisch, Austro-Hungarian.

Ottoman—e [ɔto'ma:nə], m., —isch, adj. Ottoman, Turk(ish).

Ozeanien [otse'a:nlən], n. Oceania, Australasia.

P

Palästin—a [palɛs'ti:na], n. Palestine- —ensisch, adj. Palestinian.

Parnaß [par'nas], m Parnassus.

Parse ['parzə], m. Parsee.

Parzen ['partsən] (die), pl. the Parcæ, Fates.

Parzival ['partsival], m. Percival.

Paul(us) ['paul(us)], m. Paul.

Pendschab [pɛn'dʒa:p], n. Punjab.

Pers—er ['pɛrzər], m., —isch, adj. Persian.

Pfalz [pfalts] (die), f. the Palatinate.

Pforte ['pfɔrtə], f. (die Hohe —) the (Sublime) Porte.

Pharao ['fa:rao], m. Pharaoh.

Pharisä—er [fari'zɛ:ər], m. (—ers, pl. —er) Pharisee. —isch, adj. pharisai- cal.

Philipp ['fi:lɪp], m. Philip.

Phöniz—ier [fø'ni:tslər], m., —isch, adj. Phœnician.

Pilatus [pi'la:tus], m. Pilate.

Polarkreis [po'la:rkraɪs], m.; nörd= licher —, Arctic Circle; südlicher —, Antarctic Circle.

Pol—e ['po:lə], m. Pole. —en, n. Poland. —nisch, adj. Polish.

Pommer ['pɔmər], m. Pomeranian. —n, n. Pomerania.

Pompei—us [pɔm'pe:jus], m. Pompey.

—aner [—'ja:nər], m., —anisch, adj. Pompeian. —i, Pompeii.

Prag [pra:k], n. Prague. —er, m. inhabitant of Prague.

Preuß—e ['prɔysə], m. Prussian. —en, n. Prussia. —isch, adj. Prussian.

Pyrenä—en [pyrə'nɛ:ən], pl. Pyrenees, pl. —isch, adj.; —ische Halbinsel, Iberian peninsula.

R

Rahel ['ra:əl], f. Rachel.

Randstaaten ['rantʃta:tən], m.pl. states formed in 1918 on the eastern frontier of Germany by people of non-Russian race.

Raubstaaten ['raupʃta:tən], pl. Barbary States (in North Africa).

Reichslande ['raɪçslandə], pl. the Im- perial Provinces of Alsace and Lor- raine (in the former German Empire).

Rein—eke ['raɪnəkə], —hard, m. Re(y)nard (the Fox).

Rhein [raɪn], m. R. Rhine. —strom, m. (the river) Rhine. —wein, m. Rhenish wine.

Rigaischer Meerbusen ['ri:ga:ɪʃər 'me:r- bu:zən], m. gulf of Riga.

Rom [ro:m], n. Rome.

Röm—er ['rø:mər], m. (—ers, pl. —er) Roman; rummer (glass); the town- hall at Frankfort-on-Main. —isch, adj. Roman.

Rosenkreuzer ['ro:zənkrɔytsər], m. Rosicrucian.

Rot—bart ['ro:tbart], m. Barbarossa. —häute, pl. red-skins. —käppchen, n. Little Red-Riding-Hood. —kehlchen, n. robin redbreast. —es Meer, n. Red Sea.

Ruben ['ru:bən], m. Reuben.

Rübezahl ['ry:bətsa:l], m. Rape-tail (name of a waggish mountain sprite in the Riesengebirge).

Rüdiger ['ry:dɪgər], m. Roger.

Rumän—ien [ru'mɛ:nlən], n. Rumania. —e, m., —isch, adj. Rumanian.

Ruprecht ['ru:prɛçt], m. Rupert; Knecht —, Santa Claus, St. Nicholas.

Russ—e ['rusə], m., —in, f., —isch, adj. Russian. —land, n. Russia.

S

Saba ['za:ba:], n. Sheba.

Sacharja [za'xarja], m. Zachariah (B.).

Sachse ['zaksə], m., Sächsin, f., sächsisch, adj. Saxon.

Salomo ['za:lomo], m. Solomon; das hohe Lied —nis, the Song of Solomon; Prediger —nis, Ecclesiastes; Sprüche —nis, Proverbs (of Solomon).

Sarazen—e [zara'tse:nə], m., —isch, adj. Saracen.

Sard—e ['zardə], —inier, m., —inisch, adj. Sardinian.

Schelde ['ʃɛldə], f. R. Scheldt.

Schlef—ien ['ʃle:zlən], n. Silesia. —ier, m., —isch, adj. Silesian.

Schneewittchen [ʃne:'vɪtçən], n. Little Snow-white.

Schott—e ['ʃɔtə] (—länder), m. Scot, Scotsman; die —en, the Scotch; the Scots (hist.). —in, (—länderin,) f. Scotswoman. —isch, adj. Scottish, Scotch.

Schwab—e ['ʃva:bə], m. Schwäbin, f., schwäbisch, adj. Swabian. —en, n. Swabia.

Schwarz—es Meer ['ʃvartsəs me:r], n. Black Sea, Euxine. —wald, m. Black Forest.

Schwed—e ['ʃve:də], m., —in, f. Swede; alter —e, old boy, old man, old chap (fam.). —en, n. Sweden. —isch, adj. Swedish; hinter —ischen Gardinen, behind iron bars, in prison.

Schweiz [ʃvarts] (die) f. Switzerland; in der —, in Switzerland. —er, m. Swiss; Switzer, member of the (French) bodyguard. —erin, f. Swiss woman. —erisch, adj. Swiss. —erbund, m. Swiss Confederation.

Sem [zɛm], m. Shem (B.).

Sepp [zɛp], Sepperl, Seppi, m. (dial. dim. of Joseph) Joe(y).

Serb—ien ['zɛrblən], n. Servia. —e, —ier, m. Serb, Servian. —isch, adj. Servian.

Sevennen [se'vɛnən], pl. the Cévennes.

Sibir—ien [zi'bi:rlən], n. Siberia. —ier, m., —isch, adj. Siberian.

Sichem ['zɪçɛm], n. Shechem.

Siebenbürg—en [zi:bən'byrgə], n. Transylvania. —e, m., —isch, adj. Transylvanian.

Silvesterabend [zɪl'vɛstər⁹a:bɛnt], m. New Year's Eve.

Simson ['zɪmzɔn], m. Samson.

Sizil—ien [zi'tsi:lən], n. Sicily. —i(an)er, m., —(ian)isch, adj. Sicilian.

Slaw—e ['sla:və], m., —in, f. Slav, Slavonian. —isch, adj. Slav, Slavonic, Slavonian.

Slowak—e [slo'va:kə], m., —isch, adj. Slovak.

Slowen—e [slo've:nə], m., —isch, adj. Slovenian.

Sophie [zo'fi:(ə)], f. Sophia.

Sowjet ['zovlɛt], m. Soviet.

Spaa [spa:], n. Spa (in Belgium).

Span—ien ['ʃpa:nlən], n. Spain. —ier, m., —ierin, f. Spaniard. —isch, adj. Spanish.

Steiermark ['ʃtarərmark], f. Styria.

Stephan ['ʃtɛfan], m. Stephen.

Stoffel ['ʃtɔfəl], m. (dim. of Christoph) Kit.

Stru(w)welpeter ['ʃtruvəlpe:tər], m. Shock-headed Peter.

Sund [zʊnt], m. (the) Sound.

Syr—(i)er ['zy:r(i)ər], m. Syrian. —isch, adj. Syrian, Syriac.

T

Tanger ['taŋər], n. Tangier.

Teuton—e [tɔy'to:nə], m., —in, f. Teuton. —isch, adj. Teutonic.

Themse ['tɛmzə], f. R. Thames.

Theodorich [te'o:dorɪç], Theodorik, m. Theodoric.

Theres—e [te're:zə], (—ia) f. T(h)eresa; Maria —ia, Maria Theresa.

Thüringen ['ty:rɪŋən], n. Thuringia.

Timotheus [ti'mo:teʊs], m. Timothy.

Tirol [ti'ro:l], n. the Tyrol. —er, m., —isch, adj. Tyrolese.

Tizian [titsi'a:n], m. Titian.

Tokaier [to'karər], m. Tokay wine.

Tri(d)ent [tri'(d)ɛnt], n. Trent.

Trier [tri:r], n. Treves.

Triest [tri'ɛst], n. Trieste.

Tripolis ['tri:polɪs], n. Tripoli.

Tro—as ['tro:as], n. the Troad. —ja ['tro:ja], n. Troy. —janer [—'ja:nər], m., —janisch, adj. Trojan.

Tschech—e ['tʃɛçə], m. Czech. —isch, adj. Czech. —o-Slowa'kei, f. Czecho-Slovakia.

Tscherkess—e [tʃɛr'kɛsə], m., —in, f., —isch, adj. Circassian.

Türk—e ['tyrkə], m. (pl. —en), —in, f. Turk, Turkish woman. —ei [—'kar] (die), f. Turkey.

Tyr—us ['ty:rʊs], n. Tyre. —(i)er, m., —isch, adj. Tyrian.

U

Undine [ʊn'diːnə], *f.* water-sprite, nymph.

Ungar ['ʊŋgar], *m.*, **—in**, *f.*, **—isch**, *adj.* Hungarian. **—n**, *n.* Hungary.

Uria(s) [u'riːa(s)], *m.* Uriah. **—brief**, *m.* treacherous letter.

Urian ['uːrlaːn], *m.*; **Herr —**, Mr. What's-his-name; the Devil; **Meister —**, Old Harry, Old Nick.

B

Valentin ['vaːlɛntiːn], *m.* Valentine.

Vene—dig [ve'neːdɪç], *n.* Venice. **—disch**, **—tianisch** [—etsɪ'aːnɪʃ], *adj.*, **—tianer**, *m.* Venetian. **—tien**, **—zien**, *n.* Venetia.

Vereinigte Staaten [fɛr'ʔaɪnɪçtə 'staːtən], *pl.* United States (of North America), U.S.A.

Vesuv [ve'zuːf], *m.* Mt. Vesuvius.

Vlissingen ['flɪsɪŋən], *n.* Flushing.

Vogesen [vo'geːzən], *pl.* Vosges Mts.

Voland ['foːlant], *m.*; **Junker —**, the Devil, Satan.

Voralpen ['foːrʔalpən], *pl.* the Lower Alps.

W

Waadt—(land) ['vaːt(lant)], *n.* (Canton de) Vaud. **—länder**, *m.*, **—isch**, *adj.* Vaudois.

Waal [vaːl], *m.* R. Vaal.

Waibling(er) ['vaɪblɪŋ(ər)], *m.* Ghibelline.

Waldenser [val'dɛnzər], *m.* Waldensian.

Walhalla [val'hala], *f.* Valhalla.

Waliser [va'liːzər], *m.* (**—s**, *pl.* **—**) Welshman.

Walküre [val'kyːrə], *f.* Valkyrie, Walkyrie, swan-maiden. **—n-ritt**, *m.* ride of the Valkyries.

Wal(l)—achei [vala'xaɪ], (die) *f.* Wallachia. **—ache** [va'laxə], *m.*, **—achisch**, *adj.* Wallachian.

Wallon—e [va'loːnə], *m.*, **—isch**, *adj.* Walloon.

Walpurgisnacht [val'pʊrgɪsnaxt], *f.* eve of May-day (*when witches hold a meeting on the Brocken*).

Walther, Walter ['valtər], *m.* Walter.

Warschau ['varʃau], *n.* Warsaw.

Weichsel ['vaɪksəl], *f.* R. Vistula.

Welf, Welfe [vɛlf], *m.* Guelph.

Welsch [vɛlʃ], *adj.* Welsh, Italian, French; **die —en**, the French, (*rarely*) the Italians. **—land**, *n.* Italy. **—tirol**, *n.* Italian Tyrol. **—tum**, *n.* foreign (*esp. French*) manners and customs.

Wend—e ['vɛndə], *m.*, **—isch**, *adj.* Wend.

Wendekreis ['vɛndəkraɪs], *m.* Tropic; **— des Krebses**, Tropic of Cancer; **— des Steinbocks**, Tropic of Capricorn.

Wenzel ['vɛntsəl], *m.* Wenceslas; knave (*at cards*).

West—falen [vɛst'faːlən], *n.* Westphalia. **—fale**, *m.*, **—fälin**, *f.*, **—fälisch**, *adj.* Westphalian.

Wien [viːn], *n.* Vienna. **—er**, *m.*, **—erisch**, *adj.* Viennese.

Wilhelm ['vɪlhɛlm], *m.* William. **—ine**, *f.* Wilhelmina.

Wladislaus ['vlaːdɪslaus], *m.* Ladislaus.

Wodan ['voːdan], *m.* Odin, Woden.

Wolga ['vɔlga], *f.* R. Volga.

Wolkenkukuksheim [vɔlkən'kukukshaɪm], *n.* Utopia; Fool's Paradise.

Württemberg ['vʏrtəmbɛrk], *n.* Wurtemberg.

Y

Ypern ['iːpərn], *n.* Ypres.

Z

Zabern ['tsaːbərn], *n.* Saverne.

Zebaoth ['tseːbaɔt], *m.* Sabaoth (*B.*).

Zuidersee ['zɔydərzeː], *m.* Zuyder Sea.

Zürich ['tsyːrɪç], *n.* Zurich.

Zypern ['tsyːpərn], *n.* Cyprus.

LIST OF GERMAN IRREGULAR VERBS

For compounds with be=, er=, ge=, miß=, ver=, zer=, emp=, ent=, voll=, and
other prefixes see the simple verbs where not otherwise given.

* Obsolete.　　　† To be avoided.

INFINITIVE.	PRESENT INDIC.	IMPERF. INDIC.	IMPERF. SUBJ.	PAST PART.
auslöschen (also trans. & weak)	lischt aus	losch aus	lösche aus	ausgeloschen
backen	3 bäckt	buk	büke	gebacken
befehlen	3 befiehlt	befahl	beföhle	befohlen
(sich) befleißen	3 befleißt (sich)	befliß (sich)	beflisse (sich)	beflissen
beginnen	3 beginnt	begann	begönne	begonnen
beißen	3 beißt	biß	bisse	gebissen
bergen	3 birgt	barg	bärge	geborgen
bersten	3 birst	barst	bärste or börste	geborsten
betrügen	3 betrügt	betrog	betröge	betrogen
bewegen	3 bewegt	bewog	bewöge	bewogen
biegen	3 biegt	bog	böge	gebogen
bieten	3 bietet	bot	böte	geboten
binden	3 bindet	band	bände	gebunden
bitten	3 bittet	bat	bäte	gebeten
blasen	3 bläst	blies	bliese	geblasen
bleiben	3 bleibt	blieb	bliebe	geblieben
bleichen	3 bleicht	blich	bliche	geblichen
braten	3 brät	briet	briete	gebraten
brechen	3 bricht	brach	bräche	gebrochen
brennen	3 brennt	brannte	brennte	gebrannt
bringen	3 bringt	brachte	brächte	gebracht
denken	3 denkt	dachte	dächte	gedacht
dingen	3 dingt	dang or dingte	dänge or dingte	gedingt or gedungen
dreschen	3 drischt	drosch	drösche	gedroschen
dringen	3 dringt	drang	dränge	gedrungen
dürfen	1 & 3 darf 2 darfst 1 wir dürfen, &c.	durfte	dürfte	gedurft
erlöschen (to become extinguished)	3 erlischt	erlosch	erlösche	erloschen
erschrecken (intrans.) (weak when trans.=to frighten)	3 erschrickt	erschrak	erschräke	erschrocken
erwägen	3 erwägt	erwog	erwöge	erwogen
essen	3 ißt	aß	äße	gegessen

INFINITIVE.	PRESENT INDIC.	IMPERF. INDIC.	IMPERF. SUBJ.	PAST PART.
fahren	3 fährt	fuhr	führe	gefahren
fallen	3 fällt	fiel	fiele	gefallen
fangen	3 fängt	fing	finge	gefangen
fechten	3 ficht	focht	föchte	gefochten
finden	3 findet	fand	fände	gefunden
flechten	3 flicht	flocht	flöchte	geflochten
fliegen	3 fliegt	flog	flöge	geflogen
fliehen	3 flieht	floh	flöhe	geflohen
fließen	3 fließt	floß	flösse	geflossen
fressen	3 frißt	fraß	fräße	gefressen
frieren	3 friert	fror	fröre	gefroren
gären (weak when used figuratively)	3 gärt	gor or gärte	göre or gärte	gegoren or gegärt
gebären	3 gebiert	gebar	gebäre	geboren
geben	3 gibt	gab	gäbe	gegeben
gedeihen	3 gedeiht	gedieh	gediehe	gediehen
gehen	3 geht	ging	ginge	gegangen
gelingen (Impers.)	3 (es) gelingt (mir)	gelang	gelänge	gelungen
gelten	3 gilt	galt	gälte or gölte	gegolten
genesen	3 genest	genas	genäse	genesen
genießen	3 genießt	genoß	genösse	genossen
geraten	3 gerät	geriet	geriete	geraten
geschehen (Impers.)	3 geschieht	geschah	geschähe	geschehen
gewinnen	3 gewinnt	gewann	gewänne or gewönne	gewonnen
gießen	3 gießt	goß	gösse	gegossen
gleichen (trans. is weak)	3 gleicht	glich	gliche	geglichen
gleiten	3 gleitet	glitt	glitte	geglitten
glimmen	3 glimmt	glomm or glimmte	glömme or glimmte	geglommen or geglimmt
graben	3 gräbt	grub	grübe	gegraben
greifen	3 greift	griff	griffe	gegriffen
haben	1 habe	hatte	hätte	gehabt
	2 hast			
	3 hat			
halten	3 hält	hielt	hielte	gehalten
hangen	3 hängt	hing	hinge	gehangen
hauen	3 haut	hieb	hiebe	gehauen
heben	3 hebt	hob	höbe	gehoben
heißen	3 heißt	hieß	hieße	geheißen
helfen	3 hilft	half	hülfe	geholfen
kennen	3 kennt	kannte	kenn(e)te	gekannt
kiesen	3 kiest	kor	köre	gekoren
klimmen	3 klimmt	klomm	klömme	geklommen
klingen	3 klingt	klang	klänge	geklungen
kneifen	3 kneift	kniff	kniffe	gekniffen
kommen	3 kommt or kömmt	kam	käme	gekommen

INFINITIVE.	PRESENT INDIC.	IMPERF. INDIC.	IMPERF. SUBJ.	PAST PART.
können	1 kann 2 kannst 3 kann 1 pl. können &c.	konnte	könnte	gekonnt
kriechen	3 kriecht	kroch	kröche	gekrochen
laden (= aufladen)	3 lädt	lud	lüde	geladen
laden (= ein= laden) (orig. only weak)	3 ladet or lädt	lud or *ladete	lüde or ladete	geladen
lassen	3 läßt	ließ	ließe	gelassen
laufen	3 läuft	lief	liefe	gelaufen
leiden	3 leidet	litt	litte	gelitten
leihen	3 leiht 2 liest	lieh	liehe	geliehen
lesen	3 liest	las	läse	gelesen
liegen	3 liegt	lag	läge	gelegen
lügen	3 lügt	log	löge	gelogen
meiden	3 meidet	mied	miede	gemieden
melken	3 melkt	melkte	melkte	gemelkt or gemolken
messen	3 mißt	maß	mäße	gemessen
mögen	1 mag 2 magst 3 mag 1 pl. mögen	mochte	möchte	gemocht
müssen	1 muß 2 mußt 3 muß 1 pl. müssen	mußte	müßte	gemußt
nehmen	3 nimmt	nahm	nähme	genommen
nennen	3 nennt	nannte	nennte	genannt
pfeifen	3 pfeift	pfiff	pfiffe	gepfiffen
pflegen	2 pflegst 3 pflegt	pflegte or *pflog	pflegte or *pflöge	gepflegt
preisen	3 preist	pries	priese	gepriesen
quellen	3 quillt	quoll	quölle	gequollen
raten	3 rät	riet	riete	geraten
reiben	3 reibt	rieb	riebe	gerieben
reißen	3 reißt	riß	risse	gerissen
reiten	3 reitet	ritt	ritte	geritten
rennen	3 rennt	rannte	renn(e)te	gerannt
riechen	3 riecht	roch	röche	gerochen
ringen	3 ringt	rang	ränge	gerungen
rinnen	3 rinnt	rann	ränne	geronnen
rufen	3 ruft	rief	riefe	gerufen
saufen	3 säuft	soff	söffe	gesoffen
saugen	3 saugt	sog	söge	gesogen (†gesaugt)
schaffen (to create) (in the meaning ' to do,' ' be busy,' the verb is weak)	3 schafft	schuf	schüfe	geschaffen

INFINITIVE.	PRESENT INDIC.	IMPERF. INDIC.	IMPERF. SUBJ.	PAST PART.
schallen	3 schallt	scholl or schallte	schölle or schallte	geschallt
scheiden	3 scheidet	schied	schiede	geschieden
scheinen	3 scheint	schien	schiene	geschienen
schelten	3 schilt	schalt	schölte	gescholten
scheren	3 schert or schiert	schor (†scherte)	schöre (†scherte)	geschoren
schieben	3 schiebt	schob	schöbe	geschoben
schießen	3 schießt	schoß	schösse	geschossen
schinden	3 schindet	schund	schünde	geschunden
schlafen	3 schläft	schlief	schliefe	geschlafen
schlagen	3 schlägt	schlug	schlüge	geschlagen
schleichen	3 schleicht	schlich	schliche	geschlichen
schleifen	3 schleift	schliff	schliffe	geschliffen
schleißen	3 schleißt	schliß	schlisse	geschlissen
schließen	3 schließt	schloß	schlösse	geschlossen
schlingen	3 schlingt	schlang	schlänge	geschlungen
schmeißen	3 schmeißt	schmiß	schmisse	geschmissen
schmelzen (v.n.)	3 schmilzt	schmolz	schmölze	geschmolzen
schnauben	3 schnaubt	schnob or schnaubte	schnöbe or schnaubte	geschnoben or geschnaubt
schneiden	3 schneidet	schnitt	schnitte	geschnitten
schrauben	3 schraubt	schraubte or *schrob	schraubte or *schröbe	geschraubt or *geschroben
schreiben	3 schreibt	schrieb	schriebe	geschrieben
schreien	3 schreit	schrie	schriee	geschrieen
schreiten	3 schreitet	schritt	schritte	geschritten
schweigen (= ' to be silent ' is intrans. & strong) (= ' to silence ' is trans. & weak)	3 schweigt	schwieg	schwiege	geschwiegen
schwellen	3 schwillt	schwoll	schwölle	geschwollen
schwimmen	3 schwimmt	schwamm	schwömme or schwämme	geschwommen
schwinden	3 schwindet	schwand	schwände	geschwunden
schwingen	3 schwingt	schwang	schwänge	geschwungen
schwören	3 schwört	schwor or schwur	schwüre	geschworen
sehen	3 sieht	sah	sähe	gesehen
sein	S 1 bin 2 bist 3 ist P 1 sind 2 seid 3 sind	war	wäre	gewesen
senden	3 sendet	sandte or sendete	sendete	gesandt or gesendet
sieden	3 siedet	sott or siedete	sötte or siedete	gesotten or gesiedet
singen	3 singt	sang	sänge	gesungen
sinken	3 sinkt	sank	sänke	gesunken
sinnen	3 sinnt	sann	sänne or sönne	gesonnen
sitzen	3 sitzt	saß	säße	gesessen

INFINITIVE.	PRESENT INDIC.	IMPERF. INDIC.	IMPERF. SUBJ.	PAST PART.
ſollen	1 ſoll 2 ſollſt 3 ſoll P 1 ſollen, &c.	ſollte	ſollte	geſollt
ſpalten	3 ſpaltet	ſpaltete	ſpaltete	geſpalten or geſpaltet
ſpeien	3 ſpeit	ſpie	ſpiee	geſpieen
ſpinnen	3 ſpinnt	ſpann	ſpönne	geſponnen
ſprechen	3 ſpricht	ſprach	ſpräche	geſprochen
ſprießen	3 ſprießt	ſproß	ſpröſſe	geſproſſen
ſpringen	3 ſpringt	ſprang	ſpränge	geſprungen
ſtechen	3 ſticht	ſtach	ſtäche	geſtochen
ſtehen	3 ſteht	ſtand	ſtände	geſtanden
ſtehlen	3 ſtiehlt	ſtahl	ſtöhle	geſtohlen
ſteigen	3 ſteigt	ſtieg	ſtiege	geſtiegen
ſterben	3 ſtirbt	ſtarb	ſtürbe	geſtorben
ſtieben	3 ſtiebt	ſtob	ſtöbe	geſtoben
ſtinken	3 ſtinkt	ſtank	ſtänke	geſtunken
ſtoßen	3 ſtößt	ſtieß	ſtieße	geſtoßen
ſtreichen	3 ſtreicht	ſtrich	ſtriche	geſtrichen
ſtreiten	3 ſtreitet	ſtritt	ſtritte	geſtritten
thun, see tun				
tragen	3 trägt	trug	trüge	getragen
treffen	3 trifft	traf	träfe	getroffen
treiben	3 treibt	trieb	triebe	getrieben
treten	3 tritt	trat	träte	getreten
triefen	3 trieft	troff	tröffe	getroffen
trinken	3 trinkt	trank	tränke	getrunken
trügen	3 trügt	trog	tröge	getrogen
tun	S 1 tue 2 tuſt 3 tut P 1 & 3 tun 2 tut	tat	täte	getan
verderben (v.n.)	3 verdirbt	verdarb	verdürbe	verdorben
verdrießen	3 verdrießt	verdroß	verdröſſe	verdroſſen
vergeſſen	3 vergißt	vergaß	vergäße	vergeſſen
verhehlen	3 verhehlt	verhehlte	verhehlte	verhehlt or verhohlen
verlieren	3 verliert	verlor	verlöre	verloren
verſchallen	3 verſchallt	verſcholl	verſchölle	verſchollen
wachſen (meaning to grow)	3 wächſt	wuchs	wüchſe	gewachſen
wägen	3 wägt	wog or wägte	wöge or wägte	gewogen or gewägt
waſchen	3 wäſcht	wuſch	wüſche	gewaſchen
weben	3 webt	webte or wob	webte or wöbe	gewebt or gewoben
weichen	3 weicht	wich	wiche	gewichen
weiſen	3 weiſt	wies	wieſe	gewieſen
wenden	3 wendet	wandte or wendete	wendete	gewendet or gewandt
werben	3 wirbt	warb	würbe	geworben
werden	3 wird	wurde (*ward)	würde	geworden (*worden)

INFINITIVE.	PRESENT INDIC.	IMPERF. INDIC.	IMPERF. SUBJ.	PAST PART.
werfen	3 wirft	warf	würfe	geworfen
wiegen (to weigh, v.n.) (wiegen, to rock, v.a. is weak)	3 wiegt	wog	wöge	gewogen
winden	3 windet	wand	wände	gewunden
wissen	S 1 & 3 weiß 2 weißt P 1 wissen	wußte	wüßte	gewußt
wollen	S 1 & 3 will 2 willst P 1 wollen	wollte	wollte	gewollt
zeihen	3 zeiht	zieh	ziehe	geziehen
ziehen	3 zieht	zog	zöge	gezogen
zwingen	3 zwingt	zwang	zwänge	gezwungen

CASSELL'S
ENGLISH-GERMAN
DICTIONARY

A

A, das A, a (**An** before a vowel or silent h), ind. art. ein, eine, ein; (used distributively) der, die, das; two minutes at — time, zwei Minuten hintereinander; many — man, mancher Mann; half — day, ein halber Tag; two shillings — pound, zwei Mark das Pfund; three shillings — day, täglich drei Mark; — hundred soldiers, hundert Soldaten; — few (some) einige; (not many) wenige; — great deal, sehr viel; — little, etwas.

Aback, adv. zurück, rückwärts, hinten; mastwärts (Naut.); taken —, überrascht, bestürzt.

Abacus, s. das Rechenbrett; die Säulenplatte (Arch.).

Abaft, adv. hinterwärts, nach hinten, hinten.

Abandon, v.a. (give up) aufgeben; (forsake, leave for ever) verlassen; (surrender, deliver up) preisgeben, überlassen. —ed, p.p. & adj. verlassen; aufgegeben; (profligate) lasterhaft, verworfen. —ment, s. das Verlassen; das Aufgeben; die Verlassenheit.

Abase, v.a. (humiliate) demütigen; (degrade) erniedrigen. —ment, s. die Demütigung, Erniedrigung.

Abash, v.a. beschämen, verlegen machen.

Abate, v. I. a. nachlassen, herabsetzen (the price); mildern (pain, etc.); (diminish) vermindern. II. n. nachlassen, an Stärke verlieren, abnehmen; the wind —s, der Wind legt sich. —ment, s. (diminution) die Verminderung, Abnahme; der Nachlaß, Abzug, die Herabsetzung (in price, etc.).

Abb—ess, s. die Äbtissin. —ey, s. die Abtei. —ot, s. der Abt.

Abbreviat—e, v.a. abkürzen. —ion, s. die Abkürzung (also Mus.).

Abdicat—e, v.a. & n. niederlegen, aufgeben, entsagen; abdanken. —ion, s. die Niederlegung, Abdankung.

Abdomen, s. der Unterleib.

Abduct, v.a. entführen. —ion, s. die Entführung. —or, s. der Abziehmuskel (Anat.); der Entführer.

Abed, adv. zu Bett, im Bette.

Aberration, s. der Irrgang, Irrweg; die Geistesverwirrung.

Abet, v.a. helfen, unterstützen. —ment, s. der Beistand, die Unterstützung. —tor, s. der Anhetzer, Anstifter.

Abhor, v.a. verabscheuen. —rence, s. der Abscheu, die Verabscheuung; to hold in —rence, verabscheuen. —rent, adj. zuwider (to, dat.), unvereinbar (mit).

Abide, ir.v. I. n. (dwell) wohnen; (remain, stay) verweilen, bleiben; (last) fortdauern; — by, verharren bei (an opinion, etc.); to — by the consequences, die Folgen auf sich (acc.) nehmen. II. a. (endure) aushalten, leiden, ertragen; I cannot — him, ich kann ihn nicht ausstehen or leiden.

Abiding, adj. dauernd. —place, s. der Wohnort.

Ability, s. das Vermögen, die Fähigkeit, die Geschicklichkeit.

Abject, adj., —ly, adv. unterwürfig; verächtlich, niedrig. —ness, s. die Niedrigkeit; die Niederträchtigkeit.

Abjure, v.a. abschwören; (give up) entsagen (einer S. Dat.), verschwören (eine S.).

Ablative, s. der Ablativ.

Able, adj., **Ably,** adv. (capable) fähig; (clever) geschickt; (efficient) tüchtig; to be —, können, imstande sein; — to pay, zahlungsfähig. —bodied, adj. stark, handfest; dienstfähig, tauglich.

Ablution, s. die Abwaschung, Abspülung.

Abnegation, s. die Ableugnung, Verneinung; self—, die Selbstverleugnung.

Abnormal, adj. regelwidrig.

Aboard, adv. an Bord; to go —, sich einschiffen; all — for Berlin! einsteigen nach Berlin!

Abode, s. (dwelling) die Wohnung; (stay) der Aufenthalt; der Aufenthaltsort, Wohnsitz.

Aboli—sh, v.a. aufheben, abschaffen; (annul) vertilgen, vernichten; (abrogate) abschaffen; (suppress) unterdrücken. **—tion,** s. die Abschaffung, Aufhebung; die Vernichtung.

Abomina—ble, adj., **—bly,** adv. abscheulich, scheußlich. **—te,** v.a. verabscheuen. **—tion,** s. (horror) die Verabscheuung, der Abscheu; object of —tion, der Greuel.

Aborigin—al, adj. ursprünglich, einheimisch. **—es,** pl. die Ureinwohner.

Aborti—on, s. die Fehlgeburt. **ve,** adj. unzeitig, zu früh geboren; (fig.) verunglückt; to prove **—ve,** fehlschlagen, mißlingen.

Abound, v.n. (possess abundantly) wimmeln von einer S.; (be abundant) im Überfluß vorhanden sein.

About, I. prep. (round) um, herum; (towards) gegen, um; (on account of) wegen, über, um; (concerning) über, in Beziehung auf, betreffend. II. adv. herum, umher, ringsherum; (round) in der Runde; (in circumference) im Umfange; (aside) abwegs; (nearly) ungefähr, etwa; (everywhere) überall; to be — to do a thing, im Begriffe sein etwas zu tun; to come —, geschehen; right —, turn! rechts um, kehrt! he is — my height, er hat etwa meine Größe; a long way —, ein grosser Umweg.

Above, I. prep. über; — all things, vor allen Dingen, vor allem. II. adv. oben; darüber; over and —, oben drein; **—mentioned,** oben erwähnt; it is — me, das ist mir zu hoch. **—board,** adv. offen, ohne Arg, unverstedt.

Abrasion, s. das Abreiben, die Abschürfung.

Abreast, adv. neben einander, Seite an Seite; formed—, in Schlachtlinie (Mil.).

Abridg—e, v.a. abkürzen, verkürzen. **—ment,** s. die Abkürzung; der Auszug (of a book, etc.).

Abroad, adv. draußen, außer dem Hause; im Freien; im Auslande; auswärts; weithin; to live —, im Ausland leben; there is a report —, es geht die Rede; the matter has got —, die Sache ist ruchbar geworden.

Abrogat—e, v.a. abschaffen. **—ion,** s. die Abschaffung.

Abrupt, adj., **—ly,** adv. abgerissen, abgebrochen; jäh; plötzlich; (curt) schroff, kurz. **—ness,** s. die Abgebrochenheit (of style); die Jähe (of a declivity); die Rauhheit (of a person's manner); die Eile, Übereilung (of someone's departure).

Abscess, s. das Geschwür.

Abscond, v.n. entweichen, sich heimlich davon machen. **—er,** s. der Flüchtling.

Absen—ce, s. die Abwesenheit; leave of —ce, der Urlaub. **—t,** I. adj. abwesend. II. v.r. (to —t oneself) sich entfernen; ausbleiben. **—tee,** s. Abwesende(r). **—t-minded,** adj. zerstreut. **—t-mindedness,** s. die Geistesabwesenheit, Zerstreutheit.

Absol—ute, adj. unumschränkt, unbeschränkt, eigenmächtig; (complete) vollkommen, vollständig; (unconditional) unbedingt; **—ute** space, der unbeziehliche Raum. **—utely,** adv. unumschränkt; (actually) in der Tat, wirklich; (unconditionally) unbedingt; (positively) bestimmt; (indispensably) durchaus; (wholly) ganz, völlig. **—uteness,** s. die Unumschränktheit. **—ution,** s. die Freisprechung. **—ve,** v.a. (acquit) lossprechen, freisprechen; entbinden (from a promise, etc.).

Absorb, v.a. verschlucken, einsaugen; (swallow up) verschlingen; in Anspruch nehmen (the attention, etc.); **—ed** in thought, in Gedanken vertieft. **—ent,** adj. einsaugend, absorbierend.

Absorption, s. das Einsaugen; die Aufsaugung; die Absorption (Chem.); die Vertiefung (in thought), das in Gedanken Versunkensein.

Abstain, v.n. sich enthalten (from, von or gen.). **—er,** s. der Enthaltsame, der Abstinenzler.

Abstemious, adj., **—ly,** adv. enthaltsam; (temperate) mäßig. **—ness,** s. die Enthaltsamkeit; die Mäßigkeit.

Abstention, s. die Enthaltung, Zurückhaltung (from, von); der Verzicht (from a thing, auf eine S.); die Entbehrung, das Fasten.

Abstinen—ce, *s.* die Enthaltsamkeit; das Fasten; day of —ce, der Fasttag. —t, *adj.* enthaltsam; mäßig.

Abstract, I. *v.a.* (withdraw) abziehen; (separate) absondern; abziehen, absondern (*Chem.*); (epitomize) in einen Abriß bringen. II. *adj.* abgezogen, abgesondert; (not concrete) abstrakt, rein begrifflich (*Log.*); (general) allgemein (*Log. etc.*); rein (*Math.*). III. *s.* der Abriß, Auszug (*from a book*). —ed, *adj.* abgesondert, getrennt; abgezogen; (refined) verfeinert; (abstruse) schwer verständlich; (inattentive) geistesabwesend, unaufmerksam, zerstreut; abstrakt. —edly, *adv.* in der Zerstreuung. —er, *s.* der Entwender, Dieb; der Verfasser eines Abrisses. —ion, *s.* die Abziehung, Absonderung; das Abziehen; das Abgesondertsein; die Abstraktion. —ly, *adv.* abstrakt, an sich.

Abstruse, *adj.*, —ly, *adv.* dunkel, schwerverständlich; (profound) tief, tiefsinnig. —ness, *s.* die Dunkelheit, Unverständlichkeit.

Absurd, *adj.*, —ly, *adv.* (foolish) albern, töricht, abgeschmackt; (unreasonable) ungereimt, vernunftwidrig; (laughable) lächerlich. —ity, *s.* die Ungereimtheit, Albernheit, Abgeschmacktheit.

Abund—ance, *s.* die Fülle; der Überfluß; in —ance (—antly), vollauf. —ant, *adj.*, —antly, *adv.* reichlich, genugsam, übergenug; (overflowing) überflüssig.

Abus—e, I. *v.a.* (scold) schimpfen; (violate) schänden; (beat, etc.) mißhandeln. II. *s.* der Mißbrauch; die Beschimpfung. —er, *s.* der Schimpfer; der Lästerer. —ive, *adj.*, —ively, *adv.* schimpfend, schmähend.

Abut, *v.n.* angrenzen. —ment, *s.* das Angrenzen; der Strebepfeiler.

Abyss, (*poet.* **Abysm,**) *s.* der Abgrund, Schlund.

Acacia, *s.* die Akazie, der Akazienbaum.

Academ—ic, *adj.*, —ically, *adv.* akademisch. —ician, *s.* der Akademiker. —y, *s.* die Akademie; die Hochschule; member of the —y, der Mitglied der Akademie.

Acanthus, *s.* die Bärenklau; der Akanthus; das Säulenlaubwerk (*Arch.*).

Accede, *v.n.* (— to) bewilligen (*a request*); besteigen (*a throne*).

Accelerat—e, *v.a.* beschleunigen. —ion, *s.* die Beschleunigung. —or, *s.* das Gaspedal (*Mach.*).

Accent, I. *v.a. see* —uate. II. *s.* der Ton, Wortton, die Betonung; der Akzent, das Tonzeichen (*Gram.*); (pronunciation) die Aussprache. —uate, *v.a.* betonen. —uation, *s.* die Betonung; die Tonbezeichnung.

Accept, *v.a.* annehmen. —able, *adj.*, —ably, *adv.* annehmbar, annehmlich; (agreeable) angenehm; (welcome) willkommen, erwünscht. —ability, —ableness, *s.* die Annehmbarkeit. —ance, *s.* die Annahme; das Akzept (*of a bill*); my proposals did not meet with —ance from him, er ging nicht auf meine Vorschläge ein. —ed, *adj.* angenommen; (sanctioned, usual) üblich. —er, —or, *s.* der Annehmer; der Akzeptant (*of a bill*).

Access *s.* der Zugang, Zutritt; (increase) der Zuwachs, die Vermehrung. —ibility, *s.* die Zugänglichkeit. —ible, *adj.* zugänglich; erreichbar. —ion, *s.* die Vermehrung, das Hinzukommen (*of property, etc.*); —ion to the crown, die Thronbesteigung. —ory, I. *adj.* (additional) hinzutommend, beiläufig, zusätzlich; beitragend; nebensächlich, untergeordnet; (abetting) teilnehmend, mitschuldig. II. *s.* der Teilnehmer, Mitschuldige; —ories, *pl.* (something added) das Zubehör; die Begleiterscheinung(en).

Accidence, *s.* die Flexionslehre (*Gram.*).

Accident, *s.* (chance occurrence) der Zufall; (mishap) der Unfall; der Unglücksfall; by —, zufälligerweise, zufällig; it was by mere — that I met him, es war der reine Zufall, daß ich ihm begegnete. —al, I. *adj.* zufällig; (non-essential) unwesentlich. II. *s.* das Zufällige; das Unwesentliche.

Acclaim, *v.a.* Beifall rufen, applaudieren.

Acclamation, *s.* der laute Beifall, Zuruf.

Accolade, *s.* der Ritterschlag.

Accommodat—e, *v.a.* (adapt) passend machen, anbequemen, anpassen (to a thing, einer S.); (lodge) unterbringen, logieren, bewirten; —e oneself to circumstances, sich in die Umstände fügen or schicken, sich den Verhältnissen anpassen; to — someone with money, einem Geld leihen; to be well —ed, bequem wohnen, eine gute Wohnung haben. **—ing,** adj. gefällig, entgegenkommend. **—ion,** s. (adaptation) die Anpassung; die Beilegung, der gütliche Vergleich (of a dispute); (conveniences) die Bequemlichkeit; (help, etc.) die Aushülfe; I found —ion for the night, ich fand ein Unterkommen für die Nacht.

Accompan—iment, s. die Begleitung. **—ist,** s. der Begleiter. **—y,** v. I. a. & n. begleiten (Mus.). II. a. (einen) begleiten, geleiten, (einem) Gesellschaft leisten.

Accomplice, s. der Mitschuldige, Teilhaber.

Accomplish, v.a. vollenden, vollführen, zustande bringen (a task); vollenden (a period); erlangen, erreichen (one's object, etc.); he has —ed his purpose, er hat seinen Zweck erreicht. **—ed,** adj. ausgebildet. **—ment,** s. die Ausführung (of an object); die Vollendung (of a task, etc.); die Erfüllung (of a prophecy, of a duty, etc.); she has many —ments, sie ist sehr fein gebildet.

Accord, I. s. (agreement in opinion) die Übereinstimmung; (union) die Eintracht, Einigkeit; with one —, einstimmig; of one's own —, freiwillig. II. v.a. übereinstimmend machen; in Einklang bringen; vergleichen vereinigen, versöhnen; bewilligen (a request); gewähren (praise). III. v.n.; — with, übereinstimmen mit. **—ance,** s. die Übereinstimmung. **—ant,** adj. gemäß, übereinstimmend. **—ing to,** prep. gemäß, zufolge, nach. **—ingly,** adv. danach, folglich, demnach, demgemäß, also.

Accost, v.a. anreden, ansprechen.

Account, I. s. die Rechnung; (report) der Bericht; (narrative) die Erzählung; die Rechenschaft (of a person's doings, etc.); (importance) der Wert, das Ansehen; profit and loss —, das Gewinn- und Verlust-konto; bank account, das Bankkonto; cash —, die Kassen-rechnung; — agreed upon, der Rechnungsabschluß; to balance an —, ein Konto faldieren; on —, auf Rechnung, auf Abschlag; payment on —, Abschlagszahlung; on no —, auf keinen Fall; on his —, um seinetwillen; on — of, wegen; on that —, darum, deswegen; of no —, unbedeutend. II. v.n.; to — for, (answer for) Rechenschaft von

einer S. ablegen or geben; (explain) erklären. **—able,** adj. verantwortlich. **—ant,** s. der Rechnungsführer; der Buchhalter; der Bücherrevisor. **—book,** s. das Rechnungsbuch, Kontobuch.

Accoutre, v.a. ausrüsten, ausstatten. **—ment,** s. (gen'lly —ments, pl.) der Anzug; die Ausrüstung, Bewaffnung (Mil.).

Accredit, v.a. beglaubigen, akkreditieren; (authorize) ermächtigen; (empower) bevollmächtigen.

Accr—etion, s. das Wachstum; der Zuwachs, Anwachs. **—ue,** v.a. anwachsen, zuwachsen; zufallen, erwachsen (as property, etc.).

Accumulat—e, v. I. a. (an)häufen, zusammenhäufen. II. n. sich anhäufen, sich ansammeln, zunehmen. **—ing,** p. & adj. zunehmend. **—ion,** s. die Anhäufung; (the act of —ing) das Anhäufen. **—or,** s. (Elec.) der Akkumulator.

Accura—cy, s. die Genauigkeit; die Pünktlichkeit (in time); (correctness) die Richtigkeit. **—te,** adj., **—tely,** adv. genau; pünktlich; getreu (as a narrative).

Accurs—ed, **—t,** p.p. & adj. verflucht, verwünscht.

Accus—ation, s. die Anklage, Beschuldigung; die Klage (Law). **—ative,** s. (—ative case) der Akkusativ. **—atory,** adj. anklagend. **—e,** v.a. anklagen (of a thing, einer or wegen einer Sache), beschuldigen. **—ed,** s. der, die Angeklagte. **—er,** s. der Ankläger.

Accustom, v.a. gewöhnen; **—ed,** p.p. & adj. (in the habit) gewohnt; (trained) gewöhnt; (usual) gewöhnlich.

Ace, s. das As, die Eins; within an —, um ein Haar.

Acerbity, s. die Herbigkeit; die Rauhheit (of manner, etc.).

Acet—ic, **—ous,** adj. essigsauer; säuerlich. **—ylene,** s. das Acetylen.

Ach—e, I. s. der Schmerz. II. v.n. schmerzen, weh tun. **—ing,** I. adj. schmerzhaft. II. s. das Schmerzen.

Achieve, v.a. (accomplish) ausführen, zustande bringen, vollenden; (perform) verrichten; (gain) gewinnen, erlangen. **—ment,** s. die Ausführung; großes Werk, die Heldentat.

Achromatic, *adj.* farblos.

Acid, I. *adj.* sauer. II. *s.* die Säure.
—**ity,** *s.* die Säure.

Acknowledg—e, *v.a.* (admit) zugeben; (confess) bekennen, gestehen; (notify) anzeigen. —**ment,** *s.* die Anerkennung; das Bekenntnis, Geständnis (*of a fault*); die Quittung, der Empfangsschein (*of payment, etc.*); (of a letter) die Bestätigung (eines Briefes); —**ments,** der Dank, die Erkenntlichkeit.

Acorn, *s.* die Eichel.

Acquaint, *v.a.* bekannt machen; (announce) berichten, melden. —**ance,** *s.* die Bekanntschaft (*with persons and things*); (knowledge) die Kenntnis; (person) der, die Bekannte.

Acquiesce, *v.n.* einwilligen (in eine S.), sich (*dat.*) (etwas) gefallen lassen, sich (in eine S.) fügen, schicken. —**nce,** *s.* (submission) die Ergebung; (consent) die Einwilligung (in), Zustimmung (zu), Genehmigung (zu). —**nt,** *adj.* ergeben, geduldig, nachgiebig.

Acquir—e, *v.a.* erlangen, erwerben; erlernen, lernen (*a language, etc.*). —**ement,** *s.* die Erwerbung, Erlangung; (object gained) das Erworbene. —**er,** *s.* der Erwerber.

Acquisit—ion, *s.* der Erwerb; die Erlernung (*of a language, etc.*); (gain) der Erwerb, das Erworbene. —**ive,** *adj.* habsüchtig.

Acquit, *v.a.* freisprechen, lossprechen (*a person accused*); abtragen, quittieren (*a debt*). —**tal,** *s.* die Lossprechung; (discharge of duties) die Erledigung. —**tance,** *s.* die Abtragung, die Quittung.

Acre, *s.* der Morgen.

Acrid, *adj.* scharf, beißend.

Acrimony, *s.* die Schärfe, die Bitterkeit.

Acrobat, *s.* der Akrobat, Seiltänzer. —**ic,** *a.* akrobatisch.

Across, I. *adv.* kreuzweise, in die Quer(e). II. *prep.* quer durch, quer über; mitten durch; to come — a person, jemandem begegnen.

Act, I. *s.* (deed) die Tat, das Werk; der Aufzug (*of a play*); — of parliament, die Parlamentsakte, das Gesetz. II. *v.a.*; to — a part, eine Rolle spielen; sich verstellen. III. *v.n.* wirken (behave) sich betragen, handeln; spielen (*on the stage, etc.*); (operate) wirken. —**ing,** I. *s.* das Handeln;

das Spiel. II. *adj.* handelnd, wirkend. —**ion,** *s.* die Wirkung; die Handlung; der Prozeß; der Gang einer Maschine; die Schlacht. —**ionable,** *adj.* prozeßfähig, klagbar. —**ive,** *adj.,* —**ively,** *adv.* tätig; emsig, geschäftig; wirkend; (agile) behend, flink. —**ivity,** *s.* die Tätigkeit; die Wirksamkeit; die Behendigkeit; in full —ivity, in vollem Gange. —**or,** *s.* der Schauspieler. —**ress,** die Schauspielerin. —**ual,** *adj.,* —**ually,** *adv.* wirklich. —**uality,** *s.* die Wirklichkeit.

Acu—men, *s.* der Scharfsinn. —**te,** *adj.* spitzig; scharf; fein. —**teness,** *s.* der Scharfsinn; die Feinheit; die Heftigkeit.

Adage, *v.n.* das Sprichwort.

Adamant, I. *s.* sehr harter Stein; die Härte. II. *adj.* unerbitterlich, felsenfest. —**ine,** *adj.* hart wie ein Diamant.

Adapt, *v.a.* anpassen, anbequemen; —er plug, der Zwischenstecker (*Elec.*). —**ability,** *s.* die Anwendbarkeit. —**able,** *adj.* anwendbar; paßlich. —**ation,** *s.* die Anwendung; die Anpassungsfähigkeit; —ation of a book, Bearbeitung eines Buches. —**ive,** *adj.* anpassungsfähig.

Add, *v.a.* beifügen, beitragen; (increase) vermehren; zusammenzählen (*Arith.*). —**ition,** *s.* die Hinzusetzung, der Zusatz; die Vermehrung; die Zusammenzählung, Addition (*Arith.*); in —ition to this, noch dazu. —**itional,** *adj.* hinzugesetzt, beigefügt, nachträglich.

Adder, *s.* die Natter.

Addict, *v.a.*; to — oneself, sich ergeben; —ed to drink, demTr unk ergeben.

Addle, *v.a.* unfruchtbar machen; —d eggs, faule Eier.

Address, I. *s.* die Anrede; die Rede; die Adresse, Aufschrift; (dexterity) die Gewandtheit, Geschicklichkeit; (manner) das Benehmen, die Haltung. II. *v.a.* anreden (einen, a person); adressieren, überschreiben (*a letter*).

Adduce, *v.a.* anführen, beibringen.

Adept, *adj.* gelehrt, erfahren; geschickt.

Adequa—cy, *s.* die Hinlänglichkeit, Angemessenheit. —**te,** *adj.* angemessen, entsprechend; hinreichend.

Adhere, *v.n.* anhangen, ankleben. —**nce,** *s.* das Anhängen, Ankleben; (attachment) die Anhänglichkeit (an). —**nt,** *s.* der Anhänger.

Adhesi—on, s. die Anhaftung; das Anhangen; der Anschluß. **—ve,** adj. anklebend; —ve plaster, das Heftpflaster. **—veness,** s. die Klebrigkeit; die Zähigkeit.

Adieu, I. adv. & int. lebe wohl! II. s. das Lebewohl.

Adipose, a. fett, feist.

Adjacen—cy, s. die Angrenzung. **—t,** adj. anliegend, angrenzend.

Adjective, I. s. das Beiwort, Adjektiv. II. adj. beiwörtlich, adjektivisch.

Adjoin, v.n. anliegen, angrenzen, anstoßen.

Adjourn, v.a. vertagen. **—ment,** s. die Vertagung, Verschiebung, der Aufschub.

Adjud—ge, v.a. zuerkennen, zusprechen. **—ication,** s. der Entscheid, das Urteil.

Adjunct, s. der Zusatz.

Adjust, v.a. zurecht machen, ordnen. **—able,** adj. stellbar, verschiebbar. **—ment,** s. das Anordnen; die Einrichtung, Zurechtmachung; die Ausgleichung, Schlichtung.

Adjutant, s. der Adjutant.

Administ—er, v.a. (manage) verwalten; handhaben (justice); erteilen, geben (relief, etc.); to —er the law, Recht sprechen; to —er an oath, einen Eid abnehmen. **—ration,** s. die Verwaltung; die Regierung; die Handhabung (of justice); die Ausspendung (of the sacraments). **—rative,** adj. verwaltend; behilflich. **—rator,** s. der Verwalter. **—ratrix,** s. die Verwalterin.

Admir—able, adj., **—ably,** adv. bewundernswert, herrlich. **—ation,** s. die Bewunderung. **—e,** v.a. bewundern. **—er,** s. der Bewunderer; der Verehrer (of a lady).

Admiral, s. der Admiral. **—ty,** s. die Admiralität; First Lord of the —ty englischer Marineminister.

Admissi—bility, s. die Zulässigkeit. **—ble,** adj. zulässig. **—on,** s. die Zulassung, Aufnahme; (concession) das Zugeständnis.

Admit, v.a. einlassen, zulassen, den Zutritt gestatten; gestehen, erkennen zugeben, gestatten; I will — that, das lasse ich gelten. **—tance,** s. der Eintritt, Eingang; no —tance, verbotener Eingang.

Admoni—sh, v.a. ermahnen; warnen.

—tion, s. die Ermahnung; die Warnung; der Verweis. **—tory,** adj. ermahnend; verweisend.

Ado, s. das Tun, der Lärm; die Mühe; much — about nothing, viel Lärm um nichts.

Adolescen—ce, s. das Jünglingsalter. **—t,** adj. jugendlich, heranwachsend.

Adopt, v.a. annehmen; his —ed country, sein neues Vaterland. **—ion,** s. die Annahme.

Ador—ation, s. die Anbetung, Verehrung. **—e,** v.a. anbeten, verehren; (love) leidenschaftlich lieben. **—er,** s. der Anbeter, Verehrer.

Adorn, v.a. schmücken, zieren, putzen. **—ment,** s. der Schmuck, Zierat; die Verzierung.

Adrift, adv. losgetrieben, treibend; (fig.) aufs Geratewohl.

Adroit, adj., **—ly,** adv. geschickt, gewandt. **—ness,** s. die Gewandtheit.

Adulation, s. die Schmeichelei.

Adult, I. adj. erwachsen. II. s. der Erwachsene.

Adulter—ate, v.a. verfälschen; (fig.) verderben. **—ation,** s. die Verfälschung. **—er,** s. der Ehebrecher. **—ess,** s. die Ehebrecherin. **—ous,** adj. ehebrecherisch. **—y,** s. der Ehebruch.

Advance, I. v.n. vorrücken, anrücken; Fortschritte machen. II. v.a. (lend) vorschießen; (push forward) vorrücken; äußern (an opinion); to — a claim, Anspruch machen auf (eine S.). III. s. das Anrücken; der Fortschritt; der Vorschuß (of money); in —, im voraus. **—ment,** s. die Beförderung; der Fortschritt.

Advantage, s. der Vorteil; die Überlegenheit; to take — of, sich etwas zunutze machen. **—ous,** adj., **—ously,** adv. vorteilhaft; günstig.

Advent, s. der Advent (Eccl.); die Ankunft.

Advent—ure, I. s. das Abenteuer. II. v.a. wagen. **—urer,** s. der Abenteurer; der Spekulant. **—urous,** adj. abenteuerlich; kühn; verwegen.

Adverb, s. das Umstandswort.

Advers—ary, s. der Gegner, Feind, Widersacher. **—e,** adj., **—ely,** adv. zuwider, widerwärtig, widrig; feindlich. **—eness,** s. die Widrigkeit. **—ity,** s. das Elend, die Not, Trübsal.

Advert—ise, v.a. öffentlich anzeigen. **—isement,** s. die Anzeige, Ankündigung. **—iser,** *s.* der Anzeiger; (newspaper) das Anzeigeblatt.

Advice, *s.* der Rat; die Meldung.

Advis—able, *adj.* ratsam. **—ability,** *s.* die Ratsamkeit. **—e,** *v.* I. *a.* raten (eine S. or zu einer S.); beraten; melden. II. *n.* überlegen, bedenken. **—edly,** *adv.* absichtlich. **—er,** *s.* der Ratgeber.

Advoca—cy, *s.* die Verteidigung. **—te,** *s.* der Advokat; der Fürsprecher.

Adze, *s.* die Krummaxt, das Breitbeil.

Aerated, *adj.* kohlensauer.

Aerial, I. *s.* die Antenne (*Radio*). II. *adj.* luftig; in der Luft; — combat, der Luftkampf; — defence, der Luftschutz; — navigation, die Luftfahrt; — race, das Wettfliegen; — warfare, der Luftkrieg.

Aerie, der (Adler=)Horst.

Aero—drome, *s.* der Flughafen, Flugplatz. **—naut,** *s.* der Luftfahrer, Luftschiffer. **—nautics,** *s.* das Flugwesen. **—plane,** *s.* das Flugzeug, die Flugmaschine.

Æsthetic, *a.* ästhetisch, geschmackvoll. **—s,** *s.* die Schönheitslehre, Ästhetik.

Afar, *adv.* fern, weit entfernt.

Affab—ility, *s.* die Leutseligkeit. **—le,** *adj.,* **—ly,** *adv.* leutselig, umgänglich.

Affair, *s.* die Angelegenheit; (matter) die Sache.

Affect, *v.a.* Eindruck machen; rühren, bewegen (*the passions, etc.*); angreifen (*injuriously*); (influence) Einfluß üben auf (einen or eine S.); (er)heucheln; it —s the eyes, es greift die Augen an. **—ation,** *s.* die Ziererei. **—ed,** *p.p.* & *adj.* (moved) gerührt; (injured) angegriffen; (full of affectation) geziert; (pretended) erheuchelt. **—edly,** *adv.* gezwungen, geziert. **—ing,** *adj.* rührend. **—ion,** *s.* die Zuneigung, Liebe. **—ionate,** *adj.,* **—ionately,** *adv.* herzlich, liebevoll.

Affiance, *v.a.* verloben.

Affidavit, *s.* schriftliche Erklärung unter Eid.

Affinity, *s.* die Verwandtschaft.

Affirm, *v.* I. *a.* (confirm) bestätigen; (assert) behaupten. II. *n.* feierlich erklären. **—ation,** *s.* die Bestätigung, Beträftigung. **—ative,** *adj.* bejahend.

Affix, *v.a.* anheften, anschlagen.

Afflict, *v.a.* betrüben; quälen, plagen, peinigen. **—ing,** *p.* & *adj.* betrübend. **—ion,** *s.* die Betrübnis, Kümmernis, Trübsal.

Afflu—ence, *s.* der Reichtum; der Überfluß. **—ent,** *adj.* wohlhabend, reich.

Afford, *v.a.* (yield) hervorbringen; (give) geben, gewähren; I can't — it, meine Mittel erlauben es mir nicht.

Affront, I. *s.* die Beleidigung. II. *v.a.* beleidigen.

Afloat, *adv.* schwimmend, flott.

Afraid, *adj.* bange; to be — of, sich fürchten vor.

Afresh, *adv.* von neuem.

After, I. *prep.* nach (*of time*); (behind) nach, hinter; the day — to-morrow, übermorgen; I'll go — him, ich will ihm nach. II. *adv.* hinterher; nachher, darauf. III. *conj.* nachdem. **—wards,** *adv.* nachher, hernach, darauf, in der Folge. **—noon,** *s.* der Nachmittag. **—thought,** *s.* nachträglicher Einfall.

Again, *adv.* wieder, wiederum, nochmals, noch einmal; (back) zurück; (moreover) ferner, außerdem; (on the other hand) dagegen; as much —, noch einmal so viel.

Against, *prep.* gegen; wider; (by) gegen, an, bis; (on, close to) an; — the wall, an der Wand.

Age, *s.* das Alter; (period) das Zeitalter, die Zeit; to be of —, mündig sein. **—d,** *adj.* alt, bejahrt.

Agen—cy, *s.* (action) die Wirkung; (intervention) die Vermittelung; (commence) die Agentur. **—t,** *s.* die wirkende Kraft; der Geschäftsträger.

Aggravat—e, *v.a.* erschweren, verschlimmern; (provoke) ärgern. **—ion,** *s.* die Verschlimmerung; die Aufreizung.

Aggregate, I. *adj.* angehäuft; vereint. II. *s.* das Aggregat.

Aggress—ion, *s.* der Anfall. **—ive,** *adj.* angreifend; streitlustig; —ive war, der Angriffskrieg.

Aghast, *adj.* entsetzt.

Agil—e, *adj.* behend, flink. **—ity,** *s.* die Behendigkeit.

Agitat—e, *v.a.* beunruhigen (*the mind, etc.*). **—ion,** *s.* die Unruhe; der Aufruhr. **—or,** *s.* der Aufwiegler.

Aglow, *adv.* glühend.

Ago, I. *adj.* (*after a noun*) vergangen, vorüber, her, vor. II. *adv.*; long —, lange her; not long —, vor kurzem.

Agoniz—e, *v.a.* quälen, martern. **—ing,** *adj.* höchst schmerzlich.

Agony, *s.* die Seelenangst; — of sorrow, unbeschreiblicher Schmerz; — column (in newspapers), die Seufzerspalte (in Zeitungen).

Agrarian, *adj.* agrarisch; the — party, die Bauernpartei.

Agree, *v.n.* übereinstimmen; übereinkommen; —d! einverstanden! —**able,** *adj.*, —**ably,** *adv.* angenehm, gefällig; —able, —ably to, zufolge, in Gemäßheit mit. —**ment,** *s.* die Übereinstimmung; der Einklang; der Vertrag; to come to an —ment, eine Verständigung erzielen.

Agricultur—al, *adj.* landwirtschaftlich. —**e,** *s.* der Feldbau, die Landwirtschaft. —**ist,** *s.* der Landwirt.

Aground, *adv.* auf dem Grunde, gestrandet; to run —, stranden.

Ague, *s.* der Fieberfrost.

Ah, *int.* ah! ach! —**Aha,** *int.* aha!

Ahead, *adv.* vorwärts, voraus; to go —, vorwärts streben; he is a go-ahead, er ist ein Streber.

Aid, I. *s.* die Hilfe, der Beistand. II. *v.a.* helfen, unterstützen, beistehen.

Aide-de-camp, *s.* der Adjutant.

Ail, *v.* I. *n.* unpäßlich sein. II. *imp.* weh tun, schmerzen; what —s him? was fehlt ihm? —**ing,** *adj.* leidend, kränklich. —**ment,** *s.* das Leiden.

Aim, I. *s.* (direction) die Richtung; das Ziel; der Zweck. II. *v.n.*; — at, zielen auf (*acc.*) or nach. —**less,** *adj.* ziellos, zwecklos.

Air, I. *s.* die Luft; die Melodie (*Mus.*), (manner) die Miene, das Ansehen; in the open —, im Freien; to give oneself —s, vornehm tun. II. *v.a.* lüften; auslüften (*a room, etc.*); wärmen (*linen, etc.*). —**y,** *adj.* luftig. —**base,** *s.* der Fliegerstützpunkt. —**craft,** *s.* das Luftfahrzeug. —**force,** *s. pl.* die Luftstreitkräfte. —**gun,** *s.* die Windbüchse. —**liner,** *s.* das Verkehrsflugzeug. —**mail,** *s.* die Luftpost. —**man,** *s.* der Flieger, Pilot. —**passenger,** *s.* der Fluggast. —**pocket,** *s.* der Luftsack. —**raid,** *s.* der Luftüberfall. —**ship,** *s.* das Luftschiff. —**tight,** *adj.* luftdicht. —**way,** *s.* die Flugstrecke. —**woman,** *s.* die Fliegerin.

Aisle, *s.* das Seitenschiff einer Kirche.

Ajar, *adv.* halb offen.

Akin, *adj.* verwandt.

Alabaster, *s.* der Alabaster.

Alacrity, *s.* die Bereitwilligkeit.

Alarm, I. *s.* (call to arms) der Lärm; (fear) die Angst. II. *v.a.* Lärm blasen; erschrecken. —**clock,** *s.* die Weckuhr.

Alas, *int.* leider! o' weh! ach!

Albumen, *s.* das Eiweiß.

Alcohol, *s.* der Alkohol. —**ic,** *adj.* alkoholisch.

Alder, *s.* die Erle.

Alderman, *s.* der Ratsherr.

Ale, *s.* englisches Bier. —**house,** *s.* das Bierhaus, die Bierkneipe.

Alert, *adj.* wachsam; on the —, auf der Hut. —**ness,** *s.* die Wachsamkeit.

Algebra, *s.* die Algebra. —**ic(al),** *adj.* —**ically,** *adv.* algebraisch.

Alien, *adj.* fremd, ausländisch. —**ate,** *v.a.* veräußern, entfremden.

1Alight, *v.n.* herabsteigen (*from a horse*); aussteigen (*from a carriage*).

2Alight, *adv.* brennend, erhellt.

Alike, I. *adj.* gleich, ähnlich. II. *adv.* gleichmäßig.

Aliment, *s.* die Speise. —**ary,** *adj.* zur Nahrung gehörig; nährend; —ary canal, der Verdauungskanal.

Alive, *adj.* lebend, lebendig, am Leben.

Alkali, *s.* das Alkali, Laugensalz.

All, I. *adj. & pronominal adj.* all; ganz; above —, vor allen Dingen; once for —, ein für allemal; for — I care, meinetwegen; not at —, durchaus nicht; — the better, desto besser. II. *adv.* or *part.* forming with another word an adverb, all-, ganz, gar, gänzlich, völlig; — bounteous, — bountiful, allgütig. III. *n.* das Ganze; das All, Alles. —**hallow eve,** *s.* der Allerheiligenabend. — **saints' day,** *s.* der Allerheiligen (tag). — **souls,** *s. pl.* Allerseelen (2 November).

Allay, *v.a.* lindern (*pain*); stillen (*thirst*); beruhigen (*fears*).

Alleg—ation, *s.* die Behauptung. —**e,** *v.a.* behaupten.

Allegiance, *s.* die Treue der Untertanen; die Ergebenheit.

Allegor—ical, *adj.* sinnbildlich, allegorisch. —**y,** *s.* die Allegorie, das Sinnbild.

Allevia—te, *v.a.* mildern. —**tion,** *s.* die Erleichterung, Linderung.

Alley, *s.* die Allee; das Gäßchen.

Alliance, *s.* (treaty) das Bündnis, der Bund; die Verwandtschaft.

Alligator, *s.* der Alligator.

Allot, *v.a.* (assign) zuteilen; (distribute)

austeilen. **—ment,** *s.* (share) der Anteil, Teil; die Landparzelle.

Allow, *v.a.* (grant) zugeben; (permit) erlauben, gestatten; (give) bestimmen; (admit) gelten lassen; to — for, Rücksicht nehmen auf. **—able,** *adj.* zulässig. **—ance,** *s.* die Zulassung; (approval) die Genehmigung; die Erlaubnis; das Taschengeld; to make —ance, Nachsicht üben.

Alloy, *s.* die Vermischung.

Allude, *v.n.* anspielen (to a thing, auf eine Sache).

Allure, *v.a.* anlocken.

Allusi—on, *s.* die Hindeutung (to a thing, auf eine S.). **—ve,** *adj.* anspielend.

Ally, I. *v.a.* verbinden, vereinigen; allied to or with, verbunden, verwandt mit. II. *s.* der Verbündete, Bundesgenosse.

Almanac, *s.* der Almanach, Kalender.

Almighty, I. *adj.* allmächtig. II. *s.* der Allmächtige.

Almond, *s.* die Mandel.

Almost, *adv.* fast, beinahe.

Alms, *s.* (often used as pl.) das Almosen. **—house,** *s.* das Armenhaus.

Aloe, *s.* die Aloe.

Aloft, *adv.* in der Höhe; empor; im Tauwerk (*Naut.*).

Alone, *adj. & adv.* allein; (solitary) einsam; (unique) einzig; let it —, lass' das bleiben.

Along, I. *adv.* längs, der Länge nach; get — with you, pack' dich. II. *prep.* längs, entlang.

Aloof, *adv.* fern, weitab; to keep — from, sich fernhalten von. **—ness,** *s.* das Sichfernhalten.

Aloud, *adv.* laut.

Alphabet, *s.* das Alphabet. **—ical,** *adj.* alphabetisch.

Alp—ine, *adj.* alpin(isch). **—inist,** *s.* der Bergsteiger. **—s,** *pl.* die Alpen.

Already, *adv.* bereits, schon.

Also, *adv.* (likewise) auch, ebenfalls, gleichfalls; (moreover) ferner.

Altar, *s.* der Altar.

Alter, *v.* I. *a.* ändern, verändern. II. *n.* sich (ver)ändern. **—able,** *adj.* veränderlich. **—ation,** *s.* die Änderung, Veränderung.

Alter—cation, *s.* der Zank. **—nate,** *s.* I. *v.a.* abwechseln lassen. II. *v.n.* abwechseln. III. *adj.* abwechselnd; wech-

selseitig; on —nate days, einen Tag um den anderen.

Although, *conj.* obgleich, obschon, wenngleich.

Altitude, *s.* die Höhe.

Altogether, *adv.* zusammen, allesamt; (wholly) gänzlich, ganz und gar, völlig, durchaus.

Alum, *s.* der Alaun.

Always, *adv.* immer, stets, beständig, allezeit.

Am, *first pers. pres. indic.* of to be, bin; I — to go, ich soll gehen.

Amain, *adv.* mit aller Kraft, heftig, frisch.

Amass, *v.a.* aufhäufen.

Amateur, *s.* der Kunstfreund; der Dilettant.

Amaz—e, *v.a.* erstaunen. **—ement,** *s.* die höchste Verwunderung. **—ing,** *adj.* höchst erstaunlich, wunderbar.

Ambassad—or, *s.* der Botschafter, Gesandte. **—orial,** *adj.* gesandtschaftlich. **—ress,** *s.* die Botschafterin.

Amber, *s.* der Bernstein.

Ambi—guity, *s.* die Zweideutigkeit. **—guous,** *adj.,* **—guously,** *adv.* zweideutig, doppelsinnig, dunkel.

Ambitio—n, *s.* die Ehrbegier, der Ehrgeiz. **—us,** *adj.,* **—usly,** *adv.* ehrbegierig, ehrgeizig.

Amble, *s.* der Paß, Paßgang.

Ambulance, *s.* das Feldlazarett (*Mil.*).

Ambuscade, Ambush, I. *s.* der Hinterhalt. II. *v.a.* aus dem Hinterhalt überfallen.

Ameliorat—e, *v.a.* verbessern. **—ion,** *s.* die Verbesserung.

Amen, *int.* Amen.

Amenable, *adj.* biegsam, leitsam; — to law, verantwortlich.

Amend, *v.* I. *a.* bessern, verbessern; (correct) berichtigen. II. *n.* sich bessern. **—ment,** *s.* die Verbesserung; der Verbesserungsantrag. **—s,** *s.* die Genugtuung.

Amethyst, *s.* der Amethyst.

Ami—able, *adj.,* **—ably,** *adv.* liebenswürdig. **—ability,** *s.* die Liebenswürdigkeit. **—cable,** *adj.,* **—cably,** *adv.* freundschaftlich.

Amid, —st, *prep.* mitten in, mitten unter (*dat.*), inmitten (*gen.*).

Amiss, *adj. & adv.* verkehrt; übel, unrecht; to take —, übelnehmen.

Ammonia, *s.* das Ammoniak; liquid —, der Salmiakgeist.

Ammunition, *s.* die Munition.

Amnesty, *s.* der (allgemeine) Straferlaß, die Begnadigung.
Among, —st, *prep.* (mitten) unter, zwischen.
Amorous, *adj.,* —ly, *adv.* verliebt. —ness, *s.* die Verliebtheit.
Amount, I. *s.* der Betrag; die Summe; der Bestand. II. *v.n.* sich belaufen (to, acc.), betragen; the whole sum —s to, die ganze Summe beträgt.
Amour, *s.* der Liebeshandel, die Liebschaft.
Ampl—e, *adj.,* —y, *adv.* weit, breit; weitläufig. —ification, *s.* die Erweiterung. —ify, *v.a.* erweitern, ausdehnen. —itude, *s.* der Umfang.
Amputat—e, *v.a.* abschneiden. —ion, *s.* die Abnahme, Amputation (*Med.*).
Amulet, *s.* das Amulett, Schutzmittel.
Amuse, *v.a.* vergnügen, unterhalten, belustigen. —ment, *s.* die Unterhaltung, der Zeitvertreib.
Anabaptist, *s.* der Wiedertäufer.
Anachronism, *s.* der Anachronismus.
Anæm—ia, *s.* die Blutarmut. —ic, *adj.* blutarm.
Anæsthe—sia, *s.* die Anästhesie. —tics, *pl.* anästhetische Mittel.
Ana—logous, *adj.* ähnlich, analog(isch). —logy, *s.* die Analogie, Ähnlichkeit.
Ana—lyse, *v.a.* analysieren, auflösen. —lysis, *s.* die Analyse, Auflösung. —lyst, *s.* der Analytiker. —lytic, —lytical, *adj.,* —lytically, *adv.* analytisch).
Ana—tomical, *adj.,* —tomically, *adv.* anatomisch. —tomist, *s.* der Anatom. —tomy, *s.* die Anatomie, Zergliederungskunst.
Anarch—ical, *adj.* anarchisch. —ist, *s.* der Anarchist. —y, *s.* die Anarchie.
Anathema, *s.* der Bannfluch. —tize, *v.a.* verfluchen.
Ancest—or, *s.* der Vorfahr; der Ahn (*Poet.*). —ral, *adj.* angestammt; altererbt. —ress, *s.* die Stamm(m)utter; die Ahne (*Poet.*). —ry, *s.* die Abstammung.
Anchor, I. *s.* der Anker. II. *v.n.* antern, vor Anker liegen. —age, *s.* der Ankergrund.
Anchovy, *s.* die Sardelle.
Ancient, *adj.* alt; ehemalig, vormalig. —ly, *adv.* ehedem, vormals.
And, *conj.* und.
Anecdote, *s.* die Anekdote.

Anew, *adv.* von neuem.
Angel, *s.* der Engel. —ic(al), *adj.* engelgleich.
Ang—er, I. *s.* der Zorn, Unwille, Ärger Verdruß. II. *v.a.* erzürnen, aufbringen; böse machen. —ered, *p.p.* & *adj.* erzürnt, aufgebracht. —rily, *adv.,* —ry, *adj.* zornig, böse.
Ang—le, I. *s.* der Winkel; (fishing) die Angel. II. *v.n.* angeln (for, nach). —ler, *s.* der Angler. —ling, *s.* das Angeln. —ular, *adj.,* —ularly, *adv.* winkelig.
Anguish, *s.* die Angst, Pein, Qual.
Anim—al, I. *s.* das Tier. II. *adj.* animalisch, tierisch. —ate, I. *v.a.* beleben, beseelen; aufmuntern. II. *adj.* lebendig. —ated, *adj.* belebt, beseelt; lebhaft, munter. —ation, *s.* die Belebung; das Leben, die Lebhaftigkeit. —osity, *s.* der Unwille; die Feindseligkeit, Erbitterung.
Ankle, *s.* der Fußknöchel, Enkel.
Annals, *pl.* die Annalen; die Jahrbücher.
Annex, I. *v.a.* anhängen, beifügen, hinzufügen. II. *s.* der Anbau. —ation, *s.* die Beifügung; die Annektierung.
Annihilat—e, *v.a.* vernichten, zerstören. —ion, *s.* die Vernichtung.
Anniversary, *s.* der Jahrestag.
Announce, *v.a.* melden. —ment, *s.* die Bekanntmachung.
Annoy, *v.a.* beunruhigen, belästigen. —ance, *s.* der Verdruß. —ing, *adj.* ärgerlich.
Annual, I. *adj.* jährlich. II. *s.* die einjährige Pflanze (*Bot.*); das Jahrbuch.
Annul, *v.a.* ungültig machen.
Annunciation, *s.* die Verkündigung.
Anoint, *v.a.* salben. —ing, *s.* die Salbung.
Anonym—ity, *s.* die Namenverschweigung. —ous, *adj.* ohne Namen, namenlos, ungenannt.
Another, *adj.* verschieden; noch ein(e); ein anderer, 2c., *see* Other; — time, ein anderes Mal; — way, anders; they injure one —, sie schaden einander; yet —? noch einer?
Answer, I. *s.* die Antwort. II. *v.a.* beantworten; to — the purpose, dem Zweck entsprechen; to — for, Rede stehen für. III. *v.n.* antworten. —able, *adj.* beantwortbar (*of a question, etc.*); (responsible) verantwortlich.

Ant, *s.* die Ameise.

Antagonis—m, *s.* der Widerstand. **—t,** *s.* der Gegner. **—tic,** *adj.* gegnerisch.

Antarctic, *adj.* antarktisch; **—** circle, der südliche Polarkreis.

Ante—cedence, *s.* das Vorhergehen. **—cedent,** I. *adj.* vorhergehend. II. *s.* das Vorhergehende.

Antediluvian, *adj.* vorsündflutlich.

Antelope, *s.* die Antilope.

Antemeridian, *adj.* vormittägig.

Antenna, *s.* die Antenne (*Radio*).

Anterior, *adj.* früher, älter.

Anteroom, *s.* das Vorzimmer.

Anthem, *s.* die Hymne.

Antic, *s.* die Posse, Fratze.

Antichrist, *s.* der Antichrist.

Anticipat—e, *v.a.* vorausnehmen. **—ion,** *s.* die Vorausnahme; das Zuvorkommen. **—ory,** *adj.* vorgriesend, vorwegnehmend.

Antidote, *s.* das Gegenmittel.

Antipathy, *s.* der Widerwille.

Antipodes, *pl.* die Gegenfüßler, Antipoden.

Anti—quarian, I. *adj.* altertümlich. II. *s.,* **—quary,** *s.* der Altertumskenner, Altertumsforscher. **—quated,** *adj.* veraltet. **—que,** I. *adj.* altmodisch. II. *s.* das Altertumsstück. **—quity,** *s.* das Altertum.

Antiseptic, I. *adj.* Fäulnisverhindernd, antiseptisch. II. *s.* das Antiseptikum.

Anti—thesis, *s.* die Entgegensetzung. **—thetical,** *adj.* entgegengestellt.

Antitoxin, *s.* das Gegengift.

Antler, *s.* das (Hirsch-)Geweih.

Anvil, *s.* der Amboß.

Anxi—ety, *s.* (fear) die Angst, Bangigkeit; (uneasiness) die Unruhe. **—ous,** *adj.* ängstlich, bange, besorgt (for, about, um, wegen); eifrig bemüht; I am **—** to see him, mir liegt etwas daran, ihn zu sehen.

Any, I. *adj.* irgend ein, eine, ein; jeder, jede, jedes; irgend welch, welche, welches; not **—,** keiner, keine, keins; are there **—** witnesses present? sind irgend welche Zeugen da? II. *adv.* irgend. **—body,** *s.* irgend einer. **—how,** *adv.* irgendwie. **—one,** *see* **—body;** not **—**one, niemand, nicht einer. **—thing,** *s.* irgend etwas. **—way,** *adv.* irgend wie. **—where,** *adv.* irgendwo. **—wise,** *adv.* (in **—**wise) auf irgend eine Weise.

Apace, *adv.* geschwind, hastig.

Apart, *adv.* beiseits, bei Seite, für sich; (separately) abgesondert, einzeln; **—** from, abgesehen von.

Apartment, *s.* das Zimmer.

Ap—e, I. *s.* der Affe. II. *v.a.* nachäffen. **—ish,** *adj.* affenmäßig.

Aperient, I. *adj.* abführend, öffnend. II. *s.* das Abführ(ungs)mittel.

Apex, *s.* die Spitze, der Gipfel.

Apiece, *adv.* für jedes Stück; für jede Person.

Apo—logetic), *adj.* entschuldigend. **—logize,** *v.n.* (sich) entschuldigen. **—logy,** *s.* die Entschuldigung. **—plexy,** *s.* der Schlagfluß. **—stasy,** *s.* die Abtrünnigkeit. **—state,** I. *s.* der Abtrünnige. II. *adj.* abtrünnig; falsch.

Apost—le, *s.* der Apostel. **—olic(al),** *adj.* apostolisch.

Apothecary, *s.* der Apotheker; **—'s** shop, die Apotheke.

Appal, *v.a.* erschrecken. **—ling,** *adj.* erschreckend, schrecklich.

Apparatus, *s.* der Apparat, die Vorrichtung, das Gerät.

Apparel, I. *s.* die Kleidung, der Anzug. II. *v.a.* kleiden, bekleiden.

Appar—ent, *adj.,* **—ently,** *adv.* scheinbar. **—ition,** *s.* die Erscheinung.

Appeal, I. *v.n.* sich berufen (to a person, auf einen); dringend bitten. II. *s.* die Appellation; die Berufung, Anrufung. **—ing,** *adj.,* **—ingly,** *adv.* flehend.

Appear, *v.n.* erscheinen, zum Vorschein kommen; auftreten; scheinen. **—ance,** *s.* das Auftreten; der Anschein; der Schein; to keep up **—**ances, den Schein wahren.

Appease, *v.a.* besänftigen, befriedigen; löschen (*thirst*).

Append, *v.a.* beifügen (a seal, etc.). **—age,** *s.* der Anhang, das Anhängsel.

Appertain, *v.n.* zugehören.

Appet—ite, *s.* der Appetit. **—izing, —ising,** *adj.* appetitlich.

Applau—d, *v.a.* einem *or* einer Sache Beifall geben. **—se,** *s.* der Beifall.

Apple, *s.* der Apfel. **—pie,** *s.* die Apfelpastete; in **—**pie order, in der größten Ordnung.

Appli—ance, *s.* die Anwendung; (thing applied) das Gerät. **—cable,** *adj.* anwendbar (to a thing, auf eine S.). **—cant,** *s.* der Bewerber. **—cation,** *s.* die Anlegung (of poultices, etc.);

die Bewerbung (*for a place, etc.*); (industry) der Fleiß. **Apply**, *v.* I. *a.* anlegen, auflegen; (employ) anwenden; (for assistance, etc.) sich an einen (um Hilfe, ꝛc.) wenden. II. *n.* passen.

Appoint, *v.a.* bestimmen (*a day, etc.*); ernennen; (equip) ausrüsten. **—ment**, *s.* die Bestimmung, Festsetzung; die Ernennung; to make an —ment with, sich verabreden mit; by special—ment to the King, Hoflieferant des Königs.

Appraise, *v.a.* schätzen.

Appreci—able, *adj.*, **—ably**, *adv.* merklich. **—ate**, *v.a.* würdigen. **—ation**, *s.* die Würdigung.

Apprehen—d, *v.a.* verhaften (*a prisoner, etc.*); begreifen (*an idea, etc.*); fürchten. **—sible**, *adj.* faßlich, begreiflich. **—sion**, *s.* (seizure) das Ergreifen; (fear) die Besorgnis. **—sive**, *adj.* besorgt, furchtsam.

Apprentice, *s.* der Lehrling. **—ship**, *s.* die Lehrjahre.

Approach, I. *v.n.* (heran)nahen, sich nähern. II. *v.a.* nähern. III. *s.* das Herannahen; die Annäherung. **—able**, *adj.* erreichbar; zugänglich.

Approbation, *s.* die Billigung.

Appropriat—e, I. *v.a.* zueignen, widmen, bestimmen (*to a special use*); to —e something (to oneself), sich (*dat.*) etwas aneignen. II. *adj.* zweckmäßig, angemessen, passend. **—eness**, *s.* die Angemessenheit. **—ion**, *s.* die Aneignung; (dedication) die Zueignung; (application) die Anwendung, Verwendung.

Approv—al, *s.* die Billigung. **—e**, *v.a. & n.* billigen, genehmigen. **—ed**, *p.p.* anerkannt, erprobt. **—er**, *s.* der Billiger. **—ing**, *adj.*, **—ingly**, *adv.* billigend.

Approximat—e, I. *adj.* annähernd; ungefähr. II. *v.n.* sich nähern *or* nahen. **—ion**, *s.* die Annäherung.

Appurtenan—ce, *s.* das Zugehör, Zubehör. **—t**, *adj.* zugehörig.

Apricot, *s.* die Aprikose.

April, *s.* der April.

Apron, *s.* die Schürze. **—string**, *s.* das Schürzenband; tied to her —string, unter ihrem Pantoffel.

Apt, *adj.* (suitable) passend; (prone to) geneigt; (capable) geschickt, fähig. **—itude**, *s.* die Geneigtheit. **—ly**, *adv.*

(suitably) passend, gemäß; (readily) schnell, fertig. **—ness**, *s.* die Paßlichkeit, Angemessenheit (*of an expression, etc.*).

Aque—duct, *s.* die Wasserleitung. **—ous**, *adj.* wässerig.

Aquiline, *adj.* adlerartig.

Arable, *adj.* pflügbar, urbar.

Arbit—er, *s.* der Schiedsrichter. **—rament**, *s.* die Entscheidung. **—rariness**, *s.* die Willkür. **—rary**, *adj.* willkürlich. **—rate**, *v.a. & n.* urteilen. **—ration**, *s.* der Schiedsspruch.

Arbour, *s.* die Laube.

Arc, *s.* der Bogen. **—lamp**, *s.* die Bogenlampe.

Arcade, *s.* die Arkade.

¹**Arch**, I. *s.* der Bogen. II. *v.a.* wölben; **—ed**, gewölbt. III. *v.n.* sich wölben. **—way**, *s.* der Bogengang.

²**Arch**, I. *adj.*, **—ly**, *adv.* schalkhaft, schelmisch. II. *adj. & pref.* oberst, erst; (*in comp. often =*) Erz-. **—ness**, *s.* die Schelmerei, Schalkhaftigkeit. **—angel**, *s.* der Erzengel. **—deacon**, *s.* der Archidiakonus.

Archæolog—ical, *adj.* archäologisch. **—ist**, *s.* der Altertumsforscher. **—y**, *s.* die Altertumskunde.

Archer, *s.* der Bogenschütze. **—y**, *s.* das Bogenschießen.

Archiepiscopal, *adj.* erzbischöflich.

Architect, *s.* der Baumeister. **—tectural**, *adj.* baukünstlerisch. **—tecture**, *s.* die Baukunst.

Archives, *pl.* das Archiv.

Arctic, *adj.* arktisch.

Ard—ent, *adj.*, **—ently**, *adv.* heiß, glühend. **—our**, *s.* die Inbrunst, der Eifer.

Arduous, *adj.*, **—ly**, *adv.* schwierig, mühsam. **—ness**, *s.* die Schwierigkeit, Mühseligkeit.

Area, *s.* der Flächeninhalt.

Arena, *s.* der Kampfplatz.

Argu—e, *v.* I. *a. & n.* erörtern. II. *n.* streiten, disputieren. **—er**, *s.* der Disputant. **—ment**, *s.* der Wortstreit, das Disputieren; (subject of dispute) die Streitfrage. **—mentative**, *adj.* streitsüchtig. **—mentativeness**, *s.* die Streitsucht.

Arid, *adj.* dürr, trocken. **—ity**, *s.* die Dürre.

Aright, *adv.* recht, richtig; zurecht.

Arise, *v.n.* sich erheben, aufstehen (*from bed, etc.*); sich empören (against, gegen); entstehen, entspringen (from, von); auferstehen (*from the dead*); aufgehen (*as the sun*).

Aristocra—cy, *s.* der Adel. **—t**, *s.* der Edelmann. **—tic**, *adj.*, **—tically**, *adv.* vornehm, edel.

Arithmetic, *s.* die Rechenkunst, Arithmetik. **—al**, *adj.* arithmetisch. **—ian**, *s.* der Rechenmeister, Rechner.

Ark, *s.* die Lade, der Kasten; Noah's **—**, die Arche Noahs.

¹**Arm**, *s.* der Arm. **—-chair**, *s.* der Lehnsessel. **—pit**, *s.* die Achselgrube.

²**Arm**, I. *s.* die Waffe; shoulder **—s**! Gewehr auf! up in **—s**, in vollem Aufruhr. II. *v.a.* waffnen (*Mil.*). III. *v.n.* sich waffnen.

Armada, *s.* die Kriegsflotte.

Armament, *s.* die Kriegsrüstung.

Armistice, *s.* der Waffenstillstand.

Arm—our, I. *s.* die Rüstung, der Harnisch. II. *v.* panzern. **—ourer**, *s.* der Waffenschmied. **—oury**, *s.* die Rüstkammer. **—our-plated**, *adj.* gepanzert.

Army, *s.* das Heer, die Armee.

Aroma, *s.* der würzige Duft, das Aroma; die Würze. **—tic**, *adj.* aromatisch, würzig.

Around, I. *adv.* rund herum, rings umher. II. *prep.* um . . . herum, (rings) um.

Arouse, *v.a.* (auf)wecken.

Arrange, *v.a.* ordnen, einrichten; (order) anordnen. **—ment**, *s.* die Anordnung, Einrichtung; (settlement) der Vergleich, die Übereinkunft. **—r**, *s.* der Anordner.

Array, I. *s.* kleiden, schmücken. II. *s.* die Kleidung, der Anzug.

Arrear, *s.* der Rückstand; **—s** of rent, rückständige Miete.

Arrest, I. *s.* der Arrest, die Verhaftung; (stoppage) die Hemmung; (check) der Einhalt, Aufhalt. II. *v.a.* in Verhaft nehmen; aufhalten (*the current of a river, etc.*).

Arriv—al, *s.* die Ankunft. **—e**, *v.n.* ankommen, anlangen; gelangen.

Arroga—nce, **—ncy**, *s.* der Übermut. **—nt**, *adj.* anmaßend, vermessen; hochmütig. **—te**, *v.a.* sich (*dat.*) aneignen or anmaßen.

Arrow, *s.* der Pfeil.

Arsenal, *s.* das Zeughaus.

Arsen—ic, *s.* der Arsenik. **—ical**, *adj.* arsenisch.

Arson, *s.* die Brandstiftung.

Art, *s.* die Kunst; (skill) die Geschicklichkeit; (cunning) die List; master of **—s** (M.A.), Magister der freien Künste. **—ful**, *adj.*, **—fully**, *adv.* listig, schlau. **—fulness**, *s.* die List, Schlauheit. **—less**, *adj.*, **—lessly**, *adv.* kunstlos; ungekünstelt; arglos. **—lessness**, *s.* die Arglosigkeit.

Artery, *s.* die Pulsader, Schlagader.

Artichoke, *s.* die Artischocke.

Artic—le, *s.* das Stück; die Klausel, Bedingung (*of an agreement*); der Aufsatz (*in a journal, etc.*); (item) der Posten; der Artikel (*Gram.*). **—u-late**, I. *v.a.* deutlich aussprechen. II. *adj.* deutlich, vernehmlich. **—ulation**, *s.* die deutliche Aussprache.

Art—ifice, *s.* der Kunstgriff; die List. **—ificer**, *s.* der Handwerker. **—ificial**, *adj.* künstlich.

Artillery, *s.* die Artillerie, das Geschütz. **—man**, *s.* der Artillerist.

Artisan, *s.* der Handwerker.

Artist, *s.* der (die) Künstler(in). **—ic(al)**, *adj.* künstlerisch.

As, *adv. & conj.* als wie; so, sowie, ebenso; sofern; da; indem; **—** well **—**, sowohl . . . als auch; **—** far **—**, soweit als; such **—**, derart, daß.

Asbestos, *s.* der Asbest.

Ascend, *v.* I. *n.* aufsteigen, auffahren. II. *a.* besteigen, ersteigen. **—ant**, *adj.* aufsteigend (*Astr.*); his star is in the **—ant**, sein Glück ist im Steigen. **—ancy**, *s.* die Überlegenheit.

Ascen—sion, **—t**, *s.* das Aufsteigen (*also Astr.*); **—sion** of Christ, die Himmelfahrt Christi.

Ascertain, *v.a.* erfahren; sich erkundigen. **—able**, *adj.* erforschbar. **—ment**, *s.* die Ermittelung.

Ascetic, *adj.*, **—ally**, *adv.* aszetisch, enthaltsam.

Ascrib—able, *adj.* zuschreibbar. **—e**, *v.a.* zuschreiben; beilegen.

¹**Ash**, *s.* die Esche.

²**Ash**, *s.*, **—es**, *pl.* die Asche. **—en**, **—y**, *adj.* aschfarben, aschgrau. **—Wednesday**, *s.* Aschermittwoch. **—tray**, *s.* der Aschbecher.

Ashamed, *adj.* beschämt.

Ashore, *adv.* am Ufer, am Lande; ans Ufer, ans Land; to run **—**, stranden.

Aside, *adv.* seitwärts, auf die Seite; bei Seite; für sich (*Theat.*).

Ask, *v.a.* fragen (*a question*); verlangen; fordern (*a price*); bitten; einladen; — about, sich erkundigen nach; to — after, fragen nach. —er, *s.* der Bittende; der Fragende.

Asleep, *adv.* schlafend; to fall —, einschlafen.

Asparagus, *s.* der Spargel.

Aspect, *s.* (sight) der Anblick; (appearance) das Ansehen, Aussehen; my house has a southern —, mein Haus liegt nach Süden.

Aspen, *s.* die Espe.

Asphalt, I. *s.* der Asphalt. II. *adj.* asphaltisch.

Aspir—ate, I. *v.a.* aspirieren. II. *adj.* aspiriert. III. *s.* der Hauchlaut. —ation, *s.* das Streben. —e, *v.n.* verlangen, trachten, streben.

Ass, *s.* der Esel.

Assail, *v.a.* angreifen. —ant, *s.* der Angreifer.

Assassin, *s.* der Meuchelmörder. —ation, *s.* der Meuchelmord.

Assault, I. *v.a.* angreifen, anfallen. II. *s.* der Angriff, Anfall.

Assay, I. *s.* die Probe, Prüfung. II. *v.a.* prüfen, probieren.

Assembl—e, *v.* I. *a.* versammeln. II. *n.* sich versammeln. —y, *s.* die Versammlung.

Assent, I. *s.* die Zustimmung, Genehmigung. II. *v.n.* beistimmen, genehmigen, billigen.

Assert, *v.a.* behaupten. —ion, *s.* die Behauptung. —ive, *adj.* bestimmt, ausdrücklich.

Assess, *v.a.* einschätzen, abschätzen, schätzen. —ment, *s.* die Einschätzung.

Assets, *pl.* die Aktiva; no —, kein Guthaben (*C.L.*).

Assidu—ity, *s.* die Emsigkeit. —ous,** *adj.* unablässig.

Assign, *v.a.* anweisen, zuteilen. —ation, *s.* das Stelldichein; die Übertragung (*C.L.*). —ment, *s.* die Anweisung, Bestimmung.

Assimilat—e, *v.* I. *a.* einverleiben. II. *n.* ähnlich werden. —ion, *s.* die Anpassung, Einverleibung.

Assist, *v.a.* beistehen. —ance, *s.* der Beistand. —ant, *s.* der Helfer.

Assize, *s.* die Assise.

Associat—e, I. *v.a.* zugesellen, gesellen. II. *v.n.* sich gesellen zu, sich verbinden. III. *s.* der Gefährte, Genosse. —ion, *s.* die Verbindung; der Verein; die Genossenschaft.

Assort, *v.* I. *a.* (zusammen)ordnen. II. *n.* übereinstimmen, passen. —ment, *s.* das Assortiment.

Assum—e, *v.* I. *a.* annehmen, sich (*dat.*) aneignen. II. *n.*; to be —ing, anmaßend sein, groß tun. —ption, *s.* die Aneignung; —ption of the Blessed Virgin Mary, Mariä Himmelfahrt.

Assur—ance, *s.* die Zusicherung, Versicherung; (confidence) die Zuversicht; (self-confidence) das Selbstvertrauen; (arrogance) Unverschämtheit. —e, *v.a.* versichern; zusichern; (make sure) sichern, sicher machen. —edly, *adv.* sicherlich, gewiß.

Aster, *s.* die Aster (*Bot.*).

Asterisk, *s.* das Sternchen (*Typ.*).

Astern, *adv.* (nach) achtern, achteraus.

Asthma, *s.* das Asthma. —tic, *adj.* engbrüstig, asthmatisch.

Astonish, *v.a.* in Erstaunen setzen. —ing, *adj.*, —ingly, *adv.* erstaunend, erstaunlich. —ment, *s.* das Erstaunen, die Verwunderung.

Astray, *adv.* irre.

Astride, *adv.* rittlings.

Astro—loger, *s.* der Astrolog. —logical, *adj.* astrologisch. —logy, *s.* die Astrologie, Sterndeuterei. —nomer, *s.* der Astronom, der Sternkundige. —nomical, *adj.* astronomisch. —nomy, *s.* die Astronomie, Sternkunde.

Astute, *adj.*, —ly, *adv.* listig, schlau. —ness, *s.* der Scharfsinn.

Asunder, *adv.* auseinander, voneinander; entzwei.

Asylum, *s.* das Asyl, der Zufluchtsort; — for the insane, das Irrenhaus.

At, *prep.* an; auf; aus; bei; für; gegen; in; mit; nach; über, um; von; vor; zu; — my expense, auf meine Kosten; — table, bei Tische; — peace, in Frieden; — pleasure, nach Belieben; what are you driving —? worauf wollen Sie hinaus?

Atheis—m, *s.* die Gottesleugnung, der Atheismus. —t, *s.* der Gottesleugner. —tic(al), *adj.*, —tically, *adv.* atheistisch.

Athlet—e, *s.* der Wettkämpfer. —ic, *adj.*, —ically, *adv.* athletisch.

Atlas, *s.* die Landkartensammlung, der Atlas.

Atmospher—e, *s.* die Atmosphäre, der Dunstkreis. —ic(al), *adj.* atmosphärisch.

Atom, *s.* das Atom. **—ic,** *adj.* atomi(sti)sch.

Atone, *v.n.* büßen (für). **—ment,** *s.* die Versöhnung (*B.*); die Buße.

Atroci—ous, *adj.* gräßlich. **—ty,** *s.* die Gräßlichkeit, Grausamkeit.

Attach, *v.a.* anbinden (to, an); (fasten) befestigen; (subjoin) beifügen. **—able,** *adj.* verknüpfbar. **—ment,** *s.* die Fesselung; die Neigung; die Verhaftung.

Attack, I. *v.a.* angreifen, anfallen. II. *s.* der Angriff (*of the enemy*), Anfall (*of influenza, etc.*).

Attain, *v.* I. *a.* erreichen, erlangen. II. *n.* gelangen (zu), erreichen. **—able,** *adj.* erreichbar. **—ment,** *s.* die Erlangung, Erreichung.

Attempt, I. *v.a.* versuchen. II. *s.* der Versuch.

Attend, *v.* I. *a.* begleiten, folgen; pflegen; (await) erwarten; (be present) beiwohnen, zugegen sein. II. *n.* merken, achten. **—ance,** *s.* die Bedienung (*at a restaurant*); die Zuhörerschaft (*at a lecture*); to be in **—ance,** den Dienst haben. **—ant,** I. *adj.* begleitend; aufwartend. II. *s.* der Aufwartende; der Diener.

Attenti—on, *s.* die Aufmerksamkeit. **—ve,** *adj.* aufmerksam.

Attest, *v.a.* bezeugen; bescheinigen. **—ation,** *s.* das Zeugnis.

Attic, *s.* die Dachstube.

Attire, I. *s.* die Kleidung. II. *v.a.* ankleiden, kleiden.

Attitude, *s.* die Stellung, Haltung.

Attorney, *s.* der Anwalt; der Sachwalter. **—general,** *s.* der Staatsanwalt.

Attract, *v.a.* anziehen. **—ion,** *s.* die Anziehung. **—ive,** *adj.,* **—ively,** *adv.* anziehend.

Attribut—able, *adj.* zuzuschreiben, beizulegen. **—e,** I. *v.a.* beilegen, zuschreiben. II. *s.* die Eigenschaft.

Auburn, *adj.* rotbraun.

Auction, *s.* die öffentliche Versteigerung. **—eer,** *s.* der öffentliche Versteigerer.

Audaci—ous, *adj.,* **—ously,** *adv.* verwegen; unverschämt. **—ty,** *s.* die Verwegenheit.

Audi—bility, *s.* die Hörbarkeit, Vernehmbarkeit. **—ble,** *adj.,* **—bly,** *adv.* hörbar, vernehmbar. **—ence,** *s.* die Audienz, das Gehör; die Zuhörerschaft.

Audit, I. *s.* die Rechnungsuntersuchung. II. *v.a.* eine Rechnung, prüfen.

Auger, *s.* der große Bohrer.

Aught, *s. pron.* etwas, irgend etwas; for — I care, meinetwegen; for — I know, soviel ich weiß.

Augment, *v.a.* vermehren, vergrößern, zunehmen.

Augur, I. *s.* der Augur, Wahrsager. II. *v.a.* weissagen. **—y,** *s.* die Wahrsagung.

August, I. *adj.* erhaben, herrlich, hehr. II. *s.* der (Monat) August.

Aunt, *s.* die Tante.

Auspicious, *adj.,* **—ly,** *adv.* günstig, glücklich.

Auster—e, *adj.,* **—ely,** *adv.* herb; streng. **—ity,** *s.* die Strenge.

Authentic, *adj.* authentisch. **—ity,** *s.* die Echtheit.

Author, *s.* der Verfasser, Autor; der Schriftsteller. **—ess,** *s.* die Verfasserin; die Schriftstellerin. **—itative,** *adj.* (authorized) bevollmächtigt; (commanding) gebieterisch. **—ity,** *s.* die Autorität. **—ization,** *s.* die Bevollmächtigung, Autorisation. **—ize,** *v.a.* bevollmächtigen; billigen; gültig machen.

Auto—biographical, *adj.* autobiographisch. **—biography,** *s.* die Autobiographie. **—cracy,** *s.* die Selbstherrschaft. **—crat,** *s.* der Selbstherrscher. **—cratic,** *adj.* selbstherrlich. **—graph,** *s.* die Selbstschrift, Urschrift. **—graphic,** *adj.* eigenhändig geschrieben, autographisch. **—matic,** *adj.* automatisch, selbstbeweglich. **—maton,** *s.* der Automat. **—mobile,** *s.* das Auto. **—nomy,** *s.* die Selbstregierung.

Autumn, *s.* der Herbst. **—al,** *adj.* herbstlich.

Auxiliary, I. *adj.* hilfend, beistehend; — engine, der Hilfsmotor. II. *s.* der Helfer, Verbündete(r).

Avail, I. *v.n.* nützen, helfen; to — oneself of, benutzen. II. *s.* der Nutzen. **—able,** *adj.,* **—ably,** *adv.* verfügbar; gültig.

Avalanche, *s.* die Lawine.

Avaric—e, *s.* die Habsucht, der Geiz. **—ious,** *adj.,* **—iously,** *adv.* habsüchtig, geizig.

Avenge, *v.a.* rächen. **—r,** *s.* der Rächer.

Avenue, *s.* die Allee.

Aver, *v.a.* behaupten.

Average, I. *adj.* durchschnittlich. **II.** *v.a.* den Durchschnitt finden. **III.** *v.n.* durchschnittlich ausmachen. **IV.** *s.* der Durchschnitt.

Avers—e, *adj.* abgeneigt. **—eness,** *s.* die Abgeneigtheit. **—ion,** *s.* die Abneigung, der Widerwille.

Avert, *v.a.* abwenden, ablenken.

Aviary, *s.* das Vogelhaus.

Aviat—ion, *s.* das Flugwesen, die Fliegerei; — ground, der Flugplatz. **—or,** *s.* der Flieger, die Fliegerin.

Avidity, *s.* die Gier, Begierde (of, for, nach).

Avoid, *v.a.* (shun) meiden, vermeiden. **—able,** *adj.* vermeidlich. **—ance,** *s.* das Meiden, Vermeiden.

Avouch, *v.a.* behaupten, versichern.

Avow, *v.a.* offen bekennen; gestehen. **—al,** *s.* das Bekenntnis, Geständnis. **—ed,** *p.p. & adj.* anerkannt; offen.

Await, *v.a.* abwarten; erwarten.

Awake, I. *v.a.* wecken, erwecken, aufwecken. **II.** *v.n.* erwachen, aufwachen. **III.** *adj.* wachend; (to be wide —, völlig wach sein; (*fig.*) schlau, auf der Hut sein. **—ning, I.** *adj.* erwachend. **II.** *s.* das Erwachen; das Erwecken.

Award, I. *v.a.* zuerkennen, gerichtlich zusprechen. **II.** *s.* das Urteil, der Ausspruch; die Belohnung, Prämie.

Aware, *adj.* gewahr.

Away, *adv.* weg, hinweg, fort; abwesend; laugh —! lacht nur drauf los!

Aw—e, I. *s.* die Furcht, Scheu; die Ehrfurcht. **II.** *v.a.* (heilige) Scheu einflößen; einschüchtern. **—ful,** *adj.,* **—fully,** *adv.* furchtbar, furchterregend; feierlich, erhaben. **—fulness,** *s.* (terribleness) die Furchtbarkeit; (venerableness) die Ehrwürdigkeit.

Awhile, *adv.* eine Weile, auf kurze Zeit.

Awkward, *adj.,* **—ly,** *adv.* ungeschickt, unbeholfen; (inconvenient) ungelegen. **—ness,** *s.* das tölpische, linkische, unbeholfene Wesen; die Ungeschicklichkeit.

Awl, *s.* die Ahle, der Pfriem.

Awning, *s.* das Schirmdach.

Awry, *adj.* schief; verkehrt (*fig.*).

Axe, *s.* die Axt, das Beil.

Axiom, *s.* das Axiom. **—atic,** *adj.,* **—atically,** *adv.* unumstößlich, zweifellos, gewiß.

Axis, die Achse.

Axle, *s.* (—le-tree, *s.*) die Achse.

1Aye, *adv.* immer.

2Aye, *adv.* ja.

Azalea, *s.* die Azalie.

Azure, *adj.* himmelblau.

B

B, b, das B, b.

Baa, *v.n.* blöcken.

Babble, I. *v.n.* schwatzen. **II.** *v.a.* ausschwatzen. **III.** *s.* das Geschwätz.

Baboon, *s.* der Pavian.

Baby, *s.* das Kindlein, Kindchen. **—hood,** *s.* erste Kindheit.

Bachelor, *s.* der Junggesell.

Back, I. *s.* der Rücken; die Rückseite. **II.** *adv.* zurück, hinterwärts. **III.** *v.n.* zurück treten, rückwärts gehen. **IV.** *adj.*; — part, der hintere Teil. **—ward, I.** *adj.* spät (*in ripening*); träge; zurückgeblieben. **II.** *adv.,* **—wards,** *adv.* rückwärts, zurück, nach dem Rücken zu; rückgängig; verkehrt. **—bite,** *v.a.* verleumden. **—biter,** *s.* der Verleumder. **—biting, I.** *adj.* verleumderisch. **II.** *s.* das Verleumden. **—bone,** *s.* der or das Rückgrat; he has no —bone, er ist schlapp, charakter-schwach. **—door,** *s.* die Hintertür. **—fire,** *s.* die Frühzündung. **—ground,** *s.* der Hintergrund. **—slide,** *v.n.* abfallen, abtrünnig werden. **—slider,** *s.* der Abtrünnige.

Bacon, *s.* der Speck.

Bad, (Worse, Worst) *adj.,* **—ly,** *adv.* schlecht; schlimm; böse; he is —ly off, es geht ihm sehr traurig. **—ness,** *s.* die Bosheit.

Badge, *s.* das Kennzeichen.

Badger, *s.* der Dachs (Zool.).

Baffle, *v.a.* vereiteln, täuschen.

Bag, *s.* der Beutel. **—gy,** *adj.* sackartig.

Bagatelle, *s.* die Kleinigkeit; das Bagatellspiel.

Baggage, *s.* das Gepäck.

Bagpipe, *s.* der Dudelsack.

Bail, I. *s.* der Bürge; die Bürgschaft. **II.** *v.a.* Bürgschaft leisten für Jemand. **—iff,** *s.* der Amtmann, Landvogt; der Gerichtsdiener.

Bait, I. *s.* der Köder. **II.** *v.a.* ködern, ankörnen; (harass) quälen.

Baize, *s.* der Boi.

Bak—e, *v.a.* backen. **—er,** *s.* der

Bäcker. —ery, *s.* die Bäckerei. —ing, *s.* das Backen.

Balance, I. *s.* die Waage; das Gleichgewicht (*also fig.*); der Saldo, die Bilanz (*C. L.*); (surplus) der Überschuß; — of trade, die Handelsbilanz; to strike a —, einen Saldo ziehen. II. *v.a.* wägen, abwägen.

Balcony, *s.* der Söller, Balkon.

Bald, *adj.*, —ly, *adv.* kahl. —ness, *s.* die Kahlheit.

1Bale, *s.* der Ballen.

2Bale, *v.a. & n.* ausschöpfen.

Balk, I. *v.a.* aufhalten, hemmen. II. *v.n.* (of horses) scheuen (at a thing, vor einer S.).

1Ball, *s.* der Ball; die Kugel (*Artil.*). —cartridge, *s.* die scharfe Patrone.

2Ball, *s.* der Ball.

Ballad, *s.* die Ballade; das Volkslied.

Ballast, *s.* der Ballast.

Ballet, *s.* das Ballett.

Balloon, *s.* der Ballon, Luftballon.

Ballot, I. *s.* das Ballotieren. II. *v.n.* wählen, ballotieren. —box, *s.* die Wahlurne.

Balsam, *s.* der Balsam.

Balust—er, *s.* die Geländersäule. —rade, *s.* die Brüstlehne.

Bamboo, *s.* der Bambus.

Ban, I. *s.* der Bann, die Acht. II. *v.a.* verfluchen.

Banana, *s.* die Banane.

Band, *s.* das Band, die Binde; (troop) die Bande, Schar; die Musik-kapelle. —age, I. *s.* die Binde, der Verband. II. *v.a.* verbinden.

Bandy, *v.a.* — words with someone, Worte mit einem wechseln. —legged, *adj.* krummbeinig.

Bane, *s.* das Gift. —ful, *adj.* verderblich.

Bang, I. *s.* der Klapp, Knall. II. *v.a.* zuwerfen (a door, etc.).

Bangle, *s.* der Arm- or Fuß-ring, -spange.

Banish, *v.a.* verbannen. —ment, *s.* die Verbannung.

Bank, I. *s.* der Damm (of a road); das Ufer Gestade (of a river); die Bank (*C. L.*). II. *v.a.* dämmen. III. *v.n.* Bankgeschäfte machen. —er, *s.* der Bankier. —ing, *s.* das Bankgeschäft. —rupt. I. *s.* der Bank(e)rottier. II. *adj.* bankerott, bankbrüchig, fallit. —ruptcy, *s.* der Bank(e)rott, —-note, *s.* die Banknote.

Banner, *s.* das Banner.

Banns, *pl.* das (kirchliche) Aufgebot (vor der Heirat).

Banquet, *s.* das Festmahl, Bankett. —-hall, *s.* der Festsaal.

Bantam, *s.* das Bantamhuhn, das Zwerghuhn.

Banter, I. *s.* die Neckerei. II. *v.a.* necken.

Bapti—sm, *s.* die Taufe. —st, *s.* der Täufer. —ze, *v.a.* taufen.

Bar, I. *s.* die Stange (of wood or metal), Barre; (bolt) der Riegel; der Takt-strich (*Mus.*); (*fig.*) das Hindernis; der Advokatenstand; der Schenktisch. II. *v.a.* sperren, versperren; (*fig.*) hemmen, hindern; riegeln.

Barb, I. *s.* der Widerhaken. II. *v.a.* mit Widerhaken versehen.

Barbar—ian, I. *adj.* barbarisch. II. *s.* der Barbar. —ity, *s.* die Unmenschlichkeit.

Barbel, *s.* die Barbe (*Icht.*).

Barber, *s.* der Barbier.

Barberry, *s.* die Berberitze.

Bard, *s.* der Barde.

Bare, I. *adj.* nackt, bloß, entblößt. II. *v.a.* entblößen. —ly, *adv.* nackt; kaum. —ness, *s.* die Nacktheit, Blöße. —-faced, *adj.* frech, schamlos.

Bargain, I. *s.* der Handel; der Vertrag; it's a —! abgemacht! topp! into the —, obendrein, noch dazu. II. *v.n.* handeln; (chaffer) feilschen. —er, der Handelnde.

Barge, *s.* das Flußschiff. —e, *s.* der Bootsmann.

Baritone, *s.* der Bariton.

1Bark, *s.* die Rinde.

2Bark, I. *v.n.* bellen; to — at, anbellen. II. *s.* das Gebell.

Barley, *s.* die Gerste.

Barn, *s.* die Scheune, Scheuer.

Barnacle, *s.* die Entenmuschel.

Barometer, *s.* das Barometer.

Baron, *s.* der Baron, Freiherr. —age, *s.* die Freiherrschaft. —ess, *s.* die Baronin, Freifrau.

Barque, *s.* die Bark.

Barrack, *s.* die Barracke. —s, *pl.* die Kaserne.

Barrel, *s.* das Faß, die Tonne. —-organ, *s.* die Drehorgel.

Barren, *adj.* unfruchtbar; wüst. —ness, *s.* die Unfruchtbarkeit.

Barricade, I. *s.* die Verschanzung. II. *v.a.* verrammeln, verschanzen.

Barrier, *s.* die Schranke.
Barrister, *s.* der Rechtsanwalt, Advokat.
Barrow, *s.* der Schubkarren.
Barter, I. *s.* der Tauschhandel. II. *v.a.* vertauschen.
Basalt, *s.* der Basalt. **—ic,** *adj.* basaltisch.
Base, I. *adj.,* **—ly,** *adv.* niedrig; (*fig.*) niederträchtig, gemein ; **—** coin, falsches Geld. II. *s.* die Grundlage, Basis. III. *v.a.* gründen. **—less,** *adj.* grundlos. **—lessness,** *s.* die Grundlosigkeit. **—ment,** *s.* das Kellergeschoß. **—ness,** *s.* die Niedrigkeit; die Gemeinheit; die Falschheit (*of coin*).
Bashful, *adj.,* **—ly,** *adv.* schamhaft; schüchtern. **—ness,** *s.* die Schüchternheit.
Basin, *s.* das Becken.
Bask, *v.n.* sich sonnen.
Basket, *s.* der Korb.
¹**Bass,** I. *s.* der Baß (*Mus.*). II. *adj.* **—** clef, der F-Schlüssel, Baßschlüssel.
²**Bass,** *s.* die Bastmatte.
³**Bass,** *s.* der Barsch.
Bastard, I. *s.* der Bastard. II. *adj.* unehelich.
¹**Baste,** *v.a.* mit Fett begießen.
²**Baste,** *v.a.* zusammenheften.
Bastinado, *s.* die Bastonnade.
Bastion, *s.* die Bastei.
¹**Bat,** *s.* die Fledermaus (*Zool.*).
²**Bat,** *s.* der Knüttel.
Bath, *s.* das Bad. **—e,** *v.n. & a.* baden. **—er,** *s.* der Badende. **—ing,** I. *adj.* badend. II. *s.* das Baden.
Battalion, *s.* das Bataillon.
¹**Batten,** *s.* die Latte.
²**Batten,** *v.n.* gedeihen.
Batter, I. *s.* der Schlagteig (*Cook.*). II. *v.a.* schlagen; zerschlagen. **—y,** *s.* die Schlägerei; die Batterie (*Mil.*); die Batterie (*Phys.*). **—ing-ram,** *s.* der Sturmbock. **—ing-train,** *s.* die Belagerungslaffette.
Battle, I. *s.* die Schlacht. II. *v.n.;* to **—** for, streiten um. **—cruiser,** *s.* der Schlachtkreuzer. **—ship,** *s.* das Linienschiff. **—field,** *s.* das Schlachtfeld. **—ments,** *s.* die Zinnen.
Bawl, *v.a. & n.* schreien, brüllen, plärren.
¹**Bay,** *adj.* rötlichbraun.
²**Bay,** *s.* der Lorbeerbaum (*Bot.*).
³**Bay,** *s.* die Bai, Bucht. **—window,** *s.* das Erkerfenster.

⁴**Bay,** *s.;* to stand at **—,** sich zur Wehre setzen; to keep at **—,** in Schach halten, hinhalten.
⁵**Bay,** *v.n.* bellen.
Bayonet, *s.* das Bajonett.
Be, *ir.v.n.* sein; bleiben; vorhanden sein, existieren; to **—** about, beschäftigt sein mit; to **—** off, weggehen, fortkommen.
Beach, *s.* der Strand, das Gestade.
Beacon, *s.* die Bake.
Bead, *s.* das Kügelchen, Perlchen. **—s,** *pl.* Perlen, der Rosenkranz.
Beadle, *s.* der Pedell, der Kirchendiener.
Beagle, *s.* der Spürhund.
Beak, *s.* der Schnabel.
Beaker, *s.* der Becher.
Beam, I. *s.* der Balken; der Strahl, Lichtstrahl; der Glanz (*of the eye*). II. *v.n.* strahlen.
Bean, *s.* die Bohne.
¹**Bear,** *s.* der Bär.
²**Bear,** *ir.v.* I. *a.* tragen (*a burden*); gebären (*children*); hegen (*ill-will, love, etc.*); **—** off, wegtragen, entführen; **—** out, bestätigen; to **—** up, standhalten, fest bleiben. II. *n.* tragen; fruchtbar werden; leiden, dulden; to bring to **—,** in Wirksamkeit setzen, zur Geltung bringen. **—able,** *adj.,* **—ably,** *adv.* erträglich. **—er,** *s.* der Träger. **—ing,** *s.* das Tragen; die Haltung; die Beziehung.
Beard, *s.* der Bart. **—ed,** *adj.* bärtig. **—less,** *adj.* bartlos.
Beast, *s.* das Tier. **—ly,** *adj.* viehisch; ekelhaft.
Beat, I. *ir.v.a.* schlagen, prügeln; to **—** the air, (*fig.*) sich vergebens bemühen; **—** back, zurückschlagen; **—** down, niederdrücken. II. *ir.v.n.* schlagen. III. *s.* der Schlag; der Taktschlag (*Mus.*). **—er,** *s.* der Schläger; der Treiber (*Sport.*). **—ing,** I. *p. & adj.* schlagend, ꝛc. II. *s.* das Schlagen, Klopfen; die Züchtigung.
Beati—fication, *s.* die Seligsprechung. **—fy,** *v.a.* selig sprechen.
Beau, *s.* der Stutzer. **—ideal,** *s.* Ideal, Vorbild.
Beaut—eous, *adj.* sehr schön. **—eousness,** *s.* die Schönheit. **—iful,** *adj.,* **—ifully,** *adv.* schön. **—ify,** *v.a.* ausschmücken. **—y,** *s.* die Schönheit.
Beaver, *s.* der Biber.
Becalm, *v.a.* bekalmen; beruhigen; be

—ed, von einer Windstille überfallen werden.

Because, *conj.* weil, auf daß; (*in comp.* = *prep.*) — of, wegen; — of you, um Ihretwillen.

Beck, *s.* der Wink. **—on,** *v.n.* mit der Hand winken.

Becloud, *v.a.* umwölfen.

Becom—e, *ir.v.* I. *n.* werden. II. *a.* geziemen; (sich) paffen, sich schicken. **—ing,** *adj.,* **—ingly,** *adv.* geziemend, passend. **—ingness,** *s.* die Schicklichkeit; das Passende.

Bed, *s.* das Bett; (flower —) das Beet. **—ding,** *s.* das Bettzeug; die Lagerstreu (*for cattle*). **—chamber,** *s.* das Schlafzimmer. **—fellow,** *s.* der Bettgenoß, die Bettgenossin. **—linen,** die Bettwäsche. **—room,** *s.* das Schlafzimmer. **—stead,** *s.* die Bettstelle.

Bedew, *v.a.* betauen.

Bee, *s.* die Biene. **—line,** *s.* der gerade Weg, die Luftlinie.

Beech, *s.* die Buche. **—en,** *adj.* buchen.

Beef, *s.* das Rindfleisch; — tea, die klare Fleischbrühe, die Bouillon. **—y,** *adj.* fleischig.

Beer, *s.* das Bier.

¹Beetle, *s.* der Schlägel.

²Beetle, *s.* der Käfer (*Ent.*).

Beet-root, *s.* die Bete, Runkelrübe.

Befall, *ir.v.a.* & *n.* widerfahren; (happen) sich ereignen.

Befit, *v.a.* sich geziemen, gebühren.

Before, I. *adv.* (in front) vorn; (on in front) voran; (previously) vorher, früher, ehemals; (sooner) eher; (already) bereits, schon. II. *conj.* bevor; ehe. III. *prep.* vor. **—hand,** *adv.* vorher, im voraus. **—mentioned,** *adj.* vorhererwähnt.

Befoul, *v.a.* beschmutzen.

Befriend, *v.a.* begünstigen.

Beg, *v.* I. *a.* bitten, ersuchen; betteln. II. *n.* betteln.

Beget, *ir.v.a.* zeugen.

Beggar, *s.* der Bettler, die Bettlerin. **—gared,** *adj.* bettelarm. **—garly,** *adj.* bettelhaft.

Begin, *ir.v.a.* & *n.* anfangen, beginnen. **—ner,** *s.* der Anfänger; der Urheber. **—ning,** *s.* der Anfang.

Begone, *int.* fort! packe dich!

Beguil—e, *v.a.* täuschen, betrügen. **—er,** *s.* der Betrüger; der Verführer.

Behalf, *s.* der Behuf, Vorteil; on — of, im Namen von, zugunsten (*with genitive*).

Behav—e, *v.* I. *n.* handeln, sich betragen. II. *r.*; to —e oneself, sich gut betragen. **—iour,** *s.* das Betragen.

Behead, *v.a.* enthaupten. **—ing,** *s.* die Enthauptung.

Behind, I. *adv.* hinten, zurück. II. *prep.* hinter. **—hand,** *adv.* im Rückstande, zurück; (in arrears) rückständig.

Behold, I. *ir.v.a.* anschauen, ansehen. II. *int.* siehe (da)! **—en,** *adj.* verpflichtet, verbunden. **—er,** *s.* der Anschauer, Zuschauer.

Behove, *v.a.* & *imp.* gebühren, sich ziemen.

Being, I. *pres. part.* of Be. II. *adj.*; for the time —, für jetzt, für den Augenblick. III. *s.* das Sein, Dasein, die Existenz; das Wesen.

Belabour, *v.a.* durchprügeln.

Beleaguer, *v.a.* belagern. **—er,** *s.* der Belagerer.

Belfry, *s.* der Glockenturm.

Belie, *v.a.* verleumden.

Belief, *s.* der Glaube; past all —, unglaublich.

Believ—able, *adj.* glaublich. **—e,** *v.a.* & *n.* glauben. **—er,** *s.* der Gläubige.

Belittle, *v.a.* verächtlich machen.

Bell, *s.* die Glocke; die Schelle, Klingel. **—founder,** *s.* der Glockengießer. **—pull,** *s.* der Schellenzug. **—ringer,** *s.* der Glöckner.

Bellow, I. *v.n.* brüllen; bellen. II. *s.* das Gebrüll.

Bellows, *pl.* der Blasebalg.

Belly, *s.* der Bauch.

Belong, *v.n.* gehören; angehören. **—ings,** *pl.* das Zubehör.

Beloved, *adj.* geliebt, teuer.

Below, I. *adv.* unten; hienieden. II. *prep.* unter.

Belt, *s.* der Gürtel.

Bemoan, *v.a.* beklagen.

Bench, *s.* die Bank; die Werkbank; die Gerichtsbank (*Law*).

Bend, I. *v.a.* beugen, biegen, krümmen. II. *v.n.* sich biegen, sich neigen (to, vor). III. *s.* die Biegung, Krümmung. **—able,** *adj.* biegsam.

Bene—diction, *s.* der Segensspruch. **—faction,** *s.* die Wohltat. **—factor,** *s.* der Wohltäter. **—factress,** *s.* die Wohltäterin. **—fice,** *s.* die Pfründe. **—ficence,** *s.* die Wohltätigkeit. **—fi-**

cent, *adj.*, —ficently, *adv.* wohltätig.
—ficial, *adj.*, —ficially, *adv.* vorteilhaft. —fit, I. *s.* die Wohltat; (advantage) der Vorteil, Nutzen. II. *v.a.*
begünstigen; nützen. —volence, *s.*
das Wohlwollen. —volent, *adj.*, —
volently, *adv.* wohlwollend; gütig.

Beneath, I. *adv.* unten. II. *prep.* unter.

Benign, *adj.*, —ly, *adv.* gutartig.
—ity, *s.* die Holdseligkeit.

Bent, I. *p.p.* & *adj.* gebogen; (inclined) geneigt. II. *s.* die Neigung;
die Richtung.

Benumb, *v.a.* erstarren.

Benz—ine, *s.* das Benzin. —oline, *s.*
das Benzol.

Bequeath, *v.a.* vermachen. —er, *s.* der
Erblasser.

Bequest, *s.* das Vermächtnis.

Bereave, *v.a.* berauben. —ment, *s.*
die Beraubung; der Verlust.

Berry, *s.* die Beere.

Berth, *s.* das Schiffsbett, die Koje.

Beseech, *ir.v.a.* dringend ersuchen,
flehentlich bitten. —ing, *adj.*, —
ingly, *adv.* flehend.

Beseem, *v.a.* & *n.* geziemen, sich schicken.

Beset, *v.a.* umlagern.

Beside, *prep.* neben, an, bei, dicht bei;
außer, über; quite — the mark, weit
vom Ziele; — the purpose, nicht zweckdienlich. —s, I. *adv.* überdies, ohne-
dies, außerdem, zudem. II. *prep.*
außer.

Besiege, *v.a.* belagern. —r, *s.* der
Belagerer.

Besmirch, *v.a.* besudeln.

Besom, *s.* der Besen.

Bespeak, *ir.v.a.* (order) sich (*dat.*)
vorher bestellen. —er, *s.* der Besteller.

Best, I. *adj.* (*sup.* of good) best. II.
adv. am besten; — man, der Braut-
führer; for the —, zum Besten. III.
s. das Beste; der, die, das Beste.

Bestial, *adj.* tierisch, viehisch.

Bestir, *v.r.*; to — oneself, sich rühren.

Bestow, *v.a.* erteilen, geben. —al, *s.*
die Schenkung, Verleihung.

Bestride, *ir.v.a.* besteigen.

Bet, I. *s.* die Wette. II. *v.a.* & *n.*
wetten.

Bethink, *ir.v.r.* sich besinnen, sich bedenken.

Betimes, *adv.* beizeiten.

Betoken, *v.a.* bezeichnen, andeuten.

Betray, *v.a.* verraten. —al, *s.* der
Verrat. —er, *s.* der Verräter.

Betroth, *v.a.* verloben. —al, *s.* die
Verlobung.

Better, I. *adj.* & *adv.* besser; to get the
— of, überwinden, besiegen; you had
— stay, es wäre besser, Sie blieben.
II. *s.* das Bessere, der, die, das Bessere.
III. *adv.* besser; mehr. IV. *v.n.* besser
werden. V. *v.a.* bessern, verbessern.

Between, I. *adv.* dazwischen; — ourselves, unter uns, unter vier Augen.
II. *prep.* zwischen.

Beverage, *s.* das Getränk.

Bevy, *s.* die Schar.

Bewail, *v.a.* beklagen, beweinen.

Beware, *v.a.* & *n.*; to — of (a person),
sich hüten vor (einem); —! nimm
dich in acht!

Bewilder, *v.a.* verirren; verwirren.
—ing, *p.* & *adj.*, —ingly, *adv.* verwirrend. —ment, *s.* die Verwirrung.

Bewitch, *v.a.* behexen, bezaubern.
—ing, *adj.*, —ingly, *adv.* bezaubernd,
reizend.

Beyond, I. *adv.* über (eine S.) hinaus.
II. *prep.* jenseits, über; außer; — dispute, außer allem Zweifel; — expression, unaussprechlich; to go —
one's depth, festen Fuß verlieren.

Bias, I. *s.* die Quere, Schräge. II.
v.a. hinneigen, bestimmen.

Bib, *s.* das Lätzchen.

Bibl—e, *s.* die Bibel. —ical, *adj.*,
—ically, *adv.* biblisch.

Bicker, *v.n.* zanken, hadern. —ing,
s. das Gezänk.

Bicycl—e, I. *s.* das Zweirad, Fahrrad.
II. *v.a.* radfahren. —ist, *s.* der
Radfahrer, die Radfahrerin.

Bid, I. *ir.v.a.* (order) befehlen, heißen;
bieten (*at auctions*, etc.); to — farewell, Lebewohl sagen. II. *s.* das
Gebot (*at auctions*, etc.). —der, *s.*
der Bieter. —ding, *s.* das Bieten
(*at auctions*); das Geheiß, der Befehl.

Biennial, *adj.*, —ly, *adv.* zweijährig.

Bier, *s.* die Bahre, Totenbahre.

Big, *adj.*, —ly, *adv.* groß; to talk —,
prahlen. —ness, *s.* die Größe, Dicke.
—wig, *s.* die vornehme Person,
(*coll.*) der großes Tier.

Bigamy, *s.* die Doppelehe.

Bight, *s.* die Bucht (*Geog.*); die Bugt
(*Naut.*).

Bigot, *s.* der Frömmler. —ed, *adj.*
frömmelnd. —ry, *s.* die Fröm-
melei.

Bilberry, *s.* die Heidelbeere.

Bil—e, *s.* die Galle. **—ious,** *adj.* gall(en)süchtig.

¹**Bill,** *s.* der Schnabel (*of a bird, etc.*). **—hook,** *s.* die Hippe.

²**Bill,** *s.* (— of sale, *etc.*) der Schein, Brief; (poster, *etc.*) der Zettel; der Gesetzentwurf (*Parl.*); der Wechsel (*C. L.*); die Rechnung (*C. L.*); — of lading, der Ladeschein; — of mortality, die Totenliste. **—broker,** *s.* der Wechselmakler. **—sticker,** *s.* der Zettelankleber.

¹**Billet,** I. *s.* das Briefchen; das Quartier. II. *v.a.* einquartieren (on, bei).

²**Billet,** *s.* das Scheit (*of wood*).

Billiards, *pl.* das Billard.

Billion, *s.* die Billion.

Billow, *s.* die Woge. **—y,** *adj.* wogend, wogig.

Bin, *s.* der Kasten.

Bin—ocle, *s.* das Doppelfernrohr. **—ocular,** *adj.* zweiäugig.

Bind, *ir.v.* I. *a.* binden; einbinden (*books*); verbinden; verpflichten; aufdingen (*apprentices, etc.*). II. *n.* binden. **—er,** *s.* der Buchbinder. **—ing,** I. *p. & adj.* bindend. II. *s.* das Binden; der Einband (*of a book*).

Binnacle, *s.* das Kompaßhaus.

Bio—grapher, *s.* der Biograph. **—graphic(al),** *adj.,* **—graphically,** *adv.* biographisch. **—graphy,** *s.* die Lebensbeschreibung.

Biplane, *s.* der Doppeldecker.

Birch, *s.* die Birke.

Bird, *s.* der Vogel; —'s eye view, die Vogelperspektive. **—cage,** *s.* das Vogelbauer, der Vogelkäfig.

Birth, *s.* die Geburt. **—day,** *s.* der Geburtstag.

Biscuit, *s.* der Zwieback.

Bisect, *v.a.* halbieren. **—ion,** *s.* die Halbierung.

Bishop, *s.* der Bischof; der Läufer (*at Chess*). **—ric,** *s.* das Bistum.

Bismuth, *s.* der Wismut.

Bit, *s.* der Bissen; das Gebiß (*of a bridle*).

Bitch, *s.* die Hündin.

Bite, I. *ir.v.a. & n.* beißen; biting cold, schneidende Kälte. II. *s.* das Beißen, der Biß.

Bitter, *adj.,* **—ly,** *adv.* bitter, herb. **—ness,** *s.* die Bitterkeit.

Bivouac, *s.* das Biwak (*Mil.*).

Blab, *v.a. & n.* schwatzen.

Black, I. *adj.,* **—ly,** *adv.* schwarz; — sheep, (*fig.*) der Taugenichts; — pudding, die Blutwurst. II. *s.* das Schwarz; (negro) der Neger. **—en,** *v.* I. *a.* schwärzen. II. *n.* schwarz werden. **—ing,** *s.* die Schuhwichse. **—ish,** *adj.* schwärzlich. **—ness,** *s.* die Schwärze. **—beetle,** *s.* die Küchenschabe. **—berry,** *s.* die Brombeere. **—bird,** *s.* die Amsel. **—board,** *s.* die Wandtafel. **—mail,** I. *s.* die Erpressung. II. *v.a.* durch Drohungen erpressen. **—smith,** *s.* der Grobschmied.

Blackguard, I. *s.* der Spitzbube, Schuft. II. *v.a.* beschimpfen. **—ly,** *adj. & adv.* gemein; schuftig.

Bladder, *s.* die Blase.

Blade, *s.* der Halm (*of grass, etc.*); die Klinge (*of a knife, etc.*); shoulder—, das Schulterblatt.

Blam—able, *adj.,* **—ably,** *adv.* tadelnswert, tadelhaft. **—e,** I. *s.* der Tadel; die Schuld. II. *v.a.* tadeln. **—eless,** *adj.,* **—elessly,** *adv.* tadellos. **—elessness,** *s.* die Tadellosigkeit; die Unschuld. **—eworthiness,** *s.* die Tadelnswürdigkeit. **—eworthy,** *adj.* tadelnswert.

Blanch, *v.n.* erbleichen.

Bland, *adj.,* **—ly,** *adv.* mild, sanft. **—ish,** *v.a.* schmeicheln; liebkosen. **—ishment,** *s.* die Schmeichelei. **—ness,** *s.* die Milde.

Blank, I. *adj.,* **—ly,** *adv.* blank; leer (*of paper, etc.*); reimlos (*of verse*); verwundert, bestürzt (*fig.*). II. *s.* der leere Raum (*in a book, etc.*).

Blanket, *s.* die Schlafdecke; a wet —, (*fig.*) der Dämpfer, der kalte Wasserstrahl.

Blasphem—e, *v.a. & n.* Gott lästern. **—er,** *s.* der Gotteslästerer. **—ous,** *adj.,* **—ously,** *adv.* (gottes)lästerlich. **—y,** *s.* die (Gottes)lästerung.

Blast, I. *s.* der Windstoß; der Schall, Stoß (*of trumpets*); die Explosion. II. *v.a.* sprengen; (destroy) vernichten; to — a person's reputation, einen um seinen guten Namen bringen; —ed corn, verbranntes Getreide; —ed hopes, vereitelte Hoffnungen. **—ing,** I. *p. & adj.,* **—ing agent,** das Sprengmittel; **—ing powder,** das Sprengpulver. II. *s.* das Sprengen. **—furnace,** *s.* der Hochofen.

Blaze, I. *s.* die Flamme. II. *v.n.* flammen, lodern.

Bleach, v.a. & n. bleichen. —er, s. der Bleicher. —ing, I. p. & adj. bleichend. II. s. das Bleichen. — green, s. die Bleiche. —ing-powder, s. das Bleichpulver.

Bleak, adj., —ly, adv. rauh, öde. —ness, s. die Rauhheit; die Öde.

Blear-eyed, adj. triefäugig.

Bleat, I. v.n. blöten. II. —ing, s. das Blöten.

Bleed, ir.v.n. bluten. —ing, I. p. & adj. blutend. II. s. der Blutfluß.

Blemish, s. der Makel, Flecken (also fig.).

Blench, v.n. zurückweichen, stutzen.

Blend, v. I. a. mischen, vermischen. II. n. sich vermischen. III. die Mischung, das Gemisch.

Bless, v.a. segnen. —ed, adj., —edly, adv. selig; gesegnet. —edness, s. die Glückseligkeit, Seligkeit; (salvation) das Heil; he is in single —edness, er ist Junggeselle. —ing, s. das Segnen.

Blight, I. s. der Brand. II. v.a. durch Meltau verderben; (fig.) vereiteln.

Blind, I. adj. blind; — man's buff, das Blindekuh-spiel. II. s. die Fensterblende, der Rollvorhang. III. v.a. blind machen; verblenden (to, gegen). —s, pl. das Blendwerk. —ly, adv. blind, blindlings. —ness, s. die Blindheit. —fold, adj. mit verbundenen Augen. —worm, s. die Blindschleiche.

Blink, I. s. das Blinzeln. II. v.n. blinken; blinzeln.

Bliss, s. die Seligkeit, Wonne. —ful, adj., —fully, adv. selig, wonnevoll.

Blister, s. die Blase.

Blithe, adj., —ly, adv. munter, lustig. —ness, s. die Fröhlichkeit, Munterkeit.

Bloat—ed, adj. aufgedunsen. —er, s. der geräucherte Häring, Büding.

Block, I. s. der Block, Klotz. II. v.a. (— up) versperren, sperren. —ade, I. s. die Blockade. II. v.a. blockieren. —head, s. der Dummkopf. —headed, adj. dumm.

Blonde, I. s. die Blondine. II. adj. hell, blond.

Blood, s. das Blut. —ily, adv. blutig. —less, adj., —lessly, adv. blutlos, unblutig. —y, adj. blutig; grausam, verdammt; (—thirsty) blutgierig; (—stained) blutbefleckt. —

curdling, adj. haarsträubend. — **horse,** s. das Vollblutpferd. — **hound,** s. der Bluthund. —relation, s. der or die Blutsverwandte. —shot, adj. blutunterlaufen. —thirsty, adj. blutdurstig.

Bloom, I. s. die Blüte. II. v.n. blühen (also fig.). —ing, p. & adj. blühend.

Blossom, I. s. die Blüte. II. v.n. blühen, Blüte treiben.

Blot, I. v.a. beflecken (also fig.); löschen (with blotting-paper). II. s. der Fleck.

Blotch, s. die Finne. —y, adj. finnig.

Blotter, s. das Löschblatt, Löschpapier.

Blouse, s. die Bluse.

¹Blow, s. der Schlag (also fig.).

²Blow, ir.v. I. n. blasen, wehen; (puff, gasp) keuchen, schnaufen. II. a. blasen; wehen; treiben; anfachen (the fire, etc.).

Blubber, I. s. der Tran. II. v.n. schluchzen.

Bludgeon, s. der Knüttel.

Blue, I. adj. blau; (fig.) trübe, schwermütig. II. s. das Blau; die Bläue (Laundry). bluish, adj. bläulich. —ness, s. die Bläue. —bell, s. die Glockenblume. —bottle, s. die Fleischfliege (Ent.). —jacket, s. die Blaujacke, der Matrose. —stocking, s. der Blaustrumpf.

Blunder, I. s. der Fehler. II. v.a. & n. einen groben Fehler machen. —er, s. der Tölpel.

Blunderbuss, s. die Donnerbüchse.

Blunt, I. adj., —ly, adv. stumpf; (fig.) derb. II. v.a. abstumpfen (also fig.). —ness, s. die Stumpfheit; die Derbheit.

Blur, I. s. der Fleck. II. v.a. beflecken, verwischen.

Blush, I. s. das Erröten. II. v.n. erröten (at a thing, über eine S.).

Bluster, I. s. das Brausen, Toben. II. v.n. brausen.

Boa, s. die Boa; der Halspelz.

Boar, s. der Eber.

Board, I. s. das Brett; die Diele; der Bord (Naut.); die Kost, Unterhalt; der Ausschuß. II. v.a. täfeln, dielen. III. v.n. in der Kost sein. —er, s. der Pensionär. —ing, s. das Dielen; die Kost. —ing-house, s. die Pension. —ing-school, *s.* das Internat; das Pensionat. **—school,** *s.* die Volksschule.

Boast, I. *v.n.* sich rühmen (of a thing, einer Sache); prahlen. II. *v.a.* rühmen, erheben. III. *s.* die Prahlerei, der Ruhm. **—er,** *s.* der Prahler, Prahlhans. **—ful,** *adj.,* **—fully,** *adv.* prahlerisch. **—fulness,** *s.* die Ruhmredigkeit.

Boat, *s.* das Boot, der Kahn. **—ing,** *s.* die Bootfahrt. **—man,** *s.* der Bootsmann.

Bob, I. *s.* der Knix. II. *v.n.* baumeln.

Bobbin, *s.* die Spule.

Bode, *v.a.* vorbedeuten.

Bod—ice, *s.* das Mieder, Schnürleibchen. **—ied,** *adj.* (*in comp.*) big—ied, dickleibig; strong—ied, nervig; able—ied, gesund, stark; dienstfähig (*of sailors*). **—iless,** *adj.* unkörperlich. **—ily,** *adj.* & *adv.* körperlich, leiblich.

Bodkin, *s.* die Schnürnadel.

Body, *s.* der Körper, Leib; in a —, zusammen, sämtlich; a dead —, eine Leiche. **—guard,** *s.* die Leibwache.

Bog, *s.* der Sumpf. **—gy,** *adj.* sumpfig.

Bogus, *adj.* falsch, unecht; — affair, die Schwindelei.

Bogy, Bogey, *s.* der Kobold.

Boil, I. *s.* die Beule, der Schwären. II. *v.a.* & *n.* sieden, kochen. **—er,** *s.* der Kessel. **—ing,** I. *p.* & *adj.* siedend. II. *s.* das Kochen, Sieden. **—ing-point,** *s.* der Siedepunkt.

Boisterous, *adj.,* **—ly,** *adv.* ungestüm. **—ness,** *s.* der Ungestüm.

Bold, *adj.,* **—ly,** *adv.* (brave) kühn, mutig; keck, dreist; (impudent) frech. **—ness,** *s.* die Kühnheit; die Dreistigkeit.

Bole, *s.* der Stamm.

Bollard, *s.* der Poller.

Bolster, *s.* das Polster.

1Bolt, I. *s.* der Bolzen; der Riegel; thunder—, der Donnerkeil. II. *v.a.* verbolzen; verriegeln, zuriegeln.

2Bolt, *v.a.* beuteln, sichten. **—ing-cloth,** *s.* das Beuteltuch.

Bomb, *s.* die Bombe. **—ard,** *v.a.* bombardieren, beschießen. **—ardment,** *s.* die Beschießung. **—proof,** *adj.* bombenfest.

Bombast, *s.* der Schwulst. **—ic,** *adj.* schwülstig.

Bond, I. *s.* (tie) das Band, der Strick; die Schuldverschreibung, Obligation

(*Law*); **—s,** die Fesseln. II. *adj.* gebunden. **—age,** *s.* die Knechtschaft. **—maid,** *s.* die Leibeigene. **—man,** *—servant,** *s.* der Leibeigene.

Bone, I. *s.* der Knochen, das Bein; die Gräte (*of fish*); — of contention, der Zankapfel. II. *adj.* beinern.

Bonfire, *s.* das Freudenfeuer.

Bonnet, *s.* der Damenhut.

Bonn—y, *adj.,* **—ily,** *adv.* hübsch.

Bony, *adj.* knöchern, beinern.

Book, *s.* das Buch. **—ish,** *adj.,* **—ishly,** *adv.* den Büchern ergeben. **—binder,** *s.* der Buchbinder. **—binding,** *s.* das Buchbinden. **—case,** *s.* der Bücherbehälter, Bücherschrank. **—ing-office,** *s.* der Schalter. **—keeper,** *s.* der Buchhalter. **—keeping,** *s.* die Buchhaltung. **—seller,** *s.* der Buchhändler. **—shelf,** *s.* das Bücherbrett. **—shop,** *s.* die Buchhandlung.

1Boom, *s.* der Baum; die Stange.

2Boom, *v.n.* dumpf schallen, dröhnen, brausen.

Boon, *s.* die Wohltat.

Boor, *s.* der Lümmel. **—ish,** *adj.,* **—ishly,** *adv.* grob. **—ishness,** *s.* die Grobheit, Tölpelei.

1Boot, *v.a.* nutzen, frommen. **—less,** *adj.* nutzlos.

2Boot, *s.* der Stiefel. **—jack,** *s.* der Stiefelknecht. **—lace,** *s.* das Schuhband. **—last,** **—tree,** *s.* der Stiefelleisten.

Booty, *s.* die Beute.

Border, I. *s.* der Rand, Saum; die Grenze. II. *v.a.* besetzen (*dresses, etc.*). III. *v.n.* ; to — on, grenzen an. **—er,** *s.* der Grenzbewohner.

Bore, I. *v.a.* bohren; langweilen. II. *s.* das Bohrloch; die Bohrung (*of a gun*). **—dom,** *s.* das Langweilige; die Lästigkeit. **—r,** *s.* der Bohrer.

Born, *p.p.* & *adj.* geboren, geborn.

Borrow, *v.a.* borgen, sich (*dat.*) leihen. **—er,** *s.* der Borger. **—ing,** *s.* das Borgen.

Bosom, *s.* der Busen; — friend, der Busenfreund.

Boss, *s.* der Knopf, Beschlag; (*sl.*) der Arbeitgeber.

Botan—ic(al), *adj.,* **—ically,** *adv.* botanisch. **—ist,** *s.* der Botaniker. **—y,** *s.* die Botanik, Pflanzenkunde.

Botch, I. *s.* das Flickwerk. II. *v.a.* hunzen, verderben. **—er,** *s.* der Flicker.

Both, I. *adj. & pron.* beide, beides; — of them, alle beide. II. *conj.*; — ... and, sowohl ... als (auch).

Bother, I. *v.a.* plagen, quälen; — it! zum Henfer damit! II. *v.n.* sich (ab)quälen (mit). III. *s.* die Plage, Beläftigung.

Bottle, *s.* die Flasche.

Bottom, I. *s.* der Boden, Grund; der Bauch (*of a ship*); to get to the — of a thing, einer Sache auf den Grund kommen. —less, *adj.* bodenlos.

Bough, *s.* der Aft; —s, das Geäst.

Boulder, *s.* der Rollstein, Felsblock.

Bounce, I. *v.n.* auffpringen. II. *s.* der Rücksprung.

¹**Bound,** *adj.* verpflichtet; I will be —, ich bürge dafür.

²**Bound,** *adj.* fertig; beftimmt.

³**Bound,** I. *s.* der Sprung; der Auffprung. II. *v.n.* fpringen.

⁴**Bound,** I. *s.*; —s, *pl.* die Grenze; die Schranke. II. *v.a.* begrenzen, einfchränken. —ary, *s.* die Grenze. —less, *adj.*, —lessly, *adv.* grenzenlos. —lessness, *s.* die Grenzenlofigkeit.

Bount-eous, *adj.*, —eously, *adv.* freigebig. —y, *s.* die Freigebigkeit, Wohltätigkeit; (*gift*) die Wohltat.

Bouquet, *s.* der Strauß; die Blume (*of wine*).

Bourgeois, I. *s.* der Bürger, Philifter. II. *adj.* bürgerlich, philifterhaft.

¹**Bow,** *s.* der Bug (*of a ship*). —sprit, *s.* das Bugfpriet (*Naut.*).

²**Bow,** *s.* der Bogen; die Schleife (*of ribbon*). —man, *s.* der Bogenfchütze.

³**Bow,** I. *s.* die Verbeugung, Verneigung. II. *v.a.* bücken, biegen, neigen (*head*). III. *v.n.* fich neigen; fich biegen.

Bowel, *s.*, der Darm; —s, das Eingeweide.

¹**Bowl,** *s.* der Napf, die Schale.

²**Bowl,** *s.* die Kugel. —s, *pl.* das Kegelfpiel. —er-hat, *s.* die Melone. —ing-alley, *s.* die Kegelbahn.

¹**Box,** *s.* der Buchsbaum (*Bot.*); die Büchfe, Schachtel, Dofe; die Loge (*in a theatre*). —keeper, der Logenfchließer. —office, die Theaterkaffe.

²**Box,** I. *s.*; — on the ear, eine Ohrfeige. II. *v.n.* fich boxen. —er, *s.* der Faufttämpfer, Boxer.

Boy, *s.* der Bube, Knabe, Junge. —hood, *s.* das Knabenalter. —ish, *adj.*, —ishly, *adv.* knabenhaft.

Brace, I. *s.* das Band, die Binde.

II. *v.a.* ftraff anziehen, fpannen; (*fig.*) ftärken, erfrifchen. —let, *s.* das Armband.

Bracken, *s.* das Farnkraut.

Bracket, I. *s.* der Tragftein, die Klammer (*Arch.*); das Wandbrettchen. II. *v.a.* einklammern.

Brackish, *adj.* falzig.

Brad, *s.* der Spiekernagel. —awl, *s.* der Spitzbohrer.

Brag, *v.n.* prahlen. —gart, I. *s.* der Prahler. II. *adj.* prahlerifch. —ging, *s.* die Prahlerei.

Braid, I. *s.* die Borte, Flechte. II. *v.a.* flechten.

Brail, *s.* das Geitau.

Brain, I. *s.* (*gen'lly*) —s, *pl.*) das Gehirn; scatter——ed, gedankenlos, toll. II. *v.a.* (einem) den Kopf zerfchmettern. —less, *adj.* ohne Verftand. —wave, *s.* der Geiftesblitz.

¹**Brake,** *s.* das Farnkraut.

²**Brake,** der Hemmfchuh, die Bremfe (*Railw.*).

Bramble, *s.* der Brombeerftrauch.

Bran, *s.* die Kleie.

Branch, I. *s.* der Aft, Zweig. II. *attrib.*; — establishment, das Nebengefchäft. III. *v.n.*; — out, fich verzweigen.

Brand, I. *s.* der (Feuer-)Brand; (*stigma*) das Brandmal, der Schandfleck; die Sorte (*of cigars, etc.*). II. *v.a.* brandmarken. —new, *adj.* funkelnagelneu.

Brandish, *v.a.* fchwingen. —er, *s.* der Schwinger.

Brandy, *s.* der Kognak, Schnaps.

Brass, *s.* das Meffing. —y, *adj.* ehern, erzartig.

Brat, *s.* der Balg, das Kindchen.

Brav-e, I. *v.a.* trotzen. II. *adj.* —ely, *adv.* tapfer, kühn, mutig. —ery, *s.* der Mut, die Tapferkeit, der Heldenmut. —o, *s. int.* bravo!

Brawl, I. *v.n.* laut zanken, lärmen. II. *s.* der Aufruhr, Auflauf. —er, *s.* der Lärmer, Zänker.

Brawn, *s.* das Eberfleifch. —iness, *s.* die Stärke. —y, *adj.* fehnig.

Bray, I. *v.n.* ia(n)en. II. *s.* das Efelgefchrei.

Braz-en, *adj.* ehern; (*fig.*) unverfchämt. —ier, *s.* der Kupferfchmied; die Kohlenpfanne.

Breach, *s.* der Bruch; die Brefche (*Fort.*); die Zwietracht.

Bread, s. das Brot; — and butter,
das Butterbrot; der Lebensunterhalt.
Breadth, s. die Breite, Weite.
Break, I. s. der Bruch, die Lücke;
der Anbruch (of day). II. ir.v.a.
brechen; zerbrechen, zerschlagen; to
— down, niederbrechen; to — off,
abbrechen, aufhören lassen; to —
open, aufbrechen, erbrechen. III.
ir.v.n. brechen, zerbrechen, zerspringen;
the school —s up, die Ferien beginnen.
to — away from a person, sich von
einem losreißen; — down, zusammenbrechen; to — forth, hervorbrechen; to — out, ausbrechen. —
able, adj. zerbrechlich. **—age,** s. das
Brechen. **—er,** s. der Brecher; die
Sturzsee (Naut.). **—ers,** pl. die
Brandung. **—down,** s. der Sturz;
die Panne (Motor.).
Breakfast, I. v.n. frühstücken. II. s.
das Frühstück.
Breakwater, s. der Hafendamm.
Bream, s. der Brassen (Icht.).
Breast, s. die Brust. **—bone,** s. das
Brustbein.
Breath, s. der Atem; der Hauch; with
bated —, mit verhaltenem Atem.
Breath—e, v.a. atmen; to —e ven-
geance, Rache schnauben. **—ing,** s. das
Atmen, Hauchen. **—less,** adj.,
lessly, adv. atemlos; außer Atem.
—lessness, s. die Atemlosigkeit.
Bred, imperf. & p.p. erzogen.
Breech, s. der Hintere; die Schwanz-
schraube (Gun.). **—es,** pl. die Reit-
hosen; die Kniehosen. **—loader,** s.
der Hinterlader.
Breed, I. ir.v.n. sich vermehren. II.
ir.v.a. erzeugen, hervorbringen; aufziehen (cattle). III. s. die Brut,
Zucht; das Geblüt (of horses). **—er,**
s. der Züchter (of cattle). **—ing,** s.
die Erziehung; die Bildung; die
Zucht (of cattle).
Breez—e, s. die Brise. **—y,** adj. windig, luftig.
Breviary, s. das Brevier.
Brevity, s. die Kürze.
Brew, I. v.a. & n. brauen. II. s. das
Gebräu. **—er,** s. der Brauer. **—ery,**
s. die Brauerei, das Brauhaus.
—ing, s. das Brauen; das Gebräu.
Bribe, I. s. die Bestechung. II. v.a.
bestechen. **—ry,** s. die Bestechung.
Brick, s. der Ziegelstein, Backstein; a
regular —, ein Prachtkerl. **—layer,**

s. der (Ziegel=)Maurer. **—work,** s.
das Backsteinmauerwerk. **—works,**
pl. die Ziegelhütte.
Brid—al, I. adj. bräutlich. II. s. die
Hochzeit, das Hochzeitsfest. **—e,** s.
die Neuvermählte; die Braut (be-
fore the wedding). **—egroom,** s.
der Bräutigam. **—esmaid,** s. die
Brautjungfer.
Bridge, I. s. die Brücke. II. v.a. eine
Brücke schlagen.
Bridle, I. s. der Zaum, Zügel. II. v.a.
zäumen; im Zaume halten. **—path,**
s. der Reitweg.
Brief, I. adj., **—ly,** adv. kurz, bündig.
II. s. das Rechtsdokument. **—ness,**
s. die Kürze.
Brier, s. der Dornstrauch; der Brom-
beerstrauch.
Brig, s. die Brigg. **—ade,** s. die
Brigade. **—adier,** s. der Brigadier.
—and, s. der Freibeuter. **—andage,**
s. die Straßenräuberei.
Bright, adj., **—ly,** adv. hell, glänzend.
—en, v. I. a. glänzend machen; (fig.)
aufhellen. II. n. hell werden, sich
aufhellen. **—ness,** s. der Glanz.
—eyed, adj. helläugig.
Brill, s. der Glattbutt (Icht.).
Brillian—cy, s. der Glanz. **—t,** I.
adj., **—tly,** adv. glänzend, funkelnd.
II. s. der Brillant.
Brim, s. der Rand. **—ful,** adj. bis
zum Rande voll. **—stone,** s. der
Schwefel.
Brindled, adj. gefleckt, schäckig.
Brin—e, s. die Lake; die Salzsole;
(Poet.) das Meer. **—y,** adj. salzig.
Bring, ir.v.a. bringen; to — about,
zustande bringen; to — away, weg-
bringen; to — back, zurückbringen or
führen; to — forth, hervorbringen,
darstellen; to — on, herbeiführen (war,
etc.); to — together, zusammenbringen; to — under, bezwingen; to
— up, heraufbringen; (fig.) aufziehen.
Brink, s. der Rand.
Brisk, adj., **—ly,** adv. lebhaft; flink.
—ness, s. die Lebhaftigkeit.
Bristl—e, I. s. die Borste. II. v.n.
sich sträuben. **—ed,** adj. struppig.
—y, adj. borstig, borstenartig.
Brittle, adj. zerbrechlich, spröde,
schwach. **—ness,** s. die Brüchigkeit.
Broach, v.a. anzapfen; to — a subject,
das Gespräch auf eine Sache bringen.
Broad, adj., **—ly,** adv. breit, weit.

—en, v. I. a. breiter machen, erweitern. II. n. breiter werden, sich ausbreiten. —cast, I. adj. ausgestreut. II. v.a. rundfunken, senden (Radio). —casting-station, s. die Sendestation (Radio). —minded, adj. weitherzig, duldsam.

Brocade, s. der Brokat. —d, adj. brokaten.

1Broil, s. der Lärm, Tumult.

2Broil, v.a. braten, rösten.

Broken, p.p. of Break (& adj.) gebrochen; to speak — English, Englisch radebrechen. —ly, adv. unterbrochen. —down, adj. gebrochen, niedergeschlagen; vereitelt. —winded, adj. kurzatmig, keuchend.

Broker, s. der Makler. —age, s. die Maklergebühr.

Bronch—ial, adj. zur Luftröhre gehörig. —itis, s. die Luftröhrenentzündung.

Bronze, s. die Bronze.

Brooch, s. die Brosche, Busennadel.

Brood, I. s. die Brut (also fig.). II. v.n. brüten.

1Brook, s. der Bach. —let, s. das Bächlein.

2Brook, v.n. ertragen, leiden.

Broom, s. der Besen. —stick, s. der Besenstiel.

Broth, s. die (Fleisch=)Brühe.

Brother, s. der Bruder, —in-law, der Schwager. —hood, s. die Brüderschaft. —ly, adj. brüderlich.

Brow, s. (eyebrow) die Augenbraue; (forehead) die Stirne.

Brown, adj. braun, bräunlich. —ness, s. die braune Farbe. —ie, s. das Heinzelmännchen.

Browse, v.n. weiden.

Bruise, I. v.a. zermalmen; wund schlagen. II. s. die Quetschung.

Brush, I. s. die Bürste; der Pinsel (Paint.). II. v.a. bürsten, abbürsten; to — up, aufbürsten; auffrischen. —wood, s. das Gestrüpp.

Brusque, adj., —ly, adv. barsch, schroff. —ness, s. die Barschheit, Schroffheit.

Brut—al, adj., —ally, adv. tierisch, viehisch; unmenschlich; grausam. — ality, s. die Unmenschlichkeit, Roheit, Brutalität. —e, s. das Vieh; der Grobian. —ish, adj. tierisch, viehisch.

Bubble, I. s. die Blase. II. v.n. aufwallen.

Buccaneer, s. der Seeräuber.

Buck, s. der Bock.

Bucket, s. der Eimer, Kübel.

Buckle, I. s. die Schnalle. II. v.a. schnallen; to — to, sich eifrig legen auf (with accus.).

Buckwheat, s. der Buchweizen.

Bud, I. s. die Knospe. II. v.n. knospen; (fig.) blühen.

Budge, v.n. sich rühren, sich regen.

Budget, s. das Budget; der Haushaltsplan; der Vorrat.

Buff, I. s. das Büffelleder. II. adj. ledergelb.

Buffalo, s. der Büffel.

Buffer, s. der Puffer.

1Buffet, I. s. der Puff, Faustschlag. II. v.a. puffen.

2Buffet, s. der Schenktisch.

Buffoon, s. der Possenreißer. —ery, s. die Possen.

Bug, s. die Wanze.

Bugle, s. das Jagdhorn, Hifthorn.

Build, I. v.a. bauen, erbauen. II. s. die Form; die Gestalt. —er, s. der Bauende; der Baumeister. —ing, s. das Bauen; (thing built) das Gebäude. —ing-ground, s. der Bauplatz.

Bulb, s. der Knollen (Bot.); die Zwiebel; electric —, die Glühlampe, Glühbirne. —ous, adj. zwiebelartig, knollig.

Bulge, I. v.n. vorragen. II. s. die Ausbauchung (Build.).

Bulk, s. der Umfang, die Größe; die Masse (of a body); (greater part) der Hauptteil; in the —, in Bausch und Bogen. —y, adj. dick. —head, s. das Schott.

1Bull, s. der Stier, Bulle. —ock, s. der Farre. —dog, s. der Bullenbeißer. —fight, s. das Stiergefecht. —finch, s. der Dompfaff. —frog, s. der Ochsenfrosch. —'s-eye, s. die Blendlaterne; das Zentrum (Mil., etc.).

2Bull, s. die Bulle (Eccles.).

Bullet, s. die Kugel.

Bullion, s. Gold oder Silber in Barren.

Bully, I. s. der Eisenfresser, Raufdegen. II. v.a. einschüchtern.

Bulrush, s. die Binse.

Bulwark, s. das Bollwerk.

Bump, I. s. der Stoß; die Beule. II. v.a. stoßen.

Bun, s. die Semmel.

Bunch, s. das Bund (of keys, etc.);

das Bündel, Bund (*of straw, etc.*); — of flowers, der Blumenstrauß. —y, *adj.* büschelig; büschelförmig; bauschig.

Bundle, *s.* das Bund, Bündel, Paket.

Bung, I. *s.* der Spund. II. *v.a.* (zu)spunden. —hole, *s.* das Spundloch.

Bungl—e, I. *s.* die Pfuscherei, Stümperei. II. *v.a.* (ver)pfuschen, verhunzen. —er, *s.* der Stümper, Pfuscher. —ing, *adj.*, —ingly, *adv.* ungeschickt, stümperhaft.

Bunion, *s.* die Schwiele.

Bunk, *s.* die Schlafbank. —er, *s.* der Kohlenraum.

Bunting, *s.* die Ammer (Orn.); das Flaggentuch.

Buoy, *s.* die Boje. —ancy, *s.* die Schwimmkraft. —ant, *adj.*, —antly, *adv.* schwimmend.

Bur, *s.* die Klette.

Burden, I. *s.* die Bürde, Last. II. *v.a.* aufbürden, belasten. —some, *adj.* drückend, lästig. —someness, *s.* die Lästigkeit.

Bureau, *s.* das Amtszimmer, Bureau; das Schreibbureau, Schreibpult. —cracy, *s.* die Beamtenherrschaft, Bureaukratie.

Burgl—ar, *s.* der Einbrecher. —arious, *adj.*, —ariously, *adv.* einbrecherisch. —e, *v.a.* einbrechen.

Burgomaster, *s.* der Bürgermeister.

Burial, *s.* das Begräbnis, die Beerdigung. —ground, *s.* der Kirchhof. —service, *s.* die Totenfeier.

Burlesque, I. *adj.* burlesk, possierlich. II. *s.* das Burleske.

Burl—iness, *s.* die Stämmigkeit. —y, *adj.* stämmig.

Burn, I. *v.a.* brennen lassen, verbrennen. II. *v.n.* brennen. III. *s.* der Brand. —er, *s.* der Brenner. —ing, I. *p. & adj.* brennend. II. *s.* das Brennen, der Brand.

Burnish, *v.a.* glätten, polieren.

Burrow, I. *s.* die Kaninchenhöhle. II. *v.n.* sich eingraben.

Burst, I. *v.n.* bersten, platzen; (explode) explodieren; — out, hervorbrechen; to — into tears, in Tränen ausbrechen; to — into flame, aufflammen. II. *v.a.* sprengen, zersprengen. —ing, *s.* das Bersten; der Bruch.

Bury, *v.a.* begraben, beerdigen. —ingground, *s.* der Kirchhof; die Begräbnisstätte.

Bush, *s.* der Busch, Strauch. —iness,

s. das Buschige. —y, *adj.* buschig; gebüschig.

Bushel, *s.* der Scheffel.

Busi—ly, *adv.* geschäftig, emsig. —ness, *s.* (calling) das Geschäft; (affair) die Angelegenheit, Sache; (trade) der Handel, das Getriebe. —nesslike, *adj.* kaufmännisch, geschäftsmäßig.

Bust, *s.* die Büste.

Bustard, *s.* die gemeine Trappe (Orn.).

¹Bustl—e, I. *v.n.* (hurry) sich regen, sich rühren. II. *s.* das Getöse. —ing, *adj.* rührig, geschäftig.

²Bustle, *s.* die Turnüre.

Busy, I. *adj.* beschäftigt; geschäftig, emsig, fleißig, tätig. II. *v.a.* beschäftigen.

But, I. *conj.* aber, allein, sondern; wenn nicht; dessen ungeachtet, indessen, nichts desto weniger; the last — one, der vorletzte; all —, fast, nahe daran; nothing —, nichts als. II. *prep. or with another part.* = prep. & negation, außer, ausgenommen. III. *adv.* nur.

Butcher, I. *s.* der Fleischer, Metzger, Schlächter. II. *v.a.* metzeln (*also fig.*). —y, *s.* die Metzgerei.

Butler, *s.* der Kellermeister.

¹Butt, *s.* das Stückfaß.

²Butt, I. *s.* der Stoß mit dem Kopfe; die Zielscheibe. II. *v.n.* mit dem Kopfe stoßen. —end, *s.* der Kolben.

Butter, I. *s.* die Butter. II. *v.a.* mit Butter bestreichen. —y, *adj.* butterig. —cup, *s.* die Butterblume. —fly, *s.* der Schmetterling. —milk, *s.* die Buttermilch.

Buttock, *s.* das Hinterteil.

Button, I. *s.* der Knopf. II. *v.a.* (— up) zuknöpfen. —hole, *s.* das Knopfloch. —hook, *s.* der Stiefelknöpfer.

Buttress, *s.* der Strebepfeiler.

Butts, *pl.* der Scheibenstand (Artil.).

Buxom, *adj.* drall.

Buy, *v.* I. *a.* kaufen; — in, einkaufen. II. *n.* handeln; kaufen. —er, *s.* der Käufer. —ing, *s.* das Kaufen, Handeln.

Buzz, I. *v.n.* summen, sumsen. II. *s.* das Summen, Gesumse.

Buzzard, *s.* der Bussard.

By, I. *prep.* (beside) neben, an; (near) nahe; (about) bei; (before, by the time of) bei, gegen, um, in;

(from, owing to) burch, von, nach, aus; (by the help of, with) burch, mit; — all means, gewiß; — the dozen, bußenbweise; — itself, für sich, allein. II. *adv.*; — and —, näch= stens, bald, nachher; by the —, gelegentlich, nebenher; hard —, close —, dicht babei; to go —, vorbei gehen. —gone, *adj.* vergangen, veraltet. —law, *s.* bas Nebengeseß. —play, *s.* bas Zwischenspiel. —road, —way, *s.* ber Nebenweg. —stander, *s.* ber Zuschauer; (*pl.*) die Umstehenden.

C

C, c, bas C, c.
Cab, *s.* die Droschke. —man, *s.* ber Droschkenkutscher. —stand, *s.* ber Droschkenhalteplaß.
Cabal, *s.* die Kabale.
Cabbage, *s.* ber Kohl. —lettuce, *s.* ber Kopfsalat.
Cabin, *s.* die Hütte, bas Häuschen (*Build.*); die Kajüte (*Naut.*). —boy, *s.* ber Schiffsjunge.
Cabinet, *s.* bas Kabinett; ber Schu= blabenschrank; bas Kabinett (*Pol.*). —maker, *s.* ber Kunsttischler. — speaker, *s.* ber Flächenlautsprecher (*Radio*).
Cable, *s.* bas Seil, Tau, Kabel.
Cacao, *s.* ber Kakao.
Cackle, I. *v.n.* gackern, gackeln (*as a hen*); schnattern (*as a goose*). II. *s.* bas Gackeln, Gegacker; bas Schnat= tern, Geschnatter.
Cactus, *s.* ber Kaktus.
Cad, *s.* ber gemeine Kerl.
Caddy, *s.* die Teebüchse, bas Tee= kästchen.
Cadence, *s.* ber Tonfall; die Kadenz.
Cadet, *s.* ber Kadett (*Mil.*).
Café, *s.* bas Café.
Cage, I. *s.* ber Käfig; bas Vogelbauer. II. *v.a.* einsperren. —aerial, *s.* die Korbantenne (*Radio*).
Cairn, *s.* ber Steinhaufen.
Caitiff, I. *s.* ber Schurke, Schuft. II. *adj.* schurkisch.
Cajole, *v.a.* schmeicheln. —r, *s.* ber Schmeichler. —ry, *s.* die Schmeichelei.
Cake, I. *s.* ber Kuchen; a — of soap, ein Stück Seife. II. *v.n.* hart werden.
Calamit—ous, *adj.*, —ously, *adv.* unheilvoll. —y, *s.* bas Unglück, Unheil.
Calcareous, *adj.* kalkig, kalkhaltig.

Calcul—able, *adj.* berechenbar. —ate, *v.* I. *a.* berechnen. II. *n.* rechnen. —ation, *s.* die Rechenkunst; die Be= rechnung.
Calendar, *s.* ber Kalender.
Calender, *s.* ber Kalander.
Calf, *s.* bas Kalb (*of leg*).
Calibre, *s.* bas Kaliber; (*fig.*) die Beschaffenheit.
Calico, *s.* ber Kaliko, Kattun.
Caliph, *s.* ber Kalif.
Call, I. *v.a.* rufen, herbeirufen; (— together) zusammenrufen; (name) heißen, (be)nennen; (summon) kom= men lassen, zitieren; to — to account, zur Rechenschaft ziehen. II. *v.n.* rufen; he —ed in this morning, heute morgen sprach er vor; to — upon a person, sich an einen wenden; (visit) einen be= suchen *or* aufsuchen. III. *s.* ber Ruf, Schrei. —ing, *s.* bas Rufen; (profession) ber Beruf, bas Gewerbe. —box, *s.* die Fernsprechzelle.
Calligraphy, *s.* die Schönschreibekunst.
Callipers, *pl.* die Tasterzirkel.
Callous, *adj.* schwielig; (*fig.*) unemp= findlich.
Callow, *adj.* unbefiebert; (*fig.*) un= erfahren.
Calm, I. *adj.*, —ly, *adv.* ruhig, still. II. die Stille, Ruhe; die Windstille (*Naut., etc.*). III. *v.a.* beruhigen, stillen.
Calomel, *s.* bas Kalomel.
Calumn—ious, *adj.*, verleumberisch. —y, *s.* die Verleumdung.
Calve, *v.n.* kalben.
Cambric, *s.* die Battistleinwand.
Camel, *s.* bas Kameel.
Camellia, *s.* die Kamelie (*Bot.*).
Cameo, *s.* die Kamee.
Camera, *s.* die Camera (*Phot.*).
Camomile, *s.* die Kamille.
Camp, I. *s.* bas Lager, Feldlager. II. *v.n.* sich lagern. —follower, *s.* ber Marketender.
Campaign, I. *s.* ber Feldzug. II. *v.n.* einen Feldzug mitmachen.
Camphor, *s.* ber Kampfer.
¹Can, *ir.v.* 1 & 3 *sing.* & 1, 2 & 3 *pl. of the pres. ind. of the old English infin.* cunnan (= können); I, he —, ich, er kann; we, you, they —, wir können, ihr könnt, sie können.
²Can, *s.* die Kanne; canned goods, die Konserven.
Canal, *s.* ber Kanal. —lock, *s.* die Kanalschleuse.

Canary, *s.* (—bird) der Kanarienvogel.

Cancel, *v.a.* durchstreichen; (annul) aufheben, vernichten; widerrufen (*an order*). —**lation**, *s.* die Entwertung.

Cancer, *s.* der Krebs. —**ous**, *adj.* krebsartig.

Candid, *adj.*, —**ly**, *adv.* aufrichtig, offen. —**ate**, *s.* der Kandidat, Bewerber. —**ature**, *s.* die Kandidatur, Bewerbung.

Candied, *adj.* überzuckert.

Candle, *s.* die Kerze. —**extinguisher**, *s.* das Lichthütchen —**light**, *s.*; Kerzenlicht. —**stick**, *s.* der Leuchter; der Armleuchter. —**wick**, *s.* der Lichtdocht.

Candour, *s.* die Biederkeit, Redlichkeit, Lauterkeit.

Candy, I. *s.* das Zuckerwerk. II. *v.a.* kandieren, kristallisieren.

Cane, I. *s.* das Rohr; der Rohrstock. II. *v.a.* prügeln.

Canine, *adj.* hündisch; — tooth, der Hundszahn.

Canister, *s.* die Blechbüchse.

Canker, I. *s.* der Krebs, Rost, Brand (*on trees, etc.*). II. *v.n.* rosten.

Cannibal, *s.* der Menschenfresser, Kannibale. —**ism**, *s.* der Kannibalismus, die Menschenfresserei.

Cannon, *s.* die Kanone, das Geschütz. —**ball**, *s.* die Kanonenkugel. —**proof**, *s.* bombenfest.

Canoe, *s.* das Kanu, der Baumkahn.

¹**Canon**, *s.* (law) der Kanon. —**ical**, *adj.* kanonisch. —**ization**, —**isation**, *s.* die Heiligsprechung. —**law**, *s.* das Kirchenrecht, kanonische Recht.

²**Canon**, *s.* der Kanoniker, Domherr.

Canopied, *adj.* bedeckt. —**y**, *s.* der Baldachin.

Cant, I. *s.* die Kante. II. *v.a.* stoßen; auf die Seite legen. —**ed**, *adj.* eckig, kantig.

Cantata, *s.* die Kantate.

Canteen, *s.* die Kantine.

Canter, I. *s.* der kurze Galopp. II. *v.n.* in kurzem, leichtem Galopp reiten.

Canticle, *s.* der Lobgesang.

Canto, *s.* der Gesang.

Canton, *s.* der Bezirk, Kanton. —**ment**, *s.* die Einlagerung.

Canvas, *s.* der Kanevas (*Text.*); das Segeltuch (*Naut.*); die Malerleinwand (*Paint.*); (*fig.*) das Gemälde.

Canvass, I. *s.* die Bewerbung, Stimmenwerbung. II. *v.a.* (examine) prüfen;

(solicit) sich um eine S. bewerben. —**er**, *s.* der Bewerber, Stimmenwerber.

Cap, I. *s.* die Kappe, Mütze (*for boys, etc.*); die Haube (*for women*). II. *v.a.* (oben) bedecken; übertreffen.

Capa—**bility**, *s.* die Fähigkeit. —**ble**, *adj.*, —**bly**, *adv.* fähig. —**cious**, *adj.*, —**ciously**, *adv.* geräumig. —**ciousness**, *s.* die Geräumigkeit. —**city**, *s.* die Weite, Geräumigkeit; (ability) die Fähigkeit, Leistungsfähigkeit, Tüchtigkeit; in the —city of, in der Eigenschaft als.

¹**Cape**, *s.* der Kragenmantel (*Tail.*).

²**Cape**, *s.* das Vorgebirge, Kap.

¹**Caper**, I. *s.* der Bocksprung, Luftsprung. II. *v.n.* springen, hüpfen.

²**Caper**, *s.* die Kaper (*Bot.*).

Capercailzie, *s.* der Auerhahn.

¹**Capit**—**al**, I. *adj.*, —**ally**, *adv.* (chief) hauptsächlich, Haupt-; (excellent) vortrefflich, prächtig, famos; —al crime, ein Todesverbrechen. II. *s.* (city) die Hauptstadt; großer Anfangsbuchstabe, Majuskel; das Kapital (*C.L.*).

²**Capital**, *s.* das Kapitäl (*Arch.*).

Capit—**alism**, *s.* die Macht des Großkapitals. —**alist**, *s.* der Kapitalist.

Capitulate, *v.a.* kapitulieren; sich auf Vertrag ergeben.

Capric—**e**, *s.* die Laune, Grille. —**ious**, *adj.*, —**iously**, *adv.* launenhaft.

Capsize, *v.* I. *a.* umwerfen. II. *n.* umfallen.

Capstan, *s.* die Erdwinde (*Mach.*); das Gangspill, Spill (*Naut.*).

Captain, *s.* der (Schiffs-)Kapitän (*Naut.*); der Hauptmann (*Mil.*). —**cy**, *s.* die Hauptmannschaft.

Captious, *adj.*, —**ly**, *adv.* zänkisch. —**ness**, *s.* die Zanksucht.

Captiv—**ate**, *v.a.* gefangen nehmen; (*fig.*) fesseln, einnehmen. —**ating**, *adj.* fesselnd, reizend. —**e**, I. *adj.* gefangen; —e balloon, der Fesselballon. II. *s.* der Kriegsgefangene. —**ity**, *s.* die Gefangenschaft.

Captor, *s.* der Fänger.

Capture, I. *s.* das Fangen; das Erbeuten. II. *v.a.* fangen; erbeuten.

Car, *s.* der Karren; der Nachen (*of a balloon*).

Carafe, *s.* die gläserne Wasserflasche, Karaffe.

Caramel, *s.* der Karamel.

Carat, *s.* das Karat.

Caravan, *s.* die Karawane. **—serai,** *s.* die Karawanserei.

Caraway, *s.* der Kümmel.

Carbine, *s.* der Karabiner. **—er,** *s.* der Karabiner.

Carbolic-acid, *s.* die Karbolsäure (*Chem.*).

Carbon, *s.* der Kohlenstoff. **—light,** *s.* das Bogenlicht.

Carbuncle, *s.* der Karfunkel (*Min.*); das Blutgeschwür (*Med.*).

Carburettor, *s.* der Karburator.

Carcass, Carcase, *s.* der Körper; (corpse) der Leichnam; das Aas (*of beasts*).

¹Card, *s.* die Karte; (playing—) Spielkarte; (visiting—) Visitenkarte; (post—) Postkarte. **—board,** *s.* der Pappdeckel.

²Card, I. *s.* die Karde, Kardätsche. II. *v.a.* (Wolle) krempeln; (Baumwolle) kardätschen.

Cardinal, I. *adj.* hauptsächlichst, Haupt-. II. *s.* der Kardinal (*Eccl.*).

Care, I. *s.* (anxiety) die Sorge, Besorgnis; (providence) die Fürsorge; (heed) die Achtsamkeit, Hut, Vorsicht; (sorrow) der Kummer; (carefulness) die Sorgfalt; (— of a patient) die Pflege; care of, c/o, per Adresse, bei. II. *v.n.* sorgen, sich bekümmern; I don't —! meinetwegen! I don't — a straw about it, ich mache mir nichts daraus. **—ful,** *adj.,* **—fully,** *adv.* (anxious) sorgenvoll, besorgt; (provident) sorgsam, achtsam, vorsichtig. **—fulness,** *s.* (solicitude) die Sorgfalt; (providence) die Wachsamkeit. **—less,** *adj.,* **—lessly,** *adv.* (without —) sorgenfrei, sorglos; (negligent) nachlässig. **—lessness,** *s.* die Sorglosigkeit; die Unachtsamkeit; die Nachlässigkeit. **—worn,** *adj.* von Sorgen gedrückt, abgehärmt.

Career, I. *s.* die Laufbahn. II. *v.n.* schnell laufen, eilen.

Caress, I. *s.* die Liebkosung. II. *a.v.* liebkosen.

Cargo, *s.* die Fracht, Ladung.

Caricature, I. *s.* das Zerrbild, die Karikatur. II. *v.a.* karikieren, verzerren.

Carmine, *s.* der Karmin.

Carn—age, *s.* das Blutbad. **—al,** *adj.,* **—ally,** *adv.* fleischlich, sinnlich.

Carnation, *s.* die Fleischfarbe; die Gartennelke (*Bot.*).

Carnelian, *s.* der Karneol.

Carnival, *s.* der Karneval.

Carnivorous, *adj.* fleischfressend.

Carol, *s.*; Christmas —, das Weihnachtslied.

Carouse, I. *s.* das Zechgelage. II. *v.n.* zechen, trinken.

¹Carp, *s.* der Karpfen (*Icht.*).

²Carp, *v.n.*; etwas bekritteln, tadeln. **—er,** *s.* der Krittler.

Carpent—er, I. *s.* der Zimmermann. II. *v.n.* zimmern. **—ry,** *s.* das Zimmerhandwerk.

Carpet, *s.* der Teppich.

Carriage, *s.* der Wagen, das Fuhrwerk; (transport) die Verfrachtung; (deportment) die Haltung; (railway —) der Eisenbahnwagen.

Carrier, *s.* der Fuhrmann. **—pigeon,** *s.* die Brieftaube.

Carrion, *s.* das Aas.

Carrot, *s.* die Karotte, Mohrrübe.

Carry, *v.* I. *a.* tragen, fahren, führen; to — interest, Zinsen tragen; to — on, fortsetzen, weiterführen. II. *n.* schießen (*as a gun*). **—ing,** *s.* das Fuhrwesen (*C.L.*); das Fahren; (trade) das Speditionsgeschäft.

Cart, *s.* der Karren, Frachtwagen. **—er,** *s.* der Fuhrmann, Kärrner. **—horse,** *s.* das Zugpferd.

Cartilage, *s.* der Knorpel.

Cartoon, *s.* der Karton, die Musterzeichnung; das Vollbild; die Karikatur.

Cartridge, *s.* die Patrone.

Carv—e, *v.* I. *a.* schneiden (*a joint, etc.*); schnitzen, meißeln (*Carp., Sculp., Engr.*). II. *n.* vorschneiden (*at table*). **—ed,** *p.p. & adj.* geschnitzt. **—er,** *s.* der Vorschneider; der Schnitzer, Bildner (*Art*). **—ing,** *s.* das Schnitzwerk; die Bildhauerarbeit.

Cascade, *s.* der Wasserfall.

¹Case, I. *s.* das Futteral, Etui, der Kasten; die Kiste. II. *v.a.* mit einem Überzug versehen.

²Case, *s.* (circumstance) der Fall, Umstand, die Sache; (event) der Vorfall; (accident) der Zufall; (condition) der Zustand.

Casement, *s.* das Fenster.

Cash, I. *s.* das Geld; (ready —) das bare Geld; payment in —, die Barzahlung; to — einwechseln. **—ier,** I. *s.* der Kassierer (*C.L.*). II. *v.a.* abbanken, entlassen.

Cashmere, *s.* der Kaschmir.

Cask, *s.* das Faß. **—et,** *s.* das Kästchen.

Casque, *s.* der Helm.

Cassock, *s.* die Soutane.

Cast, I. *ir.v.a.* werfen; wegwerfen; gießen (*iron*); ausrechnen (*accounts*); to — lots for, losen um. II. *s.* der Wurf, das Werfen; der Guß (*Metall.*); (squint) das Schielen. III. *adj.*; — steel, — iron, der Gußstahl, das Gußeisen. **—off,** *adj.* abgelegt.

Castanets, *pl.* die Kastagnetten.

Caste, *s.* die Kaste.

Caster, *s.* der Werfer; die Streubüchse. **—sugar,** *s.* der Streuzucker.

Casting, *s.* das Gießen; (cast) der Abguß.

Castle, *s.* die Burg, das Schloß; der Turm (*Chess*).

Castor, *s.* der Biber (*Zool.*). **—oil,** *s.* das Rizinusöl.

Casu—al, *adj.*, **—ally,** *adv.* zufällig. **—alty,** *s.* der Unglücksfall. **—alties,** *s.* Unfälle; der Verlust (*in battle*).

Cat, *s.* die Katze; tom—, der Kater. **—gut,** die Darmsaite. **—whisker,** *s.* die Detektorfeder (*Radio*).

Cata—logue, *s.* das Verzeichnis, der Katalog. **—pult,** *s.* die Katapulte. **—ract,** I. *s.* der Stromsturz; der Star (*of the eye*).

Catarrh, *s.* der Katarrh. **—al,** *adj.* Schnupfen-.

Catastrophe, *s.* die Katastrophe; der Zusammenbruch.

Catch, I. *ir.v.a.* fangen, fassen, ergreifen; to — cold, sich erkälten; to — it, eine Tracht Prügel erhalten; a —y tune, eine ins Ohr fallende Melodie. II. *v.n.* in einander greifen; einspringen (*as a spring*); to be —ing, ansteckend sein. III. *s.* das Fangen, der Fang; der Haken, Griff (*Mech.*). **—penny,** *s.* der Lockartikel, die Schleuderware. **—word,** *s.* das Stichwort.

Catch—etical, *adj.*, **—etically,** *adv.* katechetisch. **—ize, —ise,** *v.a.* katechisieren.

Categor—ical, *adj.*, **—ically,** *adv.* kategorisch. **—y,** *s.* die Kategorie.

Cater, *v.n.* (to — for) einkaufen. **—er,** *s.* der Proviantmeister.

Caterpillar, *s.* die Raupe.

Cathedral, *s.* die Kathedrale, Domkirche, der Dom.

Catholic, *adj.* katholisch. **—ism,** der Katholizismus.

Cattle, *s.* & *pl.* das Vieh.

Caul, *s.* die Netzhaut.

Cauldron, *s.* der (große) Kessel.

Cauliflower, *s.* der Blumenkohl.

Caulk, Calk, *v.a.* kalfatern. **—ing,** *s.* das Kalfatern.

Cause, I. *s.* die Ursache, der Grund. II. *v.a.* verursachen, veranlassen. **—less,** *adj.*, **—lessly,** *adv.* grundlos. **—r,** *s.* der Urheber.

Causeway, *s.* die Chaussee.

Caustic, I. *adj.* kaustisch, ätzend. II. *s.* das Ätzmittel.

Cautio—n, I. *s.* die Vorsicht, Behutsamkeit. II. *v.a.* warnen (vor einer S., against a thing). **—nary,** *adj.* warnend. **—us,** *adj.*, **—usly,** *adv.* behutsam, vorsichtig.

Caval—cade, *s.* der Reiterzug. **—ier,** *s.* der Reiter. **—ry,** *s.* die Kavallerie, Reiterei.

Cave, *s.* die Höhle; to — in, einstürzen; (*fig.*) klein beigeben.

Cavern, *s.* die Höhle. **—ous,** *adj.* hohl; höhlenreich.

Caviare, *s.* der Kaviar.

Cavil, I. *v.n.* (to — at) kritteln, bekritteln. II. *s.* die Spitzfindigkeit. **—ler,** *s.* der (Be)krittler. **—ling,** *p. & adj.* tadelnd, spitzfindig; without —, zweifellos.

Cavity, *s.* die Höhlung.

Caw, I. *v.n.* krächzen. II. *interj.* krah, krah!

Cayenne-pepper, *s.* der Cayennepfeffer.

Cease, *v.* I. *n.* (— from) aufhören (mit). II. *a.* aufhören; einstellen. **—less,** *adj.*, **—lessly,** *adv.* unaufhörlich, unablässig.

Cedar, *s.* die Zeder.

Cede, *v.a.* abtreten, überlassen, nachgeben.

Ceiling, *s.* die Decke.

Celebr—ate, *v.a.* feiern (a *birthday, etc.*). **—ated,** *adj.* berühmt. **—ation,** *s.* die Feier, das Fest. **—ity,** *s.* die Berühmtheit; (person) die berühmte Persönlichkeit.

Celerity, *s.* die Geschwindigkeit, Schnelligkeit.

Celery, *s.* der Sellerie (*Bot.*).

Celestial, *adj.*, **—ly,** *adv.* himmlisch.

Celiba—cy, *s.* die Ehelosigkeit. **—te,** I. *s.* der Ehelose. II. *adj.* ehelos, unverheiratet.

Cell, *s.* die Zelle. **—ar,** *s.* der Keller;

salt——ar, die Salzbüchſe. —arage, s. das Kellergeſchoß.

Cement, I. s. der and das Zement; der Kitt. II. v.a. zementieren, verkitten.

Cemetery, s. der Kirch=, Fried=hof.

Cenotaph, s. das Ehrengrabmal.

Censer, s. das Rauchfaß, Weihrauchfaß.

Cens—or, s. der Zenſor. —orious, adj., —oriously, adv. ſtreng, tadelſüchtig. —oriousness, s. die Tadelſucht. —ure, I. s. (blame) der Tadel; (reproof) der Verweis. II. v.a. tadeln.

Census, s. die Volkszählung; der Zenſus.

Cent, s. das Hundert; der Zent (Amer.); per —, Prozent. —igram, s. das Zentigramm. —ipede, s. der Tauſendfuß. —ner, s. der Zentner.

Central, adj. zentral.

Centre, s. der Mittelpunkt, das Zentrum.

Century, s. das Jahrhundert.

Cereal, adj. Getreide=. —s, pl. das Getreide.

Ceremon—ial, I. adj. feierlich. II. s. das Zeremoniell. —ious, adj., —iously, adv. feierlich. —iousness, s. die Feierlichkeit. —y, s. die Zeremonie; die Feier.

Certain, adj. (sure) ſicher, gewiß; (indubitable) unzweifelhaft; (trustworthy) zuverläſſig; (unchanging) unveränderlich. —ly, adv. gewiß. —ty, s. die Gewißheit.

Certi—ficate, s. das Zeugnis. —fication, s. die Beſcheinigung. —fy, v.a. beſcheinigen, bezeugen. —tude, s. die Gewißheit.

Cess—ation, s. das Aufhören. —ion, s. die Überlaſſung.

Chafe, v. I. a. warm reiben; wund reiben (the skin, etc.). II. n. ſich entrüſten.

Chafer, s. der Käfer.

Chaff, s. die Spreu.

Chaffer, v.n. ſchachern.

Chaffinch, s. der Buchfink.

Chain, I. s. die Kette. II. v.a. (— up) anketten; (fig.) feſſeln.

Chair, s. der Stuhl, Seſſel. —man, s. der Vorſitzende.

Chalice, s. der Kelch.

Chalk, s. die Kreide. —y, adj. freidig.

Challenge, I. s. die Herausforderung (to fight, etc.); die Aufforderung (to

a contest); die Anrufung (of a sentry, etc.). II. v.a. herausfordern; anrufen (Mil.).

Chamber, s. die Kammer. —lain, s. der Kammerherr. —maid, s. das Zimmermädchen.

Chameleon, s. das Chamäleon.

Chamois, s. die Gemſe.

Champagne, s. der Champagner.

Champion, I. s. der Vorkämpfer. II. v.a. beſchützen, verteidigen.

Chance, I. s. der Zufall; by —, von ungefähr; to take a —, eine Sache wagen, es darauf ankommen laſſen. II. v.n. ſich ereignen. III. adj. zufällig.

Chancel, s. der Altarplatz. —lor, s. der Kanzler.

Chancery, s. das Kanzleigericht.

Chand—elier, s. der Hängeleuchter. —ler, s. der Lichtzieher.

Change, I. v.a. (alter) ändern, verändern; (exchange) vertauſchen, wechſeln. II. v.n. ſich ändern. III. s. die Veränderung; der Wechſel; (small money) das Kleingeld. —able, adj., —ably, adv. veränderlich, wandelbar. —ableness, s. die Unbeſtändigkeit; der Wankelmut. —ful, adj. unbeſtändig; unzuverläſſig. —less, adj. unveränderlich. —over switch, s. der Umſchalter (Radio).

Channel, s. der Kanal.

Chant, I. s. der Geſang. II. v.a. beſingen.

Chao—s, s. das Chaos; (fig.) der Wirrwarr. —tic, adj. chaotiſch.

1Chap, I. s. der Spalt. II. v.a. aufſpringen, ſpalten. —ped, p.p. & adj. geſpalten, offen.

2Chap, s. der Kinnbacken.

3Chap, s. der Burſche.

Chapel, s. die Kapelle.

Chaperon, s. die Anſtandsdame.

Chaplain, s. der Kaplan.

Chapter, s. das Kapitel.

1Char, Chare, v.n. im Tagelohn arbeiten. — woman, s. die Tagelöhnerin.

2Char, v.a. verkohlen.

Character, s. (sign) das Zeichen; (figure) die Ziffer; (moral character) der Charakter, die Gemütsart; (written —) das Zeugnis. —istic, I. adj., —istically, adv. charakteriſtiſch. II. s. das Merkmal, Kennzeichen. —ize, —ise, v.a. charakteriſieren; kennzeichnen. —less, adj. charakterlos.

Charade, *s.* die Scharade, das Silben-rätsel.

Charcoal, *s.* die Holzkohle. **—burner,** *s.* der Kohlenbrenner.

Charge, I. *s.* die Ladung (*of a gun, etc.*); (care) die Verwahrung; (person under —) der Schützling; (expense) die Kosten; (command) der Befehl; der Angriff (*Mil.*); (accusation) die Beschuldigung. II. *v.a.* beladen, belasten (*also fig.*); laden (*a gun, etc.*); beauftragen (*with a duty, etc.*); (command) befehlen; (accuse) beschuldigen; (demand) fordern; (attack) angreifen. III. *v.n.* einen Angriff machen. **—able,** *adj.* (—able to) zuzuschreiben, zuzurechnen. **—r,** *s.* das Schlachtroß. **—s,** *pl.* die Kosten, Unkosten, Spesen (*C.L.*).

Char—ily, *adv.* behutsam; sparsam. **—iness,** *s.* die Behutsamkeit.

Chariot, *s.* der Wagen.

Charit—able, *adj.*, **—ably,** *adv.* wohltätig, freigebig. **—ableness,** *s.* die Mildtätigkeit, Wohltätigkeit. **—y,** *s.* die Mildtätigkeit; die Freigebigkeit; (alms) die Almosen; sister of —y, barmherzige Schwester.

Charm, I. *s.* das Zaubermittel. II. *v.a.* bezaubern, behexen. **—ing,** *adj.*, **—ingly,** *adv.* bezaubernd, reizend.

Chart, *s.* die Karte; die Seekarte. **—er,** I. *s.* der Vertrag; (privilege) der Freibrief; die Schiffsmiete (*Naut.*). II. *v.a.* privilegieren, bevorrechtigen; mieten (*a ship*).

Chary, *adj.* sparsam, knapp; (cautious) vorsichtig.

Chase, I. *s.* die Jagd; wild-goose —, die nutzlose Verfolgung. II. *v.a.* jagen, Jagd machen auf (*acc.*); (— away) verjagen.

Chasm, *s.* die Kluft.

Chassis, *s.* das Fahrgestell, der Chassis (*Motor.*).

Chast—e, *adj.*, **—ely,** *adv.* keusch, züchtig. **—en,** *v.a.* züchtigen. **—ening,** *s.* die Züchtigung. **—ise,** *v.a.* züchtigen, strafen. **—ity,** *s.* die Keuschheit.

Chat, I. *v.n.* plaudern, schwatzen. II. *s.* das Geplauder.

Chattel, *s.*; goods and —s, Hab und Gut.

Chatter, I. *v.n.* schnattern. II. *s.* das Geschwätz. **—box,** *s.* die Plaudertasche.

Chauffeur, *s.* der Chauffeur, Kraftwagenführer.

Cheap, *adj.*, **—ly,** *adv.* wohlfeil, billig. **—ness,** *s.* die Wohlfeilheit.

Cheat, I. *s.* der Betrug; (person) der Betrüger. II. *v.a.* betrügen. **—ing,** *s.* die Betrügerei.

Check, I. *s.* (reprimand) der Verweis; (hindrance) das Hindernis, die Hemmung; das Schach (*Chess*); to keep a person in —, einen im Zaume halten; II. *v.a.* einhalten, hemmen. III. *v.n.* Schach bieten. **—er, chequer,** I. *s.* das gewürfelte Zeug. II. *v.a.* scheckig, würfelig, bunt machen. **—book,** *s.* das Kontrollbuch (*C.L.*); *see* Cheque. **—mate,** I. *s.* das Schachmatt. II. *v.a.* schachmatt machen. **—rein,** *s.* kurzer Pferdezügel. **—string,** *s.* die Zugschnur (*in carriages, etc.*). **—taker,** *s.* der Kontramarkenabnehmer (*Theat.*).

Cheek, *s.* die Backe, Wange; (*fig.*) die Unverschämtheit. **—y,** *adj.* frech; a —y fellow, ein frecher Dachs.

Cheer, I. *s.* der Beifallsruf; to be of good —, guter Dinge sein. II. *v.a.* aufmuntern. III. *v.n.* Vivat rufen; — up! frischen Mut! **—ful,** *adj.*, **—fully,** *adv.* heiter, munter, froh. **—fulness,** *s.* die Heiterkeit, der Frohsinn. **—ing,** *adj.*, **—ingly,** *adv.* erfreuend, erheiternd. **—less,** *adj.*, **—lessly,** *adv.* unerfreulich. **—lessness,** *s.* die Freud(en)losigkeit. **—y,** *adj.* heiter, froh.

Cheese, *s.* der Käse.

Chemical, *adj.*, **—ly,** *adv.* chemisch.

Chemise, *s.* das Frauenhemd.

Chemist, *s.* der Chemiker; (druggist) der Apotheker. **—ry,** *s.* die Chemie.

Cheque, Check, *s.* die Bankanweisung, der Scheck.

Cherish, *v.a.* pflegen; to — a thought, einen Gedanken hegen.

Cherry, *s.* die Kirsche. **—brandy,** *s.* das Kirschwasser.

Cherub, *s.* der Cherub.

Chess, *s.* das Schach(spiel). **—board,** *s.* das Schachbrett. **—man,** *s.* die Schachfigur. **—player,** *s.* der Schachspieler.

Chest, *s.* die Kiste; die Brust (*Anat.*); — of drawers, die Kommode.

Chestnut, I. *s.* die Kastanie. II. *adj.* kastanienbraun.

Chew, *v.a.* kauen.

Chiaroscuro, *s.* das Helldunkel.

Chicane, *v.n.* schikanieren. **—ry,** *s.* die Haarspalterei.

Chicken, *s.* das Hühnchen, Küchlein. **—pox,** *s.* die Windpocken (*Med.*).

Chicory, *s.* die Zichorie.

Chid—e, *v.a.* (aus)schelten, verweisen. **—er,** *s.* der Scheltende. **—ing,** *adj.,* **—ingly,** *adv.* scheltend.

Chief, I. *adj.,* **—ly,** *adv.* höchst, vornehmst, erst; (principal) hauptsächlich(st). II. *s.* (head) das Haupt, Oberhaupt. **—tain,** *s.* der Häuptling.

Chilblain, *s.* die Frostbeule.

Child, I. *s.* das Kind; from a —, von Kindheit an. II. *attrib.;* — murder, der Kindermord. **—hood,** *s.* die Kindheit. **—ish,** *adj.,* **—ishly,** *adv.* kindisch. **—ishness,** *s.* das kindische Wesen. **—less,** *adj.* kinderlos. **—like,** *adj.* kindlich.

Chill, I. *s.* die Erkältung. II. *adj.* kalt, frostig. III. *v.a.* durchkälten. **—iness,** *s.* die Kälte. **—y,** *adj.* frostig, kalt.

Chime, I. *s.* das Glockenspiel. II. *v.a.* ertönen lassen.

Chimney, *s.* der Kamin, Schornstein. **—piece,** *s.* das Kaminsims. **—sweep,** *s.* der Schornsteinfeger.

Chimpanzee, *s.* der Schimpanse (*Zool.*).

Chin, *s.* das Kinn.

China, *s.,* (**—ware,** *s.,*) das Porzellan.

¹**Chink,** *s.* die Ritze.

²**Chink,** *s.* der Klang (*of money, etc.*).

Chintz, *s.* der Möbelkattun.

Chip, I. *s.* das Schnitzchen, der Span. II. *v.a.* schnitzeln. **—s,** *pl.* die Späne, Splitter.

Chirp, *v.n.* zirpen, zwitschern. **—ing,** *s.* das Zirpen, Gezirpe.

Chisel, I. *s.* der Meißel. II. *v.a.* meißeln.

Chivalr—ic, *adj.,* **—ous,** *adj.,* **—ously,** *adv.* ritterlich. **—y,** *s.* die Ritterschaft; (—ousness) die Ritterlichkeit.

Chive, *s.* der Schnittlauch.

Chock-full, *adv.* ganz voll.

Chocolate, I. *s.* die Schokolade. II. *adj.* schokoladenfarbig.

Choice, I. *s.* die Wahl; die Auswahl; (object of —) das Ausgewählte. II. *adj.* auserlesen; vorzüglich. **—ness,** *s.* die Erlesenheit.

Choir, *s.* der (Sänger)chor; der Chor (*Arch.*).

Choke, *v.* I. *a.* ersticken; erwürgen. II. *n.* sich würgen, ersticken (an einer S.).

Choler, *s.* die Galle; (*fig.*) der Zorn. **—ic,** *adj.* jähzornig.

Cholera, *s.* die Cholera, asiatische Brechruhr.

Choose, *v.* I. *a.* wählen, auswählen. II. *n.* wählen. **—r,** *s.* der Wähler.

Chop, I. *s.* die Schnitte; das Kotelett. **—ping and changing,** steter Wechsel. II. *v.a.* hacken. **—-house,** *s.* das Speisehaus. **—stick,** *s.* das Eßstäbchen der Chinesen.

Chopp—er, *s.* das Hackbeil. **—ing,** *p. & adj.* hauend.

Chord, *s.* die Saite.

Chor—ister, *s.* der Chorsänger, Chorist. **—us,** *s.* der Chor; der Kehrreim.

Chosen, *adj.* erwählt, auserlesen.

Chough, *s.* die Dohle.

Christen, *v.a.* taufen; (name) benennen. **—dom,** *s.* die Christenheit. **—ing,** *s.* die Taufe.

Christian, I. *adj.* christlich; — era, das christliche Zeitalter. — name, der Vorname, Taufname. II. *s.* der Christ. **—ity,** *s.* die christliche Religion, das Christentum. **—ize,** *v.a.* zum Christen machen.

Christmas, *s.* das (also die) Weihnachten. **—box,** *s.* das Weihnachtsgeschenk. **—eve,** *s.* der Heiligabend.

Chron—ic, *adj.* chronisch, **—icle,** I. *s.* die Chronik. II. *v.a.* aufzeichnen, verzeichnen. **—icler,** *s.* der Chronik(en)schreiber. **—icles,** *pl.* Bücher der Chronika (*B.*). **—ological,** *adj.,* **—ologically,** *adv.* chronologisch. **—ology,** *s.* die Chronologie.

Chrys—alis, *s.* die Puppe. **—anthemum,** *s.* die Wucherblume.

Chub, *s.* der Döbel (*Icht.*).

Chubby(-faced), *adj.* pausbackig.

Chuck, I. *v.n.* glucken (*as a hen*). II. *v.a.* sanft schlagen; werfen; to — under the chin, unters Kinn fassen. **—le,** *v.n.* kichern.

Chum, *s.* der Kamerad.

Church, *s.* die Kirche. **—warden,** *s.* der Kirchenvorsteher. **—yard,** *s.* der Kirchhof.

Churl, *s.* der Grobian. **—ish,** *adj.,* **—ishly,** *adv.* roh; grob. **—ishness,** *s.* die Grobheit.

Churn, I. *s.* das Butterfaß. II. *v.a.* Butter stoßen. **—ing,** *s.* das Buttern.

Cicada, *s.* die Heuschrecke.

Cicatrice, *s.* die Narbe.

Cider, *s.* der Apfelwein.

Cigar, *s.* die Zigarre. **—ette,** *s.* die Zigarette.

Cinder, *s.* die ausgebrannte Kohle. **—ella,** *s.* (das) Aschenbrödel.

Cinematograph, *s.* der Kinematograph.

Cinnamon, *s.* der Zimmt.

Cipher, I. *s.* die Ziffer. II. *v.n.* rechnen. **—ing,** *s.* das Rechnen.

Circ—le, I. *s.* der Zirkel (*also fig.*), Kreis. II. *v.n.* sich freisen. **—uit,** *s.* der Kreislauf; (circle) der Umkreis, Umfang; der Stromkreis (*Tele.*). **—uitous,** *adj.,* **—uitously,** *adv.* weitläufig. **—ular,** I. *adj.* kreisförmig; **—ular railway,** die Ringbahn. II. *s.* das Rundschreiben, Zirkularschreiben. **—ulate,** *v.* I. *n.* umlaufen. II. *a.* in Umlauf bringen; to **—ulate bills,** Wechsel girieren. **—ulating,** *p. & adj.* umlaufend; **—ulating library,** eine Leihbibliothek. **—ulation,** *s.* der Umlauf, Kreislauf.

Circum—ference, *s.* der Kreisumfang. **—scribe,** *v.a.* beschränken. **—spect,** *adj.,* **—spectly,** *adv.* umsichtig, vorsichtig. **—spection,** *s.* die Umsicht. **—stance,** *s.* der Umstand. **—stantial,** *adj.,* **—stantially,** *adv.* umständlich.

Circumvent, *v.a.* überlisten.

Circus, *s.* der Zirkus.

Cistern, *s.* der Behälter.

Citadel, *s.* die Zitadelle (*Fort.*).

Citizen, *s.* der Bürger; (inhabitant) der Einwohner. **—ship,** *s.* das Bürgerrecht.

Cithern, *s.* die Zither.

Citrate, *s.* das Zitrat.

Citron, *s.* die Zitrone.

City, I. *s.* die Stadt. II. *adj.* städtisch.

Civic, *adj.* bürgerlich, Bürger-.

Civil, *adj.* (not military) zivil; (courteous) artig, höflich; (mannerly) gesittet; (intestine) einheimisch. **—ian,** *s.* der Bürger. **—ity,** *s.* die Artigkeit, Höflichkeit. **—ization,** *s.* die Zivilisation. **—ize,** *v.a.* zivilisieren.

Clack, *v.n.* klappern.

Claim, I. *v.a.* in Anspruch nehmen, fordern. II. *s.* der Anspruch. **—ant,** *s.* der Anspruchmacher.

Clam, *s.* die Venusmuschel.

Clamber, *v.a. & n.* klettern.

Clamm—iness, *s.* die Klebrigkeit. **—y,** *adj.,* **—ily,** *adv.* kaltfeucht, klebrig.

Clamorous, *adj.,* **—ly,** *adv.* lärmend; ungestüm.

Clamour, I. *s.* das Geschrei, Getöse. II. *v.n.* schreien (for a thing, nach einer S.).

Clamp, I. *s.* die Klampe, Klammer. II. *v.a.* klammern, festklammern.

Clan, *s.* der Stamm. **—sman,** *s.* der Stammverwandte.

Clandestine, *adj.,* **—ly,** *adv.* heimlich, verstohlen. **—ness,** *s.* die heimlichkeit.

Clang, I. *s.* der Klang, Schall. II. *v.a.* schallen lassen.

Clank, I. *s.* das Gerassel, Klirren. II. *v.n.* rasseln.

Clap, I. *v.a. & n.* klappen, klatschen; to **— one's hands,** Beifall klatschen. II. *s.* der Klapp(s). **—per,** *s.* der Klöppel.

Claret, *s.* der Rotwein.

Clari—fy, *v.a.* abklären, läutern. **—ty,** *s.* die Klarheit.

Clari(o)net, *s.* die Klarinette.

Clash, I. *v.n.* zusammenschlagen; schmettern. II. *s.* das Gerassel, Geschmetter.

Clasp, I. *v.a.* (hook together *or* in) zuhäkeln; umfassen (*the knees, etc.*); to **— in one's arms,** umarmen. II. *v.n.* festhalten. III. *s.* die Schnalle (*of a belt*); die Spange, der Verschluß.

Class, *s.* die Klasse.

Classic, I., **—al,** *adj.,* **—ally,** *adv.* klassisch. II. *s.* der Klassiker. **—s,** *pl.* die alten Sprachen.

Classif—ication, *s.* die Einteilung, Anordnung. **—y,** *v.a.* (in Klassen) einteilen.

Clatter, I. *v.n.* klappern. II. *v.a.* klirren, rasseln lassen. III. *s.* das Gerassel.

Clause, *s.* das Satzglied.

Claw, I. *s.* die Klaue, Kralle (*of birds*). II. *v.a.* kratzen, zerkratzen.

Clay, *s.* der Ton, Lehm. **—ey,** *adj.* tonig, lehmig.

Clean, I. *adj.* rein, reinlich, sauber. II. *adv.* rein. III. *v.a.* reinigen, säubern, blank machen, putzen. **—liness,** *s.* die Reinlichkeit, Sauberkeit. **—ly,** *adj. & adv.* reinlich, sauber, säuberlich. **—ness,** *s.* die Reinheit. **—shaven,** *adj.* glattrasiert.

Clear, I. *adj.,* **—ly,** *adv.* (bright) klar, hell; (acute) scharfsichtig; (free from blame) schuldlos; (evident) deutlich; to get **— of,** loswerden. II. *adv.* offenbar; gänzlich, völlig. III.

v.a. flar, hell machen, erhellen, aufflären; säubern; lichten (*a wood, etc.*); to — the coast, sich von der Küste fernhalten; to — one's throat, sich räuspern. IV. *v.n.* (— up) sich aufhellen, hell *or* flar werden. **—ance,** *s.* das Reinigen; (—ing up) die Abräumung; die Ausräumung (eines Warenlagers). **—ing,** *s.* das Reinmachen; die Lichtung (*in a wood*). **—ness,** *s.* die Klarheit, Helle.

¹Cleave, *ir.v.* I. *a.* spalten, zerspalten. II. *n.* sich spalten. **—r,** *s.* das Hackmesser.

²Cleave, *ir.v.n.* kleben, ankleben.

Clef, *s.* der Schlüssel (*Mus.*).

Clemen—cy, *s.* die Gnade. **—t,** *adj.,* **—tly,** *adv.* gnädig; mild, gütig.

Clench, *v.a.;* to — one's fist, die Faust ballen.

Clergy, *s.* die Geistlichkeit. **—man,** *s.* der Geistliche.

Clerk, *s.* der Schreiber; der Kommis. **—ly,** *adj. & adv.* gelehrt. **—ship,** *s.* die Schreiberstelle; die Kommisstelle.

Clever, *adj.,* **—ly,** *adv.* klug, gescheit. **—ness,** *s.* die Klugheit; die Geschicklichkeit.

Clew, *s.* der Leitfaden.

Click, I. *s.* der Tick-Tack. II. *v.n.* schlagen, ticken.

Client, *s.* der Klient, die Klientin.

Cliff, *s.* die Klippe, der Felsen.

Climat—e, *s.* das Klima. **—ic,** *adj.* klimatisch, Klima-.

Climax, *s.* die Klimax, der Höhepunkt.

Climb, *v.* I. *a.* erklimmen (*a tree, etc.*); (mount) hinaufsteigen, besteigen. II. *n.* klettern, klimmen. **—er.** *s.* der Steiger, Kletterer.

Clinch, I. *v.a.* nieten, vernieten. II. *v.n.* festhalten. III. *s.* die Klinke.

Cling, *ir.v.n.* sich klammern; anhangen (*as a dress*). **—ing,** *adj.* anhängend, anhänglich.

Clink, I. *s.* das Geklirr. II. *v.n.* klirren. III. *v.a.* rasseln; to — glasses, (mit den Gläsern) anstoßen.

Clip, *v.a.* scheren (*sheep, etc.*). **—pers,** *pl.* die Stutzschere. **—ping,** *s.* die Beschneidung, Abstutzung; (*pl.*) die Abfälle.

Cloak, *s.* der Mantel; (*fig.*) der Deckmantel. **—room,** *s.* die Garderobe.

Clock, *s.* die Schlaguhr, Pendeluhr. **—dial, —face,** *s.* das Zifferblatt. **—hand,** *s.* der (Uhr=)zeiger. —

maker, *s.* der Uhrmacher. **—movement, —work,** *s.* das Uhrwerk; like -work, pünktlich; automatisch.

Clod, *s.* die Erdscholle.

Clog, I. *v.a.* hindern, hemmen. II. *v.n.* verkleben (vor Schmutz). III. *s.* der Klotz; der Holzschuh.

Cloister, *s.* das Kloster. **—s,** *pl.* der Klostergang.

Close, I. *adj.* (shut) verschlossen, zugemacht; (hidden) verborgen; schwül, trüb (*as the air*); (near) enganschließend, anliegend; (alike, nearly equal) ziemlich gleich. II. *adv.* nicht offen, verschlossen, zu; (near to) nahe daran, dicht dabei, an einander; (exactly) genau; (secretly) verborgen, heimlich. III. *s.* der Schluß; das Ende; der Domhof. IV. *v.a.* schließen, zuschließen, zumachen, zutun; night is closing in, die Nacht bricht herein. **—ness,** *s.* die Eingeschlossenheit; die Dumpfheit (*of a room, etc.*); (nearness) die Nähe. **—fisted,** *adj.* geizig, karg.

Closet, *s.* das Geheimzimmer, Kabinett.

Clot, I. *s.* das Klümpchen. II. *v.n.* sich verdichten.

Cloth, *s.* das Tuch; the —, der geistliche Stand; to lay the —, den Tisch decken; bound in —, in Leinwand gebunden. **—ier,** *s.* der Kleiderhändler, Tuchhändler. **—ing,** *s.* die Kleidung, der Anzug.

Clothe, *reg. & ir.v.a.* kleiden, ankleiden, bekleiden. **—s,** *pl.* die Kleider, die Kleidung. **—s-line.** *s.* die Waschleine. **—s-man,** *s.;* old- —s-man, der Kleidertrödler. **—s-peg, —s-pin,** *s.* die Waschklammer.

Cloud, I. *s.* die Wolke; to be under a —, im Unglück sein. II. *v.a.* bewölken. III. *v.n.* sich umwölken. **—ily,** *adv.* wolkig; dunkel. **—iness,** *s.* die Umwölkung. **—less, —lessly,** *adv.* wolkenlos, unbewölkt. **—y,** *adj.* wolkig, bewölkt.

¹Clove, **—n,** *p.p. & adj.* gespalten. **—n-footed,** *adj.* spaltfüßig.

²Clove, *s.* die Gewürznelke (*Bot.*).

Clover, *s.* der Klee; to be in —, sorgenfrei, glücklich sein.

Clown, *s.* der Hanswurst. **—ish,** *adj.,* **—ishly,** *adv.* roh, grob. **—ishness,** *s.* die Grobheit.

Cloy, *v.a.* anekeln.

Club, I. *s.* (thick, short stick) die

Keule, der Knüttel; das Treff (*Cards*); der Klub; das Kasino. II. *v.n.* sich versammeln; beisteuern. —**foot**, *s.* der Klumpfuß. —**house**, *s.* das Klublokal, Kasino.

Cluck, *v.n.* glucken.

Clue, *s.* der Knäuel (*of thread, etc.*); der Leitfaden.

Clump, *s.* die Gruppe.

Clums—**iness**, *s.* die Plumpheit. —**y**, *adj.* plump, ungeschickt.

Cluster, *s.* die Traube, der Büschel.

Clutch, I. *s.* (seizing) der Griff; die Kuppelung (*Mach.*); in his —es, in seinen Krallen. II. *v.a.* greifen, packen.

Coach, *s.* die Kutsche, der Wagen; der Privatlehrer; to —, (teach) einpauken, eintrichtern. —**house**, *s.* die Wagenremise. —**man**, *s.* der Kutscher.

Coal, *s.* die Kohle (*Min.*). —**box**, *s.* das Kohlenbecken. —**bunker**, *s.* der Kohlenraum. —**dust**, *s.* der Kohlenstaub. —**field**, *s.* das Kohlenfeld. —**gas**, *s.* das Leuchtgas. —**heaver**, *s.* der Kohlenträger. —**mine**, *s.* das Kohlenbergwerk. —**pit**, *s.* die Kohlengrube.

Coal—**esce**, *v.n.* sich vereinigen. —**escence**, *s.* das Zusammenfließen.

Coalition, *s.* die Verbindung.

Coarse, *adj.*, —**ly**, *adv.* grob; roh, plump. —**ness**, *s.* die Grobheit.

Coast, *s.* die Küste, das Seeufer.

Coat, *s.* der Rock. —**ing**, *s.* der Überzug, der Anstrich; der Rockstoff; der Pelz, das Fell; — of arms, das Wappen.

Coax, *v.a.* streicheln; to — a person into a thing, jemand zu etwas überreden. —**er**, *s.* (flatterer) der Schmeichler, die Schmeichlerin. —**ingly**, *adv.* schmeichelnd.

Cob, *s.* ein kleines dickes Pferdchen.

1**Cobble**, *v.a.* flicken. —**r**, *s.* der Schuster.

2**Cobble**, *s.* (—**stone**) der Stromstein.

Cobra, *s.* die Brillenschlange.

Cobweb, *s.* das Spinnweb(e).

Cocaine, *s.* das Kokain.

Cochineal, *s.* die Cochenille; das Scharlachrot.

1**Cock**, I. *s.* der Hahn. II. *v.a.* (— up) in die Höhe richten; den Hahn spannen (*of a gun*). —**ed**, *p.p. & adj.* gestülpt. —**crow(ing)**, *s.* der Hahnenschrei.

2**Cock**, (—**boat**,) *s.* die Schaluppe.

Cockswain, **Coxswain**, *s.* der Steuermann.

Cockade, *s.* die Kokarde.

Cockatoo, *s.* der Kakadu.

Cockchafer, *s.* der Maikäfer.

Cockle, *s.* die Herzmuschel (*Mollusc*).

Cockpit, *s.* der Führersitz (*Aviation*).

Cockroach, *s.* die Sch(w)abe.

1**Cocoa**, *s.* der Kakao.

2**Cocoa**, *s.* (—**nut** tree) die Kokospalme. —**nut**, *s.* die Kokosnuß.

Cocoon, *s.* der Kokon.

Cod, (—**fish**,) *s.* der Kabeljau, Dorsch; dried —, der Stockfisch; —**liver oil**, der Lebertran.

Code, I. *s.* der Kodex; das Gesetzbuch. II. *attrib.*; — telegram, das Ziffertelegram.

Coer—**ce**, *v.a.* zwingen, nötigen. —**cion**, *s.* der Zwang.

Coffee, *s.* der Kaffee. —**pot**, *s.* die Kaffeekanne.

Coffer, *s.* der Koffer, Kasten.

Coffin, I. *s.* der Sarg. II. *v.a.* einsargen.

Cog, *s.* der Kamm, Zahn. —**ged**, *adj.* gezahnt. —**wheel**, *s.* das Kammrad, Zahnrad.

Cogitate, *v.n.* nachdenken.

Cohe—**rence**, —**rency**, *s.* der Zusammenhang, die Kohäsion. —**rent**, *adj.*, —**rently**, *adv.* zusammenhängend. —**sion**, *s.* der Zusammenhalt.

Coiffure, *s.* der Kopfputz.

Coil, I. *s.* die Windung, der Wickel. II. *v.a.* ringförmig wickeln. III. *v.n.* sich winden.

Coin, I. *s.* die Münze. II. *v.a.* Münzen schlagen, prägen. —**age**, *s.* das Münzen. —**er**, *s.* der Münzer.

Coincide, *v.n.* zusammentreffen; (*fig.*) übereinstimmen. —**nce**, *s.* das Zusammentreffen; (*fig.*) die Übereinstimmung.

Coke, *s.* der Koks.

Cold, I. *adj.*, —**ly**, *adv.* kalt (*also fig.*); — meat, kalte Küche; to give a person the — shoulder, jemanden kühl behandeln. II. *s.* die Kälte; (— in the head) der Schnupfen; die Erkältung (*Med.*). —**ness**, *s.* die Kälte (*also fig.*). —**blooded**, *adj.* kaltblütig; (*fig.*) gefühllos.

Cole, *s.* der Kohl.

Colic, *s.* die Kolik.

Collaborator, *s.* der Mitarbeiter.

Collapse, I. *s.* der Zusammenbruch.
II. *v.n.* zusammenfallen; zusammenbrechen.

Collar, I. *s.* (dog-collar) das Halsband; der Kragen (*of a dress, etc.*).
II. *v.a.* beim Kragen anpacken. —
bone, *s.* das Schlüsselbein (*Anat.*).

Collateral, *adj.* nebenseitig.

Colleague, *s.* der Kollege.

Collect, I. *v.a.* sammeln; versammeln, zusammenbringen (*of people*).
II. *v.n.* sich sammeln. III. *s.* die
Kollekte. **—ed,** *adj.* **—edly,** *adv.*
gesammelt; (*fig.*) gefaßt, ruhig. —
edness, *s.* die Fassung. **—ion,** *s.* die
Sammlung (*of coins, etc.*). **—ive,**
adj. gesammelt; zusammengefaßt. —
ively, *adv.* insgesamt, im Ganzen.
—or, *s.* der Sammler; der Einnehmer (*of tolls, etc.*).

College, *s.* das College.

Collegian, *s.* der Student.

Collide, *v.n.* zusammenstoßen, -schlagen.

Collie, *s.* der schottische Schäferhund.

Collier, *s.* der Kohlenarbeiter; das
Kohlenschiff. **—y,** *s.* das Kohlenbergwerk.

Collision, *s.* der Zusammenstoß.

Coll—oquial, *adj.,* **—oquially,** *adv.*
gesprächsweise. **—oquy,** *s.* die Unterredung.

Collusion, *s.* das heimliche Einverständnis.

Colon, *s.* das Kolon, der Doppel-
punkt.

Colonel, *s.* der Oberst; lieutenant- —,
der Oberstleutnant.

Colon—ial, *adj.* Kolonial-. **—ist,** *s.*
der Ansiedler. **—ization,** *s.* das
Kolonisieren, die Besiedelung. **—ize,**
v. I. *a.* kolonisieren, besiedeln. II. *n.*
sich ansiedeln.

Colonnade, *s.* der Säulengang.

Colony, *s.* die Kolonie, Ansiedlung.

Colossal, *adj.* riesenhaft, kolossal.

Colour, I. *s.* die Farbe; (complexion)
Gesichtsfarbe; (dye) die Färbung.
II. *v.a.* färben. III. *v.n.* erröten.
—able, *adj.,* **—ably,** *adv.* scheinbar,
annehmbar. **—ed,** *adj.* gefärbt; bunt,
farbig. **—ing,** *s.* das Färben. —
less, *adj.,* **—lessly,** *adv.* farblos.
—blind, *adj.* farbenblind.

Colt, *s.* das Füllen.

Colter, Coulter, *s.* das Pflugeisen, die
Pflugschar.

Column, *s.* die Säule (*Arch.*); die

Kolonne (*Mil.*); die Kolumne, Spalte
(*Typ.*). **—ar,** *adj.* säulenförmig.

Coma, *s.* die Schlafsucht (*Med.*).
—tose, *adj.* schlafsüchtig.

Comb, I. *s.* der Kamm; (curry—)
der Striegel; (honey—) die Honigscheibe. II. *v.a.* kämmen; striegeln.

Com—bat, I. *s.* der Kampf. II. *v.a.*
bestreiten (*an opinion, etc.*). III.
v.n. sich streiten, kämpfen (with, mit).
—batant, *s.* der Kämpfer; der
Verfechter. **—bative,** *adj.* streitsüchtig. **—bination,** *s.* die Vereinigung;
die Hemdhose. **—bine,** *s.* I. *a.*
vereinigen. II. *n.* sich verbinden, sich
vereinigen. **—bustible,** *adj.* brennbar. **—bustion,** *s.* die Verbrennung.

Come, *ir.v.n.* kommen; to — about,
sich ereignen (*as events*); to — across
a person, auf einen stoßen; to — by,
(get) erlangen, erwerben; to — for,
abholen; to — forth, heraus-, hervor-
kommen; to — from, herkommen; to
— in, hereinkommen; to — off, davon
kommen, entkommen; to — out,
auskommen; (be published) veröf-
fentlicht werden; to — to, zu, auf,
in *or* an etwas kommen; to — to one's
senses, wieder zu sich kommen. **—ing**
of age, das Mündigwerden. **—liness,**
s. die Schönheit, Anmut. **—ly,** *adj.*
anmutig; hübsch. **—r,** *s.* der, die,
das Kommende; new —rs, neue
Ankömmlinge.

Comed—ian, *s.* der Schauspieler.
—y, *s.* das Lustspiel.

Comet, *s.* der Komet.

Comfort, I. *s.* die Behaglichkeit,
Bequemlichkeit; der Trost. II. *v.a.*
trösten. **—able,** *adj.,* **—ably,** *adv.*
behaglich, gemütlich, bequem. **—er,**
s. der Tröster. **—less,** *adj.,* **—lessly,**
adv. trostlos; unbehaglich.

Comical, *adj.* komisch, lustig, drollig.

Comma, *s.* der Beistrich, das Komma.

Command, I. *v.a.* (einem) befehlen,
gebieten; beherrschen; kommandieren
(*Mil.*). II. *v.n.* den Befehl führen;
kommandieren. III. *s.* die Herrschaft;
(order) das Gebot, der Befehl; das
Kommando (*Mil.*). **—ant,** *s.* der Befehlshaber, Kommandant. **—er,** *s.* der
Gebieter; der Kapitän (*Naut.*); —er
in chief, der Oberbefehlshaber. **—ing,**
adj. gebietend. **—ment,** *s.* das Gebot.

Commemor—ate, *v.a.* feiern. —
ation, *s.* die Gedächtnisfeier.

Commence, *v.a. & n.* anfangen. — **ment,** *s.* der Anfang.

Commend, *v.a.* (praise) rühmen, loben; (recommend) empfehlen; (entrust to) anvertrauen. **—able,** *adj.* löblich.

Comment, I. *v.n.* Bemerkungen machen (upon, über). II. *s.* die Bemerkung, Anmerkung. **—ary,** *s.* der Kommentar.

Commerc—e, *s.* der Handel. **—ial,** *adj.* den Handel betreffend, kommerziell; —ial traveller, der Geschäftsreisende; —ial broadcast, der Wirtschaftsrundfunk (*Radio*). **—ially,** *adv.* kaufmännisch.

Commiserate, *v.a.* bemitleiden.

Commiss—ariat, *s.* das Kommissariat. **—ion,** I. *s.* (order) der Auftrag; (act of committing) die Begehung; (percentage) die Kommissionsgebühr; das Offizierspatent (*Mil.*); (board) die Behörde. II. *attrib.;* —ion business, das Kommissionsgeschäft. III. *v.a.* beauftragen; anvertrauen; abordnen. **—ionaire,** *s.* der Dienstmann. **—ioner,** *s.* der Beauftragte.

Comm—it, *v.a.* begehen, verüben (*a sin, etc.*); (consign) übergeben; to —it to prison, verhaften lassen. **—ittal,** *s.* die Begehung. **—ittee,** *s.* der Ausschuß. **—odious,** *adj.,* **—odiously,** *adv.* bequem; gemächlich. **—odity,** *s.* die Ware. **—odore,** *s.* der Kommodore.

Common, I. *adj.,* **—ly,** *adv.* (usual) gewöhnlich, gemein; (general) allgemein; (vulgar) gemein; of — gender, beiderlei Geschlechts. II. *s.* die Gemeindeweide. **—er,** *s.* der Bürgerliche. **—ness,** *s.* die Gewöhnlichkeit; die Gemeinheit. **—s,** *pl.* die Gemeindeweiden; the (House of) —s, das Unterhaus des Parlaments. **— noun,** *s.* der Sachname. **—place,** *adj.* alltäglich. **— sense,** *s.* der gesunde Menschenverstand. **—wealth,** *s.* der Staat.

Com—motion, *s.* der Aufruhr, Aufstand. **—munal,** *adj.* Kommunal-. **—mune,** I. *v.n.* sich unterreden. II. *s.* die Gemeinde. **—municable,** *adj.* mitteilbar. **—municate,** *v.a.* mitteilen, benachrichtigen. **—munication,** *s.* die Mitteilung, Bekanntmachung. **—munion,** *s.* die Glaubensgemeinschaft; das heilige Abendmahl. **—munism,** *s.* der Kommunismus. **—**

munist, *s.* der Kommunist. **—munity,** *s.* die Gemeinschaft. **—mute,** *v.a.* verändern; to —mute a sentence, eine Strafe mildern. **—pact,** I. *adj.,* **—pactly,** *adv.* dicht, fest; (succinct) gedrungen, bündig. II. *s.* der Vergleich, Vertrag. **—pactness,** *s.* die Dichtheit, Festigkeit. **—panion,** *s.* der Kamerad, Genoß. **—panionable,** *adj.,* **—panionably,** *adv.* gesellig. **—panionship,** *s.* die Gesellschaft, Genossenschaft. **—pany,** *s.* die (Gesellschaft; die Kompagnie (*Mil., C.L.*); die Handelsgesellschaft (*C.L.*). **—parative,** *adj.,* **—paratively,** *adv.* vergleichsweise. **—pare,** I. *v.a.* vergleichen. II. *v.n.* sich vergleichen. **—parison,** *s.* die Vergleichung; (simile) das Gleichnis. **—partment,** *s.* die Abteilung; der Abteil (*Railw.*).

Com—pass, I. *s.* (circuit, range) der Umfang, Umkreis; mariner's —pass, der Seekompaß; point of the —pass, der Kompaßstrich. II. *v.a.* umgehen; (contrive) bewerkstelligen. **—passes,** *pl.* der Zirkel.

Com—passion, *s.* das Mitleid, Erbarmen. **—passionate,** *adj.,* **—passionately,** *adv.* mitleidig. **—pel,** *v.a.* zwingen, nötigen. **—pensate,** *v.* I. *a.* ersetzen; ausgleichen. II. *n.* einen Ersatz geben (for, für). **—pensation,** *s.* (amends) der Ersatz; (set-off) die Ausgleichung. **—pete,** *v.n.* sich mitbewerben (um). **—petence, —petency,** *s.* (livelihood) das Auskommen; (capability) die Befähigung. **—petent,** *adj.,* **—petently,** *adv.* zulänglich, hinreichend. **—petition,** *s.* die Konkurrenz, der Wettbewerb. **—petitive,** *adj.* konkurrierend. **—petitor,** *s.* der Mitbewerber, Konkurrent. **—plain,** *v.n.* klagen, sich beklagen. **—plaint,** *s.* die Klage. **—plement,** *s.* die Ergänzung. **—plementary,** *adj.* ergänzend. **—plete,** I. *adj.,* **—pletely,** *adv.* vollkommen. II. *v.a.* ergänzen; erfüllen; vollenden. **—pleteness,** *s.* die Vollkommenheit. **—pletion,** *s.* die Vollendung. **—plex,** *adj.* vielteilig; (*fig.*) verwickelt. **—plexion,** *s.* die Gesichtsfarbe. **—plexity,** *s.* die Verflechtung. **—pliance,** *s.* die Einwilligung; in —pliance with, gemäß. **—pliant,** *adj.,* **—pliantly,** *adv.* nachgiebig. **—plicate,** *v.a.* verflechten, verwickeln. **—plication,** *s.* die Ver-

flechtung, Verwickelung. —**plicity**, *s.*
die Mitschuld. —**pliment**, I. *s.* das
Kompliment. II. *v.a.* einem ein
Kompliment machen. —**plimentary**,
adj. höflich. —**ply**, *v.n.* einwilligen
in eine S. —**pose**, *v.a.* bilden;
verfassen, dichten (*a poem, etc.*);
komponieren (*Mus.*); setzen (*Typ.*);
beruhigen (*the mind, etc.*); gütlich
beilegen (*a quarrel*). —**posed**, *adj.*,
—**posedly**, *adv.* gefaßt. —**poser**, der
Komponist (*Mus.*). —**posing**, I. *adj.*
beruhigend. II. *s.* das Bilden; das
Komponieren. —**posite**, *adj.* zusammengesetzt. —**position**, *s.* die Zusam-
mensetzung, Mischung; die Beschaffenheit; die Zusammenstellung (*of a
picture*); das Verfassen; die Komposi-
tion (*Chem., Metall.*); die Setzkunst
(*Typ.*). —**positor**, *s.* der Schriftsetzer.
—**posure**, *s.* die Fassung, Gelassenheit.
—**pound**, I. *adj.* zusammengesetzt.
II. *s.* die Mischung, Zusammen-
setzung; das Gemisch. III. *v.a.* zu-
sammensetzen. —**prehend**, *v.a.* (include) in sich fassen; (understand) begreifen. —**prehensible**, *adj.*, —**pre-
hensibly**, *adv.* faßlich, begreiflich.
—**prehension**, *s.* die Fassungskraft.
—**prehensive**, *adj.*, —**prehensively**,
adv. umfassend. —**press**, I. *v.a.* zusammendrücken. II. *s.* die Kom-
presse (*Surg.*). —**pressibility**, *s.* die
Preßbarkeit. —**pressible**, *adj.* zusam-
mendrückbar. —**pression**, *s.* das
Zusammendrücken, Pressen. —**prise**,
v.a. in sich fassen, einschließen. —
promise, I. *s.* die Übereinkunft, der
Ausgleich. II. *v.a.* gütlich abmachen;
kompromittieren. —**pulsion**, *s.* der
Zwang. —**pulsory**, *adj.* zwingend.
—**punction**, *s.* die Gewissensbisse.
—**putation**, *s.* die Berechnung,
Rechnung. —**pute**, *v.a.* berechnen.

Comrade, *s.* der Kamerad, Genoß,
Gefährte. —**ship**, *s.* die Kamerad-
schaft.

1**Con**, *v.a.* fleißig studieren; lenten
(*Naut.*); —ning tower, der Komman-
doturm.

2**Con**, *s.* (*abbr. of contra*) pro and con, für
und wider; the pros and —s, die Gründe.

Concav—**e**, *adj.* konkav. —**ity**, *s.* die
Hohlründung.

Conceal, *v.a.* verhehlen, verbergen.
—**ed**, *adj.*, —**edly**, *adv.* verborgen.
—**er**, *s.* der Verhehler. —**ment**, *s.*

die Verheimlichung; (place of —
ment) das Versteck.

Concede, *v.a.* einräumen, zugestehen.

Conceit, *s.* (opinion) die Meinung;
(vanity) die Eitelkeit, Einbildung, der
Eigendünkel. —**ed**, *adj.* eingebildet;
(vain) dünkelhaft, eitel. —**edness**,
s. der (Eigen)dünkel.

Conceiv—**able**, *adj.*, —**ably**, *adv.*
denkbar. —**e**, *v.* I. *a.* (imagine) sich
(*dat.*) denken, sich vorstellen; (understand) fassen, begreifen. II. *n.* empfangen, schwanger werden (*of women*);
begreifen, sich (*dat.*).

Concentra—**te**, *v.a.* konzentrieren;
verdichten. —**tion**, *s.* die Konzentra-
tion; die verdichtung.

Conception, *s.* das Erfassen; die
Empfängnis; der Entwurf, die Idee.

Concern, I. *v.a.* (affect) betreffen, angehen; Kummer, Teilnahme er-
wecken; to — oneself with, sich
kümmern um. II. *s.* (affair) die
Angelegenheit; (care) die Sorge,
Kummer; (business) das Geschäft.
—**ed**, *p.p.* & *adj.*, —**edly**, *adv.*
beteiligt, interessiert; —ed at *or* about
or for, bekümmert, besorgt. —**ing**,
prep. in Betreff, betreffend, betreffs,
hinsichtlich; —ing him, was ihn betrifft;
—ing it, mit Bezug darauf.

Concert, I. *v.a.* (heimlich) verabreden.
II. *s.*; das Einverständnis; das
Konzert (*Mus.*). —**ina**, *s.* die Kon-
zertina (*Mus.*). —**ed**, *adj.*; —ed
action, gemeinschaftliches Vorgehen;
—ed music, die Konzertmusik. —
pitch, *s.* der Kammerton. —**room**,
s. der Konzertsaal.

Concession, *s.* (permission) die
Gestattung; (thing conceded) das
Zugeständnis.

Conciliat—**e**, *v.a.* gewinnen, versöhnen. —**ion**, *s.* die Versöhnung.

Concise, *adj.*, —**ly**, *adv.* kurz, knapp.
—**ness**, *s.* die Kürze; die Bündigkeit.

Conclave, *s.* das Konklave.

Conclu—**de**, *v.* I. *a.* (end) (be)schließen,
endigen; (infer) schließen, folgern;
(abschließen (*a peace, etc.*). II. *n.*
endigen, schließen. —**ding**, *p.* & *adj.* schließ-
end. —**sion**, *s.* der Schluß. —**sive**,
adj., —**sively**, *adv.* entscheidend.

Concord, *s.* die Eintracht. —**ant**, *adj.*,
—**antly**, *adv.* einhellig; harmonisch.
—**at**, *s.* das Konkordat.

Concourse, *s.* der Zusammenlauf.

Concrete, I. *adj.,* —**ly,** *adv.* konkret, dicht. II. *s.* der Steinmörtel.

Concur, *v.n.* übereinstimmen. —**rence,** *s.* die Übereinstimmung. —**rent,** *adj.,* —**rently,** *adv.* begleitend, mitwirkend.

Concussion, *s.* die Erschütterung.

Condemn, *v.a.* verdammen; verurteilen; mißbilligen. —**able,** *adj.* verwerflich. —**ation,** *s.* die Verurteilung, Verdammung.

Condens—ation, *s.* die Verdichtung. —**e,** *v.* I. *a.* verdichten. II. *n.* sich verdichten. —**ed,** *p.p.* & *adj.* verdichtet. —**er,** *s.* der Kondensator.

Condescen—d, *v.n.* sich herablassen. —**ding,** *adj.,* —**dingly,** *adv.* herablassend. —**sion,** *s.* die Herablassung.

Condiment, *s.* die Würze.

Condition, *s.* (state) der Zustand; (rank) der Rang, Stand; (stipulation) die Bedingung. —**al,** *adj.* bedingt; konditionell (*Gram.*). —**ally,** *adv.* unter (gewissen) Bedingungen. —**ed,** *adj.* beschaffen, geartet.

Condole, *v.n.* Beileid bezeigen. —**nce,** *s.* das Beileid.

Conduct, I. *s.* das Betragen, Benehmen; — of war, die Kriegsführung. II. *v.a.* leiten, führen; to — oneself, sich führen, sich benehmen. —**or,** *s.* der Führer, Anführer; der Leiter (*Phys.*); der Kapellmeister (*Mus.*); der Schaffner (*Railw.*).

Cone, *s.* der Kegel (*Geom.*); der Tannenzapfen (*of firs*).

Confectioner, *s.* der Konditor, Zuckerbäcker. —**y,** *s.* das Zuckerwerk; (shop) die Konditorei.

Confedera—cy, *s.* das Bündnis, der Bund. —**te,** I. *adj.* verbündet, verbunden. II. *s.* der Verbündete, Bundesgenoß; (accomplice) der Mitschuldige. III. *v.a.* verbünden. IV. *v.n.* sich verbünden.

Confer, *v.* I. *a.* geben, erteilen. II. *n.* unterhandeln, sich besprechen. —**ence,** *s.* die Beratung; (meeting) die Konferenz.

Confess, *v.* I. *a.* (acknowledge) zugestehen, einräumen; beichten (*sins*). II. *n.* beichten. —**edly,** *adv.* unleugbar. —**ion,** *s.* das Geständnis, Bekenntnis; die Beichte. —**ional,** *s.* der Beichtstuhl. —**or,** *s.* der Glaubensbekenner; father —or, der Beichtvater.

Confid—ant, *s.* der Vertraute. —**ante,** *s.* die Vertraute. —**e,** *v.* I. *a.* anvertrauen (something to a person, einem etwas). II. *n.* vertrauen, sich verlassen. —**ence,** *s.* (trust) das Vertrauen, Zutrauen; (communication) die vertrauliche Mitteilung; (forwardness) die Dreistigkeit. —**ent,** *adj.,* —**ently,** *adv.* vertrauend; zuversichtlich; keck, dreist. —**ential,** *adj.,* —**entially,** *adv.* vertraulich. —**ing,** *adj.* vertrauensvoll.

Confine, I. *v.a.* einschränken; einsperren; to be —ed to bed, das Bett hüten müssen. II. *s.* (*gen'lly* —**s,** *pl.*) die Grenze. —**ment,** *s.* die Einsperrung; (childbirth) die Entbindung.

Confirm, *v.a.* (strengthen) bestärken; (corroborate) bestätigen. —**ation,** *s.* die Bestätigung, Bekräftigung; die Einsegnung (*Theol.*). —**ed,** *p.p.* & *adj.* fest, bestimmt; (ingrained) eingewurzelt, unverbesserlich.

Confiscat—e, *v.a.* in Beschlag nehmen. —**ion,** die Beschlagnahme.

Conflagration, *s.* der große Brand, die Feuersbrunst.

Conflict, *s.* der Zusammenstoß. —**ing,** *adj.* entgegengesetzt.

Conform, *v.n.;* to — to, sich fügen, sich richten nach. —**ably,** *adv.* gemäß, angemessen. —**ity,** *s.* die Gleichförmigkeit; in —ity with, gemäß.

Confound, *v.a.* verwechseln (one person or thing with another); (confuse) verwirren; (overthrow) vernichten; — it! verdammt! —**ed,** *adj.* verwirrt; verwünscht.

Confront, *v.a.* gegenüberstellen.

Confus—e, *v.a.* verwirren. —**ed,** *adj.,* —**edly,** *adv.* verwirrt, wirr, bestürzt. —**ion,** *s.* die Verwirrung, Unordnung; die Verlegenheit.

Confut—ation, *s.* die Widerlegung. —**e,** *v.a.* widerlegen.

Congenial, *adj.* geistesverwandt. —**ity,** *s.* die Gleichartigkeit.

Conger, *s.* (— -**eel**) der Meeraal.

Congestion, *s.* die Anhäufung, die (Blut-)Überfüllung (*Med.*); — of population, die Übervölkerung.

Congratulat—e, *v.a.* beglückwünschen, gratulieren. —**ory,** *adj.* glückwünschend.

Congregat—e, *v.* I. *a.* versammeln. II. *n.* sich versammeln. —**ion,** *s.* das

Sammeln; die Versammlung; die Kirchengemeinde.

Congress, s. die Tagung.

Conic, —al, adj., **—ally,** adv. kegelförmig, konisch; — section, der Kegelschnitt.

Conjectur—able, adj., **—al,** adj., **—ally,** adv. mutmaßlich. **—e,** I. s. die Mutmaßung. II. v.a. mutmaßen, vermuten.

Conjuga—l, adj., **—ally,** adv. ehelich. **—te,** v.a. (ein Zeitwort) abwandeln. **—tion,** s. die Abwandlung (der Zeitwörter), Konjugation.

Conjunct, adj. verbunden. **—ion,** s. (union) die Verbindung; das Bindewort (Gram.).

Conjur—ation, s. die Zauberformel; die Zauberei. **—e,** v. I. a. beschwören; (implore) ernst anflehen; **—ing** trick, das Zauberkunststück. II. n. Zauberei treiben. **—er, —or,** s. der Beschwörer; der Zauberer.

Connect, v.a. verknüpfen, verbinden. **—ed,** adj., **—edly,** adv. verbunden. **—ion,** s. die Verbindung; (coherence) der Zusammenhang; (person —ed) der, die Verwandte; (relationship) die Verwandtschaft.

Connoisseur, s. der Kenner.

Conquer, v. I. a. erobern, besiegen. II. n. siegen. **—ing,** adj., **—ingly,** adv. siegend. **—or,** s. der Eroberer; der Sieger.

Conquest, s. die Eroberung.

Conscien—ce, s. das Gewissen; in all —, sicherlich, wahrhaftig; out of all —, unverschämt. **—celess,** adj. gewissenlos. **—tious,** adj., **—tiously,** adv. gewissenhaft. **—tiousness,** s. die Gewissenhaftigkeit.

Conscious, adj., **—ly,** adv. bewußt. **—ness,** s. das Bewußtsein.

Conscript, s. der Dienstpflichtige (Mil.). **—ion,** s. die (Zwangs-)Aushebung.

Consecrat—e, I. v.a. weihen; widmen. II. adj., **—ed,** adj. geweiht, heilig. **—ion,** s. die Einweihung, Weihe; die Heiligsprechung (at the Mass). **—or,** s. der Einsegnende.

Consecutive, adj. aufeinanderfolgend. **—ly,** adv. fortlaufend. **—ness,** s. die Aufeinanderfolge.

Consent, I. s. die Einwilligung, Zustimmung, Genehmigung; with one —, einstimmig. II. v.n. (— to) einwilligen, genehmigen, beistimmen.

Conservatory, s. das Treibhaus; (music, etc.) das Konservatorium.

Consequen—ce, s. das Ergebnis; (effect) die Wirkung (einer Ursache); (importance) die Wichtigkeit. **—t,** adj. folgend. **—tly,** adv. folglich.

Conservati—sm, s. der Konservatismus. **—ve,** I. adj. erhaltend; konservativ (Pol.). II. s. der Konservative.

Consider, v. I. a. bedenken, in Betracht ziehen; schätzen, halten für. II. n. nachdenken, überlegen. **—able,** adj., **—ably,** adv. ansehnlich, bedeutend, wichtig. **—ate,** adj., **—ately,** adv. rücksichtsvoll. **—ateness,** s. die Rücksicht. **—ation,** s. die Betrachtung, Überlegung; (payment) die Vergütung; (motive) der Beweggrund.

Consign, v.a. übergeben, überliefern. **—ee,** s. der Warenempfänger. **—er, —or,** s. der Übersender. **—ment,** s. die Übersendung, Versendung.

Consist, v.a. bestehen (of, aus; in, in einer S.). **—ence, —ency,** s. die Konsistenz; (durability) die Dauer, der Bestand. **—ent,** adj., **—ently,** adv. fest, dicht; (—ent with) übereinstimmend, gemäß.

Console, v.a. trösten. **—r,** s. der Tröster.

Consolidate, v.a. fest machen, verdichten.

Consonan—ce, s. die Konsonanz (Mus.); die Übereinstimmung. **—t,** I. adj., **—tly,** adv. übereinstimmend. II. s. der Konsonant.

Consort, I. s. der Gemahl, die Gemahlin. II. v.n. sich gesellen (with, zu).

Conspicuous, adj. sichtbar; hervorragend.

Conspir—acy, s. die Verschwörung. **—ator,** s. der Verschwörer. **—e,** v.n. sich verschwören.

Constable, s. der Polizist, Schutzmann, Polizeidiener.

Constan—cy, s. die Beständigkeit, Beharrlichkeit. **—t,** adj., **—tly,** adv. beständig, unverändert.

Constellation, s. die Konstellation, das Gestirn, Sternbild (also fig.).

Consternation, s. die Bestürzung.

Constitu—ency, s. die Wählerschaft. **—ent,** I. adj. wesentlich. II. s. der Wähler; Bestandteil. **—te,** v.a. (establish) festsetzen; (set up) errichten. **—tion,** s. (act of —ting) die

Errichtung; (nature) die Beschaffenheit; (government) die Staatsverfassung. —tional, I. *adj.*, —tionally, *adv.* temperamentsmäßig; konstitutionell.

Constrain, *v.a.* zwingen, nötigen. —ed, *adj.*, —edly, *adv.* gezwungen. —t, *s.* der Zwang.

Constrict, *v.a.* zusammenziehen.

Construct, *v.a.* errichten, aufbauen. —ion, *s.* das Erbauen; (manner of —ing) die Form, Bauart. —ive, *adj.* aufbauend, bildend. —or, *s.* der Erbauer.

Construe, *v.a.* konstruieren (*Gram.*); (translate) übersetzen; (interpret) auslegen, deuten.

Consul, *s.* der Konsul. —ar, *adj.* konsularisch.

Consult, *v.* I. *n.* sich beraten (mit einem über eine S.). II. *a.* um Rat fragen; (consider) berücksichtigen. —ation, *s.* die Beratung.

Consum—e, *v.a.* verzehren, aufzehren. —er, *s.* der Verzehrer, Verbraucher.

Consumpt—ion, *s.* (use) der Verbrauch; die Schwindsucht (*Med.*). —ive, *adj.* schwindsüchtig.

Contact, *s.* die Berührung.

Contagio—n, *s.* die Ansteckung, Seuche. —us, *adj.*, —usly, *adv.* ansteckend.

Contain, *v.a.* enthalten, in sich (*dat.*) halten. —able, *adj.* enthaltbar.

Contemplat—e, *v.* I. *a.* betrachten; (intend) beabsichtigen. II. *n.* (über eine S.) nachsinnen. —ion, *s.* die Betrachtung. —ive, *adj.*, —ively, *adv.* nachdenklich; beschaulich.

Contempora—neousness, *s.* die Gleichzeitigkeit. —ry, I. *adj.* gleichzeitig. II. *s.* der Zeitgenosse.

Contempt, *s.* die Verachtung; in — of, trotz. —ible, *adj.*, —ibly, *adv.* verächtlich. —ibleness, *s.* die Verächtlichkeit. —uous, *adj.*, —uously, *adv.* verachtend, höhnisch).

Conten—d, *v.* I. *n.* streiten. II. *a.* bestreiten. —tion, *s.* der Streit. —tious, *adj.*, —tiously, *adv.* streitig.

Content, I. *adj.* zufrieden. II. *v.a.* befriedigen. —ed, *adj.*, —edly, *adv.* zufrieden. —edness, —ment, *s.* die Zufriedenheit. —s, *pl.* der Inhalt.

Contest, *s.* der Streit.

Context, *s.* der Zusammenhang. —ure, *s.* der Bau, das System.

Continen—ce, *s.* die Enthaltsamkeit. —t, I. *s.* der Kontinent. II. *adj.*, —tly, *adv.* enthaltsam.

Continu—al, *adj.*, —ally, *adv.* fortwährend. —ance, *s.* die Fortdauer. —ation, *s.* die Fortsetzung. —e, *v.* I. *a.* fortsetzen; to —e reading, weiter lesen; to be —ed, Fortsetzung folgt. —ous, *adj.*, ununterbrochen.

Contort, *v.a.* verdrehen. —ion, *s.* die Krümmung.

Contour, *s.* der Umriß.

Contraband, *adj.* verboten; — trade, der Schleichhandel.

Contract, I. *v.a.* (narrow) verengen; sich (*dat.*) zuziehen (*disease, etc.*); sich (*dat.*) aneignen (*habits, etc.*). II. *v.n.* sich zusammenziehen, zusammenschrumpfen; (bargain) einen Vertrag schließen. III. *s.* der Kontrakt, Vertrag. —ion, *s.* die Zusammenziehung. —or, *s.* der Unternehmer.

Contra—dict, *v.a.* widersprechen (someone, einem). —diction, *s.* der Widerspruch. —dictory, *adj.* —dictorily, *adv.* unvereinbar.

Contralto, *s.* die tiefe Altstimme (*Mus.*).

Contrar—iety, *s.* der Widerspruch. —y, I. *adj.* entgegengesetzt; (perverse) widerwärtig; (with to = prep.) zuwider, entgegen, gegen, im Gegensatz zu. II. *s.* das Gegenteil.

Contrast, I. *v.a.* einander entgegenstellen. II. *v.n.*; to — with, einen Gegensatz bilden zu *or* mit. III. *s.* der Gegensatz.

Contravene, *v.a.* überschreiten; (*fig.*) verstoßen gegen.

Contribut—e, *v.a.* beitragen, beisteuern. —ion, *s.* der Beitrag, die Beisteuer. —ive, *adj.* beitragend. —or, *s.* der Beitragende.

Contrite, *adj.* zerknirscht, reuevoll.

Contriv—ance, *s.* die Vorrichtung. —e, *v.a.* veranstalten. —er, *s.* der Erfinder; der Veranstalter.

Control, I. *s.* das Hemmnis; die Aufsicht. II. *v.a.* (overlook) beaufsichtigen, leiten; (restrain) einschränken. —ler, *s.* der Leiter, Geschäftsführer.

Controversy, *s.* der Streit; die Streitfrage.

Contum—acious, *adj.*, —aciously, *adv.* hartnäckig, trotzig. —acy, *s.* die Halsstarrigkeit. —ely, *s.* die Beschimpfung.

Conundrum, s. das Scherzrätsel.

Convalesce, v.n. genesen. —nce, s. die Genesung. —nt, I. adj. genesend. II. s. der Genesende.

Conven—e, v.a. versammeln. —ience, s. die Bequemlichkeit, Gemächlichkeit; at your earliest —ience, umgehend. —ient, adj., —iently, adv. schicklich, passend; bequem.

Convent, s. das Kloster.

Conventional, adj. üblich, herkömmlich.

Convers—ation, s. die Unterredung. —e, v.n. sich mit einem unterhalten.

Conversion, s. (change) die Umwandelung; die Bekehrung (Theol.).

Convert, I. v.a. (change) umändern, umwandeln; bekehren (Theol., etc.). II. v.n. sich umändern. III. s. der Bekehrte. —er, s. der Bekehrer, Proselytenmacher. —ible, adj. verwandelbar, verkäuflich.

Convex, adj., —ly, adv. konvex.

Convey, v.a. (fort)bringen, wegschaffen; mitteilen. —ance, s. das Fortschaffen; (transport) die Spedition (C.L.); (carriage) das Fuhrwerk.

Convict, I. v.a. überweisen, überführen. II. s. der Sträfling. —ion, s. (act of —ing) die Überweisung, Überführung; (belief) die Überzeugung.

Convinc—e, v.a. überzeugen. —ing, adj., —ingly, adv. überzeugend.

Convivial, adj., festlich. —ity, s. die Geselligkeit.

Convoy, I. v.a. geleiten. II. s. das Geleit.

Convuls—e, v.a. (fig.) erschüttern. —ion, s. der Krampf. —ive, adj., —ively, adv. krampfhaft, zuckend.

Coo, v.n. girren.

Cook, I. s. der Koch; (female —) die Köchin. II. v.a. & n. kochen. —ery, s. das Kochen.

Cool, I. adj., —ly, adv. kühl, frisch. II. s. die Kühle, Frische. III. v.a. (ab-) kühlen. IV. v.n. kühl werden; (fig.) erkalten. —ing, p. & adj. kühlend, erfrischend. —ish, adj. ziemlich kühl. —ness, s. die Kühle. —headed, adj. besonnen.

Coop, I. v.a. — up, einsperren. II. s. der Hühnerkäfig. —er, s. der Küfer, Böttcher.

Co-operate, v.n. mitwirken.

Coot, s. das Wasserhuhn.

1Cop—e, I. s. (vestment) der Priester-

rock; (top) der Gipfel. II. v.a. decken, abdachen. —ing, s. die Mauerkappe.

2Cope, v.n. wetteifern.

Copious, adj., —ly, adv. reich, reichlich. —ness, s. der Überfluß.

Copper, I. s. das Kupfer. II. adj. kupfern. —y, adj. kupferig. —plate, s. der Kupferstich.

Coppice, Copse, s. das Dickicht.

Copy, I. s. die Abschrift, Kopie. II. v.a. abschreiben, kopieren; (imitate) nachbilden. III. v.n. kopieren, nachahmen. —ist, s. der Abschreiber. —book, s. das Schreibheft. —right, s. das Verlagsrecht.

Coquet, v.n. kokettieren. —ry, s. die Koketterie. —te, s. die Kokette. —tish, adj., —tishly, adv. kokett.

Coral, I. s. die Koralle. II. adj. korallen.

Cord, s. der Strick.

Cordial, adj., —ly, adv. herzlich.

Core, s. der Kern.

Cork, I. s. der Kork. II. v.a. (zu-) korken. —screw, s. der Pfropfenzieher.

Cormorant, s. die Scharbe.

1Corn, s. das Getreide.

2Corn, s. das Hühnerauge.

Cornelian, s. der Karneol (Min.).

Corner, s. der Winkel, die Ecke. —ed, adj., eckig; three—ed, dreieckig.

Cornice, s. das Gesims.

Coronation, s. die Krönung.

Coroner, s. der Leichenbeschauer.

Coronet, s. die kleine Krone.

1Corporal, s. der Unteroffizier, Korporal (Mil.).

2Corp—oral, adj., —orally, adv. körperlich, leiblich. —oration, s. die Körperschaft. —oreal, adj., —orally, adv. körperlich.

Corps, s. (also pl.) das Korps (Mil.).

Corpse, s. die Leiche, der Leichnam.

Corp—ulence, —ulency, s. die Dickleibigkeit. —ulent, adj. dickleibig.

Correct, I. adj., —ly, adv. richtig, fehlerfrei; regelrecht, tadellos; to be —, richtig sein, stimmen. II. v.a. berichtigen, verbessern. —ion, n. die Berichtigung, Verbesserung. —ness, s. die Fehlerfreiheit, Richtigkeit. —or, s. der Berichtigende.

Correspond, v.n. (agree, answer) übereinstimmen, entsprechen; (write) in Briefwechsel stehen. —ence, s. die

Übereinstimmung; der Briefwechsel.
—ent, I. *adj.* übereinstimmend, entsprechend. II. *s.* der Korrespondent.

Corridor, *s.* der Korridor, Gang.

Corrobor—ate, *v.a.* bestätigen. —ation, *s.* die Bestätigung.

Corro—de, *v.a.* zerfressen. —sion, *s.* die Ätzung. —sive, I. *adj.* fressend, ätzend. II. *s.* das Ätzmittel.

Corrupt, I. *v.a.* verderben (*also fig.*). II. *v.n.* faulen, verderben. III. *adj.*, —ly, *adv.* (putrid) faul, verdorben; (depraved) verderbt. —er, *s.* der Verführer; (briber) der Bestecher. —ible, *adj.*, —ibly, *adv.* verderblich. —ion, *s.* die Verwesung. —ness, *s.* die Verdorbenheit.

Cors(e)let, *s.* das Brustüttück.

Corset, *s.* das Korsett.

Cosiness, *s.* die Behaglichkeit.

Cosmetic, I. *adj.* verschönernd. II. *s.* das Schönheitsmittel.

Cosmic(al), *adj.* kosmisch.

Cosmopolit—an *or* —e, I. *adj.* weltbürgerlich. II. *s.* der Weltbürger.

Cossack, *s.* der Kosak.

Cost, I. *s.* die Kosten; — price, der Selbstkostenpreis, Einkaufspreis; free of —, kostenfrei. II. *v.a. & n.* kosten. —liness, *s.* die Kostbarkeit. —ly, *adj.* kostspielig, teuer.

Costermonger, *s.* der Höker.

Costum—e, *s.* das Kostüm; die Tracht. —ier, *s.* der Kostümschneider.

Cosy, *adj.* gemütlich.

Cot, *s.* das kleine Bett.

Cottage, *s.* das Häuschen.

Cotton, *s.* die Baumwolle; (calico) der Kattun. —wool, *s.* die (Roh=)Baumwolle.

Couch, I. *s.* das Ruhelager, Ruhebett. II. *v.a.* (nieder)legen. III. *v.n.* sich legen.

Cough, I. *s.* der Husten. II. *v.n.* husten.

Council, *s.* der Rat. —lor, *s.* der Ratsherr; privy-—lor, Geheimrat.

Counsel, I. *s.* die Beratung, Beratschlagung; (advice) der (erteilte) Rat; der Rechtsanwalt (*Law*). II. *v.a.* raten, beraten. —lor, *s.* der Ratgeber; der Advokat.

1Count, *s.* der Graf. —ess, *s.* die Gräfin. —y, *s.* die Grafschaft.

2Count, I. *v.a.* zählen; rechnen; berechnen (*a sum, etc.*). II. *v.n.* (to — on) rechnen, zählen (auf). III. *s.*

(reckoning) die Rechnung. —ing, *s.* das Rechnen, Zählen. —less, *adj.* unzählig, zahllos. —ing-house, *s.* das Kontor.

Countenance, I. *s.* das Gesicht. II. *v.a.* begünstigen.

1Counter, *s.* der Rechner; der Zähltisch, Zahltisch.

2Counter, *adv.* entgegen, zuwider, entgegengesetzt.

Counter—act, *v.a.* entgegenwirken. —action, *s.* die Entgegenwirkung, der Widerstand. —balance, *s.* das Gegengewicht.

Counterfeit, I. *v.a.* (forge) verfälschen; (feign) erheucheln. II. *v.a.* sich verstellen. III. *adj.* falsch, unecht (*as a document*); (feigned) verstellt, erheuchelt. IV. *s.* das Verfälschte, Unechte.

Counterfoil, *s.* das Kontrollblatt.

Countermand, I. *s.* die Widerrufung. II. *v.a.* widerrufen, abbestellen.

Counter—march, *s.* der Rückmarsch. —mine, *s.* die Gegenmine (*Fort.*).

Counterpane, *s.* die Bett(stepp)decke.

Counter—part, *s.* das Gegenbild. —poise, *s.* das Gegengewicht. —sign, I. *s.* die Losung (*Mil.*). II. *v.a.* mitunterschreiben.

Country, I. *s.* das Land; (native —) das Vaterland. II. *adj.* Land=, vom Lande, auf dem Lande. —man, *s.* der Landsmann. —woman, *s.* die Landsmännin.

County, *s.* die Grafschaft.

Couple, *s.* das Paar.

Courage, *s.* der Mut, die Tapferkeit. —ous, *adj.*, —ously, *adv.* mutig, herzhaft, tapfer.

Courier, *s.* der Eilbote.

Course, I. *s.* (running) das Laufen; (track) die Laufbahn, Rennbahn; (direction) der Lauf; in due —, zu rechter Zeit; of —, natürlich. II. *v.n.* laufen, rennen, jagen. III. *v.a.* jagen. —r, *s.* der Renner.

Coursing, *s.* die Hetzjagd.

Court, I. *s.* (—yard) der Hof; der Hof (*of a prince*); das Gericht (*of justice*). II. *v.a.* (einer Person) den Hof machen. —eous, *adj.*, —eously, *adv.* höflich, artig. —er, *s.* der Bewerber. —esy, *s.* die Höflichkeit, Artigkeit. —ier, *s.* der Höfling. —liness, *s.* der feine Ton. —ly, *adj.* & *adv.* höfisch; höflich. —ship, *s.*

das Freien. — **martial,** *s.* das Kriegsgericht.

Cousin, *s.* der Vetter; (female —) die Base, die Cousine. **—ly,** *adj.* vetterlich. **—ship,** *s.* die Vetterschaft.

Cove, *s.* die kleine Bucht.

Covenant, I. *s.* der Vertrag. II. *v.n.* übereinkommen. III. *v.a.* geloben; (aus)bedingen.

Cover, I. *v.a.* bedecken, decken. II. *s.* die Decke. **—ing,** *adj.* deckend. **—let, —lid,** *s.* die Bettdecke. **—t,** I. *adj.,* **—tly,** *adv.* bedeckt. II. *s.* der bedeckte Ort; der Wildpark (*for game*).

Covet, *v.a.* begehren. **—ous,** *adj.,* **—ously,** *adv.* begehrlich, gierig (of, nach). **—ousness,** *s.* die Begierde.

Covey, *s.* die Brut.

Cow, *s.* die Kuh. **—house,** *s.* der Kuhstall.

Coward, *s.* der Feigling. **—ice,** *s.* die Feigheit. **—ly,** *adj. & adv.* feig(e).

Cower, *v.n.* kauern.

Cowl, *s.* die Mönchskappe, Kapuze.

Cowslip, *s.* die Schlüsselblume.

Coxcomb, *s.* der Geck.

Coxswain, *s.* der Bootsführer, Steuermann.

Coy, *adj.,* **—ly,** *adv.* scheu, spröde. **—ness,** *s.* die Sprödigkeit.

Crab, *s.* die Krabbe. **—bed,** *adj.* mürrisch, verworren.

Crack, I. *v.a.* (burst) (zer)spalten, zersprengen; to — a joke, einen Witz reißen; to — a nut, eine Nuß knacken; a little —ed (*sl.*), nicht recht gescheit. II. *v.n.* sich spalten. III. *s.* der Krach, Knall. **—er,** *s.* der Knacker, Knallbonbon.

Cradle, *s.* die Wiege.

Craft, *s.* (trade) das Handwerk, Gewerbe; (vessel) die Fahrzeuge. **—ily,** *adv.,* **—y,** *adj.* listig; (cleverly) geschickt. **—iness,** *s.* die List, Schlauheit. **—sman,** *s.* der Handwerker.

Crag, *s.* die Klippe. **—gy,** *adj.* schroff.

Cram, *v.a.* vollstopfen.

Cramp, *s.* der Krampf. **—ed,** *adj.* krampfig; beengt.

Cranberry, *s.* die Preiselbeere.

Crane, *s.* der Kranich (*Orn.*); der Kran (*Mach.*).

Crank, *s.* die Kurbel (*Mech.*).

Cranny, *s.* der Riß, Spalt.

Crape, *s.* der Flor.

Crash, I. *s.* das Gekrach. II. *v.n.* krachen, platzen.

Crate, *s.* der große geflochtene Korb.

Crater, *s.* der Krater.

Cravat, *s.* die Krawatte.

Crave, *v.a.* flehen.

Craven, I. *adj.* feig. II. *s.* die Memme.

Crawl, *v.n.* kriechen. **—ing,** I. *p. & adj.,* **—ingly,** *adv.* kriechend. II. *s.* das Kriechen.

Crayfish, *s.* der Krebs.

Crayon, *s.* der Zeichenstift.

Craze, I. *s.* die Manie (for something, für eine S.). II. *v.a.* verwirrt machen. **—d,** *adj.* verrückt.

Creak, *v.n.* knarren.

Cream, *s.* der Rahm, die Sahne; cold —, die Hautsalbe. **—y,** *adj.* sahnig.

Crease, I. *s.* die Falte. II. *v.a.* falten. III. *v.n.* Falten werfen.

Creat—e, *v.a.* schaffen, erschaffen. **—ion,** *s.* die Schöpfung. **—ive,** *adj.* schaffend, erschaffend. **—or,** *s.* der Schöpfer. **—ure,** *s.* das Geschöpf.

Cred—ence, *s.* der Glaube. **—ibility,** *s.* die Glaubwürdigkeit. **—ible,** *adj.,* **—ibly,** *adv.* glaublich (of things); glaubwürdig (of persons). **—it,** I. *s.* (reputation) der (gute) Ruf; (trust reposed) das Zutrauen; (balance in a person's favour) das Guthaben. II. *v.a.* (believe) glauben; (trust) trauen; kreditieren (*C.L.*). **—itable,** *adj.,* **—itably,** *adv.* ehrbar, ehrenwert. **—itor,** *s.* der Gläubiger (*C.L.*). **—ulity,** *s.* die Leichtgläubigkeit. **—ulous,** *adj.,* **—ulously,** *adv.* leichtgläubig.

Creed, *s.* das Glaubensbekenntnis.

Creek, *s.* die Bucht.

Creel, *s.* der Weidenkorb, Fischkorb.

Creep, *v.n.* kriechen. **—er,** *s.* der Kriecher. **—y,** *adj.* kriechend; fröstelnd, gruselig.

Cremat—e, *v.a.* einäschern. **—ion,** *s.* die Einäscherung.

Crescent, I. *adj.* wachsend, zunehmend. II. *s.* der Halbmond.

Cress, *s.* die Kresse (*Bot.*).

Crest, *s.* der Kamm (of a cock); der Helmschmuck (*Her.*). **—fallen,** *adj.* mutlos.

Cretonne, *s.* die Kretonne.

Crev—asse, *s.* die Gletscherspalte. **—ice,** *s.* der Riß.

Crew, *s.* die Schiffsmannschaft.

Crib, *s.* die Krippe; das Kinderbett; (*sl.*) die Eselsbrücke.

Cricket, *s.* die Grille.

Crim—e, *s.* das Verbrechen. —inal,
I. *adj.,* —inally, *adv.* verbrecherisch.
II. *s.* der Verbrecher.

Crimson, I. *s.* das Karmesin. II. *adj.*
karmesin.

Cringe, *v.n.* sich krümmen, kriechen.
—r, *s.* der Fuchsschwänzer.

Crinkle, I. *s.* die Falte. II. *v.a.*
kräuseln.

Cripple, *s.* der Krüppel.

Crisis, *s.* die Krise, Notlage.

Crisp, *adj.,* —ly, *adv.* kraus (*of hair*);
bröckelig, knusperig (*of cakes*).

Criterion, *s.* das Kennzeichen, der
Prüfstein.

Critic, *s.* der Kritiker. —al, *adj.,*
—ally, *adv.* kritisch. —ism, *s.* die
Kritik.

Croak, *v.n.* krächzen (*as a raven*);
quaken (*of frogs*). —ing, *s.* das
Quaken, Gequake.

Crochet, I. *s.* die Häkelei. II. *v.a. &
n.* häkeln. —ed, *adj.* gehäkelt. —
ing, *s.* das Häkeln.

Crock, *s.* der Topf. —ery, *s.* die
Töpferware, das Steingut.

Crocodile, *s.* das Krokodil.

Crocus, *s.* der Krokus (*Bot.*).

Cron—e, *s.* das alte Weib. —y, *s.*
(old —y) vertrauter Freund.

Crook, *s.* die Krümmung; (shepherd's —) der Schäferstab; (*sl.*) der
Schwindler. —ed, *adj.,* —edly, *adv.*
krumm. —edness, *s.* die Krummheit.

Croon, *v.a.* wimmern, leise singen.

Crop, *s.* der Kropf (*of a fowl*); die
Ernte; das kurz abgeschnittene Haar;
Eton — der Herrenschnitt. —ped,
p.p. & adj. kurz (ab)geschnitten.

Crosier, *s.* der Bischofsstab.

Cross, I. *s.* das Kreuz. II. *adj.* kreuzweise; (ill-humoured) mürrisch. III.
adv. quer, schief. IV. *v.a.* kreuzen;
to — oneself, sich bekreuzen. —ing,
s. der Übergang, die Überfahrt; der
Kreuzweg. —ly, *adv.* mürrisch, ärgerlich. —ness, *s.* die Quere; das
mürrische Wesen. —bow, *s.* die
Armbrust. —breed, *s.* der Mischling;
die Mischrasse. —examination, *s.*
das Kreuzverhör. —eyed, *adj.*
schielend. —road, *s.* der Scheideweg.

Crotchet, *s.* die Grille; die Viertelnote
(*Mus.*).

Crouch, *v.n.* sich ducken.

Croup, *s.* der Krupp (*Med.*); die Kruppe.

Crow, I. *s.* die Krähe (*Orn.*); das
Krähen (*of a cock*). II. *v.n.* krähen.
—bar, *s.* das Brecheisen.

Crowd, I. *s.* das Gedränge. II. *v.a.*
(fill) anfüllen. III. *v.n.* sich drängen.

Crown, I. *s.* die Krone; der Gipfel;
der Scheitel, Kopf. II. *v.a.* krönen.
—prince, *s.* der Kronprinz.

Cruci—fix, *s.* das Kruzifix. —fixion,
s. die Kreuzigung. —fy, *v.a.* kreuzigen.

Crude, *adj.,* —ly, *adv.* roh. —ness,
s. das Rohe.

Cruel, *adj.,* —ly, *adv.* grausam. —ty,
s. die Grausamkeit.

Cruet, *s.* das Fläschchen.

Cruise, I. *v.n.* kreuzen (*Naut.*). II. die
Seefahrt; pleasure —, die Ver-
gnügungsfahrt (zu Wasser). —r, *s.*
der Kreuzer; armoured —r, der
Panzerkreuzer.

Crumb, I. *s.* die Krume, Brosame.
II. *v.a.* krümeln. —le, *v.* I. *a.*
zerbröckeln, krümeln. II. *n.* sich
zerbröckeln, krümeln.

Crumpet, *s.* der Teekuchen.

Crumple, *v.a.* zerknüllen.

Crunch, *v.a.* zerknirschen.

Crupper, *s.* die Kruppe.

Crusade, *s.* der Kreuzzug, die Kreuz-
fahrt. —r, *s.* der Kreuzfahrer.

Crush, I. *v.a.* drücken. II. *v.n.* zu-
sammengedrückt werden. III. *s.* das
Gedränge.

Crust, *s.* die Kruste, Rinde. —y,
adj. krustig; (surly) grämlich, mürrisch.

Crutch, *s.* die Krücke.

Cry, I. *v.n.* schreien. II. *s.* der Schrei.

Crypt, *s.* die Krypta, Gruft.

Crystal, I. *s.* der Kristall. II. *adj.*
kristallen.

Cub, *s.* das Junge.

Cub—e, *s.* der Kubus; der Würfel.
—ic(al), *adj.* kubisch. —e-root, *s.* die
Kubikwurzel.

Cuckoo, *s.* der Kuckuck. —clock, *s.*
die Kuckucksuhr.

Cucumber, *s.* die Gurke.

Cuddle, *v.a.* verhätscheln, liebkosen.

Cudgel, *s.* der Knüttel.

Cue, *s.* das Stichwort (*Theat.*); der
Billardstock (*Bill.*); to give a person
his —, einem die Worte in den
Mund legen.

¹Cuff, I. *s.* der Schlag. II. *v.a.* (mit
Fäusten) schlagen, knuffen.

²Cuff, *s.* die Manschette; der Aufschlag
(*of a sleeve*).

Cuirass, *s.* der Küraß.

Cull, *v.a.* auslesen.

Culp—able, *adj.,* **—ably,** *adv.* strafbar. **—rit,** *s.* der Schuldige.

Cult, *s.* der Kultus. **—ivate,** *v.a.* anbauen, bebauen. **—ivation,** *s.* der Bau, Anbau. **—ivator,** *s.* der Anbauer, Landwirt. **—ure,** I. *s.* die Kultur (*also fig.*). II. *v.a.* kultivieren, ausbilden.

Cunning, I. *adj.,* **—ly,** *adv.* listig. II. *s.* die List.

Cup, *s.* der Becher; die Tasse (*for tea, etc.*). **—board,** *s.* der Schrank.

Cupidity, *s.* die Begierde.

Cupola, *s.* die Kuppel.

Cur, *s.* der Köter. **—rish,** *adj.,* **—rishly,** *adv.* hündisch.

Curable, *adj.* heilbar.

Curate, *s.* der Unterpfarrer.

Curative, *adj.* heilend.

Curator, *s.* der Aufseher.

Curb, I. *s. see* Kerb; die Kinnkette; (*fig.*) der Zaum. II. *v.a.* zäumen; zügeln.

Curd, *s.* der Käsequark. **—le,** *v.a.* & *n.* gerinnen lassen.

Cure, I. *s.* die Heilung, Kur. II. *v.a.* heilen.

Curio, *s.* die Kuriosität. **—sity,** *s.* die Neugier(de). **—us,** *adj.,* **—usly,** *adv.* neugierig.

Curl, I. *s.* der (Haar=)Ringel. II. *v.a.* kräuseln. III. *v.n.* sich kräuseln. **—iness,** *s.* das Lockige, Krause. **—ing,** *adj.,* **—ingly,** *adv.* kräuselnd. **—y,** *adj.* lockig, gekräuselt.

Curlew, *s.* der Brachvogel.

Currant, *s.* die Johannisbeere; (dried —) die Korinthe.

Curren—cy, *s.* der Umlauf, die Gangbarkeit. **—t,** I. *adj.,* **—tly,** *adv.* laufend (*of time*); umlaufend; to pass **—t,** für gültig angenommen werden. II. *s.* der Strom (*of water, etc.*); der Luftzug (*of air*); der Lauf, Gang (*of events, etc.*).

Curr—ier, *s.* der Gerber. **—y,** *v.a.* Leder zurichten; striegeln (*a horse*).

Curs—e, I. *v.a.* verfluchen, verwünschen. II. *v.n.* fluchen. III. *s.* der Fluch. **—ed,** **—t,** *adj.,* **—edly,** *adv.* verflucht.

Curt, *adj.,* **—ly,** *adv.* kurz, knapp, barsch. **—ail,** *v.a.* abkürzen.

Curtain, *s.* der Vorhang, die Gardine.

Curts(e)y, *s.* die Verbeugung, der Knicks.

Curv—e, I. *s.* die Krümmung. II. *v.a.* krümmen, biegen. **—ilinear,** *adj.* krummlinig.

Cushion, *s.* das Kissen, Polster.

Custod—ian, *s.* der Hüter. **—y,** *s.* die Haft; die Aufsicht.

Custom, *s.* (habit) die Gewohnheit; die Sitte. **—ary,** *adj.* (usual) gebräuchlich; (traditional) herkömmlich. **—er,** *s.* der Kunde. **—s,** *pl.* die Zölle. **—house,** *s.* das Zollamt.

Cut, I. *v.a.* (*also imperf. & p.p.*) schneiden; to — a person, jemanden nicht sehen wollen (beim Begegnen); to — teeth, zahnen; to — short, plötzlich unterbrechen; — and dried, fix und fertig; to — to the quick, auf's tiefste verwunden; that won't — any ice, das wird sich nicht machen lassen. II. *v.n.* schneiden, hauen. III. *s.* der Schnitt, Hieb. IV. *p.p. & adj.* geschnitten. **—ter,** *s.* der Schneidende; der Zuschneider (*Tail.*); der Kutter (*Naut.*). **—ting,** I. *adj.* schneidend. II. *s.* das Schneiden. **—glass,** *s.* das geschliffene Glas. **—throat,** *s.* der Meuchelmörder.

Cutler, *s.* der Messerschmied. **—y,** *s.* die Messerschmiedewaren.

Cutlet, *s.* das Kotelett, die Kotelette.

Cycle, *s.* der Zirkel, Kreis.

Cyclone, *s.* der Zyklon, Wirbelsturm.

Cylinder, *s.* der Zylinder.

Cymbal, *s.* die Zimbel (*Mus.*).

Cynic, I. *adj.,* **—al,** *adj.,* **—ally,** *adv.* zynisch; menschenfeindlich. II. *s.* der Zyniker.

Cypress, *s.* die Zypresse.

Czar, *s. see* Tsar.

D

D, d, das D, b, D (*Mus.*).

Dabble, I. *v.a.* benetzen, bespritzen. II. *v.n.* hineinpfuschen. **—r,** *s.* der Plätscherer; (*fig.*) der Stümper.

Dace, *s.* der Weißfisch, Häsling.

Dado, *s.* die Täfelung.

Daffodil, *s.* die gelbe Narzisse (*Bot.*).

Dagger, *s.* der Dolch.

Dahlia, *s.* die Georgine (*Bot.*).

Daily, *adj. & adv.* täglich.

Daint—ies, *pl.* das Naschwerk. **—ily,** *adv.* lecker, zierlich. **—iness,** *s.* die Leckerhaftigkeit. **—y,** *adj.* lecker, delikat (*of food*); (nice) fein, zierlich.

Dairy, *s.* die Milchkammer (*in a house*); die Molkerei; die Milchwirtschaft. —-farm, *s.* die Meierei.

Daisy, *s.* das Marienblümchen.

Dale, *s.* das Tal.

Dall—iance, *s.* das Schäfern. —y, *v.n.* schäfern, tändeln.

¹**Dam,** I. *s.* der Deich, Damm. II. *v.a.* (— in, — up) abdämmen, eindämmen.

²**Dam,** *s.* die Mutter (der vierfüßigen Tiere).

Damage, I. *s.* der Schaden, Nachteil. II. *v.a.* beschädigen. —d, *p.p. & adj.* beschädigt. —s, *pl.* der Schadenersatz.

Damask, I. *s.* der Damast. II. *adj.* damasten.

Dame, *s.* die Frau.

Damn, *v.a.* verdammen. —able, *adj.,* —ably, *adv.* verdammlich; verdammt. —ation, I. *s.* die Verdammnis, Verdammung. II. *int.* Donnerwetter! verwünscht!

Damp, I. *adj.* feucht. II. *s.* die Feuchtigkeit. III. *v.a.* (be)feuchten, anfeuchten; to — a person's spirits, einen niederdrücken. —er, *s.* die Zugklappe.

Damsel, *s.* die Jungfrau.

Damson, *s.* die Damaszener Pflaume.

Danc—e, I. *v.a.* tanzen; tanzen lassen. II. *v.n.* tanzen. III. *s.* der Tanz. —er, *s.* der Tänzer, die Tänzerin. —ing, *s.* das Tanzen. —ing-room, *s.* der Tanzsaal.

Dandelion, *s.* der Löwenzahn (*Bot.*).

Dandle, *v.a.* hüpfen lassen.

Dandy, *s.* der Stutzer.

Danger, *s.* die Gefahr. —ous, *adj.,* —ously, *adv.* gefährlich. —ousness, *s.* die Gefährlichkeit.

Dangle, *v.n.* baumeln.

Dapper, *adj.,* —ly, *adv.* niedlich, behend, gewandt.

Dapple, *adj.* getupft, fleckig, scheckig.

Dar—e, *v.n.* dürfen, wagen; I — say, das glaube ich wohl. —ing, I. *adj.,* —ingly, *adv.* kühn, tapfer. II. *s.* die Kühnheit.

Dark, I. *adj.,* —ly, *adv.* dunkel, finster. II. *s.* das Dunkel, die Dunkelheit. —en, *v.* I. *a.* verfinstern. II. *n.* dunkel werden. —ish, *adj.* schwärzlich (*of colour*). —ness, *s.* die Finsternis, Dunkelheit. —some, *adj.,* dunkel. —eyed, *adj.* dunkeläugig.

Darling, I. *adj.* teuer, lieb. II. *s.* der Liebling.

Darn, I. *v.a.* stopfen. II. *s.* der Stopffleck. —ing, *s.* das Stopfen; —ing needle, die Stopfnadel.

Dart, I. *s.* der Wurfspieß. II. *v.a.* werfen. III. *v.n.* sich stürzen (at, on a person, auf einen).

Dash, I. *v.a.* (— to pieces) zerschmettern; (— out) ausschlagen. II. *v.n.* stoßen, schlagen; stürzen; to — off, schnell abfahren, dahinsprengen. III. *s.* der Streich; (rush) der Sturz, Anlauf; (— of the pen) der Federstrich. —ing, *adj.* platschend, rauschend; (*fig.*) flott, fesch. —board, *s.* das Schmutzbrett (am Wagen).

Dastard, I. *s.* die Memme. II. —ly, *adj. & adv.* feig.

¹**Date,** I. *s.* das Datum. II. *v.a.* datieren.

²**Date,** *s.* die Dattel (*Bot.*).

Daub, I. *v.a.* beschmieren, besudeln.

Daughter, *s.* die Tochter; —-in-law, Schwiegertochter; step——, Stieftochter. —ly, *adj.* töchterlich.

Daunt, *v.a.* entmutigen. —less, *adj.,* —lessly, *adv.* unerschrocken.

Dauphin, *s.* der Dauphin. —ess, *s.* die Dauphine.

Davit, *s.* die Jütte (*Naut.*).

Daw, *s.* die Dohle (*Orn.*).

Dawdle, *v.n.* schlendern. —r, *s.* der Tagedieb, die Schlafmütze.

Dawn, I. *s.* die Morgendämmerung. II. *v.n.* dämmern, tagen.

Day, I. *s.* der Tag; the other —, neulich; this — week, heute über 8 Tage. —break, *s.* der Tagesanbruch. —dream, *s.* die Träumerei. —time, *s.* der Tag.

Daz—e, *v.a.* (dazzle) blenden; (stupefy) betäuben. —zle, *v.a.* blenden. —zling, *p. & adj.,* —zlingly, *adv.* blendend (*also fig.*).

Deacon, *s.* der Diakonus. —ess, *s.* die Diakonissin. —ry, *s.* das Diakonat.

Dead, *adj.* tot; to come to a — stop, plötzlich anhalten; a — shot, ein nie fehlender Schütze; in the — of winter, im tiefsten Winter. —en, *v.a.* abstumpfen. —liness, *s.* die Tödlichkeit, das Tödliche. —ly, *adj. & adv.* tödlich. —lock, *s.* der Stillstand.

Deaf, *adj.,* taub. —en, *v.a.* betäuben (with, von, durch). —ness, *s.* die Taubheit. —and-dumb, *adj.* taubstumm. —mute, *s.* der Taubstumme.

¹**Deal,** I. *v.a.* (divide) teilen; geben (*Cards*). II. *v.n.* handeln, Handel treiben (*in goods, etc.*). III. *s.* die Menge; das Kartengeben (*Cards*); a great —, sehr viel. **—er,** *s.* der Handelsmann, Händler; der Geber (*Cards*); double **—er,** ein falscher Mensch. **—ing,** *s.* das Teilen.

²**Deal,** *s.* die Diele, Bohle.

Dean, *s.* der Dechant, Dekan. **—ery,** *s.* die Dekanei; (*office*) das Dekanat.

Dear, I. *adj. & adv.,* **—ly,** *adv.* teuer; (beloved) lieb; — me! verwünscht! ach herrje! II. *s.* der Liebling. **—ness,** *s.* die Teuerung.

Dearth, *s.* der Mangel.

Death, *s.* der Tod. **—less,** *adj.* unsterblich. **—like,** *adj.* totenähnlich. **—bed,** *s.* das Sterbebett, Totenbett. **—blow,** *s.* der Todesstoß. **—'s-head,** *s.* der Totenkopf. **—warrant,** *s.* das Todesurteil.

Debar, *v.a.*; to — from, ausschließen von.

Debas—e, *v.a.* erniedrigen. **—ing,** *adj.,* **—ingly,** *adv.* erniedrigend, entwürdigend.

Debat—able, *adj.* streitig. **—e,** I. *s.* der Redekampf, die Debatte. II. *v.n.* erörtern. III. *v.a.* streitig machen.

Debauch, I. *v.a.* verführen. II. *s.* die Ausschweifung. **—ed,** *adj.* liederlich. **—ee,** *s.* der Wüstling, Schwelger.

Debenture, *s.* der Schuldschein.

Debit, I. *s.* das Soll. II. *v.a.* in das Soll eintragen.

Débris, *s.* die Trümmer.

Debt, *s.* die Schuld; to contract —s, Schulden machen. **—or,** *s.* der Schuldner.

Decaden—ce, *s.* der Verfall. **—t,** *adj.* verfallend.

Decamp, *v.n.* sich davon machen.

Decant, *v.a.* umfüllen. **—er,** *s.* die Karaffe.

Decapitat—e, *v.a.* enthaupten, köpfen. **—ion,** *s.* die Enthauptung, das Köpfen.

Decay, I. *v.n.* verfallen. II. *s.* der Verfall.

Decease, I. *s.* das Hinscheiden, der Tod. II. *v.n.* sterben.

Deceit, *s.* die Täuschung, der Trug. **—ful,** *adj.,* **—fully,** *adv.* betrügerisch. **—fulness,** *s.* die Betrüglichkeit.

Deceive, *v.a.* betrügen. **—r,** *s.* der Betrüger.

December, *s.* der Dezember.

Decen—cy, *s.* der Anstand. **—t,** *adj.,* **—tly,** *adv.* schicklich, anständig.

Decepti—on, *s.* der Betrug. **—ve,** *adj.* betrüglich.

Decide, *v.* I. *a.* entscheiden. II. *n.* (sich) entscheiden. **—d,** *adj.,* **—dly,** *adv.* entschieden, bestimmt.

Decimal, *adj.* zehnteilig, dezimal.

Decipher, *v.a.* entziffern.

Decisi—on, *s.* die Entscheidung. **—ve,** *adj.,* **—vely,** *adv.* entscheidend, ausschlaggebend; entschieden (*of persons*). **—veness,** *s.* die Entschiedenheit.

Deck, I. *v.a.* schmücken. II. *s.* das Deck, Verdeck. **—chair,** *s.* der Liegestuhl.

Declaim, *v.* I. *a.* laut vortragen. II. *n.* deklamieren.

Declamat—ion, *s.* die Deklamation. **—ory,** *adj.* rednerisch.

Declar—ation, *s.* die Erklärung; die Angabe (*Customs*). **—e,** *v.* I. *a.* erklären. II. *n.*; to —e (for, against), sich erklären (für, gegen). **—ed,** *adj.* offen.

Declension, *s.* die Abweichung, der Verfall; die Deklination (*Gram.*).

Declin—able, *adj.* veränderlich, beklinierbar. **—e,** I. *v.a.* (bend down) neigen, biegen; deklinieren (*Gram.*); (refuse) ablehnen. II. *v.n.* sich niederbeugen; (refuse) sich weigern; fallen (*as prices*); abnehmen (*as strength*). III. *s.* der Niedergang, Verfall.

Decliv—ity, *s.* der Abhang. **—itous, —ous,** *adj.* abhängig, abschüssig.

Decode, *v.a.* entziffern.

Decompose, *v.n.* verwesen.

Decor—ate, *v.a.* schmücken, zieren. **—ation,** *s.* die Verzierung; der Schmuck, Zierrat. **—ative,** *adj.* verschönernd. **—ator,** *s.* der Verzierer. **—ous,** *adj.,* **—ously,** *adv.* schicklich, anständig. **—um,** *s.* der Anstand.

Decoy, I. *v.a.* locken; (*fig.*) (ver-)locken. II. *s.* die Lockung; der Köder. **—bird,** *s.* der Lockvogel.

Decrease, I. *v.n.* abnehmen. II. *v.a.* verringern, vermindern. III. *s.* die Abnahme, Verminderung.

Decree, I. *s.* die Vorschrift, das Dekret. II. *v.a.* (einen Beschluß) erlassen; verordnen.

Decrepit, *adj.* abgelebt. **—ude,** *s.* die Abgelebtheit.

Decry, *v.a.* verschreien, verrufen, tadeln.

Dedicat—e, I. *v.a.* weihen; widmen. II. *adj.*, **—ed,** *adj.* geweiht; gewidmet. **—ion,** *s.* die Widmung; die Zueignung (*of a book*). **—ory,** *adj.* widmend, zueignend.

Deduc—e, *v.a.* schließen. **—t,** *v.a.* abziehen. **—tion,** *s.* das Abziehen; der Abzug.

Deed, *s.* die Tat; (document) die Urkunde, der Kontrakt.

Deem, *v.n.* urteilen, vermuten, halten für, denken, beurteilen.

Deep, I. *adj.*, **—ly,** *adv.* tief. II. *s.* die Tiefe. **—en,** *v.* I. *a.* vertiefen. II. *n.* sich vertiefen. **—ness,** *s.* die Tiefe. **—sea,** *s.* die Tiefsee.

Deer, *s.* das Rotwild, Wild. **—stalking,** *s.* Pirschen auf Rotwild.

Deface, *v.a.* entstellen.

Defam—ation, *s.* die Verleumdung. **—atory,** *adj.* verleumderisch. **—e,** *v.a.* verleumden. **—er,** *s.* der Verleumder, Lästerer.

Default, *s.* (omission) die Vernachlässigung; (fault) der Fehler; in — whereof, in Ermangelung dessen. **—er,** *s.* der Pflichtvergessene.

Defeat, I. *s.* die Niederlage. II. *v.a.* schlagen, überwinden (*an army*).

Defect, *s.* der Makel, Flecken. **—ion,** *s.* die Abtrünnigkeit. **—ive,** *adj.* mangelhaft. **—iveness,** *s.* die Fehlerhaftigkeit.

Defen—ce, *s.* die Verteidigung. **—celess,** *adj.* schutzlos, wehrlos. **—celessness,** *s.* die Schutzlosigkeit. **—d,** *v.a.* schützen, verteidigen. **—dant,** *s.* der (die) Angeklagte (*Law*). **—der,** *s.* der Verteidiger. **—sive,** I. *adj.*, **—sively,** *adv.* verteidigend, schützend. II. *s.* die Defensive.

¹Defer, *v.a.* aufschieben. **—ment,** *s.* der Aufschub, die Verschiebung.

²Defer, *v.a.* dem Urteile eines andern überlassen. **—ence,** *s.* die Achtung, Ehrerbietung; in —ence to, aus Rücksicht gegen. **—ential,** *adj.*, **—entially,** *adv.* ehrerbietig.

Defi—ance, *s.* der Trotz, Hohn. **—ant,** *adj.*, **—antly,** *adv.* trotzig, herausfordernd. **—er,** *s.* der Trotzende.

Deficien—cy, *s.* die Mangelhaftigkeit. **—t,** *adj.*, **—tly,** *adv.* ungenügend (in a thing, an einer S.); to be —t in, Mangel haben an (*dat.*).

¹Defile, I. *v.n.* defilieren (*Mil.*). II. *s.* der Engpaß.

²Defile, *v.a.* beflecken, besudeln; (violate) schänden, entehren. **—ment,** *s.* die Befleckung; die Schändung. **—r,** *s.* der Entweiher; der Schänder.

Defin—e, *v.a.* (fix bounds) begrenzen; erklären (*words*); bestimmen, definieren (*ideas, etc.*). **—er,** *s.* der Bestimmende. **—ite,** *adj.*, **—itely,** *adv.* bestimmt; ausdrücklich, deutlich. **—iteness,** *s.* die Bestimmtheit. **—ition,** *s.* die Begriffsbestimmung. **—itive,** *adj.*, **—itively,** *adv.* (positive) bestimmt, entschieden; (final) endgültig.

Deflect, *v.* I. *a.* ablenken. II. *n.* abweichen.

Deform, I. *v.a.* verunstalten. **—ed,** *adj.* entstellt, verunstaltet, mißgestaltet. **—ity,** die Mißgestalt.

Defraud, *v.a.* betrügen. **—er,** *s.* der Betrüger.

Defray, *v.a.*; to — expenses, die Kosten tragen.

Deft, *adj.*, **—ly,** *adv.* geschickt, gewandt. **—ness,** *s.* die Gewandtheit.

Defunct, I. *adj.* verstorben. II. *s.* der Verstorbene.

Defy, *v.a.* trotzen.

Degenera—cy, *s.* die Entartung. **—te,** I. *v.n.* entarten. II. *adj.*, **—tely,** *adv.* entartet; (depraved) verkommen.

Degrad—ation, *s.* (removal from office, *etc.*) die Absetzung, Entsetzung; (debasement) die Erniedrigung, Herabwürdigung; die Degradation (*Mil.*). **—e,** *v.a.* absetzen, entsetzen; herabwürdigen, entehren. **—ed,** *adj.* erniedrigt; (*fig.*) heruntergekommen. **—ing,** *adj.* entehrend.

Degree, *s.* der Grad; (rank) der Rang, Stand; by —s, allmählich; to a —, bis zu einem gewissen Grade; to take one's —, einen akademischen Grad erlangen.

Dei—fication, *s.* die Vergötterung. **—fy,** *v.a.* vergöttern (*also fig.*).

Deign, *v.* I. *n.* geruhen. II. *a.* (grant) gewähren; (think worthy of) würdigen.

Deity, *s.* die Gottheit; der Gott.

Deject—ed, *adj.*, **—edly,** *adv.* niedergeschlagen. **—ion,** *s.* die Niedergeschlagenheit, die Schwermut.

Delay, I. *v.a.* verzögern, aufschieben, verschieben; (keep back) hindern, hinhalten. II. *v.n.* zögern, zaudern. III. *s.* die Verzögerung; der Aufschub.

Delegat—e, I. *v.a.* überweisen, übertragen. II. *adj.* abgeordnet. III. *s.* der Beauftragte, Abgeordnete. **—ion,** *s.* die Überweisung, Übertragung.

Delf, *s.* das Delfter Porzellan.

Deliberat—e, I. *v.a. & n.* erwägen, bedenken. II. *v.n.* (hesitate) sich bedenken. III. *adj.,* **—ely,** *adv.* besonnen; umsichtig. **—eness,** *s.* die Bedachtigkeit. **—ion,** *s.* die Überlegung; die Berat(schlag)ung. **—ive,** *adj.* beratschlagend.

Delica—cy, *s.* die Köstlichkeit; der Leckerbissen, die Delikatesse; die Feinheit, Zartheit; die Schwächlichkeit (*of health*). **—te,** *adj.,* **—tely,** *adv.* (pleasing to the taste) schmackhaft, köstlich; (refined) fein, zart; (sickly, weak) schwächlich; (difficult, nice) kitzlich, bedenklich.

Delicious, *adj.,* **—ly,** *adv.* köstlich. **—ness,** *s.* die Köstlichkeit.

Delight, I. *s.* die Lust, das Vergnügen. II. *v.a.* ergötzen, erfreuen. III. *v.n.* sich erfreuen, sich ergötzen (in, an). **—ed,** *adj.* höchst erfreut, entzückt. **—ful,** *adj.,* **—fully,** *adv.* höchst erfreulich, entzückend. **—fulness,** *s.* die Ergötzlichkeit; die Wonne.

Delineat—e, *v.a.* entwerfen, malen, schildern. **—ion,** *s.* der Entwurf, die Schilderung.

Delinquent, *s.* der Missetäter, Verbrecher.

Deliri—ous, *adj.,* **—ously,** *adv.* wahnsinnig. **—um,** *s.* der Wahnsinn, Irrsinn.

Deliver, *v.a.* (set free) befreien; (— up) übergeben, überreichen; (hand over, give) abliefern; abgeben (*letters*); überbringen (*a message*); äußern (*an opinion*); halten (*a speech, etc.*). **—ance,** *s.* die Befreiung, Erlösung. **—er,** *s.* der Befreier; der Erretter, Erlöser. **—y,** *s.* die Befreiung; die Ablieferung, Abgabe (*of goods*).

Delta, *s.* das Delta (*Geog.*).

Delude, *v.a.* betrügen, täuschen, verleiten.

Deluge, I. *s.* die Überschwemmung; die Sündflut (*B.*). II. *v.a.* überfluten.

Delus—ion, *s.* die Täuschung, Verblendung. **—ive,** *adj.,* **—ively,** *adv.* (be)trügerisch, täuschend.

Delve, *v.n.* graben; (*fig.*) untersuchen.

Demagog—ic(al), *adj.* demagogisch. **—ue,** *s.* der Demagoge; der Aufwiegler.

Demand, I. *v.a.* verlangen, fordern. II. *s.* das Verlangen, Begehren; in —, begehrt, gesucht; on —, auf Verlangen. **—er,** *s.* der Forderer.

Demean, *v.r.* sich benehmen. **—our,** *s.* das Benehmen.

Demented, *adj.* wahnsinnig, toll.

Demi— (*in comp.* =) halb. **—god,** *s.* der Halbgott.

Demobiliz—ation, *s.* (*Mil.*) die Abrüstung, Demobilisierung. **—e,** *v.a.* abrüsten (Truppen).

Democra—cy, *s.* die Demokratie. **—t,** *s.* der Demokrat. **—tic(al),** *adj.,* **—tically,** *adv.* demokratisch.

Demoli—sh, *v.a.* niederreißen. **—tion,** *s.* die Zerstörung, Vernichtung.

Demon, *s.* der Dämon. **—iac,** *s.* der Besessene. **—iacal,** *adj.* dämonisch.

Demonstra—ble, *adj.,* **—bly,** *adv.* beweisbar. **—te,** *v.* I. *a.* beweisen (from, aus). II. *a. & n.* durch Vorzeigen erklären. **—tion,** *s.* (proving) das Beweisen; (proof) der Beweis. **—tive,** *adj.,* **—tively,** *adv.* beweiskräftig. **—tor,** *s.* der Beweisführer.

Demoraliz—ation, *s.* die Entsittlichung. **—e,** *v.a.* entsittlichen.

Demur, I. *v.n.* Anstand nehmen. II. *s.* der Zweifel, Skrupel.

Demure, *adj.,* **—ly,** *adv.* gesetzt; (prim) zimperlich, spröde. **—ness,** *s.* die Gesetztheit; die Sprödigkeit.

Den, *s.* die Höhle; das Lager.

Deni—able, *adj.,* verneinbar, zu verneinen. **—al,** *s* die Verneinung. **—er,** *s.* der Leugner.

Denizen, *s.* der Bewohner.

Denominat—e, *v.a.* (be)nennen. **—ion,** *s.* die Benennung; (sect) die Sekte. **—ional,** *adj.* sektiererisch. **—or,** *s.* der Nenner (*Arith.*).

Denote, *v.a.* bedeuten, bezeichnen.

Dénouement, *s.* die Entwickelung.

Denounce, *v.a.* anzeigen, denunzieren.

Dens—e, *adj.,* **—ely,** *adv.* dicht, fest; dick (*as a fog*). **—eness,** *s.* die Dichtigkeit; (*fig.*) die Beschränktheit. **—ity,** *s.* die Dichtheit.

Dent, I. *s.* die Kerbe. II. *v.a.* (aus-) kerben, zacken.

Dent—al, *adj.* zu den Zähnen ge=
hörig, Zahn=. **—ifrice,** *s.* das Zahn=
pulver. **—ist,** *s.* der Zahnarzt. **—
istry,** *s.* die Zahnheilkunde.

Denude, *v.a.* entblößen; (*fig.*) berauben.

Denunciat—ion, *s.* das Angeben,
die Angabe; der Tadel. **—ory,** *adj.*
tadelnd, rügend.

Deny, *v.a.* verneinen; (disavow) leug=
nen; (refuse) verweigern, abschlagen;
to — oneself a pleasure, einem Ver=
gnügen entsagen.

Depart, *v.* I. *n.* abreisen, abfahren (for,
nach); scheiden, sich trennen (from,
von); sterben; the —ed, die Hinge=
schiedenen. II. *a.* verlassen. **—ment,**
s. der Geschäftskreis, das Fach; die
Abteilung. **—mental,** *adj.* Abtei=
lungs=, Fach=. **—ure,** *s.* die Abreise,
Abfahrt; das Verscheiden, Abscheiden
(*from this world*).

Depend, *v.a.* (ab)hängen, abhängig
sein (on, von); (rely on) sich verlassen,
sich stützen (upon a person, auf einen);
it —s, es kommt darauf an. **—able,**
adj. zuverlässig. **—ant,** *s.* der Ab=
hängige. **—ence, —ency,** *s.* das
Herabhängen; der Zusammenhang;
die Abhängigkeit (upon, von); (re=
liance) das Vertrauen (on, auf). **—
ent,** *adj.*, **—ently,** *adv.* abhängig (on,
von).

Depict, *v.a.* (ab)malen; (*fig.*) schildern,
beschreiben.

Deplet—e, *v.a.* entleeren; (*fig.*)
erschöpfen. **—ion,** *s.* (*fig.*) die Er=
schöpfung.

Deplor—able, *adj.*, **—ably,** *adv.* jam=
mervoll, kläglich. **—e,** *v.a.* beweinen,
betrauern, bejammern. **—er,** *s.* der
Bejammernde.

Deploy, *v.a.* & *n.* aufmarschieren
(*Mil.*). **—ment,** *s.* das Deployieren.

Depone, *v.a.* deponieren. **—nt,** I. *adj.*
deponierend. II. *s.* der Deponent.

Depopulat—e, *v.a.* entvölkern. **—ion,**
s. die Entvölkerung.

Deport, *v.a.* verbannen; to — oneself,
sich benehmen. **—ation,** *s.* die Ver=
bannung. **—ment,** *s.* das Benehmen,
Betragen.

Depos—able, *adj.* absetzbar. **—e,** *v.a.*
(*fig.*) absetzen, entsetzen; entthronen
(*a king, etc.*).

Deposit, I. *s.* der Niederschlag (*Geol.,
Phys., Chem.*); die Einlage (*C.L.*).
II. *v.a.* absetzen; einlegen (*money*).

Deposition, *s.* die eidliche Zeugenaus=
sage; die Absetzung, Entsetzung (*from
an office, etc.*); die Entthronung.

Depos—itor, *s.* der Depositor, Einleger.
—itory, *s.* der Niederlageort.

Depot, *s.* die Niederlage (*C.L.*), das
Lagerhaus.

Deprav—e, *v.a.* verführen, verschlech=
tern. **—ed,** *adj.* moralisch verdorben.
—ity, *s.* die Verdorbenheit; die Ver=
worfenheit.

Deprecat—e, *v.a.* abbitten; (regret)
bedauern. **—ion,** *s.* die Abbitte.
—ory, *adj.* abbittend.

Depreciat—e, *v.* I. *a.* herabsetzen
(*prices*); (*fig.*) herabwürdigen, gering=
schätzen. II. *n.* im Werte sinken.
—ion, *s.* die Verringerung (*of the
value, etc.*); die Entwertung. **—ory,**
adj. geringschätzig.

Depredat—ion, *s.* das Rauben, Plün=
dern. **—or,** *s.* der Plünderer. **—ory,**
adj. plündernd, verheerend.

Depress, *v.a.* niederdrücken; nieder=
schlagen (*one's spirits*). **—ed,** *p.p.*
& *adj.* niedergeschlagen. **—ion,** *s.*
die Niederdrückung; die Flauheit
(*of trade*); die Abspannung.

Depriv—ation, *s.* der Verlust. **—e,**
v.a. (einem etwas) benehmen, entzie=
hen.

Depth, *s.* die Tiefe (*also fig.*).

Deput—ation, *s.* die Abordnung.
—e, *v.a.* abordnen. **—y,** *s.* der Ab=
geordnete, Abgesandte; der Stellver=
treter (*Law*).

Derail, *v.a.* entgleisen lassen.

Derange, *v.a.* verwirren, stören. **—
ment,** *s.* die Unordnung; die Geistes=
störung.

Derelict, I. *adj.* verlassen. II. *s.*
treibendes Wrack. **—ion,** *s.* das
Verlassen; —ion of duty, die Pflicht=
vergessenheit.

Deri—de, *v.a.* verlachen, verhöhnen,
verspotten. **—der,** *s.* der Spötter,
Verhöhner. **—sion,** *s.* die Verspot=
tung. **—sive,** *adj.*, **—sively,** *adv.*
spöttisch, höhnisch.

Deriv—able, *adj.* ableitbar. **—ation,**
s. die Ableitung. **—ative,** I. *adj.*,
—atively, *adv.* abgeleitet, hergeleitet.
II. *s.* das Derivatum (*Gram.*). **—e,**
v.a. ableiten, herleiten; to —e profit
from, Nutzen ziehen aus.

Derogat—ion, *s.* die Herabwürdigung.
—ory, *adj.* beeinträchtigend.

Dervish, *s.* der Derwisch.

Descend, *v.n.* (get down from) herab=, herunter=steigen, =kommen (von); (spring) abstammen, herkommen; (abase oneself) sich herablassen, sich erniedrigen. **—ant,** der Abkömmling.

Descen—sion, *s.* das Herabsteigen. **—t,** *s.* das Herabsteigen; das Fallen; die Neigung (*Surv., Build.*); (ancestry) die Abstammung; (slope) der Abhang.

Describ—able, *adj.* beschreiblich. **—e,** *v.a.* beschreiben; schildern, darstellen.

Descripti—on, *s.* die Beschreibung; die Schilderung, Darstellung. **—ve,** *adj.* beschreibend, schildernd.

Descry, *v.a.* entdecken.

Desecrat—e, *v.a.* entweihen, entheiligen. **—ion,** *s.* die Entweihung, Entheiligung.

¹**Desert,** I. *adj.* wüst, öde. II. *s.* die Wüste, Einöde. III. *v.a.* verlassen; to — a cause, einer Sache untreu werden. IV. *v.n.* fahnenflüchtig werden, desertieren. **—er,** *s.* der Ausreißer. **—ion,** *s.* das Verlassen (*of a place, etc.*); die Fahnenflucht, Desertion.

²**Desert,** *s.* (*also* —s) das Verdienste, der Lohn.

Deserv—e, *v.a.* verdienen. **—ed,** *adj.* verdient. **—edly,** *adv.* verdienter Weise, nach Verdienst. **—ing,** *adj.* verdient.

Design, I. *v.a.* (sketch) entwerfen; (intend) beabsichtigen, vorhaben. II. *s.* (intention) die Absicht; die Anordnung, Einteilung (*of a work*); (drawing) die Zeichnung; (pattern) das Muster; with the —, in der Absicht; school of —, die Zeichenschule. **—ed,** *adj.,* **—edly,** *adv.* absichtlich. **—er,** *s.* der Zeichner; (planner) der Projektenmacher; (plotter) der Ränkeschmied. **—ing,** *adj.* hinterlistig, ränkevoll.

Designat—e, *v.a.* bezeichnen. **—ion,** *s.* die Bezeichnung; die Ernennung.

Desir—able, *adj.,* **—ably,** *adv.* wünschenswert; erwünscht. **—ability,** — **ableness,** *s.* die Erwünschtheit. **—e,** I. *v.a.* verlangen, begehren; (beg) ersuchen; (bid) befehlen, heißen. II. *s.* das Verlangen, die Sehnsucht. **—ous,** *adj.* begierig (of, nach).

Desist, *v.n.* ablassen.

Desk, *s.* das Pult.

Desolat—e, I. *adj.,* **—ely,** *adv.* einsam; (waste) wüst, öde; (sad) traurig; (uninhabited) unbewohnt. II. *v.a.* verwüsten, verheeren. **—ion,** *s.* die Verödung, Verwüstung; das Elend.

Despair, I. *s.* die Verzweiflung. II. *v.n.;* to — of, verzweifeln an (*dat.*). **—ing,** *adj.,* **—ingly,** *adv.* verzweifelnd.

Desperado, *s.* der Wagehals.

Despera—te, *adj.,* **—tely,** *adv.* verzweifelt; (reckless) verwegen. **—tion,** *s.* die Verzweiflung.

Despicabl—e, *adj.,* **—y,** *adv.* verächtlich, jämmerlich.

Despise, *v.a.* verachten, geringschätzen.

Despite, I. *s.* die Verachtung; in his own —, sich selbst zum Trotz. II. *prep.* (*or comp. prep.* — of) trotz.

Despoil, *v.a.* plündern, berauben.

Despond, *v.n.* verzagen. **—ency,** *s.* die Verzagtheit. **—ent,** **—ing,** *adj.,* **—ently,** **—ingly,** *adv.* ganz verzagt.

Despot, *s.* der Zwingherr, Despot. **—ic,** *adj.,* **—ically,** *adv.* despotisch. **—ism,** *s.* der Despotismus.

Dessert, *s.* der Nachtisch.

Destin—ation, *s.* der Bestimmungsort. **—e,** *v.a.* bestimmen. **—y,** *s.* das Schicksal; the **—ies,** die Schicksalsgöttinnen, die Parzen.

Destitut—e, *adj.* verlassen, hilflos. **—ion,** *s.* die bittere Not.

Destroy, *v.a.* zerstören, vernichten. **—er,** *s.* der Zerstörer. **—ing,** I. *p. & adj.* vernichtend, verheerend. II. *s.* die Zerstörung, Vernichtung.

Destructi—bility, *s.* die Zerstörbarkeit. **—ble,** *adj.* zerstörbar. **—on,** *s.* die Zerstörung, Vernichtung, Verwüstung. **—ve,** *adj.,* **—vely,** *adv.* zerstörend. **—veness,** *s.* der Zerstörungssinn.

Detach, *v.a.* losmachen, ablösen. **—able,** *adj.* abnehmbar. **—ed,** *adj.* alleinstehend; abgeschnitten, abgesondert; —ed house, ein freistehendes Haus. **—ment,** *s.* die Absonderung, Trennung; die Abteilung (*Mil.*).

Detail, I. *v.a.* umständlich darstellen; abkommandieren (*Mil.*). II. *s.* das Einzelne, die Einzelheit. **—ed,** *p.p. & adj.* eingehend, umständlich, ausführlich.

Detain, *v.a.* zurückhalten, verhindern; festhalten (*in prison*). **—er,** *s.* der Zurückhaltende.

Detect, *v.a.* ertappen, entdecken. **—ion,** *s.* die Entdeckung. **—ive,** *s.* der Geheimpolizist. **—or-valve,** *s.* die Audionröhre (*Radio*).

Detention, *s.* die Zurückhaltung, Vorenthaltung; (confinement) der Verhaft.

Deter, *v.a.* verhindern. **—ment,** *s.* das Hindernis. **—rent,** *adj.* abschreckend.

Deteriorat—e, *v.n.* sich verschlimmern, an wert verlieren. **—ion,** *s.* die Verschlimmerung, Entartung.

Determin—able, *adj.* bestimmbar. **—ate,** *adj.,* **—ately,** *adv.* festgesetzt. **—ation,** *s.* die Entschlossenheit, Entschiedenheit; (resolve) der Entschluß. **—e,** *v.a.* bestimmen, entscheiden. **—ed,** *adj.* entschlossen.

Detest, *v.a.* verabscheuen, hassen. **—able,** *adj.,* **—ably,** *adv.* abscheulich. **—ation,** *s.* der Abscheu (of, vor).

Dethrone, *v.a.* entthronen. **—ment,** *s.* die Entthronung.

Detonat—e, *v.n.* verpuffen. **—ion,** *s.* die Verpuffung. **—or,** *s.* der Puffer.

Detour, *s.* der Umweg.

Detract, *v.a.* abziehen, entziehen. **—ion,** *s.* die Herabsetzung, Beeinträchtigung. **—ive,** *adj.* verleumderisch. **—or,** *s.* der Verleumder.

Detriment, *s.* der Nachteil. **—al,** *adj.,* **—ally,** *adv.* schädlich, nachteilig.

Deuce, *s.* die Zwei; (tennis) der Einstand; der Teufel. **—d,** *adj.* verteufelt.

Devastat—e, *v.a.* verwüsten. **—ion,** *s.* die Verwüstung, Verheerung.

Develop, *v.* I. *a.* entwickeln, entfalten; entwickeln (a photograph). II. *n.* sich entwickeln. **—er,** *s.* das Entwickelungsmittel (*Phot.*). **—ment,** *s.* die Entwickelung, Entfaltung.

Deviat—e, *v.n.* abweichen (from, von). **—ion,** *s.* die Abweichung.

Device, *s.* die Erfindung; der Plan; der Kunstgriff.

Devil, *s.* der Teufel. **—ish,** *adj.,* **—ishly,** *adv.* teuflisch. **—may-care,** *adj.* sorglos, verwegen.

Devious, *adj.,* **—ly,** *adv.* herumirrend. **—ness,** *s.* das Umherschweifen.

Devis—able, *adj.,* erdenkbar, erfindbar. **—e,** *v.a.* ersinnen, erdenken, erfinden. **—er,** *s.* der Erfinder.

Devoid, *adj.* ohne (acc.), leer (an einer S.), **-los.**

Devol—ution, *s.* die Abwälzung. **—ve,** *v.* I. *a.* abwälzen; übertragen. II. *n.* zufallen.

Devot—e, *v.a.* widmen, weihen. **—ed,** *adj.* geweiht. **—edly,** *adv.* ergeben. **—ion,** *s.* die Frömmigkeit; (prayer) die Andacht; (affection) die Ergebenheit. **—ional,** *adj.,* **—ionally,** *adv.* andächtig, fromm.

Devour, *v.a.* verschlingen.

Devout, *adj.,* **—ly,** *adv.* andächtig, fromm. **—ness,** *s.* die Frömmigkeit.

Dew, *s.* der Tau.

Dexter—ity, *s.* die Behendigkeit. **—ous,** *adj.,* **—ously,** *adv.* behende; gewandt; geschickt.

Diabetes, *s.* die Zuckerkrankheit.

Diaboli—c(al), *adj.,* **—cally,** *adv.* teuflisch.

Dia—dem, *s.* das Diadem. **—gnosis,** *s.* die Diagnose. **—gonal,** I. *adj.,* **—gonally,** *adv.* diagonal, schräg. II. *s.* die Diagonale. **—gram,** *s.* die Figur.

Dial, *s.* die Sonnenuhr; das Zifferblatt (of a clock, etc.).

Dia—lect, *s.* die Mundart. **—logue,** *s.* das Zwiegespräch. **—meter,** *s.* der Durchmesser. **—metrical,** *adj.,* **—metrically,** *adv.* diametrisch.

Diamond, *s.* der Diamant; das Karo (*Cards*).

Dia—phragm, *s.* das Zwerchfell (*Anat.*). **—rrhœa,** *s.* der Durchfall.

Diary, *s.* das Tagebuch.

Dice, I. *s. pl.* (see Die) die Würfel. II. *v.a.* würfeln.

Dict—ate, *v.* I. *a.* vorschreiben; diktieren. II. *n.* in die Feder diktieren; befehlen. **—ates,** *pl.* die Eingebungen. **—ation,** *s.* das Diktieren. **—ator,** *s.* der Diktator. **—atorial,** *adj.,* **—atorially,** *adv.* gebieterisch. **—atorship,** *s.* die Diktatur. **—ion,** *s.* die Ausdrucksweise. **—ionary,** *s.* das Wörterbuch.

Didactic, *adj.,* **—ally,** *adv.* didaktisch.

¹Die, *v.n.* sterben (of, an (dat.); from, vor); never say **—!** verzweifle nie! to **— away,** schwächer werden, verhallen.

²Die, *s.* der Würfel; (stamp) der (Münz-)Stempel.

Diet, I. *s.* die Lebensweise; die Speise; (public assembly) der Landtag, Reichstag. II. *v.a.* (einem) Diät vorschreiben; (feed) beköstigen. III. *v.n.* Diät halten.

Differ, *v.n.* (be different) sich unterscheiden, verschieden sein; (not agree)

nicht übereinstimmen (with, mit).
—ence, *s.* der Unterschied, die Verschiedenheit. —ent, *adj.,* —ently,
adv. verschieden.

Difficult, *adj.* schwer, schwierig.

Diffiden—ce, *s.* die Schüchernheit.
—t, *adj.,* —tly, *adv.* schüchtern, bescheiden, mißtrauisch.

Diffus—e, I. *adj.,* —ely, *adv.* weitschweifig, weitläufig. II. *v.a.* aus-
schütten, ausgießen. —ed, *adj.* verbreitet, zerstreut. —eness, *s.* die
Weitläufigkeit. —ion, *s.* die Verbreitung. —ive, *adj.,* —ively, *adv.*
weitschweifig; ausgedehnt.

Dig, I. *ir.v.a.* graben; ausgraben.
II. *ir.v.n.* graben; to — for (a thing),
(einer S.) nachgraben. —ger, *s.* der
Grabende, Gräber. —ging, *s.* das
Graben.

Digest, *v.a.* verdauen. —ible, *adj.*
verdaulich. —ibility, *s.* die Ver-
daulichkeit. —ion, *s.* die Verdauung.

Digni—fied, *adj.* würdevoll. —fy,
v.a. verherrlichen, ehren. —tary, *s.*
der Würdenträger. —ty, *s.* die
Würde.

Digress, *v.n.* abschweifen. —ion, *s.*
die Abschweifung. —ive, *adj.,* —
ively, *adv.* abschweifend.

Dike, I. *s.* der Deich, Damm. II. *v.a.*
eindeichen, eindämmen.

Dilapidat—e, *v.n.* verfallen. —ed,
adj. baufällig. —ion, *s.* der Verfall.

Dilat—ion, *s.* die Erweiterung. —e,
v. I. *a.* ausdehnen, erweitern. II. *n.*
sich ausdehnen, erweitern; to — upon
a thing, weitläufig über eine Sache
sprechen. —orily, *adv.,* —ory, *adj.*
aufschiebend, verzögernd. —oriness,
s. die Saumseligkeit.

Dilemma, *s.* das Dilemma (*Log.*); die
Verlegenheit, Klemme.

Diligen—ce, *s.* die Emsigkeit, der
Fleiß. —t, *adj.,* —tly, *adv.* fleißig,
emsig.

Dilu—te, I. *v.a.* verdünnen; (*fig.*)
schwächen. II. *adj.,* —ted, *adj.* ver-
dünnt; geschwächt. —tion, *s.* die
Verdünnung. —vial, —vian, *adj.*
diluvianisch, Diluvial-.

Dim, I. *adj.,* —ly, *adv.* trübe, düster,
dunkel; (not clear) undeutlich. II.
v.a. verdunkeln; (*fig.*) trüben. —
ness, *s.* die Düsterheit.

Dimension, *s.* die Ausdehnung; der
Umfang.

Dimin—ish, *v.* I. *a.* vermindern, verringern. II. *n.* sich vermindern.
—ution, *s.* die Verkleinerung. —
utive, I. *adj.,* —utively, *adv.* klein,
winzig. II. *s.* das Verkleinerungs-
wort (*Gram.*). —utiveness, *s.* die
Geringfügigkeit.

Dimple, *s.* das Grübchen.

Din, *s.* das Getöse.

Din—e, *v.* I. *n.* zu Mittag essen. II.
a. zu Mittag bewirten. —er, *s.* der
Speisende.

Ding—ily, *adv.,* —y, *adj.* schwärzlich.
—iness, *s.* die düstere Farbe.

Dinner, *s.* das Mittagessen. —jacket,
s. der Smoking.

Dint, I. *s.* der Schlag; by — of, kraft,
vermöge. II. *v.a.* eindrücken.

Dioces—an, I. *adj.* Diözesan-. II. *s.*
der Diözesan (=Bischof). —e, *s.* der
Kirchensprengel.

Dip, I. *v.a.* (ein)tauchen, eintunken (in,
into, in). II. *v.n.* (unter)tauchen.
III. *s.* (—ping) das Eintauchen;
(slope) der Abhang. —ping, *s.* das
Eintauchen.

Diphtheri—a, *s.* die Diphtheritis.
—tic, *adj.* diphtheritisch.

Diphthong, *s.* der Diphthong, Dop-
pellaut.

Diploma, *s.* das Diplom. —cy, *s.*
die Diplomatie. —tic, *adj.,* —tically, *adv.* diplomatisch. —tist, *s.*
der Diplomat.

Dire, *adj.* schrecklich, grausam.

Direct, I. *adj.* gerade, direkt. II. *v.a.*
richten (*one's course, etc.*); zielen;
(point out) hinweisen; (conduct) einrichten, leiten, führen; (order) anordnen. —ion, *s.* die Richtung (*also fig.*).
—ion-finder, *s.* der Peiler (*Radio*).
—ly, *adv.* gerade; gleich, unmittelbar; (promptly) ohne Verzug; geradezu. —ness, *s.* die Bestimmtheit;
die Geradheit. —or, *s.* der Direktor,
Leiter, Führer, Vorsteher. —orate,
s. das Direktorat; der Vorstand.
—ory, *s.* das Adreßbuch. —ress, *s.*
die Vorsteherin.

Dirge, *s.* das Klagelied.

Dirigible, *s.* ein lenkbares Luftschiff.

Dirt, *s.* der Schmutz, Kot. —y, I.
adj. schmutzig, unflätig. II. *v.a.* beschmutzen, besudeln.

Disab—ility, *s.* die Unfähigkeit, Untüchtigkeit. —le, *v.a.* unfähig, untüchtig, unbrauchbar machen. —led,

adj. unfähig, untauglich; —led soldier, der Invalide. **—lement,** *s.* die Entkräftung.

Disabuse, *v.a.* enttäuschen.

Disaccustom, *v.a.* abgewöhnen.

Disadvantage, *s.* der Nachteil; to sell to —, mit Verlust verkaufen. **—ous,** *adj.,* **—ously,** *adv.* nachteilig, schädlich.

Disaffect, *v.a.* abgeneigt, abspenstig machen; (cause to desert) abtrünnig machen. **—ed,** *adj.* unzufrieden. **—ion,** *s.* (discontentment) das Mißvergnügen; (ill will) der Widerwille, die Abgeneigtheit.

Disagree, *v.n.* (differ in opinion) verschiedener Meinung sein; (quarrel) streiten; the food —s with me, die Speise bekommt mir nicht, ist mir zuwider. **—able,** *adj.,* **—ably,** *adv.* unangenehm; (annoying) verdrießlich. **—ableness,** *s.* das Unangenehme, Widrige. **—ment,** *s.* die Verschiedenheit (*in form, etc.*); (quarrel) der Streit.

Disallow, *v.a.* nicht gelten lassen, verwerfen.

Disappear, *v.n.* verschwinden. **—ance,** *s.* das Verschwinden.

Disappoint, *v.a.* täuschen, vereiteln (*hopes, etc.*); enttäuschen (a person); to — a person, jemanden im Stich lassen. **—ment,** *s.* die Täuschung; —ment in love, unglückliche Liebe.

Disapprobation, *s.* die Mißbilligung.

Disapprov—al, *s.* die Mißbilligung. **—e,** *v.a.* mißbilligen.

Disarm, *v.* I. *a.* entwaffnen. II. *n.* abrüsten. **—ament,** *s.* die Entwaffnung; die Abrüstung.

Disarrange, *v.a.* in Unordnung bringen. **—ment,** *s.* die Unordnung, Verwirrung.

Disast—er, *s.* das Unglück, Mißgeschick, der Unfall. **—rous,** *adj.,* **—rously,** *adv.* unglücklich, unheilvoll. **—rousness,** *s.* die Un(glück)seligkeit.

Disavow, *v.a.* (ab)leugnen. **—al,** *s.* die Nichtanerkennung, das Ableugnen.

Disband, *v.a.* abdanken.

Disbelie—f, *s.* der Unglaube. **—ve,** *v.a.* nicht glauben. **—ver,** *s.* der Ungläubige.

Disburden, *v.a.* entbürden, entlasten.

Disburse, *v.a.* auszahlen, ausgeben. **—ment,** *s.* die Ausgabe, Auszahlung.

Discard, *v.a.* entlassen (*men*); ablegen (*prejudices, etc.*).

Discern, *v.* I. *a.* (discriminate) unterscheiden; (see) sehen; (judge) beurteilen. II. *n.* unterscheiden. **—ible,** *adj.,* **—ibly,** *adv.* unterscheidbar. **—ing,** *adj.,* **—ingly,** *adv.* scharfsinnig. **—ment,** *s.* das Unterscheiden; die Einsicht; der Scharfsinn.

Discharge, I. *v.a.* entladen, ausladen, ausschiffen (*goods, etc.*); abfeuern, losschießen (*gun*); abmachen, bezahlen (*debts, etc.*); verabschieden entlassen (*servants*); abdanken (*soldiers*); entlassen (a *jury, etc.*); erfüllen (one's duty, seine Pflicht). II. *s.* die Ausladung, Löschung; das Losschießen (*of firearms*); der Ausfluß; die Eiterung; die Bezahlung, Entrichtung (*C.L. etc.*); die Verabschiedung; die Entlassungsschrift; die Leistung (*of a duty*).

Discipl—e, *s.* der Jünger. **—inarian,** I. *adj.* disziplinarisch. II. *s.* der Zuchtmeister. **—ine,** I. *s.* die Zucht. II. *v.a.* in (die) Zucht nehmen.

Disclaim, *v.a.* nicht anerkennen, verleugnen. **—er,** *s.* der Verleugner; (renunciation) die Verzichtleistung; der Widerruf.

Disclos—e, *v.a.* enthüllen. **—er,** *s.* der Entdecker. **—ure,** *s.* die Enthüllung, Offenbarung.

Discolo—ration, *s.* die Verfärbung. **—ur,** *v.a.* die Farbe ändern; (*fig.*) entstellen.

Discomfit, *v.a.* verwirren. **—ure,** *s.* die Verwirrung.

Discomfort, *s.* das Mißbehagen.

Disconcert, *v.a.* verlegen machen, außer Fassung bringen.

Disconnect, *v.a.* trennen; entkuppeln (*Mach.*).

Disconsolate, *adj.,* **—ly,** *adv.* trostlos, untröstlich.

Discontent, *s.* die Unzufriedenheit, das Mißvergnügen. **—ed,** *adj.,* **—edly,** *adv.* unzufrieden, mißvergnügt.

Discontinu—ance, *s.* das Aufhören. **—e,** *v.* I. *a.* unterlassen, unterbrechen. II. *n.* aufhören, nachlassen.

Discord, *s.* die Zwietracht; der Mißklang (*Mus.*). **—ant,** *adj.,* **—antly,** *adv.* mißhellig, uneinig; mißklingend.

Discount, I. *s.* der Abzug, Rabatt (*C.L.*). II. *v.a.* diskontieren. **—er,** *s.* der Diskontierer.

Discourage, *v.a.* entmutigen. **—ment,** *s.* die Entmutigung.

Discourse, I. *s.* das Gespräch, die Abhandlung, der Vortrag. II. *v.n.* sich unterhalten.

Discourte—ous, *adj.,* **—ously,** *adv.* unhöflich, unmanierlich. **—sy,** *s.* die Unhöflichkeit.

Discover, *v.a.* entdecken, enthüllen, ertappen. **—able,** *adj.* entdeckbar. **—er,** *s.* der Entdecker. **—y,** *s.* die Entdeckung, Enthüllung (*of a plot*); die Offenbarung (*of a secret*).

Discredit, I. *s.* der schlechte Ruf. II. *v.a.* nicht glauben; in übeln Ruf bringen, verunglimpfen. **—able,** *adj.* entehrend, schimpflich.

Discreet, *adj.,* **—ly,** *adv.* verständig, umsichtig, verschwiegen.

Discrepan—cy, *s.* die Verschiedenheit. **—t,** *adj.,* **—tly,** *adv.* verschieden; widerstreitend.

Discretion, *s.* die Besonnenheit, der feine Takt; to surrender at —, sich auf Gnade und Ungnade ergeben. **—ary,** *adj.* willkürlich.

Discriminat—e, *v.a.* & *n.* unterscheiden. **—ing,** *adj.* unterscheidend. **—ion,** *s.* die Unterscheidung. **—ive,** *adj.,* **—ively,** *adv.* unterscheidend.

Discursive, *adj.,* **—ly,** *adv.* flüchtig, unzusammenhängend.

Discuss, *v.a.* erörtern, besprechen. **—ion,** *s.* die Erörterung.

Disdain, I. *s.* die Verachtung, Verschmähung, Geringschätzung. II. *v.a.* verachten, verschmähen. **—ful,** *adj.,* **—fully,** *adv.* verächtlich, verachtend.

Disease, *s.* die Krankheit. **—d,** *adj.* krank.

Disembark, *v.a.* & *n.* ausschiffen, landen. **—ation,** *s.* das Ausschiffen, die Landung.

Disembod—ied, *adj.* entkörpert. **—y,** *v.a.* entkörpern.

Disenchant, *v.a.* entzaubern. **—ment,** *s.* die Entzauberung.

Disengage, *v.a.* befreien. **—d,** *adj.* frei, unbeschäftigt.

Disentangle, *v.a.* entwirren. **—ment,** *s.* die Entwirrung.

Disfavour, *s.* die Ungunst, Ungnade.

Disfigur—ation, *s.* die Verunstaltung. **—e,** *v.a.* entstellen, verunstalten.

Disfranchise, *v.a.* (einem) das Wahlrecht nehmen. **—ment,** *s.* die Entziehung des Wahlrechts.

Disgorge, *v.a.* auswerfen.

Disgrace, I. *s.* die Ungnade; (dishonour) die Unehre, Schande. II. *v.a.* in Ungnade bringen; entehren. **—d,** *p.p.* & *adj.* in Ungnade (gefallen). **—ful,** *adj.,* **—fully,** *adv.* entehrend schändlich.

Disguise, I. *v.a.* verkleiden, vermummen; (*fig.*) verstellen. II. *s.* die Verkleidung.

Disgust, I. *s.* der Ekel, Widerwille. II. *v.a.* anekeln; to be —ed with, ärgerlich sein über (*Acc.*), Ekel haben an (*Dat.*). **—ing,** *adj.,* **—ingly,** *adv.* ekelhaft, widerlich.

Dish, I. *s.* die Schüssel. II. *v.a.*; to — up, anrichten, auftragen. **—cloth, —clout,** *s.* der Wischlappen. **—cover,** *s.* der Schüsseldeckel. **—water,** *s.* das Spülicht.

Dishearten, *v.a.* entmutigen.

Dishevel, *v.a.* auflösen (*hair*).

Dishonest, *adj.,* **—ly,** *adv.* unehrlich, unredlich. **—y,** *s.* die Unredlichkeit, Unehrlichkeit.

Dishonour, I. *s.* die Unehre, Schmach, Schande. II. *v.a.* entehren, schänden. **—able,** *adj.,* **—ably,** *adv.* entehrend, schändlich.

Disillusion, **—ize,** *v.a.* enttäuschen.

Disinclin—ation, *s.* die Abneigung. **—ed,** *adj.* abgeneigt.

Disinfect, *v.a.* desinfizieren. **—ant,** *s.* das Desinfektionsmittel. **—ing,** **—ion,** *s.* die Desinfektion.

Disinherit, *v.a.* enterben.

Disinter, *v.a.* ausgraben. **—ment,** *s.* das Ausgraben.

Disinterested, *adj.,* **—ly,** *adv.* uneigennützig. **—ness,** *s.* die Uneigennützigkeit.

Disjoin, *v.a.* trennen.

Disjoint, *v.a.* verrenken. **—ed,** *adj.* abgebrochen. **—edness,** *s.* der Mangel an Zusammenhang.

Disk, *s.* die Scheibe.

Dislike, I. *s.* die Abneigung. II. *v.a.* mißbilligen; (not like) nicht mögen, nicht lieben, nicht leiden mögen.

Dislocat—e, *v.a.* verrenken, ausrenken. **—ion,** *s.* die Verrenkung.

Dislodge, *v.a.* vertreiben.

Disloyal, *adj.,* **—ly,** *adv.* treulos, pflichtvergessen. **—ty,** *s.* die Untreue.

Dismal, *adj.,* **—ly,** *adv.* trübe, düster.

Dismast, *v.a.* entmasten.

Dismay, I. *s.* der Schreck(en), die Bestürzung. II. *v.a.* erschrecken.

Dismember, *v.a.* zergliedern zerſtückeln. **—ment,** *s.* die Zergliederung.

Dismiss, *v.a.* verabſchieden, entlaſſen. **—al,** *s.* die Entlaſſung.

Dismount, *v.n.* abſteigen.

Disobe—dience, *s.* der Ungehorſam. **—dient,** *adj.,* **—diently,** *adv.* ungehorſam (to, gegen). **—y,** *v.a.* (einem) nicht gehorchen.

Disoblig—e, *v.a.* (gegen einen) ungefällig ſein. **—ing,** *adj.,* **—ingly,** *adv.* unfreundlich. **—ingness,** *s.* die Ungefälligkeit.

Disorder, I. *s.* die Unordnung, Verwirrung. II. *v.a.* in Unordnung bringen. **—liness,** *s.* die Unordnung. **—ly,** I. *adj.* unordentlich; (riotous), liederlich, aufrührerisch. II. *adv.* in Unordnung.

Disorganiz—ation, *s.* die Zerſtörung. **—e,** *v.a.* in Verwirrung bringen.

Disown, *v.a.* verleugnen, ableugnen.

Disparag—e, *v.a.* herabſetzen. **—ment,** *s.* die Beeinträchtigung. **—ing,** *adj.,* **—ingly,** *adv.* geringſchätzend, geringſchätzig.

Dispassionate, *adj.,* **—ly,** *adv.* leidenſchaftslos; unparteiiſch.

Dispatch, I. *v.a.* (send off) abfertigen, abſenden; (do speedily) erledigen. II. *s.* (prompt execution) die Erledigung; (sending away) die Abfertigung; (haste) die Eile; (killing) das Töten. **—er,** *s.* der Abſender; bearer of **—es,** der Eilbote. **—es,** *pl.* die Depeſchen.

Dispel, *v.a.* vertreiben.

Dispensable, *adj.* erläßlich; verteilbar.

Dispens—ary, *s.* die Armenapotheke. **—ation,** *s.* (dealing out) die Austeilung, Ausſpendung; die Dispenſation. **—e,** *v.* I. *a.* austeilen, verteilen, ſpenden. II. *n.* (do without) verzichten auf (*acc.*); to **—e** with, etwas nicht verlangen, einem etwas erſparen.

Dispers—e, *v.* I. *a.* zerſtreuen. II. *n.* auseinandergehen. **—ion,** *s.* die Zerſtreuung.

Dispirit, *v.a.* entmutigen, niederſchlagen. **—ed,** *adj.,* **—edly,** *adv.* entmutigt, niedergeſchlagen.

Displace, *v.a.* verlegen, verſetzen. **—ment,** *s.* das Verſchiebung; die Abſetzung; das Deplacement (*of ships*).

Display, I. *v.a.* ausſtellen, auslegen. II. *s.* die Schauſtellung.

Displeas—e, *v.a.* mißfallen. **—ed,** *adj.* mißvergnügt; unbefriedigt (von), unzufrieden (mit). **—ing,** *adj.* mißfällig, unangenehm. **—ure,** *s.* das Mißfallen.

Dispos—able, *adj.* verfügbar, disponibel. **—al,** *s.* die Anordnung, Einrichtung. **—e,** *v.* I. *a.* (an)ordnen, einrichten; (incline) ſtimmen, lenken. II. *n.* to **—e** of, verfügen, gebieten. (über eine S.); (use) brauchen; (get rid of) abſchaffen, wegſchaffen; to **—** of a thing by will, eine Sache vermachen. **—ed,** *adj.* geneigt; well **—ed,** gut gelaunt. **—er,** *s.* der Anordner; der Herrſcher. **—ition,** *s.* (arrangement) die Anordnung, Einrichtung; (control) die Disposition, Verfügung; (temperament) die Gemütsart.

Dispossess, *v.a.* entſetzen (*gen.*), berauben (*gen.*).

Disproof, *s.* die Widerlegung.

Disproportion, *s.* das Mißverhältnis. **—able,** *adj.,* **—ably,** *adv.* unverhältnißmäßig.

Disprove, *v.a.* widerlegen.

Disput—able, *adj.* beſtreitbar. **—ant,** *s.* der Streiter, Disputant. **—e,** I. *s.* der Streit. II. *v.a.* beſtreiten. III. *v.n.* ſtreiten.

Disqualif—ication, *s.* die Unfähigmachung. **—y,** *v.a.* unfähig, untauglich machen.

Disquiet, *v.a.* beunruhigen, ſtören. **—ing,** *adj.* beunruhigend. **—ude,** *s.* die Unruhe.

Disregard, *v.a.* mißachten; (neglect) vernachläſſigen.

Disreput—able, *adj.,* **—ably,** *adv.* verrufen. **—e,** *s.* der üble Ruf.

Disrespect, *s.* der Mangel an Ehrerbietung, die Geringſchätzung. **—ful,** *adj.,* **—fully,** *adv.* unehrerbietig, unhöflich.

Disruption, *s.* das Abreißen.

Dissatisf—action, *s.* die Unzufriedenheit (mit). **—ied,** *adj.* unzufrieden, mißvergnügt.

Dissect, *v.a.* zerlegen, zergliedern; ſezieren (*Anat.*). **—ion,** *s.* die Zerlegung; die Sektion (*Anat.*); (*fig.*) die Zergliederung.

Dissemble, *v.* I. *a.* verhehlen. II. *n.* heucheln; ſich verſtellen. **—r,** *s.* der Verhehler, Heuchler.

Dissen—sion, *s.* die Mißhelligkeit,

Zwietracht. —t, I. *s.* die Meinungs=
verschiedenheit. II. *v.n.* nicht über=
einstimmen. —tient, I. *adj.* miß=
billigend. II. *s.* der Andersdenkende.
Dissertation, *s.* die Auseinander=
setzung; die Abhandlung.
Dissever, *v.a.* trennen; (divide) zer=
teilen.
Dissimilar, *adj.* unähnlich, ungleich.
—ity, *s.* die Unähnlichkeit, Verschie=
denartigkeit.
Dissimulat—e, *v.a.* verhehlen, ver=
decken, verstellen. —ion, *s.* die Ver=
stellung, Heuchelei.
Dissipat—e, *v.* I. *a.* zerstreuen;
(squander) vergeuden, verschwenden.
II. *n.* sich zerstreuen. —ed, *adj.* aus=
schweifend, liederlich. —ion, *s.* die
Zerstreuung (*also fig.*); (disorderli=
ness) die Liederlichkeit.
Dissol—uble, *adj.* (auf)löslich. —ute,
adj., —utely, *adv.* ausschweifend, lie=
derlich. —uteness, *s.* die Lieder=
lichkeit. —ution, *s.* die Auflösung.
—vable, *adj.* auflösbar, auflöslich.
—ve, *v.* I. *a.* auflösen. II. *n.* sich
auflösen; to —ve into tears, in
Tränen ausbrechen. —ving, *adj.*
auflösend; —ving views, (*pl.*) die
Nebelbilder.
Dissonan—ce, *s.* der Mißklang. —t,
adj. dissonierend; mißhellig.
Dissua—de, *v.a.* (einem von einer S.)
abraten. —sion, *s.* die Abratung.
—sive, *adj.*, —sively, *adv.* abratend.
Distaff, *s.* der Spinnrocken.
Distan—ce, I. *s.* die Entfernung,
Weite; die Ferne. II. *v.a.* hinter
sich zurücklassen. —t, *adj.* fern, ent=
fernt (*in time or space*); entfernt,
zurückhaltend (*in feeling, etc.*).
Distaste, *s.* der Ekel (vor); der
Widerwille (gegen). —ful, *adj.* miß=
fällig. —fulness, *s.* die Mißfällig=
keit, Widrigkeit.
¹**Distemper,** *s.* die Krankheit. —ed,
adj. krank, unpäßlich.
²**Distemper,** I. *s.* die Wasserfarbe.
II. *v.a.* mit Wasserfarben streichen.
Disten—d, *v.a.* ausdehnen. —tion, *s.*
die Ausdehnung.
Distich, *s.* das Distichon.
Distil, *v.a.* destillieren (*Chem.*); bren=
nen (*spirits*). —lation, *s.* die
Destillierung. —lery, *s.* die Brannt=
weinbrennerei.
Distinct, I. *adj.*, —ly, *adv.* (different)

verschieden; (clear) vernehmlich; (de=
cided) bestimmt. II. *adv.* klar, deutlich.
—ion, *s.* die Unterscheidung; (differ=
ence) der Unterschied; (eminence) die
Auszeichnung. —ive, *adj.* unter=
scheidend. —ively, *adv.* klar, deutlich.
—ness, *s.* die Deutlichkeit, Bestimmt=
heit.
Distinguish, *v.* I. *a.* unterscheiden; to
— oneself, sich auszeichnen. II. *n.*
unterscheiden; to be —ed by, sich
unterscheiden durch. —able, *adj.*
unterscheidbar. —ed, *adj.* ausgezeich=
net. —ing, *adj.* unterscheidend; (char=
acteristic) eigentümlich, bezeichnend.
Distort, *v.a.* verrenken (*the limbs*);
verzerren (*the features*). —ion, *s.*
die Verdrehung, Verrenkung.
Distract, *v.a.* abziehen, ablenken;
(disturb) beunruhigen; (craze) der
Verstand zerrütten. —ed, *adj.* zer=
streut, wahnsinnig; —ed with pain,
außer sich vor Schmerz. —ion, *s.*
die Zerstreuung (*of mind*); der
Wahnsinn. —ing, *adj.* abziehend;
wahnsinnig machend.
Distrain, *v.a.* in Beschlag nehmen.
—t, *s.* die Beschlagnahme.
Distress, I. *s.* die Not, Trübsal.
II. *v.a.* betrüben, quälen. —ed, *adj.*
bekümmert, bedrängt. —ful, *adj.*,
—fully, *adv.* kummervoll. —ing,
adj., —ingly, *adv.* peinlich, qualvoll.
Distribut—able, *adj.* verteilbar. —e,
v.a. verteilen, austeilen (among, unter,
to, an, *acc.*). —ion, *s.* die Verteilung,
Austeilung; die Abteilung, Eintei=
lung (*into classes*), die Anordnung der
Teile; die Verbreitung (*of plants,
etc.*). —ive, *adj.* austeilend, ver=
teilend; distributiv (*Gram.*).
District, *s.* der Bezirk, Kreis.
Distrust, I. *v.a.* mißtrauen. II. *s.*
das Mißtrauen, der Argwohn. —ful,
adj., —fully, *adv.* mißtrauisch.
Disturb, *v.a.* (disarrange) in Unord=
nung bringen; (trouble) stören. —
ance, *s.* die Störung, Beunruhi=
gung; der Aufruhr. —er, *s.* der
Störer.
Disuni—on, die Entzweiung, die
Zwietracht. —te, *v.* I. *a.* entzweien,
trennen. II. *n.* sich trennen.
Disuse, *s.* der Nichtgebrauch; to fall
into —, außer Gebrauch kommen.
Disyllab—ic, *adj.* zweisilbig. —le, *s.*
zweisilbiges Wort.

Ditch, *s.* der Graben.

Ditto, *adv.* desgleichen, ditto.

Ditty, *s.* das Liedchen.

Divan, *s.* der Diwan.

Dive, *v.n.* tauchen; to make a — at, langen nach. —**r,** *s.* der Taucher (*also Orn.*).

Diverg—**e,** *v.n.* abweichen. —**ence,** *s.* das Auseinanderlaufen. —**ent,** *adj.* divergierend.

Divers, *adj.*; *pl.* etliche, verschiedene, mehrere. —**e,** *adj.* verschieden. —**e-ly,** *adv.* verschieden. —**ification,** *s.* die Verschiedenheit. —**ified,** *adj.* mannigfaltig. —**ify,** *v.a.* verschieden machen. —**ion,** *s.* die Ablenkung (*of a stream, etc.*); die Diversion (*Mil.*); (amusement) die Zerstreuung. —**ity,** *s.* die Verschiedenheit, Ungleichheit; (variety) die Mannigfaltigkeit.

Divert, *v.a.* abwenden, ablenken, abziehen; (amuse) zerstreuen, ergötzen.

Divest, *v.a.* entkleiden; berauben (*of rights, etc.*); to — oneself of, (*fig.*) verzichten auf (*acc.*).

Divid—**e,** *v.* I. *a.* teilen; (separate) absondern, trennen; (partition) abteilen; (cut through) durchschneiden, zerteilen; (set at variance) uneinig machen; (part among) austeilen, verteilen; einteilen (*one's time, etc.*); dividieren (*Arith.*). II. *n.* sich trennen. —**end,** *s.* die Dividende. —**ing,** *adj.* teilend.

Divin—**ation,** *s.* die Weissagung. —**atory,** *adj.* weissagend. —**e,** I. *adj.*, —**ely,** *adv.* göttlich. II. *v.a.* & *n.* weissagen, wahrsagen; (have a presentiment of) ahnen. III. *s.* der Geistliche. —**eness,** *s.* die Göttlichkeit. —**er,** *s.* der Weissager; der Errater. —**ity,** *s.* die Gottheit; (theology, *etc.*) die Theologie. —**ing-rod,** *s.* die Wünschelrute.

Diving, *adj.* tauchend. —**bell,** *s.* die Taucherglocke.

Divis—**ibility,** *s.* die Teilbarkeit. —**ible,** *adj.* teilbar. —**ion,** *s.* die Teilung; die Abteilung, Einteilung (*of time, etc.*); (partition) die Abteilung. —**or,** *s.* der Divisor (*Arith.*).

Divorce, I. *s.* die Scheidung, Ehescheidung. II. *v.a.* scheiden.

Divulge, *v.a.* entdecken, ausschwatzen. —**r,** *s.* der Verbreiter.

Dizz—**iness,** *s.* der Schwindel. —**y,**

I. *adj.* schwind(e)lig. II. *v.a.* schwindlig machen; (confuse) verwirren.

Do, I. *ir.v.a.* tun, machen, verrichten; (effect) bewirken; (accomplish) ausführen, vollbringen, zustande bringen; (execute) ausrichten. II. *ir.v.n.* tun, handeln; (be in a state) sich befinden; (answer) dem Zwecke entsprechen; (suit) tauglich sein, passen. III. *aux. v.* 1. (in interrogations, bei einer Frage) did you see him? sahen Sie ihn? 2. (in negative sentences, bei einer Verneinung) I — not know him, ich kenne ihn nicht. 3. (emphatic, verstärkend) send it, —! schicke es doch! 4. (*for yes*) — you see him? I —, sehen Sie ihn? Jawohl; to — London, London besehen; to — a person credit, einem Ehre machen; that will —, das genügt, so ist's recht; that won't —, das geht nicht; to — badly, schlechte Geschäfte machen; I — feel better, ich fühle mich wirklich besser; to — without, fertig werden ohne, entbehren. —**er,** *s.* der Täter; der Verrichter.

Docil—**e,** *adj.* gelehrig, lenksam. —**ity,** *s.* die Gelehrigkeit.

¹**Dock,** *s.* das Ampferkraut (*Bot.*).

²**Dock,** *v.a.* stutzen (*dogs' or horses' tails, etc.*).

³**Dock,** *s.* das Dock (*Naut.*). —**gate,** *s.* das Docktor, die Dockschleuse. —**yard,** *s.* die Werft.

Docket, I. *s.* der Zettel; der Abriß. II. *v.a.* kurz angeben.

Doct—**or,** *s.* der Doktor (*of Laws, etc.*); (medical man) der Arzt, Doktor. —**orate,** *s.* die Doktorwürde.

Doct—**rinaire,** I. *s.* der Doktrinär. II. *adj.* doktrinär. —**rine,** *s.* die Lehre.

Document, *s.* die Beweisschrift; die Urkunde. —**ary,** *adj.* dokumentarisch.

Dodge, I. *v.a.* entschlüpfen, ausweichen. II. *s.* der Kniff (*sl.*). —**r,** *s.* der Ränkeschmied.

Doe, *s.* das Reh. —**skin,** *s.* das Rehleder.

Doff, *v.a.* ablegen (*clothes, etc.*).

Dog, I. *s.* der Hund. II. *v.a.* (einen) unablässig verfolgen. —**days,** *s.* die Hundshitze. —**'s-ear,** *s.* das Eselsohr (*in book*). —**fish,** *s.* der Dornhai. —**rose,** *s.* die Hagerose.

Dogged, *adj.*, —**ly,** *adv.* unverdrossen, zäh. —**ness,** *s.* die Zähigkeit.

Doggerel, s. die Knittelverſen.

Doggish, adj. hündiſch.

Dogma, s. das Dogma. **—tic(al),** adj., **—tically,** adv. dogmatiſch. **—tics,** pl. die Dogmo⸱ti̇́f. **—tism,** s. der Dogmatismus. **—tist,** s. der Dogmatiſt.

Doing, s. das Tun; **—s,** pl. Dinge, Begebenheiten.

Dole, I. s. das Almoſen; die Arbeitsloſenunterſtützung. II. v.a. verteilen.

Dol—eful, adj., **—efully,** adv. kummervoll, traurig. **—efulness,** s. die Traurigkeit.

Doll, s. die Puppe.

Dollar, s. der Dollar.

Dolman, s. der Dolman (also for ladies).

Dolphin, s. der Delphin.

Dolt, s. der Tölpel. **—ish,** adj., **—ishly,** adv. dumm, tölpelhaft. **—ishness,** s. die Tölpelhaftigkeit.

Domain, s. das Gebiet; (estate) das Gut; die Herrſchaft.

Dome, s. der Dom (Arch.), die Kuppel.

Domestic, I. adj., **—ally,** adv. häuslich; Haus⸗, Familien⸗. II. s. der Diener, die Dienerin. **—ate,** v.a. zähmen (beasts).

Domicile, I. s. die Wohnung. II. v.a. wohnhaft, anſäſſig machen. **—d** adj. wohnhaft, anſäſſig.

Domin—ant, adj. herrſchend. **—ate,** v.a. beherrſchen. **—ation,** s. die Herrſchaft. **—eer,** v.n. tyranniſieren. **—eering,** adj., **—eeringly,** adv. herriſch, gebieteriſch. **—ion,** s. (rule) die Herrſchaft, Gewalt; (district governed) das Gebiet, der Staat.

Domino, s. (mask) der Domino. **—es,** pl. das Dominoſpiel.

Don, v.a. I. antun, anlegen. II. s. ein Graduierter an der Univerſität.

Don—ate, v.a. verleihen. **—ation,** s. (giving) das Schenken; (gift) die Schenkung. **—ee,** s. der Beſchenkte.

Done, adj. & p.p. of Do. **—!** (to a bet) topp! done, abgetan, abgemacht, fertig; well —, gut gekocht; he is —for, es iſt aus mit ihm.

Donkey, s. der Eſel. **—engine,** s. die Hilfsmaſchine.

Donor, s. der Schenkende.

Doom, I. v.a. verurteilen. II. s. die Verurteilung. **—sday,** s. der Tag des jüngſten Gerichts.

Door, s. die Tür(e); (fig.) der Ein-

gang; next —, nebenan; in—s, zu Hauſe; out of —s, im Freien. **—bell,** s. die Türklingel, Türſchelle. **—handle,** s. der Türgriff. **—keeper,** s. der Pförtner, Portier. **—knocker,** s. der Türklopfer. **—latch,** s. die Türklinke.

Doric, adj. doriſch.

Dorm—ancy, s. die Betäubung. **—ant,** adj. ſchlafend; ungebraucht.

Dormer-window, s. das Dachfenſter.

Dormitory, s. der Schlafſaal.

Dormouse, s. die Haſelmaus.

Dose, I. s. die Doſis. II. v.a. Arznei (in Doſen) beibringen.

Dot, I. s. der kleine Punkt. II. v.a. tüpfeln. **—ted,** p.p. & adj. tüpfelig, punktiert.

Dot—age, s. die geiſtige Altersſchwäche. **—ard,** s. der kindiſche Greis. **—e,** v.n. faſeln. **—ing,** adj., **—ingly,** adv. faſelnd, kindiſch; innig verliebt.

Double, I. adj. doppelt, zwiefach; — flowers, gefüllte Blumen. II. s. das Doppelte, Zwiefache; (second self) der Doppelgänger; (duplicate) die Abſchrift; at the —, im Geſchwindſchritt or Sturmſchritt. III. v.a. (ver)doppeln; (fold) zuſammenlegen; ballen (the fist). IV. v.n. ſich verdoppeln; Kreuzſprünge machen (of hares); to — up with pain, ſich vor Schmerz zuſammenkrümmen.

Double-barrelled, adj. doppelläufig. **—bass,** s. die Baßgeige. **—dealing,** s. die Falſchheit.

Doublet, s. das or der Wams.

Doubly, adj. doppelt, zwiefach, zweifach.

Doubt, I. v.n. zweifeln. II. v.a. bezweifeln, in Zweifel ziehen; (suspect) mißtrauen. III. s. der Zweifel; (uncertainty) die Ungewißheit; (dubiousness) die Bedenklichkeit; no —, ohne Zweifel. **—er,** s. der Zweifler. **—ful,** adj. zweifelnd, unſchlüſſig, bedenklich; (dubious) zweifelhaft; unbeſtimmt (as a colour); zweideutig (as an expression); to be —ful of something, an (dat.) etwas zweifeln. **—fully,** adv. auf zweifelhafte Weiſe. **—fulness,** s. die Zweifelhaftigkeit. **—ingly,** adv. zweifelnd, mißtrauiſch. **—less,** adv. ohne Zweifel.

Douche, s. die Duſche.

Dough, s. der Teig. **—y,** adj. teigig.

Dought—ily, adv., **—y,** adj. tapfer,

mannhaft, tüchtig. **—iness,** *s.* die Tapferfeit.

Dove, *s.* die Taube. **—cote,** *s.* der Taubenschlag. **—tail,** I. *s.* der Schwalbenschwanz (*Carp.*). II. *v.a.* einschwalben. **—tailing,** *s.* die Verzinfung.

Dowager, *s.* die Witwe; the queen —, die Königin-Witwe.

Dowdy, I. *s.* eine altmodisch gefleidete Frau. II. *adj.* schlumpig.

Dower, I. *s.* (*fig.*) die Begabung. II. *v.a.* begaben; ausstatten.

¹Down, *s.* der Flaum (*also fig.*); die Daunen. **—y,** *adj.* flaumig.

²Down, *s.* die Düne; das dürre Hügelland.

³Down, I. *adv.* nieder, herunter *or* hinunter, unten, herab *or* hinab; to turn upside —, auf den Kopf stellen; the ups and **—s** of life, die Wechselfälle des Lebens. II. *prep.* herab, herunter, hinab, hinunter. III. *int.* nieder! hinab! **—ward,** I. *adj.* sich senfend, herabfommend. II. *adv.* (**—wards**) niederwärts, hinab, abwärts. **—cast,** *adj.* niedergeschlagen. **—fall,** *s.* der Sturz; (*fig.*) der Verfall, Untergang. **—hearted,** *adj.* niedergeschlagen. **—hill,** I. *adj.* abschüssig. II. *adv.* den Hügel hinab, bergab. **—pour,** *s.* der Regenguß. **—right,** I. *adj.* offen, offenherzig, redlich; a **—right** fool, ein völliger Narr. II. *adv.* (right down) senfrecht; geradezu; (thoroughly) tüchtig, völlig. **—rightness,** *s.* die Offenheit, Geradheit. **—stairs,** *adj.,* *adv.* treppab, die Treppe hinab *or* hinunter. **—trodden,** *adj.* niedergetreten; zertreten.

Dowry, *s.* die Mitgift.

Doze, *v.n.* schlummern, duseln.

Dozen, *s.* das Dutzend.

Drab, *adj.* mattbraun, schmutzfarben.

Draft, I. *s.* die Tratte (*C.L.*); das Detachement (*Mil.*); der Umriß. II. *v.a.* (Zeichnungen, Risse) entwerfen; schriftlich entwerfen (*a lease, etc.*); detachieren (*soldiers*).

Drag, I. *v.a.* schleppen. II. *v.n.* schleifen. III. *s.* die Schleife (*for dragging burdens*); (brake) der Hemmschuh; (grapnel) der Dreghafen; das Hemmende. **—net,** *s.* das Schleppnetz. **—wheel,** *s.* das Schlepprad.

Draggle, *v.n.* sich beschmutzen.

Dragon, *s.* der Drache. **—fly,** *s.* die See- *or* Wasser-jungfer, Libelle (*Ent.*).

Dragoon, *s.* der Dragoner. **—guard,** *s.* der Gardedragoner.

Drain, I. *v.a.* (draw off) abziehen, ableiten; (empty) ausleeren. II. *v.n.* ablaufen, abfließen. III. *s.* der Abzug; (gutter) die Gosse; a — on the purse, starfe Inanspruchnahme des Geldbeutels. **—age,** *s.* das Ablaufen, Abfließen; der Abzugsfanal (*Build.*). **—ing,** I. *p.* & *adj.* abziehend (*in cpds.*). II. *s.* die Entwässerung, Trockenlegung. **—pipe,** *s.* das Abzugsrohr.

Drake, *s.* der Enterich.

Dram, *s.* der Trunf, Schluck.

Drama, *s.* das Schauspiel, Drama. **—tic(al),** *adj.,* **—tically,** *adv.* dramatisch. **—tist,** *s.* der Dramatifer. **—tize,** *v.a.* dramatisieren.

Drape, *v.a.* behängen. **—r,** *s.* der Tuchhändler. **—ry,** *s.* der Tuchhandel; (cloths) das Tuch, wollene Zeug.

Drastic, *adj.* derb, drastisch.

Draught, *s.* der Tiefgang (*of a ship*); (drink) der Zug, Schluck; der Zug (*of air*); die Zeichnung, der Abriß (*Draw.*); (sketch) das Konzept, der Entwurf. **—s,** *pl.* das Damenspiel. **—y,** *adj.* zugig. **—horse,** *s.* das Zugpferd. **—sman,** *s.* der Zeichner; der Stein (*in draughts*).

Draw, I. *ir.v.a.* (pull) ziehen; (drag) schleppen, schleifen; (attract) anziehen; abziehen (beer, wine, *etc.*); zuziehen (the curtain); losen (lots); zeichnen (*Draw.*); schildern (a picture); ausstellen (a bill); to — a sigh, einen Seufzer ausstoßen; to — breath, Luft schöpfen; to — comparisons, Vergleiche anstellen. II. *ir.v.n.* ziehen (upon, auf); zeichnen (*Draw.*). III. *s.* das Ziehen, der Zug; das Los; die unentschiedene Partie. **—er,** *s.* der Zieher; der Zeichner; der Trassant (*C.L.*); die Schublade. **—ers,** *pl.* die Unterhosen; a chest, set of **—ers,** die Kommode. **—ing,** *s.* das Ziehen; das Zeichnen; die Zeichnung; die Ausstellung (eines Wechsels). **—back,** *s.* (customs) der Rückzoll; (disadvantage) der Mißstand, die Schattenseite, der Nachteil. **—bridge,** *s.* die Zugbrücke. **—ing-board,** *s.* das Zeichenbrett. **—ing-pen,** *s.* die

Reißfeder. **—ing-room,** *s.* der Salon. **—well,** *s.* der Ziehbrunnen.

Drawl, I. *v.a.* dehnen (die Worte). II. *v.n.* dehnen. III. *s.* die schleppende Sprechweise.

Dray, *s.* der niedrige Karren.

Dread, I. *s.* die Furcht. II. *adj.* schrecklich, furchtbar. III. *v.a.* fürchten, ein Grauen empfinden (vor). **—ful,** *adj.,* **—fully,** *adv.* schrecklich, furchtbar. **—fulness,** *s.* die Schrecklichkeit.

Dream, I. *s.* der Traum. II. *v.a. & n.* träumen; I —t, mir träumte. **—er,** *s.* der Träumer. **—ily,** *adv.,* **—y,** *adj.* träumerisch. **—ing,** *s.* die Träumerei. **—less,** *adj.* traumlos.

Drear, *adj.,* **—ily,** *adv.,* **—y,** *adj.* traurig, öde. **—iness,** *s.* die Traurigkeit, Öde.

¹Dredge, I. *s.* das Schleppnetz. II. *v.a.* ausbaggern (*Hydr.*); draggen (*Naut.*). **—r,** *s.* der Bagger.

²Dredge, *v.a.* bestreuen (*Cook.*). **—r,** *s.* die Streubüchse.

Dregs, *pl.* die Hefe, der Bodensatz.

Drench, *v.a.* durchnässen.

Dress, I. *v.a.* kleiden; anrichten (*food*); behauen (*stones*). II. *v.n.* sich (an-)kleiden. III. *s.* die Kleidung; das Kleid; full —, die Galakleidung; — circle, erster Rang. IV. *attrib.*; — shirt, das (Herren-)Oberhemd; — suit, der Frackanzug. **—er,** *s.* der Ankleider; die Ankleiderin; (kitchen —er) der Anrichtetisch. **—ing,** *s.* das Ankleiden; der Verband, Umschlag (*Surg.*). **—y,** *adj.* prunkhaft. **—ing-case,** *s.* das Toilettenkästchen. **—coat,** *s.* der Frack. **—ing-gown,** *s.* der Schlafrock. **—ing-room,** *s.* das Ankleidezimmer. **—ing-table,** *s.* die Toilette, der Toilettentisch. **—jacket,** *s.* der Smoking. **—maker,** *s.* die Kleidermacherin, Damenschneiderin.

Drift, I. *s.* das Getriebene; (aim) der Zweck, das Ziel; snow- —, die Schneewehe. II. *v.a.* zusammen-treiben, -wehen. III. *v.n.* dahin treiben; sich aufhäufen; triftig sein (*Naut.*). **—ing,** *adj.* triftig. **—ice,** *s.* das Treibeis. **—wood,** *s.* das Treibholz.

Drill, I. *v.a.* bohren, drillen (*holes, etc.*); exerzieren, drillen (*Mil.*). II. *s.* das Exerzieren (*Mil.*); (furrow) die Furche, Rille. III. *attrib.*; **—bore,** der Drillbohrer; — ground, der

Exerzierplatz. **—ing,** *s.* das Bohren; das Exerzieren. **—hall,** *s.* das Exerzierhaus.

²Drill, Drilling, *s.* der Drillich (*Text.*).

Drink, I. *ir.v.a.* trinken; saufen (*of beasts*); to — in, einsaugen; (*fig.*) einatmen; to — off, austrinken, ausleeren. II. *v.n.* trinken; übermäßig, trinken, zechen. III. *s.* der Trank, Trunk; (strong —) das geistige Getränk. **—able,** *adj.* trinkbar. **—er,** *s.* der Trinker; der Zecher; (drunkard) der Trunkenbold. **—ing,** *s.* das Trinken. **—ing bout,** das Trinkgelage.

Drip, I. *v.n.* tröpfeln. II. *s.* die Traufe. **—ping,** I. *p. & adj.* tröpfelnd. II. *s.* das Bratenfett, Schmalz.

Drive, I. *ir.v.a.* treiben (*away, etc.*); (force) zwingen; fahren (*a carriage*); führen (*an engine*); to — away, vertreiben; to — back, zurück treiben; to — in, einschlagen (*as nails, etc.*); to — into, hineintreiben; to — off, wegtreiben; to — on, vorwärts treiben; to — out, hinaustreiben, forttreiben. II. *ir.v.n.* treiben (*also Naut.*); fahren; what are you driving at? was haben Sie im Sinn? was wollen Sie damit sagen? III. *s.* die Spazierfahrt; (way) der Fahrweg. **—r,** *s.* der Fuhrmann, Kutscher; engine—r, Lokomotivführer.

Drivel, *v.n.* geifern (*as infants*); (*fig.*) faseln. **—ler,** *s.* der Geiferer; der Faselhans.

Driving, *s.* das Treiben. **—box,** *s.* der Kutsch(er)bock. **—gear,** *s.* das Getriebe. **—shaft,** *s.* die Treibachse (*Locom., etc.*). **—wheel,** *s.* das Treibrad (*Locom.*).

Drizzl—e, I. *s.* der Sprühregen. II. *v.n.* rieseln. **—ing,** *adj.,* **—y,** *adj.* rieselnd.

Droll, *adj.* drollig. **—ery,** *s.* die Posse.

Dromedary, *s.* das Dromedar.

¹Drone, I. *s.* das Gebrumme. II. *v.n.* summen, brummen.

²Drone, *s.* die Drohne; (*fig.*) der Faulenzer.

Droop, I. *v.a.* sinken lassen. II. *n.* verwelten (*as flowers*); verschmachten. **—ing,** *adj.,* **—ingly,** *adv.* matt, hinfällig.

Drop, I. *s.* der Tropfen. II. *v.a.* tropfen, tröpfeln; to — a line, eine Zeile schreiben. III. *v.n.* tröpfeln, triefen; (herab) fallen, sinken; to —

asleep, einschlafen; to — in, vor-
sprechen (bei). **—ping,** s. das Tröp-
feln. **—scene,** s. der Vorhang
(*Theat.*).
Drops—ical, adj. wassersüchtig. **—y,**
s. die Wassersucht.
Dross, s. das Gekräß, die Schlacke
(*Metall.*).
Drought, s. die Dürre, Trockenheit.
—y, adj. dürr, trocken.
Drove, I. imperf. of Drive. II. s. die
Viehherde, Trift (Vieh). **—r,** s. der
Viehtreiber.
Drown, v. I. a. ertränken, ersäufen.
II. n. ertrinken, ersaufen. **—ing,** s.
das Ertrinken.
Drows—e, v.n. schlummern. **—ily,**
adv., **—y,** adj. schläfrig. **—iness,** s.
die Schläfrigkeit.
Drub, v.a. prügeln.
Drudge, I. s. der Packesel. II. v.n.
sich (ab)placken. **—ry,** s. die Plackerei.
Drug, I. s. die Droge. II. v.a. mit
Zutaten vermischen; (stupefy) durch
ein Schlafmittel betäuben. **—gist,**
s. der Drogist.
Drugget, s. der Droget(t).
Druid, s. der Druide. **—ic(al),** adj.
druidisch.
Drum, I. s. die Trommel (*Mil., Mech.,
Anat.*). II. v.n. trommeln. **—mer,** s.
der Trommler. **—ming,** s. das Trommeln. **—stick,** s. der Trommelschlä-
gel.
Drunk, adj. betrunken, trunken; (*fig.*)
berauscht. **—ard,** s. der Trunkenbold.
—enness, s. die Trunkenheit.
Dry, I. adj. (not wet) trocken; durstig;
(sapless) dürr; (uninteresting) kahl,
abgeschmackt; — goods, die Schnitt-
waren. II. v.a. trocknen, abtrocknen.
III. v.n. trocknen, trocken werden;
(— up) eintrocknen, vertrocknen, verdorren. **—ing,** adj. trocknend. **—ly,**
adv. trocken. **—ness,** s. die Trockenheit; (*fig.*) die Dürre. **—dock,** s. das
Trockendock. **—nurse,** s. das Kindermädchen.
Dubi—ous, adj., **—ously,** adv. zweifelhaft. **—ousness,** s. die Zweifelhaftigkeit, Ungewißheit.
Ducal, adj. herzoglich.
Ducat, s. der Dukaten.
Duchess, s. die Herzogin.
Duchy, s. das Herzogtum.
1Duck, s. die Ente. **—ling,** s. das
Entchen.

2Duck, v.n. (unter-)tauchen; sich bücken.
—ing, s. das (Unter-)Tauchen.
Duct, s. der Gang, die Röhre. **—ile,**
adj. dehnbar; biegsam. **—ility,** s.
die Dehnbarkeit.
Dudgeon, s. der Groll, Zorn.
Due, I. adj. gebührend, geziemend,
schuldig, angemessen; fällig (*C.L.*);
in — time, zur rechten Zeit; the train
is —, der Zug ist fällig. II. adv. gerade.
III. s. die Gebühr, das Recht; (debt) die
Schuld.
Duel, s. der Zweikampf, das Duell.
—ling, s. das Duellieren. **—list,** s.
der Duellant.
Duet, s. das Duett.
1Dug, s. die Zitze (of cows, etc.).
2Dug, imperf. & p.p. of Dig.
Duke, s. der Herzog. **—dom,** s. das
Herzogtum.
Dulcet, adj. wohlklingend.
Dulcimer, s. das Hackbrett.
Dull, I. adj. (stupid) dumm; (sluggish)
träge, schwerfällig; (obtuse) stumpf-
sinnig; (blunt) stumpf; (dry) platt,
schal, abgeschmackt; (uninteresting)
langweilig; (gloomy) trübsinnig,
glanzlos, matt (as eyes); schwach (as
the fire); matt (as colours or metals);
trübe (as weather); dumpf (of sounds);
flau, stockend (as trade); — weather,
trübes Wetter. II. v.a. stumpf machen,
abstumpfen. **—ness,** s. die Stumpfheit; die Stumpfsinnigkeit; die Schwerfälligkeit; die Schwäche (of the hearing, etc.); die Mattheit (of the colour,
etc.).
Dumb, adj., **—ly,** adv. stumm. **—
ness,** s. die Stummheit. **—bell,**
s. die Hantel (*Gymn.*).
Dumfound, v.a. betäuben. **—ed,** adj.
wie vom Donner gerührt.
Dummy, s. der Stumme; (*fig.*) der
Strohmann; die Attrappe, Nachbildung.
1Dump, v.a. umstürpen. **—ling,** s.
der Kloß. **—y,** adj. kurz und dick.
—ing-ground, s. der Ablageplatz.
2Dump, s. (usually in the plural **—s**)
schlechte Laune.
1Dun, adj. schwarzbraun.
2Dun, I. s. der drängende Gläubiger.
II. v.a. ungestüm mahnen; **—ning**
letter, der Mahnbrief.
Dunce, s. der Dummkopf.
Dune, s. die Düne.
Dung, s. der Mist; der Kot. **—heap,**
—hill, s. der Misthaufen.

Dungeon, *s.* der Bergfried; das Burgverließ.

Dupe, I. *s.* der Gimpel. II. *v.a.* betrügen. **—ry,** *s.* die Prellerei.

Dupl—ex, *adj.* doppelt, zweifach. **—icate,** I. *adj.* doppelt. II. *s.* das Duplikat. III. *v.a.* verdoppeln. **—ication,** *s.* die Verdoppelung. **—icity,** *s.* die Falschheit, Doppelzüngigkeit.

Dur—ability, *s.* die Dauerhaftigkeit. **—able,** *adj.,* **—ably,** *adv.* dauerhaft. **—ation,** *s.* die Dauer, Fortdauer. **—ess,** *s.* der Zwang. **—ing,** *prep.* während.

Dusk, *s.* die Dämmerung. **—iness,** *s.* die Dunkelheit. **—y,** *adj.,* **—ily,** *adv.* düster, trüb.

Dust, I. *s.* der Staub. II. *v.a.* ausab-stäuben. **—er,** *s.* der Wischlappen. **—iness,** *s.* die Staubigkeit. **—y,** *adj.* staubig. **—bin,** *s.* der Kehrichtbehälter. **—cloak,** *s.* der Staubmantel.

Dut—eous, *adj.,* **—eously,** *adv.* pflichtgetreu. **—iable,** *adj.* zollpflichtig. **—iful,** *adj.,* **—ifully,** *adv.* pflichtgetreu, gehorsam. **—ifulness,** *s.* die Ehrerbietigkeit, Ehrerbietung. **—y,** *s.* (obligation) die Pflicht, Schuldigkeit; der Dienst, Kriegsdienst (*of an officer, etc.*); (impost) die Auflage, der Zoll; on **—y,** im Dienst; off **—y,** dienstfrei; in **—y** bound, von Rechts wegen. **—y-free,** *adj.* zollfrei.

Dwarf, I. *s.* der Zwerg. II. *adj.* Zwerg-. **—ed,** *p.p. & adj.* verbuttet. **—ish,** *adj.,* **—ishly,** *adv.* zwerghaft, winzig.

Dwell, *v.n.* wohnen; to **—** on a subject, bei einem Thema verweilen. **—er,** *s.* der Bewohner. **—ing,** *s.* die Wohnung. **—ing-place,** *s.* der Wohnort.

Dwindle, *v.n.* abnehmen.

Dye, I. *v.a.* färben. II. *v.n.* sich färben lassen. III. *s.* die Farbe, Färbung, der Farbstoff. **—ing,** *s.* das Färben. **—r,** der Färber. **—works,** *pl.* die Färberei.

Dying, I. *adj.* sterbend. II. *s.* das Sterben.

Dynam—ic(al), *adj.* dynamisch. **—ics,** *pl.* die Dynamik. **—ite,** *s.* der Dynamit. **—o,** *s.* die Dynamomaschine.

Dynast—ic, *adj.* dynastisch. **—y,** *s.* die Dynastie.

Dys—entery, *s.* die Ruhr. **—pepsia,** **—pepsy,** *s.* die Dyspepsie. **—peptic,** I. *adj.* magenschwach. II. *s.* der Dyspeptiker.

E

E, e, das E, e (*also Mus.*); E-flat, Es; E-minor, E-moll; E-sharp, Eis.

Each, I. *adj.* jed(-er, -c.); — one, jeder, ein jeder; — other, einander, sich. II. *pron.* jeder, jede, jedes, ein jeder, eine jede, ein jedes.

Eager, *adj.,* **—ly,** *adv.* eifrig, hitzig. **—ness,** *s.* die Heftigkeit; die Begierde.

Eagle, *s.* der Adler.

¹**Ear,** *s.* die Ähre (*Bot.*).

²**Ear,** *s.* das Ohr. **—mark,** I. *s.* das Ohrenzeichen (*on sheep*); (*fig.*) das Eigentumszeichen. II. *v.a.* mit einem Kennzeichen versehen. **—piece,** *s.* die Hörermuschel (*Radio*). **—piercing,** *adj.* ohrzerreißend. **—shot,** *s.* die Hörweite. **—trumpet,** *s.* das Hörrohr.

Earl, *s.* der Graf. **—dom,** *s.* die Grafschaft.

Earl—iness, *s.* die Frühzeitigkeit. **—y,** *adj. & adv.* früh, (früh)zeitig.

Earn, *v.a.* erwerben, verdienen. **—ings,** *pl.* der Erwerb, Verdienst.

¹**Earnest,** I. *adj.,* **—ly,** *adv.* ernst, ernsthaft. II. *s.* der Ernst. **—ness,** *s.* die Ernstlichkeit.

²**Earnest,** *s.* das Handgeld.

Earth, *s.* die Erde. **—en,** *adj.* irden. **—ly,** *adj.* erdig; (unspiritual) irdisch; körperlich, sinnlich. **—y,** *adj.* erdig; erdfarben; irdisch. **—enware,** *s.* das Steingut. **—quake,** *s.* das Erdbeben. **—work,** *s.* der Erdbau. **—worm,** *s.* der Regenwurm.

Earwig, *s.* der Ohrwurm.

Eas—e, I. *s.* die Gemächlichkeit, Bequemlichkeit, Behaglichkeit, das Behagen; ill at —, unruhig; to take one's —, es sich bequem machen; at —, gemächlich. II. *v.a.* erleichtern, lindern. **—ily,** *adv.* leicht. **—iness,** *s.* die Bequemlichkeit, Gemächlichkeit; die Leichtigkeit.

Easel, *s.* die Staffelei.

East, I. *s.* der Osten, Ost (*poet.*); der Orient, das Morgenland. II. *adj. & adv.* ost-, östlich. **—erly,** I. *adj.* östlich. II. *adv.,* **—ward,** *adv.* ostwärts. **—ern,** *adj.* östlich, morgenländisch.

Easter, s. die Oftern (pl.).

Easy, I. adj. leicht; bequem, behaglich; in —y circumstances, wohlhabend; take it —y! nur ruhig! II. adv. leicht. **—chair,** s. der Lehnftuhl. **—going,** adj. gemütlich. **—tempered,** adj. gutmütig.

Eat, ir.v. I. a. effen; freffen (of beasts). II. n. effen; (taste) fchmecken. **—able,** adj. eßbar. **—ables,** pl. die Eßwaren, Lebensmittel. **—er,** s. der Effer. **—ing,** s. das Effen. **—ing-house,** s. das Speifehaus.

Eau-de-Cologne, s. Rölnifches Waffer.

Eaves, pl. die Dachrinne. **—drop,** v.n. laufchen. **—dropper,** s. der Laufcher. **—dropping,** s. das Laufchen, Horchen.

Ebb, I. s. die Ebbe. II. v.a. ebben. **—tide,** s. die Ebbe.

Ebony, s. das Ebenholz.

Eccentric, I. adj., exzentrifch. II. s. der Sonderling. **—ity,** s. die Exzentrizität, Überspanntheit.

Ecclesiastic, s. der Geiftliche. **—al,** adj., **—ally,** adv. kirchlich, geiftlich.

Echo, I. s. das Echo, der Widerhall. II. v.a. widerhallen; (fig.) nachfprechen. III. v.n. widerhallen, wiederfchallen. **—less,** adj. ohne Echo.

Éclat, s. das Auffehen; die Auszeichnung, der Ruhm.

Eclectic, I. adj. eklektifch, wählerifch, auswählend. II. s. der Eklektiker.

Eclip—se, I. s. die Verfinfterung, Finfternis; —se of the sun, die Sonnenfinfternis. II. v.a. verfinftern; verdunkeln (also fig.). **—tic,** s. die Elliptik, Sonnenbahn.

Eclogue, s. das Hirtengedicht, die Ekloge.

Econom—ic, adj., **—ical,** adj., **—ically,** adv. ökonomifch; haushälterifch, wirtfchaftlich; (frugal) fparfam. **—ics,** pl. die Haushaltungskunft; die Staatshaushaltslehre, Volkswirtfchaft (slehre), Staatswirtfchaft. **—ist,** s. der fparfame Ausnutzer, gute Wirtfchafter; political **—ist,** der Staatswirtfchaftslehrer, Nationalökonom. **—ize,** v. I. n. fparen (in, an, with, mit). II. a. fparfam umgehen mit.

Economy, s. die Haushaltung, Wirtfchaft; die Sparfamkeit; political **—y,** die Volkswirtfchaft (slehre), Nationalökonomie.

Ecsta—sy, s. die übergroße Erregung; das Entzücken, die Wonne; (religious rapture) die Verzückung; (enthusiasm) die Begeifterung. **—tic,** adj., **—tically,** adv. entzückend; (enraptured) entzückt, hingeriffen.

Eczema, s. das Hautbläschen.

Eddy, I. s. der Wirbel, Wirbelftrom; (back current) die Gegenftrömung. II. v.n. wirbeln.

Edge, I. s. die Schärfe, Schneide (of a knife, etc.); (ledge) die fcharfe Kante; (brink) der Rand; (border) der Rand, Saum; die Ecke (of a table); der Schnitt (of a book); (keenness) die Schärfe, Stärke, Heftigkeit; die Feinheit (of wit, etc.); to put an — on, fchärfen; to set the teeth on —, die Zähne ftumpf machen. II. v.a. fäumen, befetzen, umgeben. III. v.n. fich feitwärts (heran) bewegen; to —in, hineinfchieben; to — forward, vorwärtsrücken; to — off, von . . . abhalten (Naut.); wegrücken, wegrutfchen. **—d,** adj. fcharf; two- —d, zweifchneidig; —d with lace, mit Spitzen eingefaßt. **—less,** adj. ftumpf. **—wise,** (—ways,) adv. feitwärts, von der Seite, hochkantig. **—tool,** s. das Schneidewerkzeug.

Edging, I. p. see Edge. II. s. die Einfaffung (Hort., Semp., etc.); (lace —) die Kantenfpitzen.

Edible, adj., eßbar. **—ness,** s. die Eßbarkeit.

Edict, s. das Edikt, die Verordnung.

Edification, s. (fig.) die Erbauung.

Edifice, s. das Gebäude.

Edif—y, v.a. erbauen. **—ying,** adj., **—yingly,** adv. erbaulich; belehrend.

Edit, v.a. herausgeben. **—ion,** s. die Auflage, Ausgabe; second **—ion,** zweite Ausgabe (of a paper); third **—ion,** dritte Auflage (of a book). **—or,** s. der Herausgeber (of a book); der Schriftleiter, Redakteur (of a journal, etc.). **—orial,** I. adj. vom Herausgeber, Redaktions-. II. s. der Leitartikel. **—orship,** s. die Schriftleitung, Redaktion; das Amt eines Herausgebers.

Educat—e, v.a. erziehen, bilden. **—ion,** s. die Erziehung, Bildung; das Erziehungswefen, Schulwefen; primary (or elementary) **—ion,** das Volksfchulwefen; secondary (or intermediate) **—ion,** das höhere Schulweſen; university —ion, die Universitätsbildung, das Hochschulweſen; liberal —ion, höhere Schulbildung, gelehrte Bildung, gute Allgemeinbildung; —ion department, das Unterrichtsminiſterium; minister of —ion, der Unterrichtsminiſter. —**ional**, *adj.* die Erziehung betreffend, erziehlich, Unterrichts-, Erziehungs-. —**ion**(al)**ist**, *s.* der Schulmann, Pädagoge. —**ive**, *adj.* erziehlich. —**or**, *s.* der Erzieher.

Educ—**e**, *v.a.* heraus-, hervor-ziehen. —**ible**, *adj.* hervorziehbar.

Eel, *s.* der Aal.

Efface, *v.n.* auswiſchen, auslöſchen; (*fig.*) vertilgen, verwiſchen. —**d**, verwiſcht. —**ment**, *s.* die Auslöſchung; (destruction) die Vertilgung.

Effect, I. *s.* die Wirkung; (result) die Folge, Wirkung, das Ergebnis; (reality) die Wirklichkeit, Wahrheit; (power) die Kraft, Gültigkeit; (purport) der Inhalt; (purpose) der Zweck, die Absicht; (use) der Nutzen; (impression) der Eindruck, Effekt, die Wirkung; die Wirkung (*Mech.*); of no —, vergeblich; to this —, zu dem Ende, in der Absicht, deshalb; a message to the — that . . ., eine Botschaft, welche beſagt(e), daß . . .; to the same —, deſſelben Inhalts; to carry into —, ausführen; to take —, wirken, Eindruck machen (on a person, auf einen). II. *v.a.* bewirken, bewerkſtelligen, ausführen; to — a junction with the army, ſich dem Heere anſchließen; the insurance is —ed on . . ., die Verſicherung validiert auf . . . —**ive**, *adj.* (operative) wirkend; (powerful) wirkſam, kräftig, effektvoll; (available) dienſtfähig, kampffähig; —ive horse-power, wirkliche Pferdekräfte. —**ively**, *adv.* (forcibly) mit Nachdruck; (efficaciously) mit Wirkung, wirkungsvoll. —**iveness**, *s.* die Wirkſamkeit. —**s**, *pl.* die Varvorräte (*C.L.*), Effekten, Güter, die Habe. —**ual**, *adj.*, —**ually**, *adv.* wirkſam; kräftig. —**uate**, *v.a.* bewerkſtelligen, bewirken, ausführen.

Effemina—**cy**, *s.* die Verweichlichung, Weichlichkeit, das weibiſche Weſen. —**te**, *adj.*, —**tely**, *adv.* weibiſch, weichlich, verzärtelt.

Effervesc—**e**, *v.n.* (auf)brauſen, gähren. —**ence**, *s.* das Aufbrauſen,

ſchäumen. —**ent**, —**ing**, *adj.* (auf)brauſend; —nt powder, das Brauſepulver.

Effete, *adj.* abgenutzt. —**ness**, *s.* die Erſchöpftheit, Kraftloſigkeit.

Effic—**acious**, *adj.*, —**aciously**, *adv.* wirkſam, kräftig. —**aciousness**, *s.* die Wirkſamkeit. —**acy**, *s.* die Wirkſamkeit, Kraft.

Effic—**iency**, *s.* der Nutzungswert, die Kraft; die Leistungsfähigkeit, Tüchtigkeit. —**ient**, I. *adj.*, —**iently**, *adv.* wirkſam, wirkend. II. *s.* die Urſache; der Urheber.

Effigy, *s.* das Bild(nis), Abbild.

Effort, *s.* die Anſtrengung, das Beſtreben; to make an —, ſich anſtrengen; to make every —, alles aufbieten, alle Kräfte anſpannen. —**less**, *adj.* ohne Anſtrengung, mühelos.

Effrontery, *s.* die Frechheit, Unverſchämtheit.

Efful—**gence**, *s.* das (Aus-)Strahlen, der Glanz. —**t**, *adj.*, —**tly**, *adv.* ſtrahlend, glänzend.

Effus—**e**, *adj.* ausgebreitet (*Bot.*). —**ion**, *s.* die Ausgießung, Vergießung; (outpouring) die Ergießung; (*fig.*) der Erguß. —**ive**, *adj.*, —**ively**, *adv.* ausgießend; vergießend; (*fig.*) überſchwenglich. —**iveness**, *s.* die Überſchwenglichkeit.

Eft, *s.* der Waſſermolch.

Egg, *s.* das Ei; fried —s, die Spiegeleier; scrambled —, das Rührei; poached —s, verlorene Eier; white, yolk of (an) —, das Eiweiß, der Eidotter. —**flip**, *s.* der Eierpunſch. —**shell**, *s.* die Eierſchale.

Eglantine, *s.* die wilde Roſe.

Ego, *s.* das Ich. —**ism**, *s.* der Egoismus. —**ist**, *s.* der Egoiſt.

Egress, *s.* der Ausgang; der Ausfluß (of water).

Eh, *interj.* he? nicht wahr? wie? ei!

Eight, I. *num. adj.* acht; — times, achtmal. II. *s.* die Acht. —**een**, *num. adj.* achtzehn. —**eenth**, *num. adj.* achtzehnt. —**fold**, *adj.* achtfach. —**h**, I. *num. adj.* (der, die, das) acht(e). II. *s.* das Achtel (*Mus.*). —**hly**, *adv.* achtens. —**ieth**, *num. adj.* (der, die, das) achtzigſt(e). —**y**, *num. adj.* achtzig.

Either, I. *adj. & pron.* einer, eine, eins; (each) jeder, jede, jedes (of two or more). II. *conj.* entweder.

Ejaculat—e, *v.a.* ausstoßen. **—ion**, *s.* der Ausruf.

Eject, *v.a.* ausstoßen. **—ion**, *s.* das Ausstoßen. **—ment**, *s.* die Vertreibung.

Elaborat—e, I. *v.a.* (sorgsam) ausarbeiten. II. *adj.*, **—ely**, *adv.* sorgfältig ausgearbeitet. **—ion**, *s.* die sorgfältige Ausarbeitung.

Elapse, *v.n.* entgleiten, verfließen.

Elastic, I. *adj.* elastisch. II. *s.* das Gummiband. **—ity**, *s.* die Elastizität, Feder-, Spann-kraft.

Elat—e, I. *v.a.* aufblähen. II. *adj.*, **—ed**, *adj.*, **—edly**, *adv.* aufgeblasen, stolz. **—ion**, *s.* die Aufgeblasenheit.

Elbow, *s.* der Ellbogen; — of a chair, die Armlehne; at one's —, nahe bei der Hand; to — one's way through, sich durchdrängen. **—room**, *s.* der Spielraum.

¹Eld—er, I. *adj.* (*comp. of Old*) älter. II. *s.* der Ältere; der Älteste (*in a church, etc.*). **—erly**, *adj.* ältlich. **—est**, *adj.* (*sup. of Old*) ältest; the **—est** (child), der Erstgeborene.

²Elder, *s.* der Holunder, Flieder (*Bot.*).

Elect, I. *v.a.* (aus)wählen (*out of several*); (er)wählen (to *or* into, zu). II. *adj.* (aus)gewählt; auserwählt. **—ion**, *s.* die Erwählung, Wahl. **—ive**, *adj.* wählend, Wahl. **—or**, *s.* der Wähler; (prince) der Kurfürst. **—ress**, *s.* die Kurfürstin.

Electr—ic(al), *adj.*, **—ically**, *adv.* elektrisch; **—ical** engineer, der Elektrotechniker. **—ician**, *s.* der Monteur. **—ocution**, *s.* die elektrische Hinrichtung. **—icity**, *s.* die Elektrizität. **—ifiable**, *adj.* elektrisierbar. **—ification**, *s.* die Elektrisierung. **—ify**, *v.a.* elektrisieren. **—otype**, I. *adj.* galvanoplastisch. II. *s.* der galvanische Abdruck.

Elegan—ce, **—cy**, *s.* die Zierlichkeit, Eleganz. **—t**, *adj.*, **—tly**, *adv.* fein, zierlich, elegant.

Eleg—iac, *adj.* elegisch. **—y**, *s.* die Elegie, das Klagelied.

Element, *s.* der Urstoff; (ingredient) der (Grund-)Bestandteil; das Element. **—al**, *adj.* natürlich, angeboren. **—ariness**, *s.* die Einfachheit. **—ary**, *adj.* elementar; (simple) urstofflich; (rudimentary) anfangsmäßig; **—ary** school, die Volksschule. **—s**, *pl.* die Grundzüge, Anfangsgründe, Elemente.

Elephant, *s.* der Elefant.

Elevat—e, *v.a.* erhöhen, emporheben; erheben (to *a dignity, etc.*). **—ed**, *p.p.* & *adj.* hoch; **—ed** with, erhoben. **—ing**, *adj.* erhebend. **—ion**, *s.* (raising) die Erhebung, Erhöhung (*also fig.*); (height) die Höhe; die Erhabenheit, der Aufschwung (*of mind, etc.*); die Erhabenheit (*of character*); die Erhebung (*of the voice, etc.*); der Aufriß (*Arch., etc.*). **—or**, *s.* der Aufzug, Fahrstuhl.

Eleven, *num.* I. *adj.* elf. II. *s.* die Elf. **—th**, *num. adj.* elft. **—thly**, *adv.* elftens.

Elf, *s.* der Elfe. **—in**, *adj.*, elfisch, Elfen-. **—ish**, **—(in-)like**, *adj.* elfengleich.

Elicit, *v.a.* entlocken, herauslocken.

Eligib—ility, *s.* die Wählbarkeit. **—le**, *adj.*, **—ly**, *adv.* wahlwürdig; passend, angemessen.

Eliminat—e, *v.a.* entfernen, eliminieren. **—ion**, *s.* die Wegschaffung.

Elision, *s.* die Elision.

Élite, *s.* der Kern, Ausbund.

Elixir, *s.* das Elixir.

Elk, *s.* der Elch, das Elentier.

Ell, *s.* die Elle.

Ellip—se, *s.* die Ellipse. **—sis**, *s.* die Ellipsis. **—tic(al)**, *adj.*, **—tically**, *adv.* elliptisch.

Elm, *s.* die Ulme. **—tree**, *s.* die Ulme.

Elocution, *s.* der Vortrag. **—ist**, *s.* der Redekünstler.

Elope, *v.n.* von Hause entfliehen. **—ment**, *s.* das Entlaufen.

Eloquen—ce, *s.* die Beredsamkeit, Beredtheit. **—t**, *adj.*, **—tly**, *adv.* beredtsam, beredt.

Else, I. *adv.* sonst, weiter; any one —, irgend ein anderer; anything —, irgend etwas anderes; what —? was sonst? no one —, niemand anders. II. *conj.* sonst, wo nicht. **—where**, *adv.* sonstwo, anderswo; anderswohin.

Elude, *v.a.* ausweichen, entschlüpfen.

Elus—ion, *s.* die List, Ausflucht. **—ive**, *adj.* (mit List) ausweichend. **—oriness**, *s.* das Trügliche. **—ory**, *adj.* trügerisch, betrüglich.

Emaciat—e, *v.n.* abmagern, mager werden. **—ion**, *s.* die Abmagerung.

Emancipat—e, *v.a.* befreien. **—ion**, *s.* die Befreiung. **—or**, *s.* der Befreier.

Embalm, *v.a.* einbalsamieren.

Embank, v.a. ein-deichen, -dämmen.

Embankment, s. die Ein-dämmung, -deichung; der (Erd=)Damm, Eisenbahndamm (*Railw.*).

Embargo, s. die Handelssperre.

Embark, v. I. a. einschiffen. II. n. sich einschiffen. —ation, Embarcation, s. die Einschiffung, Verladung.

Embarrass, v.a. in Verlegenheit setzen. —ed, adj. verlegen. —ment, s. die Verlegenheit.

Embassy, s. die Botschaft (*in the larger capitals*); die Gesandtschaft.

Embed, v.a. betten, einbetten.

Embellish, v.a. verschöne(r)n.

Ember, s. (*usually pl.* —s) glimmende Kohle; — days, die Quatembertage.

Embezzle, v.a. veruntreuen, unterschlagen. —ment, s. die Veruntreuung, Unterschlagung. —r, s. der Veruntreuende.

Embitter, v.a. verbittern; to — a person's life, einem das Leben sauer machen.

Emblem, s. das Sinnbild. —atic(al), adj., —atically, adv. emblematisch, sinnbildlich.

Embod—iment, s. die Verkörperung. —y, v.a. verkörpern.

Embolden, v.a. ermutigen.

Embrace, I. v.a. umarmen; to — a profession, einen Beruf ergreifen. II. v.n. sich or einander umarmen. III. s. die Umarmung.

Embrasure, s. die Fenster-, Tür-Vertiefung.

Embrocat—e, v.a. einreiben. —ion, s. das Einreibemittel (*Pharm.*).

Embroider, v.a. sticken. —er, s. der (die) Sticker(in). —y, s. die Stickerei.

Embroil, v.a. verwickeln.

Embryo, s. der Fruchtkeim; in —, im Werden.

Emend, v.a. (Texte) verbessern or berichtigen. —ation, s. die Textbesserung.

Emerald, I. s. der Smaragd. II. adj. smaragden.

Emerge, v.n. auftauchen, emporkommen. —nce, s. das Auftauchen.

Emergency, s. das unerwartete Ereignis; in case of—, im Notfalle; — exit, der Notausgang. — plant, die Notanlage (*Elec.*).

Emery, s. der Schmirgel.

Emetic, s. das Brechmittel.

Emigra—nt, I. adj. auswandernd. II. s. der Auswanderer. —te, v.n. auswandern. —tion, s. die Auswanderung.

Eminen—ce, s. (hill, *etc.*) die Erhöhung, Anhöhe; (elevation) die Erhabenheit; (high station) der hohe Rang; (title) die Eminenz. —t, adj., —tly, adv. hoch, erhaben.

Emir, s. der Emir.

Emissary, s. der Sendling, Abgesandte.

Emission, s. das Aussenden; die Ausströmung (*Phys.*).

Emit, v.a. ausströmen (rays, *etc.*).

Emolument, s. das Gehalt; —s, die Einkünfte.

Emotion, s. die Aufregung, Rührung. —al, adj. leicht aufgeregt or gerührt.

Emperor, s. der Kaiser.

Empha—sis, s. der Nachdruck. size, v.a. betonen, mit Nachdruck aussprechen. —tic(al), adj., —tically, adv. nachdrücklich.

Empire, s. das Reich, Kaiserreich.

Empiric, I., —al, adj., —ally, adv. empirisch. II., —ist, s. der Empiriker.

Employ, I. v.a. (use) brauchen, anwenden; (engage in service) anstellen; to be — ed in, sich beschäftigen mit. II. s. das Geschäft, die Beschäftigung. —é, s. der Angestellte. —ee, s. der Arbeiter. —er, s. der Anwender; der Arbeitgeber, Dienstherr. —ment, s. die Beschäftigung; (office) die Anstellung; (service) der Dienst.

Emporium, s. der Stapelplatz (town); das Magazin (shop).

Empower, v.a. ermächtigen.

Empress, s. die Kaiserin.

Emptiness, s. die Leere, Leerheit.

Empty, I. adj. leer; (—ied) ausgeleert. II. v.a. leeren, entleeren, ausleeren. —headed, adj. gedankenarm.

Emul—ate, v.a. nacheifern (einem). —ation, s. der Wetteifer, die Nacheiferung. —ous, adj. (mit einem) wetteifernd, (einem) nacheifernd.

Emulsion, s. die Emulsion (*Pharm.*).

Enable, v.a. befähigen.

Enact, v.a. verordnen. —ment, s. die Verordnung.

Enamel, I. s. der Schmelz. II. v.a. emaillieren.

Enamour, *v.a.* verliebt machen.

Encamp, *v.* I. *a.* lagern. II. *n.* sich lagern. —ment, *s.* das Lager.

Enchant, *v.a.* bezaubern. —er, *s.* der Zauberer. —ing, *adj.*, —ingly, *adv.* bezaubernd. —ment, *s.* die Bezauberung. —ress, *s.* die Zauberin.

Encircle, *v.a.* umringen; (*fig.*) umfassen.

Enclos—e, *v.a.* (fence in) einzäunen, einfriedigen; beifügen (*a letter, etc.*). —ure, *s.* die Einzäunung; der Einschluß (*in a letter*).

Encompass, *v.a.* umringen.

Encore, *int.* noch einmal!

Encounter, I. *s.* das Zusammentreffen; (fight) das Treffen. II. *v.a.* begegnen, treffen; to—difficulties, auf Schwierigkeiten stoßen.

Encourag—e, *v.a.* ermutigen, ermuntern. —ement, *s.* die Ermutigung; die Beförderung. —ing, *adj.*, —ingly, *adv.* ermutigend, aufmunternd.

Encroach, *v.n.* eingreifen (upon, in, *acc.*); to — upon a person's kindness, jemandes Güte mißbrauchen. —ment, *s.* der Eingriff (on rights, in Rechte).

Encumb—er, *v.a.* belasten. —rance, *s.* die Last; das Hindernis.

Encyclop—ædia, —edia, *s.* die Enzyklopädie. —ædian, —edic, *adj.* enzyklopädisch.

End, I. *s.* das Ende; in the —, am Ende, auf die Dauer; on —, aufrecht; to the — that, damit; to no —, vergebens; to this —, zu dem Zweck; to make both —s meet, mit dem Einkommen auskommen, sich nach der Decke strecken. II. *v.a.* endigen, zu Ende bringen, beendigen. III. *v.n.* sich endigen. —ing, *s.* das Ende, der Schluß; die Endung (*Gram.*).

Endanger, *v.a.* gefährden.

Endear, *v.a.* lieb, wert, teuer machen. —ing, *adj.* zärtlich. —ment, *s.* die Liebkosung, Zärtlichkeit.

Endeavour, I. *s.* die Bestrebung. II. *v.n.* sich bestreben.

End—less, *adj.*, —lessly, *adv.* endlos, unendlich. —lessness, *s.* die Endlosigkeit, Unendlichkeit.

Endorse, *v.a.* indossieren. —ment, *s.* das Indossement. —r, *s.* der Indossant, Girant.

Endow, *v.a.* begaben, ausstatten. — ment, *s.* die Begabung.

Endue, *v.a.* ausstatten.

Endur—able, *adj.* erträglich, leiblich. —ance, *s.* die Dauer, Fortdauer; past —ance, unerträglich. —e, *v.* I. *a.* aushalten, ausdauern; erdulden, leiden. II. *n.* (continue) fortdauern; aushalten; dulden. —ing, *adj.* dauernd; duldend, duldsam; power of —ing, die Ausdauer.

End—way(s), —wise, *adv.* aufrecht, gerade.

Enemy, *s.* der Feind, Gegner.

Energ—etic, *adj.*, —etically, *adv.* tatkräftig, energisch. —y, *s.* die Tatkraft, Energie.

Enervat—e, *v.a.* entkräften. —ing, *adj.* entkräftend, schwächend. —ion, *s.* die Entkräftigung.

Enfeeble, *v.a.* schwächen.

Enfilade, I. *s.* das Seitenfeuer. II. *v.a.* der Länge nach beschießen (*Mil.*).

Enfold, *v.a.* einhüllen.

Enforce, *v.a.* erzwingen; zur Geltung bringen (*the law, etc.*).

Enfranchise, *v.a.* befreien. —ment, *s.* die Freilassung.

Engag—e, *v.* I. *a.* (pledge) verpfänden, (bind) verpflichten, verbinden; (employ) beschäftigen; dingen, in Dienst nehmen (*a servant, etc.*); beteiligen (an), hineinbringen (in); angreifen (*the enemy*). II. *n.* sich verpflichten; unternehmen; (fight) sich schlagen. —ement, *s.* die Verpflichtung; die Verlobung (*of lovers*); die Einladung (*to dinner, etc.*); (appointment) die Verabredung; (fight) das Handgemenge. —ing, *adj.*, —ingly, *adv.* einnehmend, gewinnend.

Engine, *s.* die Maschine; (steam —) die Dampfmaschine; die Lokomotive (*Railw.*); (fire —) die Feuerspritze; marine —, Schiffsmaschine; traction —, die Zuglokomobile.

Engine—er, *s.* der Ingenieur. —ering, I. *attrib.*; —ering drawing, die Maschinenzeichnung. II. *s.*; civil —ering, die Ingenieurkunst; electrical —ering, die Elektrotechnik; mechanical —ering, die Maschinenbaukunst. —builder, *s.* der Maschinenbauer. —driver, *s.* der Lokomotivführer (*Railw.*); der Maschinenführer. —fitter, *s.* der Monteur. —house, *s.* der Lokomotivschuppen (*Railw.*); das

Maschinengestell. **—man,** s. der Maschinenwärter.

Engrain, v.a. tief färben, unauslöschlich einprägen.

Engrav—e, v.a. gravieren. **—ed,** p.p. & adj. gestochen. **—er,** s. der Graveur, Bildstecher. **—ing,** s. das Gravieren; (picture) der Kupferstich, Holzschnitt.

Engross, v.a. ganz in Anspruch nehmen; mundieren (Law); to — the conversation, das Gespräch völlig an sich reißen. **—ing,** adj. fesselnd.

Enhance, v.a. erhöhen, vergrößern.

Enigma, s. das Rätsel. **—tic(al),** adj., **—tically,** adv. rätselhaft; (obscure) zweideutig, dunkel.

Enjoin, v.a. (— upon a person, einem) auferlegen, anbefehlen, einschärfen.

Enjoy, v.a. genießen, sich erfreuen (einer S. or an einer S.); to — oneself, sich gut unterhalten, sich amüsieren. **—able,** adj. genießbar (of food); genußreich, erfreulich. **—ment,** s. der Genuß, die Freude.

Enlarge, v. I. a. erweitern, ausdehnen. II. n. sich vergrößern, sich ausdehnen. **—ment,** s. die Vergrößerung, Erweiterung.

Enlighten, v.a. erleuchten, aufklären. **—ment,** s. die Aufklärung.

Enlist, v. I. a. anwerben (soldiers). II. n. sich anwerben lassen.

Enliven, v.a. beleben, ermuntern.

Enmity, s. die Feindschaft; die Feindseligkeit.

Ennoble, v.a. adeln, veredeln. **—ment,** s. das Adeln.

Ennui, s. die Langeweile.

Enorm—ity, s. (atrocity) die Abscheulichkeit. **—ous,** adj., **—ously,** adv. ungeheuer; (atrocious) abscheulich, unerhört. **—ousness,** s. die Ungeheuerlichkeit.

Enough, I. adv. genug; sure —! freilich, gewiß! well —, recht wohl, ziemlich gut. II. adj. genug, hinlänglich. III. s. das Genügende.

Enrage, v.a. wütend machen; —d at, entrüstet über.

Enrapture, v.a. entzücken.

Enrich, v.a. bereichern.

Enrol, v.a. einschreiben; to — oneself, sich anwerben lassen. **—ment,** s. das Eintragen.

Ensconce, v.r. sich niederlassen.

Enshroud, v.a. umhüllen, einhüllen.

Ensign, s. die Fahne, Standarte.

Enslave, v.a. unterjochen. **—ment,** s. die Knechtung.

Ensnare, v.a. (in einer Schlinge) fangen; (fig.) verführen.

Ensue, v.n. (result) folgen, sich ergeben; (succeed, follow) nachfolgen, erfolgen.

Ensure, v.a. sichern, befestigen.

Entail, s. das Fideikommiß.

Entangle, v.a. verwickeln (in); verlegen machen. **—ment,** s. die Verwickelung.

Enter, v. I. a. hineingehen, eintreten, gehen, ziehen, treten, kommen in; (write down) einschreiben, eintragen. II. n.; to — into, hinein-, hereinkommen, hineingehen, eintreten (in); to — on, upon, vornehmen, sich einlassen in or auf (eine S.); eintreten in (an office, ein Amt); antreten (one's duties, sein Amt). **—ing,** s. der Eintritt.

Enterpris—e, s. die Unternehmung; die Spekulation (risk). **—ing,** adj. unternehmend; (daring) kühn.

Entertain, v.a. unterhalten; (treat as guest) gastlich bewirten; hegen (an opinion); annehmen (a proposal). **—ing,** adj., **—ingly,** adv. unterhaltend, ergötzlich. **—ment,** s. die Unterhaltung.

Enthrone, v.a. auf den Thron setzen; (fig.) thronen. **—ment,** s. die Thronerhebung.

Enthusias—m, s. die Begeisterung. **—t,** s. der Begeisterte, Schwärmer. **—tic,** adj., **—tically,** adv. enthusiastisch, begeistert; (about, für) schwärmerisch (in religion, etc.).

Entic—e, v.a. (an)locken. **—ement,** s. die Lockung. **—er,** s. der Anlocker, Verlocker. **—ing,** adj., **—ingly,** adv. verführerisch, reizend.

Entire, adj., **—ly,** adv. ganz, unversehrt. **—ty,** s. die Ganzheit.

Entitle, v.a. betiteln (books & persons); berechtigen zu.

Entity, s. die Wesenheit, das Wesen.

Entomb, v.a. begraben.

Entomolog—ical, adj., **—ically,** adv. entomologisch. **—ist,** s. der Insektenkenner. **—y,** s. die Insektenkunde.

Entrails, pl. die Eingeweide.

Entrain, v. I. a. verschiffen (auf der Eisenbahn). II. n. sich in einen Zug begeben (of troops).

¹**Entrance,** s. (entry) der Eintritt,

Einzug; (door, etc.) der Eingang; (— into office) Amtsantritt; (— hall) der Hausflur.

²**Entrance**, v.a. entzücken, hinreißen.

Entreat, v.a. ersuchen. —ingly, adv. flehendlich. —y, s. die dringende Bitte.

Entrench, v. I. a. mit Graben versehen (Mil.). II. n. (— upon) sich (dat.) etwas aneignen. —ment, s. die Verschanzung.

Entrust, v.a. anvertrauen (something to a person, einem eine S.).

Entry, s. der Eingang (to a house, etc.); der feierliche Einzug; das Einschreiben (in a book, in ein Buch); die Einfuhr (of goods); to make an —, (bookkeeping) eine Sache buchen; bookkeeping by double —, doppelte Buchführung.

Entwine, v. I. a. herumwickeln. II. n. sich um eine S. winden.

Entwist, v.a. verflechten.

Enumerat—e, v.a. aufzählen. —ion, s. die Aufzählung.

Envelop, v.a. einwickeln, einhüllen. —e, s. der Briefumschlag. —ment, s. die Einhüllung.

Envenom, v.a. vergiften.

Env—iable, adj. beneidenswert. —ier, s. der Neider. —ious, adj., —iously, adv. neidisch (of a person, auf einen). —iousness, s. die Mißgunst.

Environ, v.a. umgeben, umringen. —ment, s. die Umschließung. —s, pl. die Umgegend.

Envoy, s. der Gesandte.

Envy, I. s. der Neid. II. v.a. (be-)neiden.

Enwrap, v.a. einwickeln.

Epaulet, s. das Achselband.

Ephemera, s. die Eintagsfliege. —l, adj. eintägig; (short-lived) schnell vorübergehend.

Epic, I. adj. episch. II. s. das Epos.

Epicure, s. der Feinschmecker. —an, I. adj. epikureisch. II. s. der Lebemann.

Epidemic, I. adj. epidemisch. II. s. die Epidemie, Seuche.

Epi—gram, s. das Epigramm. —grammatic, adj. epigrammatisch.

Epilepsy, s. die Fallsucht.

Epilogue, s. der Epilog, das Nachwort.

Epiphany, s. das Dreikönigsfest.

Episcopa—cy, s. die bischöfliche Verfassung. —l, adj. bischöflich. —te, s. die Bischofswürde.

Episode, s. der Zwischenfall, Vorfall.

Epist—le, s. das Sendschreiben. —olary, adj. brieflich.

Epitaph, s. die Grabschrift.

Epithet, s. die Benennung.

Epi—tome, s. der Abriß. —tomize, v.a. abkürzen.

Epoch, s. die Epoche.

Equa—bility, s. der Gleichmut (of temper, etc.). —ble, adj., —bly, adv. gleichförmig, gleich.

Equa—l, I. adj., —lly, adv. gleich; (uniform) gleichmäßig. II. s. der Gleiche; my —s, meinesgleichen. III. v.n. (einem) gleich kommen, gleichen; not to be —led, nicht seinesgleichen haben. —lity, s. die Gleichheit. —lization, s. die Gleichmachung. —lize, v.a. gleichmachen.

Equanimity, s. der Gleichmut.

Equation, s. die Gleichung.

Equator, s. der Äquator. —ial, adj. äquatorial.

Equerry, s. der Stallmeister.

Equestrian, I. adj. reitend, beritten. II. s. der Reiter.

Equi—angular, adj. gleichwinkelig. —lateral, adj. gleichseitig.

Equilibrium, s. das Gleichgewicht; to be in —librium, sich das Gleichgewicht halten.

Equine, adj. pferdeartig, Pferde-.

Equinox, s. die Tag- und Nacht-gleiche.

Equip, v.a. ausrüsten. —age, s. die Equipage. —ment, s. die Ausrüstung; das Betriebsmaterial.

Equit—able, adj., —ably, adv. billig, gerecht, unparteiisch. —y, s. die Billigkeit; die Gerechtigkeit.

Equivalent, I. adj., gleichwertig. II. s. der Gleichwert, Gegenwert.

Equivocal, adj., —vocally, adv. doppelsinnig. —vocate, v.a. zweideutig reden.

Era, s. die Ära, die Zeitrechnung.

Eradica—ble, adj. ausrottbar. —te, v.a. entwurzeln, ausrotten. —tion, s. die Entwurzelung.

Eras—e, v.a. auskratzen, auslöschen. —ement, s. das Auskratzen. —er, s. der Radiergummi. —ure, s. das Auskratzen.

Ere, I. conj. ehe, bevor. II. prep. vor; — this, schon vorher; — long, in kurzem; bald; — now, vormals.

Erect, I. *adj.* aufrecht, gerade. II. *v.a.* aufrichten; errichten (*a monument, etc.*). **—er,** *s.* der Erbauer. **—ion,** *s.* das Aufrichten; (building) das Gebäude. **—ly,** *adv.* aufrecht. **—ness,** *s.* die Geradheit.

Ergo, *adv. & conj.* also, folglich, daher.

Ermine, *s.* das Hermelin.

Ero—de, *v.a.* zerfressen. **—sion,** *s.* die Zerfressung.

Erotic, *adj.* sinnlich.

Err, *v.n.* herumirren; (*fig.*) sich irren.

Errand, *s.* die Botschaft, der Auftrag; to go on **—s,** Botschaften ausrichten. **—boy,** *s.* der Laufbursche.

Errant, *adj.* irrend; knight **—,** fahrender Ritter.

Erratic, *adj.,* **—ally,** *adv.* regellos, wandelbar.

Erratum, *s.* der Druckfehler.

Erroneous, *adj.,* **—ly,** *adv.* fehlhaft, irrig, unrichtig.

Error, *s.* der Irrtum, Fehler.

Erudit—e, *adj.,* **—ely,** *adv.* gelehrt. **—ion,** *s.* die Gelehrsamkeit.

Erupti—on, *s.* der Ausbruch. **—ve,** *adj.* ausbrechend.

Escapade, *s.* der Streich.

Escape, I. *v.a.* entwischen, entkommen. II. *v.n.* entkommen, entrinnen. III. *s.* das Entrinnen, die Flucht; to have a narrow **—,** mit genauer Not davon kommen.

Escort, I. *s.* die Begleitung (*also Mil.*), das Geleit. II. *v.a.* geleiten.

Escutcheon, *s.* der *and* das Wappenschild.

Espalier, *s.* das Spalier.

Especial, *adj.* besonder. **—ly,** *adv.* besonders, hauptsächlich.

Esplanade, *s.* die Esplanade.

Espous—als, *pl.* die Vermählung. **—e,** *v.a.* vermählen, verheiraten (to, an (*acc.*)).

Espy, *v.a.* erspähen.

Essay, I. *v.a.* versuchen, probieren. II. *s.* der Versuch; der Aufsatz; (trial) die Probe. **—ist,** *s.* der Essayist.

Essen—ce, *s.* das Wesen einer S.; (perfume) die Essenz. **—tial,** *adj.,* **—tially,** *adv.* wesentlich; (important) wichtig.

Establish, *v.a.* festsetzen; (found) errichten, gründen; verordnen (*laws, rules, etc.*); (confirm) bestätigen; **—ed** Church, die Staatskirche. **—er,** *s.* der

Stifter. **—ment,** *s.* die Festsetzung, Gründung, Errichtung.

Estate, *s.* (position) der Rang, Stand; (fortune) das Besitztum; (property) das Gut; personal **—,** bewegliche Habe; real **—,** unbewegliche Habe.

Esteem, I. *v.a.* hochschätzen, achten; (deem) erachten, dafür halten. II. *s.* die Hochachtung.

Estima—ble, *adj.* (that can be **—ted**) schätzbar; (worthy of esteem) wertvoll, achtungswert, schätzbar. **—bleness,** *s.* die Schätzbarkeit. **—te,** I. *v.a.* schätzen, würdigen. II. *s.* die Schätzung; der (Vor)anschlag. **—tion,** *s.* die Achtung. **—tor,** *s.* der Schätzer, Taxator.

Estrange, *v.a.* entfremden (from a person, einem). **—ment,** *s.* die Entfremdung.

Estuary, *s.* der Meeresarm.

Etcetera = und so weiter, und so fort.

Etch, *v.a.* ätzen. **—er,** *s.* der Radierer, Ätzer. **—ing,** *s.* das Ätzen; (pen & ink drawing) die Radierung.

Etern—al, I. *adj.,* **—ally,** *adv.* ewig. II. *s.* das Ewige. **—ity,** *s.* die Ewigkeit.

Ether, *s.* der Äther. **—eal,** *adj.,* **—eally,** *adv.* ätherisch (*also fig.*). **—ealize,** *v.a.* vergeistigen.

Ethic—al, *adj.,* **—ally,** *adv.* sittlich, ethisch. **—s,** *s.* die Ethik, die Sittenlehre.

Ethnography, *s.* die Völkerkunde.

Etiquette, *s.* die Sitte, Etikette.

Etymolog—ical, *adj.,* **—ically,** *adv.* etymologisch. **—ist,** *s.* der Etymolog(e). **—y,** *s.* die Wortableitung, Etymologie.

Eucharist, *s.* das heilige Abendmahl.

Eu—logistic, *adj.,* **—logistically,** *adv.* lobrednerisch. **—logium,** *s.,* **—logy,** *s.* die Lobrede. **—logize,** *v.a.* loben, preisen.

Eunuch, *s.* der Verschnittene.

Euphony, *s.* der Wohlklang, Wohllaut.

Evacuat—e, *v.a.* räumen (*Mil.*). **—ion,** *s.* die Räumung.

Evade, *v.a.* entwischen, entrinnen (einem).

Evangel, *s.* das Evangelium. **—ic(al),** *adj.,* **—ically,** *adv.* evangelisch. **—ist,** *s.* der Evangelist.

Evaporat—e, *v.* I. *n.* verdunsten, verdampfen (*also fig.*). II. *a.* abdampf-

fen laſſen. **—ion,** s. die Ausdün=
ſtung.

Evaſi—on, s. die Ausflucht. **—ve,**
adj., **—vely,** adv. ausweichend.

Eve, s. der Abend; Christmas —, der
Weihnachtsabend, heilige Abend.

Even, I. adj., **—ly,** adv. eben, gerade,
gleich; to make — with the ground,
dem Boden gleich machen; to be —
with a person, mit einem quitt ſein;
odd or —, gerade oder ungerade. II.
adv. (just) gerade, eben; ſelbſt, ſogar;
— though, wenn auch; not —, nicht
einmal. III. v.a. gleich machen. **—
ness,** die Ebenheit, Geradheit,
Gleichheit. **—tempered,** adj. gleich=
mütig, gelaſſen.

Evening, I. s. der Abend. II. adj.
Abend=.

Event, s. die Begebenheit, das Er=
eignis; at all —s, auf alle Fälle. **—
ful,** adj. ereignisvoll. **—ual,** adj.
(resultant) erfolgend; (final) ſchließlich,
endlich. **—ually,** adv. am Ende. **—
uate,** v.n. auslaufen, endigen.

Ever, adv. (always) immer; (con=
tinually) ſtets, beſtändig; (at any
time) je, jemals, zu irgend einer Zeit;
(in any degree) noch, irgend; — so,
noch ſo; — since, von der Zeit an;
for —, immer und ewig; liberty for
—, es lebe die Freiheit. **—y,** adj.
jed(=er, =e, =es) alle; — one, ein
jeder, jeder(mann); **—y** now and
then, dann und wann; **—y** other day,
einen Tag um den andern. **—green,**
I. s. das Immergrün. II. adj. immer=
grün. **—lasting,** adj., **—lastingly,**
adv. immerdauernd. **—more,** adv.
immerfort. **—ybody,** pron. jeder=
(mann), ein jeder. **—yday,** adj.
alltäglich. **—ything,** pron. alles. **—
ywhere,** adv. überall.

Evict, v.a. vertreiben.

Eviden—ce, s. das Zeugnis (in a
court of law, etc.); (documentary
—ce) das Beweisſtück. **—t,** adj.,
—tly, adv. (visible) augenſcheinlich;
(obvious) offenbar, deutlich.

Evil, I. adj. übel, böſe, ſchlimm.
II. adv. übel. III. s. das Übel, Böſe.
—ly, adv. übel. **—ness,** s. die
Böſartigkeit. **—doer,** s. der Übel=
täter, Miſſetäter. **—minded,** adj.
übelgeſinnt, boshaft. **—speaking,** s.
die Verleumdung, üble Nachrede.

Evince, v.a. dartun, erweiſen, zeigen.

Evo—cation, s. die Hervorrufung.
—ke, v.a. hervorrufen; beſchwören
(spirits).

Evol—ution, s. die Entwickelung, Ent=
faltung (also Phys.). **—utionary,**
adj. Evolutions=.

Evolve, v. I. a. entwickeln, entfalten.
II. n. ſich entfalten.

Ewe, s. das Mutterſchaf.

Ewer, s. die Waſſerkanne.

Ex, I. prep. = out (of), aus; — officio,
von Amts wegen. II. pref. = out of,
out, formerly, ehemalig, früher.

Exact, I. adj., **—ly,** adv. genau, pünkt=
lich. II. v.a. eintreiben (payment);
(demand) fordern, verlangen. **—ing,**
adj. anſpruchsvoll. **—ion,** s. die
Beitreibung, Eintreibung (of money,
debts, etc.). **—itude,** s. die Genauig=
keit, Pünktlichkeit. **—or,** s. der Bei=
treiber.

Exaggerat—e, v.a. übertreiben. **—
ion,** s. die Übertreibung.

Exalt, v.a. erhöhen, erheben. **—ation,**
s. die Erhebung, Erhöhung. **—ed,**
adj., erhaben, hoch.

Examin—ation, s. die Prüfung, das
Examen. **—e,** v.a. unterſuchen; prü=
fen; verhören (Law); (question
closely) ausfragen; (look into) be=
trachten. **—er,** s. der Prüfende,
Unterſuchende; der Examinator.

Example, s. das Beiſpiel; for —, zum
Beiſpiel.

Exasperat—e, v.a. aufreizen. **—ion,**
s. die Erbitterung; die Entrüſtung.

Excavat—e, v.a. ausgraben. **—ion,**
s. die Aushöhlung.

Exceed, v. I. a. (go beyond) über=
ſchreiten; (surpass) übertreffen (in a
thing, an einer S.); to — one's credit,
ſein Guthaben überſchreiten. II. n.
zu weit gehen. **—ing,** adj. übermäßig.
—ingly, adv. außerordentlich, überaus.

Excel, v. I. n. ſich auszeichnen. II. a.
übertreffen. **—lence, —lency,** s. die
Vortrefflichkeit, Vorzüglichkeit; (title)
die Excellenz. **—lent,** adj., **—lently,**
adv. vortrefflich, vorzüglich.

Except, I. v.a. ausſchließen, vorbe=
halten. II. conj. außer, es ſei denn
daß, wenn nicht. III. prep. mit
Ausnahme von, ausgenommen. **—
ion,** s. die Ausnahme; (objection)
der Einwurf. **—ionable,** adj. anfecht=
bar. **—ional,** adj. außergewöhnlich.
—ionally, adv. ausnahmsweiſe.

Excess, I. *s.* das Übermaß; to carry to —, übertreiben. II. *adj.* übermäßig; — fare, der Zuschlag; — luggage, die Überfracht. **—ive,** *adj.,* **—ively,** *adv.* übermäßig.

Exchange, I. *v.a.* (aus=, ein=, um=, ver=)tauschen, (ver=, aus=)wechseln (for, gegen). II. *s.* der Tausch, Austausch; der Wechsel, Umsatz (*of money*); (rate of —) der Kurs; (place of —) die Börse; — of prisoners, die Auswechselung von Gefangenen. **—able,** *adj.* austauschbar, auswechselbar. **—r,** *s.* der Tauscher.

Exchequer, *s.* das Finanzamt; Chancellor of the —, der Finanzminister.

Excisable, *adj.* steuerbar.

¹**Excise,** I. *s.* die Akzise. II. *v.a.* besteuern. **—man,** —officer, *s.* der Akziseeinnehmer, Zollbeamte.

²**Excise,** *v.a.* (her)ausschneiden.

Excision, *s.* die Ausschneidung.

Excit—ability, *s.* die Erregbarkeit. **—able,** *adj.* erregbar, reizbar. **—e,** *v.a.* erregen, aufregen. **—ed,** *adj.,* **—edly,** *adv.* aufgeregt. **—ement,** *s.* die Erregung, Aufregung. **—er,** *s.* der Erreger. **—ing,** *adj.* aufregend.

Exclaim, *v.* I. *n.* ausrufen. II. *a.* ausrufen. **—er,** *s.* der Schreier; der Eiferer.

Exclamat—ion, *s.* der Ausruf; **—ion** mark, das Ausrufzeichen. **—ory,** *adj.* ausrufend.

Exclude, *v.a.* ausschließen.

Exclusi—on, *s.* die Ausschließung, der Ausschluß. **—ve,** *adj.,* **—vely,** *adv.* ausschließend; ausschließlich (*as privileges, etc.*); (select) wählerisch, exklusiv.

Excommunicat—e, I. *v.a.* in den Kirchenbann tun. II. *adj.,* **—ed,** *adj.* gebannt. **—ion,** *s.* der Kirchenbann, die Exkommunikation.

Excrement, *s.* der Kot.

Excrescence, *s.* der Auswuchs.

Excruciat—e, *v.a.* martern. **—ing,** *adj.,* **—ingly,** *adv.* peinigend.

Excursion, *s.* der Ausflug; — train, der Vergnügungszug. **—ist,** *s.* der Ausflügler.

Excurs—ive, *adj.,* **—ively,** *adv.* umherschweifend.

Excus—able, *adj.,* **—ably,** *adv.* entschuldbar. **—ableness,** *s.* die Entschuldbarkeit. **—e,** I. *v.a.* entschuldigen. II. *s.* die Entschuldigung.

Execra—ble, *adj.,* **—bly,** *adv.* ab-

scheulich. **—bleness,** *s.* die Abscheulichkeit. **—te,** *v.a.* verabscheuen. **—tion,** *s.* die Verwünschung.

Execut—e, *v.a.* ausführen, vollführen, vollziehen, verrichten, ausrichten; (put to death) hinrichten. **—er,** *s.* der Vollzieher, Vollstrecker. **—ion,** *s.* die Ausführung, Vollstreckung, Vollziehung; die Hinrichtung. **—ioner,** *s.* der Scharfrichter. **—ive,** I. *adj.,* vollziehend, ausübend. II. *s.* die Obrigkeit. **—or,** *s.* der (Testaments=)Vollstrecker. **—ory,** *adj.* vollziehend; exekutorisch. **—rix,** *s.* die Testamentsvollstreckerin.

Exemplar, *s.* das Muster, Vorbild. **—iness,** *s.* der Musterhaftigkeit. **—y,** *adj.* musterhaft.

Exempt, I. *v.a.* ausschließen (from, von). II. *adj.* befreit (from, von). **—ion,** *s.* die Befreiung, Freiheit.

Exercis—able, *adj.* anwendbar. **—e,** I. *v.a.* üben (*the body or mind*); ausüben (*power, an art*); (practise) einüben; exerzieren, drillen (*soldiers*). II. *v.n.* exerzieren (*Mil.*); sich (*dat.*) Bewegung machen. III. *s.* die Übung; die Ausübung (*of an art, etc.*).

Exert, *v.a.* (employ) anwenden; to — oneself, sich anstrengen. **—ion,** *s.* die Anstrengung.

Exhalation, *s.* die Ausdünstung.

Exhaust, I. *v.a.* erschöpfen. **—ed,** *p.p. & adj.* erschöpft; (*fig.*) abgemattet. **—ing,** *adj.* anstrengend. **—ion,** *s.* die Erschöpfung. **—ive,** *adj.,* — **ively,** *adv.* erschöpfend. **—less,** *adj.* unerschöpflich.

Exhibit, I. *v.a.* zeigen; ausstellen (*for inspection, etc.*). II. *s.* das Exhibitum. **—ion,** *s.* die Ausstellung; (manifestation) die Darlegung, Äußerung. **—or,** *s.* der Aussteller.

Exhilarat—e, *v.a.* erheitern, aufheitern. **—ing,** *adj.,* **—ingly,** *adv.* erheiternd. **—ion,** *s.* die Erheiterung.

Exhort, *v.a.* ermahnen. **—ation,** *s.* die Ermahnung, Mahnung.

Exigen—ce, **—cy,** *s.* (necessity) das Bedürfnis; (emergency) der Notfall. **—t,** *adj.* dringend.

Exile, I. *s.* die Verbannung; (—d person) der Verbannte. II. *v.a.* verbannen.

Exist, *v.n.* sein. **—ence,** *s.* das

Dasein. **—ent,** **—ing,** *adj.* vorhanden, bestehend.

Exit, *s.* der Abgang; (way out) der Ausgang.

Exodus, *s.* der Auszug; zweites Buch Mosis (*B.*).

Ex officio, *adj. & adv.* amtlich, von Amtswegen.

Exonerat—e, *v.a.* entlasten. **—ion,** *s.* die Entlassung, Befreiung. **—ive,** *adj.* entlastend.

Exorbitan—ce, **—cy,** *s.* die Maßlosigkeit. **—t,** *adj.*, **—tly,** *adv.* maßlos, übermäßig.

Exorcis—e, *v.a.* (Geister, 2c.) beschwören. **—er,** **—t,** *s.* der Geisterbeschwörer. **—m,** *s.* die Geisterbeschwörung; (charm) die Beschwörungsformel.

Exotic, *adj.* ausländisch, exotisch.

Expan—d, *v.* I. *a.* ausbreiten. II. *n.* sich ausbreiten, sich ausspannen. **—se,** *s.* die Ausdehnung. **—sible,** *adj.* (aus) dehnbar. **—sion,** *s.* die Ausbreitung; (the —ding) die Erweiterung. **—sive,** *adj.* (—ding) ausdehnend; (—sible) ausdehnungsfähig. **—siveness,** *s.* die Ausdehnungsfähigkeit, Mitteilsamkeit.

Expect, *v.a.* erwarten; (look forward to) entgegensehen. **—ancy,** *s.* die Erwartung. **—ation,** *s.* die Erwartung, Hoffnung.

Expedi—ence, **—ency,** *s.* die Schicklichkeit. **—ent,** I. *adj.*, **—ently,** *adv.* (fitting) schicklich, füglich; (advisable) ratsam; (advantageous) zuträglich. II. *s.* das Mittel; (shift) der Ausweg. **—te,** *v.a.* beschleunigen. **—tion,** *s.* (haste) die Geschwindigkeit; (journey etc.) die Reise, Expedition. **—tionary,** *adj.* Expeditions-. **—tious,** *adj.*, **—tiously,** *adv.* schnell, hurtig.

Expel, *v.a.* vertreiben, wegtreiben (from, von, aus).

Expen—d, *v.a.* ausgeben (*money*); verwenden (*labour*); (use up) verbrauchen. **—diture,** **—se,** *s.* die Ausgabe; die Kosten; —diture of time, der Zeitaufwand. **—sive,** *adj.*, **—sively,** *adv.* kostspielig, teuer. **—siveness,** *s.* die Kostspieligkeit.

Exper—ience, I. *s.* die Erfahrung; by —ience, aus Erfahrung. II. *v.a.* erfahren. **—ienced,** *adj.* erfahren, erprobt.

Exper—iment, I. *s.* der Versuch, das Experiment. II. *v.n.* Versuche an-

stellen (upon, mit), experimentieren. **—imental,** *adj.*, **—imentally,** *adv.* auf Erfahrung gegründet.

Expert, I. *adj.*, **—ly,** *adv.* geschickt, gewandt. II. *s.* der Sachverständige, Fachmann. **—ness,** *s.* die Gewandtheit.

Expir—ation, *s.* (breathing out) das Ausatmen; (termination) der Ablauf, Verlauf; at the time of **—ation** (*C.L.*), zur Verfall(s)zeit. **—atory,** *adj.* ausatmend. **—e,** *v.n.* aushauchen; (die) sterben, verscheiden; erlöschen (*as time, etc.*).

Explain, *v.* I. *a.* erklären. II. *n.* sich erklären. **—able,** *adj.* erklärbar. **—er,** *s.* der Erklärer.

Explanat—ion, *s.* die Erklärung, Auslegung; to demand an **—ion** from a person, sich mit einem auseinandersetzen. **—ory,** *adj.* erklärend.

Explicit, *adj.*, **—ly,** *adv.* ausdrücklich. **—ness,** *s.* die Deutlichkeit, Bestimmtheit.

Explode, *v.* I. *a.* zerspringen lassen. II. *n.* explodieren, zerplatzen.

Exploit, I. *s.* die Großtat, Heldentat. II. *v.a.* ausbeuten. **—able,** *adj.* ausnutzbar. **—ation,** *s.* die Ausbeutung.

Explor—ation, *s.* die Erforschung. **—e,** *v.a.* er=, ausforschen, unterfuchen. **—er,** *s.* der Erforscher.

Explosi—on, *s.* die Explosion, Zersprengung. **—ve,** I. *adj.*, **—vely,** *adv.* losknallend. II. *s.* der Sprengstoff. **—veness,** *s.* die Explodierbarkeit.

Exponent, *s.* der Erklärer, Ausleger.

Export, I. *v.a.* ausführen. II. *s.* die Ausfuhr. **—able,** *adj.* ausführbar. **—ation,** *s.* die Ausfuhr. **—er,** *s.* der Exporthändler.

Expos—e, *v.a.* ausstellen; belichten (*Phot.*); (disclose) darlegen; (subject) bloßstellen. **—ition,** *s.* (interpretation) die Auslegung; (exhibition) die Ausstellung.

Expostulat—e, *v.n.* to **—e** with a person upon, on *or* for, einem ernste Vorstellungen machen über (*acc.*). **—ion,** *s.* der Verweis, Wortwechsel.

Exposure, *s.* die Ausstellung; die Bloßstellung (*to danger*); die Belichtung (*Phot.*).

Expound, *v.a.* auslegen, erklären.

Express, I. *v.a.* ausdrücken, aussprechen (*thoughts, etc.*); (show, exhibit) bezeigen, zu erkennen geben (*love, etc.*), darstellen (*in art*);

to — thoughts, Gedanken äußern.
II. *adj.* ausdrücklich, klar. III. *s.* der
Eil-, Eigenbote, die Stafette. —**ible**,
adj. ausdrückbar. —**ion**, *s.* der Aus=
druck. —**ionless**, *adj.* ausdruckslos.
—**ive**, *adj.*, —**ively**, *adv.* ausdrucksvoll.
—**ly**, *adv.* ausdrücklich.

Expropriat—**e**, *v.a.* enteignen. —**ion**,
s. die Enteignung.

Expulsi—**on**, *s.* die Vertreibung.
—**ve**, *adj.* vertreibend, austreibend.

Expunge, *v.a.* auslöschen.

Exquisite, *adj.*, —**ly**, *adv.* (aus)er=
lesen, vortrefflich, vorzüglich. —**ness**,
s. die Vorzüglichkeit, Vortrefflichkeit.

Extant, *adj.* vorhanden.

Extempor—**aneous**, *adj.*, —**aneously**,
adv., —**ary**, *adj.*, —**e**, *adj. & adv.* aus
dem Stegreife, unvorbereitet. —**ize**,
v.a. & n. aus dem Stegreife reden.

Extend, *v.* I. *a.* ausdehnen (*limits*,
etc.); ausstrecken (*the hand*, *etc.*);
erweitern (*one's dominions*, *etc.*);
verlängern (*time*); (offer) erteilen,
anbieten. II. *n.* sich erstrecken.

Extensibility, *s.* die Dehnbarkeit.

Extensible, *adj.* dehnbar, streckbar.

Extension, *s.* die Ausdehnung; (com=
pass) der Umfang, die Ausdehnung;
University —, die Volkshochschule.

Exten—**sive**, *adj.*, —**sively**, *adv.* weit
ausgedehnt.

Extent, *s.* die Ausdehnung, Weite,
Größe; to a certain —, gewisser=
maßen, bis zu einem gewissen Grade;
to the — of, bis zum Betrage von.

Extenuat—**e**, *v.a.* verringern. —**ion**,
s. die Milderung, Verringerung.

Exterior, I. *adj.* äußerlich. II. *s.*
das Äußere.

Exterminat—**e**, *v.a.* vertilgen. —**ion**,
s. die Vernichtung.

External, *adj.*, —**ly**, *adv.* äußerlich,
außer, auswärtig. II. *s.*, —**s**, *pl.*
das Äußere, Äußerliche.

Extinct, *adj.* ausgestorben. —**ion**,
s. das Auslöschen, Erlöschen.

Extinguish, *v.a.* auslöschen (*fire, etc.*).
—**er**, *s.* das Löschhütchen.

Extol, *v.a.* preisen, loben. —**ler**, *s.*
der Lobpreiser.

Extort, *v.a.* erpressen. —**er**, *s.* der
Erpresser. —**ion**, *s.* die Erpressung.
—**ionate**, *adj.* erpressend.

Extra, I. *adj.* nachträglich. II. *s.* das
Außergewöhnliche; —**s**, die Neben=
ausgaben.

Extract, I. *v.a.* ausziehen (*a tooth, etc.*);
einen Auszug machen (*from books*).
II. *s.* der Auszug (*from a book, etc.*);
der Auszug, Extrakt (*Chem., etc.*).
—**ion**, *s.* das Heraus=, Aus=ziehen;
(descent) die Abstammung.

Extradit—**e**, *v.a.* ausliefern. —**ion**,
s. die Auslieferung.

Extraordinar—**ily**, *adv.* außerordent=
lich. —**iness**, *s.* das Außerordent=
liche. —**y**, *adj.* außerordentlich.

Extravagan—**ce**, —**cy**, *s.* (excess) die
Ausschweifung; (prodigality) die Ver=
schwendung. —**t**, *adj.*, —**tly**, *adv.*
verschwenderisch.

Extrem—**e**, I. *adj.*, —**ely**, *adv.*
äußerst; (*fig.*) äußerst, höchst; (last)
letzt; (ultra) übertrieben. II. *s.* das
Äußerste. —**ity**, *s.* das Äußerste, die
äußerste Grenze; (straits) äußerste
Verlegenheit. —**ities**, *pl.* die Glied=
maßen; to proceed to —ities, zum
Äußersten schreiten; to be reduced to
—ities, in höchster Not sein.

Extrica—**ble**, *adj.* herauswickelbar. —
te, *v.a.* heraus=wickeln, =winden.

Exuberan—**ce**, —**cy**, *s.* der Überfluß.
—**t**, *adj.*, —**tly**, *adv.* überflüssig;
überschwenglich.

Exult, *v.n.* frohlocken. —**ant**, *adj.*
frohlockend; triumphierend. —**ation**,
s. das Frohlocken.

Eye, I. *s.* das Auge (*also fig.*); das
Öhr (*of a needle*); to — ansehen,
betrachten. —**d**, *adj.*; black-—d,
schwarzäugig. —**ball**, *s.* der Aug=
apfel. —**brow**, *s.* die Augenbraue.
—**glass**, *s.* der Kneifer, Zwicker,
Klemmer. —**lash**, *s.* die Augen=
wimper. —**lid**, *s.* das Augenlid.
—**sight**, *s.* das Gesicht; (power of
vision) die Sehkraft. —**tooth**, *s.*
der Augenzahn. —**witness**, *s.* der
Augenzeuge.

Eyrie, *s.* der Horst.

* * *

F

F, f, *s.* das F, f; das F (*Mus.*).

Fable, *s.* die Fabel.

Fabric, *s.* das Fabrikat, Gewebe, der
Stoff. —**ate**, *v.a.* verfertigen, her=
stellen, fabrizieren; (invent) erfinden.
—**ation**, *s.* die Herstellung, Fabrikation
(*of cloth, etc.*); die Erdichtung. —**ator**,
s. der Verfertiger; der Lügenerfinder.

Fabul—ist, *s.* der Fabeldichter. **—ous,** *adj.,* **—ously,** *adv.* fabelhaft.

Façade, *s.* die Fassade.

Face, I. *s.* das Gesicht, das Angesicht; Antlitz (*high style*); on the — of it, auf den ersten Blick; double-—d, falsch; shame-—d, beschämt. II. *v.a.* (einem) ins Gesicht sehen; (be opposite) gegenüber liegen *or* stehen; (brave) trotzen; verbrämen, besetzen (*a dress, etc.*); this window —s the street, dieses Fenster geht auf die Straße. III. *v.n.;* to — about, sich (um)drehen, sich wenden; right-about —! kehrt euch!

Facet, *s.* die Facette.

Facetious, *adj.,* **—ly,** *adv.* lustig. **—ness,** *s.* die Drolligkeit.

Facial, *adj.* gesichts-.

Facil—e, *adj.* leicht. **—itate,** *v.a.* erleichtern. **—itation,** *s.* die Erleichterung, Nachgiebigkeit. **—ity,** *s.* die Gewandtheit; (opportunity) die günstige Gelegenheit; die Nachgiebigkeit.

Facsimile, *s.* das Faksimile.

Fact, *s.* (reality) die Wirklichkeit; (matter of —) die Tatsache; in —, in der Tat, ja sogar.

Factio—n, *s.* die Partei, Faktion; (dissension) die Zwietracht. **—us,** *adj.,* **—usly,** *adv.* (turbulent) aufrührerisch; (disloyal) ungehorsam. **—usness,** *s.* der Parteigeist; der aufrührerische Sinn.

Factor, *s.* der Faktor.

Factory, *s.* die Fabrik, das Fabrikgebäude.

Faculty, *s.* die Fähigkeit; die Fakultät (*Univ.*).

Fad, *s.* die Grille, Laune; it's a — of mine, das ist meine Liebhaberei. **—dy,** *adj.* grillenhaft, launisch.

Fad—e, *v.n.* (ver)welken; (lose colour) verbleichen; to — away, vergehen. **—ing,** *adj.,* **—ingly,** *adv.* vergänglich.

Fag, *v.n.* sich abmühen. **—ged,** *adj.* erschöpft.

Faggot, *s.* das Holzbündel.

Fail, I. *v.n.* (be wanting) fehlen, mangeln; (miss) fehlschlagen; stocken; versagen (voice); nachlassen (strength); ermangeln (*in a duty*); Bankerott machen (*C.L.*); she cannot — to, sie kann nicht umhin zu. II. *v.a.* verlassen; he —ed me, er hat mich im Stich gelassen; my courage —ed me, mir sank der Mut. III. *s.;* without

—, unfehlbar, ganz gewiß. **—ing,** *s.* der Fehler, die Schwäche. **—ure,** *s.* das Fehlen; die Ermangelung; das Fehlschlagen, Mißlingen (*of an enterprise, etc.*); der Bank(e)rott (*C.L.*).

Fain, *adv.* gern.

Faint, I. *adj.,* **—ly,** *adv* schwach, kraftlos, ohnmächtig; blaß (*as a colour*). II. *v.n.* ohnmächtig werden; (grow weak) ermatten. III. *s.* die Ohnmacht. **—ness,** *s.* die Schwäche. **—hearted,** *adj.* schwachherzig. **—heartedness,** *s.* der Kleinmut.

¹**Fair,** I. *adj.* (beautiful) schön, hübsch; (blonde) hellfarbig, blond; (clear) hell. II. *adj. & adv.* günstig (*as wind*); (equitable) ehrlich, redlich; (just) billig; — chances, gute Aussichten; — copy, die Reinschrift; — play, ehrliches Spiel; — dealing, die Redlichkeit. **—ly,** *adv.* ehrlich, billig; (legibly) leserlich. **—ness,** *s.* die Schönheit (*of a form*); die Redlichkeit, Billigkeit. **—haired,** *adj.* mit blondem Haar. **—spoken,** *adj.* höflich, artig.

²**Fair,** *s.* die Messe, der Jahrmarkt.

Fairy, I. *adj.* feenhaft. II. *s.* die Fee. **—land,** *s.* das Feenland, Elfenreich. **—like,** *adj.* feenartig; feenhaft. **—tale,** *s.* das Märchen.

Faith, *s.* (trust) das Vertrauen; (belief) der Glaube (*also Theol.*); —! fürwahr! in good —, auf Treu und Glauben, ehrlich. **—ful,** I. *adj.,* **—fully,** *adv.* treu; ehrlich. II. *s.;* the —ful, die Rechtgläubigen. **—fulness,** *s.* die Treue. **—less,** *adj.,* **—lessly,** *adv.* treulos. **—lessness,** *s.* die Treulosigkeit.

Fake, *s.* der Betrug, Schwindel.

Falcon, *s.* der Falke. **—er,** *s.* der Falkner. **—ry,** *s.* die Falkenjagd.

Fall, I. *ir.v.n.* fallen, (nieder-)stürzen; to — asleep, einschlafen; to — away, abfallen; to — back, zurückfallen; to — down, niederfallen; to — due, fällig, zahlbar werden; to — in, einfallen; — in! angetreten! (*Mil.*); to — off, herab-, herunterfallen; abfallen (von einem) (fig.); to — out, ausfallen; zanken; (chance) vorfallen, sich ereignen; to — under, unter (eine S.) fallen, dazu gerechnet werden; to — upon, auf (eine S.) fallen, (einen) anfallen; to — ill, krank werden; to — in love with, sich

verlieben in; his face fell, er machte
ein langes Gesicht. II. *s.* das Fallen,
der Fall, Sturz; der Herbst. **—ing,**
s. das Fallen. **—ing-star,** *s.* die
Sternschnuppe.

Fallac—ious, *adj.,* **—iously,** *adv.* trü=
gerisch. **—iousness,** *s.* die Trüg=
lichkeit. **—y,** *s.* die Täuschung; der
Trugschluß.

Fallib—ility, *s.* die Fehlbarkeit. **—le,**
adj., **—ly,** *adv.* fehlbar.

Fallow, I. *adj.* fahl, falb; brach (*Agr.*).
II. *s.* das Brachfeld.

Fals—e, I. *adj. & adv.,* **—ely,** *adv.*
falsch; **—e key,** der Nachschlüssel. II.
s. das Falsche, Unwahre. **—ehood,**
s. die Lüge; die Falschheit. **—eness,**
s. die Falschheit. **—etto,** *s.* das
Falsett (*Mus.*). **—ification,** *s.* die
Verfälschung. **—ifier,** *s.* der Ver=
fälscher. **—ify,** *v.a.* fälschen (*coin*);
verfälschen (*writings, etc.*). **—ity,** *s.*
die Falschheit.

Falter, *v.* I. *a.* stammeln. II. *n.* wan=
ken (*in walking*); stocken (*in a speech*).

Fam—e, *s.* der Ruhm. **—ed,** *adj.*
berühmt. **—ousness,** *s.* die Berühmt=
heit.

Famil—iar, I. *adj.,* **—iarly,** *adv.* ver=
traut, vertraulich, intim; wohlbe=
kannt (with, mit); (affable) leutselig,
umgänglich; (habitual) gewohnt, ge=
wöhnlich; (unceremonious) zu ver=
traut, frei. II. *s.* der Vertraute. **—
iarity,** *s.* die Vertraulichkeit; die
Leutseligkeit, Zugänglichkeit; (freedom) die Ungezwungenheit. **—iarize,**
v.a. sich gewöhnen an (*acc.*), sich
bekannt machen mit.

Family, I. *s.* die Familie. II. *adj.*
zur Familie gehörig.

Fami—ne, *s.* die Hungersnot. **—sh,** *v.*
I. *a.* verhungern lassen. II. *n.* ver=
hungern; (*fig.*) verschmachten.

Famous, *adj.,* **—ly,** *adv.* berühmt.

Fan, I. *s.* der Fächer; der Ventilator;
(*sl.*) der Liebhaber; film-—,
Filmschwärmer. II. *v.a.* anfachen (*a
flame*); (*fig.*) entfachen, entflammen.

Fanatic, I. *adj.,* **—al,** *adj.,* **—ally,** *adv.*
fanatisch. II. *s.* der Fanatiker. **—
ism,** *s.* die (religiöse) Schwärmerei.

Fanc—ier, *s.* der Liebhaber. **—iful,**
adj., **—ifully,** *adv.* phantastisch,
schwärmerisch. **—ifulness,** *s.* das
grillenhafte Wesen. **—y,** I. *s.* die
Phantasie, Einbildungskraft. II. *v.a.*

sich (*dat.*) einbilden. III. *v.n.* sich
(*dat.*) einbilden, sich (*dat.*) vorstellen.
—y-(dress-)ball, *s.* der Kostümball.
—y-goods, *pl.* Galanteriewaren. **—
y-price,** *s.* der Liebhaberpreis, ein sehr
hoher Preis. **—y-work,** *s.* feine
Handarbeit.

Fane, *s.* der Tempel.

Fang, *s.* der Fangzahn, die Klaue.

Fantastic, **—al,** *adj.,* **—ally,** *adv.*
phantastisch, eingebildet; (odd) gril=
lenhaft. **—alness,** *s.* die Grillen=
fängerei.

Fantasy, *s.* die Phantasie.

Far, I. *adj.* fern, entfernt, weit; on
the **— side,** jenseits; **— from it,** weit
davon entfernt; **by —,** bei weitem;
—-fetched, weit hergeholt, gezwungen,
bei den Haaren herbeigezogen. II.
adv. fern, weit. **—ness,** *s.* die Ent=
fernung. **—-fetched,** *adj.* gesucht.
—-reaching, *adj.* weittragend. **—-
sighted,** *adj.* weitsichtig.

Farc—e, *s.* die Posse (*also Theat.*).
—ical, *adj.* possenhaft, drollig.

Fare, I. *v.n.* (get on) ergehen, sich be=
finden; (feed) essen; he **—d badly,**
es ist ihm schlecht ergangen. II. *s.* das
Fahrgeld; (passenger) der Passagier;
(food) die Speise; **bill of —,** die
Speisekarte; **poor —,** schmale Kost.
—well, I. *s.* Abschieds=; **—well
letter,** der Abschiedsbrief. II. *s.* das
Lebewohl. III. *interj.* lebewohl!

Farm, I. *s.* der Pachthof; (— land)
das Gut. II. *v.a.* bauen; (— out)
verpachten. **—er,** *s.* der Pächter,
Meier; der Landwirt. **—ing,** *s.* die
Landwirtschaft. **—-house,** *s.* der
Meierhof, die Meierei, der Bauernhof.
—-yard, *s.* der Hof.

Farrier, *s.* der Hufschmied.

Farthe—r, *adj. & adv.* (*comp. of* Far)
ferner, weiter. **—st,** I. *adj.* (*sup. of*
Far) fernst, weitest, entferntest. II.
adv.; **at —st,** am fernsten, am weite=
sten.

Farthing, *s.* der Heller.

Fascinat—e, *v.a.* bezaubern. **—ion,**
s. die Bezauberung.

Fashion, I. *s.* die Mode; **people of —,**
Leute von gutem Tone; **to set the
—,** den Ton angeben. II. *v.a.* bilden,
gestalten. **—able,** *adj.,* **—ably,** *adv.*
modisch; **it is —able,** es ist die Mode.

1Fast, *adj. & adv.* fest; fest, tief (*as
sleep*); schnell; **my watch is —,**

meine Uhr geht vor; she is —, sie ist flott, fesch; — train, der Schnellzug.

²Fast, I. *v.n.* fasten. II. *s.,* **—ing,** *s.* das Fasten. **—-day,** *s.* der Fasttag.

Fasten, *v.* I. *a.* fest machen, befestigen (to, an). II. *n.* sich festhalten, sich ansetzen (upon, an, *acc.*). **—er,** *s.* der Befestiger. **—ing,** *s.* das Befestigungsmittel.

Fastidious, *adj.,* **—ly,** *adv.* wählerisch. **—ness,** *s.* das wählerische Wesen.

Fat, I. *adj.* fett (*also fig.*). II. *s.* das Fett. **—ness,** *s.* die Fettigkeit.

Fat—al, *adj.,* **—ally,** *adv.* verhangnisvoll; tödlich (*as wounds, etc.*). **—alism,** *s.* der Fatalismus. **—alist,** *s.* der Fatalist. **—alistic,** *adj.* fatalistisch. **—ality,** *s.* das Verhängnis; (*fig.*) das Mißgeschick.

Fate, *s.* das Schicksal, Verhängnis. **—d,** *adj.* bestimmt. **—ful,** *adj.,* **—fully,** *adv.* verhängnisvoll.

Father, *s.* der Vater; — Christmas, der Weihnachtsmann; the early —s, die Kirchenväter. **—hood,** *s.* die Vaterschaft. **—less,** *adj.* vaterlos. **—ly,** *adj.* väterlich. **—-in-law,** *s.* der Schwiegervater. **—land,** *s.* das Vaterland.

Fathom, I. *s.* die Klafter. II. *v.a.* ergründen. **—able,** *adj.* meßbar; ergründlich.

Fatigue, I. *s.* die Ermüdung; die Erschöpfung. II. *v.a.* ermüden, abmatten. **—-duty,** *s.* der Arbeitsdienst (*Mil.*).

Fatt—en, *v.* I. *a.* fett machen, mästen. II. *n.* fett werden. **—y,** *adj.* fettig.

Fatuous, *adj.* albern, nichtig.

Faucet, *s.* der Zapfen, Hahn.

Fault, *s.* der Fehler; to find — with, tadeln, bemängeln; it is my —, es ist meine Schuld. **—iness,** *s.* die Fehlerhaftigkeit. **—less,** *adj.,* **—lessly,** *adv.* fehlerfrei, tadellos. **—lessness,** *s.* die Fehlerlosigkeit. **—y,** *adj.* fehlerhaft, mangelhaft.

Faun, *s.* der Faun. **—a,** *s.* die Tierwelt.

Favour, I. *s.* die Gunst; your —, Ihr geehrtes Schreiben; do me a —, tun Sie mir einen Gefallen; to be in great —, sehr begehrt sein. II. *v.a.* begünstigen, (einem) geneigt sein. **—able,** *adj.,* **—ably,** *adv.* günstig. **—ed,** *adj.* begünstigt. **—ite,** *s.* der Günstling.

¹Fawn, *s.* das Rehkalb. **—-coloured,** *adj.* rehfarben.

²Fawn, *v.n.* schwänzeln (*as a dog*). **—ing,** *adj.,* **—ingly,** *adv.* kriecherisch.

Fay, *s.* die Fee.

Fear, I. *s.* die Furcht; to stand in — of, sich fürchten vor. II. *v.a.* fürchten. III. *v.n.* sich fürchten; no need to —, da ist nichts zu befürchten; never —! seien Sie unbesorgt. **—ful,** *adj.,* **—fully,** *adv.* (timid) furchtsam; (dreadful) furchtbar. **—fulness,** *s.* die Furchtbarkeit, Fürchterlichkeit; die Furchtsamkeit, Furcht. **—less,** *adj.,* **—lessly,** *adv.* furchtlos, unbesorgt. **—lessness,** *s.* die Furchtlosigkeit.

Feasib—ility, *s.* die Tunlichkeit. **—le,** *adj.,* **—ly,** *adv.* tunlich.

Feast, I. *s.* das Gastmahl, der Schmaus. II. *v.a.* (einen) festlich bewirten, speisen. III. *v.n.* sich weiden, sich ergötzen (upon a thing, an einer S.). **—er,** *s.* der Schmauser; der Festgeber.

Feat, *s.* die Heldentat; (— of agility, *etc.*) das Kunststück, Kraftstück.

Feather, *s.* die Feder; to show the white —, Feigheit zeigen; to — one's nest, sein Schäfchen ins trockene bringen. **—ed,** *adj.* befiedert, gefiedert. **—-bed,** *s.* das Federbett. **—brained,** *adj.* unbesonnen, töricht.

Feature, *s.* der Gesichtszug, Zug; —s of a landscape, der Charakter einer Landschaft. **—less,** *adj.* ohne bestimmte Züge.

February, der Februar.

Fecund, *adj.* fruchtbar. **—ate,** *v.a.* befruchten. **—ity,** *s.* die Fruchtbarkeit.

Fed, *imperf. & p.p.* of Feed; to get — up with a thing, eine Sache satt bekommen.

Feder—acy, *s.* der Bund. **—al,** *adj.* bundesmäßig, Bundes-. **—ation,** *s.* die Verbündung.

Fee, I. *s.* die Gebühr, der Lohn; das Honorar (*of a doctor, etc.*). II. *v.a.* bezahlen.

Feebl—e, *adj.,* **—y,** *adv.* schwach. **—e-minded,** *adj.* geistesschwach. **—eness,** *s.* die Schwäche.

Feed, I. *ir.v.a.* füttern (*cattle*); speisen (*people*). II. *ir.v.n.* essen (*as men*); fressen, weiden (*as beasts*); to — the eye upon a thing, die Augen weiden an einer Sache. III. *s.* das Futter.

—er, *s.* der Fütterer; der Babylatz. —ing, *s.* die Nahrung; die Fütterung (*of cattle*). —ing-bottle, *s.* die Saugflasche.

Feel, I. *ir.v.a.* fühlen, befühlen, betasten; (be sensible of) empfinden; to — one's way, vorsichtig gehen. II. *ir.v.n.* fühlen, empfinden; I — cold, ich friere; I — for him, er tut mir leid. III. *s.* das Fühlen. —ing, I. *adj.,* —ingly, *adv.* fühlend; gefühlvoll. II. *s.* das Gefühl, die Empfindung.

Feign, *v.* I. *a.* heucheln. II. *n.* heucheln, sich verstellen. —ed, *adj.* falsch, verstellt. —ing, *s.* die Heuchelei.

Feint, *s.* die Verstellung; die Finte (*fig. & Fenc.*).

Felicit—ate, *v.a.* beglückwünschen. —ation, *s.* die Beglückwünschung. —ous, *adj.,* —ously, *adv.* glücklich; gut gewählt (*expressions*). —y, *s.* die Glückseligkeit.

Feline, *adj.* katzenartig, Katzen-.

¹Fell, *v.a.* fällen. —er, *s.* der Holzfäller.

²Fell, *adj.* grausam.

Felloe, *s.* die (Rad-)Felge.

Fellow, *s.* der Gefährte, Genosse, Kamerad; Mit- (*in compounds*); (equal for one) das Gleiche von einem Paar (*e.g. stockings, gloves*); das Mitglied eines Kollegiums; der Kerl, Gesell, Bursche (*coll.*); the — of a shoe, der andere Schuh; to be —s, zusammen gehören; good —, guter Kerl. —ship, *s.* die Genossenschaft. —citizen, *s.* der Mitbürger. —countryman, *s.* der Landsmann. —creature, *s.* der Mitmensch. —feeling, *s.* das Mitgefühl. —labourer, *s.* der Mitarbeiter. —traveller, *s.* der Reisegefährte.

Felon, *s.* der Verbrecher. —ious, *adj.,* —iously, *adv.* verbrecherisch. —y, *s.* Staatsverbrechen.

Felt, *s.* der Filz; —ed cloth, das Filztuch.

Fem—ale, I. *adj.* weiblich. II. *s.* das Weib; das Weibchen (*of beasts, etc.*). —inine, *adj.* weiblich (*also Gram.*).

Fen, *s.* der Sumpf. —land, *s.* das Marschland.

Fenc—e, I. *s.* der Zaun, das Gehege. II. *v.a.* einfriedigen, einhegen, umzäunen. III. *v.n.* fechten, kämpfen. —er, *s.* der Fechter. —ing, *s.* das

Fechten; die Fechtkunst. —ing-master, *s.* der Fechtmeister. —ing-school, *s.* die Fechtschule.

Fend, *v.a.*; to — off, abwehren; she must — for herself, sie ist auf sich selbst angewiesen. —er, *s.* der Kaminvorsatz.

Fennel, *s.* der Fenchel.

Ferment, I. *s.* die Gärung. II. *v.a.* gären lassen. III. *v.n.* gären. —able, *adj.* gärungsfähig. —ation, *s.* die Gärung. —ing, *adj.* gärend.

Fern, *s.* das Farnkraut.

Feroci—ous, *adj.,* —ously, *adv.* grimmig. —ty, *s.* die Grimmigkeit.

Ferret, *s.* das Frett(chen); to — out, ausspüren.

Ferry, I. *s.* die Fähre. II. *v.a. & n.* fahren. —man, *s.* der Fährmann.

Fertil—e, *adj.,* —ely, *adv.* fruchtbar. —ity, *s.* die Fruchtbarkeit (*also fig.*). —ization, *s.* die Befruchtung. —ize, *v.a.* befruchten. —izer, *s.* das Düngmittel.

Ferv—ency, *s.* die Inbrunst. —ent, *adj.,* —ently, *adv.* inbrünstig; —ent prayer, das innige Gebet. —id, *adj.,* —idly, *adv.* glühend. —idness, *s.* (*fig.*) der Eifer, das Feuer. —our, *s.* die Hitze; die Inbrunst, der Eifer.

Festal, *adj.,* —ly, *adv.* festlich.

Fester, *v.n.* eitern.

Fest—ival, *s.* der Festtag, das Fest. —ive, *adj.,* —ively, *adv.* festlich. —ivity, *s.* die Festlichkeit.

Festoon, *s.* die Girlande.

Fetch, *v.a.* holen, bringen; to — a high price, einen hohen Preis erzielen; to — away, wegholen; to — down, herunterholen; to — from, herholen aus; to — in, hereinbringen; to — up, heraufholen.

Fetid, *adj.* stinkend.

Fetish, *s.* der Fetisch.

Fetter, I. *v.a.* fesseln. II. *s.* die Fessel.

Feud, *s.* die Fehde. —al, *adj.,* lehnbar. —alism, *s.* der Feudalismus.

Fever, *s.* das Fieber. —ed, *adj.* fieberisch. —ish, *adj.* fieberhaft. —ishness, *s.* die Fieberhaftigkeit.

Few, *adj.* wenig, wenige; a —, some —, einige wenige. —ness, *s.* die geringe Anzahl.

Fiancé, *s.* der Verlobte, Bräutigam. —e, die Braut, Verlobte.

Fiasco, *s.* der Mißerfolg, das Fiasko.

Fib, I. *s.* die (kleine) Lüge. II. *v.n.* lügen. —ber, *s.* der Flunkerer.

Fibr—e, *s.* die Fiber, Faser. **—eless,**
adj. ohne Fibern. **—ous,** *adj.* fiberig,
faserig.

Fickle. *adj.,* wankelmütig. **—ness,** *s.*
der Wankelmut.

Ficti—on, *s.* die Erdichtung; work of
—, der Roman. **—tious,** *adj.,* —
tiously, *adv.* erdichtet; (false) unecht,
nachgemacht.

Fiddle, I. *s.* die Fiedel, Geige, Violine;
to play first —, (*fig.*) die Hauptrolle
spielen. **II.** *v.n.* geigen; (*coll.*) tändeln;
— about, zwecklos geschäftig sein.
III. *v.a.* fiedeln, (auf der) Geige
spielen. **—r,** *s.* der Geiger; Fiedler;
der Spielmann. **—stick,** *s.* der
Geigenbogen. **—sticks!** *int.* Un=
sinn! Possen! **—string,** *s.* die
Geigensaite.

Fidelity, *s.* die Pflichttreue.

Fidget, I. *v.n.* unruhig sein. **II.** *v.a.*
nervös machen. **III.** *s.* nervöse Aufre=
gung; he is a —, er ist ein Zappel=
philipp. **—iness,** *s.* die Aufgeregtheit.
—y, *adj.* unruhig.

Fie, *int.* pfui!

Fief, *s.* das Lehen.

Field, *s.* das Feld (*also fig.*); in the
—, (*fig.*) im Wettbewerb; — of vision,
der Gesichtskreis. **—marshal,** *s.* der
Feldmarschall. **—officer,** *s.* der
Stabsoffizier.

Fiend, *s.* der Unhold. **—ish,** *adj.,*
—ishly, *adv.* teuflisch. **—ishness,** *s.*
die Bosheit.

Fierce, *adj.,* **—ly,** *adv.* wild, grim=
mig. **—ness,** *s.* die Wildheit, Wut.

Fier—iness, *s.* die Hitze, das Feuer.
—y, *adj.* **—ily,** *adv.* feurig, glühend
(*also fig.*).

Fife, *s.* die (Quer=)Pfeife. **—r,** *s.* der
Pfeifer.

Fifteen, *num. adj.* fünfzehn. **—**
th, I. *num. adj.* (der, die, das)
fünfzehnt(e). **II.** *s.* das Fünfzehntel.

Fift—h, I. *num. adj.* (der, die, das)
fünft(e). **II.** *s.* das Fünftel. **—hly,**
adv. fünftens. **—ieth, I.** *num. adj.*
(der, die, das) fünfzigst(e). **II.** *s.* das
Fünfzigstel.

Fifty, *num. adj.* fünfzig.

Fig, *s.* die Feige; (—tree) der Feigen=
baum; I don't care a — for it, ich
mache mir nichts daraus; in full —,
(*coll.*) in vollem Wichs.

Fight, I. *ir.v.n.* fechten, kämpfen,
streiten. **II.** *ir.v.a.* fechten, kämpfen

(mit *or* gegen), schlagen (*a battle*); to
— shy of a person, einen vermeiden;
to — one's way, sich durchschlagen.
III. *s.* das Gefecht, der Kampf. **—er,**
s. der Fechter, Kämpfer. **—ing, I.**
adj. streitbar, kampffähig; Kampf=.
II. *s.* das Gefecht, der Kampf.

Figurative, *adj.,* **—ly,** *adv.* bildlich,
vorbildlich.

Figure, I. *s.* die Figur, Gestalt, Form;
die Ziffer (*Arith.*); to make a —,
eine Rolle spielen. **II.** *v.a.* bilden,
gestalten; (represent) darstellen; I —
to myself, ich stelle mir vor. **III.** *v.n.*
eine Rolle spielen. **—d,** *adj.* figuriert.
—head, *s.* die Bugfigur (*Naut.*);
(*fig.*) die Dekorationsfigur.

Filament, *s.* die Faser.

Filbert, *s.* die Lambertsnuß.

File, I. *s.* die Feile; die Reihe (*Mil.*),
der Draht; die Liste; in single —,
im Gänsemarsch; in rank and —,
in Reih' und Glied. **II.** *v.a.* feilen;
anreihen. **—leader,** *s.* der Flügel=
mann.

Filial, *adj.* kindlich.

Filibuster, *s.* der Freibeuter.

Filigree, *s.* das Filigran.

Fill, I. *v.a.* (an)füllen; to — in, ein=
schalten; to — out, ausfüllen; to
— up, auf=, aus=füllen; to — a post,
eine Stelle bekleiden. **II.** *v.n.* sich
füllen. **III.** *s.* die Fülle, Genüge; to
eat one's —, sich satt essen. **—er,** *s.*
der Trichter (*for wine, etc.*). **—ing,**
s. die Füllung.

Fillet, *s.* die Kopfbinde; — of veal,
das Kalbsfilet.

Filly, *s.* das Stutenfüllen.

Film, *s.* die Membrane; der Film
(*Photo.*); first night of a —, die
Uraufführung eines Films. **—y,** *adj.*
häutig. **—actor,** *s.* **—actress,** *s.*
der (die) Filmschauspieler(in).

Filter, I. *s.* das Filter. **II.** *v.a.*
filtrieren.

Filth, *s.* der Schmutz. **—ily,** *adv*
schmutzig. **—iness,** *s.* die Unreinlich=
keit. **—y,** *adj.* unflätig (*also fig.*).

Fin, *s.* die Finne, Flosse.

Fin—al, *adj.* endlich, schließlich; (de=
cisive) entscheidend; — cause, die
Endursache. **—ality,** *s.* die Finalität.
—ally, *adv.* zuletzt, zum Schluß.

Financ—e, I. *s.* das Finanzwesen.
II. *v.a.* finanziell unterstützen. **—es,**
pl. die Finanzen. **—ial,** *adj.,* **—ially,**

adv. finanziell, Finanz-; —ial position, die Vermögensverhältnisse. —ier, *s.* der Finanzmann.

F nch, *s.* der Fink.

Find, I. *ir.v.a.* finden; to — oneself, sich befinden; to — fault with, tadeln; all found, alles frei, volle Beköstigung. II. *s.* der Fund. —er, *s.* der Finder, Entdecker. —ing, *s.* die Entdeckung; the —ing of the jury, der Ausspruch der Geschworenen.

¹**Fine**, *adj.*, —ly, *adv.* schön, fein; dünn (*as hair, silk, etc.*); scharf (*as an edge*); you are a — fellow! du bist mir ein netter Kerl; the — arts, die schönen Künste. —ness, *s.* die Feinheit; die Zartheit (*of feelings, etc.*). —ry, *s.* der Putz, Staat.

²**Fine**, I. *s.* die Geldstrafe, Geldbuße. II. *v.a.* um Geld strafen.

³**Fine**, *s.*; in —, endlich.

Finesse, I. *s.* die Schlauheit, List. II. *v.n.* Kunstgriffe anwenden.

Finger, I. *s.* der Finger (*also fig.*). II. *v.a.* betasten. —ed, *adj.* gefingert. —board, *s.* die Klaviatur (*of a piano*). —post, *s.* der Wegweiser.

Finis, *s.* das Ende.

Finish, I. *v.a.* endigen, beendigen, vollenden; (stop) aufhören; to put the —ing touch to a thing, die letzte Hand an eine Sache legen. II. *v.n.* aufhören; enden. III. *s.* die Vollendung; (end) der Schluß.

Finite, *adj.*, —ly, *adv.* begrenzt. —ness, *s.* die Eingeschränktheit.

Fir, *s.* (—-tree) die Tanne, Fichte, der Tannenbaum. —cone, *s.* der Tannenzapfen.

Fire, I. *s.* das Feuer (*also fig.*). II. *v.a.* in Brand stecken, anzünden; (*fig.*) anfeuern, entflammen. III. *v.n.* Feuer geben, feuern, schießen (at, upon, auf). —arms, *pl.* Feuerwaffen. —brand, *s.* der Feuerbrand. —brigade, *s.* die Feuerwehr. —engine, *s.* die Feuerspritze. —escape, *s.* die Rettungsleiter. —fly, *s.* der Leuchtkäfer. —irons, *pl.* die Schüreisen. —place, *s.* der Kamin; (*fig.*) der Familienkreis. —side, *s.* der Kamin; (*fig.*) der Familienkreis. —works, *pl.* das Feuerwerk.

Firm, I. *adj.*, —ly, *adv.* fest, hart; standhaft (*fig.*). II. *s.* die (Handels-) Firma (*C.L.*). —ament, *s.* das Firmament. —ness, *s.* die Festigkeit.

First, I. *adj.* erst; in the — place, — of all, zuerst, erstens, erstlich. II. *adv.* erst (*in time*), zuerst (*in time, rank, order*); erstlich, erstens, fürs erste; (previously) erst; — come, — served, wer zuerst kommt, mahlt zuerst. III. *s.* der, die, das Erste; die erste Klasse (*Railw.*); from the —, von Anbeginn. —ly, *adv.* erstlich, erstens, zum Ersten, zuerst. —born, I. *adj.* erstgeboren. II. *s.* der Erstgeborene. —class, *adj.* erstklassig. —rate, *adj.* vorzüglich, vortrefflich, famos.

Fiscal, *adj.* fiskalisch.

Fish, I. *s.* der Fisch; queer —, wunderlicher Kauz. II. *v.a. & n.* fischen; to — for compliments, nach Komplimenten haschen. —er, *s.* der Fischer. —ery, *s.* die Fischerei. —ing, I. *pr.p.*; to go —ing, auf den Fischfang ausgehen. II. *s.* das Fischen, der Fischfang. III. *adj.* fischend. —y, *adj.* fischartig; that sounds —y, das klingt verdächtig. —bone, *s.* die Gräte. —hook, *s.* die Fischangel. —ing-boat, *s.* das Fischerboot. —ing-line, *s.* die Angelschnur. —ing-rod, *s.* die Angelrute. —ing-tackle, *s.* das Angelgerät. —monger, *s.* der Fischhändler.

Fissure, *s.* der Spalt.

Fist, *s.* die Faust; close —ed, geizig. —icuffs, *pl.* Faustschläge.

¹**Fit**, I. *adj.*, —ly, *adv.* (appropriate) tauglich, passend; (qualified) fähig; (proper) angemessen, schicklich. II. *s.* das genaue Passen, Anschließen; it is a bad —, es paßt schlecht. III. *v.a.* (einem einen Anzug) anpassen (*Tail., etc.*); einrichten; (answer) passen für *or* zu, angemessen sein; to — out, ausrüsten, ausstatten; to — up, einrichten; montieren (*mach.*). IV. *v.n.* sich schicken; passen. —ness, *s.* die Füglichkeit, Schicklichkeit, Tauglichkeit. —ted, *p.p. & adj.* ausgestattet; montiert. —ter, *s.* der Installateur, Monteur. —ting, *adj.*, —tingly, *adv.* schicklich, passend; it is not —ting, es schickt sich nicht. —tings, *pl.* die Ausstattung.

²**Fit**, *s.* der Anfall; by —s and starts, ruckweise, dann und wann. —ful, *adj.*, —fully, *adv.* abwechselnd, unterbrochen. —fulness, *s.* die Unbeständigkeit.

Five, *num. adj.* fünf.

Fix, I. *v.a.* befestigen, festmachen, anheften; bestimmen, festsetzen (*a time, a price, etc.*). II. *v.n.*; to — on, sich entschließen für, wählen; to — one's eyes upon, seine Aufmerksamkeit heften auf. III. *s.* die Klemme (*coll.*); I'm in a —, ich bin in Verlegenheit. **—ed,** *adj.* fest; bestimmt; —ed salary, festes Gehalt. **—edly,** *adv.* fest. **—ture,** *s.* die Festsetzung; das Pertinenzstück.

Fizz, I. *v.a.* zischen. II. *s.* das Gezisch. **—le,** *v.n.* zischen.

Flabb—iness, *s.* die Schlaffheit. **—y,** *adj.* schlaff.

¹Flag, *s.* die Flagge (*Naut.*); die Fahne (*Mil.*). **—officer,** *s.* der Flaggenoffizier. **—ship,** *s.* das Flagg(en)schiff. **—staff,** *s.* die Flaggenstange.

²Flag, *v.n.* ermatten, erschlaffen.

³Flag, I. *s.,* **—stone,** *s.* die Fliese, der Fliesstein. II. *v.a.* mit Fliesen belegen. **—ging,** *s.* das Pflastern mit Fliesen.

⁴Flag, *s.* die Schwertlilie (*Bot.*).

Flagon, *s.* das Fläschchen.

Flagran–cy, *s.* die Schändlichkeit. **—t,** *adj.,* **—tly,** *adv.* abscheulich, entsetzlich.

Flail, *s.* der Dreschflegel.

Flak—e, *s.* die Flocke. **—y,** *adj.* flockig.

Flam—e, I. *s.* die Flamme. II. *v.n.* flammen, lodern. **—eless,** *adj.* flammenlos. **—ing,** *adj.,* **—ingly,** *adv.* flammend. **—e-coloured,** *adj.* feuerfarbig, feuerfarben.

Flamingo, *s.* der Flamingo.

Flange, *s.* der Flan(t)sch, die Flan(t)sche.

Flank, I. *s.* die Seite, Weiche (*of animals*); die Flanke (*Mil.*). II. *v.a.* flankieren. III. *v.n.* angrenzen.

Flannel, *s.* der Flanell.

Flap, I. *s.* der Klaps; die Klappe; das Läppchen (*of the ear*); der Flügelschlag (*of wings*). II. *v.a. & n.* klappen, schlagen. III. *v.n.* lose herabhängen. **—per,** *s.* (*coll.*) der Backfisch.

Flar—e, I. *v.n.* flackern; to —e up, aufbrausen. II. *s.* das flackernde Licht. **—ing,** *adj.* auffackernd.

Flash, I. *s.* der Blitz (*of lightning*); (*fig.*) das Auflodern. II. *v.n.* auflodern, blitzen. **—ily,** *adv.* **—light,** *s.* (*Phot.*) das Blitzlicht; **—light photo,** die Blitzlicht-fotografie, -aufnahme. **—y,** *adj.* bunt.

Flask, *s.* die Flasche.

Flat, I. *adj.* platt, flach. II. *adv.*; to sing —, falsch singen; I —ly refused it, ich habe es rundweg abgelehnt; to fall —, (*fig.*) keinen Eindruck machen. III. *s.* die Fläche, Ebene; das Be, ♭ (*Mus.*); die Etage (*of a house*); die Fläche (*of a sword*). **—ness,** *s.* die Fläche. **—ten,** *v.a.* platt, flach machen. **—fish,** *s.* der Flachfisch. **—footed,** *adj.* plattfüßig. **—iron,** *s.* das Bügeleisen.

Flatter, *v.a.* schmeicheln. **—er,** *s.* der Schmeichler. **—ing,** *adj.,* **—ingly,** *adv.* schmeichelhaft, schmeichlerisch. **—y,** *s.* die Schmeichelei.

Flaunt, *v.n.* prangen.

Flavour, I. *s.* der Geschmack. II. *v.a.* würzen. **—ed,** *adj.* schmackhaft, würzig. **—less,** *adj.* geschmacklos.

Flaw, *s.* die Blase (*in cast metal, etc.*). **—less,** *adj.* fleckenlos; fehlerfrei.

Flax, *s.* der Flachs. **—en,** *adj.* flachsen. **—dresser,** *s.* der Flachshechler. **—en-haired,** *adj.* flachshaarig.

Flay, *v.a.* schinden, die Haut abziehen. **—ing,** *s.* das Schinden, die Schinderei.

Flea, *s.* der Floh. **—bite,** *s.* der Flohstich; (*coll.*) eine unbedeutende Wunde.

Fleck, I. *v.a.* flecken, sprenkeln. II. *s.* der kleine Fleck(en).

Fledge, *v.n.* flügge werden. **—d,** *p.p. & adj.* flügge; befiedert.

Flee, *v.a. & n.* fliehen.

Fleec—e, I. *s.* das Vlies. II. *v.a.* scheren; to —e a person, (*fig.*) jemand ausplündern. **—y,** *adj.* wollig.

Fleet, I. *adj.,* **—ly,** *adv.* schnell. II. *v.n.* dahin eilen. III. *s.* die Flotte. **—ing,** *adj.* flüchtig, vergänglich. **—ness,** *s.* die Schnelligkeit.

Flesh, *s.* das Fleisch (*also fig.*). **—iness,** *s.* die Fleischigkeit. **—less,** *adj.* fleischlos, mager. **—ly,** *adj.* fleischlich.

Flex, *s.* der Isolierdraht.

Flexib—ility, *s.* die Biegsamkeit (*also fig.*). **—le,** *adj.,* **—ly,** *adv.* biegsam; a —le mind, ein lenksames Gemüt.

Flick, I. *s.* der leichte Schlag. II. *v.a.* leicht schlagen.

Flicker, I. *v.n.* flackern. II. *s.* das Flackern.

Flight, *s.* die Flucht; (flying) das Fliegen, der Flug; der Flug (*of time, etc.*); — of stairs, — of steps, der

Treppenlauf. **—iness,** s. die Flüchtigkeit (*als. fig.*). **—y,** *adj.,* **—ily,** *adv.* flüchtig; a **—y** person, eine faselige Person.

Flims—iness, s. das Lockere. **—y,** *adj.* locker, dünn; **—y** excuse, nichtige Entschuldigung.

Flinch, *v.n.* (zurück-)weichen.

Fling, I. *ir.v.a.* werfen, schleudern. II. s. der Wurf; he had his **—,** er hat sich amüsiert, ausgetobt.

Flint, s. der Feuerstein. **—y,** *adj.* kieselig, steinhart.

Flippan—cy, s. die Leichtigkeit, der Leichtsinn. **—t,** *adj.,* **—tly,** *adv.* vorlaut, leichtsinnig.

Flirt, I. *v.n.* kokettieren. II. s. die Kokette. **—ation,** s. das Kokettieren.

Flit, *v.n.* hin und her flattern.

Flitch, s. die Speckseite.

Flitter, *v.n.* flattern.

Float, I. s. (raft) das Floß; die Flöße (*of anglers*). II. *v.n.* obenauf schwimmen; (— in the air) in der Luft schweben. III. *v.a.* flott machen (*a ship, etc.*). **—ing,** *adj.* zirkulierend, im Umlaufe; schwimmend; **—ing** dock, schwimmendes Dock; **—ing** ice, das Treibeis; **—ing** rumours, umlaufende Gerüchte.

¹**Flock,** s. die Flocke, Locke (*of wool*). **—paper,** s. das Flockpapier.

²**Flock,** I. s. die Herde (*of sheep, also fig.*). II. *v.n.* sich gesellen.

Floe, s. das Tafeleis.

Flog, *v.a.* peitschen, stäupen. **—ging,** s. das Prügeln.

Flood, I. s. die Flut; die Sündflut (*B.*). II. *v.a.* überfluten, überschwemmen. **—ing,** s. das Überfluten. **—gate,** s. die Schleuse. **—tide,** s. die Flut.

Floor, s. der Fußboden, Flur, Estrich; ground-**—,** das Parterre, Erdgeschoß; second **—,** zweiter Stock. **—ing,** s. die Dielung.

Flop, I. *v.n.* (*coll.*) hinplumpsen. II. *int.* plumps!

Flor—a, s. die Flora. **—al,** *adj.* Blüten-, Blumen-.

Florid, *adj.* blühend.

Florin, s. der Gulden.

Florist, s. der Blumenhändler.

Flotilla, s. die Flotille.

Flotsam, s. das Strandgut.

¹**Flounce,** *v.n.* plätschern.

²**Flounce,** s. die Falbel.

¹**Flounder,** *v.n.* sich abarbeiten, umhertappen.

²**Flounder,** s. der Flunder, die Scholle (*Icht.*).

Flour, s. das Mehl.

Flourish, I. *v.n.* blühen, gedeihen; Schnörkel machen (*in writing*); schmettern (*of trumpets*). II. *v.a.* schwingen (*a sword*). III. s. der Schnörkel. **—ing,** *adj.,* **—ingly,** *adv.* blühend; gedeihend; a **—ing** business, ein blühendes Geschäft.

Flow, I. *v.n.* fließen. II. s. der Fluß. **—ing,** *adj.* fließend; **—ing** beard, wallender Bart.

Flower, I. s. die Blume; cut **—s,** Schnittblumen. II. *v.n.* blühen (*also fig.*). **—iness,** s. das Blumige. **—y,** *adj.* blumenreich. **—bed,** s. das Blumenbeet. **—pot,** s. der Blumentopf.

Fluctuat—e, *v.n.* schwanken; **—ing** prices, schwankende Preise. **—ing,** *adj.* veränderlich. **—ion,** s. das Schwanken.

¹**Flue,** s. der Rauchfang.

²**Flue,** s. die Staubflocke.

Flu—ency, s. der Fluß. **—ent,** *adj.,* **—ently,** *adv.* fließend.

Fluff, s. Federflocke. **—y,** *adj.* flaumig.

Fluid, I. s. die Flüssigkeit; electric (magnetic) **—,** das elektrische (magnetische) Fluidum. II. *adj.* flüssig.

Fluke, s. die Ankerhand; by a **—,** (*sl.*) durch glücklichen Zufall.

Flunkey, s. der Livreebediente.

Flurry, I. s. die Verwirrung. II. *v.a.* verwirren; to get flurried, außer Fassung geraten; don't **—** yourself, reg' dich nicht auf.

Flush, I. *v.n.* plötzlich erröten. II. *v.a.*; to **—** the sewers, die Schleusen ausspülen. III. s. das Erröten. IV. *adj.* gleich (*Carp.*).

Fluster, *v.a.* erhitzen, verwirren.

Flute, s. die Flöte (*Mus.*).

Flutter, I. *v.n.* flattern. II. *v.a.* beunruhigen. III. s. das Geflatter.

Fly, I. *ir.v.n.* fliegen; entfliehen (*as time*); to **—** about, umherfliegen; to **—** at, anfahren, herfallen über (*acc.*); to **—** in (— in pieces) zerspringen; to **—** into a passion, in Zorn geraten; to **—** open, auffliegen. II. *ir.v.a.* fliegen lassen (*a kite, etc.*). III. s. die Fliege. **—wheel,** s. das Schwungrad (*Mach.*).

Flyer, *s.* der Fliegende; der Flieger (*Aviat.*).

Flying, *adj.* fliegend, Flug-; a — visit, ein kurzer Besuch; —-field, der Flugplatz; —-machine, der Flugapparat, die Flugmaschine; —-week, die Flugwoche.

Foal, *s.* das Fohlen, Füllen.

Foam, I. *s.* der Schaum. II. *v.n.* schäumen.

Fob, *s.* die Uhrtasche.

Foc—al, *adj.*; —al distance, die Brennweite. —**us,** I. *s.* der Brennpunkt. II. *v.a.* fixieren, den Fokus suchen.

Fodder, I. *s.* das Futter. II. *v.a.* füttern.

Foe, *s.* der Feind, die Feindin, der Gegner, die Gegnerin.

Fog, *s.* der Nebel. —**giness,** *s.* die Nebligkeit. —**gy,** *adj.* nebelig, dicht; I have only a —gy recollection of it, ich besinne mich nicht klar darauf. —**bank,** *s.* die Nebelschicht. —**horn,** *s.* das Nebelhorn.

Fogey, *s.*; old —, der altmodische wunderliche Mensch.

Foible, *s.* die Schwäche.

Foil, *v.a.* vereiteln, vernichten.

Foist, *v.a.* unterschieben; to — a thing upon a person, jemand mit etwas betrügen.

¹**Fold,** I. *s.* die Falte (*in cloth, etc.*); (*in comp.* =) -fach, -fältig. II. *v.a.* falten; übereinanderlegen (*the arms, etc.*). III. *v.n.* schließen; to — in one's arms, in die Arme schließen. —**ing-chair,** *s.* der Klappstuhl. —**ing-door,** *s.* die Flügeltür. —**ing-hat,** *s.* der Klapphut.

²**Fold,** *s.* I. der Pferch, Schafstall. II. *v.a.* einpferchen (*sheep, etc.*).

Foliage, *s.* das Laub(werk).

Folio, *s.* das Folio; book in —, der Foliant.

Folk, *s.* die Leute, das Volk. —**lore,** *s.* die Sagenkunde.

Follow, *v.a. & n.* (einem) folgen (*also fig.*); to — the fashion, die Mode mitmachen; it —s from this, daraus folgt; to — a profession, einen Beruf ausüben. —**er,** *s.* der Nachfolger (*also fig.*); (adherent) der Anhänger. —**ers,** *pl.* das Gefolge; (adherents) der Anhang. —**ing,** I. *adj.* folgend. II. *s.* das Folgen; (what —s) das Folgende, Folgendes.

Folly, *s.* die Torheit, Narrheit.

Fond, *adj.*, —**ly,** *adv.* liebevoll, zärtlich; to be — of, gern haben, gern essen; I am — of dancing, ich tanze gern. —**le,** *v.a.* liebkosen. —**ness,** *s.* die Liebe (for, zu), Vorliebe (für), Zärtlichkeit (für).

Font, *s.* der Taufstein.

Food, *s.* die Speise. —**stuffs,** *pl.* Nahrungsmittel.

Fool, I. *s.* der Narr, Tor; (female —) die Närrin, Törin. II. *v.a.* zum Narren haben; to make a — of oneself, eine Torheit begehen. III. *v.n.* den Narren machen; to — about, Unsinn treiben. —**ery,** *s.* die Torheit. —**ish,** *adj.*, —**ishly,** *adv.* närrisch, töricht, albern. —**ishness,** *s.* die Torheit, Narrheit. —**hardiness,** *s.* die Tollkühnheit. —**hardy,** *adj.* tollkühn.

Foot, *s.* der Fuß; to put one's — in it, etwas völlig verderben; to fall on one's feet, Glück haben. —**ed,** *adj.* (*in comp.* =) -füßig; flat- —ed, plattfüßig. —**ing,** *s.* der Grund, Halt; (state) der Zustand; der Raum für den Fuß; to gain a —ing, festen Fuß fassen; to lose one's —ing, ausgleiten. —**ball,** *s.* der Fußball; das Fußballspiel. —**prints,** *pl.* Fußtapfen. —**soldier,** *s.* der Infanterist. —**stool,** *s.* der Schemel. —**wear,** *s.* das Schuhwerk.

Fop, *s.* der Geck, Stutzer. —**pish,** *adj.*, —**pishly,** *adv.* geckenhaft.

For, I. *prep.* (in place of) für, anstatt; (in exchange —) für, um; (as) als, für; (— the sake of) um (einer Sache) willen; — example, zum Beispiel; as — me, was mich anbelangt; — all that, trotz alledem; — life, lebenslänglich. II. *conj.* denn; (because) weil, da.

Forag—e, I. *s.* die Furage. II. *v.n.* furagieren. —**er,** *s.* der Furier. —**ing,** *s.* das Furagieren.

Forbear, I. *ir.v.a.* Geduld haben mit; I cannot — smiling, ich kann nicht umhin zu lächeln. II. *ir.v.n.* sich enthalten. —**ance,** *s.* die Geduld. —**ing,** *adj.*, —**ingly,** *adv.* geduldig, langmütig.

Forbid, *ir.v.a.* verbieten; God —! Gott bewahre! —**den,** *adj.* verboten. —**ding,** *adj.*, —**dingly,** *adv.*, widerwärtig; his —ding behaviour, sein abstoßendes Wesen.

Force, I. *s.* die Kraft, Macht, Stärke, Gewalt; military —, die Kriegsmacht; the law is in —, das Gesetz ist in Kraft. II. *v.a.* zwingen, nötigen. **—d,** *adj.* erzwungen; (unnatural) gezwungen. **—s,** *pl.* Truppen. **—ful,** *adj.* kräftig.

Forceps, *s.* die Zange (*Surg.*).

Forcibl—e, *adj.,* **—y,** *adv.* kräftig, mächtig. **—eness,** *s.* die Gewaltsamkeit.

Ford, I. *s.* die Furt. II. *v.a.* durchwaten.

Fore, I. *adv.* vorn; — and aft, vorn und hinten. II. *adj.* vorder. **— arm,** *s.* der Vorderarm. **—bear,** *s.* der Vorfahr. **—bode,** *v.a.* vorbedeuten. **—boding,** *s.* die Ahnung. **—cast,** I. *s.* die Vorhersagung. II. *v.a.* vorbedeuten, vorhersehen. **—castle,** *s.* das Vorderkastell. **—deck,** *s.* das Vorderdeck. **—father,** *s.* der Ahnherr. **—finger,** *s.* der Zeigefinger. **—ground,** *s.* der Vordergrund. **—head,** *s.* die Stirn. **—know,** *ir.v.a.* vorherwissen.

Foreign, *adj.* ausländisch, fremd; this remark is — to the subject, diese Äußerung gehört nicht zur Sache. **—er,** *s.* der Ausländer. **—ness,** *s.* die Fremdheit; (*fig.*) das Ungehörige.

Fore—man, *s.* der Obmann (*of a jury*); der Vorsteher, Aufseher (*Manuf.*). **mast,** *s.* der Fockmast. **—most,** I. *adj.* vorderst. II. *adv.* zuerst; voran. **—noon,** *s.* der Vormittag. **—sail,** *s.* das Focksegel. **—see,** *v.a.* vorhersehen. **—sight,** *s.* die Vorsicht.

Forest, *s.* der Forst, Wald. **—er,** *s.* der Förster.

Fore—stall, *v.a.* (einem) zuvorkommen. **—tell,** *ir.v.a.* vorhersagen; (*fig.*) vorbedeuten. **—thought,** *s.* der Vorbedacht. **—warn,** *v.a.* vorher warnen.

Forfeit, I. *v.a.* verwirken. II. *adj.* verwirkt, verfallen. III. *s.* das Verlustigwerden. **—s,** *pl.* das Pfänderspiel. **—ure,** *s.* die Verwirkung.

Forge, I. *v.a.* schmieden; fälschen (*a document*). II. *s.* die Schmiede. **—r,** *s.* der Schmiedende, der Verfälscher. **—ry,** *s.* die Verfälschung.

Forget, *ir.v.a.* & *n.* vergessen; I —, ich weiß nicht mehr. **—ful,** *adj.* vergeßlich. **—fulness,** *s.* die Vergeßlichkeit. **—me-not,** *s.* das Vergißmeinnicht.

Forgiv—able, *adj.* verzeihlich. **—e,**

ir.v.a. vergeben, verzeihen; not to be **—en,** unverzeihlich. **—eness,** *s.* die Vergebung, Verzeihung. **—er,** *s.* der Vergebende. **—ing,** *adj.* versöhnlich. **—ingness,** *s.* die Versöhnlichkeit.

Forgo, *v.a.* verzichten auf (*acc.*). **—ne,** *adj.* vorherbestimmt.

Fork, I. *s.* die Gabel. II. *v.a.* gabeln, aufgabeln. III. *v.n.* sich spalten, sich gabeln. **—ed,** *adj.* gabelig.

Forlorn, *adj.* verloren.

Form, I. *s.* die Gestalt, Form (*of a body*); (ceremony) die Formalität; (bench) die Schulbank; to be in —, tüchtig sein; that is bad —, das verstößt gegen den guten Ton; in due —, vorschriftsmäßig; a matter of —, Formsache. II. *v.a.* formen, bilden, gestalten; erdenken (*a plan, etc.*); aufstellen (*a line of battle*). **—al,** *adj.,* **—ally,** *adv.* förmlich; (exact) pünktlich; (ceremonious) formell, umständlich. **—ality,** *s.* die Formalität. **—ation,** *s.* das Bilden; die Formation (*Geol.*); der Verband (*Mil.*). **—ative,** *adj.* bildend. **—less,** *adj.* formlos.

Former, *adj.* vorig, früher; (late) ehemalig; (aforementioned) vorher erwähnt; ersterer, dieser (*opp. to* letzterer, jener, *latter*). **—ly,** *adv.* ehemals, früher.

Formidabl—e, *adj.,* **—y,** *adv.* furchtbar, fürchterlich, schrecklich.

Formula, *s.* die Formel. **—te,** *v.a.* formulieren.

Forsake, *ir.v.a.* aufgeben; verlassen (*a country*); preisgeben (*friends*). **—n,** *adj.* verlassen.

Forswear, *ir.v.a.* abschwören; to — oneself, meineidig werden. **—er,** *s.* der (die) Meineidige.

Fort, *s.* die Schanze.

Forth, *adv.* fort, weiter; vorwärts (*of time*); her, vor, hervor (*of place and rank*); (out) heraus, hinaus; (abroad, out) draußen; from this day —, von heute an; and so —, und so weiter. **—coming,** *adj.* bevorstehend; vorhanden sein; to be — coming, zum Vorschein kommen, erscheinen. **—with,** *adv.* sogleich, sofort.

Fortieth, *adj.* vierzigst.

Forti—fication, *s.* die Befestigung. **—fied,** *adj.* befestigt, verschanzt. **—fy,** *v.a.* befestigen (*also fig.*).

Fortitude, *s.* der Mut.

Fortnight, *s.* vierzehn Tage; this day —, heute über 14 Tage; a — ago, heute vor 14 Tagen; —ly review, die Halbmonatsschrift.

Fortress, *s.* die Festung.

Fortunate, *adj.* glücklich. —ly, *adv.* glücklicherweise.

Fortune, *s.* das Glück; (fate) das Geschick, Schicksal; (wealth) das Vermögen; to marry a —, eine reiche Partie machen. —hunter, *s.* der Mitgiftjäger. —teller, *s.* der Wahrsager, die Wahrsagerin. —telling, *s.* die Wahrsagerei.

Forty, *num. adj.* vierzig.

Forward, I. *adj.* (fore) vorn; (over ready) voreilig; (early) frühzeitig; (advanced) vorgerückt. II. *adv.* vorwärts; balance carried —, Saldo vorgetragen. III. *v.a.* absenden, spedieren; please —, bitte nachzusenden. —ness, *s.* die Bereitwilligkeit; die Voreiligkeit. —ing-agent, *s.* der Spediteur. —ing-note, *s.* der Frachtbrief.

Fosse, *s.* der Graben.

Fossil, I. *adj.* fossil, versteinert. II. *s.* das Fossil.

Foster, *v.a.* nähren, pflegen; to — a thought, einen Gedanken hegen. —brother, *s.* der Milchbruder. —child, *s.* das Pflegekind. —father, *s.* der Pflegevater.

Foul, I. *adj.* schmutzig; — tongue, belegte Zunge; (*fig.*) loses Maul; — deeds, ruchlose Taten; to fall — of a person, ungestüm über einen herfallen. II. *v.a.* beschmutzen. —ness, *s.* die Unreinigkeit. —ly, *adv.* schändlich; unredlich.

1Found, *v.a.* gründen. —ation, *s.* der Grund, Grundbau (*of a building*); (*fig.*) der Ursprung, Anbeginn. —ation-stone, *s.* der Grundstein.

2Found, *v.a.* gießen.

1Founder, *s.* der Gründer, Begründer, Stifter.

2Founder, *s.* der Schmelzer, Gießer.

3Founder, *v.n.* scheitern (*Naut., fig.*).

Foundling, *s.* der Findling.

Foundress, *s.* die Stifterin, Begründerin.

Foundry, die Gießerei.

Fount, *s.* die Quelle, der Quell; der Guß (*Typ.*). —ain, *s.* die Quelle (*also fig.*); der Springbrunnen. —ain-head, *s.* der Urquell. —ain-pen, *s.* die Füllfeder.

Four, *num. adj.* vier. —fold, *adj.* vierfach. —teen, *num. adj.* vierzehn. —teenth, *num. adj.* vierzehnt. —th, I. *num. adj.* viert. II. *s.* das Viertel. —thly, *adv.* viertens, zum vierten. —footed, *adj.* vierfüßig.

Fowl, *s.* das Huhn. —er, *s.* der Vogler, Vogelsteller.

Fox, *s.* der Fuchs. —y, *adj.* (*fig.*) schlau, listig.

Fract—ion, *s.* das Bruchstück; der Bruch (*Arith.*). —ional, *adj.* gebrochen.

Fractious, *adj.*, —ly, *adv.* ärgerlich. —ness, *s.* die Reizbarkeit.

Fracture, I. *s.* der Knochenbruch. II. *v.a.* (zer)brechen.

Fragil—e, *adj.* zerbrechlich. —ity, *s.* die Zerbrechlichkeit.

Fragment, *s.* das Bruchstück. —ary, *adj.* bruchstückartig.

Fragran—ce, *s.* der Wohlgeruch. —t, *adj.*, —tly, *adv.* wohlriechend, duftig.

Frail, *adj.* gebrechlich. —ness, *s.* die Gebrechlichkeit.

Fram—e, I. *v.a.* bilden, bauen; einrahmen (*of a picture, etc.*). II. *s.* das Gebält (*of a house, etc.*); der Rahmen (*of a picture*). —ing, *s.* die Einrahmung, Einfassung. —ework, *s.* das Fachwerk.

Franchise, *s.* das Wahlrecht.

Frank, *adj.*, —ly, *adv.* offenherzig. —incense, *s.* der Weihrauch. —ness, *s.* die Offenheit.

Frantic, *adj.*, —ally, *adv.* rasend, wahnsinnig; — with rage, außer sich vor Wut.

Frat—ernal, *adj.*, —ernally, *adv.* brüderlich. —ernity, *s.* die Brüderschaft. —ricide, *s.* der Brudermord; der Brudermörder.

Fraud, *s.* der Trug, Betrug. —ulent, *adj.*, —ulently, *adv.* betrügerisch, betrüglich.

Fraught, *adj.* beladen; — with meaning, bedeutungsschwer.

Fray, I. *v.a.* abreiben. II. *v.n.* sich ausfasern.

Freak, *s.* das Sonderbare; die Laune, Grille. —ish, *adj.*, —ishiy, *adv.* launenhaft.

Freckle, I. *s.* die Sommersprosse. II. *v.n.* sich sprenkeln. —d, *adj.* (—e-faced) sommersprossig.

Free, I. *adj.* frei; he is — to go, es steht ihm frei zu gehen; — from care,

sorgenfrei; to set —, frei geben. II.
v.a. befreien. —booter, s. der Frei=
beuter. —dom, s. die Freiheit. —ly,
adv. frei. —-handed, adj. freigebig.
—hold, s. das Freigut. —mason,
s. der Freimaurer. —masonry, s. die
Freimaurerei. —stone, s. der Sand=
stein. —thinker, s. der Freidenker.
—thinking, s. das Freidenken. —
trade, s. der Freihandel.

Freez—e, v. I. a. gefrieren machen
(water); erfrieren machen (living
beings); (fig.) erstarren machen. II.
n. frieren; (fig.) erstarren; to —e to
death, erfrieren. —ing, I. adj.
gefrierend; —ing machine, die Eis=
maschine. II. s. das Gefrieren. —
ing-point, s. der Gefrierpunkt.

Freight, I. s. die Fracht (C.L.); die
Befrachtung, Ladung (Naut.); (—
cost) das Frachtgeld; bill of —, der
Frachtbrief. II. v.a. befrachten, be=
laden (a ship).

Frenz—ied, adj. wahnsinnig. —y, s.
die Raserei.

Frequen—cy, s. die Häufigkeit. —t,
I. adj., —tly, adv. häufig. II. v.a.
häufig, öfters besuchen.

Fresco, s. das Freskogemälde.

Fresh, adj., —ly, adv. frisch; —
arrivals, neue Ankömmlinge. —en,
v. I. a. erfrischen. II. n. frisch wer=
den. —ness, s. die Frische. —
looking, adj. frisch aussehend. —
water, adj. Süßwasser=. —man,
s. (univ. sl.) der Fuchs.

Fret, I. v.a. abreiben; (vex) ärgern.
II. v.n. sich quälen, sich grämen. III.
s. der Ärger. —ful, adj., —fully,
adv. mürrisch, verdrießlich. —ful=
ness, s. der Unmut.

Fret-saw, s. die Laub=, Loch=säge.
—work, s. die durchbrochene Arbeit.

Friar, s. der Mönch.

Friction, s. die Reibung. —al, adj.;
—al electricity, die Reibungselektri=
zität.

Friday, s. der Freitag; Good —, Kar=
freitag.

Friend, s. der Freund, die Freundin;
to make —s, Freundschaft schließen;
a — at court, ein einflußreicher
Freund. —less, adj. freundlos. —
lessness, s. die Freundlosigkeit. —li=
ness, s. die Freundlichkeit. —ly, adj.
freundlich. —ship, s. die Freund=
schaft.

¹Frieze, s. der Fries (cloth).

²Frieze, s. der Fries (Arch.).

Frigate, s. die Fregatte.

Fright, I. s. der Schrecken; the horse
takes —, das Pferd scheut; to look a
—, äußerst häßlich aussehen. II. —,
v.a. erschrecken. —ful, adj.,
—fully, adv. schrecklich, fürchterlich.
—fulness, s. die Schrecklichkeit.

Frigid, adj., —ly, adv. kalt; (fig.)
gefühllos. —ity, s. die Kälte.

Frill, I. s. die Hals= or Hand=krause.
II. v.a. fälteln, kräuseln.

Fringe, s. die Franse; (of hair) die
Ponyfrisur.

Frisk, v.n. umherhüpfen. —iness, s.
die Lebendigkeit. —y, adj., —ily,
adv. lebhaft.

Frit, s. die Fritte. —ter, s. das
Schnittchen; apple=ters, Apfelschnitt=
chen.

Frivol—ity, s. die Leichtfertigkeit.
—ous, adj., —ously, adv. leichtsinnig.

Frizzle, I. v.a. kräuseln. II. v.n. sich
kräuseln.

Fro, adv.; to and —, hin und her, auf
und ab.

Frock, s. das Kinderröckchen. —
coat, s. der Gehrock.

Frog, s. der Frosch.

Frolic, I. s. die Posse. II. v.n. Possen
treiben. —some, adj. ausgelassen.

From, prep. von; (out of) aus; (be=
cause of) aus; (judging from) nach;
vor; — above, von oben herab; — a
child, von Kindheit an.

Front, s. die Vorderseite; die Front
(of a battalion, etc.); to show a bold
—, die Stirne bieten. —age, s. die
Vorderfront (Arch.). —al, adj. von
vorn kommend. —ier, s. die Grenze.
—ispiece, s. das Titelbild (Typ.).

Frost, s. der Frost; —ed cake, der
Kuchen mit Zuckerguß; —ed glass, das
Milchglas. —iness, s. die (Eis=)
Kälte (also fig.). —y, adj. frostig.
—bite, s. das Erfrieren. —bitten,
adj. erfroren.

Froth, I. s. der Schaum. II. v.n.
schäumen. —y, adj. schäumig.

Froward, adj., —ly, adv. widerspen=
stig.

Frown, I. s. das Stirnrunzeln. II.
v.n. die Stirne runzeln.

Frowzy, adj. muffig; schmutzig.

Frugal, adj., —ly, adv. sparsam.
—ity, s. die Sparsamkeit.

Fruit, *s.* die Frucht (*also fig.*); die Früchte, das Obst (*collect.*); stewed —, das Kompott; to bear —, Früchte tragen. **—ful,** *adj.*, **—fully,** *adv.* fruchtbar. **—fulness,** *s.* die Fruchtbarkeit. **—less,** *adj.*, **—lessly,** *adv.* fruchtlos. **—lessness,** *s.* (*fig.*) die Fruchtlosigkeit; **—-tree,** *s.* der Obstbaum.

Frump, *s.* das wunderliche altmodisch gekleidete Frauenzimmer; old —, die alte Schachtel.

Frustrat—e, *v.a.* vereiteln. **—ion,** *s.* die Vereitelung.

¹Fry, *v.a. & n.* braten, schmoren; fried eggs, Spiegeleier. **—ing-pan,** *s.* die Bratpfanne; out of the —ing pan into the fire, vom Regen in die Traufe.

²Fry, *s.* die Fischbrut.

Fuchsia, *s.* die Fuchsie.

Fuel, *s.* die Feuerung.

Fugitive, I. *adj.* flüchtig (*also fig.*). II. *s.* der Flüchtling.

Fugue, *s.* die Fuge (*Mus.*).

Fulcrum, *s.* die Stütze.

Fulfil, *v.a.* vollziehen, vollbringen. **—ment,** *s.* die Erfüllung, Vollführung.

Fulgen—cy, *s.* der Glanz. **—t,** *adj.* glänzend.

¹Full, I. *adj.* voll; at — length, ausführlich; — stop, der Punkt; to be — of oneself, von sich eingenommen sein; to have one's hands —, vollauf zu tun haben. II. *adv.* völlig, ganz; genau, gerade; recht, sehr. III. *s.* die Fülle, Genüge; — of the moon, Vollmond. **—y,** *adv.* voll, völlig, gänzlich. **—dress,** *s.* der Gesellschaftsanzug. **—grown,** *adj.* ausgewachsen.

²Full, *v.a.* walken. **—er,** *s.* der Walker. **—er's-earth,** *s.* die Walkererde.

Fullness, *s.* die Fülle.

Fulsome, *adj.*, **—ly,** *adv.* widrig, ekelhaft. **—ness,** *s.* die Ekelhaftigkeit.

Fumbl—e, *v.n.* umhertappen. **—ing,** *adj.*, **—ingly,** *adv.* tappend.

Fume, I. *s.* der Dunst, Dampf. II. *v.n.* dampfen, dunsten; (*fig.*) toben vor Wut.

Fumiga—te, *v.a.* räuchern. **—tion,** *s.* die Räucherung.

Fun, *s.* der Scherz, Spaß; to make — of a person, einen zum besten haben.

Function, *s.* die Funktion. **—al,** *adj.* funktionell.

Fund, I. *s.* der Fonds. II. *v.a.* kapitalisieren; —ed debts, fundierte Staatsschulden.

Fundament, *s.* der Grund; das Gesäß. **—al,** *adj.* Grund=.

Funer—al, I. *s.* das Begräbnis. II. *adj.* Leichen=, Trauer=. **—eal,** *adj.*, **—eally,** *adv.* wehklagend.

Fung—ous, *adj.* schwammartig. **—us,** *s.* der Schwamm.

Funk, *s.* (*sl.*) die große Angst; der Feigling; he got into a —, ihm wurde angst und bange.

Funnel, *s.* der Trichter.

Funn—ily, *adv.*, **—y,** *adj.* komisch.

Fur, *s.* der Pelz; a —red tongue, eine belegte Zunge.

Furbish, *v.a.* polieren, putzen.

Furious, *adj.*, **—ly,** *adv.* wütend, rasend. **—ness,** *s.* die Wut, Raserei.

Furl, *v.a.* beschlagen (*sails*); to — a flag, eine Fahne aufrollen.

Furlough, *s.* der Urlaub.

Furnace, *s.* der Ofen, Schmelzofen.

Furnish, *v.a.* versehen, versorgen (with, mit); möblieren (*rooms*), ausmöblieren (*houses*). **—er,** *s.* der Lieferant; (house- —er) der Möblierer.

Furniture, *s.* das Hausgerät, die Möbel (*pl.*), das Mobiliar. **—-van,** *s.* der Möbelwagen.

Furrier, *s.* der Kürschner. **—y,** *s.* das Pelzwerk.

Furrow, I. *s.* die Furche (*also fig.*). II. *v.a.* furchen.

Furry, *adj.* pelzig.

Further, I. *adj.* weiter, ferner. II. *adv.* weiter, ferner; (besides) überdies; what —? was sonst noch? nothing —? weiter nichts? III. *v.a.* (be=)fördern. **—ance,** *s.* die Förderung.

Furthest, I. *adj.* weitest, fernst. II. *adv.* am weitesten.

Furtive, *adj.* verstohlen. **—ly,** *adv.* heimlich.

Fury, *s.* die Raserei; die Furie (*Myth.*).

Furze, *s.* der Stechginster.

¹Fuse, *v.a. & n.* schmelzen. **—wire,** *s.* der Schmelzdraht (*Radio*).

²Fuse, *s.* der Zünder, Brander.

Fusil—ier, *s.* der Füsilier. **—lade,** *s.* die Erschießung.

Fusion, *s.* die Verschmelzung.

Fuss, *s.* I. das Wesen, Getue. II. *v.n.* (to make much — about a thing) viel Aufhebens machen (von einer S.). **—iness,** *s.* übertriebene Umständlichkeit. **—y,** *adj.,* **—ily,** *adv.* viel Wesens um nichts machend.

Fust—iness, *s.* das Muffige. **—y,** *adj.* muffig.

Futil—e, *adj.,* **—ely,** *adv.* unnütz, wirkungslos. **—ity,** *s.* die Nichtigkeit.

Future, I. *adj.* künftig, zukünftig; — tense, das Futurum. II. *s.* die Zukunft.

Fuzz, I. *s.* der feine Flaum. II. *v.n.* sich fasern. **—y,** *adj.* flockig, zottig, struppig.

G

G, g, *s.* das g, G (*also Mus.*); G sharp, das Gis; G flat, das Ges; key of G, G-Schlüssel.

Gab, *s.* das Geplauder; the gift of the —, ein gutes Mundwerk.

Gabble, I. *v.n.* schnattern; schwatzen. II. *s.* das Geschnatter; das Geschwätz.

Gable, *s.* der Giebel.

Gad, *v.n.*; to — about, umherlaufen. **—fly,** *s.* die Viehfliege.

Gaff, *s.* der Haken; die Gaffel (*Naut.*).

Gag, I. *v.a.* den Mund knebeln. II. *s.* der Knebel.

Gage, *s.* das Pfand; die Bürgschaft (*also fig.*).

Gai—ly, *adv.,* see Gay. **—ety,** *s.* die Heiterkeit.

Gain, I. *s.* der Gewinn. II. *v.a.* gewinnen; to — one's bread, sein Brot verdienen; to — possession, Besitz ergreifen. III. *v.n.* gewinnen; vorgehen (*Horol.*). **—s,** *pl.* der Gewinn.

Gainsay, *v.a.* widersprechen.

Gait, *s.* der Gang, die Gangart.

Gaiter, *s.* die Gamasche.

Galaxy, *s.* die Milchstraße; (*fig.*) die glänzende Versammlung.

Gale, *s.* der Sturm(wind); a — is raging, ein Sturm wütet. **—day,** *s.* der Rentenzahltag.

¹**Gall,** *s.* die Galle (*also fig.*).

²**Gall,** *s.* (—-nut) der Gallapfel.

³**Gall,** I. *s.* das Wundreiben. II. *v.a.* wundreiben. **—ing,** I. *adj.* verletzend; it is —ing, es ist ärgerlich. II. *s.* das Aufreiben.

Gallant, I. *adj.,* **—ly,** *adv.* tapfer, brav; (courtly) höflich, artig. II. *s.* der Galan, Liebhaber. **—ry,** *s.* die Tapferkeit; der Edelmut; die Galanterie.

Gallery, *s.* die Galerie.

Galley, *s.* die Galeere.

Gallipot, *s.* der Apothekertopf.

Gallop, I. *s.* der Galopp (*also Mus., Danc.*). II. *v.n.* galoppieren.

Gallows, *s. & pl.* der Galgen.

Galosh, *s.* der Gummischuh.

Galvan—ic, *adj.* galvanisch. **—ism,** *s.* der Galvanismus. **—ize,** *v.a.* galvanisieren.

Gam—ble, *v.* I. *n.* (hoch) spielen. II. *a.*; to —ble away, verspielen. **—bler,** *s.* der Spieler. **—bling,** *s.* das Spielen (um Geld). **—bling-hell,** *s.* die Spielhölle.

Gamboge, *s.* das Gummigutt.

Gambol, *s.* der Luftsprung.

Game, I. *s.* das Spiel (*also fig.*). II. *v.n.* spielen. **—bag,** *s.* die Jagdtasche. **—cock,** *s.* der Kampfhahn. **—keeper,** *s.* der Förster. **—licence,** *s.* der Jagdschein.

Gammon, *s.* der Schinken.

Gamut, *s.* die Tonleiter.

Gander, *s.* der Gänserich.

Gang, *s.* die Horde, Rotte. **—way,** *s.* der Durchgang, Quergang; die Laufplanke (*Naut.*).

Gap, *s.* die Öffnung.

Gape, *v.n.* gähnen; to — at, angaffen.

Garage, *s.* die Garage, der Autoschuppen.

Garb, *s.* die Tracht, Kleidung.

Garbage, *s.* der Abfall, Auswurf.

Garble, *v.a.* verstümmeln.

Garden, I. *s.* der Garten. II. *v.n.* im Garten arbeiten. **—er,** *s.* der Gärtner. **—ing,** *s.* der Gartenbau.

Gargle, *v.n.* sich gurgeln.

Gargoyle, *s.* der Wasserspeier.

Garish, *adj.* grell.

Garland, I. *s.* der (Blumen-)Kranz. II. *v.a.* bekränzen.

Garlic, *s.* der Knoblauch.

Garment, *s.* das Gewand.

Garner, I. *s.* der Kornboden. II. *v.a.* aufspeichern.

Garnet, *s.* der Granat.

Garnish, *v.a.* zieren, schmücken.

Garret, *s.* die Dachstube.

Garrison, I. *s.* die Garnison, Besatzung. II. *v.a.* mit einer Besatzung versehen.

Garrul—ity, *s.* die Geschwätzigkeit. **—ous,** *adj.* geschwätzig.

Garter, *s.* das Strumpfband; Order of the —, der Hosenbandorden.

Gas, *s.* das Gas (*also Chem.*, *Phys.*); poison —, (*Mil.*) das Giftgas. — **eous,** *adj.* gas-artig, -förmig. — **burner,** *s.* der Gasbrenner. —**works,** *s.* die Gasanstalt.

Gash, I. *v.a.* schneiden. II. *s.* die Schnittwunde.

Gasometer, *s.* der Gasmesser.

Gasp, I. *s.* das schwere Atmen. II. *v.a.* to — out, ausatmen, aushauchen. III. *v.n.* schwer atmen; to — for breath, nach Luft schnappen.

Gastric, *adj.* gastrisch; — trouble, Magenbeschwerden.

Gate, *s.* das Tor; die Pforte (*also fig.*). —**way,** *s.* der Torweg, die Einfahrt.

Gather, I. *v.a.* sammeln (*also fig.*); to — together, versammeln; to — up, aufnehmen (*clothes, etc.*). II. *v.n.* sich sammeln; sich versammeln (*as people*). III. *s.* die Kräusel, Falte. —**ing,** I. *s.* die Versammlung; das Kräuseln (*Semp.*). II. *adj.* (stets) zunehmend.

Gauche, *adj.* unbeholfen, tölpisch.

Gaud—**ily,** *adv.*, *see* —**y.** —**iness,** *s.* geschmacklose Geputztheit. —**y,** *adj.* prunkhaft.

Gauge, I. *v.a.* abmessen, ausmessen. II. *s.* das Maß, der Maßstab; die Spurweite; weather —, der Wettermesser. —**r,** *s.* der Eichmeister.

Gaunt, *adj.*, —**ly,** *adv.* mager. —**ness,** *s.* die Hagerkeit.

Gauntlet, *s.* der Panzerhandschuh; to throw down the —, die Fehde ansagen.

Gauz—**e,** *s.* die Gaze. —**y,** *adj.* gazeartig.

Gavot(**te**)**,** *s.* die Gavotte.

Gay, *adj.* heiter, lustig; bunt (*as colours*).

Gaze, *v.n.* starren.

Gazelle, *s.* die Gazelle.

Gazette, *s.* die Zeitung.

Gear, *s.* das Geschirr; das Triebwerk (*Mach.*); das Zubehör, Geschirr (*Naut.*); in —, im Gange; out of —, in Unordnung; (*fig.*) verwirren. —**ing,** *s.* das Triebwerk, Getriebe (*Mach.*).

Gelatin—**e,** *s.* die Gallerte. —**ous,** *adj.* gallertartig.

Gem, *s.* der Edelstein.

Gender, *s.* das Geschlecht (*also Gram.*).

Genealog—**ical,** *adj.* genealogisch. —**y,** *s.* die Genealogie; der Stammbaum.

General, I. *adj.* allgemein. II. *s.* der General, der Feldherr (*Mil.*). —**issimo,** *s.* der Oberbefehlshaber. —**ity,** *s.* die Allgemeinheit. — **ization,** *s.* die Verallgemeinerung. — **ize,** *v.a.* verallgemeinern. — **ly,** *adv.* im allgemeinen; (in —) überhaupt; meistens, gewöhnlich; — ly speaking, im Ganzen genommen. —**ship,** *s.* die Feldherrnkunst; (*fig.*) die Leitung.

Generat—**e,** *v.a.* zeugen; (*fig.*) erzeugen. —**ion,** *s.* das Zeugen; die Erzeugung, Hervorbringung; die Generation, das Geschlecht; (period) das Zeitalter. —**ive,** *adj.* zeugend.

Gener—**osity,** *s.* die Großmut; die Freigebigkeit. —**ous,** *adj.*, —**ously,** *adv.* großmütig; (liberal) freigebig.

Genesis, *s.* die Zeugung; das erste Buch Mosis.

Genetive, *adj.* Zeugungs-; — case, der Wesfall, Genitiv.

Genial, *adj.*, —**ly,** *adv.* leutselig. —**ity,** *s.* die Leutseligkeit.

Genius, *s.* der Genius.

Gentile, I. *s.* der Heide. II. *adj.* heidnisch.

Gentility, *s.* die edle Abkunft.

Gent—**le,** *adj.*, —**ly,** *adv.* mild, sanft; gelind (*as a breeze*); fromm, zahm (*as beasts*). —**leness,** *s.* die Milde, Güte; die Sanftmut. —**lefolk,** —**lefolks,** *pl.* vornehme Leute. —**leman,** der Herr, der Mann von Stand; — lemen! meine Herren! he is no — leman, er hat keine Lebensart. — **lemanlike,** —**lemanly,** *adj.* ritterlich, anständig, ehrenhaft. —**lewoman,** *s.* vornehme Dame.

Gentry, *s.* der niedere Adel; nobility and —, der Adel und die Vornehmen.

Genuine, *adj.*, —**ly,** *adv.* echt, wahr, unverfälscht. —**ness,** *s.* die Echtheit.

Gen—**us,** *s.* (pl. —era) die Gattung.

Geo—**grapher,** *s.* der Geograph. — **graphical,** *adj.*, —**graphically,** *adv.* erdkundlich, geographisch. —**graphy,** *s.* die Geographie, die Erdkunde. — **logical,** *adj.* geologisch. —**logist,** *s.* der Geolog. —**logy,** *s.* die Geologie. —**meter,** —**metrician,** *s.* der Geometer. —**metric(al),** *adj.*, —**metrically,** *adv.* geometrisch. —**metry,** *s.* die Erdmeßkunst, Geometrie.

Geranium, *s.* der Storchschnabel, das Geranium.

Germ, *s.* der Keim (*also fig.*). **—an,**
—ane, *adj.* (der Sache) zugehörig;
verwandt. **—inate,** *v.n.* keimen.
—ination, *s.* das Keimen.

Gerund, *s.* das Gerundium. **—ial,**
adj. Gerundial=.

Gest—iculate, *v.n.* Gebärden machen.
—iculation, *s.* das Gebärdenspiel.
—ure, *s.* die Gebärde.

Get, *ir.v.* I. *a.* erhalten, bekommen; erlangen, sich (*dat.*) verschaffen. II. *n.*
(arrive) gelangen, ankommen, anlangen; to — back, zurückkommen; to —
down, hinunterkommen; absteigen;
to — home, nach Hause kommen *or* gelangen; to — off, davonkommen; to
— over, hinwegkommen über, überwinden (*difficulties*); to — up, aufsteigen, (rise) aufstehen; I — my hair
cut, ich lasse mir die Haare schneiden;
to — a wife, sich eine Frau nehmen;
— me the book! besorge mir das Buch!
to — out of one's depth, den Boden
unter den Füßen verlieren. **—at-**
able, *adj.* erreichbar.

Gewgaw, *s.* der Tand.

Geyser, *s.* der Geyser; der Badeofen.

Ghastl—iness, *s.* das Grausen. **—y,**
adj. totenbleich; (dreadful) gräßlich.

Gherkin, *s.* die Essiggurke.

Ghetto, *s.* die Judengasse.

Ghost, *s.* der Geist, das Gespenst; not
the — of a chance, nicht die geringste
Aussicht. **—ly,** *adj.* geistlich.

Giant, I. *s.* der Riese. II. *adj.* riesenhaft, riesig. **—ess,** *s.* die Riesin.

Gibber, *v.n.* schnattern. **—ish,** *s.* das
Geschnatter, Kauderwelsch.

Gibbet, *s.* der Galgen.

Gib—e, I. *s.* der Spott. II. *v.a.*
höhnen. **—ing,** *adj.*, **—ingly,** *adv.*
spöttisch.

Giblets, *s.* das Klein.

Gidd—ily, *adv.*, *see* **—y.** **—iness,** *s.*
der Schwindel. **—y,** *adj.* schwindelig;
(*fig.*) gedankenlos.

Gift, *s.* die Gabe, das Geschenk. **—ed,**
adj. begabt.

Gig, *s.* das Kabriolett; der Schiffs-
nachen (*Naut.*).

Gigantic, *adj.* riesenhaft, gigantisch.

Giggle, I. *v.n.* kichern. II. *s.* das
Gekicher.

Gild, *ir.v.a.* vergolden; to — the pill,
die bittere Pille versüßen. **—er,** *s.* der
Vergolder. **—ing,** *s.* die Vergoldung.

¹**Gill,** *s.* die Kieme (*Icht.*).

²**Gill,** *s.* die Viertelpinte.

Gilt, *s.* die Vergoldung. **—edged,**
adj. mit Goldschnitt; (*C.L.*) hochfein.

Gimbals, *pl.* die Bügel.

Gimcrack, *s.* der Tand.

Gimlet, *s.* der (Zwick=)Bohrer.

Gin, *s.* der Wacholderbranntwein.

Ginger, *s.* der Ingwer; — hair, das
rotbraune Haar. **—ly,** *adv.* behutsam.
—bread, *s.* der Pfefferkuchen. **—nut,**
s. die Pfeffernuß.

Gipsy, I. *s.* der (die) Zigeuner(in).
II. *adj.* zigeunerartig, Zigeuner=.

Giraffe, *s.* die Giraffe.

¹**Gird,** *ir.v.a.* gürten.

²**Gird,** *v.a.* to — at, verhöhnen.

Girder, *s.* der Binde=, Trag=balken.

Girdle, *s.* der Gurt, Gürtel.

Girl, *s.* das Mädchen. **—hood,** *s.*
die Mädchenjahre. **—ish,** *adj.*, —
ishly, *adv.* mädchenhaft, jugendlich.

Girth, *s.* der Gurt.

Gist, *s.* das Wesentliche.

Give, *ir.v.* I. *a.* geben; hergeben, hin-
geben; to — battle, eine Schlacht liefern;
to — offence, Anstoß erregen. II. *n.*
geben; (— way) nachgeben, weichen;
to — credit to, Glauben schenken; to
— away the bride, Brautvater sein;
a —n time, eine bestimmte Zeit.
—r, *s.* der Geber.

Gizzard, *s.* der Magen (des Vogels).

Glaci—al, *adj.* eisig, Gletscher=. **—er,**
s. der Gletscher.

Glad, *adj.* froh, erfreut (of, at a thing,
über eine S.); I am — of it, das
freut mich. **—den,** *v.a.* erfreuen.
—ly, *adv.* gern. **—ness,** *s.* die
Freude, Fröhlichkeit.

Glade, *s.* die Lichtung.

Gladiator, *s.* der Gladiator.

Glamour, *s.* der Zauber.

Glance, I. *s.* der flüchtige Blick; at a
—, auf den ersten Blick. II. *v.n.*
to — at, Blicke werfen auf (*acc.*);
to — off, abprallen; to — over,
flüchtig überblicken.

Gland, *s.* die Drüse (*Anat.*, *Bot.*).
—ular, *adj.* drüsig.

Glar—e, I. *s.* der blendende Glanz,
Schimmer; der wilde, durchbohrende
Blick. II. *v.n.* funkeln, glänzen; to
—e at *or* upon a person, einen
anstarren, anglotzen. **—ing,** *adj.*, —
ingly, *adv.* grell brennend; schreiend
(*as a crime*); auffallend, grell (*as
colours*).

Glass, I. *s.* das Glas; (tumbler) Trink=
glas; (looking-—) der Spiegel;
(weather-—) das Barometer; —
beads, die Glasperlen. II. *adj.* gläsern,
Glas=. **—es,** *pl.* die Brille, der
Kneifer. **—y,** *adj.* gläsern; glasig,
glasartig. **—blower,** *s.* der Glas=
bläser. **—works,** *pl.* die Glashütte.

Glaz—e, I. *v.a.* mit Glasscheiben ver=
sehen; glasieren (*a cake, etc.*; *also
Paint., Pott.*); **—ed paper,** das Glanz=
papier. II. *s.* die Glasur. **—ier,** *s.*
der Glaser.

Gleam, I. *s.* der Lichtstrahl. II. *v.n.*
strahlen, funkeln, schimmern.

Glean, *v.a.* nachlesen; (*fig.*) auflesen.
—er, *s.* der Ährenleser; (*fig.*) der
Sammler. **—ings,** *pl.* die Nachlese.

Glee, *s.* die Freude. **—ful,** *adj.*
fröhlich.

Glen, *s.* die Bergschlucht.

Glib, *adj.,* **—ly,** *adv.* glatt. **—ness,**
s. die Zungengeläufigkeit.

Glide, I. *v.n.* gleiten. II. *s.* das
Gleiten.

Glider, *s.* das Segelflugzeug (*Av.*).

Glimmer, *v.n.* flimmern, glimme(r)n.

Glimpse, *s.* der flüchtige Blick; **to
catch a — of,** flüchtig zu sehen bekom=
men.

Glint, *v.n.* glänzen.

Glisten, *v.n.* glitzern, schimmern.

Glitter, *v.n.* funkeln (*also fig.*). **—ing,**
adj., **—ingly,** *adv.* glänzend, glitzernd.

Gloaming, *s.* die Dämmerung.ˋ

Gloat, *v.n.* glotzen.

Globe, *s.* die Kugel; (earth) die
Erdkugel. **—trotter,** *s.* der vielgereiste
Mensch.

Globul—ous, —ar, *adj.* kugelförmig.

Gloom, *s.* die Dunkelheit; (*fig.*) der
Trübsinn. **—y,** *adj.* dunkel; trübsinnig.

Glor—ify, *v.a.* verherrlichen. **—ious,**
adj., **—iously,** *adv.* herrlich, prächtig.
—y, I. *s.* die Herrlichkeit. II. *v.n.*
sich (einer Sache) rühmen; **to —y in**
a thing, sich einer Sache rühmen.

Gloss, I. *s.* der Glanz (*also fig.*). II.
v.a. glänzend machen; **to — over,**
beschönigen. **—y,** *adj.* glänzend.

Glove, *s.* der Handschuh; **to be hand**
in — with, sehr vertraut sein mit.

Glow, I. *s.* die Glut, das Glühen.
II. *v.n.* glühen. **—worm,** *s.* der
Leuchtkäfer.

Glower, *v.n.* **to — at,** einen finster
ansehen.

Glue, I. *s.* der Leim. II. *v.a.* leimen
(*Carp.*).

Glum, *adj.* mürrisch.

Glut, I. *v.a.* übersättigen. II. *s.* die
Überfülle. **—ton,** *s.* der Schwelger.
—tonous, *adj.,* **—tonously,** *adv.*
gefräßig. **—tony,** *s.* die Schwel=
gerei.

Glycerine, *s.* das Glyzerin.

Gnash, *v.a.* knirschen.

Gnat, *s.* die Mücke.

Gnaw, *v.a.* nagen.

Gneiss, *s.* der Gneiß.

Gnome, *s.* der Gnom.

Go, *ir.v.n.* gehen; (— on) fortgehen;
(— away) abgehen; **to let —,** fahren
lassen, loslassen; **by which train do
you —?** mit welchem Zuge fahren
Sie? **to —** for a walk (drive), spa=
zieren gehen (fahren); **to — shares,**
teilen; **go!** vorwärts! los! **it is all
the —,** es ist Mode; **he goes in for
languages,** er spezialisiert in Sprachen;
that won't — down with me, das
lasse ich mir nicht gefallen; **—ahead,**
rührig, energisch; **a —ing concern,**
ein schwunghaftes Geschäft; **to keep
—ing,** im Gange erhalten; **—ing,
—ing, gone!** zum ersten, zum zweiten,
zum dritten! **—between,** *s.* der
Vermittler. **—by,** *s.*; **to give someone the —-by,** einen unbeachtet
lassen, ignorieren. **—cart,** *s.* der
Gängelwagen.

Goad, I. *s.* der Stachelstock. II. *v.a.*
anstacheln, (*fig.*) anregen.

Goal, *s.* das Ziel.

Goat, *s.* die Ziege; **he—,** der Ziegen=
bock.

Gobble, *v.a.* (— up) hastig verschlingen.

Goblet, *s.* der Becher, Pokal.

Goblin, *s.* der Kobold, Gnom; der Elf.

God, *s.* der Gott; (idol) der Abgott.
—dess, *s.* die Göttin. **—head,** *s.* die
Gottheit. **—less,** *adj.,* **—lessly,** *adv.*
gottlos. **—liness,** *s.* die Frömmig=
keit, Gottesfurcht. **—ly,** *adj.,* fromm,
gottesfürchtig. **—child,** *s.* das Paten=
kind. **—father,** *s.* der Taufpate,
Gevatter. **—fearing,** *adj.* gottes=
fürchtig. **—like,** *adj.* göttlich; er=
haben. **—mother,** *s.* die Pate,
Patin, Gevatterin. **—send,** *s.* die
unerwartete Wohltat; **that is a —send,**
das ist ein unerhoffter Fund.

Goggle, *v.n.* die Augen verdrehen.
—s, *s.* die Schutzbrille. **—eye,** *s.*

das Glotauge. **—eyed**, *adj.* starr=, glot=äugig.

Goitre, *s.* der Kropf.

Gold, I. *s.* das Gold; (*fig.*) das Geld. II. *adj.* golden, Gold=. **—en**, *adj.* golden. **—finch**, *s.* der Diſtelfink. **—fish**, *s.* der Goldfiſch. **—lace**, *s.* die Goldtreſſe. **—smith**, *s.* der Goldſchmied.

Golliwog, *s.* die Grotestpuppe.

Gondol—a, *s.* die Gondel. **—ier**, der Gondelführer.

Gong, *s.* der Gong.

Good, I. (Better, Best) *adj.* gut; in — earnest, in vollem Ernſte; in — time, zur rechten Zeit; for —, auf immer; that's no —, das nüt nichts; for your own —, zu Ihrem Beſten. II. *adv.* gut; as — as, ſo gut wie. III. *s.* (benefit) das Gute, Wohl, Beſte. IV. *int.* gut! **—ly**, *adj.* ſchön, anmutig. **—ness**, *s.* die Güte; (piety) die Frömmigkeit; for —ness' sake, um Himmelswillen. **—bye**, *s.* das Lebewohl. **— day**, *int.* guten Tag. **—Friday**, *s.* der Karfreitag. **—natured**, *adj.* gutmütig. **— night**, I. *s.* der Nachtgruß. II. *adj.* gute Nacht. **—will**, *s.* das Wohlwollen; die Kundschaft (*C.L.*).

Goose, *s.* die Gans; wild — chase, unnüte Verfolgung. **—flesh**, (*fig.*) die Gänsehaut.

Gooseberry, *s.* die Stachelbeere.

¹**Gore**, I. *s.* der Zwickel (*Semp.*). II. *v.a.* vergehren (*Semp.*); durchbohren (*as bulls*).

²**Gor—e**, *s.* geronnenes Blut. **—y**, *adj.* blutig.

Gorge, I. *s.* die Gurgel; (pass) die (Berg=)Schlucht. II. *v.a.* verschlingen.

Gorgeous, *adj.*, **—ly**, *adv.* prächtig. **—ness**, *s.* die Pracht.

Gorget, *s.* die Halsberge.

Gorilla, *s.* der Gorilla.

Gorse, *s.* der Stechginster.

Gosling, *s.* das Gänschen.

Gospel, *s.* das Evangelium.

Gossamer, *s.* der Altweibersommer; die leichte Gaze (*coll.*).

Gossip, I. *s.* (tattler) die Schwätzerin, Klatschbase; (male) der Klätscher; (tattle) der Klatsch. II. *v.n.* schwaten. **—ing**, *s.* das Geklatsch.

Gouge, I. *s.* der Hohlmeißel. II. *v.a.* ausmeißeln.

Gourd, *s.* der Kürbiß.

Gourmand, *s.* der Freſſer.

Gourmet, *s.* der Feinſchmecker.

Gout, *s.* die Gicht. **—y**, *adj.* gichtiſch.

Govern, *v.* I. *a.* regieren, beherrſchen, verwalten. II. *n.* regieren, herrſchen. **—ess**, *s.* die Erzieherin. **—ing**, *adj.* herrſchend; leitend. **—ment**, *s.* die Regierung. **—mental**, *adj.* Regierungs=. **—or**, *s.* (ruler) der (Be=)Herrſcher; der Statthalter (*of a province, etc.*); (administrator) der Verwalter.

Gown, *s.* das Frauenkleid; der Talar (*university*).

Grab, I. *v.a.* ergrapſen. II. *v.n.* haſchen, greifen (at, nach).

Grace, I. *s.* die Gunſt, Gnade; (pleasingness) die Anmut, der Reiz; (—fulness) die Grazie; with a good —, bereitwillig; to say —, das Tiſchgebet ſprechen. II. *v.a.* ſchmücken. **—ful**, *adj.*, **—fully**, *adv.* anmutig. **—less**, *adj.* reizlos; (depraved) verworfen. **—s**, *pl.* Grazien (*Myth.*).

Gracious, *adj.*, **—ly**, *adv.* gütig, huldreich; good —! ach du meine Güte! **—ness**, *s.* die Gnade (*also of God*).

Grad—e, *s.* der Grad. **—ient**, *s.* (ascending) die Steigung; (descending) die Neigung. **—ual**, *adj.*, **—ually**, *adv.* allmählich.

Graft, I. *v.a.* pfropfen. II. *s.* das Pfropfreis.

Grain, *s.* das Korn, Getreide; der Strich (*in leather*); against the —, gegen den Strich.

Gramma—r, *s.* die Grammatik. **—tical**, *adj.*, **—tically**, *adv.* grammatiſch.

Gramme, *s.* das Gramm.

Gramophone, *s.* das Grammophon.

Granary, *s.* der Speicher.

Grand, *adj.*, **—ly**, *adv.* groß, vornehm. **—eur**, *s.* die Größe, Pracht. **—ness**, *s.* die Erhabenheit. **—child**, *s.* der Enkel, die Enkelin. **—duke**, *s.* der Großherzog. **—father**, *s.* der Großvater. **—mother**, *s.* die Großmutter. **—piano**, *s.* der Flügel. **—stand**, *s.* die Tribüne.

Grange, *s.* der Meierhof.

Granite, *s.* der Granit.

Granny, *s.* das Großmütterchen.

Grant, I. *v.a.* bewilligen, gewähren; God — it! Gott gebe es! I take it for —ed, ich nehme es für ausgemacht an. II. *s.* die Bewilligung, Gewährung. **—ee**, *s.* der Begünstigte. **—er**, *s.* der Bewilliger.

Granu—lar, *adj.* förnig. **—lated,** *adj.* feinförnig.

Grape, *s.* die (Wein-)Traube, Weinbeere. **—shot,** *s.* (Trauben-)Kartätschen. **—stone,** *s.* der Traubenkern.

Grapnel, *s.* der Enterhaken (*Naut.*).

Grapple, *v.a.* anhaken (*Naut.*); to **—** with a thing, sich ernstlich an eine Sache machen.

Grasp, I. *v.a.* greifen; I cannot **—** it, ich kann es nicht begreifen. II. *v.n.* (*fig.*) to **—** at, nach einer S. greifen, streben. III. *s.* der Griff.

Grass, *s.* das Gras, der Rasen. **—y,** *adj.* grasig. **—hopper,** *s.* die Heuschrecke. **—widow,** *s.* die Strohwitwe.

¹Grate, *s.* der (Feuer-)Rost.

²Grate, *v.* I. *a.* kratzen, raspeln. II. *n.* knarren, knirschen; it **—s** upon my nerves, das geht mir auf die Nerven.

Grateful, *adj.,* **—ly,** *adv.* dankbar; (pleasing) angenehm, zusagend. **—ness,** *s.* die Dankbarkeit, Erkenntlichkeit.

Grater, *s.* das Reibeisen.

Grating, *s.* das Gitter.

Grati—fication, *s.* die Befriedigung (*of the palate, etc.*); (satisfaction) der Genuß. **—fy,** *v.a.* befriedigen; to **—fy** a wish, einen Wunsch erfüllen. **—fying,** *adj.* erfreulich.

Gratis, *adv.* unentgeltlich, umsonst.

Gratitude, *s.* die Dankbarkeit, Erkenntlichkeit.

Gratuity, *s.* das Trinkgeld.

Gravamen, *s.* der Beschwerdepunkt, Klagepunkt.

¹Grave, *adj.,* **—ly,** *adv.* ernst(haft); wichtig.

²Grave, *s.* das Grab. **—yard,** *s.* der Friedhof.

Gravel, *s.* der Kies, Gries.

Gravitat—e, *v.n.* gravitieren. **—ion,** *s.* die Schwerkraft, Gravitation.

Gravity, *s.* die Schwere (*Phys.*); die Wichtigkeit, Bedenklichkeit (*of a fact, etc.*); die Würde (*of bearing*).

Gravy, *s.* der Fleischsaft.

¹Graz—e, *v.* I. *a.* weiden. II. *n.* grasen. **—ier,** *s.* der Viehmäster.

²Graze, I. *v.a.* streifen. II. *s.* die Schramme.

Greas—e, I. *s.* das Fett, (der) Schmer. II. *v.a.* schmieren. **—iness,** *s.* das Schmierige, die Fettheit. **—y,** *adj.* schmierig, fettig.

Great, I. *adj.* groß; a **—** deal, sehr viel; a **—** friend, ein intimer Freund. II. *pl.* die Großen, Vornehmen. **—ly,** *adv.* in hohem Grade, beträchtlich. **—ness,** *s.* die Größe. **—grandchild,** *s.* der Urenkel, die Urenkelin. **—grandfather,** *s.* der Urgroßvater. **—grandfather,** *s.* der Ururgroßvater.

Greed—iness, *s.* die Gierigkeit (*also fig.*). **—y,** *adj.,* **—ily,** *adv.* gierig (*also fig.*), gefräßig.

Green, I. *adj.* grün; to be **—** in one's memory, noch in frischem Andenken sein. II. *s.* das Grün. **—gage,** *s.* die Reneklode. **—grocer,** *s.* der Grünkramhändler. **—horn,** *s.* unerfahrener Junge. **—house,** *s.* das Gewächshaus.

Greet, *v.a.* (be)grüßen. **—ing,** *s.* die Begrüßung.

Grenad—e, *s.* die Granate. **—ier,** *s.* der Grenadier.

Grey, I. *adj.* grau. II. *s.* das Grau. **—haired,** *adj.* grauhaarig. **—hound,** *s.* das Windspiel.

Grid, *s.* das Gitter; *see* Gridiron.

Gridiron, *s.* der Bratrost.

Grief, *s.* der Kummer, Gram, das Weh.

Griev—ance, *s.* die Beschwerde, der Verdruß. **—e,** *v.* I. *a.* kränken, betrüben, (einem) Weh tun. II. *n.* sich grämen, trauern; I am much **—ed,** es tut mir sehr leid. **—ous,** *adj.,* **—ously,** *adv.* schmerzlich, empfindlich, verdrießlich.

Grill, I. *v.a.* rösten. II. *v.n.* braten, schmoren. III. *s.* das geröstete Fleisch.

Grim, *adj.,* **—ly,** *adv.* grimmig. **—ness,** *s.* die Scheußlichkeit.

Grimace, *s.* die Grimasse, Fratze.

Grim—e, I. *s.* der tiefe Schmutz. II. *v.a.* beschmutzen, berußen. **—y,** *adj.* schmutzig, rußig.

Grin, I. *v.n.* grinsen; we must **—** and bear it, wir müssen gute Miene zum bösen Spiel machen. II. *s.* das Grinsen, Fletschen.

Grind, *ir.v.a.* reiben, zerreiben; mahlen (*corn, coffee, etc.*); (whet) schleifen, wetzen; to **—** the teeth, mit den Zähnen knirschen. **—er,** *s.* der Schleifer; der Backenzahn. **—ing,** *s.* das Mahlen, Schleifen. **—stone,** *s.* der Mühlstein; der Schleif-, Wetzstein.

Grip, I. *s.* der Griff; to lose one's **—,** den Halt verlieren. II. *v.a.* ergreifen, fassen. **—ing,** *adj.* kneipend, nagend.

Grisly, *adj.* ſcheußlich, entſeßlich.

Grist, *s.* das Gemahlene.

Gristl—e, *s.* der Knorpel. **—y,** *adj.* knorpelig.

Grit, *s.* das Schrot; der Kies; he has **—,** er hat Mut. **—s,** *pl.* Grütze. **—ty,** *adj.* griesig, kiesig.

Grizzl—ed, *adj.* grauſprenklich. **—y,** *adj.,* grau, graulich; **—y** bear, der graue Bär.

Groan, I. *v.n.* ſtöhnen, ächzen. II. *s.* das Stöhnen, Ächzen.

Groats, *pl.* die Hafergrütze.

Grocer, *s.* der Materialwarenhändler. **—ies,** *pl.* die Materialwaren. **—y,** *s.* der Kolonialwarenhandel.

Grog, *s.* der Grog.

Groin, *s.* der Schambug (*Anat.*); der Grat, die Rippe (*Arch.*).

Groom, I. *s.* der Stallknecht, Reitknecht. II. *v.a.* (Pferde) pußen, beſorgen.

Groove, I. *s.* die Rinne, Auskehlung, Furche; to get into a **—,** in demſelben Geleiſe bleiben. II. *v.a.* auskehlen, furchen.

Grope, *v.n.* taſtend fühlen (for, nach).

Gross, *adj.,* **—ly,** *adv.* grob, roh; in the **—,** in Bauſch und Bogen; **—** amount, der Bruttobetrag.

Grot, —to, *s.* die Felſenhöhle, Grotte.

Grotesque, *adj.,* **—ly,** *adv.* grotesk. **—ness,** *s.* das Groteske.

Ground, I. *s.* der Grund, Boden; on the **—** that, aus dem Grunde, weil; to hold one's **—,** ſeinen Plaß behaupten; to lose **—,** Boden verlieren. II. *v.a.* niederſeßen (*arms*); (*fig.*) begründen (auf eine S.); in den Anfangsgründen unterrichten. **—less,** *adj.,* **—lessly,** *adv.* grundlos; unbegründet. **—s,** *pl.* (dregs) der Bodenſaß, die Hefen; (rudiments, elements) die Grundſäße. **—sel,** *s.* das Kreuzkraut. **—floor,** *s.* das Erdgeſchoß, Parterre. **—plan,** *s.* der Grundriß.

Group, I. *s.* die Gruppe. II. *v.a.* gruppieren. **—ing,** *s.* die Gruppierung.

Grouse, *s.* das Waldhuhn.

Grove, *s.* das Gehölz.

Grovel, *v.n.* auf der Erde kriechen. **—ler,** *s.* der Kriecher. **—ling,** *adj.* kriechend.

Grow, *ir.v.* I. *n.* wachſen; (become) werden; to **—** dark, dunkel werden; **—ing** weather, fruchtbares Wetter. II. *ir.v.a.* bauen, ziehen (*Agr.*): he

grew a beard, er ließ ſich einen Bart wachſen. **—er,** *s.* der, die, das Wachſende; der Pflanzer, Bauer (*Agr.*).

Growl, I. *s.* das Knurren, Brummen. II. *v.n.* knurren, brummen. III. *v.a.* herausbrummen. **—er,** *s.* der knurrige Hund; (person) der Brummbart.

Grown, *p.p. & adj.* (—n up) erwachſen.

Growth, *s.* der Wuchs, das Wachstum; (increase) die Zunahme, der Anwuchs.

Grub, I. *v.a.*; to **—** up, ausjäten, ausreuten. II. *s.* der Engerling, die Made.

Grudg—e, I. *v.a.* mißgönnen (a person a thing, einem etwas). II. *s.* (enmity) der Groll, die Mißgunſt; (reluctance) der Widerwille; to bear a **—e** against, Groll hegen gegen. **—er,** *s.* der Mißgünſtige. **—ingly,** *adv.* grollend, ungern.

Gruel, *s.* der Haferſchleim.

Gruesome, *adj.* greulich.

Gruff, *adj.,* **—ly,** *adv.* mürriſch. **—ness,** *s.* die Barſchheit.

Grumble, I. *v.n.* murren. II. *s.* das Murren. **—r,** *s.* der Murrende, Mißvergnügte.

Grunt, I. *v.n.* grunzen. II. *s.* das Grunzen.

Guarant—ee, I. *s.* die Bürgſchaft. II. *v.a.* Gewähr leiſten (für), bürgen (für), garantieren; **—eed** genuine, für Echtheit wird gebürgt. **—or,** *s.* der Bürge.

Guard, I. *v.a.* (be)hüten, bewahren, (be)ſchüßen, bewachen (from, vor). II. *v.n.* auf der Hut ſein. III. *s.* die Wache, Bewachung, Hut; die Wache, Wachmannſchaft (*Mil.*); der Schaffner (*Railw.*); der Bügel (*Gun.*); das Stichblatt (*of a sword*); to put someone on his **—,** einen warnen; be off one's **—,** unachtſam ſein. **—ed,** *adj.,* **—edly,** *adv.* vorſichtig, behutſam. **—s,** *pl.* die Garde (truppen). **—house,** *s.* die Wache, das Wachthaus (*Mil.*). **—sman,** *s.* der Gardiſt.

Guardian, I. *s.* der Vormund (*Law*). II. *adj.* ſchüßend, Schuß-. **—angel,** *s.* der Schußengel.

Gudgeon, *s.* der Gründling.

Guelder-rose, *s.* der Schneeball.

Guess, I. *v.a.* erraten (*a riddle*). II. *v.n.* **—** (at) mutmaßen, raten. III. *s.* die Mutmaßung, Vermutung; to make a **—,** raten.

Guest, *s.* der Gaſt; paying —, der Penſionär. **—chamber, —room,** *s.* das Fremdenzimmer (*in a private house*); das Gaſtzimmer (*at an inn*).

Guffaw, *s.* lautes, ſchallendes Gelächter.

Guid—able, *adj.* lenkſam, lenkbar. **—ance,** *s.* die Führung, Leitung. **—e,** I. *s.* der Führer (*also fig.*), Wegweiſer; girl —e, die Pfadfinderin. II. *v.a.* führen, leiten (*also fig.*); —ing star, der Leitſtern. **—e-book,** *s.* das Reiſehandbuch. **—e-post,** *s.* der Wegweiſer.

Guild, *s.* die Gilde, Zunft, Innung. **—hall,** *s.* das Innungshaus; das Rathaus.

Guile, *s.* die Liſt, Argliſt. **—ful,** *adj.* **—fully,** *adv.* argliſtig, trügeriſch. **—less,** *adj.,* **—lessly,** *adv.* arglos. **—lessness,** *s.* die Argloſigkeit, Unſchuld.

Guillotine, I. *s.* die Guillotine. II. *v.a.* guillotinieren.

Guilt, *s.* die Schuld. **—ily,** *adv.* ſchuldig. **—iness,** *s.* die Strafbarkeit. **—less,** *adj.,* **—lessly,** *adv.* ſchuldlos, unſchuldig. **—y,** *adj.* ſchuldig; to find —y, für ſchuldig erklären; to plead —y, ſein Verbrechen eingeſtehen.

Guise, *s.* das äußere Anſehen; under the — of, unter der Maske (des, der).

Guitar, *s.* die Guitarre.

Gulf, *s.* der Meerbuſen, Golf, die Bucht. **—stream,** *s.* der Golfſtrom.

1Gull, *s.* die Möve.

2Gull, I. *s.* der Einfaltspinſel. II. *v.a.* zum beſten haben.

Gullet, *s.* die Gurgel, der Schlund.

Gullib—ility, *s.* die Leichtgläubigkeit. **—le,** *adj.* einfältig.

Gully, *s.* die Waſſerrinne.

Gulp, I. *v.a.* gierig (ver-)ſchlucken. II. *s.* der Schluck, das Schlucken.

1Gum, I. *s.* das Gummi. II. *v.a.* zukleben.

2Gum, *s.* das Zahnfleiſch. **—boil,** *s.* das Zahngeſchwür.

Gun, *s.* (firearm) das Feuergewehr; (musket, *etc.*) die Flinte, Büchſe; (cannon) das Geſchütz. **—ner,** *s.* der Kanonier, Artilleriſt. **—nery,** *s.* die Geſchützkunſt, Artillerie (wiſſenſchaft). **—barrel,** *s.* der Flintenlauf. **—carriage,** *s.* die Lafette. **—cotton,** *s.* die Schießbaumwolle. **—metal,** *s.*

das Kanonenmetall, Stückmetall. **—powder,** *s.* das Schießpulver. **—shot,** I. *s.* der Schuß; die Schußweite (distance). II. *adj.;* Schuß-; **—shot wound,** die Schußwunde. **—smith,** *s.* der Büchſenmacher. **—stock,** *s.* der Kolben.

Gunwale, *s.* das Dollbord (on rowboats).

Gurgl—e, I. *v.n.* gluckſen. II. *s.,* **—ing,** *s.* das Gemurmel, Gurgeln.

Gush, I. *v.n.* hervorſtrömen; (fig.) ſchwärmen. II. *s.* der Guß, Strom. **—ing,** *adj.* ſich ergießend; (fig.) überſchwenglich.

Gusset, *s.* der Zwickel.

Gust, *s.* der Windſtoß. **—y,** *adj.* ſtürmiſch, ungeſtüm.

Gut, I. *s.* der Darm. II. *v.a.* ausweiden; (fig.) ausleeren.

Gutter, I. *s.* die Waſſerrinne, die Goſſe; die Dach-, Trauf-rinne (Build.). II. *v.n.* ablaufen (as a candle). **—snipe,** *s.* das Straßenkind.

Guttural, *adj.* zur Kehle gehörig; Kehl-.

Guy, *s.* der Achterholer (Naut.); die Vogelſcheuche.

Guzzle, *v.n.* gierig eſſen *or* zechen.

Gymkhana, *s.* die athletiſche Schauſtellung.

Gymn—asium, *s.* die Turnhalle, der Turnplatz. **—ast,** *s.* der Turner. **—astic,** *adj.,* **—astically,** *adv.* gymnaſtiſch, Turn-. **—astics,** *pl.* das Turnen.

Gyrat—e, *v.n.* wirbeln. **—ion,** *s.* das Drehen.

Gyves, *pl.* Feſſeln.

H

H, h, das H, h.

Haberdasher, *s.* der Poſamentier. **—y,** *s.* Kurzwaren; der Kurzwarenhandel.

Habit, *s.* der Gebrauch, die Gewohnheit; I do it from —, ich tue es aus Gewohnheit; to fall into bad —s, in ſchlechte Gewohnheiten verfallen. **—able,** *adj.* bewohnbar. **—ation,** *s.* der Wohnort. **—ual,** *adj.,* **—ually,** *adv.* gewöhnlich, Gewohnheits-.

1Hack, I. *v.a.* (zer)hacken. II. *s.* der Hieb. **—ing,** *adj.;* —ing cough, kurzer, trockener Huſten.

2Hack, I. *s.* das Reitpferd. II. *adj.* gemein.

Hackle, *v.a.* hecheln.

Hackney, I. *s.* der Gaul. II. — carriage, die Droschke, der Mietwagen. —ed, *adj.* abgenutzt; —ed expression, die abgedroschene Redensart.

Haddock, *s.* der Schellfisch.

Haft, *s.* der Griff.

Hag, *s.* das häßliche alte Weib.

Haggard, *adj.* abgemagert.

Haggle, *v.n.* feilschen.

¹Hail, I. der Hagel. II. *v.n.* hageln. —stone, *s.* das Hagelkorn. —storm, *s.* das Hagelwetter.

²Hail, *int.* Heil! Glück.

³Hail, I. *v.a.* (call to) anrufen; (salute) beglückwünschen, begrüßen; to —from, stammen aus. II. *s.* der Anruf.

Hair, *s.* das Haar; die Haare. —ed, *adj.* haarig. —iness, *s.* die Haarigkeit, Behaartheit. —less, *adj.* unbehaart, kahl. —y, *adj.* haarig, behaart. —breadth, *s.*; within a —breadth, um ein Haar, ums Haar, beinah. —brush, *s.* die Haarbürste. —dresser, *s.* der Friseur. —pin, *s.* die Haarnadel. —splitting, I. *adj.* haarspaltend. II. *s.* die Haarspalterei. —spring, *s.* die Haarfeder, Schnecken-, Spiral-feder. —tonic, *s.* das Haarwasser.

Hake, *s.* der Hechtdorsch (*Ichth.*).

Halberd, *s.* die Hellebarde. —ier, *s.* der Hellebardier.

Hale, *adj.* frisch und gesund.

Half, I. *s.* die Hälfte; by halves, nicht gründlich. II. *adj.* halb; — a pound, ein halbes Pfund; a pound and a —, anderthalb Pfund; two pounds and a —, zwei und ein halbes Pfund; at —price, zum halben Preise; —past one, halb zwei. —bred, *adj.* halbbürtig, Halbblut-. —breed, *s.* der Mischling. —brother, *s.* der Halb-, Stiefbruder. —hearted, *adj.* mattherzig, gleichgültig. —way, I. *adv.* halbwegs. II. *adj.* auf halbem Wege liegend, in der Mitte; to meet a person —way, einem auf halbem Wege entgegenkommen.

Halibut, *s.* die Heilbutte.

Hall, *s.* (room) die Halle, der Saal; (entrance-) der Hausflur. —mark, *s.* der Stempel der Echtheit (für Gold-, Silberwaren 2c.).

Hallelujah, *s.* & *int.* (das) Hallelujah.

Hallow, *v.a.* heiligen. —eve, —e'en, *s.* der Allerheiligenabend.

Hallucination, *s.* die Sinnestäuschung (also *Med.*).

Halo, *s.* der Hof (round the moon, etc.); der Heiligenschein (*Paint.*).

Halt, I. *v.n.* Halt machen. II. *v.a.* Halt machen lassen (troops, etc.). III. *s.* der Halt. IV. *adj.* lahm, hinkend; in a —ing voice, mit schwankender Stimme. —ingly, *adv.* hinkend; langsam.

Halter, *s.* die Halfter (for a horse, etc.); (rope) der Strick.

Halve, *v.a.* zur Hälfte teilen.

Halyard, *s.* das Fall.

Ham, *s.* der Schinken. —sandwich, *s.* das Schinkenbröttchen.

Hamlet, *s.* der Weiler, das Dörfchen.

Hammer, I. *s.* der Hammer; der Hahn (of a percussion-lock); to bring to the —, versteigern lassen. II. *v.a.* & *n.* hämmern.

Hammock, *s.* die Hängematte.

¹Hamper, *s.* der Packkorb.

²Hamper, *v.a.* (obstruct) hemmen, belästigen.

Hand, I. *s.* die Hand; der Zeiger (*Horol.*); at first —, aus erster Quelle; to lend a helping —, Hilfe leisten; to change —s, den Besitzer wechseln; second —, antiquarisch, aus zweiter Hand; the letter has come to —, der Brief ist eingelaufen; to shake —s with a person, einem die Hand schütteln. II. *v.a.* einhändigen, geben, überreichen. —ful, *s.* eine Handvoll (also *fig.*). —book, *s.* das Handbuch. —breadth, *s.* die Handbreite. —cuff, *s.* die Handschelle.

Handicap, I. *s.* das Handicap (rennen). II. *v.a.* (*fig.*) hemmen, behindern.

Handi-craft, *s.* das Handwerk, Gewerbe. —craftsman, *s.* der Handwerker. —ness, *s.* die Behendigkeit, Gewandtheit.

Handiwork, *s.* die Handarbeit.

Handkerchief, *s.* das Taschentuch.

Handle, I. *v.a.* anfassen; behandeln (a subject). II. *s.* die Handhabe, der Griff; das Heft (of sword, etc.); der Henkel (of a vessel). —bar, *s.* die Lenkstange (*Cycl.*).

Handrail, *s.* die Geländerstange.

Handsel, *s.* das Handgeld.

Handshake, *s.* der Händedruck.

Handsome, *adj.*, —ly, *adv.* hübsch, schön. —ness, *s.* die Schönheit.

Handwriting, *s.* die Handschrift.

Handy, *adj.* gewandt, geschickt.

Hang, I. *reg.* (& *ir.*) *v.a.* (auf)hängen; tapezieren (rooms); — it! hol's der Henker! II. *ir.v.n.* hangen; hängen, schweben (over a thing, über einer S.); to — about, umherlungern, faulenzen. —ing, *s.* das Hangen, Hängen. — man, *s.* der Henker.

Hangar, *s.* der Luftzeugschuppen.

Hanger, *s.* der Aufhänger. —on, *s.* der Anhänger.

Hank, *s.* die Docke.

Hanker, *v.n.*; to — after a thing, sich nach einer S. sehnen. —ing, I. *adj.*, —ingly, *adv.* sehnsüchtig. II. *s.* die Sehnsucht.

Hap, *s.* der Zufall. —less, *adj.* unglücklich. —ly, *adv.* vielleicht.

Haphazard, *s.* das Geratewohl; at —, aufs Geratewohl.

Happen, *v.n.* sich ereignen; I —ed to meet him, ich traf ihn zufällig.

Happ—ily, *adv.* glücklicherweise; glücklich. —iness, *s.* die Glückseligkeit. —y, *adj.* glücklich. —y-go-lucky, *adj.* unbekümmert, sorglos.

Harangue, I. *v.a.* feierlich anreden. II. *v.n.* eine feierliche Ansprache halten. III. *s.* die (An-)Rede.

Harass, *v.a.* quälen, plagen.

Harbinger, *s.* der Vorbote.

Harbour, I. *s.* der Hafen. II. *v.a.* beherbergen.

Hard, I. *adj.* hart; (difficult) schwer; — of hearing, schwerhörig; to be — up, in Geldnot sein; — at work, fleißig bei der Arbeit; to be —ly dealt with, übel behandelt werden. II. *adv.* (forcibly) heftig, stark; (diligently) fleißig, tüchtig; (with difficulty) mit Mühe. —en, *v.* I. *a.* härten. II. *n.* hart werden, sich verhärten. —i-hood, *s.* die Unerschrockenheit. —ily, *adv.* kühn, dreist. —ly, *adv.* mühsam; (scarcely) kaum, schwerlich. —ness, *s.* die Härte; (difficulty) die Schwierigkeit. —ship, *s.* die Beschwerde. —y, *adj.* stark; abgehärtet. —headed, *adj.* verständig. —hearted, *adj.* hartherzig. —ware, *s.* die Eisenwaren. —working, *adj.* fleißig.

Hare, *s.* der Hase. —lip, *s.* die Hasenscharte.

Harem, *s.* der Harem, das Serail.

Haricot, *s.* die welsche Bohne.

Hark, I. *v.n.* horchen. II. *int.* horch!

Harlequin, *s.* der Harlekin. —ade, *s.* das Possenspiel.

Harm, I. *s.* der Schaden, Nachteil; he doesn't mean any —, er meint es nicht böse; it won't do us any —, es wird uns nichts schaden; to keep out of —'s way, sich vorsehen. II. *v.a.* beschädigen, verletzen. —ful, *adj.*, —fully, *adv.* nachteilig, schädlich, verderblich. —less, *adj.*, —lessly, *adv.* harmlos, unschädlich. —lessness, *s.* die Harmlosigkeit.

Harmon—ic, *adj.* harmonisch (*Mus.*). —ious, *adj.*, —iously, *adv.* wohlklingend. —iousness, *s.* der Einklang; die Übereinstimmung; das Ebenmaß. —ium, *s.* das Harmonium. —ize, *v.* I. *n.* übereinstimmen. II. *a.* in Einklang bringen. —izer, *s.* der Harmonist. —y, *s.* die Harmonie, Übereinstimmung (*Mus., Paint.*); to be in —y with, im Einklang stehen mit.

Harness, I. *s.* das Geschirr. II. *v.a.* anschirren.

Harp, I. *s.* die Harfe (*Mus.*). II. *v.n.* harfen; he is always —ing on the same string, er bleibt immer bei der alten Leier. —er, —ist, *s.* der Harfner.

Harpoon, I. *s.* die Harpune. II. *v.a.* harpunieren.

Harrier, *s.* der Hasenhund.

Harrow, I. *s.* die Egge. II. *v.a.* eggen. —ing, *adj.* herzzerreißend.

Harry, *v.a.* verheeren.

Harsh, *adj.*, —ly, *adv.* rauh (to the touch); herb, streng (to the taste); mißklingend (to the ear); (severe) streng, barsch. —ness, *s.* die Rauheit.

Hart, *s.* der Hirsch.

Harum-scarum, I. *adj.* wild, leichtsinnig. II. *adv.* Hals über Kopf.

Harvest, I. *s.* die Ernte. II. *v.a.* ernten; einheimsen.

Hash, I. *s.* gehacktes Fleisch. II. *v.a.* klein hacken; to make a — of a thing, eine Sache verderben.

Hasp, *s.* die Haspe, Klampe.

Hassock, *s.* das Betkissen.

Hast—e, I. *s.* die Hast, Eile. II. —en, *v.a.* beschleunigen. III. —en, *v.n.* & *r.* eilen, sich beeilen. —ily, *adv.* eilig. —iness, *s.* die Übereilung. —y, *adj.* hastig, eilig; voreilig, überschnell.

Hat, *s.* der Hut; top —, der Zylinder.
—ter, *s.* der Hutmacher.

Hatch, I. *v.a.* aushecken, ausbrüten
(*also fig.*). II. *v.n.* brüten. III. *s.*
die Luke (*Naut.*).

Hatchet, *s.* das Beil.

Hate, I. *s.* der Haß (to, towards,
gegen, wider, auf einen). II. *v.a.*
hassen. —ful, *adj.*, —fully, *adv.*
(—d) verhaßt; gehässig. —fulness,
s. die Gehässigkeit. —r, *s.* der Hasser.

Hatred, *s.* der Haß, Groll, Abscheu,
die Feindseligkeit.

Haught—ily, *adv.* hochmütig. —iness,
s. der Hochmut, Stolz. —y, *adj.*
hochmütig, stolz.

Haul, *v.a.* ziehen, schleppen.

Haunch, *s.* die Keule.

Haunt, I. *v.a.* heimsuchen. II. *s.* der
gewohnte Aufenthalt. —ed, *p.p.* &
adj.; the —ed house, das Spukhaus.

Hautboy, *s.* die Hoboe, Oboe.

Have, I. *ir.v.a.* (possess) haben, besitzen; (cause) lassen; (be obliged)
müssen; I — my hair washed, ich
lasse mir die Haare waschen; I would
— you know, Sie müssen wissen; to
— rather, vorziehen. II. *ir.v.aux.*
haben; sein; we — seen, wir haben
gesehen; he has come, er ist gekommen.

Haven, *s.* der Hafen (*also fig.*).

Haversack, *s.* der Brotbeutel, Futterbeutel (*Mil.*).

Havoc, *s.* die Verwüstung; to make —
of a thing, etwas zerstören.

¹Hawk, I. *s.* der Habicht, Falke. II.
v.n. mit Falken jagen. —er, *s.* der
Falkenjäger. —ing, *s.* die Falken-
beize.

²Hawk, *v.a.* hökern, hausieren. —er,
s. der Höker, Hausierer.

Hawse—r, *s.* das Kabeltau. —holes,
pl. die Klüsen.

Hay, *s.* das Heu; make — while the
sun shines, schmiede das Eisen solange
es noch heiß ist. —cock, *s.* der
Heuhaufen. —rick, —stack, *s.* der
Heuschober.

Hazard, I. *s.* das Wagestück, Wagnis;
at all —s, auf alle Fälle. II. *v.a.*
wagen, aufs Spiel setzen. —ous, *adj.*
gewagt, gefährlich.

Haz—e, *s.* der leichte Nebel. —iness,
s. die Nebeligkeit. —y, *adj.* nebelig,
dunstig.

Hazel, I. *s.* die Hasel(-staude). II. *adj.*
nußbraun. —nut, *s.* die Haselnuß.

He, I. *pers. pron.* er; der, derjenige;
— who, derjenige, welcher. II. *in
comp.* = das männliche Tier, Männchen.

Head, I. *s.* der Kopf; das Haupt (*high
style*); to come to a —, eitern; — over
heels, Hals über Kopf; I cannot make
— or tail of it, ich kann daraus nicht
klug werden. II. *adj.* (*in comp.*) der,
die, das vordere, erste, vorzüglichste,
Haupt-, Ober-. III. *v.a.* (an)führen,
befehligen (*an army, etc.*); (be at
the —) of) an der Spitze stehen. —ing,
s. der Titelkopf (*Typ.*); (inscription)
die Überschrift. —less, *adj.* ohne
Kopf, kopflos (*also fig.*). —y, *adj.*
berauschend. —ache, *s.* das Kopfweh.
—dress, *s.*, —gear, *s.* der Kopfputz.
—land, *s.* das Vorgebirge. —light,
s. die Kopflaterne (*vehicle*). —long,
I. *adj.* jäh, abschüssig. II. *adv.* köpf-
lings-; kopfüber. —master, *s.* der
Direktor. —phone, *s.* der Kopfhörer
(*Radio*). —quarters, *pl.* das Haupt-
quartier. —sman, *s.* der Scharfrichter. —stall, *s.* das Kopfstück (*of
a bridle*); die Halfter. —stone, *s.* der
Kopfstein (*Arch.*). —strong, *adj.*
starrköpfig, halsstarrig. —way, *s.*
der Fortschritt; to make —way,
vorankommen, Fortschritte machen.

Heal, *v.a. & n.* heilen; (*fig.*) versöhnen.
—er, *s.* der Heiler. —ing, I. *adj.*
heilend, heilsam; (*fig.*) versöhnend.
II. *s.* das Heilen.

Health, *s.* die Gesundheit (*also in
drinking*); good —! Gesundheit!
Prosit! —ful, *adj.*, —fully, *adv.*,
—y, *adj.* gesund. —iness, *s.* die Gesundheit. —resort, *s.* der Kurort.

Heap, I. *s.* der Haufe(n). II. *v.a.*
häufen; to — on, hinzutun; to —
up, aufhäufen.

Hear, I. *ir.v.a.* hören; anhören; (listen to) zuhören; abhören (*a witness,
reading, a fact*); let me — from you,
laß von Dir hören. II. *ir.v.n.* hören;
horchen. III. *int.* horch! hört! —er,
s. der Hörer; der Zuhörer (*of a
preacher, etc.*). —ing, *s.* das Hören;
(sense of —ing) das Gehör; das
Verhör (*Law*); die Hörweite; the
—ing of witnesses, das Zeugen-
verhör. —say, *s.* das Hörensagen.

Hearken, *v.n.* horchen.

Hearse, *s.* der Leichenwagen.

Heart, *s.* das Herz (*also fig.*); to lose

—, den Mut verlieren; to have at —, etwas auf dem Herzen haben; by —, auswendig; in the — of China, im Innersten von China; to speak from one's —, frisch von der Leber weg sprechen; with all my —, von Herzen gern. **—en**, *v.a.* aufmuntern. **—ily**, *adv.* herzlich. **—iness**, *s.* die Herzlichkeit. **—less**, *adj.*, **—lessly**, *adv.* herzlos. **—lessness**, *s.* die Herzlosigkeit. **—y**, *adj.* herzlich, aufrichtig; stark, tüchtig. **—-ache**, *s.* das Herzweh. **—beat**, *s.* der Herzschlag.

Hearth, *s.* der Herd (*also fig.*).

Heat, I. *s.* die Hitze; die Wärme, Glut (*Phys.*); (*fig.*) die Hitze, Heftigkeit; die Partie, das Rennen (*Sport*); dead —, unentschiedenes Rennen. II. *v.a.* heiß machen, heizen; erhitzen (*also fig.*). III. *v.n.* heiß, warm werden. **—er**, *s.* der Bügelstahl (*of an iron*). **—ing**, *s.* die Heizung; die Anheizung (*of a furnace, etc.*).

Heath, *s.* die Heide.

Heathen, I. *s.* der Heide. II. *adj.* heidnisch.

Heather, *s.* das Heidekraut.

Heave, I. *v.a.* (auf-, er-)heben; (swell) schwellen; ausstoßen (*a sigh*). II. *v.n.* sich heben; schwellen (*as the sea*). III. *s.* das Heben; das Schwellen (*of the breast*); (throw) der Aufwärtsstoß.

Heaven, *s.* der Himmel; oh —s! ach du lieber Himmel. **—ly**, *adj.* himmlisch. **—ward**, *adv.* himmelwärts.

Heaviness, *s.* die Schwere, das Gewicht (*of a body*); (—iness of spirit) die Schwermut.

Heav—y, I. *adj.* schwer. II. **—ily**, *adv.* schwer; drückend, lästig.

Hectic, *adj.* hektisch.

Hectogramme, *s.* das Hektogramm.

Hedge, I. *s.* die Hecke, der Zaun. II. *v.a.* einzäunen, einfriedigen. **—hog**, *s.* der Igel.

Heed, I. *v.a.* (be)achten, Acht geben auf (*acc.*). II. *v.n.* achten. III. *s.* die Achtung. **—ful**, *adj.*, **—fully**, *adv.* achtsam, aufmerksam. **—less**, *adj.*, **—lessly**, *adv.* achtlos. **—lessness**, *s.* die Unachtsamkeit, Achtlosigkeit.

¹**Heel**, *s.* die Ferse; der Absatz (*on shoes, etc.*); he is close at my —s, er ist mir dicht auf den Fersen; to take to one's —s, die Flucht ergreifen.

²**Heel**, *v.n.* sich neigen, krengen (*Naut.*).

Heifer, *s.* die Färse.

Height, *s.* die Höhe (*also fig.*); (size) die Größe. **—en**, *v.a.* erhöhen.

Heir, *s.* der Erbe (*also fig.*). **—ess**, *s.* die Erbin. **—loom**, *s.* das Erbstück.

Hell, *s.* die Hölle. **—ish**, *adj.* höllisch. **—ishness**, *s.* das Höllische. **—fire**, *s.* das Höllenfeuer.

Helm, *s.* der Steuer(ruder); (*fig.*) das Ruder. **—sman**, *s.* der Steuermann.

Helmet, *s.* der Helm; spiked —, die Pickelhaube.

Help, I. *v.a.* (einem) helfen, beistehen, Hilfe leisten; — yourself! langen Sie zu! we cannot — weeping, wir müssen weinen; so — me God! so wahr mir Gott helfe! II. *v.n.* helfen, dienen (to, zu). III. *s.* die Hilfe(leistung), der Beistand. **—er**, *s.* der Helfer. **—ful**, *adj.*, **—fully**, *adv.* hilfreich, behilflich, dienlich. **—fulness**, *s.* die Dienlichkeit, Nützlichkeit. **—less**, *adj.*, **—lessly**, *adv.* hilflos. **—lessness**, *s.* die Hilflosigkeit. **—mate**, **—meet**, *s.* die Helferin.

Helter-skelter, *adv.* holterdipolter, Hals über Kopf.

Helve, *s.* der Stiel.

¹**Hem**, I. *s.* der Saum. II. *v.a.* säumen. **—stitch**, *s.* der Hohlsaum.

²**Hem**, I. *s.* das Räuspern. II. *v.n.* sich räuspern.

Hemispher—e, *s.* die Halbkugel, Hemisphäre. **—ical**, *adj.* halbkugelig.

Hemlock, *s.* der Schierling.

Hemorrhage, *s.* der Blutabgang, Blutfluß, das Bluten.

Hemp, *s.* der Hanf. **—en**, *adj.* hanfen, hänsen.

Hen, *s.* die Henne. **—roost**, *s.* die Hühnerstange.

Hence, *adv.* (away) von hinnen, weg, hinweg, fort; (from this) hieraus, von da; daher, deshalb; (from now) von jetzt an; (off) von hier entfernt; a year —, heute übers Jahr. **—forth**, **—forward**, *adv.* hinfort, von nun an.

Henchman, *s.* der Leibdiener.

Hepta—gon, *s.* das Siebeneck. **—gonal**, *adj.* siebeneckig. **—ngular**, *adj.* siebenwinklig.

Her, I. *pers. pron.* (acc. and dat. of She) sie; ihr. II. *poss. adj.* ihr; (*referring to masc. & neuter nouns*) sein.

Herald, *s.* der Herold. **—ry,** *s.* die Wappenkunde.

Herb, *s.* das Kraut. **—age,** *s.* Futterkräuter.

Herd, I. *s.* die Herde; one of the common —, ein ganz gewöhnlicher Mensch. II. *v.a.* eine Herde hüten. III. *v.n.* in Herden gehen. **—sman,** *s.* der Hirt.

Here, *adv.* hier; that's neither — nor there, das gehört nicht zur Sache; here's to you! auf dein Wohl! **—about(s),** *adv.* hier herum. **—after,** I. *adv.* hernach, künftighin. II. *s.* das künftige Leben. **—at,** *adv.* hierbei, hierüber. **—by,** *adv.* (by this) hierdurch; (close by) nebenbei, nebenan. **—in,** *adv.* hierin. **—of,** *adv.* hiervon. **—on,** *adv.* hierauf, hierüber. **—to,** *adv.* hierzu. **—tofore,** *adv.* vormals, vor diesem. **—upon,** *adv.* hierauf, darauf. **—with,** *adv.* hiermit.

Heredit—ary, *adj.* erblich. **—y,** *s.* die Erblichkeit.

Heresy, *s.* die Ketzerei.

Heretic, *s.* der Ketzer. **—al,** *adj.* ketzerisch.

Heritage, *s.* die Erbschaft.

Hermit, *s.* der Einsiedler, Eremit, Klausner. **—age,** *s.* die Einsiedelei.

Hero, *s.* der Held. **—ical,** *adj.,* **—ically,** *adv.* heldenmäßig; (brave) tapfer, heldenmütig. **—ine,** *s.* die Heldin. **—ism,** *s.* der Heldenmut. **—worship,** *s.* die Heldenverehrung.

Heron, *s.* der Reiher.

Herring, *s.* der Hering; pickled —, marinierter Hering; red —, der Bückling.

Her—s, *poss. pron.* ihr, der, die, das ihrige. **—self,** *pron.* selbst, sie selbst; ihr selbst; sich (selbst).

Hesita—ncy, *s.* das Zögern. **—te,** *v.n.* zögern, zaudern. **—ting,** *adj.,* **—tingly,** *adv.* unschlüssig, zögernd — **tion,** *s.* das Zaudern; without any **—tion,** ohne jedes Bedenken.

Hetero—dox, *adj.* heterodox; irrgläubig. **—doxy,** *s.* die Heterodoxie; der Irrglaube. **—geneous,** *adj.,* **—geneously,** *adv.* ungleich-, verschiedenartig.

Hew, *v.a.* hauen.

Hexa—gon, *s.* das Sechseck. **—gonal,** *adj.* sechseckig. **—meter,** *s.* der Hexameter.

Hiatus, *s.* die Lücke.

Hiccup, I. *s.* der Schlucken, Schluckauf. II. *v.n.* den Schlucken *or* Schluckauf haben.

¹Hid—e, *ir.v.* I. *a.* verbergen; to play —e and seek, Verstecken spielen. II. *n.* sich verbergen. **—ing,** *s.* das Verbergen.

²Hide, *s.* das Fell.

Hideous, *adj.,* **—ly,** *adv.* schrecklich, scheußlich. **—ness,** *s.* die Scheußlichkeit.

Hier—archy, *s.* die Priesterherrschaft. **—oglyphic,** *adj.* hieroglyphisch. **—oglyphics,** *pl.* die Hieroglyphen.

Higgle, *v.n.* schachern. **—dy-piggledy,** *adv.* wirr durcheinander.

High, I. *adj.* hoch; — school for girls, die höhere Mädchenschule. II. *adv.* hoch; stark, mächtig. **—er,** *comp. of* — I. & II. höher. **—est,** *sup. of* —, höchst, **—ly,** *adv.* hoch, höchlich; I think —ly of him, ich halte viel von ihm. **—ness,** *s.* die Höhe; (*fig.*) die Hoheit; His (Your) Royal **—ness,** Seine (Eure, Ew.) Königliche Hoheit. **—born,** *adj.* hochgeboren. **—brow,** *s.* (*coll.*) der Aufgeklärte, Gebildete; the **—s,** die Intelligenz. **—handed,** *adj.* hochfahrend. **—land,** *s.* das Hochland. **—lander,** *s.* der Hochländer. **—minded,** *adj.* hochgesinnt. **—mindedness,** *s.* der Hochsinn. **—placed,** *adj.* hochgestellt. **—pressure,** *s.* der Hochdruck. **—road,** *s.* die Landstraße. **—sheriff,** *s.* der Oberrichter. **—spirited,** *adj. adv.,* munter, lustig, ausgelassen. **—tension,** *s.* die Hochspannung (*Radio*). **—tide,** *s.* hohe Flut. **—treason,** *s.* der Hochverrat. **—water,** *s.* die Fluthöhe. **—wayman,** *s.* der Straßenräuber.

Hike, *v.n.* wandern. **—r,** *s.* der Wandervogel.

Hilari—ous, *adj.,* **—ously,** *adv.* lustig. **—ty,** *s.* die Heiterkeit.

Hill, *s.* der Hügel; as old as the **—s,** steinalt. **—ock,** *s.* der kleine Hügel. **—y,** *adj.* hügelig.

Hilt, *s.* das Heft; up to the —, durch und durch.

Him, *pers. pron.* (acc. of He) ihn; (*dat. of* He, to —) ihm; den, dem (-jenigen). **—self,** selbst, (er, sich) selbst, sich; he is not **—self,** er ist nicht ganz wohl; er ist nicht wie sonst.

¹Hind, *s.* die Hindin, Hirschkuh.

²Hind, *s.* der Knecht, Bauer.

3**Hind,** *adj. (especially in compounds)*
hinter, Hinter=; — leg, das Hinter=
bein. **—er,** I. *adj. (comp. of* —)
hinter. II. *v.a.* hindern (from, an
einer G.). **—rance,** *s.* das Hin=
dernis. **—most,** *adj.* hinterst.

Hinge, I. *s.* die Angel, Haspe. II.
v.n.; to — upon, (*fig.*) sich drehen
um, ankommen auf (*acc.*).

Hint, I. *v.a. & n.* andeuten. II. *s.* der
Wink; a broad —, ein Wink mit dem
Zaunpfahl.

1**Hip,** *s.* die Hüfte. **—bone,** *s.* das
Hüftbein. **—joint,** *s.* das Hüft=
gelenk.

2**Hip,** *s.* die Hagebutte (*Bot.*).

Hippo—drome, *s.* die Rennbahn, der
Rennplatz. **—potamus,** *s.* das Fluß=
pferd.

Hire, I. *v.a.* mieten (*a horse, house,
etc.*); dingen, mieten (*a servant, etc.*).
II. *s.* das Mieten; (cost of —) die
Miete. **—ling,** I. *s.* der Mietling,
Lohnarbeiter. II. *adj.* feil. **—r,** *s.*
der Mieter. **—purchase,** *s.* der Kauf
mit Ratenzahlung.

His, I. *poss. pron.* sein, seine, seines;
der, die, das seinige; a book of —,
eins seiner Bücher. II. *poss. adj.*
sein, seine, sein.

Hiss, I. *v.a.* auszischen. II. *v.n.* zi=
schen. III. *s.* das Zischen.

Histor—ian, *s.* der Geschichtschreiber.
—ic(al), *adj.,* **—ically,** *adv.* geschicht=
lich, Geschichts=. **—y,** *s.* die Geschichte.

Hit, I. *ir.v.a. & n.* schlagen; treffen
(*the mark, the note, etc.*). II. *s.* der
Schlag, Stoß.

Hitch, I. *s.* der Haken; der Knoten
(*Naut.*); without a —, ohne Störung.
II. *v.a.* (an)haken.

Hither, *adv.* hierher; — and thither,
hierher und dorthin. **—to,** *adv.* bis=
her, bisjetzt.

Hive, I. *s.* der Bienenkorb, Bienen=
stock; (— of bees) der Bienenschwarm;
(*fig.*) der Schwarm. II. *v.a.* (Bienen)
in einen Stock tun.

Hoar, *adj.* weiß; weißgrau. **—y,**
adj. weiß; (alters=)grau, eisgrau.
—frost, *s.* der (Rauh=)Reif.

Hoard, I. *s.* der Schatz; der Hort
(*poet.*). II. *v.a.* aufhäufen.

1**Hoarding,** *s.* das Schätzesammeln.

2**Hoarding,** *s.* der Bauzaun.

Hoarse, *adj.,* **—ly,** *adv.* heiser. **—ness,**
s. die Heiserkeit.

Hoax, I. *s.* der Betrug. II. *v.a.*
foppen.

Hob, *s.* der Kaminvorsprung.

Hobbl—e, I. *v.n.* hinken (*also fig.*). II.
v.a. fesseln. **—ing,** *adj.,* **—ingly,**
adv. humpelnd.

Hobby, *s.* das Steckenpferd.

Hob-nob, *v.n.* vertraulich zusammen=
plaudern.

1**Hock,** *s.* die Kniekehle (*of horses*).

2**Hock,** *s.* der Hochheimer.

Hod, *s.* der Mörteltrog.

Hoe, I. *s.* die Haue. II. *v.a.* behacken.

Hog, *s.* das Schwein (*also fig.*). **—
gish,** *adj.,* **—gishly,** *adv.* schweinisch.

Hogshead, *s.* das Oxhoft.

Hoist, *v.a.* hissen.

Hold, I. *ir.v.a.* halten, festhalten; (contain) enthalten; (keep) anhalten;
(believe) glauben; (maintain) be=
haupten; (consider) halten für; to lay
— of, ergreifen; to — one's own, (sich)
behaupten; to — forth, Reden halten;
to — one's breath, den Atem anhalten;
to — an office, ein Amt bekleiden.
II. *ir.v.n.* halten; (— on) festhalten.
III. *s.* der Halt, Griff; der Laderaum
(*Naut.*). IV. *int.* halt! **—er,** *s.* der,
die, das Haltende; der Inhaber
(*of a bill, stock, etc.*); der Halter,
Griff (*of a pen, etc.*).

Hole, *s.* das Loch.

Holiday, *s.* der Feiertag; (*pl.*) die
Ferien. **—makers,** *s.* die Ausflügler.

Holloa, I. *int. & s.* (das) Hallo. II.
v.n. halloen, hallo or holla rufen.

Hollow, I. *adj.* hohl. II. *s.* die
Höhle, Höhlung. **—ness,** *s.* die
Hohlheit. **—cheeked,** *adj.* hohlwan=
gig.

Holly, *s.* die Stechpalme.

Hollyhock, *s.* die Rosenpappel.

Holster, *s.* die Halfter.

Holy, *adj.* heilig; — Week, die
Karwoche. **—stone,** I. *s.* der
Scheuerstein. II. *v.a.* scheuern.

Homage, *s.* die Huldigung (*also fig.*).

Home, I. *s.* das Heim; at —, zu
Hause; — Secretary, der Minister
des Innern; — trade, der Binnen=
handel; charity begins at —, ein
jeder ist sich selbst der Nächste. II.
adj. heimisch, häuslich, inländisch. III.
adv. heim, nach Hause. **—less,** *adj.*
heimatlos. **—liness,** *s.* die Einfach=
heit, Schlichtheit. **—ly,** *adj.* heimisch;
einfach. **—stead,** *s.* die Heimstätte.

—ward(s), adv. heimwärts. **—sick,** adj. heimwehkrank. **—sickness,** s. das Heimweh.

Homicid—al, adj. mörderisch. **—e,** s. der Mord.

Homœopath—ic, adj., **—ically,** adv. homöopathisch. **—y,** s. die Homöopathie.

Homogeneous, adj. gleichartig.

Hone, s. der Wetzstein.

Honest, adj., **—ly,** adv. redlich, ehrbar. **—y,** s. die Ehrlichkeit, Redlichkeit; **—y** is the best policy, ehrlich währt am längsten.

Honey, s. der Honig. **—comb,** s. die Honigscheibe. **—moon,** s. die Flitterwochen. **—suckle,** s. das Geißblatt.

Honk, v.n. tuten.

Honorary, adj. ehrend; Ehren=.

Honour, I. s. die Ehre; a feast in his —, ein Fest ihm zu Ehren; man of —, der Ehrenmann; word of —, das Ehrenwort; I have the —, ich habe die Ehre. II. v.a. ehren; beehren (with, mit); akzeptieren (C.L.). **—able,** adj., **—ably,** adv. ehrenvoll.

Hood, s. die Kapuze.

Hoof, s. der Huf. **—ed,** adj. gehuft.

Hook, I. s. der Haken. II. v.a. haken; fangen (also fig.). III. v.n. sich festhaken; a —ed nose, eine Habichtsnase. **—ed,** adj. hakig.

Hoop, s. der Reif(en).

Hoot, I. v.n. schreien; tuten (motor). II. s. der Schrei.

¹Hop, s. der Hopfen (Bot.).

²Hop, I. s. der Hupf, Sprung. II. v.n. hüpfen.

Hope, I. s. die Hoffnung; there is no — for him, es ist aus mit ihm. II. v.a. & n. hoffen. **—ful,** adj., **—fully,** adv. hoffnungsvoll; hoffnungsreich. **—less,** adj., **—lessly,** adv. hoffnungslos. **—lessness,** s. die Hoffnungslosigkeit.

Horde, s. die Horde.

Horizon, s. der Gesichtskreis, Horizont. **—tal,** adj., **—tally,** adv. horizontal.

Horn, s. das Horn. **—ed,** adj. gehörnt. **—less,** adj. hornlos. **—y,** adj. hornig, hörnern. **—pipe,** s. die Hornpfeife.

Hornet, s. die Hornisse.

Horr—ible, adj., **—ibly,** adv. entsetzlich, schrecklich. **—ibleness,** s. die Entsetzlichkeit. **—id,** adj., **—idly,** adv. schrecklich, entsetzlich. **—ify,** v.a.

erschrecken, entsetzen. **—or,** s. das Entsetzen, Grausen, Grauen; —ors of war, die Greuel des Krieges.

Horse, s. das Pferd, Roß; to —! zu Pferde! aufsitzen! **—artillery,** s. reitende Artillerie. **—back,** s.; on —back, zu Pferde, beritten. **—collar,** s. das Kummet. **—dealer,** s. der Pferdehändler. **—man,** s. der Reiter. **—manship,** s. die Reitkunst. **—power,** s. die Pferdekraft, Pferdestärke (abbrev.: P.S.). **—radish,** s. der Meerrettich. **—shoe,** s. das Hufeisen. **—woman,** s. die Reiterin.

Horticulture, s. der Gartenbau.

Hosanna, s. das Hosianna.

Hos—e, s. der Schlauch; der Strumpf. **—ier,** s. der Strumpfwarenhändler. **—iery,** s. die Strumpfwaren.

Hospitabl—e, adj., **—y,** adv. gastfreundlich.

Hospital, s. das Krankenhaus, Hospital.

Hospitality, s. die Gastfreundschaft; to show —, gastfrei sein.

¹Host, s. der Wirt. **—ess,** s. die Wirtin.

²Host, s. das Heer, die Schar.

³Host, s. die (geweihte) Hostie (R. C.).

Hostage, s. der Geisel.

Hostil—e, adj., **—ely,** adv. feindlich; feindselig. **—ity,** s. die Feindseligkeit (to, gegen).

Hot, adj., **—ly,** adv. heiß; (fig.) hitzig, feurig. **—ness,** s. die Hitze. **—house,** s. das Treibhaus.

Hotchpotch, s. der Mischmasch.

Hotel, s. der Gasthof, das Hotel.

Hound, s. der Jagdhund; (fig.) Hund.

Hour, s. die Stunde; working —s, die Arbeitszeit; small —s of the night, die frühen Morgenstunden; to keep good —s, zeitig schlafen gehen.

House, I. s. das Haus; neither — nor home, weder Dach noch Fach. II. v.a. beherbergen (people); stallen (cattle). **—breaker,** s. der Einbrecher. **—hold,** I. s. der Haushalt. II. adj. häuslich, Haus=, Familien=. **—holder,** s. der Hausvater, Hausherr. **—keeper,** s. die Haushälterin. **—keeping,** s. das Haushalten. **—maid,** s. das Stubenmädchen. **—wife,** s. die Hausfrau.

Hovel, s. die elende Hütte.

Hover, v.n. schweben.

How, adv. & int. wie; — do you do?

wie geht es Ihnen? I know — to swim, ich kann schwimmen; I don't know — to say it, ich weiß nicht wie ich es sagen soll. **—ever,** I. *adv.* wie sehr auch; (at least) wenigstens; (at all events) jedenfalls. II. *conj.* doch, dennoch, gleichwohl.

Howitzer, *s.* die Haubitze.

Howl, I. *v.n.* heulen (*also fig.*). II. *v.a.*; to — out, losheulen. III. *s.* das Geheul.

Hoyden, *s.* die Range.

Hub, *s.* die Nabe (*of a wheel*).

Hubbub, *s.* der Lärm, Tumult.

Huckster, I. *s.* der Höker. II. *v.n.* hökre(r)n.

Huddle, *v.n.* sich drängen.

¹Hue, *s.* die Farbe.

²Hue, *s.* das Geschrei; — and cry, das Zetergeschrei.

Huff, *s.* die üble Laune; to be in a —, schmollen.

Hug, I. *v.a.* umarmen. II. *s.* die Umarmung.

Huge, *adj.*, **—ly,** *adv.* ungeheuer, kolossal. **—ness,** *s.* ungeheure Größe.

Hulk, *s.* der Rumpf; der Holk (*Naut.*). **—ing,** *adj.* schwerfällig, plump.

Hull, I. *s.* der Rumpf (*Naut.*). II. *v.a.* schälen.

Hullo! *int.* holla! he!

Hum, I. *v.a. & n.* summen, sumsen. II. *s.* das Summen. **—ming-bird,** *s.* der Kolibri.

Humar, *adj.*, **—ly,** *adv.* menschlich. **—e,** *adj.*, **—ely,** *adv.* menschenfreundlich. **—kind,** *s.* das Menschengeschlecht.

Humanit—arian, *s.* der Menschenfreund. **—y,** *s.* die Menschheit.

Humbl—e, I. *adj.*, **—y,** *adv.* bescheiden, demütig; to eat — pie, Abbitte tun, sich demütigen. II. *v.a.* erniedrigen, demütigen. **—eness,** *s.* die Niedrigkeit (*of birth, etc.*); die Demut.

Humbug, *s.* der Schwindel, Blödsinn.

Humdrum, *adj.* alltäglich, langweilig.

Humid, *adj.* feucht, naß. **—ity,** *s.* die Feuchtigkeit.

Humili—ation, *s.* die Demütigung, Erniedrigung. **—ty,** *s.* die Demut, Bescheidenheit.

Humor—ist, *s.* der Humorist. **—ous,** *adj.*, **—ously,** *adv.* humoristisch.

Humour, I. *s.* der Humor; to be in the — for, aufgelegt sein zu. II. *v.a.* (einem) willfahren, gefällig sein;

— him a little, gib ihm ein wenig nach. **—some,** *adj.* launisch.

Hump, *s.* der Buckel; he has the —, (*coll.*) er ist verdrießlich.

Hunchback, *s.* der Buck(e)lige.

Hundred, I. *num. adj.* hundert. II. *s.* das Hundert. **—fold,** *adj.* hundertfältig, hundertfach. **—th,** *num. adj.* hundertst. **—weight,** *s.* der Zentner.

Hung—er, I. *s.* der Hunger. II. *v.n.* hungern. **—rily,** *adv.*, **—ry,** *adj.* hungrig.

Hunt, I. *v.a.* jagen, hetzen; to — out, ausspüren. II. *v.n.* jagen, Jagd machen (for wolves, auf Wölfe). III. *s.* die Jagd. **—er,** *s.* der Jäger. **—ing,** *s.* das Jagen.

Hurdle, *s.* die Hürde.

Hurdy-gurdy, *s.* die Drehleier.

Hurl, I. *v.a.* werfen. II. *v.r. & n.* sich schnell bewegen.

Hurricane, *s.* der Orkan.

Hurr—ied, *adj.*, **—iedly,** *adv.* übereilt. **—y,** I. *v.a.* beschleunigen. II. *v.n.* eilen, sich beeilen. III. *s.* die große Eile. **—y-scurry,** *s.* die Unruhe, der Strudel.

Hurt, I. *ir.v.a.* verletzen. II. *ir.v.n.* wehe tun; to be — at, sich verletzt fühlen über. III. *s.* die Verletzung, Wunde. **—ful,** *adj.*, **—fully,** *adv.* schädlich, nachteilig.

Husband, I. *s.* der Ehemann, Mann, Gatte. II. *v.a.* sparen. **—man,** *s.* der Ackerbauer; der Landwirt.

Hush, I. *int.* still. II. *s.* die Stille. III. *v.a.* stillen. **—money,** *s.* das Schweigegeld.

Husk, *s.* die Hülse, Schale.

Husk—iness, *s.* die Rauheit. **—y,** *adj.* rauh, heiser.

Hussar, *s.* der Husar.

Hussy, *s.* das Weibsbild; die Dirne.

Hustle, *v.* I. *a.* drängen. II. *n.* sich drängen.

Hut, *s.* die Hütte.

Hutch, *s.* der Kasten.

Hyacinth, *s.* die Hyazinthe.

Hybrid, I. *adj.* zwitterhaft. II. *s.* der Zwitter, Mischling.

Hydra, *s.* die Hydra (*Myth. & fig.*).

Hydrant, *s.* der Hydrant.

Hydraulic, *adj.* hydraulisch. **—s,** *s.* die Wasserkraftlehre.

Hydro-, (*in comp.* =) Wasser-. **—chloric,** *adj.* salzsauer. **—gen,** *s.*

der Wasserstoff. —**pathic,** *s.* die
Kaltwasserheilanstalt. —**pathy,** *s.* die
Wasserkur. —**phobia,** *s.* die Hundswut. —**phobic,** *adj.* hydrophobisch.
—**plane,** *s.* das Wasserflugzeug.
—**statics,** *pl.* die Hydrostatik.

Hyena, *s.* die Hyäne.

Hygien—e, *s.* die Gesundheitslehre.
—**ic,** *adj.* gesundheitlich, Gesund-
heits-.

Hymn, I. *s.* das Kirchenlied. II. *v.a.*
lobpreisen. —**al,** *adj.* hymnenartig.
—**book,** *s.* das Gesangbuch.

Hyper (*pref.* = über). —**bole,** *s.* die
Übertreibung, Hyperbel. —**bolical,**
adj., —**bolically,** *adv.* übertreibend,
hyperbolisch. —**critic,** *s.* der Hyper-
kritiker, Nörgler. —**critical,** *adj.*
überkritisch.

Hyphen, *s.* der Bindestrich.

Hypnoti—c, *adj.* hypnotisch. —**ze,** *v.a.*
hypnotisieren. —**sm,** *s.* Hypnotis-
mus.

Hypo (*pref.* = unter). —**chondria**(sis),
s. die Schwermut, Hypochondrie.
—**chondriac,** I. *adj.* schwermütig,
hypochondrisch. II. *s.* der Grillen-
fänger, Hypochonder. —**crisy,** *s.* die
Heuchelei. —**crite,** *s.* der Heuchler.
—**critical,** *adj.,* —**critically,** *adv.*
heuchlerisch. —**thesis,** *s.* die Vermutung, Hypothese. —**thetic**(al),
adj. vermeintlich, vorausgesetzt,
angenommen.

Hyster—ia, *s.* die Hysterie. —**ical,**
adj. hysterisch.

I

¹**I, i,** *s.* das J, i.

²**I,** *pers. pron.* ich; it is —, ich bin es.

Iambic, I. *adj.* iambisch. II. *s.* Jambus.

Ibex, *s.* der Steinbock.

Ibis, *s.* der Ibis.

Ice, I. *s.* das Eis; to skate on thin
—, auf der Messerschneide tanzen.
II. *v.a.* gefrieren machen; überzuckern
(*Conf.*). —**berg,** *s.* der Eisberg.

Ici—cle, *s.* der Eiszapfen. —**ness,** *s.*
die Eisigkeit. —**ng,** *s.* die Über-
zuckerung.

Icy, *adj.* eisig; (*fig.*) kalt, frostig.

Idea, *s.* die Idee, der Begriff; I can't
form any — of it, ich kann mir keinen
Begriff davon machen. —**l,** I. *adj.*
—**lly,** *adv.* ideal, vorbildlich. II. *s.* das
Musterbild, Ideal. —**lism,** *s.* der

Idealismus. —**list,** *s.* der Idealist.
—**listic,** *adj.* idealistisch.

Identi—cal, *adj.,* —**cally,** *adv.*
identisch. —**fication,** *s.* die Identi-
fikation. —**fy,** *v.a.* identifizieren. —
ty, *s.* die Identität; mistaken —ty,
die Personenverwechselung.

Idiocy, *s.* der Blödsinn, Irrsinn.

Idiom, *s.* die Sprechweise. —**atical,**
adj., —**atically,** *adv.* idiomatisch.

Idiot, *s.* der Schwachsinnige. —**ic,**
adj. schwachsinnig, idiotisch, blödsinnig.

Idle, I. *adj.,* **Idly,** *adv.* (unoccupied)
müßig; (indolent) träge, faul; —
words, unnütze Worte. II. *v.n.* faul-
lenzen. —**ness,** *s.* der Müßiggang;
die Faulheit, Trägheit. —**r,** *s.* der
Faulenzer, Müßiggänger.

Idol, *s.* das Götzenbild. (*fig.*) der
Abgott. —**ater,** *s.* der Götzendiener.
—**atress,** *s.* die Götzendienerin. —
atrous, *adj.,* —**atrously,** *adv.* ab-
göttisch. —**atry,** *s.* der Götzendienst.
—**ize,** *v.a.* vergöttern, anbeten.

Idyll, *s.* die Idylle. —**ic,** *adj.* idyllisch.

If, I. *conj.* wenn, wofern; ob. II.
s. das Wenn.

Ignit—e, *v.a.* anzünden. —**ion,** *s.* die
Anzündung.

Ignobl—e, *adj.,* —**y,** *adv.* gemein,
unedel. —**eness,** *s.* die Gemeinheit.

Ignomin—ious, *adj.,* —**iously,** *adv.*
schmählich. —**y,** *s.* die Schmach.

Ignor—amus, *s.* der Ignorant. —
ance, *s.* die Unwissenheit. —**ant,**
adj. unwissend, ununterrichtet. —**e,**
v.a. nicht wissen; nicht beachten.

Iliad, *s.* die Ilias, Iliade.

Ill, I. *adj.* & *adv.* übel, böse; schlimm,
schlecht; (sick) krank; — at ease,
unbehaglich. II. *adv.* schwerlich. III.
s. das Übel, Böse. —**advised,** *adj.*
unbesonnen. —**behaved,** *adj.* unartig, unhöflich. —**bred,** *adj.* ungebildet. —**luck,** *s.* das Unglück; as
—-luck would have it, unglücklicherweise. —**matched,** *adj.* schlecht
zusammenpassend. —**nature,** *s.* die
Bösartigkeit, Böswilligkeit. —
natured, *adj.* boshaft, bösartig. —
timed, *adj.* ungelegen. —**treat,** —
use, *v.a.* mißhandeln. —**will,** *s.*
das Übelwollen.

Illegal, *adj.,* —**ly,** *adv.* gesetzwidrig.

Illegib—ility, —**leness,** *s.* die Unleser-
lichkeit. —**le,** *adj.,* —**ly,** *adv.* unleserlich.

Illegitima—cy, *s.* die Unehelichkeit.
—te, *adj.*, **—tely**, *adv.* unehelich;
(*unjustified*) unberechtigt.

Illicit, *adj.* unerlaubt.

Illitera—cy, *s.* die Ungelehrtheit.
—te, *adj.*, **—tely**, *adv.* ungelehrt.

Illness, *s.* das Unwohlsein, die Krankheit.

Illuminat—e, *v.a.* beleuchten. **—ion**,
s. die Beleuchtung; die Illuminierung.

Illusi—on, *s.* die Täuschung. **—ve**,
adj. täuschend.

Illustr—ate, *v.a.* erläutern, erklären;
illustrieren (*a book*). **—ation**, *s.*
(*elucidation*) die Erläuterung, Erklärung; die Illustration. **—ator**,
s. der Illustrierer; der Erläuterer.

Illustrious, *adj.*, **—ly**, *adv.* berühmt.

Image, I. *s.* das Bild (*also Rhet. &
Opt.*). II. *v.a.* abbilden, vorstellen.
—ry, *s.* (**—s**) das Bildwerk.

Imagin—able, *adj.*, **—ably**, *adv.* erdenklich, denkbar. **—ary**, *adj.* eingebildet. **—ation**, *s.* die Einbildung, Vorstellung; (*power of —ation*)
die Einbildungskraft. **—ative**, *adj.*
erfinderisch. **—e**, *v.* I. *a.* sich (*dat.*)
einbilden, sich (*dat.*) denken. II. *n.*
sich vorstellen; **—e!** denke dir!

Imbecil—e, *adj.* blödsinnig. **—ity**, *s.*
der Blödsinn.

Imbibe, *v.a.* einsaugen.

Imita—te, *v.a.* nachahmen. **—tion**,
s. die Nachahmung. **—tor**, *s.* der
Nachahmer.

Immaculate, *adj.*, **—ly**, *adv.* unbefleckt;
— conception, die unbefleckte Empfängnis.

Immaterial, *adj.*, **—ly**, *adv.* unkörperlich; unbedeutend.

Immature, *adj.*, **—ly**, *adv.* unreif.

Immediate, *adj.* unmittelbar. **—ly**,
adv. unmittelbar; sogleich.

Immens—e, *adj.*, **—ely**, *adv.* ungeheuer; **—ely** rich, steinreich. **—ity**, *s.*
die Unermeßlichkeit.

Immers—e, *v.a.* eintauchen; **—ed** in
work, in Arbeit vertieft. **—ion**, *s.*
das Ein-, Unter-tauchen.

Immigra—nt, *s.* der Einwanderer.
—te, *v.n.* einwandern. **—tion**, *s.*
die Einwanderung.

Imminen—ce, *s.* das Bevorstehen.
—t, *adj.*, **—tly**, *adv.* bevorstehend.

Immoderate, *adj.*, **—ly**, *adv.* unmäßig.

Immodest, *adj.*, **—ly**, *adv.* unsittlich.
—y, *s.* die Unsittlichkeit.

Immoral, *adj.*, **—ly**, *adv.* sittenlos.
—ity, *s.* die Unsittlichkeit.

Immortal, *adj.*, **—ly**, *adv.* unsterblich.
—ity, *s.* die Unsterblichkeit.

Immovab—ility, *s.* die Unbewegbarkeit. **—le**, *adj.*, **—ly**, *adv.* unbewegbar.

Immun—e, *adj.* frei. **—ity**, *s.* die
Freiheit; die Immunität (*Med.*).

Imp, *s.* das Teufelchen, der Kobold.
—ish, *adj.* schelmisch.

Impact, *s.* der (Zusammen-)Stoß.

Impair, *v.a.* schwächen (*health, etc.*).

Impart, *v.a.* mitteilen.

Impartial, *adj.*, **—ly**, *adv.* unparteiisch.
—ity, *s.* die Unparteilichkeit.

Impassable, *adj.* ungangbar.

Impassible, *adj.* unempfindlich.

Impassioned, *adj.* leidenschaftlich.

Impatien—ce, *s.* die Ungeduld; die
Unduldsamkeit. **—t**, *adj.*, **—tly**, *adv.*
ungeduldig; unduldsam.

Impeach, *v.a.* anklagen (*of high treason,
etc.*). **—ment**, *s.* die Anklage.

Impecunio—sity, *s.* der Geldmangel.
—us, *adj.* mittellos, geldlos.

Imped—e, *v.a.* (ver)hindern. **—iment**,
s. das Hindernis (*to, für*); **—iment** in
the speech, der Zungenfehler.

Impel, *v.a.* (an)treiben; anregen (*to,
zu*).

Impend, *v.n.* überhangen.

Impenetrabl—e, *adj.*, **—y**, *adv.* undurchdringlich.

Impenitent, *adj.*, **—ly**, *adv.* reuelos.

Imperative, I. *adj.*, **—ly**, *adv.* befehlend, zwingend. II. *s.* (**— mood**) der
Imperativ, die Befehlsform.

Imperceptib—le, *adj.*, **—ly**, *adv.*
unmerklich.

Imperfect, *adj.*, **—ly**, *adv.* unvollkommen; **— tense**, das Imperfektum.
—ion, *s.* die Unvollkommenheit.

Imperi—al, *adj.*, **—ally**, *adv.* kaiserlich,
Reichs-. **—alism**, *s.* der Imperialismus.

Imperil, *v.a.* gefährden.

Imperious, *adj.*, **—ly**, *adv.* gebieterisch.

Impersonal, *adj.*, **—ly**, *adv.* unpersönlich (*also Gram.*).

Impertinen—ce, **—cy**, *s.* die Frechheit, Unverschämtheit. **—t**, *adj.*, **—tly**,
adv. frech, grob.

Impetu—osity, *s.* das Ungestüm.
—ous, *adj.*, **—ously**, *adv.* ungestüm,
heftig. **—s**, *s.* der Trieb, Antrieb
(*also fig.*).

Impi—ety, s. die Gottlosigkeit. **—ous,** adj., **—ously,** adv. gottlos.

Implement, s. das Gerät.

Implore, v.a. (einen) anflehen; **I —** you, ich beschwöre dich.

Imply, v.a. andeuten.

Impolite, adj., **—ly,** adv. unhöflich, ungesittet, grob. **—ness,** s. die Unhöflichkeit, Grobheit.

Import, I. v.a. ein-, zu-führen, importieren (*C.L.*); (denote) bedeuten. II. s. die Einfuhr; (purport) der Inhalt, die Bedeutung. **—ance,** s. die Wichtigkeit; to attach much **—ance** to a thing, viel Gewicht auf eine Sache legen. **—ant,** adj., **—antly,** adv. wichtig. **—ation,** s. die Wareneinfuhr. **—s,** pl. Einfuhrwaren.

Importunate, adj., **—ly,** adv. lästig.

Impos—e, v. I. a. auflegen, erheben (*a tax; the hands*). II. n.; to **—e** upon (a person), (einen) betrügen, täuschen; to **—e** on a person's good nature, jemandes Gutherzigkeit mißbrauchen; **—ing,** adj. eindrucksvoll.

Impossib—ility, s. die Unmöglichkeit. **—le,** adj., **—ly,** adv. unmöglich.

Impost—or, s. der Betrüger. **—ure,** s. der Betrug, die Betrügerei.

Impoten—ce, —cy, s. das Unvermögen. **—t,** adj., **—tly,** adv. unvermögend.

Impracticab—ility, —leness, s. die Untunlichkeit. **—le,** adj., **—ly,** adv. untunlich.

Imprecat—e, v.a. verwünschen. **—ion,** s. die Verwünschung.

Impregnabl—e, adj., **—y,** adv. unbezwinglich.

Impregnate, v.a. schwängern; **—d** with, durchtränkt mit.

Impress, v.a. ein-, auf-drücken, prägen (on, auf); (enjoin) einprägen; Eindruck machen (on, auf). **—ion,** s. (mental and physical **—ion**) der Eindruck, die Spur; der Druck, Abdruck (*Print.*). **—ive,** adj., **—ively,** adv. nachdrucksvoll.

Imprint, v.a. aufdrücken, einprägen.

Imprison, v.a. verhaften. **—ment,** s. die Haft, Gefangenschaft.

Improbab—ility, s. die Unwahrscheinlichkeit. **—le,** adj., **—ly,** adv. unwahrscheinlich.

Impromptu, I. adj. & adv. aus dem Stegreif. II. s. das Impromptu.

Improp—er, adj., **—erly,** adv. unpassend, untauglich; (indecent) unanständig. **—riety,** s. die Unschicklichkeit; die Unrichtigkeit.

Improve, v. I. a. verbessern. II. n. sich verbessern. **—ment,** s. die Verbesserung.

Improvise, v.a. improvisieren, aus dem Stegreif machen.

Impruden—ce, s. die Unklugheit. **—t,** adj., **—tly,** adv. unklug, unbedachtsam.

Impuden—ce, s. die Unverschämtheit. **—t,** adj., **—tly,** adv. unverschämt, schamlos, frech.

Impuls—e, s. (**—ion**) der Trieb; die Anregung. **—ive,** adj., **—ively,** adv. leidenschaftlich; (impellent) (an)treibend. **—iveness,** s. die Erregbarkeit.

Impunity, s. die Straflosigkeit.

Impur—e, adj., **—ely,** adv. unrein (*also fig.*). **—ity,** s. die Unreinheit.

Imput—ation, s. die Beimessung. **—e,** v.a. zurechnen, beimessen.

In, I. *prep.* in; an; auf; bei; aus; nach; unter; zu; von; über; mit; durch; **—** the morning, am Morgen, morgens; **—** appearance, dem Anschein nach; **—** the country, auf dem Lande; **—** the daytime, bei Tage; **—** my opinion, meiner Meinung nach; **—** this manner, auf diese Weise; **—** time, zu rechter Zeit, rechtzeitig; **—** turn, der Reihe nach; **—** no way, durchaus nicht; **—** writing, schriftlich; to be **—** for a thing, etwas zu erwarten haben; **—** good health, gesund; **—** poor health, kränklich; to go **—** for a thing, sich mit einer Sache beschäftigen; the **—s** and outs, alle Einzelheiten. II. *adv.* hinein; herein; (with**—**) drinnen.

Inability, s. die Unfähigkeit.

Inaccura—cy, s. die Ungenauigkeit. **—te,** adj., **—tely,** adv. ungenau.

Inadvertenc—e, —y, s. die Unachtsamkeit.

Inan—e, adj., **—ely,** adv. leer; nichtig (*fig.*). **—ity,** s. (*fig.*) die Leere, Albernheit.

Inanimate, adj. leblos.

Inapproachable, adj. unnahbar.

Inappropriate, adj., **—ly,** adv. ungeeignet.

Inapt, adj., **—ly,** adv. unpassend. **—ness, —itude,** s. die Untauglichkeit.

Inarticulate, adj., **—ly,** adv. undeutlich. **—ness,** s. die Unvernehmlichkeit.

Inasmuch, *adv.*; — as, da, weil, in so fern als.

Inaudibl—e, *adj.*, —y, *adv.* unhörbar. —eness, *s.* die Unhörbarkeit.

Inaugura—l, *adj.* Einweihungs=, Antritts=. —te, *v.a.* einweihen. —tion, *s.* die Einweihung.

Inborn, Inbred, *adj.* angeboren.

Incandescen—ce, *s.* das Weißglühen. —t, *adj.* weißglühend.

Incantation, *s.* der Zauberspruch.

Incapa—bility, *s.* die Unfähigkeit, Untüchtigkeit. —ble, *adj.*, —bly, *adv.* unfähig (zu), ungeeignet (für). —citate, *v.a.* unfähig machen.

Incarnat—e, *adj.* (*fig.*) eingefleischt. —ion, *s.* die Fleischwerdung; (*fig.*) die Verkörperung.

Incautious, *adj.*, —ly, *adv.* unvorsichtig. —ness, *s.* die Unvorsichtigkeit.

Incendiary, I. *adj.* brandstifterisch. II. *s.* der Brandstifter.

¹Incense, *s.* der Weihrauch.

²Incense, *v.a.* entrüsten, erzürnen.

Incentive, *s.* der Antrieb.

Incessant, *adj.*, —ly, *adv.* unaufhörlich.

Inch, *s.* der Zoll; — by —, allmählich; I shall not move an —, ich werde keinen Zollbreit weichen.

Inciden—ce, *s.* der Einfall. —t, I. *adj.* einfallend (*Phys.*). II. *s.* der Zwischenfall. —tal, *adj.*, —tally, *adv.* zufällig, gelegentlich; (subordinate) beiläufig; it is —tal to, es gehört zu.

Incis—ion, *s.* der Einschnitt. —ive, *adj.*, —ively, *adv.* einschneidend; (*fig.*) schneidend, scharf. —ors, *pl.* die Schneidezähne.

Incite, *v.a.* anreizen. —ment, *s.* der Antrieb.

Incivility, *s.* die Unhöflichkeit.

Inclemen—cy, *s.* die Unfreundlichkeit (*of the weather*). —t, *adj.* rauh.

Inclin—ation, *s.* die Neigung (*also fig.*). —e, I. *v.n.* sich neigen (*also fig.*); he doesn't feel —ed to work, er hat keine Lust zu arbeiten; —ed plane, die schiefe Ebene. II. *v.a.* neigen, beugen. III. *s.* die Neigung; der Abhang. —ed, *adj.* geneigt, abschüssig.

Include, *v.a.* einschließen, umfassen.

Inclusi—on, *s.* die Einschließung. —ve, *adj.*, —vely, *adv.* einschließend.

Incoheren—ce, —cy, *s.* die Zusammenhangslosigkeit. —t, *adj.*, —tly, *adv.* inkonsequent; he speaks —tly, er faselt.

Incombustible, *adj.* unverbrennbar.

Income, *s.* das Einkommen. —tax, *s.* die Einkommensteuer.

Incomparabl—e, *adj.*, —y, *adv.* unvergleichlich.

Incompatib—ility, *s.* die Unverträglichkeit. —le, *adj.*, —ly, *adv.* unverträglich (*as tempers*); unvereinbar.

Incompeten—ce, —cy, *s.* die Unfähigkeit. —t, *adj.*, —tly, *adv.* unfähig.

Incomplete, *adj.*, —ly, *adv.* unvollendet, unvollständig. —ness, *s.* die Unvollständigkeit.

Incomprehensib—ility, *s.* die Unbegreiflichkeit. —le, *adj.*, —ly, *adv.* unbegreiflich.

Inconceivabl—e, *adj.*, —y, *adv.* unbegreiflich. —eness, *s.* die Unbegreiflichkeit.

Incongru—ity, *s.* die Unangemessenheit. —ous, *adj.*, —ously, *adv.* unangemessen.

Inconsidera—ble, *adj.* unbedeutend. —te, *adj.*, —tely, *adv.* unbedachtsam. —teness, *s.* die Rücksichtslosigkeit.

Inconsisten—cy, *s.* die Inkonsequenz (*of a person*). —t, *adj.*, —tly, *adv.* unverträglich; —t with his views, unvereinbar mit seinen Anschauungen.

Inconspicuous, *adj.*, —ly, *adv.* unmerklich.

Inconstan—cy, *s.* der Wankelmut. —t, *adj.* unbeständig, wankelmütig.

Inconvenien—ce, I. *s.* die Unbequemlichkeit. II. *v.a.* belästigen. —t, *adj.*, —tly, *adv.* unbequem; it is —t to me, es ist mir ungelegen.

Incorporate, *v.a.* vereinigen; einverleiben.

Incorrect, *adj.*, —ly, *adv.* unrichtig. —ness, *s.* die Unrichtigkeit.

Incorrigib—le, *adj.*, —ly, *adv.* unverbesserlich.

Increas—e, I. *v.n.* wachsen, zunehmen. II. *v.a.* vermehren. III. *s.* das Zunehmen, die Zunahme; —e of trade, das Aufblühen des Handels. —ing, *adj.*, —ingly, *adv.* zunehmend.

Incredib—ility, *s.* die Unglaublichkeit. —le, *adj.*, —ly, *adv.* unglaublich.

Incredul—ity, *s.* die Ungläubigkeit, der Unglaube. —ous, *adj.*, —ously, *adv.* ungläubig.

Increment, *s.* die Zunahme.

Incubat—e, *v.a.* brüten. **—or**, *s.* der Brütofen.

Inculcate, *v.a.* einschärfen.

Inculpate, *v.a.* beschuldigen.

Incumben—cy, *s.* die Obliegenheit. **—t**, *adj.*, **—tly**, *adv.* aufliegend; (*fig.*) obliegend.

Incur, *v.a.* sich (*dat.*) zuziehen; sich aussetzen (*danger*).

Indebted, *adj.* schuldig; (*fig.*) verpflichtet; to be —to a person, jemandem zu Dank verpflichtet sein.

Indecen—cy, *s.* die Unanständigkeit. **—t**, *adj.*, **—tly**, *adv.* unanständig.

Indecipherable, *adj.* unentzifferbar.

Indecisi—on, *s.* die Unentschlossenheit. **—ve**, *adj.*, **—vely**, *adv.* nicht entscheidend (*as a battle*); (undecided) unentschieden.

Indecorous, *adj.*, **—ly**, *adv.* unschicklich.

Indeed, I. *adv.* in der Tat, wirklich; (certainly) wahrlich, fürwahr. II. *part. of concession*: allerdings, freilich, zwar. III. *int.* wirklich! ist es möglich?

Indefatigab—ility, *s.* die Unermüdlichkeit. **—le**, *adj.*, **—ly**, *adv.* unermüdlich.

Indefin—able, *adj.*, **—ably**, *adv.* unbestimmbar. **—ite**, *adj.*, **—itely**, *adv.* unbestimmt (*also Gram.*). **—iteness**, *s.* die Unbestimmtheit.

Indelib—ility, *s.* die Unvertilgbarkeit. **—le**, *adj.*, **—ly**, *adv.* unvertilgbar, unauslöschlich; —le pencil, der Kopierstift.

Indelica—cy, *s.* die Unzartheit. **—te**, *adj.*, **—tely**, *adv.* unzart, unfein.

Indemni—fy, *v.a.* entschädigen. **—ty**, *s.* die Entschädigung.

Indent, *v.a.* einschneiden.

Independen—ce, *s.* die Unabhängigkeit. **—t**, *adj.*, **—tly**, *adv.* unabhängig; to be —t, auf eigenen Füßen stehen; to act —tly, auf eigene Faust handeln.

Indescribabl—e, *adj.*, **—y**, *adv.* unbeschreiblich.

Index, *s.* der Anzeiger; das Inhaltsverzeichnis (*of a book*). **—finger**, *s.* der Zeigefinger.

India-rubber, *s.* das Gummi.

Indicat—e, *v.a.* anzeigen, andeuten, ankündigen. **—ion**, *s.* die Anzeige. **—ive**, *adj.*, **—ively**, *adv.* anzeigend; —ive mood, der Indikativ.

Indict, *v.a.* (schriftlich) anklagen. **—able**, *adj.* anklagbar. **—ment**, *s.* die (schriftliche) Anklage.

Indifferen—ce, *s.* die Gleichgültigkeit. **—t**, *adj.*, **—tly**, *adv.* gleichgültig; I am in —t health, mit meiner Gesundheit steht es schlecht.

Indigen—ce, *s.* die Dürftigkeit, Armut. **—t**, *adj.* dürftig, ärmlich.

Indigesti—ble, *adj.* unverdaulich. **—on**, *s.* die Verdauungsstörung.

Indign—ant, *adj.* entrüstet, aufgebracht; I felt —ant at his words, seine Worte empörten mich. **—antly**, *adv.* mit Entrüstung. **—ation**, *s.* die Entrüstung. **—ity**, *s.* die Beleidigung.

Indigo, *s.* der Indigo.

Indirect, *adj.*, **—ly**, *adv.* indirekt; — way, der Umweg.

Indiscreet, *adj.*, **—ly**, *adv.* unbedachtsam, unbesonnen.

Indiscretion, *s.* die Unklugheit, Unbedachtsamkeit.

Indispensable, *adj.* unentbehrlich; unerläßlich.

Indistinct, *adj.*, **—ly**, *adv.* unklar (*to the eye*); undeutlich (*of sounds*).

Indistinguishabl—e, *adj.*, **—y**, *adv.* ununterscheidbar.

Individual, I. *adj.* persönlich, individuell. II. *s.* das Einzelwesen, Individuum; a private —, eine Privatperson. **—ity**, *s.* die Individualität. **—ly**, *adv.* einzeln genommen, für sich; —ly and collectively, einzeln und insgesamt.

Indolen—ce, *s.* die Trägheit, Indolenz. **—t**, *adj.*, **—tly**, *adv.* träge.

Indoor, *adj.*, **—s**, *adv.* im Hause, zu Hause; — aerial, die Zimmerantenne (*Radio*); — games, Zimmerspiele.

Indubitable, *adj.*, **—y**, *adv.* unzweifelhaft.

Induce, *v.a.* herbeiführen, verursachen; nothing could — him to answer, nichts konnte ihn zu einer Antwort bewegen. **—ment**, *s.* die Veranlassung, der Anlaß, Beweggrund.

Indulge, *v.* I. *a.* (yield) nachgeben; (pamper) verwöhnen. II. *n.* sich (*dat.*) erlauben; to — in something, sich etwas gönnen; to — in vice, dem Laster frönen. **—nce**, *s.* die Nachsicht (*of children*); die Verzärtelung (*of children*); die Befriedigung (*of appetites*). **—nt**, *adj.*, **—ntly**, *adv.* mild, nachgiebig.

Industr—ial, adj. industriell; —ial school, die Gewerbeschule. —ious, adj., —iously, adv. fleißig. —y, s. der Fleiß; das Gewerbe; (—ial arts) die Industrie.

Ineffect—ive, —ual, adj., —ively, —ually, adv. wirkungslos.

Ineffic—acy, s. die Unwirksamkeit. —iency, s. die Unfähigkeit.

Inept, adj., —ly, adv. untüchtig. —i-tude, —ness, s. die Untüchtigkeit.

Inequality, s. die Ungleichheit.

Inequitable, adj., ungerecht, unbillig.

Ineradicab—le, adj., —ly, adv. un-ausrottbar.

Inert, adj., —ly, adv. träge. —ia, s. die Trägheit.

Inevitabl—e, adj., —y, adv. unver-meidlich. —eness, s. die Unver-meidlichkeit.

Inexact, adj., —ly, adv. ungenau. —ness, s. die Ungenauigkeit.

Inexcusab—le, adj., —ly, adv. unent-schuldbar, unverzeihlich. —ility, s. die Unverzeihlichkeit.

Inexhausti—bility, s. die Unerschöpf-lichkeit. —ble, —ve, adj., —bly, adv. unerschöpflich.

Inexorable, adj. unerbittlich.

Inexpedien—cy, s. das Unpassende. —t, adj., —tly, adv. unangemessen, unpassend, unschicklich.

Inexpensive, adj., —ly, adv. nicht teuer, billig.

Inexperience, s. die Unerfahrenheit. —d, adj. unerfahren.

Inexpert, adj. ungeübt.

Inexplicabl—e, adj., —y, adv. uner-klärlich.

Infallibi—ility, s. die Unfehlbarkeit. —le, adj., —ly, adv. unfehlbar.

Infam—ous, adj., —ously, adv. ehrlos, verrufen. —y, s. die Ehrlosigkeit; der üble Ruf.

Infan—cy, s. die Kindheit; die Un-mündigkeit (Law). —t, I. s. das kleine Kind; der, die Unmündige. II. adj. kindlich; —t school, die Kleinkinderschule.

Infantry, s. das Fußvolk, die Infan-terie.

Infatuat—e, v.a. betören. —ed, adj. betört. —ion, s. die Betörung.

Infect, v.a. anstecken (also fig.). —ion, s. die Ansteckung. —ious, adj. an-steckend.

Infer, v.a. schließen. —ence, s. die

Folgerung; to draw an —ence from, einen Schluß ziehen aus.

Inferior, I. adj. (lower) unter, nied-riger; minderwertig (in quality); geringer (in rank); schwächer (in number). II. s. der Untere, Gerin-gere; der Untergeordnete (in office, etc.). —ity, s. die niedrigere Lage; (fig.) die Niedrigkeit; —ity complex, der Minderwertigkeitskomplex.

Infernal, adj., —ly, adv. Höllen-, höllisch.

Infest, v.a. überschwemmen (as ver-min, etc.).

Infidel, I. adj. ungläubig. II. s. der Ungläubige. —ity, s. der Unglaube.

Infinit—e, adj., —ely, adv. unendlich, endlos. —y, s. die Unendlichkeit, Endlosigkeit.

Infinitive, s. die Nennform, der Infinitiv.

Infirm, adj. schwach. —ary, s. das Krankenhaus. —ity, s. die Schwäche.

Inflam—e, v.a. entzünden, entflammen. —mable, adj., —mably, adv. entzünd-bar. —mation, s. die Entzündung (also Med.).

Inflate, v.a. aufblasen, aufblähen (also fig.).

Inflict, v.a. auferlegen; to — oneself upon a person, sich jemandem auf-bürden.

Influen—ce, I. s. der Einfluß, die Einwirkung. II. v.a. beeinflussen. —tial, adj., —tially, adv. einflußreich.

Influenza, s. die Influenza, Grippe.

Inform, v.a. benachrichtigen; I am —ed, ich habe vernommen. —al, adj., —ally, adv. zwanglos, ohne Förmlichkeit. —ant, s. der Berichter-statter. —ation, s. die Erkundigung; to gather —ation, Erkundigungen einziehen. —ation-office, s. die Aus-kunftsstelle.

Infrequen—cy, s. die Seltenheit. —t, adj., —tly, adv. selten.

Infringe, v. I. a. verletzen (contracts, etc.). II. n.; to — upon, beeinträchti-gen. —ment, s. die Übertretung, Verletzung (of a patent, contract, etc.).

Infuriate, v.a. erzürnen.

Infus—e, v.a. (instil) einflößen, einge-ben; aufgießen (tea, etc.). —ion, s. (—ing) das Aufgießen; (decoction) der Aufguß.

Ingen—ious, adj., —iously, adv. sinnreich, geistreich. —uity, s. die

Erfindungskraft. —**uous**, *adj.*, —uously, *adv.* freimütig, unbefangen.

Ingot, *s.* der Barren.

Ingratiate, *v.a.*; to — oneself, sich beliebt machen, sich einschmeicheln.

Ingratitude, *s.* die Undankbarkeit, der Undank.

Ingredient, *s.* der Bestandteil.

Ingress, *s.* der Eintritt.

Inhabit, *v.* I. *a.* bewohnen. II. *n.* wohnen. —**able**, *adj.* bewohnbar. —**ant**, *s.* der Bewohner, Einwohner.

Inhale, *v.a.* einatmen. —**r**, *s.* der Einatmer.

Inharmonious, *adj.*, —**ly**, *adv.* unharmonisch.

Inhere, *v.n.* (einem *or* einer S.) anhaften. —**nce**, —**ncy**, *s.* die innewohnende Eigenschaft, Inhärenz. —**nt**, *adj.*, —**ntly**, *adv.* anhaftend.

Inherit, *v.* I. *a.* (be)erben. II. *n.* erben. —**ance**, *s.* das Erbgut, Erbe, Erbteil.

Inhospita—**ble**, *adj.*, —**bly**, *adv.* ungastlich. —**lity**, *s.* die Ungastlichkeit.

Inhuman, *adj.*, —**ly**, *adv.* unmenschlich. —**ity**, *s.* die Unmenschlichkeit.

Iniquit—**ous**, *adj.*, —**ously**, *adv.* frevelhaft, lasterhaft. —**y**, *s.* die Ungerechtigkeit.

Initial, I. *adj.* anfänglich, Anfangs-. II. *s.* der Anfangsbuchstabe. III. *v.a.* mit dem *or* den Anfangsbuchstaben unterschreiben.

Initiat—**e**, *v.a.* einweihen (*into a society*, etc.). —**ion**, *s.* die Einweihung.

Initiative, *s.* die erste Einleitung zu; to take the —, die ersten Schritte tun.

Inject, *v.a.* einspritzen (*Med.*). —**ion**, *s.* die Einspritzung (*Med.*, *Locom.*, etc.).

Injur—**e**, *v.a.* beschädigen (*things*); beeinträchtigen, schaden (*people*); this will —e his reputation, das wird seinem guten Ruf schaden. —**ious**, *adj.*, —**iously**, *adv.* schädlich, nachteilig. —**y**, *s.* der Nachteil; die Verletzung.

Injustice, *s.* die Ungerechtigkeit, das Unrecht.

Ink, *s.* die Tinte; as black as —, pechschwarz. —**y**, *adj.* tintig; (black) tintenschwarz. —**bottle**, *s.* die Tintenflasche. —**stand**, *s.* das Tintenfaß.

Inkling, *s.* eine Ahnung.

Inland, I. *adj.* inländisch; — revenue, die Steuereinnahmen. II. *adv.* land-einwärts; im Inlande. III. *s.* das Binnenland.

Inlay, *v.a.* einlegen; täfeln, parkettieren (*a floor*).

Inlet, *s.* der Einlaß; die Bucht.

Inmate, *s.* der Insasse.

Inmost, *adj.* innerst; the — thoughts, die geheimsten Gedanken.

Inn, *s.* der Gasthof, das Wirtshaus. —**keeper**, *s.* der Wirtshausbesitzer, Gastwirt.

Innate, *adj.*, —**ly**, *adv.* angeboren.

Inner, *adj.* inner, inwendig.

Innocen—**ce**, *s.* die Unschuld; die Schuldlosigkeit (*of a crime*, etc.). —**t**, *adj.*, —**tly**, *adv.* schuldlos; unschuldig.

Innovat—**e**, *v.n.* Neuerungen einführen. —**ion**, *s.* die Neuerung. —**or**, *s.* der Neuerungstifter.

Innuendo, *s.* die Anspielung.

Innumerabl—**e**, *adj.*, —**y**, *adv.* unzählig, unzählbar, zahllos.

Inoculat—**e**, *v.a.* impfen (*also fig.*). —**ion**, *s.* die Einimpfung.

Inopportune, *adj.*, —**ly**, *adv.* ungelegen.

Inordinate, *adj.* regellos; unmäßig.

Inorgani—**c**, —**zed**, *adj.* unorganisch.

Inquest, *s.* die Leichenschau.

Inquietude, *s.* die Unruhe.

Inquir—**e**, *v.* I. *n.* (nach einer S.) fragen, (einer S.) nachfragen, sich (nach einer S.) erkundigen; —e within, Näheres im Hause; to —e into a thing, eine Sache erforschen. II. *a.* erfragen, erforschen. —**er**, *s.* der Fragende. —**ing**, *adj.*, —**ingly**, *adv.* forschend. —**y**, *s.* die Nachfrage, Erkundigung; (—y into) die Untersuchung; to make —ies, sich erkundigen; I thank you for the kind —ies, ich danke Ihnen für die gütige Nachfrage.

Inquisit—**ion**, *s.* die Inquisition. —**ive**, *adj.*, —**ively**, *adv.* neugierig. —**iveness**, *s.* die Neugier.

Insan—**e**, I. *adj.*, —**ely**, *adv.* wahnsinnig, toll. II. *pl.* die Wahnsinnigen, Irrsinnigen; hospital for the —e, die Irrenanstalt. —**ity**, *s.* der Wahnsinn, Irrsinn.

Inscribe, *v.a.* einschreiben.

Inscription, *s.* die Inschrift.

Insect, *s.* das Kerbtier, Insekt.

Insecur—**e**, *adj.*, —**ely**, *adv.* unsicher. —**ity**, *s.* die Unsicherheit.

Insensib—**ility**, *s.* die Unempfindlichkeit, Gefühllosigkeit; state of —**ility**,

die Bewußtlosigkeit. **—le,** *adj.,* **—ly,**
adv. unempfindlich, gefühllos (of,
to, für); (unconscious) bewußtlos; he
is —le to the danger, **er ist sich der
Gefahr nicht bewußt.**

Inseparabl—e, *adj.,* **—y,** *adv.* untrenn-
bar, unzertrennlich.

Insert, *v.a.* einsetzen, einschalten;
einrücken (*an advertisement*). **—ion,**
s. die Einsetzung; das Inserat.

Inside, I. *adj.* inner, inwendig. II.
adv. im innern, drinnen; hinein.
III. *prep.* innerhalb, im Innern.
IV. *s.* innere Seite, das Innere.

Insidious, *adj.,* **—ly,** *adv.* hinterlistig;
heimtückisch.

Insight, *s.* die Einsicht (into a thing, in
eine S.).

Insignifican—ce, —cy, *s.* die Bedeu-
tungslosigkeit. **—t,** *adj.,* **—tly,** *adv.*
unbedeutend, geringfügig.

Insincer—e, *adj.,* **—ely,** *adv.* unaufrich-
tig. **—ity,** *s.* die Unaufrichtig-
keit.

Insinuat—e, *v.* I. *a.* sich in jemandes
Gunst einschmeicheln. II. *n.* auf eine
S. anspielen. **—ing,** *adj.,* **—ingly,**
adv. einschmeichelnd. **—ion,** *s.* die
Einschmeichelung; die Einflüsterung.

Insipid, *adj.,* **—ly,** *adv.* unschmackhaft;
(*fig.*) schal, abgeschmackt. **—ity,** *s.* die
Unschmackhaftigkeit.

Insist, *v.n.*; to — upon, bestehen auf
(*dat.*); beharren auf (*dat.*); (lay
stress on) Gewicht legen auf (*acc.*).
—ence, *s.* die Beharrlichkeit, das
Bestehen auf (*dat.*). **—ent,** *adj.*
beharrlich; eindringlich.

Insolen—ce, *s.* die Unverschämtheit.
—t, *adj.,* **—tly,** *adv.* unverschämt.

Insomnia, *s.* die Schlaflosigkeit.

Insomuch, *adv.* so, dergestalt.

Inspect, *v.a.* besichtigen. **—ion,** *s.*
die Besichtigung; der Appell (*Mil.*);
for —, zur Ansicht. **—or,** *s.* der
Inspektor, Aufseher.

Inspir—ation, *s.* die Inspiration, Begeisterung. **—e,** *v.a.* einhauchen (*life*);
einatmen (*air*); (*fig.*) begeistern; to
—e a person with awe, einem Ehrfurcht einflößen.

Instability, *s.* die Unbeständigkeit.

Install, *v.a.* einsetzen. **—ation,** *s.*
die Einführung; die (technische) Anlage
(*e.g. of electricity*).

Instalment, *s.* die Rate; by **—s,**
terminweise, ratenweise.

Instance, *s.* das Beispiel, der Fall;
for —, zum Beispiel.

Instant, I. *adj.* (urgent) inständig, dringend; (current) gegenwärtig, laufend;
on the 10th —, am zehnten dieses
(Monats) *or* d. M. II. *s.* der Augenblick; in an —, im Nu. **—ly,** *adv.*
sogleich. **—aneous,** *adj.,* **—aneously,**
adv. augenblicklich.

Instead, *adv.* dafür; — of, anstatt,
statt; — of writing, anstatt zu schreiben.

Instep, *s.* die Fußbiege.

Instigat—e, *v.a.* anreizen. **—ion,** *s.*
der Antrieb.

Instil, *v.a.* einflößen.

Instinct, I. *adj.* bewegt, belebt (with,
durch), voll. II. *s.* der Naturtrieb,
Instinkt. **—ive,** *adj.,* **—ively,** *adv.*
instinktmäßig.

Institut—e, I. *v.a.* einsetzen, stiften,
einrichten. II. *s.* das Institut. **—ion,**
s. das Einsetzen; die Stiftung; die
Anstalt; benevolent **—ion,** milde
Stiftung.

Instruct, *v.a.* (be)lehren, unterweisen.
—ion, *s.* der Unterricht; course of —
ion, der Lehrplan; contrary to **—ions,**
gegen ausdrückliche Anweisung. **—ive,**
adj., **—ively,** *adv.* belehrend, lehrreich.
—or, *s.* der Lehrer. **—ress,** *s.* die
Lehrerin.

Instrument, *s.* das Werkzeug, Instrument.

Insubordinat—e, *adj.* widerspenstig.
—ion, *s.* die Widersetzlichkeit.

Insufferabl—e, *adj.,* **—y,** *adv.* unerträglich.

Insufficien—cy, *s.* die Unzulänglichkeit.
—t, *adj.,* **—tly,** *adv.* unzulänglich.

Insular, *adj.* insular(isch), Insular=.

Insulat—e, *v.a.* isolieren (*also Elect.*).
—ion, *s.* die Isolierung (*Elect.*). **—
or,** *s.* der Isolator. **—ing-tape,** *s.*
das Isolierband (*Elect.*).

Insult, I. *s.* die Beleidigung, der
Schimpf. II. *v.a.* beleidigen, beschimpfen. **—ing,** *adj.,* **—ingly,** *adv.*
beschimpfend; **—ing** language, die
Schmähreden (*pl.*).

Insuperable, *adj.* unüberwindlich.

Insurance, *s.* die Assekuranz, Versicherung; general —, die allgemeine
Versicherung. **—company,** *s.* die
Versicherungsgesellschaft. **—policy,** *s.*
die Police.

Insure, *v.a.* sichern, gewiß machen;
versichern (*C.L.*); the **—d** person,

der Versicherte. **—r,** s. der Ver-
sicherer.
Insurgent, I. adj. aufrührerisch. II.
s. der Aufrührer, Empörer.
Insurrection, s. die Empörung, der
Aufstand.
Intact, adj. unberührt; unversehrt,
unverletzt.
Integ—er, s. die ganze Zahl, das
Ganze. **—ral,** adj. ganz, vollständig;
integral (Arith.).
Integrity, s. die Integrität (of the
empire); (uprightness) die Redlichkeit.
Intellect, s. der Verstand. **—ual,** adj.,
—ually, adv. verständig, einsichtsvoll.
—uality, s. die Intellektualität.
Intellig—ence, s. das Verständnis;
(news) die Nachricht. **—ent,** adj.,
—ently, adv. verständig, intelligent.
—ible, adj., **—ibly,** adv. verständlich,
klar. **—ibility,** **—ibleness,** s. die
Verständlichkeit. **—ence-department,**
s. das Nachrichtenamt.
Intemper—ance, s. die Unmäßigkeit;
die Trunksucht. **—ate,** adj., **—ately,**
adv. unmäßig; trunksüchtig; (language)
hitzig, leidenschaftlich.
Intend, v.a. meinen, beabsichtigen;
this was not —ed, das war nicht
beabsichtigt.
Intens—e, adj. angestrengt (as study,
application, etc.); (extreme) stark,
heftig; —e desire, sehnlichster Wunsch.
—ity, s. die Heftigkeit.
Intent, adj., **—ly,** adv. (— on) gespannt.
—ion, s. die Absicht, das Vorhaben.
—ional, adj., **—ionally,** adv. absichtlich. **—ioned,** adj.; well —ed,
gut gesinnt. **—ness,** s. die (An)span-
nung (des Geistes), der Eifer, Fleiß.
Inter, v.a. beerdigen, begraben.
Intercede, v.a. Fürbitte einlegen.
—r, s. der Vermittler, Fürsprecher.
Intercept, v.a. auffangen.
Intercession, s. die Fürbitte; to make
— for, Fürbitte einlegen für.
Interchange, I. v.a. gegenseitig
austauschen; (alternate) abwechseln
lassen. II. s. der Tausch, Austausch;
die Abwechslung.
Intercourse, s. der Verkehr, Umgang.
Interdict, I. v.a. untersagen. II. s.
das Verbot; das Interdikt.
Interest, I. v.a. interessieren; (concern) (einen) angehen; (give a share
in) einen Anteil geben (an); I am
—ed in it, das interessiert mich, ich

bin dabei beteiligt; the parties —ed,
die Beteiligten. II. s. (sympathy)
die Teilnahme (in a thing, für eine
S.); (profit) der Vorteil; (share) der
Anteil (in a business, etc.); der Zins,
die Zinsen; compound —, Zinseszinsen.
— `l, adj. angeregt; beteiligt; (selfish)
eigennützig. **—ing,** adj., **—ingly,** adv.
unterhaltend, interessant.
Interfere, v.n. sich (in eine S.) einmischen or einmengen. **—nce,** s. die
Einmischung.
Interim, I. s. die Zwischenzeit. II.
adj. & adv. einstweilig, vorläufig; —
report, vorläufiger Bericht.
Interior, I. adj. inner, innerlich; in-
wendig; (inland) binnenländisch. II.
s. das Innere.
Interjection, s. die Interjektion, der
Ausruf.
Interline, v.a. zwischen den Zeilen
schreiben.
Interloper, s. der Eindringling.
Interlude, s. das Zwischenspiel.
Intermarr—iage, s. die Wechselheirat.
—y, v.n. Wechselheiraten schließen.
Intermedia—ry, s. der Vermittler.
—te, adj. in der Mitte liegend, Mittel-,
Zwischen-.
Interminable, adj. endlos, unendlich.
Intermission, s. die Unterbrechung;
without —, unablässig.
Intermit, v. I. a. unterbrechen, einstel-
len. II. n. nachlassen. **—tent,** adj.
nachlassend.
Intern, v.a. internieren. **—al,** adj.,
—ally, adv. inner(-lich); (domestic)
einheimisch. **—ment,** s. die Inter-
nierung.
International, adj., zwischen Völkern,
International-; — exhibition, die
Weltausstellung.
Interpolat—e, v.a. einschalten. **—ion,**
s. die Einschiebung.
Interpose, I. v. I. a. dazwischen stellen.
II. n. dazwischentreten.
Interposition, s. das Dazwischentreten,
die Vermittlung.
Interpret, v.a. erklären (dreams, etc.);
übersetzen, verdolmetschen. **—ation,**
s. die Auslegung. **—er,** s. der
Dolmetscher; der Darsteller.
Interregnum, s. die Zwischenregierung.
Interrogat—e, v. I. a. fragen, befragen,
II. n. (einem) Fragen stellen. **—ion,**
s. das Befragen; note of —ion, das
Fragezeichen.

Interrupt, *v.a.* unterbrechen; to — a person, einem in die Rede fallen. **—ed,** *adj.* unterbrochen, gestört. **—er,** *s.* der Unterbrecher, Störer. **—ion,** *s.* die Unterbrechung.

Intersect, *v.n.* sich durchschneiden, kreuzen. **—ion,** *s.* das Durchschneiden.

Interstice, *s.* die Lücke.

Interval, *s.* der Zwischenraum; (space of time) die Zwischenzeit; at —s, dann und wann.

Interven—e, *v.n.* dazwischenkommen; (lie between) dazwischen liegen (*also of time*). **—tion,** *s.* das Dazwischenliegen; (*fig.*) die Dazwischenkunft; die Vermittelung.

Interview, *s.* die Unterredung.

Intesta—cy, *s.* das Fehlen eines Testaments. **—te,** *adj.* ohne Testament.

Intestin—al, *adj.* die Darm-, Eingeweide betreffend. **—e,** I. *adj.* inner, einheimisch. II. *s.* (*usually pl.* —s) das Gedärm, Eingeweide.

Intimacy, *s.* die Vertrautheit.

¹**Intimate,** I. *adj.,* **—ly,** *adv.* vertraut, intim. II. *s.* der, die Vertraute.

²**Intimat—e,** *v.n.* andeuten. **—ion,** *s.* die Andeutung.

Intimidat—e, *v.a.* einschüchtern. **—ion,** *s.* die Einschüchterung.

Into, *prep.* in (with acc.); to get — trouble, in Unannehmlichkeiten geraten; to put — execution, ausführen.

Intolera—ble, *adj.,* **—bly,** *adv.* unerträglich. **—nce,** *s.* die Unduldsamkeit; die Intoleranz (*Theol.*). **—nt,** *adj.,* **—ntly,** *adv.* unduldsam; intolerant.

Intoxica—nt, *s.* berauschendes Getränk. **—te,** *v.a.* berauschen (*also fig.*). **—tion,** *s.* die Berauschung (*also fig.*).

Intractab—ility, **—leness,** *s.* die Starrsinnigkeit. **—le,** *adj.,* **—ly,** *adv.* widerspenstig; unbändig (*as beasts*).

Intransitive, I. *adj.,* **—ly,** *adv.* intransitiv. II. *s.* (— verb) das Intransitivum.

Intrench, *v.a.* verschanzen (*Fort.*). **—ment,** *s.* die Verschanzung, Schanze.

Intrepid, *adj.,* **—ly,** *adv.* unerschrocken. **—ity,** *s.* die Unerschrockenheit.

Intrica—cy, *s.* die Verwicklung. **—te,** *adj.,* **—tely,** *adv.* verwickelt.

Intrigue, I. *s.* die Intrigue. II.

v.n. Ränke schmieden. **—r,** *s.* der Ränkeschmied, Intrigant.

Intrinsic, *adj.,* innerlich, wahr, wesentlich.

Introduc—e, *v.a.* einführen (*also to a club, etc.*); bekannt machen, vorstellen (*people*); to —e changes, Veränderungen vornehmen. **—er,** *s.* der Einführer. **—tion,** *s.* die Einführung; die Vorstellung, das Bekanntmachen; die Einleitung, Vorrede; letter of —tion, das Empfehlungsschreiben.

Intru—de, *v.* I. *n.* sich eindrängen, sich aufdrängen; am I —ding? störe ich? II. *a.* eindrängen. **—der,** *s.* der Eindringling. **—sion,** *s.* das Aufbringen. **—sive,** *adj.,* **—sively,** *adv.* zudringlich. **—siveness,** *s.* die Zudringlichkeit.

Intrust, *v.a.* anvertrauen.

Intuiti—on, *s.* die (geistige) Anschauung. **—ve,** *adj.,* **—vely,** *adv.* anschauend.

Inundate, *v.a.* überschwemmen.

Inure, *v.a.* gewöhnen (to, an eine S.).

Invade, *v.a.* einfallen in (ein Land). **—r,** *s.* der Angreifer.

Invalid, I. (of no force) kraftlos; ungültig; hinfällig (*of arguments*); (ill) schwach; (*in comp.*) Kranken-. II. *s.* der, die Kranke. **—ity,** *s.* die Hinfälligkeit.

Invaluabl—e, *adj.,* **—y,** *adv.* unschätzbar. **—eness,** *s.* die Unschätzbarkeit.

Invariabl—e, *adj.,* **—y,** *adv.* unveränderlich.

Invasion, *s.* der Einfall, Überfall.

Invective, *s.* die Schmähung, Schimpfrede.

Inveigle, *v.a.* verleiten, verführen. **—ment,** *s.* das Verlocken, Verführen.

Invent, *v.a.* erfinden; to — an excuse, eine Entschuldigung aussinnen. **—ion,** *s.* die Erfindung. **—ive,** *adj.,* **—ively,** *adv.* erfinderisch. **—or,** *s.* der Erfinder.

Inventory, *s.* das Inventar (ium); to take an — of a thing, ein Inventar einer Sache aufnehmen.

Inver—se, *adj.,* **—sely,** *adv.* umgekehrt. **—sion,** *s.* die Umkehrung (*also Math., Mus., Log., Gram.*). **—t,** *v.a.* umkehren; umwandeln. **—ted,** *adj.* umgekehrt.

Invertebrat—a, *pl.* wirbellose Tiere. **—e,** *adj.* wirbellos, ohne Rückgrat.

Invest, *v.a.* bekleiden (with, mit); anlegen (*money*); blockieren (*Mil.*).
Investigat—e, *v.a.* erforschen, untersuchen. **—ion,** *s.* die Erforschung, Untersuchung. **—or,** *s.* der Forscher, Untersucher.
Investiture, *s.* die Einkleidung.
Investment, *s.* die Blockade (*Mil.*); das Anlegen (*of money*); die Geldanlage; to make an —, Geld anlegen.
Invetera—cy, *s.* das Eingewurzeltsein. **—te,** *adj.,* **—tely,** *adv.* eingewurzelt.
Invidious, *adj.,* **—ly,** *adv..* gehässig. **—ness,** *s.* die Gehässigkeit.
Invigorat—e, *v.a.* kräftigen. **—ing,** *adj.* belebend.
Invincib—le, *adj.* unbesiegbar. **—ility, —leness,** *s.* die Unbezwinglichkeit, Unbesiegbarkeit.
Inviolab—ility, *s.* die Unverletzbarkeit. **—le,** *adj.,* **—ly,** *adv.* unverletzlich; unverbrüchlich (*of a promise, etc.*).
Invisib—ility, *s.* die Unsichtbarkeit. **—le,** *adj.,* **—ly,** *adv.* unsichtbar.
Invit—ation, *s.* die Einladung. **—e,** *v.a.* einladen. **—ing,** *adj.* einladend, verlockend.
Invoice, I. *s.* die Faktur(a); as per —, laut Faktura. II. *v.a.* fakturieren.
Invoke, *v.a.* anrufen, anflehen.
Involuntar—ily, *adv. see* **—y. —iness,** *s.* die Unfreiwilligkeit. **—y,** *adv.* unfreiwillig.
Involve, *v.a.* verwickeln (*in difficulties, etc.*); (connect) verbinden; **—d** in debt, verschuldet.
Inward, I. *adj.* inner, inwendig. II. *adv.* einwärts, nach innen; (within) im Inneren. **—ly,** *adv.* innerlich, im Innern (*also fig.*).
Iodi—de, *s.* das Jodid. **—ne,** *s.* das Jod.
Iota, *s.* das Jota; not an —, nicht die geringste Kleinigkeit.
Ipecacuanha, *s.* die Ipekakuanha, die Brechwurzel.
Irate, *adj.* erzürnt, ärgerlich.
Ire, *s.* der Zorn, die Wut.
Iridescen—ce, *s.* das Schillern in den Regenbogenfarben. **—t,** *adj.* regenbogenfarbig.
Iris, *s.* die Regenbogenhaut (*Anat.*); die Schwertlilie (*Bot.*).
Irk, *v.a.* (*usually impers.*) ärgern. **—some,** *adj.,* **—somely,** *adv.* lästig, beschwerlich. **—someness,** *s.* die Beschwerlichkeit.

Iron, I. *s.* das Eisen (*also fig.*). II. *adj.* eisern (*also fig.*). III. *v.a.* plätten, ausbügeln. **—s,** *pl.* Fesseln. **—clad,** I. *adj.* gepanzert. II. *s.* das Panzerschiff. **—foundry,** *s.* die Eisengießerei. **—monger,** *s.* der Eisenhändler. **—ore,** *s.* das Eisenerz. **—works,** *pl.* die Eisenhütte.
Iron—ical, *adj.* spöttelnd, ironisch. **—y,** *s.* die Ironie.
Irrecognizable, *adj.* nicht erkennbar.
Irregular, *adj.,* **—ly,** *adv.* unregelmäßig. **—ity,** *s.* die Unregelmäßigkeit. **—s,** *pl.* irreguläre Truppen.
Irrelevan—cy, *s.* die Unanwendbarkeit. **—t,** *adj.,* **—tly,** *adv.* unanwendbar.
Irreligious, *adj.,* **—ly,** *adv.* irreligiös; gottlos.
Irremovabl—e, *adj.,* **—y,** *adv.* unbeweglich.
Irrepressibl—e, *adj.,* **—y,** *adv.* ununterdrückbar.
Irreproachabl—e, *adj.,* **—y,** *adv.* untadelhaft.
Irresistib—ility, *s.* die Unwiderstehlichkeit. **—le,** *adj.,* **—ly,** *adv.* unwiderstehlich.
Irresolut—e, *adj.,* **—ely,** *adv.* unentschlossen, schwankend. **—eness, —ion,** *s.* die Unentschlossenheit, Unschlüssigkeit.
Irrespective, *adj.,* **—ly,** *adv.;* — of, ohne Rücksicht auf (*acc.*), abgesehen von.
Irreveren—ce, *s.* die Mißachtung. **—t,** *adj.,* **—tly,** *adv.* unehrerbietig.
Irrevocabl—e, *adj.,* **—y,** *adv.* unwiderruflich.
Irrigat—e, *v.a.* bewässern. **—ion,** *s.* die Bewässerung.
Irrita—bility, *s.* die Reizbarkeit. **—ble,** *adj.,* **—bly,** *adv.* reizbar. **—nt,** I. *adj.* aufreizend. II. *s.* das Reizmittel. **—te,** *v.a.* (an)reizen; (make angry) reizen, erzürnen; entzünden (*a wound*). **—tion,** *s.* die Reizung; die Entzündung (*of a wound*).
Is, *3d sing. of* Be, ist; wird; how — he? wie geht es ihm?
Island, Isle, *s.* die Insel.
Isolat—e, *v.a.* absondern. **—ion,** *s.* die Abgesondertheit.
Iso—sceles, *adj.* gleichschenkelig. **—therm,** *s.* die Isotherme.
Issue, I. *s.* das Heraus-gehen, -kommen, -strömen (*of water, etc.*); der Erlaß (*of orders*); die Ausgabe

(*of shares, books, etc.*); das Austeilen (*of provisions, etc.*); (result) der Ausgang; point at —, der strittige Punkt; the matter lies at —, die Sache schwebt; side —s, nebensächliche Punkte. II. *v.a.* auslassen, erlassen, ergehen lassen (*an order*); austeilen (*provisions, etc.*). III. *v.n.* herauskommen; (spring) herkommen, entspringen; abstammen (*as offspring*); (end) ausgehen.

Isthmus, *s.* die Landenge, der Isthmus.

It, *pron.* es; 1. (*as nom.*). 2. (*as acc.*). 3. (*as subject of imp. verb*). —s, I. *poss. pron.* 3 *sing. neuter*, sein, dessen. —self, *pron.* es selbst, selbst, sich; of —self, von selbst; in —self, in sich, an sich.

Itch, I. *s.* das (Haut=)Jucken. II. *v.n.* jucken. —y, *adj.*, krätzig.

Item, *s.* die Einzelheit; der Artikel, Posten; —s of interest, interessante Punkte.

Itinerant, *adj.* reisend.

Ivory, I. *s.* das Elfenbein. II. *adj.* elfenbeinern.

Ivy, *s.* der Efeu.

J

J, j, *s.* das J, j.

Jabber, I. *v.a.* & *n.* schnattern, plappern. II. *s.* das Geschnatter.

Jackal, *s.* der Schakal.

Jackdaw, *s.* die Dohle.

Jacket, *s.* die Jacke; potatoes in their —s, die Pellkartoffeln.

¹**Jade**, I. *s.* die (Schind=)Mähre. II. *v.a.* abmatten, ermüden.

²**Jade**, *s.* der Nierenstein.

Jag, I. *s.* die Zacke. II. *v.a.* kerben. —gy, *adj.* zackig, gekerbt.

Jaguar, *s.* der Jaguar.

Jail, *s.* der Kerker, das Gefängnis. —er, *s.* der Gefängniswärter.

¹**Jam**, *s.* das Eingemachte.

²**Jam**, I. *v.a.* hineinzwängen. II. *s.* das Gedränge; das Quetschen; traffic —, die Verkehrsstockung.

Jamb, *s.* der Pfosten (*of a door*).

Jangle, I. *v.n.* rasseln, kreischen. II. *v.a.* unharmonisch klingen lassen. III. *s.* der Mißklang.

Janitor, *s.* der Pförtner.

Janizary, *pl.* der Janitschar.

January, *s.* der Januar.

Japan, *s.* der Lackfirnis; —ned wares, lackierte Sachen.

¹**Jar**, I. *v.n.* schnarren; to — upon the ear, das Ohr unangenehm berühren. II. *s.* das Knarren.

²**Jar**, *s.* der Krug.

Jargon, *s.* das Kauderwelsch.

Jasmine, *s.* der Jasmin.

Jasper, *s.* der Jaspis.

Jaundice, *s.* die Gelbsucht. —d, *adj.* gelbsüchtig.

Jaunt, I. *v.n.* bummeln (*coll.*). II. *s.* der Ausflug. —y, *adj.* munter; lebhaft; flott.

Javelin, *s.* der Wurfspieß.

Jaw, *s.* der Kinnbacken, Kiefer; to —, (*sl.*) schwatzen. —s, *pl.* der Rachen.

Jay, *s.* der (Eichel=)Häher.

Jealous, *adj.*, —ly, *adv.* eifersüchtig (of a person, auf einen). —y, *s.* die Eifersucht.

Jeer, I. *v.a.* & *n.* spotten (über einen). II. *s.* der Spott. —er, *s.* der Spötter. —ing, *s.* die Spötterei.

Jelly, *s.* das Gelee. —fish, *s.* die Qualle.

Jeopard—ize, *v.a.* gefährden. —y, *s.* die Gefahr; to be in —y, in Gefahr stehen.

Jerk, I. *s.* der plötzliche Stoß; with a —, plötzlich. II. *v.a.* stoßen. III. *v.n.* zusammenzucken, auffahren. —y, *adj.* stoßweise.

Jersey, *s.* der Wams, Sweater.

Jest, I. *s.* der Scherz, Spaß. II. *v.n.* scherzen, spaßen. —er, *s.* der Possenreißer; king's —er, der Hofnarr. —ing, I. *adj.* spaßhaft; this is no —ing matter, das ist nichts zum Scherzen. II. *s.* das Scherzen.

¹**Jet**, *s.* der Gagat, Jet; der Erguß, Wurf; — of water, der Wasserstrahl; — of gas, der Gasstrahl. —black, *adj.* pechschwarz.

²**Jet**, I. *v.n.* hervorragen, vorspringen. II. *v.a.* herausspeien.

Jetty, *s.* der Hafendamm.

Jewel, I. *s.* die Juwele, das (der) Juwel, das Kleinod. II. *v.a.* mit Juwelen schmücken *or* versehen. —ler, *s.* der Juwelenhändler, Juwelier. —ry, —lery *s.* die Juwelen, Schmucksachen (*pl.*), der Schmuck, das Geschmeide.

Jib, *s.* der Kluver (*Naut.*).

Jiffy, *s.*; in a jiffy, (*coll.*) im Nu.

Jig, *s.* die Gigue (*Mus.*).

Jigsaw-puzzle, *s.* das Zusammen=
setzspiel.

Jilt, I. *s.* die Kokette. II. *v.n.* koket=
tieren; he —ed his girl, er hat seinem
Mädchen den Laufpaß gegeben.

Jingle, I. *v.n.* klingeln. II. *v.a.*
klingeln lassen. III. *s.* das Geklingel.

Jingo, *s.* der Hurrapatriot. **—ism,** *s.*
der Hurrapatriotismus.

Job, *s.* die kleine (Lohn=)Arbeit; a good
— he came, wie gut daß er kam; I
lost my —, ich habe meine Stellung
verloren; that was a hard —, das war
ein schweres Stück Arbeit. **—master,**
s. der Pferdevermieter. **—work,** *s.* die
Akkordarbeit, Stückarbeit.

Jockey, *s.* der Jockei.

Joc=ose, *adj.,* **—osely,** *adv.* scherz=
haft, heiter. **—oseness, —ularity,** *s.*
die Scherzhaftigkeit, Lustigkeit. **—u=
lar,** *adj.,* **—ularly,** *adv.* spaßhaft,
scherzhaft.

Jog, *v.a.* stoßen, rütteln; to — a
person's memory, dem Gedächtnis
nachhelfen. **—trot,** I. *s.* der Schlen=
drian. II. *adj.* schlendernd.

Joggle, *v.a.* rütteln.

Join, I. *v.a.* verbinden, vereinigen,
zusammenfügen (one thing to another,
eine Sache mit einer andern); to — a
club, einem Klub beitreten. II. *v.n.*
sich verbinden, sich vereinigen. III.
s. die Verbindungsstelle. **—er,** *s.*
der Tischler, Schreiner. **—ery,** *s.*
die Tischlerei; die Tischlerarbeit.

Joint, I. *s.* die Verbindung, Fuge; der
Stoß (*Carp.*); das Gelenk (*Anat.*);
die Bratenkeule (*Butch.*); to put a
person's nose out of —, einen aus
dem Sattel heben; out of —, (*fig.*)
außer Rand und Band. II. *v.a.*
zusammenfügen. **—ed,** *adj.* geglie=
dert; (divided) zergliedert. **—ly,** *adv.*
gemeinschaftlich. **—owner,** *s.* der
Mitbesitzer.

Jointure, *s.* das Wittum, Leibgedinge.

Joist, *s.* der Querbalken.

Jok=e, I. *s.* der Scherz, Spaß; he
cannot take a —, er versteht keinen
Spaß; to play a — upon a person,
einem einen Streich spielen. II.
v.a. aufziehen, necken (a person about
a thing, einen über etwas). III. *v.n.*
scherzen, spaßen. **—er,** *s.* der Witz=
bold, Spaßvogel. **—ing,** *adj.,* —
ingly, *adv.* scherzend, spaßhaft.

Joll=iness, —ity, *s.* die Lustigkeit,

Munterkeit. **—y,** *adj.* lustig, munter,
fidel.

Jolt, I. *v.a.* & *n.* schütteln. II. *s.*
der plötzliche Stoß.

Jostle, *v.a.* & *n.* anstoßen.

Jot, I. *s.* das Jota. II. *v.a.* (— down)
flüchtig hinwerfen.

Journ=al, *s.* (diary) das Tagebuch,
Journal; (periodical) die Zeitschrift.
—alist, *s.* der Journalist. **—alistic,**
adj. journalistisch.

Journey, I. *s.* die Reise; a day's —,
eine Tagereise. II. *v.n.* reisen, wan=
dern. **—ing,** *s.* das Reisen. **—man,**
s. der (Handwerks=)geselle.

Jovial, *adj.,* **—ly,** *adv.* frohsinnig.
—ity, *s.* die Lustigkeit.

Jowl, *s.* der Backen.

Joy, I. *s.* die Freude; I wish you —,
ich wünsche Ihnen Glück. II. *v.n.*
sich freuen. **—ful,** *adj.,* **—fully,** *adv.*
freudvoll, freudig. **—fulness,** *s.* die
Fröhlichkeit. **—less,** *adj.,* **—lessly,**
adv. freudlos, freudenleer. **—ous,**
adj., **—ously,** *adv.* freudevoll, froh,
erfreulich.

Jubil=ant, *adj.* jubelnd, frohlockend.
—ation, *s.* das Jubeln. **—ee,** *s.* die
Jubelfeier.

Judge, I. *s.* der Richter; I am no — of
these things, ich habe kein Urteil über
diese Sachen. II. *v.n.* urteilen (from,
nach). III. *v.a.* richten; beurteilen
(über einen).

Judgment, *s.* das Urteil; a man of
great —, ein scharfsinniger Mann;
to act with great —, sehr vernünftig
handeln. **—day,** *s.* der jüngste Tag.
—hall, *s.* die Gerichtshalle.

Judici=al, *adj.,* **—ally,** *adv.* gericht=
lich. **—ous,** *adj.,* **—ously,** *adv.*
verständig. **—ousness,** *s.* die Klug=
heit, die Einsicht.

Jug, *s.* der Krug.

Juggle, *v.n.* gaukeln. **—r,** *s.* der
Gaukler, Taschenspieler. **—ry,** *s.* die
Gaukelei.

Jugular, *adj.* Gurgel=; — vein, die
Gurgelader.

Juice, *s.* der Saft.

July, *s.* der Juli.

Jumble, I. *v.a.* vermengen. II. *v.n.*
unordentlich gemengt sein. III. *s.* der
Wirrwarr; a — sale, ein Ramsch=
verkauf.

Jump, I. *v.n.* springen. II. *v.a.*
hinüberspringen. III. *s.* der Sprung,

Satz; to give a —, einen Sprung tun.
—er, s. der Springer; (garment) der
Jumper, die Stridbluse.

Junct—ion, s. die Verbindung. —
ure, s. der Verbindungspunkt. **—ion-
line,** s. die Verbindungsbahn (Railw.).

June, s. der Juni.

Jungle, s. das Dschungel.

Junior, I. adj. jünger. II. s. der (die)
Jüngere; she is my — by two years,
sie ist zwei Jahre jünger als ich.

Juniper, s. der Wachholder.

Junk, s. die Dschunke.

Junket, s. die dicke, geronnene Milch.

Juris—diction, s. die Rechtsprechung.
—t, s. der Rechtsgelehrte, Jurist.

Jur—or, s. der Geschwor(e)ne. **—y,**
s. das Schwurgericht. **—y-box,** s.
die Geschworenenbank.

Jury-mast, s. der Notmast.

Just, I. adj. gerecht. II. adv. gerade,
genau; eben (of time) —; now, soeben;
— tell me, sage mir einmal.

Justice, s. die Gerechtigkeit.

Just—ifiable, adj., **—ifiably,** adv.
rechtmäßig. **—ification,** s. die Rechtfertigung. **—ify,** v.a. rechtfertigen.
—ly, adv. mit Recht.

Jut, v.n. (— out) hervorstehen.

Jute, s. die Jute.

Juvenile, I. adj. jung, jugendlich.
II. s. der junge Mensch.

Juxtaposition, s. die Nebeneinander-
stellung.

K

K, k, s. das K, k.

Kafir, Kaffir, s. der Kaffer.

Kaleidoscope, s. das Kaleidoskop.

Kali, s. das Kali (Chem.).

Kangaroo, s. das Känguruh.

Kedge, s. der Wurfanker.

Keel, s. der Kiel.

Keen, adj., **—ly,** adv. scharf (as an
edge); (eager) eifrig, erpicht (for a
thing, auf eine S.). **—ness,** s. die
Schärfe; die Heftigkeit. **—edged,**
adj. scharf geschliffen. **—eyed,** adj.
scharfsichtig. **—witted,** adj. scharfsinnig.

Keep, I. ir.v.a. halten; (guard) (aufbewahren; (preserve from) abhalten
(von); (support) erhalten, ernähren,
unterhalten; (observe) beobachten
(festivals, silence); feiern (a festival);
erfüllen, halten (a promise, etc.);

hüten (the house); befolgen (rules); to
— one's temper, sich beherrschen; —
on reading, fortfahren mit dem
Lesen; to — clear, sich freihalten von;
to — time, Schritt halten, im Takt
bleiben. II. ir.v.n. sich halten; (stay)
sich aufhalten, bleiben; sich halten (as
fruit, meat, etc.). III. s. die Kost.
—er, s. der Verwahrer; der Inhaber (of an hotel, etc.); (jailer) der
Gefängniswärter; (maintainer) der
Unterhalter; (game) der Jäger, Wild-
hüter. **—ing,** s. die Verwahrung,
Aufsicht, Pflege; to be in —ing with,
übereinstimmen mit. **—sake,** s. das
(Geschenk zum) Andenken.

Keg, s. das Fäßchen.

Kelp, s. das Salzkraut (Bot.).

Kennel, s. der Hundestall.

Kerb, —stone, s. der Prellstein.

Kernel, s. der Kern.

Kerosene, s. das Kerosin.

Kettle, s. der Kessel. **—drum,** s. die
Kesselpauke.

Key, s. der Schlüssel (of a door, watch,
etc.); die Taste (of a piano, etc.);
die Tonart (Mus.). **—board,** s. die
Tastatur. **—hole,** s. das Schlüsselloch.
—note, s. der Grundton.

Kick, I. v.a. ausschlagen (as horses);
(einem) einen Fußtritt geben. II. v.n.
mit den Füßen ausschlagen; to —
against, (fig.) sich auflehnen gegen.
III. s. der Fußstoß, Fußtritt.

Kid, I. s. das Zicklein; (coll.) das Kind.
II. adj.; — gloves, Glacéhandschuhe.

Kidnap, v.a. (Kinder, Menschen)
stehlen, entführen. **—per,** s. der
Kinderdieb; der Seelenverkäufer.

Kidney, s. die Niere. **—bean,** s.
türkische Bohne.

Kill, v.a. töten (also fig.), umbringen;
schlachten (cattle). **—joy,** s. der
Freudenstörer, Störenfried.

Kiln, s. der Brennofen; lime- —, der
Kalkofen.

Kilo—gramme, s. das Kilogramm.
—litre, s. das Kiloliter.

Kilt, I. s. das kurze Röckchen der
Bergschotten. II. v.a. in Falten
legen (Semp.); (— up) aufschürzen
(one's skirts, etc.).

Kin, s. die (Bluts-)Verwandtschaft;
(relation) der, die Verwandte.

Kind, I. adj. gut, gütig, freundlich.
II. s. die Art, Gattung, das Geschlecht;
to pay in —, mit gleicher Münze

zahlen. —**liness,** s. die Freundlichkeit.
—**ly,** adj. & adv. gütig, freundlich. —
ness, s. die Güte, die Gütigkeit.

Kindle, v. I. a. anzünden. II. n.
sich entzünden; (fig.) entbrennen.

Kindred, I. s. die Verwandtschaft;
(relations) die Verwandten. II. adj.
verwandt.

King, s. der König (also Cards &
Chess); die Dame (Draughts). —
dom, s. das Königreich. —**ly,** adj.
& adv. königlich. —**ship,** s. die
Königswürde.

Kingfisher, s. der Eisvogel.

Kink, s. die Kink; (coll.) der närrische
Einfall.

Kinsfolk, pl. die Sippe, Sippschaft.

Kipper, s. der geräucherte Häring.

Kiss, I. v.a. küssen. II. s. der Kuß.

Kit, s. das Handwerksgerät; die
Ausrüstung (of a soldier, etc.).

Kitchen, s. die Küche. —**garden,** s.
der Gemüsegarten. —**range,** s. der
Kochofen.

Kite, s. die Weihe; (paper —) der
Drache.

Kith, s.; — and kin, die Sippschaft.

Kitten, s. das Kätzchen. —**ish** adj.
kätzchenhaft.

Kleptomania, s. die Diebssucht.

Knack, s. die Fertigkeit, Kunst (at,
of, in, in (dat.)).

Knacker, s. der Abdecker.

Knapsack, s. der Tornister; der
Rucksack.

Knarl, s. der Knorren (wood). —**ed,**
adj. knorrig.

Knav—e, s. der Schelm, Schalk; der
Bube (Cards). —**ery,** s. die Schurkerei, der Schurkenstreich. —**ish** adj.,
—**ishly,** adv. spitzbübisch, schurkisch.

Knead, v.a. kneten. —**ing-trough,** s.
der Backtrog.

Knee, s. das Knie. —**breeches,** pl.
kurze Kniehosen. —**pan,** s. die
Kniescheibe.

Kneel, ir.v.n. knieen. —**er,** s. der
Knieende.

Knell, s. die Totenglocke.

Knick—ers, s. die (Unter)hosen; die
Kniehosen. —**erbockers,** pl. die
Kniehosen. —**knack,** s. das Spiel-
zeug, der Tand.

Knife, s. das Messer; clasp —,
das Schnappmesser; carving —, das
Vorlegemesser; pocket —, das
Taschenmesser.

Knight, I. s. der Ritter; der Springer
(Chess). II. v.a. zum Ritter schlagen.
—**hood,** s. die Ritterwürde. —**liness,** s. die Ritterlichkeit. —**ly,** adj.
ritterlich. —**errant,** s. der fahrende Ritter.

Knit, ir.v. I. a. stricken (stockings);
to — the brows, die Stirn runzeln.
II. n. sich verbinden; stricken. —**ter,**
s. der Stricker, die Strickerin. —**ting,** s.
das Strickzeug. —**ting-needle,** s.
die Stricknadel. —**ting-yarn,** s. das
Strickgarn.

Knob, s. der Knopf.

Knock, I. v.n. klopfen; pochen; to —
about, (coll.) sich umher treiben. II. v.a.
klopfen, stoßen, schlagen. III. s. der
Schlag, Stoß; das Anklopfen, Pochen
(at the door). —**er,** s. der Klopfende;
der (Haustür-)Klopfer. —**kneed,** adj.
X-beinig.

Knoll, s. der kleine Hügel.

Knot, I. s. der Knoten; sailor's —,
der Schifferknoten. II. v.a. verb.
knüpfen (fig.) verbinden. —**ted,** adj.
knotig, knorrig. —**ty,** adj. knotig,
knorrig; verwickelt.

Knout, s. die Knute.

Know, ir.v. I. a. wissen; (be acquainted)
kennen; (recognize) erkennen; unterscheiden (one thing or person from
another); (experience) erleben, erfahren; to come to —, erfahren; to
make —, bekannt machen. II. n.
wissen. —**ing,** I. adj. (skilful) geschickt; (cunning) schlau, durchtrieben;
(intelligent) verständig. II. s. das
Wissen. —**ingly,** adv. (purposely)
wissentlich; geschickt. —**ingness,** s. die
Schlauheit, Durchtriebenheit.

Knowledge, s. das Wissen; (information) die Kenntnis, Kunde; (learning,
etc.) die Wissenschaft; die Bekanntschaft
(of a person, mit einem).

Known, adj. gewußt; bekannt.

Knuckle, s. der Knöchel, das Gelenk.

Koran, s. der Koran.

Kudos, s. der Ruhm, das Ansehen.

L

L, l, s. das L, l.

Label, I. s. die Etikette, der Zettel, das
Schildchen. II. v.a. etikettieren; bekleben.

Labial, I. adj. Lippen-. II. s. der
Lippenlaut.

Laboratory, *s.* das Laboratorium.
Laborious, *adj.,* **—ly,** *adv.* mühsam,
mühevoll.
Labour, I. *s.* die Arbeit, das Werk;
— exchange, das Arbeitsnachweis-
bureau; — market, der Arbeitsmarkt;
hard —, die Zuchthausarbeit. II. *v.n.*
arbeiten; (toil) sich anstrengen, sich
bemühen. **—er,** *s.* der Handarbeiter,
Handlanger; day—er, der Tagelöhner.
—saving, *adj.* arbeitsparend.
Laburnum, *s.* der Goldregen.
Labyrinth, *s.* das Labyrinth.
Lace, I. *s.* die Spitze(n); (gold, etc.,
—) die Tresse; (cord) die Schnur.
II. *v.a.* (zu-)schnüren. **—maker,** *s.*
der Spitzenklöppler, die Spitzen-
klöpplerin.
Lacerat—e, *v.a.* zerreißen. **—ion,** *s.*
die Zerreißung.
Lack, I. *v.a.* ermangeln (einer S.),
bedürfen entbehren, Mangel leiden
an (*dat.*). II. *v.n.* Mangel leiden.
III. *s.* der Mangel.
Lackadaisical, *adj.* schmachtend;
(affected) geziert.
Lackey, *s.* der Lakai.
Laconic, *adj.,* **—ally,** *adv.* lakonisch.
Lacquer, I. *v.a.* lackieren; —ed work,
die Lackarbeit. II. *s.* der Lack.
Lact—eal, **—ic,** *adj.* milchig.
Lad, *s.* der Junge, Bursch(e), Jüng-
ling.
Ladder, *s.* die Leiter.
Lad—e, *v.a.* laden. **—ing,** *s.* die
Ladung; bill of —ing, der Ver-
ladungsschein.
Ladle, *s.* der Schöpflöffel.
Lady, *s.* die Dame; Our (blessed) —,
unsere liebe Frau; ladies! meine
Damen!; my —, gnädige Frau; —
in waiting, die Hofdame; —'s maid,
das Kammermädchen. **—bird,** *s.* der
Marienkäfer. **—day,** *s.* Mariä Ver-
kündigung (der 25ste März). **—like,**
adj. damenhaft. **—killer,** *s.* der
Damenheld.
Lag, *v.n.* zaudern. **—gard,** I. *adj.*
zaudernd. II. *s.* der Zauderer.
Lagoon, *s.* die Lagune.
Laic, I. *s.* der Laie. II. *adj.* weltlich,
laienhaft.
Lair, *s.* das Lager (eines wilden
Tieres).
Laity, *s.* der Laienstand.
Lake, *s.* der See. **—dwellings,** *s.*
die Pfahlbauten.

Lama, *s.* der Lama. **—ism,** *s.* der
Lamaismus.
Lamb, *s.* das Lamm. **—skin,** *s.* das
Lammfell, Lämmerfell.
Lame, I. *adj.,* **—ly,** *adv.* lahm. II.
v.a. lähmen, lahm machen. **—ness,**
s. die Lahmheit, Lähmung.
Lament, I. *v.a.* beklagen. II. *v.n.* (weh-)
klagen; trauern (for, um). III. *s.* das
Klagelied. **—able,** *adj.,* **—ably,** *adv.*
beklagenswert. **—ation,** *s.* die Wehklage.
Lamp, *s.* die Lampe. **—chimney,**
—post, *s.* der Laternenpfahl. **—
glass,** *s.* der Lampenzylinder. **—
light,** *s.* das Lampenlicht. **—lighter,**
s. der Laternenanzünder. **—oil,** *s.* das
Brennöl. **—shade,** *s.* die Lampen-
glocke. **—wick,** *s.* der Lampendocht.
Lampoon, *s.* die Schmähschrift.
Lamprey, *s.* das Neunauge.
Lance, I. *s.* die Lanze. **—r,** *s.* der
Lanzenreiter, Ulan. II. *v.a.* auf-
schneiden (*Surg.*). **—corporal,** *s.*
der Gefreite.
Lancet, *s.* die Lanzette. **—window,**
s. das Spitzbogenfenster.
Land, I. *s.* das feste Land; (country)
das Land. II. *v.a.* landen; löschen
(*of a ship's cargo*). III. *v.n.* landen;
(arrive) ankommen. **—ing,** *s.* die
Landung; der Treppenabsatz (*of stairs*);
—ing place, der Landungsplatz. **—
lady,** *s.* die Gutsbesitzerin; die Wirtin
(*of an inn*); my —lady, meine Haus-
wirtin. **—lord,** *s.* der Gutsherr; der
Wirt (*of an inn, etc.*); my —lord, mein
Hauswirt. **—mark,** *s.* der Grenz-
stein; (*fig.*) das Merkmal; die Land-
marke (*Naut.*). **—slide,** **—slip,** *s.*
der Bergsturz. **—steward,** *s.* der
Gutsverwalter. **—tax,** *s.* die Grund-
steuer.
Landau, *s.* der Landauer.
Landgrav—e, *s.* der Landgraf. **—
ine,** *s.* die Landgräfin.
Landscape, *s.* die Landschaft.
Lane, *s.* die Gasse.
Lang-syne, *adv.* lange her.
Language, *s.* die Sprache.
Langui—d, *adj.,* **—dly,** *adv.* schlaff,
erschlafft. **—dness,** *s.* die Mattig-
keit, Schlaffheit. **—sh,** *v.n.* ver-
schmachten; schmachten (for, nach).
Languor, *s.* die Schlaffheit, die Mattig-
keit.
Lank, *adj.,* **—ly,** *adv.* dünn, mager.

Lantern, s. die Laterne; dark —, die Blendlaterne.

Lanyard, s. das Taljereep.

¹Lap, s. der Schoß. **—dog,** s. der Schoßhund.

²Lap, v.a. umschlagen.

³Lap, v.a. auflecken.

Lapidary, I. adj. lapidarisch. II. s. der Steinschneider.

Lapis-lazuli, s. der Lasurstein.

Lapse, I. s. der Verlauf (of time); das Verfallen (into indolence, etc.); der Heimfall (Law); (fault) der Fehler. II. v.n. fallen, gleiten; verfließen (as time).

Lapwing, s. der Kibitz.

Larboard, s. das Backbord.

Larceny, s. der Diebstahl.

Larch, s. die Lärche.

Lard, I. s. das Schweineschmalz. II. v.a. picken.

Larder, s. die Speisekammer.

Large, adj. groß. **—ly,** adv. reichlich; (greatly) großenteils, größtenteils; at —, frei; to talk at —, in den Tag hineinreden. **—ness,** s. die Größe.

¹Lark, s. die Lerche. **—spur,** s. der Rittersporn.

²Lark, I. s. der Schabernack (sl.). II. v.n. necken (sl.).

Larva, s. die Larve, Puppe (Entom.).

Larynx, s. der Kehlkopf.

Lascivious, adj., **—ly,** adv. wollüstig.

Lash, I. s. die Schmitze (of a whip); (stroke) der Hieb, Streich; die Augenwimper. II. v.a. peitschen, hauen, geißeln; to — out, ausschlagen; to — in, anbinden. **—ing,** s. das Peitschen; der Bändsel (Naut.).

Lass, s. das Mädchen.

Lassitude, s. die Mattigkeit.

Lasso, s. der Lasso.

¹Last, I. adj. letzt; (next before) vorig; (extreme) äußerst, höchst. II. adv. zuletzt; am Letzten; at —, endlich; — but one, vorletzt; to breathe one's —, sterben. **—ly,** adv. zum Letzten, schließlich.

²Last, I. v.n. dauern, währen; halten (as colour); ausreichen (as provisions). **—ing,** adj., **—ingly,** adv. dauerhaft.

³Last, s. der Leisten.

Latch, I. s. die Klinke, der Drücker (on doors). II. v.a. (zu)klinken, zuschließen. **—key,** s. der Hausschlüssel, der Drücker.

Late, I. adj. (not early) spät; (tardy) zu

spät, verspätet; (dead) selig; (former) ehemalig, vormalig; (recent) jüngst; of — years, seit einigen Jahren; to keep — hours, spät aufbleiben. II. adv. spät. **—ly,** adv. kürzlich, vor kurzem. **—ness,** s. die Verspätung.

Latent, adj. verborgen.

Lateral, adj. seitlich, Seiten=.

Lath, s. die Latte.

Lathe, s. die Drechselbank.

Lather, I. s. der (Seifen=)Schaum. II. v.a. einseifen.

Latitude, s. die Breite, Polhöhe (Geog., Astr.); (laxity) die Freiheit.

Latter, adj. später; (modern) neuer, modern; dieser Letzterer, dieses Letztere(s) (of two). **—ly,** adv. neuerdings.

Lattice, s. das Gitter, Gitterwerk. **—window,** s. das Gitterfenster.

Laud, v.a. loben, preisen. **—able,** adj., **—ably,** adv. löblich.

Laudanum, s. die Opiumtinktur.

Laugh, I. v.n. lachen (also Poet., fig.); to — at, lachen über (eine S.), (eine S.) belachen; to — at a person, jemanden auslachen; he —ed it off, er setzte sich lachend darüber hinweg. II. s. das Lachen, Gelächter. **—able,** adj., **—ably,** adv. lächerlich. **—able- ness,** s. die Lächerlichkeit. **—er,** s. der Lacher. **—ing,** adj., **—ingly,** adv. lachend. **—ter,** s. das Gelächter.

Launch, I. v.a. (hurl) schleudern, wer- fen; vom Stapel laufen lassen (a ship); aussetzen (a boat); (fig.) in Gang setzen. II. v.n. sich in (eine S.) hineinbegeben; in See gehen (Naut.). III. s. der Stapellauf; steam —, die Dampfpinasse.

Laundr—ess, s. die Wäscherin. **—y,** s. die Waschanstalt, das Waschhaus.

Laureate, adj. lorbeergekrönt.

Laurel, s. der Lorbeer.

Lava, s. die Lava.

Lavatory, s. das Waschzimmer; (W.C.) der Abort; public —, die Bedürfnisanstalt.

Lave, v.a. waschen, baden.

Lavender, s. der Lavendel.

Lavish, I. adj., **—ly,** adv. (of, in) freigebig (mit). II. v.a. verschwend- en. **—ness,** s. die Verschwend- ung.

Law, s. (rule) das Gesetz; die Gesetze, das Recht (Law); to go to —, vor Gericht gehen. **—ful,** adj., **—fully,**

adv. geſetzlich, geſetzmäßig; (permitted) erlaubt. **—fulness,** *s.* die Geſetzlichkeit, Rechtmäßigkeit. **—less,** *adj.,* **—lessly,** *adv.* geſetzlos; (illegal) geſetzwidrig, unrechtmäßig; (licentious) zügellos. **—lessness,** *s.* die Geſetzloſigkeit; die Zügelloſigkeit. **—breaker,** *s.* der Geſetzesübertreter. **—court,** *s.* der Gerichtshof. **—suit,** *s.* der Prozeß.

¹**Lawn,** *s.* der Raſenplatz. **—tennis,** *s.* das Tennis.

²**Lawn,** *s.* der Batiſt.

Lawyer, *s.* der Rechtsgelehrte, Rechtsanwalt, Juriſt, Advokat.

Lax, *adj.* ſchlaff (*as a cord*); loſe, locker (*also fig.*).

¹**Lay,** *adj.* laienhaft, Laien-. **—man,** *s.* der Laie.

²**Lay,** *s.* das Lied.

³**Lay,** *ir.v.a.* legen (*eggs; a cable, etc.*); to — hold of, ergreifen.

Layer, *s.* der Legende; (stratum) die Schicht, das Lager.

Laz—iness, *s.* die Faulheit, Trägheit. **—y,** *adj.* faul, träge.

¹**Lead,** I. *s.* das Blei (*Min., Metall., Chem.*). II. *v.a.* verbleien. **—en,** *adj.* bleiern; bleifarben. **—pencil,** *s.* der Bleiſtift. **—pipe,** *s.* die Bleiröhre.

²**Lead,** I. *ir.v.a.* leiten, führen; anführen (*a party, an army*); (— the way) vorangehen. II. *ir.v.n.* (go before) voraus-, vorangehen; (conduct) anführen. III. *s.* die Führung, Leitung; die Vorhand (*Cards*). **—er,** *s.* der (An-)Führer, Leiter; der Leitartikel (*in a newspaper*). **—ership,** *s.* die Führerſchaft; (guidance) die Leitung. **—in,** *s.* der Mauerdurchlaß (*Radio*). **—ing,** *adj.* leitend; —ing lady, (*Theat.*) die Hauptſängerin. **—ing-strings,** *pl.* das Gängelband.

Leaf, *s.* (*pl.* Leaves) das Blatt (*of a tree or book, of a table*); der Flügel (*of a door, gate*). **—less,** *adj.* blattlos, entblättert, unbelaubt. **—y,** *adj.* blattreich, belaubt. **—let,** *s.* das Blättchen.

¹**League,** I. *s.* das Bündnis, der Bund; — of nations, der Völkerbund. II. *v.n.* ſich verbinden.

²**League,** *s.* die Seemeile, Meile (= 3 engliſche Meilen).

Leak, I. *s.* das Leck; to spring a —, ein Leck bekommen. II. *v.n.* leck werden; leck ſein; to — out, auslaufen; ruchbar werden. **—y,** *adj.* leck.

¹**Lean,** *ir.v.* I. *n.* lehnen (against a thing, an einer S.), ſich lehnen (against a thing, an eine S.); ſich neigen (to one side, auf eine Seite). II. *a.* ſtützen.

²**Lean,** *adj.* mager. **—ness,** *s.* die Magerkeit.

Leap, I. *v.a.* ſpringen, hüpfen. II. *s.* der Sprung, Satz. **—er,** *s.* der Springer. **—frog,** *s.* das Bockſpringen. **—year,** *s.* das Schaltjahr.

Learn, *v.a.* (*pret. & p.p.* —ed *or* —t) lernen. **—ed,** *adj.,* **—edly,** *adv.* gelehrt. **—er,** *s.* der Lernende. **—ing,** *s.* (knowledge) die Gelehrſamkeit, die Kenntniſſe (*pl.*); (act of —ing) das Lernen, die Erlernung.

Lease, I. *s.* (letting) die Verpachtung, Pacht, Miete; (deed) der Pachtbrief; to take a — of, pachten. II. *v.a.* verpachten; (rent) pachten. **—holder,** *s.* der Pächter.

Leash, *s.* die Koppelleine.

Least, I. *adj.* geringſt, kleinſt, mindeſt. II. *adv.* am wenigſten; at (the) —, wenigſtens.

Leather, I. *s.* das Leder. II. *adj. s.* ledern, Leder-.

¹**Leave,** *s.* die Erlaubnis, Einwilligung; (farewell) der Abſchied; (— of absence) der Urlaub. **—taking,** *s.* das Abſchiednehmen.

²**Leave,** *ir.v.* I. *a.* verlaſſen; laſſen; (bequeath) vermachen. II. *n.* ablaſſen; (depart) abreiſen, weggehen.

Leaven, I. *s.* der Sauerteig (*also fig.*), die Hefe. II. *v.a.* ſäuern.

Leavings, *pl.* die Überbleibſel, Reſte.

Lectern, *s.* das Leſepult.

Lecture, I. *s.* die Vorleſung (on, über, *acc.*); (reproof) die Strafpredigt. II. *v.n.* ein Vorleſung, einen Vortrag halten (on, über) die. III. *v.a.* (einem) den Text leſen. **—r,** *s.* der Vortragende, Vorleſer. **—room,** *s.* der Hörſaal.

Ledge, *s.* der Sims.

Ledger, *s.* das Hauptbuch (*C.L.*).

Lee, *s.* die Lee (ſeite). **—ward,** *adj. & adv.* leewärts, unter dem Winde. **—way,** *s.* die Abtrift.

Leech, *s.* der Blutegel (*Zool.*).

Leek, *s.* der Lauch.

Leer, I. *s.* der ſchiefe Blick. II. *v.n.* ſchielen.

Lees, *pl.* die Hefen, der Bodensaß.

Left, I. *adj.,* linf; — hand, linfe Hand. II. *s.* die Linfe; on the —, to the —, links. III. *adv.* links; right and —, rechts und links; — turn! linksum! IV. *adj. & adv.* verlaffen; vermacht; abgereift. — **handed,** *adj.* linfhändig. —**luggage office,** *s.* die Gepäck-annahme, -auf-nahme.

Leg, *s.* das Bein; die Keule (*of mutton, etc.*). —**ged,** *adj.* (*in comp.*) beinig, mit Beinen.

Legacy, *s.* das Vermächtnis.

Legal, *adj.,* —**ly,** *adv.* gefeßlich, ge-feßmäßig. —**ity,** *s.* die Gefeßlich-feit, Gefeßmäßigfeit. —**ize,** *v.a.* rechtsfräftig machen.

Legat—**e,** *s.* der (päpftliche) Legat. —**ion,** *s.* die Gefandtfchaft.

Legatee, *s.* der Erbe.

Legend, *s.* die Sage. —**ary,** *adj.* fagenhaft; märchenhaft; fabelhaft.

Legerdemain, *s.* das Kunftftück, Ta-fchenfpielerftück.

Leggings, *pl.* Gamafchen.

Legib—**ility,** *s.* die Lesbarkeit, Lefer-lichfeit. —**le,** *adj.,* —**ly,** *adv.* le-ferlich, lesbar.

Legion, *s.* die Legion.

Legislat—**e,** *v.n.* Gefeße geben *or* machen. —**ion,** *s.* die Gefeßgebung. —**ive,** *adj.* gefeßgebend. —**or,** *s.* der Gefeßgeber. —**ure,** *s.* die Legislative.

Legitim—**acy,** *s.* die Berechtigung (*of conclusions, etc.*); (—acy of birth) eheliche Geburt. —**ate,** *adj.,* —**ately,** *adv.* wohlbegründet, berechtigt (*as arguments*); ehelich geboren.

Legum—**e,** *s.* die Hülfe. —**es,** *pl.* die Hülfenfrüchte.

Leisure, I. *s.* die Muße; to be at —, Muße haben; at your —, wenn es Ihnen paßt. II. *adj.* müßig. —**ly,** *adj. & adv.* mit Muße, gemächlich, behaglich.

Lemon, *s.* die Zitrone. —**ade,** *s.* die Limonade. —**juice,** *s.* der Zit-ronenfaft. —**peel,** *s.* die Zitronen-fchale.

Lend, *ir.v.a.* (ver-)leihen; gewähren, leiften (*aid*); ausleihen (*money on interest*). —**er,** *s.* der (Aus-)Leiher, Verleiher.

Length, *s.* die Länge; die Zeitdauer, Dauer (*of time*); at —, ausführlich;

(at last) endlich, zuleßt; to go to great —s, fehr weit gehen; full —, in voller Länge; in Lebensgröße. —**en,** *v.* I. *a.* verlängern, ausdehnen. II. *n.* fich verlängern, fich ausdehnen. —**ening,** *s.* die Verlängerung. — **wise,** *adv.* der Länge nach, längelang. —**y,** *adj.* lang; (spun out) langwierig, gedehnt.

Lenient, *adj.* mild, gelind.

Lens, *s.* das Linfenglas, die Linfe.

Lent, *s.* die Faften (*pl.*), Faftenzeit. —**en,** *adj.* Faften-.

Lentil, *s.* die Linfe.

Leopard, *s.* der Leopard.

Lep—**er,** *s.* der Ausfäßige. —**rosy,** *s.* der Ausfaß. —**rous,** *adj.* aus-fäßig.

Lese-majesty, *s.* die Majeftätsbeleidi-gung.

Less, I. *adj. & adv.* fleiner, geringer, weniger; no — a person than, fein Geringerer als. II. *s.* der, die, das Geringere, Wenigere. —**en,** *v.* I. *a.* verfleinern, verringern; fchmälern (*one's reputation, etc.*); ermäßigen (*prices*); mildern (*pain*). II. *n.* abnehmen.

Less—**ee,** *s.* der Mieter, Pächter. —**or,** *s.* der Vermieter, Verpachtende.

Lesson, *s.* die Aufgabe, Leftion; (in-struction) der Unterricht, die (Schul-) Stunde; home —s, häusliche Aufgaben.

Lest, *conj.* damit nicht, daß nicht.

Let, *ir.v.* I. *a.* laffen (permit) zulaffen, geftatten, erlauben; vermieten, ver-pachten (*a house, etc.*); to — on, fich merfen laffen (*fam.*); to — alone, verlaffen, zufrieden laffen; — me see, zeigen Sie mir. II. *n.* fich vermieten (at, for, für).

Lethargy, *s.* die Lethargie, die Schlaf-fucht; (*fig.*) die Stumpfheit.

Letter, *s.* der Buchftabe; (epistle) der Brief; by —, brieflich; to the —, buchftäblich. —**ed,** *adj.* gelehrt. — **box,** *s.* der Brieffaften. —**card,** *s.* die Brieffarte. —**press,** *s.* der Druck, Text. —**weight,** *s.* der Brief-fchwerer.

Lettuce, *s.* der Lattich.

Levee, *s.* das Lever.

Level, I. *s.* die ebene Fläche; (equal height) die gleiche Höhe, Gleichheit; (carpenter's, etc.—) die Seß-, Waffer-, Blei-wage; on a — with, auf gleicher Höhe; to be on the —, offen, ehrlich fein. II. *v.a.* gleich, gerade, eben, wafferrecht machen; einebnen (*roads, etc.*); (point) zielen, richten (at, auf, nach)). III. *v.n.* zielen, gerichtet fein. IV. *adj.* eben, gleich, flach, gerade, wagerecht. —**crossing,** *s.* der Niveauübergang.

Lever, *s.* der Hebel. —**age,** *s.* die Hebekraft.

Leviathan, *s.* der Leviathan.

Levity, *s.* der Leichtfinn.

Levy, I. *v.a.* erheben (*taxes*); ausheben (*troops*). II. *s.* die Erhebung; die Aushebung.

Lewd, *alj.,* —**ly,** *adv.* liederlich, unzüchtig. —**ness,** *s.* die Unzucht, Liederlichkeit.

Lexicon, das Lexikon, Wörterbuch.

Liab—**ility,** *s.* die Verantwortlichkeit. —**le,** *adj.* ausgesetzt, geneigt; —**le** to duty, (excise) zollpflichtig.

Liar, *s.* der Lügner, die Lügnerin.

Libel, I. *s.* die Verleumdung; das Libell (*Law*). II. *v.a.* schmähen, beschimpfen. —**ler,** *s.* der (Schmäh-)schriftschreiber, der Verleumder. —**lous,** *adj.,* —**lously,** *adv.* verleumderisch.

Liber—**al,** I. *adj.,* —**ally,** *adv.* freigebig; weitherzig, aufgeklärt (*as education, views*); liberal (*as politics*). II. *s.* der Liberale, Freisinnige. —**ality,** *s.* die Großmut, Liberalität; die Freigebigkeit.

Liberat—**e,** *v.a.* befreien (from, von). —**ion,** *s.* die Befreiung (von). —**or,** *s.* der Befreier.

Libertine, *s.* der Wüstling.

Libert—**y,** *s.* die Freiheit; I am not at —y to disclose, ich darf nicht enthüllen; to take —ies, sich (*dat.*) Freiheiten erlauben; —y of the Press, die Preßfreiheit.

Librar—**ian,** *s.* der Bibliothekar. —**y,** *s.* die Bibliothek.

Licen—**ce,** *s.* (leave) die Erlaubnis, Genehmigung. —**se,** *v.a.* mit einem Erlaubnisschein versehen.

Licentious, *adj.,* —**ly,** *adv.* liederlich. —**ness,** *s.* die Ausschweifung, Liederlichkeit.

Lichen, *s.* die Flechte.

Lick, I. *v.a.* lecken. II. *s.* das Lecken; to give a good —ing, gehörig durchprügeln (*sl.*).

Lid, *s.* der Deckel; das Augenlid.

¹**Lie,** I. *s.* die Lüge. II. *v.n.* lügen.

²**Lie,** I. *s.* die Lage. II. *ir.v.n.* liegen; to — about, umherliegen; to — near, neben liegen; to — down, sich niederlegen; to — under, unterliegen; to — in wait for, jemandem auflauern.

Lieu, *s.*; in — of, anstatt. —**tenancy,** *s.* die Leutnantsstelle. —**tenant,** *s.* der Leutnant. —**tenant-colonel,** *s.* der Oberstleutnant. —**tenant-general,** *s.* der Generalleutnant.

Life, *s.* das Leben; (way of living) der Lebenswandel; (biography) die Lebensbeschreibung. —**less,** *adj.,* —**lessly,** *adv.* leblos; unbelebt. —**lessness,** *s.* die Leblosigkeit. —**belt,** *s.* der Rettungsgürtel. —**boat,** *s.* das Rettungsboot. —**buoy,** *s.* die Rettungsboje. —**guardsman,** *s.* der Leibgardist. —**insurance,** *s.* die Lebensversicherung. —**like,** *adj.* lebenswahr.—**long,** *adj.* lebenslänglich. —**size,** *s.* die Lebensgröße. —**time,** *s.* die Lebenszeit.

Lift, I. *v.a.* (auf-)heben; (*fig.*) erheben. II. *s.* das (Auf-)Heben; passenger —, der Fahrstuhl; to give a person a lift, jemandem helfen; jemanden mitfahren lassen.

¹**Light,** I. *s.* das Licht (*also fig. &* *Paint.*); to come to —, an den Tag kommen. II. *adj.* licht, hell; (*fig.*) leuchtend. III. *ir.v.a.* anzünden. —**house,** *s.* der Leuchtturm. —**ship,** *s.* das Feuer-, Leucht-schiff.

²**Light,** I. *adj. & adv.* leicht (*also of troops, food, character, etc.*). II. *v.n.*; to — on, (fall) fallen auf, sich niederlassen auf (*as birds*). —**ly,** *adv.* leicht. —**ness,** *s.* die Leichtigkeit. —**fingered,** *adj.* langfingerig, diebisch. —**headed,** *adj.* wirr im Kopf. —**hearted,** *adj.* lustig, fröhlich. —**heartedness,** *s.* der Frohsinn.

¹**Lighten,** *v.n.* blitzen; (brighten) sich aufhellen.

²**Lighten,** *v.a.* leichter machen; löschen (*Naut.*); (*fig.*) erleichtern.

¹**Lighter,** *s.* der Anzünder; das Feuerzeug (*for cigarettes, etc.*).

²**Lighter,** *s.* das Lichterfahrzeug.

Lightning, *s.* der Blitz. —**conductor,** —**rod,** *s.* der Blitzableiter.

Lights, *pl.* die Lungen.

Likable, *adj.* liebenswürdig.

Like, I. *adj. & adv.* gleich, ähnlich; such—, dergleichen; I don't feel — it, ich fühle mich nicht dazu aufgelegt; his —, seinesgleichen. II. *s.* das Gleiche, das Ähnliche. III. *v.a.* leiden, mögen, gern haben. IV. *v.n.* belieben, wollen, Lust haben. **—livelihood,** *s.* die Wahrscheinlichkeit. **—ly,** *adj. & adv.* wahrscheinlich. **—ness,** *s.* die Ähnlichkeit; (portrait) das Bild, Porträt. **—wise,** *adv.* ebenso, gleichfalls, auch.

Liking, *s.* das Gefallen.

Lilac, I. *s.* der Flieder. II. *adj.* lila.

Lily, *s.* die Lilie; — of the valley, das Maiglöckchen.

Limb, *s.* das Glied; der Ast (*of a tree*).

1Limber, *adj.* biegsam.

2Limber, *s.* die Protze (*Artill.*); **— up,** aufprotzen.

1Lime, *s.* der Leim (*for birds, etc.*); der Kalk (*Chem., Min., etc.*). **—kiln,** *s.* der Kalkofen. **—light,** *s.* das Kalklicht. **—stone,** *s.* der Kalkstein.

2Lime, *s.* die Linde; (—tree) der Lindenbaum.

3Lime, *s.* der Limonen-, Zitronenbaum.

Limit, I. *s.* die Grenze, Schranke. II. *v.a.* begrenzen, beschränken. **—ation,** *s.* die Beschränkung, Begrenzung. **—ed,** *adj.* beschränkt (to, auf, *acc.*); **—ed liability company,** Aktiengesellschaft mit beschränkter Haftpflicht (or Haftung). **—less,** *adj.* grenzenlos, schrankenlos.

1Limp, I. *v.n.* hinken (*also fig.*). II. *s.* das Hinken. **—ing,** *adj.,* **—ingly,** *adv.* hinkend.

2Limp, *adj.* weich, welk, schlaff.

Limpet, *s.* die Napf-muschel, -schnecke.

Limpid, *adj.* klar, hell.

1Line, *v.a.* füttern (*of clothes*); spicken (*one's purse*); a well—d purse, eine gut gespickte Börse.

2Line, I. *s.* die Linie; (*fig.*) die Richtschnur, Regel; die Zeile (*Print.*); (lineage) die Geschlechtslinie, das Geschlecht; the —, der Äquator (*Geog.*); das Fußvolk (*Mil.*); der Schienenweg, das Geleise (*Railw.*); that is not in my —, das schlägt nicht in mein Fach; hard —s, hartes Los. II. *v.a.* in eine Linie formieren.

Lineage, *s.* das Geschlecht.

Lineament, *s.* der (Gesichts-)Zug.

Linen, I. *s.* die Leinwand, das Leinen. II. *adj.* leinen, aus Leinwand. **—draper,** *s.* der Leinwandhändler.

Liner, *s.* das Passagierboot.

1Ling, *s.* der Leng (*Ichth.*).

2Ling, *s.* die gemeine Besenheide, das Heidekraut.

Linger, *v.n.* weilen, harren. **—ing,** *adj.,* **—ingly,** *adv.* langwierig (as *diseases*); (slow) langsam.

Lingo, *s.* das Rauderwelsch.

Lingu—al, *adj.* Zungen-. **—ist,** *s.* der Sprachkenner. **—istic,** *adj.* sprachwissenschaftlich.

Liniment, *s.* die Einreibung, die Salbe.

Lining, *s.* das Futter, die Fütterung (*of dresses, etc.*).

Link, I. *s.* das Gelenk, Glied (*of a chain*). II. *v.a.* verketten, verbinden.

Links, *s.* der Golfspielplatz.

Linnet, *s.* der Hänfling, Flachsfink.

Linoleum, *s.* das Linoleum.

Linseed, *s.* der Leinsamen.

Lint, *s.* die Scharpie.

Lintel, *s.* die Oberschwelle (*Arch.*).

Lion, *s.* der Löwe. **—ess,** *s.* die Löwin. **—s' den,** *s.* die Löwengrube.

Lip, *s.* die Lippe; der Rand (*of a vessel*).

Liquefy, *v.* I. *a.* schmelzen, flüssig machen. II. *n.* flüssig werden.

Liquid, I. *adj.* flüssig, fließend. II. *s.* die Flüssigkeit. **—ate,** *v.a.* liquidieren, saldieren (*debts*). **—ation,** *s.* die Abwickelung, Liquidation. **—ator,** *s.* der Liquidator.

Liquor, *s.* die Flüssigkeit; (spirits) das geistige Getränk.

Liquorice, *s.* die Lakritze.

Lisp, I. *v.a. & n.* lispeln. II. *s.* das Lispeln. **—ing,** *adj.,* **—ingly,** *adv.* lispelnd.

1List, *s.* die Liste.

2List, **—en,** *v.n.* horchen, lauschen (to, auf (*acc.*)). **—ener,** *s.* der Horcher, Lauscher; der Teilnehmer (*Radio*).

3List, *s.* die Schlagseite (*Naut.*).

Listless, *adj.,* **--ly,** *adv.* träge, apathisch. **—ness,** *s.* die Achtlosigkeit.

Lists, *pl.* die Schranken.

Litany, *s.* die Litanei.

Litera—l, *adj.,* **—lly,** *adv.* buchstäblich. **—lness,** *s.* die Wörtlichkeit, Buchstäblichkeit. **—ry,** *adj.* schriftstellerisch, literarisch. **—te,** *adj.* gelehrt. **—ti,** *pl.* Literaten, Gelehrte. **—ture,** *s.* die Literatur.

Lithe, *adj.* biegsam, gelenkig.

Lithograph, I. *s.* der Stein-druck.

=abbruch. II. *v.a.* & *n.* lithograph=
ieren. —y, *s.* die Steindruckerkunst,
die Lithographie.
Litig—ant, I. *adj.* streitend. II. *s.* der
Prozessierende. **—ate,** *v.n.* pro=
zessieren. **—ation,** *s.* der Rechts=
streit, Prozeß. **—ious,** *adj.*, **—iously,**
adv. prozeßsüchtig.
Litre, *s.* das (*or* der) Liter.
¹Litter, I. *s.* die Sänfte; (straw) die
Streu; (shreds) die Papierschnitzel (*pl.*).
II. *v.a.* mit Streu versehen (*beasts*); to
— a room, ein Zimmer in Unordnung
bringen.
²Litter, *s.* die Brut, Tracht.
Little, I. *adj.* klein, gering; kurz (*of
time, sleep, etc.*). II. *adv.* wenig.
III. *s.* das Wenige, die Kleinigkeit;
— by —, nach und nach. **—ness,**
s. die Kleinheit.
Liturg—ic(al), *adj.* liturgisch. **—y,** *s.*
die Liturgie.
¹Live, I. *v.n.* leben; (dwell) wohnen,
sich aufhalten; he won't — to see it,
er wird das nicht mehr erleben. II
v.a. leben, durchleben.
²Live, *adj.* lebendig; (burning) glü=
hend. **—d,** *adj.*; short—=d, von
kurzer Dauer; long—=d, langlebig.
Livelihood, *s.* der Unterhalt, das
Auskommen.
Liveliness, *s.* die Lebhaftigkeit, Munter=
keit.
Livelong, *adj.* dauernd; ganz, lebens=
länglich.
Lively, *adj.* lebhaft, munter, heiter.
Liver, *s.* die Leber; der Lebende (*living
person*); a fast —, ein Lebemann.
Livery, *s.* die Livree. **—stable,** *s.*
der Mietstall.
Livid, *adj.* bleifarbig, fahl. **—ness,** *s.*
die Totenblässe.
Living, I. *adj.* lebendig, lebend. II. *s.*
das Leben; (livelihood) der Unterhalt.
III. *attrib.*; — room, das Wohn=
zimmer.
Lizard, *s.* die Eidechse.
Lo, *int.* siehe! sieh! schau!
Loach, *s.* die Schmerle.
Load, I. *s.* die Last, Ladung, Bürde.
II. *v.a.* laden (*also guns*), beladen,
belasten. **—er,** *s.* der Lader, Ver=
lader. **—line,** *s.* die Ladewasserlinie.
¹Loaf, *s.* der Laib (Brot). **—sugar,**
s. der Zuckerhut.
²Loaf, *v.n.* umherbummeln. **—er,** *s.*
der Müßiggänger, Taugenichts.

Loam, *s.* der Lehm.
Loan, *s.* die Anleihe, das Darlehen;
(lending) das Leihen.
Loath, *adj.* abgeneigt, widerwillig.
—e, *v.a.* mit Ekel ansehen. **—ing,** *s.*
der Ekel, Abscheu. **—ly, —some,**
adj. gehässig, ekelhaft. **—someness,**
s. der Widerwille.
Lobby, *s.* die Vorhalle; das Foyer
(*Theat.*).
Lobe, *s.* der Lappen; — of the ear, das
Ohrläppchen.
Lobelia, *s.* die Lobelie.
Lobster, *s.* der Hummer.
Loca—l, *adj.*, **—lly,** *adv.* örtlich, Orts=;
the —l school, die hiesige Schule.
—lity, *s.* der Ort. **—tion,** *s.* die
Lage, Stellung.
Loch, *s.* der See; die Bucht (*Scotch*).
¹Lock, I. *s.* das Schloß; die Schleuse
(*in a canal*). II. *v.a.* (zu=)schließen
(*a door, etc.*); verschließen (*a secret,
etc.*); hemmen (*a wheel*). III. *v.n.*
(sich) schließen; in einander eingreifen
(*as wheels*). **—out,** *s.* die Aus=
sperrung. **—smith,** *s.* der Schlosser.
—stitch, *s.* der Sperrstich.
²Lock, *s.* die Locke (*of hair*).
Locker, *s.* der Back (Naut.).
Locket, *s.* das Medaillon.
Lockjaw, *s.* der Kinnbackenkrampf.
Locomoti—on, *s.* die Ortsveränd=
erung; aerial —on, die Luftschiffahrt.
—ve, I. *adj.* beweglich. II. *s.* die
Lokomotive.
Locust, *s.* die Heuschrecke.
Locution, *s.* das Sprechen; der
Ausdruck.
Lode, *s.* die Ader (*Min.*); der Minen=
gang.
Lodestar, *s.* der Leitstern; (polar star)
der Polarstern. **—stone,** *s.* der
Magnet.
Lodg—e, I. *v.a.* (place) niederlegen;
(harbour) aufnehmen; einquartieren
(*troops*); einzahlen (*money*). II. *v.n.*
wohnen, logieren. III. *s.* das Häus=
chen, Forst=, Park=, Pförtner=Haus.
—e-keeper, *s.* der Pförtner. **—er,**
s. der Mieter. **—ings,** *pl.* die (Miets=)
Wohnung. **—ing-house,** *s.* das
Mietshaus.
Loft, *s.* der Dachboden. **—iness,** *s.*
(height) die Höhe; (pride) der Hoch=
mut; (grandeur) die Erhabenheit.
—y, *adj.* hoch; hochmütig; erhaben.
Log, *s.* der (Holz=)Klotz; das Log, die

Logge (*Naut.*). **—book,** *s.* das
Logbuch, Schiffsjournal. **—cabin,**
—hut, *s.* das Blockhaus.
Logarithm, *s.* der Logarithmus.
Loggerhead, *s.* der Dummkopf; to be
at —s, sich in den Haaren liegen.
Logic, *s.* die Logik. **—al,** *adj.,* **—ally,**
adv. logisch, folgerichtig. **—ian,** *s.*
der Logiker.
Loin, *s.* die Lende; das Lendenstück
(*of meat*).
Loiter, *v.n.* bummeln, tändeln. **—er,**
s. der Müßiggänger, Faulenzer.
Loll, *v.n.* sich träge *or* bequem lehnen.
Lollipop, *s.* das Zuckerwerk.
Lonel—iness, *s.* die Einsamkeit. **—y,**
adj. einsam.
¹**Long,** I. *adj.* lang; in the — run,
am Ende; — ago, vor langer Zeit;
ere —, in Kurzem. II. *adv.* lang;
lange (*of time*). **—er,** *adj. compar.*
länger; mehr. **—hand,** *s.* die Kur-
rentschrift. **—sighted,** *adj.* weitsichtig, fernsichtig.
²**Long,** *v.n.* verlangen, sich sehnen (for,
after, nach). **—ing,** I. *adj.,* **—ingly,**
adv. sehnsüchtig, sehnsuchtsvoll. II.
s. die Sehnsucht.
Longitude, *s.* die Länge; degree of
—, der Längengrad.
Look, I. *v.n.* schauen, blicken, sehen
(at, on, auf (*acc.*), nach (*dat.*)); (appear) scheinen; to — much better,
viel besser aussehen, ein viel besseres
Aussehn haben; to — forward to,
erwarten. II. *v.a.;* to — someone
in the face, einem ins Gesicht sehen.
III. *s.* der Blick; das Ansehen, Aussehen. **—er,** *s.* der Schauer, Beschauer. **—er-on,** *s.* der Zuschauer.
—ing-glass, *s.* der Spiegel. **—out,**
s. der Ausguck, die Wache.
¹**Loom,** *s.* der Webstuhl, Stuhl.
²**Loom,** *v.n.* sichtbar werden.
Loon, *s.* großer Eistaucher (*Orn.*).
Loop, I. *s.* die Schlinge, Schleife. II.
v.a. schlingen. III. *v.n.* sich winden;
to — the —, (*Aviat.*) ein Looping
machen, sich in der Luft umschlagen.
—hole, *s.* die Schießscharte (*Fort.*);
(*fig.*) die Ausflucht. **—line,** *s.* die
Verbindungsbahn (*Railw.*).
Loose, I. *v.a.* (auf-)lösen, aufbinden;
(undo) auftun, losbinden; (set free)
loslassen, befreien; to — one's hold
on a thing, etwas loslassen. II. *adj.,*
—ly, *adv.* los; locker, lose. **—n,** *v.*

I. *a.* losmachen, losbinden (*a string,*
etc.). II. *n.* losgehen, sich lösen.
Loot, I. *v.n.* plündern. II. *v.a.* erbeuten. III. *s.* die Kriegsbeute,
Beute.
Lop, *v.a.* beschneiden, behauen. **—**
eared, *adj.* mit Hängeohren. **—sided,**
adj. schief; (*fig.*) einseitig.
Loquaci—ous, *adj.* geschwätzig, schwatzhaft. **—ty,** *s.* die Geschwätzigkeit.
Lord, I. *s.* der Herr, Gebieter; (noble)
der Edelmann, Pair; the —'s Prayer,
das Vaterunser; the —'s Supper, das
letzte Abendmahl. II. *v.a.;* to — it,
den großen Herrn spielen. **—liness,**
s. die Würde; (pride) der Hochmut.
—ly, *adj.* edel, großmütig; (*also*
adv.) (proud) vornehm; (haughty)
herrisch, gebieterisch.
Lore, *s.* die Wissenschaft.
Lorgnette, *s.* die Lorgnette.
Lorry, *s.* die Lore (*Railw.*).
Lose, *ir.v.* I. *a.* verlieren. II. *n.*
verlieren; nachgehen (*as a watch*).
—r, *s.* der Verlierende, Verlierer.
Loss, *s.* der Verlust; at a —, (*fig.*) in
Verlegenheit.
Lot, *s.* das Los; (share) der Teil,
Anteil; das Stück (*of land*); to draw
—s, losen, Lose ziehen.
Lotion, *s.* das Waschmittel.
Lottery, *s.* die Lotterie. **—ticket,** *s.*
das Lotterielos.
Lotus, *s.* die Lotos, Lotus.
Loud, *adj.,* **—ly,** *adv.* laut; (noisy)
lärmend. **—ness,** *s.* der Lärm, das
laute Geräusch. **—speaker,** *s.* der
Lautsprecher (*Radio*).
Lounge, I. *v.n.* faulenzen. II. *s.*
die Chaiselongue. **—r,** *s.* der Faul-
enzer. **—suit,** *s.* der Straßenanzug.
Lour, *v.n.* finster aussehen; (frown) die
Stirne runzeln. **—ing,** *adj.,* **—**
ingly, *adv.* trübe, düster, finster.
Louse, *s.* die Laus; *pl.* **lice,** die
Läuse.
Lout, *s.* der Tölpel. **—ish,** *adj.,* **—**
ishly, *adv.* tölpisch.
Lovable, *adj.* liebenswürdig, liebens-
wert. **—ness,** *s.* die Liebenswür-
digkeit.
Love, I. *v.a.* lieben. II. *v.n.* lieben.
III. *s.* die Liebe; for the — of God,
um Gottes willen; to play for —,
nichts spielen; neither for — nor
money, weder für Geld noch gute
Worte. **—less,** *adj.* lieblos. **—li-**

ness, *s.* die Lieblichkeit, der Reiz.
—ly, *adj.* lieblich, hold, reizend.
—r, *s.* der Liebende, Verliebte; der Liebhaber (*of flowers, etc.*). **—affair,** *s.* die Liebschaft, der Liebeshandel.
—lorn, *adj.* liebeverlassen. **—making,** *s.* das Hofmachen. **—match,** *s.* die Heirat aus Liebe. **—potion,** *s.* der Liebestrank. **—sick,** *adj.* liebeskrank.

Loving, I. *adj.,* **—ly,** *adv.* liebend; (affectionate) liebevoll. II. *s.* das Lieben.

¹**Low,** *adj. & adv.* niedrig; (deep) tief, leise (*as a voice*); kärglich (*as a diet*); schwach (*as a pulse*); niedergeschlagen, gedrückt (*as the spirits*); wohlfeil (*in price*); (mean) gemein, niederträchtig; — spirits, die Niedergeschlagenheit; — water, die niedrigste Ebbe. **—land,** *s.* die Niederung.

²**Low,** I. *v.n.* brüllen, muhen. II. *s.* das Gebrüll, Gemuh, Muhen.

Lower, I. *adj.* (*comp. of* Low); the — House, das Unterhaus; the — classes, die untern Stände. II. *v.a.* nieder-, herab-, hinab-lassen; niederschlagen (*the eyes*); to — one's voice, leise(r) sprechen; streichen (*flags, etc.*). **—ing,** *adj.* niederschlagend; drückend. **—most,** I. *adj.* niedrigst. II. *adv.* am niedrigsten.

Lowest, *adj.* (*sup. of* Low); the — bidder, der Mindestbietende.

Low—liness, *s.* die Demut; (state) die Niedrigkeit. **—necked,** *adj.*; —necked dress, tief ausgeschnittenes Kleid. **—spirited,** *adj.* niedergeschlagen. **—tension,** *s.* die Niederspannung (*Radio*).

Lowness, *s.* die Niedrigkeit.

Loyal, *adj.,* **—ly,** *adv.* treu, getreu, pflichttreu. **—ist,** *s.* der Treugesinnte. **—ty,** *s.* die Treue.

Lozenge, *s.* die Raute (*Geom., Her.*); das Zuckerplätzchen; cough —, die Hustenpastille.

Lubber, *s.* der Lümmel.

Lubrica—nt, *s.* das Schmiermittel. **—te,** *v.a.* schmieren (*Mach.*). **—tion,** *s.* das Einschmieren.

Lucid, *adj.,* **—ly,** *adv.* klar; — intervals, lichte Momente. **—ity, —ness,** *s.* die Klarheit.

Luck, *s.* das Glück, der Glücksfall; good —, das Glück; ill —, das Unglück; a run of —, immerwährendes Glück.

—ily, *adv.* glücklicherweise. **—less,** *adj.* unglücklich; a —less beggar, ein armer Teufel. **—y,** *adj.* glücklich; günstig; he is a —y fellow, er ist ein Glückspilz.

Lucr—ative, *adj.,* **—atively,** *adv.* einträglich, gewinnbringend. **—e,** *s.* der Gewinn.

Ludicrous, *adj.,* **—ly,** *adv.* lächerlich. **—ness,** *s.* das Lächerliche.

Luff, *s.* I. das (der) Luv, die Luvseite (*Naut.*). II. *v.n.* luven.

Lug, I. *v.a.* (— out, heraus-, — in, herein-) schleppen, -zerren. II. *s.* das Ohr.

Luggage, *s.* das Gepäck. **—label,** *s.* der Gepäckzettel. **—van,** *s.* der Gepäckwagen.

Lugger, *s.* der Lugger, Logger (*Naut.*).

Lug-sail, *s.* das Luggersegel.

Lugubrious, *adj.* kläglich, weinerlich.

Lukewarm, *adj.* lau, lauwarm; (*fig.*) lau, gleichgültig.

Lull, I. *v.a.* einlullen, einsingen (*to sleep*); (calm) beruhigen. II. *s.* die Windstille. **—aby,** *s.* das Wiegenlied.

Lumba—go, *s.* der Hexenschuß. **—r,** *adj.* zu den Lenden gehörig.

Lumber, I. *s.* der Polterkram; (timber) das Bauholz, Stabholz. II. *v.a.* mit Gerumpel 2c. vollpacken. III. *v.n.* poltern. **—ing,** *adj.* schwerfällig, schleppend. **—room,** *s.* die Rumpelkammer.

Lumin—ary, *s.* das Lichtkörper. **—ous,** *adj.,* **—ously,** *adv.* leuchtend.

Lump, *s.* der Klumpen; in the —, in Bausch und Bogen. **—y,** *adj.* klumpig, klümperig. **—sugar,** *s.* der Würfelzucker.

Luna—cy, *s.* der Wahnsinn. **—tic,** I. *adj.* wahnsinnig, verrückt. II. *s.* der Wahnsinnige; —tic asylum, das Irrenhaus.

Lunch, I. *s.* das Mittagessen. II. *v.n.* zu Mittag essen.

Lung, *s.* die Lunge.

Lunge, I. *s.* der plötzliche Stoß. II. *v.n.* stoßen.

Lupine, *s.* die Lupine (*Bot.*).

¹**Lurch,** *s.*; to leave in the —, im Stiche lassen.

²**Lurch,** I. *s.* das Rollen (*of a ship*). II. *v.n.* schlingern; taumeln.

Lurcher, *s.* der Spürhund.

Lure, I. *s.* der Köder, die Lockspeise. II. *v.a.* ködern, anlocken.

Lurid, *adj.* schwarzgelb; düster; — sky, finsterer Himmel.

Lurk, *v.n.* (auf einen) lauern. **—ing-place,** *s.* das Versteck.

Luscious, *adj.,* **—ly,** *adv.* saftig.

Lust, I. *s.* die Brunst, Wollust. **II.** *v.n.* (ge)lüsten (after, nach), begehren. **—ful,** *adj.* wollüstig. **—fulness,** *s.* die Wollust, Geilheit.

Lust—ily, *adv.* munter, rüstig. **—iness,** *s.* die Rüstigkeit, Stärke. **—y,** *adj.* rüstig, stämmig.

Lustre, *s.* der Glanz, Schimmer (of silk, etc.); der Kronleuchter. **—less,** *adj.* glanzlos.

Lut—(an)ist, *s.* der Lautenspieler. **—e,** *s.* die Laute.

Luxur—iance, *s.* die Üppigkeit. **—iant,** *adj.,* **—iantly,** *adv.* üppig. **—ious,** *adj.,* **—iously,** *adv.* schwelgerisch. **—iousness,** **—y,** *s.* der Luxus, die Üppigkeit; **—ies,** Luxusartikel.

Lye, *s.* die Lauge.

¹**Lying,** *s.* das Lügen.

²**Lying,** *s.* das Liegen. **—in hospital,** *s.* die Entbindungsanstalt.

Lymph, *s.* die Lymphe; der Impfstoff. **—atic,** *adj.* lymphatisch.

Lynch, *v.a.* lynchen. **—law,** *s.* das Lynchgesetz, die Volksjustiz.

Lynx, *s.* der Luchs.

Lyr—e, *s.* die Leier. **—ic, I.** *adj.* lyrisch. **II.** *s.* lyrisches Gedicht.

M

M, m, *s.* das M, m.

Macaroni, *s.* die Nudel.

Macaroon, *s.* die Makrone.

Macaw, *s.* der Makao.

¹**Mace,** *s.* der Amtsstab.

²**Mace,** *s.* die Muskatblüte.

Machination, *s.* die Anzettelung; **—s,** die Ränke.

Machin—e, *s.* die Maschine. **—ery,** *s.* die Maschinerie. **—ist,** *s.* der Maschinist.

Mackerel, *s.* die Makrele.

Mackintosh, *s.* der Gummimantel.

Mad, *adj.,* **—ly,** *adv.* verrückt, wahnsinnig, toll; that noise is driving me —, der Lärm macht mich verrückt; to go —, verrückt werden; she is — on dancing, sie ist aufs Tanzen erpicht. **—den,** *v.a.* toll *or* verrückt machen. **—dening,** *adj.* wütend. **—ness,** *s.*

der Wahnsinn, die Tollheit. **—cap,** *s.* der Tollkopf. **—house,** *s.* das Tollhaus, Irrenhaus. **—man,** *s.* der Verrückte, Wahnsinnige.

Madam, *s.* gnädige Frau! gnädiges Fräulein!

Madder, *s.* der Krapp.

Magazine, *s.* die Niederlage; powder —, das Pulvermagazin; literary —, die Zeitschrift.

Magenta, *s.* das Magenta-Rot.

Maggot, *s.* die Made.

Mag—ic, I. *s.* die Magie, Zauberei. **II.** *adj.,* **—ical,** *adj.,* **—ically,** *adv.* magisch, zauberhaft. **—ician,** **—us,** *s.* der Zauberer.

Magistra—cy, *s.* die Magistratur. **—te,** *s.* richterlicher Beamter.

Magnanim—ity, *s.* die Großmut. **—ous,** *adj.,* **—ously,** *adv.* groß-, hochherzig.

Magnate, *s.* der Magnat.

Magnesi—a, *s.* die Magnesia. **—um,** *s.* das Magnesium.

Magnet, *s.* der Magnet. **—ic,** *adj.,* **—ically,** *adv.* magnetisch. **—ism,** *s.* der Magnetismus. **—ize,** *v.a.* magnetisieren. **—o-electricity,** *s.* der Elektromagnetismus.

Magnif—icence, *s.* die Herrlichkeit. **—icent,** *adj.,* **—icently,** *adv.* herrlich, prächtig.

Magnify, *v.a.* vergrößern; **—ing glass,** das Vergrößerungsglas.

Magnitude, *s.* die Größe, die Wichtigkeit.

Magnolia, *s.* die Magnolie.

Magpie, *s.* die Elster.

Mahogany, *s.* der Mahagoni.

Maid, *s.* das Mädchen; old —, alte Jungfer. **—en, I.** *s.,* see Maid. **II.** *adj.* jungfräulich, mädchenhaft. **—servant,** *s.* das Dienstmädchen, das Mädchen. **—en-hair,** *s.* das Frauenhaar.

¹**Mail,** *s.* der Panzer; coat of —, das Panzerhemd, der Harnisch. **—ed,** *adj.* gepanzert.

²**Mail, I.** *s.* der Briefsack; die Briefpost. **II.** *v.a.* mit der Post verschicken. **—bag,** *s.* der Briefbeutel. **—boat,** *s.* das Paketboot. **—train,** *s.* der Postzug.

Maim, *v.a.* verstümmeln, lähmen. **—ed,** *adj.* verstümmelt.

Main, I. *adj.* hauptsächlich, wichtigst, größt, Haupt-; by — force, mit

voller Kraft; with might and —,
mit voller Macht. II. *s.* der Hauptteil;
(ocean) das Meer; (pipe) das Haupt-
rohr. **—ly,** *adj.* hauptsächlich. —
land, *s.* das Festland. **—mast,** *s.*
der Großmast. **—spring,** *s.* die
Hauptfeder. **—stay,** *s.* das Großstag
(*fig.*) die Hauptstütze.

Maint—ain, *v.a.* erhalten; unterhalten
(*a conversation*); (support) ernähren,
unterhalten; behaupten (*one's
ground*). **—enance,** *s.* die Erhaltung,
Unterhaltung; (sustenance) der Unterhalt; (support) die Aufrecht(er)-
haltung; die Behauptung.

Maize, *s.* der Mais.

Majest—ic, *adj.,* **—ically,** *adv.* ma-
jestätisch, würdevoll. **—y,** *s.* die
Majestät.

Majolica, *s.* die Majolika.

Major, I. *adj.* größer; — key, die
Dur-Tonart (*Mus.*); — part, der
größte Teil. II. *s.* der Major (*Mil.*);
sergeant —, der Oberfeldwebel. **—
ity,** *s.* die Mehrheit, Mehrzahl; die
Mündigkeit (*Law*); die Majorsstelle
(*Mil.*). **—domo,** *s.* der Haushof-
meister. **—general,** *s.* der General-
major.

Make, I. *ir.v.a.* machen; führen (*a
complaint*); schließen (*peace*); halten
(*a speech*); to — a port, einen Hafen
anlaufen; II. *ir.v.n.* the tide —s,
die Flut tritt ein; to — off, sich fort-
machen; to — sure, sich vergewissern;
to — up one's mind, einen Entschluß
fassen (*etc.*). **—r,** *s.* der Macher; (creator)
der Schöpfer; der Fabrikant (*C.L.*).
—believe, I. *s.* die Verstellung; der
Vorwand. II. *adj.* verstellt. **—shift,**
I. *s.* der Notbehelf. II. *adj.* als
Notbehelf dienend. **—up,** *s.* das
Schminken; der Aufputz. **—weight,**
s. die Zulage, Zugabe.

Maladroit, *adj.* ungeschickt, linkisch.

Malady, *s.* die Krankheit.

Malaria, *s.* das Sumpffieber.

Malcontent, *s.* der Mißvergnügte.

Male, I. *s.* der Mann; das Männchen (*of birds, etc.*). II. *adj.* männlich.

Malediction, *s.* die Verwünschung.

Malefactor, *s.* der Übeltäter.

Malevolent, *adj.,* **—ly,** *adv.* böswillig,
feindselig.

Malic—e, *s.* die Bosheit, Arglist. —

ious, *adj.,* **—iously,** *adv.* boshaft,
schadenfroh, heimtückisch.

Malign, I. *adj.* schädlich. II. *v.a.*
verleumden, verlästern.

Malinger, *v.n.* Krankheit heucheln.

Mallard, *s.* der wilde Enterich.

Mallet, *s.* der Schlägel.

Mallow, *s.* die Malve.

Malmsey, *s.* der Malvasier(wein).

Malt, *s.* das Malz. **—er, —ster,** *s.*
der Mälzer, Malzer.

Maltreat, *v.a.* mißhandeln. **—ment,**
s. die Mißhandlung.

Mammal, *s.* das Säugetier. **—ian,**
adj. Säugetier-.

Mammoth, I. *s.* das Mammut. II.
adj. Riesen-.

Man, I. *s.* (*pl.* Men) der Mann; (human creature) der Mensch; (—kind)
die Menschen, das Menschengeschlecht;
der Stein (*Draughts*); die Figur
(*Chess*); to a —, bis auf den letzten
Mann. II. *v.a.* bemannen, **—ful,**
adj., **—fully,** *adv.* mannhaft, tapfer.
—hood, *s.* die Mannheit. **—ikin,**
s. das Männchen, der Zwerg. **—kind,**
s. das Menschengeschlecht. **—liness,**
s. die Männlichkeit, Mannhaftigkeit.
—ly, *adj. & adv.* männlich, mannhaft.
—eater, *s.* der Menschenfresser (*tiger,*
etc.). **—of-war,** *s.* das Kriegsschiff.

Manacle, *s.* die Handschelle.

Manage, *v.* I. *a.* handhaben (*a sword,*
etc.); führen, leiten, verwalten (*a
business, etc.*). II. *n.* die Geschäfte
führen; (contrive) es einrichten,
zustande bringen; he just —d it,
es gelang ihm noch eben. **—able,** *adj.*
lenksam. **—ment,** *s.* die Handhabung,
Führung, Leitung, Verwaltung. **—r,**
s. der Verwalter, Leiter, Vorsteher,
Direktor. **—ress,** *s.* die Vorsteherin.

Mandate, *s.* der Erlaß, das Mandat.

Mandolin, *s.* die Mandoline.

Mandrill, *s.* der Mandrill (*Zool.*).

Mane, *s.* die Mähne. **—d,** *adj.* ge-
mähnt.

Mang—e, *s.* die Räude. **—y,** *adj.*
räudig.

Mangel-wurzel, *s.* die Mangoldwurzel.

Manger, *s.* die Krippe.

¹Mangle, I. *s.* die Rolle, der Kalander. II. *v.a.* mangen, rollen (*clothes*).

²Mangle, *v.a.* zerstücken, verstümmeln.

Mango, *s.* der Mangobaum; die Man-
gobeere.

Mangrove, *s.* der Mangelbaum.

Mania, *s.* die Manie, Sucht (*for gambling, etc.*). **—c,** I. *s.* der Wahnsinnige, Tolle. II. *adj.,* **—cal,** *adj.* wahnsinnig, wahnwitzig, verrückt, toll.

Manicure, *s.* die Hand= und Nägelpflege.

Manifest, I. *adj.,* **—ly,** *adv.* offenbar. II. *v.a.* offenbaren. III. *s.*; ship's —, das Ladungsmanifest. **—ation,** *s.* die Offenbarung.

Manifesto, *s.* die öffentliche Kundmachung *or* Kundgebung, das Manifest.

Manifold, *adj.* mannigfaltig, mannigfach.

Manipulat—e, *v.a.* behandeln. **—ion,** *s.* die Behandlung.

Manna, *s.* das Manna.

Mannequin, *s.* die Gliederpuppe; die Vorführdame.

Manner, *s.* die Art, Weise; (custom) die Gewohnheit; in a —, gewissermaßen; no — of doubt, gar kein Zweifel. **—ed,** *adj.* (*in comp.* =) gesittet. **—ism,** *s.* die Maniertheit. **—liness,** *s.* die Manierlichkeit. **—ly,** *adj.* höflich, artig. **—s,** *pl.* die Manieren, Sitten.

Manœuvre, I. *s.* das Manöver (*Mil.*). II. *v.n.* manövrieren. III. *v.a.* manövrieren lassen.

Manometer, *s.* der Druckmesser.

Manor, *s.* das Rittergut. **—house,** *s.* der Herrensitz.

Mansion, *s.* das Herrenhaus.

Manslaughter, *s.* der Totschlag.

Mantel, *s.* der Kaminmantel. **—piece,** *s.* der Kaminsims.

Mantilla, *s.* die Mantille.

Mantle, *s.* der Mantel; der Glühstrumpf (*in incandescent gaslight*).

Manual, I. *adj.* mit der Hand verrichtet, Hand=. II. *s.* das Handbuch.

Manufact—ory, *s.* die Fabrik. **—ure,** I. *s.* die Fabrikation; (—ured stuff) das Fabrikat; costs of —ure, die Herstellungskosten. II. *v.a.* fabrizieren. **—urer,** *s.* der Fabrikant. **—uring,** *adj.* Fabrik=.

Manure, I. *v.a.* düngen. II. *s.* der Dünger.

Manuscript, I. *s.* die Handschrift. II. *adj.* handschriftlich.

Many, *adj.* viel(e); (— a) mancher, manche, manches; — a time, oft. **—-sided,** *adj.* vielseitig.

Map, I. *s.* die Karte, Landkarte. II.

v.a. eintragen; to — out, aufzeichnen, genau beschreiben.

Maple, *s.* der Ahorn.

Mar, *v.a.* zerstören.

Maraud, *v.n.* marodieren plündern. **—er,** *s.* der Marodeur, Plünderer.

Marble, I. *s.* der Marmor; die Murmel (*toy*). II. *adj.* marmorn.

Marbling, *s.* das Marmorieren.

¹March, I. *s.* der Marsch (*also Mus.*); to steal a — on a person, einem zuvorkommen. II. *v.n.* marschieren, ziehen (*Mil.*); to be —ed off, abgeführt werden. III. *v.a.* marschieren lassen.

²March, *s.* der März.

Marchioness, *s.* die Marquise.

Marchpane, *s.* der Marzipan.

Marconigram, *s.* die drahtlose Depesche, der Funkspruch.

Mare, *s.* die Stute.

Margarine, *s.* die Margarine.

Margin, *s.* der Rand; der Spielraum.

Margrave, *s.* der Markgraf.

Marigold, *s.* die Dotterblume.

Mari—ne, I. *adj.* zur See gehörig; See=. II. *s.* der Seesoldat. **—ner,** *s.* der Seemann, Matrose.

Marionette, *s.* die Marionette, die Drahtpuppe.

Marital, *adj.* ehelich.

Maritime, *adj.* zur See gehörig.

Marjoram, *s.* der Majoran, Meiran.

¹Mark, *s.* die Mark (*German coin of account*).

²Mark, I. *s.* die Marke, das (Renn=) Zeichen, Merkmal; (trade-—) die Fabrik=, Schutz=marke; up to the —, einer Sache gewachsen; to hit the —, das Ziel treffen. II. *v.a.* (be=)zeichnen; (observe) sich (*dat.*) merken; andeuten (*the time, etc.*). III. *v.n.* Acht geben auf (*acc.*); —! Achtung! (*mil.*) **—ed,** *adj.,* **—edly,** *adv.* auffallend. **—er,** *s.* der Marqueur (*Bill.*); (book-—) das (Buch=)Zeichen.

Market, I. *s.* der Markt; der Marktplatz; der Absatz; (trade) der Handelsverkehr. II. *v.n.* einkaufen. **—able,** *adj.* verkäuflich, gangbar. **—price,** *s.* der Marktpreis.

Marking, *s.* die Markierung. **—ink,** *s.* die Zeichentinte.

Marksman, *s.* der Schütze.

Marl, *s.* der Mergel.

Marline, *s.* die Marlleine, Marling.

Marmalade, *s.* die Marmelade, das Apfelsinenmus.

Marmot, *s.* das Murmeltier.
Maroon, *adj.* kastanienbraun.
Marquee, *s.* das Zelt.
Marri—age, *s.* die Heirat, Ehe; (wedding) die Hochzeit. **—ageable,** *adj.* heiratsfähig. **—ed,** *adj.* ehelich; (wedded) verheiratet; —ed state, der Ehestand. **—age-tie,** *s.* das Eheband. **—age-vow,** *s.* das Ehegelöbnis.
Marrow, *s.* das Mark; vegetable —, der eiförmige Kürbis.
Marry, *v.* I. *a.* heiraten; verheiraten, vermählen (*a daughter, etc.*); trauen (*as the clergyman*). II. *n.* heiraten, sich verheiraten.
Marsh, *s.* der Morast, Sumpf. **—y,** *adj.* sumpfig. **—mallow,** *s.* die Sammetpappel.
Marshal, *s.* der Marschall. II. *v.a.* ordnen, führen.
Mart, *s.* der Markt.
Marten, *s.* der Marder.
Martial, *adj.,* **—ly,** *adv.* kriegerisch, Kriegs-; — law, das Kriegsrecht.
Martin, *s.* die Mauerschwalbe.
Martyr, I. *s.* der Märtyrer. II. *v.a.* zum Märtyrer machen. **—dom,** *s.* das Märtyrertum, der Märtyrertod.
Marvel, I. *s.* das Wunder. II. *v.n.* sich wundern (at a thing, über eine S.). **—lous,** *adj.,* **—lously,** *adv.* wunderbar.
Masculine, I. *adj.* männlich. II. *s.* das Maskulinum.
Mash, I. *s.* das Gemisch. II. *v.a.* mischen; —ed potatoes, der Kartoffelbrei.
Mask, I. *s.* die Maske, Larve. II. *v.a.* maskieren, vermummen. III. *v.n.* sich maskieren; (*fig.*) sich verstellen.
Mason, *s.* der Maurer, Steinmetz. **—ic,** *adj.* freimaurerisch. **—ry,** *s.* die Maurerei; das Mauerwerk.
Masquerade, I. *s.* der Maskenball. II. *v.n.* maskiert gehen.
¹Mass, *s.* die Messe; to say —, die heilige Messe lesen. **—book,** *s.* das Meßbuch.
²Mass, I. *s.* die Masse. II. *v.a.* (an-) häufen; in Massen aufstellen (*troops*). III. *v.n.* sich in Massen vereinigen.
Massacre, I. *s.* das Blutbad. II. *v.a.* niedermetzeln.
Mass—age, I. *s.* die Massage. II. *v.a.* massieren. **—eur,** *s.* der Masseur.
Mass—ive, *adj.,* massiv, dicht, gediegen.

—ively, *adv.,* **—y,** *adj.* massiv. **—iveness,** *s.* das Massiv.
¹Mast, *s.* der Mast. **—ed,** *adj.* (*in comp.*) -gemastet. **—head,** *s.* der Masttopp.
²Mast, I. *s.* die Mast. II. *v.a.* mästen.
¹Master, *s.*; three— —er, der Dreimaster.
²Master, I. *s.* der Meister; (owner) der Herr; der Lehrer (*of a school*). II. *v.a.* (be)meistern, überwältigen. **—ful,** *adj.* herrisch, großartig. **—ly,** *adj.* meisterhaft, gebieterisch. **—less,** *adj.* herrenlos, unbändig. **—y,** *s.* die Herrschaft, Gewalt. **—builder,** *s.* der Baumeister. **— key,** *s.* der Hauptschlüssel. **—piece,** *s.* das Meisterstück.
Masticate, *v.a.* kauen.
Mastiff, *s.* der Bullenbeißer, Kettenhund.
Mat, *s.* die Matte.
¹Match, *s.* das Zünd-, Streich-hölzchen.
²Match, I. *s.* der, das Gleiche, Passende; (competition) die Partie, das Spiel, Wettspiel; to be (quite) a — for someone, einem gewachsen sein; to meet one's —, seinen Mann finden. II. *v.a.* gleichen; (suit) zusammenpassen; (compare) vergleichen; (oppose) sich messen mit. III. *v.n.* zusammenpassen. **—less,** *adj.* unvergleichlich, ohnegleichen. **—lessness,** *s.* die Unvergleichlichkeit. **—maker,** *s.* der Ehestifter, die Ehestifterin. **—making,** I. *adj.* ehestiftend. II. *s.* das Ehestiften.
¹Mate, I. *s.* der Gefährte; (spouse) der Gatte, die Gattin; das Männchen, Weibchen (*of birds*); der Maat (*Naut.*). II. *v.a.* heiraten; paaren. III. *v.n.* sich paaren, sich gatten.
²Mate, I. *adj.* matt. II. *v.a.* (chess) matt machen.
Material, I. *s.* das Material, der Stoff. II. *adj.,* **—ly,** *adv.* materiell; (essential) wesentlich. **—ism,** *s.* der Materialismus. **—ist,** *s.* der Materialist. **—istic,** *adj.* materialistisch. **—ize,** *v.n.* verkörpern.
Matern—al, *adj.,* **—ally,** *adv.* mütterlich; von mütterlicher Seite. **—ity,** *s.* die Mutterschaft.
Mathematic—al, *adj.,* **—ally,** *adv.* mathematisch. **—ian,** *s.* der Mathematiker. **—s,** *s.* die Mathematik.
Matriculat—e, *v.n.* sich immatriku-

lieren lassen. **—ion,** *s.* die Imma-
tritulation.
Matrimon—ial, *adj.,* **—ially,** *adv.*
ehelich. **—y,** *s.* die Ehe.
Matron, *s.* die Matrone, Frau; die Vorsteherin (*of hospital, etc.*). **—ly,** *adj.*
matronenhaft, gesetzt.
Matter, I. *s.* die Materie, der Stoff;
(contents) der Inhalt; (subject) der
Gegenstand; (ground) die Ursache;
(affair) die Sache, Angelegenheit;
what's the —? was gibt es?; what's
the — with you? was fehlt Ihnen?;
— in hand, vorliegende Sache. II.
v.n. von Bedeutung sein, daran gelegen sein; it — s little what he does,
es ist wenig daran gelegen *or* ziemlich
einerlei, was er tut. **—of-course,**
adj. (*only predic.*) selbstverständlich.
—of-fact, *adj.* tatsächlich.
Mattock, *s.* die Haue.
Mattress, *s.* die Matratze.
Matur—e, I. *adj.,* **—ely,** *adv.* reif.
II. *v.a.* reifen; (*fig.*) zur Reife
bringen. III. *v.n.* reifen; verfallen (*as
a bill*). **—eness,** **—ity,** *s.* die Reife.
Maudlin, *adj.* benebelt, weinerlich,
überempfindlich.
Maul, I. *v.a.* der Schlägel. II. *v.a.*
durchprügeln.
Mauve, *adj.* hellviolett, malven.
Mawkish, *adj.* ekelhaft, abgeschmackt.
Maxim, *s.* die Maxime, der Grundsatz.
Maximum, I. *s.* das Maximum. II. *adj.*
höchst, größt; — output, die Höchstleistung.
¹May, *s.* der Mai(monat). **—flower,**
s. der Weißdorn. **—pole,** *s.* der
Maibaum.
²May, *aux. v.* können, dürfen; mögen.
—be, *adv.* vielleicht.
Mayor, *s.* der Bürgermeister. **—ess,**
s. die Frau Bürgermeisterin.
Maze, *s.* das Labyrinth, der Irrgarten;
die Verwirrung (*of thought, etc.*).
Mazurka, *s.* die Masurka.
Me, *s. pers. pron.* mich; (to —) mir;
he was ashamed of —, er schämte sich
meiner.
¹Mead, *s.* der Met.
²Mead, —ow, *s.* die Wiese, der Anger.
Meagre, *adj.,* **—ly,** *adv.* mager, dürr.
—ness, *s.* die Magerkeit.
¹Meal, *s.* das Mahl, die Mahlzeit.
—time, *s.* die Essenszeit.
²Meal, *s.* das grob gemahlene Mehl.
—y, *adj.* mehlig.

¹Mean, *adj.,* **—ly,** *adv.* gemein, niedrig,
armselig. **—ness,** *s.* die Gemeinheitt
Niedrigkeit. **—spirited,** *adj.* niederträchtig.
²Mean, I. *adj.* mittel, mittler, mittelmäßig; durchschnittlich (*Math.*); in
the — time, (**—time,** **—while**) unter-
dessen, indessen, inzwischen, einst-
weilen. II. *s.* die Mitte, der Mittelpunkt. **—s,** *pl.* (income) die Mittel,
Vermögensumstände; (*also sing.*) das
Mittel, der Weg (*to an end*); by this
—s, hierdurch, dadurch; by —s of,
mittels, vermittelst; by all —s, jedenfalls; ganz gewiß; by no (manner of)
—s, auf keine Weise, keineswegs,
durchaus nicht.
³Mean, *ir.v.a.* (intend) meinen; (signify) bedeuten. **—ing,** I. *adj.,* **—ingly,**
adv. bedeutungsvoll; well —ing,
wohlwollend. II. *s.* die Meinung,
Absicht, das Vorhaben; (significance)
der Sinn, die Bedeutung. **—ingless,**
adj. bedeutungslos.
Meander, I. *v.n.* sich schlängeln. II.
s. der Schlängelweg.
Measle—d, *adj.* finnig (*as pigs*). **—s,**
s. die Masern; German **—s,** die
Röteln.
Measur—able, *adj.,* **—ably,** *adv.*
meßbar. **—e,** I. *s.* das Maß (*also
fig.*); in some —, gewissermaßen,
—e of capacity, das Hohlmaß. II.
v.a. messen, abmessen. III. *v.n.*
messen. **—eless,** *adj.* unermeßlich.
—ement, *s.* das Maß, die Messung.
Meat, *s.* das Fleisch; roast —, der
Braten. **—safe,** *s.* der Fliegen-
schrank.
Mechani—c, I. *adj.,* **—cal,** *adj.,*
cally, *adv.* mechanisch. II. *s.* der
Handwerker. **—cian,** *s.* der Mecha-
niker. **—cs,** *s.* die Mechanik. **—sm,** *s.*
der Mechanismus, das Getriebe.
Medal, *s.* die Denkmünze. **—lion,** *s.*
das Medaillon.
Meddle, *v.n.* sich (unberufen)(ein)meng-
en (in, in); sich abgeben (with,
mit). **—r,** *s.* einer, der sich in fremde
Dinge mischt. **—some,** *adj.* auf-
dringlich.
Mediat—e, I. *adj.* mittelbar. II. *v.n.*
vermitteln (between, zwischen (*dat.*)).
—ion, *s.* die Fürbitte. **—or,** *s.* der
Vermittler. **—rix,** *s.* die Vermittlerin.
Medic—al, *adj.,* **—ally,** *adv.* ärztlich,
Heil-. **—inal,** *adj.,* **—inally,** *adv.*

mediziniſch, heilkräftig. **—ine,** s. die Arznei, Medizin, das Heilmittel.

Medieval, adj. mittelalterlich.

Mediocr—e, adj. mittelmäßig. **—ity,** s. die Mittelmäßigkeit.

Meditat—e, v. I. n. (—e on) nachdenken, nachſinnen (über eine S.), überlegen. II. a. beabſichtigen. **—ion,** s. das Nachdenken, Nachſinnen. **—ive,** adj., **—ively,** adv. nachdenklich, ernſt.

Medium, I. adj. mittel, mittler. II. s. der Mittelweg; (agency) das Mittel; das Medium, Mittel (Phys.).

Medlar, s. die Miſpel.

Medley, s. das Gemiſch, Gemengſel.

Meek, adj., **—ly,** adv. ſanft (mütig); (humble) demütig, beſcheiden. **—ness,** s. die Sanftmut; die Demut.

Meerschaum, s. der Meerſchaum.

¹Meet, adj. paßlich, ſchicklich, gelegen.

²Meet, I. ir.v.a. begegnen; (fall in with) (be)treffen, zuſammentreffen (mit). II. ir.v.n. ſich or einander begegnen, ſich treffen, zuſammentreffen; (unite) ſich vereinigen; (assemble) ſich verſammeln; to — with an accident, verunglücken; to make both ends —, mit ſeinen Einkünften auskommen. **—ing,** s. die Verſammlung; (coming together) die Zuſammenkunft; die Sitzung (of a council, etc.); das Zuſammentreffen (of two lines); (rendezvous) das Stelldichein. **—ing-place,** s. der Sammelplatz.

Melanchol—ia, s. die Melancholie. **—ic,** adj. ſchwermütig, melancholiſch. **—y,** I. s. die Schwermut, der Trübſinn. II. adj. ſchwermütig.

Mêlée, s. das Handgemenge.

Mellow, adj. (ripe) reif; ſanft (in tone). **—ness,** s. die Mürbigkeit (of fruit); die Sanftheit, Weichheit (of tone).

Melod—ious, adj., **—iously,** adv. melodiſch, wohlklingend. **—iousness,** s. der Wohlklang. **—y,** s. die Melodie.

Melon, s. die Melone.

Melt, v. I. a. ſchmelzen; to — down, einſchmelzen. II. n. ſchmelzen; to — away, verſchmelzen; to — into tears, in Tränen zerfließen.

Member, s. das Glied; das Mitglied, der Abgeordnete (of Parliament). **—ship,** s. die Mitgliedſchaft.

Membran—e, s. das Häutchen. **—ous,** adj. häutig.

Memento, s. das Denkzeichen.

Memoir, s. die Denkſchrift; **—s,** Memoiren.

Memorabl—e, adj., **—y,** adv. denkwürdig. **—eness,** s. die Denkwürdigkeit.

Memorandum, s. das Memorandum.

Memorial, I. adj. zum Andenken bienend. II. s. das Denkmal; (petition) die Bittſchrift.

Memorize, v.a. aufzeichnen, auswendig lernen.

Memory, s. das Gedächtnis; beyond the — of man, ſeit Menſchengedenken.

Menac—e, I. s. die Drohung. II. v.a. (be)drohen. **—ing,** adj., **—ingly,** adv. drohend.

Menagerie, s. die Menagerie.

Mend, v. I. a. (ver)beſſern. II. v.n. beſſer werden, geneſen. **—er,** s. der Flicker, Ausbeſſerer.

Mendaci—ous, adj. lügneriſch, verlogen. **—ty,** s. die Verlogenheit.

Mendican—cy, s. die Bettelei. **—t,** I. adj. bettelnd. II. s. der Bettler.

Menial, I. adj. knechtiſch. II. s. der Knecht; **—s,** das Geſinde.

Mental, adj., **—ly,** adv. geiſtig, Geiſtes-.

Mention, I. s. die Erwähnung. II. v.a. erwähnen.

Menu, s. die Speiſekarte.

Mercantile, adj. den Handel betreffend, Handels-.

Mercenar—iness, s. die Feilheit. **—y,** adj., **—ily,** adv. feil, käuflich, gewinnſüchtig.

Mercer, s. der Seidenhändler.

Merchandise, s. die Ware; die Waren (pl.).

Merchant, s. der Kaufmann. **—service,** s. die Handelsmarine. **—vessel, —man,** s. das Kauffahrteiſchiff.

Merc—iful, adj., **—ifully,** adv. barmherzig. **—iless,** adj., **—ilessly,** adv. unbarmherzig, mitleidlos.

Mercur—ial, adj. von Queckſilber, merkurialiſch. **—y,** s. der Merkur (Myth., Astr.); das Queckſilber (Chem.).

Mercy, s. die Barmherzigkeit, das Mitleid; to be at someone's —, in jemandes Gewalt ſein; at the — of the waves, den Wellen preisgegeben.

¹Mere, adj. rein, bloß, lauter. **—ly,** adv. allein, nur, bloß.

²Mere, s. der Teich.

Merge, v. I. a. versenken (in, mit).
II. n. (sich) verschmelzen (in, mit).

Meridian, I. s. der Meridian. II. adj.
Mittags-, mittägig.

Merino, s. der Merino.

Merit, I. s. das Verdienst; on the
—s of the case, aus materiellen
Gründen. II. v.a. verdienen. —ed,
adj. verdient, wohlverdient. —orious,
adj., —oriously, adv. verdienstlich.
—oriousness, s. die Verdienstlichkeit.

Mer—maid, s. die Seejungfer. —man,
s. der Triton, Wassermann.

Merr—ily, adv. lustig, fröhlich. —i-
ment, s. die Fröhlichkeit, Lustigkeit,
Belustigung. —y, adj. lustig, ver-
gnügt, fröhlich. —y-go-round, s. das
Karussel. —y-making, s. die Lust-
barkeit; das Fest.

Mesh, s. die Masche. —work, s. das
Netzwerk, das Gespinst.

Mesmeri—c, adj. mesmerisch. —sm,
s. der Mesmerismus. —ze, v.a. magnetisieren.

1Mess, I. s. die Offizierstafel (Mil., etc.);
die Back (Naut.). II. v.n. zusammen-
speisen.

2Mess, s. das Gemengsel; (state of
dirt) der Schmutz; he is in a —, (fig.)
er sitzt in der Tinte.

Message, s. die Botschaft.

Messenger, s. der Bote. —boy, s.
der Ausläufer. —pigeon, s. die
Brieftaube.

Messmate, s. der Tischgenoß.

Metal, s. das Metall. —lic, adj.
metallisch, metallen, Metall-.

Metamorphosis, s. die Verwandlung,
Umgestaltung.

Metaphor, s. der bildliche Ausdruck,
die Metapher. —ic, —ical, adj.
bildlich, metaphorisch; übertragen.

Mete, v.a. (ab)messen.

Meteor, s. das Meteor. —ic, adj.
Meteor-. —ological, adj. meteoro-
logisch, Wetter-.

Meter, s. der Messer; (gas —r) die
Gasuhr.

Method, s. die Methode. —ical, adj.,
—ically, adv. planmäßig, method. sch.

Methylated, adj.; — spirit, denu-
turierter Spiritus.

Met—re, s. das Versmaß, Metrum;
(measure) das Meter. —ric, adj.;
—ric system, das Metermaß. —ri-
cal, adj., —rically, adv. metrisch.

Metropoli—s, s. die Hauptstadt. —

tan, adj. hauptstädtisch; erzbischöflich (Eccl.).

Mettle, s. der Eifer, das Feuer; to put
a person on his —, einen anspornen,
sein Möglichstes zu leisten. —d,
—some, adj. feurig, mutig.

Mew, I. s. das Miau. II. v.n. miauen.

Mews, s. das Gäßchen mit Stallungen.

Microbe, s. die Mikrobe, die Bakterie.

Microphone, s. das Mikrophon.

Microscope, s. das Mikroskop.

Mid, —st, adj. mitten. —dle, I. s. die
Mitte. II. adj. mittel, mittler, in der
Mitte. —dling, I. adj. mittelmäßig.
II. adv. ziemlich, leidlich. —st, I.
s. die Mitte. II. adv. in der Mitte.
—day, I. s. der Mittag. II. adj.
mittäglich. —dle-aged, adj. in mitt-
lerem Alter. —dle Ages, pl. das
Mittelalter. —dle class, s. der Mit-
telstand. —dleman, s. der Zwischen-
händler. —land, adj. binnenländisch,
mittelländisch. —night, I. adj. mitter-
nächtig. II. s. die Mitternacht. —
shipman, s. der Seekadett. —ships,
adv. mitschiffs. —summer, s. der
Hochsommer; —summer Day, der
Johannistag. —way, adj. unterwegs,
auf halbem Wege.

Midge, s. die Mücke.

Midwife, s. die Hebamme.

Mien, s. die Miene.

Might, s. die Macht, Gewalt; with
— and main, mit aller Gewalt. —ily,
adv. (strongly) gewaltig, heftig, stark;
(greatly) sehr. —y, adj. mächtig;
groß; gewaltsam.

Mignonette, s. die Reseda.

Migrat—e, v.n. (aus-)wandern. —
ion, s. die Wanderung. —ory, adj.
(aus)wandernd; —ory bird, der Zug-
vogel.

Mild, adj., —ly, adv. mild, gelind(e).
—ness, s. die Milde, Gelindigkeit (of
the climate); die Sanftheit (of temper).

Mildew, I. s. der Mehltau; der Brand
(in grain). II. v.a. mit Mehltau
überziehen, brandig machen.

Mile, s. die Meile. —stone, s. der
Meilen-stein, -zeiger.

Milit—ancy, s. der Kriegsstand. —
ant, adj. kriegführend; streitend.
—ary, I. adj. militärisch, kriegerisch;
Kriegs-. II. s. das Militär, die Soldaten. —ate, v.n. widersprechen,
widerstreiten (dat.).

Militia, *s.* die Miliz, der Landsturm.
—**man,** *s.* der Landwehrmann.

Milk, I. *s.* die Milch; unskimmed —,
die Vollmilch; skimmed —, die
Magermilch. II. *v.a.* melken. —**y,**
adj. milchig, Milch=; — y Way, die
Milchstraße. —**jug,** *s* der Milchtopf.
—**man,** *s.* der Milchhändler. —**sop,**
s. der Weichling.

Mill, I. *s.* die Mühle. —**er,** *s.* der
Müller. —**dam,** *s.* das Mühlwehr.
—**race,** *s.* das Mühlgerinne. —
stone, *s.* der Mühlstein.

Millet, *s.* die Hirse.

Milliard, *s.* die Milliarde.

Milliner, *s.* die Putzmacherin. —**y,** *s.*
die Modewaren, die Putzwaren.

Million, *s.* die Million. —**aire,** *s.* der
Millionär.

1Milt, *s.* die Milch der Fische.

2Milt, *s.* die Milz.

Mim—ic, I. *adj.* nachahmend, mimisch.
II. *s.* der Mimiker. III. *v.a.* nach=
ahmen, nachäffen. —**icry,** *s.* pos=
senhafte Nachahmung, die Angleichung.

Minaret, *s.* das Minaret.

Minc—e, I. *v.a.* hacken (*meat*); he does
not — e matters, er nimmt kein Blatt
vor den Mund. II. *v.n.* zimperlich
gehen. III. *s.* gehacktes Fleisch. —**ing,**
adj., —**ingly,** *adv.* geziert, affektiert.
—**e-meat,** *s.* gehacktes Fleisch. - -**ing-
machine,** *s.* die Hackmaschine.

Mind, I. *s.* (disposition) das Gemüt,
der Sinn; (intention) die Absicht, das
Vorhaben; (inclination) die Neigung,
Lust, der Wille; (opinion) die Meinung,
Ansicht; (memory) das Gedächt=
nis, die Erinnerung, die Gedanken;
(understanding) der Verstand, Geist;
to have a — to, Lust haben zu; to
make up one's —, einen Entschluß
fassen. II. *v.a.* achten, merken (auf,
acc.), beobachten; (take care of) sich be=
schäftigen mit, sich bekümmern um;
never — ! es tut nichts! III. *v.n.*
achtgeben (auf, *acc.*); I don't —, ich
habe nichts dagegen. —**ed,** *adj.*
geneigt, gesinnt. —**ful,** *adj.* (einer
Sache) eingedenk. —**fulness,** *s.* die
Achtsamkeit. —**less,** *adj.* achtlos.

1Mine, *poss. pron.* mein, meiner; der,
die, das Meinige.

2Mine, I. *s.* das Bergwerk, die Grube
(*Min.*); die Mine (*Fort.*). II. *v.n.*
minieren, Gruben graben. —**r,** *s.*
der Bergmann; der Minierer (*Fort.*).

Mineral, I. *s.* das Mineral. II. *adj.*
mineralisch, Mineral=.

Mingle, *v.* I. *a.* (ver)mischen, mengen.
II. *n.* sich mengen (in (*acc.*)), sich
mischen (unter (*acc.*)).

Miniature, *s.* die Miniatur.

Minim, I. *s.* die halbe Note (*Mus.*);
der Tropfen. —**ize,** *v.a.* verringern.
—**um,** *s.* das Kleinste.

Mining, I. *adj.* Bergbau=, Berg=. II.
s. der Bergbau; das Minieren (*Mil.*).

Minion, *s.* der Günstling.

Minist—er, I. *s.* der Geistliche; der
(Staats=)Minister (*Pol.*); prime —er,
der Ministerpräsident. II. *v.n.* be=
hilflich sein; den Gottesdienst, das
Amt halten. III. *v.a.* geben, dar=
reichen. —**erial,** *adj.,* —**erially,** *adv.*
ministeriell, Minsterial=. —**rant,** *adj.*
dienend. —**ration,** *s.* der Dienst,
das Amt. —**ry,** *s.* das geistliche
Amt, Predigeramt; das Ministerium
(*Pol.*).

Mink, *s.* der Nerz.

Minnow, *s.* die Elritze.

Minor, I. *adj.* geringer; (unimportant) klein, unbedeutend; (under age)
unmündig; moll, weich (*Mus.*). II.
s. der, die Minderjährige, Unmündige
(*Law*); das Moll (*Mus.*). —**ity,** *s.*
die Minderjährigkeit, Unmündigkeit
(*Law*); die Minderheit.

Minster, *s.* das Münster.

Minstrel, *s.* der Sänger, der Spielmann.

1Mint, *s.* die Minze (*Bot.*).

2Mint, I. *s.* die Münze. II. *v.a.* Geld
prägen, münzen. —**er,** *s.* der
Münzer.

Minuet, *s.* das Menuett.

Minus, *adv.* weniger.

Minute, I. *adj.,* —**ly,** *adv.* winzig;
umständlich (*as details*). II. *s.* die
Minute; (*fig.*) ein Augenblick. —
ness, *s.* die Kleinheit; die Genauigkeit.
—**s,** *pl.* das Protokoll.

Minx, *s.* das naseweise Mädchen,
ausgelassenes Mädchen.

Mira—cle, *s.* das Wunder. —**culous,**
adj., —**culously,** *adv.* wunderbar.

Mirage, *s.* die Luftspiegelung, die
Fata Morgana.

Mire, *s.* der Schlamm, Kot.

Mirror, I. *s.* der Spiegel (*also fig.*).
II. *v.n.* abspiegeln; (*fig.*) darstellen.

Mirth, *s.* der Frohsinn, die Fröhlichkeit, Heiterkeit. —**ful,** *adj.,* —**fully,**

adv. fröhlich, heiter, lustig. —**ful-ness**, *s.* die Fröhlichkeit, Lustigkeit.
Misadventure, *s.* das Unglück.
Misalliance, *s.* die Mißheirat.
Misanthrop—e, —**ist**, *s.* der Menschenfeind. —**ic(al)**, *adj.*, —**ically**, *adv.* menschenfeindlich, misanthropisch. —y, *s.* der Menschenhaß.
Misapplication, *s.* die falsche Anwendung.
Misapprehen—d, *v.n.* mißverstehen. —**sion**, *s.* das Mißverständnis.
Misappropriat—e, *v.a.* sich (*dat.*) mit Unrecht aneignen. —**ion**, *s.* die Unterschlagung.
Misbehav—e, *v.n. & r.* sich schlecht betragen. —**iour**, *s.* die Unart.
Miscalculat—e, *v.* I. *a.* falsch berechnen. II. *n.* sich verrechnen. —**ion**, *s.* der Rechnungsfehler (*in an account, etc.*).
Miscarr—**iage**, *s.* das Mißlingen, Fehlschlagen; die Fehlgeburt. —**y**, *v.n.* mißlingen, fehlschlagen, mißglücken.
Miscellan—**eous**, *adj.*, —**eously**, *adv.* gemischt. —**y**, *s.* das Gemisch.
Mischance, *s.* das Mißgeschick, der Unfall.
Mischie—f, *s.* der Unfug, das Unheil. —**f-loving**, *adj.* mutwillig. —**f-maker**, *s.* der Unheilstifter. —**vous**, *adj.*, —**vously**, *adv.* schädlich, nachteilig, verderblich, boshaft.
Misconduct, I. *s.* schlechtes Benehmen. II. *v.r.* sich schlecht aufführen.
Misconstru—**ction**, *s.* die Mißdeutung. —e, *v.a.* mißdeuten.
Miscount, *v.a.* falsch rechnen, sich verrechnen.
Miscreant, *s.* der Bösewicht.
Misdeed, *s.* die Missetat, das Vergehen.
Misdemeanour, *s.* das Vergehen.
Misdirect, *v.a.* irre leiten; falsch adressieren.
Misdoing, *s.* die Missetat.
Miser, *s.* der Geizhals. —**liness**, *s.* der Geiz. —**ly**, *adv.* filzig, geizig.
Miserabl—e, *adj.*, —**y**, *adv.* elend, jämmerlich.
Misery, *s.* das Elend, der Jammer, die Not.
Misfire, I. *v.n.* versagen. II. *s.* der Blindgänger, die Versagung.
Misfit, *s.* das Nichtpassen (von Kleidern).
Misfortune, *s.* das Unglück; der Unglücksfall; das Mißgeschick.
Misgiv—e, *ir.v.a.*; my mind —es me

with regard to . . ., es scheint mir bedenklich, daß. —**ing**, *s.* die böse Ahnung.
Misgovern, *v.a.* schlecht regieren. —**ment**, *s.* die schlechte Verwaltung; (misconduct) das üble Verhalten, die Unordnung.
Mishap, *s.* der Unfall, das Unglück.
Misjudge, *v.a.* falsch beurteilen.
Mislay, *v.a.* verlegen.
Mislead, *ir.v.a.* irre leiten, verleiten. —**ing**, *p. & adj.* irreführend.
Mismanage, *v.a.* schlecht verwalten *or* einrichten. —**ment**, *s.* die schlechte Verwaltung *or* Handhabung.
Misprint, I. *v.a.* verdrucken, falsch drucken. II. *s.* der Druckfehler.
Misrepresent, *v.a.* verdrehen. —**a-tion**, *s.* die falsche Darstellung, Verdrehung.
Misrule, *s.* die schlechte Regierung.
1**Miss**, *s.* das Fräulein.
2**Miss**, I. *v.a.* missen; (feel want) vermissen; verfehlen (*the way*); verfehlen, nicht treffen (*a mark*); (not get) verfehlen; to — fire, versagen; to — one's footing, ausgleiten. II. *v.n.* fehlgehen, verfehlen; nicht treffen. III. *s.* der Fehler. —**ing**, *adj.* abwesend.
Missal, *s.* das Meßbuch.
Misshapen, *adj.* mißgestalt.
Missile, *s.* das Wurfgeschoß.
Mission, *s.* die Sendung; die Bestimmung (*in life*); die Mission (*Rel.*). —**ary**, I. *adj.* Missions=. II. *s.* der Missionär.
Missive, *s.* das Sendschreiben.
Misspell, *v.a.* falsch buchstabieren oder schreiben.
Misstate, *v.a.* unrichtig angeben. —**ment**, *s.* falsche Angabe.
Mist, *s.* der Nebel. —**ily**, *adv.*, —**y**, *adj.* nebelig. —**iness**, *s.* die Trübheit, Nebeligkeit.
Mistak—**able**, *adj.*, —**ably**, *adv.* verkennbar. —**e**, I. *ir.v.a.* verwechseln, verkennen (*a person*). II. *ir.v.n.* sich irren. III. *s.* der Irrtum, Fehler. —**en**, *adj.*, —**enly**, *adv.* irrig.
Mister, *s.* Herr.
Mistime, *v.a.* zur Unzeit tun. —**d**, *adj.* unzeitig.
Mistle-thrush, *s.* die Misteldrossel.
Mistletoe, *s.* die Mistel.
Mistress, *s.* die Herrin, Gebieterin;

(— of the house) die Hausfrau; (school—) die Lehrerin.

Mistrust, I. *v.a.* (einem) mißtrauen. II. *s.* das Mißtrauen. **—ful,** *adj.,* **—fully,** *adv.* mißtrauisch.

Misunderstand, *ir.v.a.* mißverstehen; sich irren in (*a person's character*). **—ing,** *s.* das Mißverständnis.

Misuse, I. *v.a.* mißbrauchen. II. *s.* der Mißbrauch.

¹Mite, *s.* die Milbe, Made.

²Mite, *s.* das Scherflein; das Kindchen.

Mitre, *s.* die Bischofsmütze.

Mitten, *s.* der Halbhandschuh.

Mix, *v.* I. *a.* mischen, mengen. II. *n.* sich (ver-)mischen; to — in society, in der Gesellschaft verkehren. **—ed,** *adj.* gemischt; —ed pickles, eingemachte pikante Gemüse. **—ture,** *s.* die Mischung.

Mizen, I. *s.* das Besansegel. II. *attrib.;* —mast, der Besanmast.

Moan, I. *s.* das Stöhnen. II. *v.n.* wehklagen, jammern. **—ing,** *adj.* wehklagend.

Moat, *s.* der Burggraben.

Mob, I. *s.* das Gesindel, der Pöbel. II. *v.a.* lärmend anfallen. **—law,** *s.* die Lynchjustiz.

Mobili—ty, *s.* die Beweglichkeit. **—zation,** *s.* die Mobilmachung. **—ze,** *v.a.* mobil machen.

Mock, I. *v.a.* verspotten, verlachen, höhnen. II. *v.n.;* to — at, spotten, spötteln über (*acc.*). III. *s.* der Spott, Hohn. IV. *adj.* falsch, Schein-. **—er,** *s.* der Spötter. **—ery,** *s.* das Gespött, der Spott. **—ing,** I. *s.* das Gespött, der Hohn. II. *adj.* neckend, verhöhnend. **—ingly,** *adv.* zum Spotte, spottweise.

Mode, *s.* die Art, Weise; (fashion) die Sitte, Mode.

Model, I. *s.* das Modell (*Sculpt. etc.*); (pattern) das Muster; (*fig.*) das Muster, Vorbild. II. *v.a. & n.* modeln. III. *adj.* vorbildlich, Muster-.

Moderat—e, I. *adj.,* **—ely,** *adv.* mäßig. II. *v.a.* mäßigen. **—ion,** *s.* die Mäßigung; (frugality) die Mäßigkeit.

Modern, I. *adj.* jetzig, heutig, modern. II. *s.;* the —s, die Neuern. **—ize,** *v.a.* modernisieren. **—ness,** *s.* die Neuheit.

Modest, *adj.,* **—ly,** *adv.* bescheiden; sittsam. **—y,** *s.* die Bescheidenheit; die Sittsamkeit.

Modif—ication, *s.* die Abänderung. **—y,** *v.a.* modifizieren; umlauten; einschränken, mildern (*Gram.*).

Modish, *adj.* modisch.

Modiste, *s.* die Putzmacherin.

Modulat—e, *v.a.* modulieren. **—ion,** *s.* die Modulation (*also Mus.*).

Moiety, *s.* die Hälfte; der Teil.

Moil, *v.n.* sich placken.

Moist, *adj.* feucht. **—en,** *v.a.* (an-) feuchten. **—ness, —ure,** *s.* die Feuchtigkeit.

Molar, *s.* (— tooth) der Backenzahn.

Molasses, *s.* die Melasse, der Sirup.

¹Mole, *s.* das (Mutter-)Mal.

²Mole, *s.* der Maulwurf (*Zool.*).

³Mole, *s.* der Hafendamm.

Molest, *v.a.* belästigen. **—ation,** *s.* die Belästigung.

Mollusc, *s.* das Weichtier; **—s,** Mollusken.

Molten, *adj.* geschmolzen.

Moment, *s.* der Augenblick. **—ariness,** *s.* die Vergänglichkeit. **—ary,** *adj.* augenblicklich. **—ous,** *adj.,* **—ously,** *adv.* wichtig. **—um,** *s.* das Moment.

Monarch, *s.* der Monarch; der König. **—ic(al),** *adj.* monarchisch. **—y,** *s.* die Monarchie; (realm) das Königreich.

Monast—ery, *s.* das Kloster. **—ic(al),** *adj.,* **—ically,** *adv.* monastisch, Mönchs-.

Monday, *s.* der Montag.

Monetary, *adj.* Geld-.

Money, *s.* das Geld; ready —, bares Geld; to make —, Geld verdienen. **—ed,** *adj.* vermögend. **—changer,** *s.* der Geldwechsler. **—grubber,** *s.* der Geizhals (*fam.*). **—order,** *s.* die Postanweisung.

Mongrel, *s.* der Mischling.

Monk, *s.* der Mönch.

Monkey, *s.* der Affe (*also fig.*).

Mono—chrome, I. *s.* das einfarbige Gemälde. II. *adj.* einfarbig. **—cle,** *s.* das Einglas, Monokel. **—gram,** *s.* das Monogramm. **—logue,** *s.* der Monolog, das Selbstgespräch. **—mania,** *s.* die fixe Idee. **—plane,** *s.* der Eindecker (*Aviat.*). **—polist,** *s.* der Monopolist. **—polize,** *v.a.* monopolisieren. **—poly,** *s.* der Alleinhandel, das Monopol. **—syllabic(al),** *adj.* einsilbig. **—syllable,** *s.* einsilbiges Wort. **—tone,** *s.* das Eintönige. **—tonous,** *adj.* eintönig; (tiresome)

langweilig. —**tony**, *s.* die Eintönig=
keit.

Monsoon, *s.* der Passatwind.

Monst—er, I. *s.* das Ungeheuer (*also
fig.*). II. *adj.* ungeheuer groß, Riesen=.
—**rance**, *s.* die Monstranz. —**rous**,
adj., —**rously**, *adv.* ungeheuer, unge=
schlacht.

Month, *s.* der Monat. —**ly**, I.
adj. & *adv.* monatlich. II. *s.* die
Monatsschrift.

Monument, *s.* das Denkmal. —**al**,
adj. Denkmal=, Denk=.

Moo, I. *v.n.* muhen. II. *s.* das
Gebrüll einer Kuh.

¹**Mood**, *s.* der Modus (*Gram.*).

²**Mood**, *s.* die Stimmung, Laune. —
ily, *adv.*, —**y**, *adj.* launisch.

Moon, *s.* der Mond. —**less**, *adj.*
mondlos, ohne Mond. —**beam**, *s.*
der Mondstrahl. —**light**, I. *adj.*
mondhell. II. *s.* der Mondschein.
—**struck**, *adj.* mondsüchtig.

¹**Moor**, *s.* das Moor. —**hen**, *s.* das
Moorhuhn.

²**Moor**, *v.* I. *a.* vor Anker legen. II. *n.*
vor Anker liegen. —**ing**, *s.* das
Ankern. —**ings**, *pl.* die Hafenanker.

Moose, *s.* (—-deer) das Elen(tier).

Moot, I. *v.a.* anregen. II. *adj.*; —
point, der strittige Punkt. III. *s.*
die Volksversammlung.

Mop, I. *s.* der Scheuerlappen. II.
v.a. to — up, aufwischen.

Mope, *v.n.* teilnahmslos, traurig sein.

Moral, I. *adj.* moralisch, sittlich;
(mental) geistig; Moral=, Sitten=.
II. *s.* die Moral. —**ist**, *s.* der
Sittenlehrer. —**ity**, *s.* die Morali=
tät, Sittlichkeit (*of a person*); die
sittliche Reinheit (*of an action*).
—**ize**, *v.n.* moralisieren (upon, über
eine S.). —**ly**, *adv.* moralisch; (vir-
tuously) sittlich, tugendhaft.

Morass, *s.* der Morast, Sumpf.

Moratorium, *s.* das Moratorium, die
Zahlungsfristverlängerung.

Morbid, *adj.*, —**ly**, *adv.* krankhaft.

Mordant, *adj.* beißend, ätzend.

More, I. *adj.* mehr; größer (*in number*); six miles —, noch sechs Meilen;
not a word —! kein Wort mehr! II.
adv. mehr; (in addition) noch (dazu);
so much the —, umso mehr; — and
—, immer mehr. —**over**, *adv.* außer=
dem, weiter.

Morn, *s.* der Morgen. —**ing**, I. *s.* der

Morgen; to-morrow —ing, morgen
früh. II. *adj.* früh, morgendlich,
Morgen=.

Morose, *adj.*, —**ly**, *adv.* mürrisch.
—**ness**, *s.* die Grämlichkeit.

Morph—ia, —ine, *s.* das Morphium.

Morrow, *s.* der Morgen.

Morsel, *s.* der Bissen.

Mort—al, *adj.*, —ally, *adv.* sterblich;
(human) menschlich; (deadly) tödlich.
—**ality**, *s.* die Sterblichkeit; (deaths)
das (Ab=)Sterben; (humanity) die
Menschheit.

Mortar, *s.* der Mörser (*Artil., Chem.*);
der Mörtel (*Build.*).

Mortgage, I. *s.* die Hypothek. II. *v.a.*
verpfänden. —**e**, *s.* der Hypothekar.
—**r**, *s.* der Pfandgeber.

Mortif—ication, *s.* die Demütigung;
(chagrin) der Verdruß. —**y**, *v.* I. *a.*
abtöten, kreuzigen (*the flesh*); demüti=
gen (*one's pride*); ärgern, kränken.
II. *n.* absterben, brandig werden.

Mortise, *s.* das Zapfenloch.

Mosaic, I. *adj.* Mosaik=. II. *s.* die
Mosaik, das Fugbild.

Mosque, *s.* die Moschee.

Mosquito, *s.* der Moskito.

Moss, *s.* das Moos (*Bot.*); (bog) das
Torfmoos. —**y**, *adj.* moosig, be=
moost.

Most, I. *adj.* (*sup. of Much*) meist;
größt; for the — part, größten=,
meisten=teils. II. *adv.* meist(ens), am
meisten; äußerst, außerordentlich. III.
s. das Meiste; (in number) die Meisten;
(utmost) das Höchste, Äußerste; to
make the — of, den höchsten Nutzen
ziehen aus. —**ly**, *adv.* meistens,
größtenteils, hauptsächlich.

Mote, *s.* das Sonnenstäubchen.

Moth, *s.* die Motte.

Mother, *s.* die Mutter. —**hood**, *s.*
die Mutterschaft. —**less**, *adj.* mut-
terlos. —**liness**, *s.* die Mütterlich-
keit. —**ly**, *adj.* mütterlich. —
country, *s.* das Vaterland. —**in-
law**, *s.* die Schwiegermutter. —**of-
pearl**, *s.* die Perlmutter. —**tongue**,
s. die Muttersprache.

Motif, *s.* das Leitmotiv (*Mus.*).

Motion, I. *s.* die Bewegung, der Gang
(*also Mach.*); (proposal) der Vor=
schlag, Antrag. II. *v.a.* hinanweisen.
III. *v.n.* zuwinken. —**less**, *adj.*
bewegungslos, regungslos, unbeweg=
lich.

Motive, I. *s.* der Beweggrund. II. *adj.*; — power, bewegende Kraft, Triebkraft. —**less,** *adj.* grundlos.

Motley, *adj.* buntscheckig.

Motor, I. *s.* die Kraftmaschine, der Motor, das Auto (*Mech.*). II. *v.n.* auteln, (im) Automobil fahren. — **ist,** *s.* der Autler, der Automobilfahrer. —**bicycle,** *s.* das Motorrad. —**car,** *s.* der Kraftwagen, das Auto; — race, das Auto-Rennen.

Mottled, *adj.* gefleckt, gesprenkelt.

Motto, *s.* der Spruch, Wahlspruch.

¹**Mould,** *s.* die Gartenerde.

²**Mould,** I. *s.* die Form; der Körperbau; (pattern) die Schablone. II. *v.a.* bilden, gestalten.

³**Mould,** *s.* der Moder. —**iness,** *s.* das Schimmelige. —**y,** *adj.* schimmelig.

¹**Moulder,** *v.n.* (ver)modern, zerstäuben; schimmelig *or* kahmig werden.

²**Moulder,** *s.* der Former, Bildner.

Moulding, *s.* das Modellieren; das Gesims (*Arch.*).

Moult, *v.n.* mausern, haaren.

Mound, *s.* der Erdhügel.

Mount, I. *s.* der Berg; die Einrahmung, -fassung (*pictures*, etc.); das Reitpferd. II. *v.a.* besteigen, reiten (*horses*); einrahmen (*pictures*); fassen (*jewels*).

Mountain, *s.* der Berg (*also fig.*); —s, Gebirge (*pl.*). —**eer,** *s.* der Bergbewohner. —**ous,** *adj.* bergig, gebirgig. —**ash,** *s.* die Vogelbeere.

Mountebank, *s.* der Marktschreier, Quacksalber.

Mourn, *v.* I. *a.* trauern (um einen), betrauern. II. *n.* traurig sein, trauern. —**er,** *s.* der Trauernde; der Leidtragende (*at funerals*). —**ful,** *adj.*, —**fully,** *adv.* traurig, Trauer-. —**ing,** I. *adj.* trauernd, Trauer-. II. *s.* das Trauern; die Trauer(kleidung).

Mouse, I. *s.* die Maus. II. *v.n.* mausen. —**trap,** *s.* die Mausefalle.

Mouser, *s.* der Mäusefänger.

Moustache, *s.* der Schnurrbart.

Mouth, *s.* der Mund; das Maul, der Rachen (*of beasts*); die Mündung (*of a river, a cannon*). —**ful,** *s.* der Mundvoll; (*fig.*) das Bißchen. — **piece,** *s.* das Mundstück.

Mov—able, *adj.*, —**ably,** *adv.* beweglich. —**ableness,** *s.* die Beweglichkeit. —**ables,** *pl.* Mobilien. —**e,** I. *v.a.* bewegen; fortbewegen (*from*

a place); rücken (*a chair, etc.*); ziehen (*a piece in Chess, etc.*); vorschlagen, vorbringen (*a resolution*). II. *v.n.* sich bewegen; (stir) sich regen, sich rühren. III. *s.* die Bewegung, das Ziehen; der Zug (*at Chess, etc.*). —**ement,** *s.* die Bewegung (*also Mech., Mil.*). —**er,** *s.* der, die (sich) Bewegende; der Antragsteller (*Parl., etc.*). —**ing,** *adj.*, —**ingly,** *adv.* bewegend; beweglich (*as clouds*); (*fig.*) rührend.

Mow, *v.* I. *a.* (ab)mähen. II. *n.* mähen. —**er,** *s.* der Mäher. —**ing-machine,** *s.* die Mähmaschine.

Much, I. *adj.* viel. II. *adv.* sehr, weit, bei weitem; as — again, noch einmal so viel; I thought as —, das dachte ich mir; to make — of, viel Wesens machen von.

Muck, *s.* der Mist. —**y,** *adj.* schmutzig.

Muc—ous, *adj.* schleimig; —ous membrane, die Schleimhaut. —**us,** *s.* der Schleim.

Mud, *s.* der Schlamm, Schmutz. —**diness,** *s.* die Schlammigkeit. —**guard,** *s.* das Schmutzblech, der Kotflügel. —**dy,** I. *adj.* schlammig; -rüb (*as water*). II. *v.a.* trüben.

Muddle, I. *v.a.* verwirren. II. *v.n.* wühlen. III. *s.* die Verwirrung, Unordnung.

Muff, *s.* der Muff.

Muffle, *v.a.* einhüllen. —**r,** *s.* das wollene Halstuch; der Dämpfer (*Mus.*).

Mufti, *s.*; in —, in Zivil.

Mug, *s.* der Krug, die Kanne.

Mulatto, *s.* der Mulatte, die Mulattin.

Mulberry, *s.* die Maulbeere.

Mule, *s.* das Maultier. —**teer,** *s.* der Mauleseltreiber.

Mullet, *s.* die Meeräsche.

Multi—farious, *adj.*, —**fariously,** *adv.* mannigfaltig. —**form,** *adj.* vielgestaltig. —**lateral,** *adj.* vielseitig. —**ple,** *s.* das Vielfache. —**plication,** *s.* die Vervielfältigung; die Multiplikation; the —plication table, das Einmaleins. —**ply,** *v.* I. *a.* vervielfachen, multiplizieren (*Arith.*). II. *n.* sich vermehren. —**tude,** *s.* der große Haufe. —**tudinous,** *adj.*, —**tudinously,** *adv.* zahlreich.

Mum, I. *adj.* stumm. II. *int.* still!

Mumbl—e, *v.* I. *n.* brummeln. II. *a.* hermurmeln; (chew) muffeln. —**ing,**

I. *adj.*, **—ingly**, *adv.* murmelnd. II. *s.* das Gemurmel.

Mummer, *s.* der Vermummte.

Mummy, *s.* die Mumie.

Mumps, *s.* der Ziegenpeter (*Med.*).

Munch, *v.a. & n.* (geräuschvoll) kauen.

Municipal, *adj.* Stadt=, Gemeinde=. **—ity**, *s.* der Gemeindebezirk.

Munificen—ce, *s.* die Freigebigkeit. **—t**, *adj.*, **—tly**, *adv.* freigebig.

Munition, *s.* der Kriegsvorrat.

Murder, I. *s.* der Mord, die Mordtat. II. *int.* Mordio! III. *v.a.* (er=) morden. **—er**, *s.* der Mörder. **—ess**, *s.* die Mörderin. **—ous**, *adj.*, **—ously**, *adv.* mörderisch.

Murk—y, *adj.*, **—ily**, *adv.* finster, trübe.

Murmur, I. *s.* das Gemurmel; das Rauschen (*of a stream*). II. *v.a. & n.* murmeln; leise rauschen. **—er**, *s.* der Murrkopf. **—ing**, I. *adj.* murmelnd; murrend. II. *s.* das Murmeln; das Gemurr(e).

Murrain, *s.* die Viehseuche.

Musc—le, *s.* der Muskel. **—ular**, *adj.*, **—ularly**, *adv.* muskelig, Muskel=.

¹Muse, *s.* die Muse.

²Muse, *v.n.* nachgrübeln (on a thing, über eine S.), in Gedanken vertieft sein.

Museum, *s.* das Museum.

Mushroom, *s.* der Pilz, Erdschwamm.

Music, *s.* die Musik; (written —) die Noten. **—al**, *adj.*, **—ally**, *adv.* musikalisch. **—ian**, *s.* der Musiker. **—book**, *s.* das Notenbuch.

Musing, I. *adj.*, **—ly**, *adv.* nachsinnend. II. *s.* das Grübeln, Nachsinnen.

Musk, *s.* der Moschus.

Musket, *s.* die Flinte, Muskete. **—eer**, *s.* der Musketier. **—ry**, *s.* das Musketenfeuer.

Muslin, *s.* der Musselin.

Mussel, *s.* die Muschel.

¹Must, *v.aux.* müssen; I — not do it, ich darf es nicht tun.

²Must, *s.* der Most.

Mustard, *s.* der Senf.

Muster, I. *s.* die Musterung (*Mil.*); to pass —, hingehen, geduldet werden. II. *v.a.* mustern (*Mil.*). III. *v.n.* sich versammeln *or* ansammeln.

Mustiness, *s.* die Dumpfigkeit.

Musty, *adj.* muffig.

Mute, I. *adj.*, **—ly**, *adv.* stumm. II. *s.* der, die Stumme. **—ness**, *s.* die Stummheit.

Mutilat—e, *v.a.* verstümmeln (*also fig.*). **—ion**, *s.* die Verstümmelung.

Mutin—eer, *s.* der Meuterer. **—ous**, *adj.*, **—ously**, *adv.* meuterisch. **—y**, I. *s.* die Meuterei. II. *v.n.* meutern.

Mutter, I. *v.a. & n.* murmeln, murren. II. *s.* das Murren, das Gemurmel.

Mutton, *s.* das Hammelfleisch. **—chop**, *s.* das Hammelrippchen.

Mutual, *adj.*, **—ly**, *adv.* gegenseitig, wechselseitig. **—ity**, *s.* die Gegenseitigkeit.

Muzzle, I. *s.* die Schnauze; die Mündung (*of a gun, etc.*); der Maulkorb (*for a dog*). II. *v.a.* knebeln, einen Maulkorb anlegen.

My, *poss. adj.* mein(e). **—self**, *pron.* ich selbst, mich, mir.

Myriad, *s.* die Myriade, Unzahl.

Myrrh, *s.* die Myrrhe.

Myrtle, *s.* die Myrte.

Myst—erious, *adj.*, **—eriously**, *adv.* geheimnisvoll. **—eriousness**, *s.* das Geheimnisvolle, Dunkel. **—ery**, *s.* das Geheimnis. **—ic(al)**, I. *adj.*, **—ically**, *adv.* mystisch. II. *s.*, der Mystiker. **—icism**, *s.* der Mystizismus. **—ify**, *v.a.* anführen, foppen.

Myth, *s.* die Mythe. **—ic(al)**, *adj.* mythisch, sagenhaft. **—ological**, *adj.*, **—ologically**, *adv.* mythologisch. **—ology**, *s.* die Mythologie, die Götterlehre.

N

N, n, *s.* das N, n.

Nab, *v.a.* erhaschen.

Nabob, *s.* der Nabob, der Krösus.

Nadir, *s.* der Nadir; (*fig.*) der Tiefstand.

Nag, I. *s.* das Pferdchen. II. *v.a.* (mit einem) keifen, nörgeln. **—ger**, *s.* der Keifer, Nörgler, die Keiferin, Nörglerin.

Nail, I. *s.* der Nagel (*on fingers, etc.*, also of metal). II. *v.a.* (an)nageln.

Naïve, *adj.*, **—ly**, *adv.* naiv. **—té**, **—ty**, *s.* die Naivität.

Naked, *adj.*, **—ly**, *adv.* nackt, bloß, unverhüllt. **—ness**, *s.* die Nacktheit, Blöße.

Name, I. *s.* der Name, to call a person —s, einem Schimpfnamen geben. II. *v.a.* (be)nennen. **—d**, *p.p.* genannt, namens. **—less**, *adj.* namenlos; (unknown) unbekannt. **—ly**, *adv.* näm-

lich. —-plate, s. das Türschild. —
sake, s. der Namensvetter.
Nanny-goat, s. die Ziege.
¹Nap, I. s. das Schläfchen. II. v.n.
nicken.
²Nap, s. die Noppe.
Nape, s. das Genick.
Napery, s. das Tischzeug.
Naphtha, s. das Bergöl, Steinöl,
die Naphtha.
Napkin, s. das Tellertuch, die Serviette.
Narcissus, s. die Narzisse (Bot.).
Narcotic, I. adj. einschläfernd; narkotisch. II. s. das Schlafmittel.
Narrat—e, v.a. erzählen. —ion, s.
die Erzählung. —ive, I. adj. erzählend. II. s. die Erzählung, Geschichte. —or, s. der Erzähler.
Narrow, I. adj. eng, schmal; to have
a — escape, mit genauer Not entkommen. II. v.a. einengen. III. v.n.
sich verengen. IV. s. der Engpaß.
—ly, adv. eng, schmal; (closely) genau,
sorgfältig; (by a little) kaum. —ness,
s. die Enge, Schmalheit; die Beschränktheit (of capacity, etc.). —s, pl.
die Meerenge. —-gauge, I. s. die
Schmalspur. II. attrib. schmalspurig.
—-minded, adj. engherzig.
Narwhal, s. der Narwal, das (See-)
Einhorn.
Nasal, adj. Nasen-.
Nast—iness, s. der Unflat; die Zotigkeit. —y, adj. unflätig, schmutzig.
Natal, adj. Geburts-.
Nation, s. die Nation, das Volk. —
al, adj. volkstümlich, national, Staats-,
National-. —ality, s. die Volksart, Nationalität.
Nativ—e, I. adj. gebürtig (of, aus),
heimisch (of, in); (natural) natürlich,
angeboren. II. s. der Eingeborene.
—ity, s. die Geburt.
Natural, I. adj. natürlich, Natur-;
(uncultivated) wild; (innate) angeboren; — philosophy, die Physik,
Naturlehre. II. s. der Blödsinnige.
—ist, s. der Naturforscher. —
ization, s. die Einbürgerung. —
ize, v.a. einbürgern. —ly, adv.
natürlich.
Nature, s. die Natur; (by —) von
Natur; (according to —) naturgemäß; wild; natürlicherweise. —d,
adj. (in comp.) -geartet, -artig; good-
—d, gutmütig; ill—d, boshaft.
Naught, I. adj. nichtig. II. adv.
keineswegs. III. s. & pron. das
Nichts; die Null.
Naught—ily, adv., —y, adj. unartig,
ungezogen. —iness, s. die Ungezogenheit, Unartigkeit.
Nau—sea, s. die Übelkeit; (fig.) der
Ekel. —seate, v. I. n. Ekel empfinden (at, vor). II. a. to be —seated,
sich ekeln. —seous, adj., —seously,
adv. ekelhaft, widrig. —seousness,
s. die Widerlichkeit.
Nautical, adj., —ly, adv. nautisch, See-.
Nautilus, s. der Nautilus.
Naval, adj. See-, Schiffs-.
¹Nave, s. der Nabel.
²Nave, s. die Nabe (of a wheel).
³Nave, s. das Schiff (Arch.).
Naviga—ble, adj. schiffbar, fahrbar;
—ble balloon, lenkbares Luftschiff.
—te, v. I. a. befahren (seas); durchschiffen (the air); steuern, führen
(a ship). II. n. segeln. —tion, I.
s. die Schiffahrt, Seefahrt; (art
of —tion) die Schiffahrtskunde. II.
attrib.; —tion laws, Schiffahrtsgesetze.
—tor, s. der Seefahrer; der Steuermann.
Navvy, s. der Erdarbeiter.
Navy, s. die Marine; (warships) die
Kriegsflotte.
Nay, adv. nein.
Neap, adj.; — tide, die Nippflut.
Near, I. adj. nah(e) (in time, space or
degree); gerade (as a way); — at
hand, dicht bei. II. prep. (— to) nahe,
nahe an or bei, bei. —ly, adv. nahe;
fast, ungefähr. —-sighted, adj. kurzsichtig.
Neat, I. adj., —ly, adv. nett, sauber;
(tidy) ordentlich. II. s. das Rindvieh.
—ness, s. die Nettigkeit.
Nebul—a, s. der Nebelfleck, Nebelstern. —ous, adj. bewölkt, nebelig.
Necess—arily, adv. notwendig, durchaus. —ariness, s. die Notwendigkeit. —ary, I. adj. notwendig. II.
s. das Bedürfnis. —itate, v.a.
erfordern. —itous, adj. dürftig,
notleidend. —ity, s. die Notwendigkeit; (inevitableness) die Unvermeidlichkeit; (constraint) der Zwang;
(want) die Armut.
Neck, s. der Hals, Nacken. —lace,
s. das Halsband, die Halskette.
—tie, s. die Halsbinde, Krawatte.
Nectar, s. der Nektar. —ine, s. die
Nektarine.

Need, I. *s.* die Not, der Bedarf, das Bedürfnis; in case of —, im Notfalle; if — be, nötigenfalls. II. *v.a.* nötig haben, brauchen, bedürfen. III. *v.n.* & *aux.* nötig sein. **—ful,** *adj.*, **—fully,** *adv.* notwendig, nötig, bedürftig. **—less,** *adj.*, **—lessly,** *adv.* unnötig, vergeblich. **—lessness,** *s.* die Unnötigkeit. **—y,** *adj.* arm, dürftig.

Needle, *s.* die Nadel; darning, knitting, sewing —, Stopf=, Strick=, Nähnadel; — of the compass, Magnetnadel; —'s eye, das Nadelöhr. **—work,** *s.* die Näharbeit, Nadelarbeit, Handarbeit.

Ne'er-do-well, *s.* der Taugenichts.

Negati—on, *s.* die Verneinung. **—ve,** I. *adj.*, **—vely,** *adv.* verneinend. II. *s.* die Negative, Verneinung. III. *v.a.* verneinen; ablehnen.

Neglect, I. *s.* die Vernachlässigung (*of duty, etc.*); (carelessness) die Nachlässigkeit; (omission to do) die Versäumnis. II. *v.a.* vernachlässigen, versäumen. **—ed,** *adj.* verwahrlost. **—ful,** *adj.*, **—fully,** *adv.* achtlos (of, auf (*acc.*)).

Negligen—ce, *s.* die Nachlässigkeit, Achtlosigkeit. **—t,** *adj.*, **—tly,** *adv.* nachlässig, unachtsam.

Nego—tiable, *adj.* verhandelbar. **—tiate,** *v.* I. *a.* verhandeln. II. *n.* handeln; unterhandeln. **—tiation,** *s.* das Verhandeln, Unterhandeln. **—tiator,** *s.* der Unterhändler, Vermittler; die Vermittlerin.

Negr—ess, *s.* die Negerin. **—o,** *s.* der Neger.

Negus, *s.* der Glühwein.

Neigh, I. *v.n.* wiehern. II. *s.* das Wiehern.

Neighbour, *s.* der Nachbar, die Nachbarin. **—hood,** *s.* die Nachbarschaft, die Nähe. **—ing,** *adj.*; —ing parts, die Umgebung. **—ly,** *adj.* nachbarlich, freundlich.

Neither, I. *pron.* keiner von beiden, keiner. II. *adj.* kein(e). III. *conj.* weder; . . . nor, weder . . . noch.

Nephew, *s.* der Neffe.

Nerv—e, *s.* der Nerv; (impudence) die Frechheit (*sl.*). **—ed,** *adj.* nervig. **—eless,** *adj.* kraftlos. **—ous,** *adj.*, **—ously,** *adv.* Nerven=, nervös. **—ousness,** *s.* die Nervenschwäche; die Schüchternheit, Befangenheit.

Nest, I. *s.* das Nest (*also fig.*); to feather one's —, sich bereichern, nisten. II. *v.n.* nisten. **—egg,** *s.* (*fig.*) der Heckpfennig.

Nestle, *v.n.* sich einnisten (*also fig.*).

¹Net, I. *s.* das Netz. II. *v.a.* mit einem Netze fangen (*fish, etc.*). **—ting,** *s.* das Netz, Netzwerk; wire —ting, das Drahtnetz.

²Net, *adj.* netto, rein.

Nether, *adj.* nieder, unter, Unter=. **—most,** I. *adj.* niedrigst, unterst. II. *adv.* zu unterst.

Nettle, I. *s.* die Nessel. II. *v.a.* ärgern.

Neur—algia, *s.* die Neuralgie. **—algic,** *adj.* neuralgisch. **—itis,** *s.* die Nervenzündung.

Neuter, I. *adj.* geschlechtslos; sächlich (*as nouns*). II. *s.* das Geschlechtslose; das Neutrum (*Gram.*).

Neutral, I. *adj.*, **—ly,** *adv.* unbeteiligt, parteilos, neutral. II. *s.* der Unparteiische, Neutrale. **—ity,** *s.* die Neutralität.

Never, *adv.* nie, niemals, nimmer. **—theless,** *conj.* nichtsdestoweniger.

New, *v.a.* neu, modern; — Year, das Neujahr; — Year's Eve, der Silvesterabend. **—ly,** *adv.* neulich, jüngst, neu. **—ness,** *s.* die Neuheit. **—s,** *s.* die Nachricht; what's the —s, was gibt's neues? **—comer,** *s.* der Ankömmling. **—spaper,** *s.* die Zeitung.

Newt, *s.* der Molch.

Next, I. *adj.* nächst; the — day, den Tag darauf; the week after —, die übernächste Woche; — door, nebenan; — to nothing, fast gar nichts. II. *adv.* (zu)nächst, gleich darauf. III. *prep.* nächst, bei, an.

Nib, *s.* die Spitze (*of a pen*).

Nibble, I. *v.a.* benagen. II. *v.n.* nagen. III. *s.* das Anbeißen, Nagen.

Nice, *adj.*, **—ly,** *adv.* niedlich, hübsch, nett, artig, einnehmend (*in appearance*); wohlschmeckend, köstlich (*as food*); lecker; (fastidious) wählerisch, heikel; genau, regelrecht (*as workmanship*). **—ness,** *s.* die Feinheit, Zartheit (*of taste*); die Schärfe (*of judgment*); die Genauigkeit; (overfastidiousness) die Ziererei; die Niedlichkeit, Anmut. **—ty,** *s.* die Feinheit, Schärfe; (exactness) die Pünktlichkeit; (— distinction) die Spitzfindigkeit.

Niche, *s.* die Nische.

Nick, I. *s.* der Einschnitt. II. *v.a.*

einschneiden. **—nack,** *s.* die Nippsache.

Nickel, I. *s.* das Nickel. II. *v.a.* vernickeln. **—plating,** *s.* die Vernickelung. **—silver,** *s.* das Neusilber.

Nickname, *s.* der Spitzname.

Nicotine, *s.* das Nikotin.

Niece, *s.* die Nichte.

Niggard, I. *s.* der Geizhals. II. *adj.*, **—ly,** *adj. & adv.* geizig (of, in, mit). **—liness,** *s.* die Knauserei.

Nigger, *s.* der Neger.

Nigh, I. *adj.* nah. II. *adv.* nahe; well —, nahezu. III. *prep.* neben.

Night, *s.* die Nacht. **—less,** *adj.* nachtlos. **—ly,** I. *adj.* nächtlich, Nacht-. II. *adv.* jede Nacht, alle Nächte. **—cap,** *s.* die Nachtmütze. **—dress, —gown,** *s.* das Nachtkleid, Nachthemd (einer Frau). **—fall,** *s.* der Einbruch der Nacht. **—ingale,** *s.* die Nachtigall. **—mare,** *s.* das Alpdrücken.

Nimbl—e, *adj.*, **—y,** *adv.* flink, gewandt. **—eness,** *s.* die Behendigkeit, Gewandtheit.

Nin—e, *num. adj.* neun. **—eteen,** *num. adj.* neunzehn. **—etieth,** *adj.* neunzigst. **—ety,** *num. adj.* neunzig. **—th,** *adj.* neunt. **—thly,** *adv.* neuntens. **—efold,** *adj.* neunfach. **—e-pins,** *s.* die Kegel.

1**Nip,** I. *v.a.* kneifen; to — in the bud, im Keime ersticken. II. *s.* der Kniff; der Frostbrand.

2**Nip,** *s.* das Schlückchen (*drink*).

Nipper, *s.* die Kralle, Krebsschere; der kleine Kerl (*sl.*).

Nipple, *s.* die Brustwarze.

Nit, *s.* die Niß.

Nitr—ate, I. *adj.* salpetersauer. II. *s.* salpetersaures Salz. **—e,** *s.* der (Natron-)Salpeter. **—ic,** *adj.* salpetersauer; **—ic acid,** die Salpetersäure. **—ogen,** I. *s.* der Stickstoff. II. *attrib.*; **—ogen gas,** das Stick-(stoff)gas. **—ogenous,** *adj.* stickstoffhaltig.

Nit-wit, *s.* der Einfaltspinsel (*sl.*).

No, I. *adj.* kein. II. *adv.* nein. III. *s.* das Nein.

Nob—ility, *s.* der Adel. **—le,** I. *adj.*, **—ly,** *adv.* adelig; (*fig.*) edel, groß, erhaben. II. *s.* der Adelige, Edle. **—leman,** *s.* der Edelmann, Adelige. **—lewoman,** *s.* die Edelfrau.

Nobody, *s.* niemand.

Nocturnal, *adj.* nächtlich, Nacht-.

Nod, I. *v.a. & n.* nicken. II. *s.* das Kopfnicken.

Nois—e, I. *s.* der Lärm, das Geräusch, Getöse. II. *v.a.*; to —e abroad, ausschreien. **—eless,** *adj.*, **—elessly,** *adv.* geräuschlos. **—elessness,** *s.* die Geräuschlosigkeit. **—ily,** *adv.* mit Geräusch. **—iness,** *s.* der Lärm. **—y,** *adj.* geräuschvoll, lärmend.

Noisome, *adj.* schädlich.

Nomad, I. *adj.* nomadisch. II. *s.* der Nomade.

Nomin—al, *adj.* angeblich, namentlich, nominal. **—ally,** *adv.* angeblich. **—ate,** *v.a.* ernennen (*to an office*); (*propose*) zur Wahl vorschlagen. **—ation,** *s.* die Ernennung, die Vorwahl. **—ative,** *s.* der Nominativ (*Gram.*). **—ee,** *s.* der Ernannte.

Non— (*in comp.*) —combatant, *s.* der Nichtkämpfer. **—commissioned,** *adj.*; **—commissioned officer,** der Unteroffizier. **—compliance,** *s.* die Unwillfährlichkeit. **— compos mentis,** *adj.* unzurechnungsfähig. **—conducting,** *adj.* nicht leitend. **—conductor,** *s.* der Nichtleiter. **—delivery,** *s.* die Nichtabgabe. **—essential,** I. *adj.* unwesentlich. II. *s.* das nicht wesentliche Ding.

Nonage, *s.* die Minderjährigkeit.

Nonagenarian, I. *adj.* neunzigjährig. II. *s.* der Neunzigjährige.

Nonce, *s.*; for the —, für den Fall, für den Augenblick.

Nonchalan—ce, *s.* die Fahrlässigkeit. **—t,** *adj.*, **—tly,** *adv.* nachlässig, gleichgültig.

None, I. *adj.* kein. II. *pron.* keiner, keine, keines. III. *adv.* nicht im Geringsten; — the less, nichtsdestoweniger.

Nondescript, *adj.* unbestimmt; seltsam.

Nonentity, *s.* das Nichtsein; ein unbedeutender Mensch.

Nonplus, I. *s.* die Verlegenheit. II. *v.a.* in die Enge treiben.

Nonsens—e, *s.* der Unsinn, das dumme Zeug. **—ical,** *adj.*, **—ically,** *adv.* unsinnig, sinnlos; (silly) albern.

Nook, *s.* der Winkel, die Ecke.

Noon, *s.* der Mittag. **—day, —tide,** I. *s.* der Mittag. II. *adj.* mittägig.

Noose, *s.* die Schleife, Schlinge.

Nor, *conj.* noch); auch nicht; neither . . . —, weder . . . noch.

Norm, *s.* die Regel, das Muster. **—al,**
adj., **—ally,** *adv.* normal, vorschriftsmäßig.

North, I. *s.* der Norden, der Nord
(*poet.*). II. *adj. & adv.* nördlich.
—erly, *adj. & adv.* nördlich. **—ern,**
adj. nordisch, nördlich. **—ward,** I.
adj. nördlich. II. *adv.* (*also* **—wards**)
nordwärts. **—east,** I. *s.* der Nord-
ost(en). II. *adj. & adv.,* **—eastern,**
adj., **—easterly,** *adj. & adv.* nord-
östlich. **—easter,** *s.* der Nordost-
wind. **—man,** *s.* der Standinavier.
—west, I. *s.* der Nordwest. II. *adj.
& adv.,* **—western,** *adj.,* **—westerly,**
adj. & adv. nordwestlich.

Nose, *s.* die Nase. **—bag,** *s.* der
Futterbeutel (für Pferde).

Nosegay, *s.* der Blumenstrauß, das
Sträußchen.

Nostril, *s.* das Nasenloch, die Nüster.

Nostrum, *s.* das Geheimmittel.

Not, *adv.* nicht.

Notwithstanding, I. *prep.* ungeachtet
(*gen.*), trotz (*gen., dat.*). II. *conj.*
dessen ungeachtet, trotzdem.

Not—able, I. *adj.,* **—ably,** *adv.* bemerkenswert, merkwürdig; (import-
ant) ansehnlich. II. *s.* die Notabilität.

Notary, *s.* der Notar(ius).

Notation, *s.* die Aufzeichnung; die
Bezeichnung (*Arith., Geom.*); die
Bezifferung (*Mus.*).

Notch, I. *s.* der Einschnitt. II. *v.a.*
kerben, einschneiden.

Not—e, I. *s.* (notice) die Notiz; (memorandum) die Anmerkung, Note;
(letter) das Briefchen, Billett. II.
v.a. bezeichnen; (—e down) anmerk-
en, notieren; (—ice) bemerken. **—ed,**
adj. berühmt. **—e-book,** *s.* das Merk-
buch, Notizbuch. **—e-paper,** *s.* das
Briefpapier. **—eworthy,** *adj.* bemerkenswert, merkwürdig.

Nothing, I. *pron. & s.* nichts; das
Nichts; for —, umsonst; good for —,
untauglich; next to —, fast nichts. II.
adv. keineswegs. **—ness,** *s.* die
Nichtigkeit.

Noti—ce, I. *s.* (observation) die Beobachtung, Bemerkung; (intimation)
die Notiz, Anzeige; (—ce to leave)
die Kündigung; (warning) die Warnung; (attention) die Aufmerksamkeit;
to give someone —ce, jemandem
fündigen. II. *v.a.* wahrnehmen, bemerken. **—ceable,** *adj.,* **—ceably,**

adv. merklich; bemerkenswert. **—ce-
board,** *s.* die Anschlagtafel.

Notif—ication, *s.* die Anzeige. **—y,**
v.a. anzeigen.

Notion, *s.* der Begriff.

Notori—ety, *s.* die Offenkundigkeit.
—ous, *adj.,* **—ously,** *adv.* notorisch;
(infamous) berüchtigt.

Noun, *s.* das Hauptwort, Nennwort.

Nourish, *v.a.* nähren; (*fig.*) ernähren,
erhalten. **—er,** *s.* der Ernährer.
—ing, *adj.* nahrhaft. **—ment,** *s.*
die Nahrung, das Nahrungsmittel.

Novel, I. *adj.* neu; (strange) ungewöhnlich. II. *s.* der Roman; short
—el, die Novelle. **—ist,** *s.* der
Romanschriftsteller. **—ty,** *s.* die
Neuheit.

November, *s.* der November.

Novice, *s.* der Neuling.

Now, *adv.* nun, jetzt; just —, soeben;
before —, schon einmal, **—adays,**
adv. heutzutage.

Nowhere, *adv.* nirgend(s), nirgendwo.

Noxious, *adj.,* **—ly,** *adv.* schädlich.
—ness, *s.* die Schädlichkeit.

Nozzle, *s.* die Schnauze, der Rüssel.

Nucleus, *s.* der Kern.

Nud—e, *adj.* nackt, bloß. **—ity,** *s.*
die Nacktheit, Blöße.

Nudge, I. *s.* leichter Stoß. II. *v.a.*
einen Rippenstoß geben.

Nugget, *s.* der Goldklumpen.

Nuisance, *s.* das Lästige, Anstößige,
der Unfug; a public —, ein öffent-
licher Standal.

Null, *adj.* nichtig. **—ify,** *v.a.* für
nichtig erklären. **—ity,** *s.* die Nichtigkeit, Ungültigkeit.

Numb, I. *adj.* erstarrt. II. *v.a.*
erstarren. **—ness,** *s.* die Erstarrung,
Betäubung.

Number, I. *s.* die Zahl (*also Gram.*);
(multitude) die Menge, Schar; die
Nummer (*of a ticket*); even (odd)
—, gerade (ungerade) Zahl; singular
(plural) —, Einzahl (Mehrzahl); das
Heft (*of a magazine*). II. *v.a.* zählen,
rechnen; numerieren (*houses, etc.*).
—less, *adj.* zahllos.

Numer—able, *adj.* zählbar. **—al,** I.
adj. bezeichnend, Zahl-. II. *s.* das
Zahlzeichen, die Ziffer. **—ation,** *s.*
das Zählen. **—ator,** *s.* der Zähler
(*of a fraction*). **—ical,** *adj.* numerisch,
Zahlen-, Zahl-. **—ous,** *adj.,* **—ously,**
adv. zahlreich.

Nun, *s.* die Nonne. **—nery,** *s.* das Nonnenkloster.

Nuptial, *adj.* hochzeitlich, Hochzeits=, ehelich. **—s,** *pl.* die Hochzeit.

Nurse, I. *s.* die Kinderwärterin, das Kindermädchen; (wet —) die Amme; sick —, die Krankenwärterin. II. *v.a.* stillen (*an infant*); (rear) aufziehen; pflegen (*the sick, etc.*). **—ry,** *s.* die Kinderstube; die Pflanz=, Baum= schule; —ry rhymes, die Kinderlieder.

Nurture, I. *s.* die Nahrung. II. *v.a.* nähren.

Nut, *s.* die Nuß (*also Mech.*); (screw —) die Schraubenmutter; der Stutzer (*sl.*). **—cracker,** *s.*; (pair of) —crackers, der Nußknacker. **—shell,** *s.* die Nußschale.

Nutmeg, *s.* die Muskatnuß.

Nutri—ment, *s.* das Futter, die Nahrung. **—tion,** *s.* die Ernährung. **—tious,** *adj.* nahrhaft.

Nymph, *s.* die Nymphe.

O

O, o, *s.* das O, o; das Ach.

Oak, *s.* die Eiche. **—en,** *adj.* eichen.

Oakum, *s.* das Werg.

Oar, *s.* das Ruder. **—sman,** *s.* der Ruderer.

Oasis, *s.* die Oase.

Oat, *s.* der Hafer (*Agr.*). *—en,* *adj.* von Hafer, aus Hafermehl. **—meal,** *s.* das Hafermehl.

Oath, *s.* der Eid, Schwur; (blasphe- mous —) der Fluch; to take an —, einen Eid leisten; to tender an — to a person, einem einen Eid zuschieben.

Obdura—cy, *s.* die Halsstarrigkeit. **—te,** *adj.,* **—tely,** *adv.* verhärtet, ver- stockt; halsstarrig.

Obedien—ce, *s.* der Gehorsam. **—t,** *adj.,* **—tly,** *adv.* gehorsam.

Obeisance, *s.* die Verbeugung.

Obelisk, *s.* die Spitzsäule.

Obey, *v.a.* gehorchen (a person, einem).

Obituary, *adj.* Toten=, Todes=; — notice, die Todesanzeige.

Object, I. *s.* der Gegenstand; (end) der Zweck, das Ziel; das Objekt (*Gram.*). II. *v.a.* & *n.* entgegen- stellen, einwenden. **—ion,** *s.* die Einwendung, der Einwand, Einwurf; there is no —ion, es ist nichts dagegen einzuwenden. **—ionable,** *adj.* —

ionably, *adv.* nicht einwandfrei; (inadmissible) unzulässig. **—ive,** I. *adj.,* **—ively,** *adv.* objektiv. II. *s.* (—ive case) der Objektsfall; das Ziel. **—less,** *adj.* zwecklos. **—or,** *s.* der Gegenredner. **—lesson,** *s.* der Anschauungsunterricht.

Oblig—ation, *s.* die Verpflichtung; to be under an — to a person, einem zu Danke verpflichtet sein. **—atory,** *adj.* verbindend, verpflichtend. **—e,** *v.a.* verbinden, verpflichten; (constrain) nötigen, zwingen; much —ed, sehr verbunden, danke bestens. **—ing,** *adj.,* **—ingly,** *adv.* verbindlich. **—ingness,** *s.* die Gefälligkeit.

Obliqu—e, *adj.,* **—ely,** *adv.* schief, schräg. **—eness,—ity,** *s.* die Schief- heit, Schrägheit.

Obliterat—e, *v.a.* auslöschen, vertil- gen. **—ion,** *s.* die Auslöschung.

Oblivio—n, *s.* die Vergeßlichkeit; (being forgotten) die Vergessenheit. **—us,** *adj.,* **—usly,** *adv.* vergeßlich.

Oblong, I. *adj.* länglich. II. *s.* das Rechteck.

Obnoxious, *adj.* verrufen; verhaßt.

Obscen—e, *adj.,* **—ely,** *adv.* schmutzig, unanständig. **—ity,** *s.* die Unzüchtig- keit.

Obscur—e, I. *adj.,* **—ely,** *adv.* düster, dunkel; unbekannt, verborgen. II. *v.a.* verfinstern. **—ity,** *s.* die Dun- kelheit.

Obsequies, *pl.* das Leichenbegängnis, die Totenfeier.

Obsequious, *adj.,* **—ly,** *adv.* unter- würfig. **—ness,** *s.* die Willfährigkeit.

Observ—able, *adj.,* **—ably,** *adv.* be- merkbar. **—ance,** *s.* die Beobachtung; (attention) die Aufmerksamkeit. **—ant,** *adj.,* **—antly,** *adv.* beobachtend, auf- merksam. **—ation,** *s.* die Beo- bachtung; (remark) die Bemerkung. **—atory,** *s.* die Sternwarte. **—e,** *v.* I. *a.* (notice) beobachten, merken (auf eine S.); bemerken, sagen. II. *n.* aufmerksam sein; bemerken. **—er,** *s.* der Beobachter.

Obsolete, *adj.* veraltet, außer Gebrauch. **—ness,** *s.* das Veraltetsein.

Obstacle, *s.* das Hindernis.

Obstina—cy, *s.* der Eigensinn. **—te,** *adj.,* **—tely,** *adv.* halsstarrig, eigen- sinnig.

Obstruct, *v.a.* versperren (*the way, etc.*); hemmen, hindern; verstopfen.

—or, *s.* der Verhinderer. —ion, *s.* die Verstopfung; die Hemmung. —ive, *adj.* hindernd.

Obtain, *v.a.* erlangen. —able, *adj.* erreichbar, erhältlich. —ment, *s.* die Erlangung.

Obtuse, *adj.,* —ly, *adv.* stumpf; — angle, stumpfer Winkel. —ness, *s.* die Stumpfheit.

Obverse, *adj.* umgekehrt.

Obvious, *adj.,* —ly, *adv.* klar, deutlich. —ness, *s.* die Augenscheinlichkeit, Unverkennbarkeit.

Occasion, I. *s.* (cause) der Anlaß; (opportunity) die Gelegenheit; (exigency) das Bedürfnis; (juncture) die Lage, die Umstände. II. *v.a.* veranlassen. —al, *adj.,* —ally, *adv.* zufällig, gelegentlich.

Occident, *s.* der Abend, Westen. —al, *adj.* abendländisch, westlich.

Occult, *adj.* magisch, geheim, verborgen.

Occup=ant, *s.* der Inhaber. —ation, *s.* der Besitz; (calling) der Beruf. —y, *v.a.* einnehmen (*a space*); bewohnen (*a house, etc.*); to be —ied with, sich beschäftigen mit, arbeiten an (*dat.*).

Occur, *v.n.* vorkommen, sich ereignen. —rence, *s.* das Vorkommen; der Vorfall, das Ereignis.

Ocean, I. *s.* das große Meer, Weltmeer. II. *adj.* Meeres=.

Octagon, *s.* das Achteck. —al, *adj.* achteckig.

Octave, *s.* die Oktave.

October, *s.* der Oktober.

Octopus, *s.* der Achtfüßler.

Ocul=ar, *adj.* Augen=. —ist, *s.* der Augenarzt.

Odd, *adj.,* —ly, *adv.* (uneven) ungerade; (strange) seltsam, wunderbar; to do at — times, dann und wann tun; —s and ends, die Schnitzel. —ity, *s.* die Seltsamkeit.

Ode, *s.* die Ode.

Odious, *adj.,* —ly, *adv.* gehässig; widerlich, abscheulich. —ness, *s.* die Verhaßtheit.

Odour, *s.* der Duft. —less, *adj.* geruchlos.

Of, *prep.* von; aus, unter, durch, über, für, auf, an, um, in, zu; to be in need —, (einer Sache) bedürfen; the battle — Waterloo, die Schlacht bei Waterloo; the best — all, das, der Beste von allen *or* unter allen; all —

them, sie alle; the city — Hanover, die Stadt Hannover; a glass — wine, ein Glas Wein; made — gold, von *or* aus Gold gemacht; to be — a party, zu einer Gesellschaft gehören; to die —, sterben an; — necessity, notwendigerweise; — yore, ehemals; to taste —, schmecken nach; a friend — mine, einer meiner Freunde (*or* eine meiner Freundinnen), ein Freund (*or* eine Freundin) von mir; the month —May, der Monat Mai; — all things, vor allen Dingen; — an afternoon, am Nachmittag; — late, neulich; — the name — . . ., mit Namen . . .; to think —, denken an (*acc.*).

Off, I. *adv.* (removed, distant) weg, davon, weit, bis dorthin, von hier; (*opp. to* on, an) aus; (away, from) weg, hinweg; (*with verbs denoting separation =*) ab, weg, los; the affair is —, die Sache ist aus; well —, wohlhabend, gut daran; I am —, ich gehe jetzt; — duty, dienstfrei; — and on, ab und zu. II. *prep.* (away from) von. III. *int.* weg! hinweg! fort!

Offal, *s.* der Abfall.

Offen=ce, *s.* (cause of —ce) die Beleidigung; (wrong, trespass) das Vergehen; (displeasure) der Verdruß; no —ce! nichts für ungut! —d, *v.a.* angreifen, beleidigen. —der, *s.* der Beleidiger, —sive, *adj.,* —sively, *adv.* anstößig, mißfällig; (disgusting) widrig, ekelhaft; (aggressive) angreifend; (insulting) beleidigend, anstößig.

Offer, *v.a.* (dar)bieten, darbringen; bieten (*a sum*); (propose) anbieten; he —ed to strike me, er machte Miene, mich zu schlagen. II. *s.* das Anerbieten, der Antrag; das Angebot. —er, *s.* der Darbietende; der Anbieter. —ing, *s.* das Opfer. —tory, *s.* die Opfergabe.

Offic=e, *s.* das Amt, die Stelle; (function) der Dienst. —er, *s.* der Beamte; der Offizier (*Mil.*). —es, *pl.* Nebengebäude, Stallungen, Speisekammer, Küche. —ial, I. *adj.,* —ially, *adv.* amtlich, Amtsoffiziell. II. *s.* der Beamte. —ialism, *s.* das Beamtentum, der Bürokratismus. —iate, *v.n.* ein Amt versehen.

Officious, *adj.,* übertrieben dienstfertig. —ly, *adv.* zudringlich. —ness, *s.* die Zudringlichkeit.

Offing, *s.*; in the —, (*Naut.*) draußen, auf hoher See.

Offshoot, *s.* der Sprößling.

Offspring, *s.* der Nachkömmling.

Oft, I. *adj.* häufig. II. *adv.,* **—en,** *adv.* oft, öfters. **—(en)times,** *adv.* oft-(mals).

Ogle, *v.a.* beäugeln.

Ogre, *s.* der Oger, Menschenfresser. **—ss,** *s.* die Ogerin.

Oh, *int.* ach! wehe mir!

Oil, I. *s.* das Öl. II. *v.a.* (ein)ölen, beschmieren. **—y,** *adj.* fett, schmierig. **—cloth,** *s.* das Wachstuch. **— painting,** *s.* das Ölgemälde. **— skin,** *s.* der Wachstaffet.

Ointment, *s.* die Salbe.

Old, *adj.* alt; (worn) abgenutzt, verbraucht. **—ish,** *adj.* ältlich. **— fashioned,** *adj.* altmodisch. **— maidish,** *adj.* altjüngferlich.

Olive, I. *s.* (fruit) die Ölbeere; (—tree) der Ölbaum. II. *adj.* olivenfarbig; Mount of —s, der Ölberg.

Omelet, *s.* der Eierkuchen.

Om—en, *s.* die Vorbedeutung. **— inous,** *adj.,* **—inously,** *adv.* bedeutungsvoll, verhängnisvoll.

Omi—ssible, *adj.* auslaßbar, auszulassen. **—ssion,** *s.* die Unterlassung, Versäumnis; (leaving out) die Aus-, Weg-lassung.

Omit, *v.a.* unterlassen, versäumen; auslassen.

Omni—bus, *s.* der Omnibus, Kraftwagen. **—potence,** *s.* die Allmacht. **—potent,** *adj.* allmächtig.

On, I. *prep.* an, auf, bei, zu, in, über, nach, von, um; to call — someone, einen anrufen; (visit) einen besuchen; — these conditions, unter diesen Bedingungen; — the contrary, im Gegenteil; — entering, beim Eintritt; — fire, in Brand, in Flammen; — the first of April, am ersten April; — foot, zu Fuß; — high, droben, hinauf; from — high, von oben herab; — my honour, auf Ehre; — horseback, zu Pferde; my book lies — the desk, mein Buch liegt auf dem Pult; — purpose, absichtlich; — receipt, bei Empfang. II. *adv.* (forward) fort, weiter, ferner, hin, zu; (not off) an, auf; (further) vorwärts, weiter, hin. III. *int.* voran! vorwärts! daran!

Once, *adv.* ein Mal, einmal; (one time) ein einziges Mal; (formerly) einst, vormals, ehedem; (sometime) dereinst; — more, noch einmal; more than —, mehrmals, mehrere Male; at —, sogleich, gleich, sofort; all at —, auf einmal, plötzlich; — and, ein für allemal; this —, dieses eine Mal.

One, I. *adj.* ein; (single) einzig; as — man, einstimmig. II. *pron.* einer, eine, ein, eins; man; — knows, man weiß. III. *s.* Einer; Eins (*Arith.*); the little —s, die Kleinen, die Kinder; — by —, einzeln, einer nach dem andern.

Onerous, *adj.* lästig, beschwerlich.

Onion, *s.* die Zwiebel.

Onlooker, *s.* der Zuschauer.

Only, I. *adj.* einzig. II. *adv.* (nothing but, not more than) nur, bloß; (not before) erst; — yesterday, erst gestern; — think! denken Sie nur! III. *conj.* allein.

Onset, *s.* der Angriff.

Onslaught, *s.* der Angriff.

Onus, *s.* die Beschwerde.

Onward, *adv.* vorwärts, weiter.

Ooze, I. *v.n.* träufeln; to — out, durchsickern. II. *s.* der Schlamm.

Opacity, *s.* die Undurchsichtigkeit.

Opal, *s.* der Opal.

Opaque, *adj.* undurchsichtig.

Open, I. *adj.,* **—ly,** *adv.* offen; (uncovered) unbedeckt, bloß, offen. II. *v.a.* öffnen, aufmachen; to — negotiations, Verhandlungen anknüpfen; to — an account, ein Konto eröffnen. III. *v.n.* sich öffnen, sich auftun. IV. *s.* freie Luft; freies Feld; in the —, im Freien. **—ing,** *s.* das Öffnen; die Eröffnung. **—ness,** *s.* die Offenheit; die Offenherzigkeit.

Opera, *s.* die Oper.

Operat—e, *v.n.* wirken (upon, auf eine S.; also *Med.*); operieren (*Surg.*). **—ic,** *adj.* opernhaft. **—ion,** *s.* die Wirkung; die Operation (*Surg.*); die Operation (*Mil., C.L.*). **—ive,** I. *adj.* wirksam, wirkend. II. *s.* der Handarbeiter, Fabrikarbeiter.

Ophthalmia, *s.* die Augenentzündung.

Opiate, I. *s.* das Einschläferungsmittel (also *fig.*). II. *adj.* einschläfernd.

Opin—e, *v.n.* meinen. **—ion,** *s.* die Meinung, Ansicht, das Urteil; in my —ion, meines Erachtens.

Opium, *s.* das Opium.

Opponent, *s.* der Gegner.

Opportun—e, *adj.,* **—ely,** *adv.* zeitgemäß. **—eness,** *s.* die Zeitgemäßheit, das Gelegene. **—ity,** *s.* die günstige Gelegenheit.

Oppose, *v.a.* entgegen=setzen, =stellen, gegenüberstellen; (object) einwenden, Widerstand leisten, sich entgegenstellen (*a person or thing*).

Opposer, *s.* der Gegner, Widersacher.

Oppos—ite, I. *adj.* entgegengesetzt; (—ed) widerstreitend, feindlich; —ite to, gegenüber. II. *s.* das Gegenteil. **—ition,** *s.* der Widerstand (to, gegen); (obstacle) das Hindernis; (contrast) der Gegensatz; (competition) die Konkurrenz; die Gegenpartei.

Oppress, *v.a.* (be)drücken, unter=, nieder-drücken. **—ion,** *s.* die Bedrückung, Unterdrückung. **—ive,** *adj.,* **—ively,** *adv.* (be=)drückend, niederschlagend. **—iveness,** *s.* die Beklemmung; die Schwüle (*of the air*). **—or,** *s.* der Bedrücker.

Opprobrious, *adj.,* **—ly,** *adv.* schimpflich. **—ness,** *s.* die Schimpflichkeit.

Optic, *adj.,* **—al,** *adj.,* **—ally,** *adv.* optisch. **—ian,** *s.* der Optiker. **—s,** *s.* die Lichtlehre, die Optik.

Optimis—m, *s.* der Optimismus. **—t,** *s.* der Optimist. **—tic,** *adj.* optimistisch.

Option, *s.* die Wahl. **—al,** *adj.,* **—ally,** *adv.* wahlfrei.

Opulent, *adj.* sehr reich, wohlhabend.

Or, *conj.* oder; — else, sonst.

Orac—le, *s.* das Orakel. **—ular,** *adj.,* **—ularly,** *adv.* orakelhaft; (*fig.*) dunkel.

Oral, *adj.,* **—ly,** *adv.* mündlich.

Orange, I. *s.* die Apfelsine. II. *adj.* orange (=gelb, =farbig).

Orat—ion, *s.* die (öffentliche) Rede. **—or,** *s.* der Redner. **—orical,** *adj.,* **—orically,** *adv.* rednerisch. **—orio,** *s.* das Oratorium (*Mus.*). **—ory,** *s.* die Redekunst, die Beredsamkeit; (*Eccles.*) die Betkapelle.

Orb, *s.* der Kreis.

Orbit, *s.* die Bahn (*Ast.*); die Augenhöhle (*Anat.*).

Orchard, *s.* der Obstgarten, Baumgarten.

Orchestra, *s.* das Orchester.

Orchid, *s.* die Orchidee.

Ordain, *v.a.* (arrange) (an)ordnen, einrichten; (establish) festsetzen; ordi-nieren (*clergymen*); (appoint) bestimmen. **—er,** *s.* der Anordner.

Ordeal, *s.* das Gottesurteil; (*fig.*) die harte Probe.

Order, I. *s.* die Ordnung; (mandate) die Anordnung, der Befehl, das Gebot, Geheiß; (precept) die Regel, Vorschrift; (rule) die Maßregel; der Auftrag; (rank) die Reihenfolge, Klasse; der Orden (*of the Garter, etc.*); in — to, um zu; to make to —, nach Bestellung anfertigen. II. *v.a.* (an)ordnen, einrichten; befehlen; (prescribe) verordnen; bestellen; (manage) leiten, regieren; (put in order) in Ordnung bringen. **—liness,** *s.* die Regelmäßigkeit; die Ordnungsliebe. **—ly,** I. *adj.* ordentlich (*of room, etc. and people*); sittsam; (regular) regelmäßig. II. *s.* die Ordonnanz (*Mil.*).

Ordinary, *adj.* (customary) gewöhnlich; (commonplace) gebräuchlich.

Ordination, *s.* die Amtseinführung (eines Geistlichen).

Ordnance, *s.* die Artillerie.

Ore, *s.* das Erz, Metall.

Organ, *s.* das Organ, Werkzeug; die Orgel (*Mus.*). **—ic,** *adj.,* **—ically,** *adv.* organisch. **—ist,** *s.* der Organist. **—ize,** *v.a.* einrichten. **—izer,** *s.* der Anordner.

Orgy, *s.* das zügellose Gelage, das Saufgelage.

Orient, I. *adj.* östlich. II. *s.* der Osten, Morgen; das Morgenland, der Orient. **—al,** I. *adj.* östlich; morgenländisch. II. *s.* der Morgenländer.

Orifice, *s.* die Öffnung.

Origin, *s.* der Ursprung. **—al,** *adj.,* **—ally,** *adv.* ursprünglich; —al sin, die Erbsünde. **—ality,** *s.* die Eigenart, Originalität. **—ate,** *v.* I. *a.* hervorrufen, ins Leben rufen. II. *n.* entstehen (in, aus; with, bei). **—ator,** *s.* der Urheber.

Ornament, I. *s.* der Schmuck; der Zierat. II. *v.a.* (ver)zieren, (aus=) schmücken. **—al,** *adj.,* **—ally,** *adv.* zierend. **—ation,** *s.* die Verzierung.

Ornate, *adj.,* **—ly,** *adv.* geziert, geschmückt.

Ornithology, *s.* die Vogelkunde.

Orphan, I. *s.* der, die Waise. II. *adj.* verwaist. III. *v.a.* zur Waise machen. **—age,** *s.* das Waisenhaus.

Ortho—dox, *adj.* rechtgläubig; strenggläubig. **—doxy,** *s.* die Rechtgläubig-

keit, Orthodoxie. —**graphic(al)**, *adj.*
schreibrichtig. —**graphy**, *s.* die Recht-
schreibung.
Oscillat—e, *v.n.* schwingen; (*fig.*)
schwanken. —**ion**, *s.* die Schwingung,
Schwankung.
Osier, *s.* die Korbweide.
Osprey, *s.* der Flußadler, Fischadler.
Osten—sible, *adj.*, —**sibly**, *adv.* vor-
geblich.
Ostentatio—n, *s.* die Prahlerei. —
us, *adj.*, —**usly** *adv.*, prangend,
prahlend.
Ostler, *s.* der Stallknecht.
Ostracize, *v.a.* in den Bann tun,
verbannen.
Ostrich, *s.* der Strauß.
Other, I. *adj.*, ander; the — day,
neulich; every — day, einen Tag um
den andern; somebody or —, irgend
deiner. II. *pron.* der, die, das andere.
—**s**, *pl.* andere. —**wise**, I. *adv.*
anders. II. *conj.* sonst.
Otter, *s.* die Otter.
Ought, *v.aux.* sollte; I — to do it,
ich sollte es eigentlich tun; you — to
have done it, Sie hätten es tun
sollen.
¹**Ounce**, *s.* die Unze.
²**Ounce**, *s.* der Irbis, Jaguar.
Our, *poss. adj.* unser. —**s**, *poss. pron.*
unser(e), der, die, das Unserige *or*
Unsere. —**selves**, *pl.* wir selbst, uns
(selbst).
Oust, *v.a.* ausstoßen.
Out, I. *adv.* (not in) aus; (*with verbs
of motion*) hinaus, heraus; (not at
home) nicht zu Hause, ausgegangen;
(outside) draußen. II. (— **of**) *prep.*
aus, aus . . . heraus; (beyond) außer;
(not in) außer; (from) aus, von; —
of service, außer Betrieb; the way
—, der Ausgang. —**break**, *s.* der
Ausbruch. —**burst**, *s.* der Ausbruch
—**cast**, *s.* der Verstoßene, Verbannte.
—**come**, *s.* die Folge. —**do**,
v.a. übertreffen. —**doors**, *adv.*
aus; hinaus, heraus. —**er**, *adj.*
äußer, äußerst, fernst, außen-. —**er-
most**, *adj.* äußerst. —**fit**, *s.* die
Ausrüstung. —**ing**, *s.* der Ausflug.
—**landish**, *adj.* fremdartig. —**law**,
I. *s.* der Geächtete, Vogelfreie.
II. *v.a.* ächten. —**lawry**, *s.* die Acht,
Achtung. —**lay**, *s.* die Auslage(n).
—**line**, *s.* der Umriß. —**live**, *v.a.*
überleben. —**look**, *s.* die Aussicht.

—**number**, *v.a.* an Zahl übertreffen.
—**post**, *s.* der Vorposten. —**put**, *s.*
die Produktion. —**rage**, I. *v.a.*
schänden, entehren. II. *s.* die Ge-
walttätigkeit. —**rageous**, *adj.*,
rageously, *adv.* (violent) wütend,
heftig; (atrocious) abscheulich. —
right, *adv.* gänzlich. —**set**, *s.* der
Anfang, Ausbruch. —**side**, I. *adj.*
äußer. II. *adv.* draußen. III. *s.*
(exterior) die Außenseite. —**skirt**,
s. die Grenze, Vorstadt. —**spoken**,
adj. freimütig, offen redend. —**standing**, *adj.* ausstehend (*debts*). —**strip**,
v.a. schneller laufen als (einer); zuvor-
laufen. —**vote**, *v.a.* überstimmen.
Outward, I. *adj.* außer, äußerlich;
(—s) nach außen. II. *adv.* (—s)
auswärts, nach außen; (—ly) im
Äußerlichen, äußerlich.
Outweigh, *v.a.* überwiegen.
Outwit, *v.a.* überlisten.
Ouzel, *s.* die Amsel.
Oval, I. *adj.* eirund. II. *s.* das
Eirund.
Ovation, *s.* die öffentliche Ehrenbe-
zeugung, die Huldigung.
Oven, *s.* der Backofen.
Over, I. *adv.* über; (to this side)
herüber; (to that side) hinüber; (on
the other side) drüben; (on the top)
darüber, darauf; (in excess) übrig,
darüber; (too) allzu; (past) vorüber;
(through) durch. II. *prep.* über.
—**bearing**, *adj.* hochfahrend, herrisch,
anmaßend. —**board**, *adv.* über Bord.
—**charge**, I. *v.a.* überladen; über-
fordern; you are —charging me, Sie
verlangen mir zu viel ab. II. *s.* die
Überladung; die Überteuerung. —
coat, *s.* der Überzieher. —**come**,
ir.v.a. überwinden. —**draw**, *v.a.*; to
—draw one's account, sein Konto
überschreiten, zu viel trassieren. —
flow, I. *s.* der Überfluß. II. *v.a.*
überfließen. —**haul**, *v.a.* gründlich
durchstöbern, untersuchen. —**head**,
adv. oben. —**hear**, *v.a.* zufällig
hören. —**land**, *adj.* über Land.
—**look**, *v.a.* überblick; (a fault)
übersehen; (neglect) vernachlässigen.
—**much**, *adj.* & *adv.* allzu viel,
übermäßig. —**power**, *v.a.* überwältigen. —**rate**, *v.a.* überschätzen.
—**ride**, *v.a.* überreiten; (*fig.*) über
den Haufen werfen; (oppress) unterdrücken. —**rule**, *v.a.* als ungültig

verwerfen. **—see**, *ir.v.a.* beauffichtigen. **—shoot**, *v.a.* übers Ziel hinausschießen; (*fig.*) sich verrechnen, zu weit gehen. **—sight**, *s.* das Versehen. **—strain**, *v.a.* zu sehr anstrengen, sich verrenken. **—take**, *ir.v.a.* einholen. **—throw**, I. *ir.v.a.* umwerfen, umstürzen. II. *s.* der Umsturz; die Niederlage (*Mil.*). **—ture**, *s.* die Einleitung. **—turn**, *v.a.* umkehren, umstürzen. **—whelm**, *v.a.* überwältigen. **—wrought**, *adj.* übermäßig erregt.

Ow—e, *v.a. & n.* schuldig sein, schulden; verdanken; **—ing to**, zufolge, infolge von, dank (*dat.*).

Owl, *s.* die Eule.

¹Own, I. *adj.* eigen; to hold one's **—**, standhalten. II. *v.a.* eigen, besitzen. **—er**, *s.* der Eigentümer, die Eigentümerin. **—ership**, *s.* das Eigentumsrecht; (possession) der Besitz.

²Own, *v.a. & n.* anerkennen; (acknowledge) bestätigen; (confess, **— to**) bekennen, gestehen.

Ox, *s.* der Ochs, das Rind.

Oxygen, *s.* der Sauerstoff.

Oyster, *s.* die Auster.

Ozone, *s.* das Ozon.

P

P, p, *s.* das P, p.

Pace, I. *s.* der Schritt; der Gang; to set the **—**, Schrittmacher sein; thorough**—d**, durchtrieben, abgefeimt. II. *v.n.* (einher)schreiten. III. *v.a.* abschreiten.

Pacif—ic, *adj.*, **—ically**, *adv.* friedlich. **—ier**, *s.* der Friedensstifter. **—y**, *v.a.* beruhigen, besänftigen.

Pack, I. *s.* (bundle) der Pack. II. *v.a.* (zusammen)packen (*goods*); (**— up**) einpacken. **—age**, *s.* der Pack, das Bündel, Paket. **—er**, *s.* der Packer, Auflader. **—et**, *s.* das Paket.

Pact, *s.* der Vertrag, Pakt.

¹Pad, I. *s.* das Polster. II. *v.a.* auspolstern.

²Pad, *s.* (**—**nag) das Reitpferd, der Gaul.

Padding, *s.* die Wattierung.

Paddle, *s.* das Ruder. **—box**, *s.* der Radkasten. **—steamer**, *s.* der Raddampfer.

Paddock, *s.* das Gehege.

Padlock, I. *s.* das Vorlegeschloß. II. *v.a.* mit einem Vorlegeschloß verschließen.

Pagan, I. *adj.* heidnisch. II. *s.* der Heide.

¹Page, *s.* die Seite (*book*).

²Page, *s.* der Page; der Botenjunge.

Pageant, *s.* der Prunk, das Gepränge; der Prunkaufzug.

Pail, *s.* der Eimer.

Pain, I. *s.* der Schmerz, das Weh; (sorrow) das Leid; upon **—**, of, bei Strafe von; to be in **—**, leiden; to take **—s**, sich Mühe geben. II. *v.a.* (hurt) (einem) weh tun. **—ful**, *adj.*, **—fully**, *adv.* schmerzlich (*of mental pain*), schmerzhaft (*of bodily pain*).

Paint, I. *v.a.* malen; (the face) schminken. II. *s.* die Farbe; die Schminke; wet **—!** frisch gestrichen! **—er**, *s.* der (die) Maler(in); das Bootstau; to cut the **—er**, (*fig.*) sich aus dem Staube machen. **—ing**, *s.* das Malen; (picture) das Gemälde.

Pair, I. *s.* das Paar. II. *v.a.* paaren. III. *v.n.* sich paaren, sich gatten.

Palace, *s.* der Palast, das Schloß.

Palat—able, *adj.* schmackhaft. **—e**, *s.* der Gaumen.

¹Pale, *adj.* blaß, bleich. **—ness**, *s.* die Blässe.

²Pale, *s.* der Pfahl.

Palette, *s.* die Malerscheibe, die Palette.

Paling, *s.* das Pfählen.

Palisade, *s.* das Pfahlwerk.

¹Pall, *s.* das Leichentuch.

²Pall, *v.n.* schal, matt werden (upon a person, einem), langweilen, den Reiz verlieren.

Pallet, *s.* das Strohbett.

Palliasse, *s.* der Strohsack.

Pallid, *adj.* bleich, blaß.

Pallor, *s.* die Blässe.

Palm, *s.* die Palme, der Palmbaum; (**—** of the hand) die flache Hand. **—er**, *s.* der Wallfahrer, Pilger. **—istry**, *s.* die Handwahrsagerei.

Palp—able, *adj.* fühlbar. **—itate**, *v.n.* klopfen; zittern.

Palt—er, *v.n.* unredlich handeln. **—riness**, *s.* die Erbärmlichkeit. **—ry**, *adj.*, **—rily**, *adv.* armselig.

Pamper, *v.a.* gütlich tun, reichlich füttern, verzärteln.

Pamphlet, *s.* die Flugschrift, Broschüre.

Pan, *s.* die Pfanne.

Panacea, *s.* das Universalheilmittel.

Pane, *s*. die Fensterscheibe.

Panel, I. *s*. die Füllung; die Tafel. II. *v.a.* täfeln. —**doctor**, *s*. der Kassenarzt. —**work**, *s*. das Fachwerk, Täfelwerk.

Pang, *s*. der Stich, der plötzliche Schmerz; (*fig.*) die Angst.

Panic, *s*. die Bestürzung, der panische Schreck.

Pannier, *s*. der Tragkorb.

Pannikin, *s*. die kleine Kanne.

Pansy, *s*. das Stiefmütterchen (*Bot.*).

Pant, *v.n.* keuchen (*also fig.*).

Pantaloon, *s*. der Hanswurst. —**s**, *pl*. lange Beinkleider.

Panther, *s*. der Panther.

Pantile, *s*. die Dachpfanne.

Pantomime, *s*. das Gebärdenspiel, die Pantomime, das Ausstattungsstück.

Pantry, *s*. die Speisekammer.

¹Pap, *s*. die Brustwarze (*Anat.*).

²Pap, *s*. der Brei.

Papa, *s*. der Papa. —**cy**, *s*. das Papsttum. —**l**, *adj.* päpstlich.

Paper, I. *s*. das Papier; (news—) die Zeitung; to read a — on, eine Vorlesung halten über. II. *adj.* papieren, Papier=. III.*v.a.* tapezieren (*a room*); to — up, in Papier verpacken. —**chase**, *s*. die Schnitzeljagd. —**currency**, *s*. das Papiergeld. —**hanger**, *s*. der Tapezierer. —**mill**, *s*. die Papierfabrik. —**weight**, *s*. der Briefbeschwerer.

Par, *s*. die Gleichheit, das Pari; at —, auf Pari, gleich an Wert; to be on a — with, ebenbürtig sein.

Parable, *s*. die Gleichnisrede.

Parachute, *s*. der Fallschirm.

Parade, I. *s*. der Prunk; die Parade (*Mil.*). II. *v.a.* paradieren lassen (*troops*); (make a — of) prunken mit. III. *v.n.* in Parade aufziehen (*Mil.*).

Paradis—**e**, *s*. das Paradies. — **aical**, *adj.* paradiesisch.

Paraffin, *s*. das Paraffin.

Paragon, *s*. das Muster, Vorbild.

Paragraph, *s*. der Absatz.

Parakeet, *s*. kleiner Papagei.

Parallel, I. *adj.* parallel. II. *s*. die Parallele, Parallellinie. III. *v.a.* entsprechen; vergleichen. —**ogram**, *s*. das Parallelogram.

Paraly—**sis**, *s*. die Gliederlähmung. —**tic**, *adj.* gelähmt, paralytisch. — **ze**, —**se**, *v.a.* lähmen.

Paramount, *adj.* höchst, oberst.

Parapet, *s*. die Brustwehr, das Geländer.

Paraphrase, I. *s*. die Umschreibung. II. *v.a.* & *n.* umschreiben.

Parasite, *s*. der Schmarotzer.

Parasol, *s*. der Sonnenschirm.

Parboil, *v.a.* halb kochen.

Parcel, *s*. das Paket, Bündel. —**post**, *s*. die Paketpost. —**s-delivery**, *s*. die Packetbeförderung.

Parch, *v.* I. *a.* (aus)dörren. II. *n.* ausgedörrt werden.

Parchment, *s*. das Pergament.

Pardon, I. *s*. die Verzeihung, Vergebung; (official —) die Begnadigung; der Ablaß (*Eccles.*). II.*v.a.* vergeben (*dat.*), verzeihen (*dat.*) (*a person*). —**able**, *adj.*, —**ably**, *adv.* verzeihlich. —**er**, *s*. der Verzeihende.

Pare, *v.a.* (be)schneiden (*nails, etc.*).

Parent, I. *s*. der Vater, die Mutter (*also fig.*). II. *adj.* Mutter=, elterlich, Ur=. —**age**, *s*. die Abstammung. —**al**, *adj.*, —**ally**, *adv.*, elterlich. —**less**, *adj.* elternlos. —**s**, *pl*. Eltern.

Parenthesis, *s*. die Parenthese.

Paring, *s*. das Schabsel. —**s**, *pl*. Schnitzel, die Späne.

Parish, *s*. das Kirchspiel. —**ioner**, *s*. das Gemeindemitglied, das Pfarrkind.

Parity, *s*. die Gleichheit, Parität.

Park, I. *s*. der Park, die Gartenanlage. II. *v.a.* zusammen aufstellen (*artillery*); to — a car, ein Auto parken.

Parley, I. *v.n.* unterhandeln; parlamentieren (*Mil.*). II. *s*. die Unterhandlung; to sound a —, Schamade schlagen.

Parliament, *s*. das Parlament. — **ary**, *adj.* Parlaments=, parlamentarisch.

Parlour, *s*. das Wohnzimmer. —**maid**, *s*. das Hausmädchen.

Parochial, *adj.* Kirchspiel=, Pfarr=, Gemeinde=.

Parody, I. *s*. die Parodie. II. *v.a.* parodieren.

Paroxysm, *s*. der Anfall.

Parquet, *s*.; — floor, der Täfelboden. —**ry**, *s*. das Täfelwerk, das Parkett.

Parricid—**al**, *adj.* vater=, muttermörderisch. —**e**, *s*. der Vater=, Mutter=mörder; (murder) der Vater= Mutter=mord.

Parrot, *s*. der Papagei.

Parry, I. *s.* die Parade. II. *v.a.* (einen Hieb, Stoß) parieren.

Pars—e, *v.a.* konstruieren, grammatisch zerlegen. **—ing,** *s.* das Analysieren.

Parsimonious, *adj.,* **—ly,** *adv.* sparsam.

Parsley, *s.* die Petersilie.

Parsnip, *s.* die Weißrübe.

Parson, *s.* der Pfarrer. **—age,** *s.* das Pfarrhaus.

Part, I. *s.* der Teil; die Rolle (*Theat. & fig.*); to take — in a thing, an einer Sache teilnehmen; for my —, was mich betrifft; to do one's —, das Seinige tun. II. *adv.* teils, zum Teile. III. *v.a.* teilen. IV. *v.n.* sich trennen; scheiden, auseinandergehen. **—ly,** *adv.* teils, zum Teile. **—s,** *pl.* die Gegend; (gifts) geistige Gaben. **—payment,** *s.* die Abschlagszahlung.

Partake, *ir.v.n.* teilnehmen. **—r,** *s.* der Teilnehmer, Teilhaber.

Parterre, *s.* das Blumenbeet (*Hort.*); das Parterre (*Theat.*).

Partial, *adj.,* **—ly,** *adv.* Teil-, teilweise, partiell; eingenommen (to, für). **—ity,** *s.* die Parteilichkeit; (predilection) die Vorliebe (to, for, für).

Particip—ant, *s.* der Teilnehmer. **—ate,** *v.n.* teil haben *or* nehmen (in a thing, an einer S.).

Participle, *s.* das Partizipium.

Particle, *s.* das Stückchen, Teilchen.

Particular, I. *adj.* besonder, einzeln; (fastidious) wählerisch. II. *s.* die Einzelheit. **—ly,** *adv.* besonders, vorzüglich, insbesondere. **—s,** *pl.* das Nähere.

Parting, I. *adj.* scheidend, Scheide-, Abschieds-. II. *s.* das Teilen; das Scheiden, der Abschied; der Scheitel (*of hair*).

Partisan, *s.* der Anhänger.

Partit—ion, *s.* die Teilung, Absonderung; die Scheidewand. II. *v.a.* (ver)teilen. **—ive,** I. *adj.,* **—ively,** *adv.* partitiv. II. *s.* das Partitivum.

Partner, *s.* der Teilhaber, Teilnehmer, (Mit-)Genoß. **—ship,** *s.* die Genossenschaft; to enter into —ship with, sich assoziieren mit.

Partridge, *s.* das Rebhuhn.

Party, I. *s.* die Partei (*Pol., etc.*); (company) die Gesellschaft, Partie. II. *adj.* Partei-.

Parvenu, *s.* der Emporkömmling.

Pass, I. *v.n.* sich fortbewegen, fortgehen (*from one place to another*), ziehen, geben, fahren; (occur) geschehen; (vanish) vergehen, verschwinden; verfließen (*as time*); durchkommen (*in an examination*); to — by, vorübergehen; to — for, gelten für; to — on, fortgehen, fortrücken. II. *v.a.* gehen, fahren, reisen, reiten, setzen ꝛc. über, durch, an, an . . . vorbei, über . . . hinaus; (overstep) überschreiten; zubringen (*the time*); bestehen (*an examination*); (surpass) übertreffen; ergehen lassen (*a law*); sprechen (*a judgment*); to — an act, ein Gesetz machen; please — the salt, bitte reichen Sie mir das Salz. III. *s.* der Paß. **—able,** *adj.* gangbar, fahrbar, **—ably,** *adv.* erträglich, leidlich. **—book,** *s.* das Privatkontobuch. **—key,** *s.* der Hauptschlüssel. **—er-by,** *s.* der Vorübergehende. **—ing,** *adj.* vorübergehend, flüchtig. **—word,** *s.* das Losungswort, die Parole.

Passage, *s.* das Durch-gehen, -ziehen; (transit) die Durchfahrt; (sea —) die Seereise, Überfahrt; der Korridor, Gang (*Build.*); die Stelle (*in a book*). **—money,** *s.* das Überfahrtsgeld.

Passenger, *s.* der Passagier, der Reisende. **—train,** *s.* der Personenzug.

Passion, *s.* das Leiden (*of Christ*); die Gemütsbewegung, Leidenschaft; (anger) der Zorn. **—ate,** *adj.,* **—ately,** *adv.* leidenschaftlich; (hot-tempered) zornig. **—ateness,** *s.* die Leidenschaftlichkeit. **—less,** *adj.* leidenschaftslos, kalt. **—flower,** *s.* die Passionsblume. **—week,** *s.* die Karwoche.

Passive, *adj.,* **—ly,** *adv.* leidend, passiv; — verb, leidendes Zeitwort.

Passport, *s.* der Paß; (safe-conduct) der Geleitsbrief (*also fig.*).

Past, I. *adj.* vergangen, ehemalig. II. *s.* die Vergangenheit. III. *adv.* vorbei, vorüber; it is — comprehension, es geht über alle Begriffe; — hope, hoffnungslos. IV. *prep.* nach, über; half—two, halb Drei; a quarter — twelve, ein Viertel auf Eins.

Paste, I. *s.* die Pappe (*Bookb. etc.*); die Paste (*Jewel.*). II. *v.a.* kleistern, pappen. **—board,** *s.* der Pappdeckel, Karton.

Pastel, *s.* der Pastellstift.

Pastern, *s.* die Fessel.

Pastime, *s.* der Zeitvertreib, die Kurzweil.

Pastor, *s.* der Seelsorger. **—al**, *adj.* Hirten=, Schäfer=; geistlich.

Pastry, *s.* die Torten. **—-cook**, *s.* der Konditor.

Pastur—age, *s.* das Weiden. **—e**, I. *s.* die Weide. II. *v.a. & n.* weiden.

¹**Pat**, *adj. & adv.* passend.

²**Pat**, I. *s.* der Klapps; (butter) das Stück, die kleine Scheibe Butter. II. *v.a.* tätscheln.

Patch, I. *s.* der Fleck, Lappen, Flicken. II. *v.a.* (zusammen)flicken. **—y**, *adj.* voller Flicken; (*fig.*) zusammengestoppelt. **—work**, *s.* das Flickwerk.

Pate, *s.* der Schädel (*fam.*).

Paten, *s.* der Napf.

Patent, I. *adj.* offen (kundig), offenbar; (—ed) patentiert; — leather, das Glanzleder; — (leather) boot, der Lackstiefel. II. *s.* das Patent. III. *v.a.* patentieren. **—ee**, *s.* der Patentinhaber. **—office**, *s.* as Patentamt.

Pater—nal, *adj.*, **—nally**, *adv.* väterlich. **—nity**, *s.* die Vaterschaft. **—noster**, *s.* das Vaterunser.

Path, *s.* der Pfad, Weg. **—less**, *adj.* pfadlos.

Path—etic, *adj.*, **—etically**, *adv.* pathetisch. **—ological**, *adj.*, **—ologically**, *adv.* pathologisch. **—ology**, *s.* die Krankheitslehre. **—os**, das Pathos.

Patien—ce, *s.* die Geduld. **—t**, I. *adj.*, **—tly**, *adv.* geduldig. II. *s.* der, die Kranke; der, die Patient(in).

Patriarch, *s.* der Patriarch, Erzvater. **—al**, *adj.* patriarchalisch.

Patrician, I. *adj.* adelig (*fig.*). II. *s.* der Patrizier.

Patrimony, *s.* das Erbgut.

Patriot, *s.* der Patriot. **—ic**, *adj.* patriotisch. **—ism**, *s.* die Vaterlandsliebe, der Patriotismus.

Patrol, I. *s.* die Runde (*Mil.*). II. *v.n.* die Runde machen, patrouillieren. III. *v.a.* durchschreiten.

Patron, *s.* der Schutzherr, Patron. **—age**, *s.* die Gönnerschaft. **—ess**, *s.* die Schutzherrin, Patronin; die Gönnerin. **—ize**, *v.a.* in Schutz nehmen, begünstigen. **—izing**, *adj.*, **—izingly**, *adv.* beschützend; gönnerhaft.

¹**Patter**, *v.n.* niederplatschen.

²**Patter**, I. *v.a.* (her)plappern. II. *s.* das Kauderwelsch (*of a class, etc.*); (chatter) das Plappern.

Pattern, *s.* das Muster (*also fig.*).

Patty, *s.* das Pastetchen.

Paunch, *s.* der Wanst. **—y**, *adj.* dickbauchig.

Pauper, *s.* der Arme.

Pause, I. *s.* die Pause. II. *v.n.* innehalten; (hesitate) zögern.

Pav—e, *v.a.* pflastern. **—ement**, *s.* das Pflaster; (footway) der Bürgersteig. **—ing-stone**, *s.* der Pflasterstein. **—iour**, *s.* der Pflasterer.

Pavilion, *s.* das Zelt; das Gartenhaus, der Pavillon (*Arch.*).

Paw, I. *s.* die Pfote, Tatze. II. *v.a. & n.* scharren, kratzen.

Pawl, *s.* der Sperrhaken.

¹**Pawn**, I. *s.* das Pfand, Unterpfand. II. *v.a.* verpfänden. **—broker**, *s.* der Pfandleiher; **—**(broker's) shop, das Leihhaus. **—-ticket**, *s.* der Pfandschein.

²**Pawn**, *s.* der Bauer (*Chess*).

Pay, I. *ir.v.a.* (be)zahlen, Zahlung leisten; erweisen (*attention, etc.*); abstatten (a visit); to — attention to, achtgeben auf; a —ing concern, ein einträgliches Geschäft. II. *ir.v.n.* sich bezahlt machen, sich lohnen; he must — for his sins, er muß für seine Sünden büßen. III. *s.* die Bezahlung; (wages) der Lohn; der Sold (of a soldier, etc.); (*fig.*) die Belohnung. **—able**, *adj.* zahlbar; fällig, abgelaufen (as bills). **—ee**, *s.* der Inhaber, der Vorzeiger eines Wechsels. **—er**, *s.* der (Be=)Zahler; der Trassat (*C.L.*). **—ment**, *s.* der (Be=)Zahlung; (*fig.*) die Belohnung; der Eingang (of a draft, etc.). **—master**, *s.* der Zahlmeister.

Pea, *s.* die Erbse. **—pod**, *s.* die Erbsenschote.

Peace, I. *s.* der Friede; die Ruhe (of mind, etc.). II. *attrib.*; — establishment, der Friedensfuß (*Mil.*). III. *int.* still! ruhig! **—able**, *adj.*, **—ably**, *adv.* fried=lich, =sam, =fertig; (quiet) ruhig, ungestört. **—ableness**, *s.* die Friedlichkeit, stille Ruhe. **—ful**, *adj.*, **—fully**, *adv. see* **—able**. **—maker**, *s.* der Friedensstifter. **—offering**, *s.* das Sühnopfer.

Peach, I. *s.* der Pfirsich. II. *v.n.* (*slang*) angeben, ausplaudern.

Pea—cock, *s.* der Pfauhahn. **—fowl,** *s.* der Pfau. **—hen,** *s.* die Pfauhenne.

Peak, *s.* die Spitze; der Gipfel. **—ed,** *adj.* spitz.

Peal, I. *s.* das Geläute (*of bells*); das Rollen (*of thunder, cannon, etc.*). II. *v.n.* krachen, donnern (*of cannon*); brausen (*of organs*). III. *v.a.* läuten.

Pear, *s.* die Birne. **—tree,** der Birnbaum.

Pearl, I. *s.* die Perle (*also fig.*). II. *adj.* von Perlen.

Peasant, I. *s.* der Bauer, Landmann. II. *adj.* bäuerlich, ländlich. **—ry,** *s.* die Bauernschaft, das Landvolk.

Peat, *s.* der (Brenn=)Torf. **—y,** *adj.* Torf=, torfähnlich. **—bog,** *s.* das Torfmoor. **—stack,** *s.* der Torfstoß.

Pebbl—e, *s.* der Kieselstein. **—y,** *adj.* kieselig, Kiesel=.

Peck, I. *s.* der Pick; ein Viertel Bushel. II. *v.a. & n.* picken.

Peculiar, *adj.,* **—ly,** *adv.* eigen (tümlich). **—ity,** *s.* die Eigenheit, Eigentümlichkeit.

Pecuniary, *adj.* Geld betreffend, Geld=.

Pedal, I. *s.* das Pedal (*Piano, Organ*); der Treter (*Cycl.*). II. *v.a.* treten (*Cycl.*).

Pedant, *s.* der Pedant, die Pedantin. **—ic,** *adj.* pedantisch. **—ry,** *s.* die Pedanterie.

Peddle, *v.n.* hausieren gehen.

Pedestal, *s.* der Säulenfuß.

Pedestrian, I. *adj.* zu Fuß gehend; zu Fuß, Fuß=. II. *s.* der Fuß-gänger, =reisende.

Peddling, *adj.* (*fig.*) geringfügig.

Pedigree, *s.* der Stammbaum.

Pedlar, *s.* der Hausierer.

Peel, I. *v.a.* (ab)schälen. II. *s.* die Schale, Rinde.

Peep, I. *v.n.* gucken. II. *s.* das Gucken.

¹Peer, *s.* der Ebenbürtige; (noble) der Pair. **—age,** *s.* der Reichsadel. **—ess,** *s.* die Gemahlin eines Pairs. **—less,** *adj.,* **—lessly,** *adv.* unvergleichlich.

²Peer, *v.a.* scharf blicken, gucken (for, nach).

Peevish, *adj.,* **—ly,** *adv.* verdrießlich, mürrisch. **—ness,** *s.* die Grämlichkeit.

Pe(e)wit, *s.* der Kiebitz.

Peg, I. *s.* der Pflock, Dübel. II. *v.a.* fest=, an=pflöcken. **—top,** *s.* der Kreisel.

Pelf, *s.* das Geld, der Reichtum.

Pelican, *s.* der Pelikan (*Orn.*).

Pelisse, *s.* der Frauenüberrock, die Pelisse.

Pellet, *s.* das Kügelchen.

¹Pelt, *s.* der Pelz. **—ry,** *s.* das Pelzwerk.

²Pelt, *v.* I. *a.* werfen (nach), bewerfen. II. *n.* niederstürzen (*rain*).

¹Pen, *s.* die Feder; steel —, Stahlfeder; fountain —, die Füllfeder. **—holder,** *s.* der Federhalter. **—knife,** *s.* das Federmesser.

²Pen, I. *s.* die Hürde; der Hühnerstall. II. *v.a.* einpferchen, einschließen (*sheep*).

Penal, *adj.* Straf=; (criminal) strafbar; — servitude, die Zuchthausstrafe. **—ize,** *v.a.* einer Strafe unterwerfen. **—ty,** *s.* die Strafe.

Penance, *s.* die Buße.

Pencil, *s.* der Bleistift.

Pend—ant, *s.* das Gehänge. **—ent,** *adj.* hängend, schwebend. **—ing,** I. *adj.* unentschieden, in der Schwebe. II. *prep.* während; (until) bis (zu).

Pendulum, *s.* das Pendel.

Penetra—ble, *adj.* durchdringlich. **—te,** *v.a. & n.* durchdringen, eindringen in (*acc.*). **—tion,** *s.* das Durchdringen, Eindringen; (discernment) die Einsicht. **—tive,** *adj.,* **—tively,** *adv.* eindringlich.

Penguin, *s.* der Pinguin.

Peninsula, *s.* die Halbinsel. **—r,** *adj.* halbinselförmig.

Peniten—ce, *s.* die Reue, Buße. **—t,** I. *adj.,* **—tly,** *adv.* reuig, bußfertig. II. *s.* der Büßer; das Beichtkind (*R. C.*). **—tial,** I. *adj.,* **—tially,** *adv.* bußfertig. II. *s.* das Bußbuch, Pönitentiale (*R. C.*). **—tiary,** *s.* das Zuchthaus.

Pennant, *s.* der Wimpel.

Penniless, *adj.* ohne Geld.

Pennon, *s.* das Fähnchen (*Mil.*).

Pension, I. *s.* das Ruhegehalt. II. *v.a.* (einem) ein Jahrgeld geben; (— off) pensionieren. **—ary,** **—er,** *s.* der Pensionär.

Pensive, *adj.,* **—ly,** *adv.* gedankenvoll, nachdenklich. **—ness,** *s.* die Nachdenklichkeit.

Pentagon, *s.* das Fünfeck.

Pentateuch, *s.* die fünf Bücher Mosis.

Pentecost, *s.* die Pfingsten.

Penur—ious, *adj.* farg, geizig. **—y,** *s.* die Armut; die Kargheit.

Peony, *s.* die Päonie, Pfingstrose.

People, I. *s.* das Volk, die Leute. II. *v.a.* bevölkern.

Pepper, I. *s.* der Pfeffer. II. *v.a.* pfeffern. **—box, —caster,** *s.* die Pfefferbüchse. **—mint,** *s.* die Pfefferminze. **—y,** *adj.* gepfeffert; (*fig.*) hitzig.

Per, *prep.* durch, für 2c.; as — account, laut Rechnung; — annum, für das Jahr, jährlich; — cent, prozent.

Perambulat—e, *v.a.* durchwandern. **—or,** *s.* der Kinderwagen.

Perceiv—able, *adj.* wahrnehmbar. **—e,** *v.a.* wahrnehmen.

Percentage, *s.* der Prozentsatz.

Percepti—ble, *adj.,* **—bly,** *adv.* wahrnehmbar. **—on,** *s.* die Wahrnehmung.

¹**Perch,** *s.* der Barsch (*Icht.*).

²**Perch,** I. *s.* die Stange (*for birds*). II. *v.n.* aufsitzen.

Perchance, *adv.* vielleicht.

Percolat—e, *v.n.* durchsickern, filtrieren. **—or,** *s.* der Filtriertrichter.

Percussion, *s.* der Schlag; der Widerhall; die Erschütterung. **—cap,** *s.* das Zündhütchen.

Perdition, *s.* das Verderben; die Verdammnis (*Rel.*).

Peremptor—ily, *adv.* geradezu. **—i-ness,** *s.* die Bestimmtheit (*of a refusal, etc.*). **—y,** *adj.* bestimmt, entschieden, peremptorisch.

Perennial, I. *adj.,* **—ly,** *adv.* perennierend (*Bot.*). II. *s.* die perennierende, dauernde Pflanze.

Perfect, I. *adj.* vollkommen. II. *s.* (— tense) das Perfektum. III. *v.a.* vervollkommen, vollenden. **—ion,** *s.* die Vollkommenheit, Vollendung.

Perfidious, *adj.,* **—ly,** *adv.* hinterlistig, treulos, verräterisch. **—ness, Perfidy,** *s.* die Treulosigkeit.

Perforat—e, I. *v.a.* durchbohren. II. *adj.,* **—ed,** *adj.* durchstochen. **—ion,** *s.* die Durchbohrung.

Perforce, *adv.* mit Gewalt, notgedrungen.

Perform, *v.* I. *a.* machen, tun, leisten, verrichten; (carry out) ausführen, vollziehen; (play) spielen, aufführen. II. *n.* spielen (*Theat., etc.*). **—ance,** *s.* die Ausführung, Verrichtung, Voll-

ziehung; die Aufführung, Vorstellung (*Theat.*); die Erfüllung (*of a duty*). **—er,** *s.* der Täter, Ausführende; der Schauspieler (*Theat.*); der Virtuos (*Mus.*).

Perfume, I. *s.* der Duft. II. *v.a.* durchdüften, parfümieren. **—r,** *s.* der Parfümeriewarenhändler. **—ry,** *s.* die Parfümerie.

Perfunctory, *adj.* nachlässig, oberflächlich.

Perhaps, *adv.* vielleicht, möglicherweise.

Peril, *s.* die Gefahr. **—ous,** *adj.,* **—ously,** *adv.* gefährlich.

Period, *s.* die Periode (*also Astr.*); (space of time) der Zeitraum, die Zeit; (pause) der Absatz; (*typ.*) der Punkt. **—ic,** *adj.,* **—ically,** *adv.* periodisch. **—ical,** *s.* die Zeitschrift.

Periscope, *s.* das Periskop, das Unterseebootfernrohr.

Perish, *v.n.* umkommen, untergehen. **—able,** *adj.* vergänglich; leicht verderbend (Eßwaren) (*as fruit, etc.*).

Periwig, *s.* die Perücke.

¹**Periwinkle,** *s.* die Uferschnecke (*Mollusc*).

²**Periwinkle,** *s.* das Immergrün (*Bot.*).

Perjur—e, *v.* I. *n.* meineidig werden. II. *a.;* to — oneself, eidbrüchig werden. **—ed,** *adj.* eidbrüchig, meineidig. **—er,** *s.* der Eidbrüchige, Meineidige. **—y,** *s.* der Eidbruch, Meineid.

Permanen—ce, **—cy,** *s.* die Fortdauer. **—t,** *adj.,* **—tly,** *adv.* (be)ständig, fortdauernd.

Permea—bility, *s.* die Durchlässigkeit. **—ble,** *adj.* durchlässig. **—te,** *v.a.* durchlassen, durchdringen.

Permissi—ble, *adj.* zulässig. **—on,** *s.* die Erlaubnis, Bewilligung.

Permit, I. *v.a.* erlauben, zulassen, gestatten. II. *s.* die Erlaubnis; (written —) der Erlaubnisschein.

Pernicious, *adj.* schädlich, verderblich.

Perpendicular, I. *adj.,* **—ly,** *adv.* senkrecht (to, auf, mit), lotrecht. II. *s.* die Senkrechte.

Perpetrat—e, *v.a.* begehen (*a crime, etc.*). **—ion,** *s.* die Verübung, Begehung. **—or,** *s.* der Begeher, Täter.

Perpetu—al, *adj.,* **—ally,** *adv.* unaufhörlich, fortwährend. **—ate,** *v.a.* verewigen. **—ation,** *s.* die Verewigung.

Perplex, *v.a.* verwirren. —ity, *s.* die Verwirrung.

Persecut—e, *v.a.* verfolgen. —ion, *s.* die Verfolgung. —or, *s.* der Verfolger.

Persever—ance, *s.* die Beharrlichkeit, Standhaftigkeit, Ausdauer. —e, *v.n.* beharren, ausdauern, standhaft fortfahren. —ing, *adj.*, —ingly, *adv.* beharrlich, standhaft.

Persist, *v.a.*; to — in, bestehen auf (*dat.*), beharren in (*dat.*) or bei. —ence, —ency, *s.* das Beharren (in, in). —ent, *adj.*, —ently, *adv.* beharrlich.

Person, *s.* die Person. —age, *s.* die Persönlichkeit. —al, *adj.*, —ally, *adv.* persönlich (*also Gram.*). —ality, *s.* die Persönlichkeit.

Personat—e, *v.a.* vorstellen; darstellen. —ion, *s.* die Vorstellung. —or, *s.* der Darstellende.

Personif—ication, *s.* die Verkörperung. —y, *v.a.* verkörpern.

Personnel, *s.* das Personal.

Perspective, I. *adj.* perspektivisch, Perspektiv=. II. *s.* die Perspektive.

Perspir—ation, *s.* der Schweiß. —e, *v.n.* schwitzen.

Persua—de, *v.a.* überreden, bereden (of, to, zu); to be —ded of, überzeugt sein von. —sion, *s.* die Überredung.

Pert, *adj.*, —ly, *adv.* naseweis, vorlaut. —ness, *s.* der Vorwitz.

Pertain, *v.n.* (an)gehören (*to a person or thing*); betreffen (*a matter*).

Pertinac—ious, *adj.* hartnäckig; beharrlich. —ity, *s.* die Standhaftigkeit.

Pertinent, *adj.* passend, angemessen; treffend (*of a remark*).

Perturb, *v.a.* beunruhigen. —ation, *s.* die Störung.

Perus—al, *s.* die Durchsicht. —e, *v.a.* (durch)lesen.

Perva—de, *v.a.* durchdringen. —sive, *adj.* durchdringend.

Perver—se, *adj.*, —sely, *adv.* verkehrt. —seness, —sity, *s.* die Verkehrtheit, der Eigensinn; die Verderbtheit. —sion, *s.* die Verkehrung. —t, I. *v.a.* verkehren. II. *s.* der Abtrünnige (in Religionssachen).

Pessimis—m, *s.* der Pessimismus. —t, I. *s.* der Pessimist, der Schwarzseher. II. *adj.*, —tic, *adj.* pessimistisch.

Pest, *s.* die Pest; (*fig.*) die Plage.

Pester, *v.a.* plagen, quälen.

Pestilen—ce, *s.* die Pest. —tial, *adj.* ansteckend.

Pestle, *s.* die Mörserkeule.

¹Pet, I. *s.* zahmes Tier. II. *attrib.* Lieblings=; — dog, der Schoßhund. III. *v.a.* hätscheln.

²Pet, *s.* die üble Laune; to be in a —, schlechter Laune sein.

Petal, *s.* das Blumenblatt.

Petition, I. *s.* die Bitte; (written —) die Bittschrift. II. *v.a.* bitten. —er, *s.* der Bittsteller, Ansucher.

Petrel, *s.* der Sturmvogel.

Petr—ifaction, *s.* die Versteinerung. —ify, *v.n.* zu Stein werden.

Petrol, *s.* das Benzin. —station, *s.* die Tankstelle.

Petroleum, *s.* das Erdöl, Petroleum.

Petticoat, *s.* der Unterrock.

Pettifogger, *s.* der Winkeladvokat.

Pettish, *adj.*, —ly, *adv.* übellaunig.

Petty, *adj.* klein, gering(fügig), unbedeutend.

Petulan—ce, —cy, *s.* der Mutwille. —t, *adj.*, —tly, *adv.* mutwillig, verdrießlich.

Pew, *s.* der Kirchen=stuhl, =sitz.

Pewter, I. *s.* das Hartzinn; (— vessel) das Zinn, das Zinngerät. II. *adj.* zinnern.

Phantasm, *s.* das Trugbild.

Phantom, *s.* das Scheinbild, Schattenbild; (spectre) das Gespenst.

Pharmacy, *s.* die Apothekerkunst.

Pharynx, *s.* der Schlundkopf, die Rachenhöhle.

Phase, *s.* die Phase (*Astr. & fig.*).

Pheasant, *s.* der Fasan.

Phenomen—al, *adj.*, —ally, *adv.* phänomenal. —on, *s.* das Phänomen, Wunder.

Phial, *s.* das Fläschchen.

Phil—ander, *v.n.* liebeln. —anthropist, *s.* der Menschenfreund. —anthropy, *s.* die Menschenliebe. —atelist, *s.* der Markensammler. —harmonic, *adj.* Musik liebend.

Philistine, I. *s.* der Philister. II. *adj.* philisterhaft.

Philo—logist, *s.* der Sprachforscher, Philolog. —logy, *s.* die Philologie. —sopher, *s.* der Philosoph. —sophical, *adj.*, —sophically, *adv.* philosophisch. —sophy, *s.* die Philosophie; natural —sophy, die Physik.

Philtre, *s.* der Liebestrank.

Phlegm, *s.* der Schleim; das Phlegma

(*Chem. & fig.*). —atic, *adj.*, —ati-cally, *adv.* phlegmatisch.

Phon—etic, *adj.*, —etically, *adv.* lautlich, phonetisch. —etics, *s.* die Phonetik. —ograph, *s.* der Phonograph.

Phosph—ate, *s.* das Phosphat. — orescence, *s.* die Phosphoreszenz. —orous, *adj.*, phosphorig. —orus, *s.* der Phosphor (*Chem.*).

Photograph, I. *s.* die Photographie. II. *v.a.* photographieren. —er, *s.* der Photograph. —ic, *adj.* photographisch. —y, *s.* die Photographie.

Phrase, *s.* die Phrase, Redensart.

Phrenology, *s.* die Schädellehre.

Phthisis, *s.* die Schwindsucht.

Physi—c, *s.* die Arznei. —cal, *adj.*, —cally, *adv.* physisch, natürlich; (bodily) körperlich; physikalisch (*as a science*). —cian, *s.* der Arzt. —cs, *s.* die Physik. —ognomy, *s.* die Gesichtsbildung. —ology, *s.* die Physiologie. —que, *s.* der Körperbau.

Pian—ist, *s.* der (die) Klavierspieler(in), Pianist(in). —oforte, *s.* das Klavier; cottage piano, das Pianino; grand piano, der Flügel.

Pick, I. *v.a.* picken; stochern (*the teeth*); pflücken (*fruit*); zupfen (*wool, oakum*); (auf)suchen (*a quarrel*); leeren (*a person's pocket*); to — up, sammeln (*information*). II. *s.* der Spitzhammer, die Hacke; (choice) die Auswahl. —ed, *adj.* auserlesen. — er, *s.* der Pflücker, Leser, Zupfer. —ing, *s.* das Picken, Pflücken 2c. —axe, *s.* die Pickhacke. —up, *s.* der Tonabnehmer (*Radio*). —lock, *s.* (instrument) der Dietrich; (person) der Dieb. —pocket, *s.* der Taschendieb.

Picket, I. *s.* der Pfahl; die Feldwache (*Mil.*). II. *v.a.* (tether) an einen Pfahl binden; ein Piket aufstellen (*Mil., etc.*).

Pickle, I. *s.* der Pökel, Salzbrühe; to be in a —, in einer mißlichen Lage sein; mixed —s, gemischte Essigfrüchte. II. *v.a.* einpökeln.

Picnic, *s.* das Picknick; die Landpartie.

Pict—orial, *adj.*, —orially, *adv.* Maler-, malerisch; illustriert, Bilder- (*as an edition*). —ure, I. *s.* das Gemälde, Bild. II. *attrib.*; —ure postcard, die Ansichtspostkarte. III. *v.a.* (ab)malen; (*fig.*) schildern. —uresque, *adj.*, —uresquely, *adv.* malerisch. —uresqueness, *s.* das

Malerische. —ure-frame, *s.* der Bilderrahmen. —ure-gallery, *s.* die Gemäldegallerie.

Pie, *s.* die Pastete; (fruit —) die Torte.

Piebald, *adj.* scheckig; — horse, der Schecke.

Piece, I. *s.* das Stück; a — of news, die Neuigkeit; all of a —, aus einem Stück. II. *v.a.* anstücken. III. *v.n.* sich verbinden. —meal, *adj. & adv.* stückweise. —work, *s.* die Akkordarbeit. —worker, *s.* der Stückarbeiter.

Pied, *adj.* bunt, scheckig.

Pier, *s.* der (Strebe-)Pfeiler; der Landungssteg (*Naut.*); das Widerlager (*of a bridge*). —glass, *s.* der Pfeilerspiegel.

Pierc—e, *v.a.* durch-stechen, -bohren. —er, *s.* der Pfriem(e), die Pfrieme (*Shoem., etc.*). —ing, *adj.* schneidend, durchdringend (*also fig.*).

Piety, *s.* die Frömmigkeit; die Pietät.

Pig, *s.* das Schwein; (young —) das Ferkel. —iron, *s.* das Roheisen. —sty, *s.* der Schweinestall. —tail, *s.* der Zopf.

Pigeon, *s.* die Taube. —hole, I. *s.* das Taubenloch. II. *v.a.* in ein Zettelfach legen; vernachlässigen.

Pigment, *s.* der Färbstoff.

Pike, *s.* die Pike (*Mil.*); der Hecht (*Icht.*).

¹Pile, I. *s.* (heap) der Haufe(n); der Stoß (*of wood*). II. *v.a.* (— up) aufhäufen.

²Pile, *s.* der Pfahl.

³Pile, *s.* der Flor (*of velvet*).

Pilfer, *v.a.* stehlen, mausen.

Pilgrim, *s.* der Pilger, die Pilgerin. —age, *s.* die Wall-, Pilger-fahrt (to, nach).

Pill, *s.* die Pille.

Pillage, I. *s.* der Raub. II. *v.a. & n.* plündern, rauben. —r, *s.* der Plünderer.

Pillar, *s.* der Pfeiler, die Säule. —box, *s.* der Briefkasten.

Pillion, *s.* das Sattelkissen.

Pillow, *s.* das Kopfkissen, der Pfühl. —slip, *s.* der Kissenbezug.

Pilot, I. *s.* der Lotse; air —, der Flieger. II. *v.a.* lotsen. —age, *s.* das Lotsen.

Pimpernel, *s.* die Bibernelle.

Pimpl—e, *s.* die Finne. —ed, —y, *adj.* finnig.

Pin, I. *s.* die Stecknadel. II. *v.a.*

(an=)heften. —cushion, s. das Nadel=
tissen.

Pinafore, s. die Schürze.

Pincers, pl. die (Kneip=, Beiß=)Zange.

Pinch, I. v.a. kneifen, kneipen. II. v.n.
drücken; sparen. III. s. das Kneipen;
Zwicken; die Prise (of snuff).

1Pine, s. die Kiefer, Föhre. —
apple, s. die Ananas.

2Pine, v.n.; to — away, sich ab=
zehren.

Pinion, I. s. die Schwinge. II. v.a.
fesseln. —ed, adj. gefesselt.

Pink, I. s. die Nelke (Bot.). II. adj.
blaßrot, rosa.

Pinnace, s. die Pinasse.

Pinnacle, s. die Zinne.

Pint, s. der Schoppen.

Pioneer, I. s. der Pionier (Mil.);
(fig.) der Bahnbrecher. II. v.a. der
Weg bahnen.

Pious, adj., —ly, adv. fromm.

1Pip, s. der Obstkern, Kern (of apples).

2Pip, s. der Pips (in fowls); (sl.)
he's got the —, er ist übel gelaunt.

1Pip—e, I. s. die Pfeife (also Mus.);
das Rohr, die Röhre (for gas). II.
v.n. & a. pfeifen. —er, s. der Pfeifer.
—ing, I. adj. pfeifend. II. s. das
Röhrenwerk.

2Pipe, s. die Pipe (of wine).

Piqu—ancy, s. die Schärfe; (fig.)
das Pikante. —ant, adj., —antly,
adv. pikant (also fig.). —e, I. s. der
Groll. II. v.a. ärgern, kränken. —et,
s. das Piquetspiel.

Pira—cy, s. die Seeräuberei. —te,
s. der Seeräuber. —tical, adj.
(see)räuberisch.

Pirouette, s. die Pirouette.

Pistil, s. der Stempel (Bot.).

Pistol, s. die Pistole.

Piston, s. der Kolben. —rod, s. die
Kolbenstange.

Pit, s. die Grube (Min., etc.). —fall,
s. die Fallgrube. —man, s. der
Bergmann.

1Pitch, I. s. das Pech. II. v.a. (ver=)
pichen; teeren (a ship). —y, adj.
pechig.

2Pitch, I. s. der Wurf; die Tonhöhe
(Mus.); — and toss, Kopf oder
Wappen. II. v.a. werfen, schleudern;
aufschlagen (a tent, etc.). III. v.n.
sich niederlassen; (encamp) sich lagern;
stampfen (Naut.). —fork, s. die
Heugabel.

Pitcher, s. der Krug.

Pit—eous, adj., —eously, adv. kläg=
lich. —eousness, s. die Kläglich=
keit.

Pith, s. das Mark (also Bot.). —y,
adj., —ily, adv. markig.

Piti—able, adj., —ably, adv. be=
mitleidenswert. —ful, adj., —fully,
adv. mitleidig. —less, adj., —lessly,
adv. erbarmungslos, unbarmherzig.

Pittance, s. die Portion; das armselige
Bißchen.

Pity, I. s. das Mitleid, Erbarmen. II.
v.a. bemitleiden, bedauern.

Pivot, s. der Drehpunkt.

Placard, s. das Plakat.

Place, I. s. der Platz, Raum; (locality)
der Ort. II. v.a. (an einen Platz)
stellen, setzen; anbringen (money).

Placid, adj., —ly, adv. ruhig. —ity,
—ness, s. die Sanftheit.

Plagiar—ism, s. das Plagiat. —ist, s.
der Abschreiber.

Plague, I. s. die Pest. II. v.a. plagen,
quälen.

Plaice, s. die Scholle.

Plaid, I. s. kariertes Wollenzeug
(C.L.). II. adj. bunt gewürfelt.

Plain, I. adj. & adv., —ly, adv. eben,
platt, flach; (simple) einfach, schlicht;
(unadorned) schmucklos; (without a
pattern, etc.) glatt, ungemustert;
nicht hübsch (as a face); (clear) klar,
verständlich; (easily seen) deutlich;
(evident) offenbar; — dealing, ehrliche
Handlungsweise. II. s. die Ebene,
Fläche. —ness, s. die Ebenheit; die
Glätte; die Schlichtheit; die Deut=
lichkeit; die Geradheit.

Plaint—iff, s. der (die) Kläger(in).
—ive, adj., —ively, adv. kläglich.

Plait, I. s. die Flechte (of hair); das
Geflecht (of straw). II. v.a. falten;
flechten.

Plan, I. s. der Plan, Entwurf, Riß
(Surv., etc.). II. v.a. entwerfen.
—ner, s. der Planmacher.

1Plane, I. adj. eben, flach. II. s. der
Hobel; die Fläche, Ebene (Geom.).
III. v.a. ebnen; (ab)hobeln (Carp.);
to — down, abwärts gleiten (Av.).

2Plane, s. (— =tree) die Platane.

Planet, s. der Planet, Wandelstern.

Planish, v.a. glätten, polieren.

Plank, s. die Planke, Bohle.

Plant, I. s. die Pflanze, das Gewächs;
Kraut; die Gerätschaften, die Betriebs=

anlage (*of a factory, etc.*). II. *v.a.* pflanzen.

¹**Plantain,** *s.* der Wegerich (*Bot.*).

²**Plantain,** *s.*, (fruit) der Pisang, die Banane.

Plant—ation, *s.* die Pflanzung (*also fig.*). **—er,** *s.* der Pflanzer.

Plaster, I. *s.* das Pflaster (*Pharm.*); der Mörtel; — of Paris, der Stuck, die feine Gipsmörtel; — cast, der Gipsabdruck. II. *v.a.* bepflastern. **—er,** *s.* der Gips=, Stuck-arbeiter.

Plate, I. *s.* die Platte (*of metal, etc.*); (silver) das Silber= (Gold=)Geschirr; (dinner, *etc.* —) der Teller. II. *v.a.* plattieren, überziehen; (silver——) versilbern. **—basket,** *s.* der Tellerkorb. **—glass,** *s.* das Spiegelglas. **—layer,** *s.* der Schienenleger (*Railw.*).

Plateau, *s.* die Hochebene.

Platform, *s.* die Platform; die Bühne (*in halls, etc.*); der Bahnsteig (*Railw.*).

Plating, *s.* die Plattierung (*Metall.*); (silver——ing) die Versilberung.

Platinum, *s.* das Platin.

Platitude, *s.* die Plattheit.

Platoon, *s.* das Peloton, die Rotte.

Platter, *s.* große, flache Schüssel.

Plaudit, *s.* der laute Beifall.

Plausibl—e, *adj.*, **—y,** *adv.* wahrscheinlich, annehmlich.

Play, I. *v.n.* spielen (*also fig.*). II. *v.a.* spielen. III. *s.* das Spiel; das Schauspiel (*Theat.*). **—er,** *s.* der Spieler; der Schauspieler. **—ful,** *adj.*, **—fully,** *adv.* spielend. **—fulness,** *s.* der Mutwille. **—fellow, —mate,** *s.* der Gespiele, die Gespielin. **—ground,** *s.* der Spielplatz. **—house,** *s.* das Schauspielhaus. **—thing,** *s.* das Spielzeug. **—time,** *s.* die Spielzeit. **—wright, —writer,** *s.* der Schauspielschreiber.

Plea, *s.* die Ausrede, Entschuldigung, der Vorwand.

Plead, *v.* I. *n.* vor Gericht reden; plaidieren. II. *a.* (Prozesse) führen (*Law*); (allege) sich berufen auf (*acc.*); to — guilty, sich schuldig bekennen. **—er,** *s.* der Advokat. **—ing,** *adj.* bittend; **—ings,** *pl.* gerichtliche Verhandlungen.

Pleasant, *adj.*, **—ly,** *adv.* angenehm; freundlich (*as a room*). **—ness,** *s.* die Annehmlichkeit, Anmut. **—ry,** *s.* der Scherz.

Pleas—e, *v.* I. *n.* gefallen; if you —e,

gefälligst, bitte. II. *a.* gefallen, Freude machen. **—ed,** *adj.* erfreut, zufrieden. **—ing,** *adj.*, **—ingly,** *adv.* angenehm, hold. **—ure,** *s.* das Vergnügen; at **—ure,** nach Belieben; to take **—ure** in, Vergnügen finden an (*dat.*).

Pleat, I. *v.a.* falten; corded and **—ed,** plissiert. II. *s.* die Falte.

Plebeian, I. *adj.* gemein, plebejisch. II. *s.* der Plebejer.

Plebiscite, *s.* der Volksbeschluß.

Pledge, I. *s.* das Pfand, Unterpfand; to take the **—,** Abstinenzler werden; II. *v.a.* (pawn) verpfänden.

Plent—eous, *adj.*, **—eously,** *adv.* ergiebig, reich(lich). **—eousness,** *s.* die Fülle. **—iful,** *adj.*, **—ifully,** *adv.* reichlich. **—y,** *s.* die Fülle, Menge.

Pleonasm, *s.* der Wortüberfluß, Pleonasmus.

Plethora, *s.* (*fig.*) die Überfülle.

Pleurisy, *s.* die Brustfellentzündung.

Pliable, Pliant, *adj.* biegsam; (*fig.*) fügsam, schmiegsam.

Pliers, *pl.* die Zange.

¹**Plight,** *s.* der Zustand.

²**Plight,** *v.a.* to — one's faith, versprechen.

Plod, *v.n.* & *a.* mühsam gehen. **—ding,** I. *adj.*, **—dingly,** *adv.* arbeitsam. II. *s.* das Büffeln.

Plop, *adv.* plumps!

¹**Plot,** *s.* der Fleck, das Stück (Land).

²**Plot,** I. *s.* die Verschwörung; die Verwickelung, Intrige (*of a play, etc.*). II. *v.a.* anstiften, Ränke schmieden. **—ter,** *s.* der Anstifter; der Verschwörer.

Plough, I. *s.* der Pflug. II. *v.a.* pflügen. **—man,** *s.* der Pflüger. **—share,** *s.* die Pflugschar.

Plover, *s.* der Kiebitz, Regenpfeifer.

Pluck, I. *v.a.* (ab)pflücken; rupfen (*birds*). II. *v.n.* zupfen, raufen (at, an); to — up courage, Mut fassen. **—ily,** *adv.*, **—y,** *adj.* mutig, beherzt, herzhaft (*coll.*).

Plug, I. *s.* der Pflock; der Stecker, Stöpsel (*Elec.*). II. *v.a.* zupflöcken.

Plum, *s.* die Pflaume. **—cake,** *s.* der Rosinenkuchen.

Plumage, *s.* das Gefieder.

Plumb, I. *s.* (plummet) das Senkblei, Lot; die Seigerschnur (*Surv.*). II. *adj.* & *adv.* senkrecht, lotrecht. III. *adv.* gerade, stracks. **—line,** *s.* di Bleischnur. **—rule,** *s.* das Richtscheit.

Plumbago, *s.* der Graphit.

Plumber, *s.* der Bleiarbeiter.

Plumbing, *s.* die Bleiarbeit.

Plume, *s.* die Feder; to — oneself on, sich brüsten mit.

Plummet, *s.* das Senkblei, Lot.

¹Plump, *adj.* dick, fett. **—ness,** *s.* die Beleibtheit.

²Plump, I. *v.a.* hinplumpen. II. *v.n.* to — down, hinplumpsen (*vulg.*). III. *adj. & adv.* plump, platsch.

Plunder, I. *s.* die Beute, der Raub. II. *v.a.* plündern, (be)rauben. **—er,** *s.* der Plünderer.

Plunge, I. *v.a.* tauchen (*into water, etc.*); stoßen (*a sword, etc.*); (*fig.*) stürzen. II. *v.n.* (unter)tauchen; springen und ausschlagen (*as a horse*). III. *s.* das Eintauchen; der Sturz; das Ausschlagen.

Pluperfect, *s.* (— tense) das Plusquamperfektum.

Plural, *s.* (— number) die Mehrzahl. **—ity,** *s.* die Mehrheit.

Plus, I. *adv.* mehr. II. *s.* das Plus.

Plush, *s.* der Plüsch. **—y,** *adj.* plüschartig.

Ply, I. *v.a.* fleißig, eifrig anwenden; (einem) zusetzen (*with questions*); (supply) reichlich, versehen mit. II. *v.n.* beschäftigt sein; verkehren (*as buses, vessels*). III. *s.* die Strähne (*in a rope*); three-—, dreifach (*wool, etc.*). **—wood,** *s.* das Sperrholz.

Pneumatic, *adj.* pneumatisch, Luft-.

Pneumonia, *s.* die Lungenentzündung.

Poach, *v.* I. *a.* Jagd machen auf (*acc.*); —ed eggs, verlorene Eier. II. *n.* Wilddieberei treiben. **—er,** *s.* der Wilddieb. **—ing,** *s.* die Wilddieberei.

Pock, *s.* die Pocke, Blatter. **—marked, —pitted,** *adj.* blatternarbig.

Pocket, I. *s.* die Tasche. II. *v.a.* in die Tasche stecken; einstecken (*also fig.*). **—book,** *s.* die Brieftasche. **—handkerchief,** *s.* das Taschentuch. **—money,** *s.* das Taschengeld.

Pod, *s.* die Hülse, Schote.

Poem, *s.* das Gedicht.

Poet, *s.* der Dichter. **—ess,** *s.* die Dichterin. **—ical,** *adj.,* **—ically,** *adv.* dichterisch, poetisch. **—ry,** *s.* die Gedichte.

Poignan—cy, *s.* die Schärfe. **—t,** *adj.* scharf, beißend.

Point, I. *s.* die Spitze; to make a — of, es sich zur Aufgabe machen; in — of, in Hinsicht auf; to speak to the —, zur Sache sprechen. II. *v.a.* (zu)spitzen; (— out) zeigen, hinweisen (auf, *acc.*); (aim) richten. III. *v.n.* stehen (*of dogs*); nachweisen, zeigen; to — at, weisen auf (*acc.*). **—ed,** *adj.,* **—edly,** *adv.* spitzig; (*fig.*) beißend; spitzfindig. **—er,** *s.* der Zuspitzer; (indicator) der Zeiger; (dog) der Weiser, Hühnerhund. **—less,** *adj.,* **—lessly,** *adv.* stumpf; (*fig.*) zwecklos. **—blank,** *adj. & adv.* schnurgerade (*as a shot*).

Poise, *v.a.* (ab)wägen.

Poison, I. *s.* das Gift. II. *v.a.* vergiften. **—er,** *s.* der Giftmischer, die Giftmischerin. **—ous,** *adj.,* **—ously,** *adv.* giftig (*also fig.*).

Poke, *v.a.* aufrühren, aufstöbern; schüren (*the fire*); to — fun at, sich über jemanden lustig machen. **—r,** *s.* der Feuerhaken.

Polar, *adj.* Polar-, Pol-; — bear, der Eisbär; — circles, Polarkreise; — axis, die Polachse.

¹Pole, *s.* der Pol (*Astr., Magnet., Elec.*).

²Pole, *s.* der Pfahl, die Stange.

Poleaxe, *s.* die Streitaxt.

Polecat, *s.* der Iltis.

Polic—e, *s.* die Polizei. **—eman,** *s.* der Schutzmann, Polizist. **—e-office,** *s.* das Polizeiamt, die Polizei.

Policy, *s.* der Versicherungsschein; die Police (*C.L.*); die Politik.

Polish, I. *s.* die Glätte, der Glanz; (*fig.*) die Geschliffenheit. II. *v.a.* glätten, polieren; bohnen (*with wax*); (*fig.*) bilden, verfeinern; to — off, wegputzen (*vulg.*). III. *v.n.* glatt werden. **—ed,** *adj.* glatt, poliert; fein (*as manners*).

Polite, *adj.,* **—ly,** *adv.* fein, gebildet, höflich. **—ness,** *s.* die Höflichkeit, Artigkeit, Verbindlichkeit.

Politic, *adj.* politisch; (*fig.*) weltklug, schlau. **—al,** *adj.,* **—ally,** *adv.* politisch; staatskundig; Staats-. **—ian,** *s.* der Staatsmann, Politiker. **—s,** *s.* die Politik, Staatswissenschaft.

Polka, *s.* die Polka.

Poll, I. *s.* der Schädel; (voting) die Abstimmung; (—ing-place) der Wahlort; (votes) die Stimmenzahl. II. *v.a.* behauen (*trees, etc.*); abschneiden

(the hair); Stimmen eintragen (Parl.).
III. v.n.; to — for, ſtimmen für.
IV. v.a. Stimmen erhalten. —book,
s. die Wählerliſte.
Pollard, s. (— tree) der gekappte
Baum.
Pollen, s. der Blütenſtaub.
Polling, s. das Wählen, die Abſtim=
mung. —booth, s. die Wahlbude,
das Wahllokal. —district, s. der
Wahlbezirk.
Pollut—e, v.a. beſlecken (also fig.).
—ion, s. die Befleckung.
Poltroon, s. der Feigling.
Poly— (in many compds. = viel).
—gamist, s. der Polygamiſt. —
gamy, s. die Vielweiberei. —glot,
adj. vielſprachig. —gon, s. das
Vieleck (Math.). —gonal, —gonous,
adj. vieleckig, Polygonal=. —syllabic,
adj. mehrſilbig, vielſilbig. —syllable,
s. vielſilbiges Wort. —technic, I.
adj. polytechniſch. II. s. die Gewer=
behochſchule. —theism, s. die Viel=
götterei.
Pom—ade, —atum, s. die Pomade.
Pomegranate, s. der Granatapfel.
Pommel, I. s. der (Degen=, Sattel=)
Knopf (of a sword, a saddle). II. v.a.
ſchlagen.
Pomp, s. der Pomp, Prunk. —osity,
s. die Prahlerei. —ous, adj., —ous=
ly, adv. prunkvoll, pomphaft; (pre-
tentious) prahleriſch.
Pond, s. der Teich, Weiher.
Ponder, I. v.a. erwägen, bedenken.
II. n. nachſinnen (on, over a thing,
über eine S.). —ous, adj., —ously,
adv. ſchwer.
Poniard, I. s. der Dolch. II. v.a.
erdolchen.
Pontiff, s. der Hohepriester.
Pontoon, s. der Ponton (Mil.); der
Brückenkahn.
Pony, s. das Pony.
Poodle, s. der Pudel.
Pool, s. der Pfuhl; (of blood) die Lache.
Poop, s. die Kampanje, das Halbdeck
(Naut.).
Poor, I. adj. arm; dürftig; elend;
(paltry) armſelig, gering; — me! ich
Armer! — health, ſchwache Gesundheit;
a — dinner, ein ſchlechtes Mittageſſen.
II. s. die Armen. —ly, adj. unwohl.
Pop, I. s. der Paff. II. int. paff! III.
v.n. ſchnalzen. —gun, s. die Knall=
büchſe.

Pope, s. der Papst.
Poplar, s. die Pappel.
Poppy, s. der Mohn.
Popul—ace, s. der Pöbel. —ar,
adj., —arly, adv. Volks=, volksmäßig;
(generally liked) volkstümlich, popu-
lär. —arity, s. die Volkstümlichkeit,
allgemeine Beliebtheit. —ate, v.a.
bevölkern. —ation, s. die Bevöl=
kerung. —ous, adj., —ously, adv.
volkreich.
Porcelain, I. s. das Porzellan. II. adj.
Porzellan=.
Porch, s. die Vorhalle, Halle.
Porcupine, s. das Stachelſchwein.
¹**Por**—e, s. die Pore. —ous, adj.
porös.
²**Pore,** v.n. brüten (over a thing, über
einer S.), eifrig ſtudieren.
Pork, s. das Schweinefleiſch.
Porpoise, s. das Meerſchwein.
Porridge, s. der Haferbrei, die Hafer=
grütze.
¹**Port,** s. der Hafen.
²**Port,** s. die Pforte, Pfortluke (Naut.).
³**Port,** I. s. das Backbord. II. v.a.;
— the helm! backbord das Ruder!
⁴**Port,** s. der Portwein.
Portable, adj. tragbar.
Portal, s. das Portal (Arch.).
Portcullis, s. das Fall=, Schutz=gatter.
Porten—d, v.a. vorbedeuten. —t, s.
die Vorbedeutung. —tous, adj.,
—tously, adv. verhängnisvoll.
Porter, s. der Last=, Pack=träger; der
Gepäckträger (Railw.); der Türhüter,
Pförtner.
Portfolio, s. die Mappe.
Portico, s. die Säulenhalle.
Portion, I. s. der Teil. II. v.a.
teilen.
Portly, adj. ſtattlich.
Portmanteau, s. der Mantelſack,
Handkoffer.
Portrait, s. das Bild(nis), Porträt.
Portray, v.a. abbilden, abmalen,
ſchildern.
Pose, s. die Stellung.
Position, s. die Stellung, Lage; (rank)
der Stand.
Positive, I. adj., —ly, adv. feſtge=
ſtellt; ausdrücklich, beſtimmt. II. s.
der Poſitiv (Gram., Phot.). —ness,
s. die Beſtimmtheit.
Possess, v.a. beſitzen, im Beſitz haben,
inne haben. —ion, s. der Beſitz;
(property) das Beſitztum. —ive, I.

adj. besitzanzeigend. II. *s.* (—ive case) der Genitiv. —or, *s.* der Besitzer.

Possib—ility, *s.* die Möglichkeit. —le, *adj.* möglich. —ly, *adv.* möglicherweise, vielleicht.

¹**Post,** *s.* der Pfahl, Pfosten (*Build.*, etc.); die Säule (*Tele.*); (winning-—) das Ziel.

²**Post,** I. *s.* der Posten (*Mil.*); (letter, *etc.* —) die Post; (courier) der Eilbote; (—-horse) das Eilpferd; by air —, durch Luftpost. II. *adv.* eilig, in Eile. III. *v.a.* eintragen, einschreiben (*C.L.*); aufgeben (*a letter*); aufstellen, postieren (*soldiers, etc.*). IV. *v.n.* eilen (*fig.*). —age, I. *s.* das Porto; —age free, portofrei. II. *attrib.*; —age stamp, die Briefmarke. —al, *adj.* Post-. —bag, *s.* der Briefbeutel. —card, *s.* die Postkarte; pictorial —card, die Ansichtspostkarte. —free, *adj.* franko, frankiert. —man, *s.* der Briefträger. —mark, *s.* der Poststempel. —master, *s.* der Postmeister. —office, *s.* das Postamt.

Postdate, *v.a.* nachdatieren.

Poster, *s.* der Anschlagzettel, das Plakat.

Posterior, *adj.* später, nachkommend. —s, *pl.* der Hintere.

Posterity, *s.* die Nachwelt.

Postern, *s.* das Türchen.

Posthumous, *adj.* nachgeboren, hinterlassen.

Postilion, *s.* der Postillon.

Post-mortem, *adj.* nach dem Tode; — examination, die Leichenöffnung, Leichenschau.

Postpone, *v.a.* aufschieben, verschieben. —ment, *s.* der Aufschub, die Verschiebung.

Postscript, *s.* die Nachschrift.

Posture, *s.* die Haltung.

Posy, *s.* der Blumenstrauß.

Pot, *s.* der Topf; —ted meat, eingemachtes Fleisch. —herb, *s.* das Küchenkraut.

Potash, *s.* die Pottasche.

Potassium, *s.* das Kalium.

Potato, *s.* die Kartoffel.

Poten—cy, *s.* die Macht, Stärke. —t, *adj.*, —tly, *adv.* mächtig, stark. —tate, *s.* der Machthaber. —tial, *adj.*, —tially, *adv.* möglich.

Potion, *s.* das Getränk.

Potsherd, *s.* die Scherbe.

Pottage, *s.* die dicke Suppe.

Potter, *s.* der Töpfer. —y, *s.* die Töpferware.

Pouch, *s.* die Tasche.

Poultice, *s.* der Breiumschlag.

Poultry, *s.* das Federvieh. —yard, *s.* der Hühnerhof.

Pounce, *v.n.*; to — upon, herfallen über (*acc.*).

¹**Pound,** *s.* (lb.) das Pfund.

²**Pound,** *v.a.* zerstoßen.

Pour, *v.a. & n.* gießen, schütten, strömen; a down-—, ein Regenguß.

Pout, *v.n.* schmollen. —ing, I. *adj.*, —ingly, *adv.* schmollend. II. *s.* das Schmollen.

Poverty, *s.* die Armut.

Powder, *s.* (dust) der Staub; der Puder (*for the face, etc.*); das Pulver (*Gun., Med.*). —y, *adj.* pulverartig. —puff, *s.* die Puderquaste.

Power, *s.* das Vermögen, die Kraft; die (bewegende) Kraft (*Mech.*); (authority, *etc.*) die Macht, Gewalt; the great European —s, die europäischen Großmächte. —ful, *adj.*, —fully, *adv.* kräftig, mächtig, gewaltig. —less, *adj.* kraftlos, machtlos. —lessness, *s.* die Kraftlosigkeit. —house, —station, *s.* das Kraftwerk. —amplifier, *s.* der Endverstärker. —current, *s.* der Starkstrom (*Radio*).

Pox, *s.* (small-—) die Pocken.

Practic—able, *adj.*, —ably, *adv.* tunlich. —ableness, —ability, *s.* die Tunlichkeit. —al, *adj.*, —ally, *adv.* tatsächlich, wirklich; praktisch; —al joke, handgreiflicher Spaß; —al chemistry, angewandte Chemie.

Practice, *s.* die Praxis (*also Med.*); die Ausübung, der Gebrauch; out of —, außer Übung.

Practise, *v.* I. *a.* (aus-)üben (*virtues, a profession, etc.*); einüben. II. *n.* sich üben, üben. —d, *adj.* geübt, bewandert.

Practitioner, *s.* der Praktiker, der Praktikant; praktischer Arzt.

Prairie, *s.* die Prärie, Grasebene.

Praise, I. *s.* das Lob, der Preis. II. *v.a.* loben, preisen (for, wegen). —worthy, *adj.*, —worthily, *adv.* lobenswert.

Prance, *v.n.* sich bäumen (*as horses*), paradieren, einherstolzieren.

Prank, *s.* der Possen, Streich.

Prat—e, I. *v.n.* schwatzen, plappern. II. *s.* das Geschwätz. **—er,** *s.* der Schwätzer. **—ing,** I. *adj.*, **—ingly,** *adv.* schwathaft. II. *s.* das Schwatzen, Geschwätz.

Prattle, I. *v.n.* schwatzen, plaudern. II. *s.* das Geschwätz. **—r,** *s.* der Schwätzer, Plauderer.

Prawn, *s.* die Steingarneele.

Pray, *v.* I. *n.* beten (to, zu; for, um, für); (beg) bitten. II. *a.* bitten, ersuchen (um eine S.). **—er,** *s.* das Gebet; die Bitte. **—ing,** I. *adj.* betend, bittend. II. *s.* das Beten, Bitten. **—er-book,** *s.* das Gebetbuch.

Preach, *v.a.* & *n.* predigen. **—er,** *s.* der Prediger. **—ing,** *s.* das Predigen.

Precarious, *adj.* unsicher.

Precaution, *s.* die Vorsichtsmaßregel.

Preced—e, *v.* I. *a.* vorher=, vorausgehen. II. *n.*; the day **—ing,** am Tage vorher, den Tag vor (*a battle, etc.*). **—ence,** **—ency,** *s.* der Vortritt, Vorrang. **—ent,** I. *adj.* vorhergehend. II. *s.* die Vorschrift, Richtschnur.

Precept, *s.* die Vorschrift. **—or,** *s.* der Lehrer. **—ory,** *s.* der Tempelhof (*of the Knights Templars*).

Precession, *s.* das Vorrücken (of the equinoxes, der Nachtgleichen).

Precinct, *s.* der Bezirk; **—s,** die Grenzen.

Precious, *adj.*, **—ly,** *adv.* kostbar, edel (*of stones, etc.*).

Precipi—ce, *s.* der Abgrund. **—tance, —tancy,** *s.* die Übereilung. **—tous,** *adj.*, **—tously,** *adv.* jäh.

Precise, *adj.*, **—ly,** *adv.* bestimmt, pedantisch, genau. **—ness,** *s.* die Genauigkeit.

Precoci—ous, *adj.*, **—ously,** *adv.* frühreif, altklug. **—ty,** *s.* die Frühreife; (*fig.*) die Vorzeitigkeit.

Precursor, *s.* der Vorläufer, der Vorbote.

Predecessor, *s.* der Vorgänger (*in office, etc.*).

Predestinat—e, *v.a.* vorherbestimmen. **—ion,** *s.* die Vorherbestimmung, die Gnadenwahl.

Predic—ament, *s.* die Verlegenheit. **—ate,** *s.* das Prädikat.

Predict, *v.a.* vorher=, weis=sagen. **—ion,** *s.* die Weissagung.

Predilection, *s.* die Vorliebe.

Predominan—ce, *s.* das Vorherrschen, das Übergewicht. **—t,** *adj.* vorherrschend.

Pre-existence, *s.* das Vorherdasein, früheres Vorhandensein.

Prefa—ce, *s.* die Vorrede. **—tory,** *adj.* einleitend, Einleitungs=.

Prefer, *v.a.* vorbringen (*a request*); (advance) befördern; (like better) bevorzugen. **—able,** *adj.* vorzuziehen; vorzüglicher (to, als). **—ence,** *s.* der Vorzug; from **—ence,** mit Vorliebe; **—ence shares,** Prioritätsaktien.

Prefix, I. *v.a.* vor(an)setzen. II. *s.* die Vorsilbe.

Pregnan—cy, *s.* die Schwangerschaft. **—t,** *adj.* schwanger (*of women*); trächtig (*of animals*); (*fig.*) inhaltschwer, fruchtbar.

Prehistoric, *adj.* vorgeschichtlich.

Prejudic—e, I. *s.* das Vorurteil. II. *v.a.* vorher einnehmen (against, gegen); **—ed,** eingenommen (gegen). **—ial,** *adj.*, **—ially,** *adv.* nachteilig, beeinträchtigend.

Prela—cy, *s.* die Prälatur. **—te,** *s.* der Prälat.

Preliminar—y, *adj.* vorläufig, einleitend. **—ies,** *pl.* die Vorverhandlungen.

Prelude, *s.* das Vorspiel.

Premature, *adj.*, **—ly,** *adv.* frühzeitig, =reif, vorschnell.

Premeditat—e, *v.a.* vorher überlegen. **—ed,** *adj.*, **—edly,** *adv.* vorbedacht. **—ion,** *s.* der Vorbedacht.

Premier, I. *adj.* erst. II. *s.* der Ministerpräsident.

Premise, *v.a.* & *n.* vorangehen lassen. **—s,** *pl.* das Gebäude.

Premium, *s.* die Prämie.

Prepar—ation, *s.* die Vorbereitung; die Zubereitung (*of food, etc.*). **—atory,** *adj.* vorbereitend, Vorbereitungs=. **—e,** *v.* *a.* & *n.* vorbereiten (for, zu, auf).

Prepay, *v.a.* im voraus bezahlen.

Preposition, *s.* das Verhältniswort.

Preposterous, *adj.*, **—ly,** *adv.* verkehrt, albern.

Prerogative, *s.* das Prärogativ, das Vorrecht.

Presage, *s.* die Vorbedeutung.

Presbyter, *s.* der Kirchenälteste.

Prescribe, *v.a.* & *n.* verordnen (*rules, etc.*); verschreiben (*Med.*).

Prescription, *s.* die Vorschrift, Verordnung.

Presence, *s.* die Gegenwart; he was brought into the — of the King, er wurde vor den König gebracht.

¹Present, I. *adj.* gegenwärtig, anwesend, zugegen. II. *s.* die Gegenwart. **—ly,** *adv.* bald, kurz darauf.

²Present, *v.a.* darstellen, zeigen; (introduce) vorstellen; präsentieren (*arms*); einreichen (*a petition, etc.*); (give) (be)schenken; to — one's compliments to a person, sich einem empfehlen. **—ation,** *s.* die Präsentation; (gift) die Schenkung.

³Present, *s.* das Geschenk.

Presentiment, *s.* die Vorahnung.

Preserv—ation, *s.* die Be=, Verwahrung (from, vor); die Erhaltung (*in good condition, etc.*); (saving) die Rettung. **—ative,** I. *adj.* verwahrend, erhaltend. II. das Verwahrungsmittel, Schutzmittel. **—e,** *v.a.* bewahren, behüten (from, vor); erhalten (*in health, etc.*); einmachen (*fruit, etc.*). **—er,** *s.* der Beschützer.

Preside, *v.n.* den Vorsitz führen. **—nt,** *s.* der Vorsitzende, der Präsident (*also of a republic*).

Press, I. *v.a.* pressen, drücken; (crowd) drängen. II. *v.n.* drücken, pressen. III. *s.* die Presse (*Print.*; also for wine, etc.); der Schrank (*for linen, etc.*); das Gedränge (*of people*); der Drang, Andrang (*of business, etc.*). **—man,** *s.* der Drucker; der Journalist.

Press—ing, I. *adj.,* **—ingly,** *adv.* dringend; eilig. II. *s.* das Pressen, Drücken. **—ure,** *s.* der Druck (*also fig.*).

Prestige, *s.* das Ansehen.

Presum—able, *adj.,* **—ably,** *adv.* vermutlich. **—e,** *v.* I. *a.* vermuten. II. *n.* vermuten. **—ing,** *adj.* anmaßend. **—ption,** *s.* die Voraussetzung; (assurance) die Vermessenheit. **—ptuous,** *adj.,* **—ptuously,** *adv.* vermessen.

Preten—ce, *s.* der Vorwand, Schein. **—d,** *v.* I. *a.* vorgeben; heucheln (zeal, etc.). II. *a. & n.* sich stellen, sich ausgeben für. **—ded,** *adj.* verstellt. **—der,** *s.* der Vorschützende; der Prätendent (*Hist.*). **—sion,** *s.* der Anspruch (to, auf eine S.). **—tious,** *adj.,* **—tiously,** *adv.* anspruchsvoll.

Preterite, *s.* (— tense) das Präteritum, die Vergangenheit.

Pretext, *s.* der Vorwand.

Prett—ily, *adv.* niedlich, artig, nett. **—iness,** *s.* die Niedlichkeit, Nettigkeit; die Artigkeit (*of behaviour*). **—y,** I. *adj.* hübsch, niedlich, nett. II. *adv.* ziemlich; **—y** much the same thing, ungefähr dasselbe; **—y** near, nahe daran.

Prevail, *v.n.* herrschen; häufig vorkommen. **—ing,** *adj.* vorherrschend.

Prevalen—ce, —cy, *s.* das Herrschen, Vorherrschen. **—t,** *adj.* überwiegend, weit verbreitet.

Prevaricat—e, *v.n.* Ausflüchte brauchen. **—ion,** *s.* die Ausflucht, Umgehung der Wahrheit.

Prevent, *v.a.* (ver)hindern. **—able,** *adj.* verhütbar. **—ion,** *s.* die Verhinderung.

Previous, *adj.,* **—ly,** *adv.* vorhergehend; — to, vor.

Prey, I. *s.* der Raub, die Beute. II. *v.n.* plündern; to — on, rauben.

Price, *s.* der Preis. **—less,** *adj.* unschätzbar.

Prick, I. *v.a.* stechen. II. *v.n.* stacheln, prickeln; to — up one's ears, die Ohren spitzen. III. *s.* der Stachel; der Stich (*of a needle, etc.*). **—ly,** *adj.* stachelig; **—ly** pear, die Feigendistel.

Pride, I. *s.* der Stolz, Hochmut, Übermut. II. *v.r.* stolz sein (auf eine S.); to — oneself on, sich brüsten mit.

Priest, *s.* der Priester. **—ess,** *s.* die Priesterin. **—hood,** *s.* das Priestertum, =amt. **—ly,** *adj.* priesterlich, Priester=.

Prig, I. *s.* der Laffe; (*slang*) der Dieb. II. *v.a.* mausen.

Prim, *adj.,* **—ly,** *adv.* zimperlich.

Prim—ary, *adj.* erst. **—e,** *adj.* erst; **—e** cost, der Einkaufspreis. **—eval,** *adj.* uranfänglich. **—ate,** *s.* der Erzbischof. **—er,** *s.* das Elementarbuch. **Priming,** *s.* die Grundierung (*Paint.*); die Zündung (*Artil.*). **—itive,** *adj.* Ur= (*of rocks, etc.*); Stamm= (*of words*); (old-fashioned) altertümlich. **—ly,** *adv.* primitiv (*as colours*).

Primrose, *s.* die Schlüsselblume, die Primel.

Prince, *s.* der Fürst (*as a title*); der Prinz. **—ly,** *adj.* fürstlich; prinzlich.

—ss, s. die Fürstin (title); die Prinzessin.

Princip—al, I. adj., —ally, adv. hauptsächlich, Haupt=. II. s. die Hauptperson. —le, s. (motive) der Beweggrund; (tenet) der Grundsatz.

Print, I. v.a. drucken; (imprint) aufdrucken. II. n. drucken; (publish) drucken lassen, herausgeben. III. s. der Druck, Abdruck. —er, s. der (Buch=, Kupfer=, Stein=, Kattun=) Drucker; —er's error, der Druckfehler; —er's devil, der Setzerjunge; —er's ink, die Druckerschwärze. —ing, s. das Drucken, die Druckerei, der Druck. —s, pl. bedruckte Kalikos. —ing-block, s. die Druckform. —ing-house, s. die Buchdruckerei. —ing-press, s. die Druckerpresse. —ing-types, pl. die Lettern.

Prior, I. adj. früher. II. adv.; — to, vor (dat.). III. s. der Prior. — ess, s. die Priorin. —ity, s. die Priorität. —y, s. die Abtei.

Prise, v.a. (— open) mit einem Hebel heben.

Prism, s. das Prisma.

Prison, s. das Gefängnis. —er, s. der, die Gefangene.

Priv—acy, s. die Heimlichkeit. —ate, I. adj., —ately, adv. heimlich, geheim; (personal) Privat=; in —ate, im geheimen. II. s. (—ate soldier) der Gemeine.

Privateer, s. das Kaperschiff. —ing, s. die Kaperei.

Privation, s. die Not; der Mangel.

Privet, s. die Rainweide.

Privilege, s. das Vorrecht.

Privy, I. adj. geheim, heimlich; mitwissend; — Council, der Staatsrat; — Councillor, der Geheimrat. II. s. der Abort.

1Prize, s. der Preis. —money, s. die Prisengelder, die Prämie.

2Prize, v.a. (hoch) schätzen, würdigen.

Probab—ility, s. die Wahrscheinlichkeit. —le, adj., —ly, adv. wahrscheinlich.

Probate, s. die Bestätigung (of a will).

Probation, s. die Probe; die Probezeit.

Probe, I. s. die Sonde (Surg.). II. v.a. sondieren (also fig.).

Probity, s. die Biederkeit, die Redlichkeit.

Problem, s. die Aufgabe, das Problem. —atic(al), adj. fraglich, zweifelhaft.

Proboscis, s. der Rüssel.

Procedure, s. das Verfahren.

Proceed, v.n. fort-schreiten, =rücken, schreiten (to, zu); to — with a journey, eine Reise fortsetzen; fortführen (a narrative, etc.); (act) handeln. —ing, s. das Fortschreiten; das Verfahren, die Handlung. —s, pl. der Ertrag, Erlös, Gewinn; net —s, der Reinertrag.

Process, s. der Verlauf (of time); der Prozeß (Chem., Law).

Procession, s. die Prozession.

Proclaim, v.a. kundgeben.

Proclamation, s. die Bekanntmachung; — of war, die Kriegserklärung.

Procrastinat—e, I. v.a. aufschieben. II. v.n. zögern. —ion, s. der Aufschub, die Verzögerung.

Proctor, s. der Geschäftsführer.

Procur—able, adj. erlangbar. —e, v.a. ver=, anschaffen, besorgen, beschaffen, erlangen.

Prod, v.a. stechen.

Prodigal, I. adj., —ly, adv. verschwenderisch. II. s.; — son, der verlorene Sohn (B.); (fig.) der Taugenichts. —ity, s. die Verschwendung.

Prodig—ious, adj. ungeheuer, erstaunlich. —y, s. das Wunder.

Produce, I. v.a. vor=, ein-führen; beibringen (witnesses, etc.), anführen (reasons, etc.). II. s. das Produkt; der Ertrag. —r, s. der Hervorbringer; (opp. to Consumer) der Produzent.

Product, s. das Erzeugnis, Produkt. —ive, adj. fruchtbar; (creative) schöpferisch.

Profan—ation, s. die Entweihung. —e, I. adj., —ely, adv. weltlich, profan (as history); (impious) gottlos. II. v.a. entweihen. —eness, —ity, s. die Gott=, Ruch-losigkeit.

Profess, v.a. bekennen; sich bekennen zu (a religion, etc.). —ed, adj., —edly, adv. bekannt, erklärt (as an enemy). —ion, s. die Erklärung, Versicherung; der Beruf; by —ion, von Beruf. —ional, I. adj., —ionally, adv. berufsmäßig, Berufs=; —ional men, Männer von Fach. II. s. der Fachmann, Kundige. —or, s. der Professor.

Proffer, I. v.a. anbieten. II. s. das Anerbieten.

Proficien—cy, *s.* die Tüchtigkeit. **—t,** I. *adj.* tüchtig, bewandert. II. *s.* der Meister.

Profile, *s.* das Profil, die Seitenansicht.

Profit, I. *s.* der Vorteil, Nutzen, Gewinn; — and loss account, das Gewinn= und Verlust=Konto. II. *v.n.;* to — by, gewinnen durch, Nutzen ziehen aus. **—able,** *adj.,* **—ably,** *adv.* vorteilhaft, einträglich. **—eer,** *s.* der (Kriegs=)Gewinnler, Schieber. **—less,** *adj.,* **—lessly,** *adv.* nutzlos.

Profliga—cy, *s.* die Verworfenheit. **—te,** I. *adj.* verworfen. II. *s.* der Bösewicht.

Profound, *adj.,* **—ly,** *adv.* tief, gründlich (*also fig.*).

Profus—e, *adj.,* **—ely,** *adv.* überflüssig. **—ion,** *s.* der Überfluß.

Progeny, *s.* die Nachkommenschaft.

Programme, *s.* das Programm.

Progress, I. *s.* der Fortschritt. II. *v.n.* fortschreiten, weiterrücken. **—ion,** *s.* das Fortschreiten. **—ive,** *adj.* vorrückend, =schreitend; (*fig.*) fortschreitend.

Prohibit, *v.a.* verbieten, verhindern. **—ion,** *s.* das Verbot. **—ionist,** *s.* der Antialkoholiker, Temperenzler.

Project, I. *v.a.* schleudern; entwerfen, ersinnen (*a plan*). II. *v.n.* vorragen (*Arch.*). III. *s.* der Entwurf, das Projekt.

Projectile, *s.* das Projektil.

Projection, *s.* das Schleudern; das Ausladen (*Arch.*).

Prolific, *adj.,* fruchtbar (*also fig.*).

Prolix, *adj.* weitschweifig. **—ity,** *s.* die Weitschweifigkeit.

Prologue, *s.* der Prolog, das Vorwort.

Prolong, *v.a.* verlängern.

Promenade, *s.* der Spaziergang.

Prominence—ce, *s.* das Hervorragen (*also fig.*). **—t,** *adj.,* **—tly,** *adv.* hervorragend (*also fig.*).

Promiscuous, *adj.,* **—ly,** *adv.* gemischt, gemein, unterschiedslos.

Promis—e, I. *s.* das Versprechen. II. *v.a. & n.* versprechen, geloben, verheißen. **—er,** *s.* der Versprecher. **—ing,** *adj.,* **—ingly,** *adv.* vielversprechend. **—sory,** *adj.* versprechend; **—sory note,** der Solawechsel.

Promontory, *s.* das Vorgebirge.

Promot—e, *v.a.* befördern. **—er,** *s.* der Anstifter (*of a plot, etc.*); der Gründer (*of a company*). **—ion,** *s.* die Förderung.

Prompt, I. *adj.,* **—ly,** *adv.* schnell, rasch. II. *v.a.* soufflieren. **—er,** *s.* der Souffleur (*Theat.*). **—itude,** **—ness,** *s.* die Schnelligkeit.

Promulgat—e, *v.a.* bekannt machen, verkündigen. **—ion,** *s.* die öffentliche Bekanntmachung.

Prone, *adj.* vorwärts geneigt; **— to,** geneigt zu.

Prong, *s.* die Zinke.

Pronoun, *s.* das Fürwort.

Pronounce, *v.a. & n.* aussprechen. **—d,** *adj.* ausgesprochen; (*fig.*) bestimmt.

Pronunciation, *s.* die Aussprache.

Proof, *s.* die Probe. **—sheet,** *s.* der Korrektur=, Aushänge=bogen.

Prop, I. *s.* die Stütze (*also fig.*). II. *v.a.* (— up) (unter)stützen.

Propag—anda, *s.* die Propaganda. **—ate,** *v.a.* fortpflanzen, verbreiten.

Propel, *v.a.* umtreiben (*a wheel*). **—ler,** *s.* die Schiffsschraube; der Propeller, die Antriebsschraube (*Aviation*).

Propensity, *s.* die Neigung.

Proper, *adj.,* **—ly,** *adv.* eigentümlich; (*real*) eigentlich; (*suitable*) passend, schicklich.

Property, *s.* das Eigentum, Besitztum.

Prophe—cy, *s.* die Prophezeiung. **—sy,** *v.a. & n.* weissagen. **—t,** *s.* der Weissager, Prophet. **—tess,** *s.* die Prophetin. **—tic,** *adj.,* **—tically,** *adv.* prophetisch.

Proportion, I. *s.* das Verhältnis; (symmetry) das Eben=, Gleich=maß. II. *v.a.* abmessen. **—able,** *adj.,* **—ably,** *adv.* (—ably to) im Verhältnisse, entsprechend (*dat.*). **—al,** *adj.,* **—ally,** *adv.* verhältnismäßig, Verhältnis=.

Propos—al, *s.* der Vorschlag, Antrag. **—e,** *v.* I. *a.* vorschlagen, antragen auf (*acc.*). II. *n.* beabsichtigen; einen Heiratsantrag machen. **—ition,** *s.* der Antrag.

Propound, *v.a.* vorstellen, vorlegen, vorschlagen.

Propriet—or, *s.* der Eigentümer, Besitzer, Inhaber. **—orship,** *s.* das Eigentumsrecht. **—ress,** *s.* die Eigentümerin.

Propriety, *s.* die Schicklichkeit.

Prorogation, *s.* die Vertagung.

Pros—aic, *adj.,* **—aically,** *adv.* prosaisch, langweilig. **—e,** *s.* die Prosa.

Prosecut—e, *v.a.* verfolgen. **—ion,** *s.* die Verfolgung. **—or,** *s.* der Verfolger.

Prospect, I. *s.* die Aussicht (*also fig.*); to have in —, im Auge haben. II. *v.n.* schürfen (*Min.*). **—ive,** *adj.* (in —) zu gewärtigen. **—us,** *s.* der Prospekt.

Prosper, *v.n.* gedeihen. **—ity,** *s.* das Gedeihen. **—ous,** *adj.*, **—ously,** *adv.* glücklich.

Prostrat—e, I. *adj.* hingestreckt am Boden. II. *v.a.* nieder-, hin-werfen. **—ion,** *s.* das Niederwerfen, die Erschlaffung.

Protect, *v.a.* (be)schirmen (vor). **—ing,** *adj.*, **—ingly,** *adv.* schützend, Schutz-. **—ion,** *s.* der Schutz. **—ive,** *adj.* schützend, Schutz-; **—ive** duty, der Schutzzoll. **—or,** *s.* der Beschützer.

Protest, I. *s.* der Einspruch. II. *v.a.* protestieren (lassen) (*a bill*). III. *v.n.* Einrede, Einspruch tun. **—ant,** I. *adj.* protestantisch. II. *s.* der (die) Protestant(in). **—ation,** *s.* die Beteurung. **—er,** *s.* der Beteurer.

Prototype, *s.* das Urbild.

Protract, *v.a.* in die Länge ziehen. **—ed,** *adj.*, **—edly,** *adv.* lang.

Protrude, *v.n.* hervorragen.

Protuberan—ce, *s.* der Auswuchs. **—t,** *adj.* hervorragend.

Proud, *adj.*, **—ly,** *adv.* stolz (of a thing, auf eine S.); (haughty) hochmütig.

Prove, *v.* I. *a.* (test) prüfen, erproben; (establish) bestätigen. II. *n.* sich ausweisen, sich ergeben; ausfallen, werden; to — true, sich bewähren; to — false, sich nicht bewähren.

Provender, *s.* das Viehfutter; der Proviant, die Nahrungsmittel (*pl.*).

Proverb, *s.* das Sprichwort. **—s,** *pl.* die Sprüche Salomonis. **—ial,** *adj.*, **—ially,** *adv.* sprichwörtlich.

Provide, *v.* I. *a.* versehen, versorgen (with, mit). II. *n.* sorgen, Vorsorge tragen (for, für). **—nce,** *s.* Vorsehung (*Theol.*). **—nt,** *adj.*, **—ntly,** *adv.* vorsichtig; **—nt** society, wirtschaftliche Genossenschaft. **—ntial,** *adj.*, **—ntially,** *adv.* durch die (göttliche) Vorsehung bewirkt (*as an escape, etc.*). **—r,** *s.* der Fürsorger, Lieferant.

Provinc—e, *s.* die Provinz; that is not in my —e, das liegt nicht in meinem Gebiet *or* Fach. **—ial,** *adj.* Provinzial-, kleinstädtisch).

Provision, I. *s.* die Verordnung,

Maßregel. II. *v.a.* mit Proviant *or* Lebensmitteln versehen. **—al,** *adj.*, **—ally,** *adv.* vorläufig. **—s,** *pl.* Lebensmittel.

Proviso, *s.* die Bedingung

Provo—cation, *s.* die (An-)Reizung. **—cative,** *adj.* (an)reizend. **—ke,** *v.a.* anregen, (an-)reizen.

Prow, *s.* das Vorschiff, der Schiffsvorderteil, Bug.

Prowess, *s.* die Tapferkeit.

Prowl, *v.n.* umher-streichen, -schleichen.

Proxim—ate, *adj.*, **—ately,** *adv.* nächst, unmittelbar. **—ity,** *s.* die Nähe. **—o** (*abbrev.* prox.), nächsten Monats (*C.L.*).

Proxy, *s.* der Stellvertreter; (document) die Vollmacht.

Prud—e, *s.* die Spröde. **—ery,** *s.* die Sprödigkeit. **—ish,** *adj.*, **—ishly,** *adv.* spröde, zimperlich.

Pruden—ce, *s.* die Klugheit. **—t,** *adj.*, **—tly,** *adv.* vorsichtig.

1Prun—e, *v.a.* ausputzen (*vines, etc.*); beschneiden (*trees*). **—ing-knife,** *s.* das Gartenmesser. **—ing,** *s.* das Ausputzen.

2Prune, *s.* die Backpflaume.

Prussic acid, *s.* die Blausäure.

Pry, *v.n.* spähen.

Psal—m, *s.* der Psalm. **—mist,** *s.* der Psalmist. **—ter,** *s.* der Psalter, das Psalmenbuch.

Pseudo, *adj.* falsch. **—nym,** *s.* falscher Name, das Pseudonym.

Psych—ic(al), *adj.* psychisch. **—ological,** *adj.*, **—ologically,** *adv.* psychologisch. **—ologist,** *s.* der Psycholog. **—ology,** *s.* die Psychologie.

Ptarmigan, *s.* das Schneehuhn.

Public, I. *adj.*, **—ly,** *adv.* Staats-, öffentlich; (notorious) offenkundig; — house, das Wirtshaus, die Schenke; — library, die Volkslesehalle; in —, öffentlich; — spirit, der Gemeinsinn. II. *s.* das Publikum. **—an,** *s.* der Schenkwirt.

Publication, *s.* die Herausgabe, Veröffentlichung (*of a work*); (book, *etc.*) die Schrift.

Publicity, *s.* die Öffentlichkeit.

Publish, *v.a.* veröffentlichen; herausgeben, verlegen (*a book, etc.*). **—er,** *s.* der Herausgeber, Verleger. **—ing,** *adj.*; **—ing** business, der Verlagshandel.

Pucker, *s.* die Falte.

Pudding, *s.* der Pudding; black —, die Blutwurst.

Puddle, *s.* der Pfuhl.

Pueril—e, *adj.* knabenhaft, kindisch. —ity, *s.* das kindische Wesen.

Puff, I. *s.* der Windstoß; (*fig.*) das Aufgeblasene; die Reklame (*coll.*); (powder —) der Puderquast; — paste, der Blätterteig. II. *v.n.* pusten. III. *v.a.* (— up) aufblähen (*also fig.*).

Puffin, *s.* der Sturmtaucher (*Orn.*).

Puffy, *adj.* aufgedunsen.

Pug, *s.* (—-dog) der Mops. —nosed, *adj.* stumpfnasig.

Pugilist, *s.* der Boxer, der Faust-kämpfer.

Pugnaci—ous, *adj.*, —ously, *adv.* kampflustig, streitsüchtig. —ty, *s.* die Streitsucht.

Pule, *v.n.* winseln, wimmern.

Pull, I. *s.* der Zug. II. *v.a.* ziehen, zerren. III. *v.n.* ziehen, reißen; rudern (*Naut.*); to — down, nieder-reißen.

Pullet, *s.* das Hühnchen.

Pulley, *s.* die Rolle.

Pulp, *s.* der Brei. —y, *adj.* breiig, breiartig.

Pulpit, *s.* die Kanzel.

Puls—ate, *v.n.* pochen. —ation, *s.* das Schlagen, Klopfen.

¹**Pulse**, *s.* der Puls.

²**Pulse**, *s.* die Hülsenfrüchte.

Pulverize, *v.a.* pulvern.

Puma, *s.* der Puma, Auguar.

Pumice-stone, *s.* der Bimsstein.

¹**Pump**, I. *s.* die Pumpe. II. *v.a.* pumpen. —-handle, *s.* der Pumpen-schwengel.

²**Pump**, *s.* der Tanzschuh.

Pumpkin, *s.* der Kürbis.

Pun, I. *s.* das Wortspiel. II. *v.n.* witzeln.

¹**Punch**, *s.* der Kasperle (*puppet*).

²**Punch**, *s.* der Punsch.

³**Punch**, I. *s.* der Stoß. II. *v.a.* stoßen.

⁴**Punch**, I. *s.* der Pfriem. II. *v.a.* durchbohren.

Punchinello, *s.* der Hanswurst.

Punctu—al, *adj.*, —ally, *adv.* pünkt-lich. —ality, *s.* die Pünktlichkeit. — ate, *v.a.* punktieren. —ation, *s.* die Interpunktion.

Puncture, I. *s.* der Stich. II. *v.a.* stechen.

Pungen—cy, *s.* das Beißende. —t, *adj.*, —tly, *adv.* beißend.

Puniness, *s.* die Winzigkeit.

Punish, *v.a.* (be)strafen (for, wegen, um); züchtigen (für), abstrafen (wegen). —able, *adj.* strafbar. —er, *s.* der Strafende. —ment, *s.* die Strafe, Bestrafung.

Punt, *s.* der Kahn.

Puny, *adj.* kümmerlich.

Pupa, *s.* die Puppe, Larve.

¹**Pupil**, *s.* der Augenstern, die Pupille (*Anat.*).

²**Pupil**, *s.* der Schüler, die Schülerin, der Zögling.

Puppet, *s.* die Puppe, Drahtpuppe, das Werkzeug. —show, *s.* das Puppen-theater, Marionettentheater.

Puppy, *s.* der junge Hund.

Purblind, *adj.* halbblind, kurzsichtig.

Purchase, I. *v.a.* (er)kaufen, einkaufen. II. *s.* die Erwerbung; (what is —d) der Kauf. —r, *s.* der Käufer. — money, *s.* das Kaufgeld.

Pure, *adj.*, —ly, *adv.* rein, lauter. —ness, *s.* die Reinheit.

Purg—ate, I. *adj.* purgierend. II. *s.* das Abführ(ungs)mittel. —atorial, *adj.*; —atorial fire, das Fegefeuer. —atory, *s.* das Fegefeuer.

Purge, *v.a.* reinigen (*also fig.*).

Puri—fy, *v.a.* reinigen. —fying, *s.* die Reinigung.

Purity, *s.* die Reinheit.

Purple, I. *s.* der Purpur. II. *adj.* purpurn; purpurrot.

Purport, I. *s.* der Zweck; (tenor) der Sinn. II. *v.a.* enthalten, bedeuten.

Purpose, I. *s.* der Vorsatz; die Absicht, der Zweck; on —, absichtlich; to the —, zweckdienlich; to no —, vergebens, zwecklos. II. *v.a.* beab-sichtigen. —less, *adj.* zwecklos. —ly, *adv.* vorsätzlich.

Purr, I. *v.n.* schnurren. II. *s.* das Schnurren.

Purse, *s.* der Geldbeutel, die Börse. —r, *s.* der Zahlmeister (*Naut.*).

Pursu—ance, *s.*; in —ance of an order, einem Befehle gemäß. —ant, *adj.*; — to, —antly, *adv.* infolge, gemäß, nach. —e, *v.* I. *a.* verfolgen; nachsetzen (a person, einem). II. *n.* fortfahren. —er, *s.* der Verfolger.

Pursuit, *s.* die Verfolgung.

Purvey, *v.a.* versorgen mit, anschaffen. —or, *s.* der Lieferant.

Pus, *s.* der Eiter.

Push, I. *v.a.* stoßen, drängen, drücken.

II. *v.n.* sich vordrängen. III. *s.* der Stoß; he has plenty of —, er ist sehr feck.

Put, *ir.v.* I. *a.* stellen, stecken (on, auf; to, an). II. *n.;* to — back, zurückfahren (*Naut.*); to — forth, auslaufen (*Naut.*); to — in, einlaufen (*at a port*); to — away, weglegen; to — money by, Geld zurücklegen; to — in order, in Ordnung bringen; to — to expense, jemandem Unkosten machen; to — to flight, in die Flucht treiben; to — up with, sich gefallen lassen, sich behelfen.

Putr—efy, *v.n.* verfaulen, verwesen. **—id,** *adj.* faul. **—idity,** *s.* die Fäulnis, Fäule.

Putty, I. *s.* der Kitt, Glaserkitt. II. *v.a.* (ver=)kitten.

Puzzl—e, I. *s.* das Rätsel; cross-word —e, das Kreuzworträtsel. II. *v.a.* verwirren, irre machen; to —e one's brains, sich den Kopf zerbrechen. III. *v.n.* in Verlegenheit sein. **—ing,** *adj.* verwirrend.

Pygmy, *s.* der Zwerg.

Pyjamas, *s.* der Schlafanzug.

Pyramid, *s.* die Pyramide.

Pyre, *s.* der Scheiterhaufen.

Q

Q, q, *s.* das Q, q.

¹Quack, I. *v.n.* quaken, quäken. II. *s.* das Quaken, Gequake (der Ente).

²Quack, *s.* der Marktschreier. **—ery,** *s.* die Quacksalberei, Kurpfuscherei.

Quadr—angle, *s.* das Viereck. **—angular,** *adj.* viereckig. **—ant,** *s.* der Quadrant. **—uped,** I. *s.* das vierfüßige Tier. II. *adj.* vierfüßig. **—uple,** I. *adj.* vierfach. II. *s.* das Vierfache. III. *v.a.* vervierfachen.

Quaff, *v.a.* trinken, zechen; to — off, hinunterstürzen.

Quag, *s.,* **—mire,** *s.* der Sumpfboden. **—gy,** *adj.* sumpfig.

¹Quail, *s.* die Wachtel (*Orn.*).

²Quail, *v.n.* verzagen, beben.

Quaint, *adj.,* **—ly,** *adv.* altmodisch; drollig. **—ness,** *s.* die Seltsamkeit; das Altmodische.

Quak—e, *v.n.* zittern und beben. **—er,** *s.* der Quäker. **—eress,** *s.* die Quäkerin. **—ing,** I. *adj.* zitternd. II. *s.* das Zittern.

Quali—fication, *s.* die Eigenschaft, Befähigung, Fähigkeit. **—fied,** *adj.* (fitted) geeignet, befähigt; (modified) eingeschränkt. **—fy,** *v.* I. *a.* befähigen, geeignet machen; beschränken. II. *n.* sich befähigt machen.

Quality, *s.* die Beschaffenheit, Eigenschaft, Art; people of —, (*pl.*) die Standespersonen.

Qualm, *s.* die Anwandlung von Übelkeit; — of conscience, die Gewissenspein.

Quandary, *s.* die Verlegenheit.

Quantity, *s.* die Menge.

Quarantine, I. *s.* die Quarantäne. II. *v.a.* (einem) Quarantäne auferlegen.

Quarrel, I. *s.* der Streit, Zank, Hader. II. *v.n.* streiten, zanken. **—some,** *adj.* zänkisch, streitsüchtig. **—someness,** *s.* die Streitsucht.

Quarrier, *s.* der Steinbrecher.

¹Quarry, *s.* der Steinbruch.

²Quarry, *s.* die Jagdbeute.

Quart, *s.* das Quart.

Quarter, *s.* das Viertel. **—ly,** I. *adj.* & *adv.* vierteljährlich. II. *s.* die Vierteljahrsschrift. **—s,** *pl.* das Nachtlager; das Quartier (*Mil.*). **—day,** *s.* der Vierteljahrstag. **—master,** *s.* der Quartiermeister (*Mil.*).

Quartet, *s.* das Quartett.

Quarto, *s.* das Quartformat.

Quartz, *s.* der Quarz.

Quash, *v.a.* unterdrücken; aufheben; zerquetschen.

Quaver, I. *v.n.* zittern. II. *s.* der Triller; die Achtelnote (*Mus.*).

Quay, *s.* der Kai, die Uferstraße.

Queen, *s.* die Königin; to — it, die Königin spielen.

Queer, *adj.,* **—ly,** *adv.* seltsam, wunderlich.

Quell, *v.a.* unterdrücken, dämpfen.

Quench, *v.a.* (aus=)löschen. **—less,** *adj.* unauslöschlich, unstillbar.

Querulous, *adj.* klagsüchtig, murrend.

Query, I. *s.* die Frage; das Fragezeichen. II. *v.a.* ausfragen, befragen. III. *v.n.* fragen, zweifeln.

Quest, *s.* die Nachforschung; in — of, auf der Suche nach.

Question, I. *s.* die Frage; beyond all —, unzweifelhaft; that is out of the —, das kommt nicht in Betracht. II. *v.a.* befragen. **—able,** *adj.,* **—ably,** *adv.* fraglich, zweifelhaft. **—ableness**

s. die Zweifelhaftigkeit. **—er,** *s.* der Frager. **—ing,** *s.* das Fragen.

Queue, *s.* die Reihe, Queue; der Zopf (*wig*); **to — up,** sich reihenweise anstellen, Schlange stehen.

Quibble, I. *s.* die Spitzfindigkeit. II. *v.n.* (einer Frage) ausweichen. **—r,** *s.* der Wortspieler, Sophist.

Quick, *adj. & adv.* rasch (*as a walk, step, etc.*), schnell, hurtig, geschwind; **to the —,** ins Fleisch, ins Herz, tief. **—en,** *v.a.* beleben; beschleunigen. **—ly,** *adv.* geschwind, schnell, hurtig; gleich. **—ness,** *s.* die Schnelligkeit, Raschheit. **—lime,** *s.* ungelöschter Kalk. **—sand,** *s.* der Flugsand. **—silver,** *s.* das Quecksilber. **—tempered,** *adj.* reizbar. **—witted,** *adj.* schlagfertig, scharfsinnig.

Quid, *s.* die Prieme (Tabak).

Quiet, I. *adj.,* **—ly,** *adv.* ruhig. II. *s.* die Ruhe. III. *v.a.* beruhigen, stillen, besänftigen.

Quill, *s.* der Federkiel.

Quilt, I. *s.* die Bettdecke. II. *v.a. & n.* steppen; **—ed petticoat,** wattierter Unterrock.

Quince, *s.* die Quitte.

Quinine, *s.* das Chinin.

Quinsy, *s.* die (Hals)Bräune.

Quip, *s.* die Stichelei.

Quire, *s.* das Buch (Papier).

Quit, *v.a.* verlassen, aufgeben, verzichten auf.

Quite, *adv.* ganz, völlig, durchaus.

Quittance, *s.* die Quittung.

¹Quiver, *s.* der Köcher.

²Quiver, I. *v.n.* beben, zucken, zittern. II. *s.* das Zucken, Zittern, Beben. **—ing,** *adj.,* **—ingly,** *adv.* bebend, zitternd, zuckend.

Quiz, *v.a.* necken.

Quoit, *s.* der Wurfring, die Wurfscheibe; **game of —s,** das Wurfscheibenspiel.

Quota, *s.* die Quote.

Quot—able, *adj.* anführbar, anzuführen. **—ation,** *s.* die Anführung, das Zitat. **—e,** *v.a.* anführen, zitieren.

R

R, r, *s.* das R, r.

Rabbi, *s.* der Rabbiner.

Rabbit, *s.* das Kaninchen.

Rabble, *s.* der Pöbel.

Rabid, *adj.,* **—ly,** *adv.* wütend, toll.

Rabies, *s.* die Hundswut, Tollwut.

¹Race, *s.* das Geschlecht, der Stamm.

²Race, I. *s.* der Lauf; (contest) der Wettlauf, die Wettfahrt, das Wettrennen; horse **—s,** das Pferderennen. II. *v.n.* wettrennen. III. *v.a.* rennen lassen. **—r,** **—horse,** *s.* das Rennpferd. **—course,** *s.* die Rennbahn.

Racial, *adj.* Rassen—.

Raciness, *s.* das Pikante.

Rack, I. *s.* (torture —) die Folter; der Rechen (*for clothes, etc.*); die Raufe (*in stables*); das Gepäcknetz (*in railway carriages*); **to go to —** and ruin, ganz und gar zugrunde gehen. II. *v.a.* foltern; **to — one's brains,** sich den Kopf zerbrechen.

¹Racket, *s.* der Schläger (*games*).

²Racket, I. *s.* der Lärm, das Getöse, der Spektakel. II. *v.n.* lärmen.

Racoon, *s.* der Waschbär.

Racy, *adj.* gewürzt, pikant.

Radi—ance, **—ancy,** *s.* der Glanz. **—ant,** *adj.,* **—antly,** *adv.* strahlend (*also fig.*). **—ate,** *v.n.* strahlen, glänzen. **—ation,** *s.* das Strahlen.

Radical, I. *adj.,* **—ly,** *adv.* wurzelhaft, Wurzel— (*also Alg., Gram., Bot.*); (*fig.*) gründlich, Grund—. II. *s.* der Radikale.

Radio, *s.* das Funkwesen.

Radish, *s.* der Rettig.

Radius, *s.* der Halbmesser.

Raffle, I. *v.a.* verlosen, würfeln. II. *s.* die Lotterie.

Raft, *s.* das Floß. **—sman,** *s.* der Flößer.

Rafter, *s.* der Sparren.

Rag, *s.* der Lumpen, Fetzen.

Ragamuffin, *s.* der Lump.

Rage, I. *s.* die Wut; der Zorn, Grimm. II. *v.n.* wüten, rasen, toben.

Ragged, *adj.* zerrissen; lumpig.

Ra zing, *adj.,* **—ly,** *adv.* wütend.

Raid, I. *s.* der feindliche Einfall; air **—,** der Luftangriff. II. *v.a.* einen Raubzug unternehmen.

¹Rail, *s.* der Riegel; die Reling; die Leiste (*for pictures*); die Schiene, das Geleise (*Railw.*). **—ing,** *s.* das Geländer, die Einfriedigung. **—road,** **—way,** *s.* die Eisenbahn. **—waycarriage,** *s.* der Eisenbahnwagen. **—way-train,** *s.* der Zug.

²Rail, *v.n.* (scoff) spotten über (*acc.*);

to — at someone, auf einen ſticheln.
—lery, s. der Spott, die Neckerei.
Raiment, s. die Kleidung; der Anzug.
Rain, I. s. der Regen. II. v.n. regnen;
it is —ing, es regnet. —y, adj.
regneriſch, Regen=. —bow, s. der
Regenbogen. —coat, s. der Regen=
mantel. —gauge, s. der Regen=
meſſer.
Raise, v.a. heben, erheben, aufheben;
erhöhen (prices; one's courage, etc.);
ziehen (plants, beasts); bauen (wheat,
etc.).
Raisin, s. die Roſine.
Raising, s. das Heben ꝛc.; see Raise.
¹**Rake,** I. s. der Rechen. II. v.a. rechen
(Agr., Hort.); verſcharren (the fire).
²**Rake,** s. das Überhangen (of a ship).
³**Rake,** s. der Wüſtling.
Rakish, adj. liederlich, ausſchweifend.
¹**Rally,** I. v.a. zum Stehen bringen
(Mil.). II. v.n. ſich wieder ſammeln
(as troops); ſich erholen. III. s.
die Sammlung.
²**Rally,** v.a.; to — someone upon a
thing, einen aufziehen mit.
Ram, I. s. der Widder (Zool., Astr.,
Naut.). II. v.a. rammen. —rod,
s. der Ladeſtock.
Rambl—e, I. v.n. umher=ſtreifen,
=wandern. II. s. die Wanderung.
—er, s. der Wanderer. —ing, adj.
—ingly, adv. umherſchweifend; ab=
ſchweifend (as a discourse).
Ramp, v.n. gewaltig ſpringen. —ant,
adj., —antly, adv. mutwillig, ausge=
laſſen; aufgerichtet.
Rampart, s. der Wall (Fort.); (fig.)
die Bruſtwehr.
Ramshackle, adj. baufällig, wackelig.
Rancid, adj. ranzig, ſtinkend. —
ity, —ness, s. die Ranzigkeit.
Rancour, s. der Groll.
Random, I. s.; at —, aufs Gerate=
wohl. II. adj. zufällig, aufs Gerate=
wohl; — shot, der Schuß ins Blaue.
Range, I. v.a. reihen, ordnen, in
Reihen ſtellen. II. v.n. umher=
ſtreifen. III. s. die (Hügel=)Kette
(of hills); (roving) die Wanderung,
der Ausflug, Lauf; der Umfang (of
ideas, etc.); die Schußweite (Artil.);
die Reichweite (Radio); (kitchen
—) der Kochherd. —r, s. der Förſter;
der leichte Reiter.
¹**Rank,** I. s. (row) die Reihe (also
Mil.); (class) die Klaſſe; (grade) der

Rang, Stand; — and file, Reihe und
Glied. II. v.a. reihen, ordnen; (class)
zählen (with, zu).
²**Rank,** adj., —ly, adv. üppig; frucht=
bar, fett (as soil); ſtark, kräftig (as
poison). —ness, s. die Üppigkeit.
Rankle, v.n. (fig.) nagen; ſich entzünden,
eitern (Med.).
Ransack, v.a. durchwühlen.
Ransom, I. s. das Löſegeld. II. v.a.
auslöſen; erlöſen (B.).
Rant, I. s. die Schwulſt. II. v.n.
toben.
Ranunculus, s. die Ranunkel.
Rap, I. s. der Tapp. II. v.n. klopfen,
pochen (at, an).
Rap—acious, adj., —aciously, adv.
raubgierig. —aciousness, —acity,
s. die Raub=gier, =ſucht.
¹**Rape,** s. (—-seed) der Rübſamen.
²**Rape,** s. der Raub; die Notzucht
(Law).
Rapid, adj., —ly, adv. ſchnell,
geſchwind, raſch (as growth); reißend
(as water); — fire, das Schnellfeuer
(Mil.). —ity, s. die Geſchwindigkeit.
Rapine, s. die Plünderung.
Rapt, adj. hingeriſſen, entzückt. —ure,
s. die Entzückung. —urous, adj.,
—urously, adv. entzückend.
Rar—e, adj., —ely, adv. ſelten, rar.
—ity, s. die Koſtbarkeit.
Rascal, s. der Schuft, Spitzbube. —
ity, s. die Schurkerei. —ly, adv.
ſchuftig.
¹**Rash,** adj., —ly, adv. haſtig, voreilig.
—ness, s. die Unbeſonnenheit.
²**Rash,** s. der Hautausſchlag.
Rasher, s. die Speckſchnitte.
Rasp, s. die Raſpel.
Raspberry, s. die Himbeere.
Rat, s. die Ratte; to smell a —,
Lunte riechen. —trap, s. die Ratten=
falle.
Ratchet, s. der Sperrkegel, Sperrhaken.
—wheel, s. das Sperrad (mit
Sperrlinke).
¹**Rate,** I. s. (price) der Preis; (tax)
die Gemeindeſteuer; der Wechſel=
kurs (C.L.); (proportion) die Rate;
at any —, auf jeden Fall; at a cheap
—, wohlfeil, preiswert. II. v.a.
ſchätzen, veranſchlagen. —payer, s.
der Steuerzahler.
²**Rate,** v.a. heftig ausſchelten.
Rather, adv. eher, lieber; (somewhat) ziemlich, etwas; — ! na und ob !

Ratifi—cation, s. die Bestätigung. —**er,** s. der Gutheißende.

Ratify, v.a. bestätigen.

Rating, s. das Schelten; (tax) die Steuereinschätzung.

Ratio, s. das Verhältnis.

Ration, s. die Ration (Mil.).

Rational, adj., —**ly,** adv. vernunftgemäß. —**ist,** s. der Rationalist. —**istic,** adj. rationalistisch. —**ness,** s. die Vernunftmäßigkeit.

Rattle, I. v.n. rasseln. II. s. das Gerassel; death —, das Todesröcheln. —**snake,** s. die Klapperschlange.

Raucous, adj. heiser, rauh.

Rav—age, I. s. die Verwüstung. II. v.a. verwüsten, verheeren. —**ager,** s. der Verwüster, Verheerer.

Rave, v.n. rasen; to — about a person, in jemand vernarrt sein.

Ravel, v.n. sich auf-drehen, -fasern.

Raven, s. der Rabe.

Ravenous, adj., gefräßig.

Ravine, s. die Schlucht, der Hohlweg.

Raving, I. adj. rasend; faselnd. II. s. das Rasen, Faseln.

Ravish, v.a. mit Gewalt wegnehmen; (fig.) entzücken. —**er,** s. der Räuber; der Notzüchtiger. —**ing,** adj., —**ingly,** adv. hinreißend, entzückend.

Raw, adj., —**ly,** adv. roh (also of products, etc.); wund (as flesh); rauh (as weather). —**ness,** s. die Rohheit; die Rauhigkeit; die Unerfahrenheit. —**-boned,** adj. hager, fleischlos.

¹**Ray,** s. der (Licht-)Strahl.

²**Ray,** s. der Roche (Icht.).

Raze, v.a. auskratzen; (destroy) vertilgen.

Razor, s. das Rasiermesser. —**-strop,** s. der Streichriemen.

Re—, prefix = wieder, nochmals, noch einmal. For verbs, etc., compounded with this prefix and not given in the following lists see the simple verbs, etc.

Reach, I. v.n. reichen, langen; sich ausdehnen (to, bis). II. v.a. reichen, langen; strecken (out, aus); (hand over) hergeben; (touch) treffen; (arrive at) ankommen, anlangen in; the letter —ed me, der Brief ist mir zu Händen gekommen. III. s. das Reichen, Erreichen.

React, v.a. gegen-, (zu)rück-wirken (also fig.); reagieren (Chem.). —

ion, s. die Rück, Gegen-wirkung; die Reaktion (Pol., Chem.); die Gegenwirkung (Mach., Chem.). —**ionary,** I. adj. reaktionär. II. s. der Reaktionär.

Read, I. ir.v.a. lesen (also fig.). II. ir.v.n. lesen, studieren; to — out, laut vorlesen; it —s well, es liest sich gut. III. adj.; well —, belesen. —**able,** adj. lesbar. —**er,** s. der Leser, die Leserin; der Vorleser; die Vorleserin. —**ing,** I. adj. lesend; studierend. II. s. das Lesen; das Vorlesen.

Read—ily, adv. bereitwillig, gern. —**iness,** s. die Bereitschaft; die Bereitwilligkeit. —**y,** I. adj. bereit, gerüstet, fertig; —**y** money, bares Geld, Bargeld. II. adv. bereit. —**y-made,** adj.; —**y-made** clothes, fertige Kleidungsstücke.

Readjust, v.a. wieder in Ordnung bringen.

Real, adj. wahrhaft, echt; (actual) wirklich, tatsächlich; — estate, Grundbesitz. —**istic,** adj. realistisch. —**ity,** s. die Wirklichkeit. —**ization,** s. die Verwirklichung, Realisierung (C.L.). —**ize,** v.a. verwirklichen, realisieren; gewinnen (a profit); (appreciate, feel as) sich (dat.) vorstellen. —**ly,** adv. wirklich, tatsächlich.

Realm, s. das Reich.

Realty, s. die unbewegliche Habe.

Ream, s. das Ries (Papier).

Reap, v.a. schneiden; (fig.) (ein)ernten. —**er,** s. der Schnitter, die Schnitterin; die Mähmaschine. —**ing,** s. das Ernten. —**ing-hook,** s. die Sichel.

Reappear, v.n. wiedererscheinen. —**ance,** s. die Wiedererscheinung.

Reappoint, v.a. wiederanstellen.

¹**Rear,** I. s. der Hintergrund; der Nachtrab (Mil.). II. adj. hinter-, Nach-. —**-ward,** adj. hinter. —**-admiral,** s. der Konteradmiral. —**guard,** s. die Nachhut, der Nachtrab.

²**Rear,** v. I. a. erheben; errichten (an edifice); erziehen (children); ziehen (plants and animals). II. n. sich aufbäumen.

Reason, I. s. die Vernunft; (understanding) der Verstand; (cause) die Ursache, der (Beweg-)Grund; (fairness) das Recht, die Billigkeit; by — of, wegen; it stands to —, es versteht sich von selbst. II. v.n. urteilen, schließen; (argue, debate) reden, debattieren; to — with oneself, mit sich selbst rechten. III. *v.a.* durchdenken, besprechen, erörtern. —**able**, *adj.*, —**ably**, *adv.* vernünftig, verständig; —able prices, mäßige Preise. —**er**, *s.* der Denker. —**ing**, *s.* das Urteilen.

Reassur—**ance**, *s.* die wiederholte Versicherung. —**e**, *v.a.* aufs neue versichern, beruhigen.

Rebate, I. *v.a.* ablassen (*from price*). II. *s.*, —**ment**, *s.* der Rabatt, Nachlaß, Abzug (*C.L.*).

Rebel, I. *s.* der Empörer, Rebell. II. *v.n.* sich empören. —**lion**, *s.* die Empörung, der Aufstand, Aufruhr. —**lious**, *adj.*, —**liously**, *adv.* aufrührerisch, rebellisch. —**liousness**, *s.* die Widerspenstigkeit.

Rebound, I. *v.n.* zurückprallen. II. *s.* der Rückprall, (*fig.*) der Umschwung.

Rebuff, *s.* der Rückstoß, die Abweisung.

Rebuke, I. *s.* der Tadel, Vorwurf, Verweis. II. *v.a.* verweisen, ausschelten.

Recall, I. *v.a.* zurückrufen (*a person*); widerrufen (*a statement*); to — to one's mind, sich ins Gedächtnis zurückrufen. II. *s.* die Zurückrufung.

Recant, *v.* I. *a.* & *n.* widerrufen. II. *n.* zurücktreten. —**ation**, *s.* der Widerruf.

Recede, *v.a.* abweichen, zurücktreten.

Receipt, I. *s.* der Empfang (*of a letter, etc.*); (prescription) das Rezept; die Quittung, der Empfangsschein (*C.L.*); —**s** and expenditures, Einnahme und Ausgabe. II. *v.a.* quittieren, eine Quittung geben.

Receiv—**able**, *adj.* annehmbar. —**e**, *v.a.* empfangen, bekommen, erhalten (*a parcel, news*); einnehmen (*money*). —**er**, *s.* der Empfänger (*also Radio*); der Einnehmer (*of customs, etc.*); der Hörtrichter (*Teleph.*); —er of stolen goods, der (Diebs=)Hehler. —**ing**, *s.* der Empfang.

Recen—**cy**, *s.* die Neuheit, Frische. —**t**, *adj.* neu, frisch. —**tly**, *adv.* neulich, vor Kurzem.

Receptacle, *s.* der Behälter.

Recept—**ion**, *s.* der Empfang, die Aufnahme. —**ive**, *adj.* empfänglich (für). —**ion-room**, *s.* das Empfangszimmer.

Recess, *s.* die Ferien; die Nische, Blende (*in a room, etc.*).

Recip—**e**, *s.* das Rezept. —**ient**, *s.* der Empfänger.

Reciproc—**al**, *adj.*, —**ally**, *adv.* wechselgegenseitig, beiderseitig. —**ate**, *v.* I. *n.* abwechseln. II. *a.* erwidern. —**ating**, *adj.* abwechselnd. —**ity**, *s.* die Wechselwirkung.

Recit—**al**, *s.* das Vorlesen (*of laws, etc.*), Hersagen, Vortragen. —**ation**, *s.* das Hersagen (*of lessons*); der Vortrag. —**e**, *v.* I. *a.* hersagen (*a lesson, etc.*); vortragen (*a poem, etc.*); (narrate) erzählen. II. *n.* deklamieren.

Reck, *v.a.* & *n.* sich kümmern. —**less**, *adj.*, —**lessly**, *adv.* rücksichtslos (gegen die Folgen). —**lessness**, *s.* die Rücksichtslosigkeit.

Reckon, *v.* I. *a.* rechnen, zählen; (estimate) schätzen. II. *n.* rechnen; to — on, sich verlassen auf. —**ing**, *s.* das Rechnen; die Rechnung (*at an inn, etc.*); (calculation) die Berechnung; to be out of one's —ing, sich verrechnet haben.

Reclaim, *v.a.* zurücklenken; zurückfordern.

Reclamation, *s.* die Besserung; die Urbarmachung (*of land*); (complaint) die Beschwerde.

Recline, *v.n.* (sich) lehnen.

Recluse, *s.* der Einsiedler, Klausner.

Recogni—**tion**, *s.* die (Wieder=) Erkennung (*of a person, etc.*); (acknowledgment) die Anerkennung. —**zable**, *adj.* erkennbar, zu erkennen. —**ze**, *v.a.* (wieder)erkennen; anerkennen.

Recoil, I. *v.n.* zurückprallen. II. *s.* der Rücklauf (*of a cannon*); (*fig.*) das Zurückprallen.

Recoin, *v.a.* umprägen.

Recollect, *v.a.* sich erinnern (einer Person or Sache). —**ion**, *s.* die Erinnerung; das Gedächtnis.

Recommend, *v.a.* empfehlen. —**ation**, *s.* die Empfehlung.

Recompense, I. *v.a.* entschädigen; (reward) belohnen. II. *s.* der Ersatz, die Vergütung.

Reconcil—**e**, *v.a.* ver=, aus=söhnen (*enemies, etc.*). —**er**, *s.* der Versöhner. —**iation**, *s.* die Versöhnung.

Reconn—**aissance**, *s.* die Rekognoszierung (*Mil.*). —**oitre**, *v.a.* rekognoszieren, auskundschaften (*Mil.*).

Reconsider, *v.a.* wiedererwägen. — **ation,** *s.* nochmalige Überlegung.

Record, I. *v.a.* aufzeichnen. II. *s.* die Urkunde; die höchste Leistung (*Sport*); gramophone —, die Schallplatte; to beat the —, die bisherige Höchstleistung übertreffen. —**er,** *s.* der Registrator. —**office,** *s.* das Staats=Archiv.

Recount, *v.a.* erzählen.

Recover, *v.* I. *a.* wieder erlangen *or* bekommen; wiedererobern (*territory, etc.*); eintreiben (*debts*). II. *n.* sich erholen, genesen. —**y,** *s.* die Wiedererlangung; die Wiederherstellung, Genesung; —y of damages, der Schadenersatz; past —y, unwiederbringlich verloren; unheilbar.

Recreant, I. *adj.* abtrünnig. II. *s.* der Abtrünnige.

Recreat—e, *v.a.* neu schaffen; erquicken. —**ion,** *s.* die Erquickung, Erfrischung.

Recruit, I. *v.a.* ergänzen (*an army, etc.*). II. *v.a. & n.* sich erholen, sich stärken. III. *v.n.* (an)werben (*Mil.*). IV. *s.* der Rekrut (*Mil.*). —**ing-officer,** *s.* der Werbeoffizier.

Rect—angle, *s.* das Rechteck. —**angular,** *adj.* rechtwinklig. —**ifier,** *s.* der Gleichrichter (*Radio*). —**ify,** *v.a.* berichtigen. —**ilinear,** —**ilineal,** *adj.* geradlinig. —**itude,** *s.* die Redlichkeit, Geradheit.

Rector, *s.* der Pfarrherr. —**y,** *s.* das Pfarrhaus.

Recumbent, *adj.* lehnend, liegend, ruhend.

Recur, *v.n.* zurückkehren (to the mind, ins Gedächtnis); wieder zurückkommen auf (*acc.*) (*to a subject*); (periodisch) wiederkehren. —**rence,** *s.* die Wiederkehr. —**rent,** *adj.* wiederkehrend.

Red, I. *adj.* rot; — herring, der Pökelhering. II. *s.* das Rot. —**den,** *v.n.* erröten. —**dish,** *adj.* rötlich. —**ness,** *s.* die Röte. —**breast,** *s.* das Rotkehlchen. —**hot,** *adj.* glühend. —**lead,** *s.* der Mennig. —**skin,** *s.* die Rothaut. —**start,** *s.* das Rotschwänzchen. —**tape,** *s.* die Beamtenwirtschaft; to wrap a thing in — tape, etwas vom grünen Tisch aus diktieren. —**wing,** *s.* die Rotdrossel.

Redeem, *v.a.* auslösen (*captives, etc.*); einlösen (*a pledge*); erfüllen (*a promise*); erlösen (*Theol.*). —**able,** *adj.*

tilgbar, einlösbar (*C.L.*). —**er,** *s.* der Erlöser, der Heiland.

Redemption, *s.* die Amortisation, der Rückkauf, die Tilgung (*C.L.*); die Erlösung (*Theol.*).

Redouble, *v.* I. *a.* verdoppeln. II. *n.* sich verdoppeln.

Redress, I. *s.* die Abhilfe. II. *v.a.* abstellen, abhelfen.

Reduce, *v.a.* zurück=bringen, =führen; verwandeln (to something else, in eine S.); versetzen, bringen (to poverty, in Armut) (diminish) vermindern; herabsetzen (*prices*); (subdue) bezwingen; (degrade) heruntersetzen; reduzieren (*fractions, also Chem.*); degradieren (*Mil.*).

Reduction, *s.* die Verwandlung (into, in); die Reduktion (*Arith.*); die Preisherabsetzung (*C.L.*); die Verminderung, Verringerung; — of 5%, 5 Prozent Rabatt.

Redundant, *adj.* überflüssig; weitschweifig.

Reed, *s.* das Rohr, Schilfrohr.

¹**Reef,** *s.* das Felsenriff.

²**Reef,** I. *s.* das Reef, Reff. II. *v.a.* reffen (*a sail*).

Reek, I. *s.* der Rauch, Dampf. II. *v.n.* dampfen.

¹**Reel,** I. *s.* der Haspel; die Rolle (für Nähgarn). II. *v.n.* taumeln, wanken. III. *v.a.* (ab)haspeln; to — off, abwinden. —**cotton,** *s.* das Nähgarn auf Röllchen.

²**Reel,** *s.* schottischer lebhafter Tanz.

Re-establish, *v.a.* wiederherstellen. —**ment,** *s.* die Wiederherstellung.

Refer, *v.* I. *a.* beziehen (to, auf (*acc.*)); verweisen an (*for information, etc.*). II. *n.* sich beziehen (auf); (allude) anspielen (auf); (— to) nachschlagen in (einem Wörterbuch). —**able,** *adj.* bezüglich (to, auf (*acc.*)). —**ee,** *s.* der Schiedsrichter. —**ence,** *s.* die Verweisung, Nachweisung, der Nachweis; der Bezug, die Anspielung, Bezugnahme; in —ence to, in Beziehung auf (*acc.*), in Betreff, hinsichtlich (einer Sache); works of —, die Nachschlagewerke; — library, die Handbibliothek. —**ences,** *pl.* die Auskunft (über eine S.); to give —ences, Adressen geben zur Auskunfterteilung. —**endum,** *s.* das Plebiszit.

Refine, *v.* I. *a.* verfeinern; raffinieren (*sugar, etc.*); läutern, raffinieren

(*Chem.*); fdjeiben (*gold or silver*); (*fig.*) verfeinern; bilden (*the taste, mind, etc.*). II. *n.* fid) verfeinern. —d, *adj.* raffiniert; geläutert; verfeinert; —d manners, verfeinerte Sitten. —ment, *s.* die Verfeinerung, Bildung (*also of language, mind, etc.*); das Raffinieren, Reinigen 2c.; (purity) die Reinheit, Lauterfeit; (nicety) die Spißfindigfeit. —r, *s.* der Läuterer; der Raffineur (*of sugar, etc.*). —ry, *s.* das Frifdfeuer, der Treibherd, die Abtreibhütte; die Siederei (*for sugar*).

Refit, *v.* I. *a.* wiederausrüften. II. *n.* fid (ein Sdiff) ausbeffern laffen.

Reflect, *v.* I. *a.* zurüdwerfen (*light, etc.*). II. *n.* zurüdftrahlen; nachdenfen (on, über (*acc.*)); (*fig.*) überlegen. —ing, *adj.* zurüdwerfend, Reflexions=. —ingly, *adv.* nachdenfend; tadelnd. —ion, *s.* die Zurüdwerfung, Reflexion; (*fig.*) das Nadjdenfen, die Betradjtung. —ive, *adj.* zurüdwerfend; nadjdenfend, überlegend. —or, *s.* der Refleftor.

Reflex, *adj.* zurüdftrahlend; rüdwärts geridjtet ; — action, die Reflex=Bewegung. —ive, *adj.* zurüdwirfend; reflexiv (*Gram.*).

Reflux, *s.* der Rüdfluß, die Ebbe.

Reform, I. *v.a.* umgeftalten; (*fig.*) (ver)beffern, reformieren ; (re-form) neu formieren (*Mil.*). II. *v.n.* fid (ver)beffern ; fid wieder bilden. III. *s.* die Verbefferung, Befferung. IV. *attrib.*; — movement, die Reformbewegung. —ation, *s.* die Befferung; die Umbildung; (Church) die Reformation. —atory, I. *adj.* reformatorifd. II. *s.* das Rettungshaus. —ed, *adj.* reformiert (*Eccl.*). —er, *s.* der Verbefferer, Reformator.

Refract, *v.a.* brechen (rays of light, Strahlen). —orily, *adv.*, —ory, *adj.* widerfpenftig.

¹**Refrain,** *v.* I. *n.* fid enthalten. II. *n.* zurüdhalten.

²**Refrain,** *s.* der Kehrreim.

Refresh, *v.a.* erfrifdjen, erquiden. —ing, *adj.*, —ingly, *adv.* erfrifdjend, erquidend. —ment, *s.* die Erfrifdung, Erquidung; —ment room, die (Bahnhofs=)Reftauration.

Refrigerat—e, *v.a.* fühlen. —ion, *s.* die Abfühlung. —or, *s.* der Kühler, Eisfdranf.

Refuge, *s.* die Zufludjt. —e, *s.* der Flüdtling.

Refus—al, *s.* die Verweigerung. —e, I. *v.a.* verweigern (*obedience, etc.*), abfdlagen. II. *v.n.* fid weigern. III. *adj.* verworfen, wertlos. IV. *s.* der Ausfduß.

Refut—ation, *s.* die Widerlegung. —e, *v.a.* widerlegen.

Regain, *v.a.* wiedergewinnen.

Regal, *adj.*, —ly, *adv.* föniglid.

Regale, *v.a.* föftlid bewirten, erquiden; ergößen.

Regalia, *s.* Zeidjen der föniglidjen Würde; die Abzeidjen.

Regard, I. *v.a.* anfehen; (heed) adjten; (consider) berüdfidjtigen; (honour) (hod)adjten; (look on) betradjten. II. *s.* der Blid; die Rüdfidjt; die (Hod=)Adjtung; (repute) das Anfehen; with — to, in Hinfidjt auf, hinfidjtlid, in Betreff (einer Sadje); with kind —s, mit herzlidjen Grüßen. —ing, *prep.* hinfidjtlid, in Betreff. —less, *adj.*, —lessly, *adv.* adjtlos, unbefümmert.

Regatta, *s.* die Regatta, Bootwettfahrt.

Regency, *s.* die Regentfdaft.

Regenerat—e, *v.a.* wiedererzeugen; (*fig.*) umbilden. —ion, *s.* die Wiederherftellung; die Wiedergeburt (*Theol.*).

Regent, I. *adj.* herrfdjend, regierend; queen —, die Königin=Regentin. II. *s.* der Regent.

Regicide, *s.* der Königsmörder; (act of —) der Königsmord.

Regimen, *s.* die Regierung, Verwaltung; die Diät.

Regiment, *s.* das Regiment (*Mil.*).

Region, *s.* die Gegend.

Regist—er, I. *s.* das Regifter. II. *v.a.* einfdjreiben. —ration, *s.* das Einfdjreiben. —ry-office, *s.* das Standesamt.

Regret, I. *s.* das Bedauern. II. *v.a.* bedauern. —table, *adj.* bedauerlid).

Regula—r, *adj.*, —rly, *adv.* ordentlid; (according to rule) regelmäßig (*also Gram.*). —rity, *s.* die Regelmäßigfeit. —te, *v.a.* regeln. —tion, I. *s.* die Ordnung. II. *attrib.* vorfdjriftsmäßig; Kommiß= (*Mil.*).

Rehears—al, *s.* die Wiederholung; die Probe (*Mus., Theat.*); dress —al, die Generalprobe. —e, *v.a.* wiederholen; probieren.

Reign, I. *v.n.* regieren, herrschen. II. *s.* die Regierung; die Herrschaft.

Rein, *s.* der Zügel, Zaum (*also fig.*).

Reindeer, *s.* das Renntier.

Reinforce, I. *v.a.* verstärken. II. *s.* die Verstärkung. —ments, *pl.* der Nachschub.

Reject, *v.a.* ausschlagen (*an offer*). —ion, *s.* die Auswerfung.

Rejoice, *v.* I. *a.* erfreuen. II. *n.* sich freuen, erfreut sein.

Rejoicing, I. *s.* die Freude; (*pl.*) die Lustbarkeiten. II. *adj.* froh.

Rejoin, *v.* I. *a.* wieder vereinigen. II. *n.* erwidern, versetzen. —der, *s.* die Erwiderung.

Rejuvenat—e, *v.a.* verjüngen. —ion, *s.* die Verjüngung.

Relapse, I. *v.n.* zurückfallen. II. *s.* der Rückfall.

Relat—e, *v.* I. *a.* erzählen, melden. II. *n.* sich beziehen (to a thing, auf eine S.); to be —ed, verwandt sein (to, mit); —ing to, in Beziehung *or* mit Bezug auf. —ion, *s.* die Erzählung; (reference) die Beziehung, Bezugnahme; (connection) das Verhältnis (*also Geom.*); (person —ed) der, die Verwandte. —ionship, *s.* die Verwandtschaft. —ive, I. *adj.,* —ively, *adv.* bezüglich, in Beziehung (to, auf); bezüglich. II. *s.* Relativum (*Gram.*).

Relax, *v.* I. *a.* erschlaffen, mildern, mäßigen. II. *n.* erschlaffen. —ation, *s.* die Erschlaffung. —ed, *adj.* schlaff, matt. —ing, *adj.* erschlaffend, weich.

¹Relay, *s.* das Relais.

²Relay, *v.a.* umlegen (*a pavement, etc.*).

Release, I. *v.a.* ent-, los-lassen, befreien. II. *s.* die Entlassung.

Relent, *v.n.* sich erweichen lassen. —less, *adj.,* —lessly, *adv.* unnachgiebig, unbarmherzig.

Relevan—cy, *s.* die Erheblichkeit. —t, *adj.* erheblich, passend; anwendbar.

Relia—bility, —bleness, *s.* die Zuverlässigkeit. —ble, *adj.* zuverlässig. —nce, *s.* der Verlaß. —nt, *adj.* vertrauensvoll.

Relic, *s.* die Reliquie (*of a saint, etc.*).

Relie—f, *s.* die Linderung (*of pain, etc.*); (help) die Hilfe; der Entsatz (*of a garrison, etc.*). —ve, *v.a.* erleichtern, lindern, mindern; helfen; ablösen (*Mil.*). —ving, *adj.* erleichternd.

Religio—n, *s.* die Religion. —us, *adj.* religiös, Religions-. —usly, *adv.* pünktlich; (conscientiously) gewissenhaft.

Relinquish, *v.a.* verlassen. —ment, *s.* das Aufgeben, der Verzicht.

Relish, *s.* der Geschmack (*also fig.*); der Beigeschmack, die Würze, Sauce.

Reluctan—ce, —cy, *s.* die Abneigung. —t, *adj.,* —tly, *adv.* unwillig.

Rely, *v.n.* sich verlassen.

Remain, *v.n.* (übrig) bleiben. —der, *s.* das Überbleibsel, Rest, Rückstand. —ing, *adj.* übrig. —s, *pl.* (corpse) die sterblichen Reste.

Remand, I. *v.a.* zurückverweisen. II. *s.* die Zurücksendung in die Untersuchungshaft.

Remark, I. *s.* die An-, Be-merkung. II. *v.a.* bemerken, beobachten. III. *v.n.* bemerken. —able, *adj.,* —ably, *adv.* merkwürdig, ausgezeichnet.

Remedy, I. *s.* das Heilmittel. II. *v.a.* helfen; abhelfen (*an evil, etc.*).

Rememb—er, *v.* I. *a.* sich erinnern (einer S. *or* an eine S.), sich besinnen auf (acc.); —er me to him! grüßen Sie ihn von mir! II. *n.* gedenken, sich erinnern. —rance, *s.* die Erinnerung, das Gedächtnis.

Remind, *v.a.* erinnern, mahnen (of a thing, an eine S.). —er, *s.* die Mahnung.

Reminiscence, *s.* die (Rück-)Erinnerung.

Remiss, *adj.,* —ly, *adv.* nachlässig, schlaff. —ion, *s.* das Nachlassen.

Remit, *v.* I. *a.* über-senden, -machen. II. *n.* nachlassen, abnehmen. —tance, *s.* die Geldsendung.

Remnant, *s.* das Überbleibsel, der Rest.

Remodel, *v.a.* umbilden.

Remonstra—nce, *s.* die Ermahnung. —nt, *adj.* Vorstellungen machend. —te, *v.n.* (einem) Vorstellungen, Einwendungen machen (on something, über eine S.).

Remorse, *s.* die Reue, Zerknirschung, der Gewissensbiß. —ful, *adj.,* —fully, *adv.* reuevoll. —less, *adj.* reuelos, hartherzig.

Remote, *adj.,* —ly, *adv.* entfernt. —ness, *s.* die Entlegenheit.

Remov—al, *s.* das Wegschaffen; die Hebung (*of a grievance, etc.*); die Entlassung (*from office*); der Umzug (*from a house, etc.*). —e, I. *v.a.* weg-, fort-ſchaffen, weg-rücken, -neh= men, -tun, entfernen, beſeitigen; ver= abſchieden, entlaſſen (*an officer*). II. *v.n.* aus=, um=ziehen, verziehen (*from a house*).

Remunerat—e, *v.a.* vergelten. **—ion,** *s.* die Belohnung.

Renaissance, *s.* die Renaiſſance.

Rend, *ir.v.a. & n.* reißen.

Render, *v.a.* vergelten (*evil for good, etc.*); leiſten (*a service*); gewähren (*help*); ablegen (*an account*); to — thanks, Dank abſtatten.

Rendezvous, *s.* das Stelldichein.

Renegade, *s.* der Abtrünnige.

Renew, *v.a.* erneue(r)n.

Rennet, *s.* das Lab.

Renounce, *v.a.* (einer S. (*dat.*)) ent= ſagen, (auf eine S.) verzichten.

Renovat—e, *v.a.* erneue(r)n. **—ion,** *s.* die Erneu(er)ung.

Renown, *s.* der Ruhm. **—ed,** *adj.* berühmt.

¹Rent, I. *s.* die Miete, der Zins (*of a house, etc.*). II. *v.a.* mieten, pachten. **—al,** *s.* der Mietertrag. **—day,** *s.* der Termin. **—free,** *adj.* zinsfrei.

²Rent, *s.* der Riß, die Spalte.

Renunciation, *s.* die Entſagung, der Verzicht.

Rep, *s.* der Rips.

¹Repair, I. *s.* die Ausbeſſerung, Wie= derherſtellung; in good —, in gutem Zuſtande; out of —, baufällig. II. *v.a.* ausbeſſern. **—er,** *s.* der Aus= beſſerer. **—s,** *pl.* die Ausbeſſerung.

²Repair, *v.n.*; to — to, hingehen.

Reparation, *s.* die Wiederherſtellung; der Erſatz.

Repast, *s.* die Mahlzeit.

Repay, *v.a.* zurückzahlen, vergelten.

Repeal, *v.a.* aufheben.

Repeat, *v.a.* wiederholen. **—ed,** *adj.,* **—edly,** *adv.* wiederholt.

Repel, *v.* I. *a.* zurückſtoßen (*also fig.*). II. *n.* abſtoßen.

Repent, *v.a.* bereuen. **—ance,** *s.* die Reue, Buße. **—ant,** *adj.,* **—antly,** *adv.* reuig, bußfertig.

Repertory, *s.* das Nachſchlagebuch, die Fundgrube.

Repetition, *s.* die Wiederholung; (*reciting*) das Herſagen.

Repin—e, *v.n.* murren. **—ing,** I. *adj.,* **—ingly,** *adv.* mürriſch, grämlich. II. *s.* das Murren.

Replace, *v.a.* wieder hinſtellen, erſetzen.

Replet—e, *adj.* gefüllt (*mit*), voll (von). **—ion,** *s.* das Vollſein, die Überfülle.

Reply, I. *v.a. & n.* antworten, erwidern (*to a question,* auf eine Frage). II. *s.* die Antwort, Erwiderung.

Report, I. *s.* der Bericht. II. *v.n.* (einen) Bericht abſtatten, berichten. III. *v.a.* berichten; melden. **—er,** *s.* der Berichterſtatter.

Repose, I. *s.* die Ruhe (*also fig.*). II. *v.n.* ruhen.

Reprehen—d, *v.a.* tadeln. **—sion,** *s.* der Verweis.

Represent, *v.a.* bildlich darſtellen. **—ation,** *s.* die Darſtellung. **—ative,** I. *adj.* ſtellvertretend. II. *s.* der Stell= vertreter; der Vertreter (*Parl., etc.*).

Repress, *v.a.* unterdrücken. **—ion,** *s.* die Unterdrückung. **—ive,** *adj.,* **—ively,** *adv.* unterdrückend.

Reprieve, I. *s.* die Begnadigung. II. *v.a.* begnadigen.

Reprimand, I. *s.* der Verweis. II. *v.a.* verweiſen.

Reprint, I. *v.a.* wieder drucken, neu drucken. II. *s.* der Neudruck.

Reprisal, *s.* die Gegenmaßregel.

Reproach, I. *s.* der Vorwurf. II. *v.a.* vorwerfen. **—ful,** *adj.,* **—fully,** *adv.* vorwurfsvoll.

Reprobate, *s.* der Verworfene.

Reproduc—e, *v.a.* wiederholen, repro= duzieren. **—tion,** *s.* die Wieder= hervorbringung; die Tonwiedergabe (*Radio*).

Reproof, *s.* der Verweis, Vorwurf.

Reprov—e, *v.a.* verweiſen. **—ing,** *adj.,* **—ingly,** *adv.* tadelnd, verweiſend.

Reptile, *s.* das Reptil; (*fig.*) der kriechende Menſch.

Republic, *s.* die Republik. **—an,** I. *adj.* republikaniſch. II. *s.* der Repu= blikaner.

Republish, *v.a.* wieder herausgeben.

Repudiat—e, *v.a.* verwerfen. **—ion,** *s.* die Verwerfung.

Repugnan—ce, **—cy,** *s.* die Abnei= gung. **—t,** *adj.* zuwider.

Repuls—e, I. *s.* das Zurückſchlagen. II. *v.a.* zurückſchlagen; (*fig.*) abweiſen. **—ion,** *s.* die Abſtoßung. **—ive,** *adj.,* **—ively,** *adv.* abſtoßend.

Reput—able, *adj.,* **—ably,** *adv.* an= ſtändig. **—ation,** *s.* der Ruf. **—e,** I. *v.a.* halten, achten für. II. *s.* der

Ruf. **—ed,** *adj.* vermeintlich. — **edly,** *adv.* dem Rufe nach.

Request, I. *s.* das Ansuchen; die Bitte. II. *v.a.* bitten, ersuchen; in —, gesucht, begehrt, geschätzt.

Requiem, *s.* das Requiem, die Totenmesse.

Require, *v.a.* verlangen, erfordern. **—ment,** *s.* die Forderung.

Requisite, I. *adj.* erforderlich, notwendig. II. *s.* das Erfordernis.

Requit—al, *s.* die Vergeltung. **—e,** *v.a.* vergelten.

Rescind, *v.a.* aufheben, für ungültig erklären, umstoßen.

Rescue, I. *v.a.* befreien; (*fig.*) retten. II. *s.* die Rettung.

Research, *s.* die Untersuchung, (Nach) Forschung.

Resembl—ance, *s.* die Ähnlichkeit. **—e,** *v.a.* (einem) ähnlich sein *or* sehen.

Resent, *v.a.* ahnen (*an insult, etc.*), übelnehmen. **—ful,** *adj.*, **—fully,** *adv.* empfindlich. **—ment,** *s.* die Empfindlichkeit.

Reserv—ation, *s.* der Vorbehalt; die Verwahrung (*of the Eucharist*); mental —, der Gedankenvorbehalt; with certain —es, mit gewissen Einschränkungen.

Reserve, I. *v.a.* aufsparen, bewahren. II. *s.* (store) der Vorrat; der Rückhalt, die Reserve (*Mil.*); (*fig.*) die Zurückhaltung, das zurückhaltende Wesen. **—d,** *adj.*, **—dly,** *adv.* zurückhaltend, verschlossen; (engaged) bestellt.

Reservoir, *s.* der Behälter (*for water, fish, etc.*).

Resid—e, *v.n.* wohnen, sich aufhalten. **—ence,** *s.* der Aufenthalt. **—ent,** I. *adj.* wohnhaft. II. *s.* der Bewohner.

Residu—e, *s.* der Rest, Überrest. **—ary,** *adj.* übrig.

Resign, *v.a.* verzichten auf (eine S.); to — one's place, abdanken; to — oneself to fate, sich in sein Schicksal ergeben. **—ation,** *s.* die Abtretung, Verzichtleistung (auf eine S.).

Resin, *s.* das Harz.

Resist, *v.a. & n.* widerstehen (einem), sich (einem) widersetzen. **—ance,** *s.* der Widerstand. **—ant,** *adj.*, widerstehend. **—less,** *adj.* unwiderstehlich.

Resolut—e, *adj.*, **—ely,** *adv.* entschlossen, entschieden, fest. **—eness,** *s.* die Entschlossenheit. **—ion,** *s.* die Entschlossenheit, Festigkeit; (resolve)

der Entschluß (zu einer S.); der Beschluß (*Parl.*).

Resolve, I. *v.a.* auflösen (into, in); lösen (*questions*); heben (*doubts*); (decide) entscheiden. II. *v.r.* sich bilden (*into a committee, etc.*). III. *v.n.* (— on) beschließen, einen Beschluß fassen; (decide) sich entschließen. IV. *s.* der Entschluß, Beschluß. **—d,** *adj.* entschlossen.

Resort, I. *s.* der Zusammenkunftsort; der Sammelplatz; health —, der Kurort, die Sommerfrische; as a last —, als letzte Zuflucht. II. *v.n.* sich begeben.

Resound, *v.n.* widerhallen, nachhallen. **—ing,** *adj.*, **—ingly,** *adv.* widernach=hallend.

Resource, *s.* die Zuflucht, das Hilfsmittel. **—s,** *pl.* Geldmittel, Fähigkeiten, Gaben.

Respect, I. *v.a.* berücksichtigen; (esteem) (hoch=)achten, schätzen. II. *s.* die Rücksicht, Hinsicht; die Achtung, Hochachtung; in — of, in Beziehung auf (*acc.*); hinsichtlich (*gen.*); in all —s, in every —, in jeder Hinsicht; to pay one's —s to someone, einem seine Aufwartung machen; **—ability,** *s.* die Achtbarkeit; die Solidität (*C.L.*). **—able,** *adj.*, **—ably,** *adv.* achtbar, achtenswert ; solid, gut (*C.L.*). **—ful,** *adj.*, **—fully,** *adv.* ehrerbietig; yours **—fully,** ergebenst, hochachtungsvoll. **—ing,** *prep.* in Betreff, in Beziehung auf (*acc.*), hinsichtlich (*gen.*). **—ive,** *adj.* bezüglich. **—ively,** *adv.* beziehungsweise.

Respir—ation, *s.* das Atmen. **—e,** *v.n.* atmen.

Respite, *s.* die Frist (*Law*).

Resplendent, *adj.* glänzend.

Respond, *v.n.* antworten. **—ent,** I. *adj.* antwortend, entsprechend. II. *s.* der, die Angeklagte (*Law*).

Respons—e, *s.* die Antwort; die Erwiderung. **—ibility,** *s.* die Verantwortlichkeit. **—ible,** *adj.* verantwortlich. **—ive,** *adj.* antwortend; entsprechend.

¹Rest, I. *s.* die Ruhe, Rast. II. *v.n.* rasten, (aus)ruhen; (lean) lehnen, sich stützen (on, auf (*acc.*)); (be supported) beruhen. III. *v.a.* ruhen lassen. **—ful,** *adj.*, **—fully,** *adv.* ruhig; beruhigend. **—ing,** *s.* das Ruhen. **—less,** *adj.*, **—lessly,** *adv.* rastlos, ruhelos; unruhig (*in disposi-*

tion); (ever-moving) unſtät. **—less-ness**, *s.* die Raſtloſigkeit, Unruhe. **—ing-place**, *s.* der Ruheplaß.

²**Rest**, *s.* der Reſt, Überreſt; for the —, übrigens, im übrigen.

Restaura—nt, *s.* das Reſtaurant, Speiſehaus. **—teur**, *s.* der Speiſewirt.

Restitution, *s.* die Wiederherſtellung; to make —, Erſaß leiſten.

Restive, *adj.*, **—ly**, *adv.* ſtörriſch. **—ness**, *s.* die Störrigkeit.

Restor—ation, *s.* die Wiederher-ſtellung. **—ative**, I. *adj.* wiederher-ſtellend. II. *s.* das Stärkungsmittel. **—e**, *v.a.* wiederherſtellen; to —e a person to liberty, jemandem die Freiheit ſchenken; to —e to life, ins Leben zurückrufen.

Restrain, *v.a.* zurück-, ab-halten. **—t**, *s.* die Zurückhaltung; die Hem-mung, der Zwang.

Restrict, *v.a.* be-, ein-ſchränken. **—ion**, *s.* die Einſchränkung.

Result, I. *s.* das Ergebnis. II. *v.n.* als Folge entſtehen, ſich ergeben.

Resume, *v.a.* wieder aufnehmen.

Résumé, *s.* die Zuſammenfaſſung.

Resurrection, *s.* die Auferſtehung.

Resuscitate, *v.a.* ins Leben zurückrufen.

Retail, I. *v.a.* im Kleinen, im Detail verkaufen (*C.L.*). II. *s.* der Klein-handel, das Detailgeſchäft. **—er**, *s.* der Kleinhändler.

Retain, *v.a.* behalten. **—er**, *s.* der Anhänger.

Retaliat—e, *v.n.* & *a.* mit Gleichem vergelten. **—ion**, *s.* die Wieder-vergeltung.

Retard, *v.a.* verſpäten.

Retch, *v.n.* ſich erbrechen wollen.

Retent—ion, *s.* die Zurückhaltung. **—ive**, *adj.* zurückhaltend. **—iveness**, *s.* die Gedächtniskraft.

Reticen—ce, *s.* die Verſchwiegenheit. **—t**, *adj.* verſchwiegen.

Retinue, *s.* das Gefolge.

Retir—e, *v.* I. *a.* zurückziehen; ab-danken (*an officer*). II. *n.* ſich zurück-ziehen; ſich entfernen (from, aus); —ed list, die Penſionsliſte; —ing allowance, das Ruhegehalt. **—ement**, *s.* das Sichzurückziehen; (seclusion) die Zurückgezogenheit. **—ing**, *adj.* zurückhaltend.

Retort, I. *v.a.* erwidern (upon a person, einem). II. *v.n.* ſcharf erwidern *or* entgegnen. III. *s.* die Erwiderung.

Retouch, *v.a.* überarbeiten; (*Phot.*) retouchieren.

Retract, *v.a.* & *n.* zurückziehen. **—ion**, *s.* die Zurücknahme.

Retreat, I. *s.* der Rückzug (*also Mil.*); (refuge) der Zufluchtsort; der Zap-fenſtreich (*Mil.*); to beat the —, den Zapfenſtreich ſchlagen (*Mil.*). II. *v.n.* ſich zurückziehen.

Retrench, *v.a.* verkürzen; (expenses) vermindern, einſchränken. **—ment**, *s.* die Verkürzung, Verminderung.

Retribut—ion, *s.* die Vergeltung. **—ive**, *adj.* vergeltend.

Retriev—able, *adj.* erſeßlich. **—e**, *v.* I. *a.* apportieren (*of dogs*); (re-cover) wiedereinbringen. **—er**, *s.* der Stöber (hund), Apportierhund.

Retrograde, *adj.* rückgängig.

Retrospect, *s.* der Rückblick.

Return, I. *v.n.* zurück-kehren, -kommen; (reply) entgegnen, erwidern. II. *v.a.* zurück-, wieder-geben; erſtatten (*one's thanks*); ausſprechen (*a verdict*). III. *s.* die Rückkehr; —s, die Einnahme; in —, dagegen, als Entgegnung. **—able**, *adj.* zurückſtellbar. **—ticket**, *s.* der Rückfahrſchein.

Reun—ion, *s.* die Wiedervereinigung; die Geſellſchaft. **—ite**, *v.a.* (& *n.* ſich) wiedervereinigen.

Reveal, *v.a.* offenbaren (*also Theol.*); verraten (*secrets*).

Revel, I. *s.* das Gelage. II. *v.n.* jubeln, ſchmauſen. **—ler**, *s.* der Schwelger. **—ry**, *s.* das Jubeln, laute Luſtbarkeit.

Revelation, *s.* die Offenbarung.

Revenge, I. *s.* die Rache. II. *v.a.* rächen. III. *v.r.* ſich rächen, Rache nehmen (on a person, an einem). **—ful**, *adj.*, **—fully**, *adv.* rachgierig, rachſüchtig. **—r**, *s.* der Rächer.

Revenue, *s.* das Einkommen, die Ein-künfte. **—officer**, *s.* der Zollbeamte.

Revere, *v.a.* (ver)ehren. **—nce**, I. *s.* die Ehrerbietung, Ehrfurcht; your —nce, Euer Ehrwürden. II. *v.a.* ehren (in *titles*). **—nd**, *adj.* ehrwürdig (in *titles*). **—nt**, *adj.*, **—ntly**, *adv.* erfurchtsvoll.

Reverie, *s.* die Träumerei.

Revers—al, *s.* die Umkehrung. **—e**, I. *v.a.* umkehren. II. *s.* die Rückſeite (of *a coin*, *etc.*); (opposite) das Gegenteil; das Mißgeſchick, die Nieder-lage. III. *adj.*, **—ely**, *adv.* umgekehrt.

—ed, *adj.* verkehrt. —ible, *adj.*
umstößlich. —ion, I. *s.* die Umkeh=
rung; der Erbanspruch (auf eine Sache)
(*Law*); der Rückschlag (*to a former
type, etc.*).

Revert, *v.n.* wiederkehren; zurück=
kommen (*to a thing,* auf eine
S.).

Review, I. *v.a.* rezensieren (*a book, etc.*);
mustern (*Mil.*). II. *v.n.* rezensieren.
III. *s.* die Besprechung, Rezension,
Kritik (*of a book, etc.*); military —,
die große Parade, Truppenschau;
naval —, die Flottenschau. —er, *s.*
der Musternde; der Rezensent.

Revil—e, *v.a.* verunglimpfen. —er,
s. der Schmäher. —ing, I. *adj.,* —
ingly, *adv.* schmähend. II. *s.* das
Schmähen.

Revis—al, *s.* die Revision. —e, *v.a.*
revidieren (*a work*). —er, *s.* der
Nachprüfer, Korrektor.

Reviv—al, *s.* die Wiederherstellung;
das Wiederaufblühen (*of learning, etc.*).
—e, *v.* I. *a.* neubeleben; (re-intro-
duce) wieder aufbringen *or* einführen.
II. *n.* wiederaufleben.

Revocation, *s.* der Widerruf, die
Zurückberufung, Aufhebung.

Revoke, *v.a.* widerrufen.

Revolt, I. *s.* die Empörung, der Auf=
ruhr. II. *v.n.* sich empören; ab=
fallen (from, von).

Revolution, *s.* die Umwälzung, der
Kreislauf; die (Staats=)Umwälzung,
Revolution (*Pol.*). —ary, *adj.*
revolutionär, Revolutions=. —ist, *s.*
der Revolutionär.

Revolv—e, *v.* I. *n.* sich umwälzen.
II. *a.* umdrehen; über=legen, =denken,
erwägen (*in one's mind*). —er, *s.*
der Revolver. —ing, *adj.* drehbar,
sich drehend.

Revulsion, *s.* der Rückschlag, Um=
schwung.

Reward, I. *s.* die Belohnung, der Lohn.
II. *v.a.* belohnen. —er, *s.* der
Belohner.

Rhapsody, *s.* die Rhapsodie.

Rhetoric, *s.* die Rhetorik. —al, *adj.,*
—ally, *adv.* rednerisch, rhetorisch.
—ian, *s.* der Redekünstler.

Rheumati—c, *adj.* rheumatisch. —
sm, *s.* der Rheumatismus.

Rhinoceros, *s.* das Nashorn.

Rhubarb, *s.* der Rhabarber.

Rhyme, I. *s.* der Reim. II. *v.n.*

(sich) reimen. III. *v.a.* Verse machen.
—less, *adj.* reimlos, ohne Reim.

Rhythm, *s.* der Rhythmus. —ic,
—ical, *adj.,* —ically, *adv.* rhythmisch.

Rib, *s.* die Rippe.

Ribbon, *s.* das Band, die Borte.

Rice, *s.* der Reis.

Rich, *adj.,* —ly, *adv.* reich (in, an).
—es, *pl.* der Reichtum, die Reichtümer.
—ly, *adv.* reich; reichlich, kostbar,
ergiebig, fruchtbar. —ness, *s.* der
Reichtum; die Reichhaltigkeit; die
Fruchtbarkeit.

Rick, *s.* der Schober.

Rickets, *pl.* die englische Krankheit.

Rickety, *adj.* gebrechlich, schwach,
baufällig.

Rid, I. *ir.v.a.* wegschaffen; to — of,
frei machen von. II. *adj.;* to be —
of, (einer Sache) los sein. —dance,
s. die Befreiung.

¹Riddle, *s.* das Rätsel.

²Riddle, I. *s.* das grobe Sieb. II.
v.a. sieben; to — with bullets, mit
Kugeln durchlöchern.

Ride, I. *ir.v.n.* reiten; fahren (*in a
carriage, etc.*). II. *ir.v.a.* reiten.
III. *s.* der Ritt; die Fahrt (*in a train,
a carriage*); der Reitweg, die Reit=
bahn; to go for a —, spazieren
reiten. —r, *s.* der Reiter; der
Fahrende.

Ridge, *s.* der Rücken, Gebirgskamm,
Grat.

Ridicul—e, I. *s.* das Lächerliche. II.
v.a. verspotten. —ous, *adj.,* —ously,
adv. lächerlich. —ousness, *s.* die
Lächerlichkeit.

Riding, *s.* das Reiten. —boots, *pl.*
Reitstiefel. —habit, *s.* das Reitkleid.

Rife, *adj.,* —ly, *adv.* weitverbreitet,
häufig, herrschend.

¹Rifle, *v.a.* berauben, plündern.

²Rifle, I. *v.a.* ziehen (*gun-barrels*).
II. *s.* die Büchse. —d, *adj.* gezogen
(*Mil.*). —men, *pl.* Jäger. —range,
s. der Schießplatz, Schießstand.

Rift, *s.* die Ritze, der Spalt.

Rig, I. *s.* die Takelung. II. *v.a.* aus=
rüsten (*a ship*). —ger, *s.* der Takler.
—ging, *s.* das Takel=, Tau=werk, die
Takelage.

Right, I. *adj. & adv.,* —ly, recht (*also
of angles, lines, the hand, etc.*);
(correct) richtig; to be —, recht haben;
all —! alles in Ordnung, sehr wohl!
by —s, von Rechts wegen. II. *adv.*

sehr, hoch (*before titles*); — ahead, geradeaus; — about *or* turn! rechts um! III. *s.* das Recht; (prerogative) das Vorrecht. IV. *v.a.* Recht widerfahren lassen (a person, einem). V. *v.n.* aufstehen (*Naut.*). —eous, *adj.*, —eously, *adv.* gerecht, rechtschaffen. —eousness, *s.* die Rechtschaffenheit. —ful, *adj.*, —fully, *adv.* recht (mäßig); (just) gerecht. —angled, *adj.* rechtwinflig. —hand, *adj.* rechts stehend. —minded, *adj.* rechtschaffen.

Rigid, *adj.*, —ly, *adv.* steif, starr. —ity, *s.* die Steife.

Rigor, *s.* die Starrheit. —ous, *adj.*, —ously, *adv.* streng, hart.

Rigour, *s.* die Strenge, Härte.

Rill, *s.* das Bächlein.

Rim, *s.* der Rand.

Rime, *s.* der Reif.

Rind, *s.* die Rinde, Schale.

¹Ring, I. *s.* der Ring (also Geom. & fig.). II. *v.a.* (be)ringen.

²Ring, I. *s.* der Klang, Schall. II. *ir.v.n.* läuten (*as a bell*); klingen (*as coins*). III. *v.a.* klingen lassen; läuten (*bells*); to — a person up, jemanden anklingeln, telefonisch anrufen. —er, *s.* der Glockenläuter.

Ringleader, *s.* der Rädelsführer.

Ringlet, *s.* der Ringel, die Haarlocke.

Rink, *s.* die Rollschuhbahn, künstliche Eisbahn.

Rinse, *v.a.* spülen.

Riot, I. *s.* der Lärm; der Aufruhr; to run —, umherschwärmen. II. *v.n.* schwelgen. —er, *s.* der Aufrührer, Meuterer. —ous, *adj.*, —ously, *adv.* schwelgerisch; aufrührerisch.

Rip, *v.a.* (auf)trennen (a seam, etc.).

Ripe, *adj.* reif. —ly, *adv.* reiflich, rechtzeitig. —n, *v.n.* reifen. —ness, *s.* die Reife.

Ripple, I. *v.n.* rieseln. II. *v.a.* träufeln (water). III. *s.* das Gerriesel.

Rise, I. *ir.v.n.* aufstehen, sich erheben (from a seat, bed, etc.), emporsteigen; in die Höhe gehen, steigen (in price, to a place; of water, temperature, etc.). II. *s.* das Steigen (in price, to a place), Aufsteigen; der Aufgang (of the sun); das Anschwellen (of the water, etc.).

Risk, I. *s.* die Gefahr; to run a —, Gefahr laufen, riskieren. II. *v.a.* wagen. —y, *adj.* gefährlich, gewagt.

Rit—e, *s.* der Ritus. —ual, I. *adj.* ritualmäßig. II. *s.* das Ritual.

Rival, I. *s.* der Nebenbuhler, die Nebenbuhlerin. II. *adj.* wetteifernd, nebenbuhlerisch. III. *v.a.* wetteifern mit, nacheifern. —ry, *s.* die Nebenbuhlerei.

River, *s.* der Fluß.

Rivet, I. *v.a.* vernieten. II. *s.* die Niete. —ing, I. *s.* das Nieten. II. *adj.* (in comp.) Niet-.

Roach, *s.* das Rotauge (Icht.).

Road, *s.* die (Land-)Straße. —stead, *s.* die Reede.

Roam, I. *v.n.* umherstreifen. II. *v.a.* durchstreifen.

Roan, I. *adj.* graurötlich; — binding, der Schaslebereinband. II. *s.* (—horse) der Rotschimmel.

Roar, I. *s.* das Gebrüll, Brüllen (of beasts). II. *v.n.* brüllen. —ing, I. *adj.* brüllend. II. *s.* das Brüllen, Heulen, Brausen.

Roast, I. *v.a.* braten, rösten. II. *s.* der Braten. III. *adj.* gebraten; gebrannt (coffee).

Rob, *v.a.* (be)rauben, bestehlen. —ber, *s.* der Räuber, Dieb. —bery, *s.* der Raub, Diebstahl; die Räuberei.

Robe, I. *s.* das Kleid. II. *v.a.* bekleiden.

Robin, *s.* das Rotkehlchen.

Robust, *adj.*, —ly, kräftig, stark. —ness, *s.* die Kraft, Stärke.

¹Rock, *s.* der Fels, Felsen; die Klippe. —oil, *s.* das Steinöl.

²Rock, *v.a.* schaukeln; wiegen (a cradle). —ing-chair, *s.* der Schaukelstuhl. —ing-horse, *s.* das Schaukelpferd.

Rocket, *s.* die Rakete (Firew., Mil.).

Rocky, *adj.* felsig.

Rod, *s.* die Rute; die Stange.

Rodent, I. *s.* das Nagetier. II. *adj.* nagend.

¹Roe, *s.* der (Fisch-)Rogen.

²Roe, *s.* das Reh. —buck, *s.* der Rehbock.

Rogu—e, *s.* der Schelm, Schalk. —ery, *s.* die Spitzbüberei. —ish, *adj.*, —ishly, *adv.* schelmisch.

Rôle, *s.* die Rolle.

Roll, I. *v.a.* rollen, wälzen. II. *v.n.* rollen (also of thunder, the eyes, etc.). III. *s.* die Rolle (of papers, etc.); der Wirbel (of drums); das Schlingern (of a ship); die Semmel (Bak.);

(list) die Rolle. **—er,** *s.* die Rolle, Walze, Welle (*Mach.*). **—er-skate,** *s.* der Rollschuh. **—call,** *s.* der Appell (*Mil.*). **—ing-pin,** *s.* das Rollholz.

Rollicking, *adj.* lärmend.

Roman—ce, I. *s.* der Roman. II. *v.n.* erdichten. **—tic,** *adj.,* **—tically,** *adv.* romantisch.

Romp, *v.n.* sich herumbalgen. **—ers,** *pl.* die Spielhose, der Spielkittel.

Roof, I. *s.* das Dach (*also fig.*); — of the mouth, der Gaumen. II. *v.a.* mit einem Dache versehen. **—ing,** *s.* die Dachung.

¹**Rook,** I. *s.* die Saatkrähe (*Orn.*). II. *v.a.* betrügen.

²**Rook,** *s.* der Turm, Roche (*Chess*).

Room, *s.* (space) der Raum, Platz; (chamber) das Zimmer, die Stube. **—ful,** *s.* das Zimmervoll. **—ily,** *adv.* geräumig. **—iness,** *s.* die Geräumigkeit. **—y,** *adj.* geräumig, weit.

Roost, *s.* der Schlafsitz (*of birds*).

¹**Root,** I. *s.* die Wurzel (*also fig. & Math.*). II.*v.n.* sich einwurzeln. **—ed,** *adj.* eingewurzelt, tief.

²**Root,** *v.a.* aufwühlen.

Rope, I. *s.* das Seil, Tau, der Strick. II. *v.a.* mit Stricken binden. III. *v.n.* sich in Fäden ziehen. **—dancer,** *s.* der Seiltänzer. **—walk,** *s.* die Seilerbahn.

Rosary, *s.* der Rosenkranz (*Rel.*).

Rose, *s.* die Rose.

Rosemary, *s.* der Rosmarin.

Rosin, *s.* das Harz.

Rosy, *adj.* rosig, rosenrot.

Rot, *v.* I. *n.* (ver)faulen. II. *a.* faul machen. III. *s.* die Fäulnis.

Rotate, *v.n.* sich herumdrehen.

Rote, *s.* die Übung; by —, durch bloße Übung.

Rotten, *adj.* verfault, faul.

Rotund, *adj.* rund.

Rouge, *s.* die Schminke.

Rough, *adj.,* **—ly,** *adv.* rauh. **—ness,** *s.* die Rauheit. **—shod,** *adj.* mit scharfen Hufeisen beschlagen; (*fig.*) rücksichtslos.

Roulette, *s.* das Roulettespiel.

Round, I. *adj.,* **—ly,** *adv.* rund. II. *adv.* rings(um). III. *prep.* rings(um), um, um ... herum. IV. *s.* die Runde. **—ness,** *s.* die Rundung. **—about,** I. *adj.* weitschweifig. II. *s.* der Umweg. **—dance,** *s.* der Reigen.

Rouse, I. *v.a.* aufwecken, erwecken (*from sleep, etc.*); (*fig.*) aufregen. II. *v.n.* aufwachen.

Rout, I. *s.* die Verwirrung. II. *v.a.* in Verwirrung setzen.

Route, *s.* der Weg.

Routine, *s.* die Routine.

Rov—e, *v.n.* umher-schweifen, -schwärmen. **—er,** *s.* der Herumstreicher. **—ing,** *adj.,* **—ingly,** *adv.* umher-schweifend.

¹**Row,** *s.* die Reihe.

²**Row,** *v.a. & n.* rudern. **—er,** *s.* der Ruderer. **—ing,** *s.* das Rudern. **—lock,** *s.* das Rudergat.

³**Row,** *s.* der Lärm, Spektakel.

Rowan-tree, *s.* die Eberesche.

Rowdy, I. *s.* der Raufbold, Strolch. II. *adj.* lärmend; händelsüchtig.

Rowel, *s.* das Spornrädchen.

Royal, *adj.,* **—ly,** *adv.* königlich, Königs-. **—ty,** *s.* das Königtum.

Rub, I. *s.* das Reiben, die Reibung; (*fig.*) der Anstoß. II. *v.a.* reiben. III. *v.n.* sich reiben; to — out, ausstreichen.

Rubber, I. *s.;* der Reiber, Frottierer; der Rubber (*Cards*); (*pl.*) die Gummischuhe; india-—, der Kautschuk, Gummi. II. *attrib.* Gummi-.

Rubbish, *s.* der Schutt. **—heap,** *s.* der Schutthaufen.

Rubble, *s.* der Steinschutt.

Rubicund, *adj.,* rötlich, rot.

Ruby, *s.* der Rubin.

Ruck, I. *s.* die Runzel, Falte. II. *v.a.* runzeln.

Rudder, *s.* das (Steuer-)Ruder.

Ruddy, *adj.* rot, rötlich.

Rude, *adj.,* **—ly,** *adv.* ungebildet; roh. **—ness,** *s.* die Roheit, Rauheit.

Rudiment, *s.* die Grundlage. **—al,** **—ary,** *adj.* Anfangs-, Elementar-.

¹**Rue,** *v.a.* bereuen, beklagen.

²**Rue,** *s.* die Raute (*Bot.*).

Ruff, *s.* der Halskragen. **—le,** *s.* die Krause.

Ruffian, I. *adj.* wüst, roh. II. *s.* der Raufbold.

Ruffle, I. *s.* die Krause. II. *v.a.* falten, kraus machen; verwirren; aufregen; (rumple) zerknittern.

Rug, *s.* die Decke.

Rugged, *adj.,* **—ly,** *adv.* rauh, uneben. **—ness,** *s.* die Rauheit, Schroffheit.

Ruin, I. *s.* (*fig.*) der Verfall, Untergang; die Ruine (*of a castle. etc.*).

II. *v.a.* zu Grunde richten. —ous,
adj., —ously, *adv.* baufällig.

Rule, I. *s.* die Regel (*also Arith.*).
II. *v.a.* liniieren (*paper, etc.*); (—
over) beherrschen, regieren. III. *v.n.*
herrschen, sich behaupten (*as prices*).
—r, *s.* der Herrscher, Regierer; das
Lineal.

Rum, *s.* der Rum.

Rumble, *s.* das Rumpeln.

Rumour, *s.* das Gerücht.

Rump, *s.* der Steiß.

Rumple, *v.a.* runzeln.

Run, *ir.v.* I. *n.* rennen, laufen. II.
a. rennen, laufen; to — short, zu
Ende gehen; two days —ning, zwei
Tage nacheinander. III. *s.* das Laufen,
Rennen, der Lauf; in the long —,
auf die Dauer, am Ende. —away, I.
adj. entlaufen. II. *s.* der Ausreißer.

Run—e, *s.* die Rune. —ic, *adj.*
runisch, Runen=.

Rung, *s.* die Sprosse (*of a ladder*).

Runner, *s.* der Renner, Läufer.

Rupture, I. *s.* das Brechen; der Bruch
(*also Med.*). II. *v.a.* brechen, spren=
gen (*a blood-vessel, etc.*).

Rural, *adj.*, —ly, *adv.* ländlich; Land=.

Ruse, *s.* die List.

1Rush, *s.* die Binse (*Bot.*).

2Rush, I. *s.* das Rauschen, Toben (*of the
waves, etc.*). II. *v.n.* stürzen, schießen.

Rusk, *s.* der Zwieback.

Russet, *adj.* braunrot.

Rust, I. *s.* der Rost (*also fig. & Bot.*).
II. *v.n.* rosten, verrosten. —iness,
s. die Rostigkeit. —y, *adj.* rostig.

Rustic, I. *adj.*, —ally, *adv.* ländlich;
Land=. II. *s.* der Landmann, Bauer.

Rustl—e, *v.n.* rascheln. —ing, I. *adj.*
rauschend. II. *s.* das Rauschen,
Geraffel.

Rut, *s.* die Spur.

Ruthless, *adj.* erbarmungslos, grausam.

Rye, *s.* der Roggen.

S

S, s, *s.* das S, s.

Sabbat—h, *s.* der Sabbat. —ic(al),
adj. sabbatisch, Sabbat=.

Sable, *s.* der Zobel.

Sabotage, *s.* die Sabotage.

Sabre, I. *s.* der Säbel. II. *v.a.* nieder=
säbeln. —tache, *s.* die Säbeltasche.

Saccharine, *s.* der Zuckerstoff.

1Sack, *s.* der Sack; to get the —,

(*slang*) den Laufpaß erhalten. —
cloth, *s.* die Sackleinwand.

2Sack, I. *s.* die Plünderung. II. *v.a.*
plündern.

Sacr—ament, *s.* das Sakrament. —
amental, *adj.* sakramentlich, Sakra=
ment=. —ed, *adj.*, —edly, *adv.*
heilig. —edness, *s.* die Heiligkeit.
—ifice, I. *s.* das Opfer (*also fig.*).
II. *v.a. & n.* opfern. —ilege, *s.* die
Entweihung. —ilegious, *adj.*, —
ilegiously, *adv.* frevelhaft. —istan,
s. der Kirchendiener. —isty, *s.* die
Sakristei.

Sad, *adj.*, —ly, *adv.* traurig, trüb.
—den, *v.* I. *a.* betrüben. II. *n.* sich
betrüben. —ness, *s.* die Trauer.

Saddle, I. *s.* der Sattel. II. *v.a.*
(auf)satteln; to — oneself with a
thing, etwas auf sich nehmen. —r, *s.*
der Sattler. —ry, *s.* die Sattler=
waren. —bag, *s.* die Satteltasche.
—bow, *s.* der Sattelbogen. —cloth,
s. die Satteldecke. —girth, *s.* der
Sattelgurt.

Safe, I. *adj.*, —ly, *adv.* sicher; glücklich
(*as a journey, etc.*); (out of danger)
außer Gefahr. II. *s.* der Kassen=
schrank. —ness, *s.* die Sicherheit.
—ty, *s.* die Sicherheit. —conduct,
s. das Sicherheitsgeleit. —guard, I.
s. der Schutz. II. *v.a.* beschützen.
—ty-fuse, *s.* die Sicherung (*Radio*).
ty-match, *s.* das Sicherheitszünd=
hölzchen. —ty-valve, *s.* das Sicher=
heitsventil.

Saffron, I. *s.* der Safran. II. *adj.*
safrangelb.

Sag, *v.n.* niederhängen, senken, sacken.

Saga, *s.* die Heldensage.

Sagac—ious, *adj.*, —iously, *adv.* klug,
scharfsinnig. —ity, *s.* der Scharfsinn.

1Sage, I. *adj.*, —ly, *adv.* weise, klug,
verständig. II. *s.* der Weise.

2Sage, *s.* der (*also die*) Salbei (*Bot.*).

Sago, *s.* der Sago.

Sail, I. *s.* das Segel; die Fahrt (*on
the sea, etc.*); der Flügel (*of a wind-
mill*). II. *v.n.* (ab)segeln, fahren
(for, nach). III. *v.a.* durchsegeln.
—er, *s.* der Segler. —ing, I. *adj.*
segelnd, Segel=. II. *s.* das Segeln.
—less, *adj.* segellos. —or, *s.* der
Matrose, Seemann. —cloth, *s.* das
Segeltuch.

Saint, *s.* der, die Heilige; Sankt=
(*in compounds*). —ed, *adj.* heilig.

—**liness,** *s.* die Heiligkeit. —**ly,** (—**like,**) *adj.* heilig, fromm.

Sake, *s.* die bewegende Ursache; for the — of, um . . . willen *or* wegen; for his —, um seinetwegen; for my —, um meinetwegen.

Sal, *s.* das Salz (*Chem.*); — ammoniac, der Salmiak.

Salad, *s.* der Salat.

Salamander, *s.* der Salamander (*Zool.*).

Salary, *s.* der Jahresgehalt, die Besoldung.

Sale, *s.* der Verkauf; (*also* —s) der Umsatz, Absatz; for —, zu verkaufen. —**able,** *adj.* verkäuflich, gangbar. —**price,** *s.* der Verkaufspreis. —**room,** *s.* das Auktionslokal. —**sman,** *s.* der Verkäufer. —**swoman,** *s.* die Verkäuferin.

Salic, *adj.* salisch.

Salient, *adj.* springend; hervorragend (*Arch., fig.*).

Saline, *adj.* Salz=.

Saliva, *s.* der Speichel.

¹**Sallow,** *s.* die Salweide.

²**Sallow,** *adj.* bleich und gelblich. —**ness,** *s.* die Blässe.

Sally, I. *s.* der Ausfall (*of the besieged*); (*fig.*) der Witzfunken. II. *v.n.*; to — forth, herausbrechen, sich aufmachen.

Salmon, *s.* der Lachs, Salm.

Saloon, *s.* der Salon.

Salt, I. *s.* das Salz (*also fig.*); old — (*sailor*), alter Seebär. II. *adj.* salzig, gesalzen. III. *v.a.* salzen; einsalzen, pökeln (*meat, etc.*). —**less,** *adj.*, ungesalzen. —**ness,** *s.* die Salzigkeit. —**s,** *pl.* die Salze. —**cellar,** *s.* das Salzfäßchen. —**petre,** *s.* der Salpeter. —**water,** *s.* das Salzwasser.

Salu—brious, —**tary,** *adj.* heilsam, gesund.

Salut—ation, *s.* die Begrüßung. —**e,** I. *s.* der Gruß; das Salutieren (*Mil.*). II. *v.a.* (be)grüßen; salutieren (*Mil., Naut.*). III. *v.n.* grüßen; salutieren.

Salvage, *s.* die Bergung (*of a ship's cargo, etc.*).

Salvation, *s.* die Rettung; die Erlösung (*Theol.*).

¹**Salve,** *v.a.* retten, bergen (*Naut.*).

²**Salve,** *s.* die Salbe.

Salver, *s.* der Präsentierteller.

Salvo, *s.* die Salve (*Mil.*).

Salvor, *s.* der Berger.

Same, *adj.* selb; the —, der=, die=, das=selbe; all the —, dessenungeachtet; it is all the — to me, es ist mir einerlei. —**ness,** *s.* die Einerleiheit.

Sample, I. *s.* die Probe, das Muster (*C.L.*). II. *v.a.* Probe nehmen. —**r,** *s.* das Stickmuster.

Sanatorium, *s.* die Heilanstalt.

Sanct—ify, *v.a.* heiligen. —**imonious,** *adj.*, —**imoniously,** *adv.* scheinheilig. —**imoniousness,** *s.* —**imony,** *s.* die Scheinheiligkeit.

Sanction, I. *s.* die Genehmigung, das Gutheißen. II. *v.a.* (to give — to a thing *or* an act) etwas gutheißen, genehmigen, bestätigen.

Sanctity, *s.* die Heiligkeit.

Sanctu—ary, *s.* das Heiligtum; die Freistätte, Freistatt; das Santuarium, Allerheiligste (*in churches*). —**m,** *s.* das Privatzimmer.

Sand, I. *s.* der Sand. II. *v.a.* mit Sand bestreuen.

Sandal, *s.* die Sandale.

Sandalwood, *s.* das Sandelholz.

Sandwich, *s.* das belegte Butterbrot. —**man,** *s.* der Plakatträger.

Sandy, *adj.* sandig.

San—e, *adj.* geistig gesund; (*also* —**ely,** *adv.*) vernünftig (*as an answer*). —**eness,** *s.* der gesunde Verstand.

Sangfroid, *s.* die Geistesgegenwart.

Sanguin—ary, *adj.*, —**arily,** *adv.* blutdürstig; blutig.

Sanguine, *adj.* vollblütig (*Med.*); sanguinisch, zuversichtlich.

Sanitary, *adj.* Gesundheits= (*measures, etc.*).

Sanity, *s.* der gesunde Verstand.

¹**Sap,** *s.* der Saft (*in plants*); (*fig.*) die Kraft, das Mark. —**less,** *adj.* saftlos.

²**Sap,** I. *s.* der Laufgraben, die Sappe (*Fort.*). II. *v.a.* untergraben (*also fig.*).

Sapient, *adj.* weise.

Sapling, *s.* das Bäumchen.

Saponaceous, *adj.* seifenartig.

Sapper, *s.* der Schanzgräber, Sappeur; —s and miners, Pioniere.

Sapphire, I. *s.* der Saphir. II. *adj.* saphiren.

Sappy, *adj.* saftig.

Sarc—asm, *s.* der Sarkasmus. —**astic,** *adj.*, —**astically,** *adv.* sarkastisch, beißend.

Sarcophagus, *s.* der Sarkophag.

Sard, *s.* der Karneol.

Sardine, *s.* die Sardine.

Sardonic, *adj.* sardonisch, hämisch.

Sardonyx, *s.* der Sardonyx.

1Sash, *s.* die Schärpe; die Feldbinde (*Mil.*).

2Sash, *s.* der Fensterrahmen. — **window,** *s.* das Schiebefenster.

Sassafras, *s.* der Sassafras.

Satchel, *s.* die Schulmappe.

Sate, *v.a.* sättigen. —**less,** *adj.* unersättlich.

Satellite, *s.* der Anhänger, Satellit, Trabant (*also Astr.*).

Sati—ate, I. *v.a.* sättigen. II. *adj.* satt, gesättigt. —**ety,** *s.* die Sättigung.

Satin, *s.* der Atlas. —**et,** *s.* der Halbatlas. —**y,** *adj.* atlasartig; glatt. —**ribbon,** *s.* das Atlasband. — **wood,** *s.* das Atlasholz.

Satir—e, *s.* die Satire; das Spottgedicht. —**ic,** *adj.,* —**ical,** *adj.,* —**ically,** *adv.* satirisch. —**ist,** *s.* der Satiriker. —**ize,** *v.a.* verspotten, bespötteln.

Satis—faction, *s.* die Genugtuung, Befriedigung; (contentment) die Zufriedenheit. —**factoriness,** *s.* das Befriedigende. —**factory,** *adj.,* —**factorily,** *adv.* befriedigend. —**fy,** *v.* I. *a.* befriedigen (*a passion, wish, etc.*); (suffice) genügen; (content) Genüge tun (einem); (convince) überzeugen (of, von); sättigen (*one's appetite*). II. *n.* Genüge leisten (einem). —**fying,** *adj.* genügend, hinlänglich.

Satrap, *s.* der Satrap. —**y,** *s.* die Satrapie.

Satura—te, *v.a.* sättigen (*Chem. & fig.*). —**tion,** *s.* die Sättigung.

Saturday, *s.* der Samstag, Sonnabend.

Satyr, *s.* der Satyr.

Sauc—e, *s.* die Soße, Brühe, Tunke; die Unverschämtheit (*sl.*). —**er,** *s.* die Untertasse. —**iness,** *s.* die Frechheit, Unverschämtheit. —**y,** *adj.* naseweis; unverschämt. —**e-boat,** *s.* die Soßenschale. —**epan,** *s.* die Schmorpfanne.

Saunter, I. *s.* das Schlendern. II. *v.n.* schlendern; to — about, herumschlendern. —**er,** *s.* der Müßiggänger.

Sausage, *s.* die Wurst, Bratwurst.

Savage, I. *adj.,* —**ly,** *adv.* wild,

ungebildet. II. *s.* der Wilde, Barbar. —**ness,** *s.* die Wildheit; die Grausamkeit. —**ry,** *s.* die Wildheit, Barbarei.

Save, I. *v.a.* (er)retten; bergen (*Naut.*); einbringen (*hay, etc.*); (keep) aufbewahren. II. *v.n.* Kosten (er)sparen; (be economical) sparsam sein. III. *prep. & conj.* außer, ausgenommen.

Saving, I. *adj.,* —**ly,** *adv.* (protecting) vor Verlust sichernd; (economical) sparsam. II. *s.* die Rettung. III. *prep.* außer, ausgenommen. —**s,** *pl.* die Ersparnisse. —**s-bank,** *s.* die Sparkasse. —**s-box,** *s.* die Sparbüchse.

Saviour, *s.* der Retter; der Erlöser, Heiland (*Theol.*).

Savour, I. *s.* der Geschmack; (smell) der Geruch. II. *v.n.* schmecken, riechen (of, nach). —**less,** *adj.* geschmacklos, geruchlos. —**y,** *adj.* schmackhaft, duftend (*also fig.*).

Savoy, *s.* der Wirsingkohl.

Saw, I. *s.* die Säge. II. *v.a.* sägen. —**dust,** *s.* die Sägespäne (*pl.*).

Saxifrage, *s.* der Steinbrech (*Bot.*).

Saxophone, *s.* das Saxhorn, das Saxophon.

Say, I. *ir.v.a.* sagen; hersagen (*one's lesson*); that is to —, das heißt. II. *s.* der Ausspruch. —**ing,** *s.* die Rede; die Redensart; to — Mass, die Messe lesen; you don't — so! warum nicht gar! let him have his —, laßt ihn seine Meinung äußern.

Scab, *s.* die Kruste (*Med.*); die Räude (*in sheep, etc.*).

Scabbard, *s.* die Scheide.

Scaffold, *s.* das Gerüst, Baugerüst; das Schafott. —**ing,** *s.* das (Bau-) Gerüst.

1Scald, I. *s.* die Brandwunde. II. *v.a.* verbrennen. —**ing,** I. *adj.* brühend; —ing hot, brühheiß. II. *s.* das Brühen.

2Scald, *s.* der Schorf, Grind.

1Scale, I. *s.* die Schale, Hülse; die Schuppe (*of fish, etc.*). II. *v.a.* abschälen, ablösen. III. *v.n.* sich schuppen, sich abblättern. —**d,** *adj.* schuppig. —**less,** *adj.* schuppenlos.

2Scale, I. *s.* die Wagschale; (usually *pl.* —s or pair of —s) die Wage. II. *v.a.* abwägen.

3Scal—e, I. *s.* (series) die Stufenfolge; die Tonleiter (*Mus.*); der Maßstab, die Skala (*Geom., Surv., etc.*); (*fig.*)

das Maß, der Maßstab. II. *v.a.*
ersteigen. —ing, *adj.* ersteigend. —
ing-ladder, *s.* die Sturmleiter.
Scallion, *s.* die Schalotte.
Scallop, I. *s.* der Ausschnitt; die
Kammuschel (*Zool.*). II. *v.a.* auszacken.
Scalp, I. *s.* die Schädelhaube. II. *v.a.*
abhäuten, stalpieren. —ing-knife, *s.*
das Stalpiermesser.
Scaly, *adj.* schuppig.
Scamp, *s.* der Schuft, der Taugenichts.
Scamper, I. *v.n.*; to — about, sich
umhertummeln. II. *s.* der Lauf.
Scan, *v.* I. *a.* standieren (*verses*);
durchforschen, untersuchen. II. *n.* sich
standieren lassen.
Scandal, *s.* (offence) das öffentliche
Ärgernis; die Verleumdung, Läster=
ung. —ize, *v.a.* Anstoß geben; to
be —ized at, Anstoß nehmen an. —
ous, *adj.*, —ously, *adv.* anstößig,
ärgerlich; (shameful) schändlich; (de=
famatory) verleumderisch. —ous=
ness, *s.* die Anstößigkeit; die Schänd=
lichkeit. —monger, *s.* der Ver=
leumber, die Verleumderin.
Scant, *adj.*, —ily, *adj.* knapp, kärglich,
eng. —iness, *s.* die Knappheit. —y,
adj. knapp.
Scape-goat, *s.* der Sündenbock. —
grace, *s.* der Taugenichts.
Scar, I. *s.* die Narbe. II. *v.n.* ver=
narben.
Scarce—e, I. *adj.* selten, rar. II. *adv.*,
—ely, *adv.* kaum; (hardly) schwerlich.
—eness, —ity, *s.* (want) der Mangel;
die Seltenheit.
Scare, I. *v.a.* (— away) (ver)scheuchen;
(alarm) erschrecken. II. *s.* der
Schrecken, die Panik. —crow, *s.* die
Vogelscheuche, das Schreckbild (*also fig.*).
Scarf, I. *s.* (sash) die Schärpe, Binde;
die Halsbinde. II. *attrib.*; —-pin,
die Schlipsnadel.
Scarl—atina, *s.* das Scharlachfieber.
—et, I. *adj.* scharlachrot. II. *s.* der
Scharlach. —et-runner, *s.* die tür=
kische Bohne.
Scarred, *adj.* genarbt, narbig.
Scathe, *s.* der Schaden.
Scath—ing, *adj.* verletzend, scharf.
—less, *adj.* unbeschädigt.
Scatter, *v.* I. *a.* ausstreuen (*seed, etc.*);
(dispel) zerstreuen. II. *n.* sich zer=
streuen. —ed, *adj.* zerstreut. —
brained, *adj.* leichtfertig, flatterhaft.
Scavenger, *s.* der Straßenkehrer.

Scene, *s.* die Szene; der Auftritt
(*in a play*); (place where something
occurs) der Schauplatz; behind the
s, hinter den Kulissen. —ry, *s.*
die Landschaft; die Szenerie, Dekora=
tion (*Theat.*). —-shifter, *s.* der
Kulissenrücker, Maschinist.
Scent, I. *s.* der Duft, Geruch; (per=
fume) die Parfümerie. II. *v.a.* riechen;
wittern. —ed, *adj.* wohlriechend,
duftend. —less, *adj.* geruchlos. —
bottle, *s.* das Riechfläschchen.
Sceptic, *s.* der Skeptiker. —al, *adj.*,
—ally, *adv.* skeptisch.
Sceptre, *s.* das Zepter.
Schedule, *s.* das Verzeichnis.
Scheme, I. *s.* das Schema; (plan) der
Entwurf. II. *v.n.* Ränke schmieden.
—r, *s.* der Planmacher; der Ränke=
schmied.
Schism, *s.* das Schisma, die Kirchen=
spaltung. —atic, I. *adj.* schismatisch.
II. *s.* der Schismatiker.
Schist, *s.* der Schiefer.
Scholar, *s.* der Schüler, die Schülerin;
(learned man) der Gelehrte. —ly,
adj. gelehrt. —ship, *s.* die Gelehr=
samkeit; das Stipendium.
Scholastic, *adj.*, —al, *adj.*, —ally,
adv. schulmäßig, scholastisch, Schul=.
School, I. *s.* die Schule (*also fig.*). II.
v.a. schulen, unterrichten. —ing, *s.*
der Schulunterricht. —boy, *s.* der
Schulknabe, Schuljunge. —days, *pl.*
die Schuljahre. —fellow, *s.* der
Schulgenosse, Mitschüler. —girl, *s.*
das Schulmädchen. —house, *s.* das
Schulgebäude. —master, *s.* der
Schulmeister, Lehrer. —mistress, *s.*
die Schullehrerin. —room, *s.* das
Schulzimmer, die Klasse.
Schooner, *s.* der Schoner.
Sciatica, *s.* das Hüftweh.
Scien—ce, *s.* die Wissenschaft, Kunde,
Lehre; (natural —ce) die Naturwis=
senschaft(en). —tific, *adj.*, —tifi=
cally, *adv.* wissenschaftlich. —tist,
s. der Gelehrte, Forscher.
Scintilla, *s.* der Funke(n). —te, *v.n.*
funkeln.
Scion, *s.* der Ableger; (*fig.*) der Spröß=
ling, Sproß.
Scissors, *pl.* (pair of —) die Schere.
Scoff, I. *s.* der Spott, Hohn. II. *v.n.*
(— at) (ver=)spotten. —er, *s.* der
Spötter. —ing, *adj.*, —ingly, *adv.*
spöttisch, höhnisch.

Scold, *v.a.* & *n.* (aus)schelten. **—er,** *s.* der Schelter. **—ing,** I. *adj.,* **—ingly,** *adv.* scheltend. II. *s.* das Schelten.

Scoop, I. *s.* die Schippe. II. *v.a.* (— out) aushöhlen.

Scope, *s.* der Gesichtskreis; (*fig.*) die Ausdehnung, der Spielraum.

Scorch, I. *v.a.* sengen, brennen. II. *v.n.* dahinsausen (*slang*).

Score, I. *s.* (notch) die Kerbe; (20) zwanzig (Stück); die Rechnung (*Tennis, etc.*); die Partitur (*Mus.*); four —, achtzig; what's the —? wie steht das Spiel? II. *v.a.* (ein)kerben, ein- schneiden; (record) anschreiben; to — out, ausstreichen.

Scorn, I. *s.* die Verachtung. II. *v.a.* verachten, verschmähen. **—er,** *s.* der Spötter; der Verächter, Verschmäher. **—ful,** *adj.,* **—fully,** *adv.* verächtlich, verachtend.

Scorpion, *s.* der Skorpion.

Scot-free, *adj.* unverletzt, sicher.

Scoundrel, *s.* der Schuft, Schurke. **—ly,** *adj.* schurkisch.

¹Scour, *v.a.* scheuern, putzen. **—ing,** *s.* das Scheuern.

²Scour, *v.n.* schnell laufen, fahren, fliegen; hinstreifen über.

Scourge, I. *v.a.* peitschen, geißeln. II. *s.* die Peitsche, Geißel.

¹Scout, I. *s.* der Späher, Kundschafter; boy —, der Pfadfinder. II. *v.n.* spähen, auskundschaften; rekognos- zieren (*Mil.*); —ing party, das Streifkorps.

²Scout, *v.a.* verächtlich abweisen.

Scow, *s.* das Lichterschiff, Fährboot.

Scowl, I. *v.n.* finster blicken. II. *s.* der finstere Blick. **—ing,** *adj.,* **—ingly,** *adv.* finster; mürrisch.

Scrabble, *v.n.* kritzeln.

Scragg—iness, *s.* die Hagerkeit. **—y,** *adj.* hager.

Scramble, I. *s.* das Klettern. II. *v.n.* sich reißen um. III. *v.a.*; to — eggs, Rühreier machen.

Scrap, *s.* das Stückchen, Bruchstück; (row) der Spektakel (*sl.*). **—book,** *s.* das Sammelbuch, Einklebebuch. **—py,** *adj.* bruchstückartig. **—s,** *pl.* Brocken.

Scrap—e, I. *s.* das Scharren, Kratzen. II. *v.a.* schaben, scharren, kratzen. III. *v.n.* scharren. **—er,** *s.* der (Fuß-)Ab- streicher; das Schabeisen (*Metall.*).

—ing, *s.* (act of —ing) das Scharren; das Schabsel.

Scratch, I. *s.* der Ritz. II. *v.a.* (zer-) kratzen, ritzen; to — out, ausradieren. III. *v.n.* kratzen.

Scrawl, I. *v.a.* & *n.* kritzeln, schmieren. II. *s.* das Gekritzel, Geschmiere.

Scream, I. *s.* der Angstschrei. II. *v.n.* schreien; kreischen. III. *v.a.* schreien. **—er,** *s.* der Schreier, Schreiende. **—ing,** *adj.* kreischend.

Screech, I. *s.* der grelle Angstschrei. II. *v.n.* schreien.

Screed, *s.* die lange Tirade, lange Rede.

Screen, I. *s.* der Schirm; (cinema) die Filmleinwand. II. *v.a.* (be)schirmen.

Screw, I. *s.* die Schraube; (miser) der Geizhals; (jade) die Schindmähre. II. *v.a.* schrauben. **—driver,** *s.* der Schraubenzieher. **—nut,** *s.* die Schraubenmutter.

Scribble, I. *v.a.* & *n.* kritzeln, schmieren. II. *s.* das Gekritzel. **—r,** *s.* der Schmierer (*also fig.*).

Scribe, *s.* der Schreiber.

Scrimmage, *s.* der Krawall; das Handgemenge; (football) der Nah- kampf, das Getümmel.

Scrip, *s.* der Zettel.

Script, *s.* die Handschrift, Schrift.

Scriptur—al, *adj.* biblisch. **—e,** *s.* die heilige Schrift.

Scroll, *s.* die (Papier-)Rolle; der Schnörkel, die Schnecke (*Arch.*). **—work,** *s.* die Arabeskenverzierung.

¹Scrub, *v.a.* abschrubben. **—bing- brush,** *s.* die Schrubbürste, der Schrubber.

²Scrub, *s.* das Gestrüpp. **—by,** *adj.* zwergig.

Scrup—le, I. *s.* der Skrupel; der Zweifel, die Bedenklichkeit. II. *v.n.* Bedenken tragen. **—ulous,** *adj.,* **—ulously,** *adv.* bedenklich; gewissenhaft, peinlich.

Scrutin—ize, *v.a.* durchforschen. **—y,** *s.* die Nachforschung, genaue Prüfung.

Scud, I. *s.* die vom Wind gejagten Wolken. II. *v.n.* eilen; treiben (*Naut.*).

Scuffle, I. *s.* das Handgemenge. II. *v.n.* sich raufen.

Scull, I. *s.* das Skull, der Riemen. II. *v.a.* & *n.* skullen.

Scullery, *s.* die Spültüche. **—maid,** *s.* die Scheuer-, Spül-magd.

Sculpt—or, *s.* der Bildhauer. **—ural,** *adj.* bildhauerisch, Bildhauer-. **—ure,**

I. *s.* die Bildhauerkunst. II. *v.a.* schnitzen, aushauen.

Scum, *s.* der Schaum; (*fig.*) der Auswurf.

Scupper, *s.* das Speigatt.

Scurf, *s.* der Schorf. —**y**, *adj.* schorfig, grindig.

Scurril—**ity**, *s.* die Gemeinheit. — **ous**, *adj.*, —**ously**, *adv.* gemein; grob verletzend.

Scurry, I. *v.n.* (fort)eilen. II. *s.* die Eile, Haft.

Scurv—**ily**, *adv.* niederträchtig. —**iness**, *s.* die Niederträchtigkeit. —**y**, I. *adj.* schorfig, grindig. II. *s.* der Skorbut (*Med.*).

Scutch, *v.a.* schwingen (*flax*).

¹**Scuttle**, *s.*; coal —, der Kohlenbehälter.

²**Scuttle**, I. *v.a.* Löcher einschneiden in (*a ship*). II. *s.* die Springluke (*Naut.*).

³**Scuttle**, *v.n.*; to — away, forteilen.

Scythe, *s.* die Sense.

Sea, *s.* die See, das Meer; at —, auf der See; (*fig.*) in Verwirrung; to put to —, in See stechen; on the high —s, auf hoher See; half —s over, benebelt (*sl.*); the — ran high, die See ging hoch; the open —, das weite Meer. —**bathing**, *s.* das Seebaden. —**coast**, *s.* die Meeresküste. —**farer**, *s.* der Seefahrer. —**faring**, *adj.* seemännisch. —**green**, *adj.* meergrün. —**gull**, *s.* die Möve. —**kale**, *s.* der Seekohl. —**level**, *s.* der Meeresspiegel. —**man**, *s.* (sailor) der Seemann, der Matrose. —**manlike**, *adj.* seemännisch. —**manship**, *s.* die Seemannskunst, Seefahrerkunst. —**port**, *s.* die Hafenstadt. —**room**, *s.* die Räumte. —**shore**, *s.* das Seeufer. —**sick**, *adj.* seekrank. —**sickness**, *s.* die Seekrankheit. —**side**, *s.* die (Meeres-)Küste; to go to the —side, an die See gehen. —**weed**, *s.* die Alge, der Seetang. —**worthy**, *adj.* seefest, seetüchtig. —**wrack**, *s.* das Seegras.

¹**Seal**, *s.* der Seehund, (die) Robbe. —**skin**, *s.* das Seehundsfell.

²**Seal**, I. *s.* das Siegel, Petschaft. II. *v.a.* (zu)siegeln (*letters*, *etc.*). —**ing-wax**, *s.* der Siegellack. —**ring**, *s.* der Siegelring.

Seam, *s.* der Saum, die Naht (*Sew.*); die Schicht, Ader (*Geol.*). —**less**, *adj.* ohne Naht. —**stress**, *s.* die Näherin.

Sear, I. *adj.* trocken. II. *v.a.* dörren; (burn) versengen.

Search, I. *v.a.* suchen, forschen nach; (seek through) unter-, durch-suchen. II. *v.n.* suchen, forschen. III. *s.* das Suchen, Durchsuchen; die Untersuchung; (exploration) das Forschen. —**er**, *s.* der Sucher; der Erforscher; der Untersucher, Prüfer; der Güterbeschauer (*at the Custom-house*). — **ing**, I. *adj.* gründlich. II. *s.* das Suchen; die Durchsuchung. —**light**, *s.* der Scheinwerfer. —**warrant**, *s.* der Haussuchungsbefehl.

Season, I. *s.* die Jahreszeit, Zeit; out of —, außer der Zeit, ungelegen. II. *v.a.* würzen. —**able**, *adj.*, —**ably**, *adv.* zeitgemäß. —**ing**, *s.* die Würze.

Seat, I. *s.* der Sitz (*also fig.*); der Wohnsitz, der Landsitz. II. *v.a.* (hin-)setzen.

Secede, *v.n.* sich zurückziehen, sich trennen.

Secession, *s.* die Abscheidung. —**ist**, *s.* der Separatist.

Seclu—**de**, *v.a.* abschließen. —**ded**, *adj.*, —**dedly**, *adv.* abgeschlossen. — **sion**, *s.* die Abgeschiedenheit.

Second, I. *adj.* zweit, ander; (next) nächst, folgend; (inferior) geringer. II. *s.* der, die, das Nächste, Zweite; der Sekundant (*in duels*); die Sekunde (*of time*); he is — to none, er steht keinem nach; to come off —, den kürzeren ziehen. III. *v.a.* (einem) beistehen, helfen. —**ary**, *adj.* nächstfolgend. —**er**, *s.* der Unterstützende. —**ly**, *adv.* zweitens. —**hand**, *adj.* aus zweiter Hand; (not new) alt. —**rate**, *adj.* zweiten Ranges.

Secrecy, *s.* die Heimlichkeit; (discretion) die Verschwiegenheit.

Secret, I. *adj.*, —**ly**, *adv.* geheim, heimlich, verborgen; verschwiegen; in —, im Vertrauen. II. *s.* das Geheimnis.

Secretary, *s.* der Geheimschreiber; der Schriftführer.

Sect, *s.* die Sekte, Partei. —**arian**, I. *adj.* sektiererisch. II. *s.* der Sektierer.

Section, *s.* die Durchschneidung. —**al**, *adj.* Teil-, Sekten-.

Sector, *s.* der Sektor.

Secular, *adj.* weltlich; hundertjährig.

Secur—**e**, I. *adj.*, —**ely**, *adv.* sicher (from, vor). II. *v.a.* sichern, schützen (from, against, vor). —**ity**, *s.* (confidence) die Ruhe, Sorglosigkeit; (safety) die Sicherheit; (guarantee) die Versicherung, Bürgschaft; to give —ity, Bürgschaft leisten; —ities, Wertpapiere.

Sed—**ate**, I. *adj.*, —**ately**, *adv.* gesetzt, ruhig. —**ateness**, *s.* die Gesetztheit. —**ative**, I. *adj.* beruhigend, besänftigend. II. *s.* beruhigendes Mittel.

Sedentary, *adj.* sitzend.

Sedge, *s.* das Schilfgras.

Sediment, *s.* der Bodensatz, Niederschlag, das Sediment.

Seditio—**n**, *s.* der Aufruhr, Aufstand. —**us**, *adj.*, —**usly**, *adv.* meuterisch.

Seduc—**e**, *v.a.* verführen. —**er**, *s.* der Verführer. —**tion**, *s.* die Verführung. —**tive**, *adj.* verführerisch.

1See, *ir.v.* I. *n.* sehen; (*fig.*) einsehen; to — about, *or* to, eine S. besorgen; I —, ich verstehe (schon); — to it, achten Sie darauf. II. *a.* sehen; (perceive) einsehen, verstehen, begreifen, gewahr werden; to go to — a person, einen besuchen; to live to —, erfahren; worth —ing, sehenswert; I'll — you home, ich will Sie nach Hause begleiten; we saw them off, wir begleiteten sie zur Bahn. —**ing**, I. *conj.*; —ing that, weil, da. II. *s.* das Sehen.

2See, *s.* der (bischöfliche) Sitz.

Seed, I. *s.* die Saat, der Same. II. *v.n.* in Samen schießen. —**ling**, *s.* der Sämling. —**iness**, *s.* (*slang*) die Schäbigkeit, der Katzenjammer. —**time**, *s.* die Sä-, Saat-zeit. —**vessel**, *s.* die Fruchthülle.

Seek, *ir.v.* I. *a.* suchen; (desire) begehren, verlangen; (strive after) streben, trachten nach. II. *n.* suchen. —**er**, *s.* der Sucher, (die) Suchende.

Seem, *v.n.* scheinen (einem) erscheinen. —**ing**, I. *adj.* anscheinend, scheinbar. II. *s.* der Anschein, Schein. —**liness**, *s.* der Anstand, die Schicklichkeit. —**ly**, *adv.* geziemend, schicklich.

Seer, *s.* der Sehende; (prophet) der Seher.

See-saw, *s.* die Wippe.

Seethe, *v.a.* & *n.* sieden; he —d with rage, er kochte vor Wut.

Segment, *s.* der Abschnitt.

Segregat—**e**, *v.a.* absondern, trennen. —**ion**, *s.* die Absonderung.

Seiz—**e**, *v.* 1. *a.* ergreifen, fassen,

packen. II. *n.*; to —e upon, sich (einer Sache) bemächtigen. —**ure**, *s.* das Ergreifen; plötzlicher Anfall (*of sickness*).

Seldom, *adv.* selten.

Select, I. *v.a.* aus-lesen, -wählen. II. *adj.* aus-erlesen, -erwählt. —**ion**, *s.* die Aus-lesung, -lese, -wahl.

Self, I. *s.* das Selbst, Ich; the love of —, die Selbst-, Eigen-liebe. II. *adj.* selb, selbig, nämlich. III. *pronom. adj.* selbst, selber; I my—, ich selber *or* selbst. —**ish**, *adj.*, —**ishly**, *adv.* selbstisch. —**ishness**, *s.* die Selbstsucht. —**acting**, *adj.* selbstwirkend. —**aggrandizement**, *s.* die Selbsterhebung. —**assertion**, die Anmaßung. —**assertive**, *adj.* anmaßend. —**assurance**, *s.* die Zuversicht(lichkeit). —**assured**, *adj.* zuversichtlich. —**command**, *s.* die Selbstbeherrschung. —**conceit**, *s.* der Eigendünkel. —**conceited**, *adj.* dünkelhaft; eingebildet. —**confidence**, *s.* das Selbstvertrauen. —**conscious**, *adj.* selbstbewußt. —**contained**, *adj.* verschlossen; —-contained house, das Einfamilienhaus; —-contained set, eingebauter Radioapparat. —**defence**, *s.* die Notwehr. —**denial**, *s.* die Selbstverleugnung. —**denying**, *adj.* selbstverleugnend. —**evident**, *adj.* selbstverständlich. —**importance**, *s.* der Eigendünkel. —**indulgence**, *s.* die zügellose Genußsucht. —**interest**, *s.* der Eigennutz. —**love**, *s.* die Selbstsucht, Eigenliebe. —**made**, *adj.* selbstgemacht. —**possessed**, *adj.* gefaßt, gelassen. —**possession**, *s.* die Selbstbeherrschung. —**preservation**, *s.* die Selbsterhaltung. —**reliance**, *s.* das Selbstvertrauen. —**respect**, *s.* die Selbstachtung. —**sacrificing**, *adj.* sich selbst aufopfernd. —**same**, *adj.*; the —same, eben der-, die-, dasselbe *or* nämliche, ein und der- 2c. selbe. —**satisfied**, *adj.* selbstbefriedigt. —**seeking**, *adj.* selbstsüchtig.

Sell, I. *ir.v.a.* verkaufen (*also fig.*). II. *ir.v.n.* sich verkaufen, Absatz finden, abgehen (*as goods*); to —, ausverkaufen. —**er**, *s.* der Verkäufer. —**ing**, I. *adj.*; —ing price, der Verkaufspreis. II. *s.* das Verkaufen, der Verkauf.

Selvage, Selvedge, *s.* die Sahlleiste.

Semaphore, *s.* der Semaphor.

Semblance, s. das (Eben)bild, der Anschein, die Gestalt.

Semi, pref. = Halb=, halb=. —circle, s. der Halbkreis. —circular, adj. halbkreisförmig. —colon, s. der Strichpunkt. —official, adj. halbamtlich. —quaver, s. die Sechszehntelnote. —tone, s. der Halbton, die halbe Stufe.

Seminal, adj. Samen=.

Seminary, s. das Seminar.

Sempstress, s. die Näherin.

Senat—e, s. der Senat. —or, s. der Senator.

Send, ir.v.a. senden, schicken; übersenden, zukommen lassen (a person money, etc., einem Geld c.); (despatch) absenden; to — word, sagen lassen; to — for a person, jemanden kommen lassen.

Seni—le, adj. greisenhaft. —lity, s. die Greisenhaftigkeit.

Senior, I. adj. älter; senior (in office). II. s. der Ältere.

Senna, s. das Sennesblatt (Med.).

Sensation, s. die Empfindung, der Eindruck, das Aufsehen. —al, adj., —ally, adv. sensationell.

Sense, s. der Sinn; (understanding) die Vernunft, der Verstand; (feeling) das Gefühl; the five —s, die fünf Sinne; common —, der gesunde Menschenverstand. —less, adj., —lessly, adv. sinnlos, unvernünftig. —lessness, s. die Unvernünftigkeit.

Sensi—bility, s. die Empfindlichkeit. —ble, adj., —bly, adv. merkbar; (prudent) verständig, vernünftig. —tive, adj., —tively, adv. empfindungsfähig, Empfindungs=; —tive soul, empfindsame Seele. —tiveness, s. die Empfindlichkeit (also Phys.).

Sensual, adj., —ly, adv. sinnlich; (voluptuous) wollüstig. —ist, s. der sinnliche Mensch. —ity, s. die Sinnlichkeit.

Sentence, I. s. der Satz (Gram.); das Urteil (Law). — of death, das Todesurteil. II. v.a. verurteilen.

Sententious, adj. spruchreich, bündig, kernig.

Sentiment, s. das Gefühl. —al, adj., —ally, adv. sentimental. —alism, —ality, die Empfindelei. —alist, s. der empfindsame Mensch.

Sentinel, Sentry, s. die Schildwache. —box, s. das Schilderhaus.

Separa—ble, adj., —bly, adv. trennbar. —te, I. v.a. absondern (also fig.); scheiden (husband & wife; also Chem.). II. v.n. sich trennen; sich scheiden. III. adj., —tely, adv. getrennt, abgeschieden. —tion, s. die Trennung, Scheidung.

Sepia, s. die Sepia.

September, s. der September.

Septe—nnial, adj. siebenjährig. —t, s. das Septett. —ntrional, adj. nördlich.

Septic, adj. septisch.

Septuagint, s. die Septuaginta.

Sepulchre, s. die Grabstätte.

Seque—l, —nce, s. die Folge, die Anordnung. —nt, adj. folgend.

Sequest—er, v.a. absondern; sequestrieren (Law). —ration, s. die Absonderung; die Sequestration.

Sequin, s. die Zechine.

Seraph, s. der Seraph. —ic, adj., —ically, adv. seraphisch.

Serenade, I. s. das Ständchen, die Serenade. II. v.a. (einem) ein Ständchen bringen.

Seren—e, adj., —ely, adv. klar, hell. —ity, s. die Heiterkeit; your —ity, Euer Durchlaucht.

Serf, s. der Sklave, die Sklavin.

Serge, s. die Serge.

Sergeant, s. der Sergeant (Mil.); colour —, der Feldwebel.

Serial, adj. heftweise erscheinend.

Series, s. die Reihe.

Serious, adj., —ly, adv. ernst, feierlich, wichtig, ernsthaft. —ness, s. der Ernst.

Sermon, s. die Predigt.

Serpent, s. die Schlange (also fig.). —ine, adj. schlangenartig.

Servant, s. der Knecht, Diener; (maid) die Magd, Dienerin.

Serve, v. I. a. dienen. II. n. dienen, dienstbar sein; dienen (Mil.); in Diensten stehen bei (as a servant, etc.); anschlagen (tennis).

Service, s. der Dienst; divine —, der Gottesdienst; dinner —, das Tafelgerät. —able, adj. dienlich, nützlich.

Serviette, s. die Serviette.

Servile, adj., —ly, adv. sklavisch.

Servitude, s. die Knechtschaft; penal —, die Zwangsarbeit.

Session, s. die Sitzung.

Set, I. ir.v.a. setzen, stellen; to — the fashion, die Mode angeben. II.

ir.v.n. (congeal, *etc.*) gerinnen; laufen (*as a current*); untergehen (*as the sun, etc.*); to — about, anfangen, sich vornehmen. III. *p.p. & adj.* fest, starr; (prescribed) vorgeschrieben; (intent) entschlossen (zu); — speech, die wohlüberlegte Rede. IV. *s.* der Untergang (*of the sun*); der Satz (*of balls, chessmen, etc.*); das Besteck (*of instruments*); (clique) die Clique; (pack, lot) die Sippschaft, Rotte; der Aufsatz (*of china, etc.*); die Partie (*games*). **—back,** *s.* das Hindernis; der Unfall. **—off,** *s.* der Abstich; die Gegenrechnung (*C.L.*). **—to,** *s.* das Geselcht, Handgemenge.

Settee, *s.* das Kanapee.

Setter, *s.* der Hühnerhund.

Setting, *s.* das Setzen; die Fassung (*of a jewel, etc.*); der Untergang (*of the sun, etc.*).

Settl—e, I. *s.* der Sessel. II. *v.n.* sich setzen; sich ansiedeln *or* niederlassen (*in a place*); (decide) entscheiden; sich aufklären (*as weather*). III. *v.a.* (fest-)setzen, feststellen; (arrange) ordnen, in Ordnung bringen; abmachen (accounts); (pay) bezahlen; schlichten (*disputes, etc.*). **—ed,** *adj.* fest, bestimmt; beständig (*as wind, weather*). **—ement,** *s.* die Festsetzung; die Niederlassung (*in a place*); (—ing) der Vergleich; die Saldierung, der Abschluß (*of an account*). **—er,** *s.* der Ansiedler.

Seven, *num. adj.* sieben. **—fold,** *adj. & adv.* siebenfach. **—teen,** *num. adj.* siebzehn. **—teenth,** *adj.* siebzehnt. **—th,** I. *adj.* siebent. II. *s.* das Siebentel. **—thly,** *adv.* siebentens. **—tieth,** *adj.* siebzigst. **—ty,** I. *num. adj.* siebzig. II. *s.* die (Zahl) Siebzig.

Sever, *v.* I. *a.* trennen. II. *n.* sich trennen, sich scheiden.

Several, *adj.* mehrere, verschiedene. **—ly,** *adv.* einzeln.

Sever—e, *adj.*, **—ely,** *adv.* streng. **—ity,** *s.* die Strenge; die Heftigkeit.

Sew, *v.a. & n.* nähen. **—ing,** *s.* das Nähen, die Näherei. **—ing-machine,** *s.* die Nähmaschine. **—ing-needle,** *s.* die Nähnadel. **—ing-silk,** *or* **-thread,** *s.* die Nähseide, das Nähgarn.

Sew—age, *s.* das Sielwasser. **—er,** *s.* der Abzugskanal.

Sex, *s.* das Geschlecht.

Sextant, *s.* der Sextant.

Sexton, *s.* der Küster.

Sexual, *adj.*, **—ly,** *adv.* geschlechtlich, Geschlechts-.

Shabb—ily, *adv.*, **—y,** *adj.* schäbig. **—iness,** *s.* die Lumpigkeit.

Shackle, I. *v.a.* fesseln hemmen (*also fig.*). II. *s.* das Kettenglied. **—s,** *pl.* Fesseln (*also fig.*).

Shad, *s.* die Alse, Else (*Icht.*).

Shad—e, I. *s.* der Schatten. II. *v.a.* be-, um-schatten. **—ily,** *adv.* schattig. **—ing,** *s.* das Schattieren.

Shadow, I. *s.* der Schatten. II. *v.a.* verdunkeln. **—less,** *adj.* schattenlos. **—y,** *adj.* schattenhaft; (dim) dämmerig.

Shady, *adj.* geschützt; dunkel; a — business, eine zweifelhafte Sache.

Shaft, *s.* der Schaft (*Arch., Weav., of an arrow, etc.*); der Kaminschacht (*of a chimney*); die Welle, der Wellbaum (*Mach.*); der Stiel (*of a hammer, etc.*); die Deichsel (*of a cart*); der Schacht (*Min.*). **—s,** *pl.* die Gabel (*of a carriage*).

Shagg—iness, *s.* das Zottige. **—y,** *adj.* zottig.

Shak—e, I. *ir.v.a.* schütteln; to — hands, sich (*dat.*) die Hände geben. II. *ir.v.n.* zittern, beben, schüttern (with, at, vor). III. *s.* das Schütteln; der Triller (*Mus.*).

Shako, *s.* der Tschako.

Shaky, *adj.* zitternd; unsicher, schwach.

Shale, *s.* der Schieferton.

Shall, *ir. aux. v.* werden; (must, ought, *etc.*) sollen; werden, wollen (*in pure questions*); sollen (*with questions asking permission, direction, etc.*).

Shallot, *s.* die Schalotte (*Bot.*).

Shallow, I. *adj.* seicht. II. *s.* die Untiefe.

Sham, I. *s.* der Trug. II. *v.n.* sich stellen, heucheln. III. *adj.* falsch, unecht; — fight, das Scheingefecht.

Shambl—e, *v.n.* schlenkern. **—ing,** *adj.* schlenkernd, schlotternd.

Shambles, *s.* die Schlachtbank.

Shame, I. *s.* die Scham. II. *v.a.* beschämen. **—ful,** *adj.*, **—fully,** *adv.* schändlich, schmachvoll. **—fulness,** *s.* die Schändlichkeit. **—less,** *adj.*, **—lessly,** *adv.* schamlos. **—lessness,** *s.* die Schamlosigkeit. **—-faced,** *adj.* schamhaft.

Shampoo, I. *v.a.* den Kopf waschen. II. *s.* das Haarwaschmittel.

Shank, *s.* der Schenkel.

Shape, I. *s.* die Gestalt, Form, Bildung. II. *v.a.* bilden, formen, gestalten. **—less,** *adj.* formlos, ungestalt. **—liness,** *s.* die Wohlgestalt. **—ly,** *adj.* wohlgestaltet.

Share, I. *s.* der Teil, Anteil; die Aktie (*in a joint-stock company*); to go **—s,** teilen mit. II. *v.a.* (ver)teilen, austeilen (*amongst,* unter, *acc.*); (divide) zerteilen. III. *v.n.* teilhaben (in a thing, an einer S.). **—r,** *s.* der Teilhaber, -nehmer. **—broker,** *s.* der Aktienmakler. **—holder,** *s.* der Aktieninhaber, Aktionär.

Shark, *s.* der Hai(fisch); (*fig.*) der Gauner.

Sharp, I. *adj.,* **—ly,** *adv.* scharf (*lit. & fig.*). II. *s.* das Kreuz (♯). **—en,** *v.a.* schärfen, schleifen, wetzen. **—er,** *s.* der Gauner. **—ness,** *s.* die Schärfe (*also fig.*); look **—!** paß auf! schnell! **—shooter,** *s.* der Scharfschütze. **—witted,** *adj.* scharfsinnig.

Shatter, *v.* I. *a.* zerschmettern. II. *n.* zerbrechen.

Shav—e, I. *v.a.* rasieren, barbieren. II. *v.n.* sich rasieren. III. *s.* das Rasieren; to have a close **—,** (*fig.*) entkommen mit knapper Not. **—er,** *s.* der Bartscherer. **—ings,** *pl.* die Späne. **—ing-brush,** *s.* der Rasierpinsel.

Shawl, *s.* der Schal, das Umschlagetuch.

She, I. *pers. pron.* sie; es (*referring to ships, names of countries, etc.*). II. *s.* das Weibchen (*animals, etc.*).

Sheaf, *s.* die Garbe.

Shear, *ir.v.a.* (ab)scheren. **—er,** *s.* der Scherer. **—ing,** *s.* das Scheren. **—s,** *s.* die große Schere.

Sheath, *s.* die Scheide. **—e,** *v.a.* einstecken.

Sheave, *s.* die Rolle, Scheibe (*Mech.*).

1Shed, *ir.v.a.* vergießen; abwerfen; to **—** light, Licht verbreiten.

2Shed, *s.* der Schuppen.

Sheen, *s.* der Glanz.

Sheep, *s.* (*also pl.*) das Schaf; to cast **—'s** eyes, einem verliebte Augen machen. **—ish,** *adj.,* **—ishly,** *adv.* schafsmäßig, einfältig. **—ishness,** *s.* die Blödigkeit. **—cot(e),** *s.* die Schafhürde. **—dog,** *s.* der Schäferhund. **—skin,** *s.* das Schafleder, Schaffell. **—walk,** *s.* die Schafweide.

Sheer, I. *adj.* bloß; out of **—** greed, aus reiner Gier. II. *adv.* gänzlich.

Sheet, *s.* die Breite, Fläche (*of water, etc.*); das Blatt (*of iron, etc.*); die Tafel, Scheibe (*of glass*); das Bettuch, Leintuch (*of linen, etc.*); der Bogen (*of paper*); die Schote (*Naut.*). **—anchor,** *s.* der Pflicht-, Not-anker. **—lightning,** *s.* das Wetterleuchten.

Sheik, *s.* der Scheif.

Shekel, *s.* der Sekel.

Sheldrake, *s.* die Brandente.

Shelf, *s.* der Sims, das Brett; das Fach (*in a cabinet, etc.*).

Shell, I. *s.* die Schale (*of eggs, crabs, etc., also fig.*); die Bombe (*Mil.*). II. *v.a.* schälen, aushülsen (*nuts, peas, etc.*); beschießen, bombardieren (*a town*). **—fish,** *s.* das Schaltier. **—proof,** *adj.* bombenfest.

Shellac, *s.* der Schellack.

Shelter, I. *s.* das Obdach, der Schirm; II. *v.a.* (be-)schützen, (be-)schirmen (from, vor). III. *v.r. & n.* Schutz suchen. **—less,** *adj.* obdachlos, schutzlos.

Shelv—e, *v.n.* abschüssig sein. **—ing,** *adj.* abschüssig.

Shepherd, *s.* der Schäfer, Hirte. **—ess,** *s.* die Schäferin, Hirtin.

Sherry, *s.* der Xereswein.

Shield, I. *s.* der Schild. II. *v.a.* schirmen, bedecken, behüten (from, vor, gegen).

Shift, I. *v.a.* verschieben; wegschieben; (move) umlegen. II. *v.n.* den Ort verändern; umlaufen (*as wind*). III. *s.* (change) das Wechseln; der Wechsel (*of clothing, etc.*); (resource) das Notmittel; die Schicht (*of work*). **—less,** *adj.* hilflos. **—lessness,** *s.* die Hilflosigkeit. **—y,** *adj.* unzuverlässig.

Shilling, *s.* der Schilling.

Shimmer, I. *v.n.* schimmern. II. *s.* der Schimmer.

Shin, *s.* das Schienbein.

Shine, I. *s.* der Schein, Glanz. II. *ir.v.n.* scheinen.

1Shingle, *s.* die (Dach=)Schindel.

2Shingle, *s.* der Meerkies; der Herrenschnitt (*hairdressing*).

Shingly, *adj.* grobkiesig, voller Kiesel.

Shining, *adj.* glänzend.

Ship, I. *s.* das Schiff. II. *v.a.* an Bord bringen, einschiffen. III. *v.n.* sich als Matrose verdingen. **—ment,** *s.* die Verladung; (goods **—ped**) die Ladung. **—per,** *s.* der Befrachter,

Schiffer. —**builder**, *s.* der Schiffsbaumeister. —**building**, *s.* der Schiffbau, die Schiffbaukunst. —**owner**, *s.* der Reeder. —**shape**, *adj.* nach Schiffsart; (*fig.*) richtig. —**wreck**, I. *s.* der Schiffbruch. II. *v.a.* scheitern lassen; to be —**wrecked**, scheitern. III. *v.n.* scheitern, verunglücken, Schiffbruch leiden. —**yard**, *s.* die Schiffswerft.

Shipping, *s.* die Schiffe; die Flotte (*of a country*). —**agent**, *s.* der Schiffsagent. —**charges**, *pl.* Verschiffungskosten. —**office**, *s.* das Speditionsbureau.

Shire, *s.* die Grafschaft.

Shirk, *v.a.* ausweichen; sich drücken (um eine S.) (*sl.*).

Shirt, *s.* das Hemd. —**cuffs**, *pl.* Manschetten. —**front**, *s.* das Vorhemd. —**sleeve**, *s.* der Hemdärmel; in one's —**sleeves**, in Hemdärmeln. —**stud**, *s.* der Hemdknopf.

Shiver, I. *s.* der Schauer. II. *v.n.* schauern, zittern. —**ing**, I. *adj.*, —**ingly**, *adv.* schauernd. II. *s.* das Schauern, der Schauer. —**y**, *adj.* fröstelnd.

¹**Shoal**, *s.* der Zug (*of fishes*).

²**Shoal**, I. die Untiefe; die Sandbank. II. *adj.* untief.

¹**Shock**, *s.* die Mandel, der Garbenhaufen (*of sheaves*).

²**Shock**, I. *s.* der Stoß, Anstoß. II. *v.a.* (an)stoßen, einen Stoß geben; Ärgernis geben; to be —**ed at**, empört sein über, verletzt sein durch. —**ing**, *adj.*, —**ingly**, *adv.* unerhört, schrecklich.

³**Shock**, *s.*; — of hair, der dichte Haarschopf.

Shoddy, I. *s.* die Trümmer-, Lumpenwolle. II. *adj.* lumpenwollen; (*fig.*) unecht.

Shoe, I. *s.* der Schuh; das Hufeisen (*of horses*). II. *ir.v.a.* beschuhen; beschlagen (*horses*). —**black**, *s.* der Schuhputzer. —**blacking**, *s.* die Schuhwichse. —**horn**, *s.* der Schuhanzieher. —**ing-smith**, *s.* der Hufschmied. —**lace**, *s.* der Schuhriemen, das Schuhband. —**maker**, *s.* der Schuhmacher, Schuster.

Shoot, I. *ir.v.n.* schießen; (*fig.*) ein-, durch-dringen; to — at, schießen nach. II. *ir.v.a.* schießen (*also fig.*); abschießen, abfeuern (*guns*); vorschieben (*a bolt*). —**er**, *s.* der Schießende.

—**ing**, I. *s.* das Schießen; to go —ing, auf die Jagd gehen. II. *adj.* stechend (*as pain*). —**ing-box**, *s.* das Jagdhäuschen. —**ing-range**, *s.* der Schießplatz. —**ing-star**, die Sternschnuppe.

Shop, I. *s.* der Laden; to talk — Fach simpeln. II. *v.n.* Einkäufe machen; to go —ping, einkaufen gehen. —**fittings**, *pl.* die Ladeneinrichtungen. — **girl**, *s.* die Verkäuferin, das Ladenfräulein. —**keeper**, *s.* der Ladeninhaber, Krämer. —**lifter**, *s.* der Ladendieb. —**man**, *s.* der Ladendiener. —**walker**, *s.* der Ladenaufseher.

Shore, *s.* das Ufer, Gestade.

Short, *adj. & adv.* kurz (*also fig.*); klein (*in figure*); — circuit, der Kurzschluß (*Elec.*); to make — work of, es kurz machen mit; to cut —, plötzlich unterbrechen; — wave, die Kurzwelle (*Radio*); nothing — of, nichts Geringeres als; — of money, knapp an Geld. —**age**, *s.* der Mangel (of, an, *dat.*). —**en**, *v.* I. *a.* (ver)kürzen; (curtail) abkürzen; stutzen (*hair*); einziehen (*sail*). II. *n.* kürzer werden; abnehmen (*as days*). —**ly**, *adv.* bald. —**ness**, *s.* die Kürze. —**coming**, *s.* die Schwäche. —**hand**, *s.* die Kurzschrift, Stenographie. —**handed**, *adj.* mit zu wenig Arbeitskräften versehen. —**sighted**, *adj.* kurzsichtig. —**sightedness**, *s.* die Kurzsichtigkeit (*also fig.*). —**tempered**, *adj.* heftig, reizbar.

¹**Shot**, *adj.* schillernd, changierend.

²**Shot**, *s.* der Schuß; das Geschoß, die Kugel (*for guns*); small —, das Schrot; like a —, sofort, blitzschnell; to make a bad —, fehlschießen; falsch raten; a dead —, ein nie fehlender Schütze. —**proof**, *adj.* kugelfest.

Should, *imperf. of* Shall; if I —, sollte ich.

Shoulder, I. *s.* die Schulter. II. *v.a.* mit der Schulter stoßen; — arms! Gewehr auf! —**blade**, *s.* das Schulterblatt. —**knot**, *s.* die Epaulette (*Mil.*). —**straps**, *pl.* die Achselklappen (*Mil.*).

Shout, I. *s.* das Geschrei. II. *v.n.* laut schreien. —**er**, *s.* der Schreier. —**ing**, *s.* das Geschrei.

Shove, I. *v.a.* schieben, stoßen. II. *s.* der Schub, Stoß.

Shovel, I. *s.* die Schaufel. II. *v.a.* schaufeln.

Show, I. *ir.v.a.* zur Schau stellen; (point out) zeigen, weisen; (prove) dartun; erzeigen, erweisen (*kindness, etc.*); zeigen, führen (*the way*). II. *ir.v.n.* erscheinen, beweisen; to — off, im besten Lichte erscheinen lassen. III. *s.* die Schau (*also fig.*): die Ausstellung; (appearance) der Anschein, Anblick; dumb —, das Gebärdenspiel; on —, zu besehen. **—ily,** *adv.,* —y, *adj.* prunkhaft, prahlend. **—iness,** *s.* der Prunk. **—card,** *s.* die Musterkarte, Geschäftsanzeige. **—case,** *s.* das Schaukästchen. **—man,** *s.* der Schausteller. **—room,** *s.* das Ausstellungszimmer. **—window,** *s.* das Schaufenster.

Shower, I. *s.* der (Regen=)Guß; das Schauer. II. *v.a.* (— down on) herabschütten auf (*acc.*). **—iness,** *s.* das Regnerische. **—y,** *adj.* regnerisch; —y weather, das Regenwetter. **—bath,** *s.* das Sturzbad, die Dusche, die Brause.

Shrapnel, *s.* die (Granat=)Kartätsche, der, das Schrapnell.

Shred, I. *s.* der Fetzen. II. *v.a.* zerfetzen.

¹Shrew, *s.* die Zänkerin. **—ish,** *adj.* zänkisch.

²Shrew, **—mouse,** *s.* die Spitzmaus.

Shrewd, *adj.,* —ly, *adv.* scharfsinnig. **—ness,** *s.* der Scharfsinn.

Shriek, I. *s.* das Gekreisch(e). II. *v.n.* (laut auf=)schreien, kreischen.

Shrill, *adj.,* —y, *adv.* gellend, grell. **—ness,** *s.* das Gellende.

Shrimp, *s.* die Garneele; (*fig.*) der Knirps.

Shrine, *s.* der Heiligen= (for relics, Reliquien=)schrein; der Altar.

Shrink, *ir.v.n.* ein=, zusammenschrumpfen; (recoil) zurückfahren; to — at, sich entsetzen vor. **—age,** *s.* das Eingehen (*of cloth, etc.*); (*fig.*) die Verminderung. **—ing,** I. *adj.* einschrumpfend. II. *s.* die Zusammenziehung; das Ausweichen.

Shrive, *irr.v.a.* (einem) die Buße abnehmen, beichten lassen.

Shrivel, *v.n.* einschrumpfen.

¹Shroud, I. *s.* die Leichenhülle. II. *v.a.* (ein)hüllen.

²Shroud, *s.* das Wanttau, Haupttau. **—s,** *pl.* die Wanten.

Shrove—tide, *s.* die Fastenzeit. — **Tuesday,** *s.* die Fastnacht.

Shrub, *s.* der Strauch, Busch.

Shrug, I. *s.* das Achselzucken. II. *v.a. & n.*; to — (the shoulders), (die Achseln) zucken.

Shudder, I. *v.n.* schaudern. II. *s.* der Schauder, das Zittern. **—ing,** *adj.,* —ingly, *adv.* schaudernd, zitternd.

Shuffl—e, I. *v.a.* mischen (*cards*). II. *v.n.* schlürfen, die Füße nachschleppen (*in walking*). III. *s.* das Mischen (*of cards*); die Ausflucht, der Kunstgriff. **—er,** *s.* der Mischer; einer, der Ausflüchte sucht. **—ing,** I. *adj.,* —ingly, *adv.* ausweichend. II. *s.* das Kartenmischen; die Ausflucht.

Shun, *v.a.* meiden.

Shunt, I. *v.a.* rangieren (*Railw.*). II. *v.n.* auf ein Nebengleis fahren, einlenken. **—ing-station,** *s.* der Rangierbahnhof.

Shut, *ir.v.* I. *a.* (ver)schließen, zumachen. II. *n.* sich schließen.

Shutter, *s.* einer, der schließt, zumacht 2c.; (window —) der Fensterladen.

Shuttle, *s.* das Schiffchen. **—cock,** *s.* der Federball.

Shy, I. *v.n.* scheu sein *or* werden; to — at, sich scheuen vor. II. *v.a.* (*slang*) werfen. III. *adj.,* —ly, *adv.* scheu (*also of beasts*), schüchtern; to fight — of, jemandem aus dem Wege gehen. **—er,** *s.* das scheue Pferd. **—ness,** *s.* die Scheu, Schüchternheit.

Sick, I. *adj.* krank. II. *s.*; the —, die Kranken. **—en,** *v.* I. *n.* siechen, erkranken, krank werden. II. *a.* Übelkeit erregen; (*fig.*) anekeln. **—liness,** *s.* die Kränklichkeit; die Ungesundheit (*of a climate*). **—ly,** *adj.* kränklich. **—ness,** *s.* die Krankheit; (nausea) die Übelkeit.

Sickle, *s.* die Sichel.

Side, I. *s.* die Seite. II. *adj.* Seiten=. III. *v.n.* Partei nehmen (with, für; against, gegen). **—d,** *adj.* =seitig. **—arms,** *pl.* das Seitengewehr (*Mil.*). **—board,** *s.* das Büffet. **—face,** *s.* die Seitenansicht, das Profil. **—saddle,** *s.* der Frauen=, Quer=sattel. **—walk,** *s.* der Bürgersteig. **—ways, —wise,** *adv.* seitwärts, von der Seite.

Sidereal, *adj.* Sternen=, Stern=.

Siding, *s.* das Nebengeleise (*Railw.*).

Siege, *s.* die Belagerung.

Sieve, *s.* das Sieb.

Sift, *v.a.* sieben, sichten.

Sigh, I. *s.* der Seufzer. II. *v.n.* seuf=
zen (after, for, nach).

Sight, *s.* das Gesicht, die Sehkraft;
(*fig.*) das Auge; das (Richt=)Korn,
Visier (*on a rifle*); second —, zweites
Gesicht, das Hellsehen; to be out of —,
aus den Augen. —ed, *adj.* =sichtig.
—less, *adj.* blind. —liness, *s.* die
Wohlgestalt. —ly, *adj.* wohlgestalt(et),
schön. —-seer, *s.* der Schaulustige;
to take —, visieren.

Sign, I. *s.* das Zeichen; (nod, *etc.*) der
Wink. II. *v.a.* unterzeichnen, =schrei=
ben. III. *v.n.* ein Zeichen geben,
winken (to someone, einem).

Signal, I. *s.* das Signal (*Naut., Railw.*).
II. *adj.,* —ly, *adv.* bemerkenswert.
III. *v.n.* Signale geben, durch Signale
anzeigen. —man, *s.* der Bahnwärter.

Signature, *s.* die eigenhändige Unter=
schrift.

Sign-board, *s.* das (Aushänge=)Schild.

Signer, *s.* der Unterzeichner.

Signet, *s.* das Siegel.

Signif—icance, —icancy, *s.* die Be=
deutung. **—icant,** *adj.,* **—icantly,**
adv. bedeutungsvoll. **—y,** *v.* I. *a.*
andeuten, anzeigen. II. *n.* it doesn't
—y, es hat nichts zu bedeuten.

Sign-post, *s.* der Wegweiser.

Silen—ce, I. *s.* das (Still=)Schweigen.
II. *int.* still! Ruhe! III. *v.a.* zum
Schweigen bringen. **—cer,** *s.* der
Störungsdämpfer (*Radio*). **—t,** *adj.,*
—tly, *adv.* still, schweigend.

Silhouette, *s.* der Schattenriß.

Silk, I. *s.* die Seide; sewing —,
Nähseide. II. *adj.* seiden. **—worm,**
s. die Seidenraupe.

Sill, *s.* das Gesims.

Sill—ily, *adv.,* **—y,** *adj.* albern. **—i-
ness,** *s.* die Albernheit.

Silt, *s.* der Schlamm.

Silver, I. *s.* das Silber. II. *adj.*
silbern. **—y,** *adj.* silbern, Silber=.
—-plating, *s.* die Silberplattierung.

Simil—ar, *adj.,* **—arly,** *adv.* ähnlich,
gleich. **—arity,** *s.* die Ähnlichkeit,
Gleichartigkeit. **—e,** *s.* das Gleichnis.

Simmer, *v.n.* gelinde kochen.

Simoom, *s.* der Samum.

Simper, I. *s.* das gezierte Lächeln.
II. *v.n.* geziert lächeln.

Simpl—e, I. *adj.* einfach (*also fig., Bot.,
Chem.*); (foolish) einfältig. II. *s.* das
Heilkraut. **—eton,** *s.* der Einfalts=
pinsel. **—icity,** *s.* die Einfachheit.

—ify, *v.a.* vereinfachen. **—y,** *adv.*
einfach. **—e-minded,** *adj.* arglos.

Simul—ate, *v.a.* (er)heucheln, nach=
machen, vorgeben. **—ated,** *adj.* ge=
heuchelt. **—ation,** *s.* die Verstellung.

Simultaneous, *adj.,* **—ly,** *adv.* gleich=
zeitig. **—ness,** *s.* die Gleichzeitigkeit.

Sin, I. *s.* die Sünde. II. *v.n.* sündigen,
sich vergehen (against a person, an
einem, gegen einen). III. *v.a.*; to —
a —, eine Sünde begehen. **—ful,** *adj.,*
—fully, *adv.* sündhaft, sündlich (as an
action, etc.). **—fulness,** *s.* die Sünd=
haftigkeit; die Sündlichkeit. **—less,**
adj., **—lessly,** *adv.* sündenfrei, sünd=
(en)los. **—lessness,** *s.* die Sünd=
losigkeit.

Since, I. *adv.* seitdem; long —, lange
her; how long —? seit wann? II.
prep. seit. III. *conj.* da (einmal),
weil; seit(dem).

Sincer—e, *adj.,* **—ely,** *adv.* aufrichtig,
redlich; yours —ely, Ihr ergebener.
—ity, *s.* die Aufrichtigkeit, Redlichkeit.

Sinew, *s.* die Sehne, Flechse. **—y,**
adj. sehnig.

Sing, *ir.v.a. & n.* singen. **—er,** *s.* der
Sänger, die Sängerin. **—ing,** I. *adj.*
singend. II. *s.* das Singen.

Singe, *v.a.* (ver)sengen.

Sing—le, I. *adj.* einzig; (individual)
einzeln; (unmarried) unverheiratet,
ledig; in —le file, im Gänsemarsch.
II. *v.a.* (—le out) aus=lesen, =wählen,
=sondern. **—ly,** *adv.* einzeln. **—-
breasted,** *adj.* einreihig. **—handed,**
adj. einhändig; allein; auf eigne
Faust. **—-hearted, —-minded,** *adj.*
aufrichtig, redlich.

Singsong, I. *s.* der Singsang. II. *adj.*
eintönig.

Singular, I. *adj.,* **—ly,** *adv.* seltsam.
II. *s.* der Singular. **—ity,** *s.* die
Sonderbarkeit.

Sinister, *adj.* link; finster, unheil=
drohend.

Sink, I. *ir.v.n.* sinken. II. *ir.v.a.*
(ver)senken. III. *s.* der Guß=, der
Ausguß-stein (*in a kitchen, etc.*). **—
ing,** *s.* das Sinken, Untergehen; das
Einsinken (*Build.*). **—ing-fund,** *s.*
der Tilgungsfonds.

Sinner, *s.* der Sünder, die Sünderin.

Sip, I. *s.* das Schlückchen. II. *v.a.*
nippen.

Siphon, *s.* der (Saug=)Heber; die
Siphonflasche (*for soda-water*).

Sir, *s.* Herr (*in addressing*). **—e,** *s.* Sire (*in addressing a sovereign, etc.*); (parent) der Vater.

Siren, *s.* die Sirene.

Sirloin, *s.* das Lendenstück.

Sirocco, *s.* der Sirokko.

Siskin, *s.* der Zeisig.

Sister, *s.* die Schwester (*also fig.*). **—ly,** *adj.* schwesterlich. **—in-law,** *s.* die Schwägerin.

Sit, *ir.v.* I. *n.* sitzen (*also Sport.*); to — down, niedersitzen, sich setzen; to — up, sich aufrichten; (not go to bed) aufbleiben. II. *a.* sitzen. **—ter,** *s.* der, die Sitzende. **—ting,** I. *s.* das Sitzen. II. *adj.* sitzend. **—ting-room,** *s.* das Wohnzimmer.

Site, *s.* die Lage; der Bauplatz.

Situa—te(d), *adj.* liegend. **—tion,** *s.* die Lage; die Stelle; (*fig.*) der Zustand.

Six, I. *num. adj.* sechs; 6 o'c., sechs Uhr. II. *s.* die Sechs; at —es and sevens, in völliger Verwirrung. **—teen,** *adj.* sechzehn. **—teenth,** I. *adj.* sechzehnt. II. *s.* das Sechzehntel. **—th,** I. *adj.* sechst. II. *s.* das Sechstel; die Sexte (*Mus.*). **—thly,** *adv.* sechstens. **—tieth,** *adj.* sechzigst. **—ty,** *s.* die Sechzig.

¹Size, *s.* (bulk, *etc.*) der Umfang, die Größe; das Format (*of a book*); middle —d, von mittlerer Größe.

²Size, I. *s.* der Leim. II. *v.a.* leimen.

¹Skat—e, I. *s.* der Schlittschuh. II. *v.n.* Schlittschuh laufen. **—ing,** *s.* das Schlittschuhlaufen. **—ing-rink,** *s.* die Eisbahn, Rollschuhbahn.

²Skate, *s.* die Glattroche (*Icht.*).

Skein, *s.* der Strang, die Strähne.

Skeleton, *s.* das Gerippe (*also Carp.*), Skelett.

Sketch, I. *s.* die Skizze. II. *v.a.* skizzieren. III. *v.n.* zeichnen. **—er,** *s.* der Skizzenzeichner. **—y,** *adj.* skizzenhaft.

Skew, *adj.* schief.

Skewer, *s.* der Speiler, der Fleischspieß.

Ski, I. *s.* der Ski, der Schneeschuh. II. *v.n.* auf Stien laufen. **—ing,** *s.* das Stilaufen.

Skid, I. *s.* der Hemmschuh. II. *v.a.* hemmen. III. *v.n.* ausrutschen (*Cycl.*).

Skiff, *s.* der Kahn, das Schiffchen.

Skil—ful, *adj.* **—fully,** *adv.* geschickt, gewandt. **—l,** (—fulness,) *s.* die Geschicklichkeit, Gewandtheit. **—less,** *adj.* ungeschickt.

Skillet, *s.* der Tiegel.

Skim, *v.a.* abrahmen (milk, *etc.*); (— over) streifen; flüchtig durchblättern (a book). **—mer,** *s.* der Schaumlöffel. **—milk,** *s.* Magermilch.

Skimp, I. *v.n.* knausern. II. *v.a.* sich (*dat.*) etwas verkneifen.

Skin, I. *s.* die Haut (of men and beasts); das Fell (of beasts); die Schale (of fruit). II. *v.a.* häuten. III. *v.n.* sich häuten. **—ned,** *adj.* -häutig. **—niness,** *s.* die Magerkeit. **—ny,** *adj.* mager. **—flint,** *s.* der Geizhals.

Skip, I. *v.a.* überhüpfen. II. *v.n.* seilhüpfen. III. *s.* der Hupf, Sprung.

¹Skipper, *s.* der Hüpfer; der, die Seilspringende (with a rope).

²Skipper, *s.* der Kapitän.

Skipping, *s.* das (Seil-)Springen ꝛc. **—rope,** *s.* das Springseil (for children).

Skirmish, I. *s.* das Scharmützel. II. *v.n.* scharmützeln. **—er,** *s.* der Plänkler.

Skirt, I. *s.* der (Unter-)Rock (of a woman's dress); der Schoß (of a coat). II. *v.a.* am Rande sein; (also *v.n.* to — along) den Saum entlang laufen. **—ing,** *s.* die Fußleiste.

Skit, *s.* die Stichelei. **—tish,** *adj.* **—tishly,** *adv.* scheu, leichtfertig, unbeständig.

Skittle, *s.* der Kegel. **—alley,** or **—ground,** *s.* die Kegelbahn; to play —s, Kegel schieben.

Skulk, *v.n.* lauern. **—er,** *s.* der Laurer, Schleicher.

Skull, *s.* die Hirnschale, der Hirnschädel.

Skunk, *s.* das Stinktier.

Sky, *s.* der Wolken-, Lufthimmel, Luftraum. **—lark,** *s.* die Feldlerche. **—larking,** *s.* das Possenreißen. **—light,** *s.* das Oberlicht, das Dachfenster. **—scraper,** *s.* der Wolkenkratzer (coll.).

Slab, *s.* die Platte; a — of chocolate, eine Tafel Schokolade.

Slack, I. *adj.,* **—ly,** *adv.* schlaff, locker; — water, das Totwasser; — tide, stilles Wasser. II. *s.* der Kohlengrus. **—en,** *v.* I. *n.* schlaff werden, erschlaffen. II. *a.* nachlassen (a rope); to —en speed, die Geschwindigkeit vermindern. **—ness,** *s.* die Schlaffheit; die Flauheit (of business).

Slag, *s.* die Schlacke (of metals, *etc.*).

Slake, *v.a.* löschen, dämpfen.

Slam, I. *v.a.* zuschlagen (*a door, etc.*); (strike down) hinschmeißen. II. *v.n.* heftig zuschlagen. III. *s.* das Zuwerfen; der Schlemm (*Cards*).

Slander, I. *s.* die Verleumdung. II. *v.a.* verleumden, verunglimpfen. —**er,** *s.* der Verleumder, Lästerer. —**ous,** *adj.,* —**ously,** *adv.* verleumderisch, Läster-.

Slang, *s.* das Rotwelsch; thieves' —, die Gaunersprache.

Slant, I. *v.a.* eine schiefe *or* schräge Richtung geben. II. *s.* die Schräge. —**ing,** *adj.,* —**ingly,** *adv.,* —**wise,** *adv.* schief, schräg.

Slap, I. *s.* der Klaps. II. *v.a.* klapsen, schlagen. —**dash,** *adv.* plötzlich; übereilt, oberflächlich, nachlässig.

Slash, I. *v.a.* aufschlitzen. II. *v.n.* (um sich) hauen. III. *s.* der Hieb, Streich.

Slat, *s.* die dünne Schiene, Leiste.

¹Slate, I. *s.* der Schiefer. II. *v.a.* mit Schiefer decken. III. *adj.* Schiefer-, schieferfarbig. —**r,** *s.* der Schieferdecker.

²Slate, *v.a.* ausschelten.

Slattern, *s.* die Schlumpe.

Slaughter, I. *s.* das Gemetzel, Blutbad. II. *v.a.* schlachten (*also cattle*). —**er,** *s.* der Schlächter. —**ous,** *adj.,* —**ously,** *adv.* mörderisch. —**house,** *s.* das Schlachthaus.

Slave, I. *s.* der (die) Sklav(in); (*fig.*) der Knecht. II. *v.n.* sich placken.

¹Slaver, *s.* das Sklavenschiff. —**y,** *s.* die Sklaverei, Knechtschaft.

²Slaver, *v.a.* begeifern.

Slavish, *adj.,* —**ly,** *adv.* sklavisch, knechtisch.

Slay, *ir.v.a.* erschlagen, töten. —**er,** *s.* der Totschläger.

¹Sledge, *s.* der Schlitten.

²Sledge, *s.,* —**hammer,** *s.* der Schmiedehammer.

Sleek, I. *adj.* glatt. II. *v.a.* glatt machen. —**ness,** *s.* die Glätte.

Sleep, I. *ir.v.n.* schlafen (*also fig.*); (go to —) einschlafen; —ing partner, stiller Teilhaber. II. *ir.v.a.* schlafen. III. *s.* der Schlaf. —**er,** *s.* der Schläfer; die Schwelle (*Railw.*). —**ily,** *adv.,* —**y,** *adj.* schläfrig. —**iness,** *s.* die Schläfrigkeit. —**less,** *adj.,* —**lessly,** *adv.* schlaflos; (*fig.*) ruhelos. —**walker,** *s.* der Nachtwandler. —**walking,** I. *s.* das Nachtwandeln. II. *adj.* nachtwandelnd.

Sleet, I. *s.* die Graupeln. II. *v.n.* graupeln.

Sleeve, *s.* der Ärmel; he has something up his —, er führt etwas im Schilde. —**link,** *s.* der Manschettenknopf.

Sleigh, *s.* der Schlitten. —**ing,** *s.* das Schlittenfahren.

Sleight, *s.* der Kunstgriff; — of hand, der Taschenspielerstreich, das Kunststück.

Slender, *adj.,* —**ly,** *adv.* schlank. —**ness,** *s.* die Schlankheit.

Sleuth-hound, *s.* der Spürhund, Bluthund.

Slice, I. *s.* der Schnitt; a — of bread, eine Scheibe Brot. II. *v.a.* zerschneiden.

Slid—e, I. *ir.v.n.* gleiten, schlüpfen. II. *ir.v.a.* gleiten, schlüpfen. III. *s.* die Schleifbahn. —**er,** *s.* der Gleitende. —**ing,** I. *adj.* gleitend; —ing doors, die Schiebetüren; —ing scale, die bewegliche Skala; —ing staircase, die bewegliche Treppe. II. *s.* das Gleiten.

Slight, I. *adj.,* —**ly,** *adv. see* Slender; gering, klein. II. *v.a.* geringschätzig behandeln. III. *s.* die Geringschätzung. —**ingly,** *adv.* geringschätzig.

Slim, *adj.,* —**ly,** *adv.* schlank. —**ness,** *s.* die Schmächtigkeit.

Slim—e, *s.* der Schlamm. —**iness,** *s.* das Schleimige. —**y,** *adj.* schlammig.

Sling, I. *s.* die Binde (*Surg., etc.*); die Schleuder (*for hurling*). II. *ir.v.a.* schleudern, werfen; anhängen (*hammocks*).

Slink, *ir.v.n.* schleichen; to — away, sich aus dem Staube machen.

Slip, I. *s.* das (Aus-)Gleiten, (Ab-)Glitschen; (false step) der Fehltritt (*also fig.*); der Streifen (*of paper, etc.*); der Überzug (*of a pillow*); die Fahne (*Typ.*); a — of a girl, schmächtiges junges Mädchen; — of the pen, der Schreibfehler; to give a person the —, einen im Stich lassen; II. *v.a.* schlüpfen, gleiten lassen; loslassen (*dogs*); schlippen lassen (*a cable*); to — in, einfließen lassen; to — on, to — off, hurtig (an)ziehen, ausziehen (*clothes, etc.*). III. *v.n.* schlüpfen, gleiten; (blunder) fehlen; (escape) entschlüpfen; to — away, sich wegstehlen. —**per,** *s.* der Pan-

toffel. **—periness,** *s.* die Schlüpfrig=
keit (*also fig.*). **—pery,** *adj.* schlüpfrig.
—shod, *adj.* nachlässig (*of style*).
Slit, I. *ir.v.a.* aufschlitzen. II. *s.*
der Schlitz, die Spalte.
Sliver, *s.* der Splitter.
Slobber, *v.* I. *n.* geifern. II. *a.* be=
geifern. **—er,** *s.* der Geiferer.
Sloe, *s.* die Schlehe, der Schwarzdorn.
Slog, *s.* der Schlag, Puff (*coll.*).
Slogan, *s.* das Kriegsgeschrei; die
Reklame (*coll.*).
Sloop, *s.* die Schaluppe.
Slop, *v.a.* verschütten (*water, etc.*).
—s, *pl.* Krankensuppen; (dirty water,
etc.) das Spülicht. **—py,** *adj.* naß,
schmutzig. **—basin,** *s.* der Spül=
napf. **—pail,** *s.* der Spüleimer.
Slop—e, I. *s.* die Schräge. II. *v.n.*
sich neigen, abhängen. III. *v.a.* ab=
schüssig machen; (incline) neigen,
senken; **—e arms!** Gewehr über!
—ewise, *adv.* schräg, abschüssig. **—**
ingly, *adv.* schräg, abschüssig.
Slot, *s.* die Ritze, der Spalt. **—**
machine, *s.* der Automat.
Sloth, *s.* das Faultier (*Zool.*); *see*
—fulness, —ful, *adj.,* **—fully,** *adv.*
träge, faul. **—fulness,** *s.* die Träg=
heit, Faulheit.
Slouch, *v.n.* schlaff einhergehen, den
Kopf hängen lassen.
¹Slough, *s.* der Morast.
²Slough, I. *s.* die abgestreifte leere
Haut (*of a serpent*); der Schorf (*of
a wound*). II. *v.n.* (— off) sich
ablösen (*from the sound flesh*); sich
häuten (*as serpents, etc.*).
Sloven, *s.* der Schmutzhammel. **—**
liness, *s.* die Nachlässigkeit. **—ly,**
adj. unordentlich.
Slow, *adj.,* **—ly,** *adv.* langsam; my
watch is —, meine Uhr geht nach.
—ness, *s.* die Langsamkeit. **—match,**
s. die Lunte (*Artil.*). **—worm,** *s.*
die Blindschleiche.
¹Slug, *s.* die Wegschnecke.
²Slug, *s.* die Kugel.
Slug—gard, I. *s.* der Faulenzer. II.
adj. träg, faul. **—gish,** *adj.,* **—**
gishly, *adv.* träg, schwerfällig.
Sluice, *s.* die Schleuse.
Slum, *s.* das Hintergäßchen.
Slumber, I. *s.* der Schlummer. II.
v.n. schlummern.
Slump, *s.* das Sinken der Preise, der
Krach.

Slur, I. *s.* der Flecken; das Schleif=
Winde=zeichen (*Mus.*). II. *v.a.* be=
flecken; schleifen (*Mus.*).
Slush, *s.* der weiche Kot, der Matsch,
der Schlamm. **—y,** *adj.* schlackerig.
Slut, *s.* die Lumpe. **—tish,** *adj.*
schlumpig, schmutzig.
Sly, *adj.,* **—ly,** *adv.* schlau, listig. **—**
ness, *s.* die Schlauheit, Verschlagen=
heit. **—boots,** *s.* der Schlauberger.
¹Smack, I. *s.* der (Bei)Geschmack. II.
v.n. schmecken.
²Smack, *s.* die Schmack(e) (*Naut.*).
³Smack, I. *s.* das Schmatzen (*with the
lips*); (kiss) der Schmatz; (blow)
der Patsch. II. *v.a.* schmatzen; (beat)
patschen. III. *int.* patsch!
Small, *adj.* klein; (narrow) schmal; to
make a person feel —, jemanden
beschämen; the — hours, die frühen
Stunden; — arms, Handfeuerwaffen.
—ish, *adj.* ziemlich klein, ziemlich
dünn. **—ness,** *s.* die Kleinheit ꝛc.
—pox, *s.* die Pocken, Blattern. **—**
talk, *s.* das Geschwätz.
Smart, I. *adj.,* **—ly,** *adv.* heftig, leb=
haft (*as pain, a blow*); witzig (*of
people, words, etc.*); (spruce) geputzt,
schmuck, schneidig, fein, elegant. II.
s. der Schmerz. III. *v.n.* weh tun
(*as a wound*), schmerzen; you shall —
for it, du sollst es büßen. **—en,**
v.a.; to **—en up, auf=, heraus=putzen**
(*coll.*). **—ness,** *s.* die Schärfe (*of
wit, etc.*); die Schneidigkeit (*of
people*); die Schmuckheit.
Smash, I. *v.a.* zerschmettern, zerschmei=
ßen. II. *v.n.* zusammenbrechen. III.
s. das Zerschmeißen.
Smattering, *s.* die Halbwisserei, ober=
flächliche Kenntnis.
Smear, *v.a.;* to — (with), beschmie=
ren (mit).
Smell, I. *s.* der Geruch, Geruchssinn.
II. *ir.v.a.* riechen (eine S., an einer
S.). III. *ir.v.n.* riechen (of, nach).
—ing, *s.* das Riechen; der Geruch.
—ing-bottle, *s.* das Riechfläschchen.
—ing-salts, *pl.* die Riechsalze.
¹Smelt, *v.a.* schmelzen. **—er,** *s.* der
Schmelzarbeiter. **—ing-furnace,** *s.*
der Schmelzofen.
²Smelt, *s.* der Stint (*Icht.*).
Smil—e, I. *s.* das Lächeln. II. *v.n.*
lächeln. III. *v.a.* (zu)lächeln (*approval, etc.*). **—ing,** I. *adj.,* **—ingly,**
adv. lächelnd. II. *s.* das Lächeln.

Smirch, *v.a.* beschmutzen.

Smirk, I. *s.* das Schmunzeln. II. *v.n.* schmunzeln.

Smit—e, *ir.v.a.* & *n.* schlagen. **—ten,** *p.p.* getroffen.

Smith, *s.* der Schmied. **—y,** *s.* die Schmiede.

Smock, I. *s.* das Frauenhemd. II. *v.a.* fälteln. **—frock,** *s.* der Arbeitskittel.

Smok—e, I. *v.n.* rauchen; Tabak rauchen. II. *v.a.* rauchen (*tobacco*); räuchern (*hams, etc.*). III. *s.* der Rauch; das Rauchen. **—eless,** *adj.* rauchlos. **—er,** *s.* der Raucher. **—ily,** *adv.*, **—y,** *adj.* rauchig, voll Rauch. **—iness,** *s.* das Rauchige. **—ing,** I. *s.*; no **—ing** allowed! das Rauchen ist verboten! II. *adj.* dampfend, rauchend.

Smooth, I. *adj.*, **—ly,** *adv.* glatt. II. *v.a.* glätten, ebnen. **—ness,** *s.* die Glätte (*also fig.*). **—ing-iron,** *s.* das Plätt=, Bügel=eisen.

Smother, *v.a.* & *n.* ersticken (*also fig.*).

Smoulder, *v.n.* glimmen (*also fig.*); qualmen, schwelen.

Smudge, I. *s.* der Schmutzfleck. II. *v.a.* beschmutzen.

Smug, *adj.* schmuck; spießbürgerlich.

Smuggl—e, *v.a.* schmuggeln, Schleich=handel treiben. **—er,** *s.* der Schmuggler, Schleichhändler. **—ing,** *s.* die Schmuggelei, der Schleichhandel.

Smut, *s.* der Schmutz. **—ty,** *adj.* schmutzig.

Snack, *s.* der Imbiß; to go **—s,** teilen (*coll.*).

Snaffle, *s.* die Trense. **—bit,** *s.* das Trensengebiß.

Snag, *s.* die Knagge.

Snail, *s.* die Schnecke. **—shell,** *s.* das Schneckenhaus.

Snak—e, *s.* die Schlange. **—y,** *adj.* schlangenartig.

Snap, I. *v.n.* schnappen (at, nach); (break) (zer=)springen. II. *v.a.* schnappen; (seize) haschen, erschnappen; (crack) klatschen; to — one's fingers at (a person), (einem) ein Schnipp=chen schlagen. III. *s.* der Knack, Klatsch; der Schnepper (*of bracelets, etc.*). **—pish,** *adj.*, **—pishly,** *adv.* bissig, beißend (*as dogs*); (*fig.*) schnippisch. **—dragon,** *s.* das Löwen=maul (*Bot.*). **—shot,** *s.* die Moment=aufnahme (*Phot.*).

Snare, I. *s.* die Schlinge, der Fallstrick.

II. *v.a.* verstricken. **—r,** *s.* der Fal=lensteller.

Snarl, *v.n.* knurren (*as a dog*); (*fig.*) mur=ren. **—ing,** *adj.* knurrend, mürrisch.

Snatch, I. *s.* das Haschen; by **—es,** dann und wann. II. *v.n.* schnappen, haschen (at, nach). III. *v.a.* erhaschen; (— away) wegreißen; (— up) schnell aufraffen.

Sneak, I. *s.* der Schleicher. II. *v.n.* schleichen. **—ing,** *adj.*, **—ingly,** *adv.* kriechend, schleichend.

Sneer, I. *s.* das Hohnlächeln. II. *v.n.* (— at) höhnisch lachen (über einen). III. *v.a.* verlachen, verhöhnen. **—ing,** I. *adj.* höhnisch. II. *s.* das Naserümpfen, Sticheln.

Sneeze, I. *s.* das Niesen. II. *v.n.* niesen.

Sniff, *v.a.* & *n.* schnüffeln.

Snigger, I. *v.n.* kichern. II. *s.* das Kichern, Gekicher.

Snip, *v.a.* schnippen. **—pings,** *pl.* die Schnitzel.

Snipe, I. *s.* die Schnepfe. II. *v.a.* aus dem Hinterhalt schießen.

Snivel, *v.n.* schnüffeln. **—ling,** I. *adj.* triefnasig. II. *s.* das Greinen, Heulen.

Snob, *s.* der Philister. **—bish,** *adj.*, **—bishly,** *adv.* aufgeblasen. **—bish=ness,** *s.* die Vornehmtuerei.

Snooze, *s.* I. das Schläfchen. II. *v.n.* schlummern.

Snore, I. *s.* das Schnarchen. II. *v.n.* schnarchen. **—r,** *s.* der Schnarcher.

Snort, *v.n.* schnauben, schnaufen (*as horses*).

Snout, *s.* die Schnauze (*of dogs*); der Rüssel (*of pigs*).

Snow, I. *s.* der Schnee. II. *v.n.* schneien. **—y,** *adj.* schneeig; (— white) schneeweiß. **—drift,** *s.* die Schneewehe. **—drop,** *s.* das Schnee=glöckchen. **—flake,** *s.* die Schneeflocke. **—storm,** *s.* der Schneesturm.

Snub, I. *v.a.* stutzen. II. *s.* der Rück=stoß. **—nose,** *s.* die Stumpfnase.

Snuff, I. *s.* der Schnupftabak; die Schnuppe (*of a candle*). II. *v.n.* (Tabak) schnupfen. III. *v.a.* (— up) (ein)schnupfen. **—ers,** *pl.* die Licht=schere, =putze. **—le,** I. *v.n.* schnüffeln. II. *s.* das Näseln. **—box,** *s.* die Schnupftabaksdose.

Snug, *adj.*, **—ly,** *adv.* angeschmiegt; bequem, behaglich.

So, I. *adv.* so; (thus) also, auf diese

Art; I hope —, ich hoffe es; I told him —, das sagte ich ihm; he speaks German, — do I, er spricht Deutsch und ich auch. II. *conj.* so; (provided that) wofern, wenn nur; — that, damit. —and—, *s.* so und so; Mr. —and—, Herr Soundso. — called, *adj.* sogenannt.

Soak, *v.* I. *a.* durch=nässen, =feuchten. II. *n.* ein=, durch=dringen.

Soap, I. *s.* die Seife. II. *v.a.* (ein=) seifen, beseifen. —y, *adj.* seifig; (like —) seifenartig. —boiler, *s.* der Seifensieder. —bubble, *s.* die Seifenblase. —suds, *s.* die Seifenlauge.

Soar, *v.n.* sich erheben, hoch fliegen; sich aufschwingen. —ing, *adj.* hoch= fliegend.

Sob, I. *v.n.* schluchzen. II. *s.* das Schluchzen. —bing, *s.* das Schluchzen.

Sob—er, I. *adj.*, —erly, *adv.* nüchtern. II. *v.a.* nüchtern machen. —riety, —erness, *s.* die Nüchternheit. —er-minded, *adj.* mäßig.

Sociabl—e, *adj.*, —y, *adv.* gesellig, umganglich.

Social, *adj.*, —ly, *adv.* gesellschaftlich, Gesellschafts=, sozial. —ism, *s.* der Sozialismus; die Sozialdemokratie. —ist, *s.* der Sozialist; der Sozialdemokrat. —istic, *adj.* sozialistisch.

Society, *s.* die Gesellschaft.

¹Sock, *s.* die Socke.

²Sock, *s.* die Pflugschar.

Socket, *s.* die Tülle, die Hülse (*of a candlestick*); die Röhre (*of tools*); die Höhlung (*of the eyes, teeth, etc.*).

Sod, *s.* der Rasen.

Soda, *s.* die Soda.

Soda, *s.* die Soda. —water, *s.* das Sodawasser.

Sodden, *adj.* verkocht; (*fig.*) aufgedunsen.

Sodium, *s.* das Sodium.

Sofa, *s.* das Sofa.

Soffit, *s.* die Gewölbdecke.

Soft, I. *adj.*, —ly, *adv.* sanft, weich (*to the touch, the ear, etc.*); sachte, leise (*as a tread*). II. *int.*, —ly! sachte! still! halt! —en, *v.* I. *a.* erweichen; mildern, lindern (*pain*); (enervate) schwächen. II. *n.* sanft(er) werden. —ening, I. *adj.* erweichend. II. *s.* das Erweichen. —ness, *s.* die Sanftheit, Weichheit.

¹Soil, *s.* der Boden, Grund.

²Soil, I. *s.* der Fleck, Schmutz. II. *v.a.* besudeln. III. *n.* fleckig werden.

Sojourn, I. *s.* der Aufenthalt, das Verweilen. II. *v.n.* sich aufhalten, verweilen.

Solace, I. *s.* der Trost. II. *v.a.* trösten.

Solar, *adj.* zur Sonne gehörig, Sonnen=.

Solder, I. *s.* das Lot, die Löte. II. *v.a.* (zusammen)löten, verlöten. —ing-iron, *s.* der Lötkolben.

Soldier, *s.* der Soldat. —like, —ly, *adj.* soldatenhaft. —y, *s.* das Kriegsvolk, das Militär.

¹Sole, *adj.* allein, einzig; ledig (*Law*). —ly, *adv.* allein, einzig; (only) nur.

²Sole, I. die Sohle (*of the foot, shoe, etc.*). II. *v.a.* besohlen.

³Sole, *s.* die Seezunge (*Icht.*).

Solecism, *s.* der Sprachfehler, die Unschicklichkeit.

Solemn, *adj.*, —ly, feierlich, —ity, *s.* die Feierlichkeit. —ize, *v.a.* feiern. —ization, *s.* die Feier.

Solicit, *v.a.* ansuchen. —ation, *s.* das Ansuchen; (supplication) das (dringende) Bitten. —or, *s.* der Anhaltende, Ansuchende; der Sachwalter, Anwalt (*Law.*). —ous, *adj.* sorgfältig. —ude, *s.* die Sorgfalt; die Besorgnis.

Solid, I. *adj.*, —ly, *adv.* fest (*also fig.*). II. *s.* der feste Körper (*Phys.*); der Körper (*Geom.*). —ity, *s.* die Festigkeit.

Soliloquy, *s.* das Selbstgespräch, der Monolog.

Solitaire, *s.* einzeln gefaßter Diamant; das Grillenspiel.

Solit—ary, *adj.*, —arily, *adv.* einsam; (single) einzeln. —ude, *s.* die Einsamkeit.

Solo, *s.* das Solo, Einzelspiel.

Solstice, *s.* die Sonnenwende.

Sol—ubility, —ubleness, *s.* die Auflösbarkeit, Löslichkeit. —uble, *adj.*, —ubly, *adv.* (auf)löslich. —ution, *s.* die (Auf=)Lösung (*also Geom. & Alg.*); die Beseitigung (*of difficulties*).

Solv—able, *adj.* auflösbar. —e, *v.a.* (auf)lösen. —ency, *s.* die Zahlungsfähigkeit, Solvenz. —ent, I. *adj.* auflösend; zahlungsfähig (*C.L.*). II. *s.* das Auflösungsmittel. —er, *s.* der, die Auflösende.

Sombre, *adj.* düster, finster, dunkel.

Some, I. *adj.* ein, irgend ein, (irgend) etwas; — person, irgend eine Person, irgend jemand; give me — bread, gib mir etwas Brot; to — extent, einigermaßen. II. *pron.* einige; etwas. —**body,** *s.* irgend einer, jemand. —**how,** *adv.* auf irgend eine Weise, irgendwie; —how or other, auf die eine oder die andere Weise. —**thing,** I. *s.* das Etwas. II. *pron. & adv.* etwas, ein wenig, einigermaßen. —**time,** I. *adv.* einst, dereinst, eines Tages. II. *adj.* ehemalig, einstig. —**times,** *adv.* zuweilen, bisweilen, dann und wann. —**what,** I. *s.* etwas. II. *adv.* etwas, ein wenig. —**where,** *adv.* irgendwo(hin).

Somersault, *s.* der Purzelbaum.

Somn-**ambulist,** *s.* der Nachtwandler, die Nachtwandlerin. —**olence,** —**olency,** *s.* die Schlafsucht. —**olent,** *adj.,* —**olently,** *adv.* schlafsüchtig.

Son, *s.* der Sohn. —**in-law,** *s.* der Schwiegersohn.

Sonata, *s.* die Sonate (*Mus.*).

Song, *s.* der Sang, Gesang; das Lied; for a mere —, spottbillig. —**ster,** *s.* der Sänger. —**stress,** *s.* die Sängerin.

Sonnet, *s.* das Sonett.

Sonorous, *adj.,* —**ly,** *adv.* (voll)tönend. —**ness,** *s.* der Wohlklang.

Soon, *adv.* bald; (early) früh; (readily) gern. —**er,** *comp. of* Soon; eher; früher; lieber.

Soot, *s.* der Ruß. —**iness,** *s.* die Rußigkeit. —**y,** *adj.* rußig.

Sooth-**e,** *v.a.* besänftigen. —**ing,** *adj.,* —**ingly,** *adv.* lindernd.

Soothsayer, *s.* der Wahrsager.

Sop, *s.* der eingetunkte Bissen.

Sophistic-**al,** *adj.,* —**ally,** *adv.* spitzfindig. —**ate,** *v.a.* verdrehen, verfälschen. —**ated,** *adj.* verfälscht; den Rummel verstehend.

Sophistry, *s.* die Spitzfindigkeit.

Soporific, I. *adj.* einschläfernd. II. *s.* das Schlafmittel.

Soprano, *s.* der Sopran; (singer) die Sopransängerin.

Sorcer-**er,** *s.* der Zauberer. —**ess,** *s.* die Zauberin, Hexe. —**y,** *s.* die Zauberei.

Sordid, *adj.,* —**ly,** *adv.* gemein. —**ness,** *s.* die Gemeinheit.

Sore, I. *adj.,* —**ly,** *adv.* schmerzhaft wund. II. *s.* das Geschwür. III.

—, —**ly,** *adv.* schwer, arg. —**ness,** *s.* die Schmerzhaftigkeit, das Wehe.

¹Sorrel, *s.* der Sauerampfer.

²Sorrel, *adj.* rötlich; — horse, der Rotfuchs.

Sorr-**iness,** *s.* die Armseligkeit. —**ow,** I. *s.* der Kummer, Gram, die Trauer, Betrübnis, das Leid. II. *v.n.* trauern, sich grämen *or* härmen (for, um). —**owful,** *adj.,* —**owfully,** *adv.* kummervoll, betrübt, traurig. —**ows,** *pl.,* die Leiden. —**y,** *adj.* bekümmert, betrübt; (pitiful) erbärmlich, kläglich; I am —y for you, es tut mir leid um Sie, Sie tun mir leid; we are —y to say, wir bedauern sagen zu müssen.

Sort, I. *s.* die Art, Gattung, Sorte; that — of thing, etwas Derartiges; out of —s, unpäßlich; verdrießlich (*coll.*). II. *v.a.* sortieren.

Sortie, *s.* der Ausfall.

Sot, *s.* der Trunkenbold, Säufer. —**tish,** *adj.,* —**tishly,** *adv.* versoffen.

Soul, *s.* die Seele. —**less,** *adj.,* —**lessly,** *adv.* seelenlos.

¹Sound, I. *adj.,* —**ly,** *adv.* gesund. II. *adv.;* — asleep, in tiefem Schlafe. —**ness,** *s.* die Gesundheit.

²Sound, *s.* der Sund, die Meerenge; die Fischblase (*Icht.*).

³Sound, I. *v.n.* schallen, ertönen. II. *v.n.* schallen, tönen, klingen, lauten. —**less,** *adj.* tonlos. —**proof,** *adj.* schallsicher. —**ing-board,** *s.* der Resonanzboden. —**box,** *s.* die Schalldose. —**film,** *s.* der Tonfilm.

⁴Sound, *v.a.* sondieren, peilen (*Naut.*). —**ing,** *s.* das Sondieren. —**ings,** *pl.* der Ankergrund. —**ing-lead,** *s.* das Senkblei, Lot. —**ing-line,** *s.* die Lotleine, Senkschnur.

Soup, *s.* die Suppe.

Sour, I. *adj.,* —**ly,** *adv.* sauer, herb. II. *v.a.* säuern. III. *v.n.* sauer werden. —**ness,** *s.* die Säure; (*fig.*) die Herbheit, Bitterkeit.

Source, *s.* die Quelle, der Ursprung.

Souse, *v.a.* (ein)pökeln; (plunge) ins Wasser werfen.

South, I. *s.* der Süden; der Süd (*poet.*). II. *adj. & adv.* südlich, südwärts. —**erly,** *adj.* südlich, Süd-. —**ward,** *adv.* südwärts. —**east,** I. *adj.* (eastern) südöstlich. II. *s.* der Südost. —**west,** I. *adj.* (—western) südwestlich. II. *s.* der Südwest.

Souvenir, *s.* das Andenken.

Sovereign, I. *adj.* allerhöchſt; (*fig.*) unübertrefflich; unfehlbar (*as a remedy*). II. *s.* der (die) Herr(in), Herrſcher(in). —ty, *s.* die Oberherrſchaft.

¹**Sow**, *s.* die Sau.

²**Sow**, *v.a. & n.* ſäen, ausſtreuen; beſäen (*a field, etc.*). —er, *s.* der Sämann, Säer. —ing, *s.* das Säen.

Spa, *s.* der Sauerbrunnen; der Kurort.

Spac—e, *s.* der Raum. —ing, *s.* die Räumung (*Typ.*). —ious, *adj.*, —iously, *adv.* geräumig. —iousness, *s.* die Geräumigkeit.

¹**Spade**, *s.* der Spaten.

²**Spade**, *s.* das Pik (*Cards*); ten of —s, die Pikzehn; to call a — a —, kein Blatt vor den Mund nehmen.

Span, I. *s.* die Spanne (*also fig.*); das Geſpann (*of horses*); — of an arch, die Spannung. II. *v.a.* (um)ſpannen, (über)ſpannen.

Spangle, I. *s.* der Flitter, Flimmer. II. *v.a.* beſflittern.

Spaniel, *s.* der Wachtelhund.

Spank, *v.a.* klapſen.

Spanker, *s.* der Beſan (*Naut.*).

Spanking, *adj.*;   breeze, lebhafte Briſe (*Naut.*).

Spanner, *s.* der Spanner, Schlüſſel, Hahn, Schraubenzieher.

¹**Spar**, *s.* der Spat (*Min.*).

²**Spar**, *s.* die Spiere, der Sparren (*Naut.*).

³**Spar**, *v.n.* boxen.

Spar—e, I. *adj.*, —ely, *adv.* (—ing) ſparſam; (scanty) ſpärlich; (lean) mager; (to —e) überzählig; enough and to —, vollauf; —e part, der Einzelteil. II. *v.a.* (use —ingly) ſparen; (lay by) aufſparen; (treat tenderly) (ver)ſchonen, nachſichtig behandeln; friſten, erhalten (*one's life, etc.*). —ing, *adj.*, —ingly, *adv.* ſparſam, ſchonend (of, mit); —ing of one's words, wortkarg.

Spark, I. *s.* der Funke(n) (*also fig.*); (dandy) der Stutzer; der Liebhaber. II. *v.n.* Funken ſprühen. —ing-plug, *s.* die Zündkerze (*Motor.*).

Sparkl—e, I. *s.* der Funke; (*fig.*) der Glanz, Schimmer. II. *v.n.* funkeln, blitzen. —ing, *adj.* funkelnd, glänzend; perlend; —ing wine, der Schaumwein.

Sparrow, *s.* der Sperling. —hawk, *s.* der Sperber.

Sparse, *adj.*, —ly, *adv.* zerſtreut, dünn.

Spasm, *s.* der Krampf. —odic, *adj.* —odically, *adv.* krampfhaft.

Spats, *pl.* kurze Gamaſchen.

Spatter, *v.n.* (be)ſpritzen.

Spavin, *s.* der Spat.

Spawn, I. *s.* der Laich. II. *v.a. & n.* laichen. —ing, *s.* das Laichen.

Speak, *ir.v.* I. *n.* ſprechen, reden; to — about, (discuss) (eine Sache) beſprechen; to — to, ſprechen (*acc.*); to — up, frei weg reden; — up! ſprich lauter! II. *a.* ſprechen; äußern, ausſagen (*one's mind, etc.*). —er, *s.* der Sprecher, die Sprecherin. —ing, *adj.* ſprechend. —ing-trumpet, *s.* das Sprachrohr.

Spear, I. *s.* der Speer, Spieß. II. *v.a.* durchſtechen.

Speci—al, *adj.*, —ally, *adv.* beſonder, eigen; ausdrücklich (*as orders*); (—ally) beſonders. —alist, *s.* der Fachmann. —ality, *s.* die Beſonderheit, Spezialität.

Specie, *s.* das Metallgeld, bare Geld. —s, *s.* die Art, Gattung, Spezies, Sorte.

Specif—ic, I. *adj.*, —ically, *adv.* eigen(artig), ſpezifiſch. II. *s.* das Eigenmittel. —ication, *s.* die Spezifizierung. —y, *v.a.* ſpezifizieren.

Specimen, I. *s.* das Exemplar (*fig., Bot.*). II. *attrib.*; — copy (*book*), das Muſterexemplar.

Specious, *adj.* oberflächlich. —ness, *s.* die Scheinbarkeit.

Speck, *s.* der Fleck. —le, I. *s.* der kleine, bunte Fleck. II. *v.a.* flecken, ſprenkeln. —led, *adj.* geſleckt.

Spec—tacle, *s.* das Schauſpiel; (sight) der Anblick. —tacled, *adj.* brillentragend. —tacles, *pl.* die Brille. —tator, *s.* der Zuſchauer.

Spectre, *s.* das Geſpenſt.

Speculat—e, *v.n.* nachdenken, nachſinnen (upon, über eine S.); ſpekulieren (*C.L.*). —ion, *s.* das Nach-ſinnen, =forſchen; die Spekulation.

Speech, *s.* die Sprache; to make a —, eine Rede halten. —less, *adj.* ſprachlos.

Speed, I. *ir.v.n.* ſich eilen. II. *v.a.* eiligſt fortſchicken. III. *s.* die Eile. —ily, *adv.*, —y, *adj.*, eilig, ſchnell. —iness, *s.* die Eile. —well, *s.* der Ehrenpreis (*Bot.*).

¹**Spell**, *s.* die Ablöſung, Reihe (*at work*); (time) die Friſt.

²**Spell,** *s.* der Zauber; der Zauberspruch. **—bound,** *adj.* (fest)gebannt.
³**Spell,** *v.a. & n. (imperf. & p.p. also*
Spelt) buchstabieren. **—ing,** *s.* das
Buchstabieren, die Rechtschreibung. —
ing book, *s.* die Fibel.
Spend, *ir.v.a.* aufwenden, ausgeben
(*money, etc.*); hin-, zu-bringen (*time*).
—er, *s.* der Aufwandmacher. —
thrift, I. *s.* der Verschwender. II. *adj.*
verschwenderisch.
Spent, I. *imp. & p.p. of* **—d.** II. *adj.*
erschöpft, entkräftet (*with watching,
etc.*); matt (*as a bullet*).
Sperm, *s.* der Same (der Tiere). **—
aceti,** *s.* der Walrat.
Spew, *v.* I. *a.* auswerfen, ausspeien.
II. *n.* sich erbrechen.
Spher—e, *s.* die Kugel; der Himmels-
körper (*Astr.*); die künstliche Erd- oder
Himmels-kugel (*for schools*); der
Kreislauf (*of a planet, etc.*); (*fig.*)
die Sphäre, der Bereich. **—ic, —
ical,** *adj.,* **—ically,** *adv.* kugelrund,
sphärisch.
Spice, I. *s.* das Gewürz, die Würze;
(*fig.*) der Beigeschmack, das Pikante.
II. *v.a.* würzen.
Spick-and-span, *adj.* blitzblank.
Spider, *s.* die Spinne; **—'s web,** das
Spinnengewebe.
Spigot, *s.* der Zapfen.
Spike, *s.* der Spieker, Bolzen.
Spikenard, *s.* das Nardenöl, Laven-
delöl.
Spill, I. *v.a. (imperf. & p.p. also*
Spilt) verschütten (*water, etc.*); ver-
gießen (*blood*); abwerfen (*from horse-
back*); umwerfen (*a carriage*). II.
v.n. verschüttet werden. III. *s.* die
Verschüttung; das Um-, Ab-werfen
(*sl.*); paper **—,** der Fidibus.
Spin, *ir.v.* I. *a.* spinnen; kreiseln (*a*
top). II. *n.* spinnen; to **—** round, sich
herumdrehen, herumwirbeln. III. *s.*
das (Herum-)Wirbeln, -Drehen.
Spinach, *s.* der Spinat.
Spindle, *s.* die Spindel.
Spindrift, *s.* der Sprühregen von
Seeschaum.
Spine, *s.* der Dorn; das (der) Rück-
grat (*Anat.*).
Spinner, *s.* der (die) Spinner(in).
Spinney, *s.* das Wäldchen.
Spinning—mill, *s.* die Spinnerei.
—wheel, *s.* das Spinnrad.
Spinster, I. *s.* ledige weibliche Person;

she is a **—,** sie ist unverheiratet. II.
attrib.; — aunt, unverheiratete Tante.
Spiral, I. *adj.,* **—ly,** *adv.* spiral-,
schnecken-förmig. II. *s.* die Spirale
(*Geom., etc.*).
Spire, *s.* die Turmspitze.
Spirit, *s.* der Geist, die Seele; der
Geist, Spiritus (*Chem., etc.*); in good
—s, heiter, gut aufgelegt; in bad **—s,**
niedergeschlagen. **—ed,** *adj.* lebhaft,
munter, voll Leben. **—less,** *adj.,*
—lessly, *adv.* mutlos, kleinmütig. **—s,**
pl. (ardent **—s**) geistige Getränke.
—ual, *adj.,* **—ually,** *adv.* (immaterial)
geistig, unkörperlich; (intellectual)
geistig; (not temporal, divine) geistlich;
(ecclesiastical) kirchlich. **—ualism,** *s.*
der Spiritualismus. **—ualist,** *s.* der
Spiritualist. **—level,** *s.* die Nivel-
lierwage.
Spirt, *v.n. & n.* spritzen.
¹**Spit,** *s.* der (Brat-)Spieß; die Land-
zunge (*Geog.*).
²**Spit,** I. *s.* der Speichel. II. *ir.v.a. &
n.* speien. **—fire,** *s.* der Hitzkopf.
Spite, I. *s.* der Ärger; die Bosheit;
in **—** of, trotz (*gen.*), ungeachtet
(*gen.*). II. *v.a.* ärgern. **—ful,** *adj.,*
—fully, *adv.* gehässig.
Spittle, *s.* der Speichel.
Spittoon, *s.* der Spucknapf.
Splash, I. *v.a.* bespritzen. II. *s.* der
Spritzfleck. **—board,** *s.* das Spritz-
brett.
Splay, **—ed,** *adj.* schief. **—footed,** *adj.*
mit auswärts gebogenen Füßen.
Spleen, *s.* die Milz.
Splend—id, *adj.,* **—idly,** *adv.* glänzend; prächtig, herrlich. **—our,** *s.*
die Pracht, Herrlichkeit.
Splic—e, I. *s.* die Splissung. II. *v.a.*
splissen, einfügen (*ropes*). **—ing,** *s.*
das Splissen.
Splint, *s.* die Schiene (*Surg.*). **—er,** I.
s. der Splitter, Span (*of wood, bone,*
etc.); das Granatstück (*Mil.*). II.
v.a. (zer)splittern, schiefern. III. *v.n.*
sich splittern.
Split, I. *s.* der Spalt; die Spaltung
(*also fig.*). II. *ir.v.a.* (*also pret. &*
p.p.) spalten; beleidigen (*the ears,*
fig.). III. *ir.v.n.* sich spalten.
Splutter, *v.n.* heraussprudeln; spritzen
(*as a pen*).
Spoil, I. *v.a.* berauben (einen einer S.);
plündern; verderben; verwöhnen
(Kinder). II. *s.* die Beute, der Raub.

—er, *s.* der Berauber, Plünderer; der
Zerstörer.

Spoke, *s.* die Speiche (*of a wheel*);
(rung) die Leitersprosse.

Spokes—man, *s.* der Wortführer. —
woman, *s.* die Wortführerin.

Spong—e, *s.* der Schwamm (*also
fig.*). —**er,** *s.* der Wischer (*Artil.*);
der Schmarotzer (*slang*). —**y,** *adj.*
schwammig.

Sponsor, *s.* der Bürge; der Pate
(*for a child*).

Spontane—ous, *adj.,* —**ously,** *adv.*
freiwillig, von selbst, aus eigenem
Antrieb. —**ity,** *s.* die Freiwilligkeit,
Spontaneität.

Spook, *s.* der Geist.

Spool, *s.* die Spule.

¹**Spoon,** *s.* der Löffel.

²**Spoon,** *v.n.* närrisch verliebt sein (*sl.*).
—(e)**y,** *adj.* töricht zärtlich (*sl.*).

Spore, *s.* die Spore, das Keimkorn.

Sport, I. *s.* das Spiel, der Sport; he is
no —, er ist ein Spielverderber. II.
v.n. spielen, sich belustigen. —**ive,**
adj., —**ively,** *adv.* scherzhaft, lustig,
spaßhaft. —**sman,** *s.* der Sportsmann.

Spot, I. *s.* der Flecken, Makel; (place)
der Fleck, Ort. II. *v.a.* flecken. —
less, *adj.* fleckenlos. —**ty,** *adj.* fleckig,
gefleckt.

Spouse, *s.* der Gatte, Gemahl, die Gattin, Gemahlin.

Spout, I. *s.* der Ausguß, die Tülle. II.
v.a. (aus)spritzen.

Sprain, I. *s.* die Verrenkung. II. *v.a.*
verrenken.

Sprat, *s.* die Sprotte.

Sprawl, *v.n.* sich spreizen.

¹**Spray,** *s.* der Zweig (*of holly, etc.*), der
Sproß.

²**Spray,** *s.* der Sprühregen, das Spritz-
wasser, der Gischt.

Spread, I. *ir.v.a.* (*also imperf. & p.p.*)
breiten (on, auf); ausbreiten (sails);
verbreiten (*a report, etc.*). II. *ir.v.n.*
sich ausbreiten, sich verbreiten. III.
s. die Ver-, Aus-breitung. —**ing,** *adj.*
ausgebreitet, weit.

Spree, *s.* (*slang*) der Spaß, Jux,
Streich (das Zechgelage; to go on the
—, auf den Bummel gehen.

Sprig, *s.* der Sproß, das Reis.

Sprightl—iness, *s.* die Lebendigkeit.
—**y,** *adj.* lebhaft, munter.

Spring, I. *ir.v.n.* springen; (arise) entspringen, quellen (from, aus), her-

kommen (from, von); to — at, los-
springen auf (*acc.*); to — over,
springen (*acc.*); to — up, aufspringen.
II. *ir.v.a.* sprengen (*mines, etc.*); (led)
werden (*a leak*). III. *s.* der Spring-
quell, Springbrunnen, die Quelle;
(jump) der Sprung, Satz; (elasticity)
die Spring-, Schnell-, Feder-kraft;
die (Spring-, Trieb-)Feder (*Mach.*);
(season of —) der Frühling; main
—, die Haupt-, Schlag-feder. —**iness,**
s. die Springkraft, Elastizität. —**y,**
adj. elastisch, prall. —**board,** *s.* das
Sprungbrett. —**tide,** *s.* die Spring-
flut. —**time,** *s.* der Frühling.

Springe, *s.* die Schlinge.

Sprinkl—e, I. *v.a.* besprengen, bestreuen (with, mit). II. *v.n.* sprühen.
—**ing,** *s.* das Sprengen; (*fig.*) der
Anflug, der Anstrich.

Sprint, I. *s.* kurzer, schneller Wettlauf.
II. *v.n.* schnell laufen. —**er,** *s.* der
Renner.

Sprit, *s.* das Spriet.

Sprite, *s.* der Kobold, Schrat.

Sprout, I. *v.n.* (— up, auf-)sprossen.
II. *s.* die Sprosse, der Sprößling;
Brussels —s, der Rosenkohl.

¹**Spruce,** *adj.,* —**ly,** *adv.* sauber, geputzt.
—**ness,** *s.* die Sauberkeit, der Putz.

²**Spruce,** *s.* die Fichte, Rottanne (*Bot.*).

Spry, *adj.* wacker (*coll.*), munter,
flink.

Spume, *s.* der Schaum.

Spunk, *s.* der Zündschwamm; der
Mut (*coll.*).

Spur, I. *s.* der Sporn. II. *v.a.* die
Sporen geben.

Spurge, *s.* die Wolfsmilch.

Spurious, *adj.,* —**ly,** *adv.* unecht, falsch.

Spurn, *v.a.* zurückweisen; (scorn)
verschmähen.

Sputter, *v.a.* ausprudeln.

Spy, I. *s.* der Kundschafter, Späher,
Spion. II. *v.a.* (er)spähen. —**glass,**
s. das Fernglas.

Squab, *adj.* dick und fett.

Squabble, I. *v.n.* hadern. II. *s.* der
Hader, Zank.

Squad, *s.* die Rotte, Korporalschaft
(*Mil.*).

Squadron, *s.* die Schwadron (*Mil.*);
das Geschwader (*Naut.*).

Squalid, *adj.,* —**ly,** *adv.* garstig,
schmutzig.

¹**Squall,** *s.* die Bö (*Naut.*). —**y,** *adj.*
stürmisch.

²**Squall,** I. v.n. laut schreien. II. s. der Aufschrei.

Squalor, s. der Smutz.

Squander, v.a. verschleudern. **—er,** s. der Verschwender.

Square, I. adj., **—ly,** adv. viereckig; Geviert=, Quadrat= (foot, mile, etc.); (fig.) ehrlich; — measure, das Flächenmaß. II. s. das Viereck, Quadrat (Geom.); die Quadratzahl (Arith.); der Platz (in a city); das Winkeleisen (Carp., etc.); das Karree (Mil.). III. v.a. viereckig machen; ausgleichen (an account); quadrieren (a number, etc.); auf den Winkel prüfen (Carp., etc.). **—ness,** s. das Viereckige. **—rigged,** adj. mit Raaen getakelt. **—sail,** s. das Raasegel.

Squash, v.a. (zer)quetschen.

Squat, I. v.n. sich hocken. II. adj. kauernd, hockend; kurz und dick.

Squeak, I. s. das Quieken. II. v.n. quieken (as pigs).

Squeal, v.n. quieken (as pigs).

Squeamish, adj., **—ly,** adv. Ekel empfindend; (fig.) zimperlich, wählerisch. **—ness,** s. die Übelkeit, die Zimperlichkeit.

Squeeze, I. s. der Druck, die Quetschung. II. v.a. drücken, (aus)pressen; (hug) in die Arme schließen. **—r,** s. der Drücker.

Squib, s. der Handschwärmer (Firew.); das Spottgedicht.

Squid, s. der Tintenfisch.

Squill, s. die Meerzwiebel (Bot., Pharm.).

Squint, I. adj. schielend. II. s. der schielende Blick. III. v.n. schielen. **—ing,** I. adj., **—ingly,** adv. schielend. II. s. das Schielen. **—eyed,** adj. schieläugig.

Squire, s. der Landjunker.

Squirm, v.n. sich krümmen.

Squirrel, s. das Eichhörnchen.

Squirt, I. s. die Spritze. II. v.a. spritzen.

Stab, I. s. der Stich, Stoß. II. v.a. erstechen, erdolchen (a person). III. v.a. stechen.

Stability, s. die Beständigkeit, Dauerhaftigkeit.

Stable, I. adj. fest, dauerhaft, stark; (durable) beständig, standhaft. II. s. der Stall. III. v.a. einstallen.

Stack, I. s. der Schober (of hay, etc.); die Schornsteinreihe (Build.). II. v.a. aufschichten; aufstellen (arms, etc.).

Stadtholder, s. der (Erb=)Statthalter.

Staff, s. der Stab (Mil.); der Stock, die Stütze; das Personal. **—officer,** s. der Stabsoffizier.

Stag, s. der Hirsch.

Stage, s. das Gerüst; die Bühne (Theat.); die (Post=)Station (on a journey). **—coach,** s. der Postwagen. **—manager,** s. der Regisseur.

Stagger, I. v.n. schwanken. II. v.a. wankend machen. **—s,** pl. der Schwindel (of horses).

Stagna—nt, adj. (still)stehend, stockend. **—te,** v.a. stocken. **—tion,** s. die Stockung.

Staid, adj., **—ly,** adv. gesetzt, ruhig. **—ness,** s. die Gesetztheit, Ruhe.

Stain, I. s. der Fleck(en). II. v.a. beflecken (also fig.). **—er,** s. der Färber. **—ing,** s.; —ing of glass, die Glasmalerei. **—less,** adj. ungefleckt; (fig.) makellos.

Stair, s. die Stufe, der Tritt; (flight of) —s, die Treppe. **—case,** s. das Treppenhaus. **—landing,** s. der Treppenabsatz. **—rod,** s. die Läuferstange.

Stake, I. s. die Stange; der Einsatz (in gaming); to be at —, auf dem Spiele stehen. II. v.a. umpfählen (ground, etc.); (ein)setzen (at play).

Stal—actite, s. der Tropfstein. **—agmite,** s. der Stalagmit.

¹**Stale,** adj. hart, altbacken (bread); (fig.) abgenutzt, veraltet. **—ness,** s. die Schalheit, Abgenutztheit.

²**Stale,** s., **—mate,** I. s. das Patt (Chess). II. v.a. patt setzen or machen.

¹**Stalk,** I. s. der Stengel, Stiel; der Halm (of corn).

²**Stalk,** I. v.n. sich anpirschen (an Wild). II. v.a. beschleichen (game). **—ing-horse,** s. (fig.) der Vorwand, die Maske.

Stall, I. s. der (Pferde=)Stand (in a stable, etc.); die Marktbude; der Parkettsitz (Theat.). II. v.a. einstallen.

Stallion, s. der Zuchthengst.

Stalwart, adj. stark, kräftig.

Stamen, s. der Staubfaden (Bot.).

Stamina, s. die Ausdauer.

Stammer, I. v.n. stammeln, stottern. II. s. das Stammeln, Stottern. **—er,** s. der Stotterer, Stammler. **—ing,** adj., **—ingly,** adv. stammelnd, stotternd.

Stamp, I. *s.* das Stampfen (*with the foot*); (mark) der Stempel; das Gepräge (*on a coin, etc.*); (postage —) die (Brief=)Marke; (character) die Art, der Schlag. II. *v.a.* stampfen; stempeln.

Stampede, I. *s.* die wilde Flucht. II. *v.n.* durchgehen (*of mules, horses*).

Stanch, I. *v.a.* hemmen, stillen (*blood*). II. *adj.* fest, tüchtig. —**ion,** *s.* die Stütze. —**ness, Staunchness,** *s.* die Festigkeit; (*fig.*) die Zuverlässigkeit.

Stand, I. *ir.v.n.* stehen. II. *ir.v.a.* aushalten, ertragen, leiden; stellen; to — aside, auf die Seite treten; to — between, Mittelsperson sein; to — for, als Kandidat auftreten; his hair stood on end, ihm standen die Haare zu Berge; it —s to reason, es ist natürlich, daß; to — a person a dinner, jemandem ein Mittagessen zum besten geben. III. *s.* der Stand, das Stehen; (post) der Standpunkt, die Stelle; (pause) der Stillstand; (resistance) der Widerstand; die Tribüne (*for spectators*); der Ständer, das Gestell (*for things to stand on*); to make a —, Halt machen, sich widersetzen. —**ard,** I. *s.* die Standarte, Fahne; der Maßstab, die Richtschnur; der Münzfuß (*Mint.*); the —ard is high, die Anforderungen sind hoch; above —ard, übergut; —ard of value, der Wertregulator. II. *adj.* musterhaft, maßgebend, Normal=. —**ard-bearer,** *s.* der Fähn(d)rich, Fahnenträger. —**ing,** I. *adj.* stehend (*of water; of an army*); fest, bestimmt (*as an order*); (lasting) bleibend; —ing orders, die Geschäftsordnung. II. *s.* das Stehen. —**ing-room,** *s.* der Stehplatz. —**still,** *s.* das Stillstehen.

Stanza, *s.* die Strophe.

¹**Staple,** I. *s.* das Haupterzeugnis (*of a country*). II. *adj.* bestimmt; Stapel=.

²**Staple,** *s.* die Krampe.

Star, *s.* der Stern (*also Typ.*), das Gestirn (*Astr.*); der Künstler, Schauspieler, die Künstlerin, Schauspielerin (*Theat.*). —**less,** *adj.* sternlos. —**like,** *adj.* sterngleich. —**red,** *adj.* besternt. —**riness,** *s.* die Sternenhelle. —**ry,** *adj.* sternenhell, Sternen=. —**fish,** *s.* der Seestern. —**light,** I. *s.* das Sternenlicht. II. *adj.* —**lit,** *adj.* sternenhell. —**spangled,** *adj.* sternbesät.

Starboard, I. *s.* das Steuerbord. II. *v.t.*; — the helm! Ruder am Steuerbord!

Starch, I. *v.a.* stärken. II. *s.* die Stärke. —**y,** *adj.*, —**ily,** *adv.* steif, förmlich; stärkehaltig.

Star—e, I. *s.* das Starren, der Starrblick. II. *v.n.* starren, stieren. III. *v.a.* starren. —**ing,** *adj.*, —**ingly,** *adv.* starrend, stier.

Stark, *adj. & adv.* völlig.

Starling, *s.* der Star.

Start, I. *v.n.* antennen (*on a race*); abgehen (*as a carriage*); aufbrechen (*on a journey*); (set out) beginnen; auffspringen (*in alarm, etc.*). II. *v.a.* hervortreiben; gründen (*a business*); erregen (*a quarrel*); in Gang bringen, anlassen (*machinery*); auf die Bahn bringen (*a subject, etc.*). III. *s.* das Auffahren, Stutzen (*from fright, etc.*); der Anfang, Anlauf (*of a race, etc.*); to get the — of a person, einem zuvorkommen. —**ing,** *s.* das Ablaufen. —**ing-point,** *s.* der Ausgangspunkt.

Startl—e, *v.a.* (unangenehm) überraschen. —**ing,** *adj.* erschreckend, Aufsehen erregend.

Starv—ation, *s.* das Verhungern. —**e,** *v.* I. *n.* verhungern, Hunger leiden. II. *a.* aushungern.

State, I. *s.* der Zustand; der Stand (*of a question*); die Lage (*of affairs*); (political body) der Staat; (civil power) die Regierung; (pomp) die Pracht, der Gepränge. II. *v.a.* angeben, erklären. —**d,** I. *p.p.*; as —d, wie erwähnt; angeblich. II. *adj.* bestimmt, fest. —**liness,** *s.* die Stattlichkeit. —**ly,** *adj.* stattlich. —**ment,** *s.* die Darstellung, Auseinandersetzung, Darlegung; der Ansatz, Anordnung (*of an account, etc.*). —**sman,** *s.* der Staatsmann. —**smanship,** *s.* die Staatsmannskunst.

Station, I. *s.* der Stand; (situation) die Stelle; (position) die Stellung; der Bahnhof (*Railw.*). II. *v.a.* aufstellen. —**ary,** *adj.* stillstehend. —**er,** *s.* der Schreibwarenhändler. —**ery,** *s.* Schreibwaren. —**house,** *s.* die Polizeiwache; das Bahnhofsgebäude. —**master,** *s.* der Stationsvorsteher.

Statis—tic(al), *adj.* statistisch. —**tics,** *s.* die Statistik.

Statu—ary, I. *s.* der Bildhauer;

Statuen. II. adj. Statuen=. —e, s. die Bildfäule.

Stature, s. der Wuchs.

Status, s. der Zustand, die Stellung, Lage.

Statut—e, s. das Statut; — of limitations, das Verjährungsgesetz. —ory, adj. gesetzlich.

Stave, I. s. die Faßdaube; der Stab (Metre, Music). II. ir.v.a.; to — in, einschlagen; to — off, abwehren, aufschieben.

¹Stay, I. v.n. stehen bleiben; bleiben, sich aufhalten (at a place); to — away, wegbleiben; to — up, aufbleiben. II. v.a. hemmen; (support), (unter)stützen. III. s. der Aufenthalt; (prop) die Stütze (also fig.).

²Stay, I. s. das Tau. II. v.n. wenden (Naut.). —sail, s. das Stagsegel.

Stays, pl. das Korsett.

Stead, s. die Stelle; in his —, an seiner Stelle. —fast, adj., —fastly, adv. standhaft. —fastness, s. die Festigkeit. —iness, s. die Festigkeit (also fig.). —y, I. adj., —ily, adv. fest; (fig.) beständig. II. v.a. fest machen.

Steak, s. die Fleischschnitte, das Beefsteak.

Steal, ir.v. I. a. stehlen (also fig.); to — a march upon a person, einem unvermerkt einen Vorsprung abgewinnen. II. n. stehlen; (slip) schleichen. —ing, s. das Stehlen.

Stealth, s. die heimliche List; by —, verstohlenerweise. —ily, adv., —y, adj. verstohlen, heimlich. —iness, s. die Heimlichkeit.

Steam, I. s. der Dampf. II. v.n. dampfen (also fig.). III. v.a. ausdünsten; dämpfen (Cook.). —er, s. see —ship. —engine, s. die Dampfmaschine; die Lokomotive (Railw.). —roller, s. die Dampfwalze. —ship, s. das Dampfschiff, der Dampfer. —tug, s. der Schleppdampfer.

Steed, s. das Roß.

Steel, I. s. der Stahl (also fig.). II. adj. stählern. III. v.a. (ver)stählen. —engraving, s. der Stahlstich.

Steelyard, s. die Schnellwage.

¹Steep, I. adj., —ly, adv. steil, jäh. II. s. der jähe Abhang. —ness, s. die Steilheit.

²Steep, v.a. eintauchen, tunken.

Steeple, s. der Kirchturm, Glockenturm. —chase, s. das Hindernisrennen.

¹Steer, s. der junge Ochs.

²Steer, v.a. & n. steuern. —age, I. s. die Steuerung; das Zwischendeck. II. attrib.; —age passenger, der Zwischendeckspassagier. —ing-wheel, s. das Steuerrad. —sman, s. der Steuermann.

Stellar, adj. Sternen=.

¹Stem, s. der Stamm (of a tree); der Stengel, Stiel (of a plant, fruit).

²Stem, s. der Schiffsschnabel.

³Stem, v.a. stemmen (water); (fig.) aufhalten, hemmen.

Stench, s. der Gestank.

Stencil, s. die Schablone.

Stenography, s. die Kurzschrift.

¹Step, I. s. der Schritt (also fig.), Tritt; die Stufe (of stairs, etc.); die Sprosse (of a ladder); die Türschwelle (at a door); der Wagentritt (of a carriage). II. v.n. schreiten. III. v.a. (pace) abschreiten; einsetzen (a mast). —s, pl. die Stufen=, Treppen-leiter. —ping-stone, s. der Schrittstein.

²Step, (in comp. =) Stief= (mother, brother, etc.).

Steppe, s. die Steppe.

Stereo—scope, s. das Stereoskop. —type, I. s. die Stereotypie. II. adj. stereotypisch, Stereotyp= (also fig.).

Steril—e, adj. unfruchtbar (also fig.). —ity, s. die Unfruchtbarkeit. —ized, adj. entkeimt.

Sterling, adj. echt; a pound —, ein Pfund Sterling.

¹Stern, s. das Heck.

²Stern, adj., —ly, adv. streng, ernst; finster. —ness, s. der Ernst, die Strenge.

Stethoscope, s. das Horchrohr.

Stevedore, s. der Stauer, (Aus=)Lader.

Stew, I. v.a. & n. dämpfen. II. s. das Schmorgericht. —pan, s. die Schmorpfanne.

Steward, s. der Verwalter (of estates); der Aufwärter (Naut.). —ess, s. die Aufwärterin (on board ship). —ship, s. das Verwalteramt.

¹Stick, s. der Stock.

²Stick, ir.v. I. a. stecken (pins, etc.); (fasten) heften, ankleben. II. ir.v.n. feststecken, kleben bleiben; to — at nothing, vor nichts zurückscheuen; to — out, hervorragen; to — up for, für jemanden Partei ergreifen. —iness, s. die Klebrigkeit. —ing-

plaster, s. das Heftpflaster. —y, adj. klebrig, zäh.

Stickleback, s. der Stichling (Icht.).

Stickler, s. der Pedant, der Eiferer (for, für).

Stiff, adj., —ly, adv. steif; starr, straff. —en, v. I. a. steif, starr machen. II. n. steif(er) werden, erstarren. —ness, s. die Steifheit. —necked, adj. halsstarrig.

Stifle, v.a. ersticken; erdrücken (with kisses, etc.); unterdrücken (resentment, etc.).

Stigma, s. das Brandmal; die Narbe. —tize, v.a. brandmarken.

Stile, s. der Zauntritt.

Stiletto, s. das Stilett.

¹**Still**, I. v.a. beruhigen, stillen. II. adj. still, ruhig. III. adv. stets, immer. IV. conj. doch, dennoch, indessen. —ness, s. die Stille, Ruhe, —born, adj. totgeboren.

²**Still**, s. der Destillierapparat, die Brennerei.

Stilt, s. die Stelze. —ed, adj. gespreizt; (fig.) hochtrabend.

Stimul—ant, I. s. das Reizmittel. II. adj. anregend. —ate, v.a. reizen; stimulieren (Med.). —ation, s. die Reizung. —us, s. der Antrieb (to, zu).

Sting, I. ir.v.a. stacheln, stechen, schmerzen. II. s. der Stachel (of insects); der Stich (inflicted by insects).

Sting—ily, adv., —y, adj. geizig, filzig. —iness, s. die Kargheit.

Stink, I. ir.v.n. stinken. II. s. der Gestank.

Stint, v.a. ein-, be-schränken.

Stipend, s. der Sold.

Stipulat—e, v.a. & n. verabreden, bedingen, festsetzen. —ion, s. die Bedingung, Übereinkunft, Klausel.

Stir, I. v.a. rühren, bewegen, regen. II. v.n. sich regen, sich rühren. III. s. die Bewegung; (bustle) das Getümmel.

Stirrup, s. der Steigbügel. —leather, s. der Steigriemen.

Stitch, I. s. der Stich; die Masche (in knitting, etc.); back, cross, chain or looped, herring-bone, running —, Stepp-, Kreuz-, Ketten-, Gräten-, Border-stich. II. v.a. & n. nähen, steppen; heften. —ing, s. die Näherei; das Heften.

Stoat, s. das Hermelin.

Stock, I. s. der Stock (of plants, etc.); der Stamm (of a tree); der Schaft (of a gun); (race) das Geschlecht, der Stamm; (neck-tie) die Halsbinde; (store) der Vorrat; die Aktie (of a bank, etc.); — in hand, der Warenbestand; to take — of, in Betracht ziehen. II. adj. auf Lager, bereit; (fig.) stehend, ständig. III. v.a. versehen; (— with) füllen (mit). —s, pl. der Stapel (Naut.); die Staatsaktien, -papiere, der Fonds (C.L.). —broker, s. der Börsenmakler. — exchange, s. die Börse. —holder, s. der Aktionär. —jobbing, s. das Börsenspiel. —still, adj. mäuschenstill. —taking, s. die Inventuraufnahme.

Stockade, s. das Staket.

Stockinet, s. das Trikot.

Stocking, s. der Strumpf.

Stodgy, adj. stopfend; (fig.) plump.

Stoic, I. s. der Stoiker. II. adj. stoisch.

Stoke, v.a. schüren. —r, s. der Heizer. —hole, s. das Schürloch.

Stole, s. die Stola (Eccl.).

Stolid, adj., —ly, adv. schwerfällig. —ity, s. die Schwerfälligkeit.

Stomach, I. s. der Magen. II. v.a. sich (dat.) gefallen lassen. —ache, s. der Leibschmerz.

Ston—e, I. s. der Stein. II. adj., von Stein, steinern; —e ware, das Steingut. —e-fruit, s. das Kernobst. —e-quarry, s. der Steinbruch. III. v.a. steinigen. —iness, s. das Steinige. —y, adj. steinig, versteinert, (stein)hart (fig.). —e-blind, adj. stockblind.

Stool, s. der Stuhl, Sessel; (foot—) der Schemel.

Stoop, I. v.n. sich bücken, sich beugen. II. s. das Beugen, Bücken, Neigen. —ing, s. das Bücken.

Stop, I. v.a. (auf)halten (in running, etc.); stillen (blood); (ver)sperren (a way, etc.); (— up) zumachen. II. v.n. (an)halten, stehen bleiben; (stay) sich aufhalten, bleiben; (cease) aufhören, innehalten; —! halt! III. s. der Halt, Einhalt; (obstruction) die Aufhaltung, Hemmung, Sperrung; (cessation) das Aufhören; (full —) der Punkt; die Pause. —page, s. das (Ver=)Stopfen; das Anhalten (of a vehicle); der Aufenthalt (on journeys). —per, s. der Stöpsel, Pfropf (of a bottle). —ping, s. die Plombe, Zahn-

füllung. —**cock,** *s.* der Sperrhahn.
—**gap,** *s.* der Notbehelf.

Stor—age, *s.* das Lagern. —**e,** I. *s.*
der Vorrat; (warehouse) das Ge=
wölbe, (Waren=)Lager; (shop) der
Laden; in —e, vorrätig, auf Lager.
II. *v.a.* aufspeichern, (ein=)lagern.
—**e-house,** *s.* das Vorrats=, Lager=haus,
Magazin. —**e-keeper,** *s.* der Magazin=
verwalter. —**e-room,** *s.* die Vorrats=
kammer.

Storied, *adj.* mit Stockwerken, =stöckig.

Stork, *s.* der Storch.

Storm, I. *s.* der Sturm; (thunder—)
das Gewitter. II. *v.a.* (be)stürmen;
(take by —) erstürmen. III. *v.n.*
stürmen. —**y,** *adj.,* —**ily,** *adv.*
stürmisch.

¹Story, *s.* die Geschichte; (narrative) die
Erzählung. —**teller,** *s.* der Erzähler,
die Erzählerin; (coll.) der Lügner.

²Story, *s.* das Stock(werk), Geschoß.

Stout, *adj.,* —**ly,** *adv.* stark, stämmig,
wacker, tapfer. —**hearted,** *adj.* herz=
haft.

Stove, *s.* der Ofen.

Stow, *v.a.* stauen. —**age,** *s.* das
Stauen. —**away,** *s.* der blinde
Passagier.

Straddle, *v.n.* sich spreizen.

Straggl—e, *v.n.* umherschweifen; (—e
off) abweichen. —**er,** *s.* der Nach=
zügler, der Herumstreifer (Mil.).
—**ing,** *adj.* umherschweifend.

Straight, I. *adj.,* —**ly,** *adv.* gerade
(also fig.). II. *adv.* stracks, gerades=
wegs; to put things, —, Dinge ordnen,
abmachen. —**edge,** *s.* der Richtscheit.
—**en,** *v.a.* gerade machen. —**ness,**
s. die Geradheit. —**forward,** *adj.,*
—**forwardly,** *adv.* gerade; (fig.) redlich.
—**forwardness,** *s.* die Redlichkeit.
—**way,** *adv.* stracks.

¹Strain, I. *v.a.* spannen; (fig.) zwingen;
(squeeze) zusammenziehen; verren=
ken (a muscle, etc.); durch=pressen,
=seihen (milk, etc.). II. *v.n.* sich
anstrengen. III. *s.* die Anstrengung,
Spannung; (pressure) der Druck; die
Verrenkung (Surg.); (lay) das Gedicht;
die Weise (Mus.). —**er,** *s.* die Seihe.

²Strain, *s.* das Geschlecht; der Hang, die
Tendenz.

Strait, I. *adj.,* —**ly,** *adv.* eng, schmal.
II. *s.* die Landenge; (—s) die Meerenge,
Straße; (fig.) die Klemme, Not.
—**jacket,** *s.* die Zwangsjacke.

¹Strand, I. *s.* (shore) der Strand. II.
v.n. stranden.

²Strand, *s.* die Strähne (of a rope, etc.).

Strange, *adj.,* —**ly,** *adv.* fremd. —
ness, *s.* die Fremdheit, das Fremde, die
Seltsamkeit. —**r,** *s.* der (die) Fremde,
der Neuling.

Strangle, *v.a.* erwürgen, erdrosseln.
—**s,** *s.* die Druse (Vet.).

Strangulation, *s.* die Erwürgung,
Einschnürung.

Strap, I. *s.* der Riemen; der Gurt. II.
v.a. umschnüren. —**ping,** *adj.* stäm=
mig.

Strat—agem, *s.* die Kriegslist (Mil.).
—**egic,** *adj.* strategisch. —**egy,** *s.*
die Strategie; (fig.) die List.

Stratum, *s.* die Schicht, Lage.

Straw, *s.* das Stroh; man of —, der
Strohmann (lit. & fig.). —**berry,** *s.*
die Erdbeere.

Stray, I. *v.n.* (sich ver)irren, abschweifen;
irre gehen. II. *adj.* verirrt.

Streak, I. *s.* der Streifen, Strich.
II. *v.a.* streifen. —**y,** *adj.* streifig.

Stream, I. *s.* der Strom (also fig.).
II. *v.n.* strömen. —**er,** *s.* der Wimpel.
—**let,** *s.* das Bächlein.

Street, I. *s.* die Straße, Gasse. II.
attrib.; — Arab, der Straßenjunge.

Strength, *s.* die Kraft, Stärke (also
fig.). —**en,** *v.* I. *a.* stärken, kräftigen.
II. *n.* erstarken.

Strenuous, *adj.,* —**ly,** *adv.* eifrig. —
ness, *s.* der Eifer.

Stress, *s.* der Drang; (emphasis) die
Betonung, die Wichtigkeit.

Stretch, I. *v.a.* strecken, recken. II.
v.n. sich (er)strecken, sich dehnen. III.
s. die Strecke, Weite; at a —, in
einem Zuge; (fig.) im Notfalle. —**er,**
s. die Fußbahr (in a boat); die Tragbahre
(for the sick, etc.). —**er-bearer,** *s.*
der Krankenträger.

Strew, *v.a.* bestreuen.

Strict, *adj.,* —**ly,** *adv.* streng; (exact)
genau. —**ness,** *s.* die Strenge. —
ure, *s.* die Anspielung, die kritische
Bemerkung.

Stride, I. *s.* der Schritt. II. *v.n.*
dahinschreiten.

Strident, *adj.* knarrend, grell, kreischend.

Strife, *s.* der Widerspruch, Hader,
Wettstreit.

Strike, I. *ir.v.a.* schlagen; streichen (a
flag, sails, etc.); einstellen (work, die
Arbeit); to — a balance, den Saldo

ziehen; to — home, jemanden empfind=
lich treffen; to — oil, eine Ölquelle
finden; (fig.) Glück haben. II. ir.v.n.
schlagen; (auf den Grund) stoßen,
geraten auf (acc.; Naut.); die Arbeit
einstellen, streifen; \c)lagen (as clocks);
einschlagen (of lightning). III. s. der
(Arbeiter=)Ausstand, Streik. —r, s.
der Schläger; der ausständische
Streiker (of work).

Striking, adj., —ingly, adv. auffallend,
treffend.

String, I. s. die Schnur, der Bindfaden;
die Sehne (of a bow); die Saite
(Mus.); — band, das Streichorchester.
II. ir.v.a. (auf)reihen; besaiten (Mus.).
—y, adj. faserig, zähe.

Stringen—cy, s. die Strenge, Knapp=
heit. —t, adj. streng.

Strip, I. v.a. abstreifen, abziehen.
II. v.n. sich ausziehen (coll.). III. s.
der Streifen.

Stripe, I. s. der Streifen, Strich;
(wale) der Striemen; (stroke) der
Schlag. II. v.a. streifen. —d, adj.
gestreift, streifig.

Stripling, s. der junge Mensch.

Strive, ir.v.n. (sich be)streben, sich
bemühen; (vie) wetteifern. —r, s.
der Strebende.

Stroke, I. s. der (Feder=, Pinsel=)
Strich; (blow) der Schlag, Streich;
— of genius, der Genieblitz. II. v.a.
streiche(l)n. —oar, s. der Vormann.

Stroll, I. s. das Herumziehen; to go
for a —, einen kleinen Spaziergang
machen. II. v.n. (— about) herum=
wandern.

Strong, adj., —ly, adv. stark; (powerful) kräftig, gewaltig. —hold, s. die
Festung. —-minded, adj. geistesstark.
—box, s. der Geldkasten. —room,
s. der feuersichere Raum.

Strop, I. s. der Streichriemen. II. v.a.
streichen.

Structur—al, adj. baulich. —e, s.
der Bau, das Gebäude; die Bauart.

Struggle, I. s. das Ringen; — for
existence, der Kampf ums Dasein.
II. v.n. sich sträuben. —r, s. der
Kämpfer, Ringer. —s, pl. Zuckungen,
Verzerrungen.

Strum, v.n. klimpern.

Strut, I. v.n. stolzen. II. s. das
Stolzieren; der stolze Gang; die
Strebe (Build.). —ting, adj., —ting=
ly, adv. stolzierend.

Strychnine, s. das Strychnin.

Stub, s. der (Baum=)Stumpf.

Stubbl—e, s. die Stoppel. —y, adj.
stoppelig, stoppelartig.

Stubborn, adj., —ly, adv. steif, starr;
(obstinate) halsstarrig. —ness, s. die
Unbiegsamkeit.

Stucco, s. der Stuck.

Stuck-up, adj. eingebildet.

¹**Stud**, s. das Gestüt.

²**Stud**, I. s. der Stift, Knauf; (shirt,
etc., —) der (Hemden= ꝛc.) Knopf.
II. v.a. beschlagen (with nails, etc.).
—ding-sail, s. das Leesegel.

Stud—ent, s. der Student, die Student=
in. —ied, adj. studiert; (deliberate)
vorgesucht, gekünstelt, bedacht. —io, s.
das Atelier. —ious, adj., —iously,
adv. fleißig, emsig. —iousness, s. der
Fleiß. —y, I. s. das Studieren;
(room) die Studierstube. II. v.n.
studieren. III. v.a. studieren.

Stuff, I. s. der Stoff; — and nonsense,
dummes Zeug. II. v.a. (voll=)
stopfen; ausstopfen (birds, etc.); pol=
stern (chairs). III. v.n. sich voll=
stopfen. —iness, s. die Schwüle. —
ing, s. die Füllung. —y, adj. dick
(air); dumpfig (a room); schwül
(weather).

Stumbl—e, I. v.n. stolpern. II. s. das
Stolpern; (fig.) der Fehltritt. —er,
s. der, die Stolpernde. —ing, I. adj.,
—ingly, adv. stolpernd. II. s. das
Stolpern; der Fehltritt. —ing-block,
s. das Hindernis; der Stein des
Anstoßes.

Stump, s. der Stumpf. —y, adj. kurz
und dick.

Stun, v.a. betäuben; (fig.) bestürzt
machen. —ning, adj. famos (coll.).

Stunt, v.a. am Wachstum hindern.
—ed, adj. verkürzt.

Stupe, I. s. der warme Umschlag. II.
v.a. bähen.

Stupe—faction, s. die Betäubung. —
fy, v.a. betäuben.

Stupendous, adj., —ly, adv. erstaun=
lich (coll.).

Stupid, adj., —ly, adv. dumm; —
fellow, der Dummkopf. —ity, s.
die Dummheit; (fig.) der Stumpf=
sinn.

Stupor, s. die Erstarrung.

Sturd—ily, adv., —y, adj. stark,
kräftig. —iness, s. die Stärke, Festig=
keit, Derbheit.

Sturgeon, *s.* der Stör.
Stutter, *v.n.* stottern, stammeln. **—er,** *s.* der Stotterer, Stammler.
Sty, *s.* der (Schweine=)Stall.
Styl—e, I. *s.* die Rede=, Ausdrucks= weise, der Stil (*also fig.*). II. *v.a.* (be)nennen, betiteln. **—ish,** *adj.,* **—ishly,** *adv.* modisch (*as dress*). **—ishness,** *s.* die Eleganz.
Suave, *adj.* sanft, gewinnend.
Suavity, *s.* die Lieblichkeit, Anmut.
Sub, I. *pref.* = unter. II. *Comp.* (*generally* = unter). **—altern,** I. *s.* der Subalternoffizier. II. *adj.* unter= geordnet, Unter=. **—committee,** *s.* der Unterausschuß. **—division,** *s.* die Unterabteilung.
Subdue, *v.a.* unterwerfen.
Subject, I. *adj.* unter=geben, =worfen, =tan, dienstbar. II. *s.* der Untertan; der Gegenstand (*of discourse, etc.*). III. *v.a.* unterlegen. **—ion,** *s.* das Unter= werfen; (state of —ion) die Unter= werfung (to, unter). **—ive,** *adj.,* **—ively,** *adv.* subjektiv.
Subjugate, *v.a.* unterjochen.
Subjunctive, *s.* der Konjunktiv.
Sublet, *v.a.* verpachten, vermieten.
Sublim—e, I. *adj.,* **—ely,** *adv.* erhaben. **—ity,** *s.* die Erhabenheit.
Submarine, I. *adj.* unterseeisch. II. *s.* das Unterseeboot.
Submer—ge, *v.a.* unter Wasser setzen; (*also v.n.*) untertauchen. **—sion,** *s.* die Überschwemmung.
Submi—ssion, *s.* die Ergebung. **— ssive,** *adj.,* **—ssively,** *adv.* unter= würfig, =tänig; gehorsam. **—t,** I. *v.a.* (lay before) vor=, dar=legen; to —t oneself, sich (einem) unterwerfen. II. *n.* sich ergeben.
Subordinat—e, I. *adj.,* **—ely,** *adv.* untergeordnet. II. *s.* der Unter= geordnete. **—ion,** *s.* der (Dienst=) Gehorsam.
Subscri—be, *v.* I. *a.* unter=schreiben, =zeichnen; zeichnen (*money*). II. *n.* abonnieren (to, auf eine S.). **— ber,** *s.* der Unterzeichner; der Abonnent. **—ption,** *s.* das Abonnement.
Subsequent, *adj.* (nach=)folgend. **— ly,** *adv.* hernach, darauf.
Subservient, *adj.* untergeordnet, dienend.
Subside, *v.n.* sich legen (*also of wind*).
Subsidiary, *adj.* behilflich.
Subsidy, *s.* das Hilfsgeld.

Subsist, *v.n.* sein; bestehen, Bestand haben; to — on, sich ernähren von. **—ence,** *s.* das Dasein; der Unter= halt.
Substan—ce, *s.* die Substanz; (real thing) das Wesen; (essence) das Wesentliche; (reality) die Wirklichkeit; (solidity) die Festigkeit. **—tial,** *adj.,* **—tially,** *adv.* wesentlich.
Substantive, I. *n.* das Hauptwort. II. *adj.* substantivisch.
Substitute, I. *v.a.* an eines andern Stelle (ein=)setzen. II. *s.* der Stell= vertreter, Amtsvertreter; (thing —d) das Ersatzmittel.
Substructure, *s.* der Unterbau.
Subterfuge, *s.* die leere Ausflucht.
Subterrane—an, —ous, *adj.* unter= irdisch.
Subtl—e, *adj.,* **—y,** *adv.* fein. **—ety,** *s.* die Feinheit.
Subtract, *v.a.* abziehen, subtrahieren. **—ion,** *s.* das Abziehen, die Subtraktion.
Suburb, *s.* die Vorstadt. **—an,** *adj.* vorstädtisch.
Subvert, *v.a.* umkehren; verkehren, umstürzen.
Subway, *s.* der unterirdische Gang, die Unterführung.
Succeed, *v.* I. *n.* folgen; nachfolgen (on the throne, auf dem Throne; to an office, in einem Amte); glücken, ge= lingen; he —s in, es gelingt ihm; to — to an estate, ein Gut erben; to — with a person, etwas bei jemanden durchsetzen. II. *a.* (einem) (nach=) folgen; to — a person, einem folgen. **—ing,** *adj.* nachfolgend.
Success, *s.* der Erfolg. **—ful,** *adj.,* **—fully,** *adv.* erfolgreich, glücklich.
Success—ion, *s.* die Reihe (n=folge); die Nachfolge (*in office, etc.*); (—ion to the throne) die Thronfolge. **—ive,** *adj.* aufeinander folgend. **—ively,** *adv.* der Reihe nach. **—or,** *s.* der Nachfol= ger; —or to the throne, der Thron= folger.
Succour, I. *s.* die Hilfe. II. *v.a.* (einem) helfen.
Succulent, *adj.* saftig.
Succumb, *v.n.* unterliegen, erliegen.
Such, I. *adj. or pron.* solch; so; — and —, der und der; no — thing, nichts dergleichen; **—like,** dergleichen. II. *adv.* so; es.
Suck, *v.a. & n.* (ein)saugen. **—er,** *s.* der Sprößling (*Hort.*); die Sauge

(Mech.). —ing, I. p. saugend, Saug=. II. s. das Saugen, Einsaugen. —ing-bottle, s. das Saugfläschlein. —ing-pig, s. das Spanferkel. —le, v.a. säugen, stillen. —ling, s. der Säug-ling.

Suction, s. das Säugen.

Sudden, adj. (on a —), —ly, adv. plötzlich. —ness, s. die Plötzlich-keit.

Suds, pl. das Seifenwasser, die Seifen-lauge.

Sue, v. I. a. gerichtlich verfolgen; mit Bitten angehen. II. n. klagen (for, auf eine S.).

Suet, s. das Nierenfett, der Talg.

Suffer, v. I. a. ertragen, erbulden; (allow) (zu)lassen, gestatten, erlauben; (undergo) erleiden. II. n. leiden. —able, adj., —ably, adv. erträglich, leidlich, zu erbulden. —ance, s. das Leiden; die Dulbung, Gebuld; on —ance, (nur eben) gebuldet, nur gebulbeterweise. —er, s. der, die Leibende. —ing, I. adj., —ingly, adv. leidend. II. s. das Leiden.

Suffic—e, v.n. genügen. —iency, s. die Hinlänglichkeit, Genüge. —ient, adj., —iently, adv. hinlänglich, genug.

Suffix, I. s. die Nachsilbe, das Suffix. II. v.a. anheften.

Suffocat—e, v.a. & n. ersticken. —ing, adj. erstickend. —ion, s. die Erstickung.

Suffrag—e, s. die (Wahl=)Stimme. —ette, —ist, s. die Frauenrechtlerin.

Suffus—e, v.a. übergießen. —ion, s. die Ergießung.

Sugar, I. s. der Zucker. II. v.a. zuckern. —y, adj. zuckerig. —basin, s. die Zuckerbüchse. —cane, s. das Zuckerrohr. —loaf, s. der Zuckerhut.

Suggest, v.a. beibringen (words, etc.); vorschlagen. —ion, s. die Einge-bung; (proposal) der Vorschlag. —ive, adj., —ively, adv. andeutend, anregend.

Suicid—al, adj., —ally, adv. selbst-mörderisch. —e, s. der Selbstmord; der Selbstmörder (person).

Suit, I. s. (petition) das Gesuch, die Bitte; (wooing) die Werbung; (— of clothes) der Anzug; die Klage, der Prozeß (Law). II. v.a. (adapt) an-passen; (become) anstehen, passen; kleiden, (einem gut) stehen (as a bonnet, etc.). III. v.n. überein-stimmen, passen; to be —ed, etwas

Passendes gefunden haben; it —s its purpose, es entspricht seinem Zweck; ill —ed, schlecht geeignet. —ability, —ableness, s. die Angemessenheit. —able, adj., —ably, adv. passend, angemessen, geeignet, gemäß, ent-sprechend.

Suite, s. das Gefolge (of a prince, etc.); die Reihe (of rooms, Zimmer).

Suitor, s. der Bittsteller; der Bewerber, Freier; der Kläger (Law).

Sulk, v.n. schmollen. —ily, adv. see —y. —iness, s. das Schmollen. —y, adj. mürrisch, launisch, verdrießlich.

Sullen, adj., —ly, adv. mürrisch; (obstinate) starrköpfig. —ness, s. die Halsstarrigkeit.

Sully, v.a. besudeln.

Sulph—ate, s. schwefelsaures Salz. —ide, s. das Sulfid. —ur, s. der Schwefel. —urous, adj. schweflig, schwefelhaltig.

Sultan, s. der Sultan. —a, s. die Sultanin.

Sultr—iness, s. die Schwüle. —y, adj. schwül.

Sum, I. s. die Summe. II. v.a. zusammenrechnen. —marily, adv. ohne Umstände. —mary, I. adj. bündig, in Bausch und Bogen. II. s. das Kompendium.

Summer, I. s. der Sommer. II. adj. Sommer=. —house, s. das Garten-haus.

Summit, s. der Gipfel, die Spitze, Höhe.

Summon, v.a. auffordern, aufrufen; to — up, aufbieten. —s, s. die Aufforderung, gerichtliche Vorladung.

Sump, s. der Sumpf.

Sumpter, I. s. das Saumroß, Packtier. II. attrib.; — mule, das Saumtier.

Sumptuous, adj. kostbar, prächtig.

Sun, I. s. die Sonne. II. v.n. (& r. sich) sonnen. —less, adj. sonnenlos. —niness, s. die Sonnigkeit. —ny, adj. sonnig. —beam, s. der Sonnen-strahl. —burn, I. v.a. bräunen. II. s. der Sonnenbrand. —dial, s. die Sonnenuhr. —down, s. der Sonnenuntergang. —flower, s. die Sonnenblume. —light, s. das Son-nenlicht. —rise, s. der Sonnenauf-gang. —set, s. der Sonnenunter-gang. —shade, s. der Sonnenschirm. —shine, s. der Sonnenschein. —stroke, s. der Sonnenstich.

Sunday, s. der Sonntag.

Sunder, *v.a.* sondern, trennen.

Sundr—ies, *pl.* verschiedenartige Gegenstände. **—y,** *adj.* verschiedene, mehrere; **—y expenses,** diverse Kosten.

Sunken, *adj.* eingesunken.

Sup, I. *s.* der Schluck=, Mund=voll. II. *v.a.* schlürfen. III. *v.n.* zu Abend essen.

Super, I. *s.* der Statist (*Theat.*). II. *pref.* (*in cpds. generally* = über=). **—abundance,** *s.* die Überfülle. — **abundant,** *adj.,* **—abundantly,** *adv.* über reichlich, =flüssig. **—annuate,** *v.a.* in den Ruhestand versetzen.

Superb, *adj.,* **—ly,** *adv.* prächtig, herrlich.

Super—cilious, *adj.,* **—ciliously,** *adv.* hochmütig. **—ficial,** *adj.,* **—ficially,** *adv.* oberflächlich. **—ficiality,** *s.* die Oberflächlichkeit. **—fine,** *adj.* extrafein. **—fluous,** *adj.,* **—fluously,** *adv.* überflüssig, reichlich. **—human,** *adj.* übermenschlich. **—intend,** *v.a.* beaufsichtigen, verwalten. **—intendence,** *s.* die Oberaufsicht. **—intendent,** *s.* der Oberaufseher.

Superior, I. *adj.* ober; (*fig.*) vortrefflicher; **— to,** jemandem überlegen. II. *s.* der Obere, Höhere, Vorgesetzte. **—ity,** *s.* die Übermacht, Überlegenheit, der Vorzug, Vorrang.

Super—lative, I. *adj.* höchst; unübertrefflich. II. *s.* (—lative degree) der höchste Grad, Superlativ. **—man,** *s.* der Übermensch. **—natural,** *adj.,* **—naturally,** *adv.* übernatürlich. — **scription,** *s.* die Überschrift, Aufschrift. **—sede,** *v.a.* aufheben. **—stition,** *s.* der Aberglaube. **—stitious,** *adj.,* **—stitiously,** *adv.* abergläubisch. **—vision,** *s.* die Beaufsichtigung. **—visor,** *s.* der Aufseher.

Supine, I. *adj.,* **—ly,** *adv.* rückwärts; nachlässig. II. *s.* das Supinum (*Gram.*).

Supper, Supping, *s.* das Abendessen, Abendbrot; the Lord's **—,** das letzte Abendmahl.

Supplant, *v.a.* verdrängen. **—er,** *s.* der Verdränger.

Suppl—e, *adj.* biegsam, geschmeidig. **—eness,** *s.* die Geschmeidigkeit, Biegsamkeit.

Supplement, I. *s.* der Nachtrag; die Beilage (*to a newspaper, etc.*). II. *v.a.* hinzufügen. **—al,** **—ary,** *adj.* ergänzend, nachträglich.

Suppli—ant, I. *adj.* bittend, flehend. II. *s.* der Bittsteller. **—cant,** *s.* der Bittsteller. **—cate,** *v.a. & n.* anflehen. **—cation,** *s.* das Anflehen.

Suppl—ies, *pl.* (money) Hilfsgelder; (provisions, *etc.*) der Mund= und Kriegsvorrat. **—y,** I. *v.a.* versehen, versorgen (with, mit); (give) darreichen; (furnish) liefern; ausfüllen, vertreten (a person's place, jemandes Stelle); ersetzen (the want of, den Mangel an einer Sache). II. *s.* (grant) der Beitrag; (store) der Vorrat; der Proviant.

Support, I. *v.a.* (unter)stützen. II. *s.* das (Unter=)Stützen; (prop) die Stütze; (aid) der Beistand, die Unterstützung. **—able,** *adj.,* **—ably,** *adv.* erträglich, leidlich. **—er,** *s.* der (Unter) Stützende, Beistehende.

Suppos—e, *v.a.* (assume) den Fall setzen, annehmen; (imagine) vermuten. **—ed,** *adj.* mutmaßlich, vermeintlich. **—ition,** *s.* die Vermutung, Meinung.

Suppress, *v.a.* unterdrücken. **—ion,** *s.* die Unterdrückung.

Suppurat—e, *v.n.* eitern. **—ion,** *s.* die Eiterung.

Suprem—acy, *s.* die Obergewalt. **—e,** *adj.,* **—ely,** *adv.* höchst.

Sur, *pref.* (= Super). **—charge,** I. *v.a.* überladen. II. *s.* die Überforderung (*C.L.*); das Zuschlagporto (*Post*).

Sure, I. *adj.* sicher, gewiß; **— enough!** sicherlich! versteht sich! II. *adv.;* **= —ly,** (coll.) doch. III. **—,** **—ly,** *adv.* sicher; sicherlich; (assuredly) wahrhaftig. **—ness,** *s.* die Sicherheit. — **ty,** *s.* die Sicherheit; Gewißheit.

Surf, *s.* die Brandung.

Surface, I. *s.* die Oberfläche, Außenseite. II. *adj.* oberflächlich, äußerlich.

Surfeit, I. *v.a.* überfüllen. II. *v.n.* sich über=laden, =füllen. III. *s.* die Überladung.

Surge, *s.* die hohe Welle, Woge, See.

Surg—eon, *s.* der Chirurg, Wundarzt. **—ery,** *s.* die Wundarzneikunst, die Chirurgie. **—ical,** *adj.* wundärztlich, chirurgisch.

Surl—ily, *adv.,* **—y,** *adj.* mürrisch. — **iness,** *s.* die Schroffheit.

Sur—mise, I. *v.a.* vermuten, mutmaßen. II. *s.* die Vermutung. **—mount,** *v.a.* übersteigen. **—name,** *s.* der Zu=

name, Familienname. **—pass,** *v.a.*
übersteigen, =treffen. **—passing,** *adj.*
& *adv.,* **—ingly,** *adv.* außerordentlich.
—plice, *s.* das Chorhemd; die Stola
(*R.C.*). **—plus,** I. *s.* der Überschuß.
II. *adj.* übrig(bleibend). **—prise,** I.
überraschen. II. *s.* die Überraschung.
—prising, *adj.,* **—prisingly,** *adv.*
überraschend. **—render,** I. *v.a.* überge=
ben, ausliefern. II. *v.r.* sich gefangen
geben (*as a prisoner*). III. *v.n.* sich
ergeben. IV. *s.* die Übergabe, Ergebung.

Surreptitious, *adj.* heimlich getan,
erschlichen.

Sur—round, *v.a.* umringen. **—
rounding,** *adj.* umgebend. **—round-
ings,** *pl.* die Umgebung. **—vey,** I.
v.a. überschauen; vermessen (*land*).
II. *s.* der Überblick; die Vermessung
(*Surv.*). **—veyor,** *s.* der Besichtiger;
der Feldmesser (*Surv.*). **—vival,** *s.*
das Überleben. **—vive,** *v.* I. *a.* über=
leben. **—vivor,** *s.* der Überlebende,
Hinterbliebene.

Suscepti—bility, *s.* die Empfänglichkeit.
—ble, *adj.* empfänglich.

Suspect, I. *v.a.* (be)argwöhnen; im
Verdacht haben (of, wegen). II. *s.* der
Verdächtige. **—ed,** *adj.* verdächtig,
im Verdacht stehend.

Suspen—d, *v.a.* (hang) aufhängen;
(put off) verschieben; einstellen (*payment, etc.*); zurückhalten mit (one's)
judgment, seinem Urteil. **—ders,**
pl. Hosenträger; Tragbänder (*for
stockings*). **—se,** *s.* die Ungewißheit.
—sion, *s.* das (Auf=)hängen; der Auf=
schub (*of judgment*); Suspension (*of
a law*). **—sion-bridge,** *s.* die Hänge=,
Ketten=brücke.

Suspicio—n, *s.* der Verdacht, Argwohn.
—us, *adj.,* **—usly,** *adv.* argwöhnisch,
mißtrauisch.

Sustain, *v.a.* (aufrecht)halten, stützen,
beistehen; ernähren; aushalten. **—
able,** *adj.* haltbar (*as a charge*).

Sutler, *s.* der (die) Marketender(in).

Swab, I. *s.* der Kehrwisch; der Schwab=
ber (*Naut.*). II. *v.a.* schwabbern,
schrubben (*Naut.*).

Swaddl—e, *s.* das Wickelband. **—ing-
clothes,** *pl.* Windeln.

Swagger, I. *v.n.* prahlen, großtun.
II. *s.* die Großtuerei, Prahlerei. **—
er,** *s.* der Prahler. **—ing,** *adj.,* **—
ingly,** *adv.* prahlerisch.

Swain, *s.* der Schäfer; der Liebhaber.

¹**Swallow,** *s.* die Schwalbe (*Ornith.*).
²**Swallow,** I. *s.* der Schlund. II. *v.a.*
(ver=)schlucken. III. *v.n.* schlucken.

Swamp, I. *s.* der Sumpf, Morast. II.
v.a. versenken. **—y,** *adj.* sumpfig.

Swan, *s.* der Schwan. **—'s-down,** *s.*
die Schwanendaunen (*pl.*). **—song,**
s. das Schwanenlied.

Swank, I. *v.n.* (*slang*) großtun. II. *s.*
die Großtuerei.

Swap, *v.a.* (ver)tauschen (*coll.*).

Sward, *s.* der Rasen.

¹**Swarm,** *s.* der Schwarm (*of bees,
etc.*); (*fig.*) das Gewimmel. II. *v.n.*
schwärmen; to—(with),wimmeln(von).
²**Swarm,** *v.n.* klettern (up, hinauf, *acc.*).

Swarth—y, (**Swart,**) *adj.* schwärzlich.
—iness, *s.* die schwärzliche, braune
(Gesichts=)Farbe.

Swashbuckler, *s.* der Säbelraßler,
Eisenfresser.

Swastika, *s.* das Hakenkreuz.

Swath, *s.* der Schwaden.

Swathe, *v.a.* wickeln, windeln.

Sway, I. *v.a.* schwingen. II. *v.n.*
sich neigen, schwanken. III. *s.* der
Schwung; (*fig.*) der Einfluß; (rule) die
Herrschaft.

Swear, *ir.v.* I. *n.* schwören; beschwören
(to a thing, etwas); (blaspheme)
fluchen; to — a person in, jemanden
vereidigen. II. *a.* schwören, durch einen
Schwur bekräftigen; (— to) beschwören.
—er, *s.* der Schwörende; der Flucher;
der Vereidigende.

Sweat, I. *s.* der Schweiß. II. *v.n.*
schwitzen. **—ed,** *adj.;* **—ed articles,**
für Hungerlöhne hergestellte Waren.
—er, *s.* einer, der schwitzt; wollene
Jacke; (employer) der Schinder.
—ing-system, *s.* das Ausbeutungs=
system. **—y,** *adj.* schweißig.

Sweep, I. *ir.v.a.* fegen, kehren; treiben
(*as wind*); wehen (*as a breeze*);
(drag) schleppen. II. *ir.v.n.* fegen,
fahren; (— past) schnell vorüber=
gehen. III. *s.* das Fegen, Kehren;
(chimney—) der Schornsteinfeger;
die Patsche (*of a boat*); to make a clean
—, reinen Tisch machen. **—er,** *s.* der
Feger. **—ing,** *adj.,* **—ingly,** *adv.* durch=
greifend. **—ings,** *pl.* das Fegsel,
Kehricht.

Sweet, I. *adj.,* **—ly,** *adv.* süß (*also fig.*).
II. *s.* das Süße; (*fig.*) das Liebchen.
—en, *v.a.* (ver=)süßen, süß machen
(*tea, etc.*). **—ish,** *adj.* süßlich. **—**

ness, s. die Süßigkeit; (fig.) die Liebenswürdigkeit. —s, pl. Bonbons, süße Speise. —bread, s. das Bröschen. —brier, s. die Heckenrose. —heart, s. das Herzchen, Schätzchen, der, die Geliebte. —meat, s. das Zuckerwerk, (der) Bonbon. — natured, adj. liebreich, hold. —oil, s. das Baumöl. —pea, s. die wohlriechende Wicke. —scented, adj. wohlriechend. —tempered, adj. sanft, mild, hold. —william, s. die Bartnelke.

Swell, I. ir.v.n. (an-, auf-)schwellen. II. ir.v.a. (an)schwellen (water); aufschwellen (sails); (increase) erhöhen, vermehren. III. s. das Schwellen (of a song, etc.); die Dünung (of the sea); der Stutzer, Modeherr (coll.). —ing, I. adj. (an)schwellend. II. s. die Geschwulst, Anschwellung.

Swelter, v.n. schmachten, vor Hitze umkommen.

Swerve, v.n. einen Seitensprung machen (a horse); abschweifen (from one's purpose).

Swift, I. adj., —ly, adv. schnell, geschwind, hurtig, rasch, flüchtig. II. s. die Turmschwalbe (Orn.). —ness, s. die Schnelligkeit, Geschwindigkeit.

Swill, I. v.a. abwaschen (the decks). II. v.n. sich betrinken. III. s. der Spültrank (for pigs).

Swim, I. ir.v.n. schwimmen (also fig.). II. ir.v.a. durchschwimmen, hinüberschwimmen (über, acc.). III. s. das Schwimmen; to be in the —, auf dem laufenden sein, eingeweiht sein. —mer, s. der Schwimmer. —ming, I. adj. schwimmend. II. s. das Schwimmen; (—ming of the head) der Schwindel.

Swindle, I. v.a. betrügen (out of, um). II. s. der Betrug. —r, s. der Schwindler, Gauner.

Swin—e, s. das Schwein (also fig.). —ish, adj., —ishly, adv. schweinisch. —eherd, s. der Schwein(e)hirt.

Swing, I. ir.v.n. schwingen, schwanken; sich schaukeln (on a swing). II. ir.v.a. schwingen, schwenken. III. s. das Schwingen, der Schwung; die Schaukel. —gate, s. das Drehtor.

Swinge, v.a. peitschen.

Swipes, s. das Dünnbier.

Swirl, I. v.n. wirbeln. II. s. der Wirbel, Strudel.

Switch, I. s. die Gerte, Rute; die Weiche (Railw.); der Kommutator (Elec.); der Zopf (of hair). II. v.a. peitschen; rangieren (Railw.); to — on (off) the electric light, das elektrische Licht an- (ab-)drehen. — board, s. das Schalterbrett, die Schalttafel.

Swivel, s. der Drehring.

Swoon, I. s. die Ohnmacht. II. v.n. in Ohnmacht fallen, ohnmächtig werden. —ing, I. adj. ohnmächtig. II. s. das Ohnmächtigwerden.

Swoop, I. v.n. (sich) stürzen. II. s. der Sturz.

Sword, s. das Schwert, der Säbel, Degen. —belt, s. das Degengehenk. —cut, s. der Säbelhieb. —fish, s. der Schwertfisch. —hilt, s. der Degengriff. —knot, s. die Degenquaste. —sman, s. der Fechter. —smanship, s. die Fechtkunst.

Sybarite, s. der Genußmensch.

Sycamore, s. der Bergahorn.

Sycophan—cy, s. die Fuchsschwänzerei. —t, s. der Schmarotzer, der Schmeichler, Angeber. —tic, adj. sykophantisch, angeberisch.

Syllab—ic, adj. syllabisch, Silben-. —le, s. die Silbe.

Syllabus, s. das kurze Verzeichnis, der Lehrplan, das Programm.

Syllogis—m, s. der Vernunftschluß. —tic, adj., —tically, adv. syllogistisch.

Sylph, s. der Luftgeist, Sylph.

Sylvan, adj. waldig, Wald-.

Symbol, s. das Sinnbild, Symbol. —ic(al), adj., —ically, adv. sinnbildlich, symbolisch. —ize, v.n. sinnbildlich darstellen.

Symmetr—ical, adj., —ically, adv. gleich-, eben-mäßig. —y, s. das Ebenmaß, die Symmetrie.

Sympath—etic, adj., —etically, adv. mitfühlend, teilnehmend, seelenverwandt. —ize, v.n. übereinstimmen, mitfühlen, mitleiden. —y, s. die Mitempfindung, Sympathie, das Mitgefühl.

Symphon—ic, adj. gleichklingend. —y, s. die Symphonie.

Symptom, s. das Zeichen, Symptom, der Vorbote (in illness).

Synagogue, s. die Synagoge.

Synchronism, s. die Gleichzeitigkeit.

Synchronize, v.a. gleichgehend machen.

Syncopat—e, *v.a.* ſynkopieren. **—ion,** *s.* das Synkopieren.

Syndicate, *s.* der Ausſchuß.

Synod, *s.* die Synode.

Synopsis, *s.* die Überſicht.

Syntax, *s.* die Satzlehre.

Synthetical, *adj.* zuſammenſetzend.

Syphon, *s.* der (Saug-)Heber; die Druckflaſche.

Syringa, *s.* der Flieder.

Syringe, I. *s.* die Spritze. II. *v.a.* einſpritzen (in, *acc.*).

Syrup, *s.* der Sirup. **—y,** *adj.* ſüß.

System, *s.* das Syſtem. **—atic(al),** *adj.,* **—atically,** *adv.* planmäßig, ſyſtematiſch.

T

T, t, *s.* das T, t.

Tab, *s.* die Laſche, der Schnürſenkel (*Shoem.*).

Tabard, *s.* der (Wappen-)Mantel.

Tabby, I. *s.* der Mohr (*Weav.*); (— cat) die (bunte) Katze. II. *adj.* ſcheckig.

Tabernacle, *s.* das Zelt, das Tabernakel.

Table, *s.* der Tiſch, die Tafel; die Tabelle (*Math., etc.*). **—cloth,** *s.* das Tiſchtuch. **—land,** *s.* das Tafelland. **— linen,** *s.* das Tiſchzeug. **—rapping,** *s.* das Geiſterklopfen. **—spoon,** *s.* der Eßlöffel.

Tablet, *s.* das Täfelchen.

Tabula—r, *adj.* tafelförmig. **—te,** *v.a.* täfeln.

Tacit, *adj.,* **—ly,** *adv.* ſtillſchweigend. **—urn,** *adj.,* **—urnly,** *adv.* ſchweigſam, wortkarg. **—urnity,** *s.* die Schweigſamkeit.

Tack, I. *v.a.* (an)heften (*Carp., etc.*). II. *v.n.* wenden, lavieren (*Naut.*). III. *s.* der Tapeziernagel (*Carp., etc.*); der Hals (*of a sail*); der Gang (beim Lavieren). **—ing,** *s.* das Lavieren.

Tackl—e, I. *s.* das Tau- und Tafelwerk (*Naut.*); das Gerät(e). II. *v.a.* (an-, auf-)takeln; in Angriff nehmen; fertig werden mit. **—ing,** *s.* das Takelwerk, die Takelage.

Tact, *s.* der Takt, die Feinfühligkeit. **—less,** *adj.* taktlos. **—lessness,** *s.* die Taktloſigkeit.

Tactic—ian, *s.* der Taktiker. **—s,** *s.* die Kriegskunſt, Taktik (*also fig.*).

Tadpole, *s.* die Kaulquappe.

Taffeta, *s.* der Taft.

Taffrail, *s.* das Hack-; Heck-bord (*Naut.*).

Tag, *s.* die Schnürnadel; der Reißnagel, das Anhängſel; das Etikett, das Namenſchild.

Tail, *s.* der Schwanz, Schweif; der Rockſchoß; der Schluß, der Anhang. **—coat,** *s.* der Leibrock.

Tailor, I. *s.* der Schneider. II. *v.n.* ſchneidern. **—ess,** *s.* die Schneiderin. **—ing,** *s.* die Schneiderei.

Taint, I. *v.a.* vergiften. II. *v.n.* verderben. III. *s.* der Makel, der Flecken.

Take, *ir.v.* I. *a.* nehmen; (accept, assume) annehmen; befragen um (*a person's opinion*); annehmen (*advice, a bribe, an impression*); (ein)nehmen, erobern (*a fortress, etc.*); zu ſich nehmen (*food*); ſchlagen (*Pawns, Chess, etc.*); fotografieren (a person's likeness, einen); to — a deep breath, tief aufatmen; to — care, ſich in acht nehmen; to — compassion on, ſich erbarmen (*gen.*); to — effect, in Kraft treten; to — fire, Feuer fangen; to — heart, Mut faſſen; to — to heart, ſich zu Herzen nehmen; to — liberties, ſich Freiheiten herausnehmen; to — root, Wurzel faſſen; to — for, halten für; this seat is —n, dieſer Platz iſt beſetzt; to be —n with a person, von jemandem entzückt ſein; to be—n ill, krank werden. II. *n.* (— effect) wirken, Eindruck machen; (please) Beifall finden, gefallen; fangen (*fire*). **—r,** *s.* der Nehmer, Abnehmer. **—in,** *s.* der Betrug (*coll.*).

Taking, I. *adj.* einnehmend, reizend. II. *s.* das Nehmen, *etc.* **—s,** *pl.* die Einnahmen (*C.L.*).

Talc, *s.* der Talk.

Tale, *s.* die Erzählung; das Märchen. **—bearer,** *s.* der Zuträger, Angeber. **—bearing,** *s.* die Ohrenbläſerei.

Talent, *s.* das Talent. **—ed,** *adj.* begabt, talentvoll.

Talisman, *s.* der Talisman. **—ic,** *adj.* zauberiſch.

Talk, I. *v.a.* & *n.* ſprechen, reden; to — over, durchſprechen. II. *s.* das Geſpräch; (idle —) das Geſchwätz. **—ative,** *adj.,* **—atively,** *adv.* geſprächig, redſelig, geſchwätzig. **—ativeness,** *s.* die Geſprächigkeit, Redſeligkeit. **—er,** *s.* der Schwätzer, Plauderer. **—ing,** *s.* das Geplauder. **—ing-picture,** *s.* der Tonfilm.

Tall, *adj.* lang, groß; hoch (*as trees, houses, etc.*). **—ness,** *s.* die Länge, Höhe, Größe.

Tallow, *s.* der Talg. **—y,** *adj.* talgig. **—candle,** *s.* das Talglicht.

Tally, *s.* I. das Kerbholz. II. *v.n.*; to — with, stimmen mit.

Tally-ho, *int.* ho! hallo!

Talon, *s.* die Klaue, Kralle (der Raubvögel).

Tamable, *adj.* (be)zähmbar.

Tamarind, *s.* die Tamarinde.

Tamarisk, *s.* die Tamariske.

Tambour—ine, *s.* das Tamburin. **—frame,** *s.* der Stick-, Trommel-rahmen. **—needle,** *s.* die Tamburiernadel.

Tame, I. *v.a.* zähmen. II. *adj.,* **—ly,** *adv.* zahm. **—ness,** *s.* die Zahmheit. **—r,** *s.* der Bändiger.

Tamper, *v.n.* sich angeben, sich einlassen (with, mit), heimlich unterhandeln.

Tan, I. *s.* die Lohe. II. *v.a.* lohen, gerben; (sunburn) bräunen.

Tandem, I. *s.* das Tandem. II. *adv.*; to drive —, mit voreinander gespannten Pferden fahren.

¹Tang, *s.* der Beigesmack, Nachgesmack.

²Tang, *s.* der Seetang.

Tang—ent, I. *s.* die Tangente. II. *adj.,* **—ent(i)al,** *adj.* tangentenartig. **—ible,** *adj.,* **—ibly,** *adv.* fühlbar, greifbar.

Tangle, I. *s.* das Gewirr. II. *v.a.* verwickeln (in).

Tank, *s.* der Behälter, die Zisterne; der Tank, Panzerwagen (*Mil.*). **—er,** *s.* das Tankschiff (*Naut.*).

Tankard, *s.* der Deckelkrug.

Tann—ed, *adj.* lohgar; sonnenverbrannt. **—er,** *s.* der (Loh-, Rot-) Gerber. **—ery,** *s.* die Gerberei. **—ing,** *s.* das Lohgerben.

Tantaliz—e, *v.a.* quälen. **—ing,** *adj.,* **—ingly,** *adv.* quälend, peinigend.

Tantamount, *adj.*; — to, gleichbedeutend mit.

Tantrum, *s.* die Grille, die Laune.

¹Tap, I. *v.a.* & *n.* leise klopfen. II. *s.* der gelinde Schlag.

²Tap, I. *v.a.* anzapfen (*a cask*); on —, vom Faß. II. *s.* der Zapfen, Hahn (*of a barrel, etc.*). **—root,** *s.* die Pfahlwurzel. **—ster,** *s.* der Kellner. **—room,** *s.* die Schenkstube.

Tape, *s.* das Zwirn-, Leinen-band; red —, der Bürokratismus; to be fond of red —, den Amtsschimmel reiten. **—line,** *s.* die Meßschnur (*Survey.*). **—measure,** *s.* das Metermaß (*of tailors*). **—worm,** *s.* der Bandwurm.

Taper, I. *s.* die Wachskerze. II. *adj.* spitz (zulaufend).

Tapestry, I. *s.* die gewirkte Tapete, Teppichtapete. II. *v.a.* mit Tapeten schmücken.

Tapioca, *s.* die Tapioka.

Tapir, *s.* der Tapir (*Zool.*).

Tar, I. *s.* der Teer. II. *v.a.* teeren. **—ry,** *adj.* teerig.

Tarant—ella, *s.* der Tarantellatanz. **—ula,** *s.* die Tarantel.

Tard—iness, *s.* die Säumigkeit. **—ily,** *adv.,* **—y,** *adj.* säumig.

¹Tare, *s.* die Wicke (*Agr.*); das Unkraut.

²Tare, *s.* die Tara, Verpackung (*C.L.*).

Target, *s.* die (Schieß-)Scheibe.

Tariff, *s.* der Tarif; (customs —) der Zolltarif.

Tarnish, *v.* I. *a.* matt machen, trüben, beflecken. II. *n.* matt werden.

Tarpaulin, *s.* das geteerte Segeltuch (*Naut.*).

Tarry, *v.* I. *n.* verweilen, zögern. II. *a.* abwarten. **—ing,** *s.* das Säumen, Weilen.

¹Tart, *adj.,* **—ly,** *adv.* scharf, sauer, herb. **—ness,** *s.* die Schärfe (*also fig.*).

²Tart, *s.* die Torte, das Pastetchen.

Tartan, I. *s.* der Tartan. II. *adj.* buntgewürfelt.

Tartar, *s.* der Weinstein; der Hitzkopf; to catch a —, an den Unrichtigen kommen.

Task, I. *s.* die Aufgabe; to take to — for, zur Rede stellen. II. *v.a.* beschäftigen; (tax) anstrengen. **—master,** *s.* der Zuchtmeister.

Tassel, *s.* die Trobbel, Quaste. **—ed,** *adj.* betrobbelt.

Taste, I. *v.a.* kosten, schmecken. II. *v.n.* kosten (of, von); schmecken (of, nach). III. *s.* der Geschmack (*also fig.*). **—d,** *adj.* -schmeckend. **—ful,** *adj.,* **—fully,** *adv.* schmackhaft; (*fig.*) geschmackvoll. **—less,** *adj.* geschmacklos. **—lessness,** *s.* die Geschmacklosigkeit.

Tatter, *v.a.* zerreißen, zerfetzen. **—demalion,** *s.* der Lumpenkerl. **—s,** *pl.* Lumpen; (*fig.*) Fetzen.

Tattle, I. *s.* das Geschwätz. II. *v.n.*
schwatzen. **—r,** *s.* der Plauderer, der
Schwätzer.

¹**Tattoo,** *s.* der Zapfenstreich (*Mil.*).

²**Tattoo,** *v.a.* (& *r.* sich) tätowieren.

Taunt, I. *s.* der Stich. II. *v.a.* (ver-)
höhnen. **—ing,** *adj.,* **—ingly,** *adv.*
höhnisch, spöttisch.

Taut, *adj.* steif, straff.

Tautology, *s.* die Tautologie, der
Wortschwall.

Tavern, *s.* die Schenke. **—keeper,** *s.*
der Schenkwirt.

Tawdr—y, *adj.,* **—ily,** *adv.* flitterhaft.
—iness, *s.* das Flitterhafte, der Kitsch.

Tawn—iness, *s.* das Gelbbraune.
—y, *adj.* gelbbraun (*also* wines).

Tax, I. *s.* die Staatssteuer, Auflage.
II. *v.a.* schätzen (at, auf, *acc.*); (impose a — on) besteuern. **—able,** *adj.*
steuerpflichtig. **—ation,** *s.* die Be-
steuerung; (tax) die Steuer. **—i-cab,**
s. die Taxameterdroschke, der, die, das
Taxi. **—i-meter,** *s.* der Taxameter.
—collector, *s.* der Steuereinnehmer.
—payer, *s.* der Steuerzahler.

Tea, *s.* der Tee; high —, frühes
Abendbrot mit Tee. **—pot,** *s.* die Tee-
kanne, der Teetopf. **—things,** *pl.*
das Teegeschirr. **—tray,** *s.* das
Teebrett. **—urn,** *s.* die Tee-urne,
-maschine.

Teach, *ir.v.a.* & *n.* lehren, unterrich-
ten. **—er,** *s.* der Lehrer, die
Lehrerin. **—ing,** *s.* das Lehren; die
Lehre, der Unterricht.

Teak, *s.* der Teakbaum, Tiekbaum.

Teal, *s.* die Krickente (*Orn.*).

Team, *s.* das Gespann (*of horses, etc.*);
die Gruppe, die Mannschaft (*Sport.*).
—ster, *s.* der Fuhrmann.

¹**Tear,** I. *ir.v.a.* reißen, zerren; zerreißen (*one's clothes, etc.*); ausraufen
(*one's hair*). II. *v.n.* stürzen, stürmen.
III. *s.* der Riß; wear and —, die
Abnutzung.

²**Tear,** *s.* die Träne. **—ful,** *adj.,* **—**
fully, *adv.* tränenvoll. **—less,** *adj.*
tränenlos.

Teas—e, I. *v.a.* kratzen (*wool*); (*fig.*)
necken. II. **—e,** (**—er,**) *s.* der Necker.
—ing, *adj.* quälerisch.

Teat, *s.* die Zitze, Brustwarze.

Technic, *s.* die Technik. **—al,** *adj.,*
—ally, *adv.* kunstmäßig, technisch.
—ality, *s.* das Technische.

Tedi—ous, *adj.,* **—ously,** *adv.* langweilig. **—ousness,** *s.* die Lang-
weiligkeit. **—um,** *s.* die Langeweile,
der Überdruß.

Teem, *v.n.* wimmeln (with, von). **—**
ing, *adj.* fruchtbar.

Teeth, *pl. of* Tooth. **—e,** *v.n.* zahnen.
—ing, *s.* das Zahnen.

Teetotaler, *s.* der Temperänzler, der
Abstinenzler.

Tele—gram, *s.* das Telegramm, die
Depesche; wireless **—gram,** drahtlose
Depesche. **—graph,** I. *v.a.* & *n.*
drahten, telegraphieren. II. *s.* der
Telegraph. III. *attrib.;* **—graph** office,
das Telegraphenamt. **—graphic,** *adj.,*
—graphically, *adv.* telegraphisch. **—**
graphy, *s.* die Telegraphie; wireless
—graphy, drahtlose Telegraphie. **—**
phone, I. *s.* der Fernsprecher, das
Telefon. II. *attrib.;* **—phone** office,
das Fernsprechamt, die Fernsprechstelle.
—phonic, *adj.* telefonisch. **—scope,**
s. das Fernrohr. **—vision,** *s.* das
Fernsehen, der Bildfunk.

Tell, *ir.v.* I. *a.* (count) zählen; (relate)
berichten, erzählen; (disclose) entdecken; (bid) heißen, befehlen; I have
been told, mir ist gesagt worden. II. *n.*
erzählen, sprechen (of, von); (produce effect) Eindruck machen. **—er,**
s. der Erzähler; der Zähler; der
Stimmenzähler (*at elections*). **—ing,**
adj. wirkungsvoll, eindrucksvoll, effektvoll. **—tale,** I. *s.* der Angeber,
Ohrenbläser. II. *adj.* schwatzhaft.

Temerity, *s.* die Verwegenheit.

Temper, I. *v.a.* mäßigen, mildern, lindern; (mit Wasser) anmachen (*colours*); härten (*steel*). II. *s.* die
Härte (*of needles, etc.*); der Härte-
grad (*Metall.*); die Beschaffenheit (*of
the body*); (*fig.*) das Gemüt; (fig.)
Reizbarkeit, Heftigkeit. **—ament,** *s.*
die Beschaffenheit, das Temperament.
—ance, I. *s.* die Mäßigkeit (*in eating,
etc.*); die Enthaltsamkeit. II. *attrib.;*
—ance Society, der Mäßigkeitsverein.
—ate, *adj.,* **—ately,** *adv.* gemäßigt
(*as a climate, also fig.*); mäßig (*in
eating, etc.*). **—ature,** *s.* die Tem-
peratur. **—ed,** *adj.;* even-**—ed,** gleichmütig; good-, ill-**—ed,** gut, schlecht
gelaunt.

Tempest, *s.* der Sturm(wind); das
Unwetter, Gewitter; (*fig.*) der Sturm.
—uous, *adj.* stürmisch, ungestüm. **—**
uousness, *s.* das Ungestüm.

Templar, *s.* der Tempelherr.

¹**Temple,** *s.* die Schläfe (*Anat.*).

²**Temple,** *s.* der Tempel.

Tempor—al, *adj.,* —**ally,** *adv.* zeitlich; (*opp. to* Spiritual) weltlich. —**ary,** *adj.,* —**arily,** *adv.* einstweilig, zeitweilig. —**ize,** *v.n.* sich in die Zeit schicken.

Tempt, *v.a.* reizen (zu einer S.), in Versuchung führen. —**ation,** *s.* die Versuchung, Reizung. —**er,** *s.* der Versucher, Verführer. —**ing,** *adj.,* —**ingly,** *adv.* verführerisch, reizend. —**ress,** *s* die Versucherin, Verführerin.

Ten, *num. adj.* zehn. —**fold,** *adj.* zehnfach. —**th,** I. *adj.* zehnt. II. *s.* das Zehntel. —**thly,** *adv.* zehntens.

Ten—able, *adj.* haltbar. —**ableness,** *s.* die Haltbarkeit. —**acious,** *adj.,* —**aciously,** *adv.* festhaltend (of, an einer S.). —**aciousness,** —**acity,** *s.* die Zähigkeit.

Tenan—cy, *s.* der Pacht=, Miet=besitz. —**t,** *s.* der Pächter (eines Gutes), Mieter (eines Hauses); (occupier) der Bewohner, Insasse. —**tless,** *adj.* unvermietet, unbewohnt. —**try,** *s.* die Pächter (eines Gutes).

Tench, *s.* die Schleie (*Icht.*).

¹**Tend,** *v.n.* sich richten, wenden (towards, nach). —**ency,** *s.* die Richtung (auf eine S.), Neigung (zu), der Hang (zu); die Tendenz (*of books, etc.*).

²**Tend,** *v.a.* aufwarten, bedienen.

¹**Tender,** I. *s.* das Anerbieten; legal —, gesetzliches Zahlungsmittel. II. *v.a.* darreichen, an=, dar=bieten; zuschieben (*an oath*).

²**Tender,** *s.* der Wärter, Pfleger; der Tender (*Railw.*); der Lichter (*Naut.*).

³**Tender,** *adj.,* —**ly,** *adv.* zart. —**ness,** *s.* die Zartheit. —**hearted,** *adj.* weichherzig.

Tendon, *s.* die Sehne, Flechse.

Tendril, *s.* die Widelranke.

Tenement, I. *s.* der Wohnsitz. II. *attrib.;* — house, die Mietkaserne.

Tenet, *s.* der Grund=, Lehr=satz.

Tennis, *s.* der Tennis.

Tenon, *s.* der Zapfen.

Tenor, *s.* der Inhalt; die Tenorstimme (*Mus.*); (—or singer) der Tenor.

¹**Tens—e,** *adj.,* —**ely,** *adv.* gespannt, straff. —**eness,** —**ity,** *s.* die Gespanntheit, Straffheit. —**ion,** *s.* die Spannung, Spannkraft. —**ion-spring,** *s.* die Zugfeder (*Radio*).

²**Tense,** *s.* die Zeitform, das Tempus.

Tent, *s.* das Zelt.

Tentac—le, *s.* der Fühlfaden (*Ent.*). —**ular,** *adj.* Fühlfaden=.

Tentative, *adj.* versuchend, probend.

Tenter, *s.* der Spannrahmen. —**hook,** *s.* der Spannhaken; to be on —-hooks, auf der Folter sein.

Tenu—ity, *s.* die Dünnheit. —**ous,** *adj.,* —**ously,** *adv.* dünn.

Tenure, *s.* die Art des Besitzes.

Tepid, *adj.* lau. —**ness,** —**ity,** *s.* die Lauheit.

Term, I. *s.* die Frist; die Zeit der Sitzung, Session (*of a law-court, of parliament*); der Termin (*for payment, etc.*); das Quartal, Trimester (*in schools, universities*); (expression) das Wort, der Ausdruck; das Glied (*Alg., Arith., Log.*); — of office, die Amtsdauer, Amtszeit. II. *v.a.* (be=) nennen.

Termagant, *s.* der Hausdrache.

Termin—able, *adj.* lösbar, kündbar. —**ate,** *v.* I. *a.* enden. II. *n.* endigen. —**ation,** *s.* das Ende; die Endung (*Gram.*). —**us,** *s.* die Endstation (*Railw.*).

Terms, *pl.* Bedingungen.

Tern, *s.* die Seeschwalbe, Meerschwalbe.

Terrace, *s.* die Terrasse; die Häuserreihe (*in towns*).

Terrestrial, *adj.* zur Erde gehörig, Erden=, Erd=.

Terribl—e, *adj.,* —**y,** *adv.* schrecklich, entsetzlich, fürchterlich. —**eness,** *s.* die Schrecklichkeit, Furchtbarkeit.

Terrier, *s.* der Pinscher.

Terrif—ic, *adj.,* —**ically,** *adv.* fürchterlich. —**y,** *v.a.* erschrecken, entsetzen.

Territor—ial, *adj.* Landes=. —**y,** *s.* das Gebiet, der Bezirk.

Terror, *s.* der Schrecken, das Entsetzen.

Terse, *adj.,* —**ly,** *adv.* bündig und geglättet. —**ness,** *s.* die Bündigkeit.

Test, I. *s.* die Probe, der Prüfstein. II. *v.a.* prüfen; untersuchen. —**tube,** *s.* die Probierröhre —**paper,** *s.* das Reagenzpapier (*Chem.*); die Extemporale.

Test—ament, *s.* das Testament. —**amentary,** *adj.* testamentarisch. —**ator,** *s.* der Erblasser, —**atrix,** *s.* die Erblasserin. —**ify,** *v.* I. *a.* bezeugen.

II. *n.* Zeugnis ablegen. **—imonial,**
s. das schriftliche Zeugnis. **—imony,**
s. das Zeugnis.

Tester, *s.* der Himmel (*of a bed, etc.*).

Test—iness, *s.* die Reizbarkeit. **—y,**
adj., **—ily,** *adv.* mürrisch, reizbar.

Tether, I. *s.* das Spannseil. II. *v.a.*
anbinden.

Text, *s.* der Text. **—ile,** *adj.* gewebt;
webbar. **—ual,** *adj.* zum Texte
dienend. **—book,** *s.* das Textbuch.

Texture, *s.* die Textur.

Than, *conj.* (*usually after comparatives*)
als.

Thank, *v.a.* (einem) danken; — you,
(ich) danke (dir *or* Ihnen); yes, —
you, bitte, wenn ich bitten darf; no,
— you, danke, (ich) danke schön. **—s,**
pl. der Dank, die Danksagung; to return **—s,** danken, Dank abstatten. **—
ful,** *adj.,* **—fully,** *adv.* dankbar. **—
fulness,** *s.* die Dankbarkeit. **—less,**
adj., **—lessly,** *adv.* undankbar. **—
offering,** *s.* das Dankopfer. **—s-giv-
ing,** *s.* die Danksagung; (festival)
das Dankfest.

That, I. *dem., adj. & pron.* jen=er, =e,
=es, dies=er, =e, =es, dies, der, die,
das(=jenige); — is, das ist, das
Heißt. II. *rel. pron.* der, die, das,
welcher, welche, welches. III. *conj.*
daß; (in order —) damit; seeing —,
insofern als, weil; not — I believe
nicht, weil ich glaube.

Thatch, I. *s.* das Strohdach. II. *v.a.*
mit Stroh 2c. decken. **—er,** *s.* der
Strohdecker.

Thaw, I. *s.* das Tauwetter. II. *v.a. &
n.* auftauen.

The, *def. art.* der, die, das; je, desto,
um so (*old instrumental, before comparatives*); — more, — better, je
mehr, desto besser.

Theatr—e, *s.* das Schauspielhaus,
Theater. **—ic(al),** *adj.,* **—ically,** *adv.*
bühnenmäßig, theatralisch. **—icals,**
pl. (Bühnen-)Aufführungen.

Thee, *pron.* dich; (to —) dir; of —,
deiner.

Theft, *s.* der Diebstahl.

Their, *poss. adj.* ihr(e). **—s,** *poss. pron.*
der, die, das ihrige, ihr, ihre, ihres.

Theis—m, *s.* der Theismus. **—t,** *s.*
der Theist.

Them, *pers. pron.* sie; (to —) ihnen;
(of —) von ihnen. **—selves,** *pron.* sie
selbst; (*used reflexively*) sich selbst.

Theme, *s.* das Thema, der Aufsatz.

Then, I. *adv.* (at that time) damals;
(after that) dann, alsdann, darauf;
there and —, sogleich. II. *adj.;* the
— king, der damalige König. III.
conj. denn, also, folglich. IV. *expletive;* now —, nun denn, wohlan
denn.

Thence, I. *adv.* daher, daraus, darum;
(from —) von da, dort *or* dannen. II.
conj. daher; — it came to pass, daher
geschah es. **—forth,** **—forward,** *adv.*
von da an, seitdem.

Theolog—ian, *s.* der Theolog. **—ical,**
adj., **—ically,** *adv.* theologisch. **—y,**
s. die Theologie.

Theor—em, *s.* der Lehrsatz, das
Theorem. **—etic(al),** *adj.,* **—etically,**
adv. theoretisch. **—ist,** *s.* der Theo-
retiker. **—y,** *s.* die Theorie.

There, *adv.* da, dort, daselbst; (thither)
dahin, dorthin; — is, es gibt; — are,
es sind. **—about(s),** *adv.* da herum;
(about that) ungefähr so viel.
—after, *adv.* da(r)nach. **—at,** *adv.*
dabei, darauf. **—fore,** *adv. & conj.*
deswegen, deshalb, darum, dafür;
deshalb, also, folglich. **—from,** **—of,**
adv. davon; dessen, deren. **—in,** *adv.*
darin. **—upon,** *adv.* darauf; deshalb,
darum. **—with,** *adv.* damit; gleich
darauf.

Therm—al, *adj.* Thermal=. **—ometer,**
s. das Thermometer.

These, *pl.* of This; diese.

Thesis, *s.* der Leitsatz, die These.

Thews, *pl.* Muskeln; (*fig.*) die Sehnen.

They, *pers. pron.* sie; — who, die
(jenigen) welche; — say, man sagt.

Thick, I. *adj.* dick; dicht (*as fog*).
II. *adv.* dick, dicht. III. *s.* das Dickste.
—en, *v.a.* dick machen, verdichten, verstärken. **—headed,** *adj.* dickköpfig.
—ness, *s.* die Dicke, Dichtheit. **—
set,** *adj.* untersetzt.

Thicket, *s.* das Dickicht.

Thief, *s.* der Dieb, die Diebin.

Thiev—e, *v.n.* stehlen. **—ery,** *s.* die
Dieberei. **—ish,** *adj.* diebisch (*also
fig.*).

Thigh, *s.* der Schenkel, die Lende. **—
bone,** *s.* das Schenkelbein.

Thimble, *s.* der Fingerhut.

Thin, I. *adj.,* **—ly,** *adv.* dünn. II. *v.a.*
verdünnen; lichten (*wool, etc.*). III.
v.n.; to — out, allmählich abnehmen. **—ness,** *s.* die Dünnheit; die

Magerkeit. **—skinned**, *adj.* (*fig.*) empfindlich.

Thine, I *poss. pron.* bei, bie, bas Deinige, bein=er, =e, =es. II. *poss. adj.* bein.

Thing, *s.* bas Ding (*also fig.*); bie Sache.

Think, *ir.v.* I. *n.* benken; benken (of, an einen, etwas; von einer Person ober S.; auf eine S.); nachbenken (upon, über eine S.); sich besinnen (of, auf eine S.); (believe) meinen, glauben (of, von); (intend) gebenken, beabsichtigen; to — out, (sich) ausbenken. II. *a.* benken, urteilen, meinen, glauben, vermuten, halten für. **—er,** *s.* ber Denker. **—ing,** I. *adj.* benkend, vernünftig. II. *s.* bas Denken; bie Meinung; to my —ing, nach meiner Meinung.

Third, I. *adj.* britt. II. *s.* ber, bie, bas Dritte; (— part) bas Drittel; bie Tertie, Terz (*Mus.*). **—ly,** *adv.* brittens. **—rate,** *adj.* britten Ranges.

Thirst, I. *s.* ber Durst (*also fig.*). II. *v.n.* bürsten, bursten (for, after, nach). **—ily,** *adv.* burstig. **—iness,** *s.* bie Durstigkeit, ber Durst. **—y,** *adj.* burstig (*also fig.*).

Thirteen, *num. adj.* breizehn. **—th,** I. *adj.* breizehnt. II. *s.* ber, bie, bas Dreizehnte.

Thirt—ieth, I. *adj.* breißigst. II. *s.* ber, bie, bas Dreißigste. **—y,** *num. adj.* breißig; breißig Jahre.

This, *dem. adj.* bies=er, =e, =es, bies; — morning, heute morgen.

Thistle, *s.* bie Distel. **—down,** *s.* bie Distelwolle.

Thither, *adv.* borthin, bahin. **—wards,** *adv.* borthin.

Thole-pin, *s.* ber Ruberpflock.

Thong, *s.* ber Riemen.

Thorn, *s.* ber Dorn. **—less,** *adj.* bornenlos. **—y,** *adj.* bornig, stachelig, beschwerlich.

Thorough, *adj.* burchgehend, burch unb burch, gänzlich, vollständig; (perfect) vollendet, vollkommen. **—ly,** *adv.* burchaus, völlig, gänzlich, gründlich. **—ness,** *s.* bie Vollständigkeit, Gründlichkeit. **—bred,** I. *adj.* vollblütig. II. *s.* bas Vollblut(pferd). **—fare,** *s.* ber Durchgang.

Those, *pl.* of That, *dem.* I. *adj.* jene, biejenigen; are — your parents? sinb bas Ihre Eltern? II. *pron.* bie=

(jenigen), solche; what (sort of) books are —? was sinb bas für Bücher?

Thou, *pers. pron.* bu; *see* Thee.

Though, *conj.* ob=schon, =gleich, =wohl, wenn auch, wenngleich; (nevertheless) boch; zwar, freilich, allerbings; as —, als ob; I see him —, ich sehe ihn bennoch.

Thought, I. *imperf. & p.p., see* Think. II. *s.* ber Gebanke; (reflection) bas Denken; (notion) ber Begriff; (idea) bie Meinung; (solicitude) bie Sorge. **—ful,** *adj.*, **—fully,** *adv.* gebankenvoll, tiefsinnig. **—fulness,** *s.* tiefes Nachbenken; bie Zuvorkommenheit. **—less,** *adj.*, **—lessly,** *adv.* gebankenlos; (careless) sorglos (of, um); (irreflective) unbesonnen. **—lessness,** *s.* bie Gebankenlosigkeit, Unbesonnenheit. **—reading,** *s.* bas Gebankenlesen.

Thousand, I. *num. adj.* tausenb. II. *s.* bas Tausenb. **—th,** I. *adj.* tausenbst. II. *s.* bas Tausendstel, Tausenbteil.

Thral—dom, *s.* bie Knechtschaft. **—l,** *s.* ber Knecht.

Thrash, *v.a.* (— out, aus=)breschen; (beat) (burch)prügeln. **—ing,** *s.* bas Dreschen; bie Tracht Prügel. **—ing-floor,** *s.* bie Dreschtenne. **—ing-machine,** *s.* bie Dreschmaschine.

Thread, I. *s.* ber Faden (*also fig.*); (linen =) ber Zwirn; bas Gewinde (of a *screw*). II. *v.a.* einfäbeln (a *needle*); anreihen (*beads*). **—bare,** *adj.* fabenscheinig.

Threat, I. *s.* bie Drohung. II. —, **—en,** *v.a. & n.* bebrohen, (einem) brohen (mit). **—ening,** *adj.*, **—eningly,** *adv.* brohenb.

Three, I. *num. adj.* brei. II. *s.* bie Drei. **—cornered,** *adj.* breieckig. **—fold,** *adj.* breifach. **—quarter,** *adj.* breiviertel. **—storied,** *adj.* breistöckig.

Threshold, *s.* bie Schwelle.

Thrice, *adv.* breimal, breifach.

Thrift, *s.* bie Sparsamkeit. **—ily,** *adv.*, **—y,** *adj.* sparsam. **—iness,** *s.* bie Wirtschaftlichkeit. **—less,** *adj.*, **—lessly,** *adv.* verschwenberisch.

Thrill, I. *s.* bas Durchschauern. II. *v.a.* burchschauern. III. *v.n.* schauern, zittern, beben. **—ing,** *adj.*, **—ingly,** *adv.* burchbringenb; ergreifend (as a *tale*).

Thriv—e, *ir.v.n.* gedeihen, geraten, Glück haben. **—ing,** *adj.,* **—ingly,** *adv.* gedeihlich.

Throat, *s.* die Gurgel, Kehle; (neck) der Hals.

Throb, I. *s.* der (Puls=)Schlag; das Stampfen *(of an engine).* II. *v.n.* schlagen, pochen.

Throe, *s.* der Schmerz.

Throne, *s.* der Thron.

Throng, I. *s.* das Gedränge. II. *v.n.* sich drängen. III. *v.a.* drängen.

Throttle, I. *s.* die Luftröhre; das Drosselventil *(Eng.).* II. *v.a.* erdrosseln; drosseln *(an engine).*

Through, I. *prep.* durch; (because of) aus, vor; (by means of) mittelst. — train, durchgehender Zug. II. *adv.* durch; (at an end) zu Ende. **—out,** I. *prep.* ganz (hin)durch. II. *adv.* durchaus, in jeder Beziehung.

Throw, I. *ir.v.a.* werfen, schleudern; abwerfen (as a horse his rider, wie ein Pferd seinen Reiter). II. *ir.v.n.* werfen; würfeln *(with dice);* to — away, wegwerfen; to — over, aufgeben, verlassen. III. *s.* der Wurf. **—ing,** *s.* das Werfen.

Thrush, *s.* die Drossel.

Thrust, I. *ir.v.a.* stoßen; to — oneself into, sich drängen in. II. *ir.v.n.* stoßen (at, nach). III. *s.* der Stoß, Stich.

Thud, *s.* der dumpfe Schlag, das Dröhnen.

Thumb, I. *s.* der Daumen; by rule of —, erfahrungsmäßig. II. *ir.v.a.* abgreifen. **—ed,** *adj.;* well —ed volumes, abgegriffene Bände. **—screw,** *s.* die Daumenschraube.

Thump, I. *s.* der Schlag, Puff. II. *v.a.* & *n.* schlagen, puffen.

Thunder, I. *s.* der Donner. II. *v.n.* donnern. **—ing,** *adj.,* **—ingly,** *adv.* donnernd. **—y,** *adj.* gewitterhaft. **—bolt,** *s.* der Donnerkeil. **—clap,** *s.* der Donnerschlag. **—cloud,** *s.* die Gewitterwolke. **—shower,** *s.* der Gewitterregen. **—storm,** *s.* das Gewitter. **—struck,** *adj.* wie vom Donner gerührt.

Thursday, *s.* der Donnerstag; on —s, every —, Donnerstags, jeden Donnerstag.

Thus, *adv.* so, daher.

Thwack, *v.a.* schlagen, durchwalken.

¹**Thwart,** I. *adj.* quer, schräg. II. *v.a.* in die Quere kommen, durchkreuzen, vereiteln.

²**Thwart,** *s.* die Sitzbank, Ducht *(Naut.).*

Thy, *poss. adj.* dein(e). **—self,** *pron.* du (selbst).

Thyme, *s.* der Thymian.

Tiara, *s.* die Tiara.

¹**Tick,** *s.* die Schaflaus.

²**Tick,** *s.* der (Bett=)Überzug. **—ing,** *s.* der Drillich.

³**Tick,** *s.;* upon —, auf Borg *(sl.).*

⁴**Tick,** I. *s.* das Ticken. II. *v.n.* ticken, picken *(as a clock);* to — off, punktieren.

Ticket, I. *s.* der Zettel; der Fahrschein; das Lotterielos; die Fahrkarte *(Railw.);* das Billet *(Theat.);* die Etikette *(on goods, etc.).* II. *v.a.* bezetteln. **—office,** *s.* der Schalter.

Tickl—o, *v.a.* kitzeln *(also fig.).* **—ing,** *s.* das Kitzeln. **—ish,** *adj.* kitzlig; kritisch, *(as times, etc.).*

Tid—al, *adj.* Flut=. **—e,** *s.* die Ebbe und Flut *(of the sea);* die Zeit *(Poet.);* high —e, die Flutzeit; the —e is going out, die Ebbe tritt ein; turn of the —e, der Flutwechsel; *(fig.)* der Glückswechsel. **—eless,** *adj.* ohne Ebbe und Flut.

Tidings, *pl.* die Nachrichten; glad —, frohe Botschaft.

Tid—y, I. *adj.,* **—ily,** *adv.* sauber, ordentlich; *(fig.)* nett, niedlich. II. *s.* das Schutzdeckchen für Möbel. III. *v.a.* (—y up) in Ordnung bringen. **—iness,** *s.* die Sauberkeit; die Ordnung.

Tie, I. *v.a.* binden; (unite) verknüpfen; to — a knot, einen Knoten schlagen, machen. II. *s.* das Band, die Schleife, Binde *(for the neck, etc.);* die Bindung *(Mus.).*

Tier, *s.* die Reihe, Lage; die Sitzreihe *(Theat.).*

Tiff, *s.* das Schmollen, der Unwille.

Tig—er, *s.* der Tiger. **—erish,** *adj.* tigerhaft. **—ress,** *s.* die Tigerin.

Tight, *adj.,* **—ly,** *adv.* dicht, fest; (taut) gespannt, straff; to hold —, fest halten. **—en,** *v.a.* zusammenziehen. **—ness,** *s.* die Dichtheit; die Straffheit. **—s,** *pl.* das Trikot. **—fitting,** *adj.* knapp anliegend. **—laced,** *adj.* festgeschnürt.

Til—e, I. *s.* der Ziegel; roof —, der Dachziegel. II. *v.a.* mit Ziegeln decken. **—er,** *s.* der Ziegeldecker. **—ing,** *s.* die Ziegel. **—e-floor,** *s.* der Fliesenfußboden. **—e(d)-roof,** *s.* das Ziegeldach.

¹**Till,** *conj. & prep.* bis (ʒu), bis (auf); — now, bisjeşt, bisher, bislang.

²**Till,** *s.* die Geldſchublade, die Ladentiſchkaſſe.

³**Till,** *v.a.* bebauen, adern. **—age,** *s.* der Ader=, Feld=bau.

¹**Tiller,** *s.* der Adersmann, Landmann.

²**Tiller,** *s.* der Helmſtod, die Ruderpinne.

¹**Tilt,** *s.* die Plane (*of a cart, etc.*).

²**Tilt,** I. *s.* die Neigung. II. *v.a.* neigen, kippen (*a barrel, etc.*); einlegen (*the lance*). III. *v.n.* Lanzen brechen, turnieren; to — up, ſich kippen, ſich neigen. **—er,** *s.* der Turnierer. **—ing,** I. *adj.* Turnier=. II. *s.* das Lanzenbrechen, Ritterſpiel.

Timber, I. *s.* das Zimmer=, Bau=holz; —s, Inhölzer, das Rippenwerk (*of a ship*). II. *attrib.;* — bridge, hölzerne Brüde. **—trade,** *s.* der Holzhandel. **—work,** *s.* das Zimmerwerk. **—yard,** *s.* der Zimmer=, Bau=hof.

Time, I. *s.* die Zeit; der Takt, das Tempo (*Danc.*); das Mal; every —, jedesmal; many a —, manchmal; three —s, breimal; at any —, ʒu jeder Zeit, (always) ſtets, immer; at no —, ʒu keiner Zeit; for a —, eine Zeitlang; for the —, für den Augenblid; in —, ʒur Zeit, ʒu ſeiner Zeit; in the day- —, bei Tage; to lose —, nachgehen (*as a clock*). II. *v.a.* der Zeit gemäß einrichten; die Zeit beſtimmen; ſehen, wieviel Zeit man ʒu einer S. gebraucht; to — a matter well, die rechte Zeit für eine S. wählen. III. *v.n.* Takt halten; ʒuſammenſtimmen (mit). **—liness,** *s.* die Rechtzeitigkeit. **—ly,** *adj.* (recht=) zeitig. **—honoured,** *adj.* altehrwürdig. **—keeper,** *s.* das Chronometer; der Kontrollbeamte (*in factories, etc.*). **—piece,** *s.* die Uhr. **—server,** *s.* der Achſelträger. **—serving,** I. *adj.* achſelträgeriſch. II. *s.* die Achſelträgerei. **—table,** *s.* der Fahrplan (*Railw.*); der Stundenplan (*in schools*); —tables, der Eiſenbahnführer (*Railw.*). **—worn,** *adj.* veraltet, abgenußt.

Timid, *adj.*, **—ly,** *adv.* furchtſam. **—ness, —ity,** *s.* die Furchtſamkeit.

Timorous, *adj.* furchtſam.

Tin, I. *s.* das Zinn. II. *v.a.* ver=, über=ʒinnen; in Blechbüchſen ver-

packen; —ned meat, fruit, konſerviertes *or* Büchſen=Fleiſch, Obſt. — **foil,** *s.* das Blattzinn, Stanniol. — **ware,** *s.* das Weißblech. **—works,** *s.* die Zinnhütte.

Tincture, *s.* die Farbe; die Tinte (*Paint.*); die Tinktur (*Chem.*); (*fig.*) der Anſtrich.

Tinder, *s.* der Zunder.

Tinge, I. *s.* die Färbung; (*fig.*) der Beigeſchmad. II. *v.a.* färben; (*fig.*) einen Anſtrich geben.

Tingl—e, *v.n.* prideln, **—ing,** *s.* das Klingen; das Prideln.

Tinker, I. *s.* der Klempner. II. *v.a.* fliden, herumpfuſchen; to — up, zuſammenfliden. **—ing,** *s.* das Keſſelfliden.

Tinkle, *v.* I. *n.* klingen. II. *a.* klingen machen.

Tinsel, I. *s.* das Flittergold. II. *adj.* Flitter=.

Tint, I. *s.* die Farbe, der Anſtrich. II. *v.a.* färben.

Tiny, *adj.* winzig, klein.

Tip, I. *s.* die Spitze; die Andeutung (*coll.*), der Wink; das Trinkgeld (*coll.*). II. *v.a.* (— up) (um=)kippen. **—toe,** *s.* die Zehenſpitze.

Tippet, *s.* die Pelerine.

Tipple, *v.n.* trinken, ſaufen, zechen. **—r,** *s.* der Trunkenbold.

Tipsy, *adj.* betrunken, berauſcht, benebelt.

Tirade, *s.* die Tirade, Scheltrede.

¹**Tire,** *v.* I. *a.* ermüden. II. *n.* müde werden. **—d,** müde, überdrüſſig. — **dness,** *s.* die Müdigkeit. **—less,** *adj.* unermüdlich. **—some,** *adj.*, **—somely,** *adv.* langweilig, verdrießlich.

²**Tire,** *s. see* Tyre.

Tissue, *s.* das Gewebe, **—paper,** *s.* das Seidenpapier.

Titbit, *s.* der Lederbiſſen.

Tithe, *s.* das Zehntel.

Title, *s.* der Titel; die Überſchrift. **—deed,** *s.* die (Eigentums=)Urkunde. **—page,** *s.* das Titelblatt.

Titmouse, *s.* die Meiſe.

Titter, I. *v.n.* kichern. II. *s.* das Kichern, Gekicher.

Tittle, *s.* das Pünktchen. **—tattle,** *s.* das Geſchwätz.

Titular, *adj.*, **—ly,** *adv.* nominell.

To, I. *part.* (sign of the inf., Zeichen des Infinitivs) ʒu. II. *prep. & adv.* ʒu; (*indicating direction towards*) ʒu, gegen

nach, an. in, auf; (towards) gegen;
(according —) nach); (in order —)
um zu; (up —, as far, high, etc., as)
bis (zu, in, an, nach, auf); — me,
you, him, etc. (*forming the dat.*) mir,
Ihnen, ihm, 2c.; he gave it — his
friend, er gab es seinem Freunde; it
happened — me, es geschah mir;
alive —, lebhaft fühlend; I weep —
think of it, ich weine, wenn ich daran
denke; — and fro, hin und her.

Toad, *s.* die Kröte. **—y,** I. *s.* der
Schmarotzer. II. *v.a.* niedrig schmeicheln. **—eater,** *s.* der Speichellecker.
—stool, *s.* der Giftschwamm.

¹Toast, I. *s.* die geröstete Brotschnitte.
II. *v.a.* rösten.

²Toast, I. *s.* der Toast, der Trinkspruch,
die ausgebrachte Gesundheit. II. *v.a.*
eine Gesundheit ausbringen auf (*acc.*),
trinken auf (*acc.*).

Tobacco, *s.* der Tabak. **—nist,** *s.* der
Tabak und Zigarren=händler; (—-
maker) der Tabaksfabrikant.

Toboggan, I. *s.* der Rodelschlitten.
II. *v.a.* rodeln, mit dem Rodelschlitten fahren.

Tocsin, *s.* die Sturmglocke.

To-day, I. *adv.* heute. II. *s.* der
heutige Tag.

Toddle, *v.n.* watscheln.

Toe, *s.* die Zehe. **—d,** *adj.,* mit
Zehen, =zehig.

Together, *adv.* zusammen, mit einander; beisammen; (at the same time)
zugleich; three days —, drei Tage
nach einander; for days —, tage-
lang.

¹Toil, I. *s.* die Mühe, Plackerei. II. *v.n.*
sich abarbeiten, sich anstrengen. **—er,**
s. einer der sich abarbeitet, abmüht,
plackt. **—some,** *adj.,* mühsam, mühselig.
—someness, *s.* die Mühsamkeit.

²Toil, *s.,* **—s,** *pl.* das Netz.

Toilet, *s.* die Toilette; to make one's
—, sich anziehen. **—table,** *s.* der
Putztisch.

Token, *s.* das Zeichen, Andenken.

Tolera—ble, *adj.,* **—bly,** *adv.* leidlich).
—bleness, *s.* die Erträglichkeit, Leid-
lichkeit. **—nce,** *s.* die Duldung; die
Duldsamkeit, Toleranz (*in religion,
etc.*). **—nt,** *adj.,* **—ntly,** *adv.* duldsam. **—te,** *v.a.* dulden, ertragen,
leiden.

¹Toll, *s.* der Zoll. **—bar,** *s.* der
Schlagbaum. **—bridge,** *s.* die Zoll-

brücke. **—gate,** *s.* das Zolltor.
—keeper, *s.* der Zolleinnehmer.

²Toll, *v.a.* & *n.* läuten.

Tomahawk, *s.* die Streitaxt.

Tomato, *s.* die Tomate, der Liebesapfel.

Tomb, *s.* das Grab. **—stone,** *s.* der
Grabstein.

Tom—boy, *s.* das wilde Mädchen, die
Range, der Wildfang. **—cat,** *s.* der
Kater. **—fool,** *s.* der Tropf. —
foolery, *s.* die Narrenspossen (*pl.*).

Tome, *s.* das Band, das Buch (*of a
work*).

To-morrow, I. *adv.* morgen; **—morning,** morgen früh; the day after
—, übermorgen. II. *s.* das Morgen,
der morgige Tag.

Tomtit, *s.* die Meise.

¹Ton, I. *s.* die Mode; bon —, feine
Lebensart.

²Ton, *s.* die Tonne.

Tone, I. *s.* der Ton (*in speaking*); der
Klang, Laut. II. *v.a.* abtönen (*Phot.*);
to — down, mildern, herabstimmen.
—d, *adj.* tönend; abgetönt (*Phot.*).
—less, *adj.* tonlos.

Tongs, *pl.* (a pair of —) die Zange;
(fire —) die Feuerzange.

Tongue, *s.* die Zunge; (language)
die Sprache.

Tonic, I. *adj.* tonisch (*Mus., Med.*).
II. *s.* die Tonika, der Grundton
(*Mus.*); das nervenstärkende Mittel
(*Med.*).

To-night, I. *adv.* heute abend. II. *s.*
der heutige Abend.

Tonnage, *s.* der Tonnengehalt (*of a
ship*).

Tonsil, *s.* die (Hals=)Mandel.

Tonsure, *s.* die Tonsur.

Too, *adv.* (all)zu; noch dazu, auch,
ebenfalls.

Tool, *s.* das Werkzeug (*also fig.*).

Toot, *v.n.* tuten, blasen.

Tooth, (*pl.* Teeth) *s.* der Zahn; to
go at it — and nail, etwas mit aller
Kraft angreifen; to show one's teeth,
die Zähne zeigen, drohen. **—ed,**
adj. gezähnt, zähnig; —ed wheel,
das Zahnrad. **—some,** *adj.* schmackhaft. **—ache,** *s.* das Zahnweh.
—brush, *s.* die Zahnbürste. **—less,**
adj. zahnlos. **—pick,** *s.* der Zahn-
stocher.

¹Top, I. *s.* der Wipfel (*of a tree*);
der Giebel (*of a house*); das Mars
(*Naut.*); der Scheitel (*of the head*);

die Stulpe (*of a boot*); der Gipfel (*of a hill*); at the — of his voice, so laut er kann; from — to toe, von Kopf zu Fuß. II. *adj.* oberst, Haupt=. III. *v.n.* steigen; hervorragen (*as mountains*). IV. *v.a.* (oben) bedecken; (rise above) über= ragen; (*fig.*) übertreffen. —**boots**, *pl.* Stulpenstiefel. —**coat**, *s.* der Überzieher. —**gallant**, *s.* das Bram= segel. —**hat**, *s.* der Zylinder (hut). —**heavy**, *adj.* oben schwerer als unten. —**mast**, *s.* der oberste Mast. —**most**, *adj.* höchst, oberst. —**sail**, *s.* das Marssegel.

²**Top**, *s.* der Kreisel; to spin a —, einen Kreisel schlagen, kreiseln.

Topaz, *s.* der Topas.

Tope, *v.n.* zechen, saufen. —**r**, *s.* der Säufer.

Top—**ic**, *s.* der Gegenstand, das Thema. —**ical**, *adj.*, —**ically**, *adv.* topisch. —**ographical**, *adj.*, —**o=** **graphically**, *adv.* topographisch. —**o=** **graphy**, *s.* die Ortsbeschreibung, Topographie.

Toque, *s.* eine Art Barett (für Frauen).

Torch, *s.* die Fackel; electric —, die elektrische Taschenlampe. —**light**, *s.* das Fackellicht; —**light** procession, der Fackelzug.

Torment, I. *s.* die Pein, Qual. II. *v.a.* martern, quälen, peinigen. —**or**, *s.* der Peiniger, Quäler.

Tornado, *s.* der Wirbelsturm.

Torpedo, I. *s.* der Zitterroche (*Icht.*); der Torpedo (*Naut.*). II. *v.a.* in die Luft sprengen. —**boat**, *s.* das Tor= pedoboot. —**catcher**, —(**-boat)-** **destroyer**, *s.* der Torpedobootzer= störer. —**tube**, *s.* das (Torpedo=) Lancierrohr.

Torp—**id**, *adj.*, —**idly**, *adv.* starr, erstarrt. —**idity**, *s.* die Erstarrung. —**or**, *s.* die Gefühl=, Reiz=losigkeit.

Torrent, *s.* der Gießbach. —**ial**, *adj.* strömend.

Torrid, *adj.* brennend, heiß; — regions, zone, die heiße Zone, heiße Gegenden.

Tortoise, *s.* die Schildkröte. —**shell**, I. *s.* die Schildkrötenschale, das Schild= patt. II. *attrib.*; —**shell** comb, der Schildpattkamm.

Tortuous, *adj.*, —**ly**, *adv.* schlangen= artig.

Tortur—**e**, I. *s.* die Folter, Marter (*also fig.*). II. *v.a.* foltern, martern. —**er**, *s.* der Folterer; (*fig.*) der Peiniger.

—**ing**, *adj.*, —**ingly**, *adv.* folternd, quälend.

Tosh, *s.* dummes Zeug! (*sl.*).

Toss, I. *v.a.* emporschleudern (*as bulls, etc.*). II. *v.n.* sich hin und her wälzen (*in sleep*); to — for, losen um. III. *s.* der Wurf, Stoß, das Werfen; das Zurückwerfen (*of the head*); to win the —, beim Losen gewinnen. —**up**, *s.* der (reine) Zufall.

¹**Tot**, *v.a.*; to — up, zusammen= rechnen.

²**Tot**, *s.* kleines Kind.

Total, I. *adj.*, —**ly**, *adv.* ganz, gänzlich, völlig. II. *s.* der Gesamtbetrag; (sum —al) die Gesammtsumme. III. *v.n.* sich belaufen auf.

Totter, *v.n.* wanken, wackeln.

Touch, I. *v.a.* be=, an=rühren, stoßen an (*acc.*); (feel) an=fühlen, =tasten; (reach) erreichen. II. *v.n.* sich be= rühren; to — at, anlanden; to — up, auffrischen; to — upon, berühren, kommen auf (*acc.*). III. *s.* die Berührung; (sense of —) der Tastsinn; an artistic —, ein künstlerischer Anflug. —**ily**, *adv.*, —**y**, *adj.* emp= findlich, reizbar. —**iness**, *s.* die Empfindlichkeit, Reizbarkeit. —**ing**, I. *adj.*, —**ingly**, *adv.* rührend. II. *prep.* betreffend, in Betreff. —**and-go**, I. *adj.* gewagt. II. *s.* knappes Ent= kommen. —**line**, *s.* die Marklinie (*Sport*). —**stone**, *s.* der Probierstein; (*fig.*) der Prüfstein.

Tough, *adj.*, —**ly**, *adv.* zäh(e). —**en**, *v.* I. *a.* zäh(e) machen. II. *n.* zäh(e) werden. —**ness**, *v.* die Zähigkeit.

Tour, I. *s.* die Reise, der Ausflug. II. *v.n.* reisen. —**ist**, *s.* der Reisende.

Tourn—**ament**, —**ey**, *s.* das Turnier.

Tourniquet, *s.* die Aderpresse (*Surg.*).

Tousle, *v.a.* (zer)zausen (*prov.*).

Tout, *s.* der Kundensucher.

¹**Tow**, I. *v.a.* (am Seile nach=)schleppen, bugsieren. II. *s.* das Schlepptau. —**boat**, *s.* das Schleppboot. —**ing=** **path**, *s.* der Lein=, Treidel=pfad. —**line**, —**rope**, *s.* das Schlepptau.

²**Tow**, *s.* das Werg, die Hede.

Toward, I., —**s**, *prep.* gegen, nach . . . zu. II. *adj.*, —**ly**, *adv.* geneigt, willig.

Towel, *s.* das Handtuch. —**horse**, —**rack**, *s.* der Handtuchständer.

Tower, I. *s.* der Turm. II. *v.n.* sich erheben.

Town, *s.* die Stadt. **—clerk,** *s.* der Stadtschreiber. **—council,** *s.* der Stadtrat. **—councillor,** *s.* der Stadtrat. **—hall,** *s.* das Rathaus.

Tox—ic, *adj.* toxisch, giftig. **—in,** *s.* das Toxin.

Toy, I. *s.* das Spielzeug. II. *v.n.* tändeln.

¹Trace, I. *s.* die Spur. II. *v.a.* zeichnen; pausen.

²Trace, *s.* der Strang, Zugriemen.

Tracery, *s.* das Maßwerk.

Trachea, *s.* die Luftröhre.

Tracing, *s.* das (Durch=)Zeichnen. (Durch=)Pausen.

Track, I. *s.* die Spur; (path) die Bahn; der Schienenweg, das Geleise (*Railw.*). II. *v.a.* der Spur folgen. **—er,** *s.* der Spürhund; der Verfolger. **—less,** *adj.* spurlos, pfadlos. **—lessness,** *s.* die Pfadlosigkeit.

¹Tract, *s.* die Strecke.

²Tract, *s.* der Traktat.

Tractab—le, *adj.,* **—ly,** *adv.* lenk=, folg=sam. **—leness, —ility,** *s.* die Lenksamkeit.

Tract—ion, *s.* das Ziehen, der Zug; electric **—ion,** elektrische Fortbewegung. **—ive,** *adj.* ziehend, Zieh=. **—or,** *s.* der Zieher. **—ion-engine,** *s.* die Straßenlokomotive.

Trad—e, I. *s.* der Handel. II. *v.a.* handeln, Handel treiben (with, mit). **—er,** *s.* der Handelsmann; das Handelsschiff (*Naut.*). **—ing,** *p. & adj.* handeltreibend, Handels=. **—e-mark,** *s.* das Fabrikzeichen, die Schutzmarke. **—e-price,** *s.* der Handels=, Engrospreis. **—esman,** *s.* der Kleinhändler, Krämer. **—e(s)-union,** *s.* der Gewerkverein. **—e-winds,** *pl.* Passatwinde.

Tradition, *s.* die Tradition (*Rel.*); popular **—,** die Volksüberlieferung, Volkssage. **—al, —ary,** *adj.* mündlich überliefert; herkömmlich; **—al** custom, althergömmlicher Brauch.

Traduce, *v.a.* verleumden. **—r,** *s.* der Verleumder.

Traffic, I. *s.* der Verkehr. II. *v.n.* handeln.

Trag—edian, *s.* der Trauerspieldichter; der tragische Schauspieler. **—edy,** *s.* das Trauerspiel. **—ic(al),** *adj.,* **—ically,** *adv.* tragisch.

Trail, I. *v.a.* (nach)schleppen; auf der Spur verfolgen (*Sport*). II. *v.n.*

kriechen (*plants*); to **—** along, sich hinschleppen. III. *s.* die Witterung, Fährte.

Train, I. *v.a.* dressieren (*animals*); (auf=)erziehen (*children, etc.*); ausbilden (*teachers*); (ein)exerzieren (*recruits*). II. *v.n.* üben, drillen, exerzieren. III. *s.* die Schleppe (*of a dress*); (procession) der Zug; der Zug (*Railw., Mil.*); (retinue) das Gefolge; das Leitfeuer (*Min., etc.*). **—ed,** *adj.* ausgebildet; abgerichtet (*animals*). **—er,** *s.* der Abrichter; der Erzieher. **—ing,** *s.* die Erziehung; das Einexerzieren. **—ing-college,** *s.* das Lehrer(innen)seminar.

Train-oil, *s.* der Tran.

Trait, *s.* der Zug, Charakterzug.

Trait—or, *s.* der Verräter. **—orous,** *adj.,* **—orously,** *adv.* verräterisch. **—ress,** *s.* die Verräterin.

Tram, *s.* die Grubenschiene (*Min.*). **—car,** *s.* der Straßenbahnwagen. **—way,** *s.* die Straßenbahn.

Trammel, *s.* das Garn; (*fig.*) die Fessel.

Tramp, I. *v.n.* trampeln; (walk) zu Fuß reisen. II. *v.a.* treten, trampeln auf. III. *s.* das Getrampel; **—** of horses, das Pferdegetrappel; (vagrant) der Landstreicher. **—le,** *v.a. & n.* trampeln.

Trance, *s.* die Verzückung; der Scheintod (*Med.*); hypnotischer Schlaf. (*fig.*)

Tranquil, *adj.,* **—ly,** *adv.* ruhig, still. **—lity,** *s.* die Ruhe, Stille; (*fig.*) die Gelassenheit. **—lize,** *v.a.* beruhigen, stillen.

Trans—act, *v.a.* verrichten, abmachen. **—action,** *s.* die Verrichtung, Verhandlung. **—atlantic,** *adj.* trans=atlantisch. **—cend,** *v.a.* übersteigen. **—cendent,** *adj.,* **—cendently,** *adv.* höchst vortrefflich. **—cendental,** *adj.* tranzendental (*Philos.*). **—cribe,** *v.a.* abschreiben. **—criber,** *s.* der Abschreiber. **—cript,** *s.* die Abschrift.

Transept, *s.* das Kreuzschiff.

Transfer, I. *v.a.* übertragen; versetzen (*to another place*). II. *s.* (change of place) die Versetzung; die Übertragung (*of a right, etc.*); **—** picture, das Abziehbild. **—able,** *adj.* versetzbar; übertragbar. **—ence,** *s.* die Übertragung. **—rer,** *s.* der Übertragende.

Transfiguration, *s.* die Verklärung (*B.*).

Transf—ix, *v.a.* durchstechen. **—orm**, *v.a.* umgestalten. **—ormation**, *s.* die Verwandlung, Umwandlung.

Transfuse, *v.a.* überleiten (*blood*); übergießen.

Transgress, *v.* I. *a.* überschreiten; (*fig.*) verstoßen gegen. II. *n.* sich vergehen. **—ion**, *s.* die Vergehung. **—or**, *s.* der Übertreter, Sünder.

Tranship, *v.a.* umladen.

Transi—ent, *adj.*, **—ently**, *adv.* vergänglich. **—t**, *s.* der Durchgang. **—tion**, *s.* der Übergang. **—tive**, *adj.* übergehend (*also fig.*); transitiv (*Gram.*).

Translat—e, *v.a.* übersetzen (*a language*). **—ion**, *s.* die Übersetzung. **—or**, *s.* der Übersetzer.

Transmigration, *s.* die Übersiedelung; der Übergang (*into another state*).

Trans—mission, *s.* die Überschickung; die (Waren=)Spedition (*C.L.*). **—mit**, *v.a.* überschicken. **—mitter**, *s.* der Übersender; der Fortpflanzende; der Sender (*Radio*). **—parency**, *s.* die Durchsichtigkeit. **—parent**, *adj.*, **—parently**, *adv.* durchsichtig.

Transom, *s.* das Querholz, der Querbalken.

Trans—pire, *v.n.* bekannt werden (*fig.*). **—plant**, *v.a.* verpflanzen, =setzen. **—port**, I. *v.a.* über=fahren, =setzen; deportieren (*criminals, etc.*). II. *s.* das Fortschaffen; der Transport; das Transportschiff; der Anfall (*of passion, etc.*).

Transpose, *v.a.* versetzen.

Transubstantiat—e, *v.a.* verwandeln. **—ion**, *s.* die Transsubstantiation (*Eccl.*).

Transvers—al, *adj.* quer, schräg. **—e**, *adj.* querlaufend, durchgehend.

Trap, I. *s.* die Falle; die leichte Kutsche; der Fallstrick (*fig.*); I pack up my **—s**, ich packe meine Siebensachen zusammen. II. *v.a.* fangen; (*fig.*) ertappen. **—door**, *s.* die Klappe, Falltür.

Trapez—e, **—ium**, *s.* das Trapez.

Trapper, *s.* der Fallensteller, Pelzjäger.

Trash, *s.* die Lumperei. **—y**, *adj.* nichtswürdig, schofel(ig), kitschig.

Travail, I. *v.n.* sich plagen; in Kindesnöten sein. II. *s.* mühevolle Arbeit; (*labour*) die Kindesnöte.

Travel, I. *v.n.* reisen. II. **—**, *s.*, **—s**, *pl.* die Reise(n). **—ler**, *s.* der Reisende.

Traverse, I. *adj.* quer, überzwerch. **-beam**, *s.* die Querschwelle.

Travesty, I. *s.* die Travestie. II. *v.a.* travestieren.

Trawl, *v.n.* mit dem Schleppnetz fischen. **—er**, *s.* der Schleppnetzfischer, das Schleppnetzfischerboot.

Tray, *s.* das Brett, Tablett, der Präsentierteller.

Treacher—ous, *adj.*, **—ously**, *adv.* verräterisch. **—ousness**, *s.* die Treulosigkeit. **—y**, *s.* der Verrat, die Falschheit.

Treacle, *s.* der Sirup.

Tread, I. *ir.v.n.* treten. II. *ir.v.a.* (be)treten, beschreiten. III. *s.* der Tritt, Schritt; die Trittstufe (*of stairs*). **—le**, *s.* der Tritt; das Pedal (*Cycl.*). **—mill**, *s.* die Tretmühle.

Treason, *s.* der Verrat, die Verräterei. **—able**, *adj.*, **—ably**, *adv.* verräterisch.

Treasur—e, I. *s.* der Schatz. II. *v.a.* (—e up) aufbewahren. **—er**, *s.* der Schatzmeister. **—y**, *s.* die Schatz=, Finanz=kammer.

Treat, I. *v.a.* behandeln, (mit einem) umgehen; (*entertain*) bewirten. II. *v.n.*; to — of, handeln von (einem Gegenstande), (einen G.) behandeln; to — with, unterhandeln. III. *s.* die Bewirtung; it is a —! es ist ein Schmaus, ein Hochgenuß; to stand —, zum besten geben. **—ise**, *s.* die Abhandlung (über eine S.). **—ment**, *s.* die Behandlung. **—y**, *s.* die Unterhandlung; (*compact*) der Vertrag.

Trebl—e, I. *adj.*, **—y**, *adv.* dreifach; Diskant=; **—e clef**, der Diskantschlüssel. II. *s.* der Diskant (*Mus.*). III. *v.a.* (& *n.* sich) verdreifachen.

Tree, *s.* der Baum.

Trefoil, *s.* der Klee.

Trellis, *s.* das Gitter, Gatter. **—work**, *s.* das Gitterwerk.

Trem—ble, *v.n.* zittern (at, with, vor). I. *adj.*, **—blingly**, *adv.* zitternd. II. *s.* das Zittern, Beben.

Tremendous, *adj.*, **—ly**, *adv.* furchtbar, fürchterlich; kolossal (*coll.*).

Trem—or, *s.* das Zittern, Beben. **—ulous**, *adj.*, **—ulously**, *adv.* zitternd, bebend.

Trench, I. *v.a.* verschanzen (*Mil.*); to — upon, (*fig.*) eingreifen, beeinträchtigen.

II. *s.* der Graben; der Laufgraben (*Fort.*). —ant, *adj.*, —antly, *adv.* schneidend. —er, *s.* das Schneidebrett.

Trend, I. *s.* die Neigung, Richtung. II. *v.n.* sich neigen.

Trepan, I. *s.* der Schädelbohrer. II. *v.a.* trepanieren.

Trepidation, *s.* das Zittern, Beben; die Bestürzung.

Trespass, I. *v.n.* sich vergehen, sündigen (against, wider); unbefugt fremdes Eigentum betreten; to — upon a person's time, jemandes Zeit zu sehr in Anspruch nehmen. II. *s.* die Eigentumsverletzung; (sin) das Vergehen, die Sünde. —er, *s.* der Übertreter, Rechtsverletzer.

Tress, *s.* die (Haar-)Flechte, Locke.

Trestle, *s.* das Gestell.

Tret, *s.* die Gewichtsvergütung, Refattie (*C.L.*).

Tri—ad, *s.* die Drei-heit, -einigkeit. —angle, *s.* das Dreieck; der Triangel (*Mus.*). —angular, *adj.* drei-edig, -seitig.

Trial, I. *s.* der Versuch; (test) die Probe, Prüfung; das Verhör; (*fig.*) die Versuchung; — by jury, das Geschwornengericht; to bring to —, vor Gericht bringen. II. *attrib.*; — trip, die Probefahrt.

Tribe, *s.* der Volksstamm.

Tribulation, *s.* die Trübsal, Drangsal.

Tribun—al, *s.* der Richterstuhl; (court of justice) das Gericht. —e, *s.* der Volkstribun. —eship, *s.* das Tribunat.

Tribut—ary, I. *adj.*, —arily, *adv.* zinspflichtig. II. *s.* der Nebenfluß. —e, *s.* der Tribut, Zins.

Trice, *s.*; in a —, im Nu, sofort.

¹Trick, I. *s.* der Kniff, Pfiff; der Streich; (clever contrivance) der Kunstgriff; der (Karten-)Stich (*at whist, etc.*); (habit) die Eigenheit. II. *v.a.* betrügen. —ery, *s.* die Betrügerei. —ster, *s.* der Gauner. —y, *adj.* listig, schlau.

²Trick, *v.a.*; to — out, aufputzen, schmücken.

Trickle, *v.n.* tröpfeln, rieseln.

Tricolour, *s.* die Tricolore. —ed, *adj.* dreifarbig.

Tricycle, *s.* das Dreirad.

Trident, *s.* der Dreizack.

Triennial, *adj.*, —ly, *adv.* dreijährig.

Trifl—e, I. *s.* die Kleinigkeit. II. *v.a.* & *n.* tändeln, scherzen. —er, *s.* der Tändler. —ing, *adj.*, —ingly, *adv.* tändelnd, spielend; (of little value) geringfügig.

Trigger, *s.* der Drücker (am Gewehr).

Trigonometry, *s.* die Trigonometrie.

Trill, I. *s.* der Triller. II. *v.a.* & *n.* trillern.

Trilogy, *s.* die Trilogie.

Trim, I. *adj.*, —ly, *adv.* ordnungsmäßig, geputzt. II. *s.* die Ausrüstung; die Gleichgewichtslage (*of a ship*). III. *v.a.* ordnen; ausputzen (*hats, etc.*); stutzen (*the beard, hair, etc.*); beschneiden (*hedges, etc.*); (an)schüren (*the fire*); zurecht machen (*a lamp*); stellen (*sails*). —mer, *s.* (*fig.*) der Wetterhahn. —ming, *s.* der Besatz, die Garnitur, das Aufputzen (*for hats, etc.*). —ness, *s.* die gute Ordnung, Nettigkeit.

Trinity, *s.* die Dreieinigkeit.

Trinket, *s.* die Schmucksache.

Trio, *s.* das Trio.

Trip, I. *s.* das Stolpern; (*fig.*) der Fehltritt; (excursion) der Ausflug. II. *v.a.* (— up) (einem) ein Bein stellen. III. *v.n.* straucheln; (*fig.*) sich irren; (move with short steps) trippeln; to catch a person —ping, einen auf einem Fehler ertappen.

Tripe, *s.* die Flecke (*Cook.*).

Tripl—e, *adj.* dreifach; —et, *s.* das Trio; —ets, die Drillinge. —icate, *adj.* dreifach.

Tripod, *s.* der Dreifuß.

Tripper, *s.* der Ausflügler (*fam.*).

Trite, *adj.* abgedroschen, platt.

Triumph, I. *s.* der Triumph, Sieg. II. *v.n.* siegen; (exult) jubeln. —al, *adj.* Triumph-, Sieges-. —ant, *adj.* —antly, *adv.* triumphierend; siegreich.

Trivet, *s.* der Dreifuß.

Trivial, *adj.*, —ly, *adv.* gering (fügig), unbedeutend, alltäglich. —ity, *s.* die Geringsfügigkeit, Unbedeutenheit.

¹Troll, *s.* der Erdgeist, das Erdmännchen.

²Troll, *v.a.* (ein Lied) trällern.

Troll(e)y, *s.* der Rollwagen, Förderkarren.

Trollop, *s.* die Dirne.

Trombone, *s.* die Posaune.

Troop, I. *s.* der Trupp, Haufe, die Schar, Truppe. II. *v.n.* sich scharen, sich sammeln. III. *v.a.* in Truppen

formieren. **—er,** *s.* der Kavallerist.
—ship, *s.* das Truppen-Transport-schiff.

Trophy, *s.* die Trophäe, das Sieges-zeichen.

Tropic, *s.* der Wendekreis (of Cancer, des Krebses, of Capricorn, des Stein-bocks). **—(al),** *adj.,* **—ally,** *adv.* tropisch, Wendekreis-. **—s,** *pl.* die Wendekreise, Tropen.

Trot, I. *s.* der Trott, Trab. II. *v.n.* trotten, traben. III. *v.a.* trotten lassen. **—ter,** *s.* der Trotter, Traber.

Troth, *s.* das Treugelöbnis.

Troubadour, *s.* der Troubadour, Minnesänger.

Trouble, I. *v.a.* stören, beunruhigen, belästigen; trüben *(waters).* II. *s.* der Kummer, Verdruß. **—some,** *adj.,* **—somely,** *adv.* störend, unruhig; (vexatious) verdrießlich, peinlich.

Trough, *s.* der Trog.

Trounce, *v.a.* durchwichsen *(sl.).*

Trousers, *pl.*; a pair of —, ein Paar Beinkleider, die Hosen.

Trousseau, *s.* die Aussteuer, Ausstat-tung.

Trout, *s.* die Forelle.

Trowel, *s.* die Mauerkelle.

Truant, I. *adj.,* **—ly,** *adv.* müßigfaul. II. *s.* der Schulschwänzer, der Müßig-gänger.

Truce, *s.* der Waffenstillstand.

¹**Truck,** I. *v.n.* (& *a.* aus-, ver-)tauschen. II. *s.* (—age) der Tausch(handel). III. *attrib.*; — system, das Tausch-wertsystem, Bezahlung der Arbeiter durch Waren.

²**Truck,** *s.* der Handwagen; der Güter-wagen *(Railw.).*

Truckle, *v.n.* sich unterwerfen, zu Kreuze kriechen. **—bed,** *s.* das Roll-, Schiebe-bett.

Truculen—ce, —cy, *s.* die Grausam-keit. **—t,** *adj.,* **—tly,** *adv.* wild, roh, verheerend.

Trudge, *v.n.* zu Fuß wandern.

Tru—e, *adj.* wahr(haft); (real) echt, wirklich. **—eness,** *s.* die Treue. — **ly,** *adv.* aufrichtig; (really) wirklich, in der Tat; wahrhaft; yours **—ly,** der Ihrige, ergebenst *(at close of letters).*

Truffle, *s.* die Trüffel.

¹**Trump,** I. *s.* der Trumpf. II. *v.a.* abtrumpfen. III. *v.n.* Trumpf spie-len, trumpfen.

²**Trump,** *v.a.*; to — up, erdichten. **—ery,** I. *s.* die Lumperei, der Plunder, Trödel. II. *adj.* wertlos, Lumpen-.

³**Trump,** *s.* die Trompete. **—et,** I. *s.* die Trompete; die Posaune *(B.).* II. *v.a.* & *n.* trompeten; (—et forth) ausposaunen. **—eter,** *s.* der Trom-peter.

Truncheon, *s.* der Knüttel; der Kommandostab.

Trundle, *v.a.* rollen, wälzen.

Trunk, *s.* der (Baum-)Stamm; der Rumpf *(of men, etc.);* der Rüssel *(of the elephant);* (travelling —) der große Koffer, die Kiste. **—line,** *s.* die Hauptlinie.

Trunnion, *s.* der Schildzapfen *(Mil.).*

Truss, I. *s.* das Bund; das Bruch-band *(Surg.).* II. *v.a.* packen; dres-sieren *(a fowl).*

Trust, I. *s.* das Vertrauen; der Ring, Trust *(C.L.);* (credit) der Kredit, Borg. II. *attrib.*; — funds, funds on —, — money, anvertrautes Geld; Stiftungsgelder. III. *v.a.* (ver-)trauen; glauben; anvertrauen. **—ee,** *s.* der Vertrauensmann, Bevollmäch-tigte *(Law).* **—ful,** *adj.,* **—fully,** *adv.* vertrauensvoll. **—fulness,** *s.* das Vertrauensvolle. **—ily,** *adv.,* **—y,** *adj.* treu, zuverlässig, getreu, sicher. **—iness,** *s.* die Zuverlässig-keit. **—ing,** *adj.,* **—ingly,** *adv.* ver-trauensvoll. **—worthiness,** *s.* die Zuverlässigkeit, Vertrauenswürdigkeit. **—worthy,** *adj.* zuverlässig, ver-trauenswürdig, Wirklichkeit, Ehrlich-keit.

Truth, *s.* die Wahrheit. **—ful,** *adj.,* **—fully,** *adv.* wahrhaft(ig). **—ful-ness,** *s.* die Wahrhaftigkeit.

Try, I. *ir.v.a.* versuchen, probieren, er-proben; verhören *(Law);* to — one's luck, sein Glück versuchen; to — one's eyes, die Augen anstrengen. II. *ir.v.n.* versuchen. III. *s.* der Versuch. **—ing,** *adj.* bedenklich, miß-lich, kritisch, schwierig. **—sail,** *s.* das Gaffelsegel.

Tryst, *s.* das Stelldichein.

Tsar, *s.* der Zar. **—evich,** *m.* der Zarewitsch. **—ina,** *s.* die Zarin(a), Zariza.

Tub, *s.* der Zuber, Kübel.

Tube, *s.* die Röhre, das Rohr; (railway) die Untergrundbahn.

Tuber, *s.* der Knollen, die Knolle. —

cle, *s.* die (Lungen=)Tuberkel. —cu-
lar, *adj.* Tuberkel=, tuberkulös. —
culosis, *s.* die Lungenschwindsucht.
—ous, *adj.* knotig, knollig.

Tuberose, *s.* die Tuberose.

Tubing, *s.* das Röhrenwerk.

Tubular, *adj.* röhrenförmig, Röh-
ren=.

Tuck, I. *s.* die (Quer=)Falte (*in dresses,
etc.*). II. *v.a.* einschlagen; to — up,
aufschürzen.

Tuesday, *s.* der Dienstag.

Tuft, *s.* der Busch, Büschel. —hunter,
s. (*slang*) gesellschaftlicher Streber, der
Schmarotzer.

Tug, I. *s.* der Zug, das Zerren; das
Schleppboot (*Naut.*). II. *v.a.* schleppen; zausen (*one's hair, etc.*). III.
v.n. stark, heftig ziehen. —of-war, *s.*
das Seilziehen (*Athletics*).

Tuition, *s.* der Unterricht.

Tulip, *s.* die Tulpe.

Tulle, *s.* der Tüll.

Tumble, I. *v.n.* fallen, stürzen. II.
v.a. (— down) (um)stürzen; (rumple)
zertrümpeln. III. *s.* der Sturz, Fall.
r, *s.* der Springer, Gaukler; (glass)
das Trinkglas.

Tumbrel, *s.* der Schutt=, Stürz=karren;
der Munitionskarren (*Artil.*).

Tum—id, *adj.*, —idly, *adv.* geschwol-
len. —our, *s.* die Schwellung; die
Geschwulst.

Tumult, *s.* der Lärm, das Getöse.
—uous, *adj.*, —uously, *adv.* lärmend,
tobend.

Tun, *s.* die Tonne.

Tun—e, I. *s.* die Weise, Melodie, das
Tonstück; out of —e, verstimmt. II.
v.a. stimmen. —eful, *adj.*, —efully,
adv. sangreich; (melodious) wohlklingend, melodisch. —efulness, *s.* der
süße Klang, Wohlklang. —eless, *adj.*
unmelodisch. —er, *s.* der (Klavier=)
Stimmer. —ing-fork, *s.* die Stimm-
gabel.

Tungsten, *s.* der Wolfram.

Tunic, *s.* der Waffenrock; der Arbeits-
rock (*Mil.*).

Tunnel, I. *s.* der Tunnel (*Build.*).
II. *v.a.* durchtunneln. —ling, *s.* der
Tunnelbau.

Tunny, *s.* der Thunfisch.

Tup, *s.* der Widder.

Turban, *s.* der Turban.

Turbid, *adj.*, trüb, dick. —ness, *s.* das
Trübe, Dicke.

Turbine, *s.* das Kreiselrad, die Turbine. —steamer, der Turbinen=
dampfer.

Turbot, *s.* der Steinbutt.

Turbulen—ce, *s.* das Ungestüm. —t,
adj., —tly, *adv.* stürmisch, ungestüm.

Tureen, *s.* die Terrine.

Turf, *s.* der Rasen; (peat) der (Brenn=)
Torf; die Rennbahn, das Pferderennen
(*Sport*).

Turkey, *s.* (—-cock) der Truthahn,
der Puter; (— -hen) die Truthenne.

Turmoil, *s.* der Aufruhr; die Unruhe,
Plackerei.

Turn, I. *v.a.* drehen (*a wheel, etc.*);
(direct) richten; wenden, richten (*one's
thoughts, etc.*); (change) (ver)ändern
(into, in); (divert) abwenden (*from,
von*); drechseln (*on a lathe*); to — a
corner, um die Ecke biegen. II. *v.n.*
sich drehen, sich wenden; (— round)
sich um=drehen, =wenden, =kehren; sich
herumwenden (*in bed, etc.*); gerinnen,
sauer werden (*as milk*); to — someone
against, einen aufbringen gegen;
to — into, verwandeln in; to — up,
sich erheben, sich zeigen, auftauchen.
III. *s.* das (Um=)Drehen, die (Um=)
Drehung, der Umschwung; (direction)
die Wendung, Richtung; (taste,
tendency) herrschende Richtung; (place
of —ing) die Wendung; (bend) die
Krümme, Krümmung; (change) der
Wechsel, die Veränderung; in —s, der
Reihe nach, abwechselnd; it is my —,
ich bin an der Reihe; a friendly —,
ein Freundschaftsdienst; does it serve
your —? entspricht das Ihren Zwecken?
—ing, *s.* das Drehen, Drechseln;
(bend) die Krümmung, Windung; die
Abweichung (*from the path of duty,
etc.*); —ing movement, die Umgehung
(*Mil.*). —ing-point, *s.* der Wendepunkt.
—coat, *s.* der Abtrünnige. —key, *s.*
der Gefangenwärter. —out, *s.* äußere
Erscheinung, die Ausstaffierung; die
Gesamtproduktion. —over, *s.* der
Umsatz (*C.L.*). —pike, *s.* der Schlag.
—pike-road, *s.* die Chaussee. —spit,
s. der Bratenwender. —stile, *s.* der
Schlagbaum, das Drehkreuz —table, *s.*
die Drehscheibe.

Turner, *s.* der Drechsler (*of wood, etc.*).
—y, *s.* die Drechslerarbeit.

Turnip, *s.* die Rübe.

Turpentine, *s.* der Terpentin.

Turquoise, *s.* der Türkis.

Turret, *s.* das Türmchen. **—ed,** *adj.* betürmt.

¹Turtle, *s.* die (Meer=)Schildkröte.

²Turtle, —dove, *s.* die Turteltaube.

Tush, *int.* pah!

Tusk, *s.* der Fang=, Hau=zahn; der Hauer, das Gewehr (*of a wild boar*); der Stoßzahn (*of an elephant*); der Zahn. **—ed,** *adj.* mit Fangzähnen.

Tussle, I. *s.* der Kampf, die Balgerei. II. *v.n.* kämpfen, ringen.

Tut, *int.* pfui! fort! weg damit!

Tut—elage, *s.* der Mündelstand. — **elary,** *adj.* schützend, Schutz=. **—or,** *s.* der Privatlehrer. **—orship,** *s.* die Hauslehrerstelle.

Twaddle, *s.* albernes Geschwätz.

Twain, *s.* zwei; in —, entzwei.

Twang, I. *s.* das Schwirren; die näselnde Aussprache (*in speaking*). II. *v.n.* (& *a.*) schwirren (lassen).

Tweak, *v.a.* zwicken.

Tweed, *s.*, **—s,** *pl.* der Tweed, der feine Halbwollstoff.

Tweezers, *pl.* (pair of —) das (Haar=) Zängelchen.

Twel—fth, I. *adj.* zwölft. II. *s.* der, die, das Zwölfte; (—fth part) das Zwölftel. **—ve,** I. *num. adj.* zwölf. II. *s.* die Zwölf. **—fth-night,** I. *s.* der Dreikönigsabend. II. *attrib.*; the —fth-night cake, der Dreikönigs=kuchen. **—vemonth(s),** *s.*; this day —vemonth(s), heute über ein Jahr.

Twent—ieth, I. *adj.* zwanzigst. II. *s.* der, die, das Zwanzigste; (—ieth part) das Zwanzigstel. **—y,** I. *num. adj.* zwanzig. II. *s.* die Zwanzig.

Twice, *adv.* zweimal; doppelt.

Twiddle, *v.a.*; to — one's thumbs, mit den Daumen spinnen; (*fig.*) die Hände in den Schoß legen.

¹Twig, *s.* der Zweig.

²Twig, *v.a.* begreifen (*coll.*).

Twilight, *s.* das Zwielicht; — of the gods, die Götterdämmerung.

Twill, I. *s.* der Köper. II. *v.a.* köpern. **—ed,** *adj.* geköpert, Köper=.

Twin, I. *s.* der Zwilling. II. *adj.* Zwil=lings=. **—screw,** *s.* die Doppel=schraube.

Twin—e, I. *s.* der Bindfaden, die Kordel. II. *v.a.* zwirnen (*threads, etc.*); (—e together) flechten; (—e about) umwinden. III. *v.n.* einander umschlin=gen. **—ing,** I. *adj.* sich windend (*Bot.*). II. *s.* das Zwirnen (*Manuf.*).

Twinge, I. *s.* der Stich, das Zwicken. II. *v.a.* & *n.* stechen.

Twinkl—e, I. *v.n.* blinzeln (*of the eyes*); flimmern, funkeln (*also fig.*), blitzen (*as stars*). II. *s.* das Blinzeln, Zwinkern. **—ing,** *adj.* blinzelnd, zwinkernd; in the —ing of an eye, in einem Nu, im Augenblick.

Twirl, I. *s.* der Wirbel. II. *v.a.* her=umdrehen. III. *v.n.* sich schnell um=drehen.

Twist, I. *v.a.* (zusammen)drehen, (ver)flechten; winden (*the body*); zwirnen (*thread, silk, etc.*). II. *v.n.* sich drehen. III. *s.* die Drehung, Windung; der Twist, das Maschinen=garn (*Spin.*). **—ing,** *s.* das Drehen. **—ing-machine,** *s.* die Drehmaschine.

Twit, *v.a.*; to — someone with, einem (etwas) vorwerfen.

Twitch, I. *v.a.* zwicken, zupfen. II. *v.n.* zucken (*Med.*). III. *s.* die Zuckung, der Krampf (*Med.*).

Twitter, I. *s.* das Gezwitscher. II. *v.n.* zwitschern. —ing, I. *adj.* zwitschernd. II. *s.* das Gezwitscher.

Two, I. *num. adj.* zwei; in a day or —, in ein paar Tagen; — and —, paar=weise; a marble statue or —, einige Marmorbildsäulen. II. *s.* die Zwei; the —, die beiden; they came out in —s and threes, sie kamen zu zweien und dreien heraus. **—fold,** *adj.* zweifach. **—handed,** *adj.* zwei=händig. **—ply,** *adj.* zweischäftig, dop=pelt.

Type, *s.* das Urbild; (figure of some=thing to come) das Vorbild; (emblem) das Sinnbild; die Type, Letter; (the —s) die Schrift, Lettern; in —, gesetzt; spaced —, gesperrter Druck; German —, die Fraktur; Roman —, die Antiqua; Italic —, der Kursivdruck. **—write,** *v.a.* & *n.* mit der Schreibmaschine schreiben. **—writer,** *s.* die Schreib=maschine; der (die) Maschinenschreiber= (in).

Typh—oid, **—ous,** *adj.* typhusartig, typhös. **—us,** *s.* der Typhus.

Typhoon, *s.* der Taifun.

Typi—cal, *adj.*, **—cally,** *adv.* (vor=) bildlich; typisch. **—fy,** *v.a.* vorbilden, bildlich darstellen.

Typograph—er, *s.* der Buchdrucker. — **ic(al),** *adj.*, **—ically,** *adv.* buch=druckerisch. **—ic error,** der Druckfehler.

Tyran—nic(al), *adj.*, **—nically,** *adv.*

tyrannisch. **—nicide,** s. der Tyrannenmord. **—nize,** v.n. tyrannisch herrschen. **—nous,** adj., **—nously,** adv. tyrannisch. **—ny,** s. die Tyrannei (also fig.). **—t,** s. der Tyrann (also fig. & Hist.).

Tyre, s. der Radreif(en), Schlauch; pneumatic —, der Luftreifen (Cycl.).

Tyro, s. der Anfänger, Neuling.

U

U, u, s. das U, u.

Ubiquit—ous, adj., **—ously,** adv. allgegenwärtig. **—y,** s. die Allgegenwart.

Udder, s. das Euter.

Ugh, interj. hu!

Ugl—iness, s. die Häßlichkeit. **—y,** adj. häßlich, garstig; an —y wound, eine schlimme Wunde.

Ulcer, s. das Geschwür. **—ate,** v.n. schwären. **—ation,** s. das Schwären. **—ous,** adj. geschwürig.

Ult—erior, adj. weiter (as a motive). **—imate,** adj. (aller-)letzt, endlich. **—imately,** adv. zuletzt. **—imatum,** s. das Ultimatum, die endgültige Aufforderung. **—imo** (abbrev. ult. read: of last month), adv.; your favour of the 23rd ult., Ihr geschätztes Schreiben vom 23. vorigen Monats.

Ultra, adj. übermäßig.

Umber, s. das Umbra, die Umbererde.

Umbr—age, s. der Anstoß, Ärger. **—ageous,** adj. schattenreich.

Umbrella, s. der Regenschirm.

Umpire, s. der Schiedsrichter.

Un— in numerous compds. = Un-, nicht. For words not given in the following lists see the simple words.

Unabashed, adj. unbeschämt.

Unabated, adj. unvermindert.

Unabbreviated, Unabridged, adj. unverkürzt.

Unable, adj. unfähig, unvermögend.

Unaccented, adj. unbetont.

Unaccompanied, adj. unbegleitet.

Unaccountable, adj. unverantwortlich; unerklärlich.

Unaccustomed, adj. ungewohnt (to); (new) ungewöhnlich, neu.

Unacquainted, adj. unbekannt (mit), unkundig (einer Sache).

Unadorned, adj. ungeschmückt.

Unaffected, adj., **—ly,** adv. unberührt; (fig.) ungerührt; (natural) unbefangen, ungekünstelt, natürlich.

Unalterabl—e, adj., **—y,** adv. unveränderlich.

Unamiable, adj. unliebenswürdig.

Unanim—ity, s. die Einstimmigkeit. **—ous,** adj., **—ously,** adv. einstimmig.

Unanswerabl—e, adj., **—y,** adv. unwiderlegbar.

Unappeasable, adj. unversöhnlich.

Unapproachable, adj. unnahbar, unzugänglich.

Unappropriated, adj. unverwendet, herrenlos.

Unarmed, adj. unbewaffnet.

Unasked, adj. unverlangt, ungebeten.

Unassisted, adj. ohne Beistand.

Unassuming, adj. anspruchslos, bescheiden.

Unattainable, adj. unerreichbar.

Unattended, adj. unbegleitet.

Unauthorized, adj. unbefugt, unerlaubt.

Unavailing, adj. vergeblich, nutzlos.

Unavenged, adj. ungerächt.

Unavoidabl—e, adj., **—y,** adv. unvermeidlich.

Unaware, adj.; to be — (of a thing), (eine S.) nicht vermuten, nicht wissen. **—s,** adv. unversehens, unvermutet.

Unbar, v.a. auf-, ent-riegeln, aufschließen.

Unbearabl—e, adj., **—y,** adv. unerträglich.

Unbecoming, adj., **—ly,** adv. schlecht kleidend; (unsuitable) ungeziemend; her bonnet is very —, ihr Hut steht ihr sehr schlecht.

Unbelie—f, s. der Unglaube. **—ver,** s. der Ungläubige. **—ving,** adj., **—vingly,** adv. ungläubig.

Unbend, I. v.a. abspannen; nachlassen; ausruhen. II. v.n. sich herablassen, freundlich werden. **—ing,** adj. unbiegsam; (fig.) entschlossen.

Unbiased, adj. vorurteilslos, unbefangen.

Unbidden, adj. uneingeladen.

Unbind, ir.v.a. losbinden; (loose) lösen.

Unbleached, adj. ungebleicht.

Unblemished, adj. unbefleckt.

Unblushing, adj., **—ly,** adv. schamlos.

Unbound, adj. geheftet, brochiert, ungebunden (of books).

Unbounded, *adj.* unbeschränkt, schrankenlos.

Unbroken, *adj.* ungebrochen; (continuous) ununterbrochen.

Unbuckle, *v.a.* auf=, los=schnallen.

Unburden, *v.a.* entlasten, entbürden.

Unburnt, *adj.* ungebrannt, unverbrannt.

Unbutton, *v.a.* los=, auf=knöpfen.

Uncalled, *adj.* nicht eingefordert; — for, unverlangt, unnötig.

Uncanny, *adj.* unheimlich.

Uncared-for, *adj.* unversorgt, vernachlässigt.

Unceasing, *adj.,* —ly, *adv.* unaufhörlich.

Unceremonious, *adj.,* —ly, *adv.* ohne Umstände, ungezwungen, schlicht.

Uncertain, *adj.* unsicher; (doubtful) ungewiß; (fickle) unzuverlässig; to be — of a thing, einer Sache nicht gewiß sein. —ty, *s.* die Ungewißheit.

Unchange—able, *adj.,* —ably, *adv.* unveränderlich. —d, *adj.* unverändert.

Uncharitabl—e, *adj.,* —y, *adv.* übeldenkend; lieblos, unbarmherzig. —eness, *s.* die Lieblosigkeit.

Unchecked, *adj.* ungehemmt, ungehindert.

Uncivil, *adj.* unhöflich.

Unclaimed, *adj.* unbestellbar, nicht beansprucht (*as letters*).

Uncle, *s.* der Onkel, Oheim.

Unclean, *adj.,* —ly, *adv.* unrein, unsauber. —ness, *s.* die Unreinheit; (*fig.*) die Unkeuschheit.

Unclose, *v.a.* aufmachen, öffnen.

Unclothe, *adj.* entkleiden, auskleiden.

Unclouded, *adj.* wolkenlos; (*fig.*) heiter, froh.

Uncocked, *adj.* ungespannt.

Uncoil, *v.a.* auf=winden, =wickeln.

Uncomfortabl—e, *adj.,* —y, *adv.* unbehaglich; unangenehm.

Uncommon, *adj.,* —ly, *adv.* ungewöhnlich, selten, ungemein; (extremely) sehr.

Uncompromising, *adj.,* —ly, *adv.* nicht nachgebend, auf keinen Vergleich eingehend.

Unconcern, *s.* die Gleichgültigkeit. —ed, *adj.,* —edly, *adv.* gleichgültig, sorglos.

Unconditional, *adj.,* —ly, *adv.* unbedingt.

Unconfined, *adj.* unbegrenzt.

Unconfirmed, *adj.* unbestätigt.

Uncongenial, *adj.* ungleichartig, unsympathisch.

Unconquer—able, *adj.,* —ably, *adv.* unbezwinglich. —ed, *adj.* unbesiegt, unbezwungen.

Unconscionabl—e, *adj.,* —y, *adv.* gewissenlos; übertrieben.

Unconscious, *adj.,* —ly, *adv.* unbewußt; bewußtlos; ohnmächtig. — ness, *s.* die Ohnmacht.

Unconsecrated, *adj.* ungeweiht.

Unconstitutional, *adj.* verfassungswidrig.

Unconstrained, *adj.,* —ly, *adv.* ungezwungen.

Uncontested, *adj.,* —ly, *adv.* unbestritten.

Uncontrollabl—e, *adj.,* —y, *adv.* unbändig, zügellos.

Unconventional, *adj.* nicht konventionell, zwanglos.

Unconvinc—ed, *adj.* unüberzeugt, nicht überzeugt. —ing, *adj.,* —ingly, *adv.* nicht überzeugend.

Uncork, *v.n.* entkorken, aufkorken.

Uncorrupted, *adj.,* —ly, *adv.* unverdorben; (*fig.*) unbestochen.

Uncouth, *adj.* ungeschlacht, roh, linkisch.

Uncover, *v.a.* aufdecken, entblößen.

Unct—ion, *s.* die Salbung; extreme —ion, die letzte Ölung. —uous, *adj.* ölig, fettig; (*fig.*) salbungsvoll.

Uncultivated, *adj.* unangebaut (*as land*); (rude) ungebildet, roh.

Undamaged, *adj.* unbeschädigt.

Undated, *adj.* undatiert.

Undaunted, *adj.* unerschrocken, unverzagt.

Undeceive, *v.a.* enttäuschen.

Undecided, *adj.* unentschieden.

Undefended, *adj.* unverteidigt.

Undeniabl—e, *adj.,* —y, *adv.* unleugbar.

Under, I. *adv.* unten; (—neath) darunter. II. *prep.* under; from — . . ., unter (*dat.*) . . . hervor; — age, unmündig; — sentence of, verurteilt zu. —clothing, *s.* die Unterkleidung, (Leib=)Wäsche. —done, *adj.* ungar. —estimate, *v.a.* unterschätzen. —fed, *adj.* unterernährt. —go, *ir.v.a.* (er)leiden, ertragen. —graduate, *s.* der Student. —ground, *adj.* & *adv.* unterirdisch; —ground railway, die Untergrundbahn. —hand, *adj.* & *adv.* listig; —hand service (tennis), der Tiefaufschlag. —line, *v.a.* unterſtreichen. —**ling**, *s.* der Untergebene. —**mine**, *v.a.* untergraben. —**most**, I. *adj.* unterſt. II. *adv.* zu unterſt. —**neath**, I. *adv.* unten. II. *prep.* unter. —**rate**, *v.a.* unterſchätzen. —**stand**, *ir.v.* I. *a.* verſtehen. II. *n.* verſtehen, vernehmen; faſſen. —**standing**, *s.* der Verſtand; (agreement) das Verſtändnis; on this —standing, unter dieſer Vorausſetzung. —**take**, *ir.v.a.* unternehmen. — **taker**, *s.* der Unternehmer; der Leichenbeſtatter. —**taking**, *s.* die Unternehmung. —**wood**, *s.* das Unterholz, Geſtrüpp. —**write**, *ir.v.a.* verſichern, aſſekurieren (*C.L.*). — **writer**, *s.* der Verſicherer, Aſſekurant.

Undeserv—**ed**, *adj.*, —**edly**, *adv.* unverdient. —**ing**, *adj.* verdienſtlos, unwert.

Undesigned, *adj.* abſichtslos.

Undesirable, *adj.* nicht wünſchenswert.

Undeveloped, *adj.* unentwickelt.

Undignified, *adj.* ohne Würde, würdelos.

Undisciplined, *adj.* zuchtlos, ohne Mannszucht, ungeſchult.

Undiscover—**able**, *adj.* unentdeckbar. —**ed**, *adj.* unentdeckt.

Undisguised, *adj.* unverkleidet, unverſtellt.

Undismayed, *adj.* unerſchrocken.

Undisturbed, *adj.* ungeſtört.

Undivided, *adj.* ungeteilt (*attention, etc.*).

Undo, *ir.v.a.* aufmachen (*a parcel, etc.*); trennen; vernichten; auflöſen (*a knot, etc.*). —**ing**, *s.* das Verderben.

Undoubted, *adj.* unbezweifelt, ohne Zweifel.

Undress, I. *v.a.* auskleiden, entkleiden, ausziehen. II. *v.r. & n.* ſich entkleiden. —**ed**, *adj.* unbekleidet.

Undu—**e**, *adj.*, —**ly**, *adv.* ungebührend.

Undulate, *v.n.* ſich wellenförmig bewegen, wogen. —**ion**, *s.* die Wellenbewegung.

Undying, *adj.* unvergänglich, unſterblich.

Unearned, *adj.* unverdient.

Unearthly, *adj.* unheimlich.

Uneas—**iness**, *s.* die Unruhe. —**ily**, *adv.*, —**y**, *adj.* unbequem; ängſtlich (*about something*).

Uneatable, *adj.* ungenießbar.

Uneducated, *adj.* ungebildet.

Unemployed, *adj.* unbeſchäftigt; the —, die Arbeitsloſen. —**ment**, *s.* die Arbeitsloſigkeit.

Unending, *adj.* endlos.

Unendurable, *adj.* unerträglich.

Unequal, *adj.*, —**ly**, *adv.* ungleich, unverhältnismäßig; — to, (einem, ꝛc.) nicht gewachſen. —**led**, *adj.* unerreicht.

Uneven, *adj.*, —**ly**, *adv.* uneben; ungerade (*as a number*).

Uneventful, *adj.* ereignislos.

Unexampled, *adj.* beiſpiellos.

Unexpected, *adj.*, —**ly**, *adv.* unerwartet, unvermutet.

Unexpired, *adj.* noch nicht abgelaufen.

Unexplained, *adj.* unerklärt.

Unfair, *adj.*, —**ly**, *adv.* unredlich, unehrlich. —**ness**, *s.* die Unbilligkeit.

Unfaithful, *adj.*, —**ly**, *adv.* ungetreu, treulos. —**ness**, *s.* die Treuloſigkeit, Untreue.

Unfamiliar, *adj.* ungewöhnlich, unbekannt.

Unfashionabl—**e**, *adj.*, —**y**, *adv.* unmodern.

Unfasten, *v.a.* los-binden, -machen, aufmachen.

Unfathomable, *adj.* unergründlich.

Unfavourabl—**e**, *adj.*, —**y**, *adv.* ungünſtig, unvorteilhaft.

Unfinished, *adj.* unvollendet, nicht fertig.

Unfit, I. *adj.*, —**ly**, *adv.* untauglich, unpaſſend. II. *v.a.* untauglich machen (für eine S.). —**ness**, *s.* die Untauglichkeit.

Unfledged, *adj.* ungefiedert; (*fig.*) zart, jung.

Unflinching, *adj.* feſt entſchloſſen, nicht nachgebend.

Unfold, *v.a.* entfalten, enthüllen; (*fig.*) erzählen.

Unforeseen, *adj.* unvorhergeſehen.

Unforgiving, *adj.* unverſöhnlich.

Unfortified, *adj.* unbefeſtigt.

Unfortunate, *adj.* unglücklich. —**ly**, *adv.* unglücklicherweiſe, leider.

Unfounded, *adj.* unbegründet, grundlos.

Unfrequented, *adj.* einſam, unbeſucht.

Unfurnished, *adj.* unmöbliert (*as houses*).

Ungainly, *adj.* ungeſchickt, linkiſch.

Ungentlemanly, *adj.* ungeſittet, ungebildet, unfein.

Ungodl—iness, *s.* die Gottlosigkeit. **—y,** *adj.* gottlos.

Ungovern—able, *adj.* unbändig, zügellos. **—ed,** *adj.* ungezähmt.

Ungrac—eful, *adj.,* **—efully,** *adv.* anmutslos, reizlos. **—ious,** *adj.,* **—iously,** *adv.* ungnädig; unhold, unfreundlich, widrig. **—iousness,** *s.* die Ungnädigkeit.

Ungrammatical, *adj.,* **—ly,** *adv.* ungrammatisch.

Ungrateful, *adj.,* **—ly,** *adv.* undankbar. **—ness,** *s.* die Undankbarkeit.

Ungratified, *adj.* unbefriedigt.

Unguarded, *adj.* unbewacht; unvorsichtig.

Unguent, *s.* die Salbe.

Unhapp—ily, *adv.* unglücklicherweise. **—iness,** *s.* das Unglück. **—y,** *adj.* unglücklich, elend, traurig.

Unharmed, *adj.* unversehrt, unbeschädigt.

Unhealth—iness, *s.* die Ungesundheit. **—y,** *adj.* ungesund, kränklich, krankhaft.

Unheard, *adj.* ungehört; **—of,** unerhört.

Unheed—ed, *adj.* unbeachtet, unbemerkt. **—ing,** *adj.,* **—ingly,** *adv.* unachtsam.

Unhesitating, *adj.* ohne Zögern.

Unhoped-for, *adj.* unverhofft.

Unhorse, *v.a.* aus dem Sattel heben, abwerfen.

Unhurt, *adj.* unbeschädigt, unverletzt.

Unicorn, *s.* das Einhorn.

Uniform, I. *adj.,* **—ly,** *adv.* ein-, gleichförmig; gemäß. II. *s.* die Uniform (*also Mil.*). **—ity,** *s.* die Ein-, Gleichförmigkeit.

Unify, *v.a.* vereinen.

Unimpaired, *adj.* unvermindert, ungeschwächt.

Unimportant, *adj.* unwichtig.

Uninfluenced, *adj.* unbeeinflußt.

Uninhabit—able, *adj.* unbewohnbar. **—ed,** *adj.* unbewohnt.

Unintelligibl—e, *adj.,* **—y,** *adv.* unverständlich.

Uninten—ded, *adj.* unbeabsichtigt. **—tional,** *adj.,* **—tionally,** *adv.* unabsichtlich.

Uninteresting, *adj.* uninteressant.

Uninterrupted, *adj.* ununterbrochen.

Unintoxicating, *adj.* nicht berauschend.

Union, *s.* die Vereinigung; die Eintracht; der Verein.

Unique, *adj.* einzig in seiner Art.

Unison, *s.* die Übereinstimmung.

Unit, *s.* die Einheit. **—e,** *v.* I. *a.* vereinigen, verbinden. II. *n.* sich vereinigen. **—y,** *s.* die Einheit (*also Math., etc.*).

Univers—al, *adj.,* **—ally,** *adv.* allgemein. **—ality,** *s.* die Allgemeinheit. **—e,** *s.* das Weltall. **—ity,** *s.* die Universität.

Unjust, *adj.,* **—ly,** *adv.* ungerecht, unbillig. **—ifiable,** *adj.,* **—ifiably,** *adv.* unverantwortlich.

Unkempt, *adj.* ungekämmt; unordentlich.

Unkind, *adj.,* **—ly,** *adv.* ungütig, unfreundlich. **—ness,** *s.* die Unfreundlichkeit.

Unknot, *v.a.* aufknüpfen, aufmachen.

Unknow—ingly, *adv.* unwissentlich. **—n,** *adj.* unbekannt; unbewußt.

Unlawful, *adj.,* **—ly,** *adv.* ungesetzlich, unerlaubt.

Unleavened, *adj.* ungesäuert.

Unless, *conj.* wofern *or* wenn nicht, ausgenommen, außer, es sei denn daß.

Unlicensed, *adj.* unberechtigt.

Unlike, *adj.* unähnlich; ungleich. **—ly,** *adv.* unwahrscheinlich.

Unlimber, *v.a.* abprotzen (*Mil.*).

Unlimited, *adj.* unbegrenzt, unbeschränkt.

Unload, *v.a.* ent-, ab-, aus-laden.

Unlock, *v.a.* aufschließen (*also fig.*).

Unlooked-for, *adj.* unerwartet, überraschend.

Unloose, *v.a.* auflösen, loslassen.

Unluck—ily, *adv.* unglücklicherweise. **—y,** *adj.* unglücklich.

Unmanageable, *adj.* unlenksam, widerspenstig. **—ness,** *s.* die Unlenksamkeit.

Unmarried, *adj.* unverheiratet, ledig.

Unmask, *v.a.* & *n.* (einem) die Maske abnehmen; (*fig.*) (einen) entlarven.

Unmeaning, *adj.* bedeutungslos, nichtssagend.

Unmerciful, *adj.,* **—ly,** *adv.* unbarmherzig.

Unmerited, *adj.* unverdient.

Unmindful, *adj.,* **—ly,** *adv.* unbedachtsam; sorglos; ohne Rücksicht auf.

Unmistakabl—e, *adj.,* **—y,** *adv.* unverkennbar.

Unmitigated, *adj.* ungemildert.

Unmoved, *adj.* ungerührt (*also fig.*), unbewegt.

Unnatural, *adj.* unnatürlich.

Unnecessar—ily, adv. unnötigerweise.
—y, adj. unnötig, überflüssig.

Unnoticed, adj. unbemerkt; vernachlässigt, nicht ausgezeichnet.

Unnumbered, adj. ungezählt, zahllos.

Unobjectionable, adj. untadelhaft.

Unobserv—ant, adj. unaufmerksam.
—ed, adj. unbemerkt.

Unobtainable, adj. nicht erhältlich, unerreichbar, nicht zu haben.

Unoccupied, adj. unbesetzt; unbeschäftigt.

Unorthodox, adj. nicht rechtgläubig.

Unpaid, adj. unbezahlt.

Unpalatable, adj. unschmackhaft; (fig.) widrig.

Unpardonabl—e, adj., —y, adv. unverzeihlich.

Unpatriotic, adj. unpatriotisch.

Unpaved, adj. ungepflastert.

Unpleasant, adj., —ly, adv. unangenehm, mißfällig. —ness, s. die Unannehmlichkeit.

Unpolished, adj. unpoliert; (fig.) ungebildet.

Unpopular, adj. unbeliebt, nicht volkstümlich. —ity, s. die Unbeliebtheit (beim Volk).

Unpractical, adj. unpraktisch.

Unpractised, adj. ungeübt.

Unprecedented, adj. beispiellos, unerhört.

Unprejudiced, adj. vorurteils-los, -frei, unbefangen.

Unpremeditated, adj. unvorbedacht, aus dem Stegreif.

Unprepared, adj. unvorbereitet.

Unprepossessing, adj. nicht einnehmend.

Unpretending, adj. bescheiden, anspruchslos.

Unprofessional, adj. nicht berufsmäßig.

Unprofitabl—e, adj., —y, adv. uneinträglich.

Unpublished, adj. unveröffentlicht.

Unpunctual, adj., —ly, adv. unpünktlich. —ity, s. die Unpünktlichkeit.

Unpunished, adj. ungestraft.

Unqualified, adj. ungeeignet, unbefähigt.

Unquestion—able, adj., —ably, adv. unzweifelhaft.

Unravel, v.a. auffase(r)n; lösen, enträtseln (a plot).

Unreadable, adj. unleserlich, undeutlich; unlesbar.

Unread—ily, adv., —y, adj. nicht bereit. —iness, s. die Unbereitschaft.

Unreal, adj. unwesentlich.

Unreason—able, adj., —ably, adv. unvernünftig; unbillig, unmäßig. — ableness, s. die Unvernünftigkeit.

Unregarded, adj. unberücksichtigt; unbeachtet, vernachlässigt.

Unrelenting, adj. unbiegsam, unerbittlich.

Unreliable, adj. unzuverlässig.

Unremitting, adj. unablässig.

Unrequited, adj. unvergolten.

Unreserved, adj., —ly, adv. rückhaltlos; nicht numeriert (seats at a theatre).

Unresisting, adj. widerstandslos.

Unrest, s. die Unruhe. —ing, adj. ruhelos.

Unrevenged, adj. ungerächt.

Unrewarded, adj. unbelohnt.

Unrhymed, adj. ungereimt, reimlos.

Unrighteous, adj., —ly, adv. ungerecht (also Theol.). —ness, s. die Ungerechtigkeit.

Unruffled, adj., glatt; gleichmütig.

Unrul—ed, adj. nicht liniert. —iness, s. die Widerspenstigkeit. —y, adj. unlenksam, widerspenstig.

Unsaddle, v.a. absatteln.

Unsafe, adj., —ly, adv. unsicher.

Unsatisfactor—iness, s. die Unzulänglichkeit. —ily, adv., —y, adj. unbefriedigend.

Unschooled, adj. ungelehrt, ungeschult.

Unscrew, v.a. auf-, ab-, zurück-schrauben.

Unscrupulous, adj., —ly, adv. gewissenlos. —ness, s. die Gewissenlosigkeit.

Unseasonable, adj. unzeitig; (fig.) ungelegen. —ness, s. die Unzeitigkeit; die Ungelegenheit.

Unseen, adj. ungesehen, unsichtbar.

Unselfish, adj., —ly, adv. uneigennützig. —ness, s. die Uneigennützigkeit, Selbstlosigkeit.

Unsentimental, adj. nicht empfindsam.

Unserviceable, adj. undienlich.

Unsettle, v.a. verwirren. —d, adj. (not fixed) nicht festgesetzt, unbestimmt; unbezahlt (as an account); (restless) unstät; (changeable) veränderlich.

Unshaven, adj. unrasiert.

Unshrinkable, adj. nicht einlaufend.

Unskilful, adj., —ly, adv. ungeschickt.

Unsolved, *adj.* ungelöst, unerklärt.

Unsophisticated, *adj.* unverfälscht, ungekünstelt.

Unsound, *adj.,* —ly, *adv.* ungesund (*in health, etc.*); (spoiled) verdorben, wurmstichig; nicht stichhaltig. —ness, *s.* die Verdorbenheit.

Unsparing, *adj.* freigebig; schonungslos, hart.

Unspoken, *adj.* ungesagt, unerwähnt.

Unstable, *adj.* wankend, schwankend, unbeständig, unsicher.

Unstead—iness, *s.* die Unstätigkeit, das Schwanken. —ily, *adv.,* —y, *adj.* unstät, schwankend.

Unstrained, *adj.* unfiltriert; (*fig.*) ungezwungen.

Unstrung, *adj.* ungespannt; (*fig.*) abgespannt.

Unsuccessful, *adj.,* —ly, *adv.* erfolg-, frucht-los.

Unsuitab—ility, *s.* das Unpassende. —le, *adj.,* —ly, *adv.* unpassend, ungeeignet.

Unsurpass—able, *adj.* unübertrefflich. —ed, *adj.* unübertroffen.

Unsusp—ected, *adj.* unverdächtig. — ecting, —icious, *adj.* arglos.

Unsweetened, *adj.* unversüßt.

Unswerving, *adj.* fest, standhaft.

Unsympath—etic, (—izing,) *adj.* teilnahmlos.

Untaught, *adj.* ungelehrt, ununterrichtet.

Untaxed, *adj.* unbesteuert.

Untena—ble, *adj.* unhaltbar. —nted, *adj.* unbewohnt, unvermietet.

Unthinking, *adj.,* —ly, *adv.* gedankenlos.

Untid—ily, *adv.,* —y, *adj.* unordentlich. —iness, *s.* die Unordnung.

Untie, *v.a.* lösen, aufmachen.

Until, I. *prep.* bis. II. *conj.* bis (daß).

Untimely, *adj.* unzeitig, ungünstig.

Unto, *prep. see* To.

Untold, *adj.* unerzählt; (unnumbered) ungezählt.

Untouched, *adj.* unberührt; (*fig.*) ungerührt.

Untoward, *adj.* widerwärtig, verdrießlich, ungeschickt.

Untrained, *adj.* ungeübt, ungebildet.

Untried, *adj.* unversucht; nicht erledigt; nicht abgeurteilt.

Untrimmed, *adj.* ungeschmückt, unbesetzt.

Untrodden, *adj.* unbetreten.

Untroubled, *adj.* ungetrübt.

Untru—e, *adj.* falsch; (faithless) treulos. —ly, *adv.* unwahr. —th, *s.* die Unwahrheit. —thful, *adj.,* —thfully, *adv.* unwahr, falsch. —thfulness, *s.* die Unwahrheit.

Untrustworthiness, *s.* die Unzuverlässigkeit.

Unus—ed, *adj.* ungebraucht. —ual, *adj.* ungewöhnlich. —ualness, *s.* die Seltenheit.

Unutter—able, *adj.,* —ably, *adv.* unaussprechlich. —ed, *adj.* unausgesprochen.

Unvalued, *adj.* nicht geachtet, ungeschätzt.

Unvar—ied, *adj.* unverändert, einförmig. —ying, *adj.* unveränderlich.

Unveil, *v.a.* entschleiern.

Unwavering, *adj.* nicht wankend, standhaft.

Unwear—ied, *adj.,* —iedly, *adv.* unermüdet. —ying, *adj.* unermüdlich.

Unwedded, *adj.* unverheiratet, ledig.

Unwelcome, *adj.* unwillkommen.

Unwell, *adj.* unwohl, nicht wohl.

Unwept, *adj.* unbeweint.

Unwholesome, *adj.* ungesund, schädlich.

Unwilling, *adj.,* —ly, *adv.* un-, widerwillig, abgeneigt. —ness, *s.* der Widerwille, die Abgeneigtheit.

Unwind, *ir.v.a.* los-, ab-winden.

Unwise, *adj.,* —ly, *adv.* unklug, töricht.

Unwished, *adj.* ungewünscht; — for, unerwünscht.

Unwonted, *adj.* ungewohnt.

Unworth—ily, *adv.,* —y, *adj.* unwürdig. —iness, *s.* die Unwürdigkeit.

Unwounded, *adj.* unverwundet, unverletzt.

Unwrap, *v.a.* auf=wickeln, -schlagen, enthüllen.

Up, I. *adv.*; (— at) auf (*dat.*,); (upwards, ascending) auf (*acc.*), in die Höhe, empor, aufwärts; (towards the speaker) herauf; (away from the speaker) hinauf; (aloft) oben, in der Höhe; it's all — with him, es ist aus mit ihm; used —, aufgebraucht, abgenutzt. II. *int.* auf! herauf! heran! III. *prep.* hinauf, auf. IV. *s.*; the —s and downs of life, die Wechselfälle des Lebens.

Upbraid, *v.a.* vorwerfen. —ing, I.

adj. vorwurfsvoll. II. *s.* der Tadel, Vorwurf.

Upbringing, *s.* die Erziehung.

Upheav—al, *s.* die Er=, Empor=hebung. **—e,** *v.a.* emporheben.

Uphill, I. *adj.* den Berg hinauf, bergauf (gehend). II. *adv.* berg=auf, =an, aufwärts; *(fig.)* mühsam.

Uphold, *ir.v.a.* auf(recht) halten; *(fig.)* aufrecht erhalten, verteidigen.

Upholster—er, *s.* der Tapezier(er). **—y,** *s.* das Zimmergerät.

Upkeep, *s.* die Instandhaltung.

Upon, *prep.* (oben) auf.

Upper, *adj.* ober, höher, Ober=. **—most,** *adj.* höchst, oberst.

Uppish, *adj.* stolz, anmaßend *(coll.).*

Upraise, *v.a.* erheben, erhöhen.

Uprear, *v.a.* aufrichten.

Upright, I. *adj.,* **—ly,** *adv.* aufrecht, gerade. II. *s.* der Ständer *(Carp., etc.).*

Uprising, *s.* das Aufstehen; der Aufgang *(of the sun)*; (revolt) der Aufstand.

Uproar, *s.* der Aufruhr. **—ious,** *adj.,* **—iously,** *adv.* lärmend, tobend.

Uproot, *v.a.* entwurzeln.

Upset, I. *v.a.* umstürzen. II. *s.* der Umsturz. III. *adj.;* — **price,** der Anschlagspreis *(at auctions).*

Upshot, *s.* der Ausgang.

Upside-down, *adv.* drunter und drüber.

Upstairs, *adv.* (above) oben; to go **—stairs,** die Treppe hinauf gehen.

Upstart, *s.* der Emporkömmling.

Up-stream, *adv.* stromauf(wärts).

Up-to-date, I. *adj.* modern, zeitgemäß. II. *adv.* bisheute.

Upward, I. *adj.* nach oben gerichtet. II. *adv.,* **—s,** *adv.* aufwärts, in die Höhe.

Urban, *adj.* Stadt=, städtisch.

Urban—e, *adj.* höflich, artig. **—ity,** *s.* die Höflichkeit, Artigkeit.

Urchin, *s.* der Balg.

Urethra, *s.* die Harnröhre.

Urge, *v.a.* (— on) drängen, (an)treiben. **—ncy,** *s.* die Dringlichkeit. **—nt,** *adj.,* **—ntly,** *adv.* dringend, dringlich.

Urine, *s.* der Harn.

Urn, *s.* die Urne; **tea** —, der Tee= kessel.

Us, *pron.* (acc. of We), uns.

Us—age, *s.* der Gebrauch. **—e,** I. *s.* der Gebrauch, die Benutzung, An= wendung. II. *v.a.* (ge)brauchen, sich (einer Sache, ꝛc.) bedienen, benutzen,

anwenden; (practise) (aus)üben; (accustom) gewöhnen. III. *v.n.* ge= wohnt sein, pflegen; to be used to, etwas gewöhnt sein. **—eful,** *adj.,* **—efully,** *adv.* nützlich, nutzbar. **—e— fulness,** *s.* die Nützlichkeit. **—eless,** *adj.,* **—elessly,** *adv.* nutzlos, unnütz. **—elessness,** *s.* die Nutzlosigkeit. **—er,** *s.* der Benutzer.

Usher, I. *s.* der Zeremonienmeister, Pedell. II. *v.a.* (— in) einführen, an= melden.

Usual, *adj.* gewöhnlich, gebräuchlich, üblich; (frequent) häufig, gemein. **—ly,** *adv.* gewöhnlich, meistens.

Usur—er, *s.* der Wucherer. **—y,** *s.* der Wucher.

Usurp, *v.a.* sich (einer S.) bemächtigen. **—ation,** *s.* die Aneignung, Anmaßung. **—er,** *s.* der Thronräuber. **—ing,** *adj.,* **—ingly,** *adv.* angemaßt, wider= rechtlich.

Utensil, *s.* das Gerät, Geschirr, Hand= werkszeug.

Utili—ty, *s.* die Nützlichkeit, der Nutzen, Vorteil. **—zation,** *s.* die Nutzbar= machung. **—ze,** *v.a.* benutzen.

Utmost, I. *adj.* höchst, äußerst. II. *s.* das Äußerste, Höchste, Möglichste.

Utopian, *adj.* utopisch.

Utter, I. *adj.* äußerst. II. *v.a.* äußern, aus=sprechen, =drücken; in Umlauf bringen, setzen *(coin, etc.).* **—ance,** *s.* die Aussprache; die Ausgabe *(of coin, etc.)*; die Äußerung *(of words).* **—ly,** *adv.* durchaus, gänzlich, völlig.

V

V, v, *s.* das V, v; V = 5.

Vac—ancy, *s.* die Leere; die Lücke; das Freiwerden *(of a post)*; —ancy of mind, die Gedankenleere. **—ant,** *adj.,* **—antly,** *adv.* leer, unbesetzt; un= bewohnt. **—ate,** *v.a.* erledigen (a throne, etc.), niederlegen *(an office, etc.).* **—ation,** *s.* die Ferien *(in schools, etc.).*

Vaccin—ate, *v.a.* impfen. **—ation,** *s.* die Einimpfung der Kuhpocken. **— ator,** *s.* der Impfarzt. **—e,** *s.* der Impfstoff.

Vacilla—te, *v.n.* schwanken. **—tion,** *s.* das Schwanken; der Wankelmut.

Vacuum, *s.* das Vacuum.

Vag—abond, s. der Landstreicher. —**ary,** s. die Grille. —**rancy,** s. die Landstreicherei. —**rant,** adj. herumschweifend.

Vague, adj., —**ly,** adv. unbestimmt, ungewiß. —**ness,** s. die Unbestimmtheit.

Vain, adj., —**ly,** adv. eitel, eingebildet; in —, umsonst, vergebens. —**glorious,** adj., —**gloriously,** adv. prahlerisch. —**glory,** s. die Großsprecherei; (pride) die Hoffart.

Valance, s. die Bettgardine.

Vale, s. das Tal.

Valedictory, adj. Abschieds-.

Valerian, s. der Baldrian.

Valet, s. der (Kammer-)Diener.

Valetudinarian, I. adj. kränkelnd. **II.** s. die kränkliche Person.

Vali—ant, adj., —**antly,** adv. tapfer, mutig, kühn.

Valid, adj., —**ly,** adv. rechtskräftig, gültig; triftig (as arguments). —**ity,** s. die Gültigkeit, Geltung.

Valise, s. das Felleisen, der Reisesack.

Valley, s. das Tal.

Valour, s. die Tapferkeit. —**ous,** adj., —**ously,** adv. tapfer, kühn.

Valu—able, adj. wertvoll, kostbar. —**ation,** s. die Abschätzung. —**ator,** s. der Taxator, Schätzer. —**e, I.** s. der Wert (also fig.); die Valuta Währung (C.L.); die Geltung (of a note, of a word, of a coin). **II.** v.a. schätzen, (ver-)anschlagen. —**eless,** adj. wertlos.

Valv—e, s. das Ventil, die Klappe; die Röhre, Lampe (Radio). —**e-holder,** s. der Lampensockel, die Röhrenfassung (Radio). —**ular,** adj. klappig.

Vamp, s. das Oberleder.

Vampire, s. der Vampir (also fig.).

¹Van, s. die Vorhut.

²Van, s. der Möbeltransport-Wagen; (luggage —) der Gepäckwagen (Railw.).

Vane, s. der Wetterhahn, die Wetterfahne.

Vanguard, s. die Vorhut.

Vanilla, s. die Vanille.

Vanish, v.n. (ver-)schwinden.

Vanity, s. die Eitelkeit.

Vanquish, v.a. besiegen, überwältigen.

Vantage, s. die günstige Gelegenheit, die Überlegenheit; der Vorteil (Tennis).

Vap—id, adj., —**idly,** adv. schal. —**orize,** v.n. verdampfen. —**orous,**

adj. dunstig, dampfig. —**our,** s. der Dunst, Dampf.

Vari—able, adj., —**ably,** adv. veränderlich, abwechselnd; (unsteady) unbeständig. —**ableness,** s. die Veränderlichkeit; der Wankelmut. —**ance,** s. die Veränderung, der Widerspruch; (disagreement) die Uneinigkeit; to be at —ance, uneinig sein; sich widersprechen. —**ation,** s. die Veränderung, Abwechselung.

Varicose, adj. krampfaderig; — vein, die Krampfader.

Varied, adj. mannigfaltig.

Variegate, v.a. vielfarbig, mannigfaltig or bunt machen. —**d,** adj. bunt (scheckig), gefleckt.

Variety, s. die Mannigfaltigkeit.

Various, adj., —**ly,** adv. verschieden(artig).

Varlet, s. der Knappe; der Schuft.

Varnish, I. s. der Firnis, Lack; (fig.) der Anstrich. **II.** v.a. (über-)firnissen.

Vary, v. **I.** a. wechseln, verändern. **II.** n. sich verändern, (ab-)wechseln. —**ing,** adj. abwechselnd, veränderlich.

Vascular, adj. Gefäß-.

Vase, s. die Vase.

Vassal, s. der Lehnsmann, Vasall.

Vast, adj. unermeßlich, ungeheuer. —**ly,** adv. ungeheuer. —**ness,** s. die Unermeßlichkeit.

Vat, s. die Kufe, der Bottich.

¹Vault, I. s. das Gewölbe, die Wölbung. **II.** v.a. wölben; überwölben. —**ed,** adj. gewölbt. —**ing,** s. die Wölbung.

²Vault, I. v.n. springen. **II.** s. der Sprung, Satz.

Vaunt, I. v.a. rühmen. **II.** v.n. prahlen.

Veal, s. das Kalbfleisch.

Veer, v.n. sich drehen; sieren (as wind).

Vegeta—ble, I. s. die Pflanze; (also —bles) das Gemüse. **II.** adj. vegetabilisch, Pflanzen-, Gewächs-. —**rian,** s. der Vegetari(an)er. —**tion,** s. die Pflanzenwelt.

Vehemen—ce, s. die Heftigkeit. —**t,** adj., —**tly,** adv. heftig, hitzig.

Vehicle, s. das Fuhrwerk.

Veil, I. s. der Schleier, die Hülle (also fig.). **II.** v.a. verschleiern; (fig.) verhüllen.

Vein, s. die (Blut-)Ader. —**ed,** adj. geädert.

Vellum, *s.* das Velin, Schreibpergament.

Velocity, *s.* die Geschwindigkeit.

Velvet, I. *s.* der Sammet, Samt. II. *adj.* Samt-. **—een,** *s.* der Baumwollsamt.

¹Venal, *adj.* venös (*Anat.*).

²Venal, *adj.* verkäuflich, feil, käuflich. **—ity,** *s.* die Feilheit.

Vend, *v.a.* verkaufen, feilbieten. **—ible,** *adj.* verkäuflich, gangbar. **—or,** *s.* der Verkäufer.

Veneer, I. *s.* das Furnier; (*fig.*) äußerer Anstrich. II. *v.a.* furnieren. **—ing,** *s.* die Furnierung.

Venera—ble, *adj.* ehr-, achtungswürdig. **—bleness,** *s.* die Ehrwürdigkeit. **—te,** *v.a.* (ver)ehren. **—tion,** *s.* die Verehrung, Hochachtung, Ehrfurcht. **—tor,** *s.* der Verehrer.

Venetian, *adj.* venetianisch; **—** blind, die Jalousie.

Venge—ance, *s.* die Rache; with a **—** ance, (*fig.*) tüchtig, ganz gehörig. **—ful,** *adj.,* **—fully,** *adv.* rachsüchtig.

Venial, *adj.,* **—ly,** *adv.* verzeihlich, erläßlich. **—ity,** **—ness,** *s.* die Erläßlichkeit, Verzeihlichkeit.

Venison, *s.* das Wildbret, Hochwild.

Venom, *s.* das Gift (*also fig.*). **—ous,** *adj.,* **—ously,** *adv.* giftig. **—ousness,** *s.* die Giftigkeit.

Vent, *s.* die Öffnung.

Ventilat—e, *v.a.* ventilieren, lüften. **—ion,** *s.* die Lüftung. **—or,** *s.* der Ventilator, Windfang, Entgaser.

Ventr—al, *adj.* Bauch-. **—iloquism,** *s.* die Bauchrednerei. **—iloquist,** *s.* der Bauchredner. **—iloquize,** *v.n.* bauchreden.

Venture, I. *s.* das Wagnis. II. *v.a.* wagen. III. *v.n.* sich erkühnen or erdreisten; I **—** to say, ich wage die Behauptung. **—some,** *adj.,* **—somely,** *adv.* kühn, verwegen. **—someness,** *s.* die Verwegenheit.

Veraci—ous, *adj.* wahrhaft. **—ty,** *s.* die Wahrhaftigkeit.

Veranda, *s.* die Veranda.

Verb, *s.* das Zeitwort, Verbum. **—al,** I. *adj.,* **—ally,** *adv.* wörtlich; mündlich; Verbal- (*Gram.*). II. *s.* (**—al** noun) das Verbal-Hauptwort. **—atim,** *adv.* Wort für Wort.

Verbena, *s.* die Verbene.

Verb—iage, *s.* der Wortschwall. **—ose,** *adj.* wortreich.

Verdant, *adj.,* **—ly,** *adv.* grün.

Verdict, *s.* der Urteilspruch, das Verdikt; die Entscheidung.

Verdigris, *s.* der Grünspan.

Verdure, *s.* das Grün.

Verge, *s.* der Rand.

Veri—est, *adj.* ärgst. **—fiable,** *adj.* beweisbar. **—fication,** *s.* die Bewahrheitung. **—fy,** *v.a.* bewahrheiten. **—ly,** *adv.* wahrlich, fürwahr. **—table,** *adj.,* **—tably,** *adv.* wahr(haftig). **—ty,** *s.* die Wahrheit.

Verjuice, *s.* der Sauerwein.

Vermicelli, *s.* Fadennudeln (*pl.*).

Vermilion, *s.* der Zinnober.

Vermin, *s.* das Ungeziefer.

Vernacular, I. *adj.* einheimisch. II. *s.* die Landessprache, Muttersprache.

Vernal, *adj.* Frühlings-; **—** equinox, Frühlings-Tag- und Nacht-gleiche.

Veronica, *s.* der Ehrenpreis.

Vers—atile, *adj.* gewandt, vielseitig, geschmeidig. **—atility,** *s.* die Geschmeidigkeit.

Vers—e, *s.* der Vers. **—ed,** *adj.* erfahren, bewandert. **—ification,** *s.* der Versbau; (art) die Verskunst. **—ify,** *v.n.* reimen.

Version, *s.* die Darstellung.

Vert—ebra, *s.* (*pl.* **—ebræ**) der Rückenwirbel, das Wirbelbein. **—ebral,** *adj.* Wirbel(bein)-; **—ebral column,** das Rückgrat. **—ebrate,** I. *adj.* **—ebrated,** *adj.* gewirbelt. II. *s.* (**—ebrate** animal) das Wirbeltier. **—ical,** *adj.,* **—ically,** *adv.* senkrecht. **—igo,** *s.* der Schwindel.

Very, I. *adv.* sehr. II. *adj.* wirklich, echt; the **—** thought, der bloße Gedanke, schon der Gedanke.

Vespers, *pl.* die Vesper, Abendbetstunde (*R. C.*).

Vessel, *s.* das Gefäß (*also Anat., Bot., fig.*); das Fahrzeug, Schiff (*Naut.*).

Vest, *s.* die Weste.

Vestibule, *s.* die Vorhalle.

Vestige, *s.* die Spur.

Vestment, *s.* das Gewand, Kleid.

Vestry, *s.* die Sakristei.

Vesture, *s.* die Kleider (*pl.*).

Vetch, *s.* die Wicke.

Veteran, I. *adj.* alt, gedient, erfahren. II. *s.* der Veteran.

Veterinary, I. *adj.* tierärztlich. II. *s.* der Tier-, Roß-arzt.

Veto, I. *s.* das Veto. II. *v.a.*; (to put one's **—** upon) sein Veto einlegen gegen.

Vex, *v.* I. *a.* plagen, quälen; —ed question, die Streitfrage. II. *n.* sich quälen, ärgern. —ation, *s.* die Beunruhigung. —atious, *adj.,* — atiously, *adv.* drückend, quälerisch, verdrießlich.

Via, *prep.* über; — London, über London. —duct, *s.* der Viadukt.

Vial, *s.* das Fläschen, die Phiole.

Viands, *pl.* die Lebensmittel, Speisen.

Vibrat—e, *v.n.* vibrieren. —ion, *s.* die Schwingung, Vibration. —ive, —ory, *adj.* schwingend.

Vicar, *s.* der Stellvertreter; der Geistliche. —age, *s.* das Pfarrhaus. —ious, *adj.* stellvertretend.

¹**Vice,** *s.* das Laster.

²**Vice,** *s.* der Schraubstock.

³**Vice,** *prep.* an Stelle von; (*in comp.* =) Unter-, Vize-. —admiral, *s.* der Vizeadmiral. —regal, *adj.* vize- königlich. —roy, *s.* der Vizekönig. — versa, *adv.* umgekehrt.

Vicious, *adj.,* —ly, *adv.* lasterhaft. —ness, *s.* die Lasterhaftigkeit.

Vicissitude, *s.* die Abwechslung.

Victim, *s.* das Opfer (*also fig.*). — ize, *v.a.* (hin-)opfern.

Victor, *s.* der Sieger. —ious, *adj.,* —iously, *adv.* siegreich. —y, *s.* der Sieg.

Victual, I. *v.a.* verproviantieren. II. *s.,* —s, *pl.* Lebensmittel. —ler, *s.* der Lieferant.

Vie, *v.n.* wetteifern.

View, I. *v.a.* besehen, besichtigen, be- trachten. II. *s.* der Blick, Anblick; (prospect) die Aussicht; (point of —) der Gesichts-, Standpunkt; (opinion) die Meinung, Ein-, Ansicht; to keep in —, im Auge behalten; to have in —, beabsichtigen. —er, *s.* der Beschauer. —finder, *s.* der Sucher (*Phot.*).

Vigil, *s.* das Wachen. —ance, *s.* die Wachsamkeit. —ant, *adj.,* —antly, *adv.* wachsam, sorgsam.

Vignette, *s.* die Vignette, Verzierung.

Vigorous, *adj.,* —ly, *adv.* stark, kräftig.

Vigour, *s.* die Lebens-kraft, -frische, Energie, der Nachdruck.

Viking, *s.* der Wiking.

Vile, *adj.,* —ly, *adv.* verächtlich, wertlos. —ness, *s.* die Gemeinheit.

Villa, *s.* das Landhaus.

Village, *s.* das Dorf. —r, *s.* der Dorfbewohner.

Villain, *s.* der Schurke, Bösewicht. — ous, *adj.,* —ously, *adv.* schurkisch. —y, *s.* die Schurkerei.

Vindic—ate, *v.a.* rechtfertigen. — ation, *s.* die Rechtfertigung. —tive, *adj.,* —tively, *adv.* rachsüchtig. — tiveness, *s.* die Rachsucht.

Vine, *s.* der Weinstock, Rebstock, die Rebe. —dresser, *s.* der Winzer. —yard, *s.* der Wein-garten, -berg.

Vinegar, *s.* der Essig.

Vinous, *adj.* weinig; weinartig.

Vintage, *s.* die Weinlese. —r, *s.* der Winzer, Weinleser.

Vintner, *s.* der Weinhändler.

Viola, *s.* die Viole, Bratsche.

Viol—ate, *v.a.* entweihen; schänden, entehren. —ation, *s.* die Verletzung; die Entehrung; der (Eides-, Bundes-, Friedens-)Bruch (*of an oath, a con- tract, peace, etc.*).

Violen—ce, *s.* die Gewaltsamkeit. —t, *adj.,* —tly, *adv.* heftig (*as a blow, wind, a fight, etc.*), ungestüm, stark; (produced by force) gewaltsam (*as a death*).

Violet, *s.* das Veilchen.

Violin, *s.* die Geige, Violine. —ist, *s.* der Geiger, Violinspieler.

Violoncello, *s.* das Violoncell, Cello.

Viper, *s.* die Natter (*also fig.*).

Virago, *s.* das Mannweib.

Virgin, I. *s.* die Jungfrau. II. *adj.* jungfräulich. —ity, *s.* die Jung- fernschaft.

Viril—e, *adj.* mannhaft; mannbar. —ity, *s.* die Männlichkeit.

Virtu—al, *adj.,* —ally, *adv.* eigent- lich. —e, *s.* die Tugend; by —e of, kraft, vermöge. —ous, *adj.,* —ously, *adv.* tugendhaft.

Virtuoso, *s.* der Virtuos, Kunstkenner.

Virulent, *adj.* giftig; (*fig.*) boshaft.

Visage, *s.* das Gesicht.

Vis-à-vis, *adv.* gegenüber. II. *s.* das Gegenüber.

Viscous, *adj.* klebrig, zäh.

Visib—ility, *s.* die Sichtbarkeit. —le, *adj.,* —ly, *adv.* sichtbar.

Vision, *s.* das Sehen; (power of —) die Sehkraft; (dream, *etc.*) das Traumbild. —ary, I. *adj.* phan- tastisch. II. *s.* der Schwärmer, die Schwärmerin.

Visit, I. *v.a.* besuchen. II. *v.n.* Be- suche machen. III. *s.* der Besuch, die Visite. —ing, I. *adj.* Besuchs-; —

ing card, die Visitenkarte. II. s. das Besuchen. —or, s. der Besuchende, Besuch(er).

Vista, s. die Aussicht.

Vital, adj. zum Leben gehörig, Lebens-; (essential) wesentlich. —ity, s. die Lebenskraft; (life) das Leben.

Vitreous, adj. gläsern.

Vitriol, s. das Vitriol.

Viv—acious, adj., —aciously, adv. lebhaft, munter. —acity, —aciousness, s. die Lebhaftigkeit. —a-voce, adv. mündlich. —id, adj., —idly, adv. lebhaft, lebendig. —idness, s. die Lebhaftigkeit, Lebendigkeit.

Vivisection, s. die Vivisektion.

Vixen, s. die Füchsin; (fig.) die böse Sieben, die Zänkerin.

Vizier, s. der Wesir.

Vocabulary, s. das Wörterverzeichnis, der Wortschatz.

Vocal, adj. Stimmen-; Vokal-.

Vocation, s. der (innere) Beruf; (talent) die Neigung, der Ruf; (occupation) der Beruf.

Vocative, s. (— case) der Vokativ.

Vogue, s. die Mode.

Voice, I. s. die Stimme; active —, das Aktivum; passive —, das Passivum. II. v.a. stimmen. —less, adj. stimmlos.

Void, I. adj. leer. II. s. die Leere.

Volatile, adj. fliegend; flüchtig (Chem.); (fig.) flatterhaft.

Volcan—ic, adj. vulkanisch. —o, s. der Vulkan.

Vole, s. die Wühlmaus.

Volition, s. das Wollen.

Volley, s. die Salve; der Flugschlag (Tennis).

Volt, s. das Volt. —age, s. die Spannung. —aic, adj. voltaisch.

Volu—bility, s. die Zungenfertigkeit. —ble, adj., —bly, adv. zungenfertig.

Volum—e, s. der Band (of a book), das Volumen (Phys., etc.); die Stärke, der Umfang (of the voice). —inous, adj., —inously, adv. umfangreich.

Volunt—arily, adv. aus freien Stücken. —ariness, s. die Freiwilligkeit. —ary, adj. freiwillig. —eer, I. s. der Freiwillige. II. v.n. freiwillig dienen.

Voluptuous, adj., —ly, adv. wollüstig, üppig. —ness, s. die Wollust, Üppigkeit.

Vomit, I. v.a. aus-brechen, -werfen.

II. v.n. (sich er-)brechen, sich übergeben.

Voraci—ous, adj., —ously, adv. gefräßig, gierig. —ty, —ousness, s. die Gefräßigkeit.

Votary, s. der Geweihte.

Vot—e, I. s. die (Wahl-)Stimme, das Votum; die Abstimmung; to put to the —e, abstimmen lassen. II. v.n. (ab)stimmen. —er, s. der Wahlmann. —ing, I. p. & adj. stimmend, Stimm-. II. s. das (Ab-)Stimmen. —ing-paper, s. der Stimmzettel.

Vouch, v.n. sich verbürgen, stehen (for, für). —er, s. der Zeuge; (written —er) der (Beleg-)Schein. —safe, v.a. gewähren; —safe, O Lord, verleih, o Herr!

Vow, I. v.a. (an)geloben. II. v.n. geloben, schwören. III. s. das Gelübde.

Vowel, I. s. der Vokal, Selbstlaut. II. adj. vokalisch.

Voyage, I. s. die Seereise. II. v.n. zur See reisen. —r, s. der, die (See-)Reisende.

Vulcanite, s. der Hartgummi.

Vulgar, I. adj., —ly, adv. gemein. II. s.; the —, gemeine Leute, das gemeine Volk, der Pöbel. —ism, s. der gemeine Ausdruck. —ity, s. die Gemeinheit.

Vulnerab—ility, s. die Verwundbarkeit. —le, adj. verwundbar.

Vulture, s. der Geier.

W

W, w, s. das W, w.

Wabbl—e, v.n. wackeln. —y, adj wackelig, schwankend.

Wad, I. s. die Schütte; der Pfropf (Artil.). II. v.a. (aus)stopfen; wattieren (a mantle, etc.). —ding, s. die Wattierung, Watte.

Waddle, v.n. watscheln.

Wade, I. v.n. waten. II. v.a. durchwaten.

Wafer, s. die Waffel; die Oblate; consecrated —, die Hostie.

Waft, v.a. wehen.

¹**Wag**, v.a. schütteln (the head); wedeln (mit dem Schwanze).

²**Wag**, s. der Spaßvogel. —gery, s. der Spaß. —gish, adj., —gishly, adv. schelmisch, possierlich.

Wage, s., —s, pl. der Lohn.

Wager, I. *s.* die Wette. II. *v.a. & n.* wetten.

Waggle, *v.n.* wackeln.

Wagon, *s.* der Wagen. —**er,** *s.* der Fuhrmann.

Wagtail, *s.* die Bachstelze.

Waif, *s.* das verwahrloste, heimatlose Kind.

Wail, I. *s.* die Wehklage. II. *v.n.* wehklagen, sich beklagen. —**ing,** *adj.,* —**ingly,** *adv.* klagend.

Wainscot, I. *s.* das Tafelwerk. II. *v.a.* (über)täfeln, (mit Tafelwerk) verkleiden.

Waist, *s.* die Taille. —**coat,** *s.* die Weste; das Wams.

Wait, *v.n.* warten, bleiben; to — for, auf (einen) warten, (einen) erwarten; to — on, upon, (einem) aufwarten; to keep —ing, warten lassen. —**er,** *s.* der Kellner. —**ress,** *s.* die Kellnerin. —**ing,** *s.* die Aufwartung, Bedienung. —**ing-room,** *s.* der Wartesaal (*Railw.*); das Wartezimmer. —**ing-woman,** *s.* die Kammerfrau.

Waive, *v.a.* verzichten auf (*acc.*), aufgeben, aufschieben.

¹**Wake,** I. *ir.v.n.* wachen; erwachen. II. *ir.v.a.* er=wecken; to — a corpse, bei einer Leiche wachen. —**ful,** *adj.,* —**fully,** *adv.* wachend. —**fulness,** *s.* die Wachsamkeit.

²**Wake,** *s.* das Kielwasser (*of a ship*).

Walk, I. *v.n.* gehen; (take a —) spazieren gehen. II. *v.a.* im Schritt gehen lassen (*a horse*); spazieren führen (*a person*). III. *s.* das Gehen, der Gang; der Spaziergang (*stroll, etc.*). —**er,** *s.* der Fuß=, Spazier= gänger. —**ing,** I. *adj.* gehend. II. *s.* das Gehen; das Spazieren. —**ing-stick,** *s.* der Spazierstock.

Wall, I. *s.* die Wand, Mauer. II. *v.a.* (enclose) mit einer Mauer umgeben; to — up, zu=, ver=mauern. —**flower,** *s.* der Goldlack. —**fruit,** *s.* das Spa= lierobst. —**map,** *s.* die Wandkarte. —**plug,** *s.* der Steckkontakt (*Elec.*). —**paper,** *s.* die Tapete.

Wallet, *s.* der Beutel; die Brieftasche.

Wallop, *v.a.* prügeln.

Wallow, *v.n.* schwelgen in (*dat.*).

Walnut, *s.* die Walnuß.

Walrus, *s.* das Walroß.

Waltz, I. *s.* der Walzer. II. *v.n.* walzen. —**er,** *s.* der, die Walzende. —**ing,** *s.* das Walzertanzen.

Wan, *adj.* bleich, blaß. —**ness,** *s.* die Bleiche, Blässe.

Wand, *s.* der Stab.

Wander, *v.n.* wandern. —**er,** *s.* der Wanderer. —**ing,** I. *adj.* wandernd; —ing Jew, der ewige Jude. II. *s.* das Wandern.

Wan—e, I. *v.n.* abnehmen. II. *s.* die Abnahme (*also fig.*). —**ing,** *adj.* abnehmend.

Want, I. *s.* der Mangel; das Be= dürfnis; (poverty) die Armut, Not; to be in — of, Mangel leiden an (*dat.*); for — of, aus Mangel an (*dat.*). II. *v.a.* bedürfen, nötig haben; (be without) ermangeln; (desire) wün= schen, verlangen; I — to know why, ich möchte gern den Grund wissen. III. *v.n.* fehlen, mangeln.

Wanton, I. *adj.* leichtfertig; üppig, liederlich. —**ly,** *adv.* liederlich. II. *s.* der Wüstling. —**ness,** *s.* der Mutwille; die Üppigkeit, die Ausge= lassenheit.

War, I. *s.* der Krieg. II. *attrib.* Kriegs=. —**cry,** *s.* der Schlachtruf. — **department,** *s.* das Kriegsministe= rium. —**horse,** *s.* das Schlachtroß. —**like,** *adj.* kriegerisch, Kriegs=. —**path,** *s.* der Kriegspfad.

Warble, *v.n.* trillern. —**r,** *s.* der Sänger; der Singvogel.

¹**Ward,** I. *v.a.* bewahren; to — off, ab= wehren. II. *s.* die Wehr, Wache; das Eingerichte (*of a lock*); der Ein= strich (*of a key*); die Abteilung (*of a hospital*); das Mündel, der, die Minderjährige. —**en,** *s.* der Hüter, Aufseher. —**er,** *s.* der Wärter, Hüter, Wächter. —**robe,** *s.* der Kleider= schrank.

²**Ward,** *adv.* =wärts.

Ware, *s.* die Ware; das Geschirr; china —, das Porzellan. —**house,** *s.* das Warenlager, der Speicher, die Niederlage.

Warfare, *s.* das Kriegsleben; der Kampf, Krieg; state of —, der Kriegszustand.

Wari—ly, *adv.* vorsichtig, bedachtsam. —**ness,** *s.* die Vorsicht.

Warm, I. *adj.,* —**ly,** *adv.* warm, heiß. II. *v.a.* (er)wärmen (*also fig.*). —**th,** *s.* die Wärme. —**hearted,** *adj.* warmherzig.

Warn, *v.a.* warnen; (admonish) er= mahnen. —**er,** *s.* der Ermahner,

Warner. —ing, I. p., —ingly, adv.
warnend, ermahnend. II. s. die
Warnung, Mahnung.

Warp, I. s. die Kette, der Zettel,
Aufzug (Weav.); das Bugsiertau
(Naut.). II. v.a. krumm machen (wood,
etc.); bugsieren (Naut.). III. v.n.
werpen, warpen (Naut.); (swerve)
abweichen, schwanken.

Warrant, I. s. die Bürgschaft; (commission) die Ermächtigung, Befugnis; (writ of arrest) der Verhafts-
befehl. II. v.a. (assure) versichern;
(empower) bevollmächtigen, ermächtigen, Befugnis erteilen. —able, adj.
zu rechtfertigen. —ably, adj. rechtmäßig, billigerweise. —ed, adj.
garantiert. —er, s. der Gewährs-
mann, Bürge. —y, s. die Garantie.

Warren, s. das Gehege.

Warrior, s. der Krieger, Kriegsmann.

Wart, s. die Warze.

Wary, adj. vorsichtig, behutsam.

Wash, I. v.a. waschen; (aus)spülen
(glasses, etc.); abspülen (a deck, etc.).
II. v.n. waschen; (— oneself) sich
waschen. —ing, s. das Waschen,
Reinigen; (linen) die Wäsche. —er, s.
die Zwischenlegscheibe, der Dichtungs-
ring. —er-woman, s. die Waschfrau,
Wäscherin. —(hand)basin, s. das
Waschbecken. —stand, s. der Wasch-
tisch. —tub, s. der Waschkübel.

Wasp, s. die Wespe.

Waste, I. v.a. verwüsten, veröden, verheeren. II. v.n.; to — away, hin-
schwinden, sich verzehren, vergehen.
III. adj. wüst, öde; (unused) un-
benutzt; (worthless) wertlos. IV. s.
die Vergeudung (of money, time,
etc.); (desert) die Wüste, Einöde. —
ful, adj., —fully, adv. verschwenderisch.
—fulness, s. die Verschwendung.

Wastrel, s. der arbeitsscheue Lump.

Watch, I. v.n. (wake) wachen; Wache
halten, wachen (with, bei, over, über
einen). II. v.a. (guard) bewachen,
hüten; (observe) beobachten. III. s.
die Wache, das Wachen; die Aufmerksamkeit; die Taschenuhr (Horol.).
—ful, adj., —fully, adv. wachsam,
achtsam. —fulness, s. die Wachsamkeit, Achtsamkeit. —ing, s. das
Wachen; das Aufpassen. —dog, s.
der Kettenhund. —maker, s. der
Uhrmacher. —man, s. der Wächter.
—word, s. die Losung.

Water, I. s. das Wasser; high (low) —,
der Hoch- (Tief-)stand des Wassers; to
be in low —, auf dem Trocknen sitzen
(fig.); a diamond of the first —, ein
Diamant vom reinsten Wasser. II.
v.a. (be-)wässern, benetzen, begießen.
III. v.n. wässern; tränen (as the eyes).
—iness, s. die Wässerigkeit. —ing,
s. das Wässern, Begießen (streets).
—y, adj. wässerig. —colours, pl.
die Aquarellfarben. —cress, s. die
Brunnenkresse. —fall, s. der Wasserfall. —ing place, s. der Badeort.
—ing-pot, s. die Gießkanne. —
proof, I. adj. wasserdicht. II. s. der
Regen-, Gummi-mantel. —shed, s.
die Wasserscheide. —way, s. die
Wasserstraße.

Wattle, s. das Flechtwerk; der Fleisch-
lappen (birds).

Wave, I. s. die Welle, Woge; permanent
—, die Dauerwelle (hair); — length,
die Wellenlänge (Radio). II. v.n.
wogen; wehen, flattern (in the wind,
etc.); zuwinken (to a person). III.
v.a. wellenförmig machen; (brandish)
schwingen, schwenken.

Waver, v.n. wanken. —er, s. der
Schwankende. —ing, adj., —ingly,
adv. schwankend, unschlüssig.

¹Wax, I. s. das Wachs; sealing —,
der Siegellack. II. v.a. bohnen (floors).
—en, adj. wächsern. —work, s. die
Wachsfigur.

²Wax, v.n. wachsen.

Way, s. der Weg; (path) die Bahn;
(manner) die Art, Weise, Manier;
— in, der Eingang; — out, der
Ausgang; this —, hierher; in a —,
in gewisser Hinsicht; —s and means,
Mittel und Wege; by the —, beiläufig;
by — of excuse, als Entschuldigung;
to lead the —, vorangehen. —bill,
s. der Frachtbrief. —farer, s. der
Wanderer, Reisende. —faring, adj.
wandernd, reisend, Reise-. —lay,
v.a. (einem) auflauern.

We, pers. pron. wir.

Weak, adj., —ly, adv. schwach, kraftlos
(also fig.). —en, v.a. schwächen.
—ling, s. der Schwächling. —ness, s.
die Schwäche, Schwachheit. —
minded, adj. schwachsinnig.

¹Weal, s. das Wohl.

²Weal, s. die Schwiele, Strieme.

Wealth, s. der Reichtum. —y, adj.
reich, wohlhabend.

Wean, *v.a.* (Kinder) entwöhnen; (*fig.*) abwöhnen (from, von).

Weapon, *s.* die Waffe; (gun) das Gewehr. **—less,** *adj.* waffenlos.

Wear, I. *ir.v.a.* anhaben, tragen (*a dress, etc.*); zerstören; to — off, abnutzen; to — out, abtragen, abnutzen; (destroy) zerstören; (exhaust) erschöpfen, ermüden. II. *s.* das Tragen. **—able,** *adj.* tragbar. **—er,** *s.* der Tragende. **—ing,** I. *attrib.*; — ing apparel, Kleidungsstücke. II. *s.* das Tragen.

Wear—ily, *adv.* müde. **—iness,** *s.* die Müdigkeit, Ermüdung. **—isome,** *adj.,* **—isomely,** *adv.* ermüdend, mühsam; (tedious) langweilig. **—y,** I. *adj.* müde. II. *v.a.* ermüden. III. *v.n.* müde werden.

Weasel, *s.* das Wiesel.

Weather, *s.* das Wetter; — permitting, bei günstiger Witterung. **—beaten,** *adj.* wetterhart, abgehärtet. **—cock,** *s.* der Wetterhahn (also *fig.*).

Weav—e, *ir.v.a.* weben. **—er,** *s.* der Weber. **—ing,** *s.* das Weben.

Web, *s.* das Gewebe.

Wed, *v.* I. *a.* heiraten. II. *n.* sich verheiraten. **—ding,** *s.* die Hochzeit. **—ding-ring,** *s.* der Trauring.

Wedge, I. *s.* der Keil. II. *v.a.* (ver-) keilen.

Wedlock, *s.* die Ehe.

Wednesday, *s.* der Mittwoch.

Wee, *adj.* klein, winzig.

Weed, *s.* das Unkraut.

Week, *s.* die Woche; this day —, heute über acht Tage. **—ly,** I. *adj.* wöchentlich. II. *s.* das Wochenblatt. **—day,** *s.* der Wochentag.

Weep, *ir.v.* I. *n.* weinen; to — for, beweinen; to — for joy, vor Freude weinen. II. *a.* vergießen (tears, etc., Tränen, 2c.). **—er,** *s.* der, die Weinende. **—ing,** I. *s.* das Weinen. II. *adj.,* **—ingly,** *adv.* weinend.

Weevil, *s.* der Kornwurm.

Weft, *s.* der Ein=schlag, =schuß, =trag.

Weigh, *v.* I. *a.* wägen; (— out something to a person, einem etwas) zuwägen; (*fig.*) (er)wägen; lichten (the anchor). II. *n.* wiegen. **—er,** *s.* der Wäger. **—t,** I. *s.* das Gewicht; (*fig.*) die Wichtigkeit. II. *v.a.* belasten, beschweren. **—tiness,** *s.* die Schwere, das Gewicht. **—ty,** *adj.,* **—tily,** *adv.* gewichtig, schwer; (*fig.*) wichtig, erheb=

lich. **—bridge,** **—ing-machine,** *s.* die Brückenwage.

Weir, *s.* das Wehr.

Weird, *adj.* unheimlich, merkwürdig, seltsam.

Welcome, I. *adj.* willkommen; you are — to it, es steht Ihnen zu Diensten, es ist gern geschehen (gegeben). II. *s.* der Willkomm. III. *v.a.* bewillkommnen, willkommen heißen. IV. *int.* willkommen!

Weld, *v.a.* (— together, zusammen=) schweißen.

Welfare, *s.* die Wohlfahrt, das Wohlergehen.

¹**Well,** I. *s.* der Brunnen. II. *v.n.* (— forth, hervor=, — up, herauf=)quellen or sprudeln.

²**Well,** I. *adv.* wohl, gut. II. *adj.* wohl, gesund. III. *part.*; — then! nun gut! wohlan! **—bred,** *adj.* feingebildet. **—educated,** *adj.* wohlerzogen. **—known,** *adj.* wohlbekannt. **—meaning,** *adj.* wohlmeinend. **—meant,** *adj.* wohlgemeint. **—off,** *adj.* in guten Verhältnissen. **—read,** *adj.* belesen. **—to-do,** *adj.* wohlhabend, reich. **—wisher,** *s.* der Gönner, Freund. **—worn,** *adj.* abgetragen.

Welt, I. *s.* der Saum. II. *v.a.* prügeln.

Welter, *v.n.* sich wälzen.

Wen, *s.* der Balg=, Fett=geschwulst.

Wench, *s.* das Mädchen.

Wend, *ir.v.n.* sich wenden; to — one's way, seinen Weg richten.

West, *s.* der Westen. **—erly,** *adj.* westlich. **—ern,** I. *adj.* westlich, abendlich, West=; abendländisch. II. *s.* der Abendländer. **—ward,** *adv.* westlich. **—wards,** *adj.* westwärts.

Wet, I. *adj.* naß, feucht; regnerisch (as weather). II. *s.* die Nässe. III. *v.a.* naß machen. **—ting,** *s.* das Naßmachen. **—nurse,** *s.* die (Säug=)Amme.

Wether, *s.* der Hammel.

Whack, I. *s.* derber Schlag. II. *v.a.* durchprügeln. **—ing,** I. *adj.* (*coll.*) kolossal. II. *s.* die Tracht Prügel.

Whale, *s.* der Walfisch.

Wharf, *s.* der Kai.

What, I. *rel. pron.* was. II. *inter. pron.* was? wie? wie viel? **—ever,** **—soever,** I. *rel. pron.* was auch (immer), was nur, alles was. II. *adj.* welch(=er, =e, =es) immer; — a man! was für ein Mann!

Wheat, *s.* der Weizen. **—en,** *adj.*
Weizen=.

Wheedle, *v.a.* & *n.* schmeicheln.

Wheel, I. *s.* das Rad. II. *v.n.* rollen,
sich drehen; sich schwenken (*Mil.*).
III. *v.a.* rollen, schieben. **—barrow,** *s.*
der Schubkarren.

Wheez—e, *v.n.* schnaufen. **—y,** *adj.*
keuchend, schnaubend.

Whelk, *s.* die Trompetenschnecke.

Whelp, *s.* das Junge.

When, I. *inter. adv.* wann. II. *conj.*
& *rel. adv.* wenn, da, als. **—ce,** I.
inter & *rel. adv.* woher, woraus.
II. *conj.* daher. **—ever,** *adv.* wann
auch immer; so oft als.

Where, I. *inter. adv.* wo. II. *rel. adv.*
& *conj.* wo; da. **—abouts,** I. *adv.*
wo herum, wo da. II. *s.* der Wohnort. **—at,** *rel. adv.* & *conj.* wobei.
—by, *rel. adv.* & *conj.* wodurch. **—
fore,** *adv.* & *conj.* weshalb. **—in,**
adv. & *conj.* worin. **—of,** *adv.* &
conj. wovon. **—on,** *rel. adv.* & *conj.*
worauf, woran. **—upon,** *rel. adv.*
& *conj.* worauf. **—to,** **—unto,** *rel.
adv.* & *conj.* wozu, wohin. **—ver,** *rel.
adv.* wo auch nur. **—with,** *rel. adv.*
& *conj.* womit, wovon. **—withal,** *s.*
das Erforderliche.

Whet, *v.a.* wetzen. **—stone,** *s.* der
Schleifstein.

Whether, *conj.* ob.

Whey, *s.* die Molken.

Which, I. *rel. pron.* der, die, das,
welcher, welche, welches; was. II.
inter. pron. welcher, welche, welches.

Whiff, *s.* der Paff.

Whil—e, I. *s.* die Weile; a long **—e**
ago, vor langer Zeit. II. **—st,** *conj.*
während; (as) indem.

Whim, *s.* der Einfall, die Grille, Laune.
—sical, *adj.* grillenhaft, wunderlich.

Whimper, *v.n.* wimmern, winseln.

¹**Whin,** *s.* der Stechginster (*Bot.*).

²**Whin,** *s.* der Basalt.

Whin—e, I. *v.n.* winseln. II. *s.* das
Gewinsel. **—er,** *s.* der Winseler.
—ing, *adj.,* **—ingly,** *adv.* winselnd;
(*fig.*) kläglich.

Whinny, I. *v.n.* wiehern. II. *s.* das
Gewieher.

Whip, I. *v.a.* peitschen, züchtigen,
geißeln; **—ped** cream, die Schlag-
sahne. II. *s.* die Peitsche, Geißel.
—ping, *s.* das Peitschen, Züchtigen.

—handle, *s.* der Peitschenstiel. **—
lash,** *s.* die Peitschenschmitze.

Whir, I. *v.n.* schwirren. II. *s.* das
Geschwirre.

Whirl, *v.a.* (& *n.*) wirbeln. **—pool,**
s. der Strudel, Wirbel. **—wind,**
s. der Wirbelwind.

Whisk, I. *s.* der (Stroh=)Wisch. II.
v.a. fegen, kehren. III. *v.n.* huschen.
—er, *s.,* usually **—ers** (*pl.*), der
Backenbart. **—ered,** *adj.* backen-
bärtig.

Whisper, I. *s.* das Geflüster. II. *v.n.*
flüstern. III. *v.a.* zuflüstern, ins Ohr
flüstern. **—er,** *s.* der Flüsterer. **—
ing,** I. *adj.,* **—ingly,** *adv.* wispernd,
flüsternd, leise. II. *s.* das Geflüster.

¹**Whist,** *int.* still! pst!

²**Whist,** *s.* das Whist(spiel).

Whistl—e, I. *v.a.* & *n.* pfeifen. II. *s.*
das Pfeifen, der Pfiff; (instrument)
die Pfeife. **—er,** *s.* der Pfeifer. **—ing,**
I. *adj.* pfeifend. II. *s.* das Pfeifen.

Whit, *s.* das Iota, die Kleinigkeit.

White, I. *adj.* weiß. II. *s.* die, das
Weiße, das Weiß. **—n,** *v.a.* weißen.
—ness, *s.* die Weiße. **—ning,** *s.* die
Schlemmkreide. **—bait,** *s.* der
Weißfisch, Breitling. **—lead,** *s.* das
Bleiweiß. **—livered,** *adj.* feige.
—smith, *s.* der Weißblechschmied. **—
wash,** I. *s.* die (weiße) Tünche. II.
v.a. (aus=)weißen, übertünchen.

Whither, *rel.* & *inter. adv.* wohin.

Whiting, *s.* die spanische Kreide; der
Weißfisch (*Icht.*).

Whitish, *adj.* weißlich.

Whitlow, *s.* das Nagelgeschwür.

Whit—Monday, *s.* der Pfingstmontag.
—sun, *adj.* Pfingst=.

Whittle, I. *s.* das Schnitzmesser. II.
v.a. schnitzeln.

Whiz, *v.n.* zischen, sausen.

Who, I. *rel. pron.* der, die, das, welcher, welche, welches. II. *inter. pron.*
wer.

Whole, I. *adj.* ganz; vollkommen;
(sound) heil, gesund. II. *s.* das
Ganze. **—sale,** I. *adj.* im Großen;
—sale manufacture, die Massen-
herstellung. II. *s.* der Großhandel.
—some, *adj.,* **—somely,** *adv.* heilsam;
nützlich, gesund.

Wholly, *adv.* gänzlich, völlig, durchaus.

Whom, I. *obj. of* who I. welchen, welche,
welches, den, die, das. II. *obj. of* who
II. wen? to **—**? wem?

Whoop, I. *v.n.* laut aufschreien. II. *s.* lautes Geschrei. **—ing-cough,** *s.* der Stichhusten.

Whortleberry, *s.* die Heidelbeere.

Whose, I. *poss. of who* I. dessen, deren, dessen, (*pl.*) deren. II. *poss. of who* II. wessen.

Why, *adv.* warum.

Wick, *s.* der Docht.

Wicked, *adj.*, **—ly,** *adv.* (spiteful) boshaft; (bad) schlecht, böse. **—ness,** *s.* die Gottlosigkeit, Bosheit.

Wicker, *adj.* (von Weidenzweigen) geflochten; — basket, der Weidenkorb. **—work,** *s.* das Flechtwerk.

Wicket, *s.* das Pförtchen.

Wide, *adj. & adv.*, **—ly,** *adv.* weit, breit. **—n,** *v.a.* (*& n.* sich) erweitern, ausdehnen. **—ness,** *s.* die Weite, Ausdehnung. **—ning,** *s.* die Erweiterung. **—awake,** *adj.* völlig wach, aufgeweckt; hellsehend, schlau.

Widgeon, *s.* die wilde Ente.

Widow, *s.* die Witwe; grass —, die Strohwitwe. **—ed,** *adj.* verwitwet. **—er,** *s.* der Witwer.

Width, *s.* die Weite, Breite.

Wield, *v.a.* handhaben, schwingen.

Wife, *s.* die Gattin, (Ehe=)Frau; my —, meine Frau.

Wig, *s.* die Perücke.

Wight, *s.* der Wicht, Kerl.

Wild, *adj.*, **—ly,** *adv.* wild. **—erness,** *s.* die Wildnis, Wüste. **—ness,** *s.* die Wildheit.

Wile, I. *s.* die List. II. *v.a.* an=, verloden.

Wilful, *adj.*, **—ly,** *adv.* eigen=willig, =sinnig, halsstarrig. **—ness,** *s.* der Eigensinn.

Will, I. *s.* der Wille; (power) die Willkür; das Testament; at —, nach Belieben; with a —, mit festem Entschlusse. II. *ir.v.a.* wollen; durch Testament verfügen. III. *ir.v.aux.* werden, wollen. **—ed,** *adj.*; self—, eigen=willig, =sinnig. **—ing,** *adj.* willig, bereit (willig). **—ingly,** *adv.* gern. **—ingness,** *s.* die Bereitwilligkeit.

Will-o'-the-wisp, *s.* das Irrlicht.

Willow, *s.* die Weide.

Willy-nilly, *adv.* gern oder ungern.

Wilt, *v.n.* verwelken.

Wily, *adj.* listig, schlau.

Win, *ir.v.a.* gewinnen (*a battle, etc.*); (*fig.*) erlangen; to — over, für sich gewinnen.

Wince, *v.n.* zusammenzucken.

Winch, *s.* der Haspel, die Winde.

¹Wind, *s.* der Wind; the — is very high, es geht ein sehr starker Wind. **—iness,** *s.* die Windigkeit. **—less,** *adj.* ohne Wind. **—ward,** I. *adj. & adv.* windwärts. II. *s.* die Wind=, Luv=seite. **—y,** *adj.* windig. **—instrument,** *s.* das Blasinstrument. **—mill,** *s.* die Windmühle. **—fall,** *s.* das Fallobst; (*fig.*) der Glücksfall. **—pipe,** *s.* die Luftröhre.

²Wind, *ir.v.a.* I. winden; blasen (*a horn*). II. *n.* sich winden, sich schlängeln. **—ing,** *adj.* sich windend. **—ing-sheet,** *s.* das Grabtuch, Totenhemd. **—ing-stair,** *s.* die Wendeltreppe. **—lass,** *s.* der Haspel.

Window, *s.* das Fenster. **—blind,** *s.* die Jalousie. **—pane,** *s.* die Fensterscheibe. **—sill,** *s.* der Fenstersims.

Wine, *s.* der Wein.

Wing, *s.* der Flügel; to take —, wegfliegen. **—ed,** *adj.* beflügelt, geflügelt.

Wink, I. *s.* das Blinzeln. II. *v.n.* winken, blinzeln.

Winkle, *s.* die Uferschnecke.

Winn—er, *s.* der Gewinner. **—ing,** I. *adj.*, **—ingly,** *adv.* einnehmend, gewinnend. II. *s.* das Gewinnen. **—ings,** *pl.* der Gewinn. **—ing-post,** *s.* das Ziel.

Winnow, *v.a.* Getreide schwingen, worfeln.

Winsome, *adj.* anziehend, reizend. **—ness,** *s.* der Reiz.

Winter, *s.* der Winter. **—ly, —y,** (**Wintry**,) *adj.* winterlich, Winter=.

Wipe, *v.a.* (ab)wischen. **—r,** *s.* der Wischer.

Wire, I. *s.* der Draht; das Telegramm; barbed —, der Stacheldraht. II. *adj.* drahten; Draht=. III. *v.a.* mit einem Draht versehen (*a lamp*). IV. *v.n.* telegraphieren, drahten (*Tele.*). **—entanglement,** *s.* das Drahthindernis. **—haired,** *adj.* mit borstigen Haaren. **—less,** *adj.*; —less telegraphy, die Funkentelegraphie, drahtlose Depeschensendung; —less set, der Radioapparat; —less telegraphy station, die Funksprechstation. **—puller,** *s.* der Marionettenspieler; der Drahtzieher, bezahlter Agitator; der Intrigant, heimliche Agent. **—pulling,** *s.* das Ziehen der Drähte für

Marionetten; (*fig.*) das Ränkeschmieden; die heimliche Leitung. **—worm,** *s.* der Drahtwurm, die schädliche Raupe. **—wove(n),** *adj.* aus Draht geflochten. **—**-wove(n) mattress, die Springfedermatratze.

Wisdom, *s.* die Weisheit; (prudence) die Klugheit; (knowledge) die Einsicht.

Wise, *adj.,* **—ly,** *adv.* weise, vernünftig, verständig.

Wish, I. *v.a.* wünschen; to — for, sich etwas wünschen; to — a person joy, jemandem Glück wünschen. II. *s.* der Wunsch. **—ful,** *adj.,* **—fully,** *adv.* wünschend.

Wisp, *s.*; a — of hay, ein Heubündel; a — of hair, eine Haarsträhne.

Wistful, *adj.,* **—ly,** *adv.* sehnlich, gedankenvoll.

Wit, I. *s.* der Witz. II. *v.n.*; to —, nämlich, das heißt.

Witch, *s.* die Hexe. **—craft,** *s.* die Hexerei, Zauberkraft. **—ery,** *s.* der Zauber.

With, *prep.* (together —) mit, nebst; angry —, böse auf; she wept — joy, sie weinte vor Freude.

Withdraw, *ir.v.* I. *a.* zurückziehen. II. *n.* sich zurückziehen, sich entfernen.

Wither, *v.n.* (ver)welken, verdorren. **—ed,** *adj.* welk, verdorrt.

Withers, *pl.* der Widerrist (*in horses*).

Withhold, *v.a.* zurückhalten; to — a thing from a person, einem etwas versagen.

Within, I. *adv.* drin(nen), darin. II. *prep.* innerhalb, binnen, in.

Without, I. *adv.* außen, draußen. II. *prep.* außerhalb; (wanting) ohne.

Withstand, *ir.v.a.* (einem) widerstehen.

Witness, I. *s.* der Zeuge; to bear — (to), Zeugnis ablegen (von), (eine S.). II. *v.a.* bezeugen.

Witt—ed, *adj.,* half —ed, albern; quick —ed, geistreich. **—icism,** *s.* der Witz. **—ily,** *adv.,* **—y,** *adj.* witzig.

Wizard, *s.* der Zauberer, Hexenmeister.

Wizen(ed), *adj.* eingeschrumpft.

Woad, *s.* der Waid.

Wobble, *v.n.* wackeln.

Woe, I. *s.* das Weh, Leid. II. *int.* wehe! **—ful,** *adj.,* **—fully,** *adv.* jammervoll. **—fulness,** *s.* der Jammer, das Elend. **—begone,** *adj.* trauervoll.

Wolf, *s.* der Wolf. **—ish,** *adj.,* — **ishly,** *adv.* wölfisch; (*fig.*) gefräßig.

Wolverine, *s.* der braune Vielfraß.

Woman, *s.* (*pl.* Women) das Weib, Frauenzimmer, die Frau. **—hood,** *s.* der Frauenstand. **—ish,** *adj.,* — **ishly,** *adv.* weibisch. **—liness,** *s.* die Weiblichkeit. **—ly,** *adj.* weiblich. — **folk, —kind,** *s.* die Frauensleute (*coll.*). **—hater,** *s.* der Weiberfeind. **—servant,** *s.* die Magd.

Womb, *s.* der Schoß, Mutterleib.

Wonder, I. *s.* das Wunder; (surprise) die Verwunderung. II. *v.n.* sich (ver)wundern (at a thing, über eine S.); (*also v.a.*) neugierig sein (if, ob); I — whether he will come, ich möchte gern wissen, ob er kommt. **—ful,** *adj.,* **—fully,** *adv.* wundervoll, -bar, erstaunlich; (strange) außerordentlich. **—fulness,** *s.* das Wunderbare. **—ing,** I. *adj.,* **—ingly,** *adv.* staunend, verwundert. II. *s.* die Verwunderung. **—ment,** *s.* das Erstaunen.

Wondrous, *adj.* & *adv.,* **—ly,** *adv.* wundersam, erstaunlich.

Wont, I. *s.* die Gewohnheit. II. *adj.* gewohnt; to be — to do a thing, etwas zu tun pflegen. **—ed,** *p.p.* & *adj.* gewöhnlich.

Woo, *v.* I. *a.* freien, werben (um). II. *n.* freien, werben. **—er,** *s.* der Freier, Bewerber. **—ing,** *s.* das Freien, Werben.

Wood, *s.* der Wald; (timber) das Holz. **—ed,** *adj.* waldig, bewaldet. **—en,** *adj.,* **—enly,** *adv.* (of—) hölzern. **—bine,** *s.* das Geißblatt. **—cut,** *s.* der Holzschnitt. **—cutter,** *s.* der Holzfäller, -hauer. **—engraver,** *s.* der Holzschneider. **—land,** *s.* die Waldung. **—pavement,** *s.* das Holzpflaster. **—pecker,** *s.* der Specht. **—pigeon,** *s.* die Holztaube. **—work,** *s.* die Holzarbeit.

Woof, *s.* der Einschlag, das Gewebe.

Wool, *s.* die Wolle (*also Bot.*). **—len,** I. *adj.* wollen. II. *s.* die Wollenware. **—ly,** *adj.* wollig. **—work,** *s.* die Wollstickerei.

Word, *s.* das Wort; to bring —, Nachricht bringen; to be as good as one's —, sein Wort halten. **—ily,** *adv.* wortreich. **—iness,** *s.* die Wortfülle. **—ing,** *s.* das Abfassen. **—less,** *adj.* stumm. **—y,** *adj.* weitschweifig.

Work, I. *v.n.* arbeiten; (take effect)

wirfen; to — hard, fleißig, eifrig arbeiten. II. *v.a.* (effect) (be)wirfen, hervorbringen, verrichten; bearbeiten. III. *s.* das Werf; at —, im Gange, im Betriebe; out of —, arbeitslos. **—able,** *adj.* bearbeitbar. **—er,** *s.* der Arbeiter, die Arbeiterin. **—ing,** *s.* das Wirfen, die Wirfung (*fig.*); das Arbeiten; der Betrieb (*of a business, etc.*). **—house,** *s.* das Armenhaus. **—man,** *s.* der Arbeiter, Handwerfer. **—manlike,** *adj.* funftgerecht, geschickt. **—people,** *pl.* die Arbeitsleute. **—shop,** *s.* die Werfstatt. **—woman,** *s.* die Arbeiterin.

World, *s.* die Welt. **—liness,** *s.* die Weltflugheit. **—ling,** *s.* das Weltfind. **—ly,** *adj.* weltlich, Welt=.

Worm, *s.* der Wurm. **—eaten,** *adj.* wurmstichig.

Wormwood, *s.* der Wermut.

Worry, I. *v.a.* würgen, zerreißen. II. *s.* die Qual, Plage. **—ing,** *adj.*, **—ingly,** *adv.* plagend, quälend.

Worse, *adj. & adv.* schlechter, schlimmer; fränfer (*Med., etc.*); to be none the —, nicht überdran sein.

Worship, I. *s.* die Verehrung, Anbetung; der Gottesdienst (*Rel.*); Your —, Ew. Gnaden, Exzellenz. II. *v.a.* ehren, achten, anbeten (*God, etc.*). **—ful,** *adj.* ehrwürdig. **—per,** *s.* der Verehrer, Anbeter.

Worst, I. *sup. adj.* schlimmft, schlechteft, ärgft. II. *s.* das Schlimmfte, Ärgfte, 2c. III. *v.a.* überwältigen.

Worsted, I. *s.* das Kammgarn. II. *adj.* wollen.

Worth, *adj.* wert. **—ily,** *adv.* würdig. **—iness,** *s.* die Würdigkeit. **—less,** *adj.*, **—lessly,** *adv.* wertlos. **—lessness,** *s.* die Wertlosigkeit; die Nichtswürdigkeit. **—y,** *adj.* würdig, wert.

Wound, I. *s.* die Wunde (*also fig.*), die Kränkung, Verwundung. II. *v.a.* verwunden.

Wrack, *s.* der Seetang.

Wraith, *s.* das Gespenst, der Geist.

Wrangl—e, I. *v.n.* zanken, streiten. II. *s.* der Zank, Streit, Hader. **—er,** *s.* der Zänker. **—ing,** *adj.* zänkisch.

Wrap, *v.a.* einwickeln, einhüllen. **—per,** *s.* der Umschlag, die Hülle.

Wrath, *s.* der Zorn, die Wut. **—ful,** *adj.*, **—fully,** *adv.* zornig, grimmig, wütend.

Wreak, *v.a.* wirfen, ausüben.

Wreath, *s.* der Kranz. **—e,** *v.a.* winden, flechten.

Wreck, I. *s.* der Schiffbruch; (*fig.*) das Verderben. II. *v.a.* zertrümmern; to be —ed, scheitern. **—age,** *s.* die Schiffstrümmer. **—er,** *s.* der Wracker, Stranddieb.

Wren, *s.* der Zaunfönig.

Wrench, I. *s.* die Verrenfung, Verftauchung. II. *v.a.* entwinden, entreißen (from someone, einem); verrenfen; to — open, mit Gewalt öffnen.

Wrest, *v.a.* entreißen, entwinden.

Wrestl—e, *v.n.* ringen. **—er,** *s.* der Ringer. **—ing,** *p.* ringend; **—ing match,** der Ringfampf.

Wretch, *s.* der Elende; (worthless —) der Wicht, Lump, Tropf. **—ed,** *adj.*, **—edly,** *adv.* elend, jämmerlich; (worthless) nichtswürdig, lumpig, verächtlich. **—edness,** *s.* das Elend; (paltriness) die Erbärmlichfeit.

Wriggl—e, *v.a.* (& *n.* sich) schlängeln, winden. **—ing,** *adj.* sich windend, sich frümmend.

Wring, *ir.v.a.* ringen (one's hands); aus(w)ringen (clothes).

Wrinkle, I. *s.* die Runzel. II. *v.a.* runzeln. **—d,** *adj.* runzelig.

Wrist, *s.* das Handgelenf. **— watch,** *s.* die Armbanduhr.

Writ, *s.* die Schrift; die Vorladung (Law).

Write, I. *ir.v.a.* schreiben; (— down, auf=, nieder=schreiben; to — out, aus=, ab=schreiben. II. *n.* schreiben; to — on, fortschreiben. **—r,** *s.* der Schreiber (of a letter); der Verfasser (of a book, etc.); der Schriftsteller (used absolutely).

Writhe, *v.n.* sich winden.

Writing, I. *p.* schreibend. II. *s.* das Schreiben, die Schrift; (hand—ing) die Handschrift; in —, schriftlich. **—desk,** *s.* das Schreibpult.

Wrong, I. *adj. & adv.* unrecht, verfehrt; (not correct) unrichtig; to be —, Unrecht haben. II. *v.a.* (einem) Unrecht tun. III. *s.* das Unrecht, die Unbill. **—ful,** *adj.*, **—fully,** *adv.* ungerecht. **—ly,** *adv.* verfehrt, auf ungerechte Weise. **—ness,** *s.* die Verfehrtheit. **—doing,** *s.* die Übeltat, das Unrechttun. **—headed,** *adj.* querföpfig.

Wroth, *adj.* ergrimmt, erzürnt.

Wry, *adj.* schief.

X

X, x, *s.* das X, x.

X-rays, *s.* X= or Röntgen=strahlen (*pl.*).

Xylophon, *s.* das Xylophon, die Strohfiedel.

Y

Y, y, *s.* das Y, y.

Yacht, *s.* die Jacht.

Yak, *s.* der Grunzochs.

¹Yard, *s.* die Rute; die Segelstange. **—stick,** *s.* der Ellenstab.

²Yard, *s.* der Hof(raum).

Yarn, *s.* das Garn; to spin a —, (*fig.*) eine Geschichte erzählen.

Yarrow, *s.* die Schafgarbe.

Yawl, *s.* die Jolle.

Yawn, I. *s.* das Gähnen. **II.** *v.n.* gähnen.

Year, *s.* das Jahr. **—ly,** *adj.* jährlich.

Yearn, *v.n.* sich sehnen. **—ing, I.** *adj.,* **—ingly,** *adv.* sehnsüchtig. **II.** *s.* die Sehnsucht.

Yeast, *s.* die Hefe. **—y,** *adj.* hefig.

Yell, I. *s.* der Schrei. **II.** *v.n.* gellen.

Yellow, I. *adj.* gelb; — press, die Hetzpresse. **II.** *s.* das Gelb. **—ish,** *adj.* gelblich.

Yelp, I. *v.n.* bellen, kläffen. **II.** *s.* das Gekläff.

Yeoman, *s.* der Freisaß.

Yes, I. *adv.* ja. **II.** *s.* das Ja.

Yesterday, I. *s.* der gestrige Tag. **II.** *adv.* gestern.

Yet, I. *adv.* jetzt noch; (till now) bis jetzt; (still) noch; (even) selbst, sogar; as —, bis jetzt, bisher; not —, noch nicht. **II.** *conj.* doch, dennoch, gleich= wohl.

Yew, *s.* die Eibe.

Yield, I. *v.a.* hergeben, einbringen, (produce) hervorbringen. **II.** *v.n.* sich ergeben. **III.** *s.* der Ertrag. **— ing,** *adj.,* **—ingly,** *adv.* willfährig, nachgiebig.

Yoke, I. *s.* das Joch (*also fig.*). **II.** *v.a. & n.* ins Joch spannen.

Yokel, *s.* der Bauerntölpel.

Yolk, *s.* das (Ei=)Dotter.

Yonder, *adv.* drüben, dort.

Yore, *s.*; (in days) of —, ehemals, weiland.

You, *pers. pron.* ihr; Sie, du; man.

Young, I. *adj.* jung. **II.** *pl.* die Jungen. **—ster,** *s.* der junge Bursche.

Your, *poss. adj.* Euer, Ihr, dein. **—s,** *poss. pron.* euer, dein, Ihr; der, die, das Eurige, Deinige, Ihrige; —s truly, Ihr ergebener. **—self,** *pron.* (*pl.* —selves) (ihr, Sie, du) selbst, euch, Sie, dich (selbst), sich selbst.

Youth, *s.* die Jugend; (lad) der Jüng- ling; in —, in der Jugend. **—ful,** *adj.,* **—fully,** *adv.* jugendlich, Jugend=. **—fulness,** *s.* die Jugendlichkeit.

Yule, *s.* das Weihnachten. **—log,** *s.* der Weihnachtsknorren.

Z

Z, z, *s.* das Z, z.

Zany, *s.* der Hanswurst, Possenreißer.

Zeal, *s.* der Eifer. **—ous,** *adj.,* — **ously,** *adv.* eifrig, hitzig, innig.

Zebra, *s.* das Zebra.

Zenith, *s.* der Zenit.

Zero, *s.* die Null; der Nullpunkt.

Zest, *s.* die Würze, der Beigeschmack; das Behagen.

Zigzag, I. *s.* der Zickzack. **II.** *adj.* im Zickzack laufend, Zickzack=.

Zinc, I. *s.* das Zink. **II.** *v.a.* ver- zinken.

Zither, *s.* die Zither.

Zodiac, *s.* der Tier=, Sonnen=kreis.

Zone, *s.* der Gürtel (*also Med.*); der Erdgürtel (*Geog.*); die Zone.

Zoo—logical, *adj.,* **—logically,** *adv.* zoologisch; —logical garden, der Tiergarten. **—logy,** *s.* die Tierkunde, Zoologie.

GEOGRAPHICAL AND OTHER PROPER NAMES

A

Abyssini—a, Abeſſinien (n.). **—an,** Abeſſinier (m.); Abeſſinierin (f.); abeſſiniſch (adj.).

Adige R., Etſch (f.).

Adolph, Adolphus, Adolf (m.).

Adrianople, Adrianopel (n.).

Adriatic, adriatiſch (adj.).

Aegean Sea, Ägäiſches Meer (n.).

Aeneid, die Äneide (f.).

Aix-la-Chapelle, Aachen (n.).

Albania, Albanien (n.).

Algiers, Algier (n.).

All Saints' Day, Allerheiligenfeſt (n.).

All Souls' Day, Allerſeelentag (m.).

Alp—ine, alpiniſch (adj.), Alpen= (in compounds). **—s,** die Alpen (pl.).

Alsace, Alsatia, Elſaß (n.). **Alsatian,** elſäſſiſch (adj.); Elſäſſer (m.); Elſäſſerin (f.).

America, Amerika (n.). **—n,** amerikaniſch (adj.); Amerikaner (m.); Amerikanerin (f.).

American cloth, Wachstuch (n.).

Andes, die Anden (pl.).

Andrew, Andreas (m.). **Merry —,** der Hanswurſt.

Anglo-Saxon, angelſächſiſch (adj.); Angelſachſe (m.).

Anne, Anna (f.).

Annie, Ännchen (n.).

Antarctic, Südpolgegend (f.).

Ant(h)ony, Anton.

Antwerp, Antwerpen (n.).

Arabia, Arabien (n.).

Aragon, Aragonien (n.).

Arctic, arktiſch (adj.); **— ocean,** nörd= liches Eismeer (n.).

Argonne; Forest of —, Argonnerwald (m.).

Aristotle, Ariſtoteles (m.).

Arminius the Cheruscan, Hermann der Cherusker.

Aryan, Arier (m.); ariſch, indo=ger= maniſch (adj.).

Asia, Aſien (n.). **—tic,** aſiatiſch (adj.).

Asia Minor, Kleinaſien (n.).

Athenian, atheniſch (adj.); Athener (m.).

Athens, Athen (n.).

Atlantic Ocean, atlantiſcher Ozean (m.).

Augustus, (Christian name) Auguſt (m.); (the Roman emperor) Auguſtus (m.).

Austria, Öſterreich (n.). **—n,** öſter= reichiſch (adj.); Öſterreicher (m.).

B

Balaam, Bileam (m.).

Bâle, Basle, Baſel (n.).

Balearic Isles, die Balearen (pl.).

Baltic, baltiſch (adj.); **— (Sea),** die Oſtſee (f.).

Barbado(e)s, Barbados (n.).

Barbary, die Berberei (f.); **— horse,** Berberroß (n.).

Bartholomew, Bartholomäus (m.); **St. Bartholomew's Eve,** die Pariſer Bluthochzeit (August 1572).

Bavaria, Bayern (n.). **—n,** bayriſch (adj.); Bayer (m.); Bay(e)rin (f.); **—n electorate,** Kurbayern (n.).

B.B.C. abbv. = **British Broadcasting Corporation,** Britiſche Rundfunk= geſellſchaft (f.).

Beauty, Sleeping —, Dornröschen (n.).

Bedouin, Beduine (m.).

Belgi—an belgiſch (adj.); Belgier (m.); Belgierin (f.). **—um,** Belgien (n.).

Belgrade, Belgrad (n.).

Belshazzar, Belſazar (m.).

Benedictine (monk), der Benediktiner (Mönch).

Bengal, Bengalen (n.); bengaliſch (adj.); **Bay of —,** der Bengaliſche Meerbuſen.

Berlin work, Wollstickerei (f.).
Bernard, Bernhard (m.); St. — dog, Bernhardiner (m.).
Bern—(e), Bern (n.); bernese, bernisch (adj.); Berner (m.); Bernerin (f.). **—ese Alps,** das Berner Oberland.
Betty, Bessie, Elschen, Lieschen (n.).
Biscay, Biscaya or Biscaia (f.); Bay of —, Meerbusen von Biscaya (m.).
Black Forest, Schwarzwald (m.).
Black Sea, das Schwarze Meer.
Blanche, Blanka (f.).
Blenheim, Blindheim (n.); battle of —, Schlacht (f.) bei Höchstädt (1704).
Blucher, Blücher (m.).
Bluebeard, Blaubart (m.).
Boer, Bur, Boer (m.); Burin (f.), Burenweib (n.); — War, Burenkrieg (m.).
Bohemia, Böhmen (n.). **—n,** böhmisch (adj.); Böhme (m.).
Bolshevik, Bolschewist (m.).
Bosnia—n, —c, bosnisch, bosniakisch (adj.); Bosnier, Bosniake (m.).
Bosphorus, Bosporus (m.).
Bothni—a, Botten (n.); Gulf of —a, Bottnischer Meerbusen (m.). **—an,** —c, bottnisch (adj.).
Brahmin, (Brahman,) der Brahmane, Brahmine. **—ic, (Brahmanic,)** brahminisch (adj.).
Brazil, Brasilien (n.), brasilianisch (adj.). **— nut,** Paranuß (f.).
Bridget, Brigitte.
Britain, Britannien (n.); Great —, Großbritannien (n.).
Brit—ish, britisch (adj.); the —ish, die Briten (pl.). **—on,** Brite (m.).
Brittany, die Bretagne.
Bruges, Brügge (n.).
Bruin, Braun, der Bär.
Brunswick, Braunschweig (n.).
Brussels, Brüssel (n.).
Brussels sprouts, Rosenkohl (m.).
Bucharest, Bukarest (n.).
Budapest, Ofenpest (n.).
Bulgaria, Bulgarien (n.).
Burgund—ian, burgundisch (adj.); Burgunder (m.); Burgunderin (f.). **—y,** Burgund (n.); (wine) Burgunder (m.).
Burm—a, Birma (n.). **—an,** —ese, birmanisch (adj.); Birmane (m.).
Byzant—ium, Byzanz (n.). **—ian,** —ine, byzantinisch (adj.); Byzantiner (m.).

C

Cæsar, Cäsar (m.). **—ean,** cäsarisch (adj.).
Cain, Kain (m.).
California, Kalifornien (n.).
Caliph, Kalif (m.). **—ate,** Kalifat (n.).
Cameroons (The), Kamerun, Kamerun (n.).
Canary Islands, die Kanarischen Inseln (pl.).
Cancer; Tropic of —, Wendekreis (m.) des Krebses.
Canute, Knut (m.).
Cape of Good Hope, Kap (n.) der guten Hoffnung.
Cape Town, Kapstadt (f.).
Capricorn ; Tropic of —, Wendekreis (m.) des Steinbocks.
Carinthia, Kärnten (n.). **—n,** kärntnisch (adj.).
Carlovingian, Karolinger (m.).
Carpathian Mts., die Karpathen (pl.).
Carthag—e, Karthago (n.). **—inian,** Karthager (m.); karthagisch (adj.).
Carthusian (friar), Kartäuser(mönch) (m.).
Cashmere, Kaschmir (n.).
Caspian Sea, Kaspisches Meer (n.).
Castil—e, Kastilien (n.). **—ian,** Kastilianer (m.); kastil(ian)isch (adj.).
Catholic, katholisch (adj.); Katholik (m.).
Caucasus, Kaukasus (m.).
Cecilia, Cäcilie (f.).
Celt, der Kelte. **—ic,** keltisch (adj.).
Champagne, (country) die Champagne; (wine) Champagner (m.), Sekt (m.).
Channel ; the English —, Kanal (m.).
Channel Islands, Normannische Inseln (pl.).
Charlemagne, Karl der Große.
Charles, (Charlie,) Karl (m.).
Chin—a, China (n.). **—ese,** Chinese (m.); Chinesin (f.); chinesisch (adj.).
Christ, Christus (m.). **—ian,** Christ (m.); Christin (f.); christlich (adj.).
Christina, Christine (f.), Tinchen (n.).
Christopher, Christoph (n.).
Cinderella, Aschenputtel, Aschenbrödel (n.).
Circassia, Tscherkessien (n.). **—n,** Tscherkesse (m.); Tscherkessin (f.); tscherkessisch (adj.).
Cisalpine, cisalpinisch (adj.).

Cistercian (monk), Cistercienser=(mönch) (m.).

Claus, Santa —, Weihnachtsmann, Sankt Nikolaus (m.).

Clement, Clemens (m.).

Clovis, Chlodwig, Chlodowech (m.).

Cluniac (monk), Cluniacenser (m.).

Cologne, Köln (n.); Eau de —, kölnisches Wasser.

Colossians, Kolosser (pl.).

Columbia, Kolumbien (n.).

Constance, (town) Konstanz (n.); (name) Konstanze (f.); Lake of —, Bodensee (m.).

Constantin—e, Konstantin (m.). —**ople,** Konstantinopel (n.).

Corinth, Korinth (n.). —**ian,** Korinther (m.); korinthisch (adj.).

Coriolanus, Coriolan (m.).

Corsica, Korsika (n.). —**n,** Korse (m.); Korsin (f.); korsisch, korsikanisch (adj.).

Cossack, Kosak (m.); kosatisch (adj.).

Courland, Kurland (n.). —**er,** Kurländer (m.).

Cracow, Krakau (n.).

Creole, Kreole (m.); Kreolin (f.); kreolisch (adj.).

Cret—e, Kreta (n.). —**an,** Kreter (m.); kretisch (adj.).

Crimea, die Krim (f.); —n war, Krimkrieg (m.).

Croat—ia, Kroatien (n.). —**ian,** Kroat (m.); Kroatin (f.); kroatisch (adj.).

Crœsus, Krösus (m.).

Cupid, Kupido (m.).

Cyclades, Cykladen (pl.).

Cyprus, Cypern (n.).

Czech, Tscheche (m.); Tschechin (f.); tschechisch (adj.).

Czechoslovakia, Tschechoslowakei (f.).

D

Dan—e, s. Däne (m.); Dänin (f.). —**ish,** dänisch (adj.); —ish war, der Dänenkrieg.

Dantzic, Dantzig, Danzig (n.).

Danube R., Donau (f.).

Dardanelles, die Dardanellen (pl.).

Denmark, Dänemark (n.).

Dervish, Derwisch (m.).

Dnieper R., Dnjepr (m.).

Dniester R., Dnjestr (m.).

Dominic; St. —, der heilige Dominicus. —**an,** Dominikaner (m.).

Dover Straits, Straße (f.) von Dover.

Drave R., Drau (f.).

Dresden china, Meißner Porzellan (n.).

Druid, Druide (m.). —**ess,** Druidin (f.). —**ical,** druidisch (adj.).

Dunkirk, Dünkirchen (n.).

Dutch, holländisch (adj.). —**man,** Holländer (m.). —**woman,** Holländerin (f.).

E

East, Osten (m.); the —, Morgenland (n.).

Edward, Eduard (m.).

Egypt, Ägypten (n.). —**ian,** ägyptisch (adj.); Ägypter (m.).

Elijah, Elias (m.).

Elisha, Elisa (m.).

Eliza, Elise (f.).

Elizabeth, Elisabeth (f.).

Elsinore, Helsingör (n.).

Elysi—an, elys(ä)isch (adj.). —**um,** Elysium (n.).

Emily, Emilie (f.).

England, England (n.).

English, englisch (adj.); Englisch (n.), englische Sprache (f.); the —, die Engländer (pl.). —**man,** Engländer (m.). —**woman,** Engländerin (f.).

Equator, Äquator (m.).

Ernest, Ernst (m.).

Esthonia, Estland (n.).

Etna, Ätna (m.).

Euphrates, Euphrat (m.).

Europe, Europa (n.). —**an,** europäisch (adj.); Europäer (m.).

F

Fascism, Faschismus (m.). **Fascist,** Faschist (m.).

Finland, Finnland (n.).

Flanders, Flandern (n.).

Flem—ing, Flam(l)änder (m.). —**ish,** flämisch, flandrisch (adj.).

Floren—ce, (city) Florenz (n.). —**tine,** florentinisch (adj.); Florentiner (m.).

Flushing, Vlissingen (n.).

France, Frankreich (n.).

Francis, Franz (m.).

Franciscan (friar), Franziskaner=(mönch) (m.).

Franconia, Franken (n.). —**n,** fränkisch (adj.); Franke (m.).

Frank (for **Francis**), (Christian name) Franz (m.).

Frankfort, Frankfurt (n.).
Fred, Fritz (m.). —eric(k), Friedrich (m.).
French, französisch (adj.). —man, Franzose (m.). —woman, Französin (f.). — bean, Schnittbohne (f.); — chalk, Schneiderkreide (f.). — casement, Fensterflügel (pl.).
Frieslander, Friese (m.); Friesin (f.).
Frisia, Friesland (n.). —n, friesisch (adj.); Friese (m.); Friesin (f.).

G

Galatians, Galater (pl.).
Galicia, Galizien (n.).
Galilee, (Galilee,) Galiläa (n.). —n, galiläisch (adj.); Galiläer (m.).
Gascon, gasconisch (adj.); Gascogner (m.). —y, die Gascogne (f.).
Gaul (country) Gallien (n.); (inhabitant) Gallier (m.). —ish, gallisch (adj.).
Genev—a, Genf (n.); Lake of —a, Genfer See (m.). —ese, Genfer (m.).
Geno—a, Genua (n.). —ese, genuesisch (adj.); Genueser (m.).
Geoffrey, Gottfried (m.).
Geor—ge, (—die, —gie,) Georg (m.).
German, deutsch (adj.); Deutsche (m. f. n.); the —s, die Deutschen.
Germanic, germanisch (adj.).
Germany, Deutschland (n.).
Ghent, Gent (n.).
G(h)ibel(l)ine, Waiblinger (m.).
Gibraltar, Straits of —, Straße (f.) von Gibraltar.
Goth, Gote (m.). —ic, gotisch (adj.).
Grain Coast, Pfefferküste (f.).
Greece, Griechenland (n.).
Greek, Grieche (m.); Griechin (f.); griechisch (adj.); that is — to me, das kommt mir spanisch vor; das sind mir böhmische Dörfer.
Greenland, Grönland (n.). —er, der Grönländer.
Gregory, Gregor, Gregorius (m.).
Grundy, Mrs. —, die Anstandstante (f.).
Guelders, Guelderland, Geldern (n.).
Guelph, Welfe (m.). —ic, welfisch, Welfen= (adj.).
Guinea; — fowl, Perlhuhn (n.); —pig, Meerschweinchen.
Gulf Stream, Golfstrom (m.).
Gunther, Günther (m.).
Guy, Veit, Guido (m.).

H

Hague : The —, der Haag.
Hainault, Hennegau (m.).
Hanover, Hannover (n.). —ian, Hannoveraner (m.); Hannoveranerin (f.); hannöversch.
Hapsburg, Habsburg (m.).
Harry, Heinz, Heini (m.).
Hartz Mts., Harzgebirge (n.), Harz (m.).
Hebraic, hebräisch (adj.).
Hebrew, Hebräer (m.); Hebräisch (n.); hebräisch (adj.).
Hebrides, Hebriden (pl.).
Hegira, Hedschra (f.).
Helen(a), Helene (f.).
Heligoland, Helgoland (n.).
Hellenic, hellenisch (adj.).
Henry, Heinrich.
Herod, Herodes (m.).
Hess—e, Hessen (n.). —ian, Hesse (m.), hessisch (adj.).
Hezekiah, Hiskia(s) (m.).
Highland—er, Bergschotte (m.). —s, Hochlande (pl.); das schottische Hochland.
Hindoo, Hindu, Hindu (m.).
Hock, Hochheimer Rheinwein (m.).
Holland, Holland (n.), die Niederlande.
Horace, Horaz (m.).
Hottentot, Hottentott(e) (m.); Hottentottin (f.).
Huguenot, Hugenott(e) (m.); Hugenottin (f.).
Hun, Hunne (m.); Hunnin (f.).
Hungar—y, Ungarn (n.). —ian, Ungar (m.); Ungarin (f.); ungarisch (adj.).
Hussite, Hussit (m.).

I

Iceland, Island (n.). —er, Isländer (m.); Isländerin (f.). —ic, isländisch (adj.).
Iliad, Ilias, Iliade (f.).
Illyrian, Illyrier (m.); illyrisch (adj.).
India, (Ost)Indien (n.). Further —, Hinterindien (n.).
Indian, (American red) Indianer (m.), Indianerin (f.), indianisch (adj.); (Asiatic) Inder, Indier (m.), Inderin, Indierin (f.); indisch (adj.).
Indies, East —, Ostindien (n.); West —, Westindien (n.).
Ireland, Irland (n.).

Irish, irisch, irländisch (*adj.*). **—man,** Irländer (*m.*). **—men,** Iren (*pl.*).

Iroquois, Irokese (*m.*); irokesisch (*adj.*).

Isaac, Isaak (*m.*).

Isaiah, Jesaias (*m.*).

Iscariot, Ischarioth (*m.*).

Ishmael, Ismael (*m.*). **—ite,** Ismaelit (*m.*).

Islam, Islam (*m.*). **—itic,** islamitisch (*adj.*).

Israelit—e, Israelit (*m.*); Israelitin (*f.*). **—ic,** israelitisch (*adj.*).

Italian, Italiener (*m.*); Italienerin (*f.*); italienisch (*adj.*).

Italic, italisch (*adj.*). **—s,** — characters, Kursivdruck (*m.*).

Italy, Italien (*n.*). **North Italy,** Oberitalien (*n.*).

J

Jack, Hans (*m.*).

James, Jakob (*m.*).

Jane, Johanna, Johanne (*f.*).

Japan, Japan (*n.*); japanisch (*adj.*). **—ese,** Japaner (*m.*); Japanerin (*f.*).

Jeremia—h, Jeremias (*m.*). **—d,** Jeremiade (*f.*).

Jew, Jude (*m.*); Jüdin (*f.*). **—ish,** (**Judaic,**) jüdisch (*adj.*).

Jezebel, Jsebel (*f.*).

Job, Hiob (*m.*).

John, Johann(es), Hans (*m.*), Hänschen (*n.*).

Jonah, Jonas, Jonas (*m.*).

Joseph, Joseph (*m.*).

Joshua, Josua (*m.*).

Josiah, Josias (*m.*).

Judaea, Judea, Judäa (*n.*).

Judah, Juda (*n.*).

Judas, Judas (*m.*); — Iscariot, Judas Ischariot.

Jude, Juda (*m.*).

Julian, julianisch (*adj.*); — Alps, Julische Alpen (*pl.*).

Juliet, Julie (*f.*).

Jutland, Jütland (*n.*). **—er,** Jüte, Jütländer (*m.*), Jütin, Jütländerin (*f.*).

K

Kaff—ir, Kaffer (*m.*). **—raria,** Kaffer(n)land (*n.*).

Kamchatka, Kamtschatka (*n.*).

Khalifa, Kalif (*m.*).

Kiev, Kiew (*n.*).

Kremlin, Kreml (*m.*).

L

Lacedemonia, Lacedämonien (*n.*).

Lapland, Lappland (*n.*). **—er,** Lappe, Lappländer (*m.*); Lappländerin (*f.*). **—ish,** lappländisch (*adj.*).

Latin, Latein (*n.*); lateinisch (*adj.*).

Laurence, Lawrence, Lorenz, St. Laurentius (*m.*).

Lebanon, Libanon (*m.*).

Leipsic, Leipzig, Leipzig (*n.*).

Leman (Lake), Genfersee (*m.*).

Leonora, Lenore (*f.*).

Leopold, Leopold, Liutpold (*m.*).

Levant, Levante (*f.*). **—ine,** levant-(in)isch (*adj.*).

Levit—e, Levit (*m.*). **—ical,** levitisch (*adj.*). **—icus,** s. das dritte Buch Mosis.

Lewis, Ludwig (*m.*).

Libyan, Libyer (*m.*); Libyerin (*f.*); libysch (*adj.*).

Liége, Lüttich (*n.*).

Lisbon, Lissabon (*n.*).

Lithuania, Litauen (*n.*). **—n,** Litauer (*m.*); Litauerin (*f.*); litauisch (*adj.*).

Livonia, Livland (*n.*). **—n,** Livländer (*m.*); Livländerin (*f.*); livländisch (*adj.*).

Livy, Livius (*m.*).

Lombardy, Lombardei (*f.*).

Loreley, Lorelei (*f.*).

Lorraine, Lothringen (*n.*); men of —, Lothringer (*pl.*); lothringisch, Lothringer (*adj.*).

Louis, Ludwig (*m.*).

Louisa, Luise (*f.*).

Louvain, Löwen (*n.*).

Lubeck, Lübeck (*n.*); lübisch, Lübecker (*adj.*).

Lucerne, (*town*) Luzern (*n.*); lake of —, Vierwaldstättersee (*m.*).

Luke, Lukas (*m.*); St. —, der heilige Lukas.

Lusatia, Lausitz (*f.*). **—n,** Lausitzer (*m.*); Lausitzerin (*f.*); lausitzisch (*adj.*).

Lutheran, lutherisch (*adj.*); Lutheraner (*m.*).

M

Maccabees, Makkabäer (*pl.*).

Macedonia, Macedonien (*n.*).

Mæcenas, Mäcen (*m.*).

Maelstrom, Mahlstrom (*m.*).

Magi, Magier (*pl.*).

Mahomet, Muhammed, Mohammed

(m.). **—an,** Mohammedan, Mo=
hammedaner (m.); Mohammedanerin
(f.); mohammedanisch (adj.).
Malines (see **Mechlin**), Mecheln (n.).
Malt—a, Malta (n.). **—ese,** Malteser
(m.); maltesisch (adj.).
Manchu, Mandschu (m.). **—ria,** die
Mandschurei (f.).
Manich—æan, —ee, Manichäer (m.).
—æan, manichäisch (adj.).
Mark, Markus (m.).
Martha, Marta, Martha (f.).
Matthew, Matthäus (Rel.); Matthias,
Matthes (m.).
Maurice, Moritz (m.).
Mayence, Mainz (n.).
Mecca, Mekka (n.).
Mechlin, Mecheln (n.).
Med—e, Meder (m.). **—ian,** medisch
(adj.).
Mediterranean (Sea), mittelländisches
Meer (n.).
Mercury, Merkur (m.).
Merovingian, Merowinger (m.); mero=
wingisch (adj.).
Messia—h, Messias (m.). **—nic,** mes=
sianisch (adj.).
Methuselah, Methusalem (m.).
Meuse R., Maas (f.).
Mexic—o, Mexiko (n.). **—an,** Mexi=
kaner (m.); Mexikanerin (f.); mexi=
kanisch (adj.).
Milan, Mailand (n.). **—ese,** Mai=
länder (m.); Mailänderin (f.); mai=
ländisch (adj.).
Milky Way, Milchstraße (f.).
Misnia, Meißen (n.).
Moabit—e, Moabiter (m.). **—ish,**
moabitisch (adj.).
Moldavia, die Moldau (f.). **—n,** Mol=
dauer (m.); moldauisch (adj.).
Mongolia, die Mongolei (f.). **—n,**
Mongole (m.); Mongolin (f.); mon=
golisch (adj.).
Montenegrin, Montenegriner (m.);
montenegrinisch (adj.).
Moor, Mohr (m.). **—ish,** maurisch
(adj.).
Moravia, Mähren (n.). **—n,** Mähre
(m.); (member of —n sect) Herrn=
huter (m.); mährisch (adj.).
Morocco, Marokko (n.).
Mosaic(al), mosaisch (adj.).
Moscow, Moskau (n.).
Moselle R., Mosel (f.).
Munich, München (n.); Münchener
(adj.).

N

Naples, Neapel (n.).
Nazarene, Nazaräer, Nazarener (m.).
Netherland—s, Niederlande (pl.). **—
isb,** niederländisch (adj.).
Newfoundland, Neufundland (n.);
(dog) Neufundländer (hund) (m.).
New South Wales, Neusüdwales (n.).
New York, Neuyork (n.).
New Zealand, Neuseeland (n.).
Nice, Nizza (n.).
Nicholas, (Nick,) Nikola(u)s, (Kla(u)s)
(m.).
Nile R., Nil(strom) (m.).
Nimeguen, Nimwegen (n.).
Nineveh, Ninive (n.).
Norman, Normanne (m.); Norman=
nin (f.); normannisch (adj.). **—dy,**
Normandie (f.).
Norse, nordisch (adj.). **—man,** Nord=
mann, Wiking (m.).
North; — Cape, Nordkap (n.); —
Sea, Nordsee (f.).
Norw—ay, Norwegen (n.). **—egian,**
Norweger (m.); Norwegerin (f.);
norwegisch (adj.).
Nova; — Scotia, Neuschottland (n.).
— Zembla, die Insel Nowaja Semlja.
Nuremberg, Nürnberg (n.).

O

Oceania, Ozeanien (n.).
Odyssey, Odyssee (f.).
Olives; Mt. of —, **Olivet,** Ölberg (m.).
Olymp—ian, Olympier (m.), **(—ic,)**
olympisch (adj.). **—us,** Olymp (m.).
Orange, Oranien (n.).
Ostend, Ostende (n.).
Ostrogoth, Ostgote (m.). **—ic,** ost=
gotisch (adj.).

P

Pacific Ocean, Stiller or Großer Ozean.
Palatinate, Pfalz (f.); Pfalzgraf=
schaft (f.); Upper —, Oberpfalz (f.);
Rhenish —, Rheinpfalz (f.).
Palatine, pfälzisch; Count —, Pfalz=
graf (m.); Countess —, Pfalzgräfin
(f.); Elector —, Kurfürst (m.) von
der Pfalz.
Palestin—e, Palästina (n.). **—ian,**
palästinisch (adj.).
Paris, (city) Paris (n.). **—ian,** Pariser
(m.); Pariserin (f.); parisisch (adj.).

Parnass—us, Parnaß (m.). **—ian,** parnassisch (adj.).

Parsee, Parse (m.).

Parthian, Parther (m.); parthisch (adj.).

Pekin, Peking (n.).

Percival, Parzival (m.).

Persian, Perser (m.); Perserin (f.).

Pharis—ee, Pharisäer (m.). **—aical,** pharisäisch (adj.).

Pharaoh, Pharao (m.).

Philip, Philipp (m.). **—pians,** Philipper (pl.).

Phœnician, Phönizier (m.); phönizisch (adj.).

Pict, Pikte (m.).

Pilate, Pilatus (m.).

Plate R., (La Plata, Rio Plata,) Platafluß (m.).

Platonist, Platoniker (m.).

Pliny, Plinius (m.).

Pol—and, Polen (n.). **—e,** Pole (m.); Polin (f.). **—ish,** polnisch (adj.).

Polar Sea, Eismeer (n.).

Pomerania, Pommern (n.).

Pompe—ian, Pompejaner (m.); pompejanisch (adj.). **—ii,** Pompeji (n.). **—y,** Pompejus (m.).

Portug—al, Portugal (n.). **—uese,** Portugiese (m.); Portugiesin (f.); portugiesisch (adj.).

Prague, Prag (m.).

Prussia, Preußen (n.). **—n,** Preuße (m.); Preußin (f.); preußisch (adj.).

Punjab, Pandschab (n.).

Pyrenees, Pyrenäen (pl.).

Pythagorean, pythagoräisch (adj.); Pythagoräer (m.).

Q

Quixote, (Don) Quichotte (m.).

R

Rachel, Rahel (f.).

Ratisbon, Regensburg (n.).

Red Riding Hood, (Little), Rotkäppchen (n.).

Red Sea, Rotes Meer.

Redskins, Rothäute (pl.).

Reynard, Reinhard (m.); — the Fox, Reineke Fuchs (m.).

Rhenish, rheinisch (adj.); — wine, Rheinwein (m.).

Rhine R., Rhein (m.). **Falls of the —,** der Rheinfall. **Lower —,** Nieder-

rhein (m.). **Palatinate of the —,** Rheinpfalz (f.).

Riga, Riga (n.). **Gulf of —,** Rigischer Busen (m.).

Rocky Mountains, Felsengebirge (n.).

Roger, Rüdiger (m.).

Roman, Römer (m.); Römerin (f.); römisch (adj.).

Romance, romanisch (adj.); — nations, Romanen (pl.).

Rome, Rom (n.).

Roumania, Rumänien (n.). **—n,** Rumäne (m.); Rumänin (f.); rumänisch (adj.).

Roumelia, Rumelien (n.). **—n,** rumelisch (adj.).

Rupert, Ruprecht (m.).

Russia, Rußland (n.). **—n,** Russe (m.); Russin (f.); russisch (adj.).

S

Sabaoth, Zebaoth (m.).

Sadducee, Sadduzäer (m.).

Sadowa, (battle) Schlacht (f.) bei Königgrätz.

St. Gall, (place) Sankt Gallen (n.).

Sal—ian, Salier (m.). **—ic,** salisch (adj.).

Samaritan, Samariter (m.).

Samson, Simson (m.).

Sanscrit, Sanskrit (n.); sanskritisch (adj.).

Santa Claus, Knecht Ruprecht.

Save R., Sau (f.).

Saverne, Zabern (n.).

Savoy, Savoyen (n.). **—ard,** Savoyarb(e) (m.); savoyardisch (adj.).

Saxe; —-Coburg, Sachsen-Koburg (n.). **—-Coburg-Gotha,** Sachsen-Koburg-Gotha (n.). **—-Meiningen,** Sachsen-Meiningen (n.). **—-Weimar,** Sachsen-Weimar (n.).

Saxon, Sachse (m.); Sächsin (f.); sächsisch (adj.). **—y,** Sachsen(land) (n.); Electorate of —y, Kursachsen (n.).

Scandinavia, Skandinavien (n.). **—n,** Skandinavier (m.); Skandinavierin (f.); skandinavisch (adj.).

Scheldt R., Schelde (f.).

Scot, Schotte (m.), Schottin (f.). **-tish,** schottisch (adj.).

Scotland, Schottland (n.).

Seltzer water, Selterswasser (n.).

Semit—e, Semit (m.). **—ic,** semitisch (adj.).

Serbia, Serbien (*n.*). —n, Serbe (*m.*); Serbin (*f.*); Serbier (*m.*); Serben (*pl.*); serbisch (*adj.*).

Seville, Sevilla (*n.*).

Sheba, Saba (*n.*).

Shechem, Sichem (*n.*).

Siberia, Sibirien (*n.*). —n, Sibirier (*m.*); sibirisch (*adj.*).

Sicil—y, Sizilien (*n.*). —ian, Sizili-(an)er (*m.*); sizil(ian)isch (*adj.*).

Silesia, Schlesien (*n.*). —n, Schlesier (*m.*); schlesisch (*adj.*).

Sistine, sixtinisch (*adj.*).

Slav, Slawe (*m.*). —ic, slawisch (*adj.*).

Slave Coast, Sklavenküste (*f.*).

Sleswig, Schleswig (*n.*); Schleswiger, schleswig(i)sch (*adj.*).

Slovak, Slowake (*m.*); slowakisch (*adj.*).

Slovene, Slowene (*m.*).

Solomon, Sol, Salomo(n) (*m.*); Song of Solomon, das hohe Lied Salomonis.

Sound, the —, der Sund.

Spain, Spanien (*n.*).

Span—iard, Spanier (*m.*); Spanierin (*f.*). —ish, spanisch (*adj.*).

Spartan, Spartaner (*m.*); spartanisch (*adj.*).

Spice Islands, Gewürzinseln, Molukken (*pl.*).

Stamboul, Stambul (*n.*).

Stephen, Stephan (*m.*).

Stoic, Stoiker (*m.*); stoisch (*adj.*).

Strasburg, Straßburg (*n.*).

Styria, Steiermark (*f.*).

Swabia, Schwaben(land) (*n.*). —n, Schwabe (*m.*); Schwäbin (*f.*); schwäbisch (*adj.*).

Swed—e, Schwede (*m.*); Schwedin (*f.*). —en, Schweden (*n.*). —ish, schwedisch (*adj.*).

Swiss, Schweizer (*m.*); Schweizerin (*f.*); schweizerisch, Schweizer (*adj.*).

Switzerland, die Schweiz (*f.*).

Syracuse, Syrakus (*n.*).

Syria, Syrien (*n.*). —c, —n, Syr(i)er (*m.*); syrisch (*adj.*).

T

Table-Mountain, Tafelberg (*m.*).

Tagus R., Tajo (*m.*) (*in Spain*), Tejo (*m.*) (*in Portugal*).

Tangier(s), Tanger (*n.*).

Tannhauser, Tannhäuser (*m.*).

Templar, Knight, Tempelritter, Tempelherr, Templer (*m.*).

Teneriffe, Teneriffa (*n.*).

Thames R., Themse (*f.*).

Theb—es, Theben (*n.*). —an, Thebaner (*m.*); thebanisch (*adj.*).

Theresa, Therese (*f.*).

Thessaly, Thessalien (*n.*).

Thuringia, Thüringen (*n.*).

Ticino R., Tessin (*m.*).

Tierra del Fuego, Feuerland (*n.*).

Tim(othy), Timotheus (*m.*).

Tokay (wine), Tokaier (*m.*).

Trans—atlantic, transatlantisch (*adj.*). —ylvania, Siebenbürgen (*n.*). —ylvanian, Siebenbürge (*m.*); Siebenbürgin (*f.*); siebenbürgisch (*adj.*).

Trebizond, Trapezunt (*n.*).

Trent, Trient, Trident (*n.*).

Trèv—es, Trier (*n.*). —iran, trierisch (*adj.*).

Trieste, Triest (*n.*).

Tripoli, Tripolis (*n.*).

Troy, Troja (*n.*).

Turk, Türke (*m.*); Türkin (*f.*). —ey, die Türkei (*f.*).

Tuscan, Toskaner (*m.*); toskanisch (*adj.*). —y, Toskana (*n.*).

Tyr—e, Tyrus (*n.*). —ian, Tyr(i)er (*m.*); tyrisch (*adj.*).

Tyrol; the —, Tirol (*n.*). —ese, Tiroler (*m.*); tirolisch, Tiroler- (*adj.*).

Tyrrhenian Sea, Tyrrhenisches Meer (*n.*).

U

United States, Vereinigte Staaten (*pl.*).

V

Valhalla, Walhalla (*f.*).

Valkyrie, Walküre (*f.*).

Vandal, Vandale (*m.*). —(ian), —(ic), vandalisch (*adj.*).

Vaud, Waadt(land) (*n.*). —ois, Waadtländer (*m.*); waadtländisch (*adj.*).

Venetia, Venetien (*n.*). —n, Venetianer (*m.*); venetianisch, venedisch (*adj.*).

Venice, Venedig (*n.*).

Verde, Cape, Grünes Vorgebirge (*n.*).

Vesuvius, Vesuv (*m.*).

Vienn—a, Wien (*n.*). —ese, Wiener (*m.*), wienerisch, Wiener (*adj.*).

Viking, Wiking (*m.*).
Vincent, Vincenz (*m.*).
Visigoth, Westgote (*m.*). —**ic,** westgotisch (*adj.*).
Vistula R., Weichsel (*f.*).
Vitus, Veit (*m.*); St. —'s dance, Veitstanz (*m.*).
Volga R., Wolga (*f.*).
Vosges, Vogesen (*pl.*).

W

Waldenses, Waldenser (*pl.*).
Wales, Wales *or* Wallis (*n.*).
Wallachia, die Walachei (*f.*). —**n,** Walache (*m.*); walachisch (*adj.*).
Walloon, Wallone (*m.*); wallonisch (*adj.*).
Warsaw, Warschau (*n.*).
Welsh, wallisisch, Walliser= (*adj.*); die Walliser (*pl.*). —**man,** Walliser (*m.*). —**woman,** Walliserin (*f.*).
Wenceslas, Wenzel (*m.*).
Wend, Wende (*m.*); Wendin (*f.*); wendisch (*adj.*).
Westphalia, Westfalen (*n.*). —**n,** Westfale (*m.*); Westfälin (*f.*); westfälisch (*adj.*).

Wilhelmina, Wilhelmine (*f.*).
William, Wilhelm (*m.*); Willi (*m.*) (*dim.*).
Wurtemberg, Württemberg (*n.*). —**ian,** Württemberger (*m.*); württembergisch (*adj.*).
Wurzburg, Würzburg (*n.*).

X

Xavier, Xaver (*m.*).

Y

Yenisei R., Jenisei (*m.*).
Yokohama, Jokohama (*n.*).
Ypres, Ypern (*n.*).
Yugoslavia, Südslawien (*n.*).

Z

Zambezi R., Sambesi (*m.*).
Zanzibar, Sansibar (*n.*).
Zealand, Seeland (*n.*). —**er,** Seeländer (*m.*). **New** —, Neuseeland (*n.*).
Zurich, Zürich (*n.*); Lake of —, Zür(i)cher See.
Zuyder Zee, Zuidersee (*m.*).

STRONG AND ANOMALOUS VERBS

PRES. INFIN.	IMPERF. INDIC.	PAST PART.	PRES. INFIN.	IMPERF. INDIC.	PAST PART.
abide	abode	abode	cry	cried	cried
arise	arose	arisen	cut	cut	cut
awake	awoke	awaked	dare	dared	dared
bake	baked	baked	deal	dealt	dealt
be *Pres.Ind.*	was	been	dig	dug	dug
am			do	did	done
bear	bore	borne, born	draw	drew	drawn
beat	beat	beaten	dream	dreamt	dreamt
become	became	become		dreamed	dreamed
beget	begot	begotten	drink	drank	drunk
begin	began	begun	drive	drove	driven
bend	bent	bent	dwell	dwelt	dwelt
bereave	bereft	bereft	eat	ate, eat	eaten
	bereaved	bereaved	fall	fell	fallen
beseech	besought	besought	feed	fed	fed
bestride	bestrode	bestridden	feel	felt	felt
bid	bade	bidden	fight	fought	fought
bind	bound	bound	find	found	found
bite	bit	bitten	flee	fled	fled
bleed	bled	bled	fling	flung	flung
blow	blew	blown	fly	flew	flown
break	broke	broken	forbear	forbore	forborne
breed	bred	bred	forbid	forbade	forbidden
bring	brought	brought		forbad	
build	built	built	forget	forgot	forgotten
burn	burnt	burnt	forgive	forgave	forgiven
	burned	burned	forsake	forsook	forsaken
burst	burst	burst	freeze	froze	frozen
buy	bought	bought	get	got	got
Pres. Ind.			gird	girt	girt
can	could	—		girded	girded
cast	cast	cast	give	gave	given
catch	caught	caught	go	went	gone
chide	chid	chidden	grind	ground	ground
choose	chose	chosen	grow	grew	grown
cleave	cleft	cleft	hang	hung	hung
	cleaved	cleaved			hanged
cling	clung	clung	have	had	had
clothe	clothed	clothed	hear	heard	heard
come	came	come	heave	heaved	heaved
cost	cost	cost	hew	hewed	hewn
creep	crept	crept			hewed
crow	crowed	crowed	hide	hid	hidden

PRES. INFIN.	IMPERF. INDIC.	PAST PART.	PRES. INFIN.	IMPERF. INDIC.	PAST PART.
hit	hit	hit	shoot	shot	shot
hold	held	held	shrink	shrank	shrunk
hurt	hurt	hurt		shrunk	
keep	kept	kept	shut	shut	shut
kneel	knelt	knelt	sing	sang	sung
know	knew	known	sink	sank	sunk
lade	laded	laden	sit	sat	sat
lay	laid	laid	slay	slew	slain
lead	led	led	sleep	slept	slept
lean	leant	leant	slide	slid	slid
leap	leapt	leapt	sling	slung	slung
	leaped	leaped	slink	slunk	slunk
learn	learnt	learnt	slit	slit	slit
		learned	smell	smelled	smelled
leave	left	left		smelt	smelt
lend	lent	lent	smite	smote	smitten
let	let	let	sow	sowed	sowed
lie	lay	lain			sown
light	lit	lit	speak	spoke	spoken
	lighted	lighted	speed	sped	sped
lose	lost	lost	spell	spelt	spelt
make	made	made		spelled	spelled
Pres. Ind. may	might	—	spend	spent	spent
			spill	spilt	spilt
mean	meant	meant		spilled	spilled
meet	met	met	spin	span	spun
Pres. Ind. must	—	—	spit	spat	spat
			split	split	split
pay	paid	paid	spread	spread	spread
put	put	put	spring	sprang	sprung
read	read	read	stand	stood	stood
rend	rent	rent	steal	stole	stolen
rid	rid	rid	stick	stuck	stuck
ride	rode	ridden	sting	stung	stung
ring	rang	rung	stink	stank	stunk
rise	rose	risen		stunk	
run	ran	run	stride	strode	stridden
saw	sawed	sawn	strike	struck	struck
		sawed	string	strung	strung
say	said	said	strive	strove	striven
see	saw	seen	strow	strowed	strown
seek	sought	sought			strowed
sell	sold	sold	swear	swore	sworn
send	sent	sent	sweep	swept	swept
set	set	set	swell	swelled	swollen
shake	shook	shaken			swelled
Pres. Ind. shall	should	—	swim	swam	swum
			swing	swang	swung
shed	shed	shed		swung	
shew, show	shewed, showed	shewn, shown	take	took	taken
		showed	teach	taught	taught
			tear	tore	torn
shine	shone	shone	tell	told	told
shoe	shod	shod	think	thought	thought

PRES. INFIN.	IMPERF. INDIC.	PAST PART.	PRES. INFIN.	IMPERF. INDIC.	PAST PART.
thrive	throve	thriven	weave	wove	woven
throw	threw	thrown		weaved	weaved
thrust	thrust	thrust	weep	wept	wept
tread	trod	trodden	will	would	—
try	tried	tried	win	won	won
wake	woke	waked	wind	wound	wound
	waked	woke	wring	wrung	wrung
wear	wore	worn	write	wrote	written